4 ENGLISH BIOGRAPHIES

4 ENGLISH

ADVENTURES IN GOOD BOOKS

BIOGRAPHIES

J. B. Priestley
O. B. Davis

HARCOURT, BRACE & WORLD, INC.

New York · Chicago · Atlanta · Dallas · Burlingame

J. B. PRIESTLEY, British novelist, essayist, and dramatist, has written extensively in all these forms. Prominent examples of each, in order, are *The Good Companions, Delight,* and *Dangerous Corner.* In addition, he has recently written a literary history, *Literature and Western Man.*

He has been a frequent visitor to this country and is known to high school readers through his editorial contribution to Harcourt, Brace & World's *Adventures in English Literature* and *Four English Novels.*

O. B. DAVIS has been head of the English Department at Kent School, Kent, Connecticut, since 1954, and has taught there since 1949. He has contributed to various professional periodicals and was Mr. Priestley's collaborator on *Four English Novels.*

Illustrations by William Hofmann

© 1961 by Harcourt, Brace & World, Inc.
Printed in the United States of America
[a · 5 · 61]

CONTENTS

Afterwords by J. B. Priestley

Study Questions by O. B. Davis

4 ENGLISH BIOGRAPHIES

Shakespeare of London

by Marchette Chute

SHAKESPEARE OF LONDON is a splendid book. It is
a firmly drawn and brightly painted panorama of Shakespeare's
life, of the Theater he worked for, of the London that applauded
him, of the Elizabethan age. It is tremendously *readable*.
(Some critics and reviewers use *readable* as a term of faint
praise, but this is not my practice. I use it positively, to suggest
that a book fastens onto the mind, defies you to leave it half
read.) It is crammed with information, the result of a hard spell
of research, but it moves easily, is not lumbering, not bogged
down by its history. No smell of the reference library has
found its way into these pages.

Marchette Chute was born in Minnesota, graduated from the
university there, a Phi Beta Kappa, and has won various
impressive awards for her studies in English literary history.
She has written other studies of great English authors, notably
Ben Jonson of Westminster and *Geoffrey Chaucer of England*.
Books of this kind are very easy to do if their authors are
content to do them badly. They are difficult to do well—and
this Shakespeare book is done superbly well.

Too many people have written books about Shakespeare, and
too many of such people have shown themselves lacking in
good sense. (A great genius acts like a kind of magnet for
nonsense.) Now Marchette Chute, in this book, shines with good
sense, of the sort that Shakespeare would have liked. For
Shakespeare, for all his astounding genius, was a sensible man.
And here is a well-informed, sensible woman writing about
him and his world. It makes a very strong and appealing
combination.

Shakespeare of London by Marchette Chute. Copyright © 1949 by
E. P. Dutton & Co., Inc.
Reprinted by permission of E. P. Dutton & Co., Inc.

✠ *Chapter* 1

There were many towns named Stratford in England, but the one that stood on the banks of the river Avon had special reason to be proud of its native sons. John of Stratford had become Archbishop of Canterbury and lay buried in a tomb of alabaster at the high altar, and Hugh Clopton had gone to the great city of London and ended by becoming its Lord Mayor.

By the middle of the sixteenth century these special glories were a thing of the past. But the stone bridge over the Avon that Sir Hugh Clopton had built at great expense for his native town had opened up a year-round traffic with London, and Stratford had become a thriving market community and was now one of the largest towns in Warwickshire. When the young men who were born in the nearby villages decided that they did not want to be farmers, they migrated to Stratford to learn a trade and settle down in one of its well-traveled streets.

Among the young men of Warwickshire who felt the pull of Stratford was one named John Shakespeare. John lived in the pleasant little village of Snitterfield, four miles to the north. His father was a tenant farmer and his brother was a tenant farmer, but John had no intention of following in their footsteps. When he left Snitterfield he probably had no higher ambition than to become a successful businessman in Stratford; but before John Shakespeare died he had achieved the highest political office in town, and had been a justice of the peace, a landowner, and a gentleman with a coat of arms. He had also become the father of a son named William who had a considerable success on the London stage; and, while this was not in itself a very dignified achievement from the Stratford point of view, John Shakespeare had the satisfaction of knowing before he died that his son was already investing his money in Stratford real estate.

The trade that young John Shakespeare selected for himself was that of making gloves. Everyone wore gloves in the sixteenth century, and since their native manufacture was protected by Act of Parliament, it was a profitable trade. The glovers were one of the most powerful trade groups in Stratford, and on market days they put up their booths and trestles in the most strategic location in town. They did their selling just under the big clock in the paved market square, where most of the customers gathered, and it was not until more than a hundred years later that another powerful trade group, the mercers, managed to take this location away from them. John Shakespeare was a "whittawer," a dealer in the fine white leather from which the best products were made, but like most of his fellow townsmen he sold other commodities, from timber to wool, in his spare time.

The Stratford that John Shakespeare knew was still a medieval town. It had never been walled, which accounted for its unusually straight and broad streets, but in spirit it was a tight, narrow little medieval community. Like every other town in England, Stratford was run on a strict, paternalistic system that had worked well for the citizens' remote ancestors and might be expected to work equally well for them. Every effort was made to protect local industry and keep away outsiders, all trade was strictly controlled and supervised, and every resident was hedged about with rules designed to keep himself and the town in order. An inhabitant of Stratford was fined if he let his dog go unmuzzled, if his duck wandered, if he played cards "or any other unlawful games," if his children were not at home by eight o'clock in the summertime, if he failed to sweep his gutters, or if he borrowed gravel from the town gravel pits. If he wanted to bring an outsider into his house, he had to have a special license from the High Bailiff, and if from a sense of compassion he gave shelter in his house to "any stranger woman" who was with child, he was heavily fined.

The natural result of Stratford's strict medieval standards of conduct was that the men of Stratford's governing body were continually obliged to fine themselves and their

fellow townsmen for breaking the rules. With so many rules to be enforced, it was impossible to avoid breaking a few of them, and there was no citizen of Stratford so virtuous or so distinguished that he escaped a fine for one offense or another.

One of the best sources of revenue was the law that forbade the residents from making private, informal dump heaps of their own instead of using the four or five official ones. Fines for making a "muckhill at chamber's door" were levied at nearly every frankpledge, for it was one of the commonest offenses in Stratford. John Shakespeare, for instance, makes his first appearance on the town records because he and two of his very respectable neighbors were fined twelvepence each for establishing a refuse heap near their houses instead of using the public one at the end of the street. John Shakespeare must have been a sober, respectable householder for he was very seldom fined for having sinned against the Stratford bylaws, but some of his fellow townsmen were always leaping in and out of the records for having done the wrong thing again.

The dealers in basic food commodities had an especially hard time in Stratford, for the town was operating on the rigid medieval system of price controls and that meant an equally strict supervision of quality. Every year two ale-tasters were elected to see that the bakers and butchers and innkeepers of Stratford were obeying the rules on prices, that the brewers were putting "no hops nor no other subtle things in their brewing," and that the numerous women who retailed beer were not serving it in unsealed pots. In the September elections of 1556, John Shakespeare was made an ale-taster and started his long climb upward through the various civic offices in Stratford.

The next year John Shakespeare entered the Council, the governing body of Stratford. He was appointed one of the fourteen Capital Burgesses and had the proud obligation of attending the meetings of the Council in the handsome old guild building. John Shakespeare wore a special gown to attend these meetings and there was a fine of twelvepence if he forgot it. There was a further fine of six shillings and eightpence if he left the meeting in any but "brotherly love"; for the citizens in that orderly little town were on the whole a rowdy and opinionated lot and it needed a direct attack on their pockets to keep them in order. More than one Council meeting was broken up for what was politely called "opprobrious words" and occasionally a member had to be expelled for having too excitable a temperament.

The following year, in 1558, John Shakespeare was made one of the constables of the borough, a position that required a strong, healthy, and determined man. Physical assaults were a commonplace in a period when every man had a right to wear a dagger but theoretically no right to use it. John Shakespeare happened to get the office at an especially difficult and contentious time, for he had been constable less than two months when Queen Mary died. As long as Mary was ruler, the official religion of England was Catholicism and every Protestant was a potential traitor. When her successor, Queen Elizabeth, came to the throne that November, the state religion became Protestant again. Most Englishmen accepted the change without any special difficulty, but in every town there was a group that did not welcome the new queen and they made the life of a constable a busy one.

The next year John Shakespeare was reappointed petty constable and he was also made affeeror. In this office he was responsible for deciding what penalties should be levied in cases that were covered by no special town statute. He must have done his work satisfactorily, for in 1561 he was given the important position of town chamberlain, and with his colleague, John Taylor, became responsible for administering the borough revenues.

Again John Shakespeare took his post in a busy period. A government order had gone out that all signs of Catholicism in the local churches and chapels were to be effaced, since the one true religion was now quite a different one, and it was the business of the local chamberlains to see that the altars were removed, the images hacked, and the old religious paintings whitewashed. John Shakespeare, for instance, paid a workman two shillings to deface the images that stood in the guild chapel, and it was probably at the same time that all the wall paintings in the chapel were whitewashed. It was rather a pity that the paintings could not have remained for Shakespeare's son to look at, since he would have enjoyed the dragons over the vicar's door, the devils with their tapirlike noses between the nave and the chancel, and St. George warring with the dragon on the other side of the nave while a horse with the horn of a unicorn did his best to be of assistance. The Reformation was responsible for removing a good deal of innocent color from the lives of the people of England, and although St. George was their patron saint, he was one of the casualties.

The chamberlains served a two-year term, with John Taylor assuming most of the responsibility the first year and John Shakespeare the second. They collected the town revenues, administered them, and turned in a full report to their fellow members on the Council. The expenditures were miscellaneous, apart from standard ones to the schoolmaster and the vicar, and ranged from seventeen shillings for mending the vicar's chimney to twelvepence for repairs of the much-repaired town clock. When the revenues fell short of the expenses, John Shakespeare made up the difference out of his own pocket. In the end the borough owed

him a substantial sum of more than four pounds, but Shakespeare asked no interest and was willing to wait some time for repayment.

It has been repeatedly suggested that John Shakespeare was an illiterate man who could not even write his own name. His handwriting does not appear in the chamberlains' accounts, which were copied out by the town clerk, and when he signed his name to documents he used either a mark or a rather delicate drawing of the compasses he used in his glover's trade. The use of a mark as a signature does not mean anything one way or the other. A close friend of Shakespeare's, Adrian Quiney, made his mark in the Council records on the same page as John Shakespeare, and he occasionally used an inverted capital Q for his signature; but there are letters of Adrian Quiney's extant to prove that he could have written his name if he wanted to. Christopher Marlowe's father signed his will with a mark, although he was a clerk in Canterbury with his signature still extant in the church register.

There is no record of a chamberlain in Stratford who did not know how to write, and an illiterate man would be a curious choice for an office that consisted of so much careful bookkeeping. John Shakespeare was such a success in the office that after his two-year term was over and William Tyler and William Smith were acting as the new chamberlains, he was retained for another year to draw up their accounts for them. This was not a normal procedure in Stratford, and indicates that John Shakespeare must have been unusually well equipped for the office of chamberlain.

In the meantime John Shakespeare had become a married man, and it is probable that his marriage was quite as gratifying to his relatives in Snitterfield as his steady business and civic advancement must have been. His wife had one of the oldest names in Warwickshire, for the Ardens had been "lords of Warwick" before William the Conqueror came. Just what connection Mary Arden may have had with the Warwickshire Ardens is not clear. When the Office of Heralds in London was obliged to wrestle with the problem, they finally linked her with another branch of the family, and the actual genealogy has never been straightened out to anyone's satisfaction. At any rate, it is clear that Mary Arden would have been considered a member of the gentry, although she lost that distinction when she became Mary Shakespeare.

But Mary Shakespeare brought her husband a gift almost as good as gentility; she brought him land. Old Robert Arden had no sons, and of all his daughters Mary seems to have been his favorite. He left her in his will not only a substantial cash payment but also a large piece of farm property in Wilmcote. What this land meant to John Shakespeare, son of one of Robert Arden's tenant farmers, can be measured by the tenacity with which he fought to get it back after he had lost it.

Mary was the youngest of Robert Arden's children and yet he made her one of the two executors of his will. It was Mary who was responsible in part for seeing that her father's feather bed and his decorative painted hangings and his colts and sheep and bees and wheat went to their new owners after his death, and that her stepmother did not war openly because she had received only part of the inheritance. Mary was evidently a competent woman, and certainly she married in John Shakespeare an intelligent and competent man.

The year that Robert Arden died, his future son-in-law himself became a landowner. This was the same year that John Shakespeare bought two houses in Stratford, one in Greenhill Street on the west edge of town, and one in Henley Street. He had been living in Henley Street for at least four years past, and he may have bought the house he had already been renting. It was probably to the house in Henley Street that he brought his bride, and it was evidently here that most of the Shakespeare children were born.

The first of the Shakespeare children was born in 1558, the same month John Shakespeare was appointed constable. It was not the hoped-for son who would carry on the family name and inherit the land. It was a little girl named Joan and she died young. It was not until four years later that a second child was born to Mary Shakespeare; this also was a little girl, and they buried her the following spring.

A year after Margaret's burial, in the same month of April, Mary Shakespeare gave birth to her third child. This time it was a son, and his father and mother named him William.

The people of Stratford had no way of peering through the mists of the future to discover that the date on which William Shakespeare was born would be of interest to the whole of the civilized world. The Stratford parish register merely recorded the date of his baptism. This was the 26th of April, 1564, and all that can be said with certainty about the day of his birth is that it was a few days earlier.

Tradition and sentiment have united to proclaim that Shakespeare was born on the 23rd of April. This was the date on which he died in Stratford, fifty-two years later. Moreover, the 23rd of April is St. George's Day, and St. George is the patron saint of England as Shakespeare is its patron writer. The pageant of St. George vanished from the streets of Stratford when Queen Elizabeth came to the throne. His dragon no longer snorted through the streets on Holy Thursday, and the two shillings that the men of Stratford had once spent for gunpowder so that

smoke and flame could come out of its mouth no doubt went to soberer and worthier objects. Still, it is pleasant to feel that the great master of make-believe was born on St. George's Day, and there is no harm in hoping that he was.

John Shakespeare was still acting as chamberlain the year his son was born, and William must have received a christening worthy of the first-born son of a town official. The ceremony took place in the handsome old Church of the Holy Trinity by the river, and John Bretchgirdle was the vicar who christened the white-clad baby in the presence of his father, his godparents, and the assembled congregation so that he could go out into the world as a properly accredited member of the Church of England. Bretchgirdle was an Oxford graduate who took equal delight in Horace and in carpentering, and when he died the following year, he had seen to it that the small boys of Stratford would inherit those of his books they would enjoy reading.

Religion was administered with a firm hand in Stratford, as it was everywhere else in England. Religion and politics were inextricably connected, and every human being in England who was loyal to the Queen was expected to be equally loyal to the Church. Since this loyalty was not in every case quite spontaneous, any citizen of Stratford was fined if he did not present himself, his family, and his servants at church every Sunday;

and government commissions were constantly on the prowl all over England to make sure that the people were obeying the Act of Uniformity and that those dreaded individuals, religious recusants, were being unearthed and properly punished. The pulpit was a useful outlet for government propaganda, and the special prayers and homilies read from the pulpit by Bretchgirdle and his successors were of great assistance in preventing the people of Stratford from making up their minds independently on any subject whatever.

The religion of John and Mary Shakespeare is not known. Mary's father made a Catholic will, but since he died in the days "of our sovereign lord and lady, Philip and Mary" it would have been odd if he had done otherwise. Little Joan Shakespeare was baptized in the Catholic fashion, in Latin and with the anointing, because Queen Mary was still on the throne; but her brother William, who was born after Elizabeth came to the throne, was baptized in the Protestant fashion, in English and at the font. Nearly two decades later, John Shakespeare's name occurs on a list, drawn up by an ecclesiastical commission, because he had not been going to church. However, his name is not listed among the six suspected of being Catholic but among those who "come not to church for fear of process for debt." In any case, whatever his parents' religion may have been, William Shakespeare was a member of the Church of England. When the Walker family of Stratford named their son William, Shakespeare acted as godfather at the baptism, and he could not have done so unless he were an accredited member of the Church of England.

Three months after William Shakespeare was born, Stratford was visited by the plague. The infection was so serious that the Council could not meet indoors in August and took up a special collection for plague victims at a meeting in the chapel garden. For once the town clerk was not there to record the meetings; his son and his daughter had just died of the plague. In six months there were more than 250 burials, and there must have been many times when John and Mary Shakespeare were frightened for the safety of their only son.

In time the plague wore itself out as it always did. Stratford resumed its normal life, and John Shakespeare continued his steady rise in the town government.

The year after William was born, the town Council found itself obliged to expel one of its members, an alderman named William Bott. Bott had indulged in too many opprobrious words, and John Shakespeare was sworn in as an alderman in his place. In his new dignity as alderman, John Shakespeare wore a black gown faced with fur, and on Sundays he had a special seat nearer the pulpit. He was entitled to hang a special lantern before his house on Henley Street during the Christmas season, and above all he had achieved the coveted social distinction of becoming "Mr. John Shakespeare.* "

Two years later, Shakespeare's name was suggested for the office of High Bailiff, the highest political office in the power of the town to give. The High Bailiff corresponded to what most towns called the mayor, and the name went back to the days when Stratford had been under the control of a lord of the manor and the lord's bailiff was responsible for administering the town affairs. Stratford had been granted a charter by Elizabeth's brother, King Edward, just before he died and now had its own self-contained government, but the name of "bailiff" instead of "mayor" remained as a sign of the town's origin.

John Shakespeare did not win the election the first time his name was suggested. But it was brought up again the following year and this time his fellow members of the Council gave him a majority. He took the oath of office on the first of October, 1568, and swore to defend the liberties of the borough and give justice to rich and poor alike. His furred robes were now of scarlet, and when he went to preside over meetings in the Council chamber he was given a special escort. When he attended the Church of the Holy

* *Mr.* was pronounced *Master,* as *Mrs.* was pronounced *Mistress.* It was not until later that the syllables were slurred into their present pronunciation.—Author's Note

Trinity (that great barometer of social prestige) he had a seat in the front pew on the north side of the nave, with Mary Shakespeare and the Chief Alderman beside him, and the lesser aldermen and their wives to his rear.

As High Bailiff, John Shakespeare became also a justice of the peace, and he presided as judge over the Court of Record as well as presiding over the meetings of the Council. The rules laid down in the instruction book of the Office of Heralds stated that he was now eligible for a coat of arms if he should request it, for the office of bailiff was one of those "divers offices of dignity" that made its owner eligible for admission into the ranks of the gentry. The son of the tenant farmer of Snitterfield had come a long way.

The son of the High Bailiff, young William Shakespeare, was now four years old and had a two-year-old brother named Gilbert to keep him company. The center of his life must have been at first the house on Henley Street, with its sturdy oak framework and slanting roof; and he must have known the premises thoroughly from the pointed gables of the attic to his father's shop with its leathers and its tools on the ground floor.

The house was on the edge of town, just south of the gravel pits that marked the northern limits of the borough, but it was only a short walk down Henley Street to the intersection where the real business of town began. Here was the pump where the Stratford housewives washed their clothes and hung them, rather improperly, on the Market Cross to dry. It was here that John Shakespeare had his stall on market days; and a square wooden structure on pillars not only supported the clock with its gilded dial but had a ledge encircling it from which a small boy could comfortably dangle his legs and watch the shoppers below.

East of Market Cross was Bridge Street, the thoroughfare that led toward Oxford and London, and most of the important shops in Stratford were concentrated along its length. Here were the smithies and the taverns, the shoemakers and the bake shops, and also Stratford's four excellent inns. An inn like the Swan could boast of leaded panes and velvet cushions, and its walls were engagingly decorated with pictures of ancient worthies like Tobias dressed in Elizabethan doublet and trunk hose.

Beyond Bridge Street a causeway led to the great stone bridge that Sir Hugh Clopton had built over the river Avon. In those days the Avon was "a river in summer and a little sea in winter," and the parapet of the bridge was low enough so that even the smallest of small boys could see over its edge. Along the riverbank between the town and the bridge was Butt Close, where the townsmen were supposed to practice their archery, and beyond that was Bank Croft, where the ducks and cattle and sheep of Stratford had their communal pasture. The practice of archery was not only supposed to distract the citizens' minds from "unlawful" games like bowling and cards but also to fit them for soldiering when the Queen needed them, although the development of gunpowder had made archers obsolete and England's own armament industry had reached such proportions that English mariners complained the enemy was destroying them with guns of English manufacture.

Each of the prosperous inhabitants of Stratford had his own barn and his own garden, and the garden that adjoined the guild buildings was noted for its apples and plums. The town was green and leafy in summer, for there were over a thousand elms in its small confines and forty ash—that wood which "being cut down green it burneth green and bright." Around Stratford was farm land, the parallel strips that were still being tilled on the communal system that had served the people well in medieval times. But as a boy grew more adventurous, there lay for his delight along the horizon what was now called the Woodland but had been known in ancient times as the Forest of Arden.

As a Stratford boy grew older, he found less time for roaming, for school was a serious business in his community. There had always been a free school in Stratford, financed before the Reformation by the Guild of the Holy Cross and since then by borough revenues. The Stratford charter stipulated that the town was to have a "free grammar school for the training and education of children" to be "continued forever," and the boys in Stratford were expected to enter it for a free education as soon as they knew how to read and write.

By the end of the century there was a man in Stratford who taught the children reading and writing while his wife taught needlework, and unless there was a similar arrangement when William Shakespeare was a small boy, he probably learned his letters from the parish clerk. The Stratford grammar school was not supposed to handle elementary work of this kind, although it was apparently sometimes forced to assume what it called the "tedious trouble" of teaching the young to read. It was a trouble to the young also, and one weak-minded English uncle of the previous decade spent twenty times as much on sugar plums as on hornbooks before his nephew succeeded in learning his letters.

The hornbook was a slab of wood on which a page full of letters had been fastened and which was covered over with a thin, transparent sheet of horn to protect it from grubby small fingers. Countless generations of children had learned to read clutching the handle of a hornbook and William Shakespeare could hardly have been an exception. From that he probably graduated to *The ABC and Little Catechism,* which gave the youth of England their letters and their religious instruction simultaneously and sold in England at the rate of ten thousand copies in eight months.

Shakespeare learned to form his letters in the way all the little boys in rural districts formed them. The new Italian hand, which corresponds roughly to the modern way of writing, had made great headway in court and city circles, but the medieval way of writing, the one called the secretary hand, was still being used in the country. Some of Shakespeare's fellow dramatists, like George Peele, used the new Italian way of writing; some of them, like Thomas Kyd and George Chapman, used both fashions interchangeably; and at least one of them, Ben Jonson, worked out an efficient compromise between the two. The few signatures which are all that remain of Shakespeare's writing are done in the old-fashioned secretary hand he was taught in Stratford, and it is probable that he did not bother to change it after he came to London.

As soon as he could read and write and knew his catechism, young William Shakespeare was ready to enter Stratford grammar school. He was the son of one of the most prominent men in Stratford, but he received the same education that was democratically open to every boy in town, and there was no charge for the instruction.

The curriculum of Stratford grammar school, like that of every other grammar school in England, was serious, thorough, and dull.

There was no attempt whatever to fit the boys for the ordinary life they were going to find when they graduated, for all school theory in England was based on the medieval system. The purpose of schools in the Middle Ages was to turn out learned clerks for church positions, and therefore what the little boys of Renaissance England learned was Latin, more Latin, and still more Latin. About a decade after Shakespeare entered the classroom, a London teacher urged that English should also be taught in the schools, but no one paid any attention to so radical a suggestion.

The chief difference between the education given Shakespeare and that given Geoffrey Chaucer two centuries earlier was that Chaucer's comparatively simple instruction book, called the Donat, had been replaced by an authorized Latin grammar written by William Lily. Lily was the first headmaster of the school at St. Paul's Cathedral, and his book must have made him more cordially hated by harassed seven-year-olds than any man before or since. The whole of the English educational system united to pound Lily's Latin grammar into the heads of the young, and if a schoolboy was wise, he resigned himself to having to memorize the whole book.

Not one boy in a hundred had any real use for Latin in his subsequent career, and it is sad to think how the young Quineys and Walkers and Shakespeares worked over their construing in the schoolroom,

in what one London teacher compassionately called "an unnatural stillness," while the whole of the sunlit world waited for them outside. One of their number was eventually to become an actor, and no doubt the strict training in memory work did him a certain amount of good, but it is hard to see how their work in the schoolroom really benefited most of them.

In the average grammar school the boys worked at their grammar about four years, although an earlier educationalist had urged a little more consideration of the boy's own point of view. "By the time he cometh to the sweet and pleasant reading of old authors, the spark of fervent desire for learning is extinct with its burden of grammar." Another reformer agreed that it was "cold and uncomfortable" for both teacher and pupil when grammar was taught without an allied course of reading, but he added gloomily that it was "the common way." It was much easier to teach rules than to give boys a real love of Latin literature, and the average teacher took the easier way.

Here and there an imaginative teacher who loved his work triumphed over Lily and kindled a love of Latin writers in the hearts of the young. William Camden, the great London teacher, lit such a fire in the heart of one of his students that Ben Jonson worshiped both Camden and the classics all his life. Somewhere at Cambridge, Christopher Marlowe evidently found a teacher who did the same, but there is no indication that any schoolmaster set off a similar spark in young William Shakespeare. Like Geoffrey Chaucer before him, Shakespeare preferred to approach his Latin authors through a translation whenever he could.

Like Chaucer, Shakespeare's one real love among the schoolroom worthies was Ovid, but it was never difficult to arouse a schoolboy's interest in Ovid. The chief difficulty, rather, was to distract his mind from that amorous and delightful storyteller. Nearly all the mythology that Shakespeare knew came from Ovid's *Metamorphoses,* as did that of most of his fellow writers, but it is evident that Shakespeare was much more familiar with the first book or two than he was with the rest of it, and even in the case of Ovid he was not above working with a translation.

Apart from learning to read Latin and write Latin, an English schoolboy was also expected to recite Latin, and here again was an aspect of the curriculum that might conceivably be of some use to a future actor. There was considerable emphasis on good public speaking and a controlled, intelligent use of the voice, and many schoolmasters let their boys act out Latin plays by Plautus and Terence to give them experience in handling the spoken word.

Richard Mulcaster, who was head for many years of the excellent school conducted by the Merchant Tailors in London, always kept the spoken word in the forefront of his mind when he taught Latin. When he expounded the mysteries of punctuation to his classes, he did it as a singing teacher might, with the emphasis on "tunable uttering." A parenthesis meant the use of a lower and quicker voice, a comma was a place to catch the breath a little, and a period was a place where the breath could be caught completely. This sort of training would have been of great use to William Shakespeare when he started work as a professional actor and had to learn to translate the words written on a cue sheet into the sound of a living voice, and if he did not learn it from some imaginative teacher in the schoolroom, it was one of the many things he had to pick up for himself after he reached London.

Apart from teaching him Latin, Stratford grammar school taught Shakespeare nothing at all. It did not teach him mathematics or any of the natural sciences. It did not teach him history, unless a few pieces of information about ancient events strayed in through Latin quotations. It did not teach him geography, for the first (and most inadequate) textbook on geography did not appear until the end of the century, and maps and atlases were rare even in university circles. It did not teach him modern languages, for when a second language was taught at a grammar school it was invariably Greek.

What Shakespeare learned about any of these subjects he learned for himself later, in London. London was the one great storehouse in England of living, contemporary knowledge, and in that great city an alert and intelligent man could find out almost anything he wanted to know. It was in London, for instance, that Shakespeare learned French; and French was taught by Frenchmen who worked in competition with each other and used oral, conversational methods that were designed to get colloquial French into the student's head as quickly as possible.

When French was finally accepted into the grammar school curriculum, it was subjected to the heavy emphasis on rules and grammar with which the Latin tongue was already burdened, and Shakespeare was probably very fortunate that no one tried to teach him English by the same system. All the rules, the ritual, and the reverent embalming were focused on Latin, and as a result the writers of the late sixteenth century had a lighthearted sense of freedom where their native tongue was concerned because it had never been laid out in the schoolroom and expounded. Much respect was given to the Latin language, but all the affection, the excited experimentation, and the warm sense of personal ownership went into the English. If a writer needed an effective word he could not go to a dictionary for it. There were no English dictionaries, although Richard Mulcaster remarked it would be a praiseworthy deed to compile one.

The writer could either reach back into his memory, a practice that forced every writer to be also an alert listener, or else he could invent a new word entirely.

There was still some doubt among thoughtful men whether it was quite respectful to the language to use it in so lighthearted a fashion. George Puttenham apologized for using such "strange and unaccustomed" new words as *idiom, method, impression, numerous, penetrate, savage,* and *obscure.* Gabriel Harvey was scolded for using such abnormalities as *theory* and *jovial* and *negotiation;* and Ben Jonson, who could never forget his classical education, was horrified by a fellow playwright who used such outlandish words as *damp, clumsy, strenuous,* and *puffy.*

This use of new words could degenerate into complete confusion in the hands of incompetent writers, but it gave Shakespeare exactly the freedom he needed. He felt at complete liberty to pick up effective new words and combinations of words wherever he could find them, and a play like *Hamlet* is so full of them that it would have made a schoolmaster turn pale if he had had any responsiblity for teaching his charges the English language. Fortunately he had no such responsibility, and young William Shakespeare was free to discover the great reaches of the English language as a free-born and independent citizen.

Every weekday, summer and

winter, from the time when he was about seven years old, young Shakespeare went to school. He walked down Henley Street, turned at the Market Cross, and went the two long blocks to the guild buildings. During most of Shakespeare's boyhood the schoolroom was upstairs over the Council room, except for a short period when it had to be repaired, and the same bell that called William to school every morning called his father about once a month to the Council meeting in one of the rooms downstairs.

No single schoolmaster can be assigned the honor of having given William Shakespeare his schooling, since there happened to be a succession of teachers in Stratford during Shakespeare's boyhood. When he entered school, the master was Walter Roche, who left because he was given a rectory. Roche's successor was Simon Hunt, who left in 1575 to become a Jesuit. The teacher for the next four years was Thomas Jenkins, and when Jenkins left his post Shakespeare was fifteen and certainly no longer in school. All these men were university graduates, each of them holding a degree from Oxford, for the pay in Stratford was excellent and the twenty pounds a year that went to the schoolmaster was almost twice what he would have received in a large town like Warwick. All three men were presumably competent and well trained, since there must have been many candidates for the post. It is to be hoped that

at least one of them had a spark of Mulcaster's imagination, but they may have been merely the routine pedagogues that the educational system of the time encouraged.

When a boy had completed the curriculum of the grammar school in Stratford, he would have his head well stocked with the principles of Latin grammar and also with a miscellaneous collection of quotations from Latin authors, designed to illustrate the different parts of speech and supply him with a little moral education besides. He had probably been taught to keep a commonplace book, in which he was encouraged to write down any quotations that pleased him in his reading from ancient authors. He had learned how to make a pen neatly, cutting off the goose feathers with his penknife and softening the nib with his tongue. He had learned to sit upright when he was writing so that the humors of the brain would not fall down into his forehead and affect his eyesight, and he had learned how to endure the discipline of long hours of labor.

The school hours for the average English boy were long, usually extending from seven in the morning to five at night, with two hours off in the middle of the day to go home for dinner. The only difference made by the coming of summer was that the school hours were generally longer because there were more hours of daylight. Since curfew was at eight in the summertime, a well-brought-up little Stratfordian had comparatively few hours to play. For the rest, each small scholar was supposed to supply his own books and satchel and pens and ink, with candles extra in the winter; and, as William Lily opened his grammar by pointing out sternly, he was also supposed to come to school with his face washed and his hair combed, and on no account was he to loiter by the way.

It has been suggested that on one hot evening in July, when William Shakespeare was eleven years old, he was taken to the castle at Kenilworth to see part of the show with which the Earl of Leicester was entertaining Queen Elizabeth. On Monday evening the water devices included a dolphin and a mermaid, and the event is therefore said to be the origin of the lovely lines in *A Midsummer Night's Dream* in which Oberon describes the mermaid singing on the dolphin's back. But the Kenilworth water show was grotesque rather than beautiful, since the mermaid was eighteen feet long and the dolphin twenty-four. Both had actors perched on their backs and were propelled by elaborate mechanical equipment, and except for the fact they both appeared in the same show, they had no connection with each other. It is very unlikely, in any case, that Shakespeare would have been allowed to leave school in July and make so long a trip. Fifteen miles in those days was a journey of real magnitude; and since no one in Stratford could

have known how charmingly suitable it would have been for England's great future dramatist to meet England's great queen, it must remain exceedingly unlikely that he ever made the trip to Kenilworth at all.

In Stratford itself, young William Shakespeare would have had many opportunities to see public entertainments. Stratford was famous for its fairs, and the people of Warwickshire came from miles around to shop at the special booths and stalls that were set up in Market Street in May and again in September. Wherever there were people in England, there were entertainers, and no fair would have been complete without its acrobats and performing animals, any more than without its pies.

Stratford also had its share of regular stage productions. The first of the touring companies of actors came to Stratford the year that Shakespeare's father was High Bailiff, and they were welcomed by him in his official capacity. After that, one of the large companies stopped there every year or so, showing plays at Stratford in their regular yearly tour through the provinces.

The acting companies were rigidly licensed under an Act of Parliament, for nothing could have been more sinister to the Elizabethan mind than any group of men traveling around the country without proper credentials. To escape being listed as vagabonds, each acting company operated under someone's patronage, the smaller groups under local dignitaries or incorporated towns and the larger ones under prominent court officials like the Earl of Leicester or the Earl of Warwick.

When a company of actors arrived in Stratford, they first presented themselves before the High Bailiff and showed their credentials so that they could be licensed for playing in town. The first show was put on at the guildhall before the Bailiff and other members of the Council. Admission to the first show was evidently free to the public, since the Council was paying the bill, and there was always an enthusiastic attendance. In Bristol, for instance, when Shakespeare was twelve years old, part of the iron bar on the guildhall door had to be repaired because of "the press of people at the play."

Since William Shakespeare was the son of one of the most prominent of the Council members, he probably always had a good place to see and hear. Perhaps, like a small boy named Willis of about his own age in Gloucester, he stood between his father's legs while John Shakespeare sat on one of the benches. The main room of the guildhall made an excellent theatre, being long and narrow, with the players acting on a platform at the south end of the hall and using the smaller room, at right angles to it, to change their costumes and wait for their cues.

There must have been a great deal of activity in this improvised

tiring room, for the touring companies were small and each actor was expected to play several characters. A company of six players thought nothing of putting on a play like *Horestes,* which called for a cast of twenty-five, and long practice had made them adept at leaping in and out of their costumes and assuming new parts. In the play of *Cambises,* for instance, two actors handled fourteen roles between them, and in *The Repentance of Mary Magdalene* four men wrestled with fourteen parts that included Carnal Concupiscence, Infidelity, Knowledge of Sin, Mary Magdalene, and Christ Jesus. The chief character here was Infidelity, who carried the comedy role known as the Vice; and since vice was always punished in the end while the better and nobler abstractions triumphed, the audience had the comfortable feeling of seeing a play that was "not only godly, learned, and fruitful, but also well furnished with pleasant mirth and pastime."

From the point of view of a small boy the whole thing was evidently pure enchantment. The little boy in Gloucester could still remember, seventy years later, every detail of the show he had seen while he stood between his father's legs. He especially remembered the scene in which the wicked hero was transformed into a swine (being a typical small boy, he took a deep interest in the way this was handled with a mask and wires) and the splendid climax in which an actor dressed in blue, portraying End-of-the-World, makes the lovely ladies like Pride and Luxury vanish from the stage and the hero is carried off howling by devils. The plots of these morality plays lent themselves to a great deal of violent physical action and to the low comedy that English audiences had been trained to expect ever since the old miracle plays were acted in carts in the town streets.

No reasonable man could object to an entertainment that was full of moral lessons and did not disturb those settled principles that the schools and the parents worked so hard to inculcate. If the plays that went on tour did not deal with moral abstractions, they dealt with equally impeccable and improving stories. The subject might be Biblical, like *The Comedy of the Most Virtuous and Godly Susanna,* or it might be classical and introduce characters like Menelaus and Clytemnestra to English country audiences. The most careful of Stratford parents would have been willing to let his son see plays like these, and even if the boys acted the plots out afterward in the elm-shaded gardens of Stratford, they could do very little injury to their moral natures.

The effect of these traveling actors on the small boys of Stratford can be measured by the effect of a similar group of English players on another small boy who was Dauphin of France. Louis managed to remain cool and dignified until a moment arrived in the plot when one of the characters had his head cut off. This made a profound impression on the small Dauphin, and for two weeks thereafter his favorite game was playing actor, costuming himself in whatever was handy, taking long strides, and announcing to his mother that he was the whole of the acting company. If the small boys of Stratford played actor for weeks after the players left, they had an advantage over the Dauphin since there were more of them to share the parts, but it is not likely they were any less excited or less impressed than the boy at Fontainebleau.

The actors were made increasingly welcome at Stratford, and soon they were coming at the rate of two companies a year. When Shakespeare was twelve, the companies of both the Earl of Warwick and the Earl of Worcester paid a visit to Stratford. When he was thirteen, the Earl of Worcester's men played a return engagement, and the town was also honored by a visit from some of the most brilliant actors in England, those under the patronage of the Earl of Leicester.

✖ Chapter 2

The head of the Earl of Leicester's company was an actor named James Burbage; and when Shakespeare was twelve years old, James Burbage built the first theatre in London.

As an actor, Burbage knew how much a theatre was needed in London. The company he headed happened to be the first to get an official license, and Burbage was well aware of the difficulties of moving from town to town with a skeleton company, with a constant packing and unpacking of theatrical properties and costumes. The greatest theatregoing population in England was not in the provinces but in London, and there was an excellent profit to be made in London by any company that could establish itself with a permanent base of operations.

At present, the arrangement in London was the same as in other English towns: the companies produced their plays in the open rectangular courtyards of the inns. The system must have been fairly satisfactory, since an inn like the Cross Keys was still being used by major acting companies when there were new theatres all over London. The shape of the innyards made it easy for them to be used as theatres, with the actors working on a scaffold at one end of the innyard and part of the audience grouped around them while the more prosperous individuals used the seats in the surrounding galleries of the upstairs rooms; and the stage arrangements must have been elaborate since the Office of the Revels was willing to pay over twenty-four shillings to borrow a property well that had been in use by the actors in the Bell Inn in Gracechurch Street.

Nevertheless, the innyards had their disadvantages. The actors had to share the yards with the carters, who brought freight and mail to London on weekly schedules. The carters used the inns on definite days of the week so that their customers would know where to find them, and the arrangement made it difficult for the actors to use the innyards more than three days out of seven. It was difficult to collect admissions, the storage of properties was not easy, and since there was no permanent tiring house the changing of costumes must have been extremely complicated. Moreover, the proprietors of the inns charged fairly high rentals, and there was every reason why an intelligent and prominent actor might decide to put up his own building and collect his own rentals.

By good fortune James Burbage had been apprenticed to a joiner in his youth and had practiced the trade of carpenter until he discovered there was much more money in acting. No man could have been better equipped to build the first theatre in England, since as an actor he knew what actors needed and as a carpenter he had the technique to supply it.

Since James Burbage had no model to guide him when he started working out the design for his theatre, he was free to adopt anything that would make for maximum efficiency in the actors and maximum comfort in the audience. One of the ideas that probably suggested itself to him was the system that he and his company used when they acted in guildhalls or in large private residences. This was not unlike the modern theatre arrangement, with a raised stage at one end of a rectangular hall and benches arranged to face it.

This kind of theatre design would have meant a fairly high scale of admission prices, since it left no room for the innyard standees who could only afford a penny to see a play. This penny public was treated rather contemptuously by the writers of the period, and when the first Italian theatre was built in the following decade, it was probably felt that the designer had done well to design it for a prosperous clientele and supply every member of the audience with a seat. James Burbage was a practical actor and he did not share this point of view. He knew that the penny public, with its willingness to stand long hours to see a production, was the backbone of the theatre business in England, and he was determined to keep his prices within the range of ordinary people.

The advantage of the innyard system was that it could accommodate these groundlings, who could pack themselves into the standing room in front of the scaffold and take up comparatively little space. The chief disadvantage of the innyard system was the extremely cramped and unsatisfactory working conditions backstage.

In solving this problem, there was one other model that Burbage could follow. Near the Thames on the other side of London Bridge were two amphitheatres in Southwark where the public went to see bearbaiting and bullbaiting. These buildings were circular, rather like the old Roman circuses, and built with curving tiers of upstairs seats. An actor was not, of course, a bear. But it might not be impossible to construct a stage that jutted out into the midst of the groundlings, with adequate backstage facilities for costuming and storage, while still keeping to the Bear Garden seating system.

A circular building would give much better visibility than could be achieved in a rectangular innyard. Moreover, the acoustics would be excellent, for the voices of the actors would be thrown back from the walls almost as though they were acting at the bottom of a padded well. It was a period when the lines spoken by the actors were much more important than the stage effects in building dramatic illusion in the minds of the audience, and people habitually spoke of "hearing" a play rather than of "seeing" it.

Burbage wanted his fellow actors to be seen, but even more he wanted every word they spoke to be heard clearly.

An amphitheatre with a jutting stage would not lend itself to intimate effects, but a smaller area behind that front stage could be curtained off and set with movable properties to be used as a bedroom or a cave or any similar scene. The height of the building would make it possible to stage the action of the play on more than one level, a feat that had already been achieved in the innyards by using the back galleries. But since the scaffolding itself did not have to be shared with carters, a much more intricate system of trap doors would be possible for the disappearance of devils and the convenience of gravediggers, and a sturdy contrivance of ropes and pulleys could be fastened to the roof to let down birds and goddesses and other aerial creatures.

A further advantage of the design was that admission money could be collected much more efficiently. The gatherer at the main door could collect the entrance penny, and anyone who could not pay more went and stood in the yard. A spectator who wished a seat went up the stairway and paid another gatherer there according to the location level he wanted. Moreover, the custom of eating and drinking during the performance, which the innyard public had come to expect as one of the pleasures of theatregoing, could be apportioned out on a concession system instead of letting the innkeeper get most of the profits.

Although an amphitheatre of this kind was open to the sky, all the seats would be protected from rain by the thatched roof under which they were built. The jutting stage was protected by a stage cover, a device rather like the sloping penthouse roofs that sheltered Elizabethan store fronts from the rain. The standees were the only ones who ran any danger of getting wet, but this had been equally true under the innyard system and by this time they must have been resigned to it.

James Burbage was doing an unheard-of thing in designing a building to be used primarily for plays, and a more cautious man would have planned a fairly small building since he could not be sure he was making a safe business investment. If such a thought passed through the mind of James Burbage, he rejected it, for Burbage was a born theatre man and caution was not one of his qualities. He planned his theatre big enough to house a crowd of Londoners on a holyday vacation, and he did not disturb himself with the thought that attendance on an ordinary working day was going to be very much less. James Burbage had no intention of turning away any potential customer for lack of room.

A building of this kind was of course expensive to erect, and it was going to cost a great deal more money than James Burbage had in the world. He signed a lease for the rental of the land on the 13th of April, 1576 (the month of Shakespeare's twelfth birthday), and then financed the payments by mortgaging the lease as soon as he had signed it. But this only paid for the rental of the land and did not bring in any money for the timber and nails and plaster and workmen's wages that somehow had to be financed.

Fortunately James Burbage had a sympathetic wife named Ellen, and Ellen had a brother named John Brayne who had prospered in the grocery business. John Brayne already had a slight connection with the theatre and he agreed to put some money into his brother-in-law's new scheme. This does not mean that James Burbage was an unusually persuasive man. There was no stock exchange in London to drain off the gambling instincts of the London merchants and they speculated informally in every project that was presented to them. Most of the great naval expeditions of the period were financed by London businessmen, eager to invest ten pounds and see fifty come back, and the great lottery that was held periodically in St. Paul's churchyard might almost serve as a symbol for the attitude of the whole of business London.

Burbage and Brayne between them shared the expense of building the theatre. Later on, the Brayne faction claimed that the venture had made him a poor man; he had poured all his savings into the building, selling even his stock of groceries, and eventually he and his wife had worked as common laborers to save the cost of two workmen's wages, while practically all that James Burbage had done was to profiteer on the lumber. This testimony came at a lawsuit after years of wrangling, and both sides were much more interested in injuring the opposition than in telling the truth. The truth seems to be that both men invested all they could, as a lawyer who worked for them both testified, and that Brayne put in most of the money because he had more to invest. Once the theatre was in operation he got an excellent return on his investment, and most of his financial difficulties arose from the fact that he subsequently went heavily into debt by building the George Inn in Whitechapel and starting a soapmaking business there.

The real trouble between the two men was not so much a matter of finances as of temperament. Burbage loved his theatre with the fierce, exclusive affection that a father might lavish on an only son, and it was impossible for him to admit to himself that Brayne had any proprietary rights in the beloved object. The two men quarreled frequently and finally went to a notary to set up a bond that they would refrain from fighting. Brayne started complaining in the notary's office about how much money he had spent and the hot-tempered Burbage struck him, with the result, as the notary reported sadly, that "they went together by the ears" and were with some difficulty finally parted.

When Brayne died in 1586, his widow carried on the feud with Burbage, and the climax came four years later in what might be called the war of the broomsticks. Margaret Brayne armed herself with a court order and some male assistance and went to install her own gatherer in the theatre that Burbage was convinced was his. Accompanying her was a friend named Robert Miles, his son Ralph, and a soapmaker named Nicholas Bishop who was to act as the gatherer. Ellen Burbage was the first to see the little procession and was quite undismayed by it. That redoubtable woman told them to leave at once or her son would break all their heads. James Burbage reinforced this information by putting his head out of one of the windows, improving on his wife's flow of fine Elizabethan invective, and adding that "if my son come he will thump you hence." At this point his son Cuthbert arrived, on cue as it were, and indulged in what the opposition called "great and horrible oaths," although Cuthbert maintained at the subsequent trial that neither he nor his father had threatened to beat Miles. The case was otherwise with Burbage's younger son, Richard, who at this point entered the fray. He seized a broomstick and fell upon Robert Miles, who was still clutching the court order, while Mrs. Burbage assisted him with enthusiasm. Nicholas Bishop, the soapmaker, ventured to suggest that Mrs. Brayne was within her legal rights and Richard Burbage threatened to beat him also, "scornfully and disdainfully playing with this deponent's nose" as Bishop later testified. Richard was evidently enjoying himself thoroughly, for when the first of the actors arrived to dress for the afternoon performance he found him still holding the broomstick and laughing. The Burbages were left in full possession of the field and their own gatherers remained in the theatre. Mrs. Brayne brought suit at once, and after a very careful and thorough investigation of the case had been made by two Masters in Chancery, James Burbage was given sole legal possession.

The Braynes were not the only source of trouble, for Burbage was also having a great deal of difficulty with the lease. He had mortgaged it to help finance the building of the theatre, and when the mortgage came due, Burbage had no money. He was faced with losing the lease and consequently his precious building with it, especially since the mortgage holder, John Hyde, was one of that predatory race of grocers and had already made plans to dispose of the mortgage elsewhere. At this time Burbage's elder son, Cuthbert, was in the service of a court official and the official's influence was used to persuade Hyde to let Cuthbert buy up the mortgage. Cuthbert had to borrow a great deal of money to make the payment, and this generous gesture toward his father put him in the theatre business for the rest of his life. Unlike his brother Richard, Cuthbert was not an actor, and he had apparently intended a non-theatrical life for himself. But since he owned the mortgage on his father's theatre, he also owned the lease, and for the rest of his long career he was an owner and operator of theatres as his brother's partner.

Apart from his financial problems, James Burbage had another source of trouble when he put up his theatre. There had always been a certain amount of opposition to the acting profession in London, and it crystallized when a whole building was put up with no other purpose but to give plays. The plaster was hardly dry on the walls of the theatre before the London preachers began to wail about the temple of sin that had been erected practically in their midst. Every current disaster that struck London, including the earthquake of 1580, could be traced to God's anger because this heathen development, with its glittering walls and rich costumes, had been allowed to flourish in the otherwise pure air of the city.

These pulpit attacks had a certain promotion value to a manager who was trying to fill a large theatre; for the London preachers depicted the sinful delights of that "gorgeous playing place," as they called it, with such fascinated horror that they must have supplied an excellent advertisement for the place. As the sober journal of Sir Roger Wilbraham indicates, the Elizabethan businessman was well aware of the value of this kind of publicity. Wilbraham tells the case of a printer at the turn of the century who found himself loaded with unsold copies of a certain book. "He caused a preacher in his sermon to inveigh against the vanity thereof; since which it hath been six times under press, so much it was in request."

On the other hand, it would be unsafe to underestimate the real fervor and conviction of these pulpit attacks or the effect they ultimately had upon the theatregoing population. The Reformation had done nothing to remove the medieval sense of sin; in fact, it had complicated the matter by putting more responsibility on the individual. An Anglican had more freedom in his search for salvation, but he also had more room to worry about possible failure; and the extreme Anglicans, who worried most about their own souls and those of their neighbors, were beginning to be called Puritans.

There were various sects of Puritans, including those who wished to purify the Church of England from the inside and those who wished another kind of state church entirely, but the distinguishing mark of any Puritan was his alarming sense of sin. In his diary he would even reproach himself for his "adulterous dreams," and his waking life was spent in a constant struggle to drown out the temptations of the flesh by hard work and prayer. Dancing was a very unsafe occupation for the godly, since it turned their thoughts in the wrong direction, and even music tended to incline the thoughts of its hearers "to all licentiousness." But nothing was better calculated to kindle the fire of inordinate lust in the tender minds of the young than to let them go to stage plays, and the Puritan opposition to the stage ultimately became implacable.

The Puritans were operating on a perfectly honest conviction. They firmly believed that "horrible enormities and swelling sins" were shown on the stage, with their glittering costumes and men dressed as women, and that the theatre as a whole was a sink of "pride and prodigality, villainy and blasphemy." To a Puritan, soberly intent upon the saving of his soul, there could hardly be a worse sin than to indulge carnal desire by going to see a play, and in time the Puritan movement gathered sufficient force to destroy the theatre of England entirely.

This Puritan attitude toward playgoing did not find much support in the people of London, but it had the full support of the London Council. The mayor and the aldermen were not at this time Puritans; but they were all businessmen who were sufficiently prosperous to be able to afford politics, and as businessmen they took a very unfavorable view of the acting profession. Actors did not sell a legitimate, visible commodity or sell it under the rules of any guild. Consequently they were parasites or, to use a favorite phrase of the period, caterpillars of the commonwealth, strutting about in fine clothes which they got by luring the pennies out of the pockets of simple-minded apprentices who should have been home working. It would even have been better for the apprentices if they had spent their money in taverns; for although the London Council did not necessarily encourage drinking, the taverners were at least selling a legitimate commodity and operating under legitimate rules. Actors, on the other hand, offered no legitimate commodity and really had no place in any well-ordered Christian society.

The opposition of the Puritans and of intense members of the clergy would have made no difference to a man like Burbage, but the opposition of the mayor and the aldermen was a serious matter. Two years before Burbage decided to build his theatre, the London Council put out a series of restrictions on actors, beginning with a stately preamble which pointed out that "the inordinate haunting of great multitudes of people, especially youths, to plays, enterludes, and shows" was very bad for the city. From that time forward no plays could be shown in an innyard unless the play had been licensed, the players had been licensed, the innyard had been approved, the owner of the inn had gone bond that order would be kept, and the actors had contributed a sum of money for the poor. The ordinance also stated that no performances were to be given on Sundays or holydays, thus removing the largest part of the potential audience at a single stroke.

The root of the difficulty was what the ordinance called the "unthrifty waste" of money that was spent in theatre admissions. The Council also had at the back of its mind a dislike of any arrangement that brought together large groups of people in a single area, where no one knew what seditious mischief might be plotted. The only time that any governing body in England could rest easy at seeing a large crowd of people gathered together was if they were listening to a sermon. There was a certain amount of justification for this point of view, since England was never free at this period from the threat of treasonous conspiracies and even the ultimate disaster of civil war. But it is likely that the Council would not have accused the innocent and patriotic contemporary theatre of encouraging "seditious matters, and many other corruptions of youth" if they did not have reason to dislike, from the business point of view, the thriving trade that the actors were conducting in the innyards.

The result of all this was that James Burbage was naturally very unwilling to erect his theatre in any district under the control of the London Council. The fields that lay northeast of the city walls were under the control of the London government, but just beyond them was a pocket of land that had once been the site of a monastery. These church lands had been taken from their owners at the time of the Reformation and had passed under the jurisdiction of the Crown. The city had no control over areas like these, which were called "liberties" and were a constant source of irritation to the mayor and the aldermen. But they were a great help to the acting profession, since the Crown approved of plays if the city did not; and it was therefore in the liberty of Holywell, east of Finsbury Fields, that Burbage decided to erect his theatre.

Like most of the suburban property around London, Holywell was something of a slum area. The land that Burbage arranged to lease from a prosperous gentleman named Giles Allen consisted of five tenements and a dilapidated barn that was being used for storage and as a slaughterhouse. Burbage had no intention of pulling down the barn, which he expected to remodel and rent to tenants. The location he planned for his theatre was an empty piece of ground surrounded on three sides by the barn, the horsepond, and the back garden of one of the tenements. On its fourth side his dream theatre would be flanked by a sewer, which would have to be bridged before the citizens of London could come across Finsbury Fields, with its windmills and its picnickers, to see the plays. Apparently unplagued by any doubts, Burbage went ahead with his elaborate plans and signed the lease. Forty pounds, the price of a whole house, was spent on the iron-work of the building alone, and Burbage probably did not lack friends who told him he was making a great and costly mistake.

It was true that the theatre was very far out of town for a casual afternoon's entertainment. Quite apart from the half-mile trip across the fields, a potential playgoer also had to cross most of London if he lived on the west side of town. It was much easier to get up a bowling match or go over to Southwark, outside the city's jurisdiction, to see the bearbaiting than it was to take the long trip to Holywell, no matter how much of a novelty the new theatre might be.

Nevertheless, Burbage was an actor of long experience and he knew Londoners. He was convinced that no amount of inconvenience would keep them from seeing a good show, and he was quite right. They came in droves, beating a path through the fields, crossing the ditch and pouring their pennies into the waiting hands of the gatherers. "Thither run the people thick and threefold," wailed the London preachers, mourning over their diminished congregations.

Burbage was of course fortunate in having erected his theatre in a prosperous time. Trade was good in London in the 1570's and 80's and the people were quite ready to spend their money. Moreover, the city was host to a great number of people who came up as tourists or on business from every county in England. Apart from the excellent shops, the great single magnet was the law courts that were held at Westminster four times a year. Nearly every adult in England either had a lawsuit pending at Westminster or was laying the foundations for one; and during each of the law terms, especially the autumn term of Michaelmas, the population of London swelled like a tidal flow of its own Thames. House-hunting in London was never easy at any time of year, for the city was chronically over-crowded; but it became nearly impossible at term time, and every householder on the west side of town could count on an excellent income by renting out spare rooms whenever court was being held at Westminster.

Moneyed visitors like these were a useful addition to Burbage's audience, but it was on the average Londoner that he really depended. Instead of making his theatre small and select and roofed in, with comfortable seats available for a few choice observers, he made it large and rather uncomfortable and available to everyone. The general admission price of one penny was the secret of Burbage's success and the success of the theatre owners that followed him. In the following century this broad base of a low general admisson was gradually destroyed. The theatres became increasingly comfortable and select and protected from the weather, and the entrance fee increased also. This was the end of the Elizabethan theatre and of the men who had worked in it, for it no longer could command the support of the ordinary middle-class London audience.

The nature of this Elizabethan audience has been much misrepresented, chiefly by nineteenth-century scholars, and among those that have been unjustly treated are the London apprentices. They have been pictured as a riotous, noisy group of young clods who, as groundlings, would only appreciate the broadest kind of ranting and horseplay, while their elders and betters in the higher-priced seats were smilingly able to appreciate the finer things that the theatre had to offer.

This point of view can be well documented, but the documentation comes from a rather prejudiced source. It was the London Council that was always viewing the youth of the city with the disapproval that an older generation usually feels for a younger one. It was the opinion of the Council that every young man should spend his time working very hard for an older one, and that any sign of independence or lack of subservience to an employer was a really serious offense. The ideal apprentice was a subservient young man who wore a wool cap and a dark coat and who kept his thoughts from silk embroidery and scarlet stockings and gold rings. He was not supposed to go to a music or dancing school, and some of his employers would have been equally pleased if he had not been allowed to go to plays. "Whosoever shall visit the chapel of Satan, I mean the Theatre, shall find there no want of young ruffians," innocent enough young lads who had become quite corrupted through seeing plays. "Many of nature honest and tractable have been altered by those shows and spectacles and become monstrous," and the Council united with the Puritans in agreeing that nothing could be worse for the morals of an apprentice than going to the theatre.

The apprentices themselves did not think so, and they flocked to the theatre. But a penny was a large sum of money to a boy who was learning a trade, and he expected good value for it. Moreover, standing places could not be reserved, and he had to arrive at the theatre early to be sure of a good location. From a complaint of the mayor's on the subject, it seems clear that the theatre began filling hours before the show started, and since the groundlings had to stand both during this period and through the whole action of the play, they demanded much more in the way of entertainment than the comfortable citizens in the seats overhead. If the groundlings felt they were being cheated, they were not slow to express themselves, and most of the contemptuous remarks about their mental incapacity came from the playwrights whose plays had not had a popular success.

As a matter of fact, the apprentices belonged as a class to one of the most privileged and intelligent groups in London. A landed gentleman did not hesitate to send his son up to London to learn to be a goldsmith or a draper, and in the ranks of the apprentices were all the future aldermen and mayors of London. Each of them was treated by his employer as a member of the household, and they belonged entirely outside the ranks of the unprotected, exploited laborers with whom London was unfortunately familiar. They were the future businessmen of London and their only crime was their youth and the fact that they loved the theatre.

Another section of the Elizabethan audience that has sometimes been misrepresented is the women. It was rather arbitrarily decided in the nineteenth century that women seldom went to plays in Elizabethan times. Occasionally a coarse tinker's wife might get in among the groundlings or a fine lady sheltered by a mask might be escorted to one of the expensive seats, but the London housewife stayed home and wove cloth and kept her house clean as a good woman should. This may have been the Victorian conception of womanhood, but it was certainly not shared by the Elizabethans.

From the first the reformers had centered their special attention on the women of London, since it was well known that few "women come from plays . . . with safe and chaste minds." One writer devoted a whole section "to the gentlewomen citizens of London" and besought them when they felt nervous and unhappy not to go to plays but to visit a neighbor or read a good book. Another writer tried to terrify them with tales of citizens' wives who sinned and then confessed on their death beds that it was the initial mistake of going to the theatre that had turned their thoughts from a contemplation of virtue and started them down the slippery path to perdition.

The citizens' wives paid no attention to all this advice, for the women of London had always done what they pleased and expected to go on doing it. England was known as "a paradise for women," and nearly every foreigner was startled by the amount of freedom they took as their right. "The womenfolk of England . . . have far more liberty than in other lands, and know just how to make good use of it." A gentleman from Kremzow noted that a throng of spectators had a great many women in it "for the womenfolk in England wish to be in at everything," and another foreigner noted it as "particularly curious" that women went into taverns alone or accompanied by other women. They evidently went without male companionship to the theatre also, for the mayor and aldermen spent a great deal of time worrying about the "inveighing and alluring of maids" at the playhouse by young gentlemen who passed them apples and hoped to escort them home when the play was over. "They give them pippins . . . they minister talk upon all occasions, and either bring them home to their houses on small acquaintance or slip into taverns when the plays are done." Sometimes this inveighing and alluring was done ahead of time, and, when John Florio wrote a conversation book in English and Italian, he included under advice on how "to speak to a damsel" a useful sentence on how to invite her to go to the theatre to see a comedy.

The playwrights themselves were very well aware that a large part of the success of a play depended on the approval of the women. There was always an epilogue spoken at the end of the show, with a request for applause, and although very few of the epilogues of Shakespeare's plays have survived, three of them are addressed to the women in the audience. For

if they smile
And say 'twill do

the play would be a success.

Fortunately for the freedom of the playwrights, the London women took a great deal of pleasure in what would now be called vaudeville jokes. A girl like Shakespeare's Rosalind took a lively interest in the subject of sex, which she considered both funny and enjoyable, and so did his Beatrice and his Portia. To that extent they are echoes of the women in Shakespeare's audience who sat and laughed comfortably at dirty jokes. An Englishman who was traveling in Germany recorded in honest amazement how a mildly off-color joke was received in a Nuremberg

inn: "I observed the women to blush, and the men also to look one upon another, as if those words were flat bawdry." He noted that in Germany "the modesty of the women is singular, and the like nowhere found." Certainly he had found nothing like it in London.

One reformer of the day rather contemptuously described the average theatre audience as "but an assembly of tailors, tinkers, cordwainers, sailors, old men, young men, women, boys, girls, and such like," and there is no doubt that it was a mixed audience of "all sorts, young and old," from carters to noblemen, that poured across Finsbury Fields whenever the playing flag of James Burbage's new theatre was hoisted. The businessmen of London were not slow to realize that the building of theatres was going to be a very profitable investment, and within the year a new theatre was built on the other side of Holywell Lane in what had once been the Prioress' pasture. This second theatre was called the Curtain, and in 1585 its owner, Henry Laneman, entered into a seven-year agreement with James Burbage to run the two theatres as a joint undertaking and pool the profits.

Meanwhile another theatre had been erected in the village of Newington, a mile from London Bridge on the other side of the Thames. The theatre of Newington Butts was never completely successful, since it was beyond Southwark and too far out of town for any but the most determined theatregoer. But in 1587 an expensive theatre was put up in Southwark itself and lavishly redecorated five years later. This theatre was called the Rose and it helped make its owner, Philip Henslowe, a wealthy man. Another Londoner, Francis Langley, also invested in Southwark real estate with the idea of putting up a theatre, and in 1595 he finished the Swan, which was handsomer even than the Rose. When a Dutch priest visited London the following summer, he reported that all four theatres, Burbage's, Laneman's, Henslowe's, and Langley's, were buildings of "notable beauty," but he felt that the largest and most magnificent "is the one of which the sign is a swan . . . for it accommodates in its seats three thousand persons."

Competition was a healthy thing for the London theatres, and the great thatched amphitheatres flourished and grew strong. In Paris the single indoor hall that was used for plays was operating under a government monopoly that prevented any competition, and when Paris finally built its second public playhouse, London was building its seventeenth.

These London builders were shrewd men who knew a good business investment when they saw it, but none was a real theatre man in the sense that James Burbage was and remained. Francis Langley was a goldsmith and a member of the Drapers' Company, and Philip Henslowe was a dyer by trade.

Henslowe was a typical Elizabethan businessman and promoter, and he was no more interested in the theatre business than he was in the starch business or, later on, in bearbaiting. He was agent for two of the most important acting companies of the period and spent a great deal of time with actors and playwrights, financing them and giving them assignments and occasionally bailing them out; and Henslowe's son-in-law, Edward Alleyn, was one of the most brilliant actors of the day. But Henslowe was chiefly in the business to make money, and he was never a theatre man in the almost violently dedicated sense that James Burbage understood the meaning of the word.

For twenty years James Burbage warred for his theatre, protecting it from the encroachments of creditors and mortgage-holders and the London Council and anything else that threatened the object of his tempestuous devotion. His building was called simply the "Theatre," and to James Burbage it was the one really important structure in England.

His two sons, Cuthbert and Richard, carried on their father's tradition and like him they were men of the theatre. Richard was the most famous actor of his day and gave the stage thirty-five years of his devotion, and his brother remained his faithful business partner and loyal friend. It was a record of which their father would have thoroughly approved.

These were the two men with whom William Shakespeare was associated during almost the whole of his career on the London stage. From 1594 to 1610, at the very least, Shakespeare was the active working partner of Richard and Cuthbert Burbage. He had part ownership of the theatres they built, and it was Richard Burbage who acted the leading roles in *Hamlet* and *Othello* and *King Lear*. Shakespeare saw these men daily, until in time they were as familiar to him as his own brothers; and it was his great good fortune that they were not business speculators like Henslowe but devoted, professional men of the theatre.

Chapter 3

When James Burbage signed the lease for his theatre, William Shakespeare was the eldest boy in a fairly large family of children. His ten-year-old brother, Gilbert, had been followed by a seven-year-old sister, named Joan after the little girl who had died. Next came Anne, now five years old, and a little boy named Richard, who was two.

John Shakespeare was a prosperous man, as well as the head of a large family, and when William was eleven years old, his father took steps to enlarge his Henley Street property. The house in which the Shakespeare family was living on Henley Street was one of a block of three buildings of which John Shakespeare owned the one to the east. In October of 1575 he bought two houses from Edmund and Emma Hall, complete with gardens and orchards, and paid forty pounds for them. The location of the two houses is not identified in the sale itself, but it must have been the two remaining houses of the block of three on Henley Street, since all three are known to have passed into John Shakespeare's hands.

Shakespeare rented the west house to a tenant, but he combined the middle one with his own residence by interior doorways, and it was evidently here that the last of his children, Edmund, was born five years later. This middle house remained in the family for a long time, and it is probably on this account that it was later believed to have been the birthplace of William Shakespeare. But if Shakespeare was born on Henley Street, it must have been in the east house, for John Shakespeare did not own the other two buildings when his eldest son was born.

Through this purchase John Shakespeare took his place as one of the prominent landholders of Stratford, and on a list of thirty-eight "freeholders" of the town his name stands sixth. But the son of a tenant farmer had greater ambitions than this. He wanted to belong to the gentry and the only way to achieve this was to be granted a coat of arms by the Office of Heralds in London.

John Shakespeare's desire to rise in the world was typically Elizabethan. He and his fellows had inherited from the Middle Ages the theory of "degrees," which meant that everyone was tucked into a definite social class; and Archbishop Whitgift was expressing the orthodox view of the period when he stated in a speech, "Equality of persons engendreth strife, which is the cause of all evil." Each Elizabethan was supposed to remain contentedly in the class for which heaven had designed him, but each Elizabethan interpreted this rule as applying to his neighbor rather than to himself. There was a scramble to leave one level of "degree" and rise to the next, and the determination of the lower classes to belong to the gentry and of the gentry to belong to the nobility was an aspect of the period that reformers viewed with special alarm. The College of Heralds did not object to it, however, since it brought them a great many fees.

John Shakespeare had a better right than many to apply for a coat of arms. He had married a daughter of the Ardens, and whatever her exact connection with the family the name was a magic one in Warwickshire. Even more to the point, he had been High Bailiff of Stratford and a justice of the peace, and this was one of the "divers offices of dignity and worship" that made a man automatically eligible for a coat of arms if he could afford to pay the fees that the Heralds demanded. John Shakespeare was obviously a prosperous man if he could afford to buy two houses; and a year after this purchase, in 1576, he sent in his application to the Office of Heralds. It was evidently considered acceptable, for Robert Cooke, King at Arms, sketched out a preliminary design for him.*

It was at this point in John Shakespeare's career, when everything seemed to be going so well for him, that something suddenly went very wrong. He attended the meeting of the Stratford Council in the normal way on September 5, 1576, as he had been doing for the past thirteen years. Since his election to the Council he had been absent on only a single occasion, and in the past eleven years he had never been absent at all. But at the meeting of the Council in the following January, John Shakespeare was absent. He was absent at the next meeting, and the one after

* The Office of Heralds stated in 1596 that Cooke made this design "in paper twenty years past" which would put the date of John Shakespeare's application in 1576, when William Shakespeare was twelve years old. The accuracy of this date has been questioned, since the Heralds' memorandum goes on to state that John Shakespeare was Bailiff "fifteen or sixteen years past," which is obviously incorrect. But the Office of Heralds would be likely to date the business routine of their own office correctly, even if they did not put down correct dates for the internal affairs of Stratford.—Author's Note

that, and in fact he never returned again as a regular member. For the rest of his life he only attended one meeting of the Council, and for five years he broke completely with the official governing body of Stratford after more than a decade of devoted, loyal attendance.

What happened to John Shakespeare at this point to make him abandon public life so suddenly and so completely will have to remain a mystery. No evidence survives to show why he left a position that he had filled worthily and that had evidently given him much happiness. It has been suggested that he suddenly became a convert to either Catholicism or Puritanism, but there would have been nothing in this to prevent his attending the regular meetings of the Council. The objection to recusants was a Crown matter rather than a local one; and the Stratford Council had both its sturdy Catholics like George Badger and George Whateley and its equally sturdy Puritans like Nicholas Barnhurst. Barnhurst was eventually "expulsed" from the Council, but for his bad behavior and not for his religious convictions. It has also been suggested that John Shakespeare suffered financial embarrassment, and it is quite true that he was less prosperous after this date than he was before. But he was never a poor man and he never had to part with the three houses he owned on Henley Street. Nor would it have cost him any money to take the short walk down Chapel Street to attend the Council meetings; the reverse would rather have been true if his fellow members had followed the usual procedure and fined him for nonattendance.

Whatever John Shakespeare's reason may have been, it did not seem a conclusive one to the other members of the Council, and they kept on hoping he would return. At every meeting from that time forward his name appears on the records, although on only one occasion, the fifth of September, 1582, was there a prick after his name to show attendance. In 1586 the members of the Council finally chose another alderman to fill his place, because Mr. Shakespeare "doth not come," but they evidently did it reluctantly. A further evidence of their regard for him is shown by the fact that an alderman was normally fined if he stayed away from meetings, and during these ten years of absence John Shakespeare was never fined.

The best guess perhaps is that sometime in the autumn or early winter of 1576 John Shakespeare suffered some sense of personal disgrace that made it impossible for him to show himself at the meetings of the Council. As for the coat of arms he had wanted, it did not come to him. He went on being plain Mr. Shakespeare instead of John Shakespeare, gentleman, and Cooke's design with its spear and its falcon crest went back into the files of the London office of the College of Heralds.

The darkening of John Shakespeare's life at this point is all the more noticeable in contrast to the increasing brilliance of Adrian Quiney's. The Shakespeares and the Quineys had known each other since the days when old Richard Quiney had been an acquaintance of Richard Shakespeare of Snitterfield, and when John Shakespeare came to live on Henley Street, Adrian Quiney was one of his close neighbors. It was together they paid a fine of twelvepence in 1552 for having an unauthorized muckheap near their houses.

Adrian Quiney was older than his friend and had started his political climb in Stratford earlier. He was High Bailiff the year John was made affeeror, and the year that John himself was elected Bailiff, Adrian Quiney went up with him to London on borough business, their trip being financed for them by the Stratford Council. When Adrian Quiney again became Bailiff in 1571, John Shakespeare was Chief Alderman and therefore his assistant; and the following January the two men again went to London, to represent Stratford in the law courts during Hilary term. The two friends evidently worked harmoniously together and for a time their careers were almost parallel.

When John Shakespeare applied for his coat of arms, Adrian Quiney was already a member of the gentry. His coat of arms consisted of a shield of gold with a hand grasping a sword, and by 1574 he was appearing in the Council records as Adrian Quiney, gentleman.

Adrian Quiney had another possession that was even more desirable than a coat of arms: he had a son who was following in his father's footsteps both in business and in politics. Young Richard Quiney was a mercer, like his father before him, and he had the unusual distinction of being appointed a Principal Burgess when he was still in his early twenties.

Richard Quiney must have been in all respects a thoroughly satisfactory son. He had evidently been a good boy at school, applying himself diligently to his studies, for he read Latin easily and for pleasure and took Tully's *Epistles* on a journey with him for relaxation. Even his marriage was impeccable, for his bride was Elizabeth Phillips, of a prominent Stratford family, and he married her the same year he became a Principal Burgess.

During the next dozen years, young Richard Quiney's career advanced steadily. He was elected to the office of chamberlain in 1586, at the same meeting in which the Council was reluctantly obliged to deprive John Shakespeare of his alderman's gown. He was elected alderman in 1588, over the heads of four senior members of the Council, the same year in which John Shakespeare was facing failure in a bitter lawsuit over land with one of his wife's relatives. And in September 1592 he was made High Bailiff of Stratford, with his proud father casting one of the many votes that swept him into office, during the same month in which John Shakespeare's son was being publicly attacked in a London pamphlet as an upstart actor who was trying to become a playwright.

Even back in 1582, when William Shakespeare was only eighteen, it seemed clear that the Quineys were advancing to a much more stable position in the community than the Shakespeares could now hope to attain. On the 27th of November, 1582, Richard Quiney attended the baptism of his first child, with his father, High Bailiff for that year, undoubtedly in attendance; and on that same 27th of November William Shakespeare's marriage license was being issued in Worcester. Young Shakespeare had not chosen his bride with any of the wisdom that Richard Quiney had shown two years earlier. Not only was Shakespeare a minor and in no position to assume the support of a family, but his bride was eight years older than he was and the child was born six months after the wedding.

Young Shakespeare's marriage may have been ill-advised, but there is no special reason to believe that his fellow townsmen considered it scandalous. Anne Hathaway came of an almost stiffly respectable background, and it is not likely that a woman of twenty-six found herself caught in a casual liaison and had to demand marriage to protect herself. Nor is it necessary to believe that she trapped an impressionable young man into marriage by seducing him. A more probable explanation is that they had what was known as a precontract and that Anne Hathaway felt free to behave as a married woman before the actual ceremony.

A precontract was taken very seriously by Elizabethan church law and was nearly as binding as the actual ceremony. If Shakespeare had a precontract with Anne and then had married someone else, his marriage would have been in a sense bigamous and could have been declared void by the Ecclesiastical Court; and if he had refused to marry after a precontract, he could have been excommunicated. Shakespeare's aunt, Agnes Arden, evidently had a precontract with her future husband, for when Robert Arden made his will in July, he spoke of her as the wife of Thomas Stringer, and Agnes did not actually marry Thomas Stringer until the following October.

Anne Hathaway's own father died a year before her marriage but he left her a marriage portion in his will. Old Richard Hathaway was a landowner in Shottery, one of the small hamlets inside the parish of Stratford, and he left most of the land to his eldest son Bartholomew with the request that he should be "a comfort unto his brethren and sisters." There was a mother-in-law in the Hathaway household, as there had been in the Arden one, and Richard Hathaway's will, like Robert Arden's, specifically requested a quiet distribution of the property. Anne was his eldest daughter by his first marriage and twenty-five years old when her father made his will.* Her brother Bartholomew married almost immediately after his father's death, and within the following year Anne was married also.

The normal way to get married in Stratford parish was to have the banns proclaimed three separate Sundays or holydays in the church, so that if there were any objections to the marriage, they could be brought forward. If for any reason the banns could not be published, the only alternative was to get a special license from the episcopal court at Worcester and have someone post a bond to indemnify the court if any objections to the marriage were made later. In the case of Shakespeare's marriage this bond was posted by two Shottery farmers named John Richardson and Fulke Sandells. Both men had been friends of Anne's father, but the posting of the bond was a normal part of the arrangement and involved no special gesture of friendship on the part of the two men. At this same time, for instance, Christopher Marlowe's father in Canterbury was acting as professional bondsman for couples who needed a license to get married. The year

Shakespeare was married there were an unusual number of these bonded marriage licenses in the Worcester Consistory Court, and the following year they reached record proportions. This was the year in which Dr. Whitgift, Bishop of Worcester, became Archbishop of Canterbury, and no man could have been more careful than he in seeing that his diocese of Worcester was obeying all the rules.

Marriages of this kind were an extra expense, but there were various reasons why the banns could not be published and a special license was required. As a bishop remarked at the end of the century: "License to marry according to the form set down without banns, are no cause to disordered marriage, but rather the contrary." An allegation normally accompanied the request for a license, explaining why the banns could not be published, but none of these allegations is extant for Worcester diocese before 1600, and the one Shakespeare entered has been lost with the rest. In his case the most probable reason why the banns could not be published was that the decision to marry was sudden and there was not time to post the banns before Advent. Between Advent and the octave of the Epiphany was a period known as "prohibited season" during which no marriages could take place, and unless William Shakespeare and Anne Hathaway wanted to wait until the middle of January the only alternative was to go to the expense of a license.

* Anne's name does not appear on the Registry of Baptism in Stratford because it was begun in 1558 after she was born. But the brass inscription on her grave says she "departed this life the 6th day of August, 1623, being of the age of 67 years."—Author's Note

The regular form was used and Dr. Cosin handled the matter in Worcester Consistory Court as part of the ordinary routine of what happened to be an extremely busy day. The clerk made an error, as clerks sometimes do, and wrote down the bride's name as "Whateley," but her name appears with reasonable correctness in the bond, where Shakespeare's name is spelled "Shagspere." * It is not known in what church the marriage took place, except that it was somewhere in Worcester diocese, which included part of Warwickshire, and that it was not in the parish church of the Holy Trinity in Stratford.

John Shakespeare gave his consent to the marriage, since otherwise the license would not have been issued. A minor could not have been married in Dr. Whitgift's diocese unless the father or guardian had given his approval. But John Shakespeare might have felt justified in disapproving of his

son's marriage or at least feeling doubtful of its wisdom. When Richard Quiney had married, he was twenty-three, with a position in the Council and an interest in his father's business. William Shakespeare was only eighteen and had apparently not settled down to any business at all.

It was the custom in Stratford for the eldest son to bring his bride back to his father's house. Richard and Elizabeth Quiney had followed this custom, and it is likely that William and Anne Shakespeare did the same. His father's property was especially suited to house an extra family, for the middle house had a wing at the back which had its own private entryway, back parlor, and kitchen, with its own stairway leading to the second floor.

It was probably in the middle house that the child was born in the following May. It was not the son for whom John Shakespeare must have been hoping. It was a little girl, and on Trinity Sunday, 1583, she was christened Susanna.

When William Shakespeare's little girl was baptized on the 26th of May, she was the third child that spring who had been given the name of Susanna. It was not a familiar name in Stratford but it was one much favored by the Puritans, following the definite Puritan prescription that children should be given Scriptural names.

It is not surprising that Anne Shakespeare's daughter was given a Puritan name. When Anne's father, Richard Hathaway, made

* In Elizabethan times spelling was still a matter of individual preference rather than rules, and surnames were still being treated almost as casually as they had been in the Middle Ages. One of the Court records under King James gives Shakespeare's name as "Shaxberd," and Christopher Marlowe's name was frequently spelled "Morley" or "Marley." The mistake in Anne Hathaway's name is, however, an outright clerical error as far as can be ascertained. Mistakes of this kind were not unusual, since the year after Shakespeare's marriage the name of a bridegroom was written in the bond as "Robert Bradeley" and on the bishop's register as "Robert Darby."—AUTHOR'S NOTE

his will, he had asked to be "honestly buried," which was a Puritan phrase. Anne's brother Bartholomew was a churchwarden, and all his sons were churchwardens after him. When Bartholomew died, he also requested a Puritan burial, "hoping to arise at the Latter Day and to receive the reward of His elect."

If Anne Hathaway had been brought up as a Puritan, that fact alone would constitute a full explanation of the estrangement that evidently arose a few years later between herself and her husband. There were doubtless many people in Stratford who were at least mildly shocked to hear that the son of a reputable man like John Shakespeare had gone into the acting profession, for many people felt that acting was respectable only when it was done by amateurs who spoke in Latin and that professional actors were little more than tinseled vagabonds. This casual contempt for actors was not shared by the Puritans, who attacked the actors as an actual threat to salvation. It was well known that through their plays they persuaded men and women to sin, and even a visitation of the plague could be explained as God's anger against the people for letting so great an evil as theatres exist in their midst.*

It would perhaps be exaggerating to say that it was a tragedy for a Puritan to be married to an actor; but it is not exaggerating to say that it created an insupportable household situation.

If the situation in the Shakespeare household had been normal, Anne Shakespeare would certainly have followed her husband to London once he became permanently settled in his acting career. Shakespeare belonged to one of the great resident London companies, and except for the yearly tours of the provinces he spent all his working time in London. But unlike the other actors in his company he had no wife and family in London, and for nearly twenty years he lived there in hired lodgings.

An actor's wife in Elizabethan times could be a great help to her husband in his profession. Although there was no actors' guild, the actors used the same system as other business and professional men in London, and each of them took a boy into his home to be trained in what was a difficult and exacting art in the Elizabethan period. It was an important part of the apprentice system that the boy should be treated as an actual member of the family, and there is still extant

* The language of some of these tracts is almost unbelievable in its violence. When Shakespeare was twenty-three, a book was published in London which described actors as "fiends that are crept into the world by stealth," "sent from their great captain Satan (under whose banner they bear arms) to deceive the world, to lead the people with enticing shows to the Devil." The author also describes them as apes, hell hounds, vipers, minotaurs, painted sepulchers, dogs, and of course caterpillars, and his book is most suitably entitled *A Mirror of Monsters.*—AUTHOR'S NOTE

a loving tribute to Mrs. Henry Condell and Mrs. Cuthbert Burbage from a boy who had worked with the company. Nearly all the actors in Shakespeare's company were settled householders, with competent wives and a large number of children, and the only exceptions were two or three men who never married, and William Shakespeare.

If Anne Shakespeare was a Puritan, she could never have brought herself to go to London and help her husband in his profession. The acting profession, which seemed so normal and natural to Elizabeth Condell or Winifred Burbage, would have been to her one of the snares of Satan. As one anxious reformer put it, actors were "crocodiles which devour the pure chastity both of single and married persons. . . . In their plays you shall learn all things that appertain to craft, mischief, deceits, and filthiness." The actors answered these attacks by parodying the Puritans on the stage and laughing at them, but to the Puritans themselves the situation was no laughing matter.

The break between Anne and William Shakespeare evidently occurred within three or four years of his marriage, probably coinciding with his decision to go on the stage. Two years after Susanna was born, Anne gave birth to twins, a boy and a girl, who were christened on the second of February, 1585, by Richard Barton, the "learned, zealous, and godly" new vicar. The twins were named Hamnet and Judith, almost certainly after friends of the Shakespeares, Hamnet and Judith Sadler of High Street. After that there were no more children and it seems probable that within the next year or two William Shakespeare had left Stratford and gone to London.

In a general way it might be said that Shakespeare's reason for leaving Stratford was the same as his father's reason for having left Snitterfield: the place was too small for him. The same thing was happening all over England, with the young men leaving the villages for the towns and the towns for the great city of London. When a widow of Stratford wrote Adrian Quiney, asking him to find a position in London for her twenty-year-old son, she said frankly, "I can get no place for him in the country." London was already so overcrowded and the smaller towns so "decayed" that the Privy Council passed measure after measure in an attempt to reverse the process. But the great city on the Thames remained the magnet that drew every hopeful and ambitious young man in England, and London's own mayors and aldermen had mostly been born in the provinces.

What was true of the ordinary professions was even more true of aspects of the luxury trade like writing or acting or publishing. A tanner named Henry Field was a neighbor of Shakespeare's, and one of his eight sons wanted to be a printer. Young Richard Field happened to be the same age as William Shakespeare, but he decided much earlier what he wanted to do; at fifteen he knew he wanted to be a printer. There were no printing presses at Stratford. There were none anywhere in England, except the fifty-three in London and one each, carefully licensed, at Oxford and Cambridge. So Richard Field went to London, apprenticed by his father to a brilliant and scholarly Flemish printer named Thomas Vautrollier. Within ten years Richard Field had married his master's widow and owned the business. Within thirteen years he was able to send back to Stratford for his younger brother Jasper to come up and be his apprentice, and that same year he was the printer and publisher of William Shakespeare's first book of narrative verse. Nothing of the sort would have happened to either Field or Shakespeare unless both of them had been living in London.

It would be pleasant to be able to report that William Shakespeare arrived in London in 1588. A series of books had been announcing that 1588 was going to be a year of special importance, a prediction that the London citizens felt was amply fulfilled by the great naval victory that year over the Spanish Armada. It would have been a graceful contribution on the part of the Muse of History if this had also been the date in which young William Shakespeare first set foot in the city, but the actual date is unknown. All that is known is that Shakespeare was established as a successful actor on the London stage by 1592, and since he was in a difficult and highly competitive profession, he must have entered it several years earlier.

Shakespeare came to London at a fortunate time. If he had been born twenty years earlier, he would have arrived in London when underpaid hacks were turning out childish dramas about brown-paper dragons. If he had been born twenty years later, he would have arrived when the drama had begun to lose its hold on ordinary people and was succumbing to a kind of self-conscious cleverness. But his arrival in London coincided with a great wave of excitement and achievement in the theatre and he rode with it to its crest. William Shakespeare brought great gifts to London, but the city was waiting with gifts of its own to offer him. The root of his genius was Shakespeare's own, but it was London that supplied him with the favoring weather.

�✗ Chapter 4

When William Shakespeare came to London in the eighties, it was still in many ways the medieval city that Geoffrey Chaucer had known. The wall that surrounded the city was still intact, and the only concession the authorities had made to the increased traffic was to open a new gate, called Moorgate, which gave access to the fields to the north. The old monastic foundations had been changed into residences and tennis courts and even into factories, and the beautiful little chapel on London Bridge had become a warehouse, but London was still a city of churches and they dominated the lives of its inhabitants. The service at St. Paul's Cathedral was now given in English, but the building was much as it had been except that its wooden spire had vanished. It had caught fire some twenty years earlier and so many citizens had gathered to watch the blaze and hamper the fire fighters that the famous steeple had burned down to its square stone base. In spite of much talk and several schemes to raise money, the steeple was never rebuilt; but the broad stone base (admission one penny) was a magnet for every tourist in town, who did not leave until he had climbed the crooked winding stairs for a view of the city from the top and who carved his initials in the leads to show he had been there.

The one really new public building in London was the Royal Exchange, which had been erected to save merchants from the inconvenience of having to do business out-of-doors in Lombard Street during the bad weather. Its builder, Sir Thomas Gresham, was as much an optimist as James Burbage, and he made the building very large with a hundred small shops in its upper corridors. At first the shops remained empty, and Gresham frantically offered them rent free to any merchants who would keep them lighted and full of goods; but the city was growing so rapidly that within the decade Gresham could ask a rent of four pounds a year for each of the little shops and they were full of apothecaries and goldsmiths and sellers of books, armor, and glassware.

In every way the tight little medieval city that Chaucer had known was pushing against its confining walls under the pressure of an expanding and increasingly excitable population. The fall of Antwerp had made London a substitute commercial center and the religious wars on the Continent had doubled the foreign population of London in thirteen years. The town historian, John Stow, watched with dismay as he saw the little farm where he had gone as a boy to fetch milk swallowed up in the creeping spread into the suburbs, and the government fought hard to keep the population within bounds by outlawing new buildings and prohibiting the subdivision of old ones. Every few years the government brought out another ordinance on the subject and the penalties were strict; the builder of a new tenement in the crowded suburb of Shoreditch, for instance, was fined twenty pounds and his tenants were allowed to use the building rent free for the rest of their lives. But in spite of the efforts of the courts, the people went on packing themselves into the overcrowded city, adding to what the citizen of a smaller town bitterly called that "vast, unwieldy, and disorderly Babel of buildings which the world calls London."

Meanwhile the city government went on gallantly trying to enforce a medieval code of behavior that had been nearly obsolete in Chaucer's day and was now little more than a wistful ideal. The mayor and the aldermen clung to the conviction that if enough laws were passed it would somehow be possible to turn their sprawling young giant of a city into something small, neat, compact, and conformable. They observed with horror the flouting of their authority in the suburbs, where men like James Burbage put up buildings that had no place at all in a Christian commonwealth, and they still struggled to keep the city in a state of mind of which their great-grandfathers would have approved.

The mayor and aldermen were heavily handicapped in this attempt by the fact they got no support at all from Queen Elizabeth. When a bill to restrict Sunday pastimes was passed by both houses of Parliament in 1585, it was promptly vetoed by the Queen, who herself went to shooting matches and plays on Sunday and saw no reason why her subjects should not do likewise. It was her opinion that no amount of ordinances would keep a Londoner from enjoying himself, and that the wisest course to pursue was to make a government profit on the money

he spent. She gave a patent for licensing gaming houses to Thomas Cornwallis in 1576, in spite of a strict law against gaming in London, and justified it with the statement that the Londoners "secretly or openly . . . do commonly play and . . . no penalty of the laws or statutes aforesaid hath heretofore restrained them." On the same basis she gave licenses for bowling alleys and the manufacture of dice and playing cards; and the fencing clubs and theatre owners could always turn to the Queen for protection when the attacks of the city fathers became especially violent. Elizabeth was a true child of the Renaissance, in this matter at least, and her attitude was one that the mayor and aldermen were incapable of understanding.

The truth was that the city authorities were trying to maintain medieval standards in a city that was no longer medieval in spirit. A new spirit of curiosity had developed, an intellectual ferment that made the old ideal of blind obedience almost impossible to enforce. London no longer lived in comparative isolation but was beginning to feel all the influences of Renaissance Europe. Above all, it felt the stirring of new winds from Italy. To the average Londoner, Italy was still the place of strange poisons and passionate love affairs, to be mistrusted as the home of the wicked Machiavelli; but English architects traveled in Italy and brought back new designs, English sportsmen did their riding and fencing in the

Italian manner, and when a poet wrote love songs he imitated Petrarch. There was a fury of translation from the Italian of novels and plays and poems, and the brilliant Italian actors penetrated England and flourished for at least a season in London.

The people of England, and especially of London, still took a rather provincial view of foreigners. Visitors from the Continent spoke with some bitterness of the self-satisfaction of the English, whose highest praise for any foreigner was that it was a pity he was not an Englishman. A popular English book frankly set out to describe "the misery of Flanders, the calamity of France, misfortune of Portugal, unquietness of Ireland, troubles of Scotland, and the blessed state of England." It was impossible for an Englishman not to feel superior to any foreigner but he was never really rude to him. He did not need to be. As one Englishman put it, "The English, contrary to the custom of all nations, give the higher place and way to women . . . out of a noble mind to give honor and support to weakness, so give they like respect to strangers."

An Englishman knew his own country was the center of the world, but he felt a deep interest in knowing how the men of lesser nations lived. Nearly every young man of birth took a tour abroad, and this was also the era of the great explorations, when boys from small English villages came back from long voyages financed by London merchants to tell of the outlandish wonders they had seen. Occasionally these wonders could be seen in London itself, like the gloomy Indians, in brown taffeta, that Walter Raleigh brought back with him. Londoners like Richard Garth and William Cope started collections of instructive curios from other lands, and in Mr. Cope's collection the respectful visitor could see costumes from Java and Arabia, African charms, porcelain from China, and a long, narrow Indian canoe hung from the ceiling, to say nothing of such special wonders as an embalmed child, a unicorn's tail, and some little flies "which glow at night in Virginia instead of lights, since there is often no day there for over a month." Some Londoners may have doubted this description of Virginia, but no one would have doubted the unicorn, except what one expert on natural history called a "vulgar sort of infidel people" who believed only in cows and sheep. Unicorns were mentioned even in the Bible and it was well known that the horn of the animal, pulverized and boiled in wine, made an excellent mouthwash.

The gardens of the Londoners echoed their interest in other parts of the world, and a prominent London surgeon like John Gerarde was able to grow tomatoes from Spain, nasturtiums from the Indies, and tiger lilies from Constantinople. His ginger plants from Barbary were winterkilled, his cotton frosted, and he accidentally murdered his Dalmatian iris by pouring cold well water on them; but his tobacco and potatoes throve and he succeeded in producing recognizable ears on what he called Turkey corn.

Since London was a great port city and deeply involved in international trading, it was a vital business matter for its citizens to know as much about foreign nations as possible. London had its teachers of almost any foreign language that could be named—Arabic, Dutch, Polish, Turkish, or Russian—and a whole colony had arrived from abroad to teach French. They charged a shilling a week and gave a good basic training in colloquial French and pronunciation, concentrating on spoken French rather than on rules of grammar. The emphasis was on business phrases, like weights and measures; but other useful aspects of the language were not forgotten, and the beginner learned to say, "Take me about the neck," "You tickle me," and "Do not meddle with her, for she is very ticklish."

This sort of thing was really an effort to supply the deficiencies of a grammar school education, which made no attempt to teach anything but Latin and assumed for all practical purposes that the modern world did not exist. There were also special lectures at Leadenhall in some of the mathematical sciences, which included astronomy, geography, and the art of navigation, but the most determined single attempt at adult education was made by Sir Thomas Gresham, builder of the Royal Exchange. Gresham founded a London college to teach law, medicine, geometry, rhetoric, and other important subjects, and he specified that the lectures were to be given in English as well as in Latin since "merchants and other citizens" would be in the audience. Emphasis was laid on the practical side of the subject, and the professor of music, for instance, was to give half the period to the theory of music and the rest to practical application, using voice and instruments. Cambridge was shocked by what it considered a misuse of money by one of its own graduates and sent Gresham a long Latin letter on the subject, although Cambridge itself did not teach subjects like music and astronomy and had no intention of beginning. When Shakespeare came to London, Gresham College was not yet in operation, but only because Gresham's widow was still inhabiting the mansion on Bishopsgate Street.

In any case, the greatest source of education to the average Londoner was not museums or language teachers or college endowments. His greatest source of education was books. It was the invention of printing that set the one deep gulf between the Middle Ages and the Renaissance, and the difference between Chaucer's audience and Shakespeare's was the difference between a period when a book was a rich man's toy and a period when it was available to the whole of the middle class.

The average Londoner did not

look upon a book primarily as entertainment for an idle hour. The purpose of reading was to tell him something he wanted to know, and books poured from the presses to tell him how to keep accounts, how to survey land, how to play the cittern without a teacher, how to take spots off velvet, or cook, or ride, or write a good hand. There was information on how to graft plants, how to compute interest, and what to do "when the physician is not present," and there were cookbooks and dream books and books on the art of navigation for amateur mariners.

Elizabethan London was the home of the short cut, with each of its inhabitants wanting to know as much as possible as quickly as he could. Not for him was the slow, laborious grounding in the classics and rhetoric on which Oxford and Cambridge spent so much time. He could buy a book of classical quotations, conveniently arranged under subject matter, to be used whenever he needed them, and to improve his vocabulary there were books that offered lists of effective similes and other aids to rhetoric. He could buy books that would tell him how to write letters, whether love letters or business communications. So great was the interest in speed and simplification that even the great field of religion was invaded by the short cut, and one book was advertised as "an easy entrance into the principal points of Christian religion very short and plain." If possible, all these books of instruction were written in dialogue, and many of them had little charts appended to help the reader still further.*

If an energetic and restless Londoner could not find time to settle down and read a book, or if he lacked the necessary sixpence or shilling, there was a still quicker and cheaper way of getting information. For a penny a Londoner could buy an illustrated ballad, a single sheet of paper with an engaging woodcut and a vigorous rhyme to be sung to some popular tune. These broadsides occasionally reported bits of history or told stories of Biblical and classical subjects, and a "proper ballad dialogue-wise between Troilus and Cressida" was not unusual. But chiefly they kept the public informed on interesting contemporary news events, especially murders, fires, and other public disasters, the death of prominent people, and monstrous births both at home and abroad. The passion

*A characteristic example of an instruction book for the London public was Gerard Legh's *Accedens of Armory*. This was a popular book on heraldry, "written down" to the general public, and it included simple drawings that could be colored by the purchaser and useful stories such as that of King Lear. Gerard Legh put the book into dialogue form by calling one of the two speakers "Gerard" and the other "Legh." "Legh" is willing to be instructed indefinitely, but "Gerard" is obliged to leave or his wife will scold him for being late to dinner. A book of this kind could make its owner an amateur expert on the subject of heraldry and amuse him at the same time, and the *Accedens of Armory* naturally had an excellent sale.—AUTHOR'S NOTE for recording local events was so pronounced that one wit remarked, "Scarce a cat can look out of a gutter but out starts a half-penny chronicler." In many Elizabethan homes and inns these broadsides were used for wallpaper and must have brightened many an infant mind with their gory details and impeccable moral conclusions. The grownups read them out of that frank desire for information mixed with entertainment that was so characteristic of the Elizabethans, and the broadsides even went so far as to supply foreign news occasionally when there had been an earthquake in Italy or a success for English arms in the Low Countries.

A more sober observer of the current scene could pay a little more money and buy news pamphlets that would keep him informed on the state of the wars in Europe—accounts of the exemplary courage of the English, or of the atrocities committed by the wicked enemies of England, or even a book with a special map of France showing all the fortresses. There were more books on news events than on any subject except religion, and the government saw to it that the approach was just as well controlled. When the English navy destroyed the Spanish Armada, one single publisher brought out over twenty pieces on the subject, but when the French king unexpectedly turned Catholic, no one mentioned it at all, in spite of the enthusiasm with which his military career up to that point had been recorded. When battles were recorded from abroad, only the Protestant successes were mentioned, and publishers had to be careful even of minor pressure groups when they issued their books. A description of Russia was dedicated to the Queen as the account of "a tyrannical state (most unlike your own) without true knowledge of God, without written law, without common justice" and was then suppressed because some of the London merchants felt it might injure trade relations.

Any of these books and broadsides could be bought in the bookstalls that were chiefly clustered together in St. Paul's churchyard. Building space was short in the city and the booksellers had first erected sheds in the area and then changed them into real shops. The bookstalls were open by seven in the morning, and here the cheap reprints of plays and the shilling novels jostled for place with translations from the French and Italian and handsome folios on law and medicine and theology.

The Cathedral of St. Paul's did what it could to supply the city's obvious need for the still nonexistent daily newspaper. Its middle aisle was the meeting place for every newsmonger in London, and not only was the news exchanged here but a great deal of informal business was transacted, especially by lawyers. Since the position of the building blocked the road that would otherwise have been used to reach Fleet Street, the Cathedral was used as a short cut even by delivery men. So many people passed through it every day instead of using Carter Lane that it was treated as an advertising agency. Anyone who was out of work posted the information so that a prospective employer could write his name and address beneath, and the west door of the Cathedral was "pasted and plastered up with serving-men's supplications." Out in the London streets there were "papers on every post for arithmetic and writing schools," and plays and fencing matches used the same way of advertising themselves.

A young man up from the country would find that London offered a series of opportunities for getting information that were undreamed of in a town like Stratford, just as he found there the variety of people that only a great port city could offer. He would find also that nowhere in England were people more intent on enjoying themselves, in spite of the twelve-hour working day and the repressive theories of the London Council.

Many London shows cost the happy population nothing at all. No one had to pay to see the Lord Mayor's show and cheer the wickerwork giants or to see the water games on the Thames. Queen Elizabeth, that great amateur showman, was given to making sudden, spectacular appearances by torchlight, and when she opened Parliament she was carried through the streets in a red velvet cloak and a gold crown, while twenty-four glittering maids of honor rode in single file behind her. It was an age of the most determined dressing-up, and a knight saw nothing undignified in appearing as Eve in a tiltyard show, with apples hanging on his armor and long hair attached to his helmet. Seats in the stands for a tiltyard show cost eighteen pence, but "many thousands of men, women, and girls" went to see knights dressed as savages or with moons on their heads, and strange carriages that seemed to be drawn along without traction; and if any Londoner failed to see it, he could always buy a pamphlet describing it in detail.

Another source of public entertainment was executions, and the criminals knew what was expected of them by the public. They went to their death like actors, delivering final speeches from the scaffolds, and a hanging at Wapping was made especially impressive because the chief performer wore breeches of crimson taffeta. When there was an important mass execution, like that which followed the Babington Conspiracy in 1586, the government made the scaffold high and railed off the place to keep horsemen away so "the people might plainly see the execution." The idea of the government was to imprint upon the popular mind the horrors of treason and the ghastly death to which it led, but the Londoners treated the occasion like an especially interesting day at the theatre. "There was no lane, street, alley, or house in London . . . out of which there issued not some of each age and sex, insomuch that the ways were pestered with people so multiplied, as they thronged and overran one another for haste, contending to the place of death for the advantage of the ground where to stand, see, and hear." Londoners who were not good at pushing and therefore missed the actual execution kept arriving at Holborn all afternoon to see the blood on the scaffold; and the unfortunate few who missed it altogether could buy "many rimes, ballads, and pamphlets" on the subject.

Important London funerals were also reported in descriptive pamphlets; and if they were further reported in woodcuts, the fortunate purchaser could attach the pictures of the various parts of the procession together, making the long strip revolve on pins and "the figures march all in order." One merchant pasted up the pictures of a London funeral of 1586 in this manner and it took up "the length of the room at least," so impressing a nine-year-old boy when the pictures began to move on their pins that he never forgot it.

If a Londoner liked to look at strange animals, there was the zoo in the Tower, where four lions, a tiger, and a porcupine could be peered at through the wooden lattices after a judicious tip to the keeper; and for a time one of the houses on London Bridge housed a melancholy camel. A traveler from Kremzow reported that he saw in London a cow with six legs and a porpoise. He also saw a woman pygmy six thumbs high, a boy with a head like a pig, and (by an association of ideas that would seem normal to any Londoner) the Earl of Arundel being led to his imprisonment in the Tower.

The Londoners especially liked their entertainment to have an element of conflict and suspense in it, and they went in large numbers to the Star Chamber hearings at Westminster. The final stages of these trials were open to the public and aroused such interest in the theatrically minded Londoners that the audience would start arriving at three o'clock in the morning to be sure of getting a good seat and the usher of the chamber made a small fortune in tips.

Betting members of the population spent much of their time watching cockfights in an arena near Smithfield, where admission was a penny and the cocks who fought on the round, straw-covered table were usually well fortified with brandy. Even more popular were the bearbaitings, which were patronized by everyone from the lowliest tinker to the loftiest of visiting noblemen, and a visit to the Bear Garden was as much standard procedure with the average London visitor as seeing the tombs at Westminster Abbey. The bears were lovingly tended by their keepers after their fights with the dogs, and the names of the best warriors among them were household words in London. As an added attraction in the eighties there was also a mechanical contrivance out of which leaped a series of performers who danced and sang, and a rocket which exploded into a rosette and showered the audience with apples and pears.

Best of all, however, there were plays, and whatever a Londoner's interests might be, there was sure to be a play in town that would suit him. If he read the gory penny broadsides and went to executions, he could go to the theatre and see the best contemporary murders reenacted on the stage, with property limbs flapping about and real blood flowing. If he liked processions, he could see kings and councilors at coronations and in battle order and at other noble events, for the plays never omitted an opportunity for pageantry "where the drums might walk and the play ruffle." If he were interested in natural wonders, he could see much of zoological interest on the stage, where pygmies warred with cranes, and dragons were as realistic as hoops and painted canvas and gunpowder could make them. If he were interested in foreign lands, he could go to a play like *The Blacksmith's Daughter* at the Theatre and shudder at the treachery of the wicked Turks; and if he were interested in politics, he could go to *Pompey and Caesar* or *Catiline's Conspiracies* and mark the danger of treason in high places. There was a whole series of plays on English history for the patriotically minded; there were plays like *The Jew*, shown at the Bull, indicating the horrors of usury to the grave and thoughtful; and for the young and giddy there were recasts of Italian comedies and romances about amorous knights and the "wooing of gentlewomen." Any popular story, from Samson to Henry V, found its way to the stage to satisfy the greatest theatregoing public in the world.

Stephen Gosson, a playwright of the period, has described the wholehearted enthusiasm with which a London audience settled down to enjoy itself in the theatre. If the play was a tragedy, the susceptible Londoners dissolved into sympathetic tears, "weeping and mourning" with a rich vicarious satisfaction at the woes portrayed on the stage. If the play was a comedy, "they generally take up a wonderful laughter, and shout together with one voice," and Gosson admits to having done the same thing himself. "Many times we laugh so extremely, that striving to bridle ourselves, we cannot." Gosson happened to be writing after he had given up making plays and abandoned the theatre, and he added that this kind of enjoyment was very unsuited to a Christian commonwealth. "When such excess of laughter bursteth out that we cannot hold it, there is no temperance. . . . Where no temperance is, there is no wisdom."

Temperance was not a virtue that interested the showmen of the Elizabethan theatre. Their policy was that anything was justified on the stage so long as it pleased the public. They brought gods and goddesses down from heaven and fiends complete with firecrackers up from hell; their plays roamed the whole world and leaped from Turkey to Babylon as blandly as though time and distance had never existed, and kings consorted with clowns as though there had never been any rigid rules of social behavior to keep each man in his place.

All well-educated men knew that this was the wrong way to do a play. Like everything else, plays had their correct set of rules and every gentleman and scholar knew what they were. A play could never mix comedy and tragedy and it "must always be presented as occurring on the same day, in the same place, and at the same time." This doctrine of the unities, which the Renaissance firmly believed in, was an expansion by French and Italian theorists of Aristotle's original theory of unity of action, and by Shakespeare's day its authority among educated men was unquestioned. An Italian critic ranked Homer well below Vergil because he did not understand the importance of such rules, and even scolded Euripides because he invented stories about Helen "which were utterly contrary to well-known history."

Out of this grew the theory of "decorum" in writing plays, which meant a judicious balance of the parts to the whole with nothing violent or out of place. Nothing could have been more ill-bred, from this point of view, than for a playwright to descend to the vulgarity of showing violent physical action on the stage, and so many messengers were used to bring in reports of off-stage murders that one otherwise orthodox French critic finally wrote rebelliously, "Much fitter is it for a renowned inn than for an excellent tragedy to be thus frequented by an abundance of messengers."

Well-educated Englishmen believed unquestioningly in these Continental standards for playwrights and tried to produce work that was equally impeccable. When a Mr. Watson of Cambridge wrote a tragedy about Absalom, his standards were so high that he was reluctant to put the play into general circulation because once or twice he had used an anapestic line instead of an iambic one. Mr. Watson could speak learnedly of the writings of Sophocles and Seneca and the precepts of Aristotle, and the young men who followed in his footsteps at Oxford and Cambridge and the London Inns of Court struggled to mount into the same rarefied atmosphere and be worthy of equal admiration. Seneca was the correct model for tragedy, as Plautus and Terence were for comedy, and everything had to be done on a fixed stage and under fixed rules. Even an admired play like *Gorboduc,* the joint product of two young gentlemen of the Inner Temple, was criticized for violating the unities, although everyone agreed that its blank verse was impressively classical and its use of messengers so correct that none of the action of the story took place on the stage at all.

A well-educated Englishman who knew all the rules about writing plays could feel nothing but pain at the wild native growth that flourished on the popular stages. Sir Philip Sidney, who had one of the most intelligent and beautiful minds of his generation, went to the public theatre occasionally, but all he could find there was a gross violation of the laws of the unities and of common sense. "You shall have Asia on the one side and Affrick on the other, and so many other under-kingdoms that the player, when he cometh on, must ever begin with telling where he is, or else the tale will not be conceived. Now we shall have three ladies walk to gather flowers, and then we must believe the stage to be a garden. By and by we hear news of shipwreck in the same place, and then we are to blame if we accept it not for a rock. Upon the back of that, comes out a hideous monster, with fire and smoke, and then the miserable beholders are bound to take it for a cave."

From Sidney's point of view the plays of the early eighties may have been ridiculous, with their complete lack of interest in the classical tradition and the heavy demands they made upon the spectator's willing imagination. But the plays made money, as James Burbage of the Theatre or Henry Laneman of the Curtain could testify, and in turn the money began to attract a new group of playwrights.

Most of these young men came from either Oxford or Cambridge, where they had been given a good education in the classics but had not been given any way of making a living. Most of them were the sons of middle-class parents who had ambitiously sent their sons to the university, either through a scholarship or at some personal sacrifice, but with no clear idea of what they should do with their expensive educations afterward. In Chaucer's day young men like these would have gone into the Church, which still controlled most of the government offices. But even by Chaucer's day the government offices were becoming secularized, and after the Reformation it was no longer the primary duty of Oxford and Cambridge to turn out churchmen. The universities gave their young graduates the education of a gentleman but with no suggestions how to put it to use; and from the practical point of view the only course open to them was either to try for a position as a teacher in a grammar school or with a private family, or else to try to negotiate a position as rector of a parish.

Some of the young men themselves had other ideas. The great city of London beckoned them, and with their excellent classical training they were sure they could make a living in London by writing books. Most of the young men discovered after they arrived that the market for serious young writers in London was not as steady as it might be. A series of plays produced at Cambridge at the turn of the century made a survey of the general problem of how a scholar could earn a living, and there was one scene that must have raised a sympathetic laugh in the audience. The young scholar's last book has not been selling well and the London publisher is extremely unwilling to accept a new one from him until he learns it has a bawdy title. This is perhaps a slightly unkind parody of the London bookseller's point of view; but he could not afford to deal in books that his customers would not buy, and if the young gentlemen of Oxford and Cambridge expected to make a steady living, they had to turn out the romances and the sensational pamphlets that the public enjoyed.

However, there was one group of paymasters in London who had just as much ready money as the London publishers and were even more in need of material. A successful company of actors needed a great many plays in a year, since they worked on the repertory system, and to keep their positions in the competitive world of the theatre, they needed good scripts and were willing to pay for them. The young men from the universities were more than willing to be paid and they had already had some experience with the academic side of playwriting. Both Oxford and Cambridge produced plays at Christmas or to entertain visiting dignitaries, and the refectory at St. John's Hall in Cambridge was famous for "its theatrical apparatus for acting plays."

The greatest of these university men to write for the common stage was Christopher Marlowe. He was the brilliant son of a Canterbury shoemaker and went to Cambridge on a scholarship. There he encountered two fine libraries and the companionship of brilliant and sympathetic minds, and the legendary glories of Greece and Rome became much more real to him than anything in his own century. Marlowe was a true son of the Renaissance in his intense ambition and his love of beauty, and when he wrote a play about a great tyrant king, he did it as much to please himself as to please the London public.

Marlowe's *Tamburlaine* was produced on the London stage in the late eighties and was given a very effective production by the Admiral's company. The title role was played, evidently from the first, by Edward Alleyn, then in his early twenties but already the most brilliant and popular actor in London. The whole city took the play to its collective heart and an equally popular sequel followed immediately.

Part of the popularity of *Tamburlaine* came from the savage effectiveness of its stage devices, for Marlowe was a born theatre man and knew how to make an audience shudder. There was a popular scene in which one of Tamburlaine's captives was carried about in a cage and used as his conqueror's footstool and another one in which the governor of Babylon was hung in chains on the wall and shot at by the besiegers. (The Admiral's company handled this scene with such realism that in a November performance a bullet miscarried and killed a pregnant woman in the audience.) Even more famous was a scene in which Tamburlaine made his entrance in a chariot drawn by two captive kings with bits in their mouths. Alleyn had a whip in his right hand to scourge the actors who played the two kings, and a delighted thrill went over the whole audience when he shouted in his wonderful voice:

Holla, ye pampered jades of Asia!
What, can ye draw but twenty miles
    a day?

A whole generation of theatregoers went around quoting the scene, and Shakespeare's Pistol was only one of many.

It was not only the stage effects that made *Tamburlaine* so popular; it was Marlowe's poetry. The Londoners loved words and they were capable of getting half-drunk on a really gorgeous flow of rhetoric. Since at least the beginning of the decade the playwrights had been showing "the majesty of their pen in tragical speeches," and the audiences had come to expect poetry with their plays. As one reformer gloomily put it, a few years earlier, "because the sweet numbers of poetry flowing in verse do wonderfully tickle the hearer's ears, the devil hath tied this to most of our plays." Most of the verse was probably not very good, but its constant use produced a series of well-trained listeners, alert and ready to be moved. Marlowe was a good theatre man but he was a great poet, and he used blank verse as it had never been used before on the London stage. The golden rhetoric caught and held the audience as a new kind of symphony would hold a musically trained audience today, and many a London apprentice must have walked home from *Tamburlaine* intoxicated with the lines singing in his head.

Another great popular success of the same period was a play by Thomas Kyd called *The Spanish Tragedy*. Kyd never quite belonged with the group of young men who came down from the universities to write plays; but he roomed for a time with Marlowe, and although he was no poet, he had some of Marlowe's theatre sense and an even better idea how to construct plays. Kyd had been educated in London under Richard Mulcaster, and Mulcaster's boys produced plays so effectively that the general public crowded to see them until the directors of the school decided that such performances were undignified and ordered them discontinued. It may have been partly from Mulcaster that Kyd learned some of the classical theories that were a commonplace at the universities and the Inns of Court, but he could just as well have found them from his own reading. The ten tragedies of Seneca, for instance, came out in an English translation at the beginning of the decade, and Kyd took some of the bloody devices that Seneca had pictured in ornate rhyme for a Roman audience and put them into action for an English one. *The Spanish Tragedy* was a success with a whole generation of theatregoers, and the revenge play, with its ghosts and its madmen, started on its long career on the London stage.

Meanwhile, other university men were turning out popular plays, and although their choice of actual subject matter was not very different from that of their predecessors in the public theatre, they brought with them a sensitive ear for words and a well-trained mind, and some of them were real poets. Most of them knew each other well, and men like Greene and Nashe and Lodge tended to congregate together in what a more academic graduate called a "riming and scribbling crew." All of them drank a good deal and were full of theories about religion, and most of them were well acquainted with the insides of the London prisons, either for their religious opinions or for street fighting or for debt. Tom Nashe gave it as his opinion that going to prison was an experience no writer could expect to miss. "I protest I should never have writ passion well, or been a piece of a poet, if I had not arrived in those quarters. Trace the gallantest youths and bravest revellers about town . . . and you shall infallibly find that once in their lifetime they have visited that melancholy habitation." Even a man's good intentions could get him into trouble with the authorities. When Thomas Watson tried to help his friend Marlowe in a fight in Hog Lane, he ended by killing Marlowe's opponent and spent five months in prison until it was decided he had acted in self-defense.

Marlowe seems to have been the leader of this writing group, if only because he was the only one who was completely in earnest. Some of his companions dabbled in free-thinking because it was currently the fashionable thing to do and they were in instinctive revolt against their conservative, middle-class backgrounds. But Marlowe hated conformity with all the passion of his free-ranging intellect, and he felt an actual sense of suffocation under the series of tight religious rules the average Englishman took for granted. In the same way Marlowe's companions respected the classics because they had been taught to honor learning and because they valued their university training as something that set them above the common herd. But Marlowe worshiped the ancient writers because beauty was more to him than life, and even the place names on a map could give his spirit a lift into another and freer world than London.

Men like Marlowe were, of course, aware that they were working in a perishable medium when they wrote plays. Once a play was sold to a company of actors, the author had no control over it at all, and it was only an accident if it got into print. A few of the plays written by George Peele and Robert Greene were eventually printed, but almost none of those written by Tom Nashe or Tom Lodge; and as for Thomas Watson, a member of this group whom his contemporaries ranked with Sidney and Spenser and who had a tremendous reputation in his own day, none of the many plays he wrote has survived at all. Even when a play was printed, it was usually given without the author's name; all of Marlowe's plays that were printed in his own lifetime appeared anonymously, and *The Spanish Tragedy* is known to have been written by Kyd only because of a casual reference by a fellow playwright more than two decades later. Even when a play succeeded in working its way into print, the text was usually a corrupt acting version and not at all what its author had originally written. Greene's *Orlando Furioso* was printed with its meter dislocated, the Italian quotations misspelled, the classical references shortened or omitted, and most of the poetry mangled and apparently quoted from memory. In the case of this particular play some of the cue sheets of the actor who played Orlando survived and with them Greene's original text; but no other original texts have survived and it is impossible to be sure that the printed versions of Marlowe's plays are exactly what Marlowe himself wrote.

The playwrights knew they were working in a perishable medium and they turned to other forms of poetry to immortalize themselves in the eyes of posterity. Marlowe did not live to finish his classical narrative poem, *Hero and Leander,* but Nashe did an imitation of Ovid in *The Choice of Valentines* and Tom Lodge made a name for himself in 1589 with *Scilla's Metamorphoses.* Lodge came of a prominent London family and had been educated at Oxford and at the Inns of Court; and he closed his classical narrative with a firm resolve to be worthy of his upbringing:

To write no more of that whence shame doth grow
  Or tie my pen to penny-knaves' delight,
  But live with fame, and so for fame to write.

Lodge was unable to keep to this noble ambition since his father's spectacular bankruptcy and his own great gifts for spending money kept him at playwriting in order to earn a living, but he could never quite forgive the penny public for forcing him to debase his art.

All this university-educated group of writers shared the conviction that they were prostituting themselves in writing plays for money and appealing to the base instincts of the "penny-knaves." If they wanted their plays to be popular, they had to disregard all the classical precepts they had learned at Oxford and Cambridge, and they could never do this without a slight sense of sin. Any of them might have echoed the complaint of Lope de Vega, the popular Spanish playwright: "When I have to write a comedy, I lock up the precepts with six keys, cast Terence and Plautus from my study . . . and I write according to the art invented by those who sought the vulgar applause. For, as the common herd pays for them, it is meet to speak to them like an ignoramus in order to please them." The playwrights consoled themselves slightly by introducing classical references into their plays whenever they could, and a writer like Robert Greene, Master of Arts from both universities, put all his stage directions in Latin to show the excellence of his education. The actors patiently removed them again, since few actors read Latin easily, and the practice survives today only in *exit* and *exeunt*.

It was a constant source of irritation to these university playwrights that the actors who bought their scripts made more money than they did. The first time that Nashe appeared in print it was to express regret that various "sweet gentlemen" of his acquaintance were in the habit of writing plays and had "tricked up a company of taffeta fools with their feathers." If the writers had not done so, the taffeta fools would not have been able to make so much money. They would be forced to go on using old-fashioned plays and would not be strutting around in satin suits in the streets of London. The average

playwright was convinced the actors owed all their popularity to the brilliant lines he and his colleagues had written for them, and he was angered to see large audiences drawn to a successful play long after its author had drunk up the whole of the purchase price in the nearest tavern.

Since no playwright had gone to the risk and expense of producing a play himself, he could hardly have been expected to realize that each acting company was carrying a heavy overhead in rentals, costumes, and properties. In the early eighties there is a reference to the cost of "these spectacles that scarce last like shoes of brown paper," and by the time Nashe was writing, all the expenses had increased. The script was only one item in a series of expenses that had to be assumed by the actors each time a script went into production, and the money that was made on a successful script was of course counterbalanced by the money that could be lost on an unsuccessful one. Although a playwright made less money than an actor, he also took fewer risks. Nevertheless, when the playwrights thought of the actors, they thought only of the successful ones, and they found it hard to forgive the "taffeta fools" for making so much money when university graduates made so little.

No one felt more strongly on this subject than Robert Greene, for Greene had a very clear idea of the commercial value of his scripts. He was the one member of the university group who was making a satisfactory living by his pen, for Greene was a born journalist and had an almost intuitive idea of what the public wanted. He was very popular with the London publishers, for whom he supplied a series of love stories and slightly fictionized exposés of the London underworld and even a diatribe against the Pope, but he had Lodge's gift for spending money rapidly and he was convinced that the actors did not really understand his worth. He was one of the most popular of all the London playwrights, but the actors neither treated him with proper respect nor paid him enough money, and he broke off in the middle of a prose romance published in 1590 to complain that the actors were "conceited," "covetous," and "insolent." When Nashe had attacked the actors, one year earlier, it had been in a preface to one of Greene's own books, and Nashe's remark about feathers reminded Greene of the fable of the crow who decked himself out in borrowed plumage. This, to Greene, was the perfect image with which to describe an actor. "Art thou proud with Aesop's crow, being pranked with the glory of others' feathers? Of thyself thou canst say nothing. . . . The invention the people applaud for excellent, that comes from the secrets of our knowledge." The actors supplied nothing but "a kind of mechanical labour" which was entitled to a mild respect only so long as the actors did not grow

conceited and think they were superior to playwrights. Greene admitted he had made a "long digression" in his novel and returned to the fortunes of Francisco that he had been recounting, but two years later his fury at the actors reappeared and with it the image of Aesop's crow.

During those two years Greene had been a familiar and spectacular figure around London, with his red hair and pointed beard, his green cloak and his silk stockings, his mistress from the underworld and her disreputable brother who served as his bodyguard. He was famous for his drinking parties and he had many friends. But in the summer of 1592 he became mortally ill and was suddenly terrified by visions of hell-fire. The Bohemian playwright had been soberly reared by devout parents, and the teachings of his childhood came back to him with a rush.

It took Greene a month to die and he spent it praying to be forgiven for his sins. He had always taken a deep interest in the repentances that were expected of Newgate criminals and he had evidently written some of their "penitent and passionate" speeches himself. When he came to his own repentance, he outdid himself, and there was hardly a bookseller in London who did not have on sale one of the pamphlets the great journalist wrote during the month he lay dying in a shoemaker's house near Dowgate. Greene's repentance was completely sincere, for, unlike Marlowe, he was not a nonconformist out of any real conviction. He had been brought up respectably and he tried to die respectably, imploring the youth of England to profit by his example and avoid blasphemy, bad company, and drink. He made what was known as a good end, and he shared it with the public only because he was a good journalist.

Of all Greene's repentance pamphlets, the one that stirred the most discussion was *Greene's Groatsworth of Wit,* the last he wrote and the most autobiographical. Calling himself Roberto, he describes his debts, his writing of plays, his desertion of his wife, his taking of a mistress, and all his other sins, and supplies a series of rules of good conduct so that others may avoid his unhappy fate. Then Greene addresses himself to three of his friends in a special warning. Greene does not call these three playwrights by name, but the references to atheism make it clear that the first of them is Marlowe. The second playwright is evidently Tom Nashe, who was getting a reputation for clever insults that made more than one writer echo Greene's description of him as "young Juvenal." The third playwright, "in some things rarer, in nothing inferior," is more difficult to identify, but it may be George Peele, whom Nashe warmly praised as "the Atlas of poetry."

The general purpose of Greene's address to his three friends was to implore them to stop writing plays and working for the actors, "for it is a pity men of such rare wits should be subject to the pleasure of such rude grooms." Greene had already made it clear two years earlier how much he disliked the men who bought plays from him, but the thought of their intolerable prosperity while he lay penniless and dying added a new edge to his fury. By now he has nothing whatever to say in the actors' favor. They are "apes," they are "peasants," they are "painted monsters"; they are puppets "that speak from our mouths" and are "garnished in our colors." Again Greene was reminded of the crow in Aesop who strutted in borrowed feathers, but this time he used the image not to attack actors in general but one actor in particular. "There is an upstart crow, beautified with our feathers, that, with his tiger's heart wrapped in a player's hide, supposes he is as well able to bombast out a blank verse as the best of you; and being an absolute *Johannes fac totum,* is in his own conceit the only Shake-scene in a country."

It is known, from the evidence of a Court document two years later, that William Shakespeare was by this time a prominent actor in London, and he also seems to be the only actor at that time who was also writing plays. The fact that Shakespeare is the actor whom Greene is attacking is further indicated by the pun on his name as "the only Shake-scene in a country," and the identification is reinforced by Greene's phrase about the "tiger's heart wrapped in a player's hide." The phrase is a slanting reference to a scene from a London success that was currently attracting large audiences. The original line reads:

O tiger's heart wrapp'd in a woman's hide!

and the play from which it comes is listed in the First Folio as the third part of Shakespeare's *Henry VI*.

It was hard enough for Robert Greene to tolerate the actors who employed him when they contented themselves merely with buying his plays. When they set up as a rival playwright one of their own number, who thought he could "bombast out a blank verse" as well as Marlowe or Nashe while still continuing his work as an actor, they had produced a *Johannes fac totum*—a "Johnny Do-Everything"—whose mere existence was more unforgivable than all the rest of their sins combined.

Greene's final repentance pamphlet was a great success on the bookstalls, where it appeared posthumously, but it inevitably had repercussions. The publisher, Henry Chettle, had been obliged to copy the semi-illegible manuscript in his neat hand to prepare it for licensing, and he took upon himself the responsibility of suppressing some of Greene's violence. Chettle was a good-natured man who eventually became a playwright himself, and he modified Greene's attack on Marlowe as an atheist. "Had it

been true, yet to publish it was intolerable."

Chettle wished later that he had modified Greene's attack on the author of *Henry VI* also. "That I did not, I am as sorry as if the original fault had been my fault, because myself have seen his demeanor no less civil than he excellent in the quality he professes." The "quality" was the Elizabethan term for the acting profession. "Besides, divers of worship have reported his uprightness of dealing, which argues his honesty, and his facetious grace in writing, that approves his art."

Of all the men writing for the London theatre, Shakespeare seems to have been almost the only one who did not take offense easily. His contemporaries called him "gentle Shakespeare" and he deserved the title. In the short-tempered Elizabethan atmosphere, where a writer almost prided himself on the vigor and variety of his insults and where even gentle scholars like William Camden and John Stow became involved in bitter arguments, Shakespeare stands almost alone for the consistent courtesy with which he behaved. His objection to Greene's attack was apparently the only protest he ever made, and it must have been a mild one or Chettle would not have spoken with admiration of his civility.

The most important thing about Greene's attack is that it establishes the fact that Shakespeare was a successful actor before he became a playwright. This, in turn, explains what he had been doing in the intervening years since the birth of his twins in Stratford in 1585. It was no easy thing to become a successful actor on the London stage. Acting was a profession that required a long, arduous period of training before a man was capable of appearing professionally before a critical metropolitan audience; and since Shakespeare was a successful actor in 1592, the year of Greene's attack on him, he must have chosen acting as his profession several years earlier.

✖ *Chapter* 5

Acting was not an easy profession on the Elizabethan stage or one to be taken lightly. An actor went through a strenuous period of training before he could be entrusted with an important part by one of the great city companies. He worked on a raised stage in the glare of the afternoon sun, with none of the softening illusions that can be achieved in the modern theatre, and in plays that made strenuous demands upon his skill as a fencer, a dancer, and an acrobat.

Many of the men in the London companies had been "trained up from their childhood" in the art, and an actor like Shakespeare, who entered the profession in his twen-

ties, had an initial handicap that could only be overcome by intelligence and rigorous discipline. Since he was a well-known actor by 1592 and Chettle says he was an excellent one, he must have had the initial advantages of a strong body and a good voice and have taught himself in the hard school of the Elizabethan theatre how to use them to advantage.

One of the most famous of the London companies, that of Lord Strange, began its career as a company of tumblers, and a standard production like *The Forces of Hercules* was at least half acrobatics. Training of this kind was extremely useful to the actors, for the normal London stage consisted of several different levels. Battles and sieges were very popular with the audiences, with the upper levels of the stage used as the town walls and turrets, and an actor had to know how to take violent falls without damaging either himself or his expensive costume.

Nearly all plays involved some kind of fighting, and in staging hand-to-hand combats, the actor's training had to be excellent. The average Londoner was an expert on the subject of fencing, and he did not pay his penny to see two professional actors make ineffectual dabs at each other with rapiers when the script claimed they were fighting to the death. A young actor like Shakespeare must have gone through long, grueling hours of practice to learn the ruthless technique of Elizabethan fencing.

He had to learn how to handle a long, heavy rapier in one hand, with a dagger for parrying in the other, and to make a series of savage, calculated thrusts at close quarters from the wrist and forearm, aiming either at his opponent's eyes or below the ribs. The actor had to achieve the brutal reality of an actual Elizabethan duel without injuring himself or his opponent, a problem that required a high degree of training and of physical coordination. The theatres and the innyards were frequently rented by the fencing societies to put on exhibition matches, and on one such occasion at the Swan a fencer was run through the eye and died, an indication of the risks this sort of work involved even with trained, experienced fencers. The actors had to be extremely skilled, since they faced precisely the same audience. Richard Tarleton, a comic actor of the eighties who was the first great popular star of the Elizabethan theatre, was made Master of Fence the year before he died, and this was the highest degree the fencing schools could award.

Not being content with savage, realistic fights in its theatre productions, the London audience also expected to see bloody deaths and mutilations; and it was necessary to find some way to run a sword through an actor's head or tear out his entrails without impairing his usefulness for the next afternoon's performance. This involved not only agility but a thorough knowledge of sleight of hand, since the players were working close to the audience and in broad daylight. Elizabethan stage management was not slavishly interested in realism, but it was always concerned with good stage effects, and when bloodshed was involved, it gave the audience real blood. It had been found by experience that ox blood was too thick to run well, and sheep's blood was generally used. To stage a realistic stabbing, one actor would use a knife with a hollow handle into which the blade would slip back when it was pressed home, and his fellow actor would be equipped with a bladder of blood inside his white leather jerkin, which could be painted to look like skin. When the bladder was pricked and the actor arched himself at the moment of contact, the blood spurted out in a most satisfactory manner. Sometimes real knives were used and a protective plate, and a juggler once staggered into St. Paul's Churchyard and died there because he had done the trick when he was drunk and forgotten his plate. In *The Battle of Alcazar* there was a disemboweling scene for which the property man supplied three vials of blood and the liver, heart, and lungs of a sheep. Then it was up to Edward Alleyn and his two fellow actors to use skillful substitution in such a way as to create the illusion, before a critical London audience in broad daylight, that their organs were being torn out.

Another test of an actor's physical control was in dancing. Apart from the dances that were written into the actual texts of the plays, it was usual to end the performance with a dance performed by some of the members of the company. A traveler from abroad who saw Shakespeare's company act *Julius Caesar* said that "when the play was over they danced very marvellously and gracefully together," and when the English actors traveled abroad, special mention was always made of their ability as dancers. The fashion of the time was for violent spectacular dances, and the schools in London taught intricate steps like those of the galliard, the exaggerated leap called the capriole, and the violent lifting of one's partner high into the air that was the volte. A visitor to one of these dancing schools of London watched a performer do a galliard and noted how "wonderfully he leaped, flung, and took on"; and if amateurs were talented at this kind of work, professionals on the stage were expected to be very much better.

In addition to all this, subordinate or beginning actors were expected to handle several roles in an afternoon instead of only one. A major company seldom had more than twelve actors in it and could not afford to hire an indefinite number of extra ones for a single production. This meant that the men who had short speaking parts or none were constantly racing about and leaping into different costumes to get on stage with a different characterization as soon as they heard their cues. In one of Alleyn's productions a single actor played a Tartar nobleman, a spirit, an attendant, a hostage, a ghost, a child, a captain, and a Persian; and while none of the parts made any special demands on his acting ability, he must have had very little time to catch his breath. The London theatre was no place for physical weaklings; and, in the same way it is safe to assume that John Shakespeare must have had a strong, well-made body or he would not have been appointed a constable in Stratford, it is safe to assume that he must have passed the inheritance on to his eldest son.

There was one more physical qualification an Elizabethan actor had to possess, and this was perhaps more important than any of the others. He had to have a good voice. An Elizabethan play was full of action, but in the final analysis it was not the physical activity that caught and held the emotions of the audience; it was the words. An audience was an assembly of listeners, and it was through the ear, not the eye, that the audience learned the location of each of the scenes, the emotions of each of the characters, and the poetry and excitement of the play as a whole. More especially, since the actors were men and boys and close physical contact could not carry the illusion of love-making, words had to be depended upon in the parts that were written for women.

An Elizabethan audience had become highly susceptible to the use of words, trained and alert to catch their exact meaning and full of joy if they were used well. But this meant, as the basis of any successful stage production, that all the words had to be heard clearly. The actors used a fairly rapid delivery of their lines, and this meant that breath control, emphasis, and enunciation had to be perfect if the link that was being forged between the emotions of the audience and the action on the stage was not to be broken. When Shakespeare first came to London, the problem of effective stage delivery was made somewhat easier by the use of a heavily end-stopped line, where the actor could draw his breath at regular intervals and proceed at a kind of jog trot. But during the following decade this kind of writing became increasingly old-fashioned, giving way to an intricate and supple blank verse that was much more difficult to handle intelligently; and no one was more instrumental in bringing the new way of writing into general use than Shakespeare himself.

Even with all the assistance given him by the old way of writing, with mechanical accenting and heavy use of rhyme, an Elizabethan actor had no easy time remembering his part. A repertory system was used and no play was given two days in succession. The actor played a different part every night, and he had no opportunity to settle into a comfortable routine while the lines of the part became second nature to him. He could expect very little help from the prompter, for that overworked individual was chiefly occupied in seeing that the actors came on in proper order, that they had their properties available, and that the intricate stage arrangements that controlled the pulleys from the "heavens" and the springs to the trap doors were worked with quick, accurate timing. These stage effects, which naturally had to be changed each afternoon for each new play, were extremely complicated. A single play in which Greene and Lodge collaborated required the descent of a prophet and an angel let down on a throne, a woman blackened by a thunderstroke, sailors coming in wet from the sea, a serpent devouring a vine, a hand with a burning sword emerging from a cloud, and "Jonah the prophet cast out of the whale's belly upon the stage." Any production that had to wrestle with as many complications as this had no room for an actor who could not remember his lines.

Moreover, an actor who forgot his lines would not have lasted long in what was a highly competitive profession. There were more actors than there were parts for them, judging by the number of people who were listed as players in the parish registers. Even the actor who had achieved the position of a sharer in one of the large London companies was not secure. Richard Jones, for instance, was the owner of costumes and properties and playbooks worth nearly forty pounds, which was an enormous sum in those days, and yet three years later he was working in the theatre at whatever stray acting jobs he could get. "Sometimes I have a shilling a day and sometimes nothing," he told Edward Alleyn, asking for help in getting his suit and cloak out of pawn.

The usual solution for an actor who could not keep his place in the competitive London theatre was to join one of the country companies, where the standards were less exacting, or to go abroad. English actors were extravagantly admired abroad, and even a second-string company with poor equipment became the hit of the Frankfort Fair, so that "both men and women flocked wonderfully" to see them. An actor like Shakespeare who maintained his position on the London stage for two decades could legitimately be praised, as Chettle praised him, for being "excellent in the quality he professes." If it had been otherwise, he would not have remained for long on the London stage.

If Shakespeare had not enjoyed his work as an actor, he could no doubt have given it up when he became a successful writer. Ben Jonson started life as an actor, but he gave the profession up as soon as he found he could make a living by his pen. Shakespeare, on the other hand, never gave up his profession. He was a successful actor in 1592, as is shown by Greene's attack on him. He was still an actor in 1598, when he appears on the list of "principal comedians" who acted in *Every Man in His Humour*. He was still an actor in 1603, when he appears on the list of "principal tragedians" who acted in *Sejanus*. He was still acting in 1608 because Cuthbert Burbage names him specifically among the "men players" who arranged to begin using the Blackfriars theatre that year; and since he evidently retired to Stratford two or three years later, it can safely be said that Shakespeare was an actor throughout the whole of his life in the London theatre.

Shakespeare was not, of course, as brilliantly successful an actor as Edward Alleyn, who could make a bad play seem good and whose name was even used on the title page of a printed play because it would increase sales. But Shakespeare's knowledge of people was infinitely greater than Alleyn's, and it is probable that none of the many audiences who saw him on the stage was ever able to deduce his own character and personality from the roles he played.

A busy actor like William Shakespeare did not have much time to write plays. The mornings were probably taken up with rehearsals and there were performances in the afternoon and sometimes special shows in the evening, to say nothing of the strenuous period when the company was on its annual tour of the provinces. A modern writer might feel it was inconceivable that anyone could write plays when he was already working in a full-time profession, but this is an echo of a more degenerate age and was not the Elizabethan point of view at all. The Elizabethans had no patience with any writer who expected to "lie in child-bed one-and-thirty weeks and eight days of three bad lines and afterward spend a whole twelve-month" trying to improve them, and Ben Jonson, who wrote one play in five weeks, was publicly jeered at because he was so "slow an inventor." Thomas Heywood, like William Shakespeare, was a full-time actor and remained one. Yet Heywood found time, in his limited leisure, to have what he called "either an entire hand, or at least a main finger" in writing two hundred and twenty plays. Shakespeare himself produced less than forty plays during twenty years' work in the theatre, a record that is not remarkable for its bulk, however incredible it may be for its quality.

The fact that Shakespeare was an actor gave him one great advantage over the average playwright of his day. Usually a playwright made a play to order and met the actors in some convenient place where it could be given a reading. Normally an alehouse served as an impromptu office since, as one foreigner remarked, there were "partitions between the tables so that one table cannot overlook the next." Once the play had been read and approved, the dramatist was paid and his contribution was over. Many of the playwrights had so little interest in the finished production that they even did not go to see it acted, and, George Chapman once remarked, "I see not mine own plays." A writer of this kind had no opportunity to judge the total emotional impact of his work on a living audience, and Chapman's plays are unactable today. But Shakespeare was an actor. He was present during every detail of the production of his own plays, and when they were acted, he almost touched hands with his audience. He was in a position to know exactly what could be achieved from the production point of view, and the quality that has kept him a living force on the stage for more than three hundred years was born, in part, of his close professional knowledge of his audience.

In the first plays he wrote, Shakespeare shows that he already had a firm grip on the art of manipulating the emotions of an audience. The plays are not masterpieces. Like every other writer, Shakespeare learned by writing. In his late twenties he was not yet ready to write *Hamlet* any more than his audience was ready to receive it. In a sense, Shakespeare and his audience grew up together, and at the beginning of his career as a playwright his approach to stagecraft was as juvenile and crude as the responses of his audience. But the important thing was that he infallibly got these responses.

The most stirring of his early

successes, to judge by contemporary reports, was a series of three plays he wrote on the Wars of the Roses. Plays on English history were very popular with Elizabethan audiences, who had not been given any history in their school days and were eager to know about former kings and queens. The Wars of the Roses made an especially good subject for a young playwright, since he could point out the horrors of civil strife and remind the audience by inference how fortunate they were to be experiencing the joys of a settled Tudor monarchy. The next time a Londoner objected to paying a special subsidy or started brooding over the cost of the war with Spain, he could always remind himself how much worse life had been under the inept rule of Henry VI.*

As far as school instruction went, Shakespeare knew no more than his audiences did about the Wars of the Roses. But there were several excellent history books available, of which the most up-to-date was a chronicle history of England, Ireland, and Scotland that Raphael Holinshed had compiled from standard sources for a syndicate of printers. Holinshed wrote a brisk, straightforward prose, and his conviction that the Tudors were the culmination of English history was an impeccable one. Ten years after the book was published the sales

* The three plays on the Wars of the Roses that are being discussed here appear in the First Folio as *Henry VI*, parts one, two, and three.—AUTHOR'S NOTE

warranted a new edition, and the publishers brought it up-to-date by including the annals of England up to the publication date of 1587. This three-volume edition became the standard history of England and was the one Shakespeare used as the general basis of all his history plays; and although it was a rather expensive publication, it must have been one of the books he eventually owned.

Only a very self-confident young man would have embarked on the confused mass of quarrels and counterquarrels recorded by Holinshed and hoped to turn it into manageable stage material; and only a young man who was experienced in the practical problems of the theatre could have succeeded. Occasionally Shakespeare found that the possibilities for drama were smothered under the weight of the material, but in general he managed to manipulate his important scenes in such a way that the audiences nearly choked in an excess of patriotic emotion.

The most successful scene in the first play of the series was the death of Lord Talbot. Talbot was the noblest kind of Englishman and he died on the battlefield at the hands of the perfidious French, clasping within his arms the dead body of his equally noble son. Talbot had a speech that the actor who played the part must have warmly appreciated—the first of a long line of bravura speeches that have made Shakespeare the beloved of actors ever since—and the audience sobbed as one man as the great warrior's soul winged its way to heaven. The play was produced at the Rose on the third of March, 1592, by Lord Strange's company, and played to enormous audiences all season. Only one play in Philip Henslowe's diary records larger grosses in the galleries, and Tom Nashe made a respectful reference to the size of the audiences in a pamphlet he wrote the same year. "How it would have joyed brave Talbot (the terror of the French) to think that after he had lain two hundred years in his tomb, he should triumph again on the stage and have his bones new embalmed with the tears of ten thousand spectators."

The young playwright was not very interested in exact historical facts. He has Talbot's death precede the capture of Joan of Arc, whereas in actual fact Joan died twenty-two years before he did. As for Joan herself, any modern reader is startled by the disrespectful, almost comic characterization that she is given, and it is difficult to remember that to the sixteenth-century Englishman she was a crafty peasant who overturned the brave English only because she was assisted by devils. Even the scholarly Gabriel Harvey saw her as nothing more than "a lusty adventurous wench," and the most that the English could feel was a certain reluctant admiration for her vigor.

The play records a series of battles and sieges that gave Shakespeare an opportunity to exploit all the resources of the stage, and he kept the actors leaping from level to level like the acrobats they were. He even made use of the rarely used top turret and had Joan ascend it to thrust out a torch, and at one point forced the actors into what must have been a twelve-foot leap from a balcony to the stage when the defenders of Orleans escape from the besieged town.

Shakespeare's second play on the Wars of the Roses gave much less opportunity for battle scenes and processions, but the young actor-dramatist did not forget his audience's love of special effects. In the first act he used three stage levels to have an actor dressed as a spirit rise up through a trap door to confront the Duchess on the balcony, with thunder to mask any noise that might be made by the machinery. Shakespeare also made a lavish use of property heads, for the rebels bring on the heads of Lord Saye and his son-in-law, Jack Cade's head is brought on stage, and Queen Margaret has a special stage direction for "mourning over Suffolk's head." These atrocity scenes were always staged with great care, and whatever company it may have been that produced the play, it was certainly prosperous enough to be able to afford four separate heads. It is not unlikely the same system was used that the French used in the Middle Ages, in which a dummy head was carved with the living actor as a model and then realistically colored. A head of this kind could even be made to bleed if a little dough kneaded with bullock's blood was pressed against it and made to look like part of the dead flesh. Suffolk's headless trunk also appears in the play, but this was a property item that even the smallest company could supply as a matter of course. When Thomas Churchyard was hired by the city of Norwich to put on a small outdoor play during Queen Elizabeth's visit, he brought along with him as a matter of course "legs and arms of men (well and lively wrought) to be let fall in numbers on the ground, as bloody as might be."

In the second play of his series, Shakespeare remained equally casual about historical facts and chronology, but this may have been because he was faced with a practical theatre difficulty. The play has nearly fifty characters, not including lords and ladies, aldermen, citizens, soldiers, and so on, and this meant that nearly every actor in the company had to play several parts. The action of the play had to be carefully arranged to make all this doubling possible, and if the historical events interfered with practical stagecraft, it was history that had to be altered.

In the third play of the trilogy, Shakespeare found himself with a large mass of undramatic material to wrestle with, and the most effective scene occurs not at the end of the play but near the beginning. At the end of the first act the Duke of York's enemies crown him with a paper crown on the battlefield before they kill him, and York turns on them in another of those wonderfully effective speeches that make Shakespeare so loved by actors. The speech is particularly directed against Queen Margaret, "she-wolf of France," and rises in a crescendo of rhetoric to its climax.

O tiger's heart wrapp'd in a woman's hide!

howls the Duke of York, and the audience evidently quivered with delight. The success of this line is shown by the fact it was the one Robert Greene chose to parody when he was attacking young "Shake-scene," and the first printed edition of the play was given the title, *The True Tragedy of Richard, Duke of York,* to capitalize on the effectiveness of York's death in the first act. According to the title page, the play was acted by the Earl of Pembroke's men, a new company that appeared for a short time in the early nineties and then collapsed. Lord Strange's men had presented the first play of the series, so it would appear that at this time Shakespeare was writing for more than one company.

The trilogy on the Wars of the Roses is the work of an ambitious young man, rather uneven in his use of words but in general deeply impressed by Marlowe, trained in a hard school of stagecraft and intent upon conquering the emotions of his audience by every means within his command. He was fascinated by the technical resources of his stage and knew exactly what the actors could do with it; and he had the courage to take a large chunk of history out of Holinshed's *Chronicles* and transmute it into real theatre material. The series is unplayable today, if only for its lack of characterization and its jingoistic view of English history, but in its own day it ranked as one of the best series of productions that the London theatre had to offer.

Another enormously successful play that Shakespeare wrote at about the same time was *Titus Andronicus*.* In the following century there were playgoers who claimed doggedly that *Titus Andronicus* and *The Spanish Tragedy* were the best plays ever written, and they certainly were, if violent and bloodthirsty action is any criterion. Shakespeare's play was a severe test of the skill of the actors in staging atrocity scenes, since Titus has a hand chopped off in full view of the audience, his sons' heads are brought on stage, and his daughter Lavinia is instructed by the stage directions to enter with

"her hands cut off, and her tongue cut out." Lavinia holds a basin between the stumps of her hands to catch the blood of the men who have raped her, and her father, Titus, serves them up in a pie for their mother to eat.

A modern reader, faced with such a wave of bloodshed, would be likely to conclude that Shakespeare had been carried away by his desire to please his audience and had packed his play with witless atrocities calculated to please the lowest element in the groundlings. As a matter of fact, the exact opposite would be much nearer the truth. Shakespeare was trying to write a "noble Roman history" and conform to the best standards of the classical drama as they were understood in his day.

The model with whom Shakespeare was wrestling at this point was Seneca. To the Renaissance mind Seneca stood for all that was impressive and valuable in ancient tragedy, and although he was unfortunately a heathen writer, many useful morals could be drawn from his work. Queen Elizabeth herself had translated parts of some of his plays, and various poets had combined to make the translation of his ten tragedies that was published in 1581. Ever since the cultured young gentlemen of the Inns of Court and the universities had been writing plays, Seneca had been one of their most revered models, and at the violent climax of a Senecan imitation put on at Trinity College, Cambridge, a gentlewoman in the

---

* The first mention of a production date for *Titus Andronicus* is January 24, 1594, when the Earl of Sussex' men played it at the Rose. But it was licensed for publication two weeks later and the title page stated that three different companies had played it, those of the Earl of Derby, the Earl of Pembroke, and the Earl of Sussex. The production date of 1594 applies only to Sussex' company, so it is evident that both the other acting companies must have played *Titus Andronicus* earlier than this. —AUTHOR'S NOTE

audience "fell distracted and never recovered."

Seneca had written his plays for a rather clever, weary Roman audience who heard them recited rather than acted, and his combination of rhetoric and horror was excellently adapted to keep his audience awake. When his plays were translated into English they were read by a young, excitable public, deeply impressed by the moral maxims and fascinated by the atrocities that were described. When Shakespeare read Seneca, he was especially impressed by the story of Thyestes, in which the hero is served a banquet of his children's flesh. It would not have occurred to him to criticize the revered Seneca, whom even the rigid French classicists took as their model; but for vulgar sensationalism there is nothing in *Titus Andronicus* to match Seneca's description of the cooking of the children, with the chunks of flesh making the broth and the livers sizzling on the spit.

Shakespeare could not transfer Seneca intact to the public stage, since no Elizabethan audience would have been content with six characters, a messenger, and a very chatty chorus. On the contrary, Shakespeare loaded his stage for *Titus Andronicus* as thoroughly as he had done for the *Henry VI* trilogy. In the first scene he used the outer and inner stage, the trap door, and the balcony, and crowded the area with processions and warriors and all the visual ex-

citement that a crowd of splendidly dressed actors could offer. Nevertheless, when an Elizabethan went to a play like *Titus Andronicus*, he would know that he had had a cultural experience. The various quotations from classical authors that Shakespeare had so earnestly imbedded in the text would have told him so. Even the rape and mutilation of Lavinia had classical justification, since it was based on Ovid's story of Philomela.

William Shakespeare was an excited, ambitious young man, eager to succeed as a writer and seizing on every kind of assistance he could get. London was the literary capital of England, and as a Londoner he was bombarded by a series of literary influences from every direction. When Geoffrey Chaucer started to write poetry, more than two centuries earlier, there was only one model he could imitate—the French school of academic love poetry. But William Shakespeare found new models wherever he turned, and the time of his youth, like that of most good writers, was spent in constant, excited experimentation with first one way of writing and then another.*

Having attempted a Roman trag-

* Youth is a comparative term, since Shakespeare was twenty-eight in 1592. But Chaucer was about the same age when he wrote his first important poem, a piece of slavish imitation of the French that shows almost no signs of his future genius. Both men developed comparatively late as writers and both men went through almost exactly the same period of imitation in their twenties.—AUTHOR'S NOTE

edy in *Titus Andronicus,* Shakespeare attempted a Roman comedy in *The Comedy of Errors.* In the same way that Seneca was the chief model for classical tragedy in the Renaissance, Plautus was the chief model for classical comedy. Nothing in Plautus was more popular than the device of the identical twins in his *Menaechmi,* and for the past fifty years the Italian dramatists had been offering complicated variations on this theme to the Italian theatregoing public. The Italian playwrights operated under a strict formula, for the stage always had to represent a city square, with a series of houses in the background, and the rules of action were as rigid as the rules of stagecraft.

Shakespeare did his best to write a correct Italian comedy in *The Comedy of Errors.* He planned the play as though it were going to be shown on a fixed set, with three doors opening off a market place. One door led to the abbey, one to the house of Antipholus, and one to the house of the courtesan. Shakespeare also kept rigidly to the classical doctrine of the three unities, and all the action takes place in the city of Ephesus in a single day. Both in staging and in construction the play is a neat, tight imitation of academic Italian comedy, which in turn was an imitation of Plautus, and the complicated intrigue is expertly handled. The one characteristically Elizabethan thing about the play is its riot of puns. Shakespeare never lost his youthful enthusiasm for wordplay, and his audience was so well trained in the art of listening that they could hear even the most complicated joke and set up a howl of recognition.

During this period of experimentation Shakespeare tried still another way of writing. Ten years earlier one of the great figures on the literary scene had been John Lyly, who had become a playwright after making a great success with a novel called *Euphues.* Popular novelists like Greene and Munday and Gosson had produced immediate imitations and even Tom Nashe admitted that he had read *Euphues* devotedly when he was "a little ape at Cambridge." The rhetorical flourishes and the mannered, ornamental style that Lyly used were not original with him, and at least one professor of Latin at Oxford had been training his students to use the same style in their Latin prose; but it struck the London public, with its greedy ear for words, as an altogether new and charming way to write. Lyly had acquired the patronage of the Earl of Oxford and had gone on to write graceful light comedies that were too slight for the public stages but very well suited to the boy companies that were acting in small private theatres at Blackfriars and at St. Paul's.

By the nineties the vein of euphuism was wearing a little thin; but Lyly's rhetoric was still the model for a good deal of fashionable writing, and Shakespeare was following what was still one of the main literary currents of the day when he wrote *Love's Labour's Lost*. The play cannot be dated but Shakespeare apparently took the names of his three young lords from the news pamphlets that were coming out about the wars in France. These pamphlets ceased when Henry of Navarre became a Catholic in 1593, but before that date printers like Richard Field brought the public news of men like the Duc de Longueville, the Duc de Mayenne, and Marechal Biron. Shakespeare's little comedy has no relation to actual French history, but he made his hero the King of Navarre and named his three lords Longaville, Dumaine, and Berowne.

In *Love's Labour's Lost* Shakespeare gave final proof that he was capable of doing almost any kind of writing and doing it well. The piece is as formal and lively as a galliard and was no more intended to be taken seriously. It is the work of a young man who was beginning to know all the literary angles and how to handle them to maintain a continuous ripple of laughter from his audience. Shakespeare plays a game with words and does a lighthearted parody of most of the literary fashions of the day, from euphuism to sonneteering. He even introduces an engaging sketch of a group of earnest amateur actors trying to present a play while their aristocratic audience makes continuous, gentle fun of them. In his aristocrats Shake-speare presents the first of his lively, mocking young men and his delightful, quick-witted girls, and although they are conventionalized sketches in comparison with what he was to do later, they manage to show the breath of life even in their endless Renaissance discussions on the subject of love. He took the stock Italian comedy figures of the Pedant and the Braggart, and in Holofernes and Armado continued them in their long and honorable tradition. Holofernes is an exact copy of what every comic schoolmaster was supposed to be on the stage, which was already an ancient tradition when Sir Philip Sidney wrote an entertainment to be given at one of the Earl of Leicester's entertainments in 1578 and had the schoolmaster start off, "Let me delicidate the very intrinsecal maribone of the matter."

Love's Labour's Lost is a Londoner's play, written for people who knew all the latest jokes with words. It was written by a man who had been watching and listening even more intently than he had been reading, and who could enter into the aristocratic life of the city with the same ease he could enter into Plautus or the court of Henry VI. But although it is a city play, few Londoners could have written the two country songs that bring it to a close. Nor would anyone but Shakespeare have dared to end his courtly dance of words with a winter song that shows a real country village in cold weather.

All these plays were written in

the early nineties and it seems reasonably clear that most of them had been produced before Robert Greene attacked the young actor-turned-playwright in September 1592. Greene's death happened to coincide with an event that created a chasm in the theatrical world and destroyed the market for new plays entirely. For on the 7th of September, 1592, the London Council put the plague orders into effect and all the theatres were closed until 1594.

The London Council had been attacking the theatres all that year. The mayor and aldermen began with a complaint to Archbishop Whitgift in February in which they asked his help to save the youth of the city, whose manners were being "infected with many evil and ungodly qualities by reason of the wanton and profane devices represented upon the stages." At the end of May there was a riot by some apprentices in Southwark, for which the Council instantly blamed the evil taught by the theatres, and in June all "profane spectacles" were forbidden until the 29th of September. By the 7th of September, however, the plague had made such inroads on the city that the plague orders were put into effect and all assemblies were suppressed within seven miles of London.

This was the same plague that had struck Stratford the year Shakespeare was born, and it had been a frequent visitor in London. The plague orders were invoked whenever the deaths passed a certain number, and represented the best the city authorities could devise. Infected houses were put under a twenty-day quarantine, every householder had to wash his part of the street twice a day, graves had to be six feet deep, two discreet women from each parish were to do the shopping and nursing for the quarantined, with the parish paying for their services if necessary, and the College of Physicians was to designate a certain number of its members to handle infected patients only. Human nature being what it is, the parish nurses were not always discreet and the graves were not always six feet deep, but the London Council had done its best with a problem that was both perennial and insoluble.

A wise and loving citizen of London named John Howes had suggested in 1587 that tax-supported public housing would go a long way to rid the city of the plague. "Let London take example of Augusta in Germany, where the citizens have builded . . . houses for the poor people, in a convenient air, with three rooms, chimneys and privies and little yards." Let London "erect three or four hundred tenements and remove the poor people out of those filthy alleys, and let the alleys be razed down to the ground and converted to open yards and gardens, and so shall the city be . . . delivered of a thousand infections." Such a suggestion must have seemed preposterous to the London Council, since it was already known what caused plagues. As a London preacher aptly phrased it during an earlier visitation of God's scourge, "The cause of plagues is sin, if you look to it well; and the cause of sin are plays; therefore the cause of plagues are plays." The restraint put upon the actors in September was certainly legitimate, since public assemblies tended to spread the infection, but it would have been a good thing for London if the Council had listened more to John Howes and less to the preachers.

The actors did the only thing left for them to do: they went on tour. They continued to hope that the London theatres might reopen shortly, and Henslowe did manage one brief winter season at the Rose. But on the 28th of January the Council repeated its order suppressing all assemblies except for divine service within seven miles of London, and theatre business did not become normal in London again until the 3rd of June, 1594.

The market for new plays was of course destroyed during this two-year period. Touring actors could not afford the risk and expense of trying out new productions. They took with them only plays that they knew would be successful and even these were heavily cut for country audiences, partly because they would not understand London illusions and partly because the companies were smaller and more parts had to be doubled.

To increase their strength, some of the companies amalgamated. Edward Alleyn, for instance, belonged to the Admiral's men, but he joined forces with the actors of Lord Strange's company and sent his wife long letters from the provinces. Like nearly all the other actors Alleyn was a very domestic man and felt his exile from his household in London keenly, one postscript imploring his wife for news. "Mouse, you send me no news of any thing; you should send me of your domestical matters, such things as happen at home, as how your distilled water proves, or this, or that, or any thing what you will. And, Jug, I pray you, let my orange-tawny stockings of woollen be dyed a very good black against I come home to wear in the winter. You sent me not word of my garden but next time you will. But remember this in any case, that all that bed which was parsley in the month of September, you sow it with spinach for then is the time. I would do it myself but we shall not come home till All Hallows tide and so, sweet mouse, farewell, and brook our long journey with patience."

Alleyn was the son-in-law of Philip Henslowe, the theatre owner, and Henslowe wrote that the spinach bed was sown but that a rival company of actors had collapsed. This was Lord Pembroke's company. In spite of a good collection of play scripts, including at least one of Shakespeare's, the company dissolved on tour in August 1593, and its members had to pawn their costumes to pay their expenses.

Many of the companies tried to help their finances by selling their stocks of playbooks to the printers, a practice they normally avoided because it cut down the potential audiences and gave other companies an opportunity to see the texts of their plays. There was an abnormal sale of play scripts during the plague period, and whereas four plays were entered for publication in 1592, twenty-three were entered in 1594. Many of these plays appeared in print with the text in a jumbled corrupt condition, showing unmistakable signs of having been reconstructed from the memories of the actors. The actors invented where they could not remember or even inserted lines from different plays altogether. But at least a great many plays were brought into print that otherwise would have vanished forever, and it is better to have them in pirated versions than not to have them at all.

Meanwhile the playwrights themselves had fallen on evil days, and one by one the great names were disappearing. Robert Greene had died four days before the plague orders went into effect and was buried in a winding sheet that cost four shillings of his landlord's money. His friend, Tom Lodge, had gone on a naval expedition to make his fortune; the voyage was a disastrous one from the beginning, and Lodge arrived back in England during the plague period, almost penniless, to start a long legal wrangle with his brother Wil-

liam. John Lyly's career as a playwright had ended when the company known as Paul's Boys was dissolved in 1590, and he tried desperately to get some kind of a position at Court for the rest of the decade, living on what he called "dead hopes."

As for the greatest of the university playwrights, his fall was the most sudden and spectacular. On the 30th of May, 1593, Christopher Marlowe was stabbed in a tavern kept by one Eleanor Bull. According to the coroner's report, there had been a quarrel over the bill between Marlowe and one Ingram Frizer. Marlowe seized Frizer's dagger and gave him two head wounds, and Frizer got his dagger back and killed Marlowe instantly with a single stab above the right eye.

The quarrel may have been over the reckoning, as the coroner's jury decided. It may have been political in origin, since Marlowe had served as a government agent. But Marlowe's own contemporaries were convinced they knew the real cause of it: it was the judgment of heaven on a wicked man who did not believe in the Christian religion. During May an informer had been drawing up a long list of Marlowe's sins as a freethinker, ranging from rowdy remarks about the Holy Ghost to his conviction that religion was only a device to hold men in bondage. Thomas Kyd, who had once roomed with Marlowe, was brought in for questioning by the Privy Council on the subject of

Marlowe's "monstrous opinions," and Kyd wrote a letter on the subject of Marlowe's wicked nature and his own pure one that reads unpleasantly today but was a natural Elizabethan reaction to the horrors of atheism. When Gabriel Harvey heard that Marlowe was dead, he concluded that the plague had killed him and saw the hand of God in the event, striking him down for "his toad conceit." By the end of the decade a new theory had turned up, that "Marlowe was stabbed to death by a bawdy servingman." But whatever the exact circumstances, it was generally agreed by Marlowe's smug contemporaries that he was a wicked man and his death was a judgment on him.

Apart from Shakespeare, almost the only playwrights that remained were Thomas Kyd and Thomas Nashe. Since there was no market for plays, Nashe's chief literary contribution to that rainy and dismal year of 1593 was a composition called *Christ's Tears over Jerusalem,* in which he pointed out with impeccable orthodoxy that the plague was a punishment for sin. "As great a desolation as Jerusalem hath London deserved," reported Nashe to his readers, recognizing a changed literary market when he saw one.

Thomas Kyd's activities as a writer in 1593 were even more peculiar. The author of the popular *Spanish Tragedy* was writing a drama called *Cornelia,* which was not intended to be acted but was designed to assist the Countess of Pembroke in her campaign to raise the artistic level of the English drama.

Mary, Countess of Pembroke, was the sister of Sir Philip Sidney, a charming, forceful, intellectual woman who considered it a duty to her dead brother to try to raise the level of English writing. The theatregoing public in its uncouth way had failed to realize that just across the Channel a great playwright was writing great plays. His name was Robert Garnier and all the best critics in France joined in admiration of his work. Garnier's taste was so civilized that he managed to be a Senecan without any of Seneca's harrowing details, and the Countess of Pembroke was convinced that nothing could be better suited to raise the current low level of English drama than a complete translation of the works of Robert Garnier.

Mary started the movement herself by translating Garnier's play on Marc Antony, which was published in 1592 in a charming little octavo volume, beautifully printed on fine paper. She encouraged her little coterie of poets to do likewise, and perhaps her greatest success was with Samuel Daniel, who did a play on Cleopatra. Daniel was exalted by his mission of helping to "chase away . . . gross barbarism" and he succeeded in avoiding any indecorous action in his play by having a messenger's report that filled nine pages.

Thomas Kyd then undertook to purge himself of the disgrace of having written popular plays for the penny public, and translated Garnier's play on Cornelia. Kyd's French was not quite perfect, but the play itself was impeccable since nothing happened in it at all. The scholars praised the book and Kyd was planning to follow it with a similar work on Portia; but he suddenly died in the winter of 1594, the last of the old popular dramatists and one who had turned his back completely on the popular drama.

A period like the plague, in which all normal theatre activity in London was at a standstill, was a good opportunity for any popular playwright to try his hand at another kind of writing. Especially was this true if he were an ambitious writer and wanted to be admired by a more select and intellectual public than the ordinary theatregoer. Shakespeare had been growing increasingly ambitious, and both *Titus Andronicus* and *The Comedy of Errors* show an attempt to write in the classical manner. The plague gave him both time and opportunity, for an actor did not go on tour during the winter months, and it was probably late in 1592 that he wrote the classical narrative he called *Venus and Adonis*.

Nothing that Shakespeare had done up to this point counted as real writing. His plays were not his property. They belonged to whatever company had bought them, to publish or not as the company saw fit, and when the first of

them began to straggle into print at the end of the plague period they appeared anonymously. No literary man took these cheap little quarto texts seriously, but *Venus and Adonis* was a different matter altogether. It was designed as a conscious work of art and written seriously and conscientiously according to the best models.

There is no mistaking the ambitious frame of mind in which the young poet wrote his first real poem. The correct thing to do was to begin a work of this kind with a Latin quotation, and the motto that Shakespeare chose from Ovid is almost touching in its arrogance.

Vilia miretur vulgus; mihi flavus Apollo
Pocula Castalia plena ministret aqua.

"Let the base mob admire what is vile; golden-haired Apollo may serve me cups filled with water from the Muses' spring." This was the same contempt for the literary taste of the "penny knaves" that was conventional with well-educated young gentlemen and that Thomas Lodge had expressed at the close of his narrative poem on Glaucus and Scilla a few years earlier. Shakespeare used the same meter that Lodge had used in his poem, but his model was not a single narrative so much as the whole flood of ornamental classical narratives in verse in which the young writers of England sought to show that they were the worthy heirs of antiquity. *Venus and Adonis* is steeped in classicism, in the rather limited Renaissance meaning of the word, and is full of the rich imagery and antique rhetorical devices that educated Renaissance readers had been taught to admire.

If *Venus and Adonis* had been written by a gentleman, it would probably not have been published at all, for gentlemen circulated their work only in manuscript and did not permit it to be handled by the general public in bookstalls. Shakespeare did not belong to this exalted group, and like the university writers he was only too anxious to find a reliable printer who would publish the book for him. Whether through friendship or for some other reason his choice was Richard Field, son of old Henry Field of Stratford who had died in the summer of 1591 and whose goods had been appraised by his neighbor, John Shakespeare. Richard Field was living at Blackfriars, where he owned his own press and was one of the twenty-two master printers that were permitted to operate in the city of London.

Richard Field was not only the printer of Shakespeare's poem but its publisher also. On the 18th of April, 1593, he filed notice with the Stationers' Company that he was the owner of "a book entitled Venus and Adonis" which had been duly licensed by Archbishop Whitgift and by one of the wardens of the Stationers' Company, and he paid the usual fee of sixpence to have the information entered on the Stationers' Register. This served as a copyright notice and made it im-

possible, or at least difficult, for another printer to steal the book and print it himself. Only about sixty-five per cent of the books that got into print were registered, but the practice protected the printer's investment and made it possible for him to pay the author a larger sum for the manuscript than if he had to run the risk of piracy. These payments to the author varied from a few free copies of the book, when the printer feared the worst, to as much as forty pounds for a really popular book on theology. It would be a fair estimate that Shakespeare got about two pounds from Field for the manuscript. Certainly he did not get more than that, since from the publishing point of view he was an unknown writer.

Field did not handle much general literature and his publications were mostly books on theology, textbooks and classics. When his master, Thomas Vautrollier, had run the press, his chief contribution to literature had been Sir Thomas North's translation of Plutarch's *Lives,* and Field in his turn had published *The Art of English Poesie* and a very elaborate English version of Ariosto's *Orlando Furioso.* But his books were mostly of the scholarly sort, and Field was equipped to set type in both Greek and Hebrew.

Venus and Adonis was a little outside the usual run of Field's printing, but he made Shakespeare's narrative poem into a handsome little volume, with good presswork and careful proofreading. Some extra copies of the title page were struck off, in the usual fashion, to be fastened to various posts around town and used as advertising, and the title page carried the information that the book could be bought "at the sign of the White Greyhound in Paul's Churchyard."

Richard Field had no retail outlet of his own in Paul's Churchyard, so he had arranged for the book to be sold through the shop of John Harrison, senior, who was one of the major London publishers. Field had printed two books in Latin for Harrison, but they would have known each other in any case as fellow members of the Company of Stationers. All the printers belonged to a regular chartered guild, with a hall on the southwest side of Paul's Churchyard and a handsome coat of arms full of books and birds and flowers. The Stationers' Company was one of the most strictly run of the London guilds, for the government had no intention of allowing seditious printing, and the slightest irregularity was severely checked. It was the Stationers' Company that was responsible for tracking down an illegal printer who was trying to do presswork in a tailor's shop while he kept his letters in a nearby henhouse, and it was the Stationers' Company that formally burned all banned books in the Hall kitchen. Discipline was handled through an elaborate organization headed by a Master, two Wardens, and a Court of Assistants, and the Master was the highest post in the company

that a printer could attain. John Harrison had twice been Master of the company when he accepted *Venus and Adonis* for sale in his shop, the White Greyhound, so that Shakespeare's first poem was launched under the best possible auspices.

Every book needed a patron to whom it could be dedicated, and an experienced man of letters like Gervase Markham could often pack several into a single book. When Markham wrote a poetic narrative on a sea fight, he opened with a dedication to Lord Mountjoy and announced that he was "eternally" his Lordship's. He then, on the next page, offered his work to the "sacred hand" of the Earl of Sussex. This was followed with a dedication to Sir Edward Wingfield and another "to the right honorable Henry Wriothesley, Earl of Southampton and Baron of Tichfield" whom he implored to favor his work.

Vouchsafe to sweet it with thy blessed
    tongue . . .
So shall my tragic lays be blest by
    thee
And from thy lips suck their eternity.

A frenzied obeisance of this kind was correct in addressing a man like the Earl of Southampton, who was one of the most glittering of the younger generation at Court. Even Tom Nashe, who was no courtier, grew almost fulsome in his dedication to Southampton: "A new brain, a new wit, a new style, a new soul will I get me, to canonize your name to posterity." Barnabe Barnes grew poetic over Southampton's "gracious eyes, those heavenly lamps which give the Muses light," and John Florio said in his dedication, "To me and many more, the glorious and gracious sunshine of your Honor hath infused light and life."

In comparison with the usual dedication to the Earl of Southampton, Shakespeare's address to him is both sober and dignified. "To the Right Honorable Henry Wriothesley, Earl of Southampton, and Baron of Tichfield. Right Honorable, I know not how I shall offend in dedicating my unpolished lines to your Lordship, nor how the world will censure me for choosing so strong a prop to support so weak a burthen: only, if your Honour seem but pleased, I account myself highly praised, and vow to take advantage of all idle hours, till I have honoured you with some graver labour. But if the first heir of my invention prove deformed, I shall be sorry it had so noble a godfather, and never after ear so barren a land, for fear it yield me still so bad a harvest. I leave it to your honorable survey, and your Honour to your heart's content; which I wish may always answer your own wish, and the world's hopeful expectation. Your Honour's in all duty, William Shakespeare."

There is nothing in this dedication to show that Shakespeare knew the Earl of Southampton personally. He merely hoped the poem would please him and offered it in a dignified way that is a pleasant contrast to the average Elizabethan dedication. He called the poem "the first heir of my invention" because it would not have occurred to the young playwright-turned-poet that his stage plays were worth mentioning, as from Southampton's point of view they certainly were not.

Shakespeare probably chose Southampton as his patron because *Venus and Adonis* was a love poem. The Earl was only nineteen years old in that spring of 1593, and the sensuous style and mild eroticism of the poem were the kind a young man would like. The Earl was a newcomer at Court, and some of his contemporaries considered him a rather unstable young man. His father and mother had become estranged when he was a small boy, and when his father died, leaving him the bulk of an enormous fortune, he also left a large sum of money to the small Earl's sister on the implacable condition that she was not to live in the same house with their mother. Lord Burghley brought the boy up, and whereas Burghley's own son Robert was a model of industry and propriety, young Southampton was more difficult to manage in spite of the beautifully written exercises he sent his guardian from Cambridge to show his progress. When he left school, he was supposed to marry Burghley's granddaughter and refused, and in 1594 a Court lady refused to marry him because he was so unstable and "so easily carried away."

The one steadfast emotion in Southampton's life was probably his reverence for the Earl of Essex, whom he worshiped with all the ardor that a young man can feel for a romantic and slightly older one.

At nineteen Southampton was a beautiful figure with his jewels and his laces and his respectful coterie of writing men, a patron young enough to enjoy a love poem and educated enough to appreciate the way it was written. Like all the young men of the day he was brought up on Ovid, and it was to "Ovid's wanton muse" that Nashe had appealed when he wrote an especially outspoken piece of eroticism in *The Choice of Valentines.* Shakespeare's poem is both innocent and dignified in comparison with Nashe's, but it belongs to the same general group and would have appealed to the same kind of reader.

When young Elizabethans read *Venus and Adonis,* it was not for its noble thoughts on the danger of lust or for its charming country descriptions, but for the detailed description of an attempted seduction and for the lush, rather overwrought Renaissance imagery. There is a risk in this kind of writing, unless the reader himself is also young and very much in earnest, that the flood of words may give an occasionally comic effect that was not intended. Even Shakespeare did not escape lapses of this kind, as in the scene where Adonis attempts to revive Venus and "wrings her nose." When Venus mourns the death of Adonis, the language gets even more out of control.

"Aye me!" she cries, and twenty times, "Woe, woe!"

As a character in one of Shakespeare's later plays remarked dryly, "This passion, and the death of a dear friend, would go near to make a man look sad." But Shakespeare was not yet at the point when he thought that unrestrained hyperbole was rather funny, and certainly his readers were not.

Venus and Adonis was an enormous success. It went through ten editions in Shakespeare's lifetime and the handsome little book was read and reread until it fell to pieces. It was lavishly quoted in anthologies, and a Cambridge play written four years later accuses one susceptible young man of keeping the poem under his pillow with a picture of "sweet Mr. Shakespeare" on his study wall.

Shakespeare at once set about writing the "graver" poem that he had promised if the first one was a success. This new poem would not appeal so much to the young and giddy, who liked love stories, but to their more reverend seniors who valued a poem for its moral instruction. It told the story of Tarquin's rape of Lucrece, and was even longer and more ornamental than the first one had been.

Shakespeare had unquestionably met Southampton after the success of *Venus and Adonis,* and Southampton must have shown his appreciation of the poem with a generous gift, since that was what a patron was for. The tone of the second dedication is much warmer and more personal, even though the word "love" had the force in the Renaissance that the word "friendship" has now. "The love I dedicate to your Lordship is without end; whereof this pamphlet, without beginning, is but a superfluous moiety. The warrant I have of your honorable disposition, not the worth of my untutored lines, makes it assured of acceptance. What I have done is yours; what I have to do is yours; being part of all I have, devoted yours. Were my worth greater, my duty would show greater; meantime, as it is, it is bound to your Lordship, to whom I wish long life, still lengthened with happiness. Your Lordship's in all duty, William Shakespeare."

Shakespeare's second narrative poem, like his first one, was in imitation of the best contemporary models. This time his chief model was Samuel Daniel, who had made a great success in 1592 with *The Complaint of Rosamund.* Daniel's poem went through two editions the year of publication, for "everyone passioneth when he readeth the afflicted death of Daniel's distressed Rosamund." Daniel's poem had the further merit of being stuffed with moral reflections, which each reader could copy out in his commonplace book, and Shakespeare could hardly have chosen a more popular model.

Shakespeare used the same meter as Daniel and expanded some of his devices. Daniel gave a brief description of a casket ornamented with pictures from classical legends which Rosamund connects with her own problem, and Shakespeare gives an extremely lengthy description of a wall painting so that Lucrece can do the same. Rosamund has fifteen stanzas of vocal lamentation before she succeeds in killing herself, and Lucrece's "sad dirge" before her suicide takes almost as long. Shakespeare included the same kind of moral observation that had been admired in Daniel, and in turn his own poem took its place as one of the most extravagantly admired productions of the decade. The narrative was more popular even than *Venus and Adonis,* with four editions called for in six years, and an anthology that was compiled at the end of the decade had ninety-one quotations from *The Rape of Lucrece.*

Richard Field did not publish *Lucrece.* That honor went to John Harrison of the White Greyhound who evidently realized at once that William Shakespeare was going to be a valuable literary commodity. Harrison retained Field to do the printing on the new book, but he took out the copyright himself, entering *Lucrece* in the Stationers' Register on the 9th of May, 1594. He also wanted to publish future editions of *Venus and Adonis,* and arranged with Field to have the copyright transferred to him the following month.

The success of his two poems found Shakespeare in an enviable position in the spring of 1594. No poet, especially a beginning poet, could have asked for more. He had a wealthy, influential, and satisfied patron who was one of the highest noblemen in the land. He had a publisher who was one of the most important men in his profession and who was obviously deeply interested in his career. He was beginning to get a chorus of commendation from the critics, especially for "all-praiseworthy Lucretia," and his position in the eyes of posterity, if he kept on as he had begun, was assured. As Richard Barnfield apostrophized him four years later, he was a poet

Whose Venus, and whose Lucrece, sweet and chaste,
Thy name in fame's immortal book have placed.

There was nothing in this to prevent Shakespeare continuing with his profession as an actor, but it gave him no special incentive to go on writing plays. The average play did not bring its author more than six pounds, and the approval of Harrison and Southampton would have guaranteed him much more than that for a new narrative poem. Moreover, a poet could not get a reputation by writing plays, which were either not printed at all in 1594 or else flooding the bookstalls in cheap, badly printed quartos that were better off anonymous. At its best a play could bring nothing but the uncritical applause of the "penny knaves," while a handsomely printed and successful book that went through several editions brought a poet not only the praise of his contemporaries but a continuing name to generations as yet unborn.

It is no exaggeration to say that the spring of 1594 was the turning point of Shakespeare's life as a writer. *Lucrece* was obviously going to be a success, as *Venus and Adonis* had been, and it was time to fulfill the promise Shakespeare had made in his last dedication to Southampton and write him another poem.

The career of every writer is strewn with various opportunities for destroying himself. If Shakespeare had continued on the course he had planned for himself, of writing for the Earl of Southampton and the better-class Elizabethan reader instead of for the penny public, his genius for characterization would have been permanently blocked. He would have gone on writing handsome, ornate poems that were as rich in detail as a well-made tapestry but equally lacked the breath of life. When the special Renaissance cult that produced such poems receded at the end of the decade, Shakespeare's work would have receded with it; he would have become one of the many minor Elizabethan writers whose works interest the literary scholar but have no life at all for the general public.

One of the qualities that make a writer great is his instinct for avoiding a pitfall that can destroy him. Whether or not Shakespeare was consciously aware of the fact, his genius depended on having complete writing freedom. More than any writer in the world's history, Shakespeare needed space around him, space to try anything he wanted without any literary rules to hamper him or any literary specialists to eye his work and pass their small judgments.

There was no space of this kind in Southampton's narrow circle, any more than there ever is in any special literary clique or fashion. The only audience that could give him that kind of liberty was the penny public of the London theatre, the ordinary London citizens who did not judge by Italian rules of the unities or French rules of diction or English rules of decorum but only by what they enjoyed. They did not want words to be treated as masters, to be respectfully arranged according to the best rules. They wanted them to be treated as servants, to bring them real people and real emotions.

In the spring of 1594, when the theatres reopened after the plague, Shakespeare turned his back forever on the literary success he had wanted so ardently when he began writing *Venus and Adonis*. He apparently made no further use of the standing he had achieved with Southampton, and after 1594 there is no document that shows any further connection between the two men at all. He made no further use of his standing with John Harrison and never offered him another manuscript. He wrote some sonnets

but he did not want to print them, and they were not published until fifteen years later in what was obviously an unauthorized edition, put into print by a minor figure in the book trade who had neither a shop nor a press. The only poem he ever again wrote for publication was a short piece called "The Phoenix and the Turtle" which appeared at the beginning of the next decade in a book called *Love's Martyr*. Shakespeare was one of four playwrights who contributed verses to the project, which was in honor of Sir John Salisbury, and the contribution seems to have been a good-natured gesture to a friend of his —about the equivalent of a nineteenth-century poet writing some verses for a memory book.

Everything else that Shakespeare wrote for the rest of his life belonged to the company of actors he joined in the spring of 1594. The company controlled the copyright of all his plays, to be published or not as it saw fit, and Shakespeare was content to be merely a working member of the company.

William Shakespeare was like his father in one thing at least: when he decided to do something, he did it thoroughly. Such complete devotion to the theatre was not merely unusual in an Elizabethan writer; it was unheard of, especially when a writer had, like Shakespeare, achieved so lofty a literary eminence in so short a time. Even if he had been unwilling to continue with narrative poems, he might have written court masques, like Ben

onson and Samuel Daniel and
Francis Beaumont. Or, like other
playwrights, he might have written
city pageants, or verses for special
public occasions, or even the complimentary poems that most writers
turned out as a matter of course to
be printed in the front of their
friends' books. Even Thomas Heywood, who spent over forty years
in the theatre as actor and playwright, wrote nondramatic works
so that his name would not be lost
to posterity, and all the other prac-
ticing playwrights, from Thomas
Dekker to George Chapman, did
the same. When the elderly Lady
Helen Branch died in the spring
of 1594, a writer suggested publicly
that an elegy from the author of
Lucrece would make a fitting memorial, and when Queen Elizabeth
died, another writer again called on
Shakespeare to write a funeral ode.
Shakespeare wrote nothing, nor did
he join the almost unanimous
chorus of poetical voices that welcomed King James to the throne.
He was the one writer of the period
who wrote for the stage and for the
stage only.

The next sixteen years of Shakespeare's life are of a creative violence unparalleled in literary history. It was as though a great wind
had suddenly found its true course
and could blow free.

❧ Chapter 6

By the spring of 1594 the plague
had worn itself out in London. The
weather improved, the splendid
shops in Goldsmiths' Row were
given a new coat of paint, and a
goldsmith named Francis Langley
began to plan a new theatre in
Southwark that would hold three
thousand people. The actors who
had survived the difficulties of the
past two years began to reorganize,
and two great acting companies
emerged that were to dominate the
London stage for the rest of the
reign.

One of these two companies was
headed by Edward Alleyn and financed by his wealthy father-in-
law, Philip Henslowe. During the
plague Alleyn had acted in the
provinces with Lord Strange's company, but in 1594 he again headed
his own company and began a long
tenancy of his father-in-law's theatre, the Rose. The patron of the
company was Charles, Lord Howard of Effingham, who had commanded the fleet against the
Spanish Armada. Since he held the
post of Lord High Admiral of England, Alleyn's company of actors
was known as the Admiral's company.

Alleyn's chief rivals were the actors with whom he had played in
the provinces during the plague. At
that time they were under the patronage of Lord Strange, and when
he died in the spring of 1594 they

found themselves a new patron in Henry, Lord Hunsdon, who was the Queen's first cousin and her closest living relative. Lord Hunsdon was a member of the Privy Council and had succeeded Lord Howard in the important court position of Lord Chamberlain, so that his group of actors was known as the Chamberlain's company.

It is known that William Shakespeare joined the Chamberlain's company when it was formed in 1594 because he is listed as one of the three actors who received payment for that year's Christmas performances at Court. It is not known whether he worked for the company earlier, when it was under the patronage of Lord Strange, since his name is on none of the scattered lists that have survived; but he remained with this group of actors for the rest of his professional life.

The men who made up this company were for all practical purposes closer to Shakespeare than his own brothers, for he worked with them summer and winter, most of the day and often well into the night, for the next sixteen years. They were his fellow craftsmen, his close personal friends, and in one sense as much the tools of his art as the words he used. They were the medium through which he operated as a playwright to reach the emotions of his audience, and it was one of the most fortunate things in Shakespeare's fortunate life that he worked with so able and intelligent a group of men.

An Elizabethan acting company was organized in such a way that each member was heavily dependent on his fellow members, and the economic life of the troupe depended on selfless and intelligent co-operation. There was joint ownership of costumes and properties and scripts, and in the case of Shakespeare's company a hitherto unheard-of step was eventually taken and there was joint ownership of a theatre building.

The success of this kind of thing depended less on legal agreement than on friendship, and each actor had to be willing to subordinate his personal interests to the welfare of the group as a whole. In the next decade a group of shareholders in another theatre company drew up elaborate articles of agreement which covered every possible contingency from the ownership of the costumes to the payment of the gatherers; but the shareholders' only interest was in making money and in less than two years the organization had collapsed in a flurry of lawsuits. Shakespeare's company had no need of rigid articles of agreement to keep it from quarreling, and it was not until the actors' shares began to be inherited by outsiders that there were any lawsuits at all.

Even the enemies of the acting profession were obliged to admit that some actors were "sober, discreet, properly learned, honest householders, and citizens well thought of among their neighbors." The description is an excellent one of the men of Shakespeare's company, who lived quietly and worked hard and saved their brilliance for the stage rather than for taverns and dice.

The leading actor of the company was Richard Burbage, who lived all his life in his father's parish of St. Leonard's, Shoreditch. There his seven children were baptized, and when thieves broke into his house on Holywell Street, five children's aprons were among the articles they stole. Richard Cowley was another member of the Chamberlain's company who lived most of his life on Holywell Street, where he and his wife Elizabeth brought up their four children. (Cowley received a posthumous fame by creating the role of Verges in Shakespeare's *Much Ado about Nothing*.) Shoreditch was a theatrical neighborhood, since both the Theatre and the Curtain were located there, and Shakespeare himself lived for a time within easy walking distance of Holywell Street.

Another major theatrical district was Southwark, where the Rose theatre stood already and where Langley was planning to build the Swan. Several members of the Chamberlain's company lived in Southwark. Augustine Phillips and his wife Anne brought up their five children in St. Savior's parish, and Robert Gough, his brother-in-law and fellow actor, brought up another family of five. Thomas Pope, who also lived in Southwark, was unmarried, but that did not mean he contented himself with a child-less household. He brought up a series of fatherless children and had help in rearing them from "goodwife Willingson, who is the keeper of my house." Will Sly, who was also a bachelor, lived most of his life in Southwark, but he died in the house of the Browne family in St. Leonard's parish, Shoreditch, leaving Cuthbert Burbage his sword.

The only two important members of the company who did not live in a theatrical district were John Heminges and Henry Condell. These two actors were neighbors in the parish of St. Mary Aldermanbury, a handsome residential district on the west side of town. John Heminges and his wife Rebecca brought up their fourteen children here and had a comfortable home whose cushions were striped with cloth of silver. In a nearby house Henry Condell and his wife Elizabeth brought up nine children. The two men were very active in parish affairs, Condell as a churchwarden and both he and Heminges as trustees, and John Heminges in particular had a well-developed business sense and a capacity for leadership. By 1600 he was handling nearly all the financial affairs of the Chamberlain's company, and he kept that position for the rest of his long life. Heminges was the one to whom other members of the company turned when they were in trouble, and he helped execute their wills and care for their children. He ended as a kind of dean of the acting profession, and a quatrain written on the death of Richard Burbage gives an oblique view of his status in the company.

Then fear not, Burbage, heaven's angry rod,
When thy fellows are angels and old Heminges is God.

Heminges and Condell were the last surviving members of the original company, and it was these two who were responsible, in 1623, for issuing the First Folio of Shakespeare's plays.

Shakespeare himself had no settled residence in London, since he had no wife and no children in the city. He lived for a time on Bishopsgate Street, which became Shoreditch Road soon after it passed the city walls and was therefore on the direct route to the Theatre and the Curtain. Later he moved to Southwark and became a neighbor of Augustine Phillips and Thomas Pope, and then he took rooms with a private family on the west side of town and lived in the next parish to Heminges and Condell. Like all the other actors, Shakespeare was a London resident and paid regular city taxes, but he was almost the only member of his company who did not have a permanent home.

Since Shakespeare had no household of his own, he was probably not in a position to keep an apprentice, since the whole theory of the apprentice system required a woman in the household. The wives of the actors brought up their husband's apprentices as members of the family; and Rebecca Heminges, with fourteen children of her own, had no trouble in making room for the series of boys to whom her husband was teaching the profession. Alexander Cooke was one of Heminges' apprentices, and when he grew up he named one of his daughters Rebecca, evidently after Heminges' wife. Another of Heminges' apprentices was John Rice, who acted with Richard Burbage in a city pageant after Heminges had given him special training for the part. Among Augustine Phillips' series of apprentices was Samuel Gilbourne, and when Phillips died he left his "late apprentice" forty shillings, some velvet hose, his white taffeta doublet, his black taffeta suit, his purple cloak, his sword, and his bass viol.

All these young men, Cooke and Rice and Gilbourne, stayed with the company whose members had trained them, and all of them are therefore listed in the First Folio as having acted in Shakespeare's plays. Another name that is listed there is that of Nicholas Tooley, who was apprenticed to Richard Burbage and who went to live with Richard's brother after his master's death. Tooley's will emphasizes how much the presence of a motherly woman in the household meant to a young man. "I do give unto Mrs. Burbage, the wife of my good friend Mr. Cuthbert Burbage (in whose house I now lodge) as a remembrance of my love, in respect of her motherly care over me, the sum of £10. . . . I give unto Mrs.

Condell, the wife of my good friend, Mr. Henry Condell, as a remembrance of my love, the sum of £5."

There is a charming survival of the relationship between an apprentice and his master's household in a letter sent back to London when the men of the Chamberlain's company were still under the patronage of Lord Strange and traveling with Edward Alleyn in the country. Alleyn wrote a letter for his apprentice, John Pyk, to send back to Mrs. Alleyn. John Pyk, who was called "Pig" even in the wardrobe lists, lavishly sent greetings to everyone in the household, from Dolly who woke him in the morning to Sara who cleaned his shoes, with a special message to the old gentleman with whom he used to fight for the best seat in the chimney corner. He signed himself "your petty, pretty, prattling, parleying pig" and announced in a postscript that the letter was written secretly "and my master knows not of it." This final piece of cheerful nonsense must have made the London household grin, since the letter is in Alleyn's handwriting.

Alleyn had been married less than a year when he went on tour with Strange's company, but he got complaints from his wife that the wives of the other actors received letters more often than she did. Alleyn seems to have been a very conscientious letter writer, but Philip Henslowe, his father-in-law, remarked plaintively, "We had no letter from you, when the other wives had letters sent." Alleyn's companions, like John Heminges and Augustine Phillips, must have spent a large amount of their time when they were on tour in writing letters back to their wives, for the actors whose company Shakespeare joined the following year were the most domestic of men. Henry Condell named three of his daughters Elizabeth because he was evidently determined to carry on the name of his "well-beloved wife." It does not need Phillips' reference in his will to "Anne Phillips, my loving wife" or Heminges' "to my loving wife Rebecca" to show the relationship that existed in most of the households of the Chamberlain's company.

The men of the company brought the same atmosphere into their dealings with each other, and the love that Heminges and Condell express in the First Folio for their "friend and fellow" Shakespeare is an inevitable echo of the affection the actors felt for each other. They left each other bequests in their wills, appointed each other as trustees and executors, and left their children and apprentices to each other's care. Any Elizabethan acting company had to practice a reasonable degree of co-operation among its members if it expected to survive as an economic unit, but only in Shakespeare's company is there so constant an expression of trust and friendship.

From a business point of view, an acting company did not of course operate merely on mutual affection. A successful acting company in London required very high professional standards, and the better the acting the more prosperous the company. Here again Shakespeare was fortunate, since his fellow actors stood high in the profession.

Richard Burbage was still in his twenties when the Chamberlain's company was formed in 1594; but his father, James Burbage, had been a successful actor before him, and Richard was already competing with the great Edward Alleyn for the position of the most popular actor in London. During his thirty-five years in the acting profession he achieved such a reputation that all London went into mourning for him when he died. He interpreted parts as varied as Hamlet, Othello, and King Lear, and one admirer went so far as to say that these characters only "lived in him" and died when he did. An actor's work has no testament but contemporary report and cannot be reconstructed, but from the enthusiastic evidence of his contemporaries it seems evident that Richard Burbage was a really great actor.

Another very brilliant member of the company was Will Kempe, who helped Burbage and Shakespeare collect the money for two Court productions in 1594. Kempe was the greatest comic actor of the nineties, and five years earlier Tom Nashe had hailed him in print as the legitimate successor of the great Tarleton himself. This was shortly after Kempe had returned from the Danish court at Elsinore, where he evidently had had a great success. Equally successful at the Danish court were Thomas Pope and George Bryan, both of whom also became members of the Chamberlain's company; and when Pope and Bryan left Elsinore, the King of Denmark sent them in a special carriage to their next place of residence, the court of the Duke of Saxony. At least two writers of the period single out Pope as a comedian, and Thomas Heywood, who was himself an actor, classes him with Augustine Phillips and Will Sly, both of whom also belonged to the Chamberlain's company. "Their deserts yet live in the remembrance of many."

Most of the members of Shakespeare's company cannot be traced in individual parts, since the whole principle of a good repertory company lies in the excellence of the performance as a whole rather than in the brilliance of individual members. But it seems safe to say that the Chamberlain's company consisted of an unusually experienced and intelligent group of actors, and that Shakespeare must have had a high standing as an actor or he would not have been asked to join them.

The effect of all this on Shakespeare as a playwright is worth considering. In the first place, when he wrote a play, he was sure that it would be given a careful, sympathetic, and intelligent interpretation by men who had worked together for a long time and knew their trade thoroughly. The best script in the world cannot survive a bad production and, as a contemporary testified, "A good play sometimes is hissed off the stage, through the fault of the player ill acting it." Shakespeare was obliged to run no such risks with his scripts, since they were all acted by the same group of intelligent men.

In the second place, Shakespeare experienced none of the financial pressure that usually weighed so heavily on any Elizabethan who tried to make a living with his pen. Shakespeare made his living in the same way that Richard Burbage or Henry Condell did—as an actor—and like them he invested in land and was able to leave a substantial sum of money to his heirs. His income was an actor's income, not a writer's, and it came from the pennies that were poured into the waiting hands of the gatherers at the Theatre and the Curtain, and, later on, at the Globe and the Blackfriars.

This money was handled as a lump sum and was divided every week among the actors after the expenses of the productions had been deducted. In the same way that each member of the company shared the expenses of buying costumes and scripts, renting the theatre, and paying the wages of the gatherers and other hired assistants, they shared weekly in the money that came in from the audiences. This meant that in bad times the Chamberlain's company had no financial reserves, since they had no wealthy backer such as the Admiral's company had in Philip Henslowe. But it also meant that in good times the members of the company had a great deal of ready cash at their disposal, and ready cash was a scarce commodity in Elizabethan England.

Shakespeare could never have made a living from writing plays. The highest price a playwright could get for a play during Elizabeth's reign was about eight pounds, and a successful writer like Thomas Heywood usually got six. Shakespeare wrote less than forty plays in twenty years' work in the theatre, and that would have meant an average income of less than twenty pounds a year. Ben Jonson once estimated that he had made less than £200 in his entire life from writing plays, and Shakespeare spent more than twice that sum on a single real-estate investment. His plays brought him a small additional income but he made his living as an actor, which was "the most excellent vocation in the world for money," as one embittered writer put it. If one of Shakespeare's plays was a success, he of course had the advantage of the increased receipts for that afternoon. But this was equally true of Heminges and Burbage and the rest, since no member of the company could have a success that was not shared by them all.

To realize the enormous advantages of Shakespeare's position, it is only necessary to compare him with the other playwrights of the decade.

When any other writer presented a play to the Chamberlain's company or to its rival, the Admiral's, he was paid a flat price for the manuscript and that was the last he saw of it. He surrendered all rights, and since he had no voice in the affairs of the company, he had no voice in any of the details of the production.

Nor did he have very much choice in the kind of play he was going to write, especially if the company was in a hurry for a script. It was the custom, in the Admiral's company at least, to divide the plot up and assign it to as many as four playwrights to do an act apiece. Under this system a sound plot constructed by an able craftsman was essential to the play as a whole, and a man like Anthony Munday, who was generally considered "our best plotter," could always find a use for his services. Remarkably good plays were occasionally turned out under this system, but the playwrights themselves apparently did not like it. In the next decade nearly all the good playwrights turned to writing for the boys' companies, which were revived about 1600, because the system under which they operated gave a writer much more room to please himself and much more opportunity to get the play into print.

It is not known if Shakespeare ever took part in this kind of collaboration. There is in existence a play on the life of Sir Thomas More, originally plotted by Anthony Munday and elaborated upon by playwrights like Thomas Dek-ker and Henry Chettle who were also in Henslowe's employ. The handwriting of one of the collaborators cannot be identified and is believed by many scholars to have been Shakespeare's. But the earliest known specimen of Shakespeare's writing dates from May 11, 1612, and is only the abbreviated scrawl of his signature. Only four other examples of his signature are extant, and the three on his will do not even look like the writing of the same man. An exact identification of his handwriting is therefore impossible, and in any case the probability that Shakespeare ever worked with this particular group of writers is extremely slight.

Men like Thomas Dekker and Henry Chettle were probably not unhappy in Henslowe's employ. Dekker wrote a share in nearly a play a month for four years and was a sufficiently quick writer both as a pamphleteer and playwright not to mind the strain, although he once remarked of his employers that "the player loves the poet so long as the sickness lies in the two-penny gallery" but was less affectionate when there was a full attendance. Dekker was not an especially ambitious man, and neither were his fellow workers for Henslowe, like Haughton and Porter and Wilson and Day.

On the other hand, Henslowe had many writers in his employ who thought of themselves as serious artists, and it must have been hard for men like these to operate under so mechanical a system.

Michael Drayton, Shakespeare's fellow poet from Warwickshire, is a case in point. Henslowe noted in his diary in 1598 that he had paid out four pounds in advance on a play called *Earl Godwin and His Three Sons* to "Mr. Drayton and Mr. Dekker, Mr. Chettle and Mr. Wilson." The play was read to Henslowe in a tavern on Fish Street and he paid out five shillings for "good cheer"; but a drink and a pound in advance must have seemed poor pay to Michael Drayton. He had been brought up as a page in an aristocratic household and came to London to be a great poet, beginning his career with a series of Spenserian pastorals. His *Heroical Epistles* were much admired; but literary fame buys no man his dinner, and Michael Drayton turned to writing for the stage. He knew that he would not achieve immortality by collaborating on plays, and in fact the only example of his work that has survived in print was mistakenly attributed to Shakespeare. But Drayton did not forget his literary ambitions, and while he worked on Earl Godwin or whatever other subject he was assigned, he dreamed of the masterpiece with which he was going to startle the world. He called it *Poly-Olbion,* and after fifteen years of devoted research he got the first section into print. He made no money on it whatever and had great difficulty in getting the next section into print. The printers were reluctant to accept any more of *Poly-Olbion*

because, as the normally gentle Drayton said bitterly, it "went not so fast away in the sale as some of their beastly and abominable trash." George Chapman had better luck, and while he was turning out popular comedies for Henslowe, he worked on his magnificent translation of the *Iliad*.

Drayton and Chapman had no special incentive to do good work for Henslowe. They wrote plays for him only because they needed the money, and there was no pride in the work or any liberty of action. Their position was exactly the reverse of Shakespeare's, who wrote his plays under no financial pressure at all and had complete freedom in his choice of material. As the enormous variety of his plays shows, he was never under any obligation, if he had a success, to follow it with another play of the same kind. He could range where he wished, experiment as he pleased, and his fellow actors followed him loyally and with devotion.

Shakespeare's company did him one further service as a playwright and this was a vitally important one. They kept the original text of all his plays intact, and in the end saw to it that they were all published. No other playwright of the period had such a service done for him, and three fourths of the plays written during this period have vanished. When Heminges and Condell presented the first complete edition of Shakespeare's plays to the public, they said of their fellow actor and well-loved friend, "His wit can no more lie hid than it could be lost." But many of Shakespeare's plays would have been lost and others would have survived only in corrupt editions if men like Heminges and Condell had never lived, and the survival of plays like *Antony and Cleopatra* and *The Tempest* is directly due to the care that was taken of them by Shakespeare's fellow actors.

All the contemporary evidence about Shakespeare unites to show that in his professional life he was a relaxed and happy man, almost incapable of taking offense. He did not participate in any of the literary feuds of the period, which recur in every century but were particularly numerous in the Elizabethan age, with its delighted talent for invective. As a contemporary of his, Sir John Davies, said admiringly of "our English Terence, Master William Shakespeare,"

Thou hast no railing but a reigning wit.

Part of this dislike of "railing" can be laid to Shakespeare's natural good temper and instinctive courtesy, which earned him the title of "gentle" Shakespeare, but some of it must have been caused by the favorable conditions that surrounded his professional life. He worked for sixteen years without friction and without restraint in the art he had chosen, sure of himself, of his tools, and of his results. Professionally he was a fortunate man, and equally fortunate were the men who had the privilege of working with him.

There is only one piece of evidence to show that Shakespeare ever took part in a London theatre quarrel, and in this case he seems to have been trying to assist a friend. A document of 1596 shows that Shakespeare and three others were placed under a bond not to break the peace because one William Wayte had testified that he was in "fear of death and mutilation of his limbs" from them. These bonds were a normal police device to prevent trouble in advance, but the customary legal phrase becomes a little comic in this particular case, since two of the four people from whom Wayte feared "death and mutilation" were women. The third was Shakespeare, and the fourth was Francis Langley, owner of the Swan theatre. It seems to have been primarily Langley's quarrel, since earlier in this same month of November Langley had sworn out a similar complaint of his own against William Wayte and against Wayte's stepfather, an unpopular local justice named William Gardiner. The writ against Langley, Shakespeare, and the two women was evidently in retaliation, and it seems probable that neither Dorothy Soer nor Anne Lee was any real threat to the peace of London. Shakespeare must have known Langley fairly well to have been willing to enter his quarrel against a rich, stubborn, and dangerous man like Justice Gardiner. No professional connection between the two men has been established, but Francis Langley was the owner of the handsomest new theatre in London and William Shakespeare was a prominent member of the Chamberlain's company which may, in 1596, have been using Langley's new theatre, the Swan.

The first theatre that is known to have been used by the newly formed Chamberlain's company was Newington Butts, a rather unsatisfactory theatre that had been built some fourteen years earlier in the village of Newington on the other side of Southwark. It was too far out of town for any but holiday crowds, and the Chamberlain's company used it for only ten days in June of 1594. It looks as though all the large London theatres remained closed for a short time after the plague period, to be cleaned and redecorated for fall reopenings; for the Chamberlain's company was obliged to share Newington Butts with the Admiral's company and only got the use of the stage for six afternoons altogether.

The Chamberlain's company presented two showings each of *Titus Andronicus* and of a Biblical drama called *Esther and Ahasuerus*. *Titus Andronicus* had been played by the Earl of Sussex' men the previous January, evidently to very good houses, and had been published by John Danter with the statement that three different acting companies had presented it. The Chamberlain's company was the fourth, so *Titus Andronicus*

was evidently sturdy acting material. A further evidence of its popularity is that Danter also issued a ballad on the same subject, and the misfortunes of Titus were sung on the London streets to the tune of "Fortune My Foe," which was normally used to accompany ballads about murders and was consequently called the "hanging tune."

The third play presented by the Chamberlain's men at Newington Butts was *Hamlet*, a popular melodrama of the period which Tom Nashe had jeered at five years earlier as a cheap imitation of Seneca. This *Hamlet* is not extant, but the fourth play put on by the Chamberlain's company had already emerged into print. This was *The Taming of a Shrew*, "as it was sundry times acted by the right honorable the Earl of Pembroke his servants," although it is not known whether the Chamberlain's company acted the same version of the text that Pembroke's did or used the one that appears in the First Folio. The brief season at Newington Butts closed with a second showing of *Titus Andronicus* and after that the company went on its regular summer tour.

By Michaelmas London was back to normal for the first time since the plague, with the town filling for the fall law term and the theatrical season in full swing. The Chamberlain's company decided to use the Cross-Keys Inn for their winter playing, since it was ideally located for the convenience of their audiences. Like the Bull and the

Bell, it stood on the great thoroughfare that was called Gracechurch and Bishopsgate Street when it ran through London and Shoreditch Road after it passed the city gate. All three inns had been used as theatres for many years past, and the carpenter work that had been done on the Bull and the Cross-Keys to make them suitable for the actors was still visible seventy years later.

All these inns were inside the city walls, and the mayor and aldermen very much disliked having them used as theatres. But the patron of the Chamberlain's company was the Queen's first cousin and consequently a persuasive man. He promised the London Council that his actors would begin their plays promptly at two o'clock in the afternoon so that the young people in the audience would be able to be home before dark. He also promised that they would forego any attempts to advertise the play with drums and trumpets through the streets and that they would make a contribution to the poor of the parish out of each day's receipts. These were the usual requirements, and equally usual was the Chamberlain's delicate reminder to the mayor that his company had to be allowed to exercise its craft before the general public or it would not be ready at Christmas with any plays to present to the Queen.

All the discussions between the Crown and the City on the subject of the theatre ended in the same way. The Queen wanted to see plays. She had no intention of undertaking the enormous expense of supporting a private company, and therefore the plays had to come from the ordinary commercial theatre, since the actors would have nothing to present at Court in the Christmas season "without their usual exercise" the rest of the year before regular London audiences. Some years earlier the Queen had selected a group of the best London actors to be under her special patronage, and although the Queen's players made no extra money, they had so much extra prestige that the London Council complained bitterly that every theatre in town was filled with acting companies calling themselves the Queen's Men. The Queen's company did not reappear in London after the plague, and for the rest of the reign the honor of opening the Christmas season at Court went to the Chamberlain's company.

Such an honor might seem inevitable to the eyes of posterity, since Shakespeare was a member of the company, but what really made it inevitable was the position at Court of the company's patron. As Chamberlain, Lord Hunsdon had complete control of the royal household, with full authority over every detail of its maintenance; and this included all Court entertainments, since the Office of the Revels with its staff of officials and workmen was directly under the supervision of the Lord Chamberlain.

Lord Hunsdon was nearly seventy when Shakespeare knew him and famous for "his custom of swearing." Like one of his successors in office he was "extremely choleric by nature, which was increased the more by the office of Lord Chamberlain," a position that involved handling a great many people. Hunsdon was an extremely tactless man and no courtier, but his cousin the Queen loved him for his honesty and faithfulness to her, and he was equally faithful "to his friends and servants." Certainly his actors prospered, for they were always given the opening date at Court for the Christmas season and presented more plays before the Queen than any other London company. On the other hand, it is equally true that Lord Hunsdon would not have given them his patronage in the first place unless they had been an exceptional group of actors.

The Chamberlain's company must have started its preparation for the Christmas season fairly early, since an enormous amount of extra work was required before the first play was presented before the Queen on December 26. Sets and costumes and properties could not be planned until it had been decided what plays were going to be given, and the Master of the Revels probably called the various acting companies to his office in Clerkenwell as soon as his summer's work of supervising the airing and sponging and brushing of the costumes had been completed,

inventory had been made, and the cobwebs in the workrooms had been cleaned out with the long-handled brushes that were kept for the purpose.

The Master of the Revels was Edmund Tilney, a pleasant, civilized man with some literary pretensions whose only regret when he died was the amount of money he had spent on his clothes. By 1594 Tilney had held the office for fifteen years and had built it up to one of great power and responsibility. His office was in the old palace of St. John's out in Clerkenwell, where he had a suite of thirteen rooms for his own use. Clerkenwell, a suburb north of Newgate, had enjoyed a theatrical reputation in the old days of the miracle plays, and when the priory of St. John's was converted into government use, much of it was taken over by the Office of the Revels. Tilney was equipped with a garden, a kitchen, storage rooms and a stable in which to keep his horses, and a "great chamber" that could be used for the rehearsal of plays.

Tilney did not choose the plays for the Queen by reading them but by seeing them acted, and the actors brought their musicians, their properties, and their costumes out with them. Tilney paid the freight charges out to Clerkenwell, and it cost him ten pounds once for "the charges of the players, the carriage and recarriage of their stuff, for examining and rehearsing of divers plays and choice making of ten of them to be shown before Her Majesty . . . and their sundry rehearsals afterwards." The plays that were finally chosen were supposed to be "the best that were to be had," and were "often perused and necessarily corrected and amended by all the aforesaid officers." In 1594, two of the plays in the stock of the Chamberlain's company survived this rigorous treatment and were selected to be played before the Queen.

Rehearsals were evidently conducted at night, so as not to interfere with the ordinary working day of the London companies. An elaborate lighting equipment was required at St. John's and a bill for one year, which was probably characteristic, included two dozen torches and fifteen dozen candles that were set around the rehearsal hall in a series of plates. Since winter was coming on, the fires had to be kept going, and the bill for rehearsals also included four thousand sticks of firewood and two loads of coal. There was also a bill for rushes, which helped to keep the floor of the rehearsal room clean and warm; and a porter and three other attendants got twelvepence each daily "for their attendance and service in the rehearsals."

Once the plays had been chosen, work could begin on the properties and costumes and sets. Some of these were probably supplied by the actors themselves, since the Office of the Revels economized where it could. But the scenic conditions were different at Court, where the players worked in a rectangular hall by artificial light, and the general arrangement was not unlike that of a modern picture stage. Elaborate backgrounds were used, apparently modeled after the Italian system of scenes done in perspective, and there was usually an order placed with some linen draper for "apt houses, made of canvas, framed, fashioned, and painted." The Revels office also used the Italian system of designing small paper models of the scenery in advance, and a typical expense was boat hire for one of the scene painters who brought the patterns to Whitehall to be approved by the Lord Chamberlain.

The painters were kept hard at work up to Christmas, since they were responsible not only for making canvas houses and castles and villages but also for gilding lions' heads and painting wool-stuffed fishes so realistically that any member of the audience could tell at a glance which was a mackerel and which was a flounder. They worked among paint pots that were a riot of gold and silver and sapphire and crimson, and one of the officers of the Revels kept a stern watch to see that none of the color was wasted and that any of the paint that was left over was replaced in the stores.

Meanwhile the costumes were being designed and executed, and the beautiful clothes to be worn by the actors were evolving out of piles of taffeta and tinsel and velvet and damask and cloth of gold. If old headpieces could be used again, they were cleaned with bread crumbs and taped to strengthen them, and if not, new ones were designed. Wigs and beards were made and carefully curled, and the chief property maker got out his bowls and rags and brown paper and plaster of paris and started to mold fruits and trees and monsters so that they could be delivered to the painters in time and be dry by opening night.

One of the Revels officers complained bitterly in the seventies because none of these workmen had private places to work. "Tailors, painters, property makers, and carpenters are all fain to work in one room, which is a very great hindrance one to another, which thing needs not for they are slack enough of themselves." Apart from the natural inclination of any Elizabethan workman to do as much chatting and as little actual work as possible, the system of a single large room must have made for a great deal of confusion. In spite of baskets and boxes used for storage, and brooms and a dust basket for neatness, the place must have been a wild confusion of properties and costumes and people, with the smell of paint and glue and the sounds of hammering rising above everything else. The actors themselves probably did not mind when they had occasion to be there; the smell was a good theatre smell and they were used to apparent confusion. If anyone was unhappy, it was probably the clerk, with his green cloth and his desk and his wax counters. The clerk was responsible for keeping the accounts and the plots of the plays and the models of the settings, and he had to know, when a property maker presented a bill for monsters and holly and horses' tails and guns and moss and "dishes for devils' eyes," that his list matched the one in the harried Revels office.

The life of this clerk was complicated by a series of outside borrowings, all of which had to be returned when the Christmas season was over. Armor was frequently borrowed, since it was an expensive item, and on one occasion at least the armorer's apprentice was also borrowed to help the actors get in and out of the equipment. Once the Revels office borrowed a cloud, presumably from a company of actors since the average London citizen had comparatively little use for a cloud, and then unfortunately they tore it. The Revels office had to go to some expense for the hoop and the blue linen cloth that were needed to mend it, and at that they had to supply their own cord and pulley for the cloud and buy a great many extra nails.

As the Christmas season grew closer, the atmosphere about the Revels office grew increasingly tense. One officer spoke feelingly of "the haste of the preparation" and added that there was "no service more troublesome for the time of the works than the service of the Revels both for the body and the mind." The officers had to be everywhere at once, and the greater the need for haste the more rapidly the expenses mounted. Sometimes the painters had to be fed while they worked because there was no time to stop off for dinner, and one year the headpiece makers had to be given a special bonus because they were still working on Christmas night. There was always some last-minute work, especially in the painting department where final touches had to be made at the Court itself; and one payment was "for coals at the court to dry the painters' work on the rock."

Meanwhile all the other equipment had to be packed in baskets and brought to Court: the scenery, the costumes, the properties, and the intricate lighting equipment that the chief wiredrawer and his assistants had to tack and wire and spike into position before opening night. Since the Queen was at Greenwich in the Christmas season of 1594, most of the material went by boat down the crowded Thames, with one hamper for farthingales and another for a frame and probably a whole boat to carry the wire and plates and ropes and branches that were used to set up the torches and candles that lit the hall. Down at Greenwich, Thomas Sheffield, the underkeeper of the palace, was paying eight men extra for night work to make the halls and galleries clean and ready.

The opening date was Thursday, December the 26th, which was St. Stephen's Day, and the performance was due to begin about ten o'clock in the evening. This was the climax of months of hard work, and if the Chamberlain's men managed to remain completely calm and relaxed in that tense atmosphere, they were a most unusual group of actors.

All the Revels officers were there, with special attendants at each door, and the seats probably began filling early. Since Greenwich was a small summer palace, the seating arrangement was more informal than at Whitehall, where the Chamberlain's men presented most of their plays in subsequent years. Whitehall had a large banqueting hall that had been erected for the sole purpose of giving entertainments, and a foreign visitor who was allowed to peer in reports that the interior was "full of benches and stools ranged one above the other." Unless special scaffoldings were used at Greenwich, it is likely that all the seats were on the same level, with a raised stage for the actors at one end of the hall and a throne for the Queen.

The Queen probably made her entrance about the time that the actor who played the Prologue began pinching his cheeks to get some color into them, and when she came in, even the most experienced member of the acting company might be permitted the cold clutch of stage fright. For Queen Elizabeth was the golden and glorious sun about whom all of England revolved. Even the greatest lords approached her kneeling, spoke to her kneeling, played cards with her kneeling, and she moved in a glitter of jewels and of homage that made her in many ways the fairy tale figure that the poets of England said she was.

Queen Elizabeth was in her sixties when Shakespeare's company faced her from the stage in the Christmas season of 1594, and very little was left of her youth except her straight back and her beautiful hands. She still dressed as a young girl in spite of her wrinkled face and false hair and missing teeth, and occasionally some self-confident male would conclude that her mind was aging also and that she was a conceited and impressionable old woman. The French ambassador who came to her Court three years later began with some such impression, but a few days later he was recording in his journal with reluctant admiration, "She is a very great princess who knows everything." The men of her Court did not altogether like being ruled by a woman, especially a brilliant woman, but most of them both loved her and were a little frightened of her.

As far as her lesser subjects were concerned, Elizabeth had decided early that the only way to get obedience from her turbulent and opinionated countrymen was to be loved. She played the courtier with her people even more than her anxious lords courted her, and the smile that was "pure sunshine" came often enough from England's greatest politician where ordinary English citizens were concerned. This was not a matter of policy alone, for she loved England more selflessly and devotedly than she ever loved anything else in her long and difficult life; but the special grace with which she handled herself before the general public was born of a very clear idea of the value of courtesy in politics. When a schoolmaster at Norwich attempted to deliver a Latin speech to her and lost his head altogether in that glorious presence, the great Queen was as concerned over his stage fright as were any of the sweating Norwich managers of the affair, and when the schoolmaster had finally staggered through to a conclusion she told him, "It is the best that ever I heard; you shall have my hand."

Elizabeth of course expected a much higher standard of performance from a group of professionals like the Chamberlain's company, especially since she had paid for their costumes and properties and was giving them a £10 fee, but in general she was the ideal theatre-goer. She hoped and expected to be amused, and from the actors' point of view it would be difficult to find any more attractive quality in a spectator than that. She and the Londoners shared the same kind of interest in the theatre and liked the same kind of things, for that vigorous woman was far too well educated to play the snob and to give her support to tenuous classical productions only. On her mother's side Elizabeth was descended from middle-class stock, and her great-grandfather, Geoffrey Boleyn, had been a merchant of London. The Londoners always felt she was one of them, since she was "descended of citizens" and her ancestor's tomb could still be seen in St. Lawrence's Church; and although her father and her successor had their court fools, Elizabeth preferred to share the great clowns like Tarleton and Kempe with the ordinary London public.

Elizabeth was much more learned than the majority of her subjects, but she did not have the exaggerated respect for learning that plagued so many of the gentlemen of the Renaissance. When the French ambassador expressed admiration at her ability to speak six languages, she remarked "that it was no marvel to teach a woman to talk; it were far harder to teach her to hold her tongue." She made translations from Cicero and Plutarch to relax her lively mind, and read Seneca to calm herself after she had been "stirred to passion" by what she considered the stupidity of her harassed Privy Council; but she was quite willing to stop off and ask the meaning of an unfamiliar word in Latin, "being of the mind of that philosopher who in his last years began with the Greek alphabet."

The actors who played before Queen Elizabeth faced a woman with a lively, critical mind and one who knew a good deal about the details of their trade. The Queen was a poet herself, and as one respectful subject put it, her "learned, delicate, noble Muse easily surmounteth all the rest . . . be it in ode, epigram, or any other kind of poem heroic or lyric." She was an expert musician who could play her own compositions, and an experienced dancer with such a strong sense of rhythm that when she watched a dance, instead of taking part in it, she followed "the cadence with her head, hand, and foot."

In her ideas on comedy Elizabeth leaned toward the same easygoing humor that her subjects did, and the strict sexual propriety that she enforced in her Court had nothing to do with her enjoyment of a bit of Shakespearian plain speaking on the stage. Elizabeth had about twenty-eight maids of honor, for whose welfare she was directly responsible to their parents, in a Court that consisted otherwise of about fifteen hundred men, and she had trouble enough with those lively and marriageable young ladies in a Court that was completely masculine down to male cooks and launderers. It is noticeable that during Elizabeth's reign the dramatists never wrote anything that condoned or encouraged sexual immorality. Adultery was a subject for tragedy, not for comedy, and when Shakespeare went to complicated lengths in *All's Well That Ends Well* to prevent the hero from committing adultery in his comedy, he was following the normal practice of Elizabethan playwrights. It was not until well into the next reign that the situation changed. By then Elizabeth was dead and the influence of her sisters in spirit, the wives of the London citizens, was receding; and it was only old-fashioned dramatists like William Shakespeare who still wrote the kind of plays that had once been popular with everyone.

The Chamberlain's company was paid twenty pounds for the two plays they presented before the Queen that first Christmas, although it was not until March that "William Kempe, William Shakespeare, and Richard Burbage, servants to the Lord Chamberlain" were able to collect the money. The payment was made, in the usual complicated way, by a warrant from the Privy Council, and the warrant states the plays were given before the Queen on the 26th and 28th of December. This must have been a clerical error, however, since the Admiral's company also received payment for a play given on Saturday the 28th.

Moreover, there is evidence that the Chamberlain's company was acting elsewhere on that particular Saturday night. On the 28th of December "a Comedy of Errors (like to Plautus his *Menechmus*) was played by the players" before the young gentlemen of Gray's Inn. This is such an accurate description of Shakespeare's play, *The Comedy of Errors,* that it must be the same; and, since the Chamberlain's company now owned all of Shakespeare's plays, it must have been this company that played at Gray's Inn on the 28th of December.

The Gray's Inn audience was not so very unlike the Court audience at Greenwich, except that the Gray's Inn gentlemen and their farthingaled guests were much younger, much livelier, and had

worked themselves up during the Christmas season to a fairly advanced state of foolishness. The whole Christmas season was a golden opportunity for nonsense, and the boys in the various Inns of Court made the most of it.

The Inns of Court were the four resident law schools west of London and trained young gentlemen in that most respectable and profitable of Elizabethan professions. It was an exceptional nobleman who escaped at least a few years' training at one of the law schools, and although it was quite true that not every name entered in the Steward's Book was that of a gentleman, the training was so expensive that a rich father was almost the first qualification for admission. Since most of the boys were at least technically members of the gentry, they were given an education "fit for persons of their station" and were taught dancing, riding, and singing, and how to stage theatrical productions. They even staged plays of their own making before the Queen and were quite capable of surmounting the technical complications of showing "Cupid descending from heaven and the Furies rising from hell."

Gray's Inn was the largest of the Inns of Court and it was generally conceded that its members excelled in dramatics; but for their Christmas entertainment of 1594 they hired professional actors. A raised scaffold at the eastern end of their seventy-foot hall was designed for the stage, but the Chamberlain's men had a hard time of it that night. The crowd of spectators at that end of the hall was "so exceeding great that thereby there was no convenient room for those that were actors."

The chief difficulty seems to have been that too many invitations had been sent out, and the Elizabethan farthingale took up a great deal of room. But a Christmas revel without "divers ladies and gentlewomen" would have been unthinkable at Gray's Inn, whose members took such a happy interest in the opposite sex that a law had to be passed "that no laundresses or women victuallers should henceforth come into the gentlemen's chambers of this Society, unless they were full forty years of age, and not send their maidservants of what age soever."

The Revels to which the Chamberlain's company gave their professional services were the first since the plague, and there was evidently a good deal of stored-up enthusiasm to be suddenly released. The evening was spent in "dancing and revelling with gentlewomen" and watching the play; but the mock formality that had been planned for the evening collapsed so thoroughly that the fledgling lawyers, who seized on every opportunity to make fun of the legal procedure they were being taught, held a mock trial the next day to find out who had been responsible for the lack of dignity in "our law sports."

When the young men of the Inns of Court were not putting on shows of their own or hiring professional actors to appear in their halls, they went across London to Southwark or Shoreditch and paid admission like everyone else to see the plays in the regular public theatres. Their presence in London made it for all practical purposes a university town, full of intelligent, well-to-do young men who wanted to be amused. From the actors' point of view, the Inns were a great improvement on Oxford and Cambridge; for the origin of these two universities was monastic and they consistently disapproved of professional actors, while the Inns of Court had originated under the guild system and their governors had no objection to plays. An Oxford boy was punished if he went to see a commercial play, but a boy at Gray's Inn or the Inner Temple could spend his seven-year residence by seeing every new show in London. Since these young men were in close touch with the Court and knew every latest joke and latest fashion, they made an excellent leaven in the average London audience and the actors appreciated them.*

There were no similar schools for girls in London, but their edu-

* Shakespeare's Justice Shallow never achieved the dignity of belonging to one of the Inns of Court, but he attended Clement's Inn, which was one of the preliminary training grounds and run on the same general system. After long years in the country, Justice Shallow still looked back wistfully to those happy days in London. "Jesu! Jesu! The mad days that I have spent."—Author's Note

cation was not neglected. Even a tax-supported institution like Christ's Hospital taught the little girls in its care how to read before they were sent out in service, and the average girl in Renaissance London could never quite convince herself that she was inferior to a man. In a book written by Edmund Tilney, Master of the Revels, a young lady remarks: "As meet it is that the husband obey the wife as the wife the husband . . . For women have souls as well as men, they have wit as well as men." The charming, independent girls in the better-class London households were to a certain extent the models for the delightful heroines of Shakespeare's later comedies, and it was girls of this kind who were the guests of the young men of Gray's Inn the night that the Chamberlain's company presented *The Comedy of Errors*.

A successful acting company like the Chamberlain's would have many calls for special productions. If the occasion was a very important one, the play might be staged in the afternoon, like the performance of Shakespeare's *Henry IV* that his company presented at the house of the Lord Chamberlain when their patron was entertaining an ambassador; but in general the performance was given in the evening so that it would not interfere with the normal daytime schedule. A fashionable supper party might conclude with a play, like the production of King Richard that was given the year after the Gray's Inn

performance and ordered by Sir Edward Hoby. A wedding frequently ended with a play, since whenever there was any special celebration, the Elizabethan mind went automatically to its favorite form of amusement, and if the house was not large enough for the production, a hall could be hired. "Weddings and other festivities" often took place in rented halls, and the Stationers' Company made a charge of ten shillings when the company hall was used for a wedding. A hall could easily be converted into a theatre by building a scaffolding at one end, and the actors were evidently well paid for their extra productions. Their chief expense was the freight charge for the transfer of costumes and properties, and Philip Henslowe notes that he paid three shillings on behalf of the Admiral's company to "the carman for carrying to and bringing of the stuff back again when they played in Fleet Street private."

It seems reasonably certain that a new play was never launched at one of these private showings. A masque could be composed for a wedding celebration, since a masque consisted of recitation and dancing and it was possible to estimate its effectiveness in advance. But the effectiveness of a play script cannot be estimated in advance; there is no way of measuring its impact upon an audience until it has actually been produced, and the London companies had no way of testing their plays except by presenting them to their regular audience. They risked their own capital when they put a new script into production, and if they had been incorrect in their estimate of the script, they shared the financial loss among themselves. If, on the other hand, the script was successful, it became a regular part of their repertoire and was available for special evening productions in the same way it was available for the Christmas season at Court. Queen Elizabeth did not see a play until it had first been applauded by the ordinary London theatregoers, and the same was probably true of all the special evening performances given by the Chamberlain's company.

✖ Chapter 7

The performances that the Chamberlain's company gave before the Queen or before private groups were important, but they were still only extras. The basis of the profession was the regular daylight performance that went on about two o'clock in the afternoon before ordinary Londoners.

A great many of these afternoon performances consisted of old plays that had achieved a permanent place in the company's repertoire, but there was also a steady supply of new scripts in which the actors were investing their time, their faith, and their money. Burbage

and Heminges and Shakespeare and Kempe hoped that each of these new scripts would be a success, but some of them of course were not. Theatrical production is an uncertain trade, and even the most experienced theatre men cannot be sure in advance of the production values of a script. But in general the Chamberlain's men chose successful scripts, since otherwise they would quickly have ceased to be a successful acting company.

One of the most successful of these scripts was produced in the middle years of the decade, not long after the company had been formed. It was written by one of their own members, William Shakespeare, and called *Romeo and Juliet*. Some of the details may be missing, but it is possible to reconstruct in a general way how the play was made ready for its first performance.

Shakespeare began, as usual, with an old plot in his head. This was normal theatre procedure, and Shakespeare differed from most of his fellow dramatists only in that he never used a plot from contemporary life. In this case, Shakespeare was using not only an old story but one which the average Londoner of his day must have known very well. In the early days the story of Romeo and Juliet had been a successful play on the London stage. Then a young man named Arthur Brooke, who had seen the stage version, was sufficiently impressed to turn it into a poem just before his unhappy death by drowning. It also appeared in a very popular collection of stories that an officer in the ordnance department, named William Painter, had collected and translated from the Italian in his spare time. Sensational Italian fiction of this type was somewhat old-fashioned by the middle years of the last decade of the century, but Shakespeare never concerned himself about being in the forefront of any literary movement. He was no innovator, and to the end of his career he was willing to take decrepit, old-fashioned stories as the basis for his plays while his colleagues dealt in glossy new inventions of their own.

One of the most curious aspects of Shakespeare as a writer was the way in which he did not seem to consider himself superior to his sources. He was making a serious tragedy out of Brooke's poem and he read the thing carefully and attentively, in some cases following the character's thoughts almost word for word as Brooke gives them. Yet it is no easy thing to read Brooke's version seriously, for his style is strongly reminiscent of Bottom's immortal production of Pyramus and Thisbe. This is the way Brooke's heroine talks to her beloved in the balcony scene:

What if your deadly foes, my kinsmen, saw you here?
Like lions wild, your tender parts asunder would they tear.
In ruth and in disdain, I, weary of my life,

With cruel hand my mourning heart would pierce with bloody knife.

Shakespeare could read this sort of thing and believe in the story wholeheartedly without being affected in the least by the childishness of the narrator. Brooke's stupidity as a poet did not irritate him in the least, as it might very well irritate a lesser man. Shakespeare's spirit accepted the whole of Brooke's with the same steady, patient courtesy that made it possible for him, as an actor, to appear in so many bad plays in the course of his life without ever becoming discouraged with his profession. His company put on about fifteen new plays a year and Shakespeare, as a regular acting member of the company, must have appeared in most of them. They were not all good plays, and some of them, to judge by the few that are extant, were very bad. For instance, the year that *King Lear* was first produced at Court, another play given on the same occasion by Shakespeare's company was *The Devil's Charter* by Barnabe Barnes. Barnes's play had an abnormally large cast and Shakespeare could probably not have avoided acting in it, even if, as a working member of the company, such a thing had crossed his mind. A good actor cannot start rehearsals by privately considering himself superior to his material, and Shakespeare must have given Barnes's play what he had given scores of similar plays in the course of his career, the courteous attention of a good professional who is anxious to make a success of the production. Barnes tenderly saw his own play into print, and the contrast between that childish melodrama and *King Lear* is probably characteristic of the gap between the plays Shakespeare himself had written and the plays in which he was only an actor. A more self-conscious artist would have been angered by such a situation. Shakespeare was as untroubled by it as he was by the childishness and vulgarity of many of the sources he chose for his plays.

Almost as irritating as Arthur Brooke's style to a modern reader is his dogged determination to point a moral. This was the normal Elizabethan practice, although it was not Shakespeare's, and the reading of stories could only be justified if they taught some useful lesson. William Painter justified translating a story of unlawful love like Romeo and Juliet's by pointing out it would teach readers "how to avoid the ruin, overthrow, inconvenience, and displeasure that lascivious desire and wanton will doth bring," and Arthur Brooke was even more concerned for the moral welfare of his reader. "To this end (good reader) is this tragical matter written, to describe unto thee a couple of unfortunate lovers, thralling themselves to dishonest desire, neglecting the authority and advice of parents and friends, conferring their principal counsels with drunken gossips and superstitious friars . . . abusing the name of lawful marriage to cloak the shame of stolen contracts, finally, by all means of unhonest life, hasting to most unhappy death."

Shakespeare's eye passed over all this moralizing without his mind accepting any of it. If he noticed anything it was Brooke's one word, "hasting," since neither Brooke nor Painter had suggested any motivation for the tragedy except due punishment for sin. Shakespeare's mind did not move in this particular pattern, however normal it may have been in his own day, and instead he made the story a tragedy of haste. The tragic flaw in the characters is that they are all in too much of a hurry, and Shakespeare made some changes in the original story to emphasize this. He cut down the action of the story from several months to less than a week, and then made it a week of "hot days" in which everything comes quickly to flower and equally soon fades. He made Juliet only fourteen, although Brooke said she was sixteen, and her love for Romeo is "like the lightning."

Brooke had done almost nothing with characterization, and in his version Mercutio appears briefly and is hardly more than a name. He made a slightly more determined effort with the Nurse, who was a stock character in fiction of this type, and he gave her a long passage describing how she nursed Juliet, which Brooke himself had to admit was a "tedious long discourse." Shakespeare also gave the Nurse a passage describing how she had nursed Juliet, and the shout of delighted laughter that went up on the opening day of the production has been echoing in audiences ever since.

Heminges and Condell made a report on Shakespeare's writing habits after they had been handling his manuscripts for nearly thirty years and they said that their fellow actor was a very rapid writer. "His mind and hand went together; and what he thought, he uttered with that easiness, that we have scarce received from him a blot in his papers." That is to say, Shakespeare was one of those writers who works everything out in his head before he puts any of it down on paper. His company later had another playwright, John Fletcher, who worked in the same way. As Fletcher's publisher said, "Whatever I have seen of Mr. Fletcher's own hand is free from interlining; and his friends affirm he never writ any one thing twice; it seems he had that rare felicity to prepare and perfect all first in his own brain." It was fortunate that Shakespeare was able to "prepare and perfect all first in his own brain," since his profession was not one that supplied him with long hours of leisure to cross out and laboriously improve his lines. Since a play is not in any case a collection of lines but an organic, swift-moving whole, Shakespeare had good use for his actor's memory, which could keep the whole gathering structure intact in his mind until it was finished and ready to be recorded on paper.

When a play was finished, the usual procedure was for the playwright to read it to the assembled actors to see if they wished to buy it. Since Shakespeare was already a prominent member of his own group of purchasers, and one of the most popular playwrights of his day, this part of the transaction was probably already a foregone conclusion. Once the average writer had been paid, his connection with the script was ended and it was left to the company of actors to produce it in any way they saw fit; but in Shakespeare's case the problem of transferring the printed words to the stage and bringing them to life was only just beginning.

The first thing that had to be done with *Romeo and Juliet* was to get it licensed. No play could be produced on the London stage until it had been certified that no seditious material had crept into it that might corrupt the susceptible public. The Crown was not concerned with suppressing indecorous or blasphemous material in the theatre and it was not until the following reign that oaths were outlawed on the London stage. It merely wished to make sure that one of the greatest popular mediums of communication, the theatre, did not lend itself to any propaganda against the dignity of the government or of the Queen.

The licenser was Edmund Tilney, Master of the Revels. Tilney had originally censored the plays that were shown before the Queen, but he had gradually extended his control to all the plays in the London area. His post was rather a profitable one, since a fee of seven shillings had to accompany the manuscript of *Romeo and Juliet* when it was sent out to his office in Clerkenwell.

Once the script had been licensed, nothing could be added to it, but the actors were free to make the abridgments that would fit into the normal playing time of two hours. In general, Shakespeare seems to have offered rather lengthy manuscripts to his company. He was not an economical writer, and he did not husband his strength or indulge in mathematical computations over a few extra words. He evidently wrote at white heat, once he had the paper in front of him, and he could not be expected to pause at intervals, with his pen in the air, to check back over his material and make sure that the play was not running too long. Many of his finished scripts needed an acting time of more than three hours and could not have been brought to an end during the brief daylight hours of a winter afternoon. The necessity for cutting a script of Shakespeare's must have been a routine part of the general problem of getting it into production, and although no evidence remains on the subject, it seems likely that the cuts were worked out at rehearsals and by general agreement. The men of Shakespeare's company all had years of practical experience in the theatre, and they could be trusted to co-operate with him intelligently in the cutting of his scripts. Nor

did these theatre cuts affect the original version, since the full-length play as Shakespeare had written it was available to the printer whenever the company authorized its publication.

Shakespeare's original script, with its suggested cuts in the margin and with Tilney's signature at the end, was apparently not copied out for the prompter. It seems to have been used just as it was, except that the loose sheets were stitched together and enclosed in some kind of wrapper. Any kind of wrapper would do, from a medieval manuscript to an expired law paper, just so that it was capable of standing hard wear. Once the play had been produced, this "book" was carefully stored, since it was the only official copy of the play the company had and the only proof that it had been properly licensed.

The next expense, after the payment for the licensing, was probably the payment to the copyist who wrote out the actors' parts for them to memorize. The only document of this kind that has survived is one made for Edward Alleyn, with corrections in Alleyn's handwriting, but they were probably more or less alike. An ordinary sheet of paper was divided lengthwise to make six-inch widths and pasted to form a long continuous strip that the actor could roll back as he worked. The closing lines of the previous speech were indicated to give the actor his cue, and directions for action were put in the left-hand margin.

The casting of *Romeo and Juliet* probably did not take very long. The actors knew each other's work intimately and could talk the problem over among themselves instead of bowing to the decree of an outside manager. Casting was controlled by a single consideration, the good of the production as a whole, and an actor's private ambitions had very little to do with the matter. Through a printer's error, one piece of casting in *Romeo and Juliet* has been preserved, and it shows that Will Kempe played Peter. The best comedy role in the play was of course that of the Nurse, and Peter, her servant, has very few effective lines. Will Kempe was the most popular comic actor of the period, but the Chamberlain's company did not use the star system. The company as a whole evidently felt that Kempe could be used to best advantage in a small role, and that was the one he played.

There is no reason to believe that the Elizabethans had any special respect for type-casting and always gave the most elderly member of the company the oldest role or the same man the low-comedy lead. Thomas Pope was famous as a clown, but the only role to which he can definitely be assigned in his long career is the dignified part of Arbactus, while the actor who played the comedy role in the same play is not identified anywhere else with a comedy characterization. Nor is it necessary to suppose that Shakespeare was always given dignified roles. He did not have his present reputation then, and like everyone else in the company he played whatever part would most clearly benefit the production as a whole. The basis of any good repertory company is intelligent, varied acting, and the Chamberlain's was a good repertory company.

Once the major roles had been cast, the minor parts like the townsmen and the guests at the ball could be handled through doubling; and if there were not enough actors in the immediate company to fill all the parts, outside actors would be hired for the occasion. There were always more actors in London than there were parts, waiting hopefully for a call from one of the theatres, and they were paid a flat rate that was usually a shilling a day.

Regret has sometimes been expressed by modern writers that there were no actresses to be cast in Shakespeare's plays and he had to undergo the grief of seeing Juliet played by a boy. But this shows a misunderstanding of the period, for a Renaissance boy was not brought up in the least like a modern one. The average man of Shakespeare's day did not consider it effeminate to write poetry or play the lute or load himself with jewels and silks and perfumes. Shakespeare's Rosalind was speaking for the normal Renaissance point of view when she said she would be "changeable, longing, and liking . . . full of tears, full of smiles . . . as boys and women." It was not until the

Puritan Commonwealth that the convention was established that men were supposed to have an entirely different life to women and many of a boy's natural qualities were choked out of him as "unmanly." The situation was different in Shakespeare's day, and the boys of his company understood perfectly what moved a young girl to laughter or to tears.

In addition, these boys had daily training by masters in the profession; and a boy who lived and worked under the watchful eye of a brilliant actor like Richard Burbage knew a great deal about acting by the time he was ready to be cast for a leading feminine role. He had been trained as a singer and dancer and in every aspect of handling his body gracefully. Above all, he had been trained in the use of his voice, since it was through the voice that the illusion could be most completely maintained. Shakespeare had this point clearly in mind when he wrote *Romeo and Juliet,* and in his great lyric tragedy of young love he lets the lines carry the illusion and keeps his actors away from much physical contact. The famous balcony scene, with the two young voices reaching out and caressing each other, would be a less useful device to a modern dramatist who could trust to the physical contact of the actors to convey the idea of sudden love. When the two lovers first meet in Brooke's poem they sit silent, dumbly holding hands at the ball; Shakespeare has them speak a sonnet. Throughout the play he had to trust to words instead of action in the love scenes, and every reader of the play should be deeply grateful to the boy actors.

A certain number of musicians were required at the ball to obey Capulet's command, "Come, musicians, play," but it was no special casting problem to find an actor who could play a musical instrument. When Shakespeare's fellow actors like Pope and Bryan appeared at the Danish court of Elsinore, part of their business was to "attend with their fiddles and instruments." After more than a decade as a successful actor Edward Alleyn was still being styled "musician," and Kempe was listed as an "instrumentalist." When Augustine Phillips died, he willed his various musical instruments to his apprentices as a natural part of their equipment as actors, and they were certainly expected to know how to use them. It was a period in which music was so vital a part of the life of the average Londoner that even a charity school like Bridewell taught music to its charges, and the right to sell ruled paper on which to copy songs was a valuable and profitable patent. The knowledge of music that Shakespeare shows in his plays was normal for the period, and was in part the result of the same knowledge and enthusiasm on the part of his audience.*

* With the single exception of *The Comedy of Errors,* music was used in all of

If the Chamberlain's company was like the Admiral's, they had an extraordinary clutter of properties stored away, from which they could choose whatever they needed for a new play. *Romeo and Juliet* required very few properties and most of these would be easy to get, like the ladder of cords for the Nurse to bring in, the basket for Friar Lawrence, and the wrenching iron for Romeo. There had to be a bed for Juliet, and the other large movable property would be the Capulet tomb. The Chamberlain's company already had the tomb they had used in *Titus Andronicus,* but the Elizabethan public evidently did not expect to see the same tomb twice unless it had been refurbished, and Henslowe's property account for 1598 lists three of them.

There was no attempt at realistic settings in *Romeo and Juliet,* since the scene changed so often that it would only have slowed up the action. Nor did a well-trained Elizabethan audience need this kind of assistance. When Romeo and his friends entered with torchbearers, the audience knew it was a street scene and that they were seeing Romeo on his way to Capulet's ball. When this group of actors left the stage and another group came on with napkins over their arms, the audience knew at once that the scene had changed and that preparations for the ball were being made in Capulet's house.

This was the sort of stagecraft that Sir Philip Sidney had once ridiculed, but Sidney was underestimating the creative power of the audience's imagination. Shakespeare never underestimated it. He knew that the imagination of the audience could build Capulet's house more quickly and effectively than all the lathe and pasteboard in London. When Shakespeare wanted to give the illusion that his two lovers, standing on the bare boards of a theatre in the glare of an afternoon sun, were in an or-

---

Shakespeare's plays. The percussion and brass instruments were used extensively in the history plays, and the actors had to be experienced in handling military music both on and off stage. The stringed instruments were too light in tone for general use in the large public theatres and mainly supplied a delicate musical background to the songs, in which the music was kept subordinate to the words. Shakespeare's songs were usually accompanied by the lute, which the actor would handle in much the same way as the modern guitar. Group singing was unusual, except for the use of choristers in *Henry VIII,* but Shakespeare introduced music to accompany group dancing at every reasonable opportunity. The chief wood instruments on the stage were the cornet and the hautboy—the Elizabethan cornet being a kind of horn and the hautboy the ancestor of the modern oboe. Shakespeare used hautboys under the stage to give an effect of supernatural music in *Antony and Cleopatra,* and he used them to supply a "lofty strain" of dance music in *Timon of Athens.* *The Tempest* calls for an especially intricate series of musical effects, but by that time Shakespeare and his colleagues had had a lifetime of experience in handling musical cues. Music was so important in the theatre that in *Cymbeline* "solemn music" is heard in the wilderness; and this unlikely event is justified by the fact the owner of a cave possesses an "ingenious instrument" that can play mechanically.—AUTHOR'S NOTE

chard at night, he turned like the excellent stage technician he was to the magic and power of his poetry; and his audience, who were the best-trained listeners in the world, saw the moonlight silver the tops of the fruit trees as they listened to Romeo's voice.

Up to this point the Chamberlain's company had not incurred any unusually heavy expenses, but an unavoidable item in any new play was the cost of the costuming. All the actors wore contemporary fashions on the stage, but they could not be expected to get up on the bare boards in their street attire and re-create the mood of legendary Verona. The splendor of the costumes gave the illusion of remoteness and glamour that a modern production can achieve through clever lighting, and the costumes were a heavy item on any company's expense account.

The Chamberlain's company did not, of course, buy a completely new set of costumes for each production. They had a fairly large stock on hand and a little ingenuity could give the illusion of a new outfit, especially for some minor actor who was only filling in as background at the ball. Old costumes were always being reused, or, as the Revels office put it, "translated." If the Revels office started with eight jerkins of purple cloth of gold for mariners, the jerkins made their next appearance translated into six costumes for Hungarians and then into four kirtles for Diana's nymphs, and so

on down until the final note was made, "not now serviceable," and they vanished out of the wardrobe department. All the London companies used old materials as far as they could, but there was a limit to this kind of economy in the case of costumes for the leading actors. Romeo and Juliet were members of the nobility and had to be costumed accordingly.

Philip Henslowe kept two tailors working for him, as well as several people who did supplemental sewing, and his bills for costuming were enormous. He spent nine pounds on taffeta for the two feminine leads in a play of Henry Porter's, and it would have taken a hired actor thirty weeks to earn as much as that. A flame-colored satin doublet cost forty-five shillings, and even the facing of a cloak cost nine. Although cheap material like buckram could be used for stiffening, the fabrics that the audience saw had to be velvets and satins and taffetas. They had to be in the brilliant colors that the London public had grown to expect, and bore imaginative names like pease-porridge tawny and popinjay blue.

From the point of view of a costumer, everything about contemporary fashions was designed to give the actors as much trouble, discomfort, and expense as possible. The basic idea of Elizabethan tailoring was a smooth, unbroken fit, and the clothes were curved with whalebone or padded with buckram to make them stand out from the body as though they had no relation to the wearer. Both men and women strove for extremely narrow waists, flaring hips, and broad shoulders, and many men were not above wearing corsets to get the desired effect. Even the sleeves were sometimes stiffened with whalebone and the doublets were so stiff their wearers could hardly bend. All tailors depended heavily on "bombast," which was a stuffing made of cotton or horsehair or even of bran or rags, to give their customers the correct bulges that fashion demanded, and the problem of how to combine this rigid shape with the violent action that was demanded on the stage, especially in dueling scenes, was one that each tailor had to solve for himself.

A quick change of costume could not have been easy, since all the clothes were held on by an intricate system of fastenings. The stockings were fastened to the doublets by a series of laces or points that must have been tiresome to fasten or small boys would not have been scolded for leaving them undone, and yet the seams of the stockings had to be as straight as though they were "set by a plumb-line." The cloak was held to the shoulders by concealed cords in the lining that were knotted under the armholes, and the jerkins had extra slits that could be buttoned to ensure a smooth fit. The costumes of the women were even more complicated because of the lavish use of pins. The various parts of a woman's costumes were made detach-able so that she could use different color combinations, and the pins were called "great farthingale pins," "middle farthingale pins," and so on, according to what part of the costume they were holding together. Wire pins cost about a penny a hundred, and costumers depended on them heavily, although by great good fortune hooks and eyes were also in general use.

Ruffs were a whole problem in themselves. They had to be stiffly starched and the pleats set in with a hot setting stick; and the larger ruffs required an underpropping of pasteboard and wire to be fastened around the owner's neck underneath. The amount of discomfort involved seems to have made no difference, and the size of the ruffs grew, as a contemporary remarked, "every day worser and worser."

The Elizabethan costume seems to have been tenderly designed to be both as unflattering to the wearer as possible and as unsuitable to the climate. A sudden rain could mean ruin, for the starch in the ruff would dissolve and leave it a limp rag around its owner's neck, and for all their brilliant colors the English dyers had not yet achieved the certainty of fast dyes. Perhaps one of the reasons for the popularity of orange tawny as a color was that it was one of the few dyes of the period that could be trusted to keep its color.

In addition to all his other problems, the costumer had to wrestle with the shopmen. He had to know if twelve shillings a yard was a fair price for satin, and be able to test velvet to make sure it was not gummed. Moreover he had to get prompt deliveries in spite of the notoriously unreliable nature of "tailors' and silkmen's promises." But in due time Romeo and Tybalt and Mercutio had costumes that were not only handsome but would hold together in the strenuous dueling scenes Shakespeare had supplied for them. In the case of lesser actors the fit of the clothes was of less importance, and much could be done with pounds of copper lace sprinkled about with a liberal hand. One of the merits of *Romeo and Juliet* from the costumer's point of view was that at least there were no battle scenes requiring armor. Armor was expensive, difficult to get on and off, and even required special underwear; and although much could be done with painted imitations, it is not likely they were ever worn by the principals.

To make sure that all the properties were ready when they should be and that the actors would remember all their cues for entrances, a large sheet of paper was pasted on a board and hung on a peg at some conspicuous point backstage to carry all this information. This action sheet was called a "plot," and it listed in two columns when each actor came on and in what character and noted the general line of the action. Notes were also made in the margin of the prompt book when new properties had to be ready backstage, and careful timing was arranged on all the technical details.

Some companies kept strict order at rehearsals by a system of fines. If an actor was late to rehearsal, he was fined twelvepence, and if he was absent, two shillings. If he was not ready in costume on the actual day of the show at a specified hour, he was fined three shillings; if he was drunk, ten shillings; and if he was absent altogether, unless by "just excuse of sickness," he was fined twenty shillings. A shilling was the price of a day's wages for a hired actor, but no company could afford lazy or unreliable performers.

The most important thing achieved at the rehearsals, apart from the smooth efficiency that comes from experienced teamwork, was the gradual creation of the reality of the characters in the minds of the actors. The men who were rehearsing *Romeo and Juliet* not only had a great deal of acting experience and an increasing knowledge of how to work effectively as a unit, but they had the final advantage of working with the man who had invented the characters and knew them better than anyone else in the world. The rehearsal period must have been one of enormous satisfaction to the Chamberlain's men, with the play coming slowly to life before their eyes and their sense of excitement deepening.

The final expense was to advertise the play, since even the most receptive London audience could not be expected to rush to a new play un-ess they had some idea of what it was going to be about. The advertising was done on single sheets, called playbills, which were posted up about the city wherever a potential member of the audience might see them. These playbills cost the actors a fair amount of money, but they had no choice where they placed their order. It had to go to James Roberts, who had married the widow of the printer who had previously held the monopoly and who consequently possessed, by decree of the Stationers' Company, the right of "the only imprinting of all manner of bills for players." The Elizabethan age was a period of monopolies, and the practice tended to keep prices high where a more competitive system might have lowered them.

It is not known how many bills were printed to advertise a single play, but a fencer who was promoting a private match put in an order for more than a hundred. Only one playbill of the period has survived and it may not be a characteristic one, since the play was not produced and its unethical promoter evidently never intended that it should be. But if the playbill for *England's Joy* represented normal procedure, it was the custom to advertise each of the big scenes in rich and detailed language that would have done credit to a circus.

A new play always attracted a large audience and was evidently not presented on a holiday when a full house could be expected whatever was played. A new production like *Romeo and Juliet* was probably given in the middle of the week, and the silk flag that had cost the company about thirty shillings was run up on the turret to show that the playhouse was open for business. The men who distributed the drinks and fruit that were sold to the audience had their stock ready, the gatherers took up their various posts, and the men with the trumpets waited for the actor who played the Prologue to give them their cue that the play was ready to begin.

The Elizabethan theatre was not based on the element of surprise but on the gratification of expectation. If anyone did not know the general plot of *Romeo and Juliet* before he entered the theatre, the speech of the Prologue solved the matter for him. The actor who played this part cannot be envied, since it was up to him to capture the attention of an excitable, individualistic audience, most of whom had been waiting for a long time, since the places were not reserved, and many of whom were probably busy chewing. Shakespeare's Prologue did not go in for mystification. He stated clearly and at once that the play was about two unlucky lovers who were eventually going to die because their parents were having a feud. Then the two minor actors who played Capulet's men came on with swords and bucklers, and the play began. If it was a success with the audience, it would be put in the regular repertoire of the company and probably played again sometime the following week. If it was a failure, it would be quietly forgotten and another play would go into rehearsal immediately.

Romeo and Juliet was an instant success. Everyone liked it, but the young people liked it especially, for it put their own dreams into poetry and gave them back again. When a satirist at the end of the decade described various young men in London—the one who collected jokes, the one who knew everything about fencing, the one who made a hobby of dancing and had "dreams of toe-turns," and so on—the young man with the craze for playgoing had just seen Shakespeare's play and was able to speak "naught but pure Juliet and Romeo." This young man's idea of making love was to quote from the latest success at the Curtain, and other young men of the period were like him in jotting down lines from the play in their commonplace books. When Robert Allot published his popular anthology, *England's Parnassus,* in 1600, he quoted more lavishly from *Romeo and Juliet* than from any other of Shakespeare's plays, and most of Allot's contemporaries would probably have agreed with his choice.

Popularity of this kind was too valuable to ignore, and a printer named John Danter, who had brought out the play and the ballad of *Titus Andronicus* in 1594, brought out the play and the ballad of *Romeo and Juliet* in 1597. Danter made the special point on the title

page that the play was a popular one, showing to "great applause.' The Londoners who had seen the play wanted to relive their experience, and the Londoners who had missed it wanted to see what the play was about, and Danter's edition probably sold well.

It did not deserve to. It was one of those corrupt editions that occurred whenever the company would not release the official text for publication and the printer had to pick up whatever version he could. This happened with the quarto editions of six or seven of Shakespeare's plays, and the text of *Romeo and Juliet* is by no means the worst. But it shows throughout what happens when a second-rate mind tries to follow a first-rate one.

The pirate who supplied Danter with his text invented his own lines of verse when he could not remember the original, and achieved such a misfortune as:

Ah, Romeo, Romeo, what disaster hap
Hath severed thee from thy true Juliet?

He was evidently working with the shortened stage version and yet he managed to make Juliet's closing speech longer than in the original because he lacked Shakespeare's gift for condensation. He had no ear for dialogue, and where Shakespeare has Capulet demand drier logs:

Call Peter, he will show thee where they are,

the individual who pirated the script was moved by vague memories of Will Kempe, who played the part of Peter, and produced a line that would turn any actor's hair gray: "Will will tell thee where thou shalt fetch them." His ability to spoil Shakespeare's stage effects shows up especially well in the balcony scene. The Nurse has been shouting "Madam" while Juliet calls Romeo again in a whisper. The pirate has Romeo also answer "Madam," a line which he could not deliver on the stage without giving the effect that he was parodying the Nurse. The text is not only inaccurate but badly printed, with an entirely new printer's type emerging suddenly in the middle of the second act, and the whole thing is a stupidly second-rate version of a great play.

Shakespeare was not the only writer whose plays were subjected to this kind of abuse. At about this same date the Rose theatre was showing a very popular play by George Chapman called *The Blind Beggar of Alexandria.* Chapman was telling the story of a tragic queen named Aegiale, but it was the comedy disguises of the blind beggar that pleased the public, and when the play was published, a year after *Romeo and Juliet,* the serious parts of the play were so heavily cut they were almost unintelligible. This mutilation may already have occurred in the stage version that was presented at the Rose, for the Admiral's company felt no responsibility for insuring a correct version of the text. The Chamberlain's company evidently felt otherwise about

Romeo and Juliet, for a new text, "augmented and amended," was published two years after Danter's corrupt version. This script was evidently the one that had been used as a prompt copy, since Will Kempe, instead of "Peter," appears in the fourth act.

The success of *Romeo and Juliet* was partly due to the brilliance of the stagecraft and the luminous beauty of the lines, but the greatest force of the play lay in its characterization. Nothing quite like Shakespeare's ability to create real people had ever appeared before on the English stage. He had shown occasional signs of it in his earlier plays, where for a moment the characters cease to be types and become individuals, but it was not until he joined the Chamberlain's company that he began peopling the stage with that incredible succession of human beings who are as real today as when the first excited audience listened to them. This power of characterization had of course lain dormant with him, but it could not have flowered unless conditions were favorable. If the actors who interpreted Romeo and Juliet had failed him, he might not have had the heart to go on to Hamlet and King Lear.

The support that Shakespeare's company gave him was not limited to *Romeo and Juliet.* The same care and intelligence must have gone into the production of each of the scripts he brought them, since they were unquestionably the best group of actors in London. Shakespeare had what every playwright needs, sympathetic and intelligent interpretation, and his genius for characterization was given the space it needed in which to grow. Even in the uncompromising field of the history play Shakespeare was able to find real people among the wars and the trumpets, and before he had spent four years with the Chamberlain's company, he had lifted the history play to such a height of reality that Falstaff himself was at home in it.

The first history play that Shakespeare wrote for his company was probably *King John*. As he often did, Shakespeare worked from an old play and in this case he followed the general line of the action so closely he must have had the original before him as he worked. Nevertheless, he used only one line from the original play in his own version, for Shakespeare did not rewrite old plays; he transformed them. The original play had no characterization in it, but Shakespeare saw an opportunity for one and seized upon it, creating what was possibly a predecessor of Mercutio in the chatty and delightful Bastard of Faulconbridge.

In another history play, Shakespeare went to his well-thumbed copy of Holinshed's *Chronicles* to conclude the Wars of the Roses that he had been recording in the *Henry VI* trilogy. The trilogy had ended with the future King Richard promising himself that he would "snarl and bite" as soon as he had the chance, and *Richard III* gave it

to him. Shakespeare did not usually use Marlowe's device of building a whole play around a single, towering villain, but Richard of York made a splendid villain with his crippled body, his bloody plots, and his violent love-making. Richard Burbage was famous for the role and evidently played it to the hilt. In the final scene of Richard's downfall he had a wonderful moment for any actor when he shouted, "A horse! a horse! My kingdom for a horse!" and he did it so well that the line became a kind of byword in the theatre and was freely parodied. There was a story of a host, "full of ale and history," who took his guests over Bosworth Field and solemnly showed them the very place where Richard Burbage had cried out the famous lines, before he had died in the battle.

Richard III was a very popular villain with Englishmen, and a popular anthology on the lives of prominent people called *The Mirror for Magistrates* had already celebrated his "fine and fatal fall." *The Mirror for Magistrates* devoted itself almost exclusively to the collapse of the great, with suitable accompanying morals, and no career lent itself better to moralizing than that of another King Richard, Richard II. Shakespeare found no moral in Richard II's career, but he was deeply interested in the temperament of that dreamy master of self-dramatization. Shakespeare's Richard II was the kind of man who could even take a certain aesthetic pleasure in his own downfall, and his tragedy is not quite a tragedy because the king is more interested in his reactions to events than he is in doing anything about them. The part is not a bravura part, like Richard III, but if Burbage played it, he must have found the development of the characterization even more interesting.

Richard II was destroyed by his practical cousin, who became Henry IV, and in the two parts of *Henry IV* Shakespeare deals with the problems he encountered by usurping the throne. Shakespeare knit his history plays very tightly to each other so that most of them form an uninterrupted sequence, and at the end of *Richard II* the new King Henry indicated that he was having difficulty with his son, who had taken to going about with "unrestrained loose companions." When Shakespeare started his new play, he found himself less interested in King Henry than in Prince Hal and his loose companions. An old play by the Queen's Men called *The Famous Victories of Henry the Fifth* had spent some time on Hal's youth and had named the leader of his disreputable followers as one Sir John Oldcastle.

The more Shakespeare thought about Sir John Oldcastle, the clearer he became. There were a great many opportunities to observe old soldiers in London, since the city supplied a fourth of the men in the entire kingdom, and Shakespeare knew the elaborate army grafts on which many an old captain had retired. He knew the cheating and the lying and the cadging of these disreputable old codgers, and he combined it with the Italian tradition of the braggart soldier; and out of this unpromising material leaped one of the greatest comedy creations in the history of the world.

As soon as Sir John Oldcastle appeared on the stage in the Chamberlain's company's production of the first part of *Henry IV*, a howl of unregenerate joy went up from the audiences, who at once took the disgraceful old gentleman to their collective hearts. The notoriety given the respectable name of Oldcastle was quite unjust, for in real life Sir John had been a renowned warrior, and someone evidently objected. The name of this individual is unknown, but it was probably Henry Brooke, eighth Lord Cobham, who was descended on his mother's side from Sir John Oldcastle. Shakespeare obligingly changed the name to Sir John Falstaff, and went on to use that name in part two of the play. There were those who objected to this name also, since it sounded too much like Sir John Fastolf, another respectable warrior of the fifteenth century, but there is no way of pleasing everyone.

Shakespeare was thorough in altering "Sir John Oldcastle" to "Sir John Falstaff," and the only sign in the play that Oldcastle had ever existed is a line in the second act that requires a three-syllable name to scan. The reference to Falstaff as "my old lad of the castle" was not necessary to omit, since that was a common slang phrase for a roisterer; Gabriel Harvey, for instance, spoke of Greene and his companions as "old lads of the castle." But many people were still calling the play *Sir John Oldcastle* at the end of the decade, and the Admiral's company capitalized on the situation by producing a play about the historical Sir John. They announced smugly that their play was not about a "pampered glutton" but about a virtuous peer, and closed the prologue by hinting pretty strongly that the Chamberlain's company had basely betrayed history.

> Let fair truth be graced
> Since forged invention former
> time disgraced.

Michael Drayton was one of the four writers who did the play for the Admiral's company, but it is to be hoped he was not the one responsible for the prologue.

Meanwhile Shakespeare had also been writing comedies; and in the comedies, as in the history plays, he came to mastership by degrees. The first romantic comedy he wrote for the Chamberlain's company was probably *The Two Gentlemen of Verona,* an elaborate study on the theme of love and friendship that was in some ways as artificial as *Love's Labour's Lost.* But this time Shakespeare did not lack for plot complications, and he packed into the play all the routine Italian devices that he was later to lift to such radiant heights. He used the device

of the girl disguised as her lover's page who is obliged to plead his suit with his rival, and later he made the scene one of the most delightful in *Twelfth Night.* He used the device of the noble band of outlaws in the forest that he later transformed in *As You Like It.* He used various devices that reappeared in *Romeo and Juliet,* like the friar, the ladder of cords, and the exile from court. The exchange of rings and the girl dressing as a man reappeared in *The Merchant of Venice,* and so did a whole scene in which the lady talks over her suitors with her maid. Shakespeare's willingness to use old material extended to material he had used himself, and he was just as capable of improving old devices as he was of improving the plays and books he used as his sources.

Shakespeare was never very interested in innovations and he even found a place in his heart for that shopworn relic of medievalism, the clown. Men like Christopher Marlowe and Ben Jonson very much disliked making a concession to popular taste by thrusting a clown into one of their carefully wrought plays, but the London audiences had been accustomed to this sort of thing for centuries and William Shakespeare saw no reason for depriving them of anything to which they had been accustomed. He thrust the usual clown into *The Two Gentlemen of Verona,* although there is no real place for him in the story and Launce and his trick dog are not much more than a vaudeville interlude to get a laugh. But Shakespeare continued to use the clown as he continued to use the cheap plot devices of Italian fiction, and Launce is the ancestor of wonderful creations like Dogberry and Bottom. Shakespeare never considered himself superior to the ordinary popular stagecraft of the period. He used it, and in using he transformed it.

Another romantic comedy that Shakespeare wrote in the same general period was *The Merchant of Venice,* and again he used the dream background of an imaginary city. Shakespeare's Venice is just as unreal as Shakespeare's Verona, and Antonio's troubles with his ships would have raised a shout of laughter in a city that had been insuring cargoes for generations. Even more unrealistic is the way the characters discuss usury, which was not only a commonplace in Venice but equally a commonplace in Shakespeare's London. A government decree at the beginning of Elizabeth's reign stated firmly that usury was a sin, but it also went on to state that ten per cent was a legal rate of interest. Half the members of Shakespeare's audience had either lent or borrowed money at high rates of interest, and they knew perfectly well that Shakespeare's *Merchant of Venice* was a folk play that had nothing to do with current economic conditions. As one contemporary remarked, "He is accounted but for a fool that doth lend his money for nothing," and although in theory the average Englishman still held to the medieval conception of usury as a wicked occupation fit only for Jews, in practice every Londoner made it a part of normal business procedure.

Shakespeare's portrait of Shylock is as unrealistic as his portrait of business conditions in Venice. It is a folk portrait, for Shakespeare had no opportunity to see any real Jews. They had all been exiled from England in the Middle Ages, and the law that kept them out was in full force. A typical incident in the eighties involved a mining expert from Prague who was working at Bristol. It was discovered he knew Hebrew and further questioning showed he was a Jew. He was arrested by the local magistrate, sent up to London for questioning by the Privy Council, and at once deported.

The crime of Joachim Gaunz was not his race but his religion, and if he had been baptized into the Christian faith, he would have been welcome in England. There had even been a home for converted Jews established in London at the time of the expulsion, and although the building in Chancery Lane was eventually annexed for government offices, any Christian of the Hebrew race was welcome in London. The point is illustrated in *The Merchant of Venice* by Shylock's daughter, who is perfectly respectable from the audience's point of view in spite of her ancestry because, as she says, "I shall be saved by my husband; he hath made me a Christian."

The only "Jews" that Shakespeare

could have met in London were baptized Christians of the Hebrew race, and none of these would have served as a model for Shylock. The model was medieval Christian tradition, and this tradition was so strong that even the greatest of writers had been unable to shake themselves loose from it. When Geoffrey Chaucer described a "cursed Jew," it was to show him murdering a little Christian boy as part of his normal behavior; and when Christopher Marlowe wrote *The Jew of Malta,* Barrabas tries to poison a whole city full of Christians and is finally plunged, to the delight of any contemporary audience, into a boiling cauldron. This was the only tradition that was available to Shakespeare when he created Shylock, and the degree to which he was able to break loose from this tradition is astonishing. Less and less as he continued his career was he able to simplify—to look at his characters through half-closed eyes and record only a few effective characteristics. Even in his folk portraits he was unable to prevent himself from seeing real human beings, and where his audiences expected only a comic villain, they got Shylock. "I am a Jew. Hath not a Jew eyes? Hath not a Jew hands, organs, dimensions, senses, affections, passions? . . . If you prick us, do we not bleed?"

The varying elements that go to make up *The Merchant of Venice* are not handled in a single key, and for a modern audience especially, the play often seems to pull apart.

Yet Shakespeare was able to take an even more varied group of characters and turn them into a perfect whole in *A Midsummer Night's Dream,* that irresistible combination of moonlight and moonshine. Again Shakespeare was economical, for he had already used the device in *Love's Labour's Lost* of the stage-struck amateurs who try to put on a play; and the production of Holofernes and the curate is a pale forerunner of the inspired nonsense of Bottom's production of Pyramus and Thisbe. The fairies were all played by children, and their rigid training as dancers must have been useful to them; but Puck, who was not technically a fairy, was played by a grown man. Incidentally, Shakespeare completely changed the character of the English fairy for future generations of readers, for they were rather malignant, earth-bound little country folk before Shakespeare housed them in flowers.

All these plays were produced in the first four years of Shakespeare's association with the Chamberlain's company and can be dated as having been written before September 1598. Attempts to find internal evidence for dating the plays are extremely risky in dealing with a mind like Shakespeare's, with its casual, gigantic leaps and its occasional carelessness. But by great good fortune a book was entered for publication in September of 1598 in which the author had written a list of Shakespeare's plays.

The book was called *Palladis*

Tamia and its author was Francis Meres. Meres was an Oxford graduate who had been mildly successful with a religious book and had been commissioned to contribute to a series of cultural handbooks called *Wits Commonwealth*. These short cuts to erudition were always popular with the London public, but, while most of the compilers kept to useful quotations from the classics, Francis Meres was more ambitious and set out to show his knowledge of the contemporary literary world of London.

Meres's knowledge of the literary world was not very extensive and he was under the impression that Marlowe had been stabbed by "a bawdy serving-man," a description of himself that would have surprised Ingram Frizer, who ended up as a churchwarden. But when Meres came to Shakespeare, whom he mentions in five different connections, he shows himself to be remarkably well informed.

It is not surprising that Meres knew about *Venus and Adonis* and *The Rape of Lucrece,* since these two narrative poems were still going into edition after edition; but unless Meres was acquainted with someone in Shakespeare's own circle, he could not have known that he was circulating "sugared sonnets among his private friends." Still less could Meres have known about Shakespeare's plays, since only a few of these were in print and most of them anonymously, and yet Meres was able to produce a long list of the plays that Shakespeare had written. "As Plautus and Seneca are accounted the best for comedy and tragedy among the Latins; so Shakespeare among the English is the most excellent in both kinds for the stage; for comedy, witness his *Gentlemen of Verona,* his *Errors,* his *Loves Labours Lost,* his *Loves Labours Won,* his *Midsummer Night's Dream,* his *Merchant of Venice;* for tragedy, his *Richard the Second, Richard the Third, Henry the Fourth, King John, Titus Andronicus,* and his *Romeo and Juliet."* If *Loves Labours Won* is another name for *The Taming of the Shrew,* this is practically a complete list. The only omission is the *Henry VI* trilogy, which can be identified as Shakespeare's from other contemporary sources.

This is the only list of its kind that was ever given for an Elizabethan playwright, just as it happens to be the only case in which all a playwright's texts have survived. It is extremely fortunate that the greatest of Elizabethan playwrights should also have been the best documented, and that Meres should have performed a service for Shakespeare that he denied to all of the rest. Meres mentioned a great many playwrights in his book, from popular playwrights like Greene and Kyd to noblemen who practiced the art like Lord Buckhurst and the Earl of Oxford, and he was sufficiently well informed to include even a newcomer like Ben Jonson. But William Shakespeare was the only one he singled out for extended comment, and the evident reason was that he admired him. "The Muses would speak with Shakespeare's fine filed phrase, if they would speak English."

Shortly after Meres wrote *Palladis Tamia* he retired to Rutland as the rector of a small parish, and it is to be hoped that he was happy there. He may not have been an important writer or made a great success of his literary career in London, but few men deserve more gratitude from any biographer of Shakespeare.

✵ *Chapter* 8

Back in Stratford the Shakespeare family had been involved for the past eighteen years in a difficulty over land that resulted in two bitter lawsuits. Going to law was a normal part of Elizabethan existence, and there was hardly a family in England in that argumentative age that did not have at least one lawsuit pending. John Shakespeare had a normal number of suits during his lifetime, mostly over the collection of debts, and won or lost as the case might be. But there was a special bitterness in the lawsuits that involved his wife's inheritance at Wilmcote.

A short time after John Shakespeare left the Council so abruptly, he found himself in need of money and borrowed forty pounds from his wife's brother-in-law, Edmund Lambert, with a mortgage on some of Mary Shakespeare's land as security. Forty pounds was a comparatively small sum for what was a fairly large piece of property, but since the transaction was kept in the family, John Shakespeare no doubt felt he was safe enough in taking out the mortgage.

The payment of the money was due in 1580, which happened to be a difficult year for John Shakespeare. He was concerned in a case involving a breach of the peace at the Court of Queen's Bench at Westminster, and when neither he nor a Nottingham hatmaker put in an appearance on a stipulated date, he had to forfeit twenty pounds for himself and another twenty for the hatmaker. Nevertheless, John Shakespeare had another forty pounds in cash for Edmund Lambert, and on Michaelmas Day he took the fifteen-mile trip south to the village where his wife's brother-in-law lived to pay off the mortgage. Lambert refused to accept the money, saying that Shakespeare owed him more than that, and when he died seven years later, Edmund Lambert was still in possession of the property.

John Shakespeare happened to be under heavy extra expenses the year Edmund Lambert died. He was being sued for ten pounds that his brother Henry owed someone and had failed to pay, and he had lost another ten pounds because he had gone surety for a Stratford coppersmith named Michael Price who had failed to make a stipulated appearance at the court in Coventry. Nevertheless, John Shakespeare was ready to shoulder the extra burden of an expensive lawsuit, and in Michaelmas term of 1588 he and his wife and his son William presented a bill of complaint against Edmund Lambert's son and heir in the Court of Queen's Bench at Warwick. The hearing was set for the following year and the Shakespeares lost the case, since the Elizabethan law in regard to mortgages was unyielding.

John Shakespeare refused to admit failure and eight years later he brought suit against John Lambert again. This time he tried the Court of Chancery, an informal court that really attempted to get to the rights of the case where a strict interpretation involved special legal hardship. The outcome of the case is unknown, but there is no evidence that John Shakespeare got back his land.

Five years after the failure of his first suit, John Shakespeare lost another of his possessions. There was a bad fire in Stratford in September 1594, and in spite of the fire ladder and the collection of buckets at Market Cross, the fire succeeded in getting as far as Henley Street. The two houses in which the Shakespeares were living were not affected, but the third house, which John Shakespeare had been renting out, was either destroyed by fire or pulled down by fire hooks. It was the opinion of the vicar of Strat-ford that the cause of the fire was the unwillingness of the citizens to observe the Sabbath, which was an entirely orthodox conclusion. His predecessor in the Stratford pulpit had read a prayer of thanksgiving, after the repulse of the Spanish Armada, which officially attributed the attempted Spanish invasion to God's punishment of various English sins, including "excess in meat and drink." Every disaster in Elizabethan England, from the greatest to the least, was always attributed to the hand of God.

Two years after the loss of a house by fire there was a tragedy in the Shakespeare family that was perhaps the most heartbreaking blow John Shakespeare ever sustained. His grandson Hamnet, the only boy in the family and the only heir of the family name, died in August 1596. Of all the hopes that must once have centered around William Shakespeare's only son there remain only two brief entries in the Stratford register, one giving the date of his baptism and the other, eleven years later, giving the date of his burial. The two surviving children were the boy's twin, Judith, and her thirteen-year-old sister, Susanna.

When Hamnet was buried in Stratford on the 11th of August, his father's company was playing at a town in Kent, forty-seven miles on the other side of London. If the boy's illness was a long one, there may have been some way to get word to his father in time, so that he could at least have reached Stratford in time for the burial. But once the actors were on tour, there was no way to reach them except to send a letter by carrier to some town on the route, with instructions to hold it there until the playing company arrived. This was not a reliable arrangement even when the letter went from London and the sender knew the company's route. Philip Henslowe knew every detail of his son-in-law's profession, and yet when Alleyn was on tour, Henslowe wrote to him, "We would write oftener to you than we do, but we know not whither to send to you." Unless word of Hamnet's illness reached his father before Shakespeare left London for the regular touring season of 1596, it is not likely that anyone in Stratford was able to get in touch with him until the company was back in London again.

From that time on there seem to have been no more tragedies in old John Shakespeare's life. The remaining five years of his life were not only undisturbed but must have been actually triumphant. The increasing splendor that spread over the Shakespeare family in Stratford was the reflected glow from the eldest son who had left the previous decade to join a despised profession but who had since become a rich and consequently respected man.

The first outward sign of the changed position of the Shakespeares in Stratford came in 1596, the otherwise tragic year of Hamnet's death. On October 20, a new draft of the Shakespeare coat of arms was made in the London office of the College of Heralds. This draft was in John Shakespeare's name, since it was he who became the gentleman, but it seems almost certain that it was William Shakespeare who arranged to have the matter reopened.

This time the grant went through and John Shakespeare received the coat of arms that had been designed for him twenty years earlier. Robert Cooke had made him a handsome, simple design: a gold shield with a band of black across it that bore a spear of gold tipped with silver, and for a crest a silver falcon with outstretched wings standing on a silver wreath and supporting a spear. John Shakespeare and his heirs could blazon the arms on their "rings, signets, edifices, utensils, liveries, tombs, and monuments," and from that time forward he walked the streets of Stratford as complete and accredited a gentleman as his friend, Adrian Quiney. In 1599 there was a move to get his wife's arms, those of the Ardens, impaled with his. The Heralds' Office went into the matter carefully and finally established her connection with the Ardens of Cheshire, but this impalement was never actually made.

After John Shakespeare's death in the next decade, when his son William had succeeded him as the "gentleman" of the family, there was a discussion in the Heralds' Office over the suitability of this grant of a coat of arms to the Shakespeares. There was nothing improper in the grant itself. John Shakespeare had been a bailiff and a justice of the peace and he had married into the great family of the Ardens. He was probably not worth the £500 attributed to him and he may not have had a great-grandfather who fought under Henry VII and thus won lands in Warwickshire, but amiable fictions of this kind were considered legitimate. What was wrong with the Shakespeare coat of arms was that it had been granted by Sir William Dethick, that brilliant, bad-tempered thunderhead of an official who so maddened some of his colleagues in the Office of Heralds that they would have gone to almost any lengths to prove him in the wrong.

Dethick's co-official in the grant to the Shakespeares was William Camden, a kindly gentleman and great scholar who had succeeded Robert Cooke; but Camden was also unpopular in the Heralds' Office because he was an outsider who had been given a high post over the heads of various experienced officials who were in line for the honor. The situation particularly maddened the York Herald, Ralph Brooke, who had a temper of his own and who had already attacked Camden's learning. In 1602 Brooke drew up a list of the mistakes Dethick and Camden had made in office and these included the granting of arms to "Shakespeare the player." The Shakespeares did not come from the upper walks of life, and in any case the coat of arms that had been granted them was too close to Lord Mauley's.

The reply that Dethick and Camden made to Brooke still exists in its original manuscript form, written out between a drawing of the Shakespeare coat of arms on one side of the page and that of Lord Mauley on the other. The two chief Heralds maintained that the two designs were not the same because the "spear on the bend" in the Shakespeare one made an obvious difference. Moreover, John Shakespeare had been worthy to receive arms. "The man was a magistrate in Stratford-upon-Avon. A justice of the peace, he married a daughter and heir of Arden and was of good substance."

This defense of the Shakespeare family made by Camden is especially interesting because of Camden's position in the literary world of his day. His *Britannia* had made him the most admired writer in England on learned matters, and since he habitually wrote in Latin, his fame was even greater on the Continent than it was in England. It was chiefly because of his fame as a writer and antiquarian that Camden had been elevated to so high a post in the Heralds' Office without previous experience in the work, and if Camden said the Shakespeares were eligible for a coat of arms, the family could not have had the backing of a more learned authority. Camden was an admirer of Shakespeare as a writer, and he once made a list of contemporary English poets, starting with Sidney and Spenser and ending with "William Shakespeare, and other most pregnant wits of these our times, whom succeeding ages may justly admire." Camden was one of the few men of the period who had connections with William Shakespeare from both the Stratford and the London end; he knew him both as John Shakespeare's son and as a writer, a fact that makes his testimony of special interest.

Less than a year after the new draft of the coat of arms had been made, the prestige of the Shakespeare family in Stratford took another enormous step forward. On the fourth of May, 1597, William Shakespeare bought the second largest house in town.

New Place was much more than just a house. It was a symbol of high social standing in Stratford and its owner had a special pew in church called the Clopton Pew. The house had been built by Sir Hugh Clopton, onetime Lord Mayor of London who also gave Stratford its great stone bridge. Sir Hugh had hoped to retire to Stratford before he died and he built what he called "my great house" opposite the Guild Chapel that his money had already beautified.

As late as 1543, in the century after Sir Hugh's death, New Place was described as "a pretty house of brick and timber." But brick was an unusual building material in Stratford, and the thin bricks of the period did not prove to be very durable. New Place was still a fine house when one of Henry VIII's physicians lived in it and collected silver, but it had a succession of tenants, and when the Underhill family took it over in Shakespeare's boyhood, it was already badly in need of repair. It was probably for this reason that Shakespeare was able to buy it for only sixty pounds, a low price for a house of this kind, especially since there had been two recent fires in Stratford and good houses were scarce. Shakespeare must have made extensive alterations, for he sold the Corporation a load of stone the following year, when the bridge was undergoing one of its frequent repairs, and since the subsoil of New Place is gravel, the stone must have come from some alterations that were being made in the foundations.

The property had its own ancient garden and included an orchard and two barns. There was nothing wrong with New Place that money could not cure, and in return its owner was assured a position of unquestioned prominence in the community. The Shakespeare family had come a long way since the previous decade, when they had been so completely outdistanced in Stratford by the Quineys.

It was almost a case of poetic justice that when Richard Quiney was in London in 1598, he tried to borrow money from William Shakespeare. Quiney was there on town business, trying to get a remission of taxes because of a depression and two fires in Stratford, but before he hurried off to Court on the 25th of October he sat down in his inn, the Bell in Carter Lane, and wrote a letter to Shakespeare in his small, swift, lawyerlike hand. Quiney wanted his "loving good friend and countryman, William Shakespeare" to lend him thirty pounds and was willing to advance excellent security.

What Quiney wanted the money for is not quite clear. He told Shakespeare he wanted to pay off "the debts I owe in London" and that these were disquieting him because he did not like to be "indebted." Since he was raising more money to do it, it would seem that Quiney did not consider a debt to Shakespeare as coming within this category. On the other hand, Richard's father, old Adrian Quiney, wrote his son that if he got any money from Shakespeare, there was an excellent bargain in knit stockings at the nearby town of Evesham and that twenty pounds invested there would bring in a good return. Probably Richard Quiney wanted part of the money to pay off old debts and part of it to make some business investments as a mercer; and since he was successful at Court in getting a remission of Stratford taxes, it is to be hoped he was equally successful in his attempt to borrow money from his "loving good friend."

By 1598 William Shakespeare had become one of the major householders in Stratford, but unlike Richard Quiney he never showed any interest in the welfare of the town or how its affairs were conducted. The town records are almost blank where his name is concerned, and Shakespeare's chief activity in Stratford, apart from the growing number of his real-estate purchases, seems to have been his lawsuits with fellow townsmen over debts. The London actor seems to have been rigidly on his dignity in his native town, in contrast to his easy, relaxed relations with his colleagues in London. He was deeply interested in the fortunes of the Shakespeare family but not in the fortunes of Stratford, and even when he finally retired to New Place to live, he sided against his native town in the great enclosure controversy. Shakespeare had many friends in Stratford, such as Hamnet Sadler, and kept them as friends all his life; and it is quite possible that he loved the town of his birth as he certainly loved the countryside around it. But it seems undeniable that he had very little interest in Stratford's welfare and very little sense of local responsibility.

One of the few occasions in which Shakespeare's name appears in the local records was in February of 1598. A survey was being made in England to see how much barley was being held in private hands, and the returns from Stratford showed every major householder in town on the list, including the owner of New Place.

For the past few years there had been an alarming succession of bad harvests in England and the Privy Council was keeping a close eye on the local price of wheat and barley, or, as the Elizabethans called it, corn and malt. To offset any tendency toward profiteering, the Privy Council ordered a survey of every barn in England so that if the owner had any extra grain, he could be forced to sell it to the general public at a set price.

The real trouble in the Stratford area was the fact that the normal flow of grain from the neighboring counties of Worcester and Gloucester was being diverted because better prices could be obtained elsewhere, and the Privy Council sent a stiff letter to both counties on the subject. But there was also a survey made of the Stratford area to make sure that no one was illegally holding grain.

The survey showed that everyone in Stratford was being illegal, or at least as illegal as possible. William Shakespeare of Chapel Street Ward had about ten quarters of malt stored in his thatched barn in Chapel Lane; ten quarters would be about eighty bushels and well over the legal limit. Shakespeare's respectable neighbor in the same ward, Alexander Aspinall, the schoolmaster, had eleven quarters. His equally respectable neighbor, Thomas Dixon, had seventeen. About a dozen residents of Stratford, many of them with smaller households than the Shakespeare family, had more malt in their barns than Shakespeare did, and the truth was that everyone in Stratford had as much barley stored away as possible and held on to it

as long as he could.

The medieval idea that prices could be controlled legally and that everything should be shared was still strong enough in England so that the Privy Council had the approval of the general public. But occasionally there was an individualist who thought otherwise, like the grain holder who announced defiantly in Star Chamber, "My goods are my own . . . I will do what I list with them." For this he was fined a hundred pounds and obliged to wear a paper cap, like a schoolboy's, which described his misdeeds.

The depression of the late nineties did more than affect the malt supply in Stratford and its roots were deeper than a few years of heavy rains and bad harvests. Ever since the Spanish Armada was overthrown, England had been paying for the war with Spain with increasingly heavy taxation and a draining off of her natural resources. Many of her European markets were closed by the war, and privateering on the high seas had raised freight costs and made a stabilization of trade almost impossible. There was a trade war with Germany and a dangerous rebellion in Ireland. Prices had been climbing steadily, with wages and rents lagging far behind, and when food began to run short, it added the final touch to the increasing gloom of the decade. Everything was "exceeding measure in price, such was our sins deserving it," and the only thing the Privy Council could suggest was that the Londoners ought to eat less.

The acting companies in London were fully aware of the depression, since they all depended on the free spending of their customers. But in 1596 they experienced a further, private disaster in the death of the Lord Chamberlain, who worked with all the companies since he controlled the Office of the Revels, but who was particularly vital to the welfare of the Chamberlain's company. Henry, Lord Hunsdon, died in July, in his seventy-first year, and was buried in Westminster Abbey; and the office of Chamberlain went to William Brooke, seventh Lord Cobham, a man who disliked plays. The mayor of London, who never missed an opportunity to harry the players, rushed to the attack as soon as their powerful protector was dead; and Tom Nashe found there was no market for new plays in London because the actors "are piteously persecuted by the Lord Mayor and however in their old lord's time they thought their state settled, it is now so uncertain they cannot build upon it."

Nevertheless, Shakespeare's company maintained its position at Court, giving all six of the plays produced before the Queen at Whitehall that year, and in the spring their prospects brightened. Lord Cobham died in March and the office of Lord Chamberlain went back into the Hunsdon family. It was given to George, second Lord Hunsdon, who had already taken over the patronage of his father's company of players and who received in April his father's position at Court. Shakespeare's company had been known since the preceding August as Lord Hunsdon's company, but now it became the Chamberlain's company again. It was during this interim that *Romeo and Juliet* was first published, since the title page stated that it had "been often (with great applause) played publicly by the Right Honorable the Lord of Hunsdon his servants."

In spite of the sympathy the new Lord Chamberlain had for the players, the mayor of London did not give up his efforts to purge the city of that sink of iniquity, the London theatre. On the 28th day of July, 1597, the mayor and aldermen wrote a long letter to the Privy Council, making a list of all the misfortunes the city was enduring by having actors in its midst. Even the heathen, the mayor said plaintively, only saw plays occasionally, but Londoners saw them all the time. "They are a special cause of corrupting youth, containing nothing but unchaste matter, lascivious devices, shifts of cosenage, and other lewd and ungodly practices," which is a fair description of a play like *Romeo and Juliet* from the Puritan point of view. In addition, they brought together thieves and contrivers of treason who would certainly corrupt by their presence any members of the audience who were not already hopelessly ruined. They attracted people who should have been in church, to the profanation of religion, and they "drew apprentices and other servants from their work," to the hindrance of trade. Moreover, if there was a plague, the Londoners tended to go to plays to comfort themselves, and thus the theatres were a threat to health as well as to everything else.

It is impossible to say what effect this powerful document might have had upon the Privy Council, for the Privy Council had just taken measures of its own to suppress the theatres. On the same day the letter was sent, the Privy Council issued a government order to have all the plays in London discontinued and every theatre in London pulled down.

The Privy Council was not interested in plays like *Romeo and Juliet*, however they might corrupt the young or hinder honest trade. The Council was interested only in the possible spread of sedition through the theatre, and it had been informed that the newly organized company of Lord Pembroke had produced a play at the Swan which contained "very seditious and slanderous matter." Three of the actors were at once sent to prison in the Marshalsea, and although the author could not be sent to join them since he had wisely left town, his lodgings were ransacked for further examples of suspicious writing.

The play was called *The Isle of Dogs* and its author was the irrepressible Tom Nashe, who had found an incautious buyer for his latest play in Pembroke's company. Nashe was the last of the old, excitable brilliant group of university men that had once gathered around Marlowe and Greene, and he was still in spirit the impish, mocking undergraduate who had once been nearly expelled from Cambridge for writing an indecorous school play.

According to Nashe himself, he wrote only the induction and the first act of *The Isle of Dogs*. The rest of the play was written by an actor in Pembroke's company, a young man in his twenties named Benjamin Johnson who had come back from the wars in what was evidently a restless state of mind and was hoping to graduate from acting to writing plays. When Johnson and his two fellow actors were packed off to the Marshalsea, the Privy Council reported of him that he "was not only an actor but a maker of part of the said play." He continued as a maker of plays, many of the best of which he wrote for Shakespeare's company, and after a time the spelling of his name altered to "Ben Jonson."

The Privy Council usually threatened much more than it actually performed where the London theatres were concerned. In spite of its grave pronouncements, no theatre in London was pulled down. But playing was discontinued for a time and all the acting companies took to the road. Summer was the normal time for touring, in any case, and the Chamberlain's company had probably planned a brief tour in the wealthy and populous counties of Sussex and Kent, very much like the one they had taken the previous year. But this year's tour was not a brief one, thanks to *The Isle of Dogs,* and the Chamberlain's company took the most extended tour of the provinces that they made in all of Elizabeth's reign.

Touring was not as comfortable or as profitable as playing in one of the large London theatres. The company acted in a series of local halls or innyards, and when they moved on to the next town, all their musical instruments and properties and costumes had to be stored in the play wagon, carefully making sure that the costumes were "folded up with the thread, not against the thread." The leading actors rode on horseback, with "their luggage and some part of their company" in the wagon, but each of them had once had the experience of being a hired actor, such as those who trudged alongside the wagon with shoes full of gravel. These hired actors were paid less than their London wages in the provinces, since the receipts were usually smaller, and Philip Henslowe paid a hired actor ten shillings a week in London and only five when he was on tour. The standard of the performances had to be kept high, since the London companies were in direct competition with excellent provincial com-

panies, but the work was not as stimulating as in London. No new plays could be launched and the ones already in existence usually had to be cut for country playing.

On the other hand, every member of Shakespeare's company had learned to expect the annual tour of the country as a normal part of his existence as an actor, and since they liked and respected each other as human beings, they probably derived a good deal of enjoyment from traveling about the countryside. The English method of forming an acting company showed to special advantage when it came to touring, since a group of experienced men and carefully trained boys could travel cheaply and live together amicably with a minimum of emotional friction. The Italian actors used women in their companies, and although some English travelers agreed that these women were almost as good as men in the parts, their presence complicated the lives of the troupe as a whole. Apart from the trouble and expense of housing the women, there were fierce rivalries between the *prima* and *secunda donna* of the company and even more savage wars between the leading actresses of rival companies. Since the whole existence of these traveling companies depended on the unity of the troupe as a whole, the great Italian actress, Vittoria, was justified in complaining bitterly when a rival whom she called simply "that woman" tried to lure her company away from her. Occasionally this rivalry resulted in furiously brilliant performances by the actresses, but it did not contribute to the economic stability of the company as a whole.

The Chamberlain's company was untroubled by any internal dissension and must have traveled very comfortably, especially since they were an unusually prosperous company and kept to well-traveled routes. The accommodations along the route were excellent, for, as one enthusiastic traveler declared, England had "the most commodious inns of all the world." The inns in cities like Bristol and Bath were actually much better than those in London, and they competed briskly for the patronage of the traveler with signs out front that cost as much as forty pounds. Some towns had a dozen inns, a few of them able to accommodate as many as three hundred travelers and their horses. Each horse was cared for "very diligently" by one of the hostlers, in wistful expectation of a large tip, and its owner was "sure to lie in clean sheets, wherein no man hath lodged since they came from the laundress." Unlike the Continental custom, the English inns did not charge a flat rate and each man was given as much food and service as he wished to pay for. The one rule laid down by the government was that each innkeeper was responsible for seeing that all his guests went to church on Sunday, for not even on the road was an Englishman free from the paternal eye of the Anglican religion.

The Chamberlain's company began their tour of 1597 by traveling through Kent toward the Channel port of Dover. Dover had its regular local audience and was also full of travelers who stayed at its numerous inns on their way to or from the Continent. They traveled abroad under a careful system of regulations, for the Privy Council did not approve of people "flying beyond the seas without license."

Dover had its own attractions for the tourist, for the castle on the hill above the town had been built by Julius Caesar, and his soldiers had left flour there that was now as hard as lime. There were cannons piled up in the port, and English warships riding at anchor, and in August the visitor could watch the samphire being gathered from the steep cliffs along the sea. The fat leaves of the samphire were gathered to be pickled and sold in the London streets as a sauce for meat, and Shakespeare has described what the gathering of it looked like:

> . . . half way down
> Hangs one that gathers samphire, dreadful trade!
> Methinks he seems no bigger than his head.
> The fishermen that walk along the beach
> Appear like mice . . .

Shakespeare visited this district more than once with his company and had many opportunities to see the samphire gathered in August before he described it in *King Lear*. It grew at Rye, and the Chamberlain's company also visited Rye in

August of 1597. Rye was an old walled town along the coast and had once had a good harbor, but its position as a port town was being gradually destroyed by the encroachment of the marshes behind it. It had a good inn but its chief distinctions were its twenty brass cannons and the fact there had just been a fascinating local murder. A London bookseller came out the following year with a full account of the deeds of one "Henry Rabson, fisherman of Rye, who poisoned his wife in the strangest manner that ever hitherto hath been heard of." Rabson used ratsbane and powdered glass and thus passed into temporary renown.

Another town that was famous for a murder was Faversham, which the Chamberlain's company had already visited at the beginning of August on their way to Dover. It was nearly half a century since Mr. Arden had been murdered in Faversham, but it was one of those striking sex murders that everyone enjoys, and even the historians gave the event their respectful attention. An excellent play called *Arden of Faversham* had been drawing large audiences, since it had the advantage of being able to show the "dissimulation of a wicked woman, the insatiable desire of filthy lust, and the shameful end of all murderers." Apart from this distinction, Faversham was a flourishing town famous for its oysters, and it had a market building with a clock that must have reminded Shakespeare very much of the one in his native Stratford. It was in May of this year that Shakespeare had bought New Place, and his thoughts must have been in Stratford oftener than usual that summer.

If the season had been a normal one, the Chamberlain's company would probably have turned back to London after touring through southeastern England. But the London theatres were still tight shut under the watchful eyes of the Privy Council and the mayor, for once in agreement, and the Chamberlain's company went west toward Bristol and Bath, which housed some of the best theatre audiences in England. On their way they stopped at Marlborough, which lay on the route. Marlborough was a market town in Wiltshire whose chief distinction was that Merlin Ambrosius, the builder of Stonehenge, may or may not have been buried there. More interesting from the actors' point of view was a local bylaw stating that "the chief officers of the borough shall not give license for the players, or using of any stageplays or interludes in the Guildhall."

The situation was very different at Bath, where every acting company was welcome. The old town had been seeing an average of fifteen to twenty plays a year for the past two decades, and the Chamberlain's company was only one of five that played there in 1597. The Guildhall, east of High Street, was not much of a building now that the cloth industry had decayed, and the actors probably preferred the innyard of one of the town's large and excellent inns.

After the collapse of its cloth industry, Bath had found a new source of revenue in its medicinal baths, which were owned by the city but brought prosperity to everyone. People flocked from all parts of England to be cured of various diseases or to participate in what was a very pleasant social season. The town had two bowling greens and a tennis court, the latter judiciously located next to the largest and most centrally located bath in town, which was called the King's Bath. There was also the New Bath and the Hot Bath, all three discreetly walled and supplied with dressing rooms. The town rented the baths out on a concession system, and each one had a bath keeper with a succession of bath guides under him. The guides manned the pumps and supplied linen for the bathers, and since they depended largely on tips they took a deeply affectionate interest in their patrons.*

Bath was a fashionable town,

* According to Elizabethan theory, these hot baths had been established in Bath in pre-Roman times by a British king named Bladud. King Bladud was not content with this distinction and "by vain trust of the art of necromancy took upon him to fly in the air, from whence he fell down and brake his neck." There were still relics in Bath of the Roman occupation, including stone images at intervals in the town wall, but Shakespeare would have seen no relics of the unlucky King Bladud, whose son was the equally unfortunate King Lear.—Author's Note

and many of the nobility owned houses there which they rented or loaned to friends when they were not in residence. The patron of the Chamberlain's company, George, second Lord Hunsdon, "kept the most honorable house that ever was kept there," and he had such faith in the curative powers of the waters that his sovereign wrote him, "I cannot but wonder, considering the great number of pails of water that I hear have been poured upon you, that you are not rather drowned than otherwise." Queen Elizabeth did not believe in anything but a careful diet and much exercise, and in another letter to the Lord Chamberlain she again expressed her doubts of the virtues of Bath's water. "I somewhat still doubt that there hath been too great abundance of the same squashed upon you."

Sometime in September the Chamberlain's company played in Bristol, another city upon the Avon that also loved the theatre. It stood northwest of Bath, on a hill, and was one of the chief cities of England. In some ways Bristol was a miniature version of London, with its cathedral and the beautiful houses that had been built by its merchants. Its stone bridge over the Avon was nearly as good as London Bridge over the Thames, for it was lined with houses in the same way and even had a chapel on it. The Avon at this point was tidal, and the ships could be brought "under sail into the very heart of the city." The merchants prospered and their place of exchange, which was called the Tolzey, was covered over for protection from the weather like the Royal Exchange in London. The fair of St. James, where actors were especially welcome, was a near rival to the great St. Bartholomew fair in London, and Bristol could lay claim to being the second city of the realm. Its citizens must have been unusually literate, since in Shakespeare's lifetime the first free public library in England was established there. The Guildhall was always open to traveling companies, and in September of 1597 the Corporation paid thirty shillings "unto my Lord Chamberlain's players playing at the Guildhall."

When the Chamberlain's company arrived that autumn, the city was not at its best. The years of depression and bad harvests had hit Bristol hard, and 1597 was the year in which the mayor decreed that all the citizens must "keep as many poor persons in their houses as their income would permit, for fear of an insurrection." Wheat was selling that year for twenty shillings a bushel, and matters might have been even worse if one intelligent alderman had not imported rye from Danzig and made it available to the people of Bristol at half the local price.

By October the Chamberlain's men had probably returned to London, a hundred and fifteen miles away. Ben Jonson had been released from the Marshalsea the eighth of October and Henslowe's

theatre, the Rose, was open by the eleventh. The Swan seems to have been the only theatre that remained closed, and the winter season was probably fairly normal.

Nevertheless, the luxury trades must all have had a hard time of it, for London was much more intricately organized than Bristol and felt the dislocation of high prices and shortages much more intensely. Moreover, the depression of the late nineties brought with it a general sense of gloom that was in noticeable contrast to the kind of lightheartedness that Shakespeare had seen in the city when he first came up to London.

The first people to register this change in the mental climate were the writers, although the *fin de siècle* mood of disillusionment that attacked literary London was of course due to more than the depression. The young writing gentlemen at the Inns of Court were not especially interested in what was going on at the Royal Exchange. Their gloom was a reaction from the overexcited optimism that had characterized London in the eighties. Men like Sidney and Marlowe had seen the world in a golden, conquering light that could hardly have been sustained indefinitely, the temperament of the average man being what it is.

The pendulum of literary fashion usually swings violently once it begins, and the disillusioned young moderns of the late nineties turned their backs on their elders under the impression that they had made a completely new discovery about the world they lived in. For that great Renaissance characteristic—love of action—they substituted the conviction that the world was a pit of iniquity and the only thing worth doing was to sit down and point out its sins. For that other great Renaissance characteristic—love of beauty—they substituted a kind of horrified fear of sex coupled with a fascinated interest in its abnormalities. And for vigor they substituted cleverness.

A young writer like John Marston might almost stand as a symbol for this new generation. His father had sent him to the Inns of Court hoping he would be a lawyer like himself, but young Marston had other dreams; he was going to be a writer. Half-Italian, emotional, ambitious, and still in his early twenties, he wrote a long, lush, erotic narrative poem and used the meter of *Venus and Adonis,* since that was still the model for hopeful young men to follow. There seems to be no doubt that Marston wrote *Pygmalion's Image* in sober emulation of a respected elder, and it was not until he finished it that he realized that no advanced young man took that sort of thing seriously any longer. So Marston promptly announced that his erotic tale had been a parody.

> Deems't that in sad seriousness
> I write
> Such nasty stuff as is Pygmalion?

Having turned his back on *Pygmalion's Image,* with its typically Renaissance glorification of physical passion, Marston launched on a series of satires in the new modern temper. The satires were very successful and Marston followed them the next year with *The Scourge of Villainy*. In his new book Marston undertook "to purge the snottery of our slimy time," and since this ambition gave him the opportunity to make a detailed study of the "slime," especially in relation to sex, he had a production for which the booksellers must have loved him well. Other young writers also started to point out the sins of the "sin-drowned world," and the craze for satires had reached such a height by 1599 that Archbishop Whitgift forbade their publication and ordered some of them burnt in the yard of Stationers' Hall. Marston's book was among those that were destroyed. He turned instead to writing for the stage, and his disappointed father in Coventry was finally obliged to admit that his son would never be a lawyer. Marston had a colorful and violent career as a playwright, with several excursions into prison, and finally ended up, as so many writers did, by entering the church.

Another young man who was deeply interested in the new fashion of writing satires was Ben Jonson, the actor who had been imprisoned for his share in writing *The Isle of Dogs.* Jonson was a boy in his teens in the great days of Spenser and Marlowe, and when he began writing, there were very few links remaining with that romantic past. Nor was Jonson in the least interested in the past, although he had been hired by Henslowe in 1597 to write conventional, old-fashioned plays and was even paid ten pounds for some "new additions" to that popular old melodrama of Kyd's, *The Spanish Tragedy.*

When Ben Jonson published a complete edition of his plays, he ignored all the work he had done for Henslowe. The first play he was willing to call his own was a satirical comedy which he wrote in the new style and which was produced by the Chamberlain's company in 1598. Jonson called the play *Every Man in His Humour,* and the changed literary atmosphere in London assured its instant success.

Jonson wrote his play as a strict Roman comedy and in the classical manner. He kept rigidly to the three unities but even more he kept to the spirit of the old classical comedy. Its purpose had always been to chastise vice, which fitted in well with the current Elizabethan craze for satire, and it never attempted to show real people but only simplified character types. This fitted in well with Jonson's natural tendency toward abstraction and simplification, for he was interested in people only for their oddities and did not have Shakespeare's gift for seeing them in the round.

Jonson's attitude toward the classics was almost one of worship, and no man in England had a greater respect for learning. He had been brought up to be a bricklayer

and was still officially listed as "citizen and bricklayer of London." But he had gone for a time to Westminster School, before his stepfather took him away to lay bricks, and there he had come under the influence of the great William Camden. That gentle, wise, and learned man had a profound influence on Ben Jonson and kindled a love of learning in him that nothing ever succeeded in quenching.

The Chamberlain's production of *Every Man in His Humour* brought Jonson into close contact with William Shakespeare, who was one of the actors in the play. Shakespeare's name heads the list of "principal comedians" in the play, with Burbage, Phillips, Heminges, and the rest of the company following. Thus began the long, although frequently interrupted, association between Ben Jonson and the company, and the long and frequently exasperated association between Ben Jonson and William Shakespeare.

Shakespeare was one of the very few writers with whom Ben Jonson never had a public quarrel. But they must have had several private arguments on the subject of how to write plays, for Ben Jonson still had the subject on his mind years after Shakespeare's death. He kept returning to it the way a man will when he feels he has not had the last word.

In his younger days Shakespeare himself had written a classical comedy in *The Comedy of Errors,* in which all the characterizations were simplified and the unities strictly obeyed. He had found that way of writing too formal and constricted for him, and since he was not comfortable in the tidy atmosphere of Plautine comedy, he saw no reason to continue with it and started instead down the road that led to Falstaff. He and Jonson had a completely different approach to the art of writing, and since Shakespeare saw no reason why everyone should be alike, he probably had no wish to discuss the matter. But Ben Jonson was a walking bundle of theories, and he was never content to let differences be.

Jonson was convinced that the correct way to write poetry was first to lay the idea out in prose. This was the way writing was taught in the schools, and the way William Camden had taught it to him. Shakespeare had apparently never heard of this rule, judging by the way his pen raced across the paper with what seemed to Jonson disgraceful ease. Jonson remarked acidly that Shakespeare "flowed with that facility that sometimes it was necessary he should be stopped," and he never quite forgave Shakespeare's fellow actors for boasting that his plays reached them without a blot or erasure in the lines. "Would he had blotted a thousand."

Jonson put a great deal of careful research into his plays, and it disturbed him deeply that his fellow playwright had so little respect for facts. Three years after Shakespeare's death Jonson had still not forgotten that he had put a seacoast in Bohemia, when "there is no sea near by some hundred miles." Shakespeare had found the seacoast in a piece of popular fiction by Robert Greene with which he was working at the moment, and it had not occurred to him to investigate the matter. What he was watching was the story. But Jonson would have gone at once to the nearest map or the nearest geographical expert and thrashed the matter out thoroughly before he added another line to his play. Moreover Shakespeare paid no attention to the unities, mixed comedy and tragedy disgracefully in the same play, and in general seemed incapable of realizing that literary rules had been made to be obeyed.

Yet in spite of all their differences Jonson loved Shakespeare and called him "my beloved." He was not a man who gave his affections lightly, but he said of Shakespeare, "I loved the man, and do honor his memory, on this side idolatry, as much as any." The highest praise Jonson could give a man was to call him honest, for the phrase had high connotations in the Renaissance and Jonson carefully saved every letter in which the word was applied to him. It was a word which in turn he applied to Shakespeare: "He was, indeed, honest, and of an open and free nature." Several men had said so, but the praise has a special force coming from a man as tempestuous as Ben Jonson.

While Jonson labored over his correctly classical lines, he was livng a life of violent extremes. He had already seen the inside of a prison the previous year for helping Nashe write *The Isle of Dogs,* and within a month of the production of *Every Man in His Humour* he was back in prison again for killing a fellow actor of Pembroke's company. He was in and out of prison during the reigns of both Elizabeth and James. He upset the authorities by turning Catholic during a prison sentence and then after twelve years turned back again with such enthusiasm that he drank all the wine in the communion cup. He had feuds with men as inoffensive as Samuel Daniel, beat John Marston and took away his pistol, frightened Michael Drayton, and insulted the great Inigo Jones for a time with such vigor that he almost made a trade of it. He was a very heavy drinker, "a great lover and praiser of himself," and a man both well loved and well hated. "Passionately kind and angry; careless either to gain or keep; vindictive, but if he be well answered, at himself."

His friend, William Shakespeare, was almost Jonson's complete opposite. As far as all the available evidence goes, he was never in prison, never fought a duel with anyone, never bore a grudge, was very careful with his money, and lived and worked for twenty harmonious years with the same group of men. Yet while Jonson labored for the classic ideal of decorum in his plays, Shakespeare went to such violent extremes in his writing that

Jonson said that some of it was "ridiculous" and "could not escape laughter." Jonson would probably have agreed that real life was occasionally ridiculous, but he saw no reason to tolerate real life on the stage.

✖ *Chapter* **9**

When the Chamberlain's company produced Ben Jonson's successful new comedy in September of 1598, they acted it at the Curtain. The Theatre was not available, for the Burbage family was at the climax of a series of difficulties over its ownership.

Ever since he built the Theatre, James Burbage had had difficulty with the owner of the land on which the Theatre was built. Giles Allen did not want the building on his land indefinitely, and when Burbage applied for a ten-year extension of the lease that would have assured him ownership until 1607, Allen refused to give it to him. This meant that the lease on the land would expire on April 13, 1597, and that the Burbage family would automatically lose the building also.

James Burbage did not have the temperament to sit down and wait helplessly for the fatal date to arrive. He was already in his sixties, but he decided that he would build a new theatre and it would be even finer than the one he was about to lose. He bought a piece of property on the west side of town for six hundred pounds, with a down payment of a hundred and a mortgage for over two hundred more. The property consisted of the major part of an old building that had once been used by the monks of Blackfriars, and although it was within the city walls, it was outside the city's jurisdiction.

Burbage spent several hundred pounds converting part of the interior into a theatre, probably using the second floor which could be reached by a huge flight of steps from the yard. In the previous decade the owners of a boys' company had maintained a theatre in Blackfriars, but it had since been reconverted into gentlemen's residences. This was in any case a select, private theatre, so that James Burbage was the first man in England to make a roofed-in, lighted interior hall into a public theatre and was again a pioneer in theatre building.

He was perhaps too much of a pioneer. From his own point of view the liberty of Blackfriars was merely a locality where the city of London could not stop him from building a theatre, and he forgot that Blackfriars might have its own objections. The liberty was an exclusive residential district of about five acres, inhabited by "noblemen and gentlemen," with a special porter to shut the four gates of Blackfriars every night. Tennis

courts were permissible, bowling alleys could be tolerated, but a public theatre was clearly insupportable. Not only would "the noise of the drums and trumpets" disturb the ladies who worshiped at the fashionable little upstairs church of St. Anne's, but the people who attended the plays would probably be "vagrant and lewd persons" who would ruin the district

It is possible that if Burbage had planned his theatre anywhere in Blackfriars but on the higher slopes of the hill in the most exclusive section, he might have been left in peace. But as it was, the hammering and carpentering for the new theatre went on in the center of the most elegant part of Blackfriars, and George, Lord Hunsdon, was actually going to be obliged to use the same passageway.

By November 1596 the new theatre was nearly finished, and it was then the residents of Blackfriars went into action. They sent a petition to the Privy Council for the suppression of the theatre that was signed by thirty-one prominent residents beginning with Lord Hunsdon and that redoubtable dowager, Lady Russell, and including such estimable citizens as the printer, Richard Field. There was never the slightest doubt that such a petition would be granted, and the Privy Council promptly agreed that a public theatre would not be permitted in Blackfriars.

It may have been this that killed James Burbage, for he had put all his hopes into the new theatre. He died less than two months later and was buried in Shoreditch. He left the now-useless Blackfriars theatre to his younger son, Richard, by deed of gift, as he left his personal property to Cuthbert, and both the sons combined in an attempt to save the Theatre in Shoreditch.

The lease on the Theatre land expired in the spring of that year, and for a year and a half following, Cuthbert Burbage wrestled with Giles Allen to try and persuade him to sign a new lease. At about the time his brother Richard was acting in Ben Jonson's successful new comedy, Cuthbert got Giles to the point where he might sign if he were paid the enormous bonus of a hundred pounds. Cuthbert hopefully drew up the lease, neatly engrossed on parchment and with the wax all ready for the sealing, and when Allen came up from his country house in Essex to collect his quarter-day rents at Michaelmas, there was a final conference at the George Inn in Shoreditch. Allen had never intended to sign, for he had already planned to tear the Theatre down and use the land for his own purposes. He suddenly refused to accept Richard Burbage as security, there was a quarrel, and all negotiations were broken off. Cuthbert's year and a half of patient diplomacy had gone for nothing.

Cuthbert and Richard Burbage were their father's own sons and they did not accept defeat easily. They might have lost the lease to the land, but they still owned the building that was on the land. There was a clause in the original lease that granted James Burbage the right "at any time or times before the end of the said term of one and twenty years, to have, take down, and carry away to his own proper use" the building he had erected, and although it was true that the twenty-one years had expired, the two Burbage brothers saw no reason why this should stand in their way.

A more serious question was how an expensive operation like the tearing down and rebuilding of a theatre could be financed, and to solve it they turned to the five actors whom Cuthbert called "those deserving men"—William Shakespeare, John Heminges, Augustine Phillips, William Kempe, and Thomas Pope. A group of actors had never before been asked to help finance the building of a theatre, but the men of the Chamberlain's company were an unusual group of actors.

The arrangement that was finally worked out between the Burbages and Shakespeare and the others was that all seven of them should join together as a syndicate and finance the undertaking by purchasing shares. The two Burbages would hold a half-interest in the new building, and the five actors the other half-interest, making Shakespeare's share, for instance, one tenth of the total. So that the actors could pass on these shares to their descendants, they turned them over to two trustees who regranted them as shares held in common. One of these trustees was William Levison, a churchwarden of John Heminges' parish, and he must have been an excellent businessman since he handled the details for one of the largest and the best run of all the London lotteries. This regranting of the shares turned out to be a mistake, since a great deal of trouble arose as the actors died and left their shares to people who were not in the theatre. But as long as the actors held the shares themselves, there was no friction whatever. William Shakespeare and the rest assumed the various expenses of a theatre landlord, from the rental of the land and the maintenance of the building to the annual fee that had to be paid to Tilney for a theatre license, and in return no longer had to pay any rent for the theatre in which they acted. This was a completely new arrangement in the history of the London theatre and must have attracted a great deal of interested attention from other actors. It worked perfectly, but that was only because the members of the Chamberlain's company were already close friends and knew how to trust one another.

The next problem was where to find a piece of land to use for the theatre. It had to be near enough London so that audiences could get home before dark, but it could not be anywhere in the city's jurisdiction. Henslowe had built the Rose in the Liberty of the Clink, which was on the Southwark side of the

Thames and in the jurisdiction of the Bishop of Winchester; and near the Rose there was a piece of land that had a few shacks on it but was chiefly being used as a dumping ground. The ground was marshy and would have to be reinforced but all the land in that district was riddled with ditches and Henslowe had to maintain a series of bridges over them to give the public access to the Rose. One site in Southwark was no worse than another, and the location was an excellent one from the point of view of the theatre-going public.*

The owner of the property was a London lawyer named Sir Nicholas Brend who again lived in the same parish as John Heminges. Brend had come into the ownership of the land through the recent death of his father and he was willing to rent it on a thirty-one-year lease at an annual rental of fourteen pounds and ten shillings. There must have been a complete meeting of minds between Brend and the new syndicate, for the lease was not signed until the following February but the new owners of the land took possession on Christmas Day.

Three days after Christmas, a small but determined company assembled in Shoreditch on the land where the Theatre was standing. The chief figure was an experienced London carpenter named Peter Street, and he brought with

* There is a difference of opinion as to the exact site of the Globe. It was near Maid Lane, but whether north or south of it is uncertain.—Author's Note

him a crew of men armed with wrecking tools. Richard and Cuthbert Burbage were there, accompanied by their indomitable mother who "liked well" the whole idea; and along with the Burbages was a friend from Waltham Cross named William Smith who had lent them some money to help with their share of the financing.

Giles Allen was in Essex but he had left two agents to keep an eye on the Theatre for him. One of these agents, a silk weaver named Henry Johnson, later testified in court that Cuthbert Burbage and Peter Street assured him they were only taking the building down to replace it on the same site and pointed out "the decays about the same as it stood there, thereby coloring their deceit." Giles Allen's own version of the affair was that he had intended to pull down the Theatre, "to convert the wood thereof to some better use," but that the Burbages and Peter Street and William Smith had come with swords and daggers and axes and in spite of the protests of all the neighbors had, in a "very riotous, outrageous, and forcible manner," pulled the building down. Allen went to law immediately, even suing Peter Street for the grass his men had trampled, but in spite of his money and influence he lost the case.

Peter Street had his own wharf down by the Thames, and the lumber from the Theatre was taken there and freighted over the river to its new destination in the Lib-erty of the Clink. Wood was scarce and expensive in England, largely because coal had not yet come into general use in the rapidly expanding industrial plants, and logs or charcoal were still being used. Richard and Cuthbert Burbage had good reason to be grateful to their father for the heavy, valuable timber he had used in the original building. They had to buy new foundations and fittings and pay the wages of carpenters and plasterers, but all this cost only about four hundred pounds, which, of course, was much less than the price of a new building. James Burbage had evidently built better than Philip Henslowe, who put up the Rose in 1587 and had to pay more than a hundred pounds for repairs five years later.

Some of the syndicate's money had to go into heavy piles for the foundation, for a network of ditches ran into the Thames, rising and falling with the tide, and the new theatre was, in Ben Jonson's phrase, "flanked with a ditch and forced out of a marsh." The yard of the theatre must have been paved or it would have been unusable in wet weather.

There were no major changes in James Burbage's original design, and the new building was still arranged with tiers of seats around a jutting stage, with a thatched roof on top and the center open to the sky. But Peter Street was able to avail himself of all the latest improvements in theatre construction, and nothing was omitted that would help the comfort of the audience or the convenience of the actors. There was probably much more room for the storage of the Chamberlain's company's large stock of costumes than there had been in the old Theatre, and all the latest devices in backstage machinery were installed. There was a system of trap doors through which the three apparitions in *Macbeth* would eventually rise, and one trap door must have had a platform that could be held a foot or so below the stage so that Richard Burbage could leap into Ophelia's grave and impress the scene on a whole generation of theatregoers. Equally intricate machinery was installed at the top of the building, just below the roof, waiting for Jove to descend on his eagle in *Cymbeline;* and there the stage crew produced the thunder and lightning that Burbage defied as King Lear.

The syndicate called its fine new theatre the Globe, and the emblem they evidently used was that of Hercules carrying the world on his shoulders. At first the alley behind the theatre was still known as Brend's Rents, but it began to be called Globe Alley and within fifteen years that became its official name. William Shakespeare was paying only one tenth of the rent to Brend, but in the eyes of Brend's lawyers he seems to have been the major member of the syndicate; the year after the Globe was built, a survey of Brend's property described the Globe as a new building in the possession of "William Shakespeare and others."

Peter Street worked quickly with the rebuilding of the theatre, and the Globe was able to run up its playing flag and be ready for public performances by the summer of 1599. It was the handsomest theatre in London and gave the Chamberlain's men a decided advantage over their nearest rivals, the Admiral's company.

The Admiral's company was quick to adjust the balance, and before the year was out they had a new theatre of their own which was called the Fortune. It was financed by Philip Henslowe and Edward Alleyn, and the contract with Peter Street stipulated that in nearly all the construction details it was to resemble "the late erected playhouse on the Bank." Even the proportions of the stage were to be the same as at the Globe, except that the posts that supported it were to be square, with carved satyrs at the top. The one great difference between the two theatres was that Alleyn wanted the Fortune to be square instead of round, a new idea that was apparently not successful, since after the building was destroyed by fire, it was rebuilt circular. The new theatre was erected in the suburbs north of town, after some delicate adjustments had been made with the local authorities; and although it attracted part of the theatregoing public northward, instead of south to the Bankside, it left the Globe the undisputed title of the finest theatre in Southwark. It remained for a generation "the glory of the Bank," and all of Shakespeare's plays from that time forward were produced in it.

One of the first of these productions was evidently *Julius Caesar*, since, in September of the year the Globe opened, a German tourist named Thomas Platter crossed the Thames to the Bankside with a party of friends "and there in the house with the thatched roof witnessed an excellent performance of the tragedy of the first emperor Julius." Platter did not understand English, and he was chiefly impressed with the way the actors danced together after the performance. He got more real enjoyment out of another play he saw during his visit to London, which had a great deal of dumb show and tussling and a comic servant who threw shoes at his master's head. But Platter thoroughly approved of the seating arrangements in all the English theatres, which were built "so that everyone has a good view." He liked the system that charged a penny for standing room in the yard, with higher prices for "the most comfortable seats which are cushioned," just as he also liked the custom of selling food and drink during the performances, and he was full of admiration for the handsome costumes of the actors. He could at least enjoy the costuming of Shakespeare's new play, even if he could not understand a word that was being said.

Shakespeare was trying some-thing new in *Julius Caesar*. Most of the sources of his plots had been cheap fiction or old plays, but in *Julius Caesar* he wrote the first of a series based on the great classic, Plutarch's *Lives*. Plutarch was greatly respected in the Renaissance, and Robert Garnier had used him as the source of all the Senecan dramas that the Countess of Pembroke had tried to transplant into England. Shakespeare had no interest in this kind of restricted closet drama and he did not read Plutarch with respect but with delight. His attitude was very like that of Sir Thomas North, the English country gentleman who had captained three hundred men against the Armada and who had translated Plutarch's *Lives* into English. North knew no Greek and frankly admitted he was working from a French version, but he had no difficulty in recognizing Plutarch's heroes as friends and contemporaries. He explained to his readers that while most classics were "fitter for universities than cities," Plutarch's work was "fit for every place" and could "reach to all persons, serve for all times." Shakespeare himself was a city man, the product of no university, and he felt very drawn to Plutarch.

It is possible that Shakespeare wrote *Julius Caesar* more slowly and with more conscious care than most of his other plays; for he restricted himself to a vocabulary almost as limited as the one for *The Comedy of Errors* at a time when most of his plays were a riot of new words. He seems to have been deliberately making an experiment in classical control, but he did not let the experiment interfere with his knowledge of people, and the results failed to please that determined classicist, Ben Jonson. Jonson was so annoyed by *Julius Caesar* that he still had it on his mind years later. One of Shakespeare's characters had said, "Caesar, thou dost me wrong," and Caesar had replied, "Caesar did never wrong but with just cause." Which was "ridiculous," said Jonson hotly. Nor was he appeased by the fact that Shakespeare evidently removed the offending lines, since they do not appear in the printed version of the play.

Jonson believed in reason and logic in the treatment of character and, unlike Shakespeare, he did not realize that dictators are not subject to reason and logic. Twentieth-century history has confirmed Shakespeare's portrait of a dictator, but it belongs to a realm of the creative imagination that Jonson could never enter. Jonson's characters were filtered through his careful mind, as his poetry was filtered through his prose. Shakespeare's characters were filtered through nothing and seem to have been born of gigantic lightning flashes of intuition. Shakespeare could describe the country of minds he had never seen as though he had been born there. Jonson cautiously required a map and even then he did not stray from well-defined paths.

During this same year of 159 the Chamberlain's company produced the second of Jonson's comedies, this one called *Every Man Out of His Humour*. Jonson called it a "comical satire" and said tha "the happier spirits in this fair-fille Globe" would not be offended b it. But in spite of a good cas headed by Richard Burbage an John Heminges the play was no popular with the Globe audience although it did well in book form and Jonson rather snappishly sug gested it was too realistic. No doub the audience would have preferre a play showing "a duke to be i love with a countess, and that coun ess to be in love with the duke son, and the son to love the lady waiting maid; some such cross wooing, with a clown to thei serving-man, better than to be thu near and familiarly allied to th time."

The operatic and unreal plot that Jonson is describing were com mon enough on the London stage but Jonson may have been thinking specifically of his friend Shake speare. It was at about this tim that Shakespeare was writing hi string of romantic comedies *Twelfth Night, As You Like I* and *Much Ado About Nothing* Will Kempe and Richard Cowle played the two comic constables i *Much Ado About Nothing,* an Kempe left the Chamberlain's com pany soon after the Globe was buil so that 1599 must be the date of tha one comedy at least.

All three of Shakespeare's com

dies are full of dukes and comic servingmen and examples of cross-wooing, and neither Illyria nor the Forest of Arden was "near and familiarly allied" to the problems of the contemporary world. Shakespeare had chosen his three plots with the same easygoing lack of dignity that maddened Jonson whenever he thought about it. Two of the plots evidently came from anthologies of cheap Italian fiction, and the third one, *As You Like It*, came from a popular prose romance called *Rosalynde* that Tom Lodge had written when he went on a voyage to the Canaries in the eighties. Shakespeare had no objection to using all the plot devices he had already found serviceable—the girl dressed as a boy, the forest outlaws, and so on—and the relaxed, giant hand took up this shoddy material and raised it into the golden light of comedy and romance. The audiences at once recognized Rosalind and Beatrice and Viola as real and delightful people, and Malvolio was so popular that *Twelfth Night* was once called by his name instead. This intimate relationship between Shakespeare and his audience was incomprehensible to an orderly mind like Jonson's, and he once remarked gloomily that "the beast, the multitude . . . love nothing that is right and proper. The farther it runs from reason and possibility, with them the better it is."

A special production of *Twelfth Night* was put on by the Chamberlain's company for the young gentlemen of the Middle Temple on the second of February, 1602. The Middle Temple had a new hall that could be used by the actors for their production, a hall so "large and stately" with its beautiful carved roof that it took its proud owners years to pay off the debt that was incurred in building it. One of the young lawyers who saw *Twelfth Night* was especially amused by Malvolio and noted in his diary all the details of that section of the plot. His name was John Manningham and being a well-educated young man he also jotted down the play's sources. In his estimation, *Twelfth Night* was "much like the Comedy of Errors, or *Menechmi* in Plautus, but most like and near to that in Italian called *Inganni.*" *Twelfth Night* does not have the remotest resemblance to a Plautine comedy, and its chief relationship with *Gl' Ingannati* is that a disguised girl is sent by her lover to further his suit with another woman, a situation that was a commonplace in popular comedy and which Shakespeare himself had already used in *Two Gentlemen of Verona*.

John Manningham's diary was really a collection of odds and ends of information he had picked up in the Middle Temple and around London, interspersed with anecdotes and with the texts of sermons he happened to admire. Later on in Manningham's diary, somewhere between notes on a new surgical instrument called a catheter and on Dr. Turner's new compound, laudanum, he jotted down an anecdote about two of the actors in the Chamberlain's company. In the days when Richard Burbage was such a success as Richard III, a citizen's wife had arranged a meeting with him before she left the playhouse. Shakespeare overheard this and went to her house instead, and when Burbage arrived and said that Richard III was at the door, Shakespeare sent down word that William the Conqueror came before Richard III. To this anecdote Manningham kindly added the note, "Shakespeare's name William," in case anyone missed the point.

When Manningham recorded an anecdote of this kind, it was his custom to jot down the name of the man who had given it to him, such as Mr. Curle or Mr. Chute. In this case the name is unfortunately not legible, making the anecdote of even less value since the source is unknown. It is not unlikely that Shakespeare had been nicknamed "William the Conqueror," considering his unbroken string of triumphs in the theatre, and it is certainly true that many women went to the theatre, both in England and on the Continent, and fell in love with the actors. But this does not mean that two close friends like Richard Burbage and William Shakespeare spent their evenings cavorting in rivalry with stray members of the audience. The anecdote is an echo of the contemporary theory that all actors were a race of painted butterflies, given to mis-

behavior because they really had little else to do with their time. In the eyes of many otherwise intelligent Elizabethans, actors led "an idle loitering life" and anyone could easily imagine all the wicked things they undoubtedly did in their spare time.

Another of Shakespeare's plays that can be dated as belonging to the early history of the Globe theatre is his chronicle play of *Henry V*. The Chorus at the beginning of the last act hopes that the Earl of Essex will soon be returning from Ireland with the rebellion crushed and asks the audience to imagine an even greater welcoming crowd waiting for Henry. Essex left for Ireland the 27th of March, 1599, and returned the 28th of the following September, so that *Henry V* was evidently produced in the summer of 1599, shortly before Thomas Platter crossed the Thames to see *Julius Caesar*.

Henry V was one of the great popular heroes of English history and the London audiences had frequently seen him acted on the stage. Knell had played the part in the eighties with the Queen's Men, and the Admiral's company had also produced him on the stage, complete with a satin doublet laid with gold lace. Shakespeare had a well-worn subject but one that could not fail to appeal to his audiences and he made his King Henry everything that an English monarch should be. He had completely reformed since the days when he was Falstaff's companion and had instead become the noblest of England's warriors.

Shakespeare for once seems a little conscious of the limitations of his stage in *Henry V*. It must have been hard on any writer of history plays to see a mighty battle blazing along the horizon of his imagination and to know that when it was transplanted into the theatre it was going to be a matter of a few drums and trumpets, some property swords, and a group of actors on foot chasing each other in one door and out another. Perhaps it was the building of the new theatre that had set Shakespeare to brooding a little on the limitations of his stage.

> May we cram
> Within this wooden O the very casques
> That did affright the air at Agincourt?

Yet Shakespeare knew that he was dealing with one factor in the Globe that had no limitation, the imagination of the audience, and it was this factor to which he appealed steadily through the actor who played the Chorus. "Piece out our imperfections with your thoughts." Shakespeare knew he could trust the imagination of his audience, and it was because he took it into full partnership that he got such remarkable results.

In *Henry V*, Shakespeare supplied the last link in his series of history plays that covered more than a hundred years in English history from the last of the Plantagenets to the first of the Tudors.

The series was not written in chronological order, and since he started writing it when he was a comparatively young man, the quality is very uneven. But each is carefully linked to the play that precedes it and the play that follows it, and all of them have the same approach to English history.

This approach was the one that had been laid down by the Tudor historians and encouraged by the Tudor monarchs, to wit, that nothing contributes to a kingdom's welfare like a strong and duly accredited monarch. The last of the Plantagenets, Richard II, was a duly accredited monarch but he was not a strong one. Henry IV, who usurped his throne, was a strong monarch but he was not an accredited one. His son, Henry V, was everything that was admirable in a king, but his premature death brought his weak son to the throne and *Henry VI* records the chaos that a weak ruler can bring. The crown is finally seized by Richard III, who was strong but not duly accredited, and the kingdom is a welter of blood until the houses of York and Lancaster are united in marriage and the new house of Tudor is born.

Shakespeare wrote the second half of the series first, but the political philosophy was not one that required any special planning. He was following the chroniclers like Hall and Holinshed, and the chroniclers were following the general temper of the times. Shakespeare was not a man to embark on detailed independent research when he was writing a play, and he could not have foreseen that his way of writing was so persuasive that future generations of Englishmen would take their views of history chiefly from him.

Shakespeare had brought Sir John Falstaff into both parts of *Henry IV* and had evidently intended to go on using him in *Henry V*. "Our humble author will continue the story, with Sir John in it," promised the actor who spoke the final lines of *Henry IV*, but Falstaff nevertheless did not appear in the new play. He dies off stage and there is only that wonderful prose piece, with its unsurpassed mixture of comedy and tragedy, describing his death.

It has been suggested that Shakespeare was unable to keep his promise because the actor who played Falstaff, presumably Will Kempe, had left the company. But there is no proof that Kempe played Falstaff, no proof he had left the company when *Henry V* was written, and certainly no proof that so competent a repertory company had only one actor who could do a certain kind of part. A more probable explanation is that Shakespeare found it would be difficult to keep the attention of the audience on his noble and warlike king as long as Sir John was on the stage to pull the eyes and the hearts of the audience in the wrong direction. That fat and altogether reasonable coward stood for everything that was disgraceful (however delightful)

and could have succeeded in making ridiculous even the glories of Agincourt. There are plenty of comic characters in the play but none of them fails to take the war with France seriously. This would have been quite beyond the powers of Falstaff, the darling of the London audiences, and so he died at the turning of the tide and went to Arthur's bosom.

However, Shakespeare did not find it as easy as that to dispose of the irresponsible old gentleman, and he evidently yielded to public demand in giving him a play of his own. This was *The Merry Wives of Windsor,* which makes no attempt to be historical and is the only middle-class domestic comedy that Shakespeare ever wrote.*

The setting of the play is not the castle of Windsor but the town of Windsor, and the chief characters are not aristocrats but townspeople. Shakespeare knew the sprawling little town well and he used it with unusual thoroughness as the background of his play. He used the Garter Inn, which stood on High

---

* John Dennis stated at the beginning of the eighteenth century that Queen Elizabeth had ordered the play to be written, but he seems to have had no authority for the story and was trying to arouse interest in his own version, which he called *The Amours of Falstaff*. Shakespeare's play needed whatever aristocratic connections it could get, since by that time it was not considered a very gentlemanly piece of work. "The plot is good, but the characters and persons of the play so mean, the wit and conversation so plain, that 'tis scarce worth reading."—AUTHOR'S NOTE

Street near Peascod Street, as Falstaff's headquarters. He used Herne's Oak, which stood on the right of the footpath from Windsor to Datchet, for Falstaff's rendezvous. And he used the creek in Datchet Mead near the ferry, where the laundresses in town took their clothes, as the place where Falstaff was dumped into the Thames along with a bundle of dirty linen. The town sets the atmosphere of the play, since at every point it is the court characters that are duped and the town characters that are successful. Queen Elizabeth unquestionably enjoyed the play when she saw it, since she had something of a middle-class background herself and shared the play's brisk contempt for the average husband. The heroines of the play are two lively and intelligent townswomen of Windsor who have a tolerant liking for their husbands but are extremely fond of each other, and the average London housewife must have given the Chamberlain's company an extra handclap when the play was over.

During this period a great many of Shakespeare's plays got into print and were available for sale in the various book stores. Occasionally they appeared in corrupt, pirated copies, like *Henry V* and *The Merry Wives of Windsor,* but in general they were good texts that must have been authorized by the company. Thirteen of Shakespeare's plays were in print by 1601, and most of the quartos were no longer anonymous but had his name as part of the advertising matter on the title page. When *Much Ado About Nothing* was registered for publication in August of 1600, it was listed as "Written by Master Shakespeare," which is the earliest appearance of his name in the Stationers' Register; and when Shakespeare's company stopped authorizing the publication of his plays, later on in the decade, the publishers began issuing plays by other writers and announcing that they were written by Shakespeare. This happened with company productions like *The London Prodigal* and *A Yorkshire Tragedy,* which the London booksellers felt should have been written by Shakespeare though they obviously were not.

Even a respectable publisher like William Jaggard was not above using Shakespeare's name to promote sales. The year the Globe was built, Jaggard got hold of a collection of verses copied out in manuscript which included five sonnets of Shakespeare's in its twenty love poems. By a judicious use of wide margins and ornamental borders and many blank pages, Jaggard managed to produce a thirty-two page booklet and called it *"The Passionate Pilgrim,* by W. Shakespeare."

The makers of anthologies also found that Shakespeare's name helped their sales. There were a great many of these anthologies around the turn of the century, and William Shakespeare was one of the writers they leaned on heavily. One of the best of the anthology editors was John Bodenham, who issued *Belvedere* and *England's Helicon* in 1600 and included Shakespeare's work in both. *Belvedere, or the Garden of the Muses* was really a dictionary of poetical phrases, helpfully divided into subheadings, "Of Virtue," "Of Patience," "Of Tyrants," and so on, and the reader could find poetical thoughts for all occasions from Shakespeare and other writers. A similar anthology that came out the same year was called *England's Parnassus* and advertised itself as containing "the choicest flowers of our modern poets," including nearly a hundred quotations from Shakespeare. Most of these quotations from Shakespeare's two narrative poems, which were still felt to have more literary value than his plays. Moreover, they were more usefully occupied with noble thoughts, and it was noble thoughts that any Renaissance anthologist was after. For generations no one in England had questioned the doctrine that the chief end of literature was to improve conduct, and the tendency to divide up poetry into "thoughts" was characteristic of a period that read Geoffrey Chaucer chiefly as a purveyor of moral maxims.

It was a literary fashion of the period, when praising Shakespeare's work, to emphasize its "sweetness." A literary judgment, once formed, travels for a long time on its own momentum, and in the same way that Chaucer's contemporaries went on praising him as the writer of pretty love songs long after he had become a vigorous realist, Shakespeare's contemporaries united to eulogize the writer that William Covell called "sweet Shakespeare." Richard Carew compared him to Catullus, and Francis Meres was echoing the general opinion of the period when he praised him as "mellifluous and honey-tongued Shakespeare." In the same year Richard Barnfield spoke of Shakespeare's "honey-flowing vein," and in the following year of 1599 John Weever wrote an epigram on "honey-tongued Shakespeare." Weever made the usual mention of *Venus and Adonis* and *The Rape of Lucrece,* but distinguished himself by being aware of the fact that Shakespeare had also created someone named Richard and someone named Romeo. He added frankly that there were "more whose names I know not," but he was quite sure they must all be "saints" with "sugared tongues" since Shakespeare begat them.

The somewhat idiotic way in which Shakespeare's admirers were praising him for one of the least of his talents tended to make the youthful intellectuals of the period look down on his work as rather old-fashioned. Some clever youngsters at Cambridge wrote a series of three plays, around the turn of the century, for university production, and the undergraduate who wrote part one of *The Return from Parnassus* included a direct attack on "sweet Mr. Shakespeare." The butt of the play is a "known fool" named Gullio who insists upon quoting *Venus and Adonis* and announces to all and sundry the virtues of his favorite poet. "Let this duncified world esteem of Spenser and Chaucer. I'll worship sweet Mr. Shakespeare." It seems hardly necessary to say that Gullio was an Oxford man, which alone would be sufficient to explain the unsoundness of his literary judgment to any young gentleman of Cambridge.

The second part of *The Return from Parnassus* was produced at Cambridge in 1601 and takes a somewhat more lenient view of Shakespeare as a poet. *Belvedere, or the Garden of the Muses* had just been published and the characters of the play have a thorough discussion of all the poets that had appeared in the popular new anthology. The chief objection to Shakespeare, incredible as it may seem, was that he always did the same kind of work.

His sweeter verse contains heart-
    throbbing line,
Could but a graver subject him content,
Without love's foolish lazy languishment.

The butt of the play is not any special writer but the Chamberlain's company as a whole. The plot concerns two Cambridge scholars who are trying to make a living after they leave school, and at one point in the play they try to hire out as actors in Shakespeare's company. Burbage and Kempe appear on stage, and Kempe is a complete illiterate who is opposed to "that writer Ovid and that writer Metamorphosis" and believes that "our fellow Shakespeare" can turn out a better play than any university-trained man. Burbage tests out one student's acting ability with a speech from *The Spanish Tragedy* and the other's with a play that evidently ranked as the equivalent of Kyd's old melodrama, Shakespeare's *Richard III*. After Shakespeare's two fellow actors leave the stage, the two Cambridge scholars decide to become fiddlers instead, since anything would be better than joining up with a company of "mimic apes."

There is an element of exaggeration here, as in most good comedy, but the Cambridge plays do mirror the contempt that most young university intellectuals felt for a popular professional writer like William Shakespeare. The plays written by the students of Oxford and Cambridge, or by their teachers, were in every way superior to the crass London product. They were quite untainted by commercialism, they appealed to educated gentlemen instead of London tinkers, and it was undeniable that they were beautifully staged. When Oxford entertained a Polish dignitary with a play, it experienced no difficulty in showing "Mercury and Iris descending and ascending" or producing an artificial snow that was "strange, marvellous, and abundant." And when Cambridge needed costumes to represent "sundry personages of greatest estate," they made a direct appeal to Lord

Burghley for the loan of some of the gorgeous robes that were housed in the Tower of London.

This superiority of the university gentlemen over the common London players was generally acknowledged, and in 1593 the Privy Council informed both universities that "common players" were not to be permitted any longer within their jurisdiction. The students of Oxford and Cambridge were the future hope of the nation and it was not fitting that their minds should become corrupted by watching these vulgar productions. There was already a university statute providing for the punishment of students who attended plays given by professionals, and throughout the last years of Elizabeth's reign the London companies were paid not to perform at the universities.

The unauthorized first edition of *Hamlet,* which was ready for publication in July 1602 and published in a very bad text the following year, announced on its title page that it had been many times acted "in the City of London, as also in the two Universities of Cambridge and Oxford." It must have been in the towns of Oxford and Cambridge, rather than in the university section, that *Hamlet* was acted, and the students who went to the innyards to see it must have gone very quietly.

Since the hero of Shakespeare's play was himself a university product, his views on the drama were those of any well-educated young intellectual of the period. Hamlet had nothing but scorn for the groundlings, and his idea of true theatre was to hear the sorrows of the characters described at secondhand in dignified and interminable blank verse. Nothing could be more distasteful to any well-educated Renaissance gentleman, from Sir Philip Sidney down, than to have an actor play Hecuba by running about the stage in indecorous agony, with a blanket about the queen's hips and Troy burning behind her. The proper thing to do was to describe her from afar, and the play from which Hamlet quotes so admiringly represents the best practices of university stagecraft, with Hecuba's agony filtered to the audience at secondhand through Senecan blank verse. It was the penny public, the groundlings, who demanded a full view on stage of Hecuba's agony and who encouraged the sprawling, violent dramas of which the universities so thoroughly disapproved. It is a sobering thought that Hamlet the playgoer would not have approved of *Hamlet* the play, with its mixture of comedy and tragedy, its failure to observe the unities, and all its other sins against decorum that any young gentleman from the universities would have noticed immediately.

The plot into which Shakespeare inserted his intellectual young student from the university of Wittenberg was a shabby old melodrama that had been in the repertoire of the Chamberlain's company for a long time and had evidently been written about the time when Shakespeare first came up to London. The ghost who went around wailing, "Hamlet, revenge," was a byword in the late eighties, and a play that Shakespeare's company produced the year the Globe was built managed to be very amusing at the expense of this kind of antiquated drama.

A filthy whining ghost
Lapt in some foul sheet, or a leather pilch,
Comes screaming in like a pig half sticked
And cries, *Vindicta*—Revenge, Revenge!

Shakespeare, as usual, knew what he was doing. It was not the first time he had used shoddy material as the springboard for a play, and in this case his actor's eye saw the special uses of the situation. The bloody, barbaric old plot gave him a dark backdrop for the unhappy young modernist who was his hero, and his hero's temperament in turn gave him a solution for the chief difficulty confronting any dramatist who worked in the field of revenge tragedy. Unless there was some reason why the revenge was delayed, the play would be over in the first act; and a revenge hero like Hamlet, caught in the general backwash of gloom and indecision that characterized the final years of Elizabeth's reign, was exactly the sort of man who was incapable of working himself up to a single course of action until he had succeeded in ruining the lives of everyone in the cast.

Hamlet was born in part of the young men who had been glooming about the universities and the Inns of Court in the *fin de siècle* atmosphere of the late nineties, passing remarks on the hollowness of life and the futility of heroic action; but he was also the product of a more specialized group that was interesting the doctors of the period. A competent London physician like Timothy Bright would have diagnosed Hamlet as a melancholic and put much of his "internal darkness" down to physical causes. Melancholics, as Dr. Bright explained, "be not so apt for action." They are "given to fearful and terrible dreams," are "exact and curious in pondering," are "sometimes furious and sometimes merry," and are "out of measure passionate." They have frequently studied too much, they mistrust their memories, and they dislike color in their clothes.

This sort of information was useful to Shakespeare as a kind of springboard, but it was no more than that. He was not like George Chapman, who was very learned in Elizabethan theories of psychology and loaded his heroes with them. Shakespeare did not work from theories but from people. He knew that Hamlet's dilemma, between the flesh and the spirit, was at the heart of every human being's private tragedy, and he made Hamlet so terrifyingly real, with his courtesy and his violence, his intelligence and his self-hatred, his inconsistencies and his terrors, that every generation since has been able to recognize in him its own image.

The actors of the Chamberlain's company must have realized, sometime during rehearsals, that they had been given the script of one of those astonishing plays that please everyone. If they did not, the reaction of the audience would have told them soon enough. Even at its lowest level, *Hamlet* is a magnificently constructed piece of melodrama, with enough blood and pageantry and swordplay to please the sleepiest ten-year-old; and at its highest it travels so far into the secret countries of the heart that even the wisest should be able to see a new landscape unfolding in front of him.

Echoes of the play's success in the contemporary theatres still exist. Anthony Scoloker introduced a book of his by remarking that any piece of writing should ideally be like Sidney's *Arcadia,* which was still the most admired work of the period. "Or, to come home to the vulgar's element, like friendly Shakespeare's tragedies. . . . Faith, it should please all, like Prince Hamlet." Gabriel Harvey, who had once argued literary theory with his friend Sidney and was still respected as a scholar, used a blank space in his copy of Chaucer to jot down in his neat handwriting a few comments on the current literary scene. He noted that "the younger sort take much delight in Shakespeare's *Venus and Adonis;* but his *Lucrece,* and his *Hamlet, Prince of Denmark,* have it in them to please the wiser sort." *Lucrece* was in its fourth edition and was generally conceded to be the best thing its author had ever written; to link it with a common play from the boards of the Globe theatre was an almost unheard-of concession for a literary man to make.

Shakespeare poured a kind of lavishness into *Hamlet* that is in direct contrast to the spareness of his *Julius Caesar. Hamlet* is the longest play he ever wrote and has by far the largest vocabulary of new words, and the cutting of the play for normal stage production must have posed a difficult problem.

Even at the risk of being obliged to omit something important, the actors who shortened the play probably did not cut Hamlet's remarks about the "aery of children" who were "most tyrannically clapped." The rivalry between the children's companies and the adult actors was very much in the public eye at the moment, and the theatregoers enjoyed any reference to it on the stage.

It was really the Burbage family that had accidentally started the boys' companies on their current cycle of prosperity. Richard Burbage still owned the empty theatre in Blackfriars his father had built, and Henry Evans offered to rent it from him in 1600. Evans had himself produced plays in the Blackfriars in the eighties, working with John Lyly under the patronage of the Earl of Oxford, and since the actors were boys and their plays were geared to attract the better class of patrons, the residents of Blackfriars had made no objection.

The upper rooms in which the boys acted had since been turned back into private residences but Burbage's theatre was still available; and in 1600 Henry Evans signed a lease with Richard Burbage to rent the theatre for forty pounds a year.

The boys' company that Evans originally managed had been a product of the Tudor custom of maintaining singing boys who occasionally put on Court plays under the guidance of their singing master. This particular company had been known as the Children of the Chapel Royal, and when Evans organized his new company in 1600, he was careful to keep the old name with all its courtly connotations. Nevertheless, the new company did not have Court patronage. It was a straight commercial proposition, run not by a single singing master but by a board of directors, and it hoped to make its money direct from the London public, as the adult companies did.

By charging more for their seats, the Chapel company was able to appeal to a more cultured and wealthy clientele than the public theatres. There was no standing room and none of the crude amphitheatre atmosphere of a large theatre like the Globe or the Fortune. There was a much greater emphasis on music, and a duke who was traveling in England reported that for an hour before the comedy began, there was a performance on "organs, lutes, pandores, mandolins, violins, and flutes." He said that he had never heard better singing "except perhaps the nuns of Milan," and he was also deeply impressed by the use of artificial light, "which produces a great effect."

At about the same time that Henry Evans revived the Children of the Chapel, Edward Pearce revived the singing school of St. Paul's Cathedral, which had also produced Lyly's plays in the eighties. Both companies evidently tried first to produce the old plays that had once been in their repertoires; but Lyly's gentle little Court pieces were hopelessly out of date and the boys' companies turned to more modern dramatists.

The new crop of playwrights like Marston and Jonson and Chapman soon found that the boys' companies gave an author much more liberty to write as he pleased than he could find under the sternly commercial eye of a man like Philip Henslowe. Henry Evans was even willing to encourage their current interest in satire and in sensationalism, and for the next seven years the Children of the Chapel at Blackfriars steered a delicate line between full houses on the one hand and entanglements with the censor on the other.

Ben Jonson quite frankly used the boys' companies to pay off old scores. Henry Evans produced his *Cynthia's Revels* late in 1600 or early in 1601, and Jonson dragged into the text a private quarrel he was having at the time with John Marston and Thomas Dekker. Marston, who loved a fight, apparently wrote a play for Paul's Boys in which he pilloried Jonson, and Jonson embarked on a new production which he called *Poetaster*. In this play he managed to insult a great many professions, but kept his chief violence for John Marston and for some of the actors of the Chamberlain's company. The Chamberlain's company then leaped into the fray by producing a play written by Thomas Dekker and called *Satiromastix, or The Untrussing of the Humourous Poet*. The "humorous poet" is of course Jonson, and Dekker's caricature of him is rather clever, if allowance is made for the usual bad manners of the period.

Within a year or two, the protagonists themselves had lost interest in what Dekker called the "merry murdering" and what was later called the "war of the theatres." Jonson offered his important new tragedy to the Globe, and Marston dedicated his own new play to Jonson as one of his dearest friends. He and Jonson collaborated with Chapman on a charming comedy for Henry Evans, and the temporary violence between the Children of the Chapel and the men of the Globe was forgotten.

Although Shakespeare mentioned this warfare in *Hamlet*, he did not take any sides. One character in the play said there had been "much to-do on both sides" and another that there had been "much throwing about of brains." Hamlet himself made the sensible suggestion that the boy actors ought not to encourage their playwrights to attack the men actors since they would some day be men actors themselves. This prophecy turned out to be correct. The boy actors who played the chief roles in Jonson's *Poetaster* were Nat Field, John Underwood, and Will Ostler, and within ten years all three of them had joined Shakespeare's company at the Globe.

During the first decade of the new century nearly every playwright of consequence wrote for the boys' companies and in general did his best work for them. The two exceptions were Thomas Heywood and William Shakespeare, both of whom were shareholders in men's companies and consequently remained faithful to their own organizations. But even if the case had been otherwise, it is doubtful if Shakespeare would have felt any interest in working for a private theatre. Unlike Jonson, he had no contempt for the average London playgoer and no wish to write plays that would appeal to a small, select audience that was relaxed and receptive after listening to an hour of good music. Shakespeare was used to a large, excitable, restless audience that had worked hard for its pennies and did not hesitate to show its feelings if it became bored. Shakespeare's audience was not bored by him, and it seems equally certain that Shakespeare was not bored by his audience.

✗ *Chapter* 10

During these years of working with the Chamberlain's company, Shakespeare had no settled place to live in London. Unlike most of the other members of the company he had no household of his own, and he moved from one part of London to another in what were apparently always hired lodgings.

When Shakespeare first joined the Chamberlain's company, he was living in St. Helen's parish on the east side of town. This might be called a theatrical neighborhood, since it extended along the length of Bishopsgate Street, the great thoroughfare that ran under various names from London Bridge to Shoreditch and had three inns that were used as theatres along its length inside the city walls. But St. Helen's was one of the most aristocratic parishes in London and was famous for its "many fair houses." The most famous was Crosby Place, which had once lodged the future Richard III and was currently the home of the Lord Mayor. The beautiful residence of Sir Thomas Gresham was also on Bishopsgate Street, and just after Shakespeare left the parish, the handsome mansion was turned into a school for London merchants.

Shakespeare worshiped on Sundays at the Church of St. Helen's, whose graceful Gothic spire could be seen from the river and whose tombs and monuments were second only to those in Westminster Abbey. Sir Thomas Gresham and Sir John Crosby both had marble tombs, but even more magnificent was the one of Sir John Pickering, who lay life-size under a canopy with his ruff and his trunk breeches and his noble Roman nose. Shakespeare could not avoid being familiar with the tombs of the titled dead, since he was a resident and taxpayer of the parish and was obliged to go to church on Sundays. A parish church like the one in Southwark had a system of passing out metal tokens to each member of the parish, which he had to deliver up to the communion table on Sunday or face severe consequences; for if any adult male taxpayer did not go to church regularly, his politics were immediately suspect.

All collection of taxes was handled through the unit of the parish, and Shakespeare went on the lists of St. Helen's for the subsidy that had been voted by Parliament in 1593. There were seventy-three taxable residents in his parish when the second assessment was made in 1596, and the value of Shakespeare's goods was rated at five pounds. This does not sound like much for a successful actor, but the most prosperous resident in St. Helen's was given an evaluation of only three hundred pounds, and in St. Leonard's parish both Richard and Cuthbert Burbage were rated as having fewer possessions than Shakespeare.

It was the policy of the government to keep the property evaluation low but the tax rate high, and when another subsidy was voted by Parliament in 1597, Shakespeare was taxed thirteen shillings and fourpence on his goods, a rate of about thirteen per cent. The two tax collectors in Shakespeare's ward were a skinner named Thomas Symons and a draper who bore the delightful name of Ferdinando Clutterbook. Their problem was not an easy one in a shifting population like London's, and about a fifth of the tax collections in St. Helen's could not be made. Shakespeare already owed five shillings on the last installment of the previous subsidy because he was among those who were either dead or "departed and gone out of the said ward," and the petty collectors of Bishopsgate ward naturally discovered they could not collect the new tax from him either.

Government offices always move slowly, but by 1599 it was decided that Shakespeare was within the tax jurisdiction of the Sheriff of Surrey and instructions were sent to the Sheriff to make the collection. Then it was finally discovered that Shakespeare's residence was in the Liberty of the Clink, which was not under the Sheriff but in the jurisdiction of the Bishop of Winchester. The Bishop of Winchester evidently included Shakespeare's back taxes in a lump sum that the Bishop accounted for in 1600, since nothing more was heard of the matter.

It is not known when Shakespeare moved across the Thames to the Liberty of the Clink, since he may not have gone there directly from St. Helen's parish, but he was evidently living there when the Globe opened. The Liberty of the Clink was a true theatrical district, and although it was not as aristocratic as St. Helen's parish, it was certainly much livelier.

The Liberty of the Clink was one of the three areas into which the ward of Southwark was divided; and although London persisted in treating Southwark as a kind of appendage across the Thames, Southwark thought of itself as an independent and extremely important borough and, in fact, did supply more soldiers than any city in the realm except London. The Liberty of the Clink had a rather unfortunate reputation in the early days of the century, since most of the disreputable establishments in London were in the Bishop of Winchester's jurisdiction; and the parish church had even been obliged to set aside a special burying ground which was courteously known as the Single Woman's Churchyard.

When Shakespeare moved to the Clink, the stews of Winchester no longer had any official sanction, but the area was still considered a doubtful one by many Londoners, if only because so many theatres had been built there by that time. The Bear Garden, the Rose, and the Globe all stood close to Maid Lane in the Liberty of the Clink, and the only really respectable building in the area was the Bishop of Winchester's handsome palace which formed the eastern boundary of the Liberty. The area was heavily built up, but mostly in a series of tenements called "rents," and the whole district was riddled with a series of large and small ditches that had to be crossed by bridges.

The water in the ditches was stirred by the tide and reminded the residents of the Clink that theirs was a watery district controlled by the Thames. More than a third of the householders in the district were watermen, who owned the hundreds of small boats that crossed and recrossed the Thames, and owed their whole living to the river.

The watermen supplied the main traffic link between London and Southwark, since London Bridge was too far down the river to be of much practical use and in any case it was quicker and cheaper to go by boat. It cost only a penny to ride from the London side of the river to the Clink or to Paris Garden, and there were many landing stairs on the Southwark side to accommodate the stream of customers. A visitor who came to London at the turn of the century said that the boats were "charmingly upholstered" and had "embroidered cushions laid across the seats, very comfortable to sit on or lean against." He added that "generally speaking the benches only seat two people next to one another," which must have seemed an extra advantage to young couples going over to Southwark to see the latest play.

The public might be well served, but the watermen felt that their life was a difficult one. About two thousand boats were engaged in a fiercely competitive business and much time was spent in jockeying for the best position at the landing stairs or trying to appeal to the better nature of potential customers. The watermen were licensed, as everyone had to be in Elizabethan England, and they resented the set fare which prevented their charging more than a penny to go straight across the river and more than sixpence for distant parts of town against the tide. They pointed out bitterly that the rate had been set by statute in the days of Queen Mary and that both rents and the price of food had more than doubled since. As a result, the watermen depended chiefly on tips to make a living and warred briskly with their customers on the subject. The Watermen's Company did its best to control the behavior of its members, but it was impossible to deny that there was a tendency in the ranks toward "abusive and unreverend speeches." Many of these watermen were old sailors who had once served under Drake or Frobisher, and a contemporary expert on mental diseases concluded it was the nature of mariners to be "tempestuous and stormy." If a customer tried to leave a penny tip with a waterman who had expected twopence, the waterman's language was vigorous even by Elizabethan standards; and Elizabethan standards of invective were very high.

The watermen and the theatre

people not only combined to give Southwark much of its color, but economically they were dependent on each other. A theatre like the Globe could not have operated at a profit unless the trip from the London side of the river was quick, easy, and inexpensive, and in turn the watermen found they made their chief living from the theatre customers. A handsome new building like the Globe multiplied the customers, and more and more sailors went into the business, "hoping that this golden stirring would have lasted ever." When Philip Henslowe decided to build the Fortune on the London side of the river, his decision must have seemed like black treachery to the Watermen's Company; and in the following decade there was a desperate petition to the government to force the actors to stay on the Southwark side of the Thames if it did not want all the watermen to starve.

The watermen themselves estimated that between three and four thousand people crossed the Thames every day to visit the Globe, the Rose, and the Swan, and they further estimated that nearly forty thousand people in Southwark were directly involved in the prosperity of the watermen. This may be an exaggeration but there is no doubt that the watermen formed a large part of Southwark's population. One list of baptisms in the parish church shows the names of four bakers, four glovers, one innkeeper, one actor, one schoolmaster, and seventy watermen.

The parish church of Southwark stood east of the Globe on the other side of the Bishop of Winchester's palace. The building had once been the old priory church of St. Mary Overy, and Chaucer's friend, the poet John Gower, was buried there with a coronet of roses around the head of his stone image. After the Reformation, St. Mary's amalgamated with another parish church to serve the whole of Southwark with a single building and the old church was renamed St. Savior's. The handsome building was still too large for the needs of a single parish, and churchwardens like Philip Henslowe found it was always needing money for repairs

The parish of St. Savior's might almost be called the actors' parish. Both Philip Henslowe and his son-in-law, Edward Alleyn, served as vestrymen in St. Savior's, and it was the following year that Henslowe became a churchwarden. Shakespeare's fellow actor, Augustine Phillips, lived at Horseshoe Court near the Globe and brought three of his children to be baptized at St. Savior's, and Thomas Pope had been on the token books of the parish since the days when he had been acting under the patronage of Lord Strange. A later member of Shakespeare's company named Lawrence Fletcher was buried in the parish church of St Savior's, and another actor to be buried in the church was Shakespeare's youngest brother, Edmund, about whom nothing else is known. Edmund died in Southwark in 1607 when he was twenty-seven years old and his burial is listed in the parochial accounts for that year: "December 31. Edmund Shakespeare, a player, buried in the church with a forenoon knell of the great bell." The bells of St. Savior's were famous, with their own special warden, and it cost twenty shillings to ring the great bell for Edmund Shakespeare where the lesser bell would only have cost twelvepence.

Apart from the beauty of the parish church and the dignity of Winchester House, Southwark was chiefly noted for its fine inns and for its many prisons. There were five prisons in Southwark, the Clink, the Counter, the Marshalsea, the King's Bench, and the White Lion, and since a great many Elizabethan Englishmen went to prison at one time or another in their lives, the prisons of Southwark were usually well filled. Shakespeare was living in Southwark in the winter of 1601 when the Marshalsea prison had its population increased suddenly by some of his friends and neighbors from Stratford. A group of the leading citizens of Stratford had been indicted for riot, which was a serious offense in the Elizabethan period. The group was headed by the High Bailiff himself and included such friends of Shakespeare as Richard Quiney and Henry Walker; and since all the men were well-to-do, they were immediately released on bail.

The men of Stratford had acted in defense of the town, for an attempt had been made to enclose some of the public pasture land so that it could be used for private grazing. All the leading citizens had at once seized shovels and mattocks, gone down to the riverbank, and personally uprooted the hedges that had been planted to fence the cattle in. They had also gone off with six loads of willows, said the aggrieved plaintiff in his complaint.

The plaintiff was Sir Edward Greville, Lord of the Manor of Stratford and a curious man even in that age of outstanding eccentrics. His father had been sent to the Marshalsea for trying to kill a man and was eventually executed for murdering one of his tenants for his money. Young Edward started on his own career by accidentally killing his brother at target practice, and his father assured him it was the best shot he had ever made. He bought the manor of Stratford after the death of the Earl of Warwick and was unable to convince himself that his position as Lord of the Manor was largely an honorary title. Stratford had its own charter and was self-governing, but Sir Edward Greville took his position so seriously that in the previous decade he had blocked the election of Richard Quiney as High Bailiff until Quiney finally asked one of Greville's influential relatives, Sir Fulke Greville, to intervene.

The war that was raging between Sir Edward and the citizens of Stratford in 1601 also involved the Stratford charter, since Sir Edward insisted that he controlled the appointment of the tollgatherer at the Stratford fair. Having been promptly released from the Marshalsea, Richard Quiney returned to London in Trinity Term to present the town's case at Westminster, and he brought with him a document that had been drawn up in consultation with four of the town's oldest inhabitants, all of whom remembered back to the days when the charter had originally been granted to Stratford.

One of these four men was John Shakespeare, who had lived in Stratford for half a century and could remember the days when young King Edward had given the town its charter just eight days before Queen Mary came to the throne. John Shakespeare had been living on Henley Street in 1553 and he was probably living there still, for he had not sold either of his two houses. Although he was now an old man in his seventies, he was still interested in his rights. Two years before he testified in regard to the charter, he had brought suit in the Court of Common Pleas against a Wiltshire man who had bought some wool from him over thirty years earlier and had failed to pay for it.

It is satisfactory to know that after his many years of political isolation from Stratford, John Shakespeare was able to do the town one final service. It was in the spring of 1601 that he helped the town steward and his old friend Adrian Quiney draw up the case against Sir Edward Greville, which was finally submitted to arbitration. A few months later he died, and he was buried in Stratford on the 8th of September, 1601.

It was now William Shakespeare who bore the title of "gentleman" after his name, who was the head of the house and the one responsible for the welfare and dignity of the Shakespeare family in Stratford. He inherited the two houses in Henley Street from his father, and rented the east house to a man from Welcombe named Lewis Hiccox, who shortly after converted it into an inn. The other house he rented to his younger sister Joan, who had married a hatmaker named William Hart and had already given birth to the first of her three sons. Shakespeare always thought of the house as belonging to Joan and he gave her life residence of it in his will, at an annual rent so small as to be only a token payment.

When John Shakespeare died, William Shakespeare had been the owner of New Place for four years, but his father's bitter experience over losing his wife's land had evidently made William Shakespeare doubly careful when it came to any real-estate transactions. New Place had been bought under somewhat peculiar circumstances, for William Underhill died shortly after he sold the house to Shakespeare and it was later discovered that his elder son had poisoned him. The son was hanged and his estates were forfeit to the crown, from which the younger son, Hercules Underhill, recovered them by paying a fee when he came of age. Hercules came of age on the 6th of June, 1602, and Shakespeare at once set out to get confirmation of his purchase of New Place. Hercules was too unwell to come up to London, and a special commission was sent to him in Northamptonshire to get his ratification. The confirmation of Shakespeare's title to New Place must have cost a great deal of money and may not have been legally necessary, but William Shakespeare, gentleman, was not a man to take any chances when it came to the ownership of land.

Shakespeare received the conveyance from Underhill during Michaelmas Term of 1602, and by that time he had made a new and even more extensive purchase of Stratford real estate. On the first of May he had bought a hundred and seven acres of land in the Stratford area and had become one of the largest property holders in the district.

The owners from whom Shakespeare bought this large acreage were a prominent local family named Combe. At one time or another Shakespeare had dealings with several members of the family, but the two men who were involved in this particular transaction were a distinguished Warwick lawyer named William Combe and his nephew John, who was a wealthy bachelor and lived near Stratford in the village of Welcombe. William Combe had invested in the property only nine years earlier, and it was typical of the purchases that had made the Combe family such

prosperous and influential members of the local gentry.

It was this group of landed gentlemen that was entered by William Shakespeare, grandson of a tenant farmer. The land he bought was the kind that his grandfather Richard had been farming when John left to make his fortune in Stratford, and that was still being farmed by his Uncle Henry until he had died six years earlier. The farm land that surrounded Stratford was laid out on the old medieval system in a series of long, narrow strips that were worked side by side by various tenant farmers, and the one real difference from the medieval period was that the rent was now paid to various private owners instead of to the lord of the manor. The system of dividing the land into strips was a wasteful one, since it made it almost impossible to improve the condition of the soil. The same difficulty applied to the communal pasturing of cattle, which made it impossible to improve the breed. But the medieval system had the sanction of all antiquity, and any effort to make a change in it met with almost hysterical local opposition.

Shakespeare's purchase from the Combes consisted of over three hundred of these farming strips, and he bought them in a single cash payment of three hundred and twenty pounds. Since Shakespeare was not in Stratford, his brother Gilbert handled the transaction for him, and the document was signed and delivered to Gilbert in the presence of witnesses. The document itself was vitally important, since in this case Shakespeare had no other proof of legal ownership. Since the deed was not recorded in the manor court, clear title was guaranteed in the deed itself in an impressive tangle of legal verbiage; but Shakespeare took the further precaution, when he bought twenty more acres from the Combes nine years later, of having his title to the original acreage confirmed.

Shakespeare made one more real-estate purchase in Stratford in this same year of 1602, but it was a comparatively small one. At the end of September he bought a cottage and about a quarter of an acre of land in Chapel Lane, just across the street from New Place. The purchase itself was simple enough but it was conducted in an atmosphere of pure medievalism, for the owner of the property, Walter Getley, held it on a copyhold tenure from the Manor of Rowington, which was in the possession of the widow of the Earl of Warwick. Walter Getley was obliged to appear at the court "of the noble Lady Anne, Countess of Warwick" and restore the cottage to her, and when William Shakespeare appeared in due time and swore fealty to her, he would receive the cottage from her hand. Getley appeared through his attorney, but Shakespeare evidently had to go through the formality of appearing in person, and he also assumed the obligation of paying the manor a token rent of a little over

two shillings a year as long as he owned the property. These relics of medievalism were familiar enough to the men of the Renaissance, and the laws that governed property rights were born of such an overlapping of ancestries that the situation was a source of great profit to the legal profession.

Shakespeare's position in the community was probably a great satisfaction to his family in Stratford, but it was not an unusual one for an Elizabethan actor to achieve. Most of the leading members of Shakespeare's company, Heminges and Burbage and Phillips and Pope, were granted coats of arms and were classified as gentlemen, although both Phillips and Pope claimed the designs of ancient houses to which they were not really entitled. All the actors in Shakespeare's company were well-to-do, and most of them made the usual Elizabethan investment and bought property. Thomas Pope owned three houses in Southwark when he died, and Richard Burbage left real estate worth over three hundred pounds. Augustine Phillips bought a country estate at Mortlake in Surrey, and Henry Condell, who already owned two houses in London, eventually retired to a home in the Cotswold Hills that was only fifteen miles from Stratford.

There were several contemporary attacks on the actors who grew wealthy "by penny-sparing and long practice of playing," and especially on the ones who "purchase land

and now esquires are made." An especially violent attack was made in 1603 by Henry Crosse, who blamed the situation on the "witless and brainsick multitude" who went to plays and thereby enriched the actors. "These copper-lace gentlemen grow rich, purchase lands by adulterous plays," and by lording it over better men than themselves, threaten the very life of the commonwealth. Crosse describes the plays of the period with the reluctant devotion of a man who must have once been a playgoer himself. "They do not only feed the air with sweet words, equally balanced, the eye with variable delight, but also with great alacrity doth swiftly run over in two hours' space the doings of many years, galloping from one country to another, whereby the mind is drawn with expectation of the sequel, and carried from one thing to another . . . when as at a lecture and holy exercise all the senses are mortified and possessed with drowsiness, so that by this we may see our corrupt nature." Crosse said that "at a play the whole faculty of the mind is altogether bent on delight," which is a fair description of the way the members of the audience felt when they saw a play like *Hamlet*, and an explanation of why the actors of Shakespeare's company made money.

None of the members of the Chamberlain's company grew as rich as Edward Alleyn of the Admiral's company. Alleyn became almost the Elizabethan equivalent of a millionaire, leaving two thousand pounds in his will after he had spent five times that amount in building Dulwich College and endowing a series of almshouses. Alleyn also acquired a coat of arms, the heralds having finally decided that he had some vague connection with the Townleys of Lancashire; and the childless man was so anxious to immortalize his name that he decreed the master and warden of Dulwich College must always be someone who bore the same name as himself. But Alleyn did not make all his money in the acting profession, since he had successful real-estate investments and a series of miscellaneous activities that ranged from starchmaking to bearbaiting; and the other actors in the Admiral's company did not become as wealthy as he or even as well-to-do as the men in the Chamberlain's company.

No group of actors in London was quite as steadily respectable as the men who made up Shakespeare's company. Homeowners, taxpayers, and hard-working professional men, they were exactly the sort of people that the mayor of London would have approved of thoroughly if he could have brought himself to approve of actors at all. Although such a record was almost inconceivable in Elizabethan London, no members of the Chamberlain's company seem to have been sent to prison. The usual reason an actor went to prison was for debt or because the play he had been appearing in displeased the government, but the men of the Chamberlain's company did not get into debt and they were politically conservative.

Only once did the Chamberlain's company come close to disaster on a matter of politics. This was in February of 1601, a month after the group of prominent Stratford men had been imprisoned in the Marshalsea for riot; and it was fortunate that Shakespeare's company had a reputation for not meddling in politics or the Privy Council would have been obliged to take a very grave view of their offense.

The difficulty had its origins back in the days when Shakespeare had written *Richard II*. The political point of view was irreproachably correct as far as the series as a whole was concerned, but Shakespeare was faced with a special dilemma in the case of Richard II. Richard had been deposed by Henry of Lancaster, who fathered that glorious monarch, Henry V; but on the other hand Richard was an anointed king of an ancient line, and there was no greater sin in the Tudor lexicon than to attempt to depose an anointed king. Shakespeare tried to minimize the problem by laying special emphasis on Richard's unfitness to rule, but this did not agree with the Tudor theory that all rulers were divinely appointed by God. "All power is of God. And therefore, whether the man be good or bad, he must be obeyed." When *Richard II* was published in 1597, the scene in which King Richard is deposed was omitted, and although there were three printings of the play in Elizabeth's reign, it was not until five years after her death that the deposition scene was finally included in a printed text.

This omission of part of the text was probably not so much a piece of voluntary discretion on the part of the publisher as of outright censorship on the part of the Crown, for Elizabeth was developing a fixed idea about the last of the Plantagenets. "I am Richard II, know ye not that?" She was convinced that some of her noblemen might see in that unlucky ruler a historical precedent for trying to depose her, and the gentleman she had especially in mind in that connection was the Earl of Essex. When an inoffensive lawyer from Cambridge wrote an account of King Richard's fall he succumbed to a kind of mad innocence and dedicated the book to Essex. "No book ever sold better," remarked its publisher, who with something less than innocence had apparently suggested the dedication in the first place. Everyone involved in the book was summoned at once before the Privy Council for questioning, and the dedication to the Earl of Essex was removed in the next printing. This was in 1599, when Essex was still high in the Queen's favor and was just setting out for Ireland to crush the rebellion.

Elizabeth was an astute politician, and her estimate of Essex was politically correct. That spoiled and sulky young nobleman knew how much the people loved him, and he found it impossible to believe that there was any reasonable limit to his ambitions. Essex was an extremely handsome young man who was convinced that he knew how to handle a doting and fading old woman, and it seems never to have occurred to him that Elizabeth had ten times his brains and twenty times his resolution. Having mismanaged everything he touched, Essex was, by 1601, in one of his periodic states of disgrace, and he conceived the unfortunate idea that in a general uprising he might destroy his enemies at Court and force the Queen to favor him.

Essex was extremely unlucky in his circle of advisers, of whom the adoring Earl of Southampton was probably as intelligent as any, and Sir Charles Percy suggested an idea that was characteristic in its impractical melodrama. It was evidently Sir Charles's theory that the population of London was a tinderbox that any spark could ignite, and he proposed that the spark should be applied by a production at the Globe of Shakespeare's *Richard II*. This evidently seemed quite reasonable to the rest of the group, and six members of the Essex group went to the Chamberlain's company and told the actors what they wanted. The Chamberlain's company tried hard to find a reasonable excuse and said that the play was so much out-of-date they could not afford to produce it for the small audiences that might be expected. Sir Charles and his friends removed this excuse by offering the

actors an outright sum of forty shillings, and Shakespeare's company agreed to produce *Richard II* on Saturday, the 7th of February.

The Essex faction had a Saturday dinner at Gunter's and then were rowed across the Thames to the Globe where they arrived early and saw the play of the "killing of Richard the second." It was expected that by Sunday the population would be in a state of seething emotion; and just as the sermon at St. Paul's was finished, the Earl of Essex at the head of two hundred young men, whose swords were wrapped in their cloaks, rushed through the streets of London calling on the citizens to arm. Essex was heading for the house of Sheriff Smith, who had promised him support, and when Smith saw him coming, he withdrew by the back door. There was no man the Londoners loved more than the Earl of Essex, and yet, as Camden says, "in all the city, then well exercised in arms, full of people, and most devoted unto him, not so much as one man of the meanest sort took arms for him." Essex had overestimated the devotion of the Londoners if he thought they would side with him against the Queen. By ten o'clock that night everyone involved in the abortive rising had surrendered. Essex and all his party were imprisoned and a searching questioning began of anyone who had any connection with the affair.

The men of the Chamberlain's company were for once in their careers in a really serious position.

If the examiners had found evidence that any of them sided with Essex or that they had produced *Richard II* deliberately, it would have gone hard with them. Sir Fulke Greville destroyed the manuscript of an inoffensive closet drama he had written about Antony and Cleopatra, for fear that someone might interpret it as an account of Elizabeth and Essex, and even in the following reign Samuel Daniel got into trouble with the government because it was thought his play of *Philotas* might be a study of the fall of Essex instead of a general study of the fall of ambition.

Augustine Phillips, who had been chosen to represent the Chamberlain's company, was searchingly questioned by the two government examiners, and according to Phillips he "and his fellows were determined to have played some other play" and only yielded with reluctance because of the extra forty shillings. Popham and Fenner were skilled examiners, and if Phillips had not been telling the truth, they would have discovered it.

Fortunately, the men of the Chamberlain's company had a spotless political record and they were Elizabeth's favorite group of actors. The government was willing to concede their innocence, and Shakespeare's company played before Elizabeth a fortnight later as though nothing had happened. The play they presented at Whitehall on Shrove Tuesday closed their regular Christmas season at Court. This was the same day that Elizabeth signed the death warrant of the Earl of Essex, and he was beheaded the following morning.

Essex died as Mary, Queen of Scots, had died, in black and scarlet and with great gallantry. But Elizabeth had loved him as she never loved her cousin of the north, and she never quite recovered from the final choice she had to make between her emotions and political necessity. The execution of Essex was the final climax of a long series of political murders that she had been obliged to countenance, and it must have seemed to her sometimes that her throne was built on blood.

Elizabeth was now nearly seventy and she had never had any life of her own except her life as queen. She had built her country from an insular little Protestant community, bankrupt and frightened, into one of the great powers of Europe, and she had loved her country with a devotion that was almost fanatical in its intentness. She had never set foot outside England and it probably had never occurred to her to do so. England was her world, the one great reason for her existence, and she served her country with a singleness of purpose that very few nations are fortunate enough to command. In turn she expected the same service from her own ministers, and those underpaid, overworked officials could get what satisfaction they might out of the fact that she honored them with such a burden.

Of all her ministers, Lord Burghley had been the most loved and the most trusted, for he had worked with her from the beginning. "God bless you," the Queen wrote him, "and long may you last." He had struggled gamely against old age and gout and increasing deafness, and had at last quietly died in 1598 when he was nearly eighty years old. His son Robert became Secretary of State, but although he was clever enough, he had none of his father's tact and experience. He managed to antagonize the Queen's last Parliament, that of 1601, so thoroughly that Elizabeth herself was obliged to take a hand. The Queen had lost none of her old magic. She summoned the hundred and forty members of the House of Commons into her presence at Whitehall and made one of the most charming and politically astute speeches of her career. "Though God hath raised me high, yet this I count the glory of my crown, that I have reigned with your loves. . . . It is not my desire to live nor reign longer than my life and reign shall be for your good."

For nearly half a century Elizabeth had played the intricate game of politics, and her enemies on the Continent waited hopefully for her death. The newsletters of Europe announced periodically that she was suffering from cancer or some other fatal disease, and the Papal Secretary stated that any loyal Catholic who tried to kill her "not only does not sin, but gains merit." But what killed Elizabeth in the end was apparently pure weariness. She had outlasted her age, and the world she had known had vanished. The men who filled her Court were the sons and grandsons of the men she had once known, and in her heart she was a stranger to them.

Elizabeth had always been a good actress, and the last years of her reign were as lively as any. She rode horseback and went on long progresses, dragging the reluctant members of her Court behind her, and a duke who saw her in 1602 said that she still walked like an eighteen-year-old. But in December of that year she told one of her godsons that she felt "creeping time" at the gate, and when Shakespeare's company played before her at Richmond, two months later, they must have noticed a great change in the Queen. She had come to Richmond on the last day of January, in a torrent of wind and rain, and she never returned to London again.

By the 19th of March it was known that the Queen's illness was mortal, and all the theatres were closed. Elizabeth sat on cushions, staring ahead of her and not speaking. All her life she had scorned medicines, and none of the twelve hovering physicians could persuade her to take any. Finally she went to bed and lay with her face to the wall, speaking to no one. Her last gesture was to keep Archbishop Whitgift on his knees beside her in prayer when the old man hoped to rise. Then she went to sleep, and at three o'clock in the morning of March 24, 1603, the great Queen died without waking, "called out of the prison of her body into an everlasting country in heaven."

The greatest of England's rulers was dead, and the Age of Elizabeth was ended.

✷ *Chapter* **11**

The new ruler of England was James VI of Scotland, henceforth to be known as James I of England. Londoners found it a curious experience to be waiting to greet a king, since no one under fifty could remember a time when there had been a man on the throne of England. There had been fear of disorder or even of civil war when Elizabeth died, since she had refused to name her successor, and when the throne went peaceably to her nearest relative, the son of Mary, Queen of Scots, the relief of the Londoners was enormous. "Every man went about his business, as readily, as peaceably, as securely, as though there had been no change, nor any news ever heard of competitors, God be thanked!"

The Londoners did not know what to expect of James, for pictures of the new King and Queen were not published until after their arrival. When James had married Anne, thirteen years earlier, his journey to Denmark to get his bride had been reported to the London public in two ballads and a "thing in prose." Another ballad had come out to describe the christening of his eldest son, but the Londoners' chief acquaintance with James came through his own writings.

James was a determined author and he had already produced a great many poems, as well as a book of advice to poets, a study of the Apocalypse, a translation of some of the Psalms, a translation of *Lepanto,* a treatise on demonology and a book of advice to his son on how to be a king. Unlike Queen Elizabeth, who wrote poems but in a gentlemanly way never permitted them to get into print, King James saw to it that his work was published. Even after he came to the throne of England, he continued his writing career, just as he continued his love of books. When he was restless at night, he could go to sleep only if someone read to him, and his idea of a pleasant way to spend the morning with a young favorite was to teach the boy Latin.

On the 7th of May, 1603, the King was met on the road to London by all the city's dignitaries and by such a crush of uninvited spectators that everyone with a cart to rent made a small fortune. Any Londoner who achieved a view of his new ruler over the heads of his neighbors saw a youngish-looking man in his late thirties, with sandy hair and a thin, feminine skin. He had none of the beauty of his mother, or even the straight-backed grace of Queen Elizabeth, for his legs were so weak he could not walk without assistance, and part of his love of hunting may have come from the fact he needed no help when he was on horseback. His forehead was too big for his face, his tongue was too big for his mouth, and he spoke with a broad Scots accent that must have sounded strange to his new subjects of the south. He was not a kingly man, for he was emotional, prying, and lacking in dignity. But he gave England twenty-two years of unbroken prosperity, "lived in peace, died in peace, and left all his kingdoms in a peaceable condition."

From the point of view of Shakespeare and his fellow actors, the most important question about the new King was how he felt about the theatre. The pressure of the Puritan bloc was increasing steadily in London, and none of the acting companies would be able to remain in existence unless they had the support of James as they had once had the support of Elizabeth. James had been brought up under the shadow of the Scottish kirk, which strongly disapproved of plays, and in his book of advice to his son he had mentioned actors only once. "Delight not to keep ordinarily in your company comedians."

Fortunately for all Shakespeare's as yet unwritten plays, the new King thoroughly enjoyed the theatre, and his point of view toward actors was quite unaffected by the way he had been brought up. His favorite actor in Scotland had been an Englishman named Lawrence Fletcher, and four years earlier there had been a brisk battle on Fletcher's account between King James and the city of Edinburgh. The deacons and elders of the city had tried to prevent Fletcher from taking a house in town and giving plays, and the King had not only forced them to withdraw the ban but had made them announce the fact from their own pulpits. Fletcher had been one of the King's favorite actors since 1594, and when James became the new King of England, he set the actor at the head of the company that was henceforth to be known as the King's Men. The warrant for the patent of the new company was dated the 17th of May, ten days after the King's arrival in London, so that no time was lost.

The new company that was called the King's Men was merely the old Chamberlain's company with Lawrence Fletcher added to it. The second name after Fletcher's was William Shakespeare's, and the other actors listed in the patent were Richard Burbage, Augustine Phillips, John Heminges, Henry Condell, William Sly, Richard Cowley, and Robert Armin.

Robert Armin had taken Will Kempe's place with the company as their major comedian when Kempe turned in his theatre shares shortly after the Globe was built. Armin must have been an excellent comedian, since according to a story in *Tarleton's Jests*, Richard

Tarleton himself had singled him out as his successor. The story went that young Armin chalked up some verses on a wainscoting and Tarleton capped them with the doggerel:

My adopted son therefore be
And enjoy my clown's suit after me.

According to the story, Armin at once resolved to be Tarleton's successor. "Private practice brought him to present playing, and at this hour performs the same where, at the Globe on the Bankside, men may see him." Whether the story is true or not, it reflects the current opinion of Armin as a comedian and was also a good piece of advertising for the Globe.

Besides Kempe, two other members of the company had left it before the royal patent was issued. George Bryan had become a member of the Court, and he served as a groom at the elaborate funeral ceremonies for Queen Elizabeth. Thomas Pope had evidently retired by 1603, for he died the year following, leaving a special sum so that a monument could be erected to him in St. Savior's.

Two years after the patent was granted, Augustine Phillips also died, and the love he bore his fellow actors is shown by the fact that he included them all in his will. Heminges and Burbage and Sly were three of his executors, and he left a silver bowl to each of them. He left thirty shillings in gold to Shakespeare and Condell; and Cowley, Armin, and Fletcher got twenty-shilling gold pieces. Although Fletcher is included in Phillips' will as one of his "fellows," he does not seem to have been a very active member of the company. He does not appear on any of the lists of working actors, although these are admittedly scattered and incomplete, and his name is not included in the First Folio list of all the actors who appeared in Shakespeare's plays.

The royal patent made Shakespeare's company the most prominent group of actors in England, and they kept that position, unchallenged, for the rest of the reign. The patronage of the Lord Chamberlain had been valuable enough, since he headed the royal household and controlled the Office of the Revels; but it was even more valuable to be under the direct patronage of the King himself. King James saw an average of five times as many plays a year as Queen Elizabeth had done, and more than half of these were presented by Shakespeare's company

The whole royal family were ardent playgoers, and the second most important company in London was put under the patronage of James's wife and given a patent as Queen Anne's Men. This was a new company that had made an elaborate start toward the end of the previous reign under the patronage of the Earl of Worcester, with Will Kempe as its chief actor, Thomas Heywood as its chief playwright, and Philip Henslowe to give it financial backing. The Admiral's company, which had once been the chief rival of the Chamberlain's, was now considered the third company in London and was put under the patronage of Prince Henry, the King's eldest son. In actual practice, the three companies performed interchangeably at Court, and Shakespeare's company did many plays before Queen Anne and Prince Henry just as the other two companies performed before James. Each company had its own set of plays, and the royal family wished to see them all.

Queen Anne in particular was an indefatigable playgoer. In Scotland she had found a certain amount of entertainment in dabbling in politics until her husband, who had a horror of women concerning themselves in men's affairs, put a stop to it. Anne was a thoroughly stupid woman whose chief assets were a pleasant manner and a good complexion, and in the twentieth century she could have spent her time quite happily in a round of motion pictures, bridge games, and beauty parlors. Living as she did in the early seventeenth century, she went to plays, and a letter is still extant that Sir Walter Cope wrote to Viscount Cranborne in 1604. "Burbage is come, and says there is no new play that the queen hath not seen, but they have revived an old one, called *Love's Labour's Lost,* which for wit and mirth he says will please her exceedingly." Shakespeare's early comedy had pleased Queen Elizabeth at a Whitehall showing, and there was no reason

why it should not please Queen Anne at a private production in the house of a nobleman. The house used was either the Viscount's own residence in the Strand or that of the Earl of Southampton, who had finally been pardoned for his part in the Essex conspiracy and was back in favor again.

The plans for the new King's coronation brought a rush of visitors up to London in the early summer of 1603. Scaffoldings were built for the triumphal procession, speeches were written, and new arrivals every day filled the inns and the theatres. "The streets were plumed with gallants, tobacconists filled up whole taverns, vintners hung out spick-and-span new ivy bushes," and so much money was being made that everyone tried to ignore the fact that the plague was again creeping into the overcrowded city. There had already been signs of trouble in Southwark when Elizabeth died in March, and as the hot weather came on, the plague increased with it until the city authorities could ignore it no longer. On the 13th of July the plague orders were sent out to all the parish churches, and when James was crowned on the 25th in a ceremony to which the general public was not admitted, over eleven hundred people a week were dying in the London area.

By the middle of the summer London was almost a ghost city. Anyone who was forced to stay in town took care to walk in the middle of the street, chewing orange peel or smoking tobacco; and the price of rosemary, which was considered a preventive, soared from twelvepence an armful to six shillings for a small bunch. Among the many who died was Ben Jonson's seven-year-old son, and among the many who were heroes was Dr. Thomas Lodge, onetime playwright and man about town, who was now a physician in London and working selflessly in the quarantined and desperate households of the city.

All the London theatres were of course closed, and the King's Men went on an extended tour that reached as far north as Coventry and as far west as Bath. By the end of November they were nearer home again, at Mortlake in Surrey, and word reached them that their royal patron wished his company to perform for him. King James was at the moment in Wiltshire, staying in the great square stone house that the Earl of Pembroke's grandfather had built near Salisbury; and it was here at Wilton House on the second of December that Shakespeare's company acted for James the first play he is known to have seen in England.

Wilton House already had its literary associations, for the uncle of the present earl was Sir Philip Sidney and it was here that he had written his greatly admired *Arcadia*. The Earl's mother was the Countess of Pembroke, that redoubtable woman who had tried to save the English theatre from "barbarism" in the nineties by transplanting the correct French dramas of Robert Garnier. Her son William, third Earl of Pembroke, was himself a famous patron of poets, and his intelligent gift to Ben Jonson, of twenty pounds a year to buy books, was characteristic of him.

The production at Wilton House may have marked the first association of the Earl of Pembroke with Shakespeare's company, but it was certainly not the last. He became a warm friend to them all, especially to Richard Burbage, and when he himself was appointed Lord Chamberlain, he was able to do a great deal for them in his official capacity. It was fitting, when Heminges and Condell brought out a complete edition of Shakespeare's plays in 1623, that the Earl of Pembroke and his brother the Earl of Montgomery were the "incomparable pair of brethren" to whom the book was dedicated.

James rewarded his company for the performance at Wilton with thirty pounds, which was a large sum even allowing for the expenses of the journey from Mortlake. James was giving money about with a right royal hand, and he later remarked that his first two and a half years in England were a "perpetual Christmas." The facts of life caught up with him and there were spasmodic attempts at economy, such as fewer meat dishes at Court. But James could never recover from the delight of spending money, after his impoverished reign in Scotland, and Parliament was always arguing with him over the huge sums of money he and his wife managed to spend.

The King celebrated Christmas that year at Hampton Court, and the handsome brick palace was the home of masques and feasting very much as it had been in the old days of Henry VIII. The Earl of Pembroke danced in a masque, and Queen Anne showed her legs freely in the costume of Pallas. Shakespeare's company had their usual opening date of December 26 and they had a particularly heavy schedule their first week. They played four times before King James and twice before Prince Henry, giving two performances on Sunday.

Prince Henry was nine years old, a grave, beautiful, self-possessed child who grew up to be adored by the people of England and the very model of a prince. Both King James and Queen Anne had endured sickly childhoods, and James still had no real control of his body; but their two eldest children, Prince Henry and Princess Elizabeth, were as beautiful as the figures in a fairy tale. The younger son, Charles, was something of a misfit after so handsome a pair, since Charles was like both his parents and could not walk unaided when he was a child. Henry was not above teasing his younger brother about his crippled legs, but Charles made no objection since like everyone else he adored Prince Henry. "Sweet, sweet brother . . . I will give anything that I have to you." Henry died young and Elizabeth made an unhappy marriage and Charles was beheaded

by his own subjects; but when the King's Men played before them that Christmas at Hampton Court they were everything that a royal family should be.

By March the plague was over in London and the postponed triumphal procession was scheduled for the 15th. The city had been presenting these pageants to their new rulers for centuries, and few people knew more about the art of welcoming kings. The scaffolds for the arches were completed and given their elaborate finishing touches, the speeches of welcome were written and rehearsed, and Edward Alleyn, who was to play the Genius of the City, was fitted for his purple buskins and tried on his long white wig.

The whole show cost the city four hundred pounds and the crowds were enormous. In spite of the railings there was a "strong stream of people," and there was so much shouting that the carefully written odes of Ben Jonson and Thomas Dekker and Michael Drayton could scarcely be heard. It was the kind of celebration Queen Elizabeth would have enjoyed thoroughly, but the new ruler of England bore it politely and without enthusiasm. James hated crowds and he never felt any temperamental affinity with his emotional Londoners. He once remarked on a visit to Oxford that he would like to "be a University man" and spend all his time in the Bodleian Library, and his idea of real pleasure was to engage in an intricate theological discussion on some minor point of doctrine. It is probable that he enjoyed nothing more thoroughly in his whole reign than his Hampton Court conference with the churchmen of England in 1604, and the English-speaking world may be glad that he did since out of this conference was born the King James Version of the Bible.

James had none of the vigor and flamboyance of his great predecessor, but he shared one quality with her: a love of peace. James was convinced that all wars were both expensive and useless, and he bent his energies to avoid them. It was an unusual point of view for the period, and a comedy was played at Brussels that parodied the English King's faith in ambassadors. As one of James's own subjects put it, the King would "rather spend £100,000 on embassies, to keep or procure peace with dishonor, than £10,000 on an army that would have forced peace with honor."

James was especially anxious to bring to an end the long, dragging, expensive war with Spain, and as soon as he was crowned, he set the peace machinery in motion. In the same March that the Londoners were shouting at his triumphal procession, the costumers of Spain were occupied with the new clothes that the Constable of Castile had ordered for his suite so that they could accompany him to England with as much splendor as possible. The English plans to receive the Spanish envoy were equally elaborate, and Queen Anne gave up Somerset House, which was her town residence and the finest palace in London, to be filled with the best furniture and the most beautiful tapestries that the royal family possessed to honor the Spanish ambassador.

Although the Constable of Castile was bringing his own suite, it was also desirable for him to have as many English attendants as possible, "people chosen for their good disposition and nobility" and also, no doubt, for their excellent carriage and general impressiveness. Among those who were chosen to be attendants were the twelve actors who made up the royal company, and John Heminges and Augustine Phillips were paid over twenty pounds "for the allowance of themselves and ten of their fellows, his Majesty's Grooms of the Chamber and players, for waiting and attending on his Majesty's service, by commandment, upon the Spanish Ambassador at Somerset House, for the space of eighteen days."

It was not a new thing for royal actors to be Grooms of the Chamber. The same posts had been held by Richard Tarleton and his fellow actors when they had been appointed the Queen's Men, and James was merely continuing the precedent she had established. When livery was granted to all the members of the King's household at the time of the coronation procession in March, the King's actors were issued livery with the rest. (This time Shakespeare was first on the list and Lawrence Fletcher third.) This livery consisted of the cloth for red doublets and cloaks, and by ancient custom it went to everyone in the royal service, even down to the perfumers and basketmakers.

If the Constable of Castile had understood English, the King's actors would probably have been used to present plays before him. Since he did not, Tilney supplied bear-baiting and acrobatics for his entertainment, and the actors became attendants at Somerset House, dressed in scarlet with the King's cypher embroidered in gold. The twelve actors probably had very little to do except look decorative, since the Spanish ambassador had brought three hundred of his own attendants with him. In return, they received board and lodging at the royal expense during their period of service, as well as nearly two pounds apiece that Phillips and Heminges collected for them.

Shakespeare was not the first major English poet to wear this kind of livery. Geoffrey Chaucer wore the royal badge as a member of the household when Richard II put on one of his greatest tournaments, and, like Shakespeare, he wore it for reasons that had nothing to do with his poetry. Chaucer wore the king's livery because at that time he was Clerk of the Works and was responsible for erecting the scaffoldings for the tournament; Shakespeare wore it because he was a professional actor in a company that was under royal patronage. It is quite probable that Juan Fernandez de Velasco, Duke de Frias and Constable of Castile, never knew

that the attendant who served him for eighteen days at Somerset House was a playwright also, much less that posterity was going to be interested in the Constable chiefly because William Shakespeare had once been paid to attend him.

The Spanish envoy had an excellent time in London, doing the usual sight-seeing around the city and buying so lavishly that the London jewelers beat a path to Somerset House. After a final grand banquet at Whitehall he went to bed with an attack of the gout, and the King visited his bedside to wish him a final farewell. He recovered sufficiently to leave London on the 25th of August, after having given "very bountifully unto all that attended him," and since the treaty had been signed in the course of the festivities, England and Spain were at last at peace.

Shakespeare and his eleven fellow actors were in service at Somerset House from the 9th of August to the 27th, and this seems to have been the first and last time they served the King in their technical capacity as Grooms of the Chamber. For the rest of the reign their services were evidently confined to acting. Two years later, for instance, the King of Denmark came over in the summer to see his sister Anne and was lavishly entertained by his royal brother-in-law. The Danes paused long enough in their drinking and feasting to see a few plays and the King's Men acted for them both at Greenwich and at Hampton Court.

The Constable of Castile had no sooner left England in the summer of 1604 than the preparations for the Christmas season began to take shape in the Office of the Revels at Clerkenwell. The King was so eager to see plays that it was decided to break with precedent and start the Christmas season on the first of November instead of the normal date of the day after Christmas. The honor of opening the season went of course to the King's Men, and the play that was assigned for the opening was Shakespeare's *Othello*.

Tilney was now Sir Edmund Tilney, for he had been knighted by James the previous year, just before the coronation. During the first excited months of his reign James had passed out knighthoods with an almost comically lavish hand, and three or four hundred knights were made the same day as Sir Edmund Tilney. A notice was posted inside St. Paul's offering a memory course so that Londoners could remember the names of the new knights, and so many jokes were made on the subject that King James himself apologized for all the knights he had made. Nevertheless, Tilney deserved the honor if some of the others did not, for he was a hard-working, intelligent official and was kept even busier in the reign of James than he had been in the reign of Elizabeth.

Tilney and four of his assistants in the Office of the Revels worked twenty days that summer overhauling the theatrical costumes that were stored at Clerkenwell, airing them and having them repaired. Richard Prescott, the porter, was kept busy earning his twelvepence a day attending to all the rehearsals and must have grown very familiar with all the actors of the King's company. Shakespeare and his group were presenting nearly all the plays that were produced at Court that Christmas. The Queen's Men were putting on one play by Heywood, the boys' company at Blackfriars was putting on one play by Chapman, and the Prince's Men had not been asked to perform that particular year at all.

Two amateur groups of actors were also busy rehearsing, for a masque was to be presented by the Earl of Pembroke and seven other gentlemen of the Court, and Queen Anne was planning to appear in a similar production with eleven of her ladies. Ben Jonson got the important assignment of writing the masque for the Queen and decided to have them appear as Moors in azure and silver costumes with feathers and pearls in their hair. Inigo Jones designed the stage machinery for the masque and it was staged at an initial cost of three thousand pounds, which was not a large sum for a woman with Anne's talent for spending money. Lady Hatton failed to get a part in the masque and Lady Hertford got the measles and the Queen was so bent on being realistic that she had everyone's arms painted black up to the elbows. The officials who were responsible for training the twelve lady-Moors in the use of their fans must occasionally have thought wistfully of the happier lot of the King's Men, who only had a single Moor to deal with in their opening production of *Othello* and had Richard Burbage for the part.

Othello was to be produced in the great Banqueting Hall at Whitehall, and Peter Wright, who was responsible for all the lighting equipment, had a complicated problem. His assistants fastened pasteboard around the columns of the hall to protect them from the wires that anchored the lights, and six men were required to haul up the great branches that held a huge array of candles and to wire them into place. Plates were set into the roof above the lights to lessen the danger of fire, for the Banqueting House was old enough and rickety enough without any added complications. It had been built in 1581 of wooden boards with a painted canvas roof, and although it was charmingly decorated, it was growing rather unsafe. King James had the building pulled down a short time later and a new Banqueting Hall, "very strong and stately," put up in its place. Even in the Christmas season of 1604, the Banqueting Hall evidently was used for *Othello* only and the rest of the plays were produced elsewhere.

When James and his Court saw *Othello* on the first of November, they saw what had once been a cheap melodrama exalted into great poetry. At the end of Elizabeth's reign, Shakespeare had been reading a group of stories that had been collected by Giraldi Cinthio, and in it he had found an ugly story of a woman whose husband went mad with jealousy and ordered her to be murdered. The casual Titan who worked with the King's Men had lifted up the bloody, old-fashioned tale, made what structural changes he thought were necessary, and added the greatness of his poetry and the reality of his people. The basic plot has been called unreal, but it never seems so when Shakespeare's version is given a good production, and it can safely be said that the production which Burbage and his fellow actors gave before King James was a good one.

The King's Men gave a Sunday production of *The Merry Wives of Windsor* and then followed it on St. Stephen's night with *Measure for Measure*. This was another rather ugly plot that had been taken from Cinthio's collection, and it had been somewhat softened when it was turned into an English play a quarter of a century earlier. The heroine of the play is forced to surrender her honor to save her brother's life, and Shakespeare manipulated the plot so that she is able to avoid the bargain and the play can end happily. The play is wonderful in sections but not very successful as a whole, since a rather complicated, mechanical plot of this kind did not give Shakespeare the space he needed for his characterization. At about this same time he turned another Italian story of this kind into a play and called it *All's Well*

That Ends Well, and here he was even less successful and for the same reason. The casual manner in which Shakespeare persisted in picking up his plots occasionally betrayed him, especially when it involved routine situations from medieval folk stories and blocked what was one of the greatest of his gifts, the gift of characterization.

After the King's Men had presented *Measure for Measure* in the palace hall, there was an interval while the Earl of Pembroke and his fellow performers presented their masque with music. Then, on Innocents' Night, the King's Men reappeared with that hardy old perennial of Shakespeare's, *The Comedy of Errors.* The plays of Heywood and Chapman followed, and then the King's Men returned with another old favorite by Shakespeare, *Love's Labour's Lost.* By this time it was Twelfth Night, and the twelve lady-Moors were ready to appear in the complicated cockleshell that Inigo Jones had designed for them.

The King's Men had the rest of the Christmas season, and among the various plays they produced were two more by Shakespeare. On the 7th of January they presented his *Henry V,* and on Shrove Sunday they did *The Merchant of Venice.* James was so pleased with *The Merchant of Venice* that he ordered a repeat performance, and it was played the following Tuesday, "again commanded by the King's Majesty."

When King James was bored by a play, he did not hesitate to say so. The following summer he attended a series of stage productions at Oxford into which the university had poured an enormous amount of time and money, even including special movable scenery and the expensive services of Inigo Jones. At the first play, James tried to leave before it was finished and only stayed because of the personal entreaty of the Chancellor. At the second one he "spoke many words of dislike" in a tone that was evidently all too audible. At the third he frankly went to sleep, for he had none of Queen Elizabeth's determination to be gracious to her subjects at whatever cost in boredom to herself. James could not have been an easy man to please, being intelligent, critical, and very restless, and it is a tribute to Shakespeare's company that they evidently pleased him enormously.

The new ruler of England was not temperamentally in sympathy with his London subjects in the way that Queen Elizabeth had been, but at least he had one characteristic in common with the thousands who flocked to the Globe playhouse each week. Neither he nor they could resist the plays of William Shakespeare.

The King's Men reopened the Globe on Easter Monday, 1604, after the plague had closed the theatre for the better part of a year. The Prince's Men returned to the Fortune, and a short time later the Queen's Men, who had been using the old Curtain, got a theatre of their own out in Clerkenwell and called it the Red Bull. This left Shakespeare's company the one major group of actors in Southwark, and for the rest of the reign they were the undisputed lords of the Bankside.

The company's royal patron had given Richard Burbage thirty pounds in February "for the maintenance and relief of himself and the rest of his company . . . till it shall please God to settle the City in a more perfect health." The company must have needed the money, for the rent on the theatre had to be paid whether the Globe was open or closed. Moreover, there is some evidence that one of the last plays that the King's Men presented before the plague closed the theatres had been an elaborately staged and expensive failure.

The play was Ben Jonson's *Sejanus,* acted by an enormous cast that was headed by Richard Burbage and William Shakespeare as the "principal tragedians." The production had evidently been planned to attract the crowds that had come up to London to see the coronation, but Jonson's play was too learned and pretentious to please the average member of the theatregoing public.

Jonson had planned a Roman tragedy in the strict Senecan model and he apologized for not having observed the unity of time, a failure that was unavoidable "in these our times, and to such auditors." He did not need to apologize for his research and was able to cite in detail an impressive array of sources, "being all in the learned tongue, save one." He wrote *Sejanus* as his first important tragedy, to fulfill all the true "offices of a tragic writer," and it was almost as though he were trying to show the rather casual author of *Julius Caesar* what could be achieved by a learned and conscientious playwright who was willing to obey the rules.

The author of *Julius Caesar* was one of the principal actors in *Sejanus.* It is not known what part Shakespeare took in Jonson's play but it makes very little difference, since all the characterizations are equally wooden. Shakespeare was accustomed to acting in pretentious plays, just as he was accustomed to acting in bad ones; and he accepted his roles in the same relaxed way he accepted the plots for his own plays and made the best of them.

It was this easygoing temperament of Shakespeare's that made him occasionally irritating to an intense and theoretical nature like Jonson's. Jonson once told a friend of his that Shakespeare lacked "art," and since by art Jonson meant the rigid, pseudoclassic theories of the Renaissance, he was quite right. Shakespeare had no special respect for theories. In his 'prentice days there had been a brief period when he tried to follow classical models, but since then he had paid no attention to rules and had used whatever dramatic technique happened to suit the story on which he was working.

The word that comes to mind in connection with Shakespeare is not "art" but freedom. He went his own way and made his own laws. By the time King James came to the throne, Shakespeare was the master of every resource of stagecraft, just as he was the master of every art of language, and a torrent of such force makes its own channels.

This is not to say that Shakespeare failed to be interested in Jonson's theories. He was interested in everything, and during this period he must have been seeing a good deal of Jonson. The year after the Globe reopened, the King's Men produced *Volpone*, which was Jonson's first real success in classic comedy. For the first time he managed to bring to life on the stage his theory that each character should have a single dominant trait or "humour," and Burbage and Heminges headed the cast in what must have been an excellent production.

It may have been at about this time that Shakespeare experimented with a play that had a classical background and in which each character symbolized a single qual-ity. The play was *Timon of Athens* and the "humour" of the hero was misanthropy. "Hate-man Timon" was a familiar name to the Renaissance, and his "strange and beastly nature" had been frequently described. It is not clear why such a stiff and unnatural figure should have attracted Shakespeare in the first place, but he evidently grew bored with the idea so quickly that he was never able to give the play the careful attention it needed.

Shakespeare made another experiment with what might be called the "well-made play," again taking his story from Plutarch, and this time he made a brilliant and almost chiseled study of the danger of pride. A good actor in the title role can make a very effective play out of *Coriolanus*. The writing is magnificent, much of it in that clipped, vivid shorthand that well-trained theatre audiences at the Globe could follow as easily as their predecessors at the Theatre could follow the rolling periods that imitated Marlowe. But Shakespeare's hero is too rigidly simplified to achieve the humanity and reality of most of his people, and *Coriolanus* is one of those plays that an audience can admire but cannot take to its heart.

Shakespeare found still another story in Plutarch, and this time his imagination took fire. The result was *Antony and Cleopatra,* which Jonson must have disapproved of even more thoroughly than he disapproved of *Julius Caesar*. No one could call *Antony and Cleopatra* a "well-made play" from the Renaissance point of view. It has thirty-two changes of scene and ranges over the whole of the ancient world with a technique not unlike that of old-fashioned plays of the eighties at which Sir Philip Sidney had once laughed. As for Cleopatra, her creator ignored the theory of the dominant "humour" with which he had been experimenting in *Coriolanus,* and he made her almost as complicated and as unpredictable as Hamlet. Cleopatra is not a consistent characterization; she is instead an enchanting woman, who cannot be held to respectable laws on paper and insists in walking off the page and into reality.

Shakespeare gave the King's Men an extremely difficult production problem in *Antony and Cleopatra* since for once the major role in a tragedy was given to a woman instead of to a man. For someone in the Globe company, the part of Cleopatra must have been the most severe test of his acting career. Shakespeare gave the actor his full assistance and let the Queen's passion for Antony be carried to a great extent by her lines or by the comments of the other players. In turn, Shakespeare trusted the capacity of his colleague at the Globe so completely that he dared to put into the mouth of Cleopatra a slighting reference to the "squeaking" boy actors of Rome. He must have known that by that time the audience would be so convinced of the reality of the story that they would have forgotten a male actor was playing the Queen and be con-

scious only of the Queen herself. The great magician knew what he was doing, and the magic did not fail him.

Shakespeare's interest in Plutarch during this period did not make him forget his old favorite, Holinshed's *Chronicles.* Shakespeare never considered himself superior to that rather old-fashioned historian, and, not long after James ascended the throne, he found in the *Chronicles* a story of a Scottish king that he transformed into the wonderful tragedy of *Macbeth.*

The mood of the play was Shakespeare's own, for he found no special hint of it in his source. Holinshed's Macbeth reigned for seventeen years, and most of these were given over to "worthy doings and princely acts." Although there are as many murders as in the play, Holinshed relates them in a singularly matter-of-fact fashion and he even manages to flatten out the three witches, who are either "the goddesses of destiny or else some nymphs or fairies endued with knowledge of prophecy by their necromantical science." It was out of such unpromising material as this that Shakespeare made a tragedy that is the color of blood and moves as steadily as the coming of darkness.

It has been repeatedly suggested that *Macbeth* was written as a compliment to King James, who once wrote a treatise on demonology. It might as well be said that the play was a compliment to Londoners, since it would have been difficult to find anyone in the audiences at the Globe who did not believe in the powers of darkness. A hardheaded businessman like Philip Henslowe could place in his diary, between notes on buying costumes and paying playwrights, the information that if a man wrote certain words on parchment with the blood of a bat and tied it around his left arm he would get whatever he wanted. This might be an especially useful formula in a chancy business like that of the theatre, but it was not theatre men only who trusted to bat's blood and incantations.

Like most normal people, King James believed in witches; but unlike most normal people he was intelligent enough to know that some of their accusers were hysterics who faked their seizures. He exposed one such case just after he came to the throne, and before the end of his reign he saved a whole group of his subjects in Leicester, who were waiting to be hanged in the regular way as witches, by proving that the boy who accused them of witchcraft had been faking. James was so completely a skeptic that he did not even believe in the curative power of the royal touch, the "healing benediction" that is described at some length in *Macbeth*. He refused to continue the ceremony when he first came to the throne, because all healing was in the hands of God and not in the hands of a king; and he only consented to it finally as a matter of policy because the French kings still kept up the custom.

Shakespeare was not a man given to complimenting royalty, and when the King ascended the throne he was almost the only writer in England who did not break out in sobs of poetical joy because so beneficent a royal sun had come to shine over England. But if he ever had wished to compliment King James, he could certainly have devised a more graceful tribute than the bloody Scottish tragedy of *Macbeth*, whose only reference to the current ruler was in the "treble sceptres" that would be carried by some of Banquo's descendants.

In the winter of 1604 the King's Men produced a play that was a direct compliment to King James. The play was called *Gowry,* and told the story of a conspiracy against James by the Earl of Gowry that had occurred four years earlier. The story included a cache of gold pieces, a loyal falconer, and a melodramatic fight on the stairway of Gowry House, and its dramatization by the King's Men attracted an "exceeding concourse of all sorts of people." One of their number played the part of King James himself, and although the King did not object, some of his Council felt it was improper to show the royal person on the stage and the play was evidently discontinued.

The custom of showing real people on the stage was common enough in the reigns of both Elizabeth and James. When Shakespeare's company presented in 1599 a drama based on the Battle of Turnhout, which had taken place two years earlier, they gave the real names of all the men who had taken part in the battle and presented Sir Francis Vere to the life with his beard, his satin doublet, and his hose trimmed with silver lace. When a breach of promise suit was tried in the London courts in the winter of 1603, one of the principals paid an outright sum to George Chapman to put the whole situation in a play, with the chief characters only faintly disguised, so that the suit could be won by ridiculing the opposition. It was a usual practice for a playwright to present someone he disliked upon the stage, ridiculing his "red beard" or his "little legs," and Lord Burghley once suggested that the best possible punishment for two cheats was to "have those that make the plays to make a comedy thereof," using their real names.

It was this custom that prompted Hamlet to tell Polonius that he should treat the actors carefully, "for they are the abstracts and brief chronicles of the time; after your death you were better have a bad epitaph than their ill report while you live." Shakespeare was almost the only playwright of the period who saw no need to comment on contemporary Londoners in his plays, and he did not share Hamlet's view that a playwright should chronicle his own times.

Hamlet was expressing a familiar opinion when he said that a play should show "the very age and body of the time his form and pressure." Nearly all the playwrights of the period, like Chapman and Middleton and Dekker, were locating their plays in contemporary London; and although Jonson's first satirical comedy, *Every Man in His Humour,* was ostensibly located in Florence, the Italian settings were only a thin disguise for real places in London and he changed the names to English ones when the play was printed in his collected works.

Shakespeare, however, did not write any play in the reign of James that had a setting in contemporary London. Instead he ranged from ancient Scotland to ancient Egypt, and when he wrote a play about England, he set it in prehistoric Britain and called it *King Lear.*

Shakespeare was a writer who was incapable of settling down mentally, and after having tried every other effect that could conceivably be achieved on a stage, he set out to orchestrate a storm. *King Lear* opened the Christmas season at Court in 1606, and if the rambling palace of Whitehall did not blow down that night, it was certainly not the fault of Shakespeare's lines. It is extremely difficult today to find an actor with the voice and the physical endurance to measure up to the part of Lear, but the Whitehall production had Richard Burbage. Burbage and Shakespeare had been growing up together, and when Shakespeare had written his youthful melodrama of *Richard III,* it was Burbage who had created the lead. They had worked for more than a decade in intimate, daily association with each other, and the actor who had already had a great success as Hamlet and Othello was able to measure up to the titanic lines of King Lear.

Like *Hamlet,* an earlier version of *King Lear* had already been a success on the London stage, but unlike *Hamlet,* the earlier version of *King Lear* is still extant. The original *King Lear* is a dull, respectable sort of play that is neatly motivated and follows the original story in Holinshed very closely. There are no disturbing characters like the Fool, and everything comes out well in the end, for Lear and Cordelia do not die and the two wicked sisters are routed. Shakespeare merely used the original play as a springboard for the action and produced a play that is not well-motivated, that does not follow the chronicles, and in which all the good characters are destroyed. The action of the characters is as senseless as life itself, and the appalling picture it conveys of the uselessness of old age, the stupidity of most mortals, and the cruelty of living would be almost unendurable to the average spectator if the greatness of its poetry did not exalt it. *King Lear* is the one play of Shakespeare's that seems to have no basis at all in any kind of Christian dogma, and it is significant that he chose a pre-Christian era and wrote of events that took place "in the days when Jeroboam ruled in Israel."

It has sometimes been said that Shakespeare's plays mirror his life.

But *King Lear* was written at a time when the country was prosperous and at peace, and Shakespeare himself seems to have had no troubles of either a business or a personal nature. It was in the difficult years of the late nineties, when a depression had gripped England and his only son had died, that Shakespeare wrote his radiant series of light lyric comedies.

During these successful years of working with the King's Men, Shakespeare moved his residence again and returned to the London side of the Thames. The exact date when he left Southwark is unknown, but it may have been at about the time of James's accession that Shakespeare left the Liberty of the Clink and took lodgings on Silver Street.

Silver Street was in St. Olave's parish, an aristocratic neighborhood on the northwest side of town that stood next to the parish in which John Heminges and Henry Condell had their homes. It was a district of handsome houses, and Shakespeare lived there as a lodger in the home of a French family named Mountjoy. Christopher Mountjoy was one of the many Huguenots who left France after the Massacre of St. Bartholomew and he had prospered in London as a maker of headdresses for women. For a long time Mountjoy had lived in St. Olave's parish as an alien and then he had finally become a naturalized citizen.

The Mountjoys had an only child, Mary, whom they had educated in the intricacies of silver wire and the art of using a twisting wheel until she knew almost as much about the business as they did. They also had an apprentice, Stephen Belott, who completed his seven years' service with them and in 1604 had just returned from a trip to Spain. A marriage between the two young people seemed both obvious and desirable, and Mrs. Mountjoy turned for assistance to her friend and lodger, William Shakespeare.

A marriage agreement was a serious matter because of the property settlement involved, and it was Shakespeare's responsibility to work out an arrangement on the dowry that would be agreeable to both sides. A married couple who were friends of Belott went formally to Shakespeare to discuss the size of the marriage portion that Mountjoy had offered, and as Shakespeare himself testified there were "many conferences" on the matter. The family servant, Joan Johnson, remembered eight years later how the lodger, "one Mr. Shakespeare," had made the arrangements whereby Stephen Belott consented to marry Mary Mountjoy, and on November 19 Mary and Stephen were married in the little church of St. Olave's across the street and came back to Christopher Mountjoy's house to live. The wedding took place in the midst of the Christmas season at Whitehall, just nineteen days after the King's Men had opened the season with a performance of Shakespeare's *Othello*.

The middle of the following summer, Shakespeare made another of his major investments in Stratford. On July 24, 1605, he spent the largest single sum of his lifetime, so far as the records go, and paid £440 for a lease on some of the Stratford tithes.

The purchase was one that involved a great deal of local prestige, for a holder of the tithes was an important man in Stratford. Seven years earlier, when Richard Quiney was in London, a Stratford businessman named Abraham Sturley had written him to suggest that, since Shakespeare had money to invest, the matter of the tithes ought to be discussed with him. "We think it a fair mark for him to shoot at, and not impossible to hit. It obtained would advance him indeed, and would do us much good. Do not fail to urge this," Sturley continued, soaring into Latin. "This would be a labor, this a work, of surpassing honor and credit."

When Shakespeare finally bought the tithes, Richard Quiney was dead, killed tragically in trying to stop a fight that had been started by some of Greville's men. But the ownership of the tithes was still a matter of surpassing honor and credit—"*et gloriae et laudis*"—and the purchase symbolizes the lofty position that the Shakespeare family had attained in Stratford.

The tithes had originally been a tax collected by the Church, but even before the Reformation the Church had fallen into the habit of selling or leasing the tithes to secular owners. In 1544 the Collegiate Church of Stratford had rented them to the Barker family on a ninety-two year lease. The Barkers sold their lease to the Hubands, retaining an annual rental fee, and the complicated holdings were gradually divided among various people who wanted to sublease them. By the time Shakespeare made his purchase from Ralph Huband, there were forty-two people who held various rights under the original ninety-two-year lease, and Shakespeare's purchase consisted of about one eighth of the entire property. The purchase gave Shakespeare the right to collect one half the tithes on "corn, grain, blade, and hay" from the three villages of Old Stratford, Welcombe, and Bishopton, and also a one-half right to various lesser tithes, such as that on wool, from the parish of Stratford as a whole.

In exchange for his £440, Shakespeare had the right to collect these tithes until the whole lease expired thirty-one years later and the property went under the control of the Stratford Corporation. In the meantime, he was obliged to pay an annual fee of £17 to the Corporation and one of £5 to John Barker. Even when these payments were deducted, the investment was an excellent one; Shakespeare was able to get a return of about ten per cent on his investment, and within twenty years the value of the property had almost doubled. Moreover, the investment carried with it additional social prestige; for in the

same way that his purchase of New Place had given him a special pew in church, the purchase of the tithes gave him a special place of burial. Shakespeare was now a lay rector and had the right to be buried within the rails of the chancel.

As the position of the Shakespeares became increasingly dignified in Stratford, it is likely that most people managed to forget that the head of the family was an actor. He did no acting in Stratford. He was William Shakespeare, gentleman, and the way he was making his money in London could be conveniently forgotten.

The acting profession had never been considered a dignified one in Stratford, although there had been a time when the people of Stratford enjoyed plays as much as the Londoners did. In Shakespeare's boyhood the acting companies had been welcome, but they were not welcome any longer. The year before Elizabeth died, the Stratford Council decided formally that no more plays were to be given in the Guildhall, and that any member of the Council who licensed the actors to perform should be fined ten shillings. Ten years later the Council decided that sterner measures should be taken in Stratford, considering the wickedness of plays "and how contrary the sufferance of them is against . . . the examples of other well-governed cities and boroughs." Therefore the Council decreed "that the penalty of ten shillings imposed in Mr. Baker's year for breaking the order shall from henceforth be ten pounds."

Like so many other towns in Warwickshire, Stratford was changing into a Puritan community, and every year the change in it became more pronounced. Within three years after Shakespeare's death, the Puritan faction had grown so strong that it was able to install a new vicar to replace the easygoing John Rogers. This set off a riot against the "sucking Puritans of Stratford," and two of Shakespeare's close friends, John Nashe and William Reynolds, ended up in the court of Star Chamber for leading an attack against Stratford's Puritan "rulers."

What had happened in Stratford was to a certain extent happening all over England, especially in the south and east. The Puritan doctrine, with its emphasis on hard work and independence of thought, made a strong appeal to the respectable middle classes; and since there is no pleasure in being respectable if someone else refuses to be, each Puritan set out vigorously to convert his neighbor to his own austere doctrine. Cambridge University and the Inns of Court produced dozens of ardent young men who had seen the light and who set out as traveling lecturers to spread the doctrine all over England.

By the time James came to the throne, the Puritan party had a majority in Parliament, and one of the early signs of their influence was a bill passed in 1606 "for the preventing and avoiding of the great abuse of the Holy Name of God in stage plays." Instead of passing a bill that called for a ten-pound fine for every oath that was permitted on the stage, the Puritan party would have liked to pass a bill outlawing the stage entirely. But too many people, from the King down, loved the English theatre, and it was not until the middle of the century that the Puritan party gained enough power to destroy its enemy, the stage.

Puritanism had of course many merits, even apart from the great contribution it made to political thought by affirming the dignity of the individual conscience and denying the old doctrine of the divine right of kings. But from the point of view of the English theatre, Puritanism was an unmitigated disaster, and if the movement had taken hold in England any earlier than it did, none of the plays of Shakespeare could have come into existence.

Shakespeare had the great good fortune to be born in a period in which he could address an audience that had no special bias; and among the many kinds of freedom that Shakespeare possessed, this freedom was by no means the least. Two centuries earlier, Geoffrey Chaucer had wrestled with the church's disapproval of love stories and of realism, and half a century later, Milton sacrificed the richness of his gifts on the altar of Puritan austerity. But in the sunny time when Shakespeare began to write, a man could say almost anything he pleased so long as he did not encroach on political matters. What have been called the spacious days of Queen Elizabeth were in many ways not spacious at all, but they did give the average Englishman a great deal of freedom when it came to the question of enjoying himself.

At the end of the eighties the playwrights had a brief skirmish with the Puritan party, during the Marprelate controversy, and had shown Martin Marprelate on the stage in what they considered a suitable costume—"a cock's comb, an ape's face, a wolf's belly." But in the next decade, the controversy died down and the attitude of the playwrights toward the Puritans was amused rather than angry. The actor who played Falstaff could be sure of a laugh when he raised his eyes heavenward and said in the Puritan singsong: "Hal, I prithee, trouble me no more with vanity." The playwrights considered the Puritans a small, distempered portion of the population, and they took much the same point of view toward them that Sir Toby Belch took toward Malvolio: "Dost thou think, because thou art virtuous, there shall be no more cakes and ale?" But in another ten years Puritan virtue was spreading over the whole land, and some of the playwrights began to be frightened. The old note of tolerant humor begins to disappear and a kind of savageness takes its place.

Meanwhile the Puritans could legitimately retort that the playwrights had lost the respect for simple morality that they had once shown in their plays. The old plays of the eighties, with their clear-cut distinctions between virtue and vice, had been replaced in the reign of James by a newer kind of drama. Although George Chapman's dramas had an ethical basis, his heroes insisted that they and their passions were above the law.

> Be free, all worthy spirits,
> And stretch yourselves.

John Marston was a savage moralist, but some of his morality consisted in presenting violent pictures of the sin he claimed to be attacking, and a play like *The Insatiate Countess* gave many normal Londoners who were not good Puritans a reason to stay away from the theatre. The final result of such an atmosphere was the plays of Beaumont and Fletcher, which have no moral base at all and are merely designed to be sensational and entertaining.

Unlike the earlier dramatists, neither John Fletcher nor Francis Beaumont was a member of the lower middle class. John Fletcher was the son of a former bishop of London, a lively, unclerical individual who was fond of horses and fine clothes and who died suddenly after a disastrous second marriage leaving eight children and a great many debts. His son was evidently given a good education, and he started his writing career in a rather lofty manner by giving the public what he felt the public ought to have. The play was a pastoral in the classical manner called *The Faithful Shepherdess,* and it was published with high praise for its "elegant propriety." But it was a complete failure on the stage, since, as Fletcher said in his arrogant preface to the printed edition, the public evidently expected to see a lot of shepherds, "sometimes laughing together, and sometimes killing one another," and were incapable of recognizing a classical tragicomedy when they saw one. The failure of *The Faithful Shepherdess* confirmed Ben Jonson's opinion that the London theatregoers were a collection of illiterate fools, and he assured Fletcher that his work would be immortal when time had destroyed "what all these fools admire."

Another writer who hastened to assure John Fletcher that the public did not understand true art was Francis Beaumont. Francis was the third son of Mr. Justice Beaumont, a prominent member of the Inner Temple, and since he was also a gentleman born, he could sympathize with the select atmosphere that Fletcher was trying to encourage on the English stage.

Moreover, Beaumont himself had written a play that was a failure because the audience could not understand it. *The Knight of the Burning Pestle* was a satire on the citizens' audience, and tells the story of a Londoner and his wife who stray into one of the private boys' theatres and suggest that their apprentice be allowed to play the lead. Their innocent and straightforward notions of dramatic art are very skillfully parodied by Beaumont, and the chief object of parody is a play that Thomas Heywood wrote in honor of London apprentices and which Heywood himself admitted was now out-of-date. But Heywood is not the only popular, old-fashioned writer to receive Beaumont's attention, for although the apprentice in Beaumont's play has won acclaim as an amateur actor in such reliable old melodramas as *Mucedorus* and *The Spanish Tragedy,* when he is asked to recite some lines from a "huffing part," he embarks on Hotspur's speech on honor from *Henry IV.* Beaumont evidently considered Shakespeare's work of the nineties sufficiently old-fashioned and sufficiently popular with a citizens' audience to ensure a laugh when it was quoted direct in the more select atmosphere of a private theatre.*

It seems almost incredible to a modern reader that two writers as

* It is hard to know exactly what Beaumont thought of Shakespeare. In a rhymed letter to Ben Jonson, Beaumont said he hoped to use simple language,

And from all learning keep these lines as clear
As Shakespeare's best are, which our heirs shall hear
Preachers apt to their auditors to show
How far sometimes a mortal man may go
By the dim light of Nature.

But just before this Beaumont has already announced what this unlearned style is to be:

. . . if this equal but the style which men
Send cheese to town with, and thanks down again
'Tis all I seek for.

dissimilar as Shakespeare and Heywood could be chosen as joint objects of parody, but it was natural enough in Beaumont's day. Shakespeare was the major playwright of the King's company, and Heywood was the major playwright of its chief rival, the Queen's company. Both men had been successful writers in the nineties, which was now considered a period of comparative barbarism, and both of them had consistently been pleasing the general London public ever since. The companies they worked for both appealed to the same group of playgoers, for when two plays of Heywood's required larger casts than a single company could produce, the King's Men and the Queen's Men united to present them at Court.

If anything, Heywood had shown himself to be a man of more ambition and more learning than Shakespeare. He had already made a good translation of Sallust, and in 1608 William Jaggard published his long and ambitious poem in the Spenserian tradition called *Troia Britannica.* Most of its seventeen cantos were devoted to a retelling of the stories in Ovid's *Metamorphoses,* and since the book did not sell particularly well, Heywood thriftily turned the same material to stage use. Both *The Golden Age* and *The Silver Age* were among the stage successes of the period, and they had the special merit of combining sensation with spectacle. Jove ascended on his eagle, Ceres and Proserpine danced with the country maidens, and so many devils filled the stage that the Queen's Men must have paid a large bill for fireworks. The cast of *The Silver Age* was an enormous one, including thirteen actors just for centaurs and planets, and this was one of the two plays that the King's Men and Queen's Men presented jointly at Court. The one other play they produced in this way was also Heywood's, and although he called it a "true Roman tragedy" *The Rape of Lucrece* was a blurred mixture of farce and of Shakespeare's youthful version of the story.

Both of these plays had been first produced at the Red Bull, where they were extremely successful, but not every play that the Queen's Men produced there was a success. Their production of John Webster's brilliant tragedy, *The White Devil,* was a failure, and Webster blamed the lack of "a full and understanding auditory." Webster did not like the atmosphere of the public theatres and complained that if a man wrote the most magnificent tragedy that was ever conceived, "observing all the critical laws," yet it would be destroyed if it were presented before the general public. "The breath that comes from the uncapable multitude is able to poison it."

Webster did not want anyone to think that his failure to please the "uncapable multitude" had made him envious of his fellow playwrights. "I have ever truly cherished my good opinion of other men's worthy labors, especially of that full and heightened style of master Chapman: the labored and understanding works of master Jonson: the no less worthy composures of the both worthily excellent master Beaumont and master Fletcher; and lastly (without wrong last to be named) the right happy and copious industry of Mr. Shakespeare, Mr. Dekker, and Mr. Heywood."

Here is another case of an intelligent writer of the period linking Shakespeare with Heywood. It seems nearly incredible today that Shakespeare could be classed with a writer like Heywood and praised chiefly for his "copious industry," but from the contemporary point of view the chief playwright of the Globe and the chief playwright of the Red Bull belonged to a different and slightly lower classification than the learned gentlemen who did most of their best work for the private theatres.

The truth of the matter was that most of the writers of the period were too close to Shakespeare to recognize his greatness, in the same way that an object held too close to the eyes cannot be seen clearly. Michael Drayton could find no higher praise for his fellow writer from Warwickshire than to say he had "as smooth a comic vein" and "as strong conception . . . as any one that trafficked with the stage." An Oxford man named Thomas Freeman wrote an enthusiastic epigram on "Master W. Shakespeare" and praised the "wit" of his plays, but his chief proof of Shakespeare's

versatility seemed to consist of the fact that his Venus was lustful and his Lucrece was chaste. Heywood included Shakespeare's name in a rhymed account of the nicknames of all the playwrights he had known, from Kit Marlowe and Tom Kyd to Jack Fletcher and Frank Beaumont. His remark on Shakespeare's nickname is charming.

Mellifluous Shakespeare, whose enchanting quill
Commanded mirth and passion, was but Will.

But the lines themselves are no more flattering than those he wrote on Jonson or Beaumont. Another Oxford student ranked Shakespeare with Chaucer and Spenser but included "rare Beaumont" as one entitled to equal honor.

There is only one piece of contemporary evidence remaining to show that any man of the Elizabethan or Jacobean age realized that a giant was walking among them, and that is the wonderful poem that Jonson wrote on Shakespeare for the First Folio. For once Jonson was able to suppress his own private theories and realize of Shakespeare:

He was not of an age, but for all time.

As a result, Jonson's magnificent lines still seem intelligent today, while the opinion of Shakespeare expressed by most of his contemporaries seems merely fantastic.

This achievement is all the more

remarkable because, in general, Jonson followed the doctrine that was held by all the learned men of his period and believed that anything the penny public loved was automatically worthless. Although Jonson and Chapman and Beaumont all wrote plays that were successful with the general public, they kept repeating in print that a really good piece of writing could attract the attention only of a chosen and initiated few. Shakespeare's plays consistently attracted enormous and enthusiastic audiences, so it seemed clear to the literary theorists of the period that there must be something wrong with them.

One of the few publishers who succeeded in getting a play of Shakespeare's into print during the reign of James followed this literary fashion and praised the play for not having been applauded by the worthless multitude. The play was *Troilus and Cressida,* which had been entered in the Stationers' Register in the previous reign as having been "acted by the Lord Chamberlain's men," but had not been published then. The editor who finally printed it in 1609 believed, rightly or wrongly, that it had never been acted, and he congratulated his readers on getting a play of unsullied purity. It had "never been staled with the stage, never clapper-clawed with the palms of the vulgar," and he bade his readers thank fortune that it had never "been sullied with the smoky breath of the multitude." This was the kind of statement that would have made the actors of the King's company smile, since they were all actively engaged in bringing as many members of the "multitude" as possible into the Globe.

The great difference between Shakespeare's point of view toward his audiences and that of writers like Jonson or Webster or Fletcher came from the fact that Shakespeare was not a writer only. He was an actor also, in constant touch with the public and closely interlocked with the economic life of his company. Shakespeare worked in a healthy, practical atmosphere in which there was little emphasis on theories and much on results. Moreover, he had no interest in any private, personal fame of his own, and while Chapman and Fletcher and Jonson and even Heywood saw their plays into print for the public to admire, Shakespeare did not. His plays belonged to his company and Shakespeare was a working member of that company, subordinating his own personal prestige to the welfare of the group as a whole.

In 1608 the group that was fortunate enough to have Shakespeare as a member took over another theatre in joint ownership. The system they had inaugurated with the Globe had worked so harmoniously for the past nine years that when the Blackfriars theatre fell empty, the men of the King's company became its joint operators.

Richard Burbage owned the Blackfriars, and Henry Evans had leased it from him in 1600 for forty pounds a year. The boys' company that Evans had installed in the theatre had been prosperous from the first, but from the first there had been trouble also. The Blackfriars theatre opened to the accompaniment of a lawsuit that had forced Evans to leave town for a time, and since then the company had plunged from crisis to crisis. In 1605 the boys of the Blackfriars presented a comedy by Jonson, Chapman, and Marston that spoke slightingly of the King's Scottish knights, and all three of its distinguished authors went to prison. The next year the Blackfriars boys put on a play of John Day's called *The Isle of Gulls* and again "sundry were committed to Bridewell." Henry Evans spoke with a resigned melancholy of what happened when the playhouse was closed, "some of the boys being committed to prison by order of his Highness, and . . . a continual rent of £40 to be paid." In 1608 the Blackfriars boys presented a play by George Chapman in which the Queen of France not only appeared on the stage but gave another lady a box on the ear. The alert French ambassador lodged a protest and succeeded in having three members of the company imprisoned, although to his regret "the principal person, the author, escaped." This final disaster proved to be too much for the company. It was dissolved, leaving a trail of lawsuits in its wake, and by August, Richard Burbage was able to buy back the lease.

Burbage saw no reason to rent his theatre to another boys' company, which would be operating in direct competition with the Globe. Instead, to use Cuthbert Burbage's words, "it was considered that house would be as fit for ourselves, and so purchased the lease remaining from Evans with our money, and placed men players, which were Heminges, Condell, Shakespeare, etc."

The actors came into the syndicate on shares, as they had with the Globe, except that the rent was paid to Richard Burbage instead of to Sir Nicholas Brend. The seven shares were divided equally between Richard Burbage, Cuthbert Burbage, William Shakespeare, John Heminges, Henry Condell, William Sly, and an outsider named Thomas Evans who was evidently some relation of Henry Evans and had to be included before Henry would surrender the lease. Each of them was responsible for one seventh of the annual rent of forty pounds, and Richard Burbage drew up a lease with each of the six men on the 9th of August, 1608.

The new syndicate was not able to open the Blackfriars theatre immediately, since it was in "decay for want of reparations" and evidently had to be extensively repaired after it was taken over. Moreover, there was a heavy visitation of the plague that winter, and even the Globe apparently had to be closed. The King's Men were on tour as late as October, and were again on tour the following spring as early as May, and for both that year and the next the King paid

John Heminges for the private practice of the company, "being restrained from public playing within the city of London in the time of infection." The exact date when the Blackfriars theatre was opened is unknown, but it does not seem likely that Shakespeare acted in it for more than a year or two before his retirement.

The residents of Blackfriars had evidently grown resigned to having a theatre in their midst, and they did not present a petition on the subject until 1618. Even then, it was merely the popularity of the theatre to which they objected. The coaches of the theatregoers clogged Ludgate Hill, blocked the entrances to residences, and broke down the stalls of the tradespeople; and the petition asked the Star Chamber to force all future theatregoers to come by foot or by the water stairs. The petition does not necessarily imply that all the audiences were aristocratic, for it makes a special point of stating that many of the coaches were "hackney coaches bringing people of all sorts."

The aristocratic nature of the Blackfriars theatre under the King's Men had been overestimated, for there is no evidence that they altered the kind of plays they had been showing at the Globe in order to conform to a new audience. The King's Men went on producing the kind of plays that had already pleased the public and the Court at the Globe and at Whitehall, and although they were able to charge higher prices at their new winter theatre, there is no evidence that they made any other changes in their general policy. The three plays that Beaumont and Fletcher wrote for them in collaboration have been described as being characteristic of a more aristocratic policy at the Blackfriars, but one of the most successful of these plays, *Philaster or Love Lies A-Bleeding,* was advertised when it was put into print as having been "acted at the Globe."

It has frequently been stated that the more select atmosphere of the Blackfriars influenced Shakespeare's last group of plays: *Cymbeline, The Winter's Tale,* and *The Tempest.* But these were not at all the kind of plays that Henry Evans had been presenting at the Blackfriars before he lost the theatre. If anything, Shakespeare's plays are much closer, from the point of view of stagecraft, to the series of plays that the rivals of the King's Men were presenting at the Red Bull. The elaborate, masquelike staging that was required for Jove's eagle in *Cymbeline* and the pastoral dances in *The Winter's Tale* are much closer to similar devices in Heywood's current series of plays than they are to anything in the productions of the children's companies.

The plot devices in Shakespeare's last group of plays are on the whole old-fashioned. He used the device of the headless corpse in *Cymbeline,* which he had once used so lavishly in *Henry VI,* and he also used the motif of the girl disguised as a page that had appeared in so many of his early comedies. In *The Winter's*

Tale he was using the plot of a popular novel that Robert Greene had written in the eighties and that probably caught his eye in a reprint of 1608. *The Winter's Tale* leaps over seas and years with such a complete disregard for the classical tradition of the unities that it might almost have inspired the stern condemnation of the English drama that George Whetstone had voiced thirty years earlier. "The Englishman . . . is most vain, indiscreet, and out of order; he first grounds his work on impossibilities; then in three hours runs he through the world, marries, gets children, makes children men."

A Dr. Forman saw both *Cymbeline* and *The Winter's Tale* produced at the Globe, and with the usual efficiency of the period he was able to find a moral in *The Winter's Tale:* "Beware of trusting feigned beggars." This seems to be the only thought that Dr. Forman was able to derive from the delightful Autolycus, and it is all too probable that he never noticed the golden poetry in which the play is written. Dr. Forman also saw a production of *Macbeth,* and jotted down a long synopsis of the plot very much as young John Manningham had once jotted down the plot of *Twelfth Night.* Forman was impressed by the sleepwalking scene and the blood on Lady Macbeth's hands, but in his uninspired prose the dismal nature of most of Shakespeare's sources for his plots becomes apparent. The question of how any man could take these limp and unin-

teresting tales, keep most of the story intact, and yet transmute the whole thing into enduring art, is one that can be explained only on the basis of alchemy. William Shakespeare had some formula for white magic that could take any kind of dross and turn it into gold.

It is generally believed that *The Tempest* was the last play Shakespeare wrote before he retired from the stage. It can be given a tentative date of 1610, because the year before there had been a spectacular shipwreck in the Bermudas and a shipload of Englishmen was obliged to spend ten months on "that dreadful coast" which was "supposed to be enchanted and inhabited with witches." Accounts of the shipwreck could be obtained in London the following year and apparently gave Shakespeare a few details for his own enchanted island. The play was certainly written by 1611, since it was chosen to open the Christmas season at Whitehall in the Banqueting Hall, and it does not seem improbable that this was the last play Shakespeare wrote while he was still an actor on the London stage.

For his last play Shakespeare returned to a device he had not used since *The Comedy of Errors;* he observed the strict dramatic unities, for all the action takes place on a single island in a single afternoon. When he wrote his first comedy, Shakespeare was an ambitious young man trying to do the right thing by imitating Plautus; when he wrote his last comedy, he was the complete master of every detail of his craft and only adopted the revered theory of the unities because for once it happened to suit his purpose.

Shakespeare also used some of the most intricate stagecraft he had demanded of his company since the early days of the history plays, and gave the stage crew this kind of direction to translate into action: "Enter Ariel like a harpy; claps his wings upon the table; and, with a quaint device, the banquet vanishes." Shakespeare was not asking anything unreasonable of the King's Men, for at about the same time Heywood was expecting the Queen's Men to show on stage the death of Hercules from a thunderbolt hurled by Jove and his soul descending as a star into the firmament. What was abnormal, or rather supernatural, about the production of *The Tempest* was the magic of the lines. The greatest of England's poets had never written more beautiful poetry.

It is a temptation to see Shakespeare himself in his fellow magician, Prospero, and it has even been suggested that when Prospero throws away his magic wand and returns to Italy, it is an image of the playwright leaving the theatre and returning to Stratford. It is doubtful, however, that anything so pretentious would have occurred to Shakespeare in connection with himself, especially since he was an objective artist and not in the habit of suddenly inserting pieces of autobiography into his plays.

Shakespeare had good reason to retire. He had been an actor for twenty years, and it was a profession that called for strenuous and unremitting physical activity, with no rest even in the summer or at Christmas. He had also spent twenty years of intense mental activity, creating the greatest series of plays and the most wonderful procession of people that one man ever fathered in the history of the world. If any single consideration made him decide to leave the theatre, it may very well have been sheer weariness. He had worked long enough and hard enough and he was entitled to a rest.

�֎ *Chapter* **13**

There had been several changes in the Shakespeare family in Stratford during Shakespeare's last years on the London stage, and one of the most important had been the marriage of his elder daughter Susanna.

On the 5th of June, 1607, Susanna married a prominent Puritan physician, Dr. John Hall. The marriage was socially satisfactory, for Dr. Hall was an Oxford graduate and a member of the local gentry. He had a large and fashionable practice in the neighborhood of Warwick and eventually numbered the Earl of Northampton, more than forty miles away in the next county, as one of his patients. In the following reign he was offered a knighthood, which he refused, and he left a medical diary in Latin which a Warwick surgeon considered sufficiently valuable to expand in English and print.

A Puritan like Dr. Hall did not normally have so large a practice in the upper classes, but, as a fellow doctor remarked, he was "in great fame for his skill both far and near . . . Such who spare not for cost, and they who have more than ordinary understanding—nay, such as hated him for his religion often made use of him." Susanna was twenty-four when she married her distinguished Puritan husband, and Dr. Hall was eight years older.

It is likely that Susanna was not so ardent a Puritan as her husband. When she was living as a widow at New Place during the Civil War, her house was chosen as the one in which to lodge the Queen. On the other hand, her epitaph says that she was "wise to salvation," and in 1649 that approving phrase in Stratford would normally have been used of a Puritan. She was, in any case, not an unduly grave and rigid member of the sect, for the epitaph calls her "witty above her sex" and adds:

Something of Shakespeare was in that.

If Susanna had something of her father in her, Dr. Hall was a fortunate man.

The married couple went to live at Hall's Croft, a house near the parish church and within easy walking distance of New Place. A daughter was born the following year and on the 21st of February was christened Elizabeth. There were no more children.

The next event in the Shakespeare household was a sad one. Little Elizabeth Hall was six months old when her great-grandmother died. Mary Shakespeare, wife of John, had outlived her husband and four of her sons and daughters, and before she died she had seen the Shakespeare family become one of consequence in the district. There had been many changes since Mary Arden married the son of a tenant farmer and bore him the first of his children on Henley Street.

It can be assumed that William Shakespeare returned to Stratford for his mother's burial, which took place on the 9th of September, 1608, since he was still in Stratford the following month. On the middle Sunday in October he stood in the parish church as godfather to a child named William Walker. The Walkers were a prominent family in Stratford, and Henry Walker had just finished a term as High Bailiff of Stratford when he asked Shakespeare to serve as godfather to his son.

Earlier in this same year of 1608 another Stratford child was christened William, but little William Greene had the further distinction that his family was actually living in New Place. He was the son of Thomas and Letitia Greene, who had been making their residence in Shakespeare's house, and he already had a four-year-old sister who had been named Anne. The father and mother of Anne and William must have been on excellent terms with Anne Shakespeare, since it was evidently her household they were sharing.*

Thomas Greene was a prosperous local lawyer who had been educated at the Middle Temple in London, where John Marston and his father had gone surety for him. He came to Stratford in 1601 and stayed for fifteen years; and although he ended as a prominent barrister in London, he always spoke affectionately of the "golden days" he had spent in the service of the men of Stratford.

Thomas Greene was living at New Place the year of Susanna's marriage, although he had bought a home of his own called St. Mary's House, just beyond Hall's Croft. Two years later he began negotiating for occupancy with the current tenant, one George Browne, and finally decided to let Browne stay another year and sow his garden. Greene noted the arrangement in his diary in his thin scrawl, making the entry on Sept. 9, 1609: "Seeing I could get no carriage to help me here with timber, I was content

to permit it without contradiction; and that rather, because I perceived I might stay another year at New Place."

Greene's diary suggests the probable time of Shakespeare's retirement. Greene asked Browne to have the house vacant by the 25th of March, 1610, so that he could use the timber he mentions in the extensive alterations he was planning, and he hoped to move into his new house by September 29. This would indicate that he expected to leave New Place by that date, and the most natural reason for Greene's planning to leave was that the master of New Place was coming home to live.

During the next six years, Greene spent the enormous sum of four hundred pounds on his new residence, converting it into what he himself called a "gentlemanlike" home, but it could never have had the social connotations that were attached to New Place.

It is not possible to reconstruct the appearance of Shakespeare's home, for it was torn down at the beginning of the eighteenth century and rebuilt in another style. But it is known from the statements on the deeds and the original foundations that the house had a sixty-foot frontage, ten fireplaces, and a bay window on the side facing the garden. A boy who had played in the original house in his youth remembered, when he was an old man in the next century, that there had been a brick wall separating New Place from the

---

* Thomas Greene speaks of Shakespeare as "my cousin Shakespeare." But no relationship has been traced between them, and since Greene also speaks of "my cousin Graves" and "my cousin Baker" he may have been using the word only as a term of affection.—Author's Note

street, with a grassed court between the wall and the house, and that the building itself was fronted with brick and had plain leaded windows. The property had two barns on the side that fronted Chapel Lane, and two orchards. The original garden that dated from Sir Hugh Clopton's day was still in existence and must have been a fine one. Fifteen years after Shakespeare's death, Sir Thomas Temple was asking for shoots from one of its vines. The house was large enough to be used for a Queen, but there is only one record of the hospitality of New Place during Shakespeare's lifetime. This is an entry in the Chamberlain's accounts for 1614, "for one quart of sack and one quart of claret given to a preacher at the New Place." It has been said this was a Puritan preacher, as there were many such traveling around Warwickshire. But it may equally well have been one of those who delivered an annual lecture before the Stratford Corporation, through an endowment. There were three such endowments by 1614, and the same year John Combe died and left provision in his will for a fourth.

William Shakespeare took very little interest in the affairs of the town, in spite of the fact that he was now a permanent resident of Stratford. The only time he concerned himself in town affairs seems to have been in 1611, when a group of local householders pledged themselves to help finance a bill for improvement of the high-ways that was coming up in Parliament. The seventy-two names on the subscription list include all the major householders of Stratford, from Dr. John Hall at Hall's Croft to Thomas Greene at St. Mary's House, and only William Shakespeare of New Place does not appear on the list. His name is added by itself on the right-hand margin, evidently as an afterthought.

It may be that Shakespeare was out of town when the subscription list was made up and asked to be included after he returned, but his frequent trips to London do not quite explain his lack of interest in the welfare of Stratford. His name is so conspicuously lacking from the Stratford records that it can only be concluded he felt no interest in the problems that were so important to fellow townsmen like Thomas Greene and Henry Walker. These men were his friends, but their interests were not his.

Before his retirement, Shakespeare's name appears twice in the Stratford records, in each case because he was bringing action for the recovery of debts. In 1604 he sued an apothecary named Philip Rogers who had run up a debt of over thirty-five shillings on some purchases of malt, with William Tetherton acting as his attorney. In 1608 he sued a member of the gentry named William Addenbrooke over a debt of six pounds. This case went to a jury, with Henry Walker presiding at the trial and Thomas Greene acting as town clerk, and Shakespeare was awarded damages.

This is an abnormally low number of lawsuits for a Stratford resident, since there was no machinery for the monthly or quarterly collection of bills, and a suit in the Stratford Court of Record had come to be regarded as a normal way to collect a debt.

Shakespeare was a careful man where money was concerned. He was not in the least like Ben Jonson, who was "careless either to gain or keep," and he went to some expense to hedge his investments in after he had made them. In 1611 he bought the twenty more acres of pasture land from the Combes, and had a special legal document drawn in Trinity Term to confirm his title to the acreage he had bought from the Combes nine years earlier, so that there could be no possible question of his full legal ownership of the land.

The same sense of caution made him join with some of the other owners of the lease on the tithes to present a bill of complaint to the Lord Chancellor. An annual fee to Henry Barker was being paid by forty-two people, of whom Shakespeare was one, and if any of them failed to contribute his share, Barker could theoretically foreclose on the whole property. The suit was really a friendly one to get the apportionment on a businesslike basis, and its chief target was Shakespeare's good friend William Combe, who owned the lease on the other half of Shakespeare's special group of tithes. Shakespeare was joined in the suit by Richard Lane, who had the largest single holding, and by Thomas Greene, who had a reversionary interest in Combe's part of the tithes. William Combe answered the bill of complaint by saying he was already paying five pounds a year to Barker but was willing to increase his contribution slightly, and he joined Shakespeare and the two others in requesting the court to make a fairer distribution of costs among the holders of the tithes.

The suit was a friendly one and Shakespeare remained on good terms with the Combes. He knew three generations of the family, starting with old William Combe, who had become High Sheriff before he died. It was William and his nephew, John Combe, who sold Shakespeare the acreage in 1602, and when John Combe died twelve years later, he remembered Shakespeare with a substantial bequest in his will. In turn, Shakespeare remembered Thomas Combe, John's nephew, in his own will. He must have known him very well, for he left Thomas Combe his sword, an intimate piece of personal property that would have gone to Shakespeare's own son if he had lived.

Most of Shakespeare's friends seem to have been among the landed gentry, like the two Nashe brothers who witnessed the Combe sale. Shakespeare left memorial rings to both of them in his will; and the wealthier of the two, Anthony Nashe, had a son Thomas who eventually married Shakespeare's granddaughter. Another county friend was Thomas Russell, Esq., a distinguished man in the district whom Shakespeare made one of the overseers of his will.

In spite of his retirement to Stratford, Shakespeare was a frequent visitor in London. He had business and personal ties in the city that he could hardly have severed even if he had wished to.

In Easter Term of 1612, Shakespeare was called to London on a rather unhappy business—a family quarrel that had turned into a lawsuit and in which he was one of the chief witnesses. The marriage of Mary Mountjoy and Stephen Belott had encountered difficulties, and most of them originated in Mary's peculiar father. Gentle Mrs. Mountjoy had died two years after Shakespeare arranged her daughter's marriage, and after she was buried in St. Olave's church, her husband's relations with his son-in-law became increasingly strained. Christopher Mountjoy refused to pay the marriage portion that he had promised, announced publicly he would leave his daughter nothing in his will, and would not even have his son-in-law "at his table." Finally Belott brought suit in the Court of Requests to force him to pay the marriage portion, and a long line of witnesses testified to such vital matters as whether Mountjoy had given Belott money to go to the barber when he was his apprentice and who had paid for the young man's stockings during the same period.

"William Shakespeare of Stratford-upon-Avon in the county of Warwick, gentleman," was given a list of only five questions to answer and was called only once. He testified he had known both men for about ten years, that Stephen Belott had been a good and faithful apprentice, that Mrs. Mountjoy had asked him to arrange the marriage, and that there had been many conferences about it. He said that Stephen had been living in Mountjoy's house at the time, but he did not recall the exact terms of the marriage settlement and he knew nothing of what Mountjoy may have promised Stephen in his will.

At Trinity Term a new set of questions was presented, and finally the court decided the case was not in its jurisdiction and referred it to the French Huguenot church in London of which both men were members. Mountjoy was ordered to pay his son-in-law twenty nobles and refused. He was twice summoned by the church elders and failed to put in an appearance, and eventually he was suspended with a request that the members of the church pray for his soul. The suspension had nothing to do with Belott's lawsuit but was caused by the fact that Mountjoy had a mistress and the French Huguenot church would not tolerate what it called *"ces scandales."* As for Stephen Belott, whom Shakespeare had described as "very good and industrious," his daughters married well and he eventually came into an inheritance from a brother who had been a schoolmaster in Holland.

It is possible that Shakespeare was in London some of the time during the winter following the trial, for the Princess Elizabeth was being married and the King's Men were involved in a heavy schedule of plays as their part in the celebration. The treasurer paid John Heminges the very large sum of £153 6s. 8d. for the plays that were produced during the season, and these included more plays by William Shakespeare than by any other writer. The Revels office had been shifted from Clerkenwell to Blackfriars, and Sir Edmund Tilney had been succeeded by a relative by marriage, Sir George Buck; but there were no changes otherwise, and the plays were selected and rehearsed as carefully as ever.

The King's Men produced a variety of Shakespeare's plays, ranging from *Othello* to *The Winter's Tale* and from *The Tempest* to *Much Ado About Nothing*. They gave *Julius Caesar,* and two plays called *Hotspur* and *Sir John Falstaff* which must be the two parts of *Henry IV*. They also gave a play called *Benedict and Beatrice,* which was evidently a repeat performance of *Much Ado About Nothing*.

Outside of Shakespeare's plays, the King's Men presented Jonson's excellent comedy, *The Alchemist,* which they had first produced in 1611 with Richard Burbage and John Heminges playing the leads. They also gave several popular plays like *The Merry Devil of Edmonton,* whose authorship is now unknown. But most strongly represented, next to Shakespeare, was that successful new team of writers, Francis Beaumont and John Fletcher.

The King's Men presented during the wedding festivities all three of the plays that Beaumont and Fletcher had written for them: *Philaster, The Maid's Tragedy,* and *A King and No King.* The new playwrights worked very well together, for they had a gift for taking a subject like sadism or incest and being able to turn it by a last-minute twist into a comedy, clothing the story in such charming language and such a variety of incidents that the spectator could forgive the artificiality of the situations and a certain lack of reality in the characterizations. The team had also written for the children's companies, but they did their best work for the King's Men, and it was a well-deserved compliment when John Heminges' grandson was named Beaumont.

Francis Beaumont was still writing at the time of the Princess Elizabeth's wedding, for he wrote the masque that was presented by the Inner Temple and Gray's Inn. It was "fraught with art, state, and delights," and when he retired to the country at about this time, having made a very correct marriage, he took with him a resplendent reputation as a writer. John Fletcher went on writing plays for many years to follow, collaborating with various writers like Massinger and Field and Rowley, but he and Beaumont had been such close riends and worked so successfully together that their names became nextricably associated with each other. When an edition of the plays was published in 1647, it came out as the joint work of Beaumont and Fletcher, in spite of the fact that Beaumont had a hand in very few of them, on the publisher's sentimental plea that since they were "never parted while they lived, I conceived it not equitable to separate their ashes." John Fletcher was not even credited with the sole authorship of *The Faithful Shepherdess* in his own lifetime, although it was a play to which Beaumont had contributed nothing but some admiring verses in the front; and very few of the plays in the folio edition can be safely attributed to both of them except the three plays that the King's Men produced during the celebrations for the Princess Elizabeth's wedding.

The King's only daughter was marrying Frederic, Elector Palatine of Bohemia, a sober, polite young Calvinist of the same age as herself. The marriage had been scheduled for the previous November, but Elizabeth's adored brother, Prince Henry, had been taken ill. He had a game of tennis one Saturday with a member of Frederic's entourage, and tennis was a game the Prince took much too seriously. He played in his shirt and contracted a chill, and the next day he began to shiver violently. From then on followed the horrible tragicomedy of a royal death, with the terrified physicians trying everything from cupping

glasses to a slit cock. The dying Prince endured their efforts patiently and said his prayers "quietly by himself," since he had no privacy otherwise, until he finally lapsed into a delirium and died on the 6th of November. The last conscious words he spoke were, "Where is my dear sister?" But they would not let her come to him, and she had gone without food for two days when they finally brought her word of her brother's death. The two of them had been so close to each other that he had secretly promised to go part of the way with her to her new home.

Elizabeth's wedding was finally held in February, on St. Valentine's Day. It was a fairy tale wedding, with the princess clad in white with a gold crown on her head and all her attendants glittering with jewels like the Milky Way, but the chief figure could have had very little satisfaction from any of it.

The next Court event that followed Elizabeth's wedding in February was the anniversary of the King's accession day on March 24. A large tournament was always held on this occasion, but the tournament of 1613 has a special interest since William Shakespeare made a contribution to it.

It had been the custom for about a century for the knights who took part in the tournaments to carry paper shields called *impresa,* which were collected afterward and hung on permanent display in a room in Whitehall. Each knight was supposed to have on his shield a picture and a motto that united to hint at his identity or his state of mind, and the guessing of these little courtly riddles was part of the fun of going to a tournament. A knight who had fallen in love could show Venus in a cloud, and one who was having difficulties at Court could show a man climbing a mountain and being pushed back by contrary winds. One knight who could think of no device at all appeared with a blank shield, except at the base there was a painter's pencil, a little shell of colors, and the motto: "Make of me what you will."

A great deal of thought and attention was lavished on these shields, and each knight tried to be more clever than his fellows. One of those who was especially anxious to distinguish himself in 1613 was Francis Manners, the new Earl of Rutland. He spent twenty-four shillings for gilt stirrups, twenty-four pounds for plumes and feathers, and four pounds, eight shillings in payment to William Shakespeare and Richard Burbage for designing a shield for him.

Shakespeare invented the motto for the Earl of Rutland's shield and Richard Burbage painted the design that went with it. Apart from his great gifts as an actor, Burbage evidently had a contemporary reputation as a painter, and for a long time a portrait he made of a woman hung in a gilt frame in Dulwich College. Each man was paid in gold, and the amount was noted in the accounts of the Earl of Rutland's steward.

A shield devised by two such talents should have made a profound impression on the spectators at the tournament, but unfortunately it did not. The only member of the audience who left a record of the event says that none of the emblems was a success except the two carried by the Earl of Pembroke and his brother, and that some of the rest were so confused "that their meaning is not yet understood." Moreover, it rained, and the Earl of Rutland's expensive plumes were very limp and wet before the tournament was over.

During this same month of March 1613 Shakespeare made another of his real-estate investments, but, for the first time, not in Stratford but in London. Shakespeare bought a house and yard in Blackfriars that stood within six hundred feet of his company's theatre. He paid £140 for it to a musician named Henry Walker, which was forty pounds more than Walker himself had paid for it at the beginning of the reign. Values were rising in a residential district as fashionable as Blackfriars, and Shakespeare could expect a good income from the property, which he had not bought for his own use but as an investment. He rented it to John Robinson, who was evidently the man of the same name who had signed the petition that had once kept James Burbage out of Blackfriars; but times had changed and Robinson was resigned to living next door to a playhouse.

The purchase of the Blackfriars

property was perhaps the most complicated of Shakespeare's many complicated purchases. He paid for it in part by taking out a £60 mortgage, and both the purchase and the mortgage involved not only Shakespeare but also three trustees whom he had taken into the transaction with him. One of these trustees, almost inevitably, was John Heminges. The second was John Jackson, another London friend, who was probably the man of the same name to whom Thomas Pope willed a diamond ring. The third was William Johnson, vintner, who is chiefly interesting because he was William Johnson of the Mermaid Tavern. This is Shakespeare's only documentary connection with the famous tavern, which incidentally seems to have been a quiet and well-run house.

The reason Shakespeare went to the complication of taking three trustees into the purchase with him was so that the property could never be claimed by Anne Shakespeare under her dower rights as his wife. Such a precaution would not have been necessary in Stratford, where there was no provision for a wife's inheritance of her husband's property, but in London it had "been observed for a custom . . . that when any citizen of London dieth, his wife shall have the third part of his goods." When Shakespeare died, a third share in the Blackfriars property would normally have gone to his wife; instead, he arranged it so that it

went into the hands of the three trustees who owned the property in joint tenancy with him; and after his death they handed it over to two other trustees, Thomas Greene's brother John and a Stratford man named Matthew Morris, so that it could be held in entail by Shakespeare's eldest daughter Susanna.

As Shakespeare's will shows, he was determined to leave all his property intact to a single male heir, and he did not want the land he had protected so carefully to be dissolved into alien hands. It was not improbable that his widow would marry again after he died; most widows of the period did, especially when they owned property, and men as unlike as Richard Field and Philip Henslowe got their business start in this fashion. In this case, whatever Anne Shakespeare had inherited as dower right might conceivably have been claimed by her new husband, and it was evidently to avoid any such complication that Shakespeare chose three trustees to go into the Blackfriars purchase with him, as a means of protecting the estate.

Shakespeare had an excellent example of the difficulties that could occur when a widow inherited property and then remarried in the case of his friend, Augustine Phillips. When Phillips died at his country home in Mortlake in 1605, Anne Phillips inherited his shares in the Globe, which had unfortunately been assigned to the actors in such a way that they could be willed like ordinary property, and therefore could be, in Cuthbert Burbage's bitter phrase, "dissolved to strangers." Phillips' widow married a Mortlake man name John Witter who "riotously spent, wasted, and consumed" his wife's property and then refused to support either her or the children. When Anne Phillips died, it was not her husband who paid for the burial; it was John Heminges. But John Witter sued Heminges on the Globe shares, which he claimed were his. Witter said he owned "a sixth part of the said galleries, ground, and gardens of the Globe playhouse," and it was not until 1620, after both Heminges and Condell had been involved in a long and expensive litigation, that the courts vindicated them completely and ordered Witter to refrain from any further suits. The whole trouble started when Anne Phillips inherited her husband's property and then remarried; and John Heminges would have been in full sympathy with Shakespeare's desire to avoid future complications when he acted as one of his three trustees in the Blackfriars purchase.

Three months after the Blackfriars transaction, the King's Men presented at the Globe what was evidently their most elaborate production of the year. It was a new play by William Shakespeare that was given the production title of *All Is True* but which later appeared in the First Folio as *Henry VIII.** The play is not one of Shakespeare's best, since it was chiefly a pageant designed to glorify the birth of Queen Elizabeth and gave him very little room for characterization. But there was a great deal of room for pageantry, and the King's Men made the most of it.

A contemporary spectator reports that the play was "set forth with many extraordinary circumstances of pomp and majesty, even to the matting of the stage; the knights of the Order, with their Georges and Garters, the guards with their embroidered coats, and the like." Rushes were normally used on the stage to protect the actors' costumes, since strips of matting were very expensive, but the King's Men were evidently determined to have the best of everything for Shakespeare's new play. Since the play was realistically costumed,

* At the end of the eighteenth century it was suggested that this play was a collaboration. By that time a theory had arisen that Shakespeare was incapable of writing a bad line, and since the play is uneven, Dr. Farmer suggested that Ben Jonson wrote part of it. In the nineteenth century, James Spedding acted on a chance suggestion from Tennyson and offered John Fletcher as the collaborator instead, and this theory became so popular it subsequently hardened into accepted fact. What Spedding offered as internal evidence of his position has been demolished by recent investigations, and there was never any external evidence in support of the idea of Fletcher's collaboration. John Heminges and Henry Condell brought out the First Folio while Fletcher was still alive, and *Henry VIII* appears in the First Folio as the work of William Shakespeare.—AUTHOR'S NOTE

he expenses that were assumed in his department must have been enormous. A single scene like the coronation of Anne Boleyn had an array of earls, dukes, bishops, judges, and so on, each one clothed in a replica of his real robe of office that was correct down to the last coronet and the last insigne.

The play was ready for showing on the 29th of June, 1613. The last play that had been shown at the Globe had been a comedy, and the actor who entered as the Prologue to Shakespeare's new play pointed out that the Globe audience, those "first and happiest hearers," must now prepare to listen to graver and more aristocratic events. The actor who played the Epilogue was prepared to ask for the special applause of the women, but on that June afternoon the play never got as far as the Epilogue.

During the first act there was an elaborate dance at Cardinal Wolsey's house in which Henry VIII first meets Anne Boleyn, and at the King's entrance the stage directions call for hautboys. These instruments had a rather shrill and reedy sound, and to give greater impressiveness, a theatre company sometimes used a combination of trumpets and cannon fire instead. Cannons had been fired from the thatched roofs of the theatres for years and so far nothing had happened, but on the 29th of June the law of averages caught up with the Globe. The thatch on the south side ignited, smoldered, and then blew into a flame, and in less than two hours the whole structure had burned to the ground. It was the most spectacular fire London had known since the burning of St. Paul's steeple, and two ballads on the great event were entered in the Stationers' Register the next day. No one was hurt, in spite of the fact that there were only two narrow doors to take care of what must have been a capacity crowd, and the absence of casualties speaks well for the orderly nature of the Globe audience.

The men who owned the Globe were the wealthiest group of actors in London, and by the following spring they were able to have it "new builded in a far fairer manner than before." John Heminges was evidently responsible for the details of the financing and he sent each member a preliminary request for money toward the rebuilding, which he raised to a higher sum when the cost of the new structure became apparent. Shakespeare owned a fourteenth interest in the Globe at the time, which would have brought his share of the expense to about a hundred pounds.

When Shakespeare died in 1616, he must have disposed of his holdings in both the Globe and the Blackfriars theatre, since they are not mentioned in his will. It may be that he disposed of his Globe holdings after the theatre was burned because he did not wish to reinvest in a new building. But the Globe was an excellent income property and a safe way to invest money, and it is more likely that Shakespeare disposed of his shares before he died because he did not wish to repeat Phillips' mistake of allowing theatre shares to be inherited by outsiders. As an actor, he knew how difficult it was to operate a theatre when outsiders could assume part of the control, and his friend John Heminges was involved in still another court suit at about this time on this same subject. When William Sly died, his share had gone back to the company since he had no wife and had been reassigned to a brilliant young actor, William Ostler. Ostler died in 1614 and his share went to his wife Thomasina, who also happened to be John Heminges' daughter. Heminges withheld the share and his daughter twice brought suit against him. Thomasina was rather quick to turn to the law for redress, and during the same period she brought suit against Sir Walter Raleigh's son for insulting her, but she seems to have had a legitimate grievance against her father. John Heminges was normally a man of the utmost probity in his business dealings, but he evidently felt that the welfare of the theatre and the continued smoothness of its operation were more important than his daughter's legal rights. The inheritance of theatre shares by outsiders had proved to be a disastrous policy from the first, and Shakespeare was probably wise to dispose of his holdings in both theatres before he died.

During the same month of June in which the Globe theatre burned, there was a flurry of excitement in Stratford in which the central figure was Shakespeare's elder daughter, Susanna Hall. There was a young man named John Lane, who belonged to a well-to-do family in town and whose sister had married a brother of Thomas Greene, and this John Lane accused Susanna Hall not only of having "the running of the reins" in Dr. Hall's household but of carrying on an affair with Rafe Smith at the house of John Palmer. Rafe Smith was a haberdasher in his thirties, who was a nephew of Hamnet Sadler's and was living at the time with his mother on Sheep Street.

The Halls did not ignore young Lane's piece of slander. They immediately filed suit against him in the Consistory Court of Worcester and, when the defendant failed to put in an appearance, the Halls won the verdict. John Lane was excommunicated, a penalty which was not as serious as it sounds; but it would have involved Lane in some personal and business inconvenience until he succeeded in getting himself reinstated and probably taught him to hold his tongue thereafter. Susanna Hall was thirty at the time, with a five-year-old daughter, and she was not going to have her reputation in the community brought into question.

The chief quality that seems to

characterize the Shakespeares in Stratford is a careful regard for their dignity and a quick eye for their rights. This was true of John Shakespeare, and it seems to have been equally true of his son and his son's daughter. Susanna Hall guarded the dignity of her name in the same spirit in which her father guarded his real-estate investments. William Shakespeare was determined to leave nothing to chance and to set a double defense about the property that was destined for Susanna and her still hoped-for son.

In 1615 Shakespeare participated in a Chancery suit to protect the property he had bought two years earlier in Blackfriars. The land he owned had been held first by the Church and then by the Crown and then by a variety of private owners, and when Shakespeare made his purchase, the documents that recorded the titles in that particular section had been in the possession of Ann Bacon. When she died, Shakespeare joined the property owners of the district in a friendly suit against Matthew Bacon, her son, to produce the old documents that established their legal rights to their own property, and Matthew Bacon told the court he was quite willing to surrender the documents to anyone the court wished to name. The Blackfriars district was a fashionable one and the petition to the court starts with a baronet and works down through several esquires before it comes to "William Shakespeare, gent."

At about this same time, Shakespeare was obliged to take action to protect another of his investments—the tithes. He had already gone to law to have a revision made in the annual payments, but now the very source of the income was being threatened. William Combe had some farming land at Welcombe that he wanted to convert into pasture for cattle, and this meant that the tenant farmers who had been renting the land would pay no more tithes. Combe hoped to annoy no one by enclosing his own land for cattle, impractical as this hope turned out to be, and he was ready to make a financial adjustment with everyone who was involved in the ownership of the tithes.

William Replingham, who seems to have been acting as Combe's agent, approached both Shakespeare and Thomas Greene in the matter. Greene had acquired the other half of the Shakespeare section of the tithes one year earlier, and both men would have been involved in an equal loss of income if Combe's plan went through. Replingham entered into an agreement with them on the 28th of October, 1614, in which they were guaranteed against any financial loss because of the proposed enclosure. Combe was prepared to do the same with the Stratford corporation, which was receiving an annual fee from each holder of the tithes and would own the whole property when the lease expired in 1636, for he was sincerely anxious to have everyone in a good mood before he started putting a ditch around his property and turning the cattle in.

The town of Stratford reacted with the utmost violence to Combe's proposal. The members of the Stratford Council felt they would be traitors to their unborn children if they permitted it, and that not even the three fires that had ravaged Stratford in the past twenty years would be as destructive as the plan to enclose the common fields at Welcombe. Eventually the whole matter became a town cause and the money to fight William Combe in the courts was voted out of town revenues, with the men of Stratford in such a fury that they must have seen themselves as a modern reincarnation of St. George with William Combe as the dragon.

Combe had stated repeatedly that the town would not lose money by the enclosures and might even make an actual profit; but the root of the difficulty was not financial but emotional. For more than a generation, any proposal to enclose land in Warwickshire had aroused an almost hysterical opposition, and seven years earlier there had been an actual crusade of three thousand men, women, and children who went through the county destroying whatever enclosures they could find, filling the ditches and cutting down the hedges. To the average villager, the word "enclosure" meant that some grasping landlord was taking the bread out of the mouths of innocent people by turning into pasture the little strips of communal farm land that had been theirs to rent since time immemorial. The medieval system was hopelessly impractical, since the ground could not be maintained in good condition or the breed of cattle improved as long as everything was handled communally; but this was considered beside the point, and there were many sympathetic readers for a "ballad of God's judgment showed upon a covetous encloser of common pasture," who was trodden to death by his own cattle.

The war of the enclosures put Thomas Greene in a difficult position. Like Shakespeare, he had signed the agreement with Replingham, but unlike Shakespeare, he was closely involved with the interests of Stratford and was in fact the town's legal adviser. When Greene was in London on the 17th of November, 1614, he went to see Shakespeare, who had arrived in London the day before, and talked the matter over with him. Shakespeare said he thought that Combe did not mean to enclose beyond Gospel Bush and would not begin surveying before the following April, and Greene added the hopeful notation in his diary, "He and Mr. Hall say they think there will be nothing done at all."

The Stratford Council thought otherwise. At a general meeting held on the 23rd of December they drafted two letters, one to Shakespeare and one to Arthur Mainwaring, Replingham's cousin, who was also working with Combe. The letter to Shakespeare is not extant, but it was probably not unlike the one that was sent Mainwaring. In it the Council listed all the tragedies that would result if the enclosure were successful, since Stratford had to support seven hundred poor out of the income from the tithes and would be utterly ruined unless "Christian meditations" caused the recipient of the letter to change his mind. Greene also sent a letter of his own to Shakespeare, giving a full account of the meeting and reinforcing the various points that had been made in the official communication.

Shakespeare seems to have ignored both letters. He took no special interest in the controversy, and since the enclosure would not hurt the town financially, he probably hoped that the whole thing would blow over. Instead, tempers grew steadily worse. William Combe's brother Thomas had already told a Stratford delegation they were "curs" (it was Thomas to whom Shakespeare willed his sword) and by January William Combe himself was in a "great passion." He started ditching his property, and the Stratford Council went out and filled the ditches up again, and the harried owner of the property said they were all Puritan knaves. The case was fought out in the London courts, and after a long and expensive litigation it was finally decreed by the Privy Council that William Combe must pay a heavy fine and put the land back as it was. It was a final triumph for medievalism, but even the most determined town council could not banish the principles of modern farming forever.

The war of the enclosures was still being fought when there was a private event of some importance in the Shakespeare family. On February 10, 1616, Shakespeare's younger daughter married Thomas Quiney. Their marriage was so sudden that it took place in a prohibited season, and they were punished by the Worcester Consistory Court because they had not obtained a special license. Like her mother, Judith married in haste, although the reason for the haste is not known. Also like her mother, she married a man younger than herself, for Judith was thirty and Thomas Quiney only twenty-seven.

Thomas was a younger son of Shakespeare's old friend, Richard Quiney, and he had been running a tavern on High Street that was called "Atwood's." At about the time of his marriage Thomas traded establishments with a brother-in-law and obtained a larger tavern in a better location that was called "the Cage." It stood at the corner of Bridge Street and High Street, near the Market Cross, and it was here that Judith went to live after her marriage.

Judith's father had already made

his will a month before her marriage, and he called his lawyer to New Place in March to make the necessary changes, since what was once Judith's dowry had now become a marriage portion. Since all the bequests to Judith were on the first page of the will, the whole of it did not have to be rewritten. The lawyer's clerk found he could get all the new material on the first page by writing the lines closer together at the bottom and adding two extra lines in the space at the top of the second page. Then he crossed out the lines on the second page that were not appropriate and left the third page as it was.

The will is a rough draft, full of corrections, and it has been suggested it was left in that state because Shakespeare was so ill there was no time to make a fair copy. But the lawyer in the case was Francis Collins of Worcester, and Collins was not in the habit of always making a fair copy of the wills he drew for his clients. He was an experienced lawyer who knew exactly what would stand in court, and the nine-page will he made for John Combe, two years earlier, is also full of deletions and corrections. It is improbable that Shakespeare was seriously ill when he made the alterations in his will on the 25th of March, for the first page opens with the statement that the testator is "in perfect health and memory." Collins would have used a different formula, "sound in mind but sick in body," if Shakespeare had been ill.

Shakespeare's will had one dominant, driving purpose: to leave all the property intact to a single male descendant. John Shakespeare's eldest and only surviving son was determined to fulfill his father's dream of a Shakespeare family established in perpetuity among the landed gentry of Warwickshire, and what sounds like a complicated series of bequests had a single end in view. The land had been bought; the land had been protected; and the land was to go to a male heir. It was true that at present there was no male heir, but Susanna was still a young woman and there was no reason why she might not still have a son. If she did not, her daughter Elizabeth might have a son, and if this failed also, there was still Judith.

The will opens with the bequests to Judith, the second-born. Since the property had to be kept intact, Judith could not be given land, and she was given instead a generous cash settlement. The money was left to her in two sections of £150 each. Part of the first section was to be paid outright and part was to be paid as soon as she surrendered her rights to the copyhold property that Shakespeare had bought on Chapel Lane from Walter Getley—a surrender that had to be made before Susanna could legally inherit this particular piece of property. The other £150 was to be paid in three years if Judith or any of her heirs were alive but otherwise was to be kept in the Shakespeare family. Her husband, Thomas Quiney, could inherit it only if he had already given his wife the equivalent of the money in land.

All Shakespeare's own land went to his first-born, Susanna. This included his residence at New Place, the cottage he had bought from Getley, the house in the Blackfriars for which John Robinson was paying rent, the two houses on Henley Street he had inherited from his father, "and all my barns, stables, orchards, gardens, lands, tenements, and hereditaments whatsoever." Susanna was to have the use of the property during her lifetime and then it was to go to her eldest son. If he was not living, it was to go to her second son; if the second son was not living, to the third son; and the succession was carefully itemized in the will up to the "fifth, sixth, and seventh sons of her body lawfully issuing." Very few wills of the period are as detailed and as insistent as Shakespeare's when it comes to the matter of entail; for if Susanna had no sons the property was to go to the sons of her daughter, Elizabeth Hall, and if Elizabeth had no sons the property was to go to the sons of Judith Quiney.

The personal bequests were thought out with as much care as the disposal of the land. Shakespeare left his only surviving sister, Joan, a life tenancy in the house she was already inhabiting on Henley Street and she was to make in return a token annual payment of twelvepence. He also left her twenty pounds in cash and all his wearing apparel, and to each of her three sons, William, Thomas, and Michael Hart, he left five pounds. He left to Judith what was evidently his most valuable single piece of plate, a bowl of gilded silver, and the rest of the plate went to his granddaughter Elizabeth. He left twenty shillings in gold to his godson, William Walker, who was about the same age as Elizabeth, and ten pounds to the poor of Stratford. Thomas Combe got Shakespeare's sword, and substantial cash bequests went to the two overseers of his will, Thomas Russell and Francis Collins. He left money for memorial rings to John and Anthony Nashe, and to two more Stratford friends, Hamnet Sadler and William Reynolds. He also left money for memorial rings "to my fellows John Heminges, Richard Burbage, and Henry Condell," who were the only three surviving members of Shakespeare's original company.

Shakespeare left his wife the second-best bed, which was probably the family one since the best bed was usually kept for visitors. When old Thomas Combe made his will, eight years earlier, he left his son William the best bed and his wife the second best, but Mrs. Combe got the rest of the household goods and Anne Shakespeare did not. All the "household stuff" went to Dr. and Mrs. Hall, whom Shakespeare had made his executors. Since Collins' clerk inserted the bequest of the second-best bed above the line, it has been said that this particular bequest was an afterthought; but the key word *house* in the bequest to Shakespeare's sister is also inserted above the line, and so is the whole of the bequest to three of Shakespeare's closest friends, Heminges, Burbage, and Condell.

It is sometimes said also that Shakespeare did not need to leave his wife any property because she automatically would get a third of the estate as her dower right. There was such a custom of dower right in London, and Shakespeare went to some trouble to circumvent it when he bought the Blackfriars property. There was no such custom in Stratford, and if there had been, the basic purpose of Shakespeare's will could have been defeated; for, if Anne inherited, the property might not have been kept intact.

The relationship between Anne and at least one of her daughters was very close. The brass plate on her tombstone bears an inscription that is unusually personal for the period: the daughter mourns that her mother gave her life while she in return had given a tombstone. She prays that Christ will come quickly and her mother will then rise again and seek the stars. It was probably Susanna rather than Judith who erected the memorial, and since Susanna was now the mistress of New Place, it is probable that she made her mother's years of widowhood happy and comfortable ones.

The tone of Shakespeare's will is impersonal throughout, although most of the wills of this period are personal and affectionate. Henry Condell's will speaks of his "well-beloved wife," and John Heminges asks to be buried "near unto my loving wife Rebecca." Augustine Phillips uses the same term, and Thomas Pope even includes in his affections "my loving friend John Jackson." But Shakespeare was one member of the company whose will does not show a flicker of personal feeling. Whatever his private emotions may have been about his family or his friends, he kept them to himself.

Shakespeare put his signature on each page of the will, with a "By me, William Shakespeare," on the third and last page. Francis Collins signed as a witness, and so did four Stratford neighbors that had been called in, Julius Shaw, John Robinson, Hamnet Sadler, and Robert Whatcott. Shaw lived next door to New Place and that year was High Bailiff of Stratford. Sadler was the old friend for whom Shakespeare had named his dead son, and Whatcott had served as a character witness for Susanna when she brought suit for slander against John Lane.

Less than a month after the revision of his will, Shakespeare died. He was only fifty-two but he had survived all his younger brothers. Edmund, the actor, had been buried in London nine years ago, and Gilbert and Richard had died a year apart, one in February 1612 and the other in February 1613. The date of William Shakespeare's death is given on his tomb as the 23rd of April, 1616, and the parish records show that he was buried two days later. He was carried out of his home in a wooden coffin, and the great bell in the tower of the Guild Chapel, just across the way, had been repaired in time to toll for his burial.

Since he was a lay rector, Shakespeare's body was interred inside the chancel rail of the parish church. The Church of the Holy Trinity is a beautiful building, but when Shakespeare died, the chancel was in a state of neglect. The rain had seeped in and blotched the paint on the walls, and the windows needed glazing. Just behind the north wall of the chancel where Shakespeare's grave had been dug, there was a room which the minister used as his study with a vault underneath that was used as a charnel house. In the crowded burial places of England, it was the custom to move old bones to the charnel house to make room for new ones, and there is a doggerel verse on Shakespeare's grave to guard against such a possibility.

Good friend, for Jesus' sake forbear
To dig the dust enclosed here.

Blest be the man that spares these stones
And curst be he that moves my bones.

Against the wall, over the grave, an elaborate monument in marble was erected. It is not known who erected Shakespeare's monument, but it was probably Dr. and Mrs. Hall since Judith certainly did not have the money for so expensive a memorial. When Shakespeare's friend, John Combe, died two years earlier, he set aside sixty pounds in his will to have his monument erected in alabaster. The London mortuary sculptor who designed the monument for Combe was also hired to design the monument for Shakespeare, and he was probably paid about the same sum for his work.

Gerard Janssen turned out one of those expensive, unimaginative pieces of work that were standard with the monument makers of the period, and the best that can be said of it is that if it had been done forty years later, when English taste was inclining even more strongly to the baroque, it would have been much worse. Between two marble columns there is a half-length statue of the poet, holding pen and paper in the conventional manner to show that he had been a writer. The carving was done in limestone, chosen because it takes paint well, and the features were done conventionally by the sculptor, who left them to the painter to be made realistic. The painter made the eyes hazel, the hair auburn, the doublet scarlet, the loose gown black, and the cushion on which the hands rest green and crimson with gilt tassels. Above the figure are Shakespeare's arms carved in stone, with a skull set above them and a cherub on either side, the one with the spade symbolizing labor and the one with the inverted torch symbolizing rest. And beneath the figure is an inscription, partly in Latin and partly in English, stating among other things that in intellect Shakespeare was a Socrates and in his art a Vergil.

When Francis Beaumont died, a month before William Shakespeare, he was buried in Westminster Abbey next to Chaucer and Spenser, and an Oxford student expressed the wish that Shakespeare could have been buried there also. William Basse ended his poem on the subject by deciding that the arrangement was better as it was:

Under this carved marble of thine own,
Sleep, rare tragedian Shakespeare, sleep alone.

The notion of burying Shakespeare in Westminster Abbey could never have occurred to anyone in Stratford, and in any case it was undoubtedly felt that he had been given a noble and worthy monument. By 1623 the chancel had been properly repaired and painted and the windows had been glazed. The bright paint and the clean marble of the Shakespeare monument must have looked very impressive, and no one in Stratford could have known that it was a pretentious, dead memorial to a living spirit.

The Shakespeare will was as much a failure as the Shakespeare monument, for the longed-for heir never made his appearance. The Halls had only one child, and although Elizabeth Hall became Lady Bernard and died old and rich, she never had any sons. Judith Quiney bore three sons and named the eldest one Shakespeare; but when Judith was buried at the age of seventy-seven, she had survived all her children, and with the death of Lady Bernard in 1670 the direct line ended. The land that Shakespeare had carefully amassed and fiercely protected went to strangers, and only a routine piece of mortuary sculpture remained to show that the greatest man in England had once walked the streets of Stratford.

Stratford had failed in its memorial to Shakespeare, but London did better. Shakespeare had never concerned himself with the safety of his plays, and it may be that he thought they were less valuable than the land. But his fellow actors thought otherwise, and seven years after his death they reared him their own kind of monument. It was the complete edition of his plays and is known as the First Folio.

✕ *Chapter* **14**

Three years after Shakespeare's death, Richard Burbage was buried in London. He died in March 1619, which was also the month of the death of Queen Anne, and Middleton scolded the Londoners for keeping all their grief for Burbage.

When he expires, lo! All lament the man,
But where's the grief should follow good Queen Anne?

Among those who mourned Burbage deeply was the Earl of Pembroke, who confessed to a friend more than two months later that he stayed away from a play that was being shown for the French ambassador, which "I . . . could not endure to see so soon after the loss of my old acquaintance Burbage."

Now that Shakespeare and Burbage were dead, the only two actors that remained of the original Chamberlain's company were John Heminges and Henry Condell. They stood at the head of the King's Men, and when a new royal patent was granted to the company at the beginning of the next reign, John Heminges was the first name on the list and Henry Condell the second.

Both men had had a lifetime of experience in the theatre, and Heminges, in particular, had become what might be called the dean of the London stage. The year before Burbage died, the London companies banded together to negotiate with the Master of the Revels, and it was John Heminges they chose to act as their agent. He had served his own company as business manager since the beginning of the century, and had been responsible for the collection and disbursement of thousands of pounds; and the work must have been well done, for in all those years there is no record of any lawsuit within the company or the complaint of any actor against him.

His closest friend in the theatre seems to have been Henry Condell, and those two neighbors and good citizens were still living in St. Mary Aldermanbury, where they were serving as parish trustees, the year that Burbage died. When the actors were in trouble, it was to these two men they usually turned. When Alexander Cooke, who had once been Heminges' apprentice, died in 1614 he left the money for the bringing-up of his "poor orphans" in the hands of Heminges and Condell; and when John Underwood, another actor in the company, died a widower ten years later, he made Condell one of the executors of his will, Heminges one of its overseers, and left the care of his five children to his "loving and kind fellows."

When Heminges and Condell gathered the plays of Shakespeare together in the First Folio, they did it with the same kind of love that made them willing to care for the orphaned children of their fellow actors. "We have but collected them, and done an office to the dead, to procure his orphans guardians; without ambition either of self-profit or fame; only to keep the memory of so worthy a friend and fellow alive as was our Shakespeare."

No better men could have been chosen to be the guardians of Shakespeare's children, for Heminges and Condell were the only two men in London who knew by personal experience what plays Shakespeare had written. It is not quite certain that Henry Condell was with the Chamberlain's company when it was formed; but John Heminges was, and he saw each script as soon as Shakespeare was finished with it for the sixteen years during which Shakespeare wrote for the company. He had discussed the scripts with Shakespeare, worked over the casting and the staging, and had acted them with him; and Shakespeare's plays were kept so constantly before the public that John Heminges would have had no reason to forget even the earliest of them.

This intimate, professional knowledge of Shakespeare's scripts was essential for anyone who planned to make a collected edition of the plays, for only the plays of his middle period were available in good printed editions and even here the list was not complete. His earlier plays had mostly been printed anonymously, if at all, and two of them were in corrupt texts that had never been corrected. As for the great series of plays he had written in the reign of James, none of these was in print except what was evidently an unauthorized edition of *King Lear*.

By the time James came to the throne, the publishers openly coveted the name of Shakespeare on their title pages, since, as the publisher of the unauthorized quarto of *Othello* remarked, "The author's name is sufficient to vent his work." The King's Men refused to release Shakespeare's plays for publication and so the publishers took the next best course: they printed other plays that had been successful at the Globe and issued them as Shakespeare's. In 1605, Nathaniel Butter published *The London Prodigal*, "as it was played by the King's Majesty's Servants. By William Shakespeare." In 1608 Thomas Pavier published *A Yorkshire Tragedy*, "acted by his Majesty's Players at the Globe. Written by W. Shakespeare." And in 1609, Henry Gosson published *Pericles*, "acted by his Majesty's Servants, at the Globe on the Bankside. By William Shakespeare."

No outsider could have found his way about in so confused a situation. It took a man as experienced as John Heminges, who had worked with Shakespeare and his scripts ever since the company had been formed, to bring order out of chaos and produce a collection of the plays that could be trusted.

A final touch of confusion was supplied the year Burbage died by

Thomas Pavier, who decided that he would bring out a collected edition of Shakespeare's plays. Pavier held the copyright to the corrupt quarto text of Shakespeare's *Henry V* and to equally corrupt texts of the second and third parts of the trilogy of *Henry VI*. He added to the list *A Midsummer Night's Dream* and *The Merchant of Venice,* which had not been republished for nineteen years and on which he evidently felt the copyright had expired. He brought two other publishers into the venture, Arthur Johnson, who held the copyright on a corrupt text of *The Merry Wives of Windsor,* and Nathaniel Butter, who had published the unauthorized version of *King Lear.* To all these he added two Globe successes, *A Yorkshire Tragedy* and *Pericles,* and since he held the copyright on *Sir John Oldcastle,* he added that also. This was the play that Drayton and three more of Henslowe's playwrights had written at the turn of the century for a rival company, but Pavier evidently felt that the London reading public had short memories and he had no hesitation at all in attributing its authorship to William Shakespeare.

Pavier was not a printer but a publisher, and to print the collection he chose a reputable Londoner named William Jaggard. The two were close friends, for Jaggard made Pavier the overseer of his will and had done printing for him back in Elizabeth's reign. Jaggard had one of the most successful printing establishments in London, and he would have had no difficulty in turning out the rather thick quarto volume that Pavier had planned.

The volume was not issued. Instead, each of the quartos was printed to be sold separately, with individual title pages, and with the exception of one group that had evidently already gone to press, all the quartos were given false dates. It was only recently discovered by experts, working with the watermarks on the paper, the kind of type used, and other technical evidence, that these dates were faked and all the quartos were issued from Jaggard's press in 1619.

In the introduction to the First Folio, Heminges and Condell spoke bitterly of the fact that Shakespeare's plays were appearing in "stolen and surreptitious copies, maimed and deformed by the frauds and stealths of injurious imposters," and it was almost certainly Pavier's edition to which they were referring. But the King's Men had a better weapon than words. They turned to the Lord Chamberlain of England, who happened to be Burbage's good friend, the Earl of Pembroke; and on the third of May, 1619, the Earl sent a letter to the Stationers' Company ordering that none of the plays in the possession of the King's Men was to be printed without their consent. Three years later two more unauthorized quartos of Shakespeare's plays were issued, and the Earl of Pembroke later sent the Stationers' Company another letter reinforcing his order.

It was not the wish of the King's Men to keep Shakespeare's plays out of the hands of the reading public. What they wished to do, as Heminges and Condell said, was to present them "absolute in their numbers as he conceived them." But this was not a very easy thing to achieve from the practical publishing point of view, for there were thirty-six plays in all. This was far too many plays to present in a quarto edition, and the only solution was the heavy expense of printing them in folio.

Folios were normally reserved for dignified books on history and theology and medicine and were not associated with ephemeral popular productions like plays. The only writer who had dared to issue his plays in a folio edition was Ben Jonson, who published what he called his "Works" the year that Shakespeare died; and although he had also included masques and poems, he had undergone a certain amount of ridicule for dignifying his plays with so august a title. Jonson had not included all his plays but only those which he felt especially merited the attention of posterity, and in any case he had achieved a rather unusual eminence in literary circles, for a playwright, and was so respected for his learning that both Oxford and Cambridge had presented him with honorary degrees.

Heminges and Condell knew very well that a folio edition of all Shakespeare's plays would be a risky venture. Shakespeare did not have Jonson's lofty reputation in cultured circles, and even Jonson's folio had not sold particularly well. In general, the kind of people who could afford to buy large folio volumes were not in the habit of reading popular plays. When Sir Thomas Bodley started his beloved library at Oxford at the beginning of the century, he said it would bring "scandal" to the library if any playbooks were admitted, and that it was highly undesirable that "such kind of books should be vouchsafed a room in so noble a library." Sir Thomas was as careful to banish books of this kind as he was to get seasoned wood for the shelves and benches, and the First Folio was only admitted to the Bodleian Library by accident. It was sent there because the Stationers' Company had made an agreement by then to supply the library with one copy of every book printed by its members.

It was a hazardous venture to print thirty-six plays in folio, and it would not be surprising if Heminges and Condell had some trouble in finding a printer. Certainly, if they could have had their choice of any printer in London, it is not likely they would have chosen the one who actually printed the First Folio. For this was William Jaggard, who had already printed in 1619 the Pavier collection that Heminges and Condell had denounced as "stolen and surreptitious."

William Jaggard was in general a reputable printer, and it was only when he was dealing with Shakespeare's work that he became at all unethical. It was Jaggard who had issued *The Passionate Pilgrim* in 1599 as Shakespeare's, although only one fourth of the poems in the book were his, and the book had rewarded Jaggard by selling so well that a third edition was called for in 1612. Jaggard padded out this third edition by blandly adding some poetry from Thomas Heywood's book *Troia Britannica,* which he had printed for Heywood three years earlier. Heywood obliged him to cancel Shakespeare's name on all the remaining title pages, and Jaggard had to issue the rest of the edition without that potent name to help the sales of the book. Six years later he printed Pavier's collection, which attributed plays like *Sir John Oldcastle* to Shakespeare, and although Jaggard showed few scruples in his use of Shakespeare's name, he showed a kind of dogged devotion to the name itself.

When Heminges and Condell began to collect Shakespeare's plays for the folio edition, they ignored the three plays, *Sir John Oldcastle, A Yorkshire Tragedy,* and *Pericles,* that Pavier had attributed to him, and they also ignored the bad texts that Pavier had used. They found only three quarto texts they could use without any changes at all, and even when an authorized quarto

was in print, they did not invariably use it. In the case of *Hamlet,* it might have been better if they had, but in general they showed excellent judgment in choosing their texts for publication. Eighteen of the plays had never been put into print at all, and for these Heminges and Condell used the scripts that had been carefully stored as the property of the King's Men.

Heminges and Condell were not acquainted with the technicalities of the publishing business and they probably had very little to do with getting the selected scripts in condition for the printer. The editor who did his work for the First Folio is unknown. It could not have been William Jaggard, for he had been blind since 1612. It might conceivably have been his son Isaac, who was made a freeman of the Stationers' Company at the early age of eighteen, the year after his father went blind, so that he could help him in the business; but it is probable that Isaac was chiefly concerned with the production rather than the editorial end of the business. When Ben Jonson's folio was published, he did his own editorial work, with such loving care that hardly a comma went unscrutinized, and Heminges and Condell expressed regret that Shakespeare had not been alive to do the same. "It had been a thing, we confess, worthy to have been wished, that the author himself had lived to have set forth and overseen his own writings."

The editor of the Folio lost his enthusiasm for the task long before he had gone through all thirty-six of the plays. The book opened with *The Tempest,* which was probably chosen for that position because it had never been published and could be trusted to attract the eye of a casual purchaser, and *The Tempest* was edited with some care. The stage directions were rewritten to make them easier to read, and the play was complete with locale and the names of the characters. As the editor advanced in his gigantic task, he began to omit the names of the characters and the locale, even when there was plenty of room for the information, and he forgot to rewrite the stage directions. Information intended for the eye of the prompter began to creep into the text, and the names of obscure members of the company like Tawyer and Sincklo and Jack Wilson were accidentally handed down to posterity. The proofreading was not carefully done, and the quotations from foreign languages in particular are full of mistakes; and the paging of the three sections of the book is so bad that in *Hamlet* page 156 leaps to page 257 and follows from there. Jaggard was often careless about page numbers, but in the First Folio he outdid himself.

The Folio had been planned for publication in 1622, and the London edition of the catalogue of the Frankfort book fair carried an announcement of it: "Plays written by Mr. William Shakespeare, all in one volume, printed by Isaac Jaggard, in folio." But there was a delay at this point and William Jaggard turned his press over to other books instead. One of these he was in a hurry to get printed, since it involved a private feud he was having with that quick-tempered member of the Office of Heralds, Ralph Brooke. But Jaggard also printed other, shorter books before he turned back to Shakespeare's, and the delay may have been caused by lack of money. When the Folio was finally published at the end of the following year, the description it bore in the Frankfort catalogue had been changed and it was now listed as having been printed by Edward Blount. Blount was not a printer but a publisher, and it looks as though the book had been refinanced in the interim.

Blount was a rather distinguished member of the profession who had once been a friend of Christopher Marlowe's, and he brought two colleagues of his into the venture with him. The Folio states on the last page that it was printed "at the charges of W. Jaggard, Ed. Blount, J. Smithweeke, and W. Aspley," so that what had evidently been Jaggard's own venture in the beginning had now become a syndicate. Blount's name appears with Isaac Jaggard's on the title page, and together they made a joint statement of ownership when they made their copyright entry in the Stationers' Register on the 8th of November, 1623. But Blount's seems to have been the dominant position, since he was able to transfer the copyrights involved as though they had been his own property when he gave them to another publisher seven years later.

An artist had to be commissioned to make the usual portrait of the author to serve as the frontispiece, and it was probably Heminges and Condell who were responsible for selecting him, since they knew, much better than anyone else involved in the venture, what their "friend and fellow" looked like. They gave the commission to a commercial artist in his early twenties named Martin Droeshout, and he gave them a stiffly correct portrait in the usual quarter view. If they had been able to pay more, they could probably have found a more talented artist, for while the art of painting was in general at a low ebb in England, there was some good work being done by portraitists. On the other hand, Ben Jonson states that the portrait was a good likeness, and at least Droeshout refrained from crowning the brow with laurel leaves and adding symbolic figures of Comedy and Tragedy. The drawing is stiff but it is straightforward and unencumbered.

It was the custom of the period to preface nearly every book, however trivial, with a series of poems from fellow writers praising the author's work. When Ben Jonson published his folio edition, it opened with nine commendatory pieces in English and Latin, and when the Beaumont and Fletcher folio was published, there were thirty-six contributions and nearly every poet in England was represented. There are only four commendatory poems in the front of the Shakespeare folio, for Shakespeare did not have quite the literary standing of either Jonson or Fletcher and it may also be that Heminges and Condell did not know many poets.

The one poet the two actors knew intimately was Ben Jonson. They had acted in all six of the plays that Jonson had written for the King's Men and had worked with him in the theatre for a period that covered thirteen years. Jonson was also a close friend of Shakespeare's, and the fact that he was now the most prominent figure in English letters made him the ideal man to write a commendatory address for the volume.

Jonson wrote eighty lines "to the memory of my beloved, the author, Master William Shakespeare, and what he hath left us." He was a warmhearted and generous man and moreover he had loved Shakespeare, and for once he was willing to forget the differences of opinion they had had on the subject of rules. He could not resist mentioning that Shakespeare had "small Latin and less Greek," but he went on to say that only the greatest of the Greek dramatists could match him and that he had outsoared all his contemporaries. He then made a statement about Shakespeare that was consistently ignored for the rest of the century, during which it was decided that Shakespeare was a child of nature who went around warbling his untutored lays and was quite without conscious art. Jonson was an experienced writer and he knew that no artist works entirely from the promptings of "nature."

Thy art,
My gentle Shakespeare, must enjoy a part . . .
For a good poet's made, as well as born.

Jonson's tribute as a whole is both beautiful and intelligent, and although his praise of Shakespeare may have seemed extravagant to the average literary gentleman of the period, the judgment of posterity has shown that Jonson was not exaggerating.

Heminges and Condell then approached Leonard Digges, a learned writer whose father had been a great mathematician. The Digges family lived in the same parish as Heminges and Condell, and Digges probably wrote his own poetical tribute as an act of friendship. Unfortunately he started off in his first line by flatly contradicting Jonson. "Poets are born, not made." He then went on to say that it was no effort at all for Shakespeare to contrive a play, a matter on which Shakespeare alone knew the truth. He then said that Shakespeare never borrowed from foreign languages, never gleaned anything from other writers, and, as a final touch of complete misinformation, that he invented all his own plots. All this was indirectly aimed at Jonson, and then Digges attacked Jonson

openly by saying that any of Shakespeare's characters, Falstaff or Iago or Malvolio or Beatrice, brought in more money for the King's Men than any of the plays Jonson had written for them.

There seems to be no doubt that this offering of Digges was intended for use in the First Folio, but Heminges and Condell could not open the volume with an attack on Jonson. Instead, they evidently asked Digges for something a little more conservative and he gave them twenty-two lines thanking Shakespeare's "pious fellows" for giving his plays to the world and expressing the conviction that the plays would outlast the Stratford monument. A few pretentious lines were supplied by Hugh Holland, whom the learned William Camden grouped with Shakespeare as one of the "pregnant wits" of the day, and another poet who may have been James Mabbe wrote eight more on the same idea of an actor reappearing before his public.

The choice of a patron for the book had been obvious from the first, for no one had done more for the King's Men than William Herbert, Earl of Pembroke. It had been at his house at Wilton, twenty years earlier, that the King's Men had made their first appearance before James, and since his appointment as Lord Chamberlain in 1615 he had protected the company against unauthorized publications of Shakespeare's plays. He had loved Richard Burbage so well he could not "endure" to see a play two months after his death, and he had looked with favor both upon Shakespeare and on his plays.

The Earl of Pembroke had a younger brother, Philip, Earl of Montgomery, who was also a patron of arts and letters. The two men came of a line that had always been interested in the theatre, for their father had been the patron of an acting company and their mother was the Countess of Pembroke who had tried to raise the level of English drama in the nineties.

The ten actors who later issued the Beaumont and Fletcher folio thanked the Earl of Montgomery for his "constant and diffuse goodness" to them, and said they had been inspired to dedicate the book to him because he and his brother had been chosen as the patrons of "the flowing compositions of the then expired sweet Swan of Avon, Shakespeare." They said they were only following the lead of the men who dedicated the Folio of Shakespeare's plays to that "most noble and incomparable pair of brethren," William Herbert, Earl of Pembroke, and Philip Herbert, Earl of Montgomery.

Heminges and Condell approached the two earls in the respectful manner that had to be employed in the seventeenth century. The dignity of their rank was much "greater than to descend to the reading of these trifles." Nevertheless, the two earls had liked the plays when they were acted.

. . . We have but collected them, and done an office to the dead, to procure his orphans guardians; without ambition either of self-profit or fame; only to keep the memory of so worthy a friend and fellow alive as was our Shakespeare, by humble offer of his plays to your most noble patronage . . . What delight is in them may be ever your Lordships', the reputation his, and the faults ours, if any be committed by a pair so careful to show their gratitude both to the living and the dead as is

Your Lordships' most bounden,
John Heminges
Henry Condell

The rather muted tone in which the two actors addressed the two earls changed considerably in the address which they sensibly entitled, "To the great variety of readers." Heminges and Condell had been working for over thirty years before a great variety of audiences at the Rose, the Theatre, the Curtain, the Globe, and the Blackfriars, and they knew two things. The first was that Shakespeare's plays could be enjoyed by a great many different kinds of people, and the second was that every audience should be ready to pay the price of admission. Anyone was free to pass judgment on the plays in the Folio, but first he must buy the book. "Read and censure . . . but buy it first." "Whatever you do, buy."

The actors continued their address to the reader with a statement of regret that the author had not lived to publish his own work, and a condemnation of the corrupt editions in which some of his plays were circulating. Then they went on to describe what Shakespeare's scripts had looked like when the actors received them from his hand. "His mind and hand went together; and what he thought, he uttered with that easiness, that we have scarce received from him a blot in his papers. But it is not our province, who only gather his works and give them to you, to praise him. It is yours that read him . . . Read him, therefore; and again and again; and if then you do not like him, surely you are in some manifest danger not to understand him." The language is not as poetic as Jonson's contribution, but there was never a truer statement about William Shakespeare.

At the end of the eighteenth century it suddenly occurred to James Boswell, son of the biographer, that Heminges and Condell did not write this address because some of the phrases are similar to some that Ben Jonson once used elsewhere. Boswell made this discovery by what he called decomposing the address, and a better name for the process could hardly be found. A great many scholars have since agreed with Boswell, although there is another group that prefers to give the credit to Edward Blount. Nevertheless, there is no reason of any kind why Heminges and Condell should not have done what they said they did. They were not illiterate men. Heminges' own son, whom he had named William, became a playwright; and when John Heminges died and left five pounds to his

grandson Richard, it was with the specific instruction the sum should be used "to buy him books."

There is only one current book review that is now extant on the First Folio. It was written, evidently at about the date of publication, in a manuscript book that belonged to the Salisburys and had been composed by someone who knew both actors since it was addressed "To my good friends Mr. John Heminges and Henry Condell."

To you that jointly with undaunted pains
Vouchsafed to chant to us these noble strains,
How much you merit by it is not said,
But you have pleased the living, loved the dead . . .

There is no question the volume "pleased the living," for a second edition was required within the decade. Nor is there any question that the two men had showed Shakespeare their love and gratitude in the one way that would have been worthy of him. Instead of a memorial of stone they made him one of his own words.

Heminges and Condell grew old and died and were buried near each other in the parish church of St. Mary Aldermanbury. The Puritans came into power and closed every playhouse in England. The last of Shakespeare's descendants died and the direct line became extinct. But Shakespeare's plays went on being read, and in every generation there was an increasing number of people who loved him. Heminges and Condell had wished him "such readers" and given him the chance to get them. Every year their number increased, and they have now built a monument to him that extends over the whole of the world.

AFTERWORD

Though I am not myself a close student of the Elizabethan age, I am no newcomer to Shakespearean studies; yet I find I have learned a good deal from Miss Chute. As an English dramatist—and I spent over twenty years not only writing plays but also helping to manage producing companies and theaters—I find myself indebted to her for the way in which she makes plain the solid opposition to the Theater during its most glorious age. I believe this opposition, which has its roots in Puritanism, to be traditional now in all English-speaking countries. So, where public money may be freely given for libraries, art galleries, museums, concerts, there is still an outcry against any money being given to the Theater. On the other hand, it is possible that the undeniable theatrical talent of the English-speaking peoples has been strengthened and burnished by this constant opposition. What is certain—and I am grateful to our author for making it so clear—is that Shakespeare was only too well acquainted with the enemies of the Theater.

There are two very important questions that lie outside the scope of this book, so that very sensibly its author has neither asked them nor answered them. Here they are. Is it possible, as many people have believed and have tried to prove, that the actor William Shakespeare, of Stratford-on-Avon, was not in fact the real author of the plays? Then, assuming he was their author, can we discover from the plays what kind of man he was?

It is a mistake to think that only crackpots have challenged Shakespeare's authorship of the plays. Among the doubters have been men like Mark Twain and H. G. Wells. It was first suggested that Bacon wrote the plays (in which case, then, somebody else wrote Bacon's works); then the Earls of Oxford, Rutland, Derby, were suggested, together with the Countess of Pembroke (as a member of a syndicate); and Marlowe, Raleigh, and even Queen Elizabeth herself, have had their advocates. We are told, by such advocates, that a mere actor, without much formal education, would have been incapable of creating these masterpieces of poetic drama. So Shakespeare was really "a front" for some more learned and aristocratic writer, wishing to avoid the hurly-burly of the Theater. And usually some final proof arrives by way of ciphers, cryptograms, and the like.

There is a strange kind of snobbery here. And with it an equally strange denial of the power of poetic and dramatic genius. The plays themselves, to anybody who understands the nature of drama, are entirely on Shakespeare's side. They do not suggest a scholar. What has drama to do with learning? They do not suggest a great aristocrat, whose rank and position would cut him off from the breadth of social experience reflected in the plays, especially in their realistic-comic scenes. Everything we know about Shakespeare—his middle-class provincial background, his modest education, his rich experience of the Theater as actor and part-manager, the references to him by his contemporaries—suggests that he and nobody else wrote the plays generally attributed to him. Instead of being the least likely author of them, as the Baconians and others have told us, he is undoubtedly the most likely.

It is said that Shakespeare cannot be the author of the plays because we know so little about him. But, as Miss Chute points out: "More is known about Shakespeare than about any other playwright of the period with the exception of Ben Jonson; and some parts of his life are better documented even than Jonson's." The people who say we know too little about him are not using their imagination. No doubt if his contemporaries had known (and how could they?) that he was destined to become a vast world figure, they would have left us all the biographical details possible to obtain and set down; but to them he was simply a popular, successful dramatist, at a time when writing for the Theater was regarded as a rough-and-tumble activity, no more to be venerated than, let us say, writing gangster serials for television is today.

It is also said that this actor Shakespeare could not have been the author of the plays because he seems to have been so careless or indifferent about the publication of them. But this is a failure to understand the mind and outlook of the working dramatist. He is aiming not at print but at performance. He feels that his primary task is getting the play onto the stage—and an urgent, hard task that can be, too—and once the piece has been performed, has gone into the playhouse's repertory, and the actors have their parts, he has had enough of it and wants to think about something else, probably another play. He is not like the nondramatic author, who can only reach the public through publication. The excitement and urgency of getting the thing onto the stage makes publication seem a faraway, dim business, which can be endlessly postponed. And in making these points I am not guessing, because I have been both a nondramatic author and a dramatist, and I know only too well the difference between the two attitudes of mind. Working as Shakespeare did, as dramatist, actor, manager, for huge, clamorous, popular playhouses, must have been murderously hard going. No wonder he retired as soon as he felt he could afford it.

Can we discover from the plays what kind of man he was? I believe that we can, but we must not be in too much of a hurry. For example, we cannot assume that what he makes his characters say is what he thought and believed himself. The characters are talking, not Shakespeare. Thus, in Act I, Scene 3, of *Hamlet,* Polonius, the old Lord Chamberlain, gives his son Laertes some parting advice, and everything he says has been quoted for generations, as if it were Shakespeare's advice to us. But this will not do. All that cautious stuff about not saying very much and not borrowing or lending money represents Polonius, the court politician, not Shakespeare. It is true there are times when we feel that Shakespeare is not writing dialogue for a character but is really saying something he wants to say; we can generally recognize such speeches because either they are rather out of character or they hold up and do not develop the dramatic situation: Hamlet, a character into which Shakespeare poured much of his own heart and mind, has a number of these speeches. But until we are familiar with the plays, we should assume that Shakespeare is making his characters speak for themselves, not for him.

Nevertheless, the plays are filled with clues to Shakespeare himself. These can be divided into three, coming under Action, Character, Imagery. Under Action, we can see how he handled the material he took from Italian novels, old plays, historical chronicles, Plutarch's *Lives:* what he left out, what he added, tell us much about him. Under Character, we can notice the kind of characters he thought important, and how he developed them. Most revealing of all is his use of Imagery, on which much contemporary Shakespearean criticism is now concentrated. His unconscious choice of images reveals the inner history of the more important plays, making plain the mood in which he wrote them. It is, however, Shakespeare the poet rather than Shakespeare the dramatist—so far as it is possible to separate them—who is the subject of this new and close examination and analysis of Imagery. When all the clues, coming under Action, Character, Imagery, are added together, Shakespeare himself, the man, begins to appear.

I will apologize in advance for what follows, if it seems too personal and too dogmatic, for lack of space makes it impossible either to amplify or to modify and qualify, and to offer evidence. (But I assure you there is plenty of evidence.) Shakespeare had of course an extraordinarily rich nature, which is why he could create so many different kinds of characters. He was often—and this is particularly true of his middle period of playwriting—a sharply divided man, at odds with himself. Outwardly and consciously, he was conservative and what we should now call "conformist"; he was anything but a bohemian and eccentric genius, an "off-beat" character; he probably appeared—and contemporary references tend to confirm this—a quiet, pleasant, sensible, businesslike sort of man, at home with people belonging to very different classes; and in company more ready to listen (and he listened to some purpose!) than to talk. He was a strong believer in order, and disliked and mistrusted rebellions and riots, hooting mobs, cheering crowds. He admired powerful, firm-minded, dependable kings and other rulers. He was always expressing what most of his contemporaries felt—and what most people still feel—and this partly explains the great popularity of his plays. This was the outward Shakespeare that his fellow actors knew in London, his neighbors knew in Stratford-on-Avon.

But, I repeat, he was until his last years a sharply divided man. In other words, there was an inner Shakespeare, who began to take charge when his creative powers were at full stretch, when he was all poet, and this inner man was the opposite of the outward one. The creator, the poet in him, instinctively sympathizes with the rebels, the nonconformers, the reckless and the disreputable, the people at odds with life as he was so often at odds with himself. All his greatest characters can be found in these disorderly ranks: the self-tormenting Hamlet; Lear, the mad old king; the immortal, raffish Falstaff; the self-destructive criminal Macbeth; the pair who tossed away an empire, Antony and Cleopatra. Here, everything esteemed and admired by the outward Shakespeare, the good citizen, the careful theater manager and property owner, is thrown into reverse, turned upside down. And it is out of the tension between these two different Shakespeares, between order and disorder, between conformity and rebellion, between cautiousness and recklessness, between sober, industrious days and wild, uproarious nights, that the best of his drama, with its wonderful richness and force, was created. Between the positive and negative poles the electricity went crackling and flashing.

His early work is very much that of an immensely clever and self-confident young man, pleased with himself and the world. While he steadily gains, both in dramatic skill and depth of insight, he loses these early high spirits; he begins to question life instead of merely accepting it; his vision of this world is stronger but darker; and weariness, scorn, disgust, all make their appearance, and finally *horror*, almost to the point of madness. (This is the period of the great tragedies.) But he rounds the danger point, no longer works in London but retires to Stratford, probably begins to lose interest in the Theater, so that his last plays suggest a smiling, elderly man telling wandering romantic tales.

Some of his likes and dislikes are quite clear. He liked music of all kinds, lively parties attended by people fond of one another, any sort of genuine wit, harmless fools and comic characters. He had a marvelous understanding of women, perhaps unmatched in all dramatic and poetic literature. He disliked coldly ambitious men, determined "go-getters," prigs and pedants, all the narrow-minded and intolerant. Like most intensely creative men, his outlook and values were as much feminine as masculine. Because he was so sharply divided in himself, he understood the importance of balance in men's character, the danger of being one-sided. He was not a conventionally religious man at all, but he was always conscious of the fact—as many great passages show us—that our life here on earth is a mystery, and that our knowledge sends only a feeble ray of light into the darkness of this mystery. He was aware, as few men have ever been, of all that is foul, disgusting, horrible in life; yet he loved life, and, I think, ended at peace with it. And this man, whose life and times Miss Chute reveals so clearly, has given to humanity more lasting satisfaction, more wonder and delight, more essential truth about itself than all the statesmen and generals of Britain and America added together. He was a marvel.

STUDY QUESTIONS

1. The story of William Shakespeare's father's life is not an unfamiliar one today: the rise of a determined, talented man from poverty and obscurity to security and success. Then as now, of course, luck and circumstance played their parts in such a success story. What important factors dominated the fortunes of John Shakespeare? What conditions of the time might have made his rise more difficult than it would be today?

2. Ben Jonson wrote that Shakespeare had "small Latin and less Greek." How might the truth of this be supported by Miss Chute's description of the usual education provided at such institutions as the Stratford grammar school? What preparation could such a school give William Shakespeare for his life's work?

3. Marchette Chute builds a great deal of her life of Shakespeare on what has been recorded about his country, his town, the city he worked in, and his business. Why do you suppose she is so dependent on this approach? Has it advantages, for example, over inferring an author's life from his own writings or from what contemporaries have said or written about him?

4. Miss Chute gives us the Stratford career of Richard Quiney in some detail. Why?

5. What various kinds of source material has Miss Chute used for information directly about William Shakespeare as an individual? Note several specific examples of each kind. Which seem to be more reliable relative to others? Why?

6. What were the conditions which led up to James Burbage's construction of the Theatre in 1576? What were the main disadvantages of using an innyard as a theater? What characteristics of the innyard were carried over to the design of the Theatre?

7. What were the objections of the Puritan faction to the theater? What were the objections of the London Council? How did the theater men get around the hostility of these groups?

8. To what kind of audience did the London public theater cater? How and why has the nature of this audience been misrepresented?

9. Miss Chute assumes that there was a real "break" between William Shakespeare and Anne Hathaway Shakespeare some three or four years after they were married. On what grounds does she make that assumption? What possible reason does she give for the estrangement of the couple?

10. "Shakespeare came to London at a fortunate time," writes Miss Chute at the end of Chapter 3. How closely can we estimate when that time was? What other events of historical importance were occurring approximately then? Why was the time so particularly fortunate for Shakespeare? Why was London the place for him to start his career?

11. List the main sources of public instruction and entertainment in London during the late sixteenth century. What was the attitude of the royal government and of the municipal government toward each of these? What can you infer from your list as to the nature of the London populace?

12. What was the attitude of such university men as Greene, Lodge, and Nashe toward the public theater? Why did they write for it? How might it be demonstrated that time has dealt ironically with them? How does *Greene's Groatsworth of Wit* pinpoint one aspect of their attitude? Why should Marlowe, also a university man, be distinguished from this group? In what relationship did the young playwright, William Shakespeare, stand to them?

13. Miss Chute emphasizes that Shakespeare was a working actor during his whole London life. Consequently, a knowledge of the necessary qualifications for the profession at that time is an important source of information about Shakespeare the man. What were these qualifications? What had an actor to be able to do? What advantages were there to being both playwright and actor?

14. Three of Shakespeare's earliest plays were *Henry VI, Titus Andronicus*, and *The Comedy of Errors*. How did these plays represent three experiments in different dramatic conventions? What was the specific appeal of each kind to Shakespeare's audience? What do these imitations suggest about the young playwright's experience and the influences on him?

15. What was the effect of the plague order of 1592 on the London theater companies? What was its effect on playwrights? Perhaps large, close gatherings did help spread the infection, but what was the London Council's reasoning about the plague and the theater?

16. What was the danger that surrounded the success of *Venus and Adonis* and *The Rape of Lucrece*? How are these works distinct from the writing Shakespeare did up to 1592? What were the circumstances of

his nontheatrical writing after 1594?

17. What were the particular advantages that Shakespeare reaped from being a member of the Chamberlain's company (afterward the King's Men)? What evidence indicates his status in the company?

18. How did the personal tastes and abilities of Queen Elizabeth affect the theater of her day? What were the special requirements and benefits of private showings at the royal Court?

19. As an example of Shakespeare's working conditions, outline the steps by which *Romeo and Juliet* was created and produced. What was his immediate source for the plot? What did he do to the existing story? What legal step had to be taken after the play was written? Why? How were the manuscripts handled? How was the casting accomplished? What were some of the important conventions and conditions of actual stage production?

20. Shakespeare not only used and improved old books and plays, he used and improved old, well-worn devices. What, specifically, are some of these devices as they appear in *Twelfth Night, As You Like It,* and *The Merchant of Venice?*

21. What light does each of the following documented circumstances throw on the life of William Shakespeare?

a. The purchase of New Place in 1597.

b. The death of Hamnet in 1596.

c. A new draft of the Shakespeare coat of arms in 1596.

d. Camden's written defense of the Shakespeare family's claims to gentility in 1602.

e. Richard Quiney's written request for a loan of thirty pounds.

22. What were the circumstances which directly led up to the opening of the Globe theater in 1599? What had William Shakespeare to do with these circumstances?

23. Ben Jonson objected to Shakespeare's line from *Julius Caesar:* "Caesar never did wrong but with just cause." How do Shakespeare's line and Jonson's criticism exemplify the difference between the two men as dramatic artists? Compare Jonson and Shakespeare as private citizens.

24. "It is a sobering thought that Hamlet the playgoer would not have approved of *Hamlet* the play." What division in early seventeenth-century opinion is Miss Chute illustrating in this sentence? How might the statement answer those who insist that the real author of Shakespeare's plays could not have been the actor from Stratford but must have been a university-educated gentleman?

25. What were the circumstances under which Shakespeare and the Chamberlain's company almost got into serious trouble during the attempted uprising of the Earl of Essex? What do these circumstances tell us about the times and about the particular status of this acting company?

26. What changes did the death of Queen Elizabeth I and the accession of King James I make in the lives and fortunes of Shakespeare and his immediate associates?

27. According to Miss Chute, if Puritanism had taken hold in England any earlier than it did, none of the plays of Shakespeare could have come into existence. What evidence does she offer to support this contention? What specific limitations were imposed on Shakespeare's writ-

ing before Puritanism took hold? What specific disabilities would the movement have imposed on Shakespeare if it could have?

28. On what evidence does Miss Chute assume William Shakespeare's natural good temper, instinctive courtesy, and dislike of quarrels?

29. What important inferences are to be drawn from Shakespeare's will?

What does it suggest about his relationships with various members of his family in the year of his death? What, according to Miss Chute, was the "dominant, driving purpose" of the document?

30. What does Miss Chute mean by the following statement? "Stratford had failed in its memorial to Shakespeare, but London did better."

The Life of Samuel Johnson, LL.D.

by James Boswell

Boswell's *Life of Johnson* is the supreme masterpiece of biography in the English language. If you develop literary taste and judgment, as you grow older, you will discover that a number of so-called great books, no matter how often they are included among the "100 Best Books" or have a place on somebody's "five-foot shelf," are in fact not as good as they are generally assumed to be. Much of the life has gone out of them.

This is not true of Boswell's *Johnson*. You may not like it at all, and if this should be the case, there is no more to be said: the loss is yours. But if you do like it, then you have made a friend for life. Indeed, you will enjoy it even more in your sixty-sixth year than you did in your sixteenth. I know because I must have been reading—and when not reading, then at least dipping into—this fat, rich masterpiece of biography for half a century. No life has gone out of this work. It is as good to read on a jet airliner as it must have been on a stagecoach.

James Boswell was born in Edinburgh, of a well-to-do family, in 1740. He first met Johnson in 1763, but it was during the period 1770–1784 (when Johnson died) that Boswell saw Johnson most frequently and carefully recorded his talk. The *Life* was first published in 1791 and was an immediate success. Boswell died four years later. Recently a great mass of hitherto unpublished Boswell material, memoirs, diaries, letters, has been acquired by Yale University, and this has led to the publication of several new Boswell books that have attracted wide attention.

What follows is an abridgment of the *Life*, too massive in its entirety for these pages, and it has been done with admirable skill by Mr. Davis.

Chapter 1

Introduction and Early Life

To write the life of him who excelled all mankind in writing the lives of others, and who, whether we consider his extraordinary endowments, or his various works, has been equalled by few in any age, is an arduous, and may be reckoned in me a presumptuous task.

Had Dr. Johnson written his own life, in conformity with the opinion which he has given, that every man's life may be best written by himself; had he employed in the preservation of his own history, that clearness of narration and elegance of language in which he has embalmed so many eminent persons, the world would probably have had the most perfect example of biography that was ever exhibited. But although he at different times, in a desultory manner, committed to writing many particulars of the progress of his mind and fortunes, he never had persevering diligence enough to form them into a regular composition. Of these memorials a few have been preserved; but the greater part was consigned by him to the flames, a few days before his death.

As I had the honour and happiness of enjoying his friendship for upwards of twenty years; as I had the scheme of writing his life constantly in view; as he was well apprised of this circumstance, and from time to time obligingly satisfied my inquiries, by communicating to me the incidents of his early years; as I acquired in recollecting, and was very assiduous in recording, his conversation, of which the extraordinary vigour and vivacity constituted one of the first features of his character; and as I have spared no pains in obtaining materials concerning him, from every quarter where I could discover that they were to be found, and have been favoured with the most liberal communications by his friends; I flatter myself that few biographers have entered upon such a work as this, with more advantages; independent of literary abilities, in which I am not vain enough to compare myself with some great names who have gone before me in this kind of writing.

Had his other friends been as diligent and ardent as I was, he might have been almost entirely preserved. As it is, I will venture to say that he will be seen in this work more completely than any man who has ever yet lived.

Having said thus much by way of introduction, I commit the following pages to the candour of the Publick.

Samuel Johnson was born at Lichfield, in Staffordshire, on the 18th of September, 1709; and his initiation into the Christian church was not delayed; for his baptism is recorded, in the register of St. Mary's parish in that city, to have been performed on the day of his birth. His father was Michael Johnson, a native of Derbyshire, of obscure extraction, who settled in Lichfield as a bookseller and stationer. His mother was Sarah Ford, descended of an ancient race of substantial yeomanry in Warwickshire. They were well advanced in years when they married, and never had more than two children, both sons; Samuel, their first born, who lived to be the illustrious character whose various excellence I am to endeavour to record, and Nathanael, who died in his twenty-fifth year.

Mr. Michael Johnson was a man of a large and robust body, and of a strong and active mind; yet, as in the most solid rocks veins of unsound substance are often discovered, there was in him a mixture of that disease, the nature of which eludes the most minute enquiry, though the effects are well known to be a weariness of life, an unconcern about those things which agitate the greater part of mankind, and a general sensation of gloomy wretchedness. From him then his son inherited, with some other qualities, 'a vile melancholy,' which in his too strong expression of any disturbance of the mind, 'made him mad all his life, at least not sober.'

Johnson's mother was a woman of distinguished understanding. I asked his old schoolfellow, Mr. Hector, surgeon, of Birmingham, if she was not vain of her son. He said, 'she had too much good sense to be vain, but she knew her son's value.' Her piety was not inferior to her understanding; and to her must be ascribed those early impressions of religion upon the mind of her son, from which the world afterwards derived so much benefit.

Young Johnson had the misfortune to be much afflicted with the scrophula, or king's evil, which disfigured a countenance naturally well formed, and hurt his visual nerves so much, that he did not see at all with one of his eyes, though its appearance was little different from that of the other. There is amongst his prayers, one inscribed *'When my eye was restored to its use,'* which ascertains a defect that many of his friends knew he had, though I never perceived it. It has been said, that he contracted this grievous malady from his nurse. His mother yielding to the superstitious notion, which, it is wonderful to think, prevailed so long in this country, as to the virtue of the regal touch; a notion, which our kings encouraged, and to which a man of such inquiry and such judgment as Carte could give credit; carried him to London, where he was actually touched by Queen Anne. Mrs. Johnson indeed, as Mr. Hector informed me, acted by the advice of the celebrated Sir John Floyer, then a physician in Lichfield. Johnson used to talk of this very frankly; and Mrs.

Piozzi has preserved his very picturesque description of the scene, as it remained upon his fancy. Being asked if he could remember Queen Anne, 'He had (he said) a confused, but somehow a sort of solemn recollection of a lady in diamonds, and a long black hood.'

He was first taught to read English by Dame Oliver, a widow, who kept a school for young children in Lichfield. He told me she could read the black letter, and asked him to borrow for her, from his father, a Bible in that character. When he was going to Oxford, she came to take leave of him, brought him, in the simplicity of her kindness, a present of gingerbread, and said he was the best scholar she had ever had. He delighted in mentioning this early compliment: adding, with a smile, that 'this was as high a proof of his merit as he could conceive.' His next instructor in English was a master, whom, when he spoke of him to me, he familiarly called Tom Brown, who, said he, 'published a spelling-book, and dedicated it to the UNIVERSE; but, I fear, no copy of it can now be had.'

He began to learn Latin with Mr. Hawkins, usher, or undermaster of Lichfield school, 'a man (said he) very skilful in his little way.' With him he continued two years, and then rose to be under the care of Mr. Hunter, the headmaster, who, according to his account, 'was very severe, and wrongheadedly severe. He used (said he) to beat us unmercifully; and he did not distinguish between ignorance and negligence; for he would beat a boy equally for not knowing a thing, as for neglecting to know it. He would ask a boy a question; and if he did not answer it, he would beat him, without considering whether he had an opportunity of knowing how to answer it. For instance, he would call up a boy and ask him Latin for a candlestick, which the boy could not expect to be asked. Now, Sir, if a boy could answer every question, there would be no need of a master to teach him.'

It is, however, but justice to the memory of Mr. Hunter to mention, that though he might err in being too severe, the school of Lichfield was very respectable in his time. Indeed Johnson was very sensible how much he owed to Mr. Hunter. Mr. Langton one day asked him how he had acquired so accurate a knowledge of Latin, in which, I believe, he was exceeded by no man of his time; he said, 'My master whipt me very well. Without that, Sir, I should have done nothing.' He told Mr. Langton, that while Hunter was flogging his boys unmercifully, he used to say, 'And this I do to save you from the gallows.' Johnson, upon all occasions, expressed his approbation of enforcing instruction by means of the rod. 'I would rather (said he) have the rod to be the general terrour to all, to make them learn, than tell a child, if you do thus, or thus, you will be more esteemed than your brothers or sisters. The rod produces an effect which terminates in itself. A child is afraid of being whipped, and gets his task, and there's an end on't; whereas, by exciting emulation and comparisons of superiority, you lay the foundation of lasting mischief; you make brothers and sisters hate each other.'

That superiority over his fellows, which he maintained with so much dignity in his march through life, was not assumed from vanity and ostentation, but was the natural and constant effect of those extraordinary powers of mind, of which he could not but be conscious by comparison; the intellectual difference, which in other cases of comparison of characters is often a matter of undecided contest, being as clear in his case as the superiority of stature in some men above others. Johnson did not strut or stand on tip-toe. He only did not stoop. From his earliest years, his superiority was perceived and acknowledged. His schoolfellow, Mr. Hector, has obligingly furnished me with many particulars of his boyish days: and assured me that he never knew him corrected at school, but for talking and diverting other boys from their business. His favourites used to receive very liberal assistance from him; and such was the submission and deference with which he was treated, such was the desire to obtain his regard, that three of the boys, of whom Mr. Hector was sometimes one, used to come in the morning as

his humble attendants, and carry him to school. One in the middle stooped, while he sat upon his back, and one on each side supported him; and thus he was borne triumphant.

He never joined with the other boys in their ordinary diversions: his only amusement was in winter, when he took a pleasure in being drawn upon the ice by a boy barefooted, who pulled him along by a garter fixed round him; no very easy operation, as his size was remarkably large. His defective sight, indeed, prevented him from enjoying the common sports; and he once pleasantly remarked to me, 'how wonderfully well he had contrived to be idle without them.'

After having resided for some time at the house of his uncle, Cornelius Ford, Johnson was, at the age of fifteen, removed to the school of Stourbridge, in Worcestershire, of which Mr. Wentworth was then master. This step was taken by the advice of his cousin, the Reverend Mr. Ford, a man in whom both talents and good dispositions were disgraced by licentiousness, but who was a very able judge of what was right. At this school he did not receive so much benefit as was expected. It has been said, that he acted in the capacity of an assistant to Mr. Wentworth, in teaching the younger boys. 'Mr. Wentworth (he told me) was a very able man, but an idle man, and to me very severe; but I cannot blame him much.'

He thus discriminated, to Dr.

Percy, Bishop of Dromore, his progress at his two grammar-schools. 'At one, I learnt much in the school, but little from the master; in the other, I learnt much from the master, but little in the school.'

The Bishop also informs me, that 'Dr. Johnson's father, before he was received at Stourbridge, applied to have him admitted as a scholar and assistant to the Reverend Samuel Lea, M.A. head-master of Newport school, in Shropshire; (a very diligent good teacher, at that time in high reputation, under whom Mr. Hollis is said, in the Memoirs of his Life, to have been also educated). This application to Mr. Lea was not successful; but Johnson had afterwards the gratification to hear that the old gentleman, who lived to a very advanced age, mentioned it as one of the most memorable events of his life, that "he was *very near* having that great man for his scholar."

The two years which he spent at home, after his return from Stourbridge, he passed in what he thought idleness, and was scolded by his father for his want of steady application. He had no settled plan of life, nor looked forward at all, but merely lived from day to day. Yet he read a great deal in a desultory manner, without any scheme of study, as chance threw books in his way, and inclination directed him through them. He used to mention one curious instance of his casual reading, when but a boy. Having imagined that his brother had hid some apples behind a large folio upon an upper shelf in his father's shop, he climbed up to search for them. There were no apples; but the large folio proved to be Petrarch, whom he had seen mentioned, in some preface, as one of the restorers of learning. His curiosity having been thus excited, he sat down with avidity, and read a great part of the book. What he read during these two years, he told me, was not works of mere amusement, 'not voyages and travels, but all literature, Sir, all ancient writers, all manly: though but little Greek, only some of Anacreon and Hesiod; but in this irregular manner (added he) I had looked into a great many books, which were not commonly known at the Universities, where they seldom read any books but what are put into their hands by their tutors; so that when I came to Oxford, Dr. Adams, now master of Pembroke College, told me, I was the best qualified for the University that he had ever known come there.'

That a man in Mr. Michael Johnson's circumstances should think of sending his son to the expensive University of Oxford, at his own charge, seems very improbable. The subject was too delicate to question Johnson upon: but I have been assured by Dr. Taylor, that the scheme never would have taken place, had not a gentleman of Shropshire, one of his schoolfellows, spontaneously undertaken to support him at Oxford, in the character of his companion;

though, in fact, he never received any assistance whatever from that gentleman.

He, however, went to Oxford, and was entered a Commoner of Pembroke College, on the 31st of October, 1728, being then in his nineteenth year.

The Reverend Dr. Adams, who afterwards presided over Pembroke College with universal esteem, told me he was present, and gave me some account of what passed on the night of Johnson's arrival at Oxford. On that evening, his father, who had anxiously accompanied him, found means to have him introduced to Mr. Jorden, who was to be his tutor. His father seemed very full of the merits of his son, and told the company he was a good scholar, and a poet, and wrote Latin verses. His figure and manner appeared strange to them; but he behaved modestly, and sat silent, till upon something which occurred in the course of conversation, he suddenly struck in and quoted Macrobius; and thus he gave the first impression of that more extensive reading in which he had indulged himself.

His tutor, Mr. Jorden, fellow of Pembroke, was not, it seems, a man of such abilities as we should conceive requisite for the instructor of Samuel Johnson, who gave me the following account of him. 'He was a very worthy man, but a heavy man, and I did not profit much by his instructions. Indeed, I did not attend him much. The first day after I came to college, I waited upon him, and then staid away four. On the sixth, Mr. Jorden asked me why I had not attended. I answered, I had been sliding in Christ-Church meadow. And this I said with as much *nonchalance* as I am now talking to you. I had no notion that I was wrong or irreverent to my tutor.' *Boswell:* 'That, Sir, was great fortitude of mind.' *Johnson:* 'No, Sir; stark insensibility.'

He had a love and respect for Jorden, not for his literature, but for his worth. 'Whenever (said he) a young man becomes Jorden's pupil, he becomes his son.'

The 'morbid melancholy,' which was lurking in his constitution, and to which we may ascribe those particularities, and that aversion to regular life, which, at a very early period, marked his character, gathered such strength in his twentieth year, as to afflict him in a dreadful manner. While he was at Lichfield, in the college vacation of the year 1729, he felt himself overwhelmed with an horrible hypochondria,[1] with perpetual irritation, fretfulness, and impatience; and with a dejection, gloom, and despair, which made existence misery. From this dismal malady he never afterwards was perfectly relieved; and all his labours, and all his enjoyments, were but temporary interruptions of its baleful influence. He told Mr. Paradise that he was sometimes so languid and ineffi-

[1] hypochondria: a morbid and depressed state of mind for which there is no direct physical cause.

cient, that he could not distinguish the hour upon the town-clock.

Johnson, upon the first violent attack of this disorder, strove to overcome it by forcible exertions. He frequently walked to Birmingham and back again, and tried many other expedients, but all in vain. His expression concerning it to me was, 'I did not then know how to manage it.'

The history of his mind as to religion is an important article. I have mentioned the early impressions made upon his tender imagination by his mother, who continued her pious care with assiduity, but, in his opinion, not with judgement. 'Sunday (said he) was a heavy day to me when I was a boy. My mother confined me on that day, and made me read "The Whole Duty of Man," from a great part of which I could derive no instruction. When, for instance, I had read the chapter on theft, which from my infancy I had been taught was wrong, I was no more convinced that theft was wrong than before; so there was no accession of knowledge.'

He communicated to me the following particulars upon the subject of his religious progress. 'I fell into an inattention to religion, or an indifference about it, in my ninth year. The church at Lichfield, in which we had a seat, wanted reparation, so I was to go and find a seat in other churches; and having bad eyes, and being awkward about this, I used to go and read in the fields on Sunday. This habit con-

tinued till my fourteenth year; and still I find a great reluctance to go to church. I then became a sort of lax *talker* against religion, for I did not much *think* against it; and this lasted till I went to Oxford, where it would not be *suffered*. When at Oxford, I took up "Law's Serious Call to a Holy Life," expecting to find it a dull book, (as such books generally are,) and perhaps to laugh at it. But I found Law quite an overmatch for me; and this was the first occasion of my thinking in earnest of religion, after I became capable of rational inquiry.' From this time forward, religion was the predominant object of his thoughts; though, with the just sentiments of a conscientious Christian, he lamented that his practice of its duties fell far short of what it ought to be.

How seriously Johnson was impressed with a sense of religion, even in the vigour of his youth, appears from the following passage in his minutes kept by way of diary: 'Sept. 7, 1736. I have this day entered upon my 28th year. Mayest thou, O God, enable me, for *Jesus Christ's* sake, to spend this in such a manner, that I may receive comfort from it at the hour of death, and in the day of judgement! Amen.'

The particular course of his reading while at Oxford, and during the time of vacation which he passed at home, cannot be traced. Enough has been said of his irregular mode of study. He told me, that from his earliest years he loved to read poetry, but hardly ever read any poem to an end; that he read Shakespeare at a period so early, that the speech of the Ghost in Hamlet terrified him when he was alone; that Horace's Odes were the compositions in which he took most delight, and it was long before he liked his Epistles and Satires. He told me what he read *solidly* at Oxford was Greek; not the Grecian historians, but Homer and Euripides, and now and then a little Epigram; that the study of which he was most fond was Metaphysicks, but he had not read much, even in that way. I always thought that he did himself injustice in his account of what he had read, and that he must have been speaking with reference to the vast portion of study which is possible, and to which a few scholars in the whole history of literature have attained. Dr. Adam Smith, than whom few were better judges on this subject, once observed to me that 'Johnson knew more books than any man alive.'

Dr. Adams told me that Johnson, while he was at Pembroke College, 'was caressed and loved by all about him, was a gay and frolicksome fellow, and passed there the happiest part of his life.' But this is a striking proof of the fallacy of appearances, and how little any of us know of the real internal state even of those whom we see most frequently; for the truth is, that he was then depressed by poverty, and irritated by disease.

When I mentioned to him this account as given me by Dr. Adams, he said, 'Ah, Sir, I was mad and violent. It was bitterness which they mistook for frolick. I was miserably poor, and I thought to fight my way by my literature and my wit; so I disregarded all power and all authority.'

The Bishop of Dromore observes in a letter to me,

'I have heard from some of his contemporaries that he was generally seen lounging at the College gate, with a circle of young students round him, whom he was entertaining with wit, and keeping from their studies, if not spiriting them up to rebellion against the College discipline, which in his maturer years he so much extolled.'

I do not find that he formed any close intimacies with his fellow-collegians. But Dr. Adams told me, that he contracted a love and regard for Pembroke College, which he retained to the last. A short time before his death he sent to that College a present of all his works, to be deposited in their library. Being himself a poet, Johnson was peculiarly happy in mentioning how many of the sons of Pembroke were poets; adding, with a smile of sportive triumph, 'Sir, we are a nest of singing birds.'

He was not, however, blind to what he thought the defects of his own College; and I have, from the information of Dr. Taylor, a very strong instance of that rigid honesty which he ever inflexibly preserved. Taylor had obtained his father's consent to be entered of Pembroke, that he might be with his schoolfellow Johnson, with whom, though some years older than himself, he was very intimate. This would have been a great comfort to Johnson. But he fairly told Taylor that he could not, in conscience, suffer him to enter where he knew he could not have an able tutor. He then made inquiry all round the University, and having found Mr. Bateman, of Christ-Church, was the tutor of highest reputation, Taylor was entered of that College. Mr. Bateman's lectures were so excellent, that Johnson used to come and get them at second-hand from Taylor, till his poverty being so extreme, that his shoes were worn out, and his feet appeared through them, he saw that this humiliating circumstance was perceived by the Christ-Churchmen, and he came no more. He was too proud to accept of money, and somebody having set a pair of new shoes at his door, he threw them away with indignation.

The *res angusta domi*[1] prevented him from having the advantage of a complete academical education. The friend to whom he had trusted for support had deceived him. His debts in College, though not great, were increasing; and his scanty remittances from Lichfield, which had all along been made with great difficulty, could be supplied no longer, his father having fallen into a state of insolvency. Compelled, therefore, by irresistible necessity, he left the College in autumn, 1731, without a degree, having been a member of it little more than three years.

And now (I had almost said *poor*) Samuel Johnson returned to his native city, destitute, and not knowing how he should gain even a decent livelihood. His father's misfortunes in trade rendered him unable to support his son; and for some time there appeared no means by which he could maintain himself. In the December of this year his father died.

In the forlorn state of his circumstances, he accepted of an offer to be employed as usher in the school of Market-Bosworth, in Leicestershire. This employment was very irksome to him in every respect, and he complained grievously of it in his letters to his friend Mr. Hector, who was now settled as a surgeon at Birmingham. The letters are lost; but Mr. Hector recollects his writing 'that the poet had described the dull sameness of his existence in these words, *"Vitam continet una dies"* (one day contains the whole of my life); that it was unvaried as the note of the cuckow; and that he did not know whether it was more disagreeable for him to teach, or the boys to learn, the grammar rules.' His general aversion to this painful drudgery was greatly enhanced by a disagreement between him and Sir Wolstan

[1] *res angusta domi:* the narrowness of his domestic affairs; poverty.

Dixey, the patron of the school, in whose house, I have been told, he officiated as a kind of domestick chaplain, so far, at least, as to say grace at table, but was treated with what he represented as intolerable harshness; and, after suffering for a few months such complicated misery, he relinquished a situation which all his life afterwards he recollected with the strongest aversion, and even a degree of horrour.

Being now again totally unoccupied, he was invited by Mr. Hector to pass some time with him at Birmingham, as his guest, at the house of Mr. Warren, with whom Mr. Hector lodged and boarded.

He continued to live as Mr. Hector's guest for about six months, and then hired lodgings in another part of the town, finding himself as well situated at Birmingham as he supposed he could be any where, while he had no settled plan of life, and very scanty means of subsistence. He made some valuable acquaintances there, amongst whom were Mr. Porter, a mercer, whose widow he afterwards married, and Mr. Taylor, who by his ingenuity in mechanical inventions, and his success in trade, acquired an immense fortune. But the comfort of being near Mr. Hector, his old schoolfellow and intimate friend, was Johnson's chief inducement to continue here.

In what manner he employed his pen at this period, or whether he derived from it any pecuniary advantage, I have not been able to ascertain. He probably got a little money from Mr. Warren; and we are certain, that he executed here one piece of literary labour, of which Mr. Hector has favoured me with a minute account. Having mentioned that he had read at Pembroke College a Voyage to Abyssinia, by Lobo, a Portuguese Jesuit, and that he thought an abridgement and translation of it from the French into English might be an useful and profitable publication, Mr. Warren and Mr. Hector joined in urging him to undertake it. He accordingly agreed; and the book not being to be found in Birmingham, he borrowed it of Pembroke College. A part of the work being very soon done, one Osborn, who was Mr. Warren's printer, was set to work with what was ready, and Johnson engaged to supply the press with copy as it should be wanted; but his constitutional indolence soon prevailed, and the work was at a stand. Mr. Hector, who knew that a motive of humanity would be the most prevailing argument with his friend, went to Johnson, and represented to him, that the printer could have no other employment till this undertaking was finished, and that the poor man and his family were suffering. Johnson upon this exerted the powers of his mind, though his body was relaxed. He lay in bed with the book, which was a quarto, before him, and dictated while Hector wrote. Mr.

Hector carried the sheets to the press, and corrected almost all the proof sheets, very few of which were even seen by Johnson. In this manner, with the aid of Mr. Hector's active friendship, the book was completed, and was published in 1735, with *London* upon the title-page, though it was in reality printed at Birmingham, a device too common with provincial publishers. For this work he had from Mr. Warren only the sum of five guineas.

Johnson returned to Lichfield early in 1734, and in August that year he made an attempt to procure some little subsistence by his pen; for he published proposals for printing by subscription the Latin Poems by Politian.

Notwithstanding the merit of Johnson, and the cheap price at which this book was offered, there were not subscribers enough to insure a sufficient sale; so the work never appeared, and, probably, never was executed.

Johnson had, from his early youth, been sensible to the influence of female charms. When at Stourbridge school, he was much enamoured of Olivia Lloyd, a young Quaker, to whom he wrote a copy of verses, which I have not been able to recover.

His juvenile attachments to the fair sex were, however, very transient; and it is certain, that he formed no criminal connection whatsoever. Mr. Hector, who lived with him in his younger days in the utmost intimacy and social freedom, has assured me, that even at that ardent season his conduct was strictly virtuous in that respect; and that though he loved to exhilarate himself with wine, he never knew him intoxicated but once.

In a man whom religious education has secured from licentious indulgences, the passion of love, when once it has seized him, is exceedingly strong; being unimpaired by dissipation, and totally concentrated in one object. This was experienced by Johnson, when he became the fervent admirer of Mrs. Porter, after her first husband's death. Miss Porter told me, that when he was first introduced to her mother, his appearance was very forbidding: he was then lean and lank, so that his immense structure of bones was hideously striking to the eye, and the scars of the scrophula were deeply visible. He also wore his hair, which was straight and stiff, and separated behind; and he often had, seemingly, convulsive starts and odd gesticulations, which tended to excite at once surprize and ridicule. Mrs. Porter was so much engaged by his conversation that she overlooked all these external disadvantages, and said to her daughter, 'this is the most sensible man that I ever saw in my life.'

Though Mrs. Porter was double the age of Johnson, and her person and manner, as described to me by the late Mr. Garrick, were by no means pleasing to others, she must have had a superiority of understanding and talents, as she certainly inspired him with a more than ordinary passion; and she having signified her willingness to accept of his hand, he went to Lichfield to ask his mother's consent to the marriage, which he could not but be conscious was a very imprudent scheme, both on account of their disparity of years, and her want of fortune. But Mrs. Johnson knew too well the ardour of her son's temper, and was too tender a parent to oppose his inclinations.

I know not for what reason the marriage ceremony was not performed at Birmingham; but a resolution was taken that it should be at Derby, for which place the bride and bridegroom set out on horseback, I suppose in very good humour. But though Mr. Topham Beauclerk used archly to mention Johnson's having told him, with much gravity, 'Sir, it was a love-marriage upon both sides,' I have had from my illustrious friend the following curious account of their journey to church upon the nuptial morn. 'Sir, she had read the old romances, and had got into her head the fantastical notion that a woman of spirit should use her lover like a dog. So, Sir, at first she told me that I rode too fast, and she could not keep up with me; and, when I rode a little slower, she passed me, and complained that I lagged behind. I was not to be made the slave of caprice; and I resolved to begin as I meant to end. I therefore pushed on briskly, till I was fairly out of her sight. The road lay between two hedges, so I was sure she could not miss it; and I contrived that she should soon come up with me. When she did, I observed her to be in tears.'

This, it must be allowed, was a singular beginning of connubial felicity; but there is no doubt that Johnson, though he thus shewed a manly firmness, proved a most affectionate and indulgent husband to the last moment of Mrs. Johnson's life: and in his 'Prayers and Meditations' we find very remarkable evidence that his regard and fondness for her never ceased, even after her death.

He now set up a private academy, for which purpose he hired a large house, well situated near his native city. In the Gentleman's Magazine for 1736, there is the following advertisement:

'At Edial, near Lichfield, in Staffordshire, young gentlemen are boarded and taught the Latin and Greek languages, by *Samuel Johnson*.'

But the only pupils that were put under his care were the celebrated David Garrick [1] and his brother George, and a Mr. Offely, a young gentleman of good fortune, who died early.

---

[1] the celebrated David Garrick (1717-1779): wit and lifelong intimate of Johnson, he became the leading and most successful actor and producer of his time.

✖ *Chapter* 2

A Profession: Literature

Johnson was not more satisfied with his situation as the master of an academy, than with that of the usher of a school; we need not wonder, therefore, that he did not keep his academy above a year and a half. From Mr. Garrick's account he did not appear to have been profoundly reverenced by his pupils. His oddities of manner, and uncouth gesticulations, could not but be the subject of merriment to them; and, in particular, the young rogues used to listen at the door of his bed-chamber, and peep through the key-hole, that they might turn into ridicule his tumultuous and aukward fondness for Mrs. Johnson, whom he used to name by the familiar appellation of *Tetty* or *Tetsey,* which, like *Betty* or *Betsy,* is provincially used as a contraction for *Elisabeth,* her Christian name, but which to us seems ludicrous, when applied to a woman of her age and appearance. Mr. Garrick described her to me as very fat, with a bosom of more than ordinary protuberance, with swelled cheeks, of a florid red, produced by thick painting, and increased by the liberal use of cordials; flaring and fantastick in her dress, and affected both in her speech and her general behaviour. I have seen Garrick exhibit her, by his exquisite talent for mimickry, so as to excite the heartiest bursts of laughter; but he, probably, as is the case in all such representations, considerably aggravated the picture.

While Johnson kept his academy, there can be no doubt that he was insensibly furnishing his mind with various knowledge; but I have not discovered that he wrote any thing except a great part of his tragedy of *Irene.* Mr. Peter Garrick, the elder brother of David, told me that he remembered Johnson's borrowing the Turkish History of him, in order to form his play from it.

Johnson now thought of trying his fortune in London, the great field of genius and exertion, where talents of every kind have the fullest scope, and the highest encouragement. It is a memorable circumstance that his pupil David Garrick went thither at the same time, with intention to complete his education, and follow the profession of the law, from which he was soon diverted by his decided preference for the stage.

Johnson had a little money when he came to town, and he knew how he could live in the cheapest manner. His first lodgings were at the house of Mr. Norris, a staymaker, in Exeter-street, adjoining Catharine-street, in the Strand. 'I dined (said he) very well for eight-pence, with very good company, at the Pine Apple in New-street, just by. Several of them had travelled. They expected to meet every day; but did not know one another's names. It used to cost the rest a shilling, for they drank wine; but I had a cut of meat for six-pence, and bread for a penny, and gave the waiter a penny; so that I was quite well served, nay, better than the rest, for they gave the waiter nothing.'

He at this time, I believe, abstained entirely from fermented liquors: a practice to which he rigidly conformed for many years together, at different periods of his life.

Amidst this cold obscurity, there was one brilliant circumstance to cheer him; he was well acquainted with Mr. Henry Hervey, one of the branches of the noble family of that name, who had been quartered at Lichfield as an officer of the army, and had at this time a house in London, where Johnson was frequently entertained, and had an opportunity of meeting genteel company. Not very long before his death, he mentioned this, among other particulars of his life, which he was kindly communicating to me; and he described this early friend, 'Harry Hervey,' thus: 'He was a vicious man, but very kind to me. If you call a dog *Hervey*, I shall love him.'

In the course of the summer he returned to Lichfield, where he had left Mrs. Johnson, and there he at last finished his tragedy, which was not executed with his rapidity of composition upon other occasions, but was slowly and painfully elaborated.

He removed, after three months, to London with Mrs. Johnson; but her daughter, who had lived with them at Edial, was left with her relations in the country. His lodg-ings were for some time in Wood-stock-street, near Hanover-square, and afterwards in Castle-street, near Cavendish-square.

His tragedy being by this time, as he thought, completely finished and fit for the stage, he was very desirous that it should be brought forward. Mr. Peter Garrick told me, that Johnson and he went together to the Fountain tavern, and read it over, and that he afterwards solicited Mr. Fleetwood, the patentee of Drury-lane theatre, to have it acted at his house; but Mr. Fleetwood would not accept it, probably because it was not patronized by some man of high rank; and it was not acted till 1749, when his friend David Garrick was manager of that theatre.

The Gentleman's Magazine, begun and carried on by Mr. Edward Cave, under the name of *Sylvanus Urban,* had attracted the notice and esteem of Johnson, in an eminent degree, before he came to London as an adventurer in literature. He told me, that when he first saw St. John's Gate, the place where that deservedly popular miscellany was originally printed, he 'beheld it with reverence.'

It appears that he was now enlisted by Mr. Cave as a regular co-adjutor in his magazine, by which he probably obtained a tolerable livelihood. At what time, or by what means, he had acquired a competent knowledge both of French and Italian, I do not know; but he was so well skilled in them, as to be sufficiently qualified for a translator. That part of his labour which consisted in emendation and improvement of the productions of other contributors, like that employed in levelling ground, can be perceived only by those who had an opportunity of comparing the original with the altered copy. What we certainly know to have been done by him in this way, was the Debates in both houses of Parliament, under the name of 'The Senate of Lilliput,' sometimes with feigned denominations of the several speakers, sometimes with denominations formed of the letters of their real names, in the manner of what is called anagram, so that they might easily be decyphered. Parliament then kept the press in a kind of mysterious awe, which made it necessary to have recourse to such devices.

Johnson's 'London' was published in May 1738; and it is remarkable, that it came out on the same morning with Pope's satire, entitled '1738.' The Reverend Dr. Douglas, now Bishop of Salisbury, to whom I am indebted for some obliging communications, was then a student at Oxford, and remembers well the effect which 'London' produced. Every body was delighted with it; and there being no name to it, the first buz of the literary circles was 'here is an unknown poet, greater even than Pope.' And it is recorded in the Gentleman's Magazine of that year, that it 'got to the second edition in the course of a week.'

Pope, who then filled the poetical throne without a rival, it may reasonably be presumed, must have been particularly struck by the sudden appearance of such a poet; and, to his credit, let it be remembered, that his feelings and conduct on the occasion were candid and liberal. He requested Mr. Richardson, son of the painter, to endeavour to find out who this new authour was. Mr. Richardson, after some inquiry, having informed him that he had discovered only that his name was Johnson, and that he was some obscure man, Pope said, 'He will soon be *déterré.*' [1]

Though thus elevated into fame, and conscious of uncommon powers, he had not that bustling confidence, or, I may rather say, that animated ambition, which one might have supposed would have urged him to endeavour at rising in life. But such was his inflexible dignity of character, that he could not stoop to court the great; without which, hardly any man has made his way to high station. He could not expect to produce many such works as his '*London,*' and he felt the hardship of writing for bread; he was, therefore, willing to resume the office of a schoolmaster, so as to have a sure, though moderate income for his life; and an offer being made to him of the mastership of a school, provided he could obtain the degree of Master of Arts, Dr. Adams was applied to, by a common friend, to know whether that could be granted him as a favour from the University of Oxford. But though he

[1] *déterré:* unearthed.

had made such a figure in the literary world, it was then thought too great a favour to be asked.

It was, perhaps, no small disappointment to Johnson that this respectable application had not the desired effect; yet how much reason has there been, both for himself and his country, to rejoice that it did not succeed, as he might probably have wasted in obscurity those hours in which he afterwards produced his incomparable works.

About this time he made one other effort to emancipate himself from the drudgery of authorship. He applied to Dr. Adams, to consult Dr. Smalbroke of the Commons, whether a person might be permitted to practice as an advocate there, without a doctor's degree in Civil Law. 'I am (said he) a total stranger to these studies; but whatever is a profession, and maintains numbers, must be within the reach of common abilities, and some degree of industry.' But here, also, the want of a degree was an insurmountable bar.

He was, therefore, under the necessity of persevering in that course, into which he had been forced.

In 1742 he wrote for the Gentleman's Magazine the 'Proposals for printing Bibliotheca Harleiana, or a Catalogue of the Library of the Earl of Oxford.' His account of that celebrated collection of books, in which he displays the importance to literature, of what the French call a *catalogue raisonné,* when the subjects of it are extensive and various, and it is executed with ability, cannot fail to impress all his readers with admiration of his philological attainments. It was afterwards prefixed to the first volume of the Catalogue, in which the Latin accounts of books were written by him. He was employed in this business by Mr. Thomas Osborne the bookseller, who purchased the library for 13,000*l.,* a sum, which Mr. Oldys says, in one of his manuscripts, was not more than the binding of the books had cost; yet, Dr. Johnson assured me, the slowness of the sale was such, that there was not much gained by it. It has been confidently related, with many embellishments, that Johnson one day knocked Osborne down in his shop, with a folio, and put his foot upon his neck. The simple truth I had from Johnson himself. 'Sir, he was impertinent to me, and I beat him. But it was not in his shop: it was in my own chamber.'

It does not appear that he wrote any thing in 1744 for the Gentleman's Magazine, but the Preface. But he produced one work this year, fully sufficient to maintain the high reputation which he had acquired. This was *'The Life of Richard Savage';* a man, of whom it is difficult to speak impartially, without wondering that he was for some time the intimate companion of Johnson; for his character was marked by profligacy, insolence, and ingratitude: yet, as he undoubtedly had a warm and vigorous, though unregulated mind, had seen life in all its varieties, and been much in the company of the statesmen and wits of his time, he could communicate to Johnson an abundant supply of such materials as his philosophical curiosity most eagerly desired; and as Savage's misfortunes and misconduct had reduced him to the lowest state of wretchedness as a writer for bread, his visits to St. John's Gate naturally brought Johnson and him together.

It is melancholy to reflect, that Johnson and Savage were sometimes in such extreme indigence, that they could not pay for a lodging; so that they have wandered together whole nights in the streets. Yet in these almost incredible scenes of distress, we may suppose that Savage mentioned many of the anecdotes with which Johnson afterwards enriched the life of his unhappy companion, and those of other Poets.

He told Sir Joshua Reynolds,[1] that one night in particular, when Savage and he walked round St. James's-square for want of a lodging, they were not at all depressed by their situation; but in high spirits and brimful of patriotism, traversed the square for several hours, inveighed against the minister, and 'resolved they would *stand by their country.*'

[1] Sir Joshua Reynolds (1723–1792): famous portrait painter and art authority; first president (1768) of the Royal Academy. He was Johnson's intimate friend and a most eminent member of Johnson's literary circle.

In Johnson's 'Life of Savage,' a very useful lesson is inculcated, to guard men of warm passions from a too free indulgence of them; and the various incidents are related in so clear and animated a manner, and illuminated throughout with so much philosophy, that it is one of the most interesting narratives in the English language. Sir Joshua Reynolds told me, that upon his return from Italy he met with it in Devonshire, knowing nothing of its authour, and began to read it while he was standing with his arm leaning against a chimney-piece. It siezed his attention so strongly, that, not being able to lay down the book till he had finished it, when he attempted to move, he found his arm totally benumbed. The rapidity with which this work was composed, is a wonderful circumstance. Johnson has been heard to say, 'I wrote forty-eight of the printed octavo pages of the "Life of Savage" at a sitting; but then I sat up all night.'

It is remarkable, that in this biographical disquisition there appears a very strong symptom of Johnson's prejudice against players; a prejudice, which may be attributed to the following causes: first, the imperfection of his organs, which were so defective that he was not susceptible of the fine impressions which theatrical excellence produces upon the generality of mankind; secondly, the cold rejection of his tragedy; and, lastly, the brilliant success of Garrick, who had been his pupil, who had come to London at the same time with him, not in a much more prosperous state than himself, and whose talents he undoubtedly rated low, compared with his own. His being outstripped by his pupil in the race of immediate fame, as well as of fortune, probably made him feel some indignation, as thinking that whatever might be Garrick's merits in his art, the reward was too great when compared with what the most successful efforts of literary labour could attain. At all periods of his life Johnson used to talk contemptuously of players; but in this work he speaks of them with peculiar acrimony; for which, perhaps, there was formerly too much reason from the licentious and dissolute manners of those engaged in that profession.

However, his old pupil and friend, David Garrick, having become joint patentee and manager of Drury-lane theatre, Johnson honoured his opening of it with a Prologue, which for just and manly dramatick criticism, on the whole range of the English stage, as well as for poetical excellence, is unrivalled.

But the year 1747 is distinguished as the epoch, when Johnson's arduous and important work, his *Dictionary of the English Language,* was announced to the world, by the publication of its Plan or *Prospectus.*

The booksellers who contracted with Johnson, single and unaided, for the execution of a work, which in other countries has not been effected but by the co-operating exertions of many, were Mr. Robert Dodsley, Mr. Charles Hitch, Mr. Andrew Millar, the two Messieurs Longman, and the two Messieurs Knapton. The price stipulated was fifteen hundred and seventy-five pounds.

The 'Plan' was addressed to Philip Dormer, Earl of Chesterfield, then one of his Majesty's Principal Secretaries of State; a nobleman who was very ambitious of literary distinction, and who, upon being informed of the design, had expressed himself in terms very favourable to its success.

It is worthy of observation that the 'Plan' has not only the substantial merit of comprehension, perspicuity, and precision, but that the language of it is unexceptionably excellent; it being altogether free from that inflation of style, and those uncommon but apt and energetick words, which in some of his writings have been censured, with more petulance than justice; and never was there a more dignified strain of compliment, than that in which he courts the attention of one who, he had been persuaded to believe, would be a respectable patron.

'With regard to questions of purity or propriety, (says he) I was once in doubt whether I should not attribute to myself too much in attempting to decide them, and whether my province was to extend beyond the proposition of the question, and the display of the suffrages on each side; but I have been since determined by your Lordship's opinion, to interpose my own judgement, and shall therefore endeavour to support what appears to me most consonant to grammar and reason. And I may hope, my Lord, that since you, whose authority in our language is so generally acknowledged, have commissioned me to declare my own opinion, I shall be considered as exercising a kind of vicarious jurisdiction, and that the power which might have been denied to my own claim, will be readily allowed me as the delegate of your Lordship.'

This passage proves, that Johnson's addressing his 'Plan' to Lord Chesterfield was not merely in consequence of the result of a report by means of Dodsley that the Earl favoured the design; but that there had been a particular communication with his Lordship concerning it. Dr. Taylor told me that Johnson sent his 'Plan' to him in manuscript, for his perusal; and that when it was lying upon his table, Mr. William Whitehead happened to pay him a visit, and being shewn it, was highly pleased with such parts of it as he had time to read, and begged to take it home with him, which he was allowed to do; that from him it got into the hands of a noble Lord, who carried it to Lord Chesterfield.

That he was fully aware of the arduous nature of the undertaking, he acknowledges; and shews himself perfectly sensible of it in the conclusion of his 'Plan;' but he had a noble consciousness of his own abilities, which enabled him to go on with undaunted spirit.

Dr. Adams found him one day busy at his Dictionary, when the following dialogue ensued. *Adams:* 'This is a great work, Sir. How are you to get all the etymologies?' *Johnson:* 'Why, Sir, here is a shelf with Junius, and Skinner, and others; and there is a Welch gentleman who has published a collection of Welch proverbs, who will help me with the Welch.' *Adams:* 'But, Sir, how can you do this in three years?' *Johnson:* 'Sir, I have no doubt that I can do it in three years.' *Adams:* 'But the French Academy, which consists of forty members, took forty years to compile their Dictionary.' *Johnson:* 'Sir, thus it is. This is the proportion. Let me see; forty times forty is sixteen hundred. As three to sixteen hundred, so is the proportion of an Englishman to a Frenchman.' With so much ease and pleasantry could he talk of that prodigious labour which he had undertaken to execute.

While the Dictionary was going forward, Johnson lived part of the time in Holborn, part in Gough-square, Fleet-street; and he had an upper room fitted up like a counting-house for the purpose, in which he gave to the copyists their several tasks. The words, partly taken from other dictionaries, and partly supplied by himself, having been first written down with spaces left between them, he delivered in writing their etymologies, definitions, and various significations. The authorities were copied from the books themselves, in which he had marked the passages with a black-lead pencil, the traces of which could easily be effaced. It is remarkable, that he was so attentive in the choice of the passages in which words were authorised, that one may read page after page of his Dictionary with improvement and pleasure; and it should not pass unobserved, that he has quoted no authour whose writings had a tendency to hurt sound religion and morality.

The necessary expence of preparing a work of such magnitude for the press, must have been a considerable deduction from the price stipulated to be paid for the copyright. I understand that nothing was allowed by the booksellers on that account; and I remember his telling me, that a large portion of it having, by mistake, been written upon both sides of the paper, so as to be inconvenient for the compositor, it cost him twenty pounds to have it transcribed upon one side only.

He is now to be considered as 'tugging at his oar,' as engaged in a steady continued course of occupation, sufficient to employ all his time for some years; and which was the best preventive of that constitutional melancholy which was ever lurking about him, ready to trouble his quiet. But his enlarged and lively mind could not be satisfied without more diversity of employment, and the pleasure of animated relaxation. He therefore not only exerted his talents in occasional composition very different from Lexicography, but formed a club in Ivy-

lane, Paternoster-row, with a view to enjoy literary discussion, and amuse his evening hours. The members associated with him in this little society were his beloved friend Dr. Richard Bathurst, Mr. Hawkesworth, afterwards well known by his writings, Mr. John Hawkins, an attorney, and a few others of different professions.

In January 1749 he published 'The Vanity of Human Wishes, being the Tenth Satire of Juvenal imitated.' Mrs. Johnson, for the sake of country air, had lodgings at Hampstead, to which he resorted occasionally, and there the greatest part, if not the whole, of this Imitation was written. The fervid rapidity with which it was produced, is scarcely credible. I have heard him say, that he composed seventy lines of it in one day, without putting one of them upon paper till they were finished.

The profits of a single poem, however excellent, appear to have been very small in the last reign, compared with what a publication of the same size has since been known to yield. I have mentioned, upon Johnson's own authority, that for his *London* he had only ten guineas; and now, after his fame was established, he got for his 'Vanity of Human Wishes' but five guineas more, as is proved by an authentick document in my possession.

His 'Vanity of Human Wishes' has less of common life, but more of a philosophick dignity than his

'London.' More readers, therefore, will be delighted with the pointed spirit of 'London,' than with the profound reflection of 'The Vanity of Human Wishes.' Garrick, for instance, observed in his sprightly manner, with more vivacity than regard to just discrimination, as is usual with wits, 'When Johnson lived much with the Herveys, and saw a good deal of what was passing in life, he wrote his "London," which is lively and easy. When he became more retired, he gave us his "Vanity of Human Wishes," which is as hard as Greek. Had he gone on to imitate another satire, it would have been as hard as Hebrew.'

Garrick being now vested with theatrical power by being manager of Drury-lane theatre, he kindly and generously made use of it to bring out Johnson's tragedy, which had been long kept back for want of encouragement. But in this benevolent purpose he met with no small difficulty from the temper of Johnson, which could not brook that a drama which he had formed with much study, should be revised and altered at the pleasure of an actor. Johnson was at first very obstinate. 'Sir, (said he) the fellow wants me to make Mahomet run mad, that he may have an opportunity of tossing his hands and kicking his heels.' He was, however, at last, with difficulty, prevailed on to comply with Garrick's wishes, so as to allow of some changes; but still there were not enough.

Dr. Adams was present the first night of the representation of *Irene,* and gave me the following account: 'Before the curtain drew up, there were catcalls whistling, which alarmed Johnson's friends. The Prologue, which was written by himself in a manly strain, soothed the audience, and the play went off tolerably, till it came to the conclusion, when Mrs. Pritchard, the heroine of the piece, was to be strangled upon the stage, and was to speak two lines with the bow-string round her neck. The audience cried out *"Murder! Murder!"* She several times attempted to speak; but in vain. At last she was obliged to go off the stage alive.' This passage was afterwards struck out, and she was carried off to be put to death behind the scenes, as the play now has it.

Notwithstanding all the support of such performers as Garrick, Barry, Mrs. Cibber, Mrs. Pritchard, and every advantage of dress and decoration, the tragedy of Irene did not please the publick. Mr. Garrick's zeal carried it through for nine nights, so that the authour had his three nights' profits; and from a receipt signed by him, now in the hands of Mr. James Dodsley, it appears that his friend Mr. Robert Dodsley gave him one hundred pounds for the copy, with his usual reservation of the right of one edition.

Johnson was wise enough to be convinced that he had not the talents necessary to write successfully for the stage, and never made another attempt in that species of composition. And let it be remembered, as an admonition to the *genus irritabile* [1] of dramatick writers, that this great man, instead of peevishly complaining of the bad taste of the town, submitted to its decision without a murmur. He had, indeed, upon all occasions, a great deference for the general opinion: 'A man (said he) who writes a book, thinks himself wiser or wittier than the rest of mankind; he supposes that he can instruct or amuse them, and the publick to whom he appeals, must, after all, be the judges of his pretensions.'

On occasion of his play being brought upon the stage, Johnson had a fancy that as a dramatick authour his dress should be more gay than what he ordinarily wore; he therefore appeared behind the scenes, and even in one of the side boxes, in a scarlet waistcoat, with rich gold lace, and a gold-laced hat. He humourously observed to Mr. Langton, 'that when in that dress he could not treat people with the same ease as when in his usual plain clothes.' His necessary attendance while his play was in rehearsal, and during its performance, brought him acquainted with many of the performers of both sexes, which produced a more favourable opinion of their profession than he had harshly expressed in his Life of Savage. With some of them he kept up an acquaintance as long as he and they lived, and was ever ready to shew them acts of kindness. He

for a considerable time used to frequent the *Green Room,* and seemed to take delight in dissipating his gloom, by mixing in the sprightly chit-chat of the motley circle then to be found there. Mr. David Hume related to me from Mr. Garrick, that Johnson at last denied himself this amusement, from considerations of rigid virtue; saying, 'I'll come no more behind your scenes, David; for the silk stockings and white bosoms of your actresses excite my amorous propensities.'

In 1750 he came forth in the character for which he was eminently qualified, a majestick teacher of moral and religious wisdom. The vehicle which he chose was that of a periodical paper, which he knew had been, upon former occasions, employed with great success. Johnson was, I think, not very happy in the choice of his title, 'The Rambler.' He gave Sir Joshua Reynolds the following account of its getting this name: 'What *must* be done, Sir, *will* be done. When I was to begin publishing that paper, I was at a loss how to name it. I sat down at night upon my bedside, and resolved that I would not go to sleep till I had fixed its title. The Rambler seemed the best that occurred, and I took it.'

The first paper of the Rambler was published on Tuesday the 20th of March, 1750; and its authour was enabled to continue it, without interruption, every Tuesday and Friday, till Saturday, the 17th

---

[1] *genus irritabile:* the irritable race.

of March, 1752, on which day it closed. This is a strong confirmation of the truth of a remark of his, which I have had occasion to quote elsewhere, that 'a man may write at any time, if he will set himself doggedly to it'; for, notwithstanding his constitutional indolence, his depression of spirits, and his labour in carrying on his Dictionary, he answered the stated calls of the press twice a week from the stores of his mind during all that time.

Posterity will be astonished when they are told, upon the authority of Johnson himself, that many of these discourses, which we should suppose had been laboured with all the slow attention of literary leisure, were written in haste as the moment pressed, without even being read over by him before they were printed. Sir Joshua Reynolds once asked him by what means he had attained his extraordinary accuracy and flow of language. He told him, that he had early laid it down as a fixed rule to do his best on every occasion, and in every company; to impart whatever he knew in the most forcible language he could put it in; and that by constant practice, and never suffering any careless expressions to escape him, or attempting to deliver his thoughts without arranging them in the clearest manner, it became habitual to him.

As the Rambler was entirely the work of one man, there was, of course, such a uniformity in its texture, as very much to exclude the charm of variety; and the grave and often solemn cast of thinking, which distinguished it from other periodical papers, made it, for some time, not generally liked. So slowly did this excellent work, of which twelve editions have now issued from the press, gain upon the world at large, that even in the closing number the authour says, 'I have never been much a favourite of the publick.' Yet, very soon after its commencement, there were who felt and acknowledged its uncommon excellence. Verses in its praise appeared in the newspapers; and the editor of the Gentleman's Magazine mentions, in October, his having received several letters to the same purpose from the learned.

Johnson told me, with an amiable fondness, a little pleasing circumstance relative to this work. Mrs. Johnson, in whose judgement and taste he had great confidence, said to him, after a few numbers of the Rambler had come out, 'I thought very well of you before; but I did not imagine you could have written any thing equal to this.'

The Rambler has increased in fame as in age. Soon after its first folio edition was concluded, it was published in six duodecimo volumes; and its authour lived to see ten numerous editions of it in London, beside those of Ireland and Scotland.

The style of this work has been censured by some shallow criticks as involved and turgid, and abounding with antiquated and hard words. So ill-founded is the first part of this objection, that I will challenge all who may honour this book with a perusal, to point out any English writer whose language conveys his meaning with equal force and perspicuity. It must, indeed, be allowed, that the structure of his sentences is expanded, and often has somewhat of the inversion of Latin; and that he delighted to express familiar thoughts in philosophical language; being in this the reverse of Socrates, who, it was said, reduced philosophy to the simplicity of common life. But let us attend to what he himself says in his concluding paper: 'When common words were less pleasing to the ear, or less distinct in their signification, I have familiarised the terms of philosophy, by applying them to popular ideas.' And, as to the second part of this objection, upon a late careful revision of the work, I can with confidence say, that it is amazing how few of those words, for which it has been unjustly characterised, are actually to be found in it; I am sure, not the proportion of one to each paper. This idle charge has been echoed from one babbler to another, who have confounded Johnson's Essays with Johnson's Dictionary; and because he thought it right in a Lexicon of our language to collect many words which had fallen into disuse, but were supported by great authorities, it has been imagined that all of these have been interwoven into his own compositions.

Though Johnson's circumstances were at this time far from being easy, his humane and charitable disposition was constantly exerting itself. Mrs. Anna Williams, daughter of a very ingenious Welsh physician, and a woman of more than ordinary talents and literature, having come to London in hopes of being cured of a cataract in both her eyes, which afterwards ended in total blindness, was kindly received as a constant visitor at his house while Mrs. Johnson lived; and after her death having come under his roof in order to have an operation upon her eyes performed with more comfort to her than in lodgings, she had an apartment from him during the rest of her life, at all times when he had a house.

In 1752 he was almost entirely occupied with his Dictionary. The last paper of his Rambler was published March 2, this year; after which, there was a cessation for some time of any exertion of his talents as an essayist.

That there should be a suspension of his literary labours during a part of the year 1752, will not seem strange, when it is considered that soon after closing his Rambler, he suffered a loss which, there can be no doubt, affected him with the deepest distress. For on the 17th of March, his wife died. Why Sir John Hawkins should unwarrantably take upon him even to *suppose* that Johnson's fondness for her was *dissembled* (meaning simulated or assumed,) and to assert, that if it was not the case, 'it was a lesson he had learned by rote,' I cannot conceive; unless it proceeded from a want of similar feelings in his own breast. To argue from her being much older than Johnson, or any other circumstances, that he could not really love her, is absurd; for love is not a subject of reasoning, but of feeling, and therefore there are no common principles upon which one can persuade another concerning it. Every man feels for himself, and knows how he is affected by particular qualities in the person he admires, the impressions of which are too minute and delicate to be substantiated in language.

That his love for his wife was of the most ardent kind, and, during the long period of fifty years, was unimpaired by the lapse of time, is evident from various passages in the series of his Prayers and Meditations, published by the Reverend Mr. Strahan, as well as from other memorials, two of which I select, as strongly marking the tenderness and sensibility of his mind.

'March 28, 1753. I kept this day as the anniversary of my Tetty's death, with prayer and tears in the morning. In the evening I prayed for her conditionally, if it were lawful.'

'April 23, 1753. I know not whether I do not too much indulge the vain longings of affection; but I hope they intenerate my heart, and that when I die like my Tetty, this affection will be acknowledged in a happy interview, and that in the mean time

I am incited by it to piety. I will, however, not deviate too much from common and received methods of devotion.'

I have been told by Mrs. Desmoulins, who, before her marriage, lived for some time with Mrs. Johnson at Hampstead, that she indulged herself in country air and nice living, at an unsuitable expence, while her husband was drudging in the smoke of London, and that she by no means treated him with that complacency which is the most engaging quality in a wife. But all this is perfectly compatible with his fondness for her, especially when it is remembered that he had a high opinion of her understanding, and that the impression which her beauty, real or imaginary, had originally made upon his fancy, being continued by habit, had not been effaced, though she herself was doubtless much altered for the worse. The dreadful shock of separation took place in the night; and he immediately dispatched a letter to his friend, the Reverend Dr. Taylor, which, as Taylor told me, expressed grief in the strongest manner he had ever read; so that it is much to be regretted it has not been preserved. The letter was brought to Dr. Taylor, at his house in the Cloysters, Westminster, about three in the morning; and as it signified an earnest desire to see him, he got up, and went to Johnson as soon as he was dressed, and found him in tears and in extreme agitation. After being a little while together, Johnson requested him to join with him in prayer. He then prayed extempore, as did Dr. Taylor; and thus, by means of that piety which was ever his primary object, his troubled mind was, in some degree, soothed and composed.

The circle of his friends, indeed, at this time was extensive and various, far beyond what has been generally imagined. To trace his acquaintance with each particular person, if it could be done, would be a task, of which the labour would not be repaid by the advantage. But exceptions are to be made; one of which must be a friend so eminent as Sir Joshua Reynolds, and with whom he maintained an uninterrupted intimacy to the last hour of his life. When Johnson lived in Castle-street, Cavendish-square, he used frequently to visit two ladies, who lived opposite to him, Miss Cotterells, daughters of Admiral Cotterell. Reynolds used also to visit there, and thus they met. Mr. Reynolds, as I have observed above, had, from the first reading of his Life of Savage, conceived a very high admiration of Johnson's powers of writing. His conversation no less delighted him; and he cultivated his acquaintance with the laudable zeal of one who was ambitious of general improvement. Sir Joshua, indeed, was lucky enough at their very first meeting to make a remark, which was so much above the commonplace style of conversation, that Johnson at once perceived that Reynolds had the habit of thinking for himself. The ladies were regretting the death of a friend, to whom they owed great obligations; upon which Reynolds observed, 'You have, however, the comfort of being relieved from a burthen of gratitude.' They were shocked a little at this alleviating suggestion, as too selfish; but Johnson defended it in his clear and forcible manner, and was much pleased with the *mind,* the fair view of human nature, which it exhibited, like some of the reflections of Rochefaucault.[1] The consequence was, that he went home with Reynolds, and supped with him.

His acquaintance with Bennet Langton, Esq., of Langton, in Lincolnshire, another much valued friend, commenced soon after the conclusion of his Rambler; which that gentleman, then a youth, had read with so much admiration, that he came to London chiefly with the view of endeavouring to be introduced to its authour. By a fortunate chance he happened to take lodgings in a house where Mr. Levet frequently visited; and having mentioned his wish to his landlady, she introduced him to Mr. Levet, who readily obtained Johnson's permission to bring Mr. Langton to him; as, indeed, Johnson, during the whole course of his life, had no shyness, real or affected, but was easy of access to all who were

[1] Rochefaucault: Duc François de La Rochefoucauld (1613–1680); French writer.

properly recommended, and even wished to see numbers at his *levee,* as his morning circle of company might, with strict propriety, be called. Mr. Langton was exceedingly surprized when the sage first appeared. He had not received the smallest intimation of his figure, dress, or manner. From perusing his writings, he fancied he should see a decent, well-drest, in short, a remarkably decorous philosopher. Instead of which, down from his bed-chamber, about noon, came, as newly risen, a huge uncouth figure, with a little dark wig which scarcely covered his head, and his clothes hanging loose about him. But his conversation was so rich, so animated, and so forcible, and his religious and political notions so congenial with those in which Mr. Langton had been educated, that he conceived for him that veneration and attachment which he ever preserved. Johnson was not the less ready to love Mr. Langton, for his being of a very ancient family; for I have heard him say, with pleasure, 'Langton, Sir, has a grant of free warren from Henry the Second; and Cardinal Stephen Langton, in King John's reign, was of this family.'

Mr. Langton afterwards went to pursue his studies at Trinity College, Oxford, where he formed an acquaintance with his fellow student, Mr. Topham Beauclerk; who, though their opinions and modes of life were so different, that it seemed utterly improbable that they should at all agree, had so ardent a love of literature, so acute an understanding, such elegance of manners, and so well discerned the excellent qualities of Mr. Langton, a gentleman eminent not only for worth and learning, but for an inexhaustible fund of entertaining conversation, that they became intimate friends.

Johnson, soon after this acquaintance began, passed a considerable time at Oxford. He at first thought it strange that Langton should associate so much with one who had the character of being loose, both in his principles and practice; but, by degrees, he himself was fascinated. Mr. Beauclerk's being of the St. Alban's family, and having, in some particulars, a resemblance to Charles the Second, contributed, in Johnson's imagination, to throw a lustre upon his other qualities; and, in a short time, the moral, pious Johnson, and the gay, dissipated Beauclerk, were companions. 'What a coalition! (said Garrick, when he heard of this;) I shall have my old friend to bail out of the Round-house.'[1] But I can bear testimony that it was a very agreeable association. Beauclerk was too polite, and valued learning and wit too much, to offend Johnson by sallies of infidelity or licentiousness; and Johnson delighted in the good qualities of Beauclerk, and hoped to correct the evil. Innumerable were the scenes in which Johnson was amused by these young men. Beauclerk could take more liberty with

[1] Round-house: jail.

him, than any body with whom I ever saw him; but, on the other hand, Beauclerk was not spared by his respectable companion, when reproof was proper. Beauclerk had such a propensity to satire, that at one time Johnson said to him, 'You never open your mouth but with intention to give pain; and you have often given me pain, not from the power of what you said, but from seeing your intention.' At another time applying to him, with a slight alteration, a line of Pope, he said,

'Thy love of folly, and thy scorn of fools—

Every thing thou dost shews the one, and every thing thou say'st the other.' At another time he said to him, 'Thy body is all vice, and thy mind all virtue.' Beauclerk not seeming to relish the compliment, Johnson said, 'Nay, Sir, Alexander the Great, marching in triumph into Babylon, could not have desired to have had more said to him.'

One night when Beauclerk and Langton had supped at a tavern in London, and sat till about three in the morning, it came into their heads to go and knock up Johnson, and see if they could prevail on him to join them in a ramble. They rapped violently at the door of his chambers in the Temple, till at last he appeared in his shirt, with his little black wig on the top of his head, instead of a nightcap, and a poker in his hand, imagining, probably, that some ruffians were coming to attack him. When he discovered who they were, and was told their errand, he smiled, and with great good humour agreed to their proposal: 'What, is it you, you dogs! I'll have a frisk with you,' He was soon drest, and they sallied forth together into Covent-Garden, where the green-grocers and fruiterers were beginning to arrange their hampers, just come in from the country. Johnson made some attempts to help them; but the honest gardeners stared so at his figure and manner, and odd interference, that he soon saw his services were not relished. They then repaired to one of the neighbouring taverns, and made a bowl of that liquor called *Bishop,* which Johnson had always liked; while in joyous contempt of sleep, from which he had been roused, he repeated the festive lines,

'Short, O short then be thy reign, And give us to the world again!'

They did not stay long, but walked down to the Thames, took a boat, and rowed to Billingsgate. Beauclerk and Johnson were so well pleased with their amusement, that they resolved to persevere in dissipation for the rest of the day: but Langton deserted them, being engaged to breakfast with some young Ladies. Johnson scolded him for 'leaving his social friends, to go and sit with a set of wretched *un-idea'd* girls.' Garrick being told of this ramble, said to him smartly, 'I heard of your frolick t'other

night. You'll be in the Chronicle.'
Upon which Johnson afterwards
observed, 'He durst not do such a
thing. His *wife* would not *let* him!'

✖ *Chapter* **3**

The Dictionary and Fame

The Dictionary, we may believe,
afforded Johnson full occupation
this year. As it approached to its
conclusion, he probably worked
with redoubled vigour, as seamen
increase their exertion and alacrity
when they have a near prospect
of their haven.

Lord Chesterfield, to whom Johnson had paid the high compliment
of addressing to his Lordship the
Plan of his Dictionary, had behaved
to him in such a manner as to
excite his contempt and indignation. The world has been for many
years amused with a story confidently told, and as confidently repeated with additional circumstances, that a sudden disgust was
taken by Johnson upon occasion
of his having been one day kept
long in waiting in his Lordship's
antechamber, for which the reason
assigned was, that he had company
with him; and that at last, when the
door opened, out walked Colley
Cibber;[1] and that Johnson was so

violently provoked when he found
for whom he had been so long
excluded, that he went away in a
passion, and never would return.
It may seem strange even to entertain a doubt concerning a story so
long and so widely current, and
thus implicity adopted, if not sanctioned, by the authority which I
have mentioned; but Johnson himself assured me, that there was not
the least foundation for it. He told
me, that there never was any particular incident which produced a
quarrel between Lord Chesterfield
and him; but that his Lordship's
continued neglect was the reason
why he resolved to have no connection with him. When the Dictionary was upon the eve of publication,
Lord Chesterfield, who, it is said,
had flattered himself with expectations that Johnson would dedicate
the work to him, attempted, in a
courtly manner, to sooth, and insinuate himself with the Sage, conscious, as it should seem, of the
cold indifference with which he
had treated its learned authour; and
further attempted to conciliate him,
by writing two papers in 'The
World,' in recommendation of the
work; and it must be confessed,
that they contain some studied compliments, so finely turned, that if
there had been no previous offence,
it is probable that Johnson would
have been highly delighted. Praise,
in general, was pleasing to him; but

---

[1] Colley Cibber (1671–1757): wit, actor,
poet, and dramatist. His facile talents made
him extremely well known in his own time,
but were not strong enough to sustain him
much past it.

by praise from a man of rank and elegant accomplishments, he was peculiarly gratified.

His Lordship says,

'I think the publick in general, and the republick of letters in particular, are greatly obliged to Mr. Johnson, for having undertaken, and executed, so great and desirable a work. Perfection is not to be expected from man; but if we are to judge by the various works of Johnson already published, we have good reason to believe, that he will bring this as near to perfection as any one man could do. The Plan of it, which he published some years ago, seems to me to be a proof of it. Nothing can be more rationally imagined, or more accurately and elegantly expressed. I therefore recommend the previous perusal of it to all those who intend to buy the Dictionary, and who, I suppose, are all those who can afford it.'

This courtly device failed of its effect. Johnson, who thought that 'all was false and hollow,' despised the honeyed words, and was even indignant that Lord Chesterfield should, for a moment, imagine, that he could be the dupe of such an artifice. His expression to me concerning Lord Chesterfield, upon this occasion, was, 'Sir, after making great professions, he had, for many years, taken no notice of me; but when my Dictionary was coming out, he fell a scribbling in "The World" about it. Upon which, I wrote him a letter expressed in civil terms, but such as might shew him that I did not mind what he said or wrote, and that I had done with him.'

'To the Right Honourable the Earl of Chesterfield

'February 7, 1755.

'My Lord,

'I have been lately informed, by the proprietor of the World, that two papers, in which my Dictionary is recommended to the publick, were written by your Lordship. To be so distinguished, is an honour, which, being very little accustomed to favours from the great, I know not well how to receive, or in what terms to acknowledge.

'When, upon some slight encouragement, I first visited your Lordship, I was overpowered, like the rest of mankind, by the enchantment of your address; and could not forbear to wish that I might boast myself *Le vainqueur du vainqueur de la terre;* [1]—that I might obtain that regard for which I saw the world contending; but I found my attendance so little encouraged, that neither pride nor modesty would suffer me to continue it. When I had once addressed your Lordship in publick, I had exhausted all the art of pleasing which a retired and uncourtly scholar can possess. I had done all that I could; and no man is well pleased to have his all neglected, be it ever so little.

'Seven years, my Lord, have now past, since I waited in your outward rooms, or was repulsed from your door; during which time I have been pushing on my work through difficulties, of which it is useless to complain, and have brought it, at last, to the verge of publication, without one act of assistance, one word of encouragement, or one smile of favour. Such treatment I did not expect, for

[1] *Le vainqueur du vainqueur de la terre:* the conqueror of the conqueror of the earth.

I never had a Patron before.

'The shepherd in Virgil grew at last acquainted with Love, and found him a native of the rocks.

'Is not a Patron, my Lord, one who looks with unconcern on a man struggling for life in the water, and, when he has reached ground, encumbers him with help? The notice which you have been pleased to take of my labours, had it been early, had been kind; but it has been delayed till I am indifferent, and cannot enjoy it; till I am solitary, and cannot impart it; till I am known, and do not want it. I hope it is no very cynical asperity not to confess obligations where no benefit has been received, or to be unwilling that the Publick should consider me as owing that to a Patron, which Providence has enabled me to do for myself.

'Having carried on my work thus far with so little obligation to any favourer of learning, I shall not be disappointed though I should conclude it, if less be possible, with less; for I have been long wakened from that dream of hope, in which I once boasted myself with so much exultation,

'My Lord,
'Your Lordship's most humble,
'Most obedient servant,
'*Sam. Johnson.*'

Johnson having now explicitly avowed his opinion of Lord Chesterfield, did not refrain from expressing himself concerning that nobleman with pointed freedom: 'This man (said he) I thought had been a Lord among wits; but, I find, he is only a wit among Lords!'

The character of a 'respectable Hottentot,' in Lord Chesterfield's letters, has been generally understood to be meant for Johnson, and I have no doubt that it was.

In 1755 we behold him to great advantage; his degree of Master of Arts conferred upon him,[1] his Dictionary published, his correspondence animated, his benevolence exercised.

The Dictionary, with a Grammar and History of the English Language, being now at length published in two volumes folio, the world contemplated with wonder so stupendous a work achieved by one man, while other countries had thought such undertakings fit only for whole academies.

A few of his definitions must be admitted to be erroneous. Thus, *Windward* and *Leeward,* though directly of opposite meaning, are defined identically the same way; as to which inconsiderable specks it is enough to observe, that his Preface announces that he was aware there might be many such in so immense a work; nor was he at all disconcerted when an instance was pointed out to him. A lady once asked him how he came to define *Pastern* the *knee* of a horse: instead of making an elaborate defence, as she expected, he at once answered, 'Ignorance, Madame, pure ignorance.'

His introducing his own opinions, and even prejudices, under general definitions of words, while

[1] Master of Arts degree was conferred by Oxford.

at the same time the original meaning of the words is not explained, as his *Tory, Whig, Pension,*[1] *Oats, Excise,* and a few more, cannot be fully defended, and must be placed to the account of capricious and humourous indulgence. Talking to me upon this subject when we were at Ashbourne in 1777, he mentioned a still stronger instance of the predominance of his private feelings in the composition of this work, than any now to be found in it. 'You know, Sir, Lord Gower forsook the old Jacobite interest.[2] When I came to the word *Renegado,* after telling that it meant "one who deserts to the enemy, a revolter," I added, *Sometimes we say a* Gower. Thus it went to the press; but the printer had more wit than I, and struck it out.'

Let it, however, be remembered, that this indulgence does not display itself only in sarcasm towards others, but sometimes in playful allusion to the notions commonly entertained of his own laborious task. Thus: '*Grub-street,* the name of a street in London, much inhabited by writers of small histories, *dictionaries,* and temporary poems; whence any mean production is called   *Grub-street.*'—'*Lexicographer,* a writer of dictionaries, a *harmless drudge.*'

[1] Johnson's definition of *Pension:* "An allowance made to anyone without an equivalent. In England it is generally understood to mean pay given to a state hireling for treason to his country."

[2] old Jacobite interest: sympathy for the exiled royal house of Stuart.

In 1756 Johnson found that the great fame of his Dictionary had not set him above the necessity of 'making provision for the day that was passing over him.'

He had spent, during the progress of the work, the money for which he had contracted to write his Dictionary. We have seen that the reward of his labour was only fifteen hundred and seventy-five pounds; and when the expence of amanuenses and paper, and other articles are deducted, his clear profit was very inconsiderable. I once said to him, 'I am sorry, Sir, you did not get more for your Dictionary.' His answer was, 'I am sorry too. But it was very well. The booksellers are generous liberalminded men.' He, upon all occasions, did ample justice to their character in this respect. He considered them as the patrons of literature; and, indeed, although they have eventually been considerable gainers by his Dictionary, it is to them that we owe its having been undertaken and carried through at the risk of great expence, for they were not absolutely sure of being indemnified.

On the first day of this year we find from his private devotions, that he had then recovered from sickness; and in February that his eye was restored to its use. The pious gratitude with which he acknowledges mercies upon every occasion is very edifying; as is the humble submission which he breathes, when it is the will of his heavenly Father to try him with afflictions.

His works this year were, an abstract or epitome, in octavo, of his folio Dictionary, and a few essays in a monthly publication, entitled, 'The Universal Visiter.' He engaged also to superintend and contribute largely to another monthly publication, entitled 'The Literary Magazine, or Universal Review'; the first number of which came out in May this year. He continued to write in it, with intermissions, till the fifteenth number; and I think that he never gave better proofs of the force, acuteness, and vivacity of his mind, than in this miscellany, whether we consider his original essays, or his reviews of the works of others.

He this year resumed his scheme of giving an edition of Shakspeare with notes. He issued Proposals of considerable length, in which he shewed that he perfectly well knew what a variety of research such an undertaking required; but his indolence prevented him from pursuing it with that diligence which alone can collect those scattered facts that genius, however acute, penetrating, and luminous, cannot discover by its own force. It is remarkable, that at this time his fancied activity was for the moment so vigorous, that he promised his work should be published before Christmas 1757. Yet nine years elapsed before it saw the light. His throes in bringing it forth had been severe and remittent; and at last we may almost conclude that the Cæsarian operation was performed by the knife of Churchill, whose upbraiding satire, I dare say, made Johnson's friends urge him to dispatch.

'He for subscribers bates his hook,
And takes your cash; but where's the book?
No matter where; wise fear, you know,
Forbids the robbing of a foe;
But what, to serve our private ends,
Forbids the cheating of our friends?'

About this period he was offered a living of considerable value in Lincolnshire, if he were inclined to enter into holy orders. It was a rectory in the gift of Mr. Langton, the father of his much valued friend. But he did not accept of it; partly I believe from a conscientious motive, being persuaded that his temper and habits rendered him unfit for that assiduous and familiar instruction of the vulgar and ignorant, which he held to be an essential duty in a clergyman; and partly because his love of a London life was so strong, that he would have thought himself an exile in any other place, particularly if residing in the country.

On the 15th of April, 1758, he began a new periodical paper, entitled 'The Idler,' which came out every Saturday in a weekly news-paper, called 'The Universal Chronicle, or Weekly Gazette,' published by Newberry. These essays were continued till April 5, 1760. Of one hundred and three, their total number, twelve were contributed by his friends.

The *Idler* is evidently the work of the same mind which produced the *Rambler,* but has less body and more spirit. It has more variety of real life, and greater facility of language. He describes the miseries of idleness, with the lively sensations of one who has felt them; and in his private memorandums while engaged in it, we find 'This year I hope to learn diligence.' Many of these excellent essays were written as hastily as an ordinary letter. Mr. Langton remembers Johnson, when on a visit at Oxford, asking him one evening how long it was till the post went out; and on being told about half an hour, he exclaimed, 'then we shall do very well.' He upon this instantly sat down and finished an Idler, which it was necessary should be in London the next day. Mr. Langton having signified a wish to read it, 'Sir, (said he) you shall not do more than I have done myself.' He then folded it up, and sent it off.

In 1759, in the month of January, his mother died at the great age of ninety, an event which deeply affected him; not that 'his mind had acquired no firmness by the contemplation of mortality,' but that his reverential affection for her was not abated by years, as indeed he retained all his tender feelings even to the latest period of his life. I have been told that he regretted much his not having gone to visit his mother for several years, previous to her death. But he was constantly engaged in literary la-

bours which confined him to London; and though he had not the comfort of seeing his aged parent, he contributed liberally to her support.

Soon after this event, he wrote his *'Rasselas, Prince of Abyssinia.'* The late Mr. Strahan the printer told me, that Johnson wrote it, that with the profits he might defray the expence of his mother's funeral, and pay some little debts which she had left. He told Sir Joshua Reynolds that he composed it in the evenings of one week, sent it to the press in portions as it was written, and had never since read it over. Mr. Strahan, Mr. Johnston, and Mr. Dodsley purchased it for a hundred pounds, but afterwards paid him twenty-five pounds more, when it came to a second edition.

Considering the large sums which have been received for compilations, and works requiring not much more genius than compilations, we cannot but wonder at the very low price which he was content to receive for this admirable performance; which, though he had written nothing else, would have rendered his name immortal in the world of literature. None of his writings has been so extensively diffused over Europe; for it has been translated into most, if not all, of the modern languages. This Tale, with all the charms of oriental imagery, and all the force and beauty of which the English language is capable, leads us through the most important scenes of human life, and shews us that this stage of our being is full of 'vanity and vexation of spirit.' Voltaire's *Candide,* written to refute the system of Optimism, which it has accomplished with brilliant success, is wonderfully similar in its plan and conduct to Johnson's *Rasselas;* insomuch, that I heard Johnson say, that if they had not been published so closely one after the other that there was not time for imitation, it would have been in vain to deny that the scheme of that which came latest was taken from the other. Though the proposition illustrated by both these works was the same, namely, that in our present state there is more evil than good, the intention of the writers was very different. Voltaire, I am afraid, meant only by wanton profaneness to obtain a sportive victory over religion, and to discredit the belief of a superintending Providence: Johnson meant, by shewing the unsatisfactory nature of things temporal, to direct the hopes of man to things eternal.

Notwithstanding my high admiration of Rasselas, I will not maintain that the 'morbid melancholy' in Johnson's constitution may not, perhaps, have made life appear to him more insipid and unhappy than it generally is; for I am sure that he had less enjoyment from it than I have. Yet, whatever additional shade his own particular sensations may have thrown on his representation of life, attentive observation and close inquiry have convinced me, that there is too much of reality in the gloomy picture.

A lady having at about this time solicited him to obtain the Archbishop of Canterbury's patronage to have her son sent to the University, one of those solicitations which are too frequent, where people, anxious for a particular object, do not consider propriety, or the opportunity, which the persons whom they solicit have to assist them, he wrote to her the following answer; with a copy of which I am favoured by the Reverend Dr. Farmer, Master of Emanuel College, Cambridge.

'Madam,
'I hope you will believe that my delay in answering your letter could proceed only from my unwillingness to destroy any hope that you had formed. Hope is itself a species of happiness, and, perhaps, the chief happiness which this world affords: but, like all other pleasures immoderately enjoyed, the excesses of hope must be expiated by pain; and expectations improperly indulged, must end in disappointment. If it be asked, what is the improper expectation which it is dangerous to indulge, experience will quickly answer, that it is such expectation as is dictated not by reason, but by desire; expectation raised, not by the common occurrences of life, but by the wants of the expectant; an expectation that requires the common course of things to be changed, and the general rules of action to be broken.

'When you made your request to me, you should have considered, Madam, what you were asking. You ask me to solicit a great man, to whom I never spoke, for a young person whom I had never seen, upon a supposition which I had no means of knowing to be true. There is no reason why, amongst all the great, I should chuse to supplicate the Archbishop, nor why, among all the possible objects of his bounty, the Archbishop should chuse your son. I know, Madam, how unwillingly conviction is admitted, when interest opposes it; but surely, Madam, you must allow, that there is no reason why that should be done by me, which every other man may do with equal reason, and which, indeed, no man can do properly, without some very particular relation both to the Archbishop and to you. If I could help you in this exigence by any proper means, it would give me pleasure; but this proposal is so very remote from all usual methods, that I cannot comply with it, but at the risk of such answer and suspicions as I believe you do not wish me to undergo.

'I have seen your son this morning; he seems a pretty youth, and will, perhaps, find some better friend than I can procure him; but, though he should at last miss the University, he may still be wise, useful, and happy. I am, Madam,

'Your most humble servant,
'*Sam. Johnson.*
'June 8, 1762.'

The accession of George the Third to the throne of these kingdoms, opened a new and brighter prospect to men of literary merit, who had been honoured with no mark of royal favour in the preceding reign. His present Majesty's education in this country, as well as his taste and beneficence, prompted him to be the patron of science and the arts; and early this year Johnson, having been repre-sented to him as a very learned and good man, without any certain provision, his Majesty was pleased to grant him a pension of three hundred pounds a year. The Earl of Bute, who was then Prime Minister, had the honour to announce this instance of his Sovereign's bounty, concerning which many and various stories, all equally erroneous, have been propagated; maliciously representing it as a political bribe to Johnson. I have taken care to have it in my power to refute them from the most authentick information. Lord Bute told me, that Mr. Wedderburne, now Lord Loughborough, was the person who first mentioned this subject to him. Lord Loughborough told me, that the pension was granted to Johnson solely as the reward of his literary merit, without any stipulation whatever, or even tacit understanding that he should write for administration. His Lordship added, that he was confident the political tracts which Johnson afterwards did write, as they were entirely consonant with his own opinions, would have been written by him, though no pension had been granted to him.

Sir Joshua Reynolds told me, that Johnson called on him after his Majesty's intention had been notified to him, and said he wished to consult his friends as to the propriety of his accepting this mark of the royal favour, after the definitions which he had given in his Dictionary of *pension* [1] and *pension-*

[1] *pension*: see footnote on page 278.

ers. He said he would not have Sir Joshua's answer till next day, when he would call again, and desired he might think of it. Sir Joshua answered that he was clear to give his opinion then, that there could be no objection to his receiving from the King a reward for literary merit; and that certainly the definitions in his Dictionary were not applicable to him. Johnson, it should seem, was satisfied, for he did not call again till he had accepted the pension, and had waited on Lord Bute to thank him. He then told Sir Joshua that Lord Bute said to him expressly, 'It is not given you for any thing you are to do, but for what you have done.' His Lordship, he said, behaved in the handsomest manner. He repeated the words twice, that he might be sure Johnson heard them, and thus set his mind perfectly at ease.

 *Chapter* 4

Enter Bozzy

1763: This is to me a memorable year; for in it I had the happiness to obtain the acquaintance of that extraordinary man whose memoirs I am now writing; an acquaintance which I shall ever esteem as one of the most fortunate circumstances in my life. Though then but two-and-twenty, I had for several years read his works with delight and instruction, and had the highest reverence for their authour, which had grown up in my fancy into a kind of mysterious veneration, by figuring to myself a state of solemn elevated abstraction, in which I supposed him to live in the immense metropolis of London.

In the summer of 1761 Mr. Thomas Sheridan was at Edinburgh, and delivered lectures upon the English Language and Publick Speaking to large and respectable audiences. I was often in his company, and heard him frequently expatiate upon Johnson's extraordinary knowledge, talents, and virtues, repeat his pointed sayings, describe his particularities, and boast of his being his guest sometimes till two or three in the morning. At his house I hoped to have many opportunities of seeing the sage, as Mr. Sheridan obligingly assured me I should not be disappointed.

When I returned to London in the end of 1762, to my surprise and regret I found an irreconcilable difference had taken place between Johnson and Sheridan. A pension of two hundred pounds a year had been given to Sheridan. Johnson, who, as has been already mentioned, thought slightingly of Sheridan's art, upon hearing that he was also pensioned, exclaimed, 'What! Have they given *him* a pension? Then it is time for me to give up mine.'

Johnson complained that a man who disliked him repeated his sarcasm to Mr. Sheridan, without telling him what followed, which was, that after a pause he added, 'However, I am glad that Mr. Sheridan has a pension, for he is a very good man.' Sheridan could never forgive this hasty contemptuous expression. It rankled in his mind; and though I informed him of all that Johnson said, and that he would be very glad to meet him amicably, he positively declined repeated offers which I made, and once went off abruptly from a house where he and I were engaged to dine, because he was told that Dr. Johnson was to be there.

Mr. Thomas Davies the actor, who then kept a bookseller's shop in Russel-street, Covent-garden, told me that Johnson was very much his friend, and came frequently to his house, where he more than once invited me to meet him; but by some unlucky accident or other he was prevented from coming to us.

Mr. Thomas Davies was a man of good understanding and talents, with the advantage of a liberal education. Though somewhat pompous, he was an entertaining companion; and his literary performances have no inconsiderable share of merit. He was a friendly and very hospitable man. Both he and his wife, (who has been celebrated for her beauty,) though upon the stage for many years, maintained an uniform decency of character; and Johnson esteemed them, and lived in as easy an intimacy with them as with any family which he used to visit. Mr. Davies recollected several of Johnson's remarkable sayings, and was one of the best of the many imitators of his voice and manner, while relating them. He increased my impatience more and more to see the extraordinary man whose works I highly valued, and whose conversation was reported to be so peculiarly excellent.

At last, on Monday the 16th of May, when I was sitting in Mr. Davies's back-parlour, after having drunk tea with him and Mrs. Davies, Johnson unexpectedly came into the shop; and Mr. Davies having perceived him through the glass-door in the room in which we were sitting, advancing towards us, —he announced his awful approach to me, somewhat in the manner of an actor in the part of Horatio, when he addresses Hamlet on the appearance of his father's ghost, 'Look, my Lord, it comes.' I found that I had a very perfect idea of Johnson's figure, from the portrait of him painted by Sir Joshua Reynolds soon after he had published his Dictionary, in the attitude of sitting in his easy chair in deep meditation, which was the first picture his friend did for him, which Sir Joshua very kindly presented to me. Mr. Davies mentioned my name, and respectfully introduced me to him. I was much agitated; and recollecting his prejudice against the Scotch, of which I had heard much, I said to Davies, 'Don't tell where I come from.'—

'From Scotland,' cried Davies, roguishly. 'Mr. Johnson, (said I) I do indeed come from Scotland, but I cannot help it.' I am willing to flatter myself that I meant this as light pleasantry to sooth and conciliate him, and not as an humiliating abasement at the expence of my country. But however that might be, this speech was somewhat unlucky; for with that quickness of wit for which he was so remarkable, he seized the expression 'come from Scotland,' which I used in the sense of being of that country; and, as if I said that I had come away from it, or left it, retorted, 'That, Sir, I find, is what a very great many of your countrymen cannot help.' This stroke stunned me a good deal; and when we had sat down, I felt myself not a little embarrassed, and apprehensive of what might come next. He then addressed himself to Davies: 'What do you think of Garrick? He has refused me an order for the play for Miss Williams, because he knows the house will be full, and that an order would be worth three shillings.' Eager to take any opening to get into conversation with him, I ventured to say, 'O, Sir, I cannot think Mr. Garrick would grudge such a trifle to you.' 'Sir, (said he, with a stern look,) I have known David Garrick longer than you have done: and I know no right you have to talk to me on the subject.' Perhaps I deserved this check; for it was rather presumptuous in me, an entire stranger, to express any

doubt of the justice of his animadversion upon his old acquaintance and pupil. I now felt myself much mortified, and began to think that the hope which I had long indulged of obtaining his acquaintance was blasted. And, in truth, had not my ardour been uncommonly strong, and my resolution uncommonly persevering, so rough a reception might have deterred me for ever from making any further attempts. Fortunately, however, I remained upon the field not wholly discomfited.

I was highly pleased with the extraordinary vigour of his conversation, and regretted that I was drawn away from it by an engagement at another place. I had, for a part of the evening, been left alone with him, and had ventured to make an observation now and then, which he received very civilly; so that I was satisfied that though there was a roughness in his manner, there was no ill-nature in his disposition. Davies followed me to the door, and when I complained to him a little of the hard blows which the great man had given me, he kindly took upon him to console me by saying, 'Don't be uneasy. I can see he likes you very well.'

A few days afterwards I called on Davies, and asked him if he thought I might take the liberty of waiting on Mr. Johnson at his Chambers in the Temple. He said I certainly might, and that Mr. Johnson would take it as a compliment. So upon Tuesday the 24th of May, after having been enlivened by the witty sallies of Messieurs Thornton, Wilkes, Churchill and Lloyd, with whom I had passed the morning, I boldly repaired to Johnson. His Chambers were on the first floor of No. 1, Inner-Temple-lane, and I entered them with an impression given me by the Reverend Dr. Blair, of Edinburgh, who had been introduced to him not long before, and described his having 'found the Giant in his den'; an expression which, when I came to be pretty well acquainted with Johnson, I repeated to him, and he was diverted at this picturesque account of himself.

He received me very courteously; but, it must be confessed, that his apartment, and furniture, and morning dress, were sufficiently uncouth. His brown suit of cloaths looked very rusty; he had on a little old shrivelled unpowdered wig, which was too small for his head; his shirt-neck and knees of his breeches were loose; his black worsted stockings ill drawn up; and he had a pair of unbuckled shoes by way of slippers. But all these slovenly particularities were forgotten the moment that he began to talk. Some gentlemen, whom I do not recollect, were sitting with him; and when they went away, I also rose; but he said to me, 'Nay, don't go.'—'Sir, (said I,) I am afraid that I intrude upon you. It is benevolent to allow me to sit and hear you.' He seemed pleased with this compliment, which I sincerely paid him, and answered, 'Sir, I am obliged to any man who visits me.'—I have preserved the following short minute of what passed this day.

'Madness frequently discovers itself merely by unnecessary deviation from the usual modes of the world. My poor friend Smart shewed the disturbance of his mind, by falling upon his knees, and saying his prayers in the street, or in any other unusual place. Now although, rationally speaking, it is greater madness not to pray at all, than to pray as Smart did, I am afraid there are so many who do not pray, that their understanding is not called in question.'

Concerning this unfortunate poet, Christopher Smart, who was confined in a mad-house, he had, at another time, the following conversation with Dr. Burney.—*Burney:* 'How does poor Smart do, Sir; is he likely to recover?' *Johnson:* 'It seems as if his mind had ceased to struggle with the disease; for he grows fat upon it.' *Burney:* 'Perhaps, Sir, that may be from want of exercise.' *Johnson:* 'No, Sir; he has partly as much exercise as he used to have, for he digs in the garden. Indeed, before his confinement, he used for exercise to walk to the alehouse; but he was *carried* back again. I did not think he ought to be shut up. His infirmities were not noxious to society. He insisted on people praying with him; and I'd as lief pray with Kit Smart as any one else. Another charge was, that he did not love clean linen; and I have no passion for it.'

When I rose a second time he again pressed me to stay, which I did.

He told me, that he generally went abroad at four in the afternoon, and seldom came home till two in the morning. I took the liberty to ask if he did not think it wrong to live thus, and not make more use of his great talents. He owned it was a bad habit. On reviewing, at the distance of many years, my journal of this period, I wonder how, at my first visit, I ventured to talk to him so freely, and that he bore it with so much indulgence.

Before we parted, he was so good as to promise to favour me with his company one evening at my lodgings; and, as I took my leave, shook me cordially by the hand. It is almost needless to add, that I felt no little elation at having now so happily established an acquaintance of which I had been so long ambitious.

My readers will, I trust, excuse me for being thus minutely circumstantial, when it is considered that the acquaintance of Dr. Johnson was to me a most valuable acquisition, and laid the foundation of whatever instruction and entertainment they may receive from my collections concerning the great subject of the work which they are now perusing.

I had learnt that his place of frequent resort was the Mitre tavern in Fleet-street, where he loved to sit up late, and I begged I might be allowed to pass an evening with him there soon, which he promised I should. A few days afterwards I met him near Temple-bar, about one o'clock in the morning, and asked if he would go to the Mitre.

Johnson agreed to meet me the following evening. I called on him, and we went thither at nine. We had a good supper, and port wine, of which he then sometimes drank a bottle. The orthodox high-church sound of the *Mitre*,—the figure and manner of the celebrated *Samuel Johnson*,—the extraordinary power and precision of his conversation, and the pride arising from finding myself admitted as his companion, produced a variety of sensations, and a pleasing elevation of mind beyond what I had ever before experienced. I find in my journal the following minute of our conversation, which, though it will give but a very faint notion of what passed, is, in some degree, a valuable record; and it will be curious in this view, as shewing how habitual to his mind were some opinions which appear in his works.

'Sir, I do not think Gray a first-rate poet. He has not a bold imagination, nor much command of words. The obscurity in which he has involved himself will not persuade us that he is sublime. His Elegy in a Church-yard has a happy selection of images, but I don't like what are called his great things. His Ode which begins

"Ruin seize thee, ruthless King, Confusion on thy banners wait!"

has been celebrated for its abruptness, and plunging into the subject all at once. But such arts as these have no merit, unless when they are original. We admire them only once; and this abruptness has nothing new in it. We have had it often before.'

Finding him in a placid humour, and wishing to avail myself of the opportunity which I fortuntely had of consulting a sage, to hear whose wisdom, I conceived in the ardour of youthful imagination, that men filled with a noble enthusiasm for intellectual improvement would gladly have resorted from distant lands;—I opened my mind to him ingenuously, and gave him a little sketch of my life, to which he was pleased to listen with great attention.

I acknowledged, that though educated very strictly in the principles of religion, I had for some time been misled into a certain degree of infidelity; but that I was come now to a better way of thinking, and was fully satisfied of the truth of the Christian revelation, though I was not clear as to every point considered to be orthodox. Being at all times a curious examiner of the human mind, and pleased with an undisguised display of what had passed in it, he called to me with warmth, 'Give me your hand; I have taken a liking to you.' He then began to descant upon the force of testimony, and the little we could know of final causes; so that the objections of, why was it so? or why was it not so? ought

not to disturb us: adding, that he himself had at one period been guilty of a temporary neglect of religion, but that it was not the result of argument, but mere absence of thought.

We talked of belief in ghosts. He said, 'Sir, I make a distinction between what a man may experience by the mere strength of his imagination, and what imagination cannot possibly produce. Thus, suppose I should think that I saw a form, and heard a voice cry "Johnson, you are a very wicked fellow, and unless you repent you will certainly be punished;" my own unworthiness is so deeply impressed upon my mind, that I might *imagine* I thus saw and heard, and therefore I should not believe that an external communication had been made to me. But if a form should appear, and a voice should tell me that a particular man had died at a particular place, and a particular hour, a fact which I had no apprehension of, nor any means of knowing, and this fact, with all its circumstances, should afterwards be unquestionably proved, I should, in that case, be persuaded that I had supernatural intelligence imparted to me.'

Here it is proper, once for all, to give a true and fair statement of Johnson's way of thinking upon the question, whether departed spirits are ever permitted to appear in this world, or in any way to operate upon human life. He has been ignorantly misrepresented as weakly credulous upon that subject;

and, therefore, though I feel an inclination to disdain and treat with silent contempt so foolish a notion concerning my illustrious friend, yet as I find it has gained ground, it is necessary to refute it. The real fact then is, that Johnson had a very philosophical mind, and such a rational respect for testimony, as to make him submit his understanding to what was authentically proved, though he could not comprehend why it was so. Being thus disposed, he was willing to inquire into the truth of any relation of supernatural agency, a general belief of which has prevailed in all nations and ages. But so far was he from being the dupe of implicit faith, that he examined the matter with a jealous attention, and no man was more ready to refute its falsehood when he had discovered it.

Our conversation proceeded. 'Sir, (said he) I am a friend to subordination, as most conducive to the happiness of society. There is a reciprocal pleasure in governing and being governed.'

'Dr. Goldsmith is one of the first men we now have as an authour, and he is a very worthy man too. He has been loose in his principles, but he is coming right.'

I mentioned Mallet's tragedy of 'Elvira,' which had been acted the preceding winter at Drury-lane, and that the Honourable Andrew Erskine, Mr. Dempster, and myself, had joined in writing a pamphlet, entitled 'Critical Strictures' against it. That the mildness of Dempster's disposition had, however, relented; and he had candidly said, 'We have hardly a right to abuse this tragedy; for bad as it is, how vain should either of us be to write one not near so good.' *Johnson:* 'Why no, Sir; this is not just reasoning. You *may* abuse a tragedy, though you cannot write one. You may scold a carpenter who has made you a bad table, though you cannot make a table. It is not your trade to make tables.'

I complained to him that I had not yet acquired much knowledge, and asked his advice as to my studies. He said, 'Don't talk of study now. I will give you a plan; but it will require some time to consider of it.' 'It is very good in you (I replied,) to allow me to be with you thus. Had it been foretold to me some years ago that I should pass an evening with the authour of the *Rambler,* how should I have exulted!' What I then expressed, was sincerely from the heart. He was satisfied that it was, and cordially answered, 'Sir, I am glad we have met. I hope we shall pass many evenings and mornings too, together.' We finished a couple of bottles of port, and sat till between one and two in the morning.

As Dr. Oliver Goldsmith will frequently appear in this narrative, I shall endeavour to make my readers in some degree acquainted with his singular character. He was a native of Ireland, and a contemporary with Mr. Burke,[1] at Trinity

---

[1] Burke, Edmund (1729–1797): great statesman and political writer. He was, as

College, Dublin, but did not then give much promise of future celebrity. He, however, observed to Mr. Malone, that 'though he made no great figure in mathematicks, which was a study in much repute there, he could turn an Ode of Horace into English better than any of them.' He afterwards studied physick at Edinburgh, and upon the Continent; and I have been informed, was enabled to pursue his travels on foot, partly by demanding at Universities to enter the lists as a disputant, by which, according to the custom of many of them, he was entitled to the premium of a crown, when luckily for him his challenge was not accepted; so that, as I once observed to Dr. Johnson, he *disputed* his passage through Europe. He then came to England, and was employed successively in the capacities of an usher to an academy, a corrector of the press, a reviewer, and a writer for a news-paper. He had sagacity enough to cultivate assiduously the acquaintance of Johnson, and his faculties were gradually enlarged by the contemplation of such a model. To me and many others it appeared that he studiously copied the manner of Johnson, though, indeed, upon a smaller scale.

His mind resembled a fertile, but thin soil. There was a quick, but not a strong vegetation, of whatever chanced to be thrown upon it. No deep root could be struck.

The oak of the forest did not grow there; but the elegant shrubbery and the fragrant parterre appeared in gay succession. It has been generally circulated and believed that he was a mere fool in conversation; but, in truth, this has been greatly exaggerated. He had, no doubt, a more than common share of that hurry of ideas which we often find in his countrymen, and which sometimes produces a laughable confusion in expressing them. His person was short, his countenance coarse and vulgar, his deportment that of a scholar aukwardly affecting the easy gentleman. Those who were in any way distinguished, excited envy in him to so ridiculous an excess, that the instances of it are hardly credible. When accompanying two beautiful young ladies with their mother on a tour in France, he was seriously angry that more attention was paid to them than to him; and once at the exhibition of the *Fantoccini* in London, when those who sat next him observed with what dexterity a puppet was made to toss a pike, he could not bear that it should have such praise, and exclaimed with some warmth, 'Pshaw! I can do it better myself.'

He boasted to me at this time of the power of his pen in commanding money, which I believe was true in a certain degree, though in the instance he gave he was by no means correct. He told me that he had sold a novel for four hundred pounds. This was his 'Vicar of Wakefield.' But Johnson informed me, that he had made the bargain

we shall see, Johnson's close friend to the end, although the two differed politically.

for Goldsmith, and the price was sixty pounds. 'And, Sir, (said he,) a sufficient price too, when it was sold; for then the fame of Goldsmith had not been elevated, as it afterwards was, by his "Traveller"; and the bookseller had such faint hopes of profit by his bargain, that he kept the manuscript by him a long time, and did not publish it till after the "Traveller" had appeared. Then, to be sure, it was accidentally worth more money.'

Mrs. Piozzi [1] and Sir John Hawkins [2] have strangely mis-stated the history of Goldsmith's situation and Johnson's friendly interference, when this novel was sold. I shall give it authentically from Johnson's own exact narration: 'I received one morning a message from poor Goldsmith that he was in great distress, and, as it was not in his power to come to me, begging that I would come to him as soon as possible. I sent him a guinea, and promised to come to him directly. I accordingly went as soon as I was drest, and found that his landlady had arrested him for his rent, at which he was in a violent passion. I perceived that he had already changed my guinea, and had got a bottle of Madeira and a glass before him. I put the cork into the bottle, desired he would be calm, and began to talk to him of the means by which

he might be extricated. He then told me that he had a novel ready for the press, which he produced to me. I looked into it, and saw its merit; told the landlady I should soon return, and having gone to a bookseller, sold it for sixty pounds. I brought Goldsmith the money, and he discharged his rent, not without rating his landlady in a high tone for having used him so ill.'

My next meeting with Johnson was on Friday the 1st of July, when he and I and Dr. Goldsmith supped together at the Mitre. I was before this time pretty well acquainted with Goldsmith, who was one of the brightest ornaments of the Johnsonian school. Goldsmith's respectful attachment to Johnson was then at its height; for his own literary reputation had not yet distinguished him so much as to excite a vain desire of competition with his great Master. He had increased my admiration of the goodness of Johnson's heart, by incidental remarks in the course of conversation, such as, when I mentioned Mr. Levet, whom he entertained under his roof, 'He is poor and honest, which is recommendation enough to Johnson'; and when I wondered that he was very kind to a man of whom I had heard a very bad character, 'He is now become miserable, and that insures the protection of Johnson.'

Dr. John Campbell, the celebrated political and biographical writer, being mentioned, Johnson said, 'Campbell is not always rigidly care-

<hr>

[1] Mrs. Piozzi: Hester Thrale upon her second marriage. Note page 427.

[2] Sir John Hawkins: Johnson's legal executor and forty-year acquaintance. Both Hawkins and Mrs. Piozzi wrote biographies of Johnson.

ful of truth in his conversation; but I do not believe there is any thing of this carelessness in his books. Campbell is a good man, a pious man. I am afraid he has not been in the inside of a church for many years; but he never passes a church without pulling off his hat. This shews that he has good principles. I used to go pretty often to Campbell's on a Sunday evening, till I began to consider that the shoals of Scotchmen who flocked about him might probably say, when any thing of mine was well done, "Ay, ay, he has learnt this of *Cawmell!*" '

He talked very contemptuously of Churchill's poetry, observing, that 'it had a temporary currency, only from its audacity of abuse, and being filled with living names, and that it would sink into oblivion. However, I will acknowledge that I have a better opinion of him now, than I once had; for he has shewn more fertility than I expected. To be sure, he is a tree that cannot produce good fruit: he only bears crabs. But, Sir, a tree that produces a great many crabs is better than a tree which produces only a few.'

Let me here apologize for the imperfect manner in which I am obliged to exhibit Johnson's conversation at this period. In the early part of my acquaintance with him, I was so wrapt in admiration of his extraordinary colloquial talents, and so little accustomed to his peculiar mode of expression, that I found it extremely difficult to recollect and record his conversation with its genuine vigour and vivacity. In

progress of time, when my mind was, as it were, *strongly impregnated with the Johnsonian æther,* I could, with much more facility and exactness, carry in my memory and commit to paper the exuberant variety of his wisdom and wit.

At this time *Miss* Williams, as she was then called, though she did not reside with him in the Temple under his roof, but had lodgings in Bolt-court, Fleet-street, had so much of his attention, that he every night drank tea with her before he went home, however late it might be, and she always sat up for him. This, it may be fairly conjectured, was not alone a proof of his regard for *her,* but of his own unwillingness to go into solitude, before that unseasonable hour at which he had habituated himself to expect the oblivion of repose. Dr. Goldsmith, being a privileged man, went with him this night, strutting away, and calling to me with an air of superiority, like that of an esoterick over an exoterick disciple of a sage of antiquity, 'I go to Miss Williams.' I confess, I then envied him this mighty privilege, of which he seemed so proud; but it was not long before I obtained the same mark of distinction.

On Wednesday, July 6, he was engaged to sup with me at my lodgings in Downing-street, Westminster. But on the preceding night my landlord having behaved very rudely to me and some company who were with me, I had resolved not to remain another night in his house. I was exceedingly uneasy at the aukward appearance I supposed

I should make to Johnson and the other gentlemen whom I had invited, not being able to receive them at home, and being obliged to order supper at the Mitre. I went to Johnson in the morning, and talked of it as of a serious distress. He laughed, and said, 'Consider, Sir, how insignificant this will appear a twelvemonth hence.'—Were this consideration to be applied to most of the little vexatious incidents of life, by which our quiet is too often disturbed, it would prevent many painful sensations. I have tried it frequently, with good effect. 'There is nothing (continued he) in this mighty misfortune; nay, we shall be better at the Mitre.'

I had as my guests this evening at the Mitre tavern, Dr. Johnson, Dr. Goldsmith, Mr. Thomas Davies, Mr. Eccles, an Irish gentleman, for whose agreeable company I was obliged to Mr. Davies, and the Reverend Mr. John Ogilvie, who was desirous of being in company with my illustrious friend, while I, in my turn, was proud to have the honour of shewing one of my countrymen upon what easy terms Johnson permitted me to live with him.

Mr. Ogilvie was unlucky enough to choose for the topick of his conversation the praises of his native country. He began with saying, that there was very rich land round Edinburgh. Goldsmith, who had studied physick there, contradicted this, very untruly, with a sneering laugh. Disconcerted a little by this, Mr. Ogilvie then took new ground, where, I suppose, he thought himself perfectly safe; for he observed, that Scotland had a great many noble wild prospects. *Johnson:* 'I believe, Sir, you have a great many. Norway, too, has noble wild prospects; and Lapland is remarkable for prodigious noble wild prospects. But, Sir, let me tell you, the noblest prospect which a Scotchman ever sees, is the high road that leads him to England!'

On Tuesday, July 18, I found tall Sir Thomas Robinson sitting with Johnson. Sir Thomas said, that the King of Prussia valued himself upon three things;—upon being a hero, a musician, and an authour. *Johnson:* 'Pretty well, Sir, for one man. As to his being an authour, I have not looked at his poetry; but his prose is poor stuff. He writes just as you might suppose Voltaire's footboy to do, who has been his amanuensis. He has such parts as the valet might have, and about as much of the colouring of the style as might be got by transcribing his works.' When I was at Ferney, I repeated this to Voltaire, in order to reconcile him somewhat to Johnson, whom he, in affecting the English mode of expression, had previously characterised as 'a superstitious dog'; but after hearing such a criticism on Frederick the Great, with whom he was then on bad terms, he exclaimed, 'An honest fellow!'

Mr. Levet this day shewed me Dr. Johnson's library, which was contained in two garrets over his Chambers, where Lintot, son of the celebrated bookseller of that name, had formerly his warehouse. I found a number of good books, but very dusty and in great confusion. The floor was strewed with manuscript leaves, in Johnson's own hand-writing, which I beheld with a degree of veneration, supposing they perhaps might contain portions of the Rambler, or of Rasselas. I observed an apparatus for chymical experiments, of which Johnson was all his life very fond. The place seemed to be very favourable for retirement and meditation.

Mr. Dempster having endeavoured to maintain that intrinsick merit *ought* to make the only distinction amongst mankind. *Johnson:* 'Why, Sir, mankind have found that this cannot be. How shall we determine the proportion of intrinsick merit? Were that to be the only distinction amongst mankind, we should soon quarrel about the degrees of it. Were all distinctions abolished, the strongest would not long acquiesce, but would endeavour to obtain a superiority by their bodily strength. But, Sir, as subordination is very necessary for society, and contentions for superiority very dangerous, mankind, that is to say, all civilised nations, have settled it upon a plain invariable principle. A man is born to hereditary rank; or his being appointed to certain offices, gives him a certain rank. Subordination tends greatly to human happiness. Were we all upon an equality, we should have no other enjoyment than mere animal pleasure.'

Next morning I found him alone, and have preserved the following fragments of his conversation. 'Hume, and other sceptical innovators, are vain men, and will gratify themselves at any expence. Truth will not afford sufficient food to their vanity; so they have betaken themselves to errour. Truth, Sir, is a cow that will yield such people no more milk, and so they are gone to milk the bull. If I could have allowed myself to gratify my vanity at the expence of truth, what fame might I have acquired. Every thing which Hume has advanced against Christianity had passed through my mind long before he wrote. Always remember this, that after a system is well settled upon positive evidence, a few partial objections ought not to shake it. The human mind is so limited, that it cannot take in all the parts of a subject, so that there may be objections raised against any thing. There are objections against a *plenum,* and objections against a *vacuum;* yet one of them must certainly be true.'

At night, Mr. Johnson and I supped in a private room at the Turk's Head coffee-house, in the Strand. 'I encourage this house (said he); for the mistress of it is a good civil woman, and has not much business.'

'Sir, I love the acquaintance of young people; because, in the first place, I don't like to think myself growing old. In the next place, young acquaintances must last longest, if they do last; and then, Sir, young men have more virtue than old men; they have more generous sentiments in every respect. I love the young dogs of this age: they have more wit and humour and knowledge of life than we had; but then the dogs are not so good scholars. Sir, in my early years I read very hard. It is a sad reflection, but a true one, that I knew almost as much at eighteen as I do now. My judgement, to be sure, was not so good; but, I had all the facts. I remember very well, when I was at Oxford, an old gentleman said to me, "Young man, ply your book diligently now, and acquire a stock of knowledge; for when years come upon you, you will find that poring upon books will be but an irksome task."'

He again insisted on the duty of maintaining subordination of rank. 'Sir, I would no more deprive a nobleman of his respect, than of his money. I consider myself as acting a part in the great system of society, and I do to others as I would have them to do to me. I would behave to a nobleman as I should expect he would behave to me, were I a nobleman and he Sam. Johnson. Sir, there is one Mrs. Macaulay in this town, a great republican. One day when I was at her house, I put on a very grave countenance, and said to her, "Madam, I am now become a convert to your way of thinking. I am convinced that all mankind are upon an equal footing; and to give you an unquestionable proof, Madam, that I am in earnest, here is a very sensible, civil, well-behaved fellow-citizen, your footman; I desire that he may be allowed to sit down and dine with us." I thus, Sir, shewed her the absurdity of the levelling doctrine. She has never liked me since.'

We walked one evening in Greenwich Park. He asked me, I suppose, by way of trying my disposition, 'Is not this very fine?' Having no exquisite relish of the beauties of Nature, and being more delighted with 'the busy hum of men,' I answered, 'Yes, Sir; but not equal to Fleet-street.' *Johnson:* 'You are right, Sir.'

We staid so long at Greenwich, that our sail up the river, in our return to London, was by no means so pleasant as in the morning; ·for the night air was so cold that it made me shiver. I was the more sensible of it from having sat up all the night before, recollecting and writing in my journal what I thought worthy of preservation; an exertion, which, during the first part of my acquaintance with Johnson, I frequently made. I remember having sat up four nights in one week, without being much incommoded in the day time.

Johnson, whose robust frame was not in the least affected by the cold, scolded me, as if my shivering had been a paltry effeminacy, saying, 'Why do you shiver?' Sir William Scott, of the Commons, told me, that when he complained of a head-ach in the post-chaise, as they were travelling together to Scotland, Johnson treated him in the same manner: 'At your age, Sir, I had no head-ach.'

We concluded the day at the Turk's Head coffee-house very socially. He was pleased to listen to a particular account which I gave him of my family, and of its hereditary estate, as to the extent and population of which he asked questions, and made calculations; recommending, at the same time, a liberal kindness to the tenantry, as people over whom the proprietor was placed by Providence.

Next day, Sunday, July 31, I told him I had been that morning at a meeting of the people called Quakers, where I had heard a woman preach. *Johnson:* 'Sir, a woman's preaching is like a dog's walking on ·his hinder legs. It is not done well; but you are surprized to find it done at all.'

On Tuesday, August 2, (the day of my departure from London having been fixed for the 5th,) Dr. Johnson did me the honour to pass a part of the morning with me at my Chambers. He said, that 'he always felt an inclination to do nothing.' I observed, that it was strange to think that the most indolent man in Britain had written the most laborious work, *The English Dictionary*.

I had now made good my title to be a privileged man, and was carried by him in the evening to drink tea with Miss Williams, whom, though under the misfortune of having lost her sight, I found to be agreeable in conversation; for she had a variety of literature, and expressed herself well; but her peculiar value was the intimacy in which she had long lived with Johnson, by which she was well acquainted with his habits, and knew how to lead him on to talk.

On Friday, August 5, we set out early in the morning in the Harwich stage coach. A fat elderly gentlewoman, and a young Dutchman, seemed the most inclined among us to conversation. At the inn where we dined, the gentlewoman said that she had done her best to educate her children; and, particularly, that she had never suffered them to be a moment idle. *Johnson:* 'I wish, Madam, you would educate me too; for I have been an idle fellow all my life.' 'I am sure, Sir, (said she) you have not been idle.' *Johnson:* 'Nay, Madam, it is very true; and that gentleman there (pointing to me,) has been idle. He was idle at Edinburgh. His father sent him to Glasgow, where he continued to be idle. He then came to London, where he has been very idle; and now he is going to Utrecht, where he will be as idle as ever.' I asked him privately how he could expose me so. *Johnson:* 'Poh, poh! They knew nothing about you, and will think of it no more.' In the afternoon the gentlewoman talked violently against the Roman Catholicks, and of the horrours of the Inquisition. To the utter astonishment of all the passengers but myself, who knew that he could talk upon any side of a question, he defended the Inquisition, and maintained, that 'false doctrine should be checked on its first appearance; that the civil power should unite with the church in punishing those who dared to attack the established religion, and that such only were punished by the Inquisition.' Though by no means niggardly, his attention to what was generally right was so minute, that having observed at one of the stages that I ostentatiously gave a shilling to the coachman, when the custom was for each passenger to give only sixpence, he took me aside and scolded me, saying that what I had done would make the coachman dissatisfied with all the rest of the passengers, who gave him no more than his due.

At supper this night he talked of good eating with uncommon satisfaction. 'Some people (said he,) have a foolish way of not minding, or pretending not to mind, what they eat. For my part, I mind my belly very studiously, and very carefully; for I look upon it, that he who does not mind his belly will hardly mind any thing else.' I never knew any man who relished good eating more than he did. When at table, he was totally absorbed in the business of the moment; his looks seemed rivetted to his plate; nor would he, unless when in very high company, say one word, or even pay the least attention to what was said by others, till he had satisfied his appetite, which was so fierce, and indulged with such intenseness, that while in the act of eating, the veins of his forehead swelled, and generally a strong perspiration was visible. But it must be owned, that

Johnson, though he could be rigidly *abstemious,* was not a *temperate* man either in eating or drinking. He could refrain, but he could not use moderately. He told me, that he had fasted two days without inconvenience, and that he had never been hungry but once. They who beheld with wonder how much he eat upon all occasions when his dinner was to his taste, could not easily conceive what he must have meant by hunger; and not only was he remarkable for the extraordinary quantity which he eat, but he was, or affected to be, a man of very nice discernment in the science of cookery. He used to descant critically on the dishes which had been at table where he had dined or supped, and to recollect very minutely what he had liked. When invited to dine, even with an intimate friend, he was not pleased if something better than a plain dinner was not prepared for him. I have heard him say on such an occasion, 'This was a good dinner enough, to be sure; but it was not a dinner to *ask* a man to.'

Next day we got to Harwich to dinner; and my passage in the packet-boat to Helvoetsluys being secured, and my baggage put on board, we dined at our inn by ourselves. I happened to say it would be terrible if he should not find a speedy opportunity of returning to London, and be confined to so dull a place. *Johnson:* 'Don't, Sir, accustom yourself to use big words for little matters. It would *not* be *terrible,* though I *were* to be detained some time here.'

We went and looked at the church, and having gone into it and walked up to the altar, Johnson, whose piety was constant and fervent, sent me to my knees, saying, 'Now that you are going to leave your native country, recommend yourself to the protection of your *Creator* and *Redeemer.*'

After we came out of the church, we stood talking for some time together of Bishop Berkeley's ingenious sophistry to prove the non-existence of matter, and that every thing in the universe is merely ideal. I observed, that though we are satisfied his doctrine is not true, it is impossible to refute it. I never shall forget the alacrity with which Johnson answered, striking his foot with mighty force against a large stone, till he rebounded from it, 'I refute it *thus.*'

My revered friend walked down with me to the beach, where we embraced and parted with tenderness, and engaged to correspond by letters. I said, 'I hope, Sir, you will not forget me in my absence.' *Johnson:* 'Nay, Sir, it is more likely you should forget me, than that I should forget you.' As the vessel put out to sea, I kept my eyes upon him for a considerable time, while he remained rolling his majestick frame in his usual manner: and at last I perceived him walk back into the town, and he disappeared.

✖ Chapter 5

The Bear

About this time he was afflicted with a very severe return of the hypochondriack disorder, which was ever lurking about him. He was so ill, as, notwithstanding his remarkable love of company, to be entirely averse to society, the most fatal symptom of that malady. Dr. Adams told me, that, as an old friend, he was admitted to visit him, and that he found him in a deplorable state, sighing, groaning, talking to himself, and restlessly walking from room to room. He then used this emphatical expression of the misery which he felt: 'I would consent to have a limb amputated to recover my spirits.'

Talking to himself was, indeed, one of his singularities ever since I knew him. I was certain that he was frequently uttering pious ejaculations; for fragments of the Lord's Prayer have been distinctly overheard. His friend Mr. Thomas Davies, of whom Churchill says,

'That Davies hath a very pretty wife':

when Dr. Johnson muttered 'lead us not into temptation,' used with waggish and gallant humour to whisper Mrs. Davies, 'You, my dear, are the cause of this.'

He had another particularity, of which none of his friends ever ventured to ask an explanation. It appeared to me some superstitious habit, which he had contracted early, and from which he had never called upon his reason to disentangle him. This was his anxious care to go out or in at a door or passage, by a certain number of steps from a certain point, or at least so as that either his right or his left foot, (I am not certain which,) should constantly make the first actual movement when he came close to the door or passage. Thus I conjecture: for I have, upon innumerable occasions, observed him suddenly stop, and then seem to count his steps with a deep earnestness; and when he had neglected or gone wrong in this sort of magical movement, I have seen him go back again, put himself in a proper posture to begin the ceremony, and, having gone through it, break from his abstraction, walk briskly on, and join his companion.

That the most minute singularities which belonged to him, and made very observable parts of his appearance and manner, may not be omitted, it is requisite to mention, that while talking or even musing as he sat in his chair, he commonly held his head to one side towards his right shoulder, and shook it in a tremulous manner, moving his body backwards and forwards, and rubbing his left knee in the same direction, with the palm of his hand. In the intervals of articulating he made various sounds with his mouth, sometimes as if ruminating, or what is called chewing the cud, sometimes giving a half

whistle, sometimes making his tongue play backwards from the roof of his mouth, as if clucking like a hen, and sometimes protruding it against his upper gums in front, as if pronouncing quickly under his breath, *too, too, too:* all this accompanied sometimes with a thoughtful look, but more frequently with a smile. Generally when he had concluded a period, in the course of a dispute, by which time he was a good deal exhausted by violence and vociferation, he used to blow out his breath like a Whale. This I suppose was a relief to his lungs; and seemed in him to be a contemptuous mode of expression, as if he had made the arguments of his opponent fly like chaff before the wind.

Trinity College, Dublin, in 1765 surprised Johnson with a spontaneous compliment of the highest academical honours, by creating him Doctor of Laws.

This unsolicited mark of distinction, conferred on so great a literary character, did much honour to the judgement and liberal spirit of that learned body.

This year was also distinguished by his being introduced into the family of Mr. Thrale, one of the most eminent brewers in England, and Member of Parliament for the borough of Southwark. Mr. Thrale had married Miss Hester Lynch Salusbury, of good Welch extraction, a lady of lively talents, improved by education. That Johnson's introduction into Mr. Thrale's family, which contributed so much to the happiness of his life, was owing to her desire for his conversation, is very probable and a general supposition: but it is not the truth. Mr. Murphy, who was intimate with Mr. Thrale, having spoken very highly of Dr. Johnson, he was requested to make them acquainted. This being mentioned to Johnson, he accepted of an invitation to dinner at Thrale's, and was so much pleased with his reception, both by Mr. and Mrs. Thrale, and they so much pleased with him, that his invitations to their house were more and more frequent, till at last he became one of the family, and an apartment was appropriated to him, both in their house in Southwark, and in their villa at Streatham.

As this family will frequently be mentioned in the course of the following pages, and as a false notion has prevailed that Mr. Thrale was inferiour, and in some degree insignificant, compared with Mrs. Thrale, it may be proper to give a true state of the case from the authority of Johnson himself, in his own words.

'I know no man, (said he,) who is more master of his wife and family than Thrale. If he but holds up a finger, he is obeyed. It is a great mistake to suppose that she is above him in literary attainments. She is more flippant; but he has ten times her learning: he is a regular scholar; but her learning is that of a schoolboy in one of the lower forms.' My readers may naturally wish for

some representation of the figures of this couple. Mr. Thrale was tall, well proportioned, and stately. As for *Madam,* or *my Mistress,* by which epithets Johnson used to mention Mrs. Thrale, she was short, plump, and brisk. She has herself given us a lively view of the idea which Johnson had of her person, on her appearing before him in a dark-coloured gown: 'You little creatures should never wear those sort of clothes, however; they are unsuitable in every way. What! Have not all insects gay colours?'

Nothing could be more fortunate for Johnson than this connection. He had at Mr. Thrale's all the comforts and even luxuries of life; his melancholy was diverted, and his irregular habits lessened by association with an agreeable and well-ordered family. He was treated with the utmost respect, and even affection. The vivacity of Mrs. Thrale's literary talk roused him to cheerfulness and exertion, even when they were alone. But this was not often the case; for he found here a constant succession of what gave him the highest enjoyment; the society of the learned, the witty, and the eminent in every way, who were assembled in numerous companies, called forth his wonderful powers, and gratified him with admiration, to which no man could be insensible.

In the October of this year he at length gave to the world his edition of Shakspeare, which, if it had no other merit but that of producing his Preface, in which the excellencies and defects of that immortal bard are displayed with a masterly hand, the nation would have had no reason to complain. A blind indiscriminate admiration of Shakspeare had exposed the British nation to the ridicule of foreigners. Johnson, by candidly admitting the faults of his poet, had the more credit in bestowing on him deserved and indisputable praise.

I returned to London in February 1766 and found Dr. Johnson in a good house in Johnson's-court, Fleet-street, in which he had accommodated Miss Williams with an apartment on the ground floor, while Mr. Levet [1] occupied his post in the garret: his faithful Francis was still attending upon him. He received me with much kindness.

At night I supped with him at the Mitre tavern, that we might renew our social intimacy at the original place of meeting. But there was now a considerable difference in his way of living. Having had an illness, in which he was advised to leave off wine, he had, from that period, continued to abstain from it, and drank only water, or lemonade.

I told him that a foreign friend of his, whom I had met with abroad, was so wretchedly perverted to infidelity, that he treated the hopes of immortality with brutal levity; and said, 'As man dies like

---

[1] Levet: one of Johnson's strange group of permanent house guests. Levet practiced medicine (among the very poor), but his professional qualifications seem to have been questioned by most of Johnson's circle.

a dog, let him lie like a dog.' *Johnson: 'If* he dies like a dog, *let* him lie like a dog.' I added, that this man said to me, 'I hate mankind, for I think myself one of the best of them, and I know how bad I am.' *Johnson:* 'Sir, he must be very singular in his opinion, if he thinks himself one of the best of men; for none of his friends think him so.'—He said, 'No honest man could be a Deist; for no man could be so after a fair examination of the proofs of Christianity.' I named Hume. *Johnson:* 'No, Sir; Hume owned to a clergyman in the bishoprick of Durham, that he had never read the New Testament with attention.' I mentioned Hume's notion, that all who are happy are equally happy; a little miss with a new gown at a dancing-school ball, a general at the head of a victorious army, and an orator, after having made an eloquent speech in a great assembly. *Johnson:* 'Sir, that all who are happy, are equally happy, is not true. A peasant and a philosopher may be equally *satisfied,* but not equally *happy.* Happiness consists in the multiplicity of agreeable consciousness. A peasant has not capacity for having equal happiness with a philosopher.' I remember this very question very happily illustrated in opposition to Hume, by the Reverend Mr. Robert Brown, at Utrecht. 'A small drinking-glass and a large one, (said he,) may be equally full; but the large one holds more than the small.'

I introduced the subject of second

sight, and other mysterious manifestations; the fulfilment of which, I suggested, might happen by chance. *Johnson:* 'Yes, Sir; but they have happened so often, that mankind have agreed to think them not fortuitous.'

Our next meeting at the Mitre was on Saturday the 15th of February, when I presented to him my old and most intimate friend, the Reverend Mr. Temple, then of Cambridge. I having mentioned that I had passed some time with Rousseau in his wild retreat, and having quoted some remark made by Mr. Wilkes, with whom I had spent many pleasant hours in Italy, Johnson said, (sarcastically,) 'It seems, Sir, you have kept very good company abroad, Rousseau [1] and Wilkes!' [2] Thinking it enough to defend one at a time, I said nothing as to my gay friend, but answered with a smile, 'My dear Sir, you don't call Rousseau bad company. Do you really think *him* a bad man?' *Johnson:* 'Sir, if you are talking jestingly of this, I don't talk with you. If you mean to be serious, I think him one of the worst of men; a rascal, who ought to be hunted out of society, as he has been. Three or four nations have expelled him; and it is a shame that he is protected in this country.'

Boswell: 'I don't deny, Sir, but that his novel may, perhaps, do harm; but I cannot think his intention was bad.' *Johnson:* 'Sir, that will not do. We cannot prove any man's intention to be bad. You may shoot a man through the head, and say you intended to miss him; but the Judge will order you to be hanged. An alleged want of intention, when evil is committed, will not be allowed in a court of justice. Rousseau, Sir, is a very bad man. I would sooner sign a sentence for his transportation, than that of any felon who has gone from the Old Bailey these many years. Yes, I should like to have him work in the plantations.' *Boswell:* 'Sir, do you think him as bad a man as Voltaire?' *Johnson:* 'Why, Sir, it is difficult to settle the proportion of iniquity between them.'

On his favourite subject of subordination, Johnson said, 'So far is it from being true that men are naturally equal, that no two people can be half an hour together, but one shall acquire an evident superiority over the other.'

In February 1767 there happened one of the most remarkable incidents of Johnson's life, which gratified his monarchical enthusiasm, and which he loved to relate with all its circumstances, when requested by his friends. This was his being honoured by a private conversation with his Majesty, in the library at the Queen's house. He had frequently visited those splendid rooms and noble collection of

[1] Rousseau, Jean Jacques (1712–1778): French philosopher whose theory that the goodness of natural man has been corrupted by organized society and organized religion was particularly repugnant to Johnson.
[2] Wilkes, John (1727–1797): English radical politician, wit, and religious skeptic.

books, which he used to say was more numerous and curious than he supposed any person could have made in the time which the King had employed. Mr. Barnard, the librarian, took care that he should have every accommodation that could contribute to his ease and convenience, while indulging his literary taste in that place; so that he had here a very agreeable resource at leisure hours.

His Majesty having been informed of his occasional visits, was pleased to signify a desire that he should be told when Dr. Johnson came next to the library. Accordingly, the next time that Johnson did come, as soon as he was fairly engaged with a book, on which, while he sat by the fire, he seemed quite intent, Mr. Barnard stole round to the apartment where the King was, and, in obedience to his Majesty's commands, mentioned that Dr. Johnson was then in the library. His Majesty said he was at leisure, and would go to him; upon which Mr. Barnard took one of the candles that stood on the King's table, and lighted his Majesty through a suite of rooms, till they came to a private door into the library, of which his Majesty had the key. Being entered, Mr. Barnard stepped forward hastily to Dr. Johnson, who was still in a profound study, and whispered him, 'Sir, here is the King.' Johnson started up, and stood still. His Majesty approached him, and at once was courteously easy.

His Majesty began by observing, that he understood he came sometimes to the library; and then mentioning his having heard that the Doctor had been lately at Oxford, asked him if he was not fond of going thither. To which Johnson answered, that he was indeed fond of going to Oxford sometimes, but was likewise glad to come back again. The King then asked him what they were doing at Oxford. Johnson answered, he could not much commend their diligence, but that in some respects they were mended, for they had put their press under better regulations, and were at that time printing Polybius. He was then asked whether there were better libraries at Oxford or Cambridge. He answered, he believed the Bodleian was larger than any they had at Cambridge; at the same time adding, 'I hope, whether we have more books or not than they have at Cambridge, we shall make as good use of them as they do.' Being asked whether All-Souls or Christ-Church library was the largest, he answered, 'All-Souls library is the largest we have, except the Bodleian.' 'Aye, (said the King,) that is the publick library.'

His Majesty enquired if he was then writing any thing. He answered, he was not, for he had pretty well told the world what he knew, and must now read to acquire more knowledge. The King, as it should seem with a view to urge him to rely on his own stores as an original writer, and to continue his labours, then said, 'I do not think you borrow much from any body.' Johnson said, he thought he had already done his part as a writer. 'I should have thought so too, (said the King,) if you had not written so well.'—Johnson observed to me, upon this, that 'No man could have paid a handsomer compliment; and it was fit for a King to pay. It was decisive.' When asked by another friend, at Sir Joshua Reynolds', whether he made any reply to this high compliment, he answered, 'No, Sir. When the King had said it, it was to be so. It was not for me to bandy civilities with my Sovereign.' Perhaps no man who had spent his whole life in courts could have shewn a more nice and dignified sense of true politeness, than Johnson did in this instance.

During the whole of this interview, Johnson talked to his Majesty with profound respect, but still in his firm manly manner, with a sonorous voice, and never in that subdued tone which is commonly used at the levee and in the drawing-room. After the King withdrew, Johnson shewed himself highly pleased with his Majesty's conversation and gracious behaviour. He said to Mr. Barnard, 'Sir, they may talk of the King as they will; but he is the finest gentleman I have ever seen.' And he afterwards observed to Mr. Langton, 'Sir, his manners are those of as fine a gentleman as we may suppose Lewis the Fourteenth or Charles the Second.'

Soon afterwards, he supped at the Crown and Anchor tavern, in the Strand, with a company whom I collected to meet him. They were Dr. Percy, now Bishop of Dromore, Dr. Douglas, now Bishop of Salisbury, Mr. Langton, Dr. Robertson the Historian, Dr. Hugh Blair, and Mr. Thomas Davies, who wished much to be introduced to these eminent Scotch literati; but on the present occasion he had very little opportunity of hearing them talk, for with an excess of prudence, for which Johnson afterwards found fault with them, they hardly opened their lips, and that only to say something which they were certain would not expose them to the sword of Goliath; such was their anxiety for their fame when in the presence of Johnson. He was this evening in remarkable vigour of mind, and eager to exert himself in conversation, which he did with great readiness and fluency; but I am sorry to find that I have preserved but a small part of what passed.

He was vehement against old Dr. Mounsey, of Chelsea College, as 'a fellow who swore and talked bawdy.' 'I have been often in his company, (said Dr. Percy,) and never heard him swear or talk bawdy.' Mr. Davies, who sat next to Dr. Percy, having after this had some conversation aside with him, made a discovery which, in his zeal to pay court to Dr. Johnson, he eagerly proclaimed aloud from the foot of the table: 'O, Sir, I have found out a very good reason why Dr. Percy never heard Mounsey swear or talk bawdy; for he tells me, he never saw him but at the Duke of Northumberland's table.' 'And so, Sir, (said Johnson loudly, to Dr. Percy,) you would shield this man from the charge of swearing and talking bawdy, because he did not do so at the Duke of Northumberland's table. Sir, you might as well tell us that you had seen him hold up his hand at the Old Bailey, and he neither swore nor talked bawdy; or that you had seen him in the cart at Tyburn, and he neither swore nor talked bawdy. And it is thus, Sir, that you presume to controvert what I have related?' Dr. Johnson's animadversion was uttered in such a manner, that Dr. Percy seemed to be displeased, and soon afterwards left the company, of which Johnson did not at that time take any notice.

Swift having been mentioned, Johnson, as usual, treated him with little respect as an authour. Some of us endeavoured to support the Dean of St. Patrick's by various arguments. One in particular praised his 'Conduct of the Allies.' *Johnson:* 'Sir, his "Conduct of the Allies" is a performance of very little ability.' 'Surely, Sir, (said Dr. Douglas,) you must allow it has strong facts.' *Johnson:* 'Why yes, Sir; but what is that to the merit of the composition? In the Sessions-paper of the Old Bailey there are strong facts. Housebreaking is a strong fact; robbery is a strong fact; and murder is a *mighty* strong fact: but is great praise due to the historian of those strong facts? No, Sir. Swift has told what he had to tell distinctly enough, but that is all. He had to count ten, and he has counted it right.'—Then recollecting that Mr. Davies, by acting as an *informer,* had been the occasion of his talking somewhat too harshly to his friend Dr. Percy, for which, probably, when the first ebullition was over, he felt some compunction, he took an opportunity to give him a hit; so added, with a preparatory laugh, 'Why, Sir, Tom Davies might have written "the Conduct of the Allies."' Poor Tom being thus suddenly dragged into ludicrous notice in presence of the Scottish Doctors, to whom he was ambitious of appearing to advantage, was grievously mortified.

When I called upon Dr. Johnson next morning, I found him highly satisfied with his colloquial prowess the preceding evening. 'Well, (said he,) we had good talk.' *Boswell:* 'Yes, Sir; you tossed and gored several persons.'

The late Alexander, Earl of Eglintoune, who loved wit more than wine, and men of genius more than sycophants, had a great admiration of Johnson; but from the remarkable elegance of his own manners, was, perhaps, too delicately sensible of the roughness which sometimes appeared in Johnson's behaviour. One evening about this time, when his Lordship did me the honour to sup at my lodgings with Dr. Robertson and several other men of literary distinction, he regretted that Johnson had not been educated with more refinement, and lived more in polished society. 'No, no, my Lord, (said Signor Baretti,) do with him what you would, he would always have been a bear.' 'True, (answered the Earl, with a smile,) but he would have been a *dancing* bear.'

To obviate all the reflections which have gone round the world to Johnson's prejudice, by applying to him the epithet of a *bear,* let me impress upon my readers a just and happy saying of my friend Goldsmith, who knew him well: 'Johnson, to be sure, has a roughness in his manner; but no man alive has a more tender heart. *He has nothing of the bear but his skin.'*

On the 30th of September we dined together at the Mitre. I attempted to argue for the superior happiness of the savage life, upon the usual fanciful topicks. *Johnson:* 'Sir, there can be nothing more false. The savages have no bodily advantages beyond those of civilised men. They have not better health; and as to care or mental uneasiness, they are not above it, but below it, like bears. No, Sir; you are not to talk such paradox: let me have no more on't. It cannot entertain, far less can it instruct. Lord Monboddo, one of your Scotch Judges, talked a great deal of such nonsense. I suffered *him;* but I will not suffer *you.'*—*Boswell:* 'But, Sir, does not Rousseau talk such nonsense?' *Johnson:* 'True, Sir; but Rousseau *knows* he is talking nonsense, and laughs at the world for staring at him.' *Boswell:* 'How so, Sir?' *Johnson:* 'Why, Sir, a man who talks nonsense so well, must know that he is talking nonsense. But I am *afraid,* (chuckling and laughing,) Monboddo does *not* know that he is talking nonsense.' *Boswell:* 'Is it wrong then, Sir, to affect singularity, in order to make people stare?' *Johnson:* 'Yes, if you do it by propagating errour: and, indeed, it is wrong in any way. There is in human nature a general inclination to make people stare; and every wise man has himself to cure of it, and does cure himself. If you wish to make people stare by doing better than others, why, make them stare till they stare their eyes out. But consider how easy it is to make people stare, by being absurd. I may do it by going into a drawing-room without my shoes. You remember the gentleman in "The Spectator," who had a commission of lunacy taken out against him for his extreme singularity, such as never wearing a wig, but a night-cap. Now, Sir, abstractedly, the night-cap was best; but, relatively, the advantage was overbalanced by his making the boys run after him.'

When I censured a gentleman of my acquaintance for marrying a second time, as it shewed a disregard of his first wife, he said, 'Not at all, Sir. On the contrary, were he not to marry again, it might be concluded that his first wife had given him a disgust to marriage; but by taking a second wife he pays the highest compliment to the first, by shewing that she made him so happy as a married man, that he wishes to be so a second time.' So ingenious a turn did he give to this delicate question. And yet, on another occasion, he owned that he once had almost asked a promise of Mrs. Johnson that she would not marry again, but had checked himself. Indeed, I cannot help thinking, that in his case the request would have been unreasonable; for if Mrs. Johnson forgot, or thought it no injury to the memory of her first love,—the husband of her youth and the father of her children,—to make a second marriage, why should she be precluded from a third, should she be so inclined? In Johnson's persevering fond appropriation of his *Tetty,* even after her decease, he seems totally to have overlooked the prior claim of the honest Birmingham trader. I presume that her having been married before had, at times, given him some uneasiness; for I remember his observing upon the marriage of one of our common friends, 'He has done a very foolish thing, Sir; he has married a widow, when he might have had a maid.'

We drank tea with Mrs. Williams. I had last year the pleasure of seeing Mrs. Thrale at Dr. Johnson's one morning, and had conversation enough with her to admire her talents, and to shew her that I was as Johnsonian as herself. Dr. Johnson had probably been kind enough to speak well of me, for this evening he delivered me a very polite card from Mr. Thrale and her, inviting me to Streatham.

On the 6th of October I complied with this obliging invitation, and found, at an elegant villa, six miles from town, every circumstance that can make society pleasing. Johnson, though quite at home, was yet looked up to with an awe, tempered by affection, and seemed to be equally the care of his host and hostess. I rejoiced at seeing him so happy.

He played off his wit against Scotland with a good humoured pleasantry, which gave me, though no bigot to national prejudices, an opportunity for a little contest with him. I having said that England was obliged to us for gardeners, almost all their good gardeners being Scotchmen:—*Johnson:* 'Why, Sir, that is because gardening is much more necessary amongst you than with us, which makes so many of your people learn it. It is *all* gardening with you. Things which grow wild here, must be cultivated with great care in Scotland.'

Mrs. Thrale praised Garrick's talent for light gay poetry; and, as a specimen, repeated his song in 'Florizel and Perdita,' and dwelt with peculiar pleasure on this line:

'I'd smile with the simple, and feed with the poor.'

Johnson: 'Nay, my dear Lady, this will never do. Poor David! Smile with the simple! What folly is that! And who would feed with the poor that can help it? No, no; let me smile with the wise, and feed with the rich.' I repeated this sally to Garrick, and wondered to find his sensibility as a writer not a little irritated by it.

On the evening of October 10, I presented Dr. Johnson to General Paoli.[1] I had greatly wished that two men, for whom I had the highest esteem, should meet. They met with a manly ease, mutually conscious of their own abilities, and of the abilities of each other. The General spoke Italian, and Dr. Johnson English, and understood one another very well, with a little aid of interpretation from me, in which I compared myself to an isthmus which joins two great continents.

Dr. Johnson went home with me, and drank tea till late in the night. He said, 'General Paoli had the loftiest port of any man he had ever seen.' He denied that military men were always the best bred men. 'Perfect good breeding,' he observed, 'consists in having no particular mark of any profession, but a general elegance of manners; whereas, in a military man, you can commonly distinguish the *brand* of a soldier.'

Dr. Johnson shunned to-night any discussion of the perplexed question of fate and free will, which I attempted to agitate: 'Sir, (said he,) we *know* our will is free, and *there's* an end on't.'

He honoured me with his company at dinner on the 16th of October, at my lodgings in Old Bond-street, with Sir Joshua Reynolds, Mr. Garrick, Dr. Goldsmith, Mr. Murphy, Mr. Bickerstaff, and Mr.

Thomas Davies. Garrick played round him with a fond vivacity, taking hold of the breasts of his coat, and, looking up in his face with a lively archness, complimented him on the good health which he seemed then to enjoy; while the sage, shaking his head, beheld him with a gentle complacency. One of the company not being come at the appointed hour, I proposed, as usual upon such occasions, to order dinner to be served; adding, 'Ought six people to be kept waiting for one?' 'Why, yes, (answered Johnson, with a delicate humanity,) if the one will suffer more by your sitting down, than the six will do by waiting.' Goldsmith, to divert the tedious minutes, strutted about, bragging of his dress, and I believe was seriously vain of it, for his mind was wonderfully prone to such impressions. 'Well, let me tell you, (said Goldsmith,) when my tailor brought home my bloom-coloured coat, he said, "Sir, I have a favour to beg of you. When any body asks you who made your clothes, be pleased to mention John Filby, at the Harrow, in Water-lane."' *Johnson:* 'Why, Sir, that was because he knew the strange colour would attract crouds to gaze at it, and thus they might hear of him, and see how well he could make a coat even of so absurd a colour.'

After dinner our conversation first turned upon Pope. Johnson said, his characters of men were admirably drawn, those of women not so well. He repeated to us, in

[1] Paoli, Pasquale (1726–1807): Corsican military and political leader. He lived in England for twenty years after France annexed Corsica in 1769.

his forcible melodious manner, the concluding lines of the Dunciad. While he was talking loudly in praise of those lines, one of the company ventured to say, 'Too fine for such a poem:—a poem on what?' *Johnson* (with a disdainful look,): 'Why, on *dunces*. It was worth while being a dunce then. Ah, Sir, hadst *thou* lived in those days! It is not worth while being a dunce now, when there are no wits.'

Mrs. Montagu, a lady distinguished for having written an Essay on Shakspeare, being mentioned; —*Reynolds:* 'I think that essay does her honour.' *Johnson:* 'Yes, Sir; it does *her* honour, but it would do nobody else honour. I have, indeed, not read it all. But when I take up the end of a web, and find it packthread, I do not expect, by looking further, to find embroidery. Sir, I will venture to say, there is not one sentence of true criticism in her book.' *Garrick:* 'But, Sir, surely it shews how much Voltaire has mistaken Shakspeare, which nobody else has done.' *Johnson:* 'Sir, nobody else has thought it worth while. And what merit is there in that? You may as well praise a schoolmaster for whipping a boy who has construed ill. No, Sir, there is no real criticism in it: none shewing the beauty of thought, as formed on the workings of the human heart.'

One day at Sir Joshua's table, when it was related that Mrs. Montagu, in an excess of compliment to the authour of a modern tragedy, had exclaimed, 'I tremble for Shakspeare'; Johnson said, 'When Shak-speare has got ——[1] for his rival, and Mrs. Montagu for his defender, he is in a poor state indeed.'

On Thursday, October 19, I passed the evening with him at his house.

I mentioned to him that I had seen the execution of several convicts at Tyburn, two days before, and that none of them seemed to be under any concern. *Johnson:* 'Most of them, Sir, have never thought at all.' *Boswell:* 'But is not the fear of death natural to man?' *Johnson:* 'So much so, Sir, that the whole of life is but keeping away the thoughts of it.' He then, in a low and earnest tone, talked of his meditating upon the aweful hour of his own dissolution, and in what manner he should conduct himself upon that occasion: 'I know not (said he,) whether I should wish to have a friend by me, or have it all between GOD and myself.'

Talking of our feeling for the distresses of others;—*Johnson:* 'Why, Sir, there is much noise made about it, but it is greatly exaggerated. No, Sir, we have a certain degree of feeling to prompt us to do good: more than that, Providence does not intend. It would be misery to no purpose.' *Boswell:* 'But suppose now, Sir, that one of your intimate friends were apprehended for an offence for which he might be hanged.' *Johnson:* 'I should do what I could to bail him, and give him any other assistance; but if he were once fairly

[1] Probably Robert Jephson (1736–1803), a minor playwright.

hanged, I should not suffer.' *Boswell:* 'Would you eat your dinner that day, Sir?' *Johnson:* 'Yes, Sir; and eat it as if he were eating it with me. Why, there's Baretti, who is to be tried for his life to-morrow; friends have risen up for him on every side; yet if he should be hanged, none of them will eat a slice of plum-pudding the less. Sir, that sympathetick feeling goes a very little way in depressing the mind.'

I told him that I had dined lately at Foote's, who shewed me a letter which he had received from Tom Davies, telling him that he had not been able to sleep from the concern which he felt on account of *'This sad affair of Baretti,'* begging of him to try if he could suggest any thing that might be of service; and, at the same time, recommending to him an industrious young man who kept a pickle-shop. *Johnson:* 'Ay, Sir, here you have a specimen of human sympathy; a friend hanged, and a cucumber pickled. We know not whether Baretti or the pickle-man has kept Davies from sleep; nor does he know himself. And as to his not sleeping, Sir; Tom Davies is a very great man; Tom has been upon the stage, and knows how to do those things: I have not been upon the stage, and cannot do those things.' *Boswell:* 'I have often blamed myself, Sir, for not feeling for others as sensibly as many say they do.' *Johnson:* 'Sir, don't be duped by them any more. You will find these very feeling people are not very ready to do you good. They *pay* you by *feeling.'*

Next day, October 20, he appeared, for the only time I suppose in his life, as a witness in a Court of Justice, being called to give evidence to the character of Mr. Baretti, who having stabbed a man in the street, was arraigned at the Old Bailey for murder.[1] Never did such a constellation of genius enlighten the aweful Sessions-House, emphatically called *Justice Hall;* Mr. Burke, Mr. Garrick, Mr. Beauclerk, and Dr. Johnson: and undoubtedly their favourable testimony had due weight with the Court and Jury. Johnson gave his evidence in a slow, deliberate, and distinct manner, which was uncommonly impressive. It is well known that Mr. Baretti was acquitted.

We went home to his house to tea. Mrs. Williams made it with sufficient dexterity, notwithstanding her blindness, though her manner of satisfying herself that the cups were full enough appeared to me a little aukward; for I fancied she put her finger down a certain way, till she felt the tea touch it. In my first elation at being allowed the privilege of attending Dr. Johnson at his late visits to this lady, I willingly drank cup after cup, as if it had been the Heliconian spring. But as the charm of novelty went off, I grew more fastidious; and besides, I discovered that she was of a peevish temper.

[1] Giuseppe Baretti was attacked in the street by three men. He attempted to escape, then turned at bay and, possibly from panic, stabbed one of them with a pocketknife.

There was a pretty large circle this evening. Dr. Johnson was in very good humour, lively, and ready to talk upon all subjects. Dominicetti being mentioned, he would not allow him any merit. 'There is nothing in all this boasted system. No, Sir; medicated baths can be no better than warm water: their only effect can be that of tepid moisture.' One of the company took the other side, maintaining that medicines of various sorts, and some too of most powerful effect, are introduced into the human frame by the medium of the pores; and, therefore, when warm water is impregnated with salutiferous substances, it may produce great effects as a bath. This appeared to me very satisfactory. Johnson did not answer it; but talking for victory, and determined to be master of the field, he had recourse to the device which Goldsmith imputed to him in the witty words of one of Cibber's comedies: 'There is no arguing with Johnson; for when his pistol misses fire, he knocks you down with the butt end of it.' He turned to the gentleman, 'Well, Sir, go to Dominicetti, and get thyself fumigated; but be sure that the steam be directed to thy *head,* for *that* is the *peccant* [1] *part.*' This produced a triumphant roar of laughter from the motley assembly of philosophers, printers, and dependents, male and female.

When we were alone, I introduced the subject of death, and endeavoured to maintain that the fear of

[1] *peccant:* offending; faulty; corrupt.

it might be got over. I told him that David Hume said to me, he was no more uneasy to think he should *not be* after this life, than that he *had not been* before he began to exist. *Johnson:* 'Sir, if he really thinks so, his perceptions are disturbed; he is mad; if he does not think so, he lies. He may tell you, he holds his finger in the flame of a candle, without feeling pain; would you believe him? When he dies, he at least gives up all he has.' *Boswell:* 'Foote, Sir, told me, that when he was very ill he was not afraid to die.' *Johnson:* 'It is not true, Sir. Hold a pistol to Foote's breast, or to Hume's breast, and threaten to kill them, and you'll see how they behave.' *Boswell:* 'But may we not fortify our minds for the approach of death?'—Here I am sensible I was in the wrong, to bring before his view what he ever looked upon with horrour; for although when in a celestial frame, in his 'Vanity of Human Wishes,' he has supposed death to be 'kind Nature's signal for retreat,' from this state of being to 'a happier seat,' his thoughts upon this aweful change were in general full of dismal apprehensions. His mind resembled the vast amphitheatre, the Colisæum at Rome. In the centre stood his judgement, which, like a mighty gladiator, combated those apprehensions that, like the wild beasts of the *Arena,* were all around in cells, ready to be let out upon him. After a conflict, he drove them back into their dens; but not killing them, they were still assailing him. To my question, whether we might not fortify our minds for the approach of death, he answered, in a passion, 'No, Sir, let it alone. It matters not how a man dies, but how he lives. The act of dying is not of importance, it lasts so short a time.' He added, (with an earnest look,) 'A man knows it must be so, and submits. It will do him no good to whine.'

I attempted to continue the conversation. He was so provoked, that he said, 'Give us no more of this'; and was thrown into such a state of agitation, that he expressed himself in a way that alarmed and distressed me; shewed an impatience that I should leave him, and when I was going away, called to me sternly, 'Don't let us meet to-morrow.'

I went home exceedingly uneasy. All the harsh observations which I had ever heard made upon his character, crowded into my mind; and I seemed to myself like the man who had put his head into the lion's mouth a great many times with perfect safety, but at last had it bit off.

Next morning I sent him a note, stating, that I might have been in the wrong, but it was not intentionally; he was therefore, I could not help thinking, too severe upon me. That notwithstanding our agreement not to meet that day, I would call on him in my way to the city, and stay five minutes by my watch. 'You are, (said I,) in my mind, since last night, surrounded with cloud and storm. Let me have a glimpse of sunshine, and go about my affairs in serenity and cheerfulness.'

Upon entering his study, I was glad that he was not alone, which would have made our meeting more aukward. There were with him, Mr. Steevens and Mr. Tyers, both of whom I now saw for the first time. My note had, on his own reflection, softened him, for he received me very complacently; so that I unexpectedly found myself at ease, and joined in the conversation.

I whispered him, 'Well, Sir, you are now in good humour.' *Johnson:* 'Yes, Sir.' I was going to leave him, and had got as far as the staircase. He stopped me, and smiling, said, 'Get you gone *in*'; a curious mode of inviting me to stay, which I accordingly did for some time longer.

This little incidental quarrel and reconciliation, which, perhaps, I may be thought to have detailed too minutely, must be esteemed as one of many proofs which his friends had, that though he might be charged with *bad humour* at times, he was always a *good-natured* man; and I have heard Sir Joshua Reynolds, a nice and delicate observer of manners, particularly remark, that when upon any occasion Johnson had been rough to any person in company, he took the first opportunity of reconciliation, by drinking to him, or addressing his discourse to him; but if he found his dignified indirect overtures sullenly neglected, he was quite indifferent, and considered himself as having done all that he ought to do, and the other as now in the wrong.

During 1770 there was a total cessation of all correspondence between Dr. Johnson and me, without any coldness on either side, but merely from procrastination, continued from day to day; and as I was not in London, I had no opportunity of enjoying his company and recording his conversation.

✖ *Chapter* **6**

Some Tossing and Goring

On the 21st of March, 1772, I was happy to find myself again in my friend's study. Dr. Johnson received me with a hearty welcome. He was engaged to dine abroad, and asked me to return to him in the evening, at nine, which I accordingly did.

We drank tea with Mrs. Williams, who told us a story of second sight, which happened in Wales where she was born.—He listened to it very attentively, and said he should be glad to have some instances of that faculty well authenticated. His elevated wish for more and more evidence for spirit, in opposition to the groveling belief of materialism, led him to a love of such mysterious disquisitions. He again justly observed, that we could

have no certainty of the truth of supernatural appearances, unless something was told us which we could not know by ordinary means, or something done which could not be done but by supernatural power; that Pharaoh in reason and justice required such evidence from Moses; nay, that our Saviour said, 'If I had not done among them the works which none other man did, they had not had sin.' He had said in the morning, that 'Macaulay's History of St. Kilda,' was very well written, except some foppery about liberty and slavery. I mentioned to him that Macaulay told me, he was advised to leave out of his book the wonderful story that upon the approach of a stranger all the inhabitants catch cold; but that it had been so well authenticated, he determined to retain it. *Johnson:* 'Sir, to leave things out of a book, merely because people tell you they will not be believed, is meanness. Macaulay acted with more magnanimity.'

We talked of the Roman Catholick religion and how little difference there was in essential matters between ours and it. *Johnson:* 'True, Sir; all denominations of Christians have really little difference in point of doctrine, though they may differ widely in external forms. There is a prodigious difference between the external form of one of your Presbyterian churches in Scotland, and a church in Italy; yet the doctrine taught is essentially the same.'

In the morning we had talked of

old families, and the respect due to them. *Johnson:* 'Sir, you have a right to that kind of respect, and are arguing for yourself. I am for supporting the principle, and am disinterested in doing it, as I have no such right.' *Boswell:* 'Why, Sir, it is one more incitement to a man to do well.' *Johnson:* 'Yes, Sir, and it is a matter of opinion, very necessary to keep society together. What is it but opinion, by which we have a respect for authority, that prevents us, who are the rabble, from rising up and pulling down you who are gentlemen from your places, and saying "We will be gentlemen in our turn"? Now, Sir, that respect for authority is much more easily granted to a man whose father has had it, than to an upstart, and so Society is more easily supported.' *Boswell:* 'Perhaps, Sir, it might be done by the respect belonging to office, as among the Romans, where the dress, the *toga,* inspired reverence.' *Johnson:* 'Why, Sir, we know very little about the Romans. But, surely, it is much easier to respect a man who has always had respect, than to respect a man who we know was last year no better than ourselves, and will be no better next year. In republicks there is not a respect for authority, but a fear of power.' *Boswell:* 'At present, Sir, I think riches seem to gain most respect.' *Johnson:* 'No, Sir, riches do not gain hearty respect; they only procure external attention. A very rich man, from low beginnings, may buy his election in a borough; but, a man of

family will be preferred. People will prefer a man for whose father their fathers have voted, though they should get no more money, or even less. That shows that the respect for family is not merely fanciful, but has an actual operation. If gentlemen of family would allow the rich upstarts to spend their money profusely, which they are ready enough to do, and not vie with them in expence, the upstarts would soon be at an end, and the gentlemen would remain: but if the gentlemen will vie in expence with the upstarts, which is very foolish, they must be ruined.'

I again visited him at night. Finding him in a very good humour, I ventured to lead him to the subject of our situation in a future state, having much curiosity to know his notions on that point. *Johnson:* 'Why, Sir, the happiness of an unembodied spirit will consist in a consciousness of the favour of GOD, in the contemplation of truth, and in the possession of felicitating ideas.' *Boswell:* 'But, Sir, is there any harm in our forming to ourselves conjectures as to the particulars of our happiness, though the scripture has said but very little on the subject? "We know not what we shall be."' *Johnson:* 'Sir, there is no harm. What philosophy suggests to us on this topick is probable: what scripture tells us is certain. Dr. Henry More has carried it as far as philosophy can. You may buy both his theological and philosophical works in two volumes folio, for about eight shillings.' *Bos-

well: 'One of the most pleasing thoughts is, that we shall see our friends again.' *Johnson:* 'Yes, Sir; but you must consider, that when we are become purely rational, many of our friendships will be cut off. Many friendships are formed by a community of sensual pleasures: all these will be cut off. We form many friendships with bad men, because they have agreeable qualities, and they can be useful to us; but, after death, they can no longer be of use to us. We form many friendships by mistake, imagining people to be different from what they really are. After death, we shall see every one in a true light. Then, Sir, they talk of our meeting our relations: but then all relationship is dissolved; and we shall have no regard for one person more than another, but for their real value. However, we shall either have the satisfaction of meeting our friends, or be satisfied without meeting them.' *Boswell:* 'As to our employment in a future state, the sacred writings say little. The Revelation, however, of St. John gives us many ideas, and particularly mentions musick.' *Johnson:* 'Why, Sir, ideas must be given you by means of something which you know: and as to musick, there are some philosophers and divines who have maintained that we shall not be spiritualized to such a degree, but that something of matter, very much refined, will remain. In that case, musick may make a part of our future felicity.'

Boswell: 'I do not know whether there are any well-attested stories of the appearance of ghosts. You know there is a famous story of the appearance of Mrs. Veal, prefixed to "Drelincourt on Death." ' *Johnson:* 'I believe, Sir, that is given up. I believe the woman declared upon her death-bed that it was a lie.' *Boswell:* 'This objection is made against the truth of ghosts appearing: that if they are in a state of happiness, it would be a punishment to them to return to this world; and if they are in a state of misery, it would be giving them a respite.' *Johnson:* 'Why, Sir, as the happiness or misery of unembodied spirits does not depend upon place, but is intellectual, we cannot say that they are less happy or less miserable by appearing upon earth.'

On Tuesday, March 31, he and I dined at General Paoli's. A question was started, whether the state of marriage was natural to man. *Johnson:* 'Sir, it is so far from being natural for a man and woman to live in a state of marriage, that we find all the motives which they have for remaining in that connection, and the restraints which civilized society imposes to prevent separation, are hardly sufficient to keep them together.' The General said, that in a state of nature a man and woman uniting together would form a strong and constant affection, by the mutual pleasure each would receive; and that the same causes of dissention would not arise between them, as occur between husband and wife in a civilized state. *Johnson:* 'Sir, they would have dissentions enough, though of another kind. One would choose to go a hunting in this wood, the other in that; one would choose to go a fishing in this lake, the other in that; or, perhaps, one would choose to go a hunting, when the other would choose to go a fishing; and so they would part. Besides, Sir, a savage man and a savage woman meet by chance; and when the man sees another woman that pleases him better, he will leave the first.'

We then fell into a disquisition whether there is any beauty independent of utility. The General maintained there was not. Dr. Johnson maintained that there was; and he instanced a coffee-cup which he held in his hand, the painting of which was of no real use, as the cup would hold the coffee equally well if plain; yet the painting was beautiful.

Dr. Johnson went home with me to my lodgings in Conduit-street and drank tea, previous to our going to the Pantheon,[1] which neither of us had seen before.

He said, 'Goldsmith's Life of Parnell is poor; not that it is poorly written, but that he had poor materials; for nobody can write the life of a man, but those who have eat and drunk and lived in social intercourse with him.'

I said, that if it was not troublesome and presuming too much, I would request him to tell me all the little circumstances of his life; what schools he attended, when he came to Oxford, when he came to London, &c. &c. He did not disapprove of my curiosity as to these particulars; but said, 'They'll come out by degrees as we talk together.'

We talked of the proper use of riches. *Johnson:* 'If I were a man of a great estate, I would drive all the rascals whom I did not like out of the county at an election.'

I asked him how far he thought wealth should be employed in hospitality. *Johnson:* 'You are to consider that ancient hospitality, of which we hear so much, was in an uncommercial country, when men being idle, were glad to be entertained at rich men's tables. But in a commercial country, a busy country, time becomes precious, and therefore hospitality is not so much valued. No doubt there is still room for a certain degree of it; and a man has a satisfaction in seeing his friends eating and drinking around him. But promiscuous hospitality is not the way to gain real influence. You must help some people at table before others; you must ask some people how they like their wine oftener than others. You therefore offend more people than you please.' *Boswell:* 'May not a man, Sir, employ his riches to advantage in educating young men of merit?' *Johnson:* 'Yes, Sir, if they fall in your way; but if it is understood that you patronize young men of merit, you will be harassed with solicitations.

[1] the Pantheon: a place for assemblies, concerts, and balls. It was generally, though not universally, admired for its magnificence.

'Were I a rich man, I would propagate all kinds of trees that will grow in the open air. A greenhouse is childish. I would introduce foreign animals into the country; for instance, the rein-deer.'

We then walked to the Pantheon. The first view of it did not strike us so much as Ranelagh.[1] However, as Johnson observed, we saw the Pantheon in time of mourning, when there was a dull uniformity; whereas we had seen Ranelagh when the view was enlivened with a gay profusion of colours. I said there was not half a guinea's worth of pleasure in seeing this place. *Johnson:* 'But, Sir, there is half a guinea's worth of inferiority to other people in not having seen it.' *Boswell:* 'I doubt, Sir, whether there are many happy people here.' *Johnson:* 'Yes, Sir, there are many happy people here. There are many people here who are watching hundreds, and who think hundreds are watching them.'

Happening to meet Sir Adam Fergusson, I presented him to Dr. Johnson. Sir Adam expressed some apprehension that the Pantheon would encourage luxury. 'Sir (said Johnson,) I am a great friend to publick amusements; for they keep people from vice. You now (addressing himself to me,) would have been with a wench, had you not been here.—O! I forgot you were married.'

Sir Adam suggested, that luxury

corrupts a people, and destroys the spirit of liberty. *Johnson:* 'Sir, that is all visionary. I would not give half a guinea to live under one form of government rather than another. It is of no moment to the happiness of an individual. Sir, the danger of the abuse of power is nothing to a private man. What Frenchman is prevented from passing his life as he pleases?' *Sir Adam:* 'But, Sir, in the British constitution it is surely of importance to keep up a spirit in the people, so as to preserve a balance against the crown.' *Johnson:* 'Sir, I perceive you are a vile Whig.—Why all this childish jealousy of the power of the crown? The crown has not power enough. When I say that all governments are alike, I consider that in no government power can be abused long. Mankind will not bear it. If a sovereign oppresses his people to a great degree, they will rise and cut off his head. There is a remedy in human nature against tyranny, that will keep us safe under every form of government. Had not the people of France thought themselves honoured as sharing in the brilliant actions of Lewis XIV, they would not have endured him; and we may say the same of the King of Prussia's people.' Sir Adam introduced the ancient Greeks and Romans. *Johnson:* 'Sir, the mass of both of them were barbarians. The mass of every people must be barbarous where there is no printing, and consequently knowledge is not generally diffused. Knowledge is diffused

---

[1] Ranelagh: a large outdoor amusement resort in Chelsea.

among our people by the newspapers.' Sir Adam mentioned the orators, poets, and artists of Greece. *Johnson:* 'Sir, I am talking of the mass of the people. We see even what the boasted Athenians were. The little effect which Demosthenes'[1] orations had upon them, shews that they were barbarians.'

On Sunday, April 5, after attending divine service at St. Paul's church, I found him alone. Of a schoolmaster of his acquaintance, a native of Scotland, he said, 'He has a great deal of good about him; but he is also very defective in some respects. His inner part is good, but his outer part is mighty aukward. You in Scotland do not attain that nice critical skill in languages, which we get in our schools in England. I would not put a boy to him, whom I intended for a man of learning. But for the sons of citizens, who are to learn a little, get good morals, and then go to trade, he may do very well.'

On Monday, April 6, I dined with him at Sir Alexander Macdonald's, where was a young officer in the regimentals of the Scots Royal, who talked with a vivacity, fluency, and precision so uncommon, that he attracted particular attention. He proved to be the Honourable Thomas Erskine, youngest brother to the Earl of Buchan, who has since risen into such brilliant reputation at the bar in Westminster-hall.

---

[1] Demosthenes (385?–322 B.C.): Athenian orator and statesman.

We talked of gaming, and animadverted on it with severity. *Johnson:* 'Nay, gentlemen, let us not aggravate the matter. It is not roguery to play with a man who is ignorant of the game, while you are master of it, and so win his money; for he thinks he can play better than you, as you think you can play better than he; and the superior skill carries it.' *Erskine:* 'He is a fool, but you are not a rogue.' *Johnson:* 'That's much about the truth, Sir. It must be considered, that a man who only does what every one of the society to which he belongs would do, is not a dishonest man. In the republick of Sparta, it was agreed, that stealing was not dishonourable, if not discovered. I do not commend a society where there is an agreement that what would not otherwise be fair, shall be fair; but I maintain, that an individual of any society, who practises what is allowed, is not a dishonest man.' *Boswell:* 'So then, Sir, you do not think ill of a man who wins perhaps forty thousand pounds in a winter?' *Johnson:* 'Sir, I do not call a gamester a dishonest man; but I call him an unsocial man, an unprofitable man. Gaming is a mode of transferring property without producing any intermediate good. Trade gives employment to numbers, and so produces intermediate good.'

I talked of the little attachment which subsisted between near relations in London. 'Sir, (said Johnson,) in a country so commercial as ours, where every man can do for himself, there is not so much occasion for that attachment. No man is thought the worse of here, whose brother was hanged. In uncommercial countries, many of the branches of a family must depend on the stock; so, in order to make the head of the family take care of them, they are represented as connected with his reputation, that, self-love being interested, he may exert himself to promote their interest. You have first large circles, or clans; as commerce increases, the connection is confined to families. By degrees, that too goes off, as having become unnecessary, and there being few opportunities of intercourse. One brother is a merchant in the city, and another is an officer in the guards. How little intercourse can these two have!'

I argued warmly for the old feudal system. Sir Alexander opposed it, and talked of the pleasure of seeing all men free and independent. *Johnson:* 'I agree with Mr. Boswell that there must be a high satisfaction in being a feudal Lord; but we are to consider, that we ought not to wish to have a number of men unhappy for the satisfaction of one.'—I maintained that numbers, namely, the vassals or followers, were not unhappy; for that there was a reciprocal satisfaction between the Lord and them: he being kind in his authority over them; they being respectful and faithful to him.

On Thursday, April 9, I called on him to beg he would go and dine with me at the Mitre tavern.

He had resolved not to dine at all this day, I know not for what reason; and I was so unwilling to be deprived of his company, that I was content to submit to suffer a want, which was at first somewhat painful, but he soon made me forget it; and a man is always pleased with himself when he finds his intellectual inclinations predominate.

He observed, that to reason too philosophically on the nature of prayer, was very unprofitable.

Talking of ghosts, he said, he knew one friend, who was an honest man and a sensible man, who told him he had seen a ghost, old Mr. Edward Cave, the printer at St. John's Gate. He said, Mr. Cave did not like to talk of it, and seemed to be in great horrour whenever it was mentioned. *Boswell:* 'Pray, Sir, what did he say was the appearance?' *Johnson:* 'Why, Sir, something of a shadowy being.'

I mentioned witches, and asked him what they properly meant. *Johnson:* 'Why, Sir, they properly mean those who make use of the aid of evil spirits.' *Boswell:* 'There is no doubt, Sir, a general report and belief of their having existed.' *Johnson:* 'Sir, you have not only the general report and belief, but you have many voluntary solemn confessions.' He did not affirm any thing positively upon a subject which it is the fashion of the times to laugh at as a matter of absurd credulity. He only seemed willing, as a candid enquirer after truth, however strange and inexplicable, to shew that he understood what might be urged for it.

On Friday, April 10, I dined with him at General Oglethorpe's, where we found Dr. Goldsmith.

Armorial bearings having been mentioned, Johnson said; they were as ancient as the siege of Thebes, which he proved by a passage in one of the tragedies of Euripides.

I started the question whether duelling was consistent with moral duty. The brave old General fired at this, and said, with a lofty air, 'Undoubtedly a man has a right to defend his honour.' *Goldsmith* (turning to me,): 'I ask you first, Sir, what would you do if you were affronted?' I answered I should think it necessary to fight. 'Why then, (replied Goldsmith,) that solves the question.' *Johnson:* 'No, Sir, it does not solve the question. It does not follow that what a man would do is therefore right.' I said, I wished to have it settled, whether duelling was contrary to the laws of Christianity. Johnson immediately entered on the subject, and treated it in a masterly manner; and so far as I have been able to recollect, his thoughts were these: 'Sir, as men become in a high degree refined, various causes of offence arise; which are considered to be of such importance, that life must be staked to atone for them, though in reality they are not so. A body that has received a very fine polish may be easily hurt. Before men arrive at this artificial refinement, if one tells his neighbour he lies, his neighbour tells him he lies; if one gives his neighbour a blow, his neighbour gives him a blow: but in a state of highly polished society, an affront is held to be a serious injury. It must, therefore, be resented, or rather a duel must be fought upon it; as men have agreed to banish from their society one who puts up with an affront without fighting a duel. Now, Sir, it is never unlawful to fight in self-defence. He, then, who fights a duel, does not fight from passion against his antagonist, but out of self-defence; to avert the stigma of the world, and to prevent himself from being driven out of society. I could wish there was not that superfluity of refinement; but while such notions prevail, no doubt a man may lawfully fight a duel.'

A question was started, how far people who disagree in any capital point can live in friendship together. Johnson said they might. Goldsmith said they could not, as they had not the same likings and the same aversions. *Johnson:* 'Why, Sir, you must shun the subject as to which you disagree. For instance, I can live very well with Burke: I love his knowledge, his genius, his diffusion, and affluence of conversation; but I would not talk to him of the Rockingham party.[1] *Goldsmith:* 'But, Sir, when

[1] the Rockingham party: a Whig group notable for its friendship for the cause of the American colonies. Burke was an important member of the Rockingham party.

people live together who have something as to which they disagree, and which they want to shun, they will be in the situation mentioned in the story of Bluebeard: "You may look into all the chambers but one." But we should have the greatest inclination to look into that chamber, to talk of that subject.' *Johnson* (with a loud voice): 'Sir, I am not saying that *you* could live in friendship with a man from whom you differ as to some point: I am only saying that *I* could do it.'

On the evening of the next day I supped with Dr. Johnson, at the Crown and Anchor tavern, in the Strand, in company with Mr. Langton and his brother-in-law, Lord Binning.

I talked of the recent expulsion of six students from the University of Oxford, who were Methodists, and would not desist from publickly praying and exhorting. *Johnson:* 'Sir, that expulsion was extremely just and proper. What have they to do at an University who are not willing to be taught, but will presume to teach? Where is religion to be learnt but at an University? Sir, they were examined, and found to be mighty ignorant fellows.' *Boswell:* 'But, was it not hard, Sir, to expel them, for I am told they were good beings?' *Johnson:* 'Sir, I believe they might be good beings; but they were not fit to be in the University of Oxford. A cow is a very good animal in the field; but we turn her out of a garden.' Lord Elibank used to

repeat this as an illustration uncommonly happy.

Mr. Langton told us he was about to establish a school upon his estate, but it had been suggested to him, that it might have a tendency to make the people less industrious. *Johnson:* 'No, Sir. While learning to read and write is a distinction, the few who have that distinction may be the less inclined to work; but when every body learns to read and write, it is no longer a distinction. A man who has a laced waistcoat is too fine a man to work; but if every body had laced waistcoats, we should have people working in laced waistcoats. There are no people whatever more industrious, none who work more, than our manufacturers; yet they have all learnt to read and write. Sir, you must not neglect doing a thing immediately good, from fear of remote evil;—from fear of its being abused. A man who has candles may sit up too late, which he would not do if he had not candles; but nobody will deny that the art of making candles, by which light is continued to us beyond the time that the sun gives us light, is a valuable art, and ought to be preserved.' *Boswell:* 'But, Sir, would it not be better to follow Nature; and go to bed and rise just as Nature gives us light or with-holds it?' *Johnson:* 'No, Sir, for then we should have no kind of equality in the partition of our time between sleeping and waking. It would be very different in different seasons and in different places. In some of the northern parts of Scotland how little light is there in the depth of winter!'

While I remained in London this spring, I was with him at several other times, both by himself and in company. I dined with him one day at the Crown and Anchor tavern, in the Strand, with Lord Elibank, Mr. Langton, and Dr. Vansittart of Oxford. Without specifying each particular day, I have preserved the following memorable things.

A gentleman having to some of the usual arguments for drinking added this: 'You know, Sir, drinking drives away care, and makes us forget whatever is disagreeable. Would not you allow a man to drink for that reason?' *Johnson:* 'Yes, Sir, if he sat next *you.*'

When one of his friends endeavoured to maintain that a country gentleman might contrive to pass his life very agreeably, 'Sir (said he,) you cannot give me an instance of any man who is permitted to lay out his own time, contriving not to have tedious hours.' This observation, however, is equally applicable to gentlemen who live in cities, and are of no profession.

A learned gentleman who in the course of conversation wished to inform us of this simple fact, that the Counsel upon the circuit at Shrewsbury were much bitten by fleas, took, I suppose, seven or eight minutes in relating it circumstantially. He in a plenitude of phrase told us, that large bales of woollen cloth were lodged in the town-hall; —that by reason of this, fleas nestled there in prodigious numbers;—that the lodgings of the Counsel were near to the town-hall;—and that those little animals moved from place to place with wonderful agility. Johnson sat in great impatience till the gentleman had finished his tedious narrative, and then burst out (playfully however,) 'It is a pity, Sir, that you have not seen a lion; for a flea has taken you such a time, that a lion must have served you a twelvemonth.'

On Saturday, April 3, the day after my arrival in London [1] this year, I went to his house late in the evening, and sat with Mrs. Williams till he came home. I found in the London Chronicle, Dr. Goldsmith's apology to the publick for beating Evans, a bookseller, on account of a paragraph in a newspaper published by him, which Goldsmith thought impertinent to him and to a lady of his acquaintance. The apology was written so much in Dr. Johnson's manner, that both Mrs. Williams and I supposed it to be his; but when he came home, he soon undeceived us. When he said to Mrs. Williams, 'Well, Dr. Goldsmith's *manifesto* has got into your paper,' I asked him if Dr. Goldsmith had written it, with an air that made him see I suspected it was his, though subscribed by Goldsmith. *Johnson:*

[1] Boswell's visits with Johnson were, at this point, intervals in his life with his family and law practice in Scotland.

'Sir, Dr. Goldsmith would no more have asked me to write such a thing as that for him, than he would have asked me to feed him with a spoon, or to do any thing else that denoted his imbecility. I as much believe that he wrote it, as if I had seen him do it. Sir, had he shewn it to any one friend, he would not have been allowed to publish it. He has, indeed, done it very well; but it is a foolish thing well done. I suppose he has been so much elated with the success of his new comedy, that he has thought everything that concerned him must be of importance to the publick.' *Boswell:* 'I fancy, Sir, this is the first time that he has been engaged in such an adventure.' *Johnson:* 'Why, Sir, I believe it is the first time he has *beat;* he may have *been beaten* before. This, Sir, is a new plume to him.'

At Mr. Thrale's, in the evening, he repeated his usual paradoxical declamation against action in publick speaking. 'Action can have no effect upon reasonable minds. It may augment noise, but it never can enforce argument. If you speak to a dog, you use action; you hold up your hand thus, because he is a brute; and in proportion as men are removed from brutes, action will have the less influence upon them.' *Mrs. Thrale:* 'What then, Sir, becomes of Demosthenes' saying? "Action, action, action!"' *Johnson:* 'Demosthenes, Madam, spoke to an assembly of brutes; to a barbarous people.'

Lord Chesterfield being mentioned, Johnson remarked, that almost all of that celebrated nobleman's witty sayings were puns. He, however, allowed the merit of good wit to his Lordship's saying of Lord Tyrawley and himself, when both very old and infirm: 'Tyrawley and I have been dead these two years; but we don't choose to have it known.'

On Thursday, April 8, I sat a good part of the evening with him, but he was very silent. Though he was not disposed to talk, he was unwilling that I should leave him; and when I looked at my watch, and told him it was twelve o'clock, he cried, 'What's that to you and me?' and ordered Frank to tell Mrs. Williams that we were coming to drink tea with her, which we did. It was settled that we should go to church together next day.

On the 9th of April, being Good Friday, I breakfasted with him on tea and cross-buns; *Doctor* Levet, as Frank called him, making the tea. He carried me with him to the church of St. Clement Danes, where he had his seat; and his behaviour was, as I had imagined to myself, solemnly devout. I never shall forget the tremulous earnestness with which he pronounced the aweful petition in the Litany: 'In the hour of death, and at the day of judgement, good Lord deliver us.'

We went to church both in the morning and evening. In the interval between the two services we did not dine; but he read in the

Greek New Testament, and I turned over several of his books.

I told him that Goldsmith had said to me a few days before, 'As I take my shoes from the shoemaker, and my coat from the taylor, so I take my religion from the priest.' I regretted this loose way of talking. *Johnson:* 'Sir, he knows nothing; he has made up his mind about nothing.'

To my great surprize he asked me to dine with him on Easter-day. I never supposed that he had a dinner at his house; for I had not then heard of any one of his friends having been entertained at his table. He told me, 'I generally have a meat pye on Sunday: it is baked at a publick oven, which is very properly allowed, because one man can attend it; and thus the advantage is obtained of not keeping servants from church to dress dinners.'

April 11, being Easter-Sunday, after having attended Divine Service at St. Paul's, I repaired to Dr. Johnson's. I had gratified my curiosity much in dining with *Jean Jacques Rousseau,* while he lived in the wilds of Neufchatel: I had as great a curiosity to dine with *Dr. Samuel Johnson,* in the dusky recess of a court in Fleet-street. I supposed we should scarcely have knives and forks, and only some strange, uncouth, ill-drest dish: but I found every thing in very good order. We had no other company but Mrs. Williams and a young woman whom I did not know. As a dinner here was considered as a singular phænomenon, and as I was frequently interrogated on the subject, my readers may perhaps be desirous to know our bill of fare. The fact was, that we had a very good soup, a boiled leg of lamb and spinach, a veal pye, and a rice pudding.

Goldsmith, he said, had great merit. *Boswell:* 'But, Sir, he is much indebted to you for his getting so high in the publick estimation.' *Johnson:* 'Why, Sir, he has, perhaps, got *sooner* to it by his intimacy with me.' Goldsmith, though his vanity often excited him to occasional competition, had a very high regard for Johnson, which he at this time expressed in the strongest manner in the Dedication of his comedy, entitled, 'She Stoops to Conquer.'

He told me, that he had twelve or fourteen times attempted to keep a journal of his life, but never could persevere. He advised me to do it. 'The great thing to be recorded, (said he), is the state of your own mind; and you should write down every thing that you remember, for you cannot judge at first what is good or bad; and write immediately while the impression is fresh, for it will not be the same a week afterwards.'

I again solicited him to communicate to me the particulars of his early life. He said, 'You shall have them all for two-pence. I hope you shall know a great deal more of me before you write my Life.'

On Monday, April 19, he called on me with Mrs. Williams, in Mr.

Strahan's coach, and carried me out to dine with Mr. Elphinston, at his academy at Kensington. A printer having acquired a fortune sufficient to keep his coach, was a good topick for the credit of literature. Mrs. Williams said, that another printer, Mr. Hamilton, had not waited so long as Mr. Strahan, but had kept his coach several years sooner. *Johnson:* 'He was in the right. Life is short. The sooner that a man begins to enjoy his wealth the better.'

Mr. Elphinston talked of a new book that was much admired, and asked Dr. Johnson if he had read it. *Johnson:* 'I have looked into it.' 'What (said Elphinston,) have you not read it through?' Johnson, offended at being thus pressed, and so obliged to own his cursory mode of reading, answered tartly, 'No, Sir; do *you* read books *through?*'

He this day again defended duelling, and put his argument upon what I have ever thought the most solid basis; that if publick war be allowed to be consistent with morality, private war must be equally so. Indeed we may observe what strained arguments are used, to reconcile war with the Christian religion. But, in my opinion, it is exceedingly clear that duelling, having better reasons for its barbarous violence, is more justifiable than war, in which thousands go forth without any cause of personal quarrel, and massacre each other.

On Wednesday, April 21, I dined with him at Mr. Thrale's. A gentleman attacked Garrick for being vain. *Johnson:* 'No wonder, Sir, that he is vain; a man who is perpetually flattered in every mode that can be conceived. So many bellows have blown the fire, that one wonders he is not by this time become a cinder.' *Boswell:* 'And such bellows too. Lord Mansfield with his cheeks like to burst: Lord Chatham like an æolus.[1] I have read such notes from them to him, as were enough to turn his head.' *Johnson:* 'True. When he whom every body else flatters, flatters me, I then am truly happy.' *Mrs. Thrale:* 'The sentiment is in Congreve, I think.' *Johnson:* 'Yes, Madam, in "The Way of the World":

"If there's delight in love, 'tis when I see
That heart which others bleed for, bleed for me."'

The modes of living in different countries, and the various views with which men travel in quest of new scenes, having been talked of, a learned gentleman who holds a considerable office in the law, expatiated on the happiness of a savage life; and mentioned an instance of an officer who had actually lived for some time in the wilds of America, of whom, when in that state, he quoted this reflection with an air of admiration, as if it had been deeply philosophical: 'Here am I, free and unrestrained, amidst the rude magnificence of

---

[1] like an æolus: Aeolus, in Greek mythology, was god of the winds.

Nature, with this Indian woman by my side, and this gun, with which I can procure food when I want it: what more can be desired for human happiness?' It did not require much sagacity to foresee that such a sentiment would not be permitted to pass without due animadversion. *Johnson:* 'Do not allow yourself, Sir, to be imposed upon by such gross absurdity. It is sad stuff; it is brutish. If a bull could speak, he might as well exclaim,—Here am I with this cow and this grass; what being can enjoy greater felicity?'

We talked of the melancholy end of a gentleman who had destroyed himself. *Johnson:* 'It was owing to imaginary difficulties in his affairs, which, had he talked with any friend, would soon have vanished.' *Boswell:* 'Do you think, Sir, that all who commit suicide are mad?' *Johnson:* 'Sir, they are often not universally disordered in their intellects, but one passion presses so upon them, that they yield to it, and commit suicide, as a passionate man will stab another.' He added, 'I have often thought, that after a man has taken the resolution to kill himself, it is not courage in him to do any thing, however desperate, because he has nothing to fear.' *Goldsmith:* 'I don't see that.' *Johnson:* 'Nay but, my dear Sir, why should not you see what every one else sees?' *Goldsmith:* 'It is for fear of something that he has resolved to kill himself; and will not that timid disposition restrain him?' *Johnson:* 'It does not signify that the fear of something made him resolve; it is upon the state of his mind, after the resolution is taken, that I argue. Suppose a man, either from fear, or pride, or conscience, or whatever motive, has resolved to kill himself; when once the resolution is taken, he has nothing to fear. He may then go and take the King of Prussia by the nose, at the head of his army. He cannot fear the rack, who is resolved to kill himself. When Eustace Budgel was walking down to the Thames, determined to drown himself, he might, if he pleased, without any apprehension of danger, have turned aside, and first set fire to St. James's palace.'

On Tuesday, April 27, Mr. Beauclerk and I called on him in the morning. As we walked up Johnson's-court, I said, 'I have a veneration for this court'; and was glad to find that Beauclerk had the same reverential enthusiasm. We found him alone. We talked of Mr. Andrew Stuart's elegant and plausible Letters to Lord Mansfield: a copy of which had been sent by the authour to Dr. Johnson. *Johnson:* 'They have not answered the end. They have not been talked of; I have never heard of them. This is owing to their not being sold. People seldom read a book which is given to them. The way to spread a work is to sell it at a low price. No man will send to buy a thing that costs even sixpence, without an intention to read it.'

He said, 'Goldsmith should not be for ever attempting to shine in conversation: he has not temper for it, he is so much mortified when he fails. Sir, a game of jokes is composed partly of skill, partly of chance. A man may be beat at times by one who has not the tenth part of his wit. Now Goldsmith's putting himself against another, is like a man laying a hundred to one who cannot spare the hundred. It is not worth a man's while. A man should not lay a hundred to one, unless he can easily spare it, though he has a hundred chances for him: he can get but a guinea, and he may lose a hundred. Goldsmith is in this state. When he contends, if he gets the better, it is a very little addition to a man of his literary reputation: if he does not get the better, he is miserably vexed.'

Johnson's own superlative power of wit set him above any risk of such uneasiness. Garrick had remarked to me of him, a few days before, 'Rabelais and all other wits are nothing compared with him. You may be diverted by them; but Johnson gives you a forcible hug, and shakes laughter out of you, whether you will or no.'

Goldsmith, however, was often very fortunate in his witty contests, even when he entered the lists with Johnson himself. Sir Joshua Reynolds was in company with them one day, when Goldsmith said, that he thought he could write a good fable, mentioned the simplicity which that kind of composition requires, and observed, that in most fables the animals introduced seldom talk in character. 'For instance, (said he,) the fable of the little fishes, who saw birds fly over their heads, and envying them, petitioned Jupiter to be changed into birds. The skill (continued he,) consists in making them talk like little fishes.' While he indulged himself in this fanciful reverie, he observed Johnson shaking his sides, and laughing. Upon which he smartly proceeded, 'Why, Dr. Johnson, this is not so easy as you seem to think; for if you were to make little fishes talk, they would talk like *whales.*'

On Thursday, April 29, I dined with him at General Oglethorpe's, where were Sir Joshua Reynolds, Mr. Langton, Dr. Goldsmith, and Mr. Thrale. I was very desirous to get Dr. Johnson absolutely fixed in his resolution to go with me to the Hebrides this year; and I told him that I had received a letter from Dr. Robertson, the historian, upon the subject, with which he was much pleased; and now talked in such a manner of his long-intended tour, that I was satisfied he meant to fulfill his engagement.

Dr. Goldsmith's new play, 'She Stoops to Conquer,' being mentioned; *Johnson:* 'I know of no comedy for many years that has so much exhilarated an audience, that has answered so much the great end of comedy—making an audience merry.'

Goldsmith having said, that Garrick's compliment to the Queen, which he introduced into the play of 'The Chances,' which he had altered and revised this year, was mean and gross flattery;—*Johnson:* 'Why, Sir, I would not *write,* I would not give solemnly under my hand, a character beyond what I thought really true; but a speech on the stage, let it flatter ever so extravagantly, is formular. It has always been formular to flatter Kings and Queens; so much so, that even in our church-service we have "our most religious King," used indiscriminately, whoever is King. Nay, they even flatter themselves;—"we have been graciously pleased to grant."—No modern flattery, however, is so gross as that of the Augustan age, where the Emperour was deified. And as to meanness, (rising into warmth,) how is it mean in a player,—a showman,—a fellow who exhibits himself for a shilling, to flatter his Queen? The attempt, indeed, was dangerous; for if it had missed, what became of Garrick, and what became of the Queen? As Sir William Temple says of a great General, it is necessary not only that his designs should be formed in a masterly manner, but that they should be attended with success. Sir, it is right, at a time when the Royal Family is not generally liked, to let it be seen that the people like at least one of them.' *Sir Joshua Reynolds:* 'I do not perceive why the profession of a player should be despised; for the great and ultimate end of all the employments of mankind is to produce amusement. Garrick produces more amusement than any body.' *Boswell:* 'You say,

Dr. Johnson, that Garrick exhibits himself for a shilling. In this respect he is only on a footing with a lawyer who exhibits himself for his fee, and even will maintain any nonsense or absurdity, if the case requires it. Garrick refuses a play or a part which he does not like; a lawyer never refuses.' *Johnson:* 'Why, Sir, what does this prove? Only that a lawyer is worse. Boswell is now like Jack in "The Tale of a Tub," who when he is puzzled by an argument, hangs himself. He thinks I shall cut him down, but I'll let him hang,' (laughing vociferously.) *Sir Joshua Reynolds:* 'Mr. Boswell thinks that the profession of a lawyer being unquestionably honourable, if he can show the profession of a player to be more honourable, he proves his argument.'

On Friday, April 30, I dined with him at Mr. Beauclerk's, where were Lord Charlemont, Sir Joshua Reynolds, and some more members of the *Literary Club,* whom he had obligingly invited to meet me, as I was this evening to be balloted for as candidate for admission into that distinguished society. Johnson had done me the honour to propose me, and Beauclerk was very zealous for me.

Goldsmith being mentioned; *Johnson:* 'It is amazing how little Goldsmith knows. He seldom comes where he is not more ignorant than any one else.' *Sir Joshua Reynolds:* 'Yet there is no man whose company is more liked.' *Johnson:* 'To be sure, Sir. When people find a man of the most distinguished abilities as a writer, their inferiour while he is with them, it must be highly gratifying to them. What Goldsmith comically says of himself is very true,—he always gets the better when he argues alone; meaning, that he is master of a subject in his study, and can write well upon it; but when he comes into company, grows confused, and unable to talk. Take him as a poet, his "Traveller" is a very fine performance; ay, and so is his "Deserted Village," were it not sometimes too much the echo of his "Traveller." Whether, indeed, we take him as a poet,—as a comick writer,—or as an historian, he stands in the first class.'

Johnson praised John Bunyan highly. 'His "Pilgrim's Progress" has great merit, both for invention, imagination, and the conduct of the story; and it has had the best evidence of its merit, the general and continued approbation of mankind. Few books, I believe, have had a more extensive sale. It is remarkable, that it begins very much like the poem of Dante; yet there was no translation of Dante when Bunyan wrote. There is reason to think that he had read Spenser.'

The gentlemen went away to their club, and I was left at Beauclerk's till the fate of my election should be announced to me. I sat in a state of anxiety which even the charming conversation of Lady Di Beauclerk could not entirely dissipate. In a short time I received the agreeable intelligence that I was chosen. I hastened to the place of meeting, and was introduced to such a society as can seldom be found. Mr. Edmund Burke, whom I then saw for the first time, and whose splendid talents had long made me ardently wish for his acquaintance; Dr. Nugent, Mr. Garrick, Dr. Goldsmith, Mr. (afterwards Sir William) Jones, and the company with whom I had dined. Upon my entrance, Johnson placed himself behind a chair, on which he leaned as on a desk or pulpit, and with humorous formality gave me a *Charge,* pointing out the conduct expected from me as a good member of this club. Goldsmith produced some very absurd verses which had been publickly recited to an audience for money.

I dined with him next day at the house of my friends, Messieurs Edward and Charles Dilly, booksellers in the Poultry: there were present, their elder brother Mr. Dilly of Bedfordshire, Dr. Goldsmith, Mr. Langton, Mr. Claxton, Reverend Dr. Mayo a dissenting minister, the Reverend Mr. Toplady, and my friend the Reverend Mr. Temple.

Hawkesworth's compilation of the voyages to the South Sea being mentioned; *Johnson:* 'Sir, if you talk of it as a subject of commerce, it will be gainful; if as a book that is to increase human knowledge, I believe there will not be much of that. Hawkesworth can tell only what the voyagers have told him; and they have found very little, only one new animal, I think.

Boswell: 'But many insects, Sir.' *Johnson:* 'Why, Sir, as to insects, Ray reckons of British insects twenty thousand species. They might have staid at home and discovered enough in that way.'

Boswell: 'I am well assured that the people of Otaheite who have the bread tree, the fruit of which serves them for bread, laughed heartily when they were informed of the tedious process necessary with us to have bread;—plowing, sowing, harrowing, reaping, threshing, grinding, baking.' *Johnson:* 'Why, Sir, all ignorant savages will laugh when they are told of the advantages of civilized life. Were you to tell men who live without houses, how we pile brick upon brick, and rafter upon rafter, and that after a house is raised to a certain height, a man tumbles off a scaffold, and breaks his neck, he would laugh heartily at our folly in building; but it does not follow that men are better without houses. No, Sir, (holding up a slice of a good loaf,) this is better than the bread tree.'

I introduced the subject of toleration. *Johnson:* 'Every society has a right to preserve publick peace and order, and therefore has a good right to prohibit the propagation of opinions which have a dangerous tendency. To say the *magistrate* has this right, is using an inadequate word: it is the *society* for which the magistrate is agent. He may be morally or theologically wrong in restraining the propagation of opinions which he thinks

dangerous, but he is politically right.' *Mayo:* 'I am of opinion, Sir, that every man is entitled to liberty of conscience in religion; and that the magistrate cannot restrain that right.' *Johnson:* 'Sir, I agree with you. Every man has a right to liberty of conscience, and with that the magistrate cannot interfere. People confound liberty of thinking with liberty of talking; nay, with liberty of preaching. Every man has a physical right to think as he pleases; for it cannot be discovered how he thinks. He has not a moral right; for he ought to inform himself, and think justly. But, Sir, no member of a society has a right to *teach* any doctrine contrary to what that society holds to be true. The magistrate, I say, may be wrong in what he thinks: but, while he thinks himself right, he may, and ought to enforce what he thinks.' *Mayo:* 'Then, Sir, we are to remain always in errour, and truth never can prevail; and the magistrate was right in persecuting the first Christians.' *Johnson:* 'Sir, the only method by which religious truth can be established is by martyrdom. The magistrate has a right to enforce what he thinks; and he who is conscious of the truth has a right to suffer. I am afraid there is no other way of ascertaining the truth, but by persecution on the one hand and enduring it on the other.' *Mayo:* 'But, Sir, is it not very hard that I should not be allowed to teach my children what I really believe to be the truth?' *Johnson:* 'Why, Sir, you might contrive to teach your children *extrà scandalum;* [1] but, Sir, the magistrate, if he know it, has a right to restrain you. Suppose you teach your children to be thieves?' *Mayo:* 'This is making a joke of the subject.' *Johnson:* 'Nay, Sir, take it thus:— that you teach them the community of goods; for which there are as many plausible arguments as for most erroneous doctrines. You teach them that all things at first were in common, and that no man had a right to any thing but as he laid his hands upon it; and that this still is, or ought to be, the rule amongst mankind. Here, Sir, you sap a great principle in society,— property. And don't you think the magistrate would have a right to prevent you? Or, suppose you should teach your children the notions of the Adamites, and they should run naked into the streets, would not the magistrate have a right to flog 'em into their doublets?' *Mayo:* 'I think the magistrate has no right to interfere till there is some overt act.' *Boswell:* 'So, Sir, though he sees an enemy to the state charging a blunderbuss, he is not to interfere till it is fired off?' *Mayo:* 'He must be sure of its direction against the state.' *Johnson:* 'The magistrate is to judge of that.—He has no right to restrain your thinking, because the evil centers in yourself. If a man were sitting at this table, and chopping off his fingers, the magistrate, as guardian of the community, has no authority to restrain him, however he might do it from kindness as a parent.—Though, indeed, upon more consideration, I think he may; as it is probable, that he who is chopping off his own fingers, may soon proceed to chop off those of other people. If I think it right to steal Mr. Dilly's plate, I am a bad man; but he can say nothing to me. If I make an open declaration that I think so, he will keep me out of his house. If I put forth my hand, I shall be sent to Newgate. This is the gradation of thinking, preaching, and acting: if a man thinks erroneously, he may keep his thoughts to himself, and nobody will trouble him; if he preaches erroneous doctrine, society may expel him; if he acts in consequence of it, the law takes place, and he is hanged.' *Mayo:* 'But, Sir, ought not Christians to have liberty of conscience?' *Johnson:* 'I have already told you so, Sir. You are coming back to where you were.' *Boswell:* 'Dr. Mayo is always taking a return post-chaise, and going the stage over again. He has it at half price.' *Johnson:* 'Dr. Mayo, like other champions for unlimited toleration, has got a set of words. Sir, it is no matter, politically, whether the magistrate be right or wrong.'

During this argument, Goldsmith sat in restless agitation, from a wish to get in and *shine*. Finding himself excluded, he had taken his hat to go away, but remained for some time with it in his hand, like a gamester, who at the close of a

[1] *extrà scandalum:* without hindrance.

long night, lingers for a little while, to see if he can have a favourable opening to finish with success. Once when he was beginning to speak, he found himself overpowered by the loud voice of Johnson, who was at the opposite end of the table, and did not perceive Goldsmith's attempt. Thus disappointed of his wish to obtain the attention of the company, Goldsmith in a passion threw down his hat, looking angrily at Johnson, and exclaiming in a bitter tone, *'Take it.'* When Toplady was going to speak, Johnson uttered some sound, which led Goldsmith to think that he was beginning again, and taking the words from Toplady. Upon which, he seized this opportunity of venting his own envy and spleen, under the pretext of supporting another person: 'Sir, (said he to Johnson,) the gentleman has heard you patiently for an hour; pray allow us now to hear him.' *Johnson:* (sternly,) 'Sir, I was not interrupting the gentleman. I was only giving him a signal of my attention. Sir, you are impertinent.' Goldsmith made no reply, but continued in the company for some time.

Johnson and I went later to *the Club,* where we found Mr. Burke, Mr. Garrick, and some other members, and amongst them our friend Goldsmith, who sat silently brooding over Johnson's reprimand to him after dinner. Johnson perceived this, and said aside to some of us, 'I'll make Goldsmith forgive me'; and then called to him in a loud voice, 'Dr. Goldsmith,—something passed to-day where you and I dined; I ask your pardon.' Goldsmith answered placidly, 'It must be much from you, Sir, that I take ill.' And so at once the difference was over, and they were on as easy terms as ever, and Goldsmith rattled away as usual.

In our way to the club to-night, when I regretted that Goldsmith would, upon every occasion, endeavour to shine, by which he often exposed himself, Mr. Langton observed, that he was not like Addison, who was content with the fame of his writings, and did not aim also at excellency in conversation, for which he found himself unfit; and that he said to a lady, who complained of his having talked little in company, 'Madam, I have but nine-pence in ready money, but I can draw for a thousand pounds.' I observed, that Goldsmith had a great deal of gold in his cabinet, but, not content with that, was always taking out his purse. *Johnson:* 'Yes, Sir, and that so often an empty purse!'

Goldsmith's incessant desire of being conspicuous in company, was the occasion of his sometimes appearing to such disadvantage as one should hardly have supposed possible in a man of his genius. When his literary reputation had risen deservedly high, and his society was much courted, he became very jealous of the extraordinary attention which was every where paid to Johnson. One evening, in a circle of wits, he found fault with me for talking of Johnson as entitled to the honour of unquestionable superiority. 'Sir, (said he,) you are for making a monarchy of what should be a republick.'

He was still more mortified, when talking in a company with fluent vivacity, and, as he flattered himself, to the admiration of all who were present; a German who sat next him, and perceived Johnson rolling himself, as if about to speak, suddenly stopped him, saying, 'Stay, stay,—Toctor Shonson is going to say something.' This was, no doubt, very provoking, especially to one so irritable as Goldsmith, who frequently mentioned it with strong expressions of indignation.

It may also be observed, that Goldsmith was sometimes content to be treated with an easy familiarity, but, upon occasions, would be consequential and important. An instance of this occurred in a small particular. Johnson had a way of contracting the names of his friends; as, Beauclerk, Beau; Boswell, Bozzy; Langton, Lanky; Murphy, Mur; Sheridan, Sherry. I remember one day, when Tom Davies was telling that Dr. Johnson said, 'We are all in labour for a name to *Goldy's* play,' Goldsmith seemed displeased that such a liberty should be taken with his name, and said, 'I have often desired him not to call me *Goldy*.' Tom was remarkably attentive to the most minute circumstance about Johnson. I recollect his telling me once, on my arrival in London, 'Sir, our great friend has made an improvement on his appellation of old Mr. Sheridan. He calls him now *Sherry derry*.'

On Monday, May 9, as I was to set out on my return to Scotland next morning, I was desirous to see as much of Dr. Johnson as I could. But I first called on Goldsmith to take leave of him. The jealousy and envy which, though possessed of many most amiable qualities, he frankly avowed, broke out violently at this interview. Upon another occasion, when Goldsmith confessed himself to be of an envious disposition, I contended with Johnson that we ought not to be angry with him, he was so candid in owning it. 'Nay, Sir, (said Johnson,) we must be angry that a man has such a superabundance of an odious quality, that he cannot keep it within his own breast, but it boils over.' In my opinion, however, Goldsmith had not more of it than other people have, but only talked of it freely.

He now seemed very angry that Johnson was going to be a traveller; said, 'he would be a dead weight for me to carry, and that I should never be able to lug him along through the Highlands and Hebrides.' Nor would he patiently allow me to enlarge upon Johnson's wonderful abilities; but exclaimed, 'Is he like Burke, who winds into a subject like a serpent?' 'But, (said I,) Johnson is the Hercules who strangled serpents in his cradle.'

I dined with Dr. Johnson at General Paoli's. He was obliged, by indisposition, to leave the company early; he appointed me, however, to meet him in the evening at Mr. (now Sir Robert) Chambers' in the Temple, where he accordingly came, though he continued to be very ill. Chambers, as is common on such occasions, prescribed various remedies to him. *Johnson:* (fretted by pain,) 'Pr'ythee don't teaze me. Stay till I am well, and then you shall tell me how to cure myself.' He grew better, and talked with a noble enthusiasm of keeping up the representation of respectable families. His zeal on this subject was a circumstance in his character exceedingly remarkable, when it is considered that he himself had no pretensions to blood. I heard him once say, 'I have great merit in being zealous for subordination and the honours of birth; for I can hardly tell who was my grandfather.' He maintained the dignity and propriety of male succession, in opposition to the opinion of one of our friends, who had that day employed Mr. Chambers to draw his will, devising his estate to his three sisters, in preference to a remote heir male. Johnson called them 'three *dowdies,*' and said, with as high a spirit as the boldest Baron in the most perfect days of the feudal system, 'An ancient estate should always go to males. It is mighty foolish to let a stranger have it because he marries your daughter, and takes your name. As for an estate newly acquired by trade, you may give it, if you will, to the dog *Towser,* and let him keep his *own* name.'

I have known him at times exceedingly diverted at what seemed to others a very small sport. He now laughed immoderately, without any reason that we could perceive, at our friend's making his will; called him the *testator,* and added, 'I dare say, he thinks he has done a mighty thing. He won't stay till he gets home to his seat in the country, to produce this wonderful deed: he'll call up the landlord of the first inn on the road; and, after a suitable preface upon mortality and the uncertainty of life, will tell him that he should not delay making his will; and here, Sir, will he say, is my will, which I have just made, with the assistance of one of the ablest lawyers in the kingdom; and he will read it to him (laughing all the time). He believes he has made this will; but he did not make it: you, Chambers, made it for him. I trust you have had more conscience than to make him say, "being of sound understanding"; ha, ha, ha! I hope he has left me a legacy. I'd have his will turned into verse, like a ballad.'

In this playful manner did he run on, exulting in his own pleasantry, which certainly was not such as might be expected from the author of 'The Rambler,' but which is here preserved, that my readers may be acquainted even with the slightest occasional characteristicks of so eminent a man.

Mr. Chambers did not by any means relish this jocularity and seemed impatient till he got rid of us. Johnson could not stop his merriment, but continued it all the way till we got without the Temple-gate. He then burst into such a fit of laughter, that he appeared to be almost in a convulsion; and, in order to support himself, laid hold of one of the posts at the side of the foot pavement, and sent forth peals so loud, that in the silence of the night his voice seemed to resound from Temple-bar to Fleet-ditch.

This most ludicrous exhibition of the aweful, melancholy, and venerable Johnson, happened well to counteract the feelings of sadness which I used to experience when parting with him for a considerable time. I accompanied him to his door, where he gave me his blessing.

 **Chapter 7**

Johnson in His Sixties

In a letter from Edinburgh, dated the 29th of May, I pressed him to persevere in his resolution to make this year the projected visit to the Hebrides, of which he and I had talked for many years, and which I was confident would afford us much entertainment.

'To James Boswell, Esq.

'Dear Sir,

'When your letter came to me, I was so darkened by an inflammation in my eye, that I could not for some time read it. I can now write without trouble, and can read large prints. My eye is gradually growing stronger; and I hope will be able to take some delight in the survey of a Caledonian loch.

'Chambers is going a Judge, with six thousand a year, to Bengal. He and I shall come down together as far as Newcastle, and thence I shall easily get to Edinburgh. Let me know the exact time when your Courts intermit. I must conform a little to Chambers' occasions, and he must conform a little to mine. The time which you shall fix, must be the common point to which we will come as near as we can. Except this eye, I am very well.

'I hope your dear lady and her dear baby are both well. I shall see them too when I come; and I have that opinion of your choice, as to suspect that when I have seen Mrs. Boswell, I shall be less willing to go away. I am, dear Sir,

'Your affectionate humble servant,
                    'Sam. Johnson.'
'Johnson's court, Fleet-street,
July 5, 1773.'

His stay in Scotland was from the 18th of August, on which day he arrived, till the 22d of November, when he set out on his return to London; and I believe ninety-four days were never passed by any man in a more vigorous exertion.

He came by the way of Berwick upon Tweed to Edinburgh, where he remained a few days, and then went by St. Andrew's, Aberdeen, Inverness, and Fort Augustus, to the Hebrides, to visit which was the principal object he had in view.

He visited the isles of Sky, Rasay, Col, Mull, Inchkenneth, and Icolmkill. He travelled through Argyleshire by Inverary, and from thence by Lochlomond and Dunbarton to Glasgow, then by Loudon to Auchinleck in Ayrshire, the seat of my family, and then by Hamilton, back to Edinburgh, where he again spent some time. He thus saw the four Universities of Scotland, its three principal cities, and as much of the Highland and insular life as was sufficient for his philosophical contemplation. I had the pleasure of accompanying him during the whole of this journey. He was respectfully entertained by the great, the learned, and the elegant, wherever he went; nor was he less delighted with the hospitality which he experienced in humbler life.

His various adventures, and the force and vivacity of his mind, as exercised during this peregrination, upon innumerable topicks, have been faithfully, and to the best of my abilities, displayed in my 'Journal of a Tour to the Hebrides,' to which, as the publick has been pleased to honour it by a very extensive circulation, I beg leave to refer, as to a separate and remarkable portion of his life, which may be there seen in detail, and which exhibits as striking a view of his powers in conversation, as his works do of his excellence in writing.

1774: He was now seriously engaged in writing an account of our travels in the Hebrides, in consequence of which I had the pleasure of a more frequent correspondence with him.

'To James Boswell, Esq.

'Streatham, June 21, 1774.
'Dear Sir,

'Yesterday I put the first sheets of the "Journey to the Hebrides" to the press. I have endeavoured to do you some justice in the first paragraph. It will be one volume in octavo, not thick.

'It will be proper to make some presents in Scotland. You shall tell me to whom I shall give; and I have stipulated twenty-five for you to give in your own name. Some will take the present better from me, others better from you. In this, you who are to live in the place ought to direct. Consider it. Whatever you can get for my purpose, send me; and make my compliments to your lady and both the young ones.

'I am, Sir, your, &c.
'Sam. Johnson.'

'To James Boswell, Esq.
'Dear Sir,

'I wish you could have looked over my book before the printer, but it could not easily be. I suspect some mistakes; but as I deal, perhaps, more in notions than in facts, the matter is not great, and the second edition will be mended, if any such there be. The press will go on slowly for a time, because I am going into Wales to-morrow.

'Of poor dear Dr. Goldsmith there is little to be told, more than the papers have made publick. He died of a fever, made, I am afraid, more violent by uneasiness of mind. His debts began to be heavy, and all his resources were exhausted. Sir Joshua is of opinion that he owed not less than two thousand pounds. Was ever poet so trusted before?

'Of your second daughter you certainly gave the account yourself, though you have forgotten it. While Mrs. Boswell is well, never doubt of a boy. Mrs. Thrale brought, I think, five girls running, but while I was with you she had a boy.

'I am obliged to you for all your pamphlets, and of the last I hope to make some use. I made some of the former.

'I am, dear Sir,
'Your most affectionate servant,
Sam. Johnson.'
'July 4, 1774.'

'My compliments to all the three ladies.'

'*To James Boswell, Esq.*

'Dear Sir,

'I long to hear how you like the book; it is, I think, much liked here. But Macpherson [1] is very furious; can you give me any more intelligence about him, or his Fingal? Do what you can, and do it quickly. Is Lord Hailes on our side?

'Pray let me know what I owed you when I left you, that I may send it to you.

'I am going to write about the Americans. If you have picked up any hints among your lawyers, who are great masters of the law of nations, or if your own mind suggests any thing, let me know. But mum, it is a secret.

'Poor Beauclerk is so ill, that his life is thought to be in danger. Lady Di nurses him with very great assiduity.

'Reynolds has taken too much to strong liquor, and seems to delight in his new character.

'This is all the news that I have; but as you love verses, I will send you a few which I made upon Inchkenneth; but remember the condition, that you shall not show them, except to Lord Hailes, whom I love better than any man whom I know so little. If he asks you to transcribe them for him, you may do it, but I think he must promise not to let them be copied again, nor to show them as mine.

'Make my compliments to dear Mrs. Boswell, and to Miss Veronica.

'I am, dear Sir,
'Yours most faithfully,
'*Sam. Johnson.*'
'Jan. 21, 1775.'

What words were used by Mr. Macpherson in his letter to the venerable Sage, I have never heard; but they are generally said to have been of a nature very different from the language of literary contest. Dr. Johnson's answer appeared in the news-papers of the day, and has since been frequently re-published; but not with perfect accuracy. I give it as dictated to me by himself, written down in his presence, and authenticated by a note in his own hand-writing, '*This, I think, is a true copy.*'

'Mr. James Macpherson,

'I received your foolish and impudent letter. Any violence offered me I

---

[1] James Macpherson professed to have discovered an ancient Gaelic epic in the Highlands of Scotland and the Western Islands. During his tour with Boswell, Johnson inquired into the authenticity of the poem and could find none. He therefore decided (and wrote) that Macpherson was an impostor.

shall do my best to repel; and what I cannot do for myself, the law shall do for me. I hope I shall never be deterred from detecting what I think a cheat, by the menaces of a ruffian.

'What would you have me retract? I thought your book an imposture; I think it an imposture still. For this opinion I have given my reasons to the publick, which I here dare you to refute. Your rage I defy. Your abilities, since your Homer are not so formidable; and what I hear of your morals inclines me to pay regard not to what you shall say, but to what you shall prove. You may print this if you will.

'Sam. Johnson.'

Mr. Macpherson little knew the character of Dr. Johnson, if he supposed that he could be easily intimidated; for no man was ever more remarkable for personal courage. He had, indeed, an aweful dread of death, or rather, 'of something after death'; and what rational man, who seriously thinks of quitting all that he has ever known, and going into a new and unknown state of being, can be without that dread? But his fear was from reflection; his courage natural. His fear, in that one instance, was the result of philosophical and religious consideration. He feared death, but he feared nothing else, not even what might occasion death. Many instances of his resolution may be mentioned. One day, at Mr. Beauclerk's house in the country, when two large dogs were fighting, he went up to them, and beat them till they separated; and at another time, when told of the danger there was that a gun might burst if charged with many balls, he put in six or seven, and fired it off against a wall. Mr. Langton told me, that when they were swimming together near Oxford, he cautioned Dr. Johnson against a pool, which was reckoned particularly dangerous; upon which Johnson directly swam into it. He told me himself that one night he was attacked in the street by four men, to whom he would not yield, but kept them all at bay, till the watch came up, and carried both him and them to the roundhouse. In the play-house at Lichfield, as Mr. Garrick informed me, Johnson having for a moment quitted a chair which was placed for him between the side-scenes, a gentleman took possession of it, and when Johnson on his return civilly demanded his seat, rudely refused to give it up; upon which Johnson laid hold of it, and tossed him and the chair into the pit. Foote, who so successfully revived the old comedy, by exhibiting living characters, had resolved to imitate Johnson on the stage, expecting great profits from his ridicule of so celebrated a man. Johnson being informed of his intention, and being at dinner at Mr. Thomas Davies' the bookseller, from whom I had the story, he asked Mr. Davies 'what was the common price of an oak stick'; and being answered sixpence, 'Why then, Sir, (said he,) give me leave to send your servant to purchase me a shilling one. I'll have a double quantity; for I am told Foote means to *take me off,* as he calls it, and I am determined the fellow shall not do it with impunity.'

Davies took care to acquaint Foote of this, which effectually checked the wantonness of the mimick. Mr. Macpherson's menaces made Johnson provide himself with the same implement of defence; and had he been attacked, I have no doubt that, old as he was, he would have made his corporal prowess be felt as much as his intellectual.

He had long before indulged most unfavourable sentiments of our fellow-subjects in America. For, as early as 1769, I was told by Dr. John Campbell, that he had said of them, 'Sir, they are a race of convicts, and ought to be thankful for any thing we allow them short of hanging.'

The doubts which, in my correspondence with him, I had ventured to state as to the justice and wisdom of the conduct of Great-Britain towards the American colonies, while I at the same time requested that he would enable me to inform myself upon that momentous subject, he had altogether disregarded; and had recently published a pamphlet, entitled, 'Taxation no Tyranny; an Answer to the Resolutions and Address of the American Congress.'

Of this performance I avoided to talk with him; for I had now formed a clear and settled opinion, that the people of America were well warranted to resist a claim that their fellow-subjects in the mother-country should have the entire command of their fortunes, by taxing them without their own consent; and the extreme violence which it breathed, appeared to me so unsuit-able to the mildness of a Christian philosopher, and so directly opposite to the principles of peace which he had so beautifully recommended in his pamphlet respecting Falkland's Islands, that I was sorry to see him appear in so unfavourable a light. Besides, I could not perceive in it that ability of argument, or that felicity of expression, for which he was, upon other occasions, so eminent. Positive assertion, sarcastical severity, and extravagant ridicule, which he himself reprobated as a test of truth, were united in this rhapsody.

That this pamphlet was written at the desire of those who were then in power, I have no doubt; and, indeed, he owned to me, that it had been revised and curtailed by some of them. His pamphlets in support of the measures of administration were published on his own account, and he afterwards collected them into a volume, with the title of 'Political Tracts, by the Authour of the Rambler.'

These pamphlets drew upon him numerous attacks. Against the common weapons of literary warfare he was hardened; but there were two instances of animadversion which I communicated to him, and from what I could judge, both from his silence and his looks, appeared to me to impress him much.

One was, 'A Letter to Dr. Samuel Johnson, occasioned by his late political Publications.' It appeared previous to his 'Taxation no Tyranny,' and was written by Dr. Joseph Towers.

It concluded thus:

'I would, however, wish you to remember, should you again address the publick under the character of a political writer, that luxuriance of imagination or energy of language will ill compensate for the want of candour, of justice, and of truth. And I shall only add, that should I hereafter be disposed to read, as I heretofore have done, the most excellent of all your performances, *"The Rambler,"* the pleasure which I have been accustomed to find in it will be much diminished by the reflection that the writer of so moral, so elegant, and so valuable a work, was capable of prostituting his talents in such productions as "The False Alarm," the "Thoughts on the Transactions respecting Falkland's Islands," and "The Patriot." '

I am willing to do justice to the merit of Dr. Towers, of whom I will say, that although I abhor his Whiggish democratical notions and propensities, (for I will not call them principles,) I esteem him as an ingenious, knowing, and very convivial man.

The other instance was a paragraph of a letter to me, from my old and most intimate friend, the Reverend Mr. Temple. The words were,

'How can your great, I will not say your *pious,* but your *moral* friend, support the barbarous measures of administration, which they have not the face to ask even their infidel pensioner Hume to defend.'

However confident of the rectitude of his own mind, Johnson may have felt sincere uneasiness that his conduct should be erroneously imputed to unworthy motives, by good men; and that the influence of his valuable writings should on that account be in any degree obstructed or lessened.

He complained to a Right Honourable friend of distinguished talents and very elegant manners, with whom he maintained a long intimacy, and whose generosity towards him will afterwards appear, that his pension having been given to him as a literary character, he had been applied to by administration to write political pamphlets; and he was even so much irritated, that he declared his resolution to resign his pension. His friend shewed him the impropriety of such a measure, and he afterwards expressed his gratitude, and said he had received good advice.

On Friday, March 24, I met him at the *Literary Club,* where were Mr. Beauclerk, Mr. Langton, Mr. Colman, Dr. Percy, Mr. Vesey, Sir Charles Bunbury, Dr. George Fordyce, Mr. Steevens, and Mr. Charles Fox. Before he came in, we talked of his 'Journey to the Western Islands,' and of his coming away, 'willing to believe the second sight,' which seemed to excite some ridicule. I was then so impressed with the truth of many of the stories of it which I had been told, that I avowed my conviction, saying, 'He is only *willing* to believe: I *do* believe. The evidence is enough for me, though not for his great mind. What will not fill a quart bottle will fill a pint bottle. I am filled with belief.' 'Are you?

(said Colman,) then cork it up.'

Johnson was in high spirits this evening at the club, and talked with great animation and success. He attacked Swift, as he used to do upon all occasions. 'The "Tale of a Tub" is so much superiour to his other writings, that one can hardly believe he was the authour of it. There is in it such a vigour of mind, such a swarm of thoughts, so much of nature, and art, and life.' I wondered to hear him say of 'Gulliver's Travels,' 'When once you have thought of big men and little men, it is very easy to do all the rest.' I endeavoured to make a stand for Swift, and tried to rouse those who were much more able to defend him; but in vain. Johnson at last, of his own accord, allowed very great merit to the inventory of articles found in the pockets of the Man Mountain, particularly the description of his watch, which it was conjectured was his GOD, as he consulted it upon all occasions.

From Swift, there was an easy transition to Mr. Thomas Sheridan. —*Johnson:* 'Sheridan is a wonderful admirer of the tragedy of Douglas, and presented its authour with a gold medal. Some years ago, at a coffee-house in Oxford, I called to him, "Mr. Sheridan, Mr. Sheridan, how came you to give a gold medal to Home, for writing that foolish play?" This, you see, was wanton and insolent; but I *meant* to be wanton and insolent. A medal has no value but as a stamp of merit. And was Sheridan to assume to himself the right of giving that stamp? If

Sheridan was magnificent enough to bestow a gold medal as an honorary reward of dramatick excellence, he should have requested one of the Universities to choose the person on whom it should be conferred. Sheridan had no right to give a stamp of merit: it was counterfeiting Apollo's coin.'

I cannot too frequently request of my readers, while they peruse my account of Johnson's conversation, to endeavour to keep in mind his deliberate and strong utterance. His mode of speaking was indeed very impressive; and I wish it could be preserved as musick is written, according to the very ingenious method of Mr. Steele, who has shown how the recitation of Mr. Garrick, and other eminent speakers, might be transmitted to posterity *in score*.

Next day I dined with Johnson at Mr. Thrale's. He attacked Gray, calling him 'a dull fellow.' *Boswell:* 'I understand he was reserved, and might appear dull in company; but surely he was not dull in poetry.' *Johnson:* 'Sir, he was dull in company, dull in his closet, dull every where. He was dull in a new way, and that made many people think him GREAT. He was a mechanical poet.'

A young lady who had married a man much her inferiour in rank being mentioned, a question arose how a woman's relations should behave to her in such a situation. While I contended that she ought to be treated with an inflexible steadiness of displeasure, Mrs. Thrale was all for mildness and forgiveness, and, according to the vulgar phrase, 'making the best of a bad bargain.' *Johnson:* 'Madam, we must distinguish. Were I a man of rank, I would not let a daughter starve who had made a mean marriage; but having voluntarily degraded herself from the station which she was originally entitled to hold, I would support her only in that which she herself had chosen; and would not put her on a level with my other daughters. You are to consider, Madam, that it is our duty to maintain the subordination of civilized society; and when there is a gross and shameful deviation from rank, it should be punished so as to deter others from the same perversion.'

On Friday, March 31, I supped with him and some friends at a tavern. One of the company attempted, with too much forwardness, to rally him on his late appearance at the theatre; but had reason to repent of his temerity. 'Why, Sir, did you go to Mrs. Abington's benefit? Did you see?' *Johnson:* 'No, Sir.' 'Did you hear?' *Johnson:* 'No, Sir.' 'Why then, Sir, did you go?' *Johnson:* 'Because, Sir, she is a favourite of the publick; and when the publick cares the thousandth part for you that it does for her, I will go to your benefit too.'

Next morning I won a small bet from Lady Diana Beauclerk, by asking him as to one of his particularities, which her Ladyship laid I durst not do. It seems he had been frequently observed at the Club to put into his pocket the Seville oranges, after he had squeezed the juice of them into the drink which he made for himself. Beauclerk and Garrick talked of it to me, and seemed to think that he had a strange unwillingness to be discovered. We could not divine what he did with them; and this was the bold question to be put. I saw on his table the spoils of the preceding night, some fresh peels nicely scraped and cut into pieces. 'O, Sir, (said I,) I now partly see what you do with the squeezed oranges which you put into your pocket at the Club.' *Johnson:* 'I have a great love for them.' *Boswell:* 'And pray, Sir, what do you do with them? You scrape them, it seems, very neatly, and what next?' *Johnson:* 'I let them dry, Sir.' *Boswell:* 'And what next?' *Johnson:* 'Nay, Sir, you shall know their fate no further.' *Boswell:* 'Then the world must be left in the dark. It must be said (assuming a mock solemnity,) he scraped them, and let them dry, but what he did with them next, he never could be prevailed upon to tell.' *Johnson:* 'Nay, Sir, you should say it more emphatically:— he could not be prevailed upon, even by his dearest friends, to tell.'

He had this morning received his Diploma as Doctor of Laws from the University of Oxford. He did not vaunt of his new dignity, but I understood he was highly pleased with it.

Dr. Johnson, as usual, spoke contemptuously of Colley Cibber. 'It is wonderful that a man, who for forty years had lived with the great and the witty, should have acquired so ill the talents of conversation: and he had but half to furnish; for one half of what he said was oaths.' He, however, allowed considerable merit to some of his comedies, and said there was no reason to believe that 'The Careless Husband' was not written by himself. Davies said, he was the first dramatick writer who introduced genteel ladies upon the stage. Johnson refuted this observation by instancing several such characters in comedies before his time. *Davies:* (trying to defend himself from a charge of ignorance,) 'I mean genteel moral characters.' 'I think (said Hicky,) gentility and morality are inseparable.' *Boswell:* 'By no means, Sir. The genteelest characters are often the most immoral. Does not Lord Chesterfield give precepts for uniting wickedness and the graces? A man, indeed, is not genteel when he gets drunk; but most vices may be committed very genteelly: a man may debauch his friend's wife genteelly: he may cheat at cards genteelly.' *Hicky:* 'I do not think *that* is genteel.' *Johnson:* 'You are meaning two different things. One means exteriour grace; the other honour. It is certain that a man may be very immoral with exteriour grace. Tom Hervey, who died t'other day, though a vicious man, was one of the genteelest men that ever lived.' Tom Davies instanced Charles the Second. *Johnson* (taking fire at any attack upon that Prince, for whom he had an extraordinary partiality,): 'Charles the Second was licentious in his practice; but he always had a reverence for what was good.'

I mentioned that Dr. Thomas Campbell had come from Ireland to London, principally to see Dr. Johnson. He seemed angry at this observation. *Davies:* 'Why, you know, Sir, there came a man from Spain to see Livy; and Corelli came to England to see Purcell, and, when he heard he was dead, went directly back again to Italy.' *Johnson:* 'I should not have wished to be dead to disappoint Campbell, had he been so foolish as you represent him; but I should have wished to have been a hundred miles off.' This was apparently perverse; and I do believe it was not his real way of thinking: he could not but like a man who came so far to see him. He laughed with some complacency, when I told him Campbell's odd expression to me concerning him: 'That having seen such a man, was a thing to talk of a century hence,'—as if he could live so long.

We got into an argument whether the Judges who went to India might with propriety engage in trade. Johnson warmly maintained that they might. 'For why (he urged) should not Judges get riches, as well as those who deserve them less?' I said, they should have sufficient salaries, and have nothing to take off their attention from the affairs of the publick. *Johnson:* 'No Judge, Sir, can give his whole attention to his office; and it is very proper that he should employ what time he has to himself, for his own advantage, in the most profitable manner.' 'Then, Sir, (said Davies, who enlivened the dispute by making it somewhat dramatick,) he may become an insurer;

and when he is going to the bench, he may be stopped,—"Your Lordship cannot go yet: here is a bunch of invoices: several ships are about to sail."' *Johnson:* 'Sir, you may as well say a Judge should not have a house; for they may come and tell him, "Your Lordship's house is on fire"; and so, instead of minding the business of his Court, he is to be occupied in getting the engine with the greatest speed. There is no end of this. Every Judge who has land, trades to a certain extent in corn or in cattle; and in the land itself, undoubtedly. His steward acts for him, and so do clerks for a great merchant. A Judge may be a farmer; but he is not to geld his own pigs. A Judge may play a little at cards for his amusement; but he is not to play at marbles, or at chuck-farthing in the Piazza. No, Sir; there is no profession to which a man gives a very great proportion of his time. It is wonderful, when a calculation is made, how little the mind is actually employed in the discharge of any profession. No man would be a Judge, upon the condition of being obliged to be totally a Judge. The best employed lawyer has his mind at work but for a small proportion of his time: a great deal of his occupation is merely mechanical.—I once wrote for a magazine: I made a calculation, that if I should write but a page a day, at the same rate, I should, in ten years, write nine volumes in folio, of an ordinary size and print.' *Boswell:* 'Such as Carte's History?' *Johnson:* 'Yes, Sir. When a man writes from his own mind, he writes very rapidly. The greatest part of a writer's time is spent in reading, in order to write: a man will turn over half a library to make one book.'

While the dispute went on, Moody once tried to say something upon our side. Tom Davies clapped him on the back, to encourage him. Beauclerk, to whom I mentioned this circumstance; said, 'that he could not conceive a more humiliating situation than to be clapped on the back by Tom Davies.'

We spoke of Rolt, to whose Dictionary of Commerce, Dr. Johnson wrote the Preface. *Johnson:* 'Old Gardner the bookseller employed Rolt and Smart to write a monthly miscellany, called "The Universal Visitor." There was a formal written contract, which Allen the printer saw. Gardner thought as you do of the Judge. They were bound to write nothing else; they were to have, I think, a third of the profits of this six-penny pamphlet; and the contract was for ninety-nine years. I wrote for some months in "The Universal Visitor," for poor Smart, while he was mad, not then knowing the terms on which he was engaged to write, and thinking I was doing him good. I hoped his wits would soon return to him. Mine returned to me, and I wrote in "The Universal Visitor" no longer.'

Friday, April 7, I dined with him at a tavern, with a numerous company.

Patriotism having become one of our topicks, Johnson suddenly uttered, in a strong determined tone, an apophthegm, at which many will start: 'Patriotism is the last refuge of a scoundrel.' But let it be considered, that he did not mean a real and generous love of our country, but that pretended patriotism which so many, in all ages and countries, have made a cloak for self-interest.

On Friday, April 14, being Good-Friday, I repaired to him in the morning, according to my usual custom on that day, and breakfasted with him. I observed that he fasted so very strictly, that he did not even taste bread, and took no milk with his tea; I suppose because it is a kind of animal food.

As we walked to St. Clement's church, and saw several shops open upon this most solemn fast-day of the Christian world, I remarked, that one disadvantage arising from the immensity of London, was, that nobody was heeded by his neighbour; there was no fear of censure for not observing Good-Friday, as it ought to be kept, and as it is kept in country-towns. He said, it was, upon the whole, very well observed even in London. He, however, owned, that London was too large; but added, 'It is nonsense to say the head is too big for the body. It would be as much too big, though the body were ever so large; that is to say, though the country were ever so extensive. It has no similarity to a head connected with a body.'

Dr. Wetherell, Master of University College, Oxford, accompanied us home from church; and after he was gone, there came two other gentlemen, one of whom uttered the commonplace complaints, that by the increase of taxes, labour would be dear, other nations would undersell us, and our commerce would be ruined. *Johnson* (smiling): 'Never fear, Sir. Our commerce is in a very good state; and suppose we had no commerce at all, we could live very well on the produce of our own country.' I cannot omit to mention, that I never knew any man who was less disposed to be querulous than Johnson. Whether the subject was his own situation, or the state of the publick, or the state of human nature in general, though he saw the evils, his mind was turned to resolution, and never to whining or complaint.

We went again to St. Clement's in the afternoon. He had found fault with the preacher in the morning for not choosing a text adapted to the day. The preacher in the afternoon had chosen one extremely proper: 'It is finished.'

After the evening service, he said, 'Come, you shall go home with me, and sit just an hour.' But he was better than his word; for after we had drunk tea with Mrs. Williams, he asked me to go up to his study with him, where we sat a long while together in a serene undisturbed frame of mind, sometimes in silence, and sometimes conversing, as we felt ourselves inclined, or more properly speaking, as *he* was inclined; for during all the course of my long intimacy with him, my respectful attention never abated, and my wish to hear him was such, that I constantly watched every dawning of communication from that great and illuminated mind.

He observed, 'All knowledge is of itself of some value. There is nothing so minute or inconsiderable, that I would not rather know it than not. In the same manner, all power, of whatever sort, is of itself desirable. A man would not submit to learn to hem a ruffle, of his wife, or his wife's maid; but if a mere wish could attain it, he would rather wish to be able to hem a ruffle.'

He again advised me to keep a journal fully and minutely, but not to mention such trifles as, that meat was too much or too little done, or that the weather was fair or rainy. He had, till very near his death, a contempt for the notion that the weather affects the human frame.

I told him that our friend Goldsmith had said to me, that he had come too late into the world, for that Pope and other poets had taken up the places in the Temple of Fame; so that as but a few at any period can possess poetical reputation, a man of genius can now hardly acquire it. *Johnson:* 'That is one of the most sensible things I have ever heard of Goldsmith. It is difficult to get literary fame, and it is every day growing more difficult. Ah, Sir, that should make a man think of securing happiness in another world, which all who try sincerely for it may attain. In comparison of that, how little are all other things! The belief of immortality is impressed upon all men, and all men act under an impression of it, however they may talk, and though, perhaps, they may be scarcely sensible of it.' I said, it appeared to me that some people had not the least notion of immortality; and I mentioned a distinguished gentleman of our acquaintance. *Johnson:* 'Sir, if it were not for the notion of immortality, he would cut a throat to fill his pockets.' When I quoted this to Beauclerk, who knew much more of the gentleman than we did, he said, in his acid manner, 'He would cut a throat to fill his pockets, if it were not for fear of being hanged.'

Dr. Johnson proceeded: 'Sir, there is a great cry about infidelity; but there are, in reality, very few infidels. I have heard a person, originally a Quaker, but now, I am afraid, a Deist, say, that he did not believe there were, in all England, above two hundred infidels.'

He was pleased to say, 'If you come to settle here, we will have one day in the week on which we will meet by ourselves. That is the happiest conversation where there is no competition, no vanity, but a calm quiet interchange of sentiments.' In his private register this evening is thus marked, 'Boswell sat with me till night; we had some serious talk.' It also appears from the same record, that after I left him he was occupied in religious duties, in 'giving Francis, his servant, some directions for preparation to communicate; in reviewing his life, and resolving on better conduct.'

On Tuesday, April 18, he and I were engaged to go with Sir Joshua Reynolds to dine with Mr. Cambridge, at his beautiful villa on the banks of the Thames, near Twickenham. Dr. Johnson's tardiness was such, that Sir Joshua, who had an appointment at Richmond, early in the day, was obliged to go by himself on horseback, leaving his coach to Johnson and me. Johnson was in such good spirits, that every thing seemed to please him as we drove along.

Our conversation turned on a variety of subjects. He thought portrait-painting an improper employment for a woman. 'Publick practice of any art, (he observed,) and staring in men's faces, is very indelicate in a female.' I happened to start a question of propriety, whether, when a man knows that some of his intimate friends are invited to the house of another friend, with whom they are all equally intimate, he may join them without an invitation. *Johnson:* 'No, Sir; he is not to go when he is not invited. They may be invited on purpose to abuse him,' (smiling).

As a curious instance how little a man knows, or wishes to know, his own character in the world, or, rather, as a convincing proof that Johnson's roughness was only external, and did not proceed from his heart, I insert the following dialogue. *Johnson:* 'It is wonderful, Sir, how rare a quality good humour is in life. We meet with very few good humoured men.' I mentioned four of our friends, none of whom he would allow to be good humoured. One was *acid,* another was *muddy,* and to the others he had objections which

have escaped me. Then, shaking his head and stretching himself at his ease in the coach, and smiling with much complacency, he turned to me and said, 'I look upon *myself* as a good humoured fellow.' I answered, also smiling, 'No, no, Sir; that will *not* do. You are good natured, but not good humoured: you are irascible. You have not patience with folly and absurdity. I believe you would pardon them, if there were time to deprecate your vengeance; but punishment follows so quick after sentence, that they cannot escape.'

He talked of Isaac Walton's Lives, which was one of his most favourite books. Dr. Donne's Life, he said, was the most perfect of them. He observed, that 'it was wonderful that Walton, who was in a very low situation in life, should have been familiarly received by so many great men, and that at a time when the ranks of society were kept more separate than they are now.' He supposed that Walton had then given up his business as a linen-draper and sempster, and was only an authour; and added, 'that he was a great panegyrist.' *Boswell:* 'No quality will get a man more friends than a disposition to admire the qualities of others. I do not mean flattery, but a sincere admiration.' *Johnson:* 'Nay, Sir, flattery pleases very generally. In the first place, the flatterer may think what he says to be true: but in the second place, whether he thinks so or not, he certainly thinks those whom he flatters of consequence enough to be flattered.'

No sooner had we made our bow to Mr. Cambridge, in his library, than Johnson ran eagerly to one side of the room, intent on poring over the backs of the books. Sir Joshua observed, (aside,) 'He runs to the books, as I do to the pictures: but I have the advantage. I can see much more of the pictures than he can of the books.' Mr. Cambridge, upon this, politely said, 'Dr. Johnson, I am going, with your pardon, to accuse myself, for I have the same custom which I perceive you have. But it seems odd that one should have such a desire to look at the backs of books.' Johnson, ever ready for contest, instantly started from his reverie, wheeled about, and answered, 'Sir, the reason is very plain. Knowledge is of two kinds. We know a subject ourselves, or we know where we can find information upon it. When we enquire into any subject, the first thing we have to do is to know what books have treated of it. This leads us to look at catalogues, and at the backs of books in libraries.'

The common remark as to the utility of reading history being made;—*Johnson:* 'We must consider how very little history there is; I mean real authentick history. That certain Kings reigned, and certain battles were fought, we can depend upon as true; but all the colouring, all the philosophy, of history is conjecture.' *Boswell:* 'Then, Sir, you would reduce all history to no better than an almanack, a mere chronological series of remarkable events.' Mr. Gibbon, who must at that time

have been employed upon his history, of which he published the first volume in the following year, was present; but did not step forth in defence of that species of writing. He probably did not like to *trust* himself with *Johnson!*

On Monday, May 8, we went together and visited the mansions of Bedlam. I had been informed that he had once been there before with Mr. Wedderburne, (now Lord Loughborough,) Mr. Murphy, and Mr. Foote; and I had heard Foote give a very entertaining account of Johnson's happening to have his attention arrested by a man who was very furious, and who, while beating his straw, supposed it to be William Duke of Cumberland, whom he was punishing for his cruelties in Scotland, in 1746. There was nothing peculiarly remarkable this day; but the general contemplation of insanity was very affecting. I accompanied him home, and dined and drank tea with him.

On Friday, May 12, as he had been so good as to assign me a room in his house, where I might sleep occasionally, when I happened to sit with him to a late hour, I took possession of it this night, found every thing in excellent order, and was attended by honest Francis with a most civil assiduity.

On Saturday, May 13, I breakfasted with him by invitation, accompanied by Mr. Andrew Crosbie, a Scotch Advocate, whom he had seen at Edinburgh, and the Hon. Colonel (now General) Edward Stopford, brother of Lord Courtown, who was desirous of being introduced to him. His tea and rolls and butter, and whole breakfast apparatus were all in such decorum, and his behaviour was so courteous, that Colonel Stopford was quite surprized, and wondered at his having heard so much said of Johnson's slovenliness and roughness. I have preserved nothing of what passed, except that Crosbie pleased him much by talking learnedly of alchymy, as to which Johnson was not a positive unbeliever, but rather delighted in considering what progress had actually been made in the transmutation of metals, what near approaches there had been to the making of gold; and told us that it was affirmed, that a person in the Russian dominions had discovered the secret, but died without revealing it, as imagining it would be prejudicial to society. He added, that it was not impossible but it might in time be generally known.

It being asked whether it was reasonable for a man to be angry at another whom a woman had preferred to him;—*Johnson:* 'I do not see, Sir, that it is reasonable for a man to be angry at another, whom a woman has preferred to him: but angry he is, no doubt; and he is loath to be angry at himself.'

I passed many hours with him on the 17th, of which I find all my memorial is, 'much laughing.' It should seem he had that day been in a humour for jocularity and merriment, and upon such occasions I never knew a man laugh more heartily. We may suppose, that the high relish of a state so different from his habitual gloom, produced more than ordinary exertions of that distinguishing faculty of man, which has puzzled philosophers so much to explain. Johnson's laugh was as remarkable as any circumstance in his manner. It was a kind of good humoured growl. Tom Davies described it drolly enough: 'He laughs like a rhinoceros.'

Chapter 8

Trips and Talk

It is to be regretted, that he did not write an account of his travels in France; for as he is reported to have once said, that 'he could write the Life of a Broomstick,' so, notwithstanding so many former travellers have exhausted almost every subject for remark in that great kingdom, his very accurate observation, and peculiar vigour of thought and illustration, would have produced a valuable work. During his visit to it, which lasted but about two months, he wrote notes or minutes of what he saw. He promised to show me them, but I neglected to put him in mind of it; and the greatest part of them has been lost, or, perhaps, destroyed in a precipitate burning of his papers a few days before his death, which must ever be lamented.

When I met him in London the following year, the account which he gave me of his French tour, was, 'Sir, I have seen all the visibilities of Paris, and around it; but to have formed an acquaintance with the people there, would have required more time than I could stay. I was just beginning to creep into acquaintance by means of Colonel Drumgould, a very high man, Sir, head of *L'Ecole Militaire,* a most complete character, for he had first been a professor of rhetorick, and then became a soldier. And, Sir, I was very kindly treated by the English Benedictines, and have a cell appropriated to me in their convent.'

He observed, 'The great in France live very magnificently, but the rest very miserably. There is no happy middle state as in England. The shops of Paris are mean; the meat in the markets is such as would be sent to a gaol in England: and Mr. Thrale justly observed, that the cookery of the French was forced upon them by necessity; for they could not eat their meat, unless they added some taste to it. The French are an indelicate people; they will spit upon any place. At Madame ——'s, a literary lady of rank, the footman took the sugar in his fingers, and threw it into my coffee. I was going to put it aside; but hearing it was made on purpose for me, I e'en tasted Tom's fingers. The same lady would needs make tea *à l'Angloise.* The spout of the tea-pot did not pour freely: she bad the footman blow into it. France is worse than Scotland in every thing but climate. Nature has done more for the French; but they have done less for themselves than the Scotch have done.'

It happened that Foote was at Paris at the same time with Dr. Johnson, and his description of my friend while there, was abundantly ludicrous. He told me, that the French were quite astonished at his figure and manner, and at his dress, which he obstinately continued exactly as in London;—his brown clothes, black stockings, and plain shirt.

While Johnson was in France, he was generally very resolute in speaking Latin. It was a maxim with him that a man should not let himself down, by speaking a language which he speaks imperfectly. Indeed, we must have often observed how inferiour, how much like a child a man appears, who speaks a broken tongue. When Sir Joshua Reynolds, at one of the dinners of the Royal Academy, presented him to a Frenchman of great distinction, he would not deign to speak French, but talked Latin, though his Excellency did not understand it, owing, perhaps, to Johnson's English pronunciation: yet upon another occasion he was observed to speak French to a Frenchman of high rank, who spoke English; and being asked the reason, with some expression of surprise,—he answered, 'because I think my French is as good as his English.'

Here let me not forget a curious anecdote, as related to me by Mr. Beauclerk, which I shall endeavour to exhibit as well as I can in that gentleman's lively manner; and in justice to him it is proper to add, that

Dr. Johnson told me I might rely both on the correctness of his memory, and the fidelity of his narrative. 'When Madame de Boufflers was first in England, (said Beauclerk,) she was desirous to see Johnson. I accordingly went with her to his chambers in the Temple, where she was entertained with his conversation for some time. When our visit was over, she and I left him, and were got into Inner Temple-lane, when all at once I heard a noise like thunder. This was occasioned by Johnson, who it seems, upon a little recollection, had taken it into his head that he ought to have done the honours of his literary residence to a foreign lady of quality, and eager to show himself a man of gallantry, was hurrying down the stair-case in violent agitation. He overtook us before we reached the Temple-gate, and brushing in between me and Madame de Boufflers, seized her hand, and conducted her to her coach. His dress was a rusty brown morning suit, a pair of old shoes by way of slippers, a little shrivelled wig sticking on the top of his head, and the sleeves of his shirt and the knees of his breeches hanging loose. A considerable crowd of people gathered round, and were not a little struck by this singular appearance.'

In the course of this year Dr. Burney informs me, that 'he very frequently met Dr. Johnson at Mr. Thrale's, at Streatham, where they had many long conversations, often sitting up as long as the fire and candles lasted, and much longer than the patience of the servants subsisted.'

A few of Johnson's sayings, which that gentleman recollects, shall here be inserted.

'I never take a nap after dinner but when I have had a bad night, and then the nap takes me.'

'The writer of an epitaph should not be considered as saying nothing but what is strictly true. Allowance must be made for some degree of exaggerated praise. In lapidary inscriptions a man is not upon oath.'

'There is now less flogging in our great schools than formerly, but then less is learned there; so that what the boys get at one end, they lose at the other.'

'I hate by-roads in education. Education is as well known, and has long been as well known, as ever it can be. Endeavouring to make children prematurely wise is useless labour. Suppose they have more knowledge at five or six years old than other children, what use can be made of it? It will be lost before it is wanted, and the waste of so much time and labour of the teacher can never be repaid. Too much is expected from precocity, and too little performed. Miss —— was an instance of early cultivation, but in what did it terminate? In marrying a little Presbyterian parson, who keeps an infant boarding-school, so that all her employment now is,

"To suckle fools, and chronicle small-beer."

She tells the children, "This is a cat, and that is a dog, with four legs and a tail; see there! you are much better than a cat or a dog, for you can speak." '

'After having talked slightingly of musick, he was observed to listen very attentively while Miss Thrale played on the harpsichord, and with eagerness he called to her, "Why don't you dash away like Burney?" Dr. Burney upon this said to him, "I believe, Sir, we shall make a musician of you at last." Johnson with candid complacency replied, "Sir, I shall be glad to have a new sense given to me." '

Having arrived in London late on Friday, the 15th of March, 1775, I hastened next morning to wait on Dr. Johnson, at his house; but found he was removed from Johnson's-court, No. 7, to Bolt-court, No. 8, still keeping to his favourite Fleet-street. My reflection at the time upon this change as marked in my Journal, is as follows: 'I felt a foolish regret that he had left a court which bore his name; but it was not foolish to be affected with some tenderness of regard for a place in which I had seen him a great deal, from whence I had often issued a better and happier man than when I went in, and which had often appeared to my imagination while I trod its pavement, in the solemn darkness of the night, to be sacred to wisdom and piety.' Being informed that he was at Mr. Thrale's, in the Borough, I hastened thither, and found Mrs. Thrale and him at breakfast. I was kindly welcomed. In a moment he was in a full glow of conversation, and I felt myself elevated as if brought into another state of being. Mrs. Thrale and I looked to each other while he talked, and our looks expressed our congenial admiration and affection for him. I shall ever recollect this scene with great pleasure. I exclaimed to her, 'I am quite restored by him, by transfusion of mind.' 'There are many (she replied) who admire and respect Mr. Johnson; but you and I *love* him.'

He seemed very happy in the near prospect of going to Italy with Mr. and Mrs. Thrale. 'But, (said he,) before leaving England I am to take a jaunt to Oxford, Birmingham, my native city Lichfield, and my old friend, Dr. Taylor's, at Ashbourn, in Derbyshire. I shall go in a few days, and you, Boswell, shall go with me.' I was ready to accompany him; being willing even to leave London to have the pleasure of his conversation.

I mentioned with much regret the extravagance of the representative of a great family in Scotland, by which there was danger of its being ruined; and as Johnson respected it for its antiquity, he joined with me in thinking it would be happy if this person should die. Mrs. Thrale seemed shocked at this, as feudal barbarity; and said, 'I do not understand this preference of the estate to its owner; of the land to the man who walks upon that land.' *Johnson*: 'Nay, Madam, it is not a preference of the land to its owner; it is the preference of a family to an individual. Here is an establishment in a country, which is of importance for ages, not only to the chief but to his people; an establishment which extends upwards and downwards; that this should be destroyed by one idle fellow is a sad thing.'

We got into a boat to cross over to Black-friars; and as we moved along the Thames, I talked to him of a little volume, which, altogether unknown to him, was advertised to be published in a few days, under the title of 'Johnsoniana, or Bon Mots of Dr. Johnson.' Johnson: 'Sir, it is a mighty impudent thing.' Boswell: 'Pray, Sir, could you have no redress if you were to prosecute a publisher for bringing out, under your name, what you never said, and ascribing to you dull stupid nonsense, or making you swear profanely, as many ignorant relaters of your bon mots do?' Johnson: 'No, Sir; there will always be some truth mixed with the falsehood, and how can it be ascertained how much is true and how much is false? Besides, Sir, what damages would a jury give me for having been represented as swearing?' Boswell: 'I think, Sir, you should at least disavow such a publication, because the world and posterity might with much plausible foundation say, "Here is a volume which was publickly advertised and came out in Dr. Johnson's own time, and, by his silence, was admitted by him to be genuine."' Johnson: 'I shall give myself no trouble about the matter.'

We landed at the Temple-stairs, where we parted.

I found him in the evening in Mrs. Williams' room. We talked of religious orders. He said, 'It is as unreasonable for a man to go into a Carthusian convent for fear of being immoral, as for a man to cut off his hands for fear he should steal. There is, indeed, great resolution in the immediate act of dismembering himself; but when that is once done, he has no longer any merit: for though it is out of his power to steal, yet he may all his life be a thief in his heart. So when a man has once become a Carthusian, he is obliged to continue so, whether he chooses it or not. Their silence, too, is absurd. We read in the Gospel of the apostles being sent to preach, but not to hold their tongues. All severity that does not tend to increase good, or prevent evil, is idle. I said to the Lady Abbess of a convent, "Madam, you are here, not for the love of virtue, but the fear of vice." She said, "She should remember this as long as she lived."' I thought it hard to give her this view of her situation, when she could not help it; and, indeed, I wondered at the whole of what he now said; because, both in his 'Rambler' and 'Idler,' he treats religious austerities with much solemnity of respect.

Finding him still persevering in his abstinence from wine, I ventured to speak to him of it.—Johnson: 'Sir, I have no objection to a man's drinking wine, if he can do it in moderation. I found myself apt to go to excess in it, and therefore, after having been for some time without it, on account of illness, I thought it better not to return to it. Every man is to judge for himself, according to the effects which he experiences. One of the fathers tells us, he found fasting made him so peevish that he did not practise it.'

Though he often enlarged upon the evil of intoxication, he was by no means harsh and unforgiving to those who indulged in occasional excess in wine. One of his friends, I well remember, came to sup at a tavern with him and some other gentlemen, and too plainly discovered that he had drunk too much at dinner. When one who loved mischief, thinking to produce a severe censure, asked Johnson, a few days afterwards, 'Well, Sir, what did your friend say to you, as an apology for being in such a situation?' Johnson answered, 'Sir, he said all that a man *should* say: he said he was sorry for it.'

I heard him once give a very judicious practical advice upon this subject: 'A man, who has been drinking wine at all freely, should never go into a new company. With those who have partaken of wine with him, he may be pretty well in unison; but he will probably be offensive, or appear ridiculous, to other people.'

He allowed very great influence to education. 'I do not deny, Sir, but there is some original difference in minds; but it is nothing in comparison of what is formed by education. We may instance the science of *numbers,* which all minds are equally capable of attaining; yet we find a prodigious difference in the powers of different men, in that respect, after they are grown up, because their minds have been more or less exercised in it: and I think the same cause will explain the difference of excellence in other things, gradations admitting always some difference in the first principles.'

I again visited him on Monday. He took occasion to enlarge, as he often did, upon the wretchedness of a sea-life. 'A ship is worse than a gaol. There is, in a gaol, better air, better company, better conveniency of every kind; and a ship has the additional disadvantage of being in danger. When men come to like a sea-life, they are not fit to live on land.'—'Then (said I) it would be cruel in a father to breed his son to the sea.' *Johnson:* 'It would be cruel in a father who thinks as I do. Men go to sea, before they know the unhappiness of that way of life; and when they have come to know it, they cannot escape from it, because it is then too late to choose another profession; as indeed is generally the case with men, when they have once engaged in any particular way of life.'

On Tuesday, March 19, which was fixed for our proposed jaunt, we met in the morning at the Somerset coffee-house in the Strand, where we were taken up by the Oxford coach. He was accompanied by Mr. Gwyn, the architect; and a gentleman of Merton College, whom we did not know, had the fourth seat. We soon got into conversation; for it was very remarkable of Johnson, that the presence of a stranger was no restraint upon his talk. I observed that Garrick, who was about to quit the stage, would soon have an easier life. *Johnson:* 'I doubt that, Sir.' *Boswell:* 'Why, Sir, he will be Atlas with the burthen off his back.' *Johnson:* 'But I know not, Sir, if he will be so steady without his load. However, he should never play any more, but be entirely the gentleman, and not partly the player: he should no longer subject himself to be hissed by a mob, or to be insolently treated by performers, whom he used to rule with a high hand, and who would gladly retaliate.' *Boswell:* 'I think he should play once a year for the benefit of decayed actors, as it has been said he means to do.' *Johnson:* 'Alas, Sir! he will soon be a decayed actor himself.'

Upon our arrival at Oxford, Dr. Johnson and I went directly to University College, but were disappointed on finding that one of the fellows, his friend Mr. Scott, who accompanied him from Newcastle to Edinburgh, was gone to the country. We put up at the Angel inn, and passed the evening by ourselves in easy and familiar conversation. Talking of constitutional melancholy, he observed. 'A man so afflicted, Sir, must divert distressing thoughts, and not combat with them.' *Boswell:* 'May not he think them down, Sir?' *Johnson:* 'No, Sir. To attempt to *think them down* is madness. He should have a lamp constantly burning in his bed-chamber during the night, and if wakefully disturbed, take a book, and read, and compose himself to rest. To have the management of the mind is a great art, and it may be attained in a considerable

degree by experience and habitual exercise.' *Boswell:* 'Should not he provide amusements for himself? Would it not, for instance, be right for him to take a course of chymistry?' *Johnson:* 'Let him take a course of chymistry, or a course of rope-dancing, or a course of any thing to which he is inclined at the time. Let him contrive to have as many retreats for his mind as he can, as many things to which it can fly from itself. Burton's "Anatomy of Melancholy" is a valuable work. It is, perhaps, overloaded with quotation. But there is great spirit and great power in what Burton says, when he writes from his own mind.'

We went to Pembroke College, and waited on his old friend Dr. Adams, the master of it, whom I found to be a most polite, pleasing, communicative man. Before his advancement to the headship of his college, I had intended to go and visit him at Shrewsbury, where he was rector of St. Chad's, in order to get from him what particulars he could recollect of Johnson's academical life. He now obligingly gave me part of that authentick information, which, with what I afterwards owed to his kindness, will be found incorporated in its proper place in this work.

Dr. Adams told us, that in some of the Colleges at Oxford, the fellows [1] had excluded the students from social intercourse with them in the common room. *Johnson:*

---

[1] fellows: members of the college faculty.

'They are in the right, Sir, for there can be no real conversation, no fair exertion of mind amongst them, if the young men are 'by; for a man who has a character does not choose to stake it in their presence.' *Boswell:* 'But, Sir, may there not be very good conversation without a contest for superiority?' *Johnson:* 'No animated conversation, Sir, for it cannot be but one or other will come off superiour. I do not mean that the victor must have the better of the argument, for he may take the weak side; but his superiority of parts and knowledge will necessarily appear: and he to whom he thus shews himself superiour is lessened in the eyes of the young men.'

We walked with Dr. Adams into the master's garden, and into the common room. *Johnson:* (after a reverie of meditation,) 'Ay! Here I used to play at draughts with Phil. Jones and Fludyer. Jones loved beer, and did not get very forward in the church. Fludyer turned out a scoundrel, a Whig, and said he was ashamed of having been bred at Oxford. He had a living at Putney, and got under the eye of some retainers to the court at that time, and so became a violent Whig: but he had been a scoundrel all along, to be sure.' *Boswell:* 'Was he a scoundrel, Sir, in any other way than that of being a political scoundrel? Did he cheat at draughts?' *Johnson:* 'Sir, we never played for *money.*'

He then carried me to visit Dr. Bentham, Canon of Christ-Church, and Divinity Professor, with whose learned and lively conversation we were much pleased. He gave us an invitation to dinner, which Dr. Johnson told me was a high honour. 'Sir, it is a great thing to dine with the Canons at Christ-Church.' We could not accept his invitation, as we were engaged to dine at University College. We had an excellent dinner there, with the Master and Fellows, it being St. Cuthbert's day, which is kept by them as a festival, as he was a saint of Durham, with which this college is much connected.

We then went to Trinity College, where he introduced me to Mr. Thomas Warton, with whom we passed a part of the evening. We talked of biography.—*Johnson:* 'It is rarely well executed. They only who live with a man can write his life with any genuine exactness and discrimination; and few people who have lived with a man know what to remark about him. The chaplain of a late Bishop, whom I was to assist in writing some memoirs of his Lordship, could tell me scarcely any thing.'

Mr. Warton, being engaged, could not sup with us at our inn; we had therefore another evening by ourselves. I asked Johnson, whether a man's being forward in making himself known to eminent people, and seeing as much of life, and getting as much information as he could in every way was not yet lessening himself by his forwardness. *Johnson:* 'No, Sir; a man always makes himself greater as he increases his knowledge.'

I censured some ludicrous fantastick dialogues between two coach-horses, and other such stuff, which Baretti had lately published. He joined with me, and said, 'Nothing odd will do long. "Tristram Shandy" did not last.' I expressed a desire to be acquainted with a lady who had been much talked of, and universally celebrated for extraordinary address and insinuation. *Johnson:* 'Never believe extraordinary characters which you hear of people. Depend upon it, Sir, they are exaggerated. You do not see one man shoot a great deal higher than another.' I mentioned Mr. Burke. *Johnson:* 'Yes; Burke is an extraordinary man. His stream of mind is perpetual.' It *is* very pleasing to me to record, that Johnson's high estimation of the talents of this gentleman was uniform from their early acquaintance. Sir Joshua Reynolds informs me, that when Mr. Burke was first elected a member of Parliament, and Sir John Hawkins expressed a wonder at his attaining a seat, Johnson said, 'Now we who know Burke, know, that he will be one of the first men in this country.' And once, when Johnson was ill, and unable to exert himself as much as usual without fatigue, Mr. Burke having been mentioned, he said, 'That fellow calls forth all my powers. Were I to see Burke now, it would kill me.' So much was he accustomed to consider conversation as a contest, and such was his notion of Burke as an opponent.

Next morning, Thursday, March 21, we set out in a post-chaise to pursue our ramble. It was a delightful day, and we drove through Blenheim Park. I observed to him, while in the midst of the noble scene around us, 'You and I, Sir, have, I think, seen together the extremes of what can be seen in Britain:—the wild rough island of Mull, and Blenheim Park.'

We dined at an excellent inn at Chapel-house, where he expatiated on the felicity of England in its taverns and inns, and triumphed over the French for not having, in any perfection, the tavern life. There is no private house, (said he,) in which people can enjoy themselves so well, as at a capital tavern. Let there be ever so great plenty of good things, ever so much grandeur, ever so much elegance, ever so much desire that every body should be easy; in the nature of things it cannot be: there must always be some degree of care and anxiety. The master of the house is anxious to entertain his guests; the guests are anxious to be agreeable to him: and no man, but a very impudent dog indeed, can as freely command what is in another man's house, as if it were his own. Whereas, at a tavern, there is a general freedom from anxiety. You are sure you are welcome: and the more noise you make, the more trouble you give, the more good things you call for, the welcomer you are. No servants will attend you with the alacrity which waiters do, who are incited by the prospect of an immediate reward in proportion as they please. No, Sir; there is nothing which has yet been contrived by man, by which so much happiness is produced as by a good tavern or inn.'

In the afternoon, as we were driven rapidly along in the post-chaise, he said to me, 'Life has not many things better than this.'

We stopped at Stratford-upon-Avon, and drank tea and coffee; and it pleased me to be with him upon the classick ground of Shakspeare's native place.

On Friday, March 22, having set out early from Henley, where we had lain the preceding night, we arrived at Birmingham about nine o'clock, and, after breakfast, went to call on his old schoolfellow Mr. Hector. A very stupid maid, who opened the door, told us, that 'her master was gone out; he was gone to the country; she could not tell when he would return.' In short, she gave us a miserable reception; and Johnson observed, 'She would have behaved no better to people who wanted him in the way of his profession.' He said to her, 'My name is Johnson; tell him I called. Will you remember the name?' She answered with rustick simplicity, in the Warwickshire pronunciation, 'I don't understand you, Sir.'—'Blockhead, (said he,) I'll write.' I never heard the word *block-head* applied to a woman before, though I do not see why it should not, when there is evident occasion for it. He, however, made another attempt to make her understand him, and roared loud in her ear, '*Johnson,*' and then she catched the sound.

We next called on Mr. Lloyd, one of the people called Quakers. He too was not at home; but Mrs. Lloyd was, and received us courteously, and asked us to dinner. Johnson said to me, 'After the uncertainty of all human things at Hector's, this invitation came very well.' We walked about the town, and he was pleased to see it increasing.

Mr. Lloyd joined us in the street; and in a little while we met *Friend Hector,* as Mr. Lloyd called him. It gave me pleasure to observe the joy which Johnson and he expressed on seeing each other again. Mr. Lloyd and I left them together, while he obligingly shewed me some of the manufactures of this very curious assemblage of artificers. We all met at dinner at Mr. Lloyd's, where we were entertained with great hospitality. Mr. and Mrs. Lloyd had been married the same year with their Majesties, and, like them, had been blessed with a numerous family of fine children, their numbers being exactly the same. Johnson said, 'Marriage is the best state for man in general; and every man is a worse man, in proportion as he is unfit for the married state.'

Dr. Johnson said to me in the morning, 'You will see, Sir, at Mr. Hector's, his sister, Mrs. Careless, a clergyman's widow. She was the first woman with whom I was in love. It dropt out of my head imperceptibly; but she and I shall always have a kindness for each other.' He laughed at the notion that a man never can be really in love but once, and considered it as a mere romantick fancy.

On our return from Mr. Bolton's, Mr. Hector took me to his house, where we found Johnson sitting placidly at tea, with his *first love;* who, though now advanced in years, was a genteel woman, very agreeable, and well-bred.

Johnson lamented to Mr. Hector the state of one of their schoolfellows, Mr. Charles Congreve, a clergyman, which he thus described: 'He obtained, I believe, considerable preferment in Ireland, but now lives in London, quite as a valetudinarian, afraid to go into any house but his own. He takes a short airing in his post-chaise every day. He has an elderly woman, whom he calls cousin, who lives with him, and jogs his elbow, when his glass has stood too long empty, and encourages him in drinking, in which he is very willing to be encouraged; not that he gets drunk, for he is a very pious man, but he is always muddy. He confesses to one bottle of port every day, and he probably drinks more. He is quite unsocial; his conversation is monosyllabical: and when, at my last visit, I asked him what o'clock it was? that signal of my departure had so pleasing an effect on him, that he sprung up to look at his watch, like a greyhound bounding at a hare.'

When he again talked of Mrs. Careless to-night, he seemed to have had his affection revived; for he said, 'If I had married her, it might have been as happy for me.' *Boswell:* 'Pray, Sir, do you not suppose that there are fifty women in the world, with any one of whom a man may be as happy, as with any one woman in particular.' *Johnson:* 'Ay, Sir, fifty thousand.' *Boswell:* 'Then, Sir, you are not of opinion with some who imagine that certain men and certain women are made for each other; and that they cannot be happy if they miss their counterparts.' *Johnson:* 'To be sure not, Sir. I believe marriages would in general be as happy, and often more so, if they were all made by the Lord Chancellor, upon a due consideration of characters and circumstances, without the parties having any choice in the matter.'

I wished to have staid at Birmingham to-night, to have talked more with Mr. Hector; but my friend was impatient to reach his native city: so we drove on that stage in the dark, and were long pensive and silent. When we came within the focus of the Lichfield lamps, 'Now (said he,) we are getting out of a state of death.' We put up at the Three Crowns, not one of the great inns, but a good old fashioned one, which was kept by Mr. Wilkins, and was the very next house to that in which Johnson was born and brought up, and which was still his own property. We had a comfortable supper, and got into high spirits. I felt all my Toryism glow in this old capital of Staffordshire.

Next morning he introduced me to Mrs. Lucy Porter, his step-daughter. She was now an old maid, with much simplicity of manner. She had never been in London. Her brother, a Captain in the navy, had left her a fortune of ten thousand pounds; about a third of which she had laid out in building a stately house, and making a handsome garden, in an elevated situation in Lichfield. Johnson, when here by himself, used to live at her house. She reverenced him, and he had a parental tenderness for her.

We dined at our inn, and had with us a Mr. Jackson, one of Johnson's schoolfellows, whom he treated with much kindness, though he seemed to be a low man, dull and untaught. He had a coarse grey coat, black waistcoat, greasy leather breeches, and a yellow uncurled wig; and his countenance had the ruddiness which betokens one who is in no haste to 'leave his can.' He drank only ale. He had tried to be a cutler at Birmingham, but had not succeeded; and now he lived poorly at home, and had some scheme of dressing leather in a better manner than common; to his indistinct account of which, Dr. Johnson listened with patient attention, that he might assist him with his advice. Here was an instance of genuine humanity and real kindness in this great man, who has been most unjustly represented as altogether harsh and destitute of tenderness. A thousand such instances might have been recorded in the course of his long life; though, that his temper was warm and hasty, and his manner often rough, cannot be denied.

He expatiated in praise of Lichfield and its inhabitants, who, he said, were 'the most sober, decent people in England, the genteelest in proportion to their wealth, and spoke the purest English.' I doubted as to the last article of this eulogy: for they had several provincial sounds; as, *there,* pronounced like *fear,* instead of like *fair; once* pronounced *woonse,* instead of *wunse,* or *wonse.* Johnson himself never got entirely free of those provincial accents. Garrick sometimes used to take him off, squeezing a lemon into a punch-bowl, with uncouth gesticulations, looking round the company, and calling out, 'Who's for *poonsh?'*

On Monday, March 25, we breakfasted at Mrs. Lucy Porter's. Johnson had sent an express to Dr. Taylor's, acquainting him of our being at Lichfield, and Taylor had returned an answer that his post-chaise should come for us this day. While we sat at breakfast, Dr. Johnson received a letter by the post, which seemed to agitate him very much. When he had read it, he exclaimed, 'One of the most dreadful things that has happened in my time.' The phrase *my time,* like the word *age,* is usually understood to refer to an event of a publick or general nature. I imagined something like an assassination of the King—like a gunpowder plot carried into execution—or like another fire of London. When asked, 'What is it, Sir?' he answered, 'Mr. Thrale has lost his only son!' This was, no doubt, a very great affliction to Mr. and Mrs. Thrale, which their friends could consider accordingly; but from the manner in which the intelligence of it was communicated by Johnson, it appeared for the moment to be comparatively small. I, however, soon felt a sincere concern, and was curious to observe, how Dr. Johnson would be affected. He said, 'This is a total extinction to their family, as much as if they were sold into captivity.' Upon my mentioning that Mr. Thrale had daughters, who might inherit his wealth;—'Daughters, (said Johnson, warmly,) he'll no more value his daughters than—' I was going to speak.—'Sir, (said he,) don't you know how you yourself think? Sir, he wishes to propagate his name.' In short, I saw male succession strong in his mind, even where there was no name, no family of any long standing. I said, it was lucky he was not present when this misfortune happened. *Johnson:* 'It is lucky for *me*. People in distress never think that you feel enough.' *Boswell:* 'And Sir, they will have the hope of seeing you, which will be a relief in the mean time; and when you get to them, the pain will be so far abated, that they will be capable of being consoled by you, which, in the first violence of it, I believe, would not be the case.' *Johnson:* 'No, Sir; violent pain of mind, like violent pain of body, *must* be severely felt.' *Boswell:* 'I own, Sir, I have not so much feeling for the distress of others, as some people have, or pretend to have: but I know this, that I would do all in my power to relieve them.' *Johnson:* 'Sir, it is affectation to pretend to feel the distress of others, as much as they do themselves. It is equally so, as if one should pretend to feel as much pain while a friend's leg is cutting off, as he does. No, Sir; you have expressed the rational and just nature of sympathy. I would have gone to the extremity of the earth to have preserved this boy.'

He was soon quite calm. The letter was from Mr. Thrale's clerk, and concluded, 'I need not say how much they wish to see you in London.' He said, 'We shall hasten back from Taylor's.'

After dinner Dr. Johnson wrote a letter to Mrs. Thrale on the death of her son. I said it would be very distressing to Thrale, but she would soon forget it, as she had so many things to think of. *Johnson:* 'No, Sir, Thrale will forget it first. *She* has many things that she *may* think of. *He* has many things that he *must* think of.' This was a very just remark upon the different effect of those light pursuits which occupy a vacant and easy mind, and those serious engagements which arrest attention, and keep us from brooding over grief.

On Tuesday, March 26, there came for us an equipage properly suited to a wealthy well-beneficed clergyman;—Dr. Taylor's large roomy post-chaise, drawn by four stout plump horses, and driven by two steady jolly postillions, which conveyed us to Ashbourne; where I found my friend's schoolfellow living upon an establishment perfectly corresponding with his substantial creditable equipage: his house, garden, pleasure-grounds, table, in short every thing good, and no scantiness appearing. I could not perceive in his character much congeniality of any sort with that of Johnson, who, however, said to me, 'Sir, he has a very strong understanding.' His size, and figure, and countenance, and manner, were that of a hearty English 'Squire, with the parson superinduced: and I took particular notice of his upper servant, Mr. Peters, a decent grave man, in purple clothes, and a large white wig, like the butler or *major domo* of a Bishop.

Dr. Johnson and Dr. Taylor met with great cordiality; and Johnson soon gave him the same sad account of their schoolfellow, Congreve, that he had given to Mr. Hector, adding a remark of such moment to the rational conduct of a man in the decline of life, that it deserves to be imprinted upon every mind: 'There is nothing against which an old man should be so much upon his guard as putting himself to nurse.' Innumerable have been the melancholy instances of men once distinguished for firmness, resolution, and spirit, who in their latter days have been governed like children, by interested female artifice.

Dr. Taylor commended a physician who was known to him and Dr. Johnson, and said, 'I fight many battles for him, as many people in the country dislike him.' *Johnson:* 'But you should consider, Sir, that by every one of your victories he is a loser; for, every man of whom you get the better, will be very angry, and will resolve not to employ him; whereas if people got the better of you in argument about him, they'll think, "We'll send for Dr. —— nevertheless." '

On Thursday, March 28, we pursued our journey. I enjoyed the luxury of our approach to London, that metropolis which we both loved so much, for the high and varied intellectual pleasure which it furnishes. I experienced immediate happiness while whirled along with such a companion, and said to him, 'Sir, you observed one day at General Oglethorpe's, that a man is never happy for the present, but when he is drunk. Will you not add,—or when driving rapidly in a post-chaise?' *Johnson:* 'No. Sir, you are driving rapidly *from* something, or *to* something.'

Talking of melancholy, he said, 'Some men, and very thinking men too, have not those vexing thoughts. Sir Joshua Reynolds is the same all the year round. Beauclerk, except when ill and in pain, is the same. But I believe most men have them in the degree in which they are capable of having them. If I were in the country, and were distressed by that malady, I would force myself to take a book; and every time I did it I should find it the easier. Melancholy, indeed, should be diverted by every means but drinking.'

We stopped at Messieurs Dillys, booksellers in the Poultry; from whence he hurried away, in a hackney coach, to Mr. Thrale's, in the Borough. I called at his house in the evening, having promised to acquaint Mrs. Williams of his safe return; when, to my surprize, I found him sitting with her at tea, and, as I thought, not in a very good humour: for, it seems, when he had got to Mr. Thrale's, he found the coach waiting at the door waiting to carry Mrs. and Miss Thrale, and Signor Baretti, their Italian master, to Bath. This was not shewing the attention which might have been expected to the 'Guide, Philosopher, and Friend,' the *Imlac* [1] who had hastened from the country to console a distressed mother, who he understood was very anxious for his return. They had, I found, without ceremony, proceeded on their intended journey. I was not pleased that his intimacy with Mr. Thrale's family, though it no doubt contributed much to his comfort and enjoyment, was not without some degree of restraint. Not, as has been grossly suggested, that it was required of him as a task to talk for the entertainment of them and their company; but that he was not quite at his ease; which, however, might partly be owing to his own honest pride—that dignity of mind which is always jealous of appearing too compliant.

On Wednesday, April 10, I dined with him at Mr. Thrale's, where were Mr. Murphy and some other company. Before dinner, Dr. Johnson and I passed some time by ourselves. I was sorry to find it was now resolved that the proposed journey to Italy should not take place this year. He said, 'I am disappointed, to be sure; but it is not a great disappointment.' I wondered to see him bear, with a philosophical calmness, what would have made most people peevish and fretful. I perceived, however, that he had so warmly cherished the hope of enjoying classical scenes, that he could not easily part

[1] *Imlac:* the friend and tutor who accompanies Prince Rasselas in Johnson's novel, *Rasselas.*

with the scheme; for he said, 'I shall probably contrive to get to Italy some other way. But I won't mention it to Mr. and Mrs. Thrale, as it might vex them.' I suggested, that going to Italy might have done Mr. and Mrs. Thrale good. *Johnson:* 'I rather believe not, Sir. While grief is fresh, every attempt to divert only irritates. You must wait till grief be *digested,* and then amusement will dissipate the remains of it.'

I said, I disliked the custom which some people had of bringing their children into company, because it in a manner forced us to pay foolish compliments to please their parents. *Johnson:* 'You are right, Sir. We may be excused for not caring much about other people's children, for there are many who care very little about their own children. It may be observed, that men, who from being engaged in business, or from their course of life in whatever way, seldom see their children, do not care much about them. I myself should not have had much fondness for a child of my own.' *Mrs. Thrale:* 'Nay, Sir, how can you talk so?' *Johnson:* 'At least, I never wished to have a child.'

Johnson mentioned Dr. Barry's System of Physick. 'He was a man (said he,) who had acquired a high reputation in Dublin, came over to England, and brought his reputation with him, but had not great success. His notion was, that pulsation occasions death by attrition; and that, therefore, the way to preserve life is to retard pulsation. But we know that pulsation is strongest in infants, and that we increase in growth while it operates in its regular course; so it cannot be the cause of destruction.' Soon after this, he said something very flattering to Mrs. Thrale, which I do not recollect; but it concluded with wishing her long life. 'Sir, (said I,) if Dr. Barry's system be true, you have now shortened Mrs. Thrale's life, perhaps, some minutes, by accelerating her pulsation.'

On Thursday, April 11, I dined with him at General Paoli's, in whose house I now resided, and where I had ever afterwards the honour of being entertained with the kindest attention as his constant guest, while I was in London, till I had a house of my own there. I mentioned my having that morning introduced to Mr. Garrick, Count Neni, a Flemish Nobleman of great rank and fortune, to whom Garrick talked of Abel Drugger as *a small part*. Garrick added, with an appearance of grave recollection, 'If I were to begin life again, I think I should not play those low characters.' Upon which I observed, 'Sir, you would be in the wrong; for your great excellence is your variety of playing, your representing so well, characters so very different.' *Johnson:* 'Garrick, Sir, was not in earnest in what he said; for, to be sure, his peculiar excellence is his variety: and, perhaps, there is not any one character which has not been as well acted by somebody else, as he could do it.' *Boswell:* 'Why then, Sir, did he talk so?' *Johnson:* 'Why, Sir, to make you answer as you did.'

Of a nobleman raised at a very early period to high office, he said, 'His parts, Sir, are pretty well for a Lord; but would not be distinguished in a man who had nothing else but his parts.'

Soon after this day, he went to Bath with Mr. and Mrs. Thrale. I had never seen that beautiful city, and wished to take the opportunity of visiting it, while Johnson was there.

On the 26th of April, I went to Bath; and on my arrival at the Pelican inn, found lying for me an obliging invitation from Mr. and Mrs. Thrale, by whom I was agreeably entertained almost constantly during my stay. They were gone to the rooms; but there was a kind note from Dr. Johnson, that he should sit at home all the evening. I went to him directly, and before Mr. and Mrs. Thrale returned, we had by ourselves some hours of tea-drinking and talk.

It having been mentioned, I know not with what truth, that a certain female political writer, whose doctrines he disliked, had of late become very fond of dress, sat hours together at her toilet, and even put on rouge:—*Johnson:* 'She is better employed at her toilet, than using her pen. It is better she should be reddening her own cheeks, than blackening other people's characters.'

A literary lady of large fortune was mentioned, as one who did good to many, but by no means 'by stealth,' and instead of 'blushing to find it fame,' acted evidently from vanity. *Johnson:* 'I have seen no beings who do as much good from benevolence, as she does, from whatever motive. If there are such under the earth, or in the clouds, I wish they would come up, or come down. No, Sir; to act from pure benevolence is not possible for finite beings. Human benevolence is mingled with vanity, interest, or some other motive.'

After Dr. Johnson's return to London, I was several times with him at his house, where I occasionally slept, in the room that had been assigned to me. I dined with him at Dr. Taylor's, at General Oglethorpe's, and at General Paoli's. To avoid a tedious minuteness, I shall group together what I have preserved of his conversation during this period also, without specifying each scene where it passed, except one, which will be found so remarkable as certainly to deserve a very particular relation.

A gentleman, whom I found sitting with him one morning, said, that in his opinion the character of an infidel was more detestable than that of a man notoriously guilty of an atrocious crime. I differed from him, because we are surer of the odiousness of the one, than of the errour of the other. *Johnson:* 'Sir, I agree with him; for the infidel would be guilty of any crime if he were inclined to it.'

When I complained of having dined at a splendid table without hearing one sentence of conversation worthy of being remembered, he said, 'Sir, there seldom is any such conversation.' *Boswell:* 'Why then meet at table?' *Johnson:* 'Why to eat and drink together, and to promote kindness; and, Sir, this is better done when there is no solid conversation; for when there is, people differ in opinion, and get into bad humour, or some of the company who are not capable of such conversation, are left out, and feel themselves uneasy. It was for this reason, Sir Robert Walpole said, he always talked bawdy at his table, because in that all could join.'

Being irritated by hearing a gentleman ask Mr. Levet a variety of questions concerning him, when he was sitting by, he broke out, 'Sir, you have but two topicks, yourself and me. I am sick of both.'

 ## Chapter 9

Wilkes, Dodd, and Others

I am now to record a very curious incident in Dr. Johnson's Life, which fell under my own observation, and which I am persuaded will, with the liberal-minded, be much to his credit.

My desire of being acquainted with celebrated men of every description, had made me, much about the same time, obtain an introduction to Dr. Samuel Johnson and to John Wilkes, Esq. Two men more different could perhaps not be selected out of all mankind. They had even attacked one another with some asperity in their writings; yet I lived in habits of friendship with both. I could fully relish the excellence of each; for I have ever delighted in that intellectual chymistry, which can separate good qualities from evil in the same person.

I conceived an irresistible wish, if possible, to bring Dr. Johnson and Mr. Wilkes together. How to manage it, was a nice and difficult matter.

My worthy booksellers and friends, Messieurs Dilly in the Poultry, at whose hospitable and well-covered table I have seen a greater number of literary men, than at any other, except that of Sir Joshua Reynolds, had invited me to meet Mr. Wilkes and some more gentlemen on Wednesday, May 15. 'Pray (said I,) let us have Dr. Johnson.'— 'What, with Mr. Wilkes? not for the world, (said Mr. Edward Dilly:) Dr. Johnson would never forgive me.'—'Come, (said I,) if you'll let me negociate for you, I will be answerable that all shall go well.' *Dilly:* 'Nay, if you will take it upon you, I am sure I shall be very happy to see them both here.'

Notwithstanding the high veneration which I entertained for Dr. Johnson, I was sensible that he was sometimes a little actuated by the spirit of contradiction, and by means of that I hoped I should gain my point. I was persuaded that if I had come upon him with a direct proposal, 'Sir, will you dine in company with Jack Wilkes?' he would have flown into a passion, and would probably have answered, 'Dine with Jack Wilkes, Sir! I'd as soon dine

with Jack Ketch.'[1] I therefore, while we were sitting quietly by ourselves at his house in an evening, took occasion to open my plan thus:—'Mr. Dilly, Sir, sends his respectful compliments to you, and would be happy if you would do him the honour to dine with him on Wednesday next along with me, as I must soon go to Scotland.' *Johnson:* 'Sir, I am obliged to Mr. Dilly. I will wait upon him—' *Boswell:* 'Provided, Sir, I suppose, that the company which he is to have, is agreeable to you.' *Johnson:* 'What do you mean, Sir? What do you take me for? Do you think I am so ignorant of the world, as to imagine that I am to prescribe to a gentleman what company he is to have at his table?' *Boswell:* 'I beg your pardon, Sir, for wishing to prevent you from meeting people whom you might not like. Perhaps he may have some of what he calls his patriotick friends with him.' *Johnson:* 'Well, Sir, and what then? What care I for his *patriotick friends?* Poh!' *Boswell:* 'I should not be surprized to find Jack Wilkes there.' *Johnson:* 'And if Jack Wilkes *should* be there, what is that to *me,* Sir? My dear friend, let us have no more of this. I am sorry to be angry with you; but really it is treating me strangely to talk to me as if I could not meet any company whatever, occasionally.' *Boswell:* 'Pray forgive me, Sir: I meant well. But you shall meet whoever comes, for me.' Thus I secured him, and told Dilly that

[1] Jack Ketch: a seventeenth-century executioner famed for his brutality.

he would find him very well pleased to be one of his guests on the day appointed.

Upon the much-expected Wednesday, I called on him about half an hour before dinner, as I often did when we were to dine out together, to see that he was ready in time, and to accompany him. I found him buffeting his books, as upon a former occasion, covered with dust, and making no preparation for going abroad. 'How is this, Sir? (said I.) Don't you recollect that you are to dine at Mr. Dilly's?' *Johnson:* 'Sir, I did not think of going to Dilly's: it went out of my head. I have ordered dinner at home with Mrs. Williams.' *Boswell:* 'But, my dear Sir, you know you were engaged to Mr. Dilly, and I told him so. He will expect you, and will be much disappointed if you don't come.' *Johnson:* 'You must talk to Mrs. Williams about this.'

Here was a sad dilemma. I feared that what I was so confident I had secured would yet be frustrated. He had accustomed himself to shew Mrs. Williams such a degree of humane attention, as frequently imposed some restraint upon him; and I knew that if she should be obstinate, he would not stir. I hastened down stairs to the blind lady's room, and told her I was in great uneasiness, for Dr. Johnson had engaged to me to dine this day at Mr. Dilly's, but that he had told me he had forgotten his engagement, and had ordered dinner at home. 'Yes, Sir, (said she, pretty peevishly,) Dr. Johnson is to dine at home.'—'Madam, (said I,) his respect for you is such, that I know he will not leave you unless you absolutely desire it. But as you have so much of his company, I hope you will be good enough to forego it for a day; as Mr. Dilly is a very worthy man, has frequently had agreeable parties at his house for Dr. Johnson, and will be vexed if the Doctor neglects him today. And then, Madam, be pleased to consider my situation; I carried the message, and I assured Mr. Dilly that Dr. Johnson was to come, and no doubt he has made a dinner, and invited a company, and boasted of the honour he expected to have. I shall be quite disgraced if the Doctor is not there.' She gradually softened to my solicitations, which were certainly as earnest as most entreaties to ladies upon any occasion, and was graciously pleased to empower me to tell Dr. Johnson, 'That all things considered, she thought he should certainly go.' I flew back to him still in dust, and careless of what should be the event, 'indifferent in his choice to go or stay'; but as soon as I had announced to him Mrs. Williams' consent, he roared, 'Frank, a clean shirt,' and was very soon drest. When I had him fairly seated in a hackney-coach with me, I exulted as much as a fortune-hunter who has got an heiress into a post-chaise with him to set out for Gretna-Green.[1]

[1] Gretna-Green: a village just over the border in Scotland; for some time known as the usual place for eloping couples to marry in haste.

When we entered Mr. Dilly's drawing room, he found himself in the midst of a company he did not know. I kept myself snug and silent, watching how he would conduct himself. I observed him whispering to Mr. Dilly, 'Who is that gentleman, Sir?'—'Mr. Arthur Lee.'—*Johnson:* 'Too, too, too,' (under his breath,) which was one of his habitual mutterings. Mr. Arthur Lee could not but be very obnoxious to Johnson, for he was not only a *patriot* but an *American*. He was afterwards minister from the United States at the court of Madrid. 'And who is the gentleman in lace?'—'Mr. Wilkes, Sir.' This information confounded him still more; he had some difficulty to restrain himself, and taking up a book, sat down upon a window-seat and read, or at least kept his eye upon it intently for some time, till he composed himself. His feelings, I dare say, were aukward enough. But he no doubt recollected his having rated me for supposing that he could be at all disconcerted by any company, and he, therefore, resolutely set himself to behave quite as an easy man of the world, who could adapt himself at once to the disposition and manners of those whom he might chance to meet.

The cheering sound of 'Dinner is upon the table,' dissolved his reverie, and we *all* sat down without any symptom of ill humour. Mr. Wilkes placed himself next to Dr. Johnson, and behaved to him with so much attention and politeness, that he gained upon him insensibly. No man

eat more heartily than Johnson, or loved better what was nice and delicate. Mr. Wilkes was very assiduous in helping him to some fine veal. 'Pray give me leave, Sir:—It is better here—A little of the brown—Some fat, Sir—A little of the stuffing —Some gravy—Let me have the pleasure of giving you some butter—Allow me to recommend a squeeze of this orange;—or the lemon, perhaps, may have more zest.'—'Sir, Sir, I am obliged to you, Sir,' cried Johnson, bowing, and turning his head to him with a look for some time of 'surly virtue,' but, in a short while, of complacency.

Foote being mentioned, Johnson said, 'He is not a good mimick.' One of the company added, 'A merry Andrew, a buffoon.' *Johnson:* 'But he has wit too, and is not deficient in ideas, or in fertility and variety of imagery, and not empty of reading; he has knowledge enough to fill up his part. One species of wit he has in an eminent degree, that of escape. You drive him into a corner with both hands; but he's gone, Sir, when you think you have got him— like an animal that jumps over your head. Then he has a great range for his wit; he never lets truth stand between him and a jest, and he is sometimes mighty coarse. Garrick is under many restraints from which Foote is free.' *Wilkes:* 'Garrick's wit is more like Lord Chesterfield's.' *Johnson:* 'The first time I was in company with Foote was at Fitzherbert's. Having no good opinion of the fellow, I was resolved not to be pleased; and it is very difficult to please a man against his will. I went on eating my dinner pretty sullenly, affecting not to mind him. But the dog was so very comical, that I was obliged to lay down my knife and fork, throw myself back upon my chair, and fairly laugh it out. No, Sir, he was irresistible. He upon one occasion experienced, in an extraordinary degree, the efficacy of his powers of entertaining. Amongst the many and various modes which he tried of getting money, he became a partner with a small-beer brewer, and he was to have a share of the profits for procuring customers amongst his numerous acquaintance. Fitzherbert was one who took his small-beer; but it was so bad that the servants resolved not to drink it. They were at some loss how to notify their resolution, being afraid of offending their master, who they knew liked Foote much as a companion. At last they fixed upon a little black boy, who was rather a favourite, to be their deputy, and deliver their remonstrance; and having invested him with the whole authority of the kitchen, he was to inform Mr. Fitzherbert, in all their names, upon a certain day, that they would drink Foote's small-beer no longer. On that day Foote happened to dine at Fitzherbert's, and this boy served at table; he was so delighted with Foote's stories, and merriment, and grimace, that when he went down stairs, he told them, "This is the finest man I have ever seen. I will not deliver your message. I will drink his small-beer." '

Mr. Wilkes remarked, that 'among all the bold flights of Shakspeare's imagination, the boldest was making Birnamwood march to Dunsinane; creating a wood where there never was a shrub; a wood in Scotland! ha! ha! ha!' And he also observed, that 'the clannish slavery of the Highlands of Scotland was the single exception to Milton's remark of "The Mountain Nymph, sweet Liberty," being worshipped in all hilly countries.'—'When I was at Inverary (said he,) on a visit to my old friend, Archibald, Duke of Argyle, his dependents congratulated me on being such a favourite of his Grace. I said, "It is then, gentlemen, truely lucky for me; for if I had displeased the Duke, and he had wished it, there is not a Campbell among you but would have been ready to bring John Wilkes's head to him in a charger." '

Mr. Arthur Lee mentioned some Scotch who had taken possession of a barren part of America, and wondered why they should choose it. *Johnson:* 'Why, sir, all barrenness is comparative. The *Scotch* would not know it to be barren.' *Boswell:* 'Come, come, he is flattering the English. You have now been in Scotland, Sir, and say if you did not see meat and drink enough there.' *Johnson:* 'Why yes, Sir; meat and drink enough to give the inhabitants sufficient strength to run away from home.' All these quick and lively sallies were said sportively, quite in jest, and with a smile, which showed that he meant only wit. Upon this topick he and Mr. Wilkes could perfectly assimilate; here was a bond of union between them, and I was conscious that as both of them had visited Caledonia, both were fully satisfied of the strange narrow ignorance of those who imagine that it is a land of famine. But they amused themselves with persevering in the old jokes. When I claimed a superiority for Scotland over England in one respect, that no man can be arrested there for a debt merely because another swears it against him; but there must first be the judgement of a court of law ascertaining its justice; and that a seizure of the person, before judgement is obtained, can take place only, if his creditor should swear that he is about to fly from the country. *Wilkes:* 'That, I should think, may be safely sworn of all the Scotch nation.' *Johnson* (to Mr. Wilkes): 'You must know, Sir, I lately took my friend Boswell and shewed him genuine civilised life in an English provincial town. I turned him loose at Lichfield, my native city, that he might see for once real civility: for you know he lives among savages in Scotland, and among rakes in London.' *Wilkes:* 'Except when he is with grave, sober, decent people like you and me.' *Johnson* (smiling): 'And we ashamed of him.'

This record, though by no means so perfect as I could wish, will serve to give a notion of a very curious interview, which was not only pleasing at the time, but had the agreeable and benignant effect of reconciling any animosity, and sweetening any acidity, which in the various

bustle of political contest, had been produced in the minds of two men, who though widely different, had so many things in common—classical learning, modern literature, wit, and humour, and ready repartee—that it would have been much to be regretted if they had been for ever at a distance from each other.

Mr. Burke gave me much credit for this successful *negociation;* and pleasantly said, that 'there was nothing to equal it in the whole history of the *Corps Diplomatique.'*

I attended Dr. Johnson home, and had the satisfaction to hear him tell Mrs. Williams how much he had been pleased with Mr. Wilkes's company, and what an agreeable day he had passed.

On the evening of the next day I took leave of him, being to set out for Scotland. I thanked him with great warmth for all his kindness. 'Sir, (said he,) you are very welcome. Nobody repays it with more.'

How very false is the notion which has gone round the world of the rough, and passionate, and harsh manners of this great and good man. That he had occasional sallies of heat of temper, and that he was sometimes, perhaps, too 'easily provoked' by absurdity and folly, and sometimes too desirous of triumph in colloquial contest, must be allowed. The quickness both of his perception and sensibility disposed him to sudden explosions of satire; to which his extraordinary readiness of wit was a strong and almost irresistible incitement. I admit that the beadle within him was often so eager to apply the lash, that the Judge had not time to consider the case with sufficient deliberation.

That he was occasionally remarkable for violence of temper may be granted: but let us ascertain the degree, and not let it be supposed that he was in a perpetual rage, and never without a club in his hand, to knock down every one who approached him. On the contrary, the truth is, that by much the greatest part of his time he was civil, obliging, nay, polite in the true sense of the word; so much so, that many gentlemen, who were long acquainted with him, never received, or even heard a strong expression from him.

The following letter concerning an Epitaph which he wrote for the monument of Dr. Goldsmith, in Westminster-Abbey, affords at once a proof of his unaffected modesty, his carelessness as to his own writings, and of the great respect which he entertained for the taste and judgement of the excellent and eminent person to whom it is addressed:

'To Sir Joshua Reynolds.

'Dear Sir,

'I have been kept away from you, I know not well how, and of these vexatious hindrances I know not when there will be an end. I therefore send you the poor dear Doctor's epitaph. Read it first yourself; and if you then think it right, shew it to the Club. I am, you know, willing to be corrected. If you think any thing much amiss, keep it to yourself, till we come together. I have sent two copies, but prefer the card. The dates must be settled by Dr. Percy.

'I am, Sir,
'Your most humble servant,
'Sam. Johnson.'

On Sunday evening, September 14, 1777, I arrived at Ashbourne, and drove directly up to Dr. Taylor's door. Dr. Johnson and he appeared before I had got out of the post-chaise, and welcomed me cordially.

I told them that I had travelled all the preceding night, and gone to bed at Leek in Staffordshire; and that when I rose to go to church in the afternoon, I was informed there had been an earthquake, of which, it seems, the shock had been felt, in some degree, at Ashbourne. *Johnson:* 'Sir, it will be much exaggerated in popular talk: for, in the first place, the common people do not accurately adapt their thoughts to the objects; nor, secondly, do they accurately adapt their words to their thoughts: they do not mean to lie; but, taking no pains to be exact, they give you very false accounts. A great part of their language is proverbial. If anything rocks at all, they say *it rocks like a cradle;* and in this way they go on.'

The subject of grief for the loss of relations and friends being introduced, I observed that it was strange to consider how soon it in general wears away. Dr. Taylor mentioned a gentleman of the neighbourhood as the only instance he had ever known of a person who had endeavoured to *retain* grief. He told

Dr. Taylor, that after his Lady's death, which affected him deeply, he *resolved* that the grief, which he cherished with a kind of sacred fondness, should be lasting; but that he found he could not keep it long. *Johnson:* 'All grief for what cannot in the course of nature be helped, soon wears away; in some sooner, indeed, in some later; but it never continues very long, unless where there is madness, such as will make a man have pride so fixed in his mind, as to imagine himself a King; or any other passion in an unreasonable way: for all unnecessary grief is unwise, and therefore will not be long retained by a sound mind. If, indeed, the cause of our grief is occasioned by our own misconduct, if grief is mingled with remorse of conscience, it should be lasting.' *Boswell:* 'But, Sir, we do not approve of a man who very soon forgets the loss of a wife or a friend.' *Johnson:* 'Sir, we disapprove of him, not because he soon forgets his grief, for the sooner it is forgotten the better, but because we suppose, that if he forgets his wife or his friend soon, he has not had much affection for them.'

I was somewhat disappointed in finding that the edition of the English Poets, for which he was to write Prefaces and Lives, was not an undertaking directed by him: but that he was to furnish a Preface and Life to any poet the booksellers pleased. I asked him if he would do this to any dunce's works, if they should ask him. *Johnson:* 'Yes, Sir; and *say* he was a dunce.' My friend seemed now not much to relish talking of this edition.

And here is the proper place to give an account of Johnson's humane and zealous interference in behalf of the Reverend Dr. William Dodd, formerly Prebendary of Brecon, and chaplain in ordinary to his Majesty; celebrated as a very popular preacher, an encourager of charitable institutions, and authour of a variety of works, chiefly theological. Having unhappily contracted expensive habits of living, partly occasioned by licentiousness of manners, he in an evil hour, when pressed by want of money, and dreading an exposure of his circumstances, forged a bond of which he attempted to avail himself to support his credit, flattering himself with hopes that he might be able to repay its amount without being detected. The person, whose name he thus rashly and criminally presumed to falsify, was the Earl of Chesterfield, to whom he had been tutor, and who, he perhaps, in the warmth of his feelings, flattered himself would have generously paid the money in case of an alarm being taken, rather than suffer him to fall a victim to the dreadful consequences of violating the law against forgery, the most dangerous crime in a commercial country; but the unfortunate divine had the mortification to find that he was mistaken. His noble pupil appeared against him, and he was capitally convicted.

Johnson told me that Dr. Dodd was very little acquainted with him, having been but once in his company, many years previous to this period (which was precisely the state of my own acquaintance with Dodd); but in his distress he bethought himself of Johnson's persuasive power of writing, if haply it might avail to obtain for him the Royal Mercy. He did not apply to him directly, but, extraordinary as it may seem, through the late Countess of Harrington, who wrote a letter to Johnson, asking him to employ his pen in favour of Dodd. Mr. Allen, the printer, who was Johnson's landlord and next neighbour in Bolt-court, and for whom he had much kindness, was one of Dodd's friends, of whom, to the credit of humanity be it recorded, that he had many who did not desert him, even after his infringement of the law had reduced him to the state of a man under sentence of death. Mr. Allen told me that he carried Lady Harrington's letter to Johnson, that Johnson read it walking up and down his chamber, and seemed much agitated, after which he said, 'I will do what I can';—and certainly he did make extraordinary exertions.

Dr. Johnson wrote in the first place, Dr. Dodd's 'Speech to the Recorder of London,' at the Old-Bailey, when sentence of death was about to be pronounced upon him.

He wrote also 'The Convict's Address to his unhappy Brethren,' a sermon delivered by Dr. Dodd, in the chapel of Newgate.

The other pieces written by Johnson in the above-mentioned collection, are two letters, one to the Lord Chancellor Bathurst, (not Lord North, as is erroneously supposed,) and one to Lord Mansfield;—A Petition from Dr. Dodd to the King;—A Petition from Mrs. Dodd to the Queen;—Observations of some length inserted in the newspapers, on occasion of Earl Percy's having presented to his Majesty a petition for mercy to Dodd, signed by twenty thousand people, but all in vain. He told me that he had also written a petition from the city of London;[1] 'but (said he, with a significant smile) they *mended* it.'

The last of these articles which Johnson wrote is 'Dr. Dodd's last solemn Declaration,' which he left with the sheriff at the place of execution. My friend marked the variations on a copy of that piece now in my possession. Dodd inserted, 'I never knew or attended to the calls of frugality, or the needful minuteness of painful œconomy'; and in the next sentence he introduced the words which I distinguish by *Italicks;* 'My life for some *few unhappy* years past has been *dreadfully erroneous.*' Johnson's expression was *hypocritical;* but his remark on the margin is 'With this he said he could not charge himself.'

On Sunday, June 22, he writes, begging Dr. Johnson's assistance in framing a supplicatory letter to his Majesty:

'If his Majesty could be moved of his royal clemency to spare me and

---

[1] city of London: represented by hard-headed businessmen who would take a harsh view of forgery.

my family the horrours and ignominy of a *publick death,* which the *publick* itself is solicitous to wave, and to grant me in some silent distant corner of the globe, to pass the remainder of my days in penitence and prayer, I would bless his clemency and be humbled.'

This letter was brought to Dr. Johnson when in church. He stooped down and read it, and wrote, when he went home, the following letter for Dr. Dodd to the King:

'Sir,

'May it not offend your Majesty, that the most miserable of men applies himself to your clemency, as his last hope and his last refuge; that your mercy is most earnestly and humbly implored by a clergyman, whom your Laws and Judges have condemned to the horrour and ignominy of a publick execution.

'I confess the crime, and own the enormity of its consequences, and the danger of its example. Nor have I the confidence to petition for impunity; but humbly hope, that publick security may be established, without the spectacle of a clergyman dragged through the streets, to a death of infamy, amidst the derision of the profligate and profane; and that justice may be satisfied with irrevocable exile, perpetual disgrace, and hopeless penury.

'My life, Sir, has not been useless to mankind. I have benefited many. But my offences against GOD are numberless, and I have had little time for repentance. Preserve me, Sir, by your prerogative of mercy, from the necessity of appearing unprepared at that tribunal, before which Kings and Subjects must stand at last together. Permit me to hide my guilt in some obscure corner of a foreign country, where, if I can ever attain confidence to hope that my prayers will be heard, they shall be poured with all the fervour of gratitude for the life and happiness of your Majesty. I am, Sir,

'Your Majesty's, &c.'

All applications for the Royal Mercy having failed, Dr. Dodd prepared himself for death; and, with a warmth of gratitude, wrote to Dr. Johnson as follows:

'June 25, *Midnight.*

'Accept, thou *great* and *good* heart, my earnest and fervent thanks and prayers for all thy benevolent and kind efforts in my behalf.—Oh! Dr. Johnson! as I sought your knowledge at an early hour in life, would to heaven I had cultivated the love and acquaintance of so excellent a man!— I pray GOD most sincerely to bless you with the highest transports—the infelt satisfaction of *humane* and benevolent exertions!—And admitted, as I trust I shall be, to the realms of bliss before you, I shall hail *your* arrival there with transport, and rejoice to acknowledge that you was my Comforter, my Advocate, and my *Friend!* GOD *be ever* with *you!*'

Dr. Johnson lastly wrote to Dr. Dodd this solemn and soothing letter:

'*To the Reverend Dr. Dodd.*

'Dear Sir,

'That which is appointed to all men is now coming upon you. Outward circumstances, the eyes and the thoughts of men, are below the notice of an immortal being about to stand the trial for eternity, before the Supreme Judge of heaven and earth. Be comforted: your crime, morally or religiously considered, has no very deep dye of turpitude. It corrupted no man's principles; it attacked no man's life. It involved only a temporary and reparable injury. Of this, and of all other sins, you are earnestly to repent; and may GOD, who knoweth our frailty, and desireth not our death accept your repentance, for the sake of His Son JESUS CHRIST our Lord.

'In requital of those well-intended offices which you are pleased so emphatically to acknowledge, let me beg that you make in your devotions one petition for my eternal welfare. I am, dear Sir,

'Your affectionate servant,
'Sam. Johnson.'
'June 26, 1777.'

Under the copy of this letter I found written, in Johnson's own hand, 'Next day, June 27, he was executed.'

Tuesday, September 16, Dr. Johnson having mentioned to me the extraordinary size and price of some cattle reared by Dr. Taylor, I rode out with our host, surveyed his farm, and was shown one cow which he had sold for a hundred and twenty guineas, and another for which he had been offered a hundred and thirty. Taylor thus described to me his old schoolfellow and friend, Johnson: 'He is a man of a very clear head, great power of words, and a very gay imagination; but there is no disputing with him. He will not hear you, and having a louder voice than you, must roar you down.'

I mentioned to Dr. Johnson, that David Hume's persisting in his infidelity, when he was dying, shocked me much. *Johnson:* 'Why should it shock you, Sir? Hume owned he had never read the New Testament with attention. Here then was a man, who had been at no pains to inquire into the truth of religion, and had continually turned his mind the other way. It was not to be expected that the prospect of death would alter his way of thinking, unless GOD should send an angel to set him right.' I said, I had reason to believe that the thought of annihilation gave Hume no pain. *Johnson:* 'It was not so, Sir. He had a vanity in being thought easy.' The horrour of death which I had always observed in Dr. Johnson, appeared strong to-night. I ventured to tell him, that I had been, for moments in my life, not afraid of death; therefore I could suppose another man in that state of mind for a considerable space of time. He said, 'he never had a moment in which death was not terrible to him.' He added, that it had been observed, that scarce any man dies in publick, but with apparent resolution; from that desire of praise which never quits us. I said, Dr. Dodd seemed to be willing to die, and full of hopes of happiness. 'Sir, (said he,) Dr. Dodd would have given both his hands and both his legs to have lived.'

Dr. Johnson was much pleased with a remark which I told him was made to me by General Paoli;— 'That it is impossible not to be afraid of death; and that those who at the time of dying are not afraid, are not thinking of death, but of applause, or something else, which keeps death out of their sight: so that all men are equally afraid of death when they see it; only some have a power of turning their sight away from it better than others.'

Talking of biography, I said, in writing a life, a man's peculiarities should be mentioned, because they mark his character. *Johnson:* 'Sir, there is no doubt as to peculiarities: the question is, whether a man's vices should be mentioned; for instance, whether it should be mentioned that Addison and Parnell drank too freely: for people will probably more easily indulge in drinking from knowing this; so that more ill may be done by the example, than good by telling the whole truth.' Here was an instance of his varying from himself in talk; for when Lord Hailes and he sat one morning calmly conversing in my house at Edinburgh, I well remember that Dr. Johnson maintained, that 'If a man is to write *A Panegyrick,*[1] he may keep vices out of sight; but if he professes to write *A Life,* he must represent it really as it was': and when I objected to the danger of telling that Parnell drank to excess, he said, that 'it would produce an instructive caution to avoid drinking, when it was seen, that even the learning and genius of Parnell could be debased

[1] *Panegyrick:* a work overtly in praise of someone.

by it.' And in the Hebrides he maintained, as appears from my 'Journal,' that a man's intimate friend should mention his faults, if he writes his life.

Johnson and Taylor were so different from each other, that I wondered at their preserving such an intimacy. Their having been at school and college together, might, in some degree, account for this; but Sir Joshua Reynolds has furnished me with a stronger reason; for Johnson mentioned to him, that he had been told by Taylor he was to be his heir. I shall not take upon me to animadvert upon this; but certain it is, that Johnson paid great attention to Taylor. He now, however, said to me, 'Sir, I love him; but I do not love him more; my regard for him does not increase. As it is said in the Apocrypha, "his talk is of bullocks"; I do not suppose he is very fond of my company. His habits are by no means sufficiently clerical: this he knows that I see; and no man likes to live under the eye of perpetual disapprobation.'

I have no doubt that a good many sermons were composed for Taylor by Johnson. Johnson was by no means of opinion, that every man of a learned profession should consider it as incumbent upon him, or as necessary to his credit, to appear as an authour. When in the ardour of ambition for literary fame, I regretted to him one day that an eminent Judge had nothing of it, and therefore would leave no perpetual monument of himself to posterity, 'Alas, Sir, (said Johnson,) what a mass of confusion should we have, if every Bishop, and every Judge, every Lawyer, Physician, and Divine, were to write books.'

On Monday, September 22, when at breakfast, I unguardedly said to Dr. Johnson, 'I wish I saw you and Mrs. Macaulay together.' He grew very angry; and after a pause, while a cloud gathered on his brow, he burst out, 'No, Sir; you would not see us quarrel, to make you sport. Don't you know that it is very uncivil to *pit* two people against one another?' Then, checking himself, and wishing to be more gentle, he added, 'I do not say you should be hanged or drowned for this; but it *is* very uncivil.' Dr. Taylor thought him in the wrong, and spoke to him privately of it; but I afterwards acknowledged to Johnson that I was to blame, for I candidly owned, that I meant to express a desire to see a contest between Mrs. Macaulay and him; but then I knew how the contest would end; so that I was to see him triumph. *Johnson:* 'Sir, you cannot be sure how a contest will end; and no man has a right to engage two people in a dispute by which their passions may be inflamed, and they may part with bitter resentment against each other. I would sooner keep company with a man from whom I must guard my pockets, than with a man who contrives to bring me into a dispute with somebody that he may hear it.'

He found great fault with a gentleman of our acquaintance for keeping a bad table. 'Sir, (said he,) when a man is invited to dinner, he is disappointed if he does not get something good. I advised Mrs. Thrale, who has no card-parties at her house, to give sweet-meats, and such good things, in an evening, as are not commonly given, and she would find company enough come to her; for every body loves to have things which please the palate put in their way, without trouble or preparation.' Such was his attention to the *minutiæ* of life and manners.

He thus characterised the Duke of Devonshire, grandfather of the present representative of that very respectable family: 'He was not a man of superiour abilities, but he was a man strictly faithful to his word. If, for instance, he had promised you an acorn, and none had grown that year in his woods, he would not have contented himself with that excuse; he would have sent to Denmark for it. So unconditional was he in keeping his word; so high as to the point of honour.' This was a liberal testimony from the Tory Johnson to the virtue of a great Whig nobleman.

Mr. Burke's 'Letter to the Sheriffs of Bristol, on the affairs of America,' being mentioned, Johnson censured the composition much, and he ridiculed the definition of a free government, *viz.,* 'For any practical purpose, it is what the people think so.—I will let the King of France govern me on those conditions, (said he,) for it is to be governed just as I please.' And when

Dr. Taylor talked of a girl being sent to a parish workhouse, and asked how much she could be obliged to work, 'Why, (said Johnson,) as much as is reasonable: and what is that? as much as *she thinks* reasonable.'

Dr. Johnson obligingly proposed to carry me to see Islam, a romantick scene, now belonging to a family of the name of Port, but formerly the seat of the Congreves. Johnson described it distinctly and vividly, at which I could not but express to him my wonder; because, though my eyes, as he observed, were better than his, I could not by any means equal him in representing visible objects. I said, the difference between us in this respect was as that between a man who has a bad instrument, but plays well on it, and a man who has a good instrument, on which he can play very imperfectly.

In the evening, a gentleman-farmer, who was on a visit at Dr. Taylor's, attempted to dispute with Johnson in favour of Mungo Campbell, who shot Alexander, Earl of Eglintoune, upon his having fallen, when retreating from his Lordship, who he believed was about to seize his gun, as he had threatened to do. He said, he should have done just as Campbell did. *Johnson:* 'Whoever would do as Campbell did, deserves to be hanged; not that I could, as a juryman, have found him legally guilty of murder; but I am glad they found means to convict him.' The gentleman-farmer said, 'A poor man has as much

honour as a rich man; and Campbell had *that* to defend.' Johnson exclaimed, 'A poor man has no honour.' The English yeoman, not dismayed, proceeded: 'Lord Eglintoune was a damned fool to run on upon Campbell, after being warned that Campbell would shoot him if he did.' Johnson, who could not bear any thing like swearing, angrily replied, 'He was *not* a *damned* fool: he only thought too well of Campbell. He did not believe Campbell would be such a *damned* scoundrel, as to do so *damned* a thing.' His emphasis on *damned,* accompanied with frowning looks, reproved his opponent's want of decorum in *his* presence.

During this interview at Ashbourne, Johnson seemed to be more uniformly social, cheerful, and alert, than I had almost ever seen him. He was prompt on great occasions and on small.

One morning after breakfast, when the sun shone bright, we walked out together, and 'pored' for some time with placid indolence upon an artificial water-fall, which Dr. Taylor had made by building a strong dyke of stone across the river behind his garden. It was now somewhat obstructed by branches of trees and other rubbish, which had come down the river, and settled close to it. Johnson, partly from a desire to see it play more freely, and partly from that inclination to activity which will animate, at times, the most inert and sluggish mortal, took a long pole which was lying on the bank, and pushed down several parcels of this wreck with painful assiduity, while I stood quietly by, wondering to behold the sage thus curiously employed, and smiling with an humorous satisfaction each time when he carried his point. He worked till he was quite out of breath; and having found a large dead cat so heavy that he could not move it after several efforts, 'Come,' said he, (throwing down the pole,) *'you* shall take it now;' which I accordingly did, and being a fresh man, soon made the cat tumble over the cascade. This may be laughed at as too trifling to record; but it is a small characteristick trait in the Flemish picture which I give of my friend, and in which, therefore, I mark the most minute particulars.

On Tuesday, September 23, Johnson was remarkably cordial to me. It being necessary for me to return to Scotland soon, I had fixed on the next day for my setting out, and I felt a tender concern at the thought of parting with him. He had, at this time, frankly communicated to me many particulars, which are inserted in this work in their proper places; and once, when I happened to mention that the expence of my jaunt would come to much more than I had computed, he said, 'Why, Sir, if the expence were to be an inconvenience, you would have reason to regret it: but, if you have had the money to spend, I know not that you could have purchased as much pleasure with it in any other way.'

During this interview at Ash-bourne, Johnson and I frequently talked with wonderful pleasure of mere trifles which had occurred in our tour to the Hebrides; for it had left a most agreeable and lasting impression upon his mind.

He found fault with me for using the phrase to *make* money. 'Don't you see (said he) the impropriety of it? To *make* money is to *coin* it: you should say *get* money.' The phrase, however, is, I think, pretty current. But Johnson was at all times jealous of infractions upon the genuine English language, and prompt to repress colloquial barbarisms; such as, *pledging myself,* for *undertaking; line,* for *department* or *branch,* as, the *civil line,* the *banking line.* He was particularly indignant against the almost universal use of the word *idea* in the sense of *notion* or *opinion,* when it is clear that *idea* can only signify something of which an image can be formed in the mind. We may have an *idea* or *image* of a mountain, a tree, a building; but we cannot surely have an *idea* or *image* of an *argument* or *proposition.* Yet we hear the sages of the law 'delivering their *ideas* upon the question under consideration'; and the first speakers in parliament 'entirely coinciding in the *idea* which has been ably stated by an honourable member';—or 'reprobating an *idea* unconstitutional, and fraught with the most dangerous consequences to a great and free country.' Johnson called this 'modern cant.'

I perceived that he pronounced the word *heard,* as if spelt with a double *e, heerd,* instead of sounding it *herd,* as is most usually done. He said, his reason was, that if it were pronounced *herd,* there would be a single exception from the English pronunciation of the syllable *ear,* and he thought it better not to have that exception.

In the evening our gentleman-farmer, and two others, entertained themselves and the company with a great number of tunes on the fiddle. Johnson desired to have 'Let ambition fire thy mind,' played over again, and appeared to give a patient attention to it; though he owned to me that he was very insensible to the power of musick. I told him, that it affected me to such a degree, as often to agitate my nerves painfully, producing in my mind alternate sensations of pathetick dejection, so that I was ready to shed tears; and of daring resolution, so that I was inclined to rush into the thickest part of the battle. 'Sir, (said he,) I should never hear it, if it made me such a fool.'

This evening, while some of the tunes of ordinary composition were played with no great skill, my frame was agitated, and I was conscious of a generous attachment to Dr. Johnson, as my preceptor and friend, mixed with an affectionate regret that he was an old man, whom I should probably lose in a short time. I said to him, 'My dear Sir, we must meet every year, if you don't quarrel with me.' *Johnson:* 'Nay, Sir, you are more likely to quarrel with me, than I with you. My regard for you is greater almost than I have words to express; but I do not choose to be always repeating it; write it down in the first leaf of your pocket-book, and never doubt of it again.'

After supper I accompanied him to his apartment, and at my request he dictated to me an argument in favour of the Negro who was then claiming his liberty, in an action in the Court of Session in Scotland. He had always been very zealous against slavery in every form, in which I with all deference thought that he discovered 'a zeal without knowledge.' Upon one occasion, when in company with some very grave men at Oxford, his toast was, 'Here's to the next insurrection of the Negroes in the West Indies.' His violent prejudice against our West Indian and American settlers appeared whenever there was an opportunity. Towards the conclusion of his 'Taxation no Tyranny,' he says, 'how is it that we hear the loudest *yelps* for liberty among the drivers of Negroes?'

When I said now to Johnson, that I was afraid I kept him too late up, 'No, Sir, (said he,) I don't care though I sit all night with you.' This was an animated speech from a man in his sixty-ninth year.

Had I been as attentive not to displease him as I ought to have been, I know not but this vigil might have been fulfilled; but I unluckily entered upon the controversy concerning the right of Great-Britain to tax America, and attempted to argue in favour of our fellow-subjects on the other side of the Atlantick. I insisted that America might be very well governed, and made to yield a sufficient revenue by the means of *influence,* as exemplified in Ireland, while the people might be pleased with the imagination of their participating of the British constitution, by having a body of representatives, without whose consent money could not be exacted from them. Johnson could not bear my thus opposing his avowed opinion, which he had exerted himself with an extreme degree of heat to enforce; and the violent agitation into which he was thrown, while answering, or rather reprimanding me, alarmed me so, that I heartily repented of my having unthinkingly introduced the subject. I myself, however, grew warm, and the change was great, from the calm state of philosophical discussion in which we had a little before been pleasingly employed.

We were fatigued by the contest, which was produced by my want of caution; and he was not then in the humour to slide into easy and cheerful talk. It therefore so happened, that we were after an hour or two very willing to separate and go to bed.

On Wednesday, September 24, I went into Dr. Johnson's room before he got up, and finding that the storm of the preceding night was quite laid, I sat down upon his bedside, and he talked with as much readiness and good-humour as ever.

After breakfast I departed, and pursued my journey northwards.

'To *James Boswell, Esq.*

'Dear Sir,

'I hope you found at your return my dear enemy and all her little people quite well, and had no reason to repent of your journey. I think on it with great gratitude.

'I was not well when you left me at the Doctor's, and I grew worse; yet I staid on, and at Lichfield was very ill. Traveling, however, did not make me worse; and when I came to London, I complied with a summons to go to Brighthelmston, where I saw Beauclerk, and staid three days.

'Our *Club* has recommenced last Friday, but I was not there. Langton has another wench.[1] Mrs. Thrale is in hopes of a young brewer. They got by their trade last year a very large sum, and their expences are proportionate.

'Mrs. Williams' health is very bad And I have had for some time a very difficult and laborious respiration; but I am better by purges, abstinence, and other methods. I am yet, however, much behind-hand in my health and rest.

'My dear friend, let me thank you once more for your visit; you did me great honour, and I hope met with nothing that displeased you. I staid long at Ashbourne, not much pleased, yet aukward at departing. I then went to Lichfield, where I found my friend at Stow-hill very dangerously diseased. Such is life. Let us try to pass it well, whatever it be, for there is surely something beyond it.

'Well, now I hope all is well, write as soon as you can to, dear Sir,

'Your affectionate servant,
'Sam. Johnson.'

'London, Nov. 25, 1777.'

---

1 wench: here, another child, a girl.

'There Is Nothing of the Old Man in My Conversation'

On Friday, March 20, I found him at his own house, sitting with Mrs. Williams, and was informed that the room formerly allotted to me was now appropriated to a charitable purpose; Mrs. Desmoulins, and I think her daughter, and a Miss Carmichael, being all lodged in it. Such was his humanity, and such his generosity, that Mrs. Desmoulins herself told me, he allowed her half-a-guinea a week. Let it be remembered, that this was above a twelfth part of his pension.

His liberality, indeed, was at all periods of his life very remarkable. Mr. Howard, of Lichfield, at whose father's house Johnson had in his early years been kindly received, told me, that when he was a boy at the Charter-House, his father wrote to him to go and pay a visit to Mr. Samuel Johnson, which he accordingly did, and found him in an upper room, of poor appearance. Johnson received him with much courteousness, and talked a great deal to him, as to a school-boy, of the course of his education, and other particulars. When he afterwards came to know and understand the high character of this great man, he recollected his condescension with wonder. He added,

that when he was going away, Mr. Johnson presented him with half-a-guinea; and this, said Mr. Howard, was at a time when he probably had not another.

We retired from Mrs. Williams to another room. Tom Davies soon after joined us. He had now unfortunately failed in his circumstances, and was much indebted to Dr. Johnson's kindness for obtaining for him many alleviations of his distress. After he went away, Johnson blamed his folly in quitting the stage, by which he and his wife got five hundred pounds a year. I said, I believed it was owing to Churchill's attack upon him,

'He mouths a sentence, as curs mouth a bone.'

Johnson: 'I believe so too, Sir. But what a man is he, who is to be driven from the stage by a line? Another line would have driven him from his shop.'

In my interview with Dr. Johnson this evening, I was quite easy, quite as his companion; upon which I find in my Journal the following reflection: 'So ready is my mind to suggest matter for dissatisfaction, that I felt a sort of regret that I was so easy. I missed that awful reverence with which I used to contemplate *Mr. Samuel Johnson,* in the complex magnitude of his literary, moral, and religious character. I have a wonderful superstitious love of *mystery.'*

He returned next day to Streatham, to Mr. Thrale's; where, as

Mr. Strahan once complained to me, 'he was in a great measure absorbed from the society of his old friends.' I was kept in London by business, and wrote to him on the 27th, that a separation from him for a week, when we were so near, was equal to a separation for a year, when we were at four hundred miles distance. I went to Streatham on Monday, March 30. Before he appeared, Mrs. Thrale made a very characteristical remark:—'I do not know for certain what will please Dr. Johnson: but I know for certain that it will displease him to praise any thing, even what he likes, extravagantly.'

I had before dinner repeated a ridiculous story told me by an old man who had been a passenger with me in the stage-coach to-day. Mrs. Thrale, having taken occasion to allude to it in talking to me, called it 'The story told you by the old *woman.*'—'Now, Madam, (said I,) give me leave to catch you in the fact: it was not an old *woman*, but an old *man*, whom I mentioned as having told me this.' I presumed to take an opportunity, in presence of Johnson, of shewing this lively lady how ready she was, unintentionally, to deviate from exact authenticity of narration.

Next morning, while we were at breakfast, Johnson gave a very earnest recommendation of what he himself practised with the utmost conscientiousness: I mean a strict attention to truth, even in the most minute particulars. 'Accustom your children (said he) constantly to this; if a thing happened at one window, and they, when relating it, say that it happened at another, do not let it pass, but instantly check them; you do not know where deviation from truth will end.' Our lively hostess, whose fancy was impatient of the rein, fidgeted at this, and ventured to say, 'Nay, this is too much. If Mr. Johnson should forbid me to drink tea, I would comply, as I should feel the restraint only twice a day; but little variations in narrative must happen a thousand times a day, if one is not perpetually watching.' *Johnson:* 'Well, Madam, and you *ought* to be perpetually watching. It is more from carelessness about truth than from intentional lying, that there is so much falsehood in the world.'

Talking of ghosts, he said, 'It is wonderful that five thousand years have now elapsed since the creation of the world, and still it is undecided whether or not there has ever been an instance of the spirit of any person appearing after death. All argument is against it; but all belief is for it.'

He said, 'John Wesley's conversation is good, but he is never at leisure. He is always obliged to go at a certain hour. This is very disagreeable to a man who loves to fold his legs and have out his talk, as I do.'

On Tuesday, April 7, I breakfasted with him at his house. He said, 'nobody was content.' I mentioned to him a respectable person in Scotland whom he knew. *Bos-*

well: 'He seems to amuse himself quite well; to have his attention fixed, and his tranquillity preserved by very small matters. I have tried this; but it would not do with me.' *Johnson* (laughing): 'No, Sir; it must be born with a man to be contented to take up with little things. Women have a great advantage that they may take up with little things, without disgracing themselves: a man cannot, except with fiddling. Had I learnt to fiddle, I should have done nothing else.' *Boswell:* 'Pray, Sir, did you ever play on any musical instrument?' *Johnson:* 'No, Sir. I once bought me a flagelet; but I never made out a tune.' *Boswell:* 'A flagelet, Sir!—so small an instrument? I should have liked to hear you play on the violoncello. *That* should have been *your* instrument.' *Johnson:* 'Sir, I might as well have played on the violoncello as another; but I should have done nothing else. No, Sir; a man would never undertake great things, could he be amused with small. I once tried knotting. Dempster's sister undertook to teach me; but I could not learn it.' He asked me to go down with him and dine at Mr. Thrale's at Streatham, to which I agreed.

Soon after our arrival at Thrale's, I heard one of the maids calling eagerly on another, to go to Dr. Johnson. I wondered what this could mean. I afterwards learnt, that it was to give her a Bible, which he had brought from London as a present to her.

He was for a considerable time occupied in reading *Mémoires de Fontenelle*, leaning and swinging upon the low gate into the court, without his hat.

At dinner, Mrs. Thrale expressed a wish to go and see Scotland. *Johnson:* 'Seeing Scotland, Madam, is only seeing a worse England. It is seeing the flower gradually fade away to the naked stalk. Seeing the Hebrides, indeed, is seeing quite a different scene.'

On Thursday, April 9, I dined with him at Sir Joshua Reynolds', with the Bishop of St. Asaph, (Dr. Shipley,) Mr. Allan Ramsay, Mr. Gibbon, Mr. Cambridge, and Mr. Langton. Mr. Ramsay had lately returned from Italy, and entertained us with his observations upon Horace's villa, which he had examined with great care. I relished this much, as it brought fresh into my mind what I had viewed with great pleasure thirteen years before. The Bishop, Dr. Johnson, and Mr. Cambridge, joined with Mr. Ramsay, in recollecting the various lines in Horace relating to the subject.

The Bishop said, it appeared from Horace's writings that he was a cheerful contented man. *Johnson:* 'We have no reason to believe that, my Lord. Are we to think Pope was happy, because he says so in his writings? We see in his writings what he wished the state of his mind to appear. Dr. Young, who pined for preferment, talks with contempt of it in his writings, and affects to despise every thing that he did not despise.' *Bishop of St. Asaph:* 'He was like other chaplains, looking for vacancies: but that is not peculiar to the clergy. I remember when I was with the army, after the battle of Lafeldt, the officers seriously grumbled that no general was killed.'

We talked of living in the country. *Johnson:* 'No wise man will go to live in the country, unless he has something to do which can be better done in the country. For instance: if he is to shut himself up for a year to study a science, it is better to look out to the fields, than to an opposite wall. Then, if a man walks out in the country, there is nobody to keep him from walking in again: but if a man walks out in London, he is not sure when he shall walk in again. A great city is, to be sure, the school for studying life; and "The proper study of mankind is man," as Pope observes.' *Boswell:* 'I fancy London is the best place in the world for society; though I have heard that the very first society of Paris is still beyond any thing that we have here.' *Johnson:* 'Sir, I question if in Paris such a company as is sitting round this table could be got together in less than half a year. They talk in France of the felicity of men and women living together: the truth is, that there the men are not higher than the women, they know no more than the women do, and they are not held down in their conversation by the presence of women. In England, any man who wears a sword and a powdered wig is ashamed to be illiterate. I believe it is not so in France. Yet there is,

probably, a great deal of learning in France, because they have such a number of religious establishments; so many men who have nothing else to do but to study. I do not know this; but I take it upon the common principles of chance. Where there are many shooters, some will hit.'

We talked of old age. Johnson (now in his seventieth year,) said, 'It is a man's own fault, it is from want of use, if his mind grows torpid in old age.' The Bishop asked, if an old man does not lose faster than he gets. *Johnson:* 'I think not, my Lord, if he exerts himself.' One of the company rashly observed, that he thought it was happy for an old man that insensibility comes upon him. *Johnson* (with a noble elevation and disdain,): 'No, Sir, I should never be happy by being less rational.'

This season there was a whimsical fashion in the news-papers of applying Shakspeare's words to describe living persons well known in the world; which was done under the title of *'Modern Characters from Shakspeare';* many of which were admirably adapted. The fancy took so much, that they were afterwards collected into a pamphlet. Somebody said to Johnson, across the table, that he had not been in those characters. 'Yes (said he) I have. I should have been sorry to be left out.' He then repeated what had been applied to him,

'I must borrow GARAGANTUA's mouth.'

Miss Reynolds not perceiving at once the meaning of this, he was obliged to explain it to her, which had something of an aukward and ludicrous effect. 'Why, Madam, it has a reference to me, as using big words, which require the mouth of a giant to pronounce them. Garagantua is the name of a giant in Rabelais.'

On Friday, April 10, I found Johnson at home in the morning. He was much pleased with my paying so great attention to his recommendation in 1763, the period when our acquaintance began, that I should keep a journal; and I could perceive he was secretly pleased to find so much of the fruit of his mind preserved; and as he had been used to imagine and say that he always laboured when he said a good thing — it delighted him, on a review, to find that his conversation teemed with point and imagery.

We dined together with Mr. Scott (now Sir William Scott, his Majesty's Advocate General,) at his chambers in the Temple, nobody else there. The company being small, Johnson was not in such spirits as he had been the preceding day, and for a considerable time little was said. At last he burst forth, 'Subordination is sadly broken down in this age. No man, now, has the same authority which his father had,—except a goaler. No master has it over his servants: it is diminished in our colleges; nay, in our grammar-schools.' Boswell: 'What is the cause of this,

Sir?' Johnson: 'Why the coming in of the Scotch,' (laughing sarcastically). Boswell: 'That is to say, things have been turned topsy turvey.—But your serious cause?' Johnson: 'Why, Sir, there are many causes, the chief of which is, I think, the great increase of money. No man now depends upon the Lord of a Manour, when he can send to another country, and fetch provisions. The shoe-black at the entry of my court does not depend on me. I can deprive him but of a penny a day, which he hopes somebody else will bring him; and that penny I must carry to another shoe-black, so the trade suffers nothing. But, besides, there is a general relaxation of reverence. No son now depends upon his father as in former times.'

I then slily introduced Mr. Garrick's fame, and his assuming the airs of a great man. Johnson: 'Sir, it is wonderful how *little* Garrick assumes. Consider, Sir: celebrated men, such as you have mentioned, have had their applause at a distance; but Garrick had it dashed in his face, sounded in his ears, and went home every night with the plaudits of a thousand in his *cranium*. Then, Sir, Garrick did not *find*, but *made* his way to the tables, the levees, and almost the bed-chambers of the great. Garrick has made a player a higher character.' Scott: 'And he is a very sprightly writer too.' Johnson: 'Yes, Sir; and all this supported by great wealth of his own acquisition. If all this had happened to me, I should have had a couple of fellows with long poles walking before me, to knock down every body that stood in the way. Yet Garrick speaks to *us*.'

We talked of war. *Johnson:* 'Every man thinks meanly of himself for not having been a soldier, or not having been at sea.' *Boswell:* 'Lord Mansfield does not.' *Johnson:* 'Sir, if Lord Mansfield were in a company of General Officers and Admirals who have been in service, he would shrink; he'd wish to creep under the table.' *Boswell:* 'No; he'd think he could *try* them all.' *Johnson:* 'Yes, if he could catch them: but they'd try him much sooner. No, Sir; were Socrates and Charles the Twelfth of Sweden both present in any company, and Socrates to say, "Follow me, and hear a lecture in philosophy"; and Charles, laying his hand on his sword, to say, "Follow me, and dethrone the Czar"; a man would be ashamed to follow Socrates. Sir, the impression is universal; yet it is strange. As to the sailor, when you look down from the quarter-deck to the space below, you see the utmost extremity of human misery; such crouding, such filth, such stench!' *Scott:* 'We find people fond of being sailors.' *Johnson:* 'I cannot account for that, any more than I can account for other strange perversions of imagination.'

He sometimes could not bear being teazed with questions. I was once present when a gentleman asked so many, as, 'What did you do, Sir?' 'What did you say, Sir?'

that he at last grew enraged, and said, 'I will not be put to the *question*. Don't you consider, Sir, that these are not the manners of a gentleman? I will not be baited with *what*, and *why*; what is this? what is that? why is a cow's tail long? why is a fox's tail bushy?' The gentleman, who was a good deal out of countenance, said, 'Why, Sir, you are so good, that I venture to trouble you.' *Johnson:* 'Sir, my being so *good* is no reason why you should be so *ill*.'

He talked with an uncommon animation of travelling into distant countries; that the mind was enlarged by it, and that an acquisition of dignity of character was derived from it. He expressed a particular enthusiasm with respect to visiting the wall of China. I catched it for the moment, and said I really believed I should go and see the wall of China had I not children, of whom it was my duty to take care. 'Sir, (said he,) by doing so, you would do what would be of importance in raising your children to eminence. There would be a lustre reflected upon them from your spirit and curiosity. They would be at all times regarded as the children of a man who had gone to view the wall of China. I am serious, Sir.'

On Wednesday, April 15, I dined with Dr. Johnson at Mr. Dilly's, and was in high spirits, for I had been a good part of the morning with Mr. Orme, the able and eloquent historian of Hindostan, who expressed a great admiration of

Johnson. 'I do not care (said he,) on what subject Johnson talks; but I love better to hear him talk than any body. He either gives you new thoughts, or a new colouring. It is a shame to the nation that he has not been more liberally rewarded. Had I been George the Third, and thought as he did about America, I would have given Johnson three hundred a year for his "Taxation no Tyranny" alone.' I repeated this, and Johnson was much pleased with such praise from such a man as Orme.

At Mr. Dilly's to-day were Mrs. Knowles, the ingenious Quaker lady, Miss Seward, the poetess of Lichfield, the Reverend Dr. Mayo, and the Rev. Mr. Beresford, Tutor to the Duke of Bedford. Before dinner Dr. Johnson seized upon Mr. Charles Sheridan's 'Account of the late Revolution in Sweden,' and seemed to read it ravenously, as if he devoured it, which was to all appearance his method of studying. 'He knows how to read better than any one (said Mrs. Knowles;) he gets at the substance of a book directly; he tears out the heart of it.' He kept it wrapt up in the tablecloth in his lap during the time of dinner, from an avidity to have one entertainment in readiness when he should have finished another; resembling (if I may use so coarse a simile) a dog who holds a bone in his paws in reserve, while he eats something else which has been thrown to him.

Mrs. Knowles affected to complain that men had much more liberty allowed them than women. *Johnson:* 'Why, Madam, women have all the liberty they should wish to have. We have all the labour and the danger, and the women all the advantage. We go to sea, we build houses, we do every thing, in short, to pay our court to the women.' *Mrs. Knowles:* 'The Doctor reasons very wittily, but not convincingly. Now, take the instance of building; the mason's wife, if she is ever seen in liquor, is ruined; the mason may get himself drunk as often as he pleases, with little loss of character; nay, may let his wife and children starve.' *Johnson:* 'Madam, you must consider, if the mason does get himself drunk, and let his wife and children starve, the parish will oblige him to find security for their maintenance. We have different modes of restraining evil. Stocks for the men, a ducking-stool for women, and a pound for beasts. If we require more perfection from women than from ourselves, it is doing them honour. And women have not the same temptations that we have: they may always live in virtuous company; men must mix in the world indiscriminately. If a woman has no inclination to do what is wrong, being secured from it is no restraint to her. I am at liberty to walk into the Thames; but if I were to try it, my friends would restrain me in Bedlam, and I should be obliged to them.' *Mrs. Knowles:* 'Still, Doctor, I cannot help thinking it a hardship that more indulgence is allowed to men than to women. It gives a superiority to men, to which I do not see how they are entitled.' *Johnson:* 'It is plain, Madam, one or other must have the superiority. As Shakspeare says, "If two men ride on a horse, one must ride behind."' *Dilly:* 'I suppose, Sir, Mrs. Knowles would have them to ride in panniers, one on each side.' *Johnson:* 'Then, Sir, the horse would throw them both.' *Mrs. Knowles:* 'Well, I hope that in another world the sexes will be equal.' *Boswell:* 'That is being too ambitious, Madam. *We* might as well desire to be equal with the angels. We shall all, I hope, be happy in a future state, but we must not expect to be all happy in the same degree. It is enough if we be happy according to our several capacities. A worthy carman will get to heaven as well as Sir Isaac Newton. Yet, though equally good, they will not have the same degrees of happiness.' *Johnson:* 'Probably not.'

Dr. Mayo having asked Johnson's opinion of Soame Jenyns' 'View of the Internal Evidence of the Christian Religion';—*Johnson:* 'I think it a pretty book; not very theological indeed; and there seems to be an affectation of ease and carelessness, as if it were not suitable to his character to be very serious about the matter.' *Boswell:* '*You* should like his book, Mrs. Knowles, as it maintains, as you *Friends* do, that courage is not a Christian virtue.' *Mrs. Knowles:* 'Yes, indeed, I like him there; but I cannot agree with him, that friendship is not a Christian virtue.' *Johnson:* 'Why, Madam, strictly speaking, he is right. All friendship is preferring the interest of a friend, to the neglect, or, perhaps, against the interest of others; so that an old Greek said, "He that has *friends* has *no friend*." Now Christianity recommends universal benevolence, to consider all men as our brethren, which is contrary to the virtue of friendship, as described by the ancient philosophers. Surely, Madam, your sect must approve of this; for, you call all men *friends.*' *Mrs. Knowles:* 'We are commanded to do good to all men, "but especially to them who are of the household of Faith."' *Johnson:* 'Well, Madam. The household of Faith is wide enough.' *Mrs. Knowles:* 'But, Doctor, our Saviour had twelve Apostles, yet there was *one* whom he *loved*. John was called "the disciple whom *Jesus* loved."' *Johnson* (with eyes sparkling benignantly): 'Very well, indeed, Madam. You have said very well.' *Boswell:* 'A fine application. Pray, Sir, had you ever thought of it?' *Johnson:* 'I had not, Sir.'

From this pleasing subject, he, I know not how or why, made a sudden transition to one upon which he was a violent aggressor; for he said, 'I am willing to love all mankind, *except an American*': and his inflammable corruption bursting into horrid fire, he 'breathed out threatenings and slaughter'; calling them, 'Rascals—Robbers—Pirates'; and exclaiming, he'd 'burn and destroy them.' Miss Seward, looking to him with mild but steady astonishment, said, 'Sir, this is an instance that we are always most violent against those whom we have injured.'—He was irritated still more by this delicate and keen reproach; and roared out another tremendous volley, which one might fancy could be heard across the Atlantick. During this tempest I sat in great uneasiness, lamenting his heat of temper; till, by degrees, I diverted his attention to other topicks.

Talking of Miss ——, a literary lady, he said, 'I was obliged to speak to Miss Reynolds, to let her know that I desired she would not flatter me so much.' Somebody now observed, 'She flatters Garrick.' *Johnson:* 'She is in the right to flatter Garrick. She is in the right for two reasons; first, because she has the world with her, who have been praising Garrick these thirty years; and secondly, because she is rewarded for it by Garrick. Why should she flatter *me?* I can do nothing for her. Let her carry her praise to a better market (then turning to Mrs. Knowles). You, Madam, have been flattering me all the evening; I wish you would give Boswell a little now. If you knew his merit as well as I do, you would say a great deal; he is the best travelling companion in the world.'

I expressed a horrour at the thought of death. *Mrs. Knowles:* 'Nay, thou should'st not have a horrour for what is the gate of life.' *Johnson:* (standing upon the hearth rolling about, with a serious, solemn, and somewhat gloomy air:) 'No rational man can die without uneasy apprehension.' *Boswell:* 'In prospect death is dreadful; but in fact we find that people die easy.' *Johnson:* 'Why, Sir, most people have not *thought* much of the matter, so cannot *say* much, and it is supposed they die easy. Few believe it certain they are then to die; and those who do, set themselves to behave with resolution, as a man does who is going to be hanged. He is not the less unwilling to be hanged.' *Miss Seward:* 'There is one mode of the fear of death, which is certainly absurd; and that is the dread of annihilation, which is only a pleasing sleep without a dream.' *Johnson:* 'It is neither pleasing, nor sleep; it is nothing. Now mere existence is so much better than nothing, that one would rather exist even in pain, than not exist.'

Mrs. Knowles mentioned, as a proselyte to Quakerism, Miss ——, a young lady well known to Dr. Johnson, for whom he had shewn much affection; while she ever had, and still retained, a great respect for him. Mrs. Knowles at the same time took an opportunity of letting him know 'that the amiable young creature was sorry at finding that he was offended at her leaving the Church of England and embracing a simpler faith'; and, in the gentlest and most persuasive manner, solicited his kind indulgence for what was sincerely a matter of conscience. *Johnson* (frowning very angrily): 'Madam, she is an odious wench. She could not have any proper conviction that it was her duty to change her religion, which is the most important of all subjects, and should be studied with all care, and with all the helps we can get. She knew no more of the Church which she left, and that which she embraced, than she did of the difference between the Copernican and Ptolemaick systems.' *Mrs. Knowles:* 'She had the New Testament before her.' *Johnson:* 'Madam, she could not understand the New Testament, the most difficult book in the world, for which the study of a life is required.' *Mrs. Knowles:* 'It is clear as to essentials.' *Johnson:* 'But not as to controversial points. The heathens were easily converted, because they had nothing to give up; but we ought not, without very strong conviction indeed, to desert the religion in which we have been educated. That is the religion given you, the religion in which it may be said Providence has placed you. If you live conscientiously in that religion, you may be safe. But errour is dangerous indeed, if you err when you choose a religion for yourself.' *Mrs. Knowles:* 'Must we then go by implicit faith?' *Johnson:* 'Why, Madam, the greatest part of our knowledge is implicit faith; and as to religion, have we heard all that a disciple of Confucius, all that a Mahometan, can say for himself?' He then rose again into passion, and attacked the young proselyte in the severest terms of reproach, so that both the ladies seemed to be much shocked.

We remained together till it was pretty late. Notwithstanding occasional explosions of violence, we were all delighted upon the whole with Johnson. I compared him at this time to a warm West-Indian climate, where you have a bright sun, quick vegetation, luxuriant foliage, luscious fruits; but where the same heat sometimes produces thunder, lightning, and earthquakes, in a terrible degree.

April 17, being Good-Friday, I waited on Johnson, as usual. I observed at breakfast that although it was a part of his abstemious discipline on this most solemn fast, to take no milk in his tea, yet when Mrs. Desmoulins inadvertently poured it in, he did not reject it.

There was a very numerous congregation to-day at St. Clement's church, which Dr. Johnson said he observed with pleasure.

And now I am to give a pretty full account of one of the most curious incidents in Johnson's life, of which he himself has made the following minute on this day: 'In my return from church, I was accosted by Edwards, an old fellow-collegian, who had not seen me since 1729. He knew me, and asked if I remembered one Edwards; I did not at first recollect the name, but gradually as we walked along, recovered it, and told him a conversation that had passed at an ale-house between us. My purpose is to continue our acquaintance.'

It was in Butcher-row that this meeting happened. Mr. Edwards, who was a decent-looking elderly man in grey clothes, and a wig of many curls, accosted Johnson with familiar confidence, knowing who he was, while Johnson returned his salutation with a courteous formality, as to a stranger. But as soon as Edwards had brought to his recollection their having been at Pembroke-College together nine-and-forty years ago, he seemed much pleased, asked where he lived, and said he should be glad to see him in Bolt-court. *Edwards:* 'Ah, Sir! we are old men now.' *Johnson* (who never liked to think of being old): 'Don't let us discourage one another.' *Edwards:* 'Why, Doctor, you look stout and hearty, I am happy to see you so; for the newspapers told us you were very ill.' *Johnson:* 'Ay, Sir, they are always telling lies of *us old fellows.*'

Wishing to be present at more of so singular a conversation as that between two fellow-collegians, who had lived forty years in London without ever having chanced to meet, I whispered to Mr. Edwards that Dr. Johnson was going home, and that he had better accompany him now. So Edwards walked along with us, I eagerly assisting to keep up the conversation. Mr. Edwards informed Dr. Johnson that he had practised long as a solicitor in Chancery, but that he now lived in the country upon a little farm, about sixty acres, just by Stevenage in Hertfordshire, and that he came to London (to Bar-

nard's Inn, No. 6), generally twice a week. Johnson appearing to be in a reverie, Mr. Edwards addressed himself to me, and expatiated on the pleasure of living in the country. *Boswell:* 'I have no notion of this, Sir. What you have to entertain you, is, I think, exhausted in half an hour.' *Edwards:* 'What? don't you love to have hope realized? I see my grass, and my corn; and my trees growing. Now, for instance, I am curious to see if this frost has not nipped my fruit-trees.' *Johnson* (who we did not imagine was attending): 'You find, Sir, you have fears as well as hopes.'

When we got to Dr. Johnson's house, and were seated in his library, the dialogue went on admirably. *Edwards:* 'Sir, I remember you would not let us say *prodigious* at College. For even then, Sir, (turning to me,) he was delicate in language, and we all feared him.' *Johnson* (to Edwards): 'From your having practised the law long, Sir, I presume you must be rich.' *Edwards:* 'No, Sir; I got a good deal of money; but I had a number of poor relations to whom I gave a great part of it. *Johnson:* 'Sir, you have been rich in the most valuable sense of the word.' *Edwards:* 'But I shall not die rich.' *Johnson:* 'Nay, sure, Sir, it is better to live rich than to *die* rich.' *Edwards:* 'I wish I had continued at College.' *Johnson:* 'Why do you wish that, Sir?' *Edwards:* 'Because I think I should have had a much easier life than mine has been. I should have been a parson, and had a good living, like Bloxam and several others, and lived comfortably.' *Johnson:* 'Sir, the life of a parson, of a conscientious clergyman, is not easy. I have always considered a clergyman as the father of a larger family than he is able to maintain. I would rather have Chancery suits upon my hands than the cure of souls. No, Sir, I do not envy a clergyman's life as an easy life, nor do I envy the clergyman who makes it an easy life.'—Here taking himself up all of a sudden, he exclaimed, 'O! Mr. Edwards! I'll convince you that I recollect you. Do you remember our drinking together at an alehouse near Pembroke gate.'

Edwards: 'You are a philosopher, Dr. Johnson. I have tried too in my time to be a philosopher; but I don't know how, cheerfulness was always breaking in. I have been twice married, Doctor. You, I suppose, have never known what it was to have a wife.' *Johnson:* 'Sir, I have known what it was to have a wife, and (in a solemn tender faultering tone) I have known what it was to *lose a wife.*—It had almost broke my heart.'

Edwards: 'How do you live, Sir? For my part, I must have my regular meals, and a glass of good wine. I find I require it.' *Johnson:* 'I now drink no wine, Sir. Early in life I drank wine: for many years I drank none. I then for some years drank a great deal.' *Edwards:* 'Some hogsheads, I warrant you.' *Johnson:* 'I then had a severe illness, and left it off, and I have never begun it again. I never felt any difference upon myself from eating one thing rather than another, nor from one kind of weather rather than another. There are people, I believe, who feel a difference; but I am not one of them. And as to regular meals, I have fasted from the Sunday's dinner to the Tuesday's dinner, without any inconvenience. I believe it is best to eat just as one is hungry: but a man who is in business, or a man who has a family, must have stated meals. I am a straggler. I may leave this town and go to Grand Cairo, without being missed here or observed there.' *Edwards:* 'Don't you eat supper, Sir?' *Johnson:* 'No, Sir.' *Edwards:* 'For my part, now, I consider supper as a turnpike through which one must pass, in order to get to bed.'

Johnson: 'You are a lawyer, Mr. Edwards. Lawyers know life practically. A bookish man should always have them to converse with. They have what he wants.' *Edwards:* 'I am grown old: I am sixty-five.' *Johnson:* 'I shall be sixty-eight next birth-day. Come, Sir, drink water, and put in for a hundred.'

Mr. Edwards mentioned a gentleman who had left his whole fortune to Pembroke College. *Johnson:* 'Whether to leave one's whole fortune to a College be right, must depend upon circumstances. I would leave the interest of the fortune I bequeathed to a College to my relations or my friends, for their lives. It is the same thing to a College, which is a permanent society, whether it gets the money now or twenty years hence; and I would wish to make my relations or friends feel the benefit of it.'

This interview confirmed my opinion of Johnson's most humane and benevolent heart. His cordial and placid behaviour to an old fellow-collegian, a man so different from himself; and his telling him that he would go down to his farm and visit him, shewed a kindliness of disposition very rare at an advanced age. He observed, 'how wonderful it was that they had both been in London forty years, without having ever once met, and both walkers in the street too!' Mr. Edwards, when going away, again recurred to his consciousness of senility, and looking full in Johnson's face, said to him, 'You'll find in Dr. Young,

"O my coevals! remnants of yourselves." '

Johnson did not relish this at all; but shook his head with impatience. Edwards walked off, seemingly highly pleased with the honour of having been thus noticed by Dr. Johnson. When he was gone, I said to Johnson, I thought him but a weak man. *Johnson:* 'Why, yes, Sir. Here is a man who has passed through life without experience: yet I would rather have him with me than a more sensible man who will not talk readily.'

Johnson once observed to me, 'Tom Tyers described me the best: "Sir (said he,) you are like a ghost: you never speak till you are spoken to." '

Johnson had a noble ambition floating in his mind, and had, undoubtedly, often speculated on the possibility of his supereminent powers being rewarded in this great and liberal country by the highest honours of the state. Sir William Scott informs me, that upon the death of the late Lord Lichfield, who was Chancellor of the University of Oxford, he said to Johnson, 'What a pity it is, Sir, that you did not follow the profession of the law. You might have been Lord Chancellor of Great Britain, and attained to the dignity of the peerage; and now that the title of Lichfield, your native city, is extinct, you might have had it.' Johnson, upon this, seemed much agitated; and, in an angry tone, exclaimed, 'Why will you vex me by suggesting this, when it is too late?'

Yet no man had a higher notion of the dignity of literature than Johnson, or was more determined in maintaining the respect which he justly considered as due to it. Of this, besides the general tenor of his conduct in society, some characteristical instances may be mentioned.

He told Sir Joshua Reynolds, that once when he dined in a numerous company of booksellers, where the room being small, the head of the table, at which he sat, was almost close to the fire, he persevered in suffering a great deal of inconvenience from the heat, rather than quit his place, and let one of them sit above him.

On Saturday, April 14, I drank tea with him. The Gentleman who had dined with us at Dr. Percy's came in. Johnson attacked the Americans with intemperate vehemence of abuse. I said something in their favour; and added, that I was always sorry when he talked on that subject. This, it seems, exasperated him; though he said nothing at the time. The cloud was charged with sulphureous vapour, which was afterwards to burst in thunder.—We talked of a gentleman who was running out his fortune in London; and I said, 'We must get him out of it. All his friends must quarrel with him, and that will soon drive him away.' *Johnson:* 'Nay, Sir, we'll send *you* to him. If your company does not drive a man out of his house, nothing will.' This was a horrible shock, for which there was no visible cause. I afterwards asked him why he had said so harsh a thing. *Johnson:* 'Because, Sir, you made me angry about the Americans.' *Boswell:* 'But why did you not take your revenge directly?' *Johnson* (smiling): 'Because, Sir, I had nothing ready. A man cannot strike till he has his weapons.' This was a candid and pleasant confession.

On Wednesday, April 29, I dined with him at Mr. Allan Ramsay's, where were Lord Binning, Dr. Robertson the historian, Sir Joshua Reynolds, and the Honourable Mrs. Boscawen. Before Johnson came we talked a good deal of him;

Ramsay said he had always found him a very polite man, and that he treated him with great respect, which he did very sincerely. *Robertson:* 'He and I have been always very gracious; the first time I met him was one evening at Strahan's, when he had just had an unlucky altercation with Adam Smith, to whom he had been so rough, that Strahan, after Smith was gone, had remonstrated with him, and told him that I was coming soon, and that he was uneasy to think that he might behave in the same manner to me. "No, no, Sir, (said Johnson) I warrant you Robertson and I shall do very well." Accordingly he was gentle and good-humoured, and courteous with me the whole evening; and he has been so upon every occasion that we have met since. I have often said (laughing) that I have been in a great measure indebted to Smith for my good reception.' *Boswell:* 'His power of reasoning is very strong, and he has a peculiar art of drawing characters, which is as rare as good portrait painting.' *Sir Joshua Reynolds:* 'He is undoubtedly admirable in this; but, in order to mark the characters which he draws, he overcharges them, and gives people more than they really have, whether of good or bad.'

No sooner did he, of whom we had been thus talking so easily, arrive, than we were all as quiet as a school upon the entrance of the head-master; and were very soon set down to a table covered with such variety of good things, as contributed not a little to dispose him to be pleased.

An ingenious gentleman was mentioned, concerning whom both Robertson and Ramsay agreed that he had a constant firmness of mind; for after a laborious day, and amidst a multiplicity of cares and anxieties, he would sit down with his sisters and be quite cheerful and good-humoured. Such a disposition, it was observed, was a happy gift of nature. *Johnson:* 'I do not think so; a man has from nature a certain portion of mind; the use he makes of it depends upon his own free will. That a man has always the same firmness of mind I do not say; because every man feels his mind less firm at one time than at another; but I think a man's being in a good or bad humour depends upon his will.' I, however, could not help thinking that a man's humour is often uncontroulable by his will.

Johnson harangued against drinking wine, 'A man (said he) may choose whether he will have abstemiousness and knowledge, or claret and ignorance.' Dr. Robertson, (who is very companionable,) was beginning to dissent as to the proscription of claret. *Johnson:* (with a placid smile): 'Nay, Sir, you shall not differ with me; as I have said that the man is most perfect who takes in the most things, I am for knowledge and claret.' *Robertson* (holding a glass of generous claret in his hand): 'Sir, I can only drink your health.' *Johnson:* 'Sir, I should be sorry if *you* should be ever in such a state as to be able to do nothing more.'

Next day, Thursday, April 30, I found him at home by himself. *Johnson:* 'Well, Sir, Ramsay gave us a splendid dinner. I love Ramsay. You will not find a man in whose conversation there is more instruction, more information, and more elegance, than in Ramsay's.' *Boswell:* 'What I admire in Ramsay, is his continuing to be so young.' *Johnson:* 'Why, yes, Sir, it is to be admired. I value myself upon this, that there is nothing of the old man in my conversation. I am now sixty-eight, and I have no more of it than at twenty-eight.' *Boswell:* 'But, Sir, would not you wish to know old age? He who is never an old man, does not know the whole of human life; for old age is one of the divisions of it.' *Johnson:* 'Nay, Sir, what talk is this?' *Boswell:* 'I mean, Sir, the Sphinx's description of it;—morning, noon, and night. I would know night, as well as morning and noon.' *Johnson:* 'What, Sir, would you know what it is to feel the evils of old age? Would you have the gout? Would you have decrepitude?'—Seeing him heated, I would not argue any farther; but I was confident that I was in the right. *Johnson:* 'Mrs. Thrale's mother said of me what flattered me much. A clergyman was complaining of want of society in the country where he lived; and said, "They talk of *runts*"; (that is, young cows). "Sir, (said Mrs. Salusbury,) Mr. Johnson would learn to talk of runts": meaning that I was a man who would make the most of my situation, whatever it was.' He added, 'I think myself a very polite man.'

On Saturday, May 2, I dined with him at Sir Joshua Reynolds', where there was a very large company, and a great deal of conversation; but owing to some circumstance which I cannot now recollect, I have no record of any part of it, except that there were several people there by no means of the Johnsonian school; so that less attention was paid to him than usual, which put him out of humour; and upon some imaginary offence from me, he attacked me with such rudeness, that I was vexed and angry, because it gave those persons an opportunity of enlarging upon his supposed ferocity, and ill treatment of his best friends. I was so much hurt, and had my pride so much roused, that I kept away from him for a week; and, perhaps, might have kept away much longer, nay, gone to Scotland without seeing him again, had not we fortunately met and been reconciled. To such unhappy chances are human friendships liable.

On Friday, May 8, I dined with him at Mr. Langton's. I was reserved and silent, which I suppose he perceived, and might recollect the cause. After dinner, when Mr. Langton was called out of the room, and we were by ourselves, he drew his chair near to mine, and said, in a tone of conciliating courtesy, 'Well, how have you done?' *Boswell*: 'Sir, you have made me very uneasy by your behaviour to me when we were last at Sir Joshua Reynolds'. You know, my dear Sir, no man has a greater respect and affection for you, or would sooner go to the end of the world to serve you. Now to treat me so—.' He insisted that I had interrupted him, which I assured him was not the case; and proceeded—'But why treat me so before people who neither love you nor me?' *Johnson*: Well, I am sorry for it. I'll make it up to you twenty different ways, as you please.' *Boswell*: 'I said to-day to Sir Joshua, when he observed that you *tossed* me sometimes—I don't care how often, or how high he tosses me, when only friends are present, for then I fall upon soft ground: but I do not like falling on stones, which is the case when enemies are present.—I think this is a pretty good image, Sir.' *Johnson*: 'Sir, it is one of the happiest I have ever heard.'

On Tuesday, May 12, I waited on the Earl of Marchmont, to know if his Lordship would favour Dr. Johnson with information concerning Pope, whose Life he was about to write. Johnson had not flattered himself with the hopes of receiving any civility from this nobleman; for he said to me, when I mentioned Lord Marchmont as one who could tell him a great deal about Pope, 'Sir, he will tell *me* nothing.' I had the honour of being known to his Lordship, and applied to him of myself, without being commissioned by Johnson. His Lordship behaved in the most polite and obliging manner, promised to tell all he recollected about Pope, and was so very courteous as to say, 'Tell Dr. Johnson I have a great respect for him, and am ready to shew it in any way I can. I am to be in the city to-morrow, and will call at his house as I return.' His Lordship however asked, 'Will he write the Lives of the Poets impartially?'

I proposed to Lord Marchmont that he should revise Johnson's Life of Pope: 'So (said his Lordship) you would put me in a dangerous situation. You know he knocked down Osborne the bookseller.'

Elated with the success of my spontaneous exertion to procure material and respectable aid to Johnson for his very favourite work, 'The Lives of the Poets,' I hastened down to Mr. Thrale's at Streatham, where he now was, that I might insure his being at home next day; and after dinner, when I thought he would receive the good news in the best humour, I announced it eagerly: 'I have been at work for you to-day, Sir. I have been with Lord Marchmont. He bade me tell you he has a great respect for you, and will call on you to-morrow at one o'clock, and communicate all he knows about Pope.'—Here I paused, in full expectation that he would be pleased with this intelligence, would praise my active merit, and would be alert to embrace such an offer from a nobleman. But whether I had shewn an over-exultation, which provoked his spleen; or whether he was seized with a suspicion that I had obtruded him on Lord Marchmont, and had humbled him too much; or whether there was any thing more than an unlucky fit of ill-humour, I know not; but, to my surprize, the result was,—*Johnson:* 'I shall not be in town to-morrow. I don't care to know about Pope.' *Mrs. Thrale* (surprized as I was, and a little angry): 'I suppose, Sir, Mr. Boswell thought, that as you are to write Pope's Life, you would wish to know about him.' *Johnson:* 'Wish! why yes. If it rained knowledge I'd hold out my hand; but I would not give myself the trouble to go in quest of it.' There was no arguing with him at the moment. Some time afterwards he said, 'Lord Marchmont will call on me, and then I shall call on Lord Marchmont.' Mr. Thrale was uneasy at his unaccountable caprice; and told me, that if I did not take care to bring about a meeting between Lord Marchmont and him, it would never take place, which would be a great pity. I sent a card to his Lordship, to be left at Johnson's house, acquainting him, that Dr. Johnson could not be in town next day, but would do himself the honour of waiting on him at another time.—I give this account fairly, as a specimen of that unhappy temper with which this great and good man had occasionally to struggle, from something morbid in his constitution. But it must not be erroneously supposed that he was, in the smallest degree, careless concerning any work which he undertook, or that he was generally thus peevish. In the following year he had a very agreeable interview with Lord Marchmont, at his Lordship's house; and this very afternoon he soon forgot any fretfulness, and fell into conversation as usual.

After Mrs. Thrale was gone to bed, Johnson and I sat up late. We resumed Sir Joshua Reynolds' argument on the preceding Sunday, that a man would be virtuous though he had no other motive than to preserve his character. *Johnson:* 'Sir, it is not true: for as to this world vice does not hurt a man's character.' *Boswell:* 'Yes, Sir, debauching a friend's wife will.' *Johnson:* 'No, Sir. A man is chosen Knight of the shire, not the less for having debauched ladies.' *Boswell:* 'What, Sir, if he debauched the ladies of gentlemen in the county, will not there be a general resentment against him?' *Johnson:* 'No, Sir. He will lose those particular gentlemen; but the rest will not trouble their heads about it,' (warmly.) *Boswell:* 'Well, Sir, I cannot think so.' *Johnson:* 'Nay, Sir, there is no talking with a man who will dispute what every body knows, (angrily.) Don't you know this?' *Boswell:* 'No, Sir: and I wish to think better of your country than you represent it.'

Next morning I stated to Mrs. Thrale at breakfast, before he came down, the dispute of last night as to the influence of character upon success in life. She said he was certainly wrong. But she would not encounter Johnson upon the subject.

I staid all this day with him at Streatham. He talked a great deal, in very good humour.

I talked of a country life.—*Johnson:* 'Were I to live in the country, I would not devote myself to the acquisition of popularity; I would live in a much better way, much more happily; I would have my time at my own command.' *Boswell:* 'But, Sir, is it not a sad thing to be at a distance from all our literary friends?' *Johnson:* 'Sir, you will by and by have enough of this conversation, which now delights you so much.'

As he was a zealous friend of subordination, he was at all times watchful to repress the vulgar cant against the manners of the great; 'High people, Sir, (said he,) are the best; take a hundred ladies of quality, you'll find them better wives, better mothers, more willing to sacrifice their own pleasure to their children, than a hundred other women. Tradeswomen (I mean the wives of tradesmen) in the city, who are worth from ten to fifteen thousand pounds, are the worst creatures upon the earth, grossly ignorant, and thinking viciousness fashionable. Farmers, I think, are often worthless fellows.

Few lords will cheat; and, if they do, they'll be ashamed of it: farmers cheat and are not ashamed of it: they have all the sensual vices too of the nobility, with cheating into the bargain.' *Boswell:* 'The notion of the world, Sir, however is, that the morals of women of quality are worse than those in lower stations.' *Johnson:* 'Yes, Sir, the licentiousness of one woman of quality makes more noise than that of a number of women in lower stations; then, Sir, you are to consider the malignity of women in the city against women of quality, which will make them believe any thing of them. No, Sir, so far as I have observed, the higher in rank, the richer ladies are, they are the better instructed and the more virtuous.'

✖ *Chapter* **11**

Johnson in His Seventies

We surely cannot but admire the benevolent exertions of this great and good man, especially when we consider how grievously he was afflicted with bad health, and how uncomfortable his home was made by the perpetual jarring of those whom he charitably accommodated under his roof. He has sometimes suffered me to talk jocularly of his group of females, and call them his

Seraglio. He thus mentions them, together with honest Levet, in one of his letters to Mrs. Thrale: 'Williams hates every body; Levett hates Desmoulins, and does not love Williams; Desmoulins hates them both; Poll loves none of them.'

In 1779, Johnson gave the world a luminous proof that the vigour of his mind in all of its faculties, whether memory, judgement, or imagination, was not in the least abated; for this year came out the first four volumes of his 'Prefaces, biographical and critical, to the most eminent of the English Poets,' published by the booksellers of London. The remaining volumes came out in the year 1780.

On Monday, March 15, at a late hour, I found Dr. Johnson sitting over his tea, attended by Mrs. Desmoulins, Mr. Levet, and a clergyman, who had come to submit some poetical pieces to his revision. It is wonderful what a number and variety of writers, some of them even unknown to him, prevailed on his good-nature to look over their works, and suggest corrections and improvements. I found that the subject under immediate consideration was a translation of Horace. When Johnson had done reading, the authour asked him bluntly, 'If upon the whole it was a good translation?' Johnson, whose regard for truth was uncommonly strict, seemed to be puzzled for a moment, what answer to make, as he certainly could not honestly commend the performance: with exquisite address he evaded the question thus, 'Sir, I do not say that it may not be made a very good translation.' Here nothing whatever in favour of the performance was affirmed, and yet the writer was not shocked. A printed 'Ode to the Warlike Genius of Britain,' came next in review; the bard was a lank bony figure, with short black hair; he was writhing himself in agitation, while Johnson read, and shewing his teeth in a grin of earnestness, exclaimed in broken sentences, and in a keen sharp tone, 'Is that poetry, Sir?' *Johnson:* 'Why, Sir, there is here a great deal of what is called poetry.'

Although I was several times with him in the course of the following days, such it seems were my occupations, such my negligence, that I have preserved no memorial of his conversation till Friday, March 26, when I visited him. He said he expected to be attacked on account of his 'Lives of the Poets.' 'However (said he) I would rather be attacked than unnoticed. For the worst thing you can do to an authour is to be silent as to his works. An assault upon a town is a bad thing; but starving it is still worse; an assault may be unsuccessful; you may have more men killed than you kill; but if you starve the town, you are sure of victory.'

During my stay in London this spring, I find I was unaccountably negligent in preserving Johnson's sayings, more so than at any time when I was happy enough to have an opportunity of hearing his wisdom and wit. There is no help for it now. I must content myself with presenting such scraps as I have. But I am nevertheless ashamed and vexed to think how much has been lost. It is not that there was a bad crop this year; but that I was not sufficiently careful in gathering it in. I, therefore, in some instances can only exhibit a few detached fragments.

On Wednesday, March 31, I visited him, and confessed an excess of which I had very seldom been guilty; that I had spent a whole night in playing at cards, and that I could not look back on it with satisfaction; instead of a harsh animadversion, he mildly said, 'Alas, Sir, on how few things can we look back with satisfaction.'

On Thursday, April 1, he commended one of the Dukes of Devonshire for 'a dogged veracity.' He said too, 'London is nothing to some people; but to a man whose pleasure is intellectual, London is the place. And there is no place where œconomy can be so well practised as in London. More can be had here for the money, even by ladies, than any where else. You cannot play tricks with your fortune in a small place; you must make an uniform appearance. Here a lady may have well-furnished apartments, and elegant dress, without any meat in her kitchen.'

I was amused by considering

with how much ease and coolness he could write or talk to a friend, exhorting him not to suppose that happiness was not to be found as well in other places as in London; when he himself was at all times sensible of its being, comparatively speaking, a heaven upon earth.

On Friday, April 2, being Good-Friday, I visited him in the morning as usual; we insensibly fell into a train of ridicule upon the foibles of one of our friends, a very worthy man. It happened also remarkably enough, that the subject of the sermon preached to us to-day by Dr. Burrows, the rector of St. Clement Danes, was the certainty that at the last day we must give an account of 'the deeds done in the body'; and, amongst various acts of culpability he mentioned evil-speaking. As we were moving slowly along in the croud from church, Johnson jogged my elbow, and said, 'Did you attend to the sermon?'—'Yes, Sir, (said I,) it was very applicable to *us*.' He, however, stood upon the defensive, 'Why, Sir, the sense of ridicule is given us, and may be lawfully used.'

On Saturday, April 3, I visited him at night, and found him sitting in Mrs. Williams' room, with her, and one who he afterwards told me was a natural son of the second Lord Southwell. The table had a singular appearance, being covered with a heterogeneous assemblage of oysters and porter for his company, and tea for himself. I mentioned my having heard an eminent physician, who was himself a Christian, argue in favour of universal toleration, and maintain, that no man could be hurt by another man's differing from him in opinion. *Johnson:* 'Sir, you are to a certain degree hurt by knowing that even one man does not believe.'

On Wednesday, April 7, I dined with him at Sir Joshua Reynolds'. I have not marked what company was there. Johnson harangued upon the qualities of different liquors; and spoke with great contempt of claret, as so weak that 'a man would be drowned by it before it made him drunk.' He was persuaded to drink one glass of it, that he might judge, not from recollection, which might be dim, but from immediate sensation. He shook his head, and said, 'Poor stuff! No, Sir, claret is the liquor for boys; port, for men; but he who aspires to be a hero (smiling) must drink brandy. In the first place, the flavour of brandy is most grateful to the palate; and then brandy will do soonest for a man what drinking *can* do for him.' I reminded him how heartily he and I used to drink wine together, when we were first acquainted; and how I used to have a head-ache after sitting up with him. He did not like to have this recalled, or, perhaps, thinking that I boasted improperly, resolved to have a witty stroke at me: 'Nay, Sir, it was not the *wine* that made your head ache, but the *sense* that I put into it.' *Boswell:* 'What, Sir! Will sense make the head ache?'

Johnson: 'Yes, Sir, (with a smile) when it is not used to it.'

On Thursday, April 8, I dined with him at Mr. Allan Ramsay's, with Lord Graham and some other company.

Lord Graham commended Dr. Drummond at Naples, as a man of extraordinary talents; and added, that he had a great love of liberty. *Johnson:* 'He is *young,* my Lord; (looking to his Lordship with an arch smile) all *boys* love liberty, till experience convinces them they are not so fit to govern themselves as they imagined. We are all agreed as to our own liberty; we would have as much of it as we can get; but we are not agreed as to the liberty of others: for in proportion as we take, others must lose. I believe we hardly wish that the mob should have liberty to govern us.' *Ramsay:* 'The result is, that order is better than confusion.' *Johnson:* 'The result is, that order cannot be had but by subordination.'

On Friday, April 16, I had been present at the trial of the unfortunate Mr. Hackman, who, in a fit of frantick jealous love, had shot Miss Ray, the favourite of a nobleman. Johnson, in whose company I dined to-day, with some other friends, was much interested by my account of what passed, and particularly with his prayer for the mercy of heaven. He said, in a solemn fervid tone, 'I hope he *shall* find mercy.'

This day a violent altercation arose between Johnson and Beauclerk, which having made much noise at the time, I think it proper, in order to prevent any future misrepresentation, to give a minute account of it.

In talking of Hackman, Johnson argued, as Judge Blackstone had done, that his being furnished with two pistols was a proof that he meant to shoot two persons. Mr. Beauclerck said, 'No; for that every wise man who intended to shoot himself, took two pistols, that he might be sure of doing it at once. Lord —— ——'s cook shot himself with one pistol, and lived ten days in great agony. Mr. ——, who loved buttered muffins, but durst not eat them because they disagreed with his stomach, resolved to shoot himself; and then he eat three buttered muffins for breakfast, before shooting himself, knowing that he should not be troubled with indigestion: *he* had two charged pistols; one was found lying charged upon the table by him, after he had shot himself with the other.' 'Well, (said Johnson, with an air of triumph,) you see here one pistol was sufficient.' Beauclerk replied smartly, 'Because it happened to kill him.' And either then, or a very little afterwards, being piqued at Johnson's triumphant remark, added, 'This is what you don't know, and I do.' There was then a cessation of the dispute; and some minutes intervened, during which, dinner and the glass went on cheerfully; when Johnson suddenly and abruptly exclaimed, 'Mr. Beauclerk, how came you to talk so petulantly to me, as "This is what you don't know, but what I know"? One thing *I* know, which *you* don't seem to know, that you are very uncivil.' *Beauclerk:* 'Because *you* began by being uncivil, (which you always are.)' The words in parenthesis, were, I believe, not heard by Dr. Johnson. Here again there was a cessation of arms. Johnson told me, that the reason why he waited at first some time without taking any notice of what Mr. Beauclerk said, was because he was thinking whether he should resent it. But when he considered that there were present a young Lord and an eminent traveller, two men of the world with whom he had never dined before, he was apprehensive that they might think they had a right to take such liberties with him as Beauclerk did, and therefore resolved he would not let it pass; adding, that 'he would not appear a coward.' A little while after this, the conversation turned on the violence of Hackman's temper. Johnson then said, 'It was his business to *command* his temper, as my friend, Mr. Beauclerk, should have done some time ago.' *Beauclerk:* 'I should learn of *you*, Sir.' *Johnson:* 'Sir, you have given *me* opportunities enough of learning, when I have been in *your* company. No man loves to be treated with contempt.' *Beauclerk* (with a polite inclination towards Johnson): 'Sir, you have known me twenty years, and however I may have treated others, you may be sure I could never treat you with contempt.' *Johnson:* 'Sir,

you have said more than was necessary.' Thus it ended; and Beauclerk's coach not having come for him till very late, Dr. Johnson and another gentleman sat with him a long time afer the rest of the company were gone; and he and I dined at Beauclerk's on the Saturday se'nnight following.

After this tempest had subsided, I recollect the following particulars of his conversation:

'I am always for getting a boy forward in his learning; for that is a sure good. I would let him at first read *any* English book which happens to engage his attention; because you have done a great deal when you have brought him to have entertainment from a book. He'll get better books afterwards.'

'To be contradicted, in order to force you to talk, is mighty unpleasing. You *shine,* indeed; but it is by being *ground.*'

I did not write to Johnson, as usual, upon my return to my family; but tried how he would be affected by my silence.

'To James Boswell, Esq.

'Dear Sir,

'What can possibly have happened, that keeps us two such strangers to each other? I expected to have heard from you when you came home; I expected afterwards. I went into the country and returned; and yet there is no letter from Mr. Boswell. No ill I hope has happened; and if ill should happen, why should it be concealed from him who loves you? Is it a fit of humour, that has disposed you to try who can hold out longest without writing? If it be, you have the victory. But I am afraid of something bad; set me free from my suspicions.

'My thoughts are at present employed in guessing the reason of your silence: you must not expect that I should tell you any thing, if I had any thing to tell. Write, pray write to me, and let me know what is, or what has been the cause of this long interruption.

'I am, dear Sir,
'Your most affectionate
humble servant,
'Sam. Johnson.
'July 13, 1779.'

'To Dr. Samuel Johnson.

'Edinburgh, July 17, 1779.
'My dear Sir,

'What may be justly denominated a supine indolence of mind has been my state of existence since I last returned to Scotland. In a livelier state I had often suffered severely from long intervals of silence on your part; and I had even been chid by you for expressing my uneasiness. I was willing to take advantage of my insensibility, and while I could bear the experiment to try whether your affection for me, would, after an unusual silence on my part, make you write first. This afternoon I have had very high satisfaction by receiving your kind letter of inquiry, for which I most gratefully thank you. I am doubtful if it was right to make the experiment; though I have gained by it. I was beginning to grow tender, and to upbraid myself, especially after having dreamt two nights ago that I was with you. I and my wife, and my four children, are all well. I would not delay one post to answer your letter; but as it is late, I have not time to do more. You shall soon hear from me, upon many and various particulars; and I shall never again put you to any test. I ever am, with veneration, my dear Sir,
'Your much obliged,
'And faithful humble servant,
'James Boswell.'

On Monday, October 4, I called at his house before he was up. He sent for me to his bedside, and expressed his satisfaction at this incidental meeting, with as much vivacity as if he had been in the gaiety of youth. He called briskly, 'Frank, go and get coffee, and let us breakfast in splendour.'

On Sunday, October 10, we dined together at Mr. Strahan's. The conversation having turned on the prevailing practice of going to the East-Indies in quest of wealth;— Johnson: 'A man had better have ten thousand pounds at the end of ten years passed in England, than twenty thousand pounds at the end of ten years passed in India, because you must compute what you give for money; and a man who has lived ten years in India, has given up ten years of social comfort and all those advantages which arise from living in England.'

We left Mr. Strahan's at seven, as Johnson had said he intended to go to evening prayers. As we walked along, he complained of a little gout in his toe, and said, 'I shan't go to prayers to-night; I shall go to-morrow. Whenever I miss church on a Sunday, I resolve to go another day. But I do not always do it.' This was a fair exhibition of that vibration between pious resolutions and indolence, which many of us have too often experienced.

I went home with him, and we had a long quiet conversation.

He said, 'Dodsley first mentioned to me the scheme of an English Dictionary; but I had long thought of it.' *Boswell:* 'You did not know what you were undertaking.' *Johnson:* 'Yes, Sir, I knew very well what I was undertaking,—and very well how to do it,—and have done it very well.' *Boswell:* 'An excellent climax! and it *has* availed you. In your Preface you say, "What would it avail me in this gloom of solitude?" You have been agreeably mistaken.'

He, I know not why, shewed upon all occasions an aversion to go to Ireland, where I proposed to him that we should make a tour. *Johnson:* 'It is the last place where I should wish to travel.' *Boswell:* 'Should you not like to see Dublin, Sir?' *Johnson:* 'No, Sir; Dublin is only a worse capital.' *Boswell:* 'Is not the Giant's-Causeway worth seeing?' *Johnson:* 'Worth seeing, yes; but not worth going to see.'

In 1781 Johnson at last completed his 'Lives of the Poets,' of which he gives this account: 'Some time in March I finished the "Lives of the Poets," which I wrote in my usual way, dilatorily and hastily, unwilling to work, and working with vigour and haste.' In a memorandum previous to this, he says of them: 'Written, I hope, in such a manner as may tend to the promotion of piety.'

This is the work which of all Dr. Johnson's writing will perhaps be read most generally, and with most pleasure. Philology and biography were his favourite pursuits, and those who lived most in intimacy with him, heard him upon all occasions, when there was a proper opportunity, take delight in expatiating upon the various merits of the English Poets: upon the niceties of their characters, and the events of their progress through the world which they contributed to illuminate. His mind was so full of that kind of information, and it was so well arranged in his memory, that in performing what he had undertaken in this way, he had little more to do than to put his thoughts upon paper, exhibiting first each Poet's life, and then subjoining a critical examination of his genius and works. But when he began to write, the subject swelled in such a manner, that instead of prefaces to each poet, of no more than a few pages, as he had originally intended, he produced an ample, rich, and most entertaining view of them in every respect. The booksellers, justly sensible of the great additional value of the copyright, presented him with another hundred pounds, over and above two hundred, for which his agreement was to furnish such prefaces as he thought fit.

This was, however, but a small recompence for such a collection of biography. As he was so good as to make me a present of the greatest part of the original, and indeed only manuscript of this admirable work, I have an opportunity of observing with wonder the correctness with which he rapidly struck off such glowing composition.

'*To James Boswell, Esq.*
'Dear Sir,
'I hoped you had got rid of all this hypocrisy of misery. What have you to do with Liberty and Necessity? Or what more than to hold your tongue about it? Do not doubt but I shall be most heartily glad to see you here again, for I love every part about you but your affectation of distress.

'I have at last finished my Lives, and have laid up for you a load of copy, all out of order, so that it will amuse you a long time to set it right. Come to me, my dear Bozzy, and let us be as happy as we can. We will go again to the Mitre, and talk old times over.

'I am, dear Sir,
'Yours affectionately,
'*Sam. Johnson.*'
'March 14, 1781.'

On Monday, March 19, I arrived in London, and on Tuesday, the 20th, met him in Fleet-street, walking, or rather indeed moving along; for his peculiar march is thus described in a very just and picturesque manner, in a short Life of him published very soon after his death:—'When he walked the streets, what with the constant roll of his head, and the concomitant motion of his body, he appeared to make his way by that motion, independent of his feet.' That he was often much stared at while he advanced in this manner, may easily be believed; but it was not safe to make sport of one so robust as he was. Mr. Langton saw him one day, in a fit of absence, by a sudden start, drive the load off a porter's back, and walk forward briskly, without being conscious of what he had done. The porter was very angry, but stood still, and eyed the huge figure with much earnestness, till he was satisfied that his wisest course was to be quiet, and take up his burthen again.

Our accidental meeting in the street after a long separation was a pleasing surprize to us both. He stepped aside with me into Falcon-court, and made kind inquiries about my family, and as we were in a hurry going different ways, I promised to call on him next day; he said he was engaged to go out in the morning. 'Early, Sir?' said I. *Johnson:* 'Why, Sir, a London morning does not go with the sun.'

I waited on him next evening, and he gave me a great portion of his original manuscript of his 'Lives of the Poets,' which he had preserved for me.

I found on visiting his friend, Mr. Thrale, that he was now very ill, and had removed, I suppose by the solicitation of Mrs. Thrale, to a house in Grosvenor-square. I was sorry to see him sadly changed in his appearance.

He told me I might now have the pleasure to see Dr. Johnson drink wine again, for he had lately returned to it. When I mentioned this to Johnson, he said, 'I drink it now sometimes, but not socially.' The first evening that I was with him at Thrale's, I observed he poured a quantity of it into a large glass, and swallowed it greedily. Every thing about his character and manners was forcible and violent; there never was any moderation; many a day did he fast, many a year did he refrain from wine; but when he did eat, it was voraciously; when he did drink wine, it was copiously. He could practise abstinence, but not temperance.

Mrs. Thrale and I had a dispute, whether Shakspeare or Milton had drawn the most admirable picture of a man. I was for Shakspeare; Mrs. Thrale for Milton; and after a fair hearing, Johnson decided for my opinion.

He said, 'Mrs. Montagu has dropt me. Now, Sir, there are people whom one should like very well to drop, but would not wish to be dropped by.' He certainly was vain of the society of ladies, and could make himself very agreeable to them, when he chose it; Sir Joshua Reynolds agreed with me that he could. Mr. Gibbon, with his usual sneer, controverted it, perhaps in resentment of Johnson's having talked with some disgust of his ugliness, which one would think a *philosopher* would not mind. Dean Marlay wittily observed, 'A lady may be vain when she can turn a wolf-dog into a lap-dog.'

On Sunday, April 1, I dined with him at Mr. Thrale's, with Sir Philip Jennings Clerk and Mr. Perkins, who had the superintendence of

Mr. Thrale's brewery, with a salary of five hundred pounds a year. Sir Philip had the appearance of a gentleman of ancient family, well advanced in life. He wore his own white hair in a bag of goodly size, a black velvet coat, with an embroidered waistcoat, and very rich laced ruffles; which Mrs. Thrale said were old fashioned, but which, for that reason, I thought the more respectable, more like a Tory; yet Sir Philip was then in Opposition in Parliament. 'Ah, Sir, (said Johnson,) ancient ruffles and modern principles do not agree.' Sir Philip defended the opposition to the American war ably and with temper, and I joined him. He said, the majority of the nation was against the ministry. *Johnson:* 'As to the American war, the *sense* of the nation is *with* the ministry. The majority of those who can *understand* is with it; the majority of those who can only *hear* is against it; and as those who can only hear are more numerous than those who can understand, and Opposition is always loudest, a majority of the rabble will be for Opposition.'

This boisterous vivacity entertained us; but the truth in my opinion was, that those who could understand the best were against the American war, as almost every man now is, when the question has been coolly considered.

One of the gentlemen said, he had seen three folio volumes of Dr. Johnson's sayings collected by me. 'I must put you right, Sir, (said I;) for I am very exact in authenticity. You could not see folio volumes, for I have none: you might have seen some in quarto and octavo. This is inattention which one should guard against.' *Johnson:* 'Sir, it is a want of concern about veracity. He does not know that he saw *any* volumes. If he had seen them he could have remembered their size.'

Mr. Thrale appeared very lethargick to-day. I saw him again on Monday evening, at which time he was not thought to be in immediate danger; but early in the morning of Wednesday the 4th, he expired. Johnson was in the house, and thus mentions the event: 'I felt almost the last flutter of his pulse, and looked for the last time upon the face that for fifteen years had never turned upon me but with respect and benignity.' Upon that day there was a *Call* of the *Literary Club;* but Johnson, apologised for his absence by the following note:

'*Mr. Johnson* knows that Sir Joshua Reynolds and the other gentlemen will excuse his incompliance with the Call, when they are told that Mr. Thrale died this morning.'

Mr. Thrale's death was a very essential loss to Johnson, who, although he did not foresee all that afterwards happened, was sufficiently convinced that the comforts which Mr. Thrale's family afforded him, would now in a great measure cease. He, however, continued to shew a kind attention to his widow and children as long as it was acceptable; and he took upon him, with a very earnest concern, the office of one of his executors, the importance of which seemed greater than usual to him, from his circumstances having been always such, that he had scarcely any share in the real business of life. His friends of the *Club* were in hopes that Mr. Thrale might have made a liberal provision for him for his life, which, as Mr. Thrale left no son, and a very large fortune, it would have been highly to his honour to have done; and, considering Dr. Johnson's age, could not have been of long duration; but he bequeathed him only two hundred pounds, which was the legacy given to each of his executors. I could not but be somewhat diverted by hearing Johnson talk in a pompous manner of his new office, and particularly of the concerns of the brewery, which it was at last resolved should be sold. Lord Lucan tells a very good story, which, if not precisely exact, is certainly characteristical: that when the sale of Thrale's brewery was going forward, Johnson appeared bustling about, with an ink-horn and pen in his button-hole, like an excise-man; and on being asked what he really considered to be the value of the property which was to be disposed of, answered, 'We are not here to sell a parcel of boilers and vats, but the potentiality of growing rich, beyond the dreams of avarice.'

On Friday, April 13, being Good-Friday, I went to St. Clement's church with him, as usual. There I saw again his old fellow-collegian,

Edwards, to whom I said, 'I think, Sir, Dr. Johnson and you meet only at Church.'—'Sir, (said he,) it is the best place we can meet in, except Heaven, and I hope we shall meet there too.' Dr. Johnson told me, that there was very little communication between Edwards and him, after their unexpected renewal of acquaintance. 'But (said he, smiling) he met me once, and said, "I am told you have written a very pretty book called *The Rambler*." I was unwilling that he should leave the world in total darkness, and sent him a set.'

Mr. Berenger visited him to-day, and was very pleasing. We talked of an evening society for conversation at a house in town, of which we were all members, but of which Johnson said, 'It will never do, Sir. There is nothing served about there, neither tea, nor coffee, nor lemonade, nor any thing whatever; and depend upon it, Sir, a man does not love to go to a place from whence he comes out exactly as he went in.' I endeavoured for argument's sake, to maintain that men of learning and talents might have very good intellectual society, without the aid of any little gratifications of the senses. Berenger joined with Johnson, and said, that without these any meeting would be dull and insipid. He would therefore have all the slight refreshments; nay, it would not be amiss to have some cold meat, and a bottle of wine upon a side-board. 'Sir, (said Johnson to me, with an air of triumph,) Mr. Berenger knows

the world. Every body loves to have good things furnished to them without any trouble.'

His disorderly habits, when 'making provision for the day that was passing over him,' appear from the following anecdote, communicated to me by Mr. John Nichols:—In the year 1763, a young bookseller, who was an apprentice to Mr. Whiston, waited on him with a subscription to his 'Shakspeare': and observing that the Doctor made no entry in any book of the subscriber's name, ventured diffidently to ask, whether he would please to have the gentleman's address, that it might be properly inserted in the printed list of subscribers.—*'I shall print no List of Subscribers';* said Johnson, with great abruptness: but almost immediately recollecting himself, added, very complacently, Sir, I have two very cogent reasons for not printing any list of subscribers;—one, that I have lost all the names,—the other, that I have spent all the money.'

Johnson could not brook appearing to be worsted in argument, even when he had taken the wrong side, to shew the force and dexterity of his talents. When, therefore, he perceived that his opponent gained ground, he had recourse to some sudden mode of robust sophistry. Once when I was pressing upon him with visible advantage, he stopped me thus:—'My dear Boswell, let's have no more of this; you'll make nothing of it. I'd rather have you whistle a Scotch tune.'

Care, however, must be taken to

distinguish between Johnson when he 'talked for victory,' and Johnson when he had no desire but to inform and illustrate.—'One of Johnson's principal talents (says an eminent friend of his) was shewn in maintaining the wrong side of an argument, and in a splendid perversion of the truth.—If you could contrive to have his fair opinion on a subject, and without any bias from personal prejudice, or from a wish to be victorious in argument, it was wisdom itself, not only convincing, but overpowering.'

I asked him if he was not dissatisfied with having so small a share of wealth, and none of those distinctions in the state which are the objects of ambition. He had only a pension of three hundred a year. Why was he not in such circumstances as to keep his coach? Why had he not some considerable office? *Johnson:* 'Sir, I have never complained of the world; nor do I think that I have reason to complain. It is rather to be wondered at that I have so much. My pension is more out of the usual course of things than any instance that I have known. Here, Sir, was a man avowedly no friend to Government at the time, who got a pension without asking for it. I never courted the great; they sent for me; but I think they now give me up. They are satisfied; they have seen enough of me.' Upon my observing that I could not believe this, for they must certainly be highly pleased by his conversation; conscious of his own superiority, he answered, 'No, Sir;

great Lords and great Ladies don't love to have their mouths stopped.' This was very expressive of the effect which the force of his understanding and brilliancy of his fancy could not but produce; and, to be sure, they must have found themselves strangely diminished in his company. When I warmly declared how happy I was at all times to hear him;—'Yes, Sir, (said he); but if you were Lord Chancellor, it would not be so: you would then consider your own dignity.'

In one of his little memorandum-books is the following minute:

'August 9, 3 P.M., in the summer-house at Streatham.

'After innumerable resolutions formed and neglected, I have retired hither, to plan a life of greater diligence, in hope that I may yet be useful, and be daily better prepared to appear before my Creator and my Judge, from whose infinite mercy I humbly call for assistance and support.

'My purpose is,

'To pass eight hours every day in some serious employment.

'Having prayed, I purpose to employ the next six weeks upon the Italian language, for my settled study.'

In 1782, his complaints increased, and the history of his life this year, is little more than a mournful recital of the variations of his illness, in the midst of which, however, the powers of his mind were in no degree impaired.

The death of Mr. Thrale had made a very material alteration with respect to Johnson's reception in that family. The manly authority of the husband no longer curbed the lively exuberance of the lady; and as her vanity had been fully gratified, by having the Colossus of Literature attached to her for many years, she gradually became less assiduous to please him. Whether her attachment to him was already divided by another object, I am unable to ascertain; but it is plain that Johnson's penetration was alive to her neglect or forced attention; for on the 6th of October this year, we find him making a 'parting use of the library' at Streatham, and pronouncing a prayer, which he composed 'On leaving Mr. Thrale's family.'

'Almighty GOD, Father of all mercy, help me by thy grace, that I may, with humble and sincere thankfulness, remember the comforts and conveniencies which I have enjoyed at this place; and that I may resign them with holy submission, equally trusting in thy protection when Thou givest, and when Thou takest away. Have mercy upon me, O LORD, have mercy upon me.

'To thy fatherly protection, O LORD, I commend this family. Bless, guide, and defend them, that they may so pass through this world, as finally to enjoy in thy presence everlasting happiness, for JESUS CHRIST's sake. Amen.'

One cannot read this prayer, without some emotions not very favourable to the lady whose conduct occasioned it.

In 1783, he was more severely afflicted than ever but still the same ardour for literature, the same constant piety, the same kindness for his friends, and the same vivacity, both in conversation and writing, distinguished him.

On Friday, March 21, having arrived in London the night before, I was glad to find him at Mrs. Thrale's house, in Argyll-street, appearances of friendship between them being still kept up. I was shewn into his room, and after the first salutation he said, 'I am glad you are come. I am very ill.' He looked pale, and was distressed with a difficulty of breathing; but after the common inquiries he assumed his usual strong animated style of conversation.

He sent a message to acquaint Mrs. Thrale that I was arrived. I had not seen her since her husband's death. She soon appeared, and favoured me with an invitation to stay to dinner, which I accepted. There was no other company but herself and three of her daughters, Dr. Johnson, and I. She too said, she was very glad I was come, for she was going to Bath, and should have been sorry to leave Dr. Johnson before I came. This seemed to be attentive and kind; and I who had not been informed of any change, imagined all to be as well as formerly. He was little inclined to talk at dinner, and went to sleep after it; but when he joined us in the drawing-room, he seemed revived, and was again himself.

I had paid a visit to General Oglethorpe in the morning, and was told by him that Dr. Johnson saw company on Saturday evenings, and he would meet me at Johnson's, that night. When I mentioned this to Johnson, not doubting that it would please him, as he had a great value for Oglethorpe, the fretfulness of his disease unexpectedly shewed itself; his anger suddenly kindled, and he said, with vehemence, 'Did not you tell him not to come? Am I to be *hunted* in this manner?' I satisfied him that I could not divine that the visit would not be convenient, and that I certainly could not take it upon me of my own accord to forbid the General.

I found Dr. Johnson in the evening in Mrs. Williams' room, at tea and coffee with her and Mrs. Desmoulins, who were also both ill; it was a sad scene, and he was not in a very good humour. He said of a performance that had lately come out, 'Sir, if you should search all the mad-houses in England, you would not find ten men who would write so, and think it sense.' I was glad when General Oglethorpe's arrival was announced, and we left the ladies. Dr. Johnson attended him in the parlour, and was as courteous as ever.

In the evening I came to him again. He was somewhat fretful from his illness. A gentleman asked him, whether he had been abroad to-day. 'Don't talk so childishly, (said he.) You may as well ask if I hanged myself to-day.' I mentioned politicks. *Johnson:* 'Sir, I'd as soon have a man to break my bones as talk to me of publick affairs, internal or external. I have lived to see things all as bad as they can be.'

Having mentioned his friend the second Lord Southwell, he said, 'Lord Southwell was the highest-bred man without insolence that I ever was in company with; the most *qualitied* I ever saw. Lord Orrey was not dignified: Lord Chesterfield was, but he was insolent.'

On Sunday, March 30, I found him at home in the evening, and had the pleasure to meet with Dr. Brocklesby, whose reading, and knowledge of life, and good spirits, supply him with a never-failing source of conversation. He mentioned a respectable gentleman, who became extremely penurious near the close of his life. Johnson said there must have been a degree of madness about him. 'Not at all, Sir, (said Dr. Brocklesby,) his judgement was entire.' Unluckily, however, he mentioned that although he had a fortune of twenty-seven thousand pounds, he denied himself many comforts, from an apprehension that he could not afford them. 'Nay, Sir, (cried Johnson,) when the judgement is so disturbed that a man cannot count, that is pretty well.'

I shall here insert a few of Johnson's sayings, without the formality of dates, as they have no reference to any particular time or place.

Sir Joshua once observed to him, that he had talked above the capacity of some people with whom they had been in company together.

'No matter, Sir, (said Johnson); they consider it as a compliment to be talked to, as if they were wiser than they are. So true is this, Sir, that Baxter made it a rule in every sermon that he preached, to say something that was above the capacity of his audience.'

Johnson's attention to precision and clearness in expression was very remarkable. He disapproved of parentheses; and I believe in all his voluminous writings, not half a dozen of them will be found. He never used the phrases *the former* and *the latter,* having observed, that they often occasioned obscurity; he therefore contrived to construct his sentences so as not to have occasion for them, and would even rather repeat the same words, in order to avoid them.

The heterogeneous composition of human nature was remarkably exemplified in Johnson. His liberality in giving his money to persons in distress was extraordinary. Yet there lurked about him a propensity to paltry saving. One day I owned to him that 'I was occasionally troubled with a fit of *narrowness.'* 'Why, Sir, (said he,) so am I. *But I do not tell it.'* He has now and then borrowed a shilling of me; and when I asked for it again, seemed to be rather out of humour. A droll little circumstance once occurred: As if he meant to reprimand my minute exactness as a creditor, he thus addressed me;—'Boswell, *lend* me sixpence—*not to be repaid.'*

Johnson, for sport perhaps, or from the spirit of contradiction, eagerly maintained that Derrick had merit as a writer. Mr. Morgann argued with him directly, in vain. At length he had recourse to this device. 'Pray, Sir, (said he,) whether do you reckon Derrick or Smart the best poet?' Johnson at once felt himself rouzed; and answered, 'Sir, there is no settling the point of precedency between a louse and a flea.'

I never shall forget the indulgence with which he treated Hodge, his cat: for whom he himself used to go out and buy oysters, lest the servants having that trouble should take a dislike to the poor creature. I am, unluckily, one of those who have an antipathy to a cat, so that I am uneasy when in the room with one; and I own, I frequently suffered a good deal from the presence of this same Hodge. I recollect him one day scrambling up Dr. Johnson's breast, apparently with much satisfaction, while my friend smiling and half-whistling, rubbed down his back, and pulled him by the tail; and when I observed he was a fine cat, saying, 'why yes, Sir, but I have had cats whom I liked better than this'; and then as if perceiving Hodge to be out of countenance, adding, 'but he is a very fine cat, a very fine cat indeed.'

This reminds me of the ludicrous account which he gave Mr. Langton, of the despicable state of a young Gentleman of good family. 'Sir, when I heard of him last, he was running about town shooting cats.' And then in a sort of kindly reverie, he bethought himself of his own favourite cat, and said, 'But Hodge shan't be shot; no, no, Hodge shall not be shot.'

On Sunday, April 20, being Easter-day, after attending solemn service at St. Paul's I came to Dr. Johnson, and found Mr. Lowe, the painter, sitting with him. Mr. Lowe mentioned the great number of new buildings of late in London, yet that Dr. Johnson had observed, that the number of inhabitants was not increased. *Johnson:* Why, Sir, the bills of mortality prove that no more people die now than formerly; so it is plain no more live. The register of births proves nothing, for not one tenth of the people of London are born there.' *Boswell:* 'I believe, Sir, a great many of the children born in London die early.' *Johnson:* 'Why, yes, Sir.' *Boswell:* 'But those who do live, are as stout and strong people as any: Dr. Price says, they must be naturally stronger to get through.' *Johnson:* 'That is system, Sir. A great traveller observes, that it is said there are no weak or deformed people among the Indians; but he with much sagacity assigns the reason of this, which is, that the hardship of their life as hunters and fishers, does not allow weak or diseased children to grow up. Now had I been an Indian, I must have died early; my eyes would not have served me to get food. I indeed now could fish, give me English tackle; but had I been an Indian I must have starved, or they would have knocked me

on the head, when they saw I could do nothing.' *Boswell:* 'Perhaps they would have taken care of you: we are told they are fond of oratory, you would have talked to them.' *Johnson:* 'Nay, Sir, I should not have lived long enough to be fit to talk; I should have been dead before I was ten years old. Depend upon it, Sir, a savage, when he is hungry, will not carry about with him a looby of nine years old, who cannot help himself. They have no affection, Sir.' *Boswell:* 'But some of the Indians have affection.' *Johnson:* 'Sir, that they help some of their children is plain; for some of them live, which they could not do without being helped.'

Talking of a man who was grown very fat, so as to be incommoded with corpulency; he said, 'He eats too much, Sir.' *Boswell:* 'I don't know, Sir, you will see one man fat who eats moderately, and another lean who eats a great deal.' *Johnson:* 'Nay, Sir, whatever may be the quantity that a man eats, it is plain that if he is too fat, he has eaten more than he should have done. One man may have a digestion that consumes food better than common; but it is certain that solidity is encreased by putting something to it.'

I have no minute of any interview with Johnson till Thursday, May 15, when I find what follows: —*Boswell:* 'I wish much to be in Parliament, Sir.' *Johnson:* 'Why, Sir, unless you come resolved to support any administration, you would be the worse for being in

Parliament, because you would be obliged to live more expensively.' *Boswell:* 'Perhaps, Sir, I should be the less happy for being in Parliament. I never would sell my vote, and I should be vexed if things went wrong.' *Johnson:* 'That's cant, Sir. It would not vex you more in the house, than in the gallery: publick affairs vex no man.' *Boswell:* 'Have not they vexed yourself a little, Sir? Have not you been vexed by all the turbulence of this reign?' *Johnson:* 'Sir, I have never slept an hour less, nor eat an ounce less meat. I would have knocked the factious dogs on the head, to be sure; but I was not *vexed.*' *Boswell:* 'I declare, Sir, upon my honour, I did imagine I was vexed, and took a pride in it; but it *was,* perhaps, cant; for I own I neither ate less, nor slept less.' *Johnson:* 'My dear friend, clear your *mind* of cant. You may *talk* as other people do: you may say to a man, "Sir, I am your most humble servant." You are *not* his most humble servant. You may say, "These are sad times; it is a melancholy thing to be reserved to such times." You don't mind the times. You tell a man, "I am sorry you had such bad weather the last day of your journey, and were so much wet." You don't care six-pence whether he was wet or dry. You may *talk* in this manner; it is a mode of talking in Society: but don't *think* foolishly.'

I asked whether a man naturally virtuous, or one who has overcome wicked inclinations is the best. *Johnson:* 'Sir, to *you,* the man who has overcome wicked inclinations is not the best. He has more merit to *himself.* I would rather trust my money to a man who has no hands, and so a physical impossibility to steal, than to a man of the most honest principles. There is a witty satirical story of Foote. He had a small bust of Garrick placed upon his bureau. "You may be surprized (said he) that I allow him to be so near my gold;—but you will observe he has no hands." '

On Friday, May 29, being to set out for Scotland next morning, I passed a part of the day with him in more than usual earnestness; as his health was in a more precarious state than at any time when I had parted from him. He, however, was quick and lively, and critical as usual. I mentioned one who was a very learned man. *Johnson:* 'Yes, Sir, he has a great deal of learning; but it never lies straight. There is never one idea by the side of another; tis all entangled: and then he drives it so aukwardly upon conversation.'

I assured him, that in the extensive and various range of his acquaintance there never had been any one who had a more sincere respect and affection for him than I had. He said, 'I believe it, Sir. Were I in distress, there is no man to whom I should sooner come than to you. I should like to come and have a cottage in your park, toddle about, live mostly on milk, and be taken care of by Mrs. Boswell. She and I are good friends now; are we not?'

✗ Chapter 12

'I'll Have No More on't'

My anxious apprehensions at parting with him this year proved to be but too well founded; for not long afterwards he had a dreadful stroke of the palsy, of which there are very full and accurate accounts in letters written by himself, which shew with what composure of mind, and resignation to the Divine Will, his steady piety enabled him to behave.

'*To Mr. Edmund Allen.*

'Dear Sir,

'It has pleased God, this morning, to deprive me of the powers of speech; and as I do not know but that it may be his further good pleasure to deprive me soon of my senses, I request you will on the receipt of this note, come to me, and act for me, as the exigencies of my case may require.

'I am,

'Sincerely yours,

'*Sam. Johnson.*'

'June 17, 1783.'

Two days after he wrote thus to Mrs. Thrale:

'On Monday, the 16th, I sat for my picture, and walked a considerable way with little inconvenience. In the afternoon and evening I felt myself light and easy, and began to plan schemes of life. Thus I went to bed, and in a short time waked and sat up, as has been long my custom, when I felt a confusion and indistinctness in my head, which lasted, I suppose, about half a minute. I was alarmed, and prayed God, that however he might afflict my body, he would spare my understanding. This prayer, that I might try the integrity of my faculties, I made in Latin verse. The lines were not very good, but I knew them not to be very good: I made them easily, and concluded myself to be unimpaired in my faculties.

'Soon after I perceived that I had suffered a paralytick stroke, and that my speech was taken from me. I had no pain, and so little dejection in this dreadful state, that I wondered at my own apathy, and considered that perhaps death itself, when it should come, would excite less horrour than seems now to attend it.

Such was the general vigour of his constitution, that he recovered from this alarming and severe attack with wonderful quickness; so that in July he was able to make a visit to Mr. Langton at Rochester, where he passed about a fortnight, and made little excursions as easily as at any time of his life. In August he went as far as the neighbourhood of Salisbury, to Heale, the seat of William Bowles, Esq. In his diary I find a short but honourable mention of this visit:—'August 28, I came to Heale without fatigue. 30. I am entertained quite to my mind.'

His fortitude and patience met with severe trials during this year. The stroke of the palsy has been related circumstantially; but he was also afflicted with the gout, and was besides troubled with a complaint which not only was attended with immediate inconvenience, but threatened him with a painful chirurgical operation, from which most men would shrink. Johnson bore this with uncommon firmness, and was not at all frightened while he looked forward to amputation.

Happily the complaint abated without his being put to the torture of amputation. But we must surely admire the manly resolution which he discovered while it hung over him.

In a letter to Dr. Mudge of Plymouth he writes, 'The gout has within these four days come upon me with a violence which I never experienced before. It made me helpless as an infant.' And in another, having mentioned Mrs. Williams, he says,—'whose death following that of Levet, has now made my house a solitude. She left her little substance to a charity-school. She is, I hope, where there is neither darkness, nor want, nor sorrow.'

He this autumn received a visit from the celebrated Mrs. Siddons.[1]

Johnson, indeed, had thought more upon the subject of acting than might be generally supposed. Talking of it one day to Mr. Kemble, he said, 'Are you, Sir, one of those enthusiasts who believe yourself transformed into the very character you represent?' Upon Mr. Kemble's answering that he had never felt so strong a persuasion himself; 'To be sure not, Sir (said Johnson;) the thing is impossible. And if Garrick really believed himself to be that monster, Richard the

Third, he deserved to be hanged every time he performed it.'

In the end of this year he was seized with a spasmodick asthma of such violence, that he was confined to the house in great pain, being sometimes obliged to sit all night in his chair, a recumbent posture being so hurtful to his respiration, that he could not endure lying in bed; and there came upon him at the same time that oppressive and fatal disease, a dropsy. It was a very severe winter, which probably aggravated his complaints; and the solitude in which Mr. Levet and Mrs. Williams had left him, rendered his life very gloomy. Mrs. Desmoulins, who still lived, was herself so very ill, that she could contribute very little to his relief. He, however, had none of that unsocial shyness which we commonly see in people afflicted with sickness. He did not hide his head from the world, in solitary abstraction; he did not deny himself to the visits of his friends and acquaintances; but at all times, when he was not overcome by sleep, was ready for conversation as in his best days.

And now I am arrived at the last year of the life of *Samuel Johnson,* a year in which, although passed in severe indisposition, he nevertheless gave many evidences of the continuance of those wondrous powers of mind, which raised him so high in the intellectual world. His conversation and his letters of this year were in no respect inferior to those of former years.

[1] Siddons, Sarah Kemble (1755–1831): a leading actress of the time.

On Wednesday, May 5, I arrived in London, and next morning had the pleasure to find Dr. Johnson greatly recovered. I but just saw him; for a coach was waiting to carry him to Islington, to the house of his friend the Reverend Mr. Strahan, where he went sometimes for the benefit of good air, which, notwithstanding his having formerly laughed at the general opinion upon the subject, he now acknowledged was conducive to health.

One morning afterwards, when I found him alone, he communicated to me, with solemn earnestness, a very remarkable circumstance which had happened in the course of his illness, when he was much distressed by the dropsy. He had shut himself up, and employed a day in particular exercises of religion,—fasting, humiliation, and prayer. On a sudden he obtained extraordinary relief, for which he looked up to Heaven with grateful devotion. He made no direct inference from this fact; but from his manner of telling it, I could perceive that it appeared to him as something more than an incident in the common course of events.

On Saturday, May 15, I dined with him at Dr. Brocklesby's, where were Colonel Vallancy, Mr. Murphy, and that ever-cheerful companion Mr. Devaynes, apothecary to his Majesty. Of these days, and others on which I saw him, I have no memorials, except the general recollection of his being able and animated in conversation, and ap-pearing to relish society as much as the youngest man. I find only these three small particulars:—One, when a person was mentioned, who said, 'I have lived fifty-one years in this world without having had ten minutes of uneasiness'; he exclaimed, 'The man who says so, lies: he attempts to impose on human credulity.' The Bishop of Exeter in vain observed, that men were very different. His Lordship's manner was not impressive, and I learnt afterwards that Johnson did not find out that the person who talked to him was a Prelate; if he had, I doubt not that he would have treated him with more respect; for once talking of George Psalmanazar, whom he reverenced for his piety, he said, 'I should as soon think of contradicting a *Bishop.*' One of the company provoked him greatly by doing what he could least of all bear, which was quoting something of his own writing, against what he then maintained. 'What, Sir, (cried the gentleman,) do you say to

"The busy day, the peaceful night,
Unfelt, uncounted, glided by"?'

Johnson finding himself thus presented as giving an instance of a man who had lived without uneasiness, was much offended, for he looked upon such quotation as unfair. His anger burst out in an unjustifiable retort, insinuating that the gentleman's remark was a sally of ebriety; 'Sir, there is one passion I would advise you to command, when you have drunk out that glass, don't drink another.' Here was exemplified what Goldsmith said of him, with the aid of a very witty image from one of Cibber's Comedies: 'There is no arguing with Johnson; for if his pistol misses fire, he knocks you down with the butt end of it.'—Another was this: when a gentleman of eminence in the literary world was violently censured for attacking people by anonymous paragraphs in newspapers; he, from the spirit of contradiction as I thought, took up his defence, and said, 'Come, come, this is not so terrible a crime; he means only to vex them a little. I do not say that I should do it; but there is a great difference between him and me.' Another, when I told him that a young and handsome Countess had said to me, 'I should think that to be praised by Dr. Johnson would make one a fool all one's life'; and that I answered, 'Madam, I shall make him a fool to-day, by repeating this to him,' he said, 'I am too old to be made a fool; but if you say I am made a fool, I shall not deny it. I am much pleased with a compliment, especially from a pretty woman.'

On Sunday, May 16, I found him alone; he talked of Mrs. Thrale with much concern, saying, 'Sir, she has done every thing wrong, since Thrale's bridle was off her neck'; and was proceeding to mention some circumstances which have since been the subject of publick discussion, when he was interrupted by the arrival of Dr. Douglas, now Bishop of Salisbury.

Johnson, talking of the fear of death, said, 'Some people are not afraid, because they look upon salvation as the effect of an absolute decree, and think they feel in themselves the marks of sanctification. Others, and those the most rational in my opinion, look upon salvation as conditional; and as they never can be sure that they have complied with the conditions, they are afraid.'

On Wednesday, May 19, I sat a part of the evening with him, by ourselves. I observed, that the death of our friends might be a consolation against the fear of our own dissolution, because we might have more friends in the other world than in this. He perhaps felt this as a reflection upon his apprehension as to death; and said, with heat, 'How can a man know *where* his departed friends are, or whether they will be his friends in the other world? How many friendships have you known formed upon principles of virtue? Most friendships are formed by caprice or by chance, mere confederacies in vice or leagues in folly.'

He charged Mr. Langton with what he thought want of judgement upon an interesting occasion. 'When I was ill, (said he) I desired he would tell me sincerely in what he thought my life was faulty. Sir, he brought me a sheet of paper, on which he had written down several texts of Scripture, recommending Christian charity. And when I questioned him what occasion I had given for such an animadversion, all that he could say amounted to this,—that I sometimes contradicted people in conversation. Now what harm does it do to any man to be contradicted?' *Boswell:* 'I suppose he meant the *manner* of doing it; roughly,—and harshly.' *Johnson:* 'And who is the worse for that? *Boswell:* 'It hurts people of weak nerves.' *Johnson:* 'I know no such weak-nerved people.' Mr. Burke, to whom I related this conference, said, 'It is well, if when a man comes to die, he has nothing heavier upon his conscience than having been a little rough in conversation.'

Johnson, at the time when the paper was presented to him, though at first pleased with the attention of his friend, whom he thanked in an earnest manner, soon exclaimed, in a loud and angry tone, 'What is your drift, Sir?' Sir Joshua Reynolds pleasantly observed, that it was a scene for a comedy, to see a penitent get into a violent passion and belabour his confessor.

He had now a great desire to go to Oxford, as his first jaunt after his illness; we talked of it for some days, and I had promised to accompany him. He was impatient and fretful tonight, because I did not at once agree to go with him on Thursday. When I considered how ill he had been, and what allowance should be made for the influence of sickness upon his temper, I resolved to indulge him, though with some inconvenience to myself, as I wished to attend the musical meeting in honour of Handel, in Westminster-Abbey, on the following Saturday.

On Thursday, June 3, the Oxford post-coach took us up in the morning at Bolt-court. The other two passengers were Mrs. Beresford and her daughter, two very agreeable ladies from America; they were going to Worcestershire, where they then resided. Frank had been sent by his master the day before to take places for us; and I found from the way-bill, that Dr. Johnson had made our names be put down. Mrs. Beresford, who had read it, whispered me, 'Is this the great Dr. Johnson?' I told her it was; so she was then prepared to listen. As she soon happened to mention in a voice so low that Johnson did not hear it, that her husband had been a member of the American Congress, I cautioned her to beware of introducing that subject, as she must know how very violent Johnson was against the people of that country. He talked a great deal, but I am sorry I have preserved little of the conversation. Miss Beresford was so much charmed, that she said to me aside, 'How he does talk! Every sentence is an essay.'

I was surprised at his talking without reserve in the publick post-coach of the state of his affairs; 'I have (said he) about the world I think above a thousand pounds, which I intend shall afford Frank an annuity of seventy pounds a year.' Indeed his openness with people at a first interview was remarkable. He said once to Mr. Langton, 'I think I am like Squire Richard in "The Journey to London." *"I'm never strange in a strange place."'*

He was truly *social*. He strongly censured what is much too common in England among persons of condition,—maintaining an absolute silence, when unknown to each other; as for instance, when occasionally brought together in a room before the master or mistress of the house has appeared. 'Sir, that is being so uncivilised as not to understand the common rights of humanity.'

At the inn where we stopped he was exceedingly dissatisfied with some roast mutton which we had for dinner. The ladies I saw wondered to see the great philosopher, whose wisdom and wit they had been admiring all the way, get into ill-humour from such a cause. He scolded the waiter, saying, 'It is as bad as bad can be: it is ill-fed, ill-killed, ill-kept, and ill-drest.'

He bore the journey very well, and seemed to feel himself elevated as he approached Oxford, that magnificent and venerable seat of Learning, Orthodoxy, and Toryism. Frank came in the heavy coach, in readiness to attend him; and we were received with the most polite hospitality at the house of his old friend Dr. Adams, Master of Pembroke College.

After dinner, when one of us talked of there being a great enmity between Whig and Tory;—*Johnson:* 'Why not so much, I think, unless when they come into competition with each other. There is none when they are only common acquaintance, none when they are of different sexes. A Tory will marry into a Whig family, and a Whig into a Tory family, without any reluctance. But indeed, in a matter of much more concern than political tenets, and that is religion, men and women do not concern themselves much about difference of opinion; and ladies set no value on the moral character of men who pay their addresses to them; the greatest profligate will be as well received as the man of the greatest virtue, and this by a very good woman, by a woman who says her prayers three times a day.' Our ladies endeavoured to defend their sex from this charge; but he roared them down! 'No, no; a lady will take Jonathan Wild [1] as readily as St. Austin, if he has threepence more; and, what is worse, her parents will give her to him. Women have a perpetual envy of our vices; they are less vicious than we, not from choice, but because we restrict them; they are the slaves of order and fashion; their virtue is of more consequence to us than our own, so far as concerns this world.'

Miss Adams mentioned a gentleman of licentious character, and said, 'Suppose I had a mind to marry that gentleman, would my parents consent?' *Johnson:* 'Yes, they'd consent, and you'd go. You'd go though they did not consent.' *Miss Adams:* 'Perhaps their opposing might make me go.' *Johnson:* 'O, very well; you'd take one whom you think a bad man, to have the

[1] Jonathan Wild (1682–1725): in his prime, the boss of the London underworld.

pleasure of vexing your parents. You put me in mind of Dr. Barrowby, the physician, who was very fond of swine's flesh. One day, when he was eating it, he said, 'I wish I was a Jew.'—'Why so? (said somebody); the Jews are not allowed to eat your favourite meat.'—'Because, (said he,) I should then have the gust of eating it, with the pleasure of sinning.'—Johnson then proceeded in his declamation.

On Friday, June 11, we talked at breakfast, of forms of prayer. *Johnson:* 'I know of no good prayers but those in the "Book of Common Prayer."' *Dr. Adams* (in a very earnest manner): 'I wish, Sir, you would compose some family prayers.' We all now gathered about him, and two or three of us at a time joined in pressing him to execute this plan. He seemed to be a little displeased at the manner of our importunity, and in great agitation called out, 'Do not talk thus of what is so aweful. I know not what time GOD will allow me in this world. There are many things which I wish to do.' Some of us persisted, and Dr. Adams said, 'I never was more serious about any thing in my life' *Johnson:* 'Let me alone, let me alone. I am overpowered.' And then he put his hands before his face, and reclined for some time upon the table.

Dr. Johnson and I went in Dr. Adams' coach to dine with Dr. Nowell, Principal of St. Mary Hall, at his beautiful villa at Iffley, on the banks of the Isis, about two miles from Oxford. While we were upon the road, I had the resolution to ask Johnson whether he thought that the roughness of his manner had been an advantage or not, and if he would not have done more good if he had been more gentle. I proceeded to answer myself thus: 'Perhaps it has been of advantage, as it has given weight to what you said: you could not, perhaps, have talked with such authority without it.' *Johnson:* 'No, Sir; I have done more good as I am. Obscenity and Impiety have always been repressed in my company.' *Boswell:* 'True, Sir; and that is more than can be said of every Bishop. Greater liberties have been taken in the presence of a Bishop, though a very good man, from his being milder, and therefore not commanding such awe. Yet, Sir, many people who might have been benefited by your conversation, have been frightened away. A worthy friend of ours has told me, that he has often been afraid to talk to you.' *Johnson:* 'Sir, he need not have been afraid, if he had any thing rational to say. If he had not, it was better he did not talk.'

When I mentioned Thomas Lord Lyttelton's vision, the prediction of the time of his death, and its exact fulfilment:—*Johnson:* 'It is the most extraordinary thing that has happened in my day. I heard it with my own ears, from his uncle, Lord Westcote. I am so glad to have every evidence of the spiritual world, that I am willing to believe it.' *Dr. Adams:* 'You have evidence enough; good evidence, which needs not such support.' *Johnson:* 'I like to have more.'

Mr. Henderson, with whom I had sauntered in the venerable walks of Merton-College, and found him a very learned and pious man, supped with us. Dr. Johnson surprised him not a little, by acknowledging with a look of horrour, that he was much oppressed by the fear of death. The amiable Dr. Adams suggested that GOD was infinitely good. *Johnson:* 'That he is infinitely good, as far as the perfection of his nature will allow, I certainly believe; but it is necessary for good upon the whole, that individuals should be punished. As to an *individual,* therefore, he is not infinitely good; and as I cannot be *sure* that I have fulfilled the conditions on which salvation is granted, I am afraid I may be one of those who shall be damned.' (looking dismally.) *Dr. Adams:* 'What do you mean by damned?' *Johnson* (passionately and loudly): 'Sent to Hell, Sir, and punished everlastingly.' *Dr. Adams:* 'I don't believe that doctrine.' *Johnson:* 'Hold, Sir; do you believe that some will be punished at all?' *Dr. Adams:* 'Being excluded from Heaven will be a punishment; yet there may be no great positive suffering.' *Johnson:* 'Well, Sir; but, if you admit any degree of punishment, there is an end of your argument for infinite goodness simply considered; for infinite goodness would inflict no punishment whatever. There is not infinite goodness physically considered; morally there is.' *Boswell:*

'But may not a man attain to such a degree of hope as not to be uneasy from the fear of death?' *Johnson:* 'A man may have such a degree of hope as to keep him quiet. You see I am not quiet, from the vehemence with which I talk; but I do not despair.' *Mrs. Adams:* 'You seem, Sir, to forget the merits of our Redeemer.' *Johnson:* 'Madam, I do not forget the merits of my Redeemer; but my Redeemer has said that he will set some on his right hand and some on his left.'—He was in gloomy agitation, and said, 'I'll have no more on't.'

From the subject of death we passed to discourse of life, whether it was upon the whole more happy or miserable. Johnson was decidedly for the balance of misery.

It was observed to Dr. Johnson, that it seemed strange that he, who has so often delighted his company by his lively and brilliant conversation, should say he was miserable. *Johnson:* 'Alas! it is all outside; I may be cracking my joke, and cursing the sun. *Sun, how I hate thy beams!*' I knew not well what to think of this declaration; whether to hold it as a genuine picture of his mind, or as the effect of his persuading himself contrary to fact, that the position which he had assumed as to human unhappiness, was true.

We talked of the casuistical question, Whether it was allowable at any time to depart from *Truth?* *Johnson:* 'The general rule is, that Truth should never be violated, because it is of the utmost importance to the comfort of life, that we should have a full security by mutual faith; and occasional inconveniencies should be willingly suffered that we may preserve it. There must, however, be some exceptions. If, for instance, a murderer should ask you which way a man is gone, you may tell him what is not true, because you are under a previous obligation not to betray a man to a murderer. But I deny the lawfulness of telling a lie to a sick man for fear of alarming him. You have no business with consequences; you are to tell the truth. Besides, you are not sure what effect your telling him that he is in danger may have. It may bring his distemper to a crisis, and that may cure him. Of all lying, I have the greatest abhorrence of this, because I believe it has been frequently practised on myself.'

In the morning of Tuesday, June 15, while we sat at Dr. Adams', we talked of a printed letter from the Reverend Herbert Croft, to a young gentleman who had been his pupil, in which he advised him to read to the end of whatever books he should begin to read. *Johnson:* 'This is surely a strange advice; you may as well resolve that whatever men you happen to get acquainted with, you are to keep to them for life. A book may be good for nothing; or there may be only one thing in it worth knowing; are we to read it all through? These Voyages, (pointing to the three large volumes of "Voyages to the South Sea," which were just come out)

who will read them through? A man had better work his way before the mast, than read them through. There can be little entertainment in such books; one set of Savages is like another.' *Boswell:* 'I do not think the people of Otaheité can be reckoned Savages.' *Johnson:* 'Don't cant in defence of Savages.' *Boswell:* 'They have the art of navigation.' *Johnson:* 'A dog or a cat can swim.' *Boswell:* 'They carve very ingeniously.' *Johnson:* 'A cat can scratch, and a child with a nail can scratch.'

After his return to London from this excursion, I saw him frequently, but have few memorandums: I shall therefore here insert some particulars which I collected at various times.

Johnson was present when a tragedy was read, in which there occurred this line:

'Who rules o'er freemen should himself be free.'

The company having admired it much, 'I cannot agree with you (said Johnson:) It might as well be said,

"Who drives fat oxen should himself be fat." '

Johnson having argued for some time with a pertinacious gentleman; his opponent, who had talked in a very puzzling manner, happened to say, 'I don't understand you, Sir': upon which Johnson observed, 'Sir, I have found you an argument; but I am not obliged to find you an understanding.'

The difference, he observed, between a well-bred and an ill-bred man is this: 'One immediately attracts your liking, the other your aversion. You love the one till you find reason to hate him; you hate the other till you find reason to love him.'

He seemed to take a pleasure in speaking in his own style; for when he had carelessly missed it, he would repeat the thought translated into it. Talking of the Comedy of 'The Rehearsal,' he said, 'It has not wit enough to keep it sweet.' This was easy;—he therefore caught himself, and pronounced a more rounded sentence; 'It has not vitality enough to preserve it from putrefaction.'

His generous humanity to the miserable was almost beyond example. The following instance is well attested: Coming home late one night, he found a poor woman lying in the street, so much exhausted that she could not walk; he took her upon his back, and carried her to his house, where he discovered that she was one of those wretched females who had fallen into the lowest state of vice, poverty, and disease. Instead of harshly upbraiding her, he had her taken care of with all tenderness for a long time, at considerable expence, till she was restored to health, and endeavoured to put her into a virtuous way of living.

On Wednesday, June 23, I visited him in the morning, after having been present at the shocking sight of fifteen men executed before Newgate. I said to him, I was sure that human life was not machinery, that is to say, a chain of fatality planned and directed by the Supreme Being, as it had in it so much wickedness and misery, so many instances of both, as that by which my mind was now clouded. Were it machinery it would be better than it is in these respects, though less noble, as not being a system of moral government. He agreed with me now, as he always did, upon the great question of the liberty of the human will, which has been in all ages perplexed with so much sophistry. 'But, Sir, as to the doctrine of Necessity, no man believes it. If a man should give me arguments that I do not see, though I could not answer them, should I believe that I do not see?' It will be observed that Johnson at all times made the just distinction between doctrines *contrary* to reason, and doctrines *above* reason.

We this day dined at Sir Joshua Reynolds' with General Paoli, Lord Eliot (formerly Mr. Eliot of Port Eliot,) Dr. Beattie, and some other company. Talking of Lord Chesterfield;—*Johnson:* 'His manner was exquisitely elegant, and he had more knowledge than I expected.' *Boswell:* 'Did you find, Sir, his conversation to be of a superiour style?' *Johnson:* 'Sir, in the conversation which I had with him I had the best right to superiority, for it was upon philology and literature.'

An addition to our company came after we went up to the

drawing-room; Dr. Johnson seemed to rise in spirits as his audience increased. He entered upon a curious discussion of the difference between intuition and sagacity; one being immediate in its effect, the other requiring a circuitous process; one he observed was the *eye* of the mind, the other the *nose* of the mind.

A young gentleman present took up the argument against him, and maintained that no man ever thinks of the *nose of the mind,* not adverting that though that figurative sense seems strange to us, as very unusual, it is truly not more forced than Hamlet's 'In my *mind's eye,* Horatio.' He persisted much too long, and appeared to Johnson as putting himself forward as his antagonist with too much presumption; upon which he called to him in a loud tone, 'What is it you are contending for, if you *be* contending?'—And afterwards imagining that the gentleman retorted upon him with a kind of smart drollery, he said, 'Mr. ——, it does not become you to talk so to me. Besides, ridicule is not your talent; you have *there* neither intuition nor sagacity.'—The gentleman protested that he had intended no improper freedom, but had the greatest respect for Dr. Johnson. After a short pause, during which we were somewhat uneasy,—*Johnson:* 'Give me your hand, Sir. You were too tedious, and I was too short.' *Mr. ——:* 'Sir, I am honoured by your attention in any way.' *Johnson:* 'Come, Sir, let's have no more of it.

We offended one another by our contention; let us not offend the company by our compliments.'

Soon after this time Dr. Johnson had the mortification of being informed by Mrs. Thrale, that 'what she supposed he never believed,' was true; namely, that she was actually going to marry Signor Piozzi, an Italian musick-master. He endeavoured to prevent it; but in vain. If she would publish the whole of the correspondence that passed between Dr. Johnson and her on the subject, we should have a full view of his real sentiments. As it is, our judgement must be biassed by that characteristick specimen which Sir John Hawkins has given us: 'Poor Thrale! I thought that either her virtue or her vice would have restrained her from such a marriage. She is now become a subject for her enemies to exult over; and for her friends, if she has any left, to forget, or pity.'

It must be admitted that Johnson derived a considerable portion of happiness from the comforts and elegancies which he enjoyed in Mr. Thrale's family; but Mrs. Thrale assures us he was indebted for these to her husband alone, who certainly respected him sincerely. Her words are,

'*Veneration for his virtue, reverence for his talents,* delight *in his conversation, and* habitual endurance of a yoke my husband first put upon me, *and of which he contentedly bore his share for sixteen or seventeen years, made me go on so long with* Mr. Johnson; *but the perpetual*

confinement I will own to have been
terrifying *in the first years of our
friendship, and* irksome *in the last;
nor could I pretend to support it
without help, when my coadjutor
was no more.'*

Alas! how different is this from
the declarations which I have heard
Mrs. Thrale make in his life-time,
without a single murmur against
any peculiarities, or against any
one circumstance which attended
their intimacy.

As a sincere friend of the great
man whose Life I am writing, I
think it necessary to guard my readers against the mistaken notion of
Dr. Johnson's character, which this
lady's 'Anecdotes' of him suggest;
for from the very nature and form
of her book, it 'lends deception
lighter wings to fly.'

I certainly, then, do not claim
too much in behalf of my illustrious
friend in saying, that however
smart and entertaining Mrs.
Thrale's 'Anecdotes' are, they must
not be held as good evidence against
him; for wherever an instance of
harshness and severity is told, I
beg leave to doubt its perfect authenticity.

The evident tendency of the following anecdote, for example, is
to represent Dr. Johnson as extremely deficient in affection, tenderness, or even common civility.

*'When I one day lamented the loss
of a first cousin killed in* America,—
*"Prithee, my dear, (said he,) have
done with canting; how would the
world be the worse for it, I may ask,
if all your relations were at once*

spitted like larks, and roasted for
Presto's *supper?"*—Presto *was the
dog that lay under the table while we
talked.'*

I allow that he made her an angry
speech; but let the circumstances
fairly appear, as told by Mr. Baretti,
who was present:

'Mrs. Thrale, while supping very
heartily upon larks, laid down her
knife and fork, and abruptly exclaimed, "O, my dear Mr. Johnson,
do you know what has happened?
The last letters from abroad have
brought us an account that our poor
cousin's head was taken off by a can-
nonball." Johnson, who was shocked
both at the fact, and her light unfeel-
ing manner of mentioning it, replied,
"Madam, it would give you very little concern if all your relations were
spitted like those larks, and drest for
Presto's supper." '

It is with concern that I find myself obliged to animadvert on the
inaccuracies of Mrs. Piozzi's 'Anecdotes,' and perhaps I may be
thought to have dwelt too long
upon her little collection. But
as from Johnson's long residence
under Mr. Thrale's roof, and his
intimacy with her, the account
which she has given of him may
have made an unfavourable and
unjust impression, my duty, as a
faithful biographer, has obliged me
reluctantly to perform this unpleasing task.

As Johnson had now very faint
hopes of recovery, and as Mrs.
Thrale was no longer devoted to
him, it might have been supposed
that he would naturally have

chosen to remain in the comfortable house of his beloved wife's daughter, and end his life where he began it. Such was his intellectual ardour even at this time, that he said to one friend, 'Sir, I look upon every day to be lost, in which I do not make a new acquaintance'; and to another, when talking of his illness, 'I will be conquered; I will not capitulate.' And such was his love of London, so high a relish had he of its magnificent extent, and variety of intellectual entertainment, that he languished when absent from it, his mind having become quite luxurious from the long habit of enjoying the metropolis; and, therefore, although at Lichfield, surrounded with friends, who loved and revered him, and for whom he had a very sincere affection, he still found that such conversation as London affords, could be found no where else. These feelings, joined, probably, to some flattering hopes of aid from the eminent physicians and surgeons in London, who kindly and generously attended him without accepting of fees, made him resolve to return to the capital.

Still his love of literature did not fail. A very few days before his death he transmitted to his friend Mr. John Nichols, a list of the authours of the Universal History, mentioning their several shares in that work. It has, according to his direction, been desposited in the British Museum, and is printed in the Gentleman's Magazine for December, 1784.

During his sleepless nights he amused himself by translating into Latin verse, from the Greek, many of the epigrams in the *Anthologia*. These translations, with some other poems by him in Latin, he gave to his friend Mr. Langton, who, having added a few notes, sold them to the booksellers for a small sum, to be given to some of Johnson's relations, which was accordingly done; and they are printed in the collection of his works.

My readers are now, at last, to behold *Samuel Johnson* preparing himself for that doom, from which the most exalted powers afford no exemption to man. Death had always been to him an object of terrour; so that, though by no means happy, he still clung to life with an eagerness at which many have wondered. At any time when he was ill, he was very much pleased to be told that he looked better. An ingenious member of the *Eumelian Club* informs me, that upon one occasion when he said to him that he saw health returning to his cheek, Johnson seized him by the hand and exclaimed, 'Sir, you are one of the kindest friends I ever had.'

It is not my intention to give a very minute detail of the particulars of Johnson's remaining days, of whom it was now evident, that the crisis was fast approaching, when he must *die like men, and fall like one of the Princes.*[1] Yet it will be instructive, as well as gratifying to the curiosity of my readers, to re-

[1] *Psalm* lxxxii, 7.

cord a few circumstances, on the authenticity of which they may perfectly rely, as I have been at the utmost pains to obtain an accurate account of his last illness, from the best authority.

Dr. Heberden, Dr. Brocklesby, Dr. Warren, and Dr. Butter, physicians, generously attended him, without accepting of any fees, as did Mr. Cruikshank, surgeon; and all that could be done from professional skill and ability, was tried, to prolong a life so truly valuable. He himself, indeed, having, on account of his very bad constitution, been perpetually applying himself to medical inquiries, united his own efforts with those of the gentlemen who attended him; and imagining that the dropsical collection of water which oppressed him might be drawn off by making incisions in his body, he, with his usual resolute defiance of pain, cut deep, when he thought that his surgeon had done it too tenderly.

About eight or ten days before his death, when Dr. Brocklesby paid him his morning visit, he seemed very low and desponding, and said, 'I have been as a dying man all night.' He then emphatically broke out in the words of Shakspeare,

'Can'st thou not minister to a mind diseas'd;
Pluck from the memory a rooted sorrow;
Raze out the written troubles of the brain;
And, with some sweet oblivious antidote,

Cleanse the stuff'd bosom of that perilous stuff,
Which weighs upon the heart?'

To which Dr. Brocklesby readily answered, from the same great poet:

'therein the patient Must minister to himself.' [1]

Having no near relations, it had been for some time Johnson's intention to make a liberal provision for his faithful servant, Mr. Francis Barber, whom he looked upon as particularly under his protection, and whom he had all along treated truly as an humble friend. Having asked Dr. Brocklesby what would be a proper annuity to bequeath to a favourite servant, and being answered that it must depend on the circumstances of the master; and, that in the case of a nobleman, fifty pounds a year was considered as an adequate reward for many years' faithful service;—'Then, (said Johnson,) shall I be *nobilissimus*,[2] for I mean to leave Frank seventy pounds a year, and I desire you to tell him so.' It is strange, however, to think, that Johnson was not free from that general weakness of being averse to execute a will, so that he delayed it from time to time; and had it not been for Sir John Hawkins' repeatedly urging it, I think it is probable that this kind resolution would not have been fulfilled.

During his last illness, Johnson

---

[1] *Macbeth*, Act V., sc. 3.

[2] *nobilissimus*: most noble; more noble than the noble.

experienced the steady and kind attachment of his numerous friends. Mr. Hoole has drawn up a narrative of what passed in the visits which he paid him during that time, from the 10th of November to the 13th of December, the day of his death, inclusive, and has favoured me with a perusal of it, with permission to make extracts, which I have done. And I think it highly to the honour of Mr. Windham, that his important occupations as an active statesman did not prevent him from paying assiduous respect to the dying Sage, whom he revered. Mr. Langton informs me, that, 'one day he found Mr. Burke and four or five more friends sitting with Johnson. Mr. Burke said to him, "I am afraid, Sir, such a number of us may be oppressive to you."—"No, Sir, (said Johnson,) it is not so; and I must be in a wretched state, indeed, when your company would not be a delight to me." Mr. Burke, in a tremulous voice, expressive of being very tenderly affected, replied, "My dear Sir, you have always been too good to me." Immediately afterwards he went away. This was the last circumstance in the acquaintance of these two eminent men.'

It is to the mutual credit of Johnson and Divines of different communions, that although he was a steady Church-of-England man, there was, nevertheless, much agreeable intercourse between him and them. Let me particularly name the late Mr. La Trobe, and Mr. Hutton, of the Moravian profession.

His intimacy with the English Benedictines, at Paris, has been mentioned; and as an additional proof of the charity in which he lived with good men of the Romish Church, I am happy in this opportunity of recording his friendship with the Reverend Thomas Hussey, D.D. His Catholick Majesty's Chaplain of Embassy at the Court of London, that very respectable man, eminent not only for his powerful eloquence as a preacher, but for his various abilities and acquisitions.—Nay, though Johnson loved a Presbyterian the least of all, this did not prevent his having a long and uninterrupted social connection with the Reverend Dr. James Fordyce, who, since his death, hath gratefully celebrated him in a warm strain of devotional composition.

Amidst the melancholy clouds which hung over the dying Johnson, his characteristical manner shewed itself on different occasions.

When Dr. Warren, in the usual style, hoped that he was better; his answer was, 'No, Sir; you cannot conceive with what acceleration I advance towards death.'

A man whom he had never seen before was employed one night to sit up with him. Being asked next morning how he liked his attendant, his answer was, 'Not at all, Sir: the fellow's an ideot; he is as aukward as a turn-spit when first put into the wheel, and as sleepy as a dormouse.'

Mr. Windham having placed a pillow conveniently to support him, he thanked him for his kindness, and said, 'That will do,—all that a pillow can do.'

As he opened a note which his servant brought to him, he said, 'An odd thought strikes me:—we shall receive no letters in the grave.'

He requested three things of Sir Joshua Reynolds:—To forgive him thirty pounds which he had borrowed of him;—to read the Bible;—and never to use his pencil on a Sunday. Sir Joshua readily acquiesced.

Johnson, with that native fortitude which, amidst all his bodily distress and mental sufferings, never forsook him, asked Dr. Brocklesby, as a man in whom he had confidence, to tell him plainly whether he could recover. 'Give me (said he) a direct answer.' The Doctor having first asked him if he could bear the whole truth, which way soever it might lead, and being answered that he could, declared that, in his opinion, he could not recover without a miracle. 'Then, (said Johnson,) I will take no more physick, not even my opiates; for I have prayed that I may render up my soul to GOD unclouded.' In this resolution he persevered, and, at the same time, used only the weakest kinds of sustenance. Being pressed by Mr. Windham to take somwhat more generous nourishment, lest too low a diet should have the very effect which he dreaded, by debilitating his mind, he said, 'I will take any thing but inebriating sustenance.'

The Reverend Mr. Strahan, who was the son of his friend, and had been always one of his great favourites, had, during his last illness, the satisfaction of contributing to soothe and comfort him.

Mr. Strahan has given me the agreeable assurance, that, after being in much agitation, Johnson became quite composed, and continued so till his death.

Having, as has been already mentioned, made his will on the 8th and 9th of December, and settled all his worldly affairs, he languished till Monday, the 13th of that month, when he expired, about seven o'clock in the evening, with so little apparent pain that his attendants hardly perceived when his dissolution took place.

A few days before his death, he had asked Sir John Hawkins, as one of his executors, where he should be buried; and on being answered, 'Doubtless, in Westminster Abbey,' seemed to feel a satisfaction, very natural to a Poet; and indeed, in my opinion, very natural to every man of any imagination, who has no family sepulchre in which he can be laid with his fathers. Accordingly, upon Monday, December 20, his remains were deposited in that noble and renowned edifice; and over his grave was placed a large blue flagstone, with this inscription:

'SAMUEL JOHNSON, LL.D.
Obiit XIII *die Decembris,*
Anno Domini
M. DCC. LXXXIV.
Ætatis suæ LXXV.'

As Johnson had abundant homage paid to him during his life, so no writer in this nation ever had such an accumulation of literary honours after his death. A sermon upon that event was preached in St. Mary's church, Oxford, before the University, by the Reverend Mr. Agutter, of Magdalen College. The Lives, the Memoirs, the Essays, both in prose and verse, which have been published concerning him, would make many volumes. The numerous attacks too upon him, I consider as part of his consequence, upon the principle which he himself so well knew and asserted. Many who trembled at his presence, were forward in assault, when they no longer apprehended danger. When one of his little pragmatical foes was invidiously snarling at his fame, at Sir Joshua Reynolds' table, the Reverend Dr. Parr exclaimed, with his usual bold animation, 'Ay, now that the old lion is dead, every ass thinks he may kick at him.'

The character of *Samuel Johnson* has, I trust, been so developed in the course of this work, that they who have honoured it with a perusal, may be considered as well acquainted with him. As, however, it may be expected that I should collect into one view the capital and distinguishing features of this extraordinary man, I shall endeavour to acquit myself of that part of my biographical undertaking, however difficult it may be to do that which many of my readers will do better for themselves.

His figure was large and well formed, and his countenance of the cast of an ancient statue; yet his appearance was rendered strange and somewhat uncouth, by convulsive cramps, by the scars of that distemper which it was once imagined the royal touch could cure, and by a slovenly mode of dress. He had the use only of one eye; yet so much does mind govern and even supply the deficiency of organs, that his visual perceptions, as far as they extended, were uncommonly quick and accurate. So morbid was his temperament, that he never knew the natural joy of a free and vigorous use of his limbs: when he walked, it was like the struggling gait of one in fetters; when he rode, he had no command or direction of his horse, but was carried as if in a balloon. That with his constitution and habits of life he should have lived seventy-five years, is a proof that an inherent *vivida vis* [1] is a powerful preservative of the human frame.

Man is, in general, made up of contradictory qualities; and these will ever shew themselves in strange succession, where a consistency in appearance at least, if not in reality, has not been attained by long habits of philosophical discipline. In proportion to the native vigour of the mind, the contradictory qualities will be the more prominent, and more difficult to be adjusted; and, therefore, we are not to wonder, that Johnson exhibited

[1] *vivida vis:* lively force.

an eminent example of this remark which I have made upon human nature. At different times, he seemed a different man, in some respects; not, however, in any great or essential article, upon which he had fully employed his mind, and settled certain principles of duty, but only in his manners, and in the display of argument and fancy in his talk. He was prone to superstition, but not to credulity. Though his imagination might incline him to a belief of the marvellous and the mysterious, his vigorous reason examined the evidence with jealousy. He was a sincere and zealous Christian, of high Church-of-England and monarchical principles, which he would not tamely suffer to be questioned; and had, perhaps, at an early period, narrowed his mind somewhat too much, both as to religion and politicks. His being impressed with the danger of extreme latitude in either, though he was of a very independent spirit, occasioned his appearing somewhat unfavourable to the prevalence of that noble freedom of sentiment which is the best possession of man. Nor can it be denied, that he had many prejudices; which, however, frequently suggested many of his pointed sayings, that rather shew a playfulness of fancy than any settled malignity. He was steady and inflexible in maintaining the obligations of religion and morality; both from a regard for the order of society, and from a veneration for the GREAT SOURCE of all order; correct, nay stern in his taste;

hard to please, and easily offended; impetuous and irritable in his temper, but of a most humane and benevolent heart, which shewed itself not only in a most liberal charity, as far as his circumstances would allow, but in a thousand instances of active benevolence. He was afflicted with a bodily disease, which made him often restless and fretful; and with a constitutional melancholy, the clouds of which darkened the brightness of his fancy, and gave a gloomy cast to his whole course of thinking: we, therefore, ought not to wonder at his sallies of impatience and passion at any time; especially when provoked by obstrusive ignorance, or presuming petulance; and allowance must be made for his uttering hasty and satirical sallies, even against his best friends. And, surely, when it is considered, that, 'amidst sickness and sorrow,' he exerted his faculties in so many works for the benefit of mankind, and particularly that he achieved the great and admirable *Dictionary* of our language, we must be astonished at his resolution. The solemn text, 'of him to whom much is given, much will be required,' seems to have been ever present to his mind, in a rigorous sense, and to have made him dissatisfied with his labours and acts of goodness, however comparatively great; so that the unavoidable consciousness of his superiority was, in that respect, a cause of disquiet. He suffered so much from this, and from the gloom which perpetually haunted him, and made solitude frightful, that it may be said of him, 'If in this life only he had hope, he was of all men most miserable.' He loved praise, when it was brought to him; but was too proud to seek for it. He was somewhat susceptible of flattery. As he was general and unconfined in his studies, he cannot be considered as master of any one particular science; but he had accumulated a vast and various collection of learning and knowledge, which was so arranged in his mind, as to be ever in readiness to be brought forth. But his superiority over other learned men consisted chiefly in what may be called the art of thinking, the art of using his mind; a certain continual power of seizing the useful substance of all that he knew, and exhibiting it in a clear and forcible manner; so that knowledge, which we often see to be no better than lumber in men of dull understanding, was, in him, true, evident, and actual wisdom. His moral precepts are practical; for they are drawn from an intimate acquaintance with human nature. His maxims carry conviction; for they are founded on the basis of common sense, and a very attentive and minute survey of real life. His mind was so full of imagery, that he might have been perpetually a poet; yet it is remarkable, that, however rich his prose is in this respect, his poetical pieces, in general, have not much of that splendour, but are rather distinguished by strong sentiment, and acute observation, conveyed in harmonious and energetick verse, particularly in heroick couplets. Though usually grave, and even aweful, in his deportment, he possessed uncommon and peculiar powers of wit and humour; he frequently indulged himself in colloquial pleasantry; and the heartiest merriment was often enjoyed in his company; with this great advantage, that as it was entirely free from any poisonous tincture of vice or impiety, it was salutary to those who shared in it. He had accustomed himself to such accuracy in his common conversation, that he at all times expressed his thoughts with great force, and an elegant choice of language, the effect of which was aided by his having a loud voice, and a slow deliberate utterance. In him were united a most logical head with a most fertile imagination, which gave him an extraordinary advantage in arguing: for he could reason close or wide, as he saw best for the moment. Exulting in his intellectual strength and dexterity, he could, when he pleased, be the greatest sophist that ever contended in the lists of declamation; and, from a spirit of contradiction, and a delight in shewing his powers, he would often maintain the wrong side with equal warmth and ingenuity; so that, when there was an audience, his real opinions could seldom be gathered from his talk; though when he was in company with a single friend, he would discuss a subject with genuine fairness: but he was too conscientious to make errour permanent and pernicious, by deliberately writing it; and, in all his numerous works he earnestly inculcated what appeared to him to be the truth; his piety being constant, and the ruling principle of all his conduct.

Such was *Samuel Johnson,* a man whose talents, acquirements, and virtues, were so extraordinary, that the more his character is considered, the more he will be regarded by the present age, and by posterity, with admiration and reverence.

AFTERWORD

Professor C. S. Lewis, who taught at Oxford for many years, is now Professor of Medieval Literature at Cambridge University. He is a fine scholar—his *Allegory of Love* is now almost a classic—and he is a brilliant and deservedly popular writer on literature and life. In his autobiography, *Surprised by Joy,* he describes how, during a troubled period of his life, he decided to keep a journal or diary in the manner of Boswell. Reading it afterward, he tells us, he suddenly realized that whatever else he might be, he was no Boswell, and that describing the day's events and talk, accurately, intimately, vividly, demands a peculiar genius, which Boswell had. This is yet another tribute, merely one of the most recent by an outstanding writer, to this peculiar genius. Well over a hundred years ago, Lord Macaulay, a very severe critic in this field, wrote of Boswell in these terms:

> The *Life of Johnson* is assuredly a great, a very great work. Homer is not more decidedly the first of heroic poets, Shakespeare is not more decidedly the first of dramatists, Demosthenes is not more decidedly the first of orators, than Boswell is the first of biographers . . .

This is very high praise indeed, but succeeding generations of critical, intelligent readers have thought it amply justified.

Writing is a very odd business. Clever, impressive men, admired by all their acquaintances, have tried to write and made a hash of it. Other men, generally thought to be fools, have made a resounding success of it. Among these surprising characters, James Boswell must be given a high place. He was anything but an impressive figure. Many of his acquaintances, perhaps most of them, thought him a rather silly little man. He was always running after important people, being very much what was called later "a lion hunter." He would risk any number of snubs to bask in the company of the great. He said and did many foolish things, and had a notable weakness for drink and dissipation, which finally killed him in his middle fifties. Everybody saw through his various pretensions; few admired him. But, although so weak in many ways, he had his own kind of determination, a Scots obstinacy. He made up his mind to attach himself to the great and formidable Dr. Johnson, at that time the dictator of the English literary world; and after many rebuffs he succeeded. But that was not half the battle, no more than a quarter of it. What has given Boswell a high place in literature is his ability, which has in it the quality of genius, to make the most of his situation.

What he saw and heard, day after day in Johnson's company, he was able to record with matchless fidelity. He might almost be said to have created the scenes of eighteenth-century literary and social life that we now associate with his name and work. Not that he invented anything; but his peculiar genius for journalizing enabled him to select, shape, color, in the best possible fashion, all that his unusually retentive memory offered him. So his *Life of Johnson* is in its way a work of art. And this explains how long, lasting, and powerful its appeal has been and is. Here we have intimate biography, showing us its subject almost day by day, raised to the level of art. It is true that Johnson himself makes a wonderful subject, only enriched by the company of his friends, themselves often remarkable men; but it is a sad mistake to imagine that it is Johnson who lifted up Boswell, that the subject is everything and the treatment of it nothing. We know this is wrong because other people wrote about Johnson too, but though what they write is not without interest, it lacks the enduring magic of Boswell's *Life*. It is Boswell who has kept Johnson alive.

This does not mean that Johnson is simply an eighteenth-century eccentric character, without any merit as a writer in our eyes. He can still be read with pleasure and profit. (If you want to try Johnson, start with his *Lives of the Poets,* which is crammed with good sense about literature and life.) But for every single person who has read more than fifty pages of Johnson, there must be several hundred, perhaps a thousand, who know him in Boswell's *Life,* where his talk, which on the whole is better than his writing, is completely captured. It is the little Scots nobody, with his notebook, who has preserved the great Englishman in the public memory. If there would have been no Boswell, as a successful author, without Johnson, it is equally true that, for ninety-nine readers out of every one hundred, there would have been no Johnson without Boswell. "Johnsons are rare," Thomas Carlyle wrote in his *Hero-Worship,* "yet, as has been asserted, Boswells perhaps still rarer—the more is the pity on both sides."

So, thanks to Boswell, we have the pleasure of Johnson's company without running the risks of those who actually met him. We can enjoy his retorts at other people's expense without dreading the moment when our own turn will come. And it must be confessed that Dr. Johnson could not only be very bad-mannered but also too often could not resist ending an argument he was losing by raising his voice and insulting his opponent. In addition to this habit of "talking for victory," as he called it, his uncertain manners, his shortsightedness, his snortings and gruntings and growlings, his tremendous prejudices, did not make him an easy and pleasant guest. But he was welcome almost everywhere, for a variety of good reasons. The publication of his dictionary, together with many essays and poems, had brought him great fame. Then, unlike many famous writers, he was a superb talker, too dogmatic and domineering to be an ideal conversationalist but, except when he was in one of his fits of depression, a man who loved good company and talk and offered his hearers a feast of sense and wit. Finally, as all his friends knew, behind the odd appearance and eccentric manners was a magnificent human being—independent, courageous, deeply religious, and filled with that compassion and that loving-kindness which should lie at the heart of religion. This huge growling bear of a fellow was a truly good man, a real Christian, a noble soul.

He was an odd mixture. He was tremendously brave, yet had a morbid fear of death. He was a High Tory, a believer in rank and class status, but was himself fiercely independent. He was genuinely pious, temperamentally inclined toward melancholy and pessimism, and yet, when he was wakened at three in the morning by two younger men, he cried: "What is it, you dogs! I'll have a frisk with you"—and out he came. On some important matters he talked sheer nonsense, as when he declared:

> I would not give half a guinea to live under one form of government rather than another. It is of no moment to the happiness of an individual.

On the other hand, he was a wonderful detector and destroyer of what he called "cant." This is the sort of solemn false stuff that people (now as well as in the eighteenth century) go on repeating, without asking themselves if there is any truth and sense in it, without bringing to it the test of experience: for example, that poverty is good for people, that work is good for them, that authors must not think about money, that windy patriotic talk should be admired, that savages are noble, romantic creatures, and so on. "Clear your mind of cant," he cried, the year before he died. It is true that sometimes he dismissed as cant various values, sentiments, and opinions that were by no means false, that happened to be in disagreement with his own prejudices and robust common-sense judgments. He was essentially a man of his time. But his talk did clear away a lot of rubbish, and much of it is often quoted to this day. It is significant that in the *Oxford Dictionary of Quotations,* no fewer than seventeen columns are given to Samuel Johnson. But about a dozen of those columns would never be there if James Boswell had not listened so carefully to Johnson's talk, and had not then set it all down for us in his *Life*.

Opening the *Life* at random, I find myself at Friday, April 3, 1778, when Johnson presided at a dinner of The Club. Among those present that night were Gibbon, the great historian, Sir Joshua Reynolds, the artist, then at the height of his fame, Edmund Burke, political philosopher and master of prose, and Sheridan, the dramatist. And these are what one casual dip into the bag can show. We meet some wonderfully good company in these pages. True, they are often not allowed to do themselves justice, not because Johnson was always shouting them down but because Boswell is always recording the scene in terms of Johnson and keeping him in the spotlight. Nevertheless, there is in this biography an astonishingly wide range of people, of all classes, of all types, famous men of genius to nameless ruffians. And here Boswell was lucky in his subject, for Dr. Johnson knew an unusually large number of people— he said he counted a day lost if during it he had not made at least one new acquaintance—and although his closest friends belonged to the professional class, authors like Goldsmith and Burke, a painter like Reynolds, an actor like Garrick, his acquaintance ranged from dukes to dustmen. And if Boswell was lucky, the rest of us have been lucky ever since, having all this huge company at our command.

Some of the best of these characters are not the celebrities but the odd nobodies who turn up. One of my favorites is Edwards, who met Johnson in the street and reminded him that they had been up at Oxford together, in the same college, Pembroke, forty-nine years before. It was Edwards, talking later in Johnson's house, who made the sublime remark:

> You are a philosopher, Dr. Johnson. I have tried too in my time to be a philosopher; but, I don't know how, *cheerfulness was always breaking in*.

As soon as we give ourselves to these pages, prepared to use a little imagination, two hundred years disappear in a flash: we are in the eighteenth century. The London of George III, of coaches and sedan chairs, of men in scarlet or sky-blue satin coats and silk stockings, of ladies wearing powdered hair and beauty patches, is magically restored to us. I do not believe that fifty colored wide-screen films and television "spectaculars" on this period, produced at a cost of 100 million dollars, could bring us as close to it as this book of Boswell's can. With them we should still be outside the scene, distant onlookers; with him we are inside the scene, taking part in it, the talk all around us. We come to know this man, old Sam Johnson, more thoroughly and intimately than we know any of the men who live down our own street. Time and space have been abolished by the book and the biographer, by the magic of literature. My friend Ed Murrow (we used to sit up together waiting to do our late-night radio talks during the bombing of London) has shown us, in his television program, *Small World,* a triumph of contemporary technique and ingenuity. But long ago, using only some notebooks, pen and ink, paper, and a printing press, Boswell did it much better. We have only to open a book—and here they are, Sam Johnson and all his friends, alive and talking!

STUDY QUESTIONS

1. Consider the details of Johnson's formal education. What, apparently, were the subjects in which he was instructed at school and college? Contrast his curriculum with that of a well-educated person in our time. How did his education fit him for the work of his maturity?

2. What were Johnson's thoughts on the instruction and disciplining of school children? Note that while he criticized Mr. Hunter, one of his old schoolmasters, he had something to say for his methods as well.

3. Johnson remarked, during his late middle age, that he had known as much at the age of eighteen as he did then. In what way should this statement be taken? Did he mean that he was as wise and competent at one time as at the other?

4. One of Johnson's longest and most interesting friendships was with the great actor, David Garrick. Under what circumstances did this relationship begin? How did the association between the two men in later life reflect this beginning?

5. In what particulars does the economic and social status of the mod-

ern writer and scholar differ from that of his eighteenth-century counterpart?

6. Often Boswell reminds us of Johnson's tremendous fondness for the city of London. Now the truth is that eighteenth-century London was dirty, crowded, and inconvenient. What was its appeal to Samuel Johnson? Did it appeal to Boswell in the same way?

7. What do we know about Johnson's marriage and his wife, Tetty? What did Johnson himself say about his courtship and married life? What picture did Garrick give of the couple? What facts can we accept about the Johnsons as fairly objective?

8. What does the history of the play *Irene* tell us about Johnson as a writer and a man? With what further insights do the circumstances surrounding the publication of *Rasselas* and the *Dictionary* provide us?

9. Johnson's letter to Lord Chesterfield (page 276) is regarded as a model of sharp rebuke written with punctilious formal courtesy. What was it that Johnson resented so much about Lord Chesterfield's behavior?

How does the courteous tone of the letter strengthen the statement of that resentment? How do certain allusions, figures of speech, and ironies add force to this famous piece of writing?

10. What contradictions were there in Johnson as a physical man? How might these combinations of strengths with weaknesses be compared with those of his character and intellect?

11. One of Johnson's moral passions was for honesty. What are some of the problems and complications that surround the proposition that one should always tell the truth? How was Johnson's concern for this subject reflected in his life?

12. What were the circumstances surrounding the first meeting of Johnson and Boswell? What does the meeting, as reported by one of the participants, reveal about them both?

13. The Boswell-Johnson friendship is one of the most famous ever to have been reported in our language. In what ways, however, does this friendship seem surprising? What was there about each man which might have reasonably seemed uninteresting or distasteful to the other? Note that this question is not concerned with what *you* might think unattractive about Johnson or Boswell.

14. Johnson, Boswell, and their friends loved conversation. They devoted time and talent to it in a way that is seldom encountered today. What are some of the subjects which they discussed? Are these subjects no longer appropriate for the sociable consideration of intelligent people? What are the requirements for good conversation?

15. During much of the *Life,* Boswell pictures himself as waiting, notebook in hand, for conversational gems. He was not, however, a passive attendant. What methods did he employ, on various occasions, in order to get Johnson to produce some material?

16. Consider Johnson's famous prejudice against Scotland and the Scots. From what source might it have developed? How serious or intense was it? To what extent did it affect his actions?

17. Compare your answers to question 16 with Johnson's attitude toward America and Americans. How might it be argued that the more violent and unpopular of these antipathies was, in fact, the more reasonably consistent with his social philosophy?

18. His conversation with King George III was, to Johnson, one of the important events of his life. What were the circumstances of this meeting? How do they reflect on Johnson and his reputation at the time? How does Johnson's own account of the meeting illustrate certain of his social and political attitudes?

19. It would be unfair and unwise for us to dismiss Johnson's passion for "subordination" as unthinking bigotry simply because it is not in accordance with many of the ideas and circumstances to which we are accustomed and to which we may feel committed. What reasoning lay behind his defense of a system in which power and position are hereditary and where privilege goes with birth? How far did he carry such ideas? Did he feel that man's individual worth entitles him to nothing?

20. What would Johnson's reaction have been to Thoreau's statement, "Any man more right than his neighbors constitutes a majority of one"?

21. How might Dr. Johnson have responded to Rousseau if the latter

had confronted him with the following assertion: "People who know little are usually great talkers, while men who know much say little"?

22. One Johnsonian remark that is more often quoted than understood is: "Patriotism is the last refuge of a scoundrel." What did Johnson obviously *not* mean? What is the most significant sense in which the statement can be taken?

23. Oliver Goldsmith remarked: "There's no arguing with Johnson; for if his pistol misses fire, he knocks you down with the butt end of it." Can you illustrate the truth of this metaphor with conversational incidents from the biography?

24. How did Johnson himself regard the fact that when he was talking for victory, he did not always play fair?

25. As most of us know, it is a good deal easier to be kind to attractive, admirable people than to unlovable or worthless ones. Indeed, our kindness in the first instance seems hardly a virtue at all. How does this reflection give significance to Johnson's relations with Mrs. Williams, his rescue of the fallen streetwalker, his attempts to assist Dr. Dodd?

26. Johnson could, on occasion, get along well with men whose interests were very different from his own. What, for example, was the basis for his long and close relationship with Dr. Taylor? What were his reactions to his cheerful old schoolfellow, Mr. Edwards?

27. What were Johnson's criticisms of French society as he encountered it on his trip to the continent with the Thrales? To what extent are these criticisms consistent with his own way of life? To what extent may the peculiarities of the French, as he saw them, be rather less eccentric than the peculiarities of Dr. Johnson himself?

28. Perhaps it is a key to Johnson's strange mixture of tolerance and prejudice to note that while he could and did hate certain ideas and institutions with inflexible violence, on the whole he liked people as individuals when he knew them as such. How does his evening with Jack Wilkes illustrate this point? How do his relationships with Edmund Burke, John Wesley, and even James Boswell further reflect on it?

29. What sustained Johnson's long relationship with the Thrales? What is significant about Boswell's account of and comments on the decline of that relationship?

30. Two purposes of biography are to give a factual record of the subject's life and to give a picture of the subject as he was in life. What were Boswell's several methods for achieving both these purposes? Do you feel that he achieved them equally well?

Queen Victoria

by Lytton Strachey

QUEEN VICTORIA, by Lytton Strachey, was first published in 1921, following three years after his *Eminent Victorians,* which was not his first book but was the one that established his reputation as a biographer. Both works were extremely successful but in a rather different way. *Queen Victoria* contains far less of the brilliant mockery and the element of caricature that are found in *Eminent Victorians* and that helped to give it a rather scandalous kind of success. *Queen Victoria* is solider, less unscrupulous, and more sympathetic in its treatment of its subject. People who objected to Strachey's methods in his *Eminent Victorians* were ready to accept and to admire his *Queen Victoria,* which is generally regarded as his finest book.

Lytton Strachey, who was born in 1880 and died in 1932, was a member of a large family of remarkable intellectual distinction and achievement. He himself was one of the central figures of the brilliant "Bloomsbury Group," which included writers like E. M. Forster and Virginia Woolf. He was a tall, stooping man, with a pale face and a big black beard (at a time when beards were far more uncommon even than they are today), and he spoke softly but with great precision. He was a gentle person, but in revolt against many of the older values, such as patriotism. In the first World War, when he was asked why he was not in the army, helping to defend civilization, he replied that he was part of the civilization that was being defended. The truth was that he was never physically robust, and this explains his comparatively early death and his limited output as a writer. He was a devoted student of French literature and one of the best English critics of that literature, which undoubtedly influenced his own work. His own influence as a biographer has been very considerable indeed, as we shall see.

To
Virginia Woolf

✖ *Chapter* 1

Antecedents

I

On November 6, 1817, died the Princess Charlotte, only child of the Prince Regent, and heir to the crown of England. Her short life had hardly been a happy one. By nature impulsive, capricious, and vehement, she had always longed for liberty; and she had never possessed it. She had been brought up among violent family quarrels, had been early separated from her disreputable and eccentric mother, and handed over to the care of her disreputable and selfish father. When she was seventeen, he decided to marry her off to the Prince of Orange; she, at first, acquiesced; but, suddenly falling in love with Prince Augustus of Prussia, she determined to break off the engagement. This was not her first love affair, for she had previously carried on a clandestine correspondence with a Captain Hess. Prince Augustus was already married, morganatically, but she did not know it, and he did not tell her. While she was spinning out the negotiations with the Prince of Orange, the allied sovereigns—it was June, 1814—arrived in London to celebrate their victory. Among them, in the suite of the Emperor of Russia, was the young and handsome Prince Leopold of Saxe-Coburg. He made several attempts to attract the notice of the Princess, but she, with her heart elsewhere, paid very little attention. Next month the Prince Regent, discovering that his daughter was having secret meetings with Prince Augustus, suddenly appeared upon the scene and, after dismissing her household, sentenced her to a strict seclusion in Windsor Park. 'God Almighty grant me patience!' she exclaimed, falling on her knees in an agony of agitation: then she jumped up, ran down the backstairs and out into the street, hailed a passing cab, and drove to her mother's house in Bayswater. She was discovered, pursued, and at length, yielding to the persuasions of her uncles, the Dukes of York and Sussex, of Brougham, and of the Bishop of Salisbury, she returned to Carlton House at two o'clock in the morning. She was immured at Windsor, but no more was heard of the Prince of Orange. Prince Augustus, too, disappeared. The way was at last open to Prince Leopold of Saxe-Coburg.

This Prince was clever enough to get round the Regent, to impress the Ministers, and to make friends with another of the Princess's uncles, the Duke of Kent. Through the Duke he was able to communicate privately with the Princess, who now declared that he was necessary to her happiness. When, after Waterloo, he was in Paris, the Duke's aide-de-camp carried letters backwards and forwards across the Channel. In January 1816 he was invited to England, and in May the marriage took place.

The character of Prince Leopold contrasted strangely with that of his wife. The younger son of a German princeling, he was at this time twenty-six years of age; he had served with distinction in the war against Napoleon; he had shown considerable diplomatic skill at the Congress of Vienna; and he was now to try his hand at the task of taming a tumultuous Princess. Cold and formal in manner, collected in speech, careful in action, he soon dominated the wild, impetuous, generous creature by his side. There was much in her, he found, of which he could not approve. She quizzed, she stamped, she roared with laughter; she had very little of that self-command which is especially required of princes; her manners were abominable. Of the latter he was a good judge, having moved, as he himself explained to his niece many years later, in the best society of Europe, being in fact 'what is called in French *de la fleur des pois.*' [1] There was continual friction, but every scene ended in the same way. Standing before him like a rebellious boy in petticoats, her body pushed forward, her hands behind her back, with flaming cheeks and sparkling eyes, she would declare at last that she was ready to do whatever he wanted. 'If you wish it, I will do

[1] *de la fleur des pois:* of the most select.

it,' she would say. 'I want nothing for myself,' he invariably answered; 'when I press something on you, it is from a conviction that it is for your interest and for your good.'

Among the members of the household at Claremont, near Esher, where the royal pair were established, was a young German physician, Christian Friedrich Stockmar. He was the son of a minor magistrate in Coburg, and, after taking part as a medical officer in the war, he had settled down as a doctor in his native town. Here he had met Prince Leopold, who had been struck by his ability, and, on his marriage, brought him to England as his personal physician. A curious fate awaited this young man; many were the gifts which the future held in store for him—many and various—influence, power, mystery, unhappiness, a broken heart. At Claremont his position was a very humble one; but the Princess took a fancy to him, called him 'Stocky,' and romped with him along the corridors. Dyspeptic by constitution, melancholic by temperament, he could yet be lively on occasion, and was known as a wit in Coburg. He was virtuous, too, and observed the royal *ménage* with approbation. 'My master,' he wrote in his diary, 'is the best of all husbands in all the five quarters of the globe; and his wife bears him an amount of love, the greatness of which can only be compared with the English national debt.' Before long he gave proof of another quality—a quality which was to colour the whole of his life—cautious sagacity. When, in the spring of 1817, it was known that the Princess was expecting a child, the post of one of her physicians-in-ordinary was offered to him, and he had the good sense to refuse it. He perceived that his colleagues would be jealous of him, that his advice would probably not be taken, but that, if anything were to go wrong, it would be certainly the foreign doctor who would be blamed. Very soon, indeed, he came to the opinion that the low diet and constant bleedings, to which the unfortunate Princess was subjected, were an error; he drew the Prince aside, and begged him to communicate this opinion to the English doctors; but it was useless. The fashionable lowering treatment was continued for months. On November 5, at nine o'clock in the evening, after a labour of over fifty hours, the Princess was delivered of a dead boy. At midnight her exhausted strength gave way. Then, at last, Stockmar consented to see her; he went in, and found her obviously dying, while the doctors were plying her with wine. She seized his hand and pressed it. 'They have made me tipsy,' she said. After a little he left her, and was already in the next room when he heard her call out in her loud voice: 'Stocky! Stocky!' As he ran back the death-rattle was in her throat. She tossed herself violently from side to side; then suddenly drew up her legs, and it was over.

The Prince, after hours of watching, had left the room for a few moments' rest; and Stockmar had now to tell him that his wife was dead. At first he could not be made to realise what had happened. On their way to her room he sank down on a chair while Stockmar knelt beside him: it was all a dream; it was impossible. At last, by the bed, he, too, knelt down and kissed the cold hands. Then rising and exclaiming, 'Now I am quite desolate. Promise me never to leave me,' he threw himself into Stockmar's arms.

II

The tragedy at Claremont was of a most upsetting kind. The royal kaleidoscope had suddenly shifted, and nobody could tell how the new pattern would arrange itself. The succession to the throne, which had seemed so satisfactorily settled, now became a matter of urgent doubt.

George III was still living, an aged lunatic, at Windsor, completely impervious to the impressions of the outer world. Of his seven sons, the youngest was of more than middle age, and none had legitimate offspring. The outlook, therefore, was ambiguous. It seemed highly improbable that the Prince Regent, who had lately been obliged to abandon his stays, and presented a preposterous figure of debauched obesity, could ever again, even on the supposition that he divorced his wife and re-married, become the father of a family. Besides the Duke of Kent, who must be noticed separately, the other brothers, in order of seniority, were the Dukes of York, Clarence, Cumberland, Sussex, and Cambridge; their situations and prospects require a brief description. The Duke of York, whose escapades in times past with Mrs. Clarke and the army had brought him into trouble, now divided his life between London and a large, extravagantly ordered and extremely uncomfortable country house where he occupied himself with racing, whist, and improper stories. He was remarkable among the princes for one reason: he was the only one of them—so we are informed by a highly competent observer—who had the feelings of a gentleman. He had been long married to the Princess Royal of Prussia, a lady who rarely went to bed and was perpetually surrounded by vast numbers of dogs, parrots, and monkeys. They had no children. The Duke of Clarence had lived for many years in complete obscurity with Mrs. Jordan, the actress, in Bushey Park. By her he had had a large family of sons and daughters, and had appeared, in effect, to be married to her, when he suddenly separated from her and offered to marry Miss Wykeham, a crazy woman of large fortune, who, however, would have nothing to say to him. Shortly afterwards Mrs. Jordan died in distressed circumstances in Paris. The Duke of Cumberland was probably the most unpopular man in England. Hideously ugly, with a distorted eye, he was bad-tempered and vindictive in private, a violent reactionary in politics, and was subsequently suspected of murdering his valet and of having carried on an amorous intrigue of an extremely scandalous kind. He had lately married a German Princess, but there were as yet no children by the marriage. The Duke of Sussex had mildly literary tastes and collected books. He had married Lady Augusta Murray, by whom he had two children, but the marriage, under the Royal Marriages Act, was declared void. On Lady Augusta's death, he married Lady Cecilia Buggin; she changed her name to Underwood; but this marriage also was void. Of the Duke of Cambridge, the youngest of the brothers, not very much was known. He lived in Hanover, wore a blonde wig, chattered and fidgeted a great deal, and was unmarried.

Besides his seven sons, George III had five surviving daughters. Of these, two—the Queen of Württemberg and the Duchess of Gloucester—were married and childless. The three unmarried princesses—Augusta, Elizabeth, and Sophia—were all over forty.

III

The fourth son of George III was Edward, Duke of Kent. He was now fifty years of age—a tall, stout, vigorous man, highly-coloured, with bushy eyebrows, a bald top to his head, and what hair he had carefully dyed a glossy black. His dress was extremely neat, and in his whole appearance there was a rigidity which did not belie his character. He had spent his early life in the army—at Gibraltar, in Canada, in the West Indies—and, under the influence of military training, had become at first a disciplinarian and at last a martinet. In 1802, having been sent to Gibraltar to restore order in a mutinous garrison, he was recalled for undue severity, and his active career had come to an end. Since then he had spent his life regulating his domestic arrangements with great exactitude, busying himself with the affairs of his numerous dependents, designing clocks, and struggling to restore order to his finances, for, in spite of his being, as someone said who knew him well *'reglé comme du papier à musique,'* [1] and in spite of an income of £24,000 a year, he was hopelessly in debt. He had quarrelled with most of his brothers, particularly with the Prince Regent, and it was only natural that he should have joined the political Opposition and become a pillar of the Whigs.

What his political opinions may actually have been is open to doubt; it has often been asserted that he was a Liberal, or even a Radical; and, if we are to believe Robert Owen, he was a necessitarian Socialist. His relations with Owen—the shrewd, gullible, high-minded, wrong-headed, illustrious and preposterous father of Socialism and Co-operation—were curious and

characteristic. He talked of visiting the Mills at New Lanark; he did, in fact, preside at one of Owen's public meetings; he corresponded with him on confidential terms, and he even (so Owen assures us) returned, after his death, from 'the sphere of spirits' to give encouragement to the Owenites on earth. 'In an especial manner,' says Owen, 'I have to name the very anxious feelings of the spirit of his Royal Highness the late Duke of Kent (who early informed me there were no titles in the spiritual spheres into which he had entered), to benefit, not a class, a sect, a party, or any particular country, but the whole of the human race through futurity.' 'His whole spirit-proceeding with me has been most beautiful,' Owen adds, 'making his own appointments; and never in one instance has this spirit not been punctual to the minute he had named.' But Owen was of a sanguine temperament. He also numbered among his proselytes President Jefferson, Prince Metternich, and Napoleon; so that some uncertainty must still linger over the Duke of Kent's views. But there is no uncertainty about another circumstance: his Royal Highness borrowed from Robert Owen, on various occasions, various sums of money which were never repaid and amounted in all to several hundred pounds.

After the death of the Princess Charlotte it was clearly important, for more than one reason, that the Duke of Kent should marry. From

---

[1] *reglé comme du papier à musique:* as precise as sheet music.

the point of view of the nation, the lack of heirs in the reigning family seemed to make the step almost obligatory; it was also likely to be highly expedient from the point of view of the Duke. To marry as a public duty, for the sake of the royal succession, would surely deserve some recognition from a grateful country. When the Duke of York had married, he had received a settlement of £25,000 a year. Why should not the Duke of Kent look forward to an equal sum? But the situation was not quite simple. There was the Duke of Clarence to be considered; he was the elder brother, and, if *he* married, would clearly have the prior claim. On the other hand, if the Duke of Kent married, it was important to remember that he would be making a serious sacrifice: a lady was involved.

The Duke, reflecting upon all these matters with careful attention, happened, about a month after his niece's death, to visit Brussels, and learnt that Mr. Creevey was staying in the town. Mr. Creevey was a close friend of the leading Whigs and an inveterate gossip; and it occurred to the Duke that there could be no better channel through which to communicate his views upon the situation to political circles at home. Apparently it did not occur to him that Mr. Creevey was malicious and might keep a diary. He therefore sent for him on some trivial pretext, and a remarkable conversation ensued.

After referring to the death of the Princess, to the improbability of the Regent's seeking a divorce, to the childlessness of the Duke of York, and to the possibility of the Duke of Clarence marrying, the Duke adverted to his own position. 'Should the Duke of Clarence not marry,' he said, 'the next prince in succession is myself, and although I trust I shall be at all times ready to obey any call my country may make upon me, God only knows the sacrifice it will be to make, whenever I shall think it my duty to become a married man. It is now seven-and twenty years that Madame St. Laurent and I have lived together: we are of the same age, and have been in all climates, and in all difficulties together, and you may well imagine, Mr. Creevey, the pang it will occasion me to part with her. I put it to your own feelings—in the event of any separation between you and Mrs. Creevey.... As for Madame St. Laurent herself, I protest I don't know what is to become of her if a marriage is to be forced upon me; her feelings are already so agitated upon the subject.' The Duke went on to describe how, one morning, a day or two after the Princess Charlotte's death, a paragraph had appeared in the *Morning Chronicle,* alluding to the possibility of his marriage. He had received the newspaper at breakfast together with his letters, and 'I did as is my constant practice, I threw the newspaper across the table to Madame St. Laurent, and began to open and read my letters. I had not done so but a very short time, when my attention was called to an extraordinary noise and a strong convulsive movement in Madame St. Laurent's throat. For a short time I entertained serious apprehensions for her safety; and when, upon her recovery, I enquired into the occasion of this attack, she pointed to the article in the *Morning Chronicle*.'

The Duke then returned to the subject of the Duke of Clarence. 'My brother the Duke of Clarence is the elder brother, and has certainly the right to marry if he chooses, and I would not interfere with him on any account. If he wishes to be king—to be married and have children, poor man—God help him! let him do so. For myself —I am a man of no ambition, and wish only to remain as I am. . . . Easter, you know, falls very early this year—the 22nd of March. If the Duke of Clarence does not take any step before that time, I must find some pretext to reconcile Madame St. Laurent to my going to England for a short time. When once there, it will be easy for me to consult with my friends as to the proper steps to be taken. Should the Duke of Clarence do nothing before that time as to marrying, it will become my duty, no doubt, to take some measures upon the subject myself.' Two names, the Duke said, had been mentioned in this connection—those of the Princess of Baden and the Princess of Saxe-Coburg. The latter, he thought, would perhaps be the better of the two, from the circumstance of Prince Leopold being so popular with the nation; but before any other steps were taken, he hoped and expected to see justice done to Madame St. Laurent. 'She is,' he explained, 'of very good family, and has never been an actress, and I am the first and only person who ever lived with her. Her disinterestedness, too, has been equal to her fidelity. When she first came to me it was upon £100 a year. That sum was afterwards raised to £400, and finally to £1000; but when my debts made it necessary for me to sacrifice a great part of my income, Madame St. Laurent insisted upon again returning to her income of £400 a year. If Madame St. Laurent is to return to live amongst her friends, it must be in such a state of independence as to command their respect. I shall not require very much, but a certain number of servants and a carriage are essentials.' As to his own settlement, the Duke observed that he would expect the Duke of York's marriage to be considered the precedent. 'That,' he said, 'was a marriage for the succession, and £25,000 for income was settled, in addition to all his other income, purely on that account. I shall be contented with the same arrangement, without making any demands grounded on the difference of the value of money in 1792 and at present. As for the payment of my debts,' the Duke concluded, 'I don't call them great. The nation, on the contrary, is greatly my debtor.' Here a clock struck, and seemed to remind the Duke that he had an appointment; he rose, and Mr. Creevey left him.

Who could keep such a communication secret? Certainly not Mr. Creevey. He hurried off to tell the Duke of Wellington, who was very much amused, and he wrote a long account of it to Lord Sefton, who received the letter 'very apropos,' while a surgeon was sounding his bladder to ascertain whether he had a stone. 'I never saw a fellow more astonished than he was,' wrote Lord Sefton in his reply, 'at seeing me laugh as soon as the operation was over. Nothing could be more first-rate than the royal Edward's ingenuousness. One does not know which to admire most—the delicacy of his attachment to Madame St. Laurent, the refinement of his sentiments towards the Duke of Clarence, or his own perfect disinterestedness in pecuniary matters.'

As it turned out, both the brothers decided to marry. The Duke of Kent, selecting the Princess of Saxe-Coburg in preference to the Princess of Baden, was united to her on May 29, 1818. On June 11, the Duke of Clarence followed suit with a daughter of the Duke of Saxe-Meiningen. But they were disappointed in their financial expectations; for though the Government brought forward proposals to increase their allowances, together with that of the Duke of Cumberland, the motions were defeated in the House of Commons. At this the Duke of Wellington was not surprised. 'There is a great deal to be said about that,' he said. 'They are the damnedest millstones about the necks of any Government that can be imagined. They have insulted—*personally* insulted—two-thirds of the gentlemen of England, and how can it be wondered at that they take their revenge upon them in the House of Commons? It is their only opportunity, and I think, by God! they are quite right to use it.' Eventually, however, Parliament increased the Duke of Kent's annuity by £6000.

The subsequent history of Madame St. Laurent has not transpired.

IV

The new Duchess of Kent, Victoria Mary Louisa, was a daughter of Francis, Duke of Saxe-Coburg-Saalfeld, and a sister of Prince Leopold. The family was an ancient one, being a branch of the great House of Wettin, which since the eleventh century had ruled over the March of Meissen on the Elbe. In the fifteenth century the whole possessions of the House had been divided between the Albertine and Ernestine branches: from the former descended the electors and kings of Saxony; the latter, ruling over Thuringia, became further subdivided into five branches, of which the duchy of Saxe-Coburg was one. This principality was very small, containing about 60,000 inhabitants, but it enjoyed independent and sovereign rights. During the disturbed years which followed the French Revolution, its affairs became terribly involved. The Duke was extravagant, and kept open house for the swarms of refugees, who fled eastward over Germany as the French power advanced. Among these was the Prince of Leiningen, an elderly beau, whose domains on the Moselle had been seized by the French, but who was granted in compensation the territory of Amorbach in Lower Franconia. In 1803 he married the Princess Victoria, at that time seventeen years of age. Three years later Duke Francis died a ruined man. The Napoleonic harrow passed over Saxe-Coburg. The duchy was seized by the French, and the ducal family were reduced to beggary, almost to starvation. At the same time the little principality of Amorbach was devastated by the French, Russian, and Austrian armies, marching and counter-marching across it. For years there was hardly a cow in the country, nor enough grass to feed a flock of geese. Such was the desperate plight of the family which, a generation later, was to have gained a foothold in half the reigning Houses of Europe. The Napoleonic harrow had indeed done its work; the seed was planted; and the crop would have surprised Napoleon. Prince Leopold, thrown upon his own resources at fifteen, made a career for himself and married the heiress of England. The Princess of Leiningen, struggling at Amorbach with poverty, military requisitions, and a futile husband, developed an independence of character and a tenacity of purpose which were to prove useful in very different circumstances. In 1814, her husband died, leaving her with two children and the regency of the principality. After her brother's marriage with the Princess Charlotte, it was proposed that she should marry the Duke of Kent; but she declined, on the ground that the guardianship of her children and the management of her domains made other ties undesirable. The Princess Charlotte's death, however, altered the case; and when the Duke of Kent renewed his offer, she accepted it. She was thirty-two years old—short, stout, with brown eyes and hair, and rosy cheeks, cheerful and voluble, and gorgeously attired in rustling silks and bright velvets.

She was certainly fortunate in her contented disposition; for she was fated, all through her life, to have much to put up with. Her second marriage, with its dubious prospects, seemed at first to be chiefly a source of difficulties and discomforts. The Duke, declaring that he was still too poor to live in England, moved about with uneasy precision through Belgium and Germany, attending parades and inspecting barracks in a neat military cap, while the English notabilities looked askance, and the Duke of Wellington dobbed him the Corporal. 'Damme!' he exclaimed to Mr. Creevey, 'd'ye know what his sisters call him? By God! they call him Joseph Surface!'[1] At

[1] Joseph Surface: a character in Richard Brinsley Sheridan's play, *A School for Scandal*. He is notable for his pose as a sensitive and fastidious man.

Valenciennes, where there was a review and a great dinner, the Duchess arrived with an old and ugly lady-in-waiting, and the Duke of Wellington found himself in a difficulty. 'Who the devil is to take out the maid of honour?' he kept asking; but at last he thought of a solution. 'Damme, Freemantle, find out the mayor and let him do it.' So the Mayor of Valenciennes was brought up for the purpose, and— so we learn from Mr. Creevey—'a capital figure he was.' A few days later at Brussels, Mr. Creevey himself had an unfortunate experience. A military school was to be inspected—before breakfast. The company assembled; everything was highly satisfactory; but the Duke of Kent continued for so long examining every detail and asking meticulous question after meticulous question, that Mr. Creevey at last could bear it no longer, and whispered to his neighbour that he was damned hungry. The Duke of Wellington heard him, and was delighted. 'I recommend you,' he said, 'whenever you start with the royal family in a morning, and particularly with *the Corporal,* always to breakfast first.' He and his staff, it turned out, had taken that precaution, and the great man amused himself, while the stream of royal inquiries poured on, by pointing at Mr. Creevey from time to time with the remark, *'Voilà le monsieur qui n'a pas déjeuné!'* [1]

[1] *Voilà le monsieur qui n'a pas déjeuné:* There is the gentleman who had no breakfast.

Settled down at last at Amorbach, the time hung heavily on the Duke's hands. The establishment was small, the country was impoverished; even clock-making grew tedious at last. He brooded— for in spite of his piety the Duke was not without a vein of superstition—over the prophecy of a gipsy at Gibraltar who told him that he was to have many losses and crosses, that he was to die in happiness, and that his only child was to be a great queen. Before long it became clear that a child was to be expected: the Duke decided that it should be born in England. Funds were lacking for the journey, but his determination was not to be set aside. Come what might, he declared, his child must be English-born. A carriage was hired, and the Duke himself mounted the box. Inside were the Duchess, her daughter Feodora, a girl of fourteen, with maids, nurses, lap-dogs, and canaries. Off they drove—through Germany, through France: bad roads, cheap inns, were nothing to the rigorous Duke and the equable, abundant Duchess. The Channel was crossed, London was reached in safety. The authorities provided a set of rooms in Kensington Palace; and there, on May 24, 1819, a female infant was born.

✗ *Chapter* 2

Childhood

I

The child who, in these not very impressive circumstances, appeared in the world, received but scant attention. There was small reason to foresee her destiny. The Duchess of Clarence, two months before, had given birth to a daughter; this infant, indeed, had died almost immediately; but it seemed highly probable that the Duchess would again become a mother; and so it actually fell out. More than this, the Duchess of Kent was young, and the Duke was strong; there was every likelihood that before long a brother would follow, to snatch her faint chance of the succession from the little princess.

Nevertheless, the Duke had other views: there were prophecies. . . . At any rate, he would christen the child Elizabeth, a name of happy augury. In this, however, he reckoned without the Regent, who, seeing a chance of annoying his brother, suddenly announced that he himself would be present at the baptism, and signified at the same time that one of the godfathers was to be the Emperor Alexander of Russia. And so when the ceremony took place, and the Archbishop of Canterbury asked by what name he was to baptise the child, the Regent replied 'Alex-

andria.' At this the Duke ventured to suggest that another name might be added. 'Certainly,' said the Regent; 'Georgina?' 'Or Elizabeth?' said the Duke. There was a pause, during which the Archbishop, with the baby in his lawn sleeves, looked with some uneasiness from one Prince to the other. 'Very well, then,' said the Regent at last, 'call her after her mother. But Alexandrina must come first.' Thus, to the disgust of her father, the child was christened Alexandrina Victoria.

The Duke had other subjects of disgust. The meagre grant of the Commons had by no means put an end to his financial distresses. It was to be feared that his services were not appreciated by the nation. His debts continued to grow. For many years he had lived upon £7000 a year; but now his expenses were exactly doubled; he could make no further reductions; as it was, there was not a single servant in his establishment who was idle for a moment from morning to night. He poured out his griefs in a long letter to Robert Owen, whose sympathy had the great merit of being practical. 'I now candidly state,' he wrote, 'that, after viewing the subject in every possible way, I am satisfied that, to continue to live in England, even in the quiet way in which we are going on, *without splendour,* and *without show, nothing short of doubling the seven thousand pounds will do,* REDUCTION BEING IMPOSSIBLE.' It was clear that he would be obliged to sell his house for £51,-

300: if that failed, he would go and live on the Continent. 'If my services are useful to my country, it surely becomes *those who have the power* to support me in substantiating those just claims I have for the very extensive losses and privations I have experienced, during the very long period of my professional servitude in the Colonies; and if this is not attainable, *it is a clear proof to me that they are not appreciated;* and under that impression I shall not scruple, in *due* time, to resume my retirement abroad, when the Duchess and myself shall have fulfilled our duties in establishing the *English* birth of my child, and giving it material nutriment on the soil of Old England; and which we shall certainly repeat, if Providence destines to give us any further increase of family.'

In the meantime, he decided to spend the winter at Sidmouth, 'in order,' he told Owen, 'that the Duchess may have the benefit of tepid sea bathing, and our infant that of sea air, on the fine coast of Devonshire, during the months of the year that are so odious in London.' In December the move was made. With the new year, the Duke remembered another prophecy. In 1820, a fortune-teller had told him, two members of the Royal Family would die. Who would they be? He speculated on the various possibilities: the King, it was plain, could not live much longer; and the Duchess of York had been attacked by a mortal disease. Probably it would be the King and the Duchess of York; or perhaps the King and the Duke of York; or the King and the Regent. He himself was one of the healthiest men in England. 'My brothers,' he declared, 'are not so strong as I am; I have lived a regular life. I shall outlive them all. The crown will come to me and my children.' He went out for a walk, and got his feet wet. On coming home, he neglected to change his stockings. He caught cold, inflammation of the lungs set in, and on January 22 he was a dying man. By a curious chance, young Dr. Stockmar was staying in the house at the time; two years before, he had stood by the death-bed of the Princess Charlotte; and now he was watching the Duke of Kent in his agony. On Stockmar's advice, a will was hastily prepared. The Duke's earthly possessions were of a negative character; but it was important that the guardianship of the unwitting child, whose fortunes were now so strangely changing, should be assured to the Duchess. The Duke was just able to understand the document, and to append his signature. Having inquired whether his writing was perfectly clear, he became unconscious, and breathed his last on the following morning. Six days later came the fulfilment of the second half of the gipsy's prophecy. The long, unhappy, and inglorious life of George the Third of England was ended.[1]

[1] King George III was declared hopelessly insane in 1811. The Prince of Wales

II

Such was the confusion of affairs at Sidmouth, that the Duchess found herself without the means of returning to London. Prince Leopold hurried down, and himself conducted his sister and her family, by slow and bitter stages, to Kensington. The widowed lady, in her voluminous blacks, needed all her equanimity to support her. Her prospects were more dubious than ever. She had £6000 a year of her own; but her husband's debts loomed before her like a mountain. Soon she learnt that the Duchess of Clarence was once more expecting a child. What had she to look forward to in England? Why should she remain in a foreign country, among strangers, whose language she could not speak, whose customs she could not understand? Surely it would be best to return to Amorbach, and there, among her own people, bring up her daughters in economical obscurity. But she was an inveterate optimist; she had spent her life in struggles, and would not be daunted now. And besides, she adored her baby. *'C'est mon bonheur, mes délices, mon existence,'* [1] she declared; the darling should be brought up as an English princess, whatever lot awaited her. Prince Leopold came forward nobly with an offer of an additional

£3000 a year; and the Duchess remained at Kensington.

The child herself was extremely fat, and bore a remarkable resemblance to her grandfather. *'C'est l'image du feu Roi!'* exclaimed the Duchess. *'C'est le Roi Georges en jupons,'* [2] echoed the surrounding ladies, as the little creature waddled with difficulty from one to the other.

Before long, the world began to be slightly interested in the nursery at Kensington. When, early in 1821, the Duchess of Clarence's second child, the Princess Elizabeth, died within three months of its birth, the interest increased. Great forces and fierce antagonisms seemed to be moving, obscurely, about the royal cradle. It was a time of faction and anger, of violent repression and profound discontent. A powerful movement, which had for long been checked by adverse circumstances, was now spreading throughout the country. New passions, new desires, were abroad; or rather old passions and old desires, reincarnated with a new potency: love of freedom, hatred of injustice, hope for the future of man. The mighty still sat proudly in their seats, dispensing their ancient tyranny; but a storm was gathering out of the darkness, and already there was lightning in the sky. But the vastest forces must needs operate through frail human instru-

---

(later George IV) was appointed that year to act in his stead as Prince Regent.

[1] *C'est mon bonheur, mes délices, mon existence:* This is my happiness, my delights, my life.

[2] *C'est l'image du feu Roi!* . . . *C'est le Roi Georges en jupons:* She is the picture of the late King! . . . She is King George in petticoats.

ments; and it seemed for many years as if the great cause of English liberalism hung upon the life of the little girl at Kensington. She alone stood between the country and her terrible uncle, the Duke of Cumberland, the hideous embodiment of reaction. Inevitably, the Duchess of Kent threw in her lot with her husband's party; Whig leaders, Radical agitators, rallied round her; she was intimate with the bold Lord Durham,[1] she was on friendly terms with the redoubtable O'Connell[1] himself. She received Wilberforce[1]—though, to be sure, she did not ask him to sit down. She declared in public that she put her faith in 'the liberties of the People.' It was certain that the young Princess would be brought up in the way that one should go; yet there, close behind the throne, waiting, sinister, was the Duke of Cumberland. Brougham, looking forward into the future in his scurrilous fashion, hinted at dreadful possibilities. 'I never prayed so heartily for a Prince before,' he wrote, on hearing that George IV had been attacked by illness. 'If he had gone, all the troubles of these villains [the Tory Ministers] went with him, and they had Fred. I [the Duke of York] their own man for his life. . . . He [Fred. I] won't live long either; that Prince of Blackguards, "Brother William," is as bad a life, so we come in the course of nature to be *assassinated* by King Ernest I or Regent Ernest [the Duke of Cumberland].' Such thoughts were not peculiar to Brougham; in the seething state of public feeling, they constantly leapt to the surface; and, even so late as the year previous to her accession, the Radical newspapers were full of suggestions that the Princess Victoria was in danger from the machinations of her wicked uncle.

But no echo of these conflicts and forebodings reached the little Drina —for so she was called in the family circle—as she played with her dolls, or scampered down the passages, or rode on the donkey her uncle York had given her along the avenues of Kensington Gardens. The fair-haired, blue-eyed child was idolised by her nurses, and her mother's ladies, and her sister Feodora; and for a few years there was danger, in spite of her mother's strictness, of her being spoilt. From time to time, she would fly into a violent passion, stamp her little foot, and set everyone at defiance; whatever they might say, she would not learn her letters—no, she *would not;* afterwards, she was very sorry, and burst into tears; but her letters remained unlearnt. When she was five years old, however, a change came, with the appearance of Fräulein Lehzen. This lady, who was the daughter of a Hanoverian clergyman and had previously been the Princess Feodora's governess, soon succeeded in instilling a new spirit into her charge. At first, indeed, she was appalled by the little

---

[1] Lord Durham, O'Connell, Wilberforce: prominent reform-minded public figures of the time.

Princess's outbursts of temper; never in her life, she declared, had she seen such a passionate and naughty child. Then she observed something else; the child was extraordinarily truthful; whatever punishment might follow, she never told a lie. Firm, very firm, the new governess yet had the sense to see that all the firmness in the world would be useless, unless she could win her way into little Drina's heart. She did so, and there were no more difficulties. Drina learnt her letters like an angel; and she learnt other things as well. The Baroness de Späth taught her how to make little board boxes and decorate them with tinsel and painted flowers; her mother taught her religion. Sitting in the pew every Sunday morning, the child of six was seen listening in rapt attention to the clergyman's endless sermon, for she was to be examined upon it in the afternoon. The Duchess was determined that her daughter, from the earliest possible moment, should be prepared for her high station in a way that would commend itself to the most respectable; her good, plain, thrifty German mind recoiled with horror and amazement from the shameless junketings at Carlton House; Drina should never be allowed to forget for a moment the virtues of simplicity, regularity, propriety, and devotion. The little girl, however, was really in small need of such lessons, for she was naturally simple and orderly, she was pious without difficulty, and her sense of propriety was keen. She understood very well the niceties of her own position. When, a child of six, Lady Jane Ellice was taken by her grandmother to Kensington Palace, she was put to play with the Princess Victoria, who was the same age as herself. The young visitor, ignorant of etiquette, began to make free with the toys on the floor, in a way which was a little too familiar; but 'You must not touch those,' she was quickly told, 'they are mine; and I may call you Jane, but you must not call me Victoria.' The Princess's most constant playmate was Victoire, the daughter of Sir John Conroy, the Duchess's majordomo. The two girls were very fond of one another; they would walk hand in hand together in Kensington Gardens. But little Drina was perfectly aware for which of them it was that they were followed, at a respectful distance, by a gigantic scarlet flunkey.

Warm-hearted, responsive, she loved her dear Lehzen, and she loved her dear Feodora, and her dear Victoire, and her dear Madame de Späth. And her dear Mamma . . . of course, she loved her too; it was her duty; and yet—she could not tell why it was—she was always happier when she was staying with her Uncle Leopold at Claremont. There old Mrs. Louis, who, years ago, had waited on her Cousin Charlotte, petted her to her heart's content; and her uncle himself was wonderfully kind to her, talking to her seriously and gently, almost as if she were a grown-up person. She and Feodora invariably wept when the too short visit was over, and they were obliged to return to the dutiful monotony, and the affectionate supervision of Kensington. But sometimes when her mother had to stay at home, she was allowed to go out driving all alone with her dear Feodora and her dear Lehzen, and she could talk and look as she liked, and it was very delightful.

The visits to Claremont were frequent enough; but one day, on a special occasion, she paid one of a rarer and more exciting kind. When she was seven years old, she and her mother and sister were asked by the King to go down to Windsor. George IV, who had transferred his fraternal ill-temper to his sister-in-law and her family, had at last grown tired of sulking, and decided to be agreeable. The old rip, bewigged and gouty, ornate and enormous, with his jewelled mistress by his side and his flaunting court about him, received the tiny creature who was one day to hold in those same halls a very different state. 'Give me your little paw,' he said; and two ages touched. Next morning, driving in his phaeton with the Duchess of Gloucester, he met the Duchess of Kent and her child in the Park. 'Pop her in,' were his orders, which, to the terror of the mother and the delight of the daughter, were immediately obeyed. Off they dashed to Virginia Water, where there was a great barge, full of lords and ladies fishing, and another barge with a band; and the King

ogled Feodora, and praised her manners, and then turned to his own small niece. 'What is your favourite tune? The band shall play it.' 'God save the King, sir,' was the instant answer. The Princess's reply has been praised as an early example of a tact which was afterwards famous. But she was a very truthful child, and perhaps it was her genuine opinion.

III

In 1827 the Duke of York, who had found some consolation for the loss of his wife in the sympathy of the Duchess of Rutland, died, leaving behind him the unfinished immensity of Stafford House and £200,000 worth of debts. Three years later George IV also disappeared, and the Duke of Clarence reigned in his stead. The new Queen, it was now clear, would in all probability never again be a mother; the Princess Victoria, therefore, was recognised by Parliament as the heir-presumptive; and the Duchess of Kent, whose annuity had been doubled five years previously, was now given an additional £10,000 for the maintenance of the Princess, and was appointed regent, in case of the death of the King before the majority of her daughter. At the same time a great convulsion took place in the constitution of the State. The power of the Tories, who had dominated England for more than forty years, suddenly began to crumble. In the tremendous struggle that followed, it seemed for a moment as if the tradition of generations might be snapped, as if the blind tenacity of the reactionaries and the determined fury of their enemies could have no other issue than revolution. But the forces of compromise triumphed: the Reform Bill was passed. The centre of gravity in the constitution was shifted towards the middle classes; the Whigs came into power; and the complexion of the Government assumed a Liberal tinge. One of the results of this new state of affairs was a change in the position of the Duchess of Kent and her daughter. From being the *protégées* of an opposition clique, they became assets of the official majority of the nation. The Princess Victoria was henceforward the living symbol of the victory of the middle classes.

The Duke of Cumberland, on the other hand, suffered a corresponding eclipse: his claws had been pared by the Reform Act. He grew insignificant and almost harmless, though his ugliness remained; he was the wicked uncle still—but only of a story.

The Duchess's own liberalism was not very profound. She followed naturally in the footsteps of her husband, repeating with conviction the catchwords of her husband's clever friends and the generalisations of her clever brother Leopold. She herself had no pretensions to cleverness; she did not understand very much about the Poor Law and the Slave Trade and Political Economy; but she hoped that she did her duty; and she

hoped—she ardently hoped—that the same might be said of Victoria. Her educational conceptions were those of Dr. Arnold, whose views were just then beginning to permeate society. Dr. Arnold's object was, first and foremost, to make his pupils 'in the highest and truest sense of the words, Christian gentlemen'; intellectual refinements might follow. The Duchess felt convinced that it was her supreme duty in life to make quite sure that her daughter should grow up into a Christian queen. To this task she bent all her energies; and, as the child developed, she flattered herself that her efforts were not unsuccessful. When the Princess was eleven, she desired the Bishops of London and Lincoln to submit her daughter to an examination, and report upon the progress that had been made. 'I feel the time to be now come,' the Duchess explained, in a letter obviously drawn up by her own hand, 'that what has been done should be put to some test, that if anything has been done in error of judgment it may be corrected, and that the plan for the future should be open to consideration and revision. . . . I attend almost always myself every lesson, or a part; and as the lady about the Princess is a competent person, she assists Her in preparing Her lessons, for the various masters, as I resolved to act in that manner so as to be Her Governess myself. . . . When she was at a proper age she commenced attending Divine Service regularly with me, and I have every feeling that she has religion at Her heart, that she is morally impressed with it to that degree, that she is less liable to error by its application to her feelings as a Child capable of reflection.' 'The general bent of Her character,' added the Duchess, 'is strength of intellect, capable of receiving with ease, information, and with a peculiar readiness in coming to a very just and benignant decision on any point Her opinion is asked on. Her adherence to truth is of so marked a character that I feel no apprehension of that Bulwark being broken down by any circumstances.' The Bishops attended at the Palace, and the result of their examination was all that could be wished. 'In answering a great variety of questions proposed to her,' they reported, 'the Princess displayed an accurate knowledge of the most important features of Scripture History, and of the leading truths and precepts of the Christian Religion as taught by the Church of England, as well as an acquaintance with the Chronology and principal facts of English History remarkable in so young a person. To questions in Geography, the use of the Globes, Arithmetic, and Latin Grammar, the answers which the Princess returned were equally satisfactory.' They did not believe that the Duchess's plan of education was susceptible of any improvement; and the Archbishop of Canterbury, who was also consulted, came to the same gratifying conclusion.

One important step, however, remained to be taken. So far, as the Duchess explained to the Bishops, the Princess had been kept in ignorance of the station that she was likely to fill. 'She is aware of its duties, and that a Sovereign should live for others; so that when Her innocent mind receives the impression of Her future fate, she receives it with a mind formed to be sensible of what is to be expected from Her, and it is to be hoped, she will be too well grounded in Her principles to be dazzled with the station she is to look to.' In the following year it was decided that she should be enlightened on this point. The well-known scene followed: the history lesson, the genealogical table of the Kings of England slipped beforehand by the governess into the book, the Princess's surprise, her inquiries, her final realisation of the facts. When the child at last understood, she was silent for a moment, and then she spoke: 'I will be good,' she said. The words were something more than a conventional protestation, something more than the expression of a superimposed desire; they were, in their limitation and their intensity, their egotism and their humility, an instinctive summary of the dominating qualities of a life. 'I cried much on learning it,' her Majesty noted long afterwards. No doubt, while the others were present, even her dear Lehzen, the little girl kept up her self-command; and then crept away somewhere to ease her heart of an inward, unfamiliar agitation, with a handkerchief, out of her mother's sight.

But her mother's sight was by no means an easy thing to escape. Morning and evening, day and night, there was no relaxation of the maternal vigilance. The child grew into the girl, the girl into the young woman; but still she slept in her mother's bedroom; still she had no place allowed her where she might sit or work by herself. An extraordinary watchfulness surrounded her every step: up to the day of her accession, she never went downstairs without someone beside her holding her hand. Plainness and regularity ruled the household. The hours, the days, the years passed slowly and methodically by. The dolls—the innumerable dolls, each one so neatly dressed, each one with its name so punctiliously entered in the catalogue—were laid aside, and a little music and a little dancing took their place. Taglioni came, to give grace and dignity to the figure, and Lablache, to train the piping treble upon his own rich bass. The Dean of Chester, the official preceptor, continued his endless instruction in Scripture history, while the Duchess of Northumberland, the official governess, presided over every lesson with becoming solemnity. Without doubt, the Princess's main achievement during her school-days was linguistic. German was naturally the first language with which she was familiar; but English and French quickly followed; and she became virtually trilingual, though her mastery of English grammar re-

mained incomplete. At the same time, she acquired a working knowledge of Italian and some smattering of Latin. Nevertheless, she did not read very much. It was not an occupation that she cared for; partly, perhaps, because the books that were given her were all either sermons, which were very dull, or poetry, which was incomprehensible. Novels were strictly forbidden. Lord Durham persuaded her mother to get her some of Miss Martineau's tales, illustrating the truths of Political Economy, and they delighted her; but it is to be feared that it was the unaccustomed pleasure of the story that filled her mind, and that she never really mastered the theory of exchanges or the nature of rent.

It was her misfortune that the mental atmosphere which surrounded her during these years of adolescence was almost entirely feminine. No father, no brother, was there to break in upon the gentle monotony of the daily round with impetuosity, with rudeness, with careless laughter and wafts of freedom from the outside world. The Princess was never called by a voice that was loud and growling; never felt, as a matter of course, a hard rough cheek on her own soft one; never climbed a wall with a boy. The visits to Claremont—delicious little escapes into male society—came to an end when she was eleven years old and Prince Leopold left England to be King of the Belgians. She loved him still; he was still 'il mio secondo padre—

or, rather, *solo* padre, for he is indeed like my real father, as I have none'; but his fatherliness now came to her dimly and indirectly, through the cold channel of correspondence. Henceforward female duty, female elegance, female enthusiasm, hemmed her completely in; and her spirit, amid the enclosing folds, was hardly reached by those two great influences, without which no growing life can truly prosper—humour and imagination. The Baroness Lehzen—for she had been raised to that rank in the Hanoverian nobility by George IV before he died—was the real centre of the Princess's world. When Feodora married, when Uncle Leopold went to Belgium, the Baroness was left without a competitor. The Princess gave her mother her dutiful regards; but Lehzen had her heart. The voluble, shrewd daughter of the pastor in Hanover, lavishing her devotion on her royal charge, had reaped her reward in an unbounded confidence and a passionate adoration. The girl would have gone through fire for her *'precious* Lehzen,' the 'best and truest friend,' she declared, that she had had since her birth. Her journal, begun when she was thirteen, where she registered day by day the small succession of her doings and her sentiments, bears on every page of it the traces of the Baroness and her circumambient influence. The young creature that one sees there, self-depicted in ingenuous clarity, with her sincerity, her simplicity, her quick affec-

tions and pious resolutions, might almost have been the daughter of a German pastor herself. Her enjoyments, her admirations, her *engouements* [1] were of the kind that clothed themselves naturally in underlinings and exclamation marks. 'It was a *delightful* ride. We cantered a good deal. SWEET LITTLE ROSY WENT BEAUTIFULLY!! We came home at a ¼ past 1. . . . At 20 minutes to 7 we went out to the Opera. . . . Rubini came on and sang a song out of 'Anna Boulena' *quite beautifully*. We came home at ½ past 11.' In her comments on her readings, the mind of the Baroness is clearly revealed. One day, by some mistake, she was allowed to take up a volume of memoirs by Fanny Kemble.[2] 'It is certainly very pertly and oddly written. One would imagine by the style that the authoress must be very pert, and not well bred; for there are so many vulgar expressions in it. It is a great pity that a person endowed with so much talent, as Mrs. Butler really is, should turn it to so little account and publish a book which is so full of trash and nonsense which can only do her harm. I stayed up till 20 minutes past 9.' Madame de Sévigné's [3] letters, which the Baroness read aloud, met with more approval. 'How truly elegant and natural her style is! It is so full of *naïveté,* cleverness, and grace.' But

[1] *engouements:* infatuations.
[2] Fanny Kemble (1809–1893): English actress.
[3] Madame de Sévigné (1626–1696): French letter-writer.

her highest admiration was reserved for the Bishop of Chester's *Exposition of the Gospel of St. Matthew.* 'It is a very fine book indeed. Just the sort of one I like; which is just plain and comprehensible and full of truth and good feeling. It is not one of those learned books in which you have to cavil at almost every paragraph. Lehzen gave it to me on the Sunday that I took the Sacrament.' A few weeks previously she had been confirmed, and she described the event as follows: 'I felt that my confirmation was one of the most solemn and important events and acts in my life; and that I trusted that it might have a salutary effect on my mind. I felt deeply repentant for all what I had done which was wrong and trusted in God Almighty to strengthen my heart and mind; and to forsake all that is bad and follow all that is virtuous and right. I went with the firm determination to become a true Christian, to try and comfort my dear Mamma in all her griefs, trials, and anxieties, and to become a dutiful and affectionate daughter to her. Also to be obedient to *dear* Lehzen, who has done so much for me. I was dressed in a white lace dress, with a white crape bonnet with a wreath of white roses round it. I went in the chariot with my dear Mamma and the others followed in another carriage.' One seems to hold in one's hand a small smooth crystal pebble, without a flaw and without a scintillation, and so transparent that one can see through it at a glance.

Yet perhaps, after all, to the discerning eye, the purity would not be absolute. The careful searcher might detect, in the virgin soil, the first faint traces of an unexpected vein. In that conventual existence visits were exciting events; and, as the Duchess had many relatives, they were not infrequent; aunts and uncles would often appear from Germany, and cousins too. When the Princess was fourteen, she was delighted by the arrival of a couple of boys from Würtemberg, the Princes Alexander and Ernst, sons of her mother's sister and the reigning duke. 'They are both *extremely tall,*' she noted; 'Alexander is *very handsome,* and Ernst has a *very kind expression.* They are both extremely *amiable.*' And their departure filled her with corresponding regrets. 'We saw them get into the barge, and watched them sailing away for some time on the beach. They were so amiable and so pleasant to have in the house; they were *always satisfied, always good-humoured;* Alexander took such care of me in getting out of the boat, and rode next to me; so did Ernst.' Two years later, two other cousins arrived, the Princes Ferdinand and Augustus. 'Dear Ferdinand,' the Princess wrote, 'has elicited universal admiration from all parties. . . . He is so very unaffected, and has such a very distinguished appearance and carriage. They are both very dear and charming young men. Augustus is very amiable, too, and, when known, shows much good sense.'

On another occasion, 'Dear Ferdinand came and sat near me and talked so dearly and sensibly. I do *so* love him. Dear Augustus sat near me and talked with me, and he is also a dear good young man, and is very handsome.' She could not quite decide which was the handsomer of the two. On the whole, she concluded, 'I think Ferdinand handsomer than Augustus, his eyes are so beautiful, and he has such a lively clever expression; *both* have such a sweet expression; Ferdinand has something *quite beautiful* in his expression when he speaks and smiles, and he is *so* good.' However, it was perhaps best to say that they were 'both very handsome and *very dear.*' But shortly afterwards two more cousins arrived, who threw all the rest into the shade. These were the Princes Ernest and Albert, sons of her mother's eldest brother, the Duke of Saxe-Coburg. This time the Princess was more particular in her observations. 'Ernest,' she remarked, 'is as tall as Ferdinand and Augustus; he has dark hair, and fine dark eyes and eyebrows, but the nose and mouth are not good; he has a most kind, honest, and intelligent expression in his countenance, and has a very good figure. Albert, who is just as tall as Ernest but stouter, is extremely handsome; his hair is about the same colour as mine; his eyes are large and blue, and he has a beautiful nose and a very sweet mouth with fine teeth; but the charm of his countenance is his expression, which is most de-

lightful; *c'est à la fois* [1] full of goodness and sweetness, and very clever and intelligent.' 'Both my cousins,' she added, 'are so kind and good; they are much more *formés* [2] and men of the world than Augustus; they speak English very well, and I speak it with them. Ernest will be 18 years old on the 21st of June, and Albert 17 on the 26th of August. Dear Uncle Ernest made me the present of a most delightful *Lory,* [3] which is so tame that it remains on your hand and you may put your finger into its beak, or do anything with it, without its ever attempting to bite. It is larger than Mamma's grey parrot.' A little later, 'I sat between my dear cousins on the sofa and we looked at drawings. They both draw very well, particularly Albert, and are both exceedingly fond of music; they play very nicely on the piano. The more I see them the more I am delighted with them, and the more I love them. . . . It is delightful to be with them; they are so fond of being occupied too; they are quite an example for any young person.' When, after a stay of three weeks, the time came for the young men and their father to return to Germany, the moment of parting was a melancholy one. 'It was our last HAPPY HAPPY breakfast, with this dear Uncle and those *dearest* beloved cousins, whom I *do* love so VERY VERY dearly; *much more dearly* than any other cousins in the *world*. Dearly as I love Ferdi-

---

[1] *c'est à la fois:* at the same time.
[2] *formés:* matured.
[3] *Lory:* a variety of parrot.

nand, and also good Augustus, I love Ernest and Albert *more* than them, oh yes, MUCH *more*. . . . They have both learnt a good deal, and are very clever, naturally clever, particularly Albert, who is the most reflecting of the two, and they like very much talking about serious and instructive things and yet are so *very very* merry and gay and happy, like young people ought to be; Albert always used to have some fun and some clever witty answer at breakfast and everywhere; he used to play and fondle Dash so funnily too. . . . Dearest Albert was playing on the piano when I came down. At 11 dear Uncle, my *dearest beloved* cousins, and Charles, left us, accompanied by Count Kolowrat. I embraced both my dearest cousins most warmly, as also my dear Uncle. I cried bitterly, very bitterly.' The Princes shared her ecstasies and her italics between them; but it is clear enough where her secret preference lay. 'Particularly Albert!' She was just seventeen; and deep was the impression left upon that budding organism by the young man's charm and goodness and accomplishments, and his large blue eyes and beautiful nose, and his sweet mouth and fine teeth.

IV

King William could not away with his sister-in-law, and the Duchess fully returned his antipathy. Without considerable tact and considerable forbearance their relative positions were well calculated to cause ill-feeling; and there was very little tact in the composition of the Duchess, and no forbearance at all in that of his Majesty. A bursting, bubbling old gentleman, with quarterdeck gestures, round rolling eyes, and a head like a pineapple, his sudden elevation to the throne after fifty-six years of utter insignificance had almost sent him crazy. His natural exuberance completely got the best of him; he rushed about doing preposterous things in an extraordinary manner, spreading amusement and terror in every direction, and talking all the time. His tongue was decidedly Hanoverian, with its repetitions, its catchwords—'That's quite another thing! That's quite another thing!'—its rattling indomitability, its loud indiscreetness. His speeches, made repeatedly at the most inopportune junctures, and filled pell-mell with all the fancies and furies that happened at the moment to be whisking about in his head, were the consternation of Ministers. He was one part blackguard, people said, and three parts buffoon; but those who knew him better could not help liking him—he meant well; and he was really good-humoured and kind-hearted, if you took him the right way. If you took him the wrong way, however, you must look out for squalls, as the Duchess of Kent discovered.

She had no notion of how to deal with him—could not understand him in the least. Occupied with her own position, her own responsibilities, her duty, and her daughter, she had no attention to spare for the peppery susceptibilities of a foolish, disreputable old man. She was the mother of the heiress of England; and it was for him to recognize the fact—to put her at once upon a proper footing—to give her the precedence of a dowager Princess of Wales, with a large annuity from the privy purse. It did not occur to her that such pretensions might be galling to a king who had no legitimate child of his own, and who yet had not altogether abandoned the hope of having one. She pressed on, with bulky vigour, along the course she had laid out. Sir John Conroy, an Irishman with no judgment and a great deal of self-importance, was her intimate counsellor, and egged her on. It was advisable that Victoria should become acquainted with the various districts of England, and through several summers a succession of tours—in the West, in the Midlands, in Wales—were arranged for her. The intention of the plan was excellent, but its execution was unfortunate. The journeys, advertised in the Press, attracting enthusiastic crowds, and involving official receptions, took on the air of royal progresses. Addresses were presented by loyal citizens; the delighted Duchess, swelling in sweeping feathers and almost obliterating the diminutive Princess, read aloud, in her German accent, gracious replies prepared beforehand by Sir John, who, bustling and ridiculous, seemed to be mingling the rôles of major-domo and Prime Minister.

Naturally the King fumed over his newspaper at Windsor. 'That woman is a nuisance!' he exclaimed. Poor Queen Adelaide, amiable though disappointed, did her best to smooth things down, changed the subject, and wrote affectionate letters to Victoria; but it was useless. News arrived that the Duchess of Kent, sailing in the Solent, had insisted that whenever her yacht appeared it should be received by royal salutes from all the men-of-war and all the forts. The King declared that these continual poppings must cease; the Premier and the First Lord of the Admiralty were consulted; and they wrote privately to the Duchess, begging her to waive her rights. But she would not hear of it; Sir John Conroy was adamant. 'As her Royal Highness's *confidential adviser,*' he said, 'I cannot recommend her to give way on this point.' Eventually the King, in a great state of excitement, issued a special Order in Council, prohibiting the firing of royal salutes to any ships except those which carried the reigning sovereign or his consort on board.

When King William quarrelled with his Whig Ministers, the situation grew still more embittered, for now the Duchess, in addition to her other shortcomings, was the political partisan of his enemies. In 1836 he made an attempt to prepare the ground for a match between the Princess Victoria and one of the sons of the Prince of Orange, and at the same time did his best to prevent the visit of the young Coburg princes to Kensington. He failed in both these objects; and the only result of his efforts was to raise the anger of the King of the Belgians, who, forgetting for a moment his royal reserve, addressed an indignant letter on the subject to his niece. 'I am really *astonished*,' he wrote, 'at the conduct of your old Uncle the King; this invitation of the Prince of Orange and his sons, this forcing him on others, is very extraordinary. . . . Not later than yesterday I got a half-official communication from England, insinuating that it would be *highly* desirable that the visit of *your* relatives *should not take place this year—qu'en dites-vous?* [1] The relations of the Queen and the King, therefore, to the God-knows-what degree, are to come in shoals and rule the land, when *your relations* are to be *forbidden* the country, and that when, as you know, the whole of your relations have ever been very dutiful and kind to the King. Really and truly I never heard or saw anything like it, and I hope it will a *little rouse your spirit;* now that slavery is even abolished in the British Colonies, I do not comprehend *why your lot alone should be to be kept a white little slavey in England,* for the pleasure of the Court, who never bought you, as I am not aware of their ever having gone to any expense on that head,

or the King's ever having *spent a sixpence for your existence.* . . . Oh, consistency and political or *other honesty,* where must one look for you!'

Shortly afterwards King Leopold came to England himself, and his reception was as cold at Windsor as it was warm at Kensington. 'To hear dear Uncle speak on any subject,' the Princess wrote in her diary, 'is like reading a highly instructive book; his conversation is so enlightened, so clear. He is universally admitted to be one of the first politicians now extant. He speaks so mildly, yet firmly and impartially, about politics. Uncle tells me that Belgium is quite a pattern for its organisation, its industry, and prosperity; the finances are in the greatest perfection. Uncle is so beloved and revered by his Belgian subjects, that it must be a great compensation for all his extreme trouble.' But her other uncle by no means shared her sentiments. He could not, he said, put up with a water-drinker; and King Leopold would touch no wine. 'What's that you're drinking, sir?' he asked him one day at dinner. 'Water, sir.' 'Damn it, sir!' was the rejoinder. 'Why don't you drink wine? I never allow anybody to drink water at my table.'

It was clear that before very long there would be a great explosion; and in the hot days of August it came. The Duchess and the Princess had gone down to stay at Windsor for the King's birthday

[1] *qu'en dites-vous:* what do you think of that?

party, and the King himself, who was in London for the day to prorogue Parliament, paid a visit at Kensington Palace in their absence. There he found that the Duchess had just appropriated, against his express orders, a suite of seventeen apartments for her own use. He was extremely angry, and, when he returned to Windsor, after greeting the Princess with affection, he publicly rebuked the Duchess for what she had done. But this was little to what followed. On the next day was the birthday banquet; there were a hundred guests; the Duchess of Kent sat on the King's right hand, and the Princess Victoria opposite. At the end of the dinner, in reply to the toast of the King's health, he rose, and, in a long, loud, passionate speech, poured out the vials of his wrath upon the Duchess. She had, he declared, insulted him—grossly and continually; she had kept the Princess away from him in the most improper manner; she was surrounded by evil advisers, and was incompetent to act with propriety in the high station which she filled; but he would bear it no longer; he would have her to know he was King; he was determined that his authority should be respected; henceforward the Princess should attend at every Court function with the utmost regularity; and he hoped to God that his life might be spared for six months longer, so that the calamity of a regency might be avoided, and the functions of the Crown pass directly to the heiress-

presumptive instead of into the hands of the 'person now near him,' upon whose conduct and capacity no reliance whatever could be placed. The flood of vituperation rushed on for what seemed an interminable period, while the Queen blushed scarlet, the Princess burst into tears, and the hundred guests sat aghast. The Duchess said not a word until the tirade was over and the company had retired; then in a tornado of rage and mortification, she called for her carriage and announced her immediate return to Kensington. It was only with the utmost difficulty that some show of a reconciliation was patched up, and the outraged lady was prevailed upon to put off her departure till the morrow.

Her troubles, however, were not over when she had shaken the dust of Windsor from her feet. In her own household she was pursued by bitterness and vexation of spirit. The apartments at Kensington were seething with subdued disaffection, with jealousies and animosities virulently intensified by long years of propinquity and spite.

There was a deadly feud between Sir John Conroy and Baroness Lehzen. But that was not all. The Duchess had grown too fond of her Major-Domo. There were familiarities, and one day the Princess Victoria discovered the fact. She confided what she had seen to the Baroness, and to the Baroness's beloved ally, Madame de Späth. Unfortunately, Madame de Späth could not hold her tongue, and was actually foolish enough to reprove the Duchess; whereupon she was instantly dismissed. It was not so easy to get rid of the Baroness. That lady, prudent and reserved, maintained an irreproachable demeanour. Her position was strongly entrenched; she had managed to secure the support of the King; and Sir John found that he could do nothing against her. But henceforward the household was divided into two camps. The Duchess supported Sir John with all the abundance of her authority; but the Baroness, too, had an adherent who could not be neglected. The Princess Victoria said nothing, but she had been much attached to Madame de Späth, and she adored her Lehzen. The Duchess knew only too well that in this horrid embroilment her daughter was against her. Chagrin, annoyance, moral reprobation, tossed her to and fro. She did her best to console herself with Sir John's affectionate loquacity or with the sharp remarks of Lady Flora Hastings, one of her maids of honour, who had no love for the Baroness. The subject lent itself to satire; for the pastor's daughter, with all her airs of stiff superiority, had habits which betrayed her origin. Her passion for carraway seeds, for instance, was uncontrollable. Little bags of them came over to her from Hanover, and she sprinkled them on her bread and butter, her cabbage, and even her roast beef. Lady Flora could not resist a caustic observation; it was repeated to the Baroness, who pursed her lips in fury; and so the mischief grew.

v

The King had prayed that he might live till his niece was of age; and a few days before her eighteenth birthday—the date of her legal majority—a sudden attack of illness very nearly carried him off. He recovered, however, and the Princess was able to go through her birthday festivities—a state ball and a drawing-room—with unperturbed enjoyment. 'Count Zichy,' she noted in her diary, 'is very good-looking in uniform, but not in plain clothes. Count Waldenstein looks remarkably well in his pretty Hungarian uniform.' With the latter young gentleman she wished to dance, but there was an unsurmountable difficulty. 'He could not dance quadrilles, and, as in my station I unfortunately cannot valse and gallop, I could not dance with him.' Her birthday present from the King was of a pleasing nature, but it led to a painful domestic scene. In spite of the anger of her Belgian uncle, she had remained upon good terms with her English one. He had always been very kind to her, and the fact that he had quarrelled with her mother did not appear to be a reason for disliking him. He was, she said, 'odd, very odd and singular,' but 'his intentions were often ill interpreted.' He now wrote her a letter, offering her an allowance of £10,-000 a year, which he proposed should be at her own disposal, and independent of her mother. Lord

Conyngham, the Lord Chamberlain, was instructed to deliver the letter into the Princess's own hands. When he arrived at Kensington, he was ushered into the presence of the Duchess and the Princess, and, when he produced the letter, the Duchess put out her hand to take it. Lord Conyngham begged her Royal Highness's pardon, and repeated the King's commands. Thereupon the Duchess drew back, and the Princess took the letter. She immediately wrote to her uncle, accepting his kind proposal. The Duchess was much displeased; £4000 a year, she said, would be quite enough for Victoria; as for the remaining £6000, it would be only proper that she should have that herself.

King William had thrown off his illness, and returned to his normal life. Once more the royal circle at Windsor—their Majesties, the elder Princesses, and some unfortunate Ambassadress or Minister's wife—might be seen ranged for hours round a mahogany table, while the Queen netted a purse, and the King slept, occasionally waking from his slumbers to observe 'Exactly so, ma'am, exactly so!' But this recovery was of short duration. The old man suddenly collapsed; with no specific symptoms besides an extreme weakness, he yet showed no power of rallying; and it was clear to everyone that his death was now close at hand.

All eyes, all thoughts, turned towards the Princess Victoria; but she still remained, shut away in the seclusion of Kensington, a small, unknown figure, lost in the large shadow of her mother's domination. The preceding year had in fact been an important one in her development. The soft tendrils of her mind had for the first time begun to stretch out towards unchildish things. In this King Leopold encouraged her. After his return to Brussels, he had resumed his correspondence in a more serious strain; he discussed the details of foreign politics; he laid down the duties of kingship; he pointed out the iniquitous foolishness of the newspaper press. On the latter subject, indeed, he wrote with some asperity. 'If all the editors,' he said, 'of the papers in the countries where the liberty of the press exists were to be assembled, we should have a *crew* to which you would *not* confide a dog that you would value, still less your honour and reputation.' On the functions of a monarch, his views were unexceptionable. 'The business of the highest in a State,' he wrote, 'is certainly, in my opinion, to act with great impartiality and a spirit of justice for the good of all.' At the same time the Princess's tastes were opening out. Though she was still passionately devoted to riding and dancing, she now began to have a genuine love of music as well, and to drink in the roulades and arias of the Italian opera with high enthusiasm. She even enjoyed reading poetry—at any rate, the poetry of Sir Walter Scott.

When King Leopold learnt that King William's death was approaching, he wrote several long letters of excellent advice to his niece. 'In every letter I shall write to you,' he said, 'I mean to repeat to you, as a *fundamental rule, to be courageous, firm, and honest, as you have been till now.*' For the rest, in the crisis that was approaching, she was not to be alarmed, but to trust in her 'good natural sense and the *truth*' of her character; she was to do nothing in a hurry; to hurt no one's *amour-propre*,[1] and to continue her confidence in the Whig administration. Not content with letters, however, King Leopold determined that the Princess should not lack personal guidance, and sent over to her aid the trusted friend whom, twenty years before, he had taken to his heart by the death-bed at Claremont. Thus, once again, as if in accordance with some preordained destiny, the figure of Stockmar is discernible—inevitably present at a momentous hour.

On June 18, the King was visibly sinking. The Archbishop of Canterbury was by his side, with all the comforts of the church. Nor did the holy words fall upon a rebellious spirit; for many years his Majesty had been a devout believer. 'When I was a young man,' he once explained at a public banquet, 'as well as I can remember, I believed in nothing but pleasure and folly—nothing at all. But when I went to sea, got into a gale, and saw the wonders of the mighty deep, then I believed; and I have been a

<hr>

[1] *amour-propre*: self-esteem.

sincere Christian ever since.' It was the anniversary of the Battle of Waterloo, and the dying man remembered it. He should be glad to live, he said, over that day; he would never see another sunset. 'I hope your Majesty may live to see many,' said Dr. Chambers. 'Oh! that's quite another thing, that's quite another thing,' was the answer. One other sunset he did live to see; and he died in the early hours of the following morning. It was on June 20, 1837.

When all was over, the Archbishop and the Lord Chamberlain ordered a carriage, and drove posthaste from Windsor to Kensington. They arrived at the Palace at five o'clock, and it was only with considerable difficulty that they gained admittance. At six the Duchess woke up her daughter, and told her that the Archbishop of Canterbury and Lord Conyngham were there, and wished to see her. She got out of bed, put on her dressing-gown, and went, alone, into the room where the messengers were standing. Lord Conyngham fell on his knees, and officially announced the death of the King; the Archbishop added some personal details. Looking at the bending, murmuring dignitaries before her, she knew that she was Queen of England. 'Since it has pleased Providence,' she wrote that day in her journal, 'to place me in this station, I shall do my utmost to fulfil my duty towards my country; I am very young, and perhaps in many, though not in all things, inexperienced, but I am sure, that very few have more real good will and more real desire to do what is fit and right than I have.' But there was scant time for resolutions and reflections. At once, affairs were thick upon her. Stockmar came to breakfast, and gave some good advice. She wrote a letter to her uncle Leopold, and a hurried note to her sister Feodora. A letter came from the Prime Minister, Lord Melbourne, announcing his approaching arrival. He came at nine, in full court dress, and kissed her hand. She saw him alone, and repeated to him the lesson which, no doubt, the faithful Stockmar had taught her at breakfast. 'It has long been my intention to retain your Lordship and the rest of the present Ministry at the head of affairs'; whereupon Lord Melbourne again kissed her hand and shortly after left her. She then wrote a letter of condolence to Queen Adelaide. At eleven, Lord Melbourne came again; and at half-past eleven she went downstairs into the red saloon to hold her first Council. The great assembly of lords and notables, bishops, generals, and Ministers of State, saw the doors thrown open and a very short, very slim girl in deep plain mourning come into the room alone and move forward to her seat with extraordinary dignity and grace; they saw a countenance, not beautiful, but prepossessing—fair hair, blue prominent eyes, a small curved nose, an open mouth revealing the upper teeth, a tiny chin, a clear complexion, and, over all, the

strangely mingled signs of innocence, of gravity, of youth, and of composure; they heard a high unwavering voice reading aloud with perfect clarity; and then, the ceremony was over, they saw the small figure rise and, with the same consummate grace, the same amazing dignity, pass out from among them, as she had come in, alone.

✖ *Chapter* **3**

Lord Melbourne

I

The new queen was almost entirely unknown to her subjects. In her public appearances her mother had invariably dominated the scene. Her private life had been that of a novice in a convent: hardly a human being from the outside world had ever spoken to her; and no human being at all, except her mother and the Baroness Lehzen, had ever been alone with her in a room. Thus it was not only the public at large that was in ignorance of everything concerning her; the inner circles of statesmen and officials and high-born ladies were equally in the dark. When she suddenly emerged from this deep obscurity, the impression that she created was immediate and profound. Her bearing at her first Council filled the whole gathering with astonishment and admiration; the Duke of Wellington, Sir Robert Peel, even the savage Croker, even the cold and caustic Greville—all were completely carried away. Everything that was reported of her subsequent proceedings seemed to be of no less happy augury. Her perceptions were quick, her decisions were sensible, her language was discreet; she performed her royal duties with extraordinary facility. Among the outside public there was a great wave of enthusiasm. Sentiment and romance were coming into fashion; and the spectacle of the little girl-queen, innocent, modest, with fair hair and pink cheeks, driving through her capital, filled the hearts of the beholders with raptures of affectionate loyalty. What, above all, struck everybody with overwhelming force was the contrast between Queen Victoria and her uncles. The nasty old men, debauched and selfish, pig-headed and ridiculous, with their perpetual burden of debts, confusions, and disreputabilities—they had vanished like the snows of winter, and here at last, crowned and radiant, was the spring. Lord John Russell, in an elaborate oration, gave voice to the general sentiment. He hoped that Victoria might prove an Elizabeth without her tyranny, an Anne without her weakness. He asked England to pray that the illustrious Princess who had just ascended the throne with the purest intentions and the justest desires might see slavery abolished, crime diminished, and education improved. He trusted that her people would henceforward derive their strength, their conduct, and their loyalty from enlightened religious and moral principles, and that, so fortified, the reign of Victoria might prove celebrated to posterity and to all the nations of the earth.

Very soon, however, there were signs that the future might turn out to be not quite so simple and roseate as a delighted public dreamed. The 'illustrious Princess' might perhaps, after all, have something within her which squared ill with the easy version of a well-conducted heroine in an edifying story-book. The purest intentions and the justest desires? No doubt; but was that all? To those who watched closely, for instance, there might be something ominous in the curious contour of that little mouth. When, after her first Council, she crossed the ante-room and found her mother waiting for her, she said, 'And now, Mamma, am I really and truly Queen' 'You see, my dear, that it is so.' 'Then, dear Mamma, I hope you will grant me the first request I make to you, as Queen. Let me be by myself for an hour.' For an hour she remained in solitude. Then she reappeared, and gave a significant order: her bed was to be moved out of her mother's room. It was the doom of the Duchess of Kent. The long years of waiting were over at last; the moment of a lifetime had come; her daughter was Queen of England; and that very moment brought her own annihilation. She found herself, absolutely and irretrievably, shut off from every vestige of influence, of confidence, of power. She was surrounded, indeed, by all the outward signs of respect and consideration; but that only made the inward truth of her position the more intolerable. Through the mingled formalities of Court etiquette and filial duty, she could never penetrate to Victoria. She was unable to conceal her disappointment and her rage. *'Il n'y a plus d'avenir pour moi,'* she exclaimed to Madame de Lieven; *'je ne suis plus rien.'* [1] For eighteen years, she said, this child had been the sole object of her existence, of her thoughts, her hopes, and now —no! she would not be comforted, she had lost everything, she was to the last degree unhappy. Sailing, so gallantly and so pertinaciously, through the buffeting storms of life, the stately vessel, with sails still swelling and pennons flying, had put into harbour at last; to find there nothing—a land of bleak desolation.

Within a month of the accession, the realities of the new situation assumed a visible shape. The whole royal household moved from Kensington to Buckingham Palace, and, in the new abode, the Duchess of Kent was given a suite of apartments entirely separate from the Queen's. By Victoria herself the change was welcomed, though, at the moment of departure, she

could afford to be sentimental. 'Though I rejoice to *go* into B. P. for many reasons,' she wrote in her diary, 'it is not without feelings of regret that I shall bid adieu *for ever* to this my birthplace, where I have been born and bred, and to which I am really attached!' Her memory lingered for a moment over visions of the past: her sister's wedding, pleasant balls and *delicious* concerts . . . and there were other recollections. 'I have gone through painful and disagreeable scenes here, 'tis true,' she concluded, 'but still I am fond of the poor old palace.'

At the same time she took another decided step. She had determined that she would see no more of Sir John Conroy. She rewarded his past services with liberality: he was given a baronetcy and a pension of £3000 a year; he remained a member of the Duchess's household, but his personal intercourse with the Queen came to an abrupt conclusion.

II

It was clear that these interior changes—whatever else they might betoken—marked the triumph of one person—the Baroness Lehzen. The pastor's daughter observed the ruin of her enemies. Discreet and victorious, she remained in possession of the field. More closely than ever did she cleave to the side of her mistress, her pupil, and her friend; and in the recesses of the palace her mysterious figure was at once invisible and omnipresent. When the

---

[1] *Il n'y a plus d'avenir pour moi. . . . je ne suis plus rien:* There is no more future for me. . . . I am no longer anything.

Queen's Ministers came in at one door, the Baroness went out by another; when they retired, she immediately returned. Nobody knew —nobody ever will know—the precise extent and the precise nature of her influence. She herself declared that she never discussed public affairs with the Queen, that she was concerned with private matters only—with private letters and the details of private life. Certainly her hand is everywhere discernible in Victoria's early correspondence. The Journal is written in the style of a child; the Letters are not so simple; they are the work of a child, rearranged—with the minimum of alteration, no doubt, and yet perceptibly—by a governess. And the governess was no fool: narrow, jealous, provincial, she might be; but she was an acute and vigorous woman, who had gained by a peculiar insight, a peculiar ascendancy. That ascendancy she meant to keep. No doubt it was true that technically, she took no part in public business; but the distinction between what is public and what is private is always a subtle one; and in the case of a reigning sovereign —as the next few years were to show—it is often imaginary. Considering all things—the characters of the persons, and the character of the times—it was something more than a mere matter of private interest that the bedroom of Baroness Lehzen at Buckingham Palace should have been next door to the bedroom of the Queen.

But the influence wielded by the Baroness, supreme as it seemed within its own sphere, was not unlimited; there were other forces at work. For one thing, the faithful Stockmar had taken up his residence in the palace. During the twenty years which had elapsed since the death of the Princess Charlotte, his experiences had been varied and remarkable. The unknown counsellor of a disappointed princeling had gradually risen to a position of European importance. His devotion to his master had been not only whole-hearted but cautious and wise. It was Stockmar's advice that had kept Prince Leopold in England during the critical years which followed his wife's death, and had thus secured to him the essential requisite of a *point d'appui*[1] in the country of his adoption. It was Stockmar's discretion which had smoothed over the embarrassments surrounding the Prince's acceptance and rejection of the Greek crown. It was Stockmar who had induced the Prince to become the constitutional Sovereign of Belgium. Above all, it was Stockmar's tact, honesty, and diplomatic skill which, through a long series of arduous and complicated negotiations, had led to the guarantee of Belgian neutrality by the Great Powers. His labours had been rewarded by a German barony and by the complete confidence of King Leopold. Nor was it only in Brussels that he was treated with

[1] *point d'appui*: point of support; a foothold.

respect and listened to with attention. The statesmen who governed England—Lord Grey, Sir Robert Peel, Lord Palmerston, Lord Melbourne—had learnt to put a high value upon his probity and his intelligence. 'He is one of the cleverest fellows I ever saw,' said Lord Melbourne—'the most discreet man, the most well-judging, and most cool man.' And Lord Palmerston cited Baron Stockmar as the only absolutely disinterested man he had come across in life. At last he was able to retire to Coburg, and to enjoy for a few years the society of the wife and children whom his labours in the service of his master had hitherto only allowed him to visit at long intervals for a month or two at a time. But in 1836 he had been again entrusted with an important negotiation, which he had brought to a successful conclusion in the marriage of Prince Ferdinand of Saxe-Coburg, a nephew of King Leopold's, with Queen Maria II of Portugal. The House of Coburg was beginning to spread over Europe; and the establishment of the Baron at Buckingham Palace in 1837 was to be the prelude of another and a more momentous advance.

King Leopold and his counsellor provide in their careers an example of the curious diversity of human ambitions. The desires of man are wonderfully various; but no less various are the means by which those desires may reach satisfaction: and so the work of the world gets done. The correct mind of Leopold craved for the whole apparatus of royalty. Mere power would have held no attractions for him; he must be an actual king—the crowned head of a people. It was not enough to do; it was essential also to be recognised; anything else would not be fitting. The greatness that he dreamt of was surrounded by every appropriate circumstance. To be a Majesty, to be a cousin of Sovereigns, to marry a Bourbon for diplomatic ends, to correspond with the Queen of England, to be very stiff and very punctual, to found a dynasty, to bore ambassadresses into fits, to live, on the highest pinnacle, an exemplary life devoted to the public service—such were his objects, and such, in fact, were his achievements. The *Marquis Peu-à-peu* [1] as George IV called him, had what he wanted. But this would never have been the case if it had not happened that the ambition of Stockmar took a form exactly complimentary to his own. The sovereignty that the Baron sought for was by no means obvious. The satisfaction of his essential being lay in obscurity, in invisibility—in passing, unobserved, through a hidden entrance, into the very central chamber of power, and in sitting there, quietly, pulling the subtle strings that set the wheels of the whole world in motion. A very few people, in very high places, and exceptionally well-informed, knew that Baron Stockmar was a most impor-

[1] *Marquis Peu-à-peu:* Lord Little-by-Little.

tant person: that was enough. The fortunes of the master and the servant, intimately interacting, rose together. The Baron's secret skill had given Leopold his unexceptionable kingdom; and Leopold, in his turn, as time went on, was able to furnish the Baron with more and more keys to more and more back doors.

Stockmar took up his abode in the Palace partly as the emissary of King Leopold, but more particularly as the friend and adviser of a queen who was almost a child, and who, no doubt, would be much in need of advice and friendship. For it would be a mistake to suppose that either of these two men was actuated by a vulgar selfishness. The King, indeed, was very well aware on which side his bread was buttered; during an adventurous and chequered life he had acquired a shrewd knowledge of the world's workings; and he was ready enough to use that knowledge to strengthen his position and to spread his influence. But then, the firmer his position and the wider his influence, the better for Europe; of that he was quite certain. And besides, he was a constitutional monarch; and it would be highly indecorous in a constitutional monarch to have any aims that were low or personal. As for Stockmar, the disinterestedness which Palmerston had noted was undoubtedly a basic element in his character. The ordinary schemer is always an optimist; and Stockmar, racked by dyspepsia and haunted by gloomy forebodings, was a constitutionally melancholy man. A schem-

er, no doubt, he was; but he schemed distrustfully, splenetically, to do good. To do good! What nobler end could a man scheme for? Yet it is perilous to scheme at all.

With Lehzen to supervise every detail of her conduct, with Stockmar in the next room, so full of wisdom and experience of affairs, with her Uncle Leopold's letters, too, pouring out so constantly their stream of encouragements, general reflections, and highly valuable tips, Victoria, even had she been without other guidance, would have stood in no lack of private counsellors. But other guidance she had; for all these influences paled before a new star, of the first magnitude, which, rising suddenly upon her horizon, immediately dominated her life.

III

William Lamb, Viscount Melbourne, was fifty-eight years of age, and had been for the last three years Prime Minister of England. In every outward respect he was one of the most fortunate of mankind. He had been born into the midst of riches, brilliance, and power. His mother, fascinating and intelligent, had been a great Whig hostess, and he had been bred up as a member of that radiant society which, during the last quarter of the eighteenth century, concentrated within itself the ultimate perfections of a hundred years of triumphant aristocracy. Nature had given him beauty and brains; the unexpected death of an elder brother brought him wealth, a peerage, and the possibility of high advancement. Within that charmed circle, whatever one's personal disabilities, it was difficult to fail; and to him, with all his advantages, success was wellnigh unavoidable. With little effort, he attained political eminence. On the triumph of the Whigs he became one of the leading members of the Government; and when Lord Grey retired from the premiership he quietly stepped into the vacant place. Nor was it only in the visible signs of fortune that Fate had been kind to him. Bound to succeed, and to succeed easily, he was gifted with so fine a nature that his success became him. His mind, at once supple and copious, his temperament, at once calm and sensitive, enabled him not merely to work, but to live with perfect facility and with the grace of strength. In society he was a notable talker, a captivating companion, a charming man. If one looked deeper, one saw at once that he was not ordinary, that the piquancies of his conversation and his manner—his free-and-easy vaguenesses, his abrupt questions, his lollings and loungings, his innumerable oaths—were something more than an amusing ornament, were the outward manifestation of an individuality that was fundamental.

The precise nature of this individuality was very difficult to gauge: it was dubious, complex, perhaps self-contradictory. Certainly there was an ironical discordance between the inner history of the man and his apparent fortunes. He owed all he had to his birth, and his birth was shameful; it was known well enough that his mother had passionately loved Lord Egremont, and that Lord Melbourne was not his father. His marriage, which had seemed to be the crown of his youthful ardours, was a long, miserable, desperate failure: the incredible Lady Caroline,

. . . with pleasures too refined to
    please,
With too much spirit to be e'er at
    ease,
With too much quickness to be ever
    taught,
With too much thinking to have common thought,

was very nearly the destruction of his life. When at last he emerged from the anguish and confusion of her folly, her extravagance, her rage, her despair, and her devotion, he was left alone with endless memories of intermingled farce and tragedy, and an only son, who was an imbecile. But there was something else that he owed to Lady Caroline. While she whirled with Byron in a hectic frenzy of love and fashion, he had stayed at home in an indulgence bordering on cynicism, and occupied his solitude with reading. It was thus that he had acquired those habits of study, that love of learning, and that wide and accurate knowledge of ancient and modern literature, which formed so unexpected a part of his mental equipment. His passion for reading never deserted him; even when he was Prime Minister he found time to master every new important book. With an incongruousness that was characteristic, his favourite study was theology. An accomplished classical scholar, he was deeply read in the Fathers of the Church; heavy volumes of commentary and exegesis he examined with scrupulous diligence; and at any odd moment he might be found turning over the pages of the Bible. To the ladies whom he most liked, he would lend some learned work on the Revelation, crammed with marginal notes in his own hand, or Dr. Lardner's *Observations upon the Jewish Errors with respect to the Conversion of Mary Magdalene*. The more pious among them had high hopes that these studies would lead him into the right way; but of this there were no symptoms in his after-dinner conversations.

The paradox of his political career was no less curious. By temperament an aristocrat, by conviction a conservative, he came to power as the leader of the popular party, the party of change. He had profoundly disliked the Reform Bill, which he had only accepted at last as a necessary evil; and the Reform Bill lay at the root of the very existence, of the very meaning, of his government. He was far too sceptical to believe in progress of any kind. Things were best as they were—or rather, they were least bad. 'You'd better try to do no good,' was one of his dictums, 'and then you'll get into no scrapes.'

Education at best was futile; education of the poor was positively dangerous. The factory children? 'Oh, if you'd only have the goodness to leave them alone!' Free Trade was a delusion; the ballot was nonsense; and there was no such thing as a democracy. Nevertheless, he was not a reactionary; he was simply an opportunist. The whole duty of government, he said, was 'to prevent crime and to preserve contracts.' All one could really hope to do was to carry on. He himself carried on in a remarkable manner—with perpetual compromises, with fluctuations and contradictions, with every kind of weakness, and yet with shrewdness, with gentleness, even with conscientiousness, and a light and airy mastery of men and of events. He conducted the transactions of business with extraordinary nonchalance. Important persons, ushered up for some grave interview, found him in a towelled bed, littered with books and papers, or vaguely shaving in a dressing-room; but, when they went downstairs again, they would realise that somehow or other they had been pumped. When he had to receive a deputation, he could hardly ever do so with becoming gravity. The worthy delegates of the tallow-chandlers, or the Society for the Abolition of Capital Punishment, were distressed and mortified when, in the midst of their speeches, the Prime Minister became absorbed in blowing a feather, or suddenly cracked an unseemly joke. How could they have guessed that he had spent the night before diligently getting up the details of their case? He hated patronage and the making of appointments—a feeling rare in Ministers. 'As for the Bishops,' he burst out. 'I positively believe they die to vex me.' But when at last the appointment was made, it was made with keen discrimination. His colleagues observed another symptom—was it of his irresponsibility or his wisdom? He went to sleep in the Cabinet.

Probably, if he had been born a little earlier, he would have been a simpler and a happier man. As it was, he was a child of the eighteenth century whose lot was cast in a new, difficult, unsympathetic age. He was an autumn rose. With all his gracious amenity, his humour, his happy-go-lucky ways, a deep disquietude possessed him. A sentimental cynic, a sceptical believer, he was restless and melancholy at heart. Above all, he could never harden himself; those sensitive petals shivered in every wind. Whatever else he might be, one thing was certain: Lord Melbourne was always human, supremely human—too human, perhaps.

And now, with old age upon him, his life took a sudden, new, extraordinary turn. He became, in the twinkling of an eye, the intimate adviser and the daily companion of a young girl who had stepped all at once from a nursery to a throne. His relations with women had been, like everything else about him, ambiguous. Nobody had ever been able quite to gauge the shifting, emotional complexities of his married life; Lady Caroline vanished; but his peculiar susceptibilities remained. Female society of some kind or other was necessary to him, and he did not stint himself; a great part of every day was invariably spent in it. The feminine element in him made it easy, made it natural and inevitable for him to be the friend of a great many women; but the masculine element in him was strong as well. In such circumstances it is also easy, it is even natural, perhaps it is even inevitable, to be something more than a friend. There were rumours and combustions. Lord Melbourne was twice a co-respondent in a divorce action; but on each occasion he won his suit. The lovely Lady Brandon, the unhappy and brilliant Mrs. Norton . . . the law exonerated them both. Beyond that hung an impenetrable veil. But at any rate it was clear that, with such a record, the Prime Minister's position in Buckingham Palace must be a highly delicate one. However, he was used to delicacies, and he met the situation with consummate success. His behaviour was from the first moment impeccable. His manner towards the young Queen mingled, with perfect facility, the watchfulness and the respect of a statesman and a courtier with the tender solicitude of a parent. He was at once reverential and affectionate, at once the servant and the guide. At the same time the habits of his life underwent a surprising change. His comfortable, unpunctual days became subject to the unaltering routine of a palace; no longer did he sprawl on sofas; not a single 'damn' escaped his lips. The man of the world who had been the friend of Byron and the regent, the talker whose paradoxes had held Holland House enthralled, the cynic whose ribaldries had enlivened so many deep potations, the lover whose soft words had captivated such beauty and such passion and such wit, might now be seen, evening after evening, talking with infinite politeness to a schoolgirl, bolt upright, amid the silence and the rigidity of Court etiquette.

IV

On her side, Victoria was instantaneously fascinated by Lord Melbourne. The good report of Stockmar had no doubt prepared the way; Lehzen was wisely propitiated; and the first highly favourable impression was never afterwards belied. She found him perfect; and perfect in her sight he remained. Her absolute and unconcealed adoration was very natural; what innocent young creature could have resisted, in any circumstances, the charm and the devotion of such a man? But, in her situation, there was a special influence which gave a peculiar glow to all she felt. After years of emptiness and dullness and suppression, she had come suddenly in the heyday of youth, into freedom and power. She was mistress of herself, of great domains and palaces; she was Queen of England. Responsibilities and difficulties she

might have, no doubt, and in heavy measure; but one feeling dominated and absorbed all others—the feeling of joy. Everything pleased her. She was in high spirits from morning till night. Mr. Creevey, grown old now, and very near his end, catching a glimpse of her at Brighton, was much amused, in his sharp fashion, by the ingenuous gaiety of 'little Vic.'—'A more homely little being you never beheld, *when she is at her ease,* and she is evidently dying to be always more so. She laughs in real earnest, opening her mouth as wide as it can go, showing not very pretty gums. . . . She eats quite as heartily as she laughs, I think I may say she gobbles. . . . She blushes and laughs every instant in so natural a way as to disarm anybody.' But it was not merely when she was laughing or gobbling that she enjoyed herself; the performance of her official duties gave her intense satisfaction. 'I really have immensely to do,' she wrote in her Journal a few days after her accession; 'I receive so many communications from my Ministers, but I like it very much.' And again, a week later, 'I repeat what I said before that I have *so many* communications from the Ministers, and from me to them, and I get so many papers to sign every day, that I have always a *very great* deal to do. I *delight* in this work.' Through the girl's immaturity the vigorous predestined tastes of the woman were pushing themselves into existence with eager velocity, with delicious force.

One detail of her happy situation deserves particular mention. Apart from the splendour of her social position and the momentousness of her political one, she was a person of great wealth. As soon as Parliament met, an annuity of £385,000 was settled upon her. When the expenses of her household had been discharged, she was left with £68,000 a year of her own. She enjoyed besides the revenues of the Duchy of Lancaster, which amounted annually to over £27,000. The first use to which she put her money was characteristic: she paid off her father's debts. In money matters, no less than in other matters, she was determined to be correct. She had the instincts of a man of business; and she never could have borne to be in a position that was financially unsound.

With youth and happiness gilding every hour, the days passed merrily enough. And each day hinged upon Lord Melbourne. Her diary shows us, with undiminished clarity, the life of the young sovereign during the early months of her reign—a life satisfactorily regular, full of delightful business, a life of simple pleasures, mostly physical—riding, eating, dancing—a quick, easy, highly unsophisticated life, sufficient unto itself. The light of the morning is upon it; and, in the rosy radiance, the figure of 'Lord M.' emerges, glorified and supreme. If she is the heroine of the story, he is the hero; but indeed they are more than hero and heroine, for there are no other characters at all.

Lehzen, the Baron, Uncle Leopold, are unsubstantial shadows—the incidental supers of the piece. Her paradise was peopled by two persons, and surely that was enough. One sees them together still, a curious couple, strangely united in those artless pages, under the magical illumination of that dawn of eighty years ago: the polished high fine gentleman with the whitening hair and whiskers and the thick dark eyebrows and the mobile lips and the big expressive eyes; and beside him the tiny Queen—fair, slim, elegant, active, in her plain girl's dress and little tippet, looking up at him earnestly, adoringly, with eyes blue and projecting, and half-open mouth. So they appear upon every page of the Journal; upon every page Lord M. is present, Lord M. is speaking, Lord M. is being amusing, instructive, delightful, and affectionate at once, while Victoria drinks in the honied words, laughs till she shows her gums, tries hard to remember, and runs off, as soon as she is left alone, to put it all down. Their long conversations touched upon a multitude of topics. Lord M. would criticise books, throw out a remark or two on the British Constitution, make some passing reflections on human life, and tell story after story of the great people of the eighteenth century. Then there would be business—a despatch perhaps from Lord Durham in Canada, which Lord M. would read. But first he must explain a little. 'He said that I must know that Canada originally belonged to the French, and was only ceded to the English in 1760, when it was taken in an expedition under Wolfe: "a very daring enterprise," he said. Canada was then entirely French, and the British only came afterwards. . . . Lord M. explained this very clearly (and much better than I have done) and said a good deal more about it. He then read me Durham's despatch, which is a very long one and took him more than ½ an hour to read. Lord M. read it beautifully with that fine soft voice of his, and with so much expression, so that it is needless to say I was much interested by it.' And then the talk would take a more personal turn. Lord M. would describe his boyhood, and she would learn that 'he wore his hair long, as all boys then did, till he was 17; (*how* handsome he must have looked!).' Or she would find out about his queer tastes and habits —how he never carried a watch, which seemed quite extraordinary. '"I always ask the servant what o'clock it is, and then he tells me what he likes," said Lord M.' Or, as the rooks wheeled about round the trees, 'in a manner which indicated rain,' he would say that he could sit looking at them for an hour, and 'was quite surprised at my disliking them. . . . Lord M. said, "The rooks are my delight."'

The day's routine, whether in London or at Windsor, was almost invariable. The morning was devoted to business and Lord M. In the afternoon the whole Court went out riding. The Queen, in her velvet riding-habit and a top-hat with a veil draped about the brim, headed the cavalcade; and Lord M. rode beside her. The lively troupe went fast and far, to the extreme exhilaration of Her Majesty. Back in the Palace again, there was still time for a little more fun before dinner—a game of battledore and shuttlecock perhaps, or a romp along the galleries with some children. Dinner came, and the ceremonial decidedly tightened. The gentleman of highest rank sat on the right hand of the Queen; on her left—it soon became an established rule—sat Lord Melbourne. After the ladies had left the dining-room, the gentlemen were not permitted to remain behind for very long; indeed, the short time allowed them for their wine-drinking formed the subject—so it was rumoured—of one of the very few disputes between the Queen and her Prime Minister; but her determination carried the day, and from that moment after-dinner drunkenness began to go out of fashion. When the company was reassembled in the drawing-room, the etiquette was stiff. For a few moments the Queen spoke in turn to each one of her guests; and during these short uneasy colloquies the aridity of royalty was apt to become painfully evident. One night Mr. Greville, the Clerk of the Privy Council, was present; his turn soon came; the middle-aged, hard-faced *viveur* was addressed by his young hostess. 'Have you been riding to-day, Mr. Greville?' asked the Queen. 'No, Madam, I have not.' replied Mr. Greville. 'It was a fine day,' continued the Queen. 'Yes, Madam, a very fine day,' said Mr. Greville. 'It was rather cold, though,' said the Queen. 'It *was* rather cold, Madam,' said Mr. Greville. 'Your sister, Lady Frances Egerton, rides, I think, doesn't she?' said the Queen. 'She does ride sometimes, Madam,' said Greville. There was a pause, after which Mr. Greville ventured to take the lead, though he did not venture to change the subject. 'Has your Majesty been riding to-day?' asked Mr. Greville. 'Oh yes, a very long ride,' answered the Queen with animation. 'Has your Majesty got a nice horse?' said Mr. Greville. 'Oh, a very nice horse,' said the Queen. It was over, Her Majesty gave a smile and an inclination of the head, Mr. Greville a profound bow, and the next conversation began with the next gentleman. When all the guests had been disposed of, the Duchess of Kent sat down to her whist, while everybody else was ranged about the round table. Lord Melbourne sat beside the Queen, and talked pertinaciously—very often à *propos* to the contents of one of the large albums of engravings with which the round table was covered—until it was half-past eleven and time to go to bed.

Occasionally, there were little diversions: the evening might be spent at the opera or at the play. Next morning the royal critic was careful to note down her impressions. 'It was Shakespeare's tragedy of *Hamlet,* and we came in at the beginning of it. Mr. Charles Kean (son of old Kean) acted the part of Hamlet, and I must say beautifully. His conception of this very difficult, and I may almost say incomprehensible, character is admirable; his delivery of all the fine long speeches quite beautiful; he is excessively graceful and all his actions and attitudes are good, though not at all good-looking in face. . . . I came away just as *Hamlet* was over.' Later on, she went to see Macready in *King Lear.* The story was new to her; she knew nothing about it, and at first she took very little interest in what was passing on the stage; she preferred to chatter and laugh with the Lord Chamberlain. But, as the play went on, her mood changed; her attention was fixed, and then she laughed no more. Yet she was puzzled; it seemed a strange, a horrible business. What did Lord M. think? Lord M. thought it was a very fine play, but to be sure, 'a rough, coarse play, written for those times, with exaggerated characters.' 'I'm glad you've seen it,' he added. But, undoubtedly, the evenings which she enjoyed most were those on which there was dancing. She was always ready enough to seize any excuse—the arrival of cousins—a birthday—a gathering of young people—to give the command for that. Then, when the band played, and the figures of the dancers swayed to the music, and she felt her own figure swaying too, with youthful spirits so close on every side—then her happiness reached its height, her eyes sparkled, she must go on and on into the small hours of the morning. For a moment Lord M. himself was forgotten.

V

The months flew past. The summer was over: 'the pleasantest summer I EVER passed in *my life,* and I shall never forget this first summer of my reign.' With surprising rapidity, another summer was upon her. The coronation came and went—a curious dream. The antique, intricate, endless ceremonial worked itself out as best it could, like some machine of gigantic complexity which was a little out of order. The small central figure went through her gyrations. She sat; she walked; she prayed; she carried about an orb that was almost too heavy to hold; the Archbishop of Canterbury came and crushed a ring upon the wrong finger, so that she was ready to cry out with the pain; old Lord Rolle tripped up in his mantle and fell down the steps as he was doing homage; she was taken into a side chapel, where the altar was covered with a table-cloth, sandwiches, and bottles of wine; she perceived Lehzen in an upper box and exchanged a smile with her as she sat, robed and crowned, on the Confessor's throne. 'I shall ever remember this day as the *proudest* of my life,' she noted. But the pride was soon merged once more in youth and simplicity. When she returned to Buckingham Palace at last she was not tired; she ran up to her private rooms, doffed her splendours, and gave her dog Dash its evening bath.

Life flowed on again with its accustomed smoothness—though, of course, the smoothness was occasionally disturbed. For one thing, there was the distressing behaviour of Uncle Leopold. The King of the Belgians had not been able to resist attempting to make use of his family position to further his diplomatic ends. But, indeed, why should there be any question of resisting? Was not such a course of conduct, far from being a temptation, simply *selon les règles?* [1] What were royal marriages for, if they did not enable sovereigns, in spite of the hindrances of constitutions, to control foreign politics? For the highest purposes, of course; that was understood. The Queen of England was his niece—more than that—almost his daughter; his confidential agent was living, in a position of intimate favour, at her court. Surely, in such circumstances, it would be preposterous, it would be positively incorrect, to lose the opportunity of bending to his wishes by means of personal influence, behind the backs of the English Ministers, the foreign policy of England.

He set about the task with becoming precautions. He continued in his letters his admirable advice. Within a few days of her accession, he recommended the young Queen to lay emphasis, on every possible occasion, upon her English birth;

---

[1] *selon les règles:* according to the rules.

to praise the English nation; 'the Established Church I also recommend strongly; you cannot, without *pledging* yourself to anything *particular, say too much on the subject.*' And then 'before you decide on anything important I should be glad if you would consult me; this would also have the advantage of giving you time'; nothing was more injurious than to be hurried into wrong decisions unawares. His niece replied at once with all the accustomed warmth of her affection; but she wrote hurriedly—and, perhaps, a trifle vaguely too. '*Your* advice is always of the *greatest importance* to me,' she said.

Had he, possibly, gone too far? He could not be certain; perhaps Victoria *had* been hurried. In any case, he would be careful; he would draw back—*pour mieux sauter,*[1] he added to himself with a smile. In his next letters he made no reference to his suggestion of consultations with himself; he merely pointed out the wisdom, in general, of refusing to decide upon important questions off-hand. So far, his advice was taken; and it was noticed that the Queen, when applications were made to her, rarely gave an immediate answer. Even with Lord Melbourne, it was the same; when he asked for her opinion upon any subject, she would reply that she would think it over, and tell him her conclusions next day.

[1] *pour mieux sauter:* the better to advance.

King Leopold's counsels continued. The Princess de Lieven, he said, was a dangerous woman; there was reason to think that she would make attempts to pry into what did not concern her; let Victoria beware. 'A rule which I cannot sufficiently recommend is *never to permit* people to speak on subjects concerning yourself or your affairs, without you having yourself desired them to do so.' Should such a thing occur, 'change the conversation, and make the individual feel that he has made a mistake.' This piece of advice was also taken; for it fell out as the King had predicted. Madame de Lieven sought an audience, and appeared to be verging towards confidential topics; whereupon the Queen, becoming slightly embarrassed, talked of nothing but commonplaces. The individual felt that she had made a mistake.

The King's next warning was remarkable. Letters, he pointed out, are almost invariably read in the post. This was inconvenient, no doubt; but the fact, once properly grasped, was not without its advantages. 'I will give you an example: we are still plagued by Prussia concerning those fortresses; now to tell the Prussian Government many things, which we *should not like* to tell them officially, the Minister is going to write a despatch to our man at Berlin, sending it *by post;* the Prussians *are sure* to read it, and to learn in this way what we wish them to hear.' Analogous circumstances might very probably occur in England. 'I tell you the *trick,*' wrote His Majesty, 'that you should be able to guard against it.' Such were the subtleties of constitutional sovereignty.

It seemed that the time had come for another step. The King's next letter was full of foreign politics— the situation in Spain and Portugal, the character of Louis Philippe; and he received a favourable answer. Victoria, it is true, began by saying that she had shown the *political part* of his letter to Lord Melbourne; but she proceeded to a discussion of foreign affairs. It appeared that she was not unwilling to exchange observations on such matters with her uncle. So far so good. But King Leopold was still cautious; though a crisis was impending in his diplomacy, he still hung back; at last, however, he could keep silence no longer. It was of the utmost importance to him that, in his manœuvrings with France and Holland, he should have, or at any rate appear to have, English support. But the English Government appeared to adopt a neutral attitude; it was too bad; not to be for him was to be against him—could they not see that? Yet, perhaps, they were only wavering, and a little pressure upon them from Victoria might still save all. He determined to put the case before her, delicately yet forcibly— just as he saw it himself. 'All I want from your kind Majesty,' he wrote, 'is, that you will *occasionally* express to your Ministers, and particularly to good Lord Melbourne, that, as far as it is *compatible* with the interests *of your own* dominions, you do *not* wish that your Government should take the lead in such measures as might in a short time bring on the *destruction* of this country, as well as that of your uncle and his family.' The result of this appeal was unexpected; there was dead silence for more than a week. When Victoria at last wrote, she was prodigal of her affection—'it would, indeed, my dearest Uncle, be *very wrong* of you, if you thought my feelings of warm and devoted attachment to you, and of great affection for you, could be changed—*nothing* can ever change them'—but her references to foreign politics, though they were lengthy and elaborate, were non-committal in the extreme; they were almost cast in an official and diplomatic form. Her Ministers, she said, entirely shared her views upon the subject; she understood and sympathised with the difficulties of her beloved uncle's position; and he might rest assured 'that both Lord Melbourne and Lord Palmerston are most anxious at all times for the prosperity and welfare of Belgium.' That was all. The King in his reply declared himself delighted, and re-echoed the affectionate protestations of his niece. 'My dearest and most beloved Victoria,' he said, 'you have written me a *very dear* and long letter, which has given me *great pleasure and satisfaction.*' He would not admit that he had had a rebuff.

A few months later the crisis came. King Leopold determined to make a bold push, and to carry Victoria with him, this time, by a display of royal vigour and avuncular authority. In an abrupt, an almost peremptory letter, he laid his case, once more, before his niece. 'You know from experience,' he wrote, 'that I *never ask anything of you*. . . . But, as I said before, if we are not careful we may see serious consequences which may affect more or less everybody, and *this* ought to be the object of our most anxious attention. I remain, my dear Victoria, your affectionate uncle, Leopold R.' The Queen immediately despatched this letter to Lord Melbourne, who replied with a carefully thought-out form of words, signifying nothing whatever, which, he suggested, she should send to her uncle. She did so, copying out the elaborate formula, with a liberal scattering of 'dear Uncles' interspersed; and she concluded her letter with a message of 'affectionate love to Aunt Louise and the children.' Then at last King Leopold was obliged to recognise the facts. His next letter contained no reference at all to politics. 'I am glad,' he wrote, 'to find that you like Brighton better than last year. I think Brighton very agreeable at this time of the year, till the east winds set in. The pavilion, besides, is comfortable; that cannot be denied. Before my marriage, it was there that I met the Regent. Charlotte afterwards came with old Queen Charlotte. How distant all

this already, but still how present to one's memory.' Like poor Madame de Lieven, His Majesty felt that he had made a mistake.

Nevertheless, he could not quite give up all hope. Another opportunity offered, and he made another effort—but there was not very much conviction in it, and it was immediately crushed. 'My dear Uncle,' the Queen wrote, 'I have to thank you for your last letter which I received on Sunday. Though you seem not to dislike my political sparks, I think it is better not to increase them, as they might finally take fire, particularly as I see with regret that upon this one subject we cannot agree. I shall, therefore, limit myself to my expressions of very sincere wishes for the welfare and prosperity of Belgium.' After that, it was clear that there was no more to be said. Henceforward there is audible in the King's letters a curiously elegiac note. 'My dearest Victoria, your *delightful* little letter has just arrived and went like *an arrow to my heart*. Yes, my beloved Victoria! I *do love you tenderly* . . . I love you *for yourself*, and I love in you the dear child whose welfare I tenderly watched.' He had gone through much; yet, if life had its disappointments, it had its satisfactions too. 'I have all the honours that can be given, and I am, politically speaking, very solidly established.' But there were other things besides politics; there were romantic yearnings in his heart. 'The only longing I still have is for the Orient, where I perhaps shall once end my life, rising in the west and setting in the east.' As for his devotion to his niece, that could never end. 'I never press my services on you, nor my councils, though I may say with some truth that from the extraordinary fate which the higher powers had ordained for me, my experience, both political and of private life, is great. I am *always ready* to be useful to you *when and where* it may be, and I repeat it, *all I want in return is some little sincere affection from you.*'

VI

The correspondence with King Leopold was significant of much that still lay partly hidden in the character of Victoria. Her attitude towards her uncle had never wavered for a moment. To all his advances she had presented an absolutely unyielding front. The foreign policy of England was not his province; it was hers and her Ministers'; his insinuations, his entreaties, his struggles—all were quite useless; and he must understand that this was so. The rigidity of her position was the more striking owing to the respectfulness and the affection with which it was accompanied. From start to finish the unmoved Queen remained the devoted niece. Leopold himself must have envied such perfect correctitude; but what may be admirable in an elderly statesman is alarming in a maiden of nineteen. And privileged observers were not without their fears. The strange mixture of ingenuous

light-heartedness and fixed determination, of frankness and reticence, of childishness and pride, seemed to augur a future that was perplexed and full of dangers. As time passed the less pleasant qualities in this curious composition revealed themselves more often and more seriously. There were signs of an imperious, a peremptory temper, an egotism that was strong and hard. It was noticed that the palace etiquette, far from relaxing, grew ever more and more inflexible. By some, this was attributed to Lehzen's influence; but, if that was so, Lehzen had a willing pupil; for the slightest infringements of the freezing rules of regularity and deference were invariably and immediately visited by the sharp and haughty glances of the Queen. Yet Her Majesty's eyes, crushing as they could be, were less crushing than her mouth. The self-will depicted in those small projecting teeth and that small receding chin was of a more dismaying kind than that which a powerful jaw betokens; it was a self-will imperturbable, impenetrable, unintelligent; a self-will dangerously akin to obstinacy. And the obstinacy of monarchs is not as that of other men.

Within two years of her accession, the stormclouds which, from the first, had been dimly visible on the horizon, gathered and burst. Victoria's relations with her mother had not improved. The Duchess of Kent, still surrounded by all the galling appearances of filial consideration, remained in Buckingham

Palace a discarded figure, powerless and inconsolable. Sir John Conroy, banished from the presence of the Queen, still presided over the Duchess's household, and the hostilities of Kensington continued unabated in the new surroundings. Lady Flora Hastings still cracked her malicious jokes; the animosity of the Baroness was still unappeased. One day, Lady Flora found the joke was turned against her. Early in 1839, travelling in the suite of the Duchess, she had returned from Scotland in the same carriage with Sir John. A change in her figure became the subject of an unseemly jest; tongues wagged; and the jest grew serious. It was whispered that Lady Flora was with child. The state of her health seemed to confirm the suspicion; she consulted Sir James Clark, the royal physician, and, after the consultation, Sir James let his tongue wag, too. On this, the scandal flared up sky-high. Everyone was talking; the Baroness was not surprised; the Duchess rallied tumultuously to the support of her lady; the Queen was informed. At last the extraordinary expedient of a medical examination was resorted to, during which Sir James, according to Lady Flora, behaved with brutal rudeness, while a second doctor was extremely polite. Finally, both physicians signed a certificate entirely exculpating the lady. But this was by no means the end of the business. The Hastings family, socially a very powerful one, threw itself into the fray with all the fury of outraged pride

and injured innocence; Lord Hastings insisted upon an audience of the Queen, wrote to the papers, and demanded the dismissal of Sir James Clark. The Queen expressed her regret to Lady Flora, but Sir James Clark was not dismissed. The tide of opinion turned violently against the Queen and her advisers; high society was disgusted by all this washing of dirty linen in Buckingham Palace; the public at large was indignant at the ill-treatment of Lady Flora. By the end of March, the popularity, so radiant and so abundant, with which the young Sovereign had begun her reign, had entirely disappeared.

There can be no doubt that a great lack of discretion had been shown by the Court. Ill-natured tittle-tattle, which should have been instantly nipped in the bud, had been allowed to assume disgraceful proportions; and the Throne itself had become involved in the personal malignities of the palace. A particularly awkward question had been raised by the position of Sir James Clark. The Duke of Wellington, upon whom it was customary to fall back, in cases of great difficulty in high places, had been consulted upon this question, and he had given it as his opinion that, as it would be impossible to remove Sir James without a public enquiry, Sir James must certainly stay where he was. Probably the Duke was right; but the fact that the peccant doctor continued in the Queen's service made the Hastings family irreconcilable and produced an unpleasant impression of unrepentant error upon the public mind. As for Victoria, she was very young and quite inexperienced; and she can hardly be blamed for having failed to control an extremely difficult situation. That was clearly Lord Melbourne's task; he was a man of the world, and, with vigilance and circumspection, he might have quietly put out the ugly flames while they were still smouldering. He did not do so; he was lazy and easy-going; the Baroness was persistent, and he let things slide. But doubtless his position was not an easy one; passions ran high in the palace; and Victoria was not only very young, she was very headstrong, too. Did he possess the magic bridle which would curb that fiery steed? He could not be certain. And then, suddenly, another violent crisis revealed more unmistakably than ever the nature of the mind with which he had to deal.

VII

The Queen had for long been haunted by a terror that the day might come when she would be obliged to part with her Minister. Ever since the passage of the Reform Bill, the power of the Whig Government had steadily declined. The General Election of 1837 had left them with a very small majority in the House of Commons; since then, they had been in constant difficulties—abroad, at home, in Ireland; the Radical group had grown hostile; it became highly doubtful how much longer they could survive. The Queen watched the development of events in great anxiety. She was a Whig by birth, by upbringing, by every association, public and private; and, even if those ties had never existed, the mere fact that Lord M. was the head of the Whigs would have amply sufficed to determine her politics. The fall of the Whigs would mean a sad upset for Lord M. But it would have a still more terrible consequence: Lord M. would have to leave her; and the daily, the hourly, presence of Lord M. had become an integral part of her life. Six months after her accession she had noted in her diary 'I shall be very sorry to lose him *even* for *one* night'; and this feeling of personal dependence on her Minister steadily increased. In these circumstances it was natural that she should have become a Whig partisan. Of the wider significance of political questions she knew nothing; all she saw was that her friends were in office and about her, and that it would be dreadful if they ceased to be so. 'I cannot say,' she wrote when a critical division was impending, '(though I feel *confident* of *our success*) HOW *low*, HOW *sad* I feel, when I think of the POSSIBILITY of this excellent and truly kind man not *remaining* my Minister! Yet I trust fervently that *He* who has so wonderfully protected me through such manifold difficulties will not *now* desert me! I should have liked to have expressed to Lord M. my anxiety, but the tears were nearer than words throughout the time I saw him, and I felt I should have choked, had I attempted to say anything.' Lord Melbourne realised clearly enough how undesirable was such a state of mind in a constitutional sovereign who might be called upon at any moment to receive as her Ministers the leaders of the opposite party; he did what he could to cool her ardour; but in vain.

With considerable lack of foresight, too, he had himself helped to bring about this unfortunate condition of affairs. From the moment of her accession, he had surrounded the Queen with ladies of his own party; the Mistress of the Robes and all the Ladies of the Bedchamber were Whigs. In the ordinary course, the Queen never saw a Tory: eventually she took pains never to see one in any circumstances. She disliked the whole tribe; and she did not conceal the fact. She particularly disliked Sir Robert Peel, who would almost certainly be the next Prime Minister. His manners were detestable, and he wanted to turn out Lord M. His supporters, without exception, were equally bad; and as for Sir James Graham, she could not bear the sight of him; he was exactly like Sir John Conroy.

The affair of Lady Flora intensified these party rumours still further. The Hastings were Tories, and Lord Melbourne and the Court were attacked by the Tory press in unmeasured language. The Queen's sectarian zeal proportionately increased. But the dreaded hour was now fast approaching. Early in May the Ministers were visibly tottering; on a vital point of policy they could only secure a majority of five in the House of Commons; they determined to resign. When Victoria heard the news she burst into tears. Was it possible, then, that all was over? Was she, indeed, about to see Lord M. for the last time? Lord M. came; and it is a curious fact that, even in this crowning moment of misery and agitation, the precise girl noted, to the minute, the exact time of the arrival and the departure of her beloved Minister. The conversation was touching and prolonged; but it could only end in one way—the Queen must send for the Duke of Wellington. When, next morning, the Duke came, he advised her Majesty to send for Sir Robert Peel. She was in 'a state of dreadful grief,' but she swallowed down her tears, and braced herself, with royal resolution, for the odious, odious interview.

Peel was by nature reserved, proud, and shy. His manners were not perfect, and he knew it; he was easily embarrassed, and, at such moments, he grew even more stiff and formal than before, while his feet mechanically performed upon the carpet a dancing-master's measure. Anxious as he now was to win the Queen's good graces, his very anxiety to do so made the attainment of his object the more difficult. He entirely failed to make any headway whatever with the haughty hostile girl before him. She coldly noted that he appeared to be un-happy and 'put out,' and, while he stood in painful fixity, with an occasional uneasy pointing of the toe, her heart sank within her at the sight of that manner, 'Oh! how different, how dreadfully different, to the frank, open, natural, and most kind warm manner of Lord Melbourne.' Nevertheless, the audience passed without disaster. Only at one point had there been some slight hint of a disagreement. Peel had decided that a change would be necessary in the composition of the royal Household: the Queen must no longer be entirely surrounded by the wives and sisters of his opponents; some, at any rate, of the Ladies of the Bedchamber should be friendly to his Government. When this matter was touched upon, the Queen had intimated that she wished her Household to remain unchanged; to which Sir Robert had replied that the question could be settled later, and shortly afterwards withdrew to arrange the details of his Cabinet. While he was present, Victoria had remained, as she herself said, 'very much collected, civil and high, and betrayed no agitation'; but as soon as she was alone she completely broke down. Then she pulled herself together to write to Lord Melbourne an account of all that had happened, and of her own wretchedness. 'She feels,' she said, 'Lord Melbourne will understand it, amongst enemies to those she most relied on and most esteemed; but what is worst of all is the being deprived of

seeing Lord Melbourne as she used to do.'

Lord Melbourne replied with a very wise letter. He attempted to calm the Queen and to induce her to accept the new position gracefully; and he had nothing but good words for the Tory leaders. As for the question of the Ladies of the Household, the Queen, he said, should strongly urge what she desired, as it was a matter which concerned her personally, 'but,' he added, 'if Sir Robert is unable to concede it, it will not do to refuse and to put off the negotiation upon it.'

On this point there can be little doubt that Lord Melbourne was right. The question was a complicated and subtle one, and it had never arisen before; but subsequent constitutional practice has determined that a Queen Regnant must accede to the wishes of her Prime Minister as to the *personnel* of the female part of her Household. Lord Melbourne's wisdom, however, was wasted. The Queen would not be soothed, and still less would she take advice. It was outrageous of the Tories to want to deprive her of her Ladies, and that night she made up her mind that, whatever Sir Robert might say, she would refuse to consent to the removal of a single one of them. Accordingly, when, next morning, Peel appeared again, she was ready for action. He began by detailing the Cabinet appointments, and then he added 'Now, ma'am, about the Ladies'—when the Queen sharply interrupted him. 'I cannot give up *any* of my Ladies,' she said. 'What, ma'am!' said Sir Robert, 'does your Majesty mean to retain them *all?*' '*All,*' said the Queen. Sir Robert's face worked strangely; he could not conceal his agitation. 'The Mistress of the Robes and the Ladies of the Bedchamber?' he brought out at last. '*All,*' replied once more her Majesty. It was in vain that Peel pleaded and argued; in vain that he spoke, growing every moment more pompous and uneasy, of the constitution, and Queens Regnant, and the public interest; in vain that he danced his pathetic minuet. She was adamant; but he, too, through all his embarrassment, showed no sign of yielding; and when at last he left her nothing had been decided—the whole formation of the Government was hanging in the wind. A frenzy of excitement now seized upon Victoria. Sir Robert, she believed in her fury, had tried to outwit her, to take her friends from her, to impose his will upon her own; but that was not all: she had suddenly perceived, while the poor man was moving so uneasily before her, the one thing that she was desperately longing for—a loophole of escape. She seized a pen and dashed off a note to Lord Melbourne.

'Sir Robert has behaved very ill,' she wrote, 'he insisted on my giving up my Ladies, to which I replied that I *never* would consent, and I never saw a man so frightened. . . . I was calm but very decided, and I think you would have been pleased to see my composure and great firmness; the Queen of England will not submit to such trickery. Keep yourself in readiness, for you may soon be wanted.' Hardly had she finished when the Duke of Wellington was announced. 'Well, Ma'am,' he said as he entered, 'I am very sorry to find there is a difficulty.' 'Oh!' she instantly replied, '*he* began it, not me.' She felt that only one thing now was needed: she must be firm. And firm she was. The venerable conqueror of Napoleon was outfaced by the relentless equanimity of a girl in her teens. He could not move the Queen one inch. At last, she even ventured to rally him. 'Is Sir Robert so weak,' she asked, 'that even the Ladies must be of his opinion?' On which the Duke made a brief and humble expostulation, bowed low, and departed.

Had she won? Time would show; and in the meantime she scribbled down another letter. 'Lord Melbourne must not think the Queen rash in her conduct. . . . The Queen felt this was an attempt to see whether she could be led and managed like a child.' The Tories were not only wicked but ridiculous. Peel, having, as she understood, expressed a wish to remove only those members of the Household who were in Parliament, now objected to her Ladies. 'I should like to know,' she exclaimed in triumphant scorn, 'if they mean to give the *Ladies* seats in Parliament?'

The end of the crisis was now fast approaching. Sir Robert returned, and told her that if she insisted upon retaining all her Ladies he could not form a Government. She replied that she would send him her final decision in writing. Next morning the late Whig Cabinet met. Lord Melbourne read to them the Queen's letters, and the group of elderly politicians were overcome by an extraordinary wave of enthusiasm. They knew very well that, to say the least, it was highly doubtful whether the Queen had acted in strict accordance with the constitution; that in doing what she had done she had brushed aside Lord Melbourne's advice; that, in reality, there was no public reason whatever why they should go back upon their decision to resign. But such considerations vanished before the passionate urgency of Victoria. The intensity of her determination swept them headlong down the stream of her desire. They unanimously felt that 'it was impossible to abandon such a Queen and such a woman.' Forgetting that they were no longer her Majesty's Ministers, they took the unprecedented course of advising the Queen by letter to put an end to her negotiation with Sir Robert Peel. She did so; all was over; she had triumphed. That evening there was a ball at the Palace. Everyone was present 'Peel and the Duke of Wellington came by looking very much put out.' She was perfectly happy; Lord M. was Prime Minister once more, and he was by her side.

VIII

Happiness had returned with Lord M., but it was happiness in the midst of agitation. The domestic imbroglio continued unabated, until at last the Duke, rejected as a Minister, was called in once again in his old capacity as moral physician to the family. Something was accomplished when, at last, he induced Sir John Conroy to resign his place about the Duchess of Kent and leave the Palace for ever; something more when he persuaded the Queen to write an affectionate letter to her mother. The way seemed open for a reconciliation, but the Duchess was stormy still. She didn't believe that Victoria had written that letter; it was not in her handwriting; and she sent for the Duke to tell him so. The Duke, assuring her that the letter was genuine, begged her to forget the past. But that was not so easy. 'What am I to do if Lord Melbourne comes up to me?' 'Do, ma'am? Why, receive him with civility.' Well, she would make an effort. . . . 'But what am I to do if Victoria asks me to shake hands with Lehzen?' 'Do, ma'am? Why, take her in your arms and kiss her.' 'What!' The Duchess bristled in every feather, and then she burst into a hearty laugh. 'No, ma'am, no,' said the Duke, laughing too. 'I don't mean you are to take *Lehzen* in your arms and kiss *her*, but the Queen.'

The Duke might perhaps have succeeded, had not all attempts at conciliation been rendered hopeless by a tragical event. Lady Flora, it was discovered, had been suffering from a terrible internal malady, which now grew rapidly worse. There could be little doubt that she was dying. The Queen's unpopularity reached an extraordinary height. More than once she was publicly insulted. 'Mrs. Melbourne,' was shouted at her when she appeared at her balcony; and, at Ascot, she was hissed by the Duchess of Montrose and Lady Sarah Ingestre as she passed. Lady Flora died. The whole scandal burst out again with redoubled vehemence; while, in the Palace, the two parties were henceforth divided by an impassable, a Stygian, gulf.

Nevertheless, Lord M. was back, and every trouble faded under the enchantment of his presence and his conversation. He, on his side, had gone through much; and his distresses were intensified by a consciousness of his own shortcomings. He realised clearly enough that, if he had intervened at the right moment, the Hastings scandal might have been averted; and, in the bedchamber crisis, he knew that he had allowed his judgment to be overruled and his conduct to be swayed by private feelings and the impetuosity of Victoria. But he was not one to suffer too acutely from the pangs of conscience. In spite of the dullness and the formality of the Court, his relationship with the Queen had come to be the dominating interest in his life; to have been deprived of it would have been heartrending; that dread eventual-

ity had been—somehow—avoided; he was installed once more, in a kind of triumph; let him enjoy the fleeting hours to the full! And so, cherished by the favour of a sovereign and warmed by the adoration of a girl, the autumn rose, in those autumn months of 1839, came to a wondrous blooming. The petals expanded, beautifully, for the last time. For the last time in this unlooked for, this incongruous, this almost incredible intercourse, the old epicure tasted the exquisiteness of romance. To watch, to teach, to restrain, to encourage the royal young creature beside him—that was much; to feel with such a constant intimacy the impact of her quick affection, her radiant vitality —that was more; most of all, perhaps, was it good to linger vaguely in humorous contemplation, in idle apostrophe, to talk disconnectedly, to make a little joke about an apple or a furbelow, to dream. The springs of his sensibility, hidden deep within him, were overflowing. Often, as he bent over her hand and kissed it, he found himself in tears.

Upon Victoria, with all her impermeability, it was inevitable that such a companionship should have produced, eventually, an effect. She was no longer the simple schoolgirl of two years since. The change was visible even in her public demeanour. Her expression, once 'ingenuous and serene,' now appeared to a shrewd observer to be 'bold and discontented.' She had learnt something of the pleasures of power and the pains of it; but that was not all. Lord Melbourne with his gentle instruction had sought to lead her into the paths of wisdom and moderation, but the whole unconscious movement of his character had swayed her in a very different direction. The hard clear pebble, subjected for so long and so constantly to that encircling and insidious fluidity, had suffered a curious corrosion; it seemed to be actually growing a little soft and a little clouded. Humanity and fallibility are infectious things; was it possible that Lehzen's prim pupil had caught them? That she was beginning to listen to siren voices? That the secret impulses of self-expression, of self-indulgence even, were mastering her life? For a moment the child of a new age looked back, and wavered towards the eighteenth century. It was the most critical moment of her career. Had those influences lasted, the development of her character, the history of her life, would have been completely changed.

And why should they not last? She, for one, was very anxious that they should. Let them last for ever! She was surrounded by Whigs, she was free to do whatever she wanted, she had Lord M.; she could not believe that she could ever be happier. Any change would be for the worse; and the worst change of all . . . no, she would not hear of it; it would be quite intolerable, it would upset everything, if she were to marry. And yet everyone seemed to

want her to—the general public, the Ministers, her Saxe-Coburg relations—it was always the same story. Of course, she knew very well that there were excellent reasons for it. For one thing, if she remained childless, and were to die, her uncle Cumberland, who was now the King of Hanover, would succeed to the Throne of England. That, no doubt, would be a most unpleasant event; and she entirely sympathised with everybody who wished to avoid it. But there was no hurry; naturally, she would marry in the end—but not just yet—not for three of four years. What was tiresome was that her uncle Leopold had apparently determined, not only that she ought to marry, but that her cousin Albert ought to be her husband. That was very like her uncle Leopold, who wanted to have a finger in every pie; and it was true that long ago, in far-off days, before her accession even, she had written to him in a way which might well have encouraged him in such a notion. She had told him then that Albert possessed 'every quality that could be desired to render her perfectly happy,' and had begged her 'dearest uncle to take care of the health of one, now *so dear* to me, and to take him under *your special* protection,' adding, 'I hope and trust all will go on prosperously and well on this subject of so much importance to me.' But that had been years ago, when she was a mere child; perhaps, indeed, to judge from the language, the letter had been dictated by Lehzen; at any rate, her feelings, and all the circumstances, had now entirely changed. Albert hardly interested her at all.

In later life the Queen declared that she had never for a moment dreamt of marrying anyone but her cousin; her letters and diaries tell a very different story. On August 27, 1837, she wrote in her journal: 'To-day is my *dearest* cousin Albert's 18th birthday, and I pray Heaven to pour its choicest blessings on his beloved head!' In the subsequent years, however, the date passes unnoticed. It had been arranged that Stockmar should accompany the Prince to Italy, and the faithful Baron left her side for that purpose. He wrote to her more than once with sympathetic descriptions of his young companion; but her mind was by this time made up. She liked and admired Albert very much, but she did not want to marry him. 'At present,' she told Lord Melbourne in April, 1839, '*my* feeling is quite against ever marrying.' When her cousin's Italian tour came to an end, she began to grow nervous; she knew that, according to a long-standing engagement, his next journey would be to England. He would probably arrive in the autumn, and by July her uneasiness was intense. She determined to write to her uncle, in order to make her position clear. It must be understood she said, that 'there is *no engagement* between us.' If she should like Albert, she could 'make *no final promise this year,* for, at the

very *earliest,* any such event could not take place till *two or three years hence.'* She had, she said, 'a *great* repugnance' to change her present position; and, if she should not like him, she was '*very* anxious that it should be understood that she would *not* be guilty of any breach of promise, for she *never gave any.'* To Lord Melbourne she was more explicit. She told him that she 'had no great wish to see Albert, as the whole subject was an odious one'; she hated to have to decide about it; and she repeated once again that seeing Albert would be 'a disagreeable thing.' But there was no escaping the horrid business; the visit must be made, and she must see him. The summer slipped by and was over; it was autumn already; on the evening of October 10 Albert, accompanied by his brother Ernest, arrived at Windsor.

Albert arrived; and the whole structure of her existence crumbled into nothingness like a house of cards. He was beautiful—she gasped—she knew no more. Then, in a flash, a thousand mysteries were revealed to her; the past, the present, rushed upon her with a new significance; the delusions of years were abolished, and an extraordinary, an irresistible certitude leapt into being in the light of those blue eyes, the smile of that lovely mouth. The succeeding hours passed in a rapture. She was able to observe a few more details—the 'exquisite nose,' the 'delicate moustachios and slight but very slight whiskers,' the 'beautiful figure, broad in the shoulders and a fine waist.' She rode with him, danced with him, talked with him, and it was all perfection. She had no shadow of a doubt. He had come on a Thursday evening, and on the following Sunday morning she told Lord Melbourne that she had 'a good deal changed her opinion as to marrying.' Next morning, she told him that she had made up her mind to marry Albert. The morning after that, she sent for her cousin. She received him alone, and 'after a few minutes I said to him that I thought he must be aware *why* I wished them to come here—and that it would make me *too happy* if he would consent to what I wished (to marry me).' Then 'we embraced each other, and he was *so* kind, *so* affectionate.' She said that she was quite unworthy of him, while he murmured that he would be very happy *'Das Leben mit dir zu zubringen.'* [1] They parted, and she felt 'the happiest of human beings,' when Lord M. came in. At first she beat about the bush, and talked of the weather, and indifferent subjects. Somehow or other she felt a little nervous with her old friend. At last, summoning up her courage, she said, 'I have got well through this with Albert.' 'Oh! you have,' said Lord M.

[1] *Das Leben mit dir zu zubringen:* To spend my life with you.

Chapter 4

Marriage

I

It was decidedly a family match. Prince Francis Charles Augustus Albert Emmanuel of Saxe-Coburg-Gotha—for such was his full title—had been born just three months after his cousin Victoria, and the same midwife had assisted at the two births. The children's grandmother, the Dowager Duchess of Coburg, had from the first looked forward to their marriage; as they grew up, the Duke, the Duchess of Kent, and King Leopold came equally to desire it. The Prince, ever since the time when, as a child of three, his nurse had told him that some day 'the little English May flower' would be his wife, had never thought of marrying anyone else. When eventually Baron Stockmar himself signified his assent, the affair seemed as good as settled.

The Duke had one other child—Prince Ernest, Albert's senior by one year, and heir to the principality. The Duchess was a sprightly and beautiful woman, with fair hair and blue eyes; Albert was very like her and was her declared favourite. But in his fifth year he was parted from her for ever. The ducal court was not noted for the strictness of its morals; the Duke was a man of gallantry, and it was rumoured that the Duchess followed her husband's example. There were scandals; one of the Court Chamberlains, a charming and cultivated man of Jewish extraction, was talked of; at last there was a separation, followed by a divorce. The Duchess retired to Paris, and died unhappily in 1831. Her memory was always very dear to Albert.

He grew up a pretty, clever, and high-spirited boy. Usually well-behaved, he was, however, sometimes violent. He had a will of his own, and asserted it; his elder brother was less passionate, less purposeful, and, in their wrangles, it was Albert who came out top. The two boys, living for the most part in one or other of the Duke's country houses, among pretty hills and woods and streams, had been at a very early age—Albert was less than four—separated from their nurses and put under a tutor, in whose charge they remained until they went to the University. They were brought up in a simple and unostentatious manner, for the Duke was poor and the duchy very small and very insignificant. Before long it became evident that Albert was a model lad. Intelligent and painstaking, he had been touched by the moral earnestness of his generation; at the age of eleven he surprised his father by telling him that he hoped to make himself 'a good and useful man.' And yet he was not over-serious; though, perhaps, he had little humour, he was full of fun—of practical jokes and mimicry. He was no milksop; he rode, and shot, and fenced; above all did he delight in being out of doors, and never was he happier than in his long rambles with his brother through the wild country round his beloved Rosenau—stalking the deer, admiring the scenery, and returning laden with specimens for his natural history collection. He was, besides, passionately fond of music. In one particular it was observed that he did not take after his father: owing either to his peculiar upbringing or to a more fundamental idiosyncrasy, he had a marked distaste for the opposite sex. At the age of five, at a children's dance, he screamed with disgust and anger when a little girl was led up to him for a partner; and though, later on, he grew more successful in disguising such feelings, the feelings remained.

The brothers were very popular in Coburg, and, when the time came for them to be confirmed, the preliminary examination which, according to ancient custom, was held in public in the 'Giants' Hall' of the Castle, was attended by an enthusiastic crowd of functionaries, clergy, delegates from the villages of the duchy, and miscellaneous onlookers. There were also present, besides the Duke and the Dowager Duchess, their Serene Highnesses the Princes Alexander and Ernest of Würtemberg, Prince Leiningen, Princess Hohenlohe-Langenburg, and Princess Hohenlohe-Schillingsfürst. Dr. Jacobi, the Court chaplain, presided at an altar, simply but appropriately decorated, which had been placed at the end of the hall; and the proceedings began by the choir singing the first verse of the hymn, 'Come, Holy Ghost.' After some introductory remarks, Dr. Jacobi began the examination. 'The dignified and decorous bearing of the Princes,' we are told in a contemporary account, 'their strict attention to the questions, the frankness, discussion, and correctness of their answers, produced a deep impression on the numerous assembly. Nothing was more striking in their answers than the evidence they gave of deep feeling and of inward strength of conviction. The questions put by the examiner were not such as to be met by a simple 'yes' or 'no.' They were carefully considered in order to give the audience a clear insight into the views and feelings of the young princes. One of the most touching moments was when the examiner asked the hereditary prince whether he intended steadfastly to hold to the Evangelical Church, and the Prince answered not only 'Yes!' but added in a clear and decided tone: 'I and my brother are firmly resolved ever to remain faithful to the acknowledged truth.' The examination having lasted an hour, Dr. Jacobi made some concluding observations, followed by a short prayer; the second and third verses of the opening hymn were sung; and the ceremony was over. The Princes, stepping down from the altar, were embraced by the Duke and the Dowager Duchess; after which the loyal inhabitants of Coburg dispersed, well satisfied with their entertainment.

Albert's mental development now proceeded apace. In his seventeenth year he began a careful study of German literature and German philosophy. He set about, he told his tutor, 'to follow the thoughts of the great Klopstock into their depths—though in this, for the most part,' he modestly added, 'I do not succeed.' He wrote an essay on the 'Mode of Thought of the Germans, and a Sketch of the History of German Civilisation,' 'making use,' he said, 'in its general outlines, of the divisions which the treatment of the subject itself demands,' and concluding with 'a retrospect of the shortcomings of our time, with an appeal to every one to correct those shortcomings in his own case, and thus set a good example to others.' Placed for some months under the care of King Leopold at Brussels, he came under the influence of Adolphe Quetelet, a mathematical professor, who was particularly interested in the application of the laws of probability to political and moral phenomena; this line of inquiry attracted the Prince, and the friendship thus begun continued till the end of his life. From Brussels he went to the University of Bonn, where he was speedily distinguished both by his intellectual and his social activities; his energies were absorbed in metaphysics, law, political economy, music, fencing, and amateur theatricals. Thirty years later his fellow-students recalled with delight the fits of laughter into which they had been sent by Prince Albert's mimicry. The *verve* with which his Serene Highness reproduced the tones and gestures of one of the professors who used to point to a picture of a row of houses in Venice with the remark, 'That is the Ponte Realte,' and of another who fell down in a race and was obliged to look for his spectacles, was especially appreciated.

After a year at Bonn, the time had come for a foreign tour, and Baron Stockmar arrived from England to accompany the Prince on an expedition to Italy. The Baron had been already, two years previously, consulted by King Leopold as to his views upon the proposed marriage of Albert and Victoria. His reply had been remarkable. With a characteristic foresight, a characteristic absence of optimism, a characteristic sense of the moral elements in the situation, Stockmar had pointed out what were, in his opinion, the conditions essential to make the marriage a success. Albert, he wrote, was a fine young fellow, well grown for his age, with agreeable and valuable qualities; and it was probable that in a few years he would turn out a strong handsome man, of a kindly, simple, yet dignified demeanour. 'Thus, externally, he possesses all that pleases the sex, and at all times and in all countries must please.' Supposing, therefore, that Victoria herself was in favour of the marriage, the further question arose as to whether Albert's mental qualities were such as to fit him for the position of husband of the Queen of England. On this point, continued the Baron, one heard much to his credit; the Prince

was said to be discreet and intelligent; but all such judgments were necessarily partial, and the Baron preferred to reserve his opinion until he could come to a trustworthy conclusion from personal observation. And then he added: 'But all this is not enough. The young man ought to have not merely great ability, but a *right* ambition, and great force of will as well. To pursue for a lifetime a political career so arduous demands more than energy and inclination—it demands also that earnest frame of mind which is ready of its own accord to sacrifice mere pleasure to real usefulness. If he is not satisfied hereafter with the consciousness of having achieved one of the most influential positions in Europe, how often will he feel tempted to repent his adventure! If he does not from the very outset accept it as a vocation of grave responsibility, on the efficient performance of which his honour and happiness depend, there is small likelihood of his succeeding.'

Such were the views of Stockmar on the qualifications necessary for the due fulfilment of that destiny which Albert's family had marked out for him; and he hoped, during the tour in Italy, to come to some conclusion as to how far the Prince possessed them. Albert on his side was much impressed by the Baron, whom he had previously seen but rarely; he also became acquainted, for the first time in his life, with a young Englishman, Lieut. Francis Seymour, who had been engaged to accompany him, whom he found *sehr liebenswürdig,*[1] and with whom he struck up a warm friendship. He delighted in the galleries and scenery of Florence, though with Rome he was less impressed. 'But for some beautiful palaces,' he said, 'it might just as well be any town in Germany.' In an interview with Pope Gregory XVI, he took the opportunity of displaying his erudition. When the Pope observed that the Greeks had taken their art from the Etruscans, Albert replied that, on the contrary, in his opinion, they had borrowed from the Egyptians: his Holiness politely acquiesced. Wherever he went he was eager to increase his knowledge, and, at a ball in Florence, he was observed paying no attention whatever to the ladies, and deep in conversation with the learned Signor Capponi. *'Voilà un prince dont nous pouvons être fiers,'* said the Grand Duke of Tuscany, who was standing by: *'la belle danseuse l'attend, le savant l'occupe.'* [2]

On his return to Germany, Stockmar's observations, imparted to King Leopold, were still critical. Albert, he said, was intelligent, kind, and amiable; he was full of the best intentions and the noblest resolutions, and his judgment was in many things beyond his years. But great exertion was repugnant to him; he seemed to be too willing to spare himself, and his good resolutions too often came to nothing. It was particularly unfortunate that he took not the slightest interest in politics, and never read a newspaper. In his manners, too, there was still room for improvement. 'He will always,' said the Baron, 'have more success with men than with women, in whose society he shows too little *empressement,*[3] and is too indifferent and retiring.' One other feature of the case was noted by the keen eye of the old physician: the Prince's constitution was not a strong one. Yet, on the whole, he was favourable to the projected marriage. But by now the chief obstacle seemed to lie in another quarter, Victoria was apparently determined to commit herself to nothing. And so it happened that when Albert went to England he had made up his mind to withdraw entirely from the affair. Nothing would induce him, he confessed to a friend, to be kept vaguely waiting; he would break it all off at once. His reception at Windsor threw an entirely new light upon the situation. The wheel of fortune turned with a sudden rapidity; and he found, in the arms of Victoria, the irrevocable assurance of his overwhelming fate.

II

He was not in love with her. Affection, gratitude, the natural reactions to the unqualified devotion of a lively young cousin who was also a queen—such feelings possessed

---

[1] *sehr liebenswürdig:* most attractive.

[2] *Voilà un prince dont nous pouvons être fiers . . . la belle danseuse l'attend, le savant l'occupe:* Here is a prince of whom we can be proud . . . the beautiful dancer awaits him; he is busy with the professor.

[3] *empressement:* eagerness.

him, but the ardours of reciprocal passion were not his. Though he found that he liked Victoria very much, what immediately interested him in his curious position was less her than himself. Dazzled and delighted, riding, dancing, singing, laughing, amid the splendours of Windsor, he was aware of a new sensation—the stirrings of ambition in his breast. His place would indeed be a high, an enviable one! And then, on the instant, came another thought. The teaching of religion, the admonitions of Stockmar, his own inmost convictions, all spoke with the same utterance. He would not be there to please himself, but for a very different purpose —to do good. He must be 'noble, manly, and princely in all things,' he would have 'to live and to sacrifice himself for the benefit of his new country'; to 'use his powers and endeavours for a great object— that of promoting the welfare of multitudes of his fellowmen.' One serious thought led on to another. The wealth and the bustle of the English Court might be delightful for the moment, but, after all, it was Coburg that had his heart. 'While I shall be untiring,' he wrote to his grandmother, 'in my efforts and labours for the country to which I shall in future belong, and where I am called to so high a position, I shall never cease *ein treuer Deutscher, Coburger, Gothaner zu sein,*'[1] And now he must part from

[1] *ein treuer Deutscher, Coburger, Gothaner zu sein:* to be a true German, Coburger, Gothaner.

Coburg for ever! Sobered and sad, he sought relief in his brother Ernest's company; the two young men would shut themselves up together, and, sitting down at the pianoforte, would escape from the present and the future in the sweet familiar gaiety of a Haydn duet.

They returned to Germany; and while Albert for a few farewell months, enjoyed, for the last time, the happiness of home, Victoria, for the last time, resumed her old life in London and Windsor. She corresponded daily with her future husband in a mingled flow of German and English; but the accustomed routine reasserted itself; the business and the pleasures of the day would brook no interruption; Lord M. was once more constantly beside her; and the Tories were as intolerable as ever. Indeed, they were more so. For now, in these final moments, the old feud burst out with redoubled fury. The impetuous sovereign found, to her chagrin, that there might be disadvantages in being the declared enemy of one of the great parties in the State. On two occasions, the Tories directly thwarted her in a matter on which she had set her heart. She wished her husband's rank to be fixed by statute, and their opposition prevented it. She wished her husband to receive a settlement from the nation of £50,-000 a year; and, again owing to the Tories, he was only allowed £30,-000. It was too bad. When the question was discussed in Parliament, it had been pointed out that the bulk of the population was suffering from great poverty, and that £30,000 was the whole revenue of Coburg; but her uncle Leopold had been given £50,000, and it would be monstrous to give Albert less. Sir Robert Peel—it might have been expected—had had the effrontery to speak and vote for the smaller sum. She was very angry; and determined to revenge herself by omitting to invite a single Tory to her wedding. She would make an exception in favour of old Lord Liverpool, but even the Duke of Wellington she refused to ask. When it was represented to her that it would amount to a national scandal if the Duke were absent from her wedding, she was angrier than ever. 'What! That old rebel! I won't have him,' she was reported to have said. Eventually she was induced to send him an invitation; but she made no attempt to conceal the bitterness of her feelings, and the Duke himself was only too well aware of all that had passed.

Nor was it only against the Tories that her irritation rose. As the time for her wedding approached, her temper grew steadily sharper and more arbitrary. Queen Adelaide annoyed her. King Leopold, too, was 'ungracious' in his correspondence; 'Dear Uncle,' she told Albert, 'is given to believe that he must rule the roost everywhere. However,' she added with asperity, 'that is not a necessity.' Even Albert himself was not impeccable. Engulfed in Coburgs, he failed to appreciate the complexity of English affairs.

There were difficulties about his household. He had a notion that he ought not to be surrounded by violent Whigs; very likely, but he would not understand that the only alternatives to violent Whigs were violent Tories; and it would be preposterous if his Lords and Gentlemen were to be found voting against the Queen's. He wanted to appoint his own Private Secretary. But how could he choose the right person? Lord M. was obviously best qualified to make the appointment; and Lord M. had decided that the Prince should take over his own Private Secretary—George Anson, a staunch Whig. Albert protested, but it was useless; Victoria simply announced that Anson was appointed, and instructed Lehzen to send the Prince an explanation of the details of the case. Then, again, he had written anxiously upon the necessity of maintaining unspotted the moral purity of the Court. Lord M.'s pupil considered that dear Albert was strait-laced, and, in a brisk Anglo-German missive, set forth her own views. 'I like Lady A. very much,' she told him, 'only she is a little *strict and particular,* and too severe towards others, which is not right; for I think one ought always to be indulgent towards other people, as I always think, if we had not been well taken care of, we might also have gone astray. That is always my feeling. Yet it is always right to show that one does not like to see what is obviously wrong; but it is very dangerous to be *too* severe, and I am certain that as a rule such people always regret that in their youth they have not been so careful as they ought to have been. I have explained this so badly and written it so badly, that I fear you will hardly be able to make it out.'

On one other matter she was insistent. Since the affair of Lady Flora Hastings, a sad fate had overtaken Sir James Clark. His flourishing practice had quite collapsed; nobody would go to him any more. But the Queen remained faithful. She would show the world how little she cared for their disapproval, and she desired Albert to make 'poor Clark' his physician in ordinary. He did as he was told; but, as it turned out, the appointment was not a happy one.

The wedding-day was fixed, and it was time for Albert to tear himself away from his family and the scenes of his childhood. With an aching heart, he had revisited his beloved haunts—the woods and the valleys where he had spent so many happy hours shooting rabbits and collecting botanical specimens; in deep depression, he had sat through the farewell banquets in the Palace and listened to the *Freischütz* performed by the State band. It was time to go. The streets were packed as he drove through them; for a short space his eyes were gladdened by a sea of friendly German faces, and his ears by a gathering volume of good guttural sounds. He stopped to bid a last adieu to his grandmother. It was a heartrending moment. 'Albert! Albert!' she shrieked, and fell fainting into the arms of her attendants as his carriage drove away. He was whirled rapidly to his destiny. At Calais a steamboat awaited him, and, together with his father and his brother, he stepped, dejected, on board. A little later, he was more dejected still. The crossing was a very rough one; the Duke went hurriedly below; while the two Princes, we are told, lay on either side of the cabin staircase 'in an almost helpless state.' At Dover a large crowd was collected on the pier, and 'it was by no common effort that Prince Albert, who had continued to suffer up to the last moment, got up to bow to the people.' His sense of duty triumphed. It was a curious omen: his whole life in England was foreshadowed as he landed on English ground.

Meanwhile Victoria, in growing agitation, was a prey to temper and to nerves. She grew feverish, and at last Sir James Clark pronounced that she was going to have the measles. But, once again, Sir James's diagnosis was incorrect. It was not the measles that were attacking her, but a very different malady; she was suddenly prostrated by alarm, regret, and doubt. For two years she had been her own mistress—the two happiest years, by far, of her life. And now it was all to end! She was to come under an alien domination—she would have to promise that she would honour and obey . . . someone, who might, after all, thwart her, oppose her—and how dreadful that would be! Why had she embarked on this hazardous experiment? Why had she not been contented with Lord M.? No doubt, she loved Albert; but she loved power too. At any rate, one thing was certain: she might be Albert's wife, but she would always be Queen of England. He reappeared, in an exquisite uniform, and her hesitations melted in his presence like mist before the sun. On February 10, 1840, the marriage took place. The wedded pair drove down to Windsor; but they were not, of course, entirely alone. They were accompanied by their suites, and, in particular, by two persons—the Baron Stockmar and the Baroness Lehzen.

III

Albert had foreseen that his married life would not be all plain sailing; but he had by no means realised the gravity and the complication of the difficulties which he would have to face. Politically, he was a cipher. Lord Melbourne was not only Prime Minister, he was in effect the Private Secretary of the Queen, and thus controlled the whole of the political existence of the sovereign. A queen's husband was an entity unknown to the British Constitution. In State affairs there seemed to be no place for him; nor was Victoria herself at all unwilling that this should be so. 'The English,' she had told the Prince when, during their engagement, a proposal had been made to give him a peerage, 'are very jealous of any foreigner interfering in the

government of this country, and have already in some of the papers expressed a hope that you would not interfere. Now, though I know you never would, still, if you were a Peer, they would all say, the Prince meant to play a political part.' 'I know you never would!' In reality, she was not quite certain; but she wished Albert to understand her views. He would, she hoped, make a perfect husband; but, as for governing the country, he would see that she and Lord M. between them could manage that very well, without his help.

But it was not only in politics that the Prince discovered that the part cut out for him was a negligible one. Even as a husband, he found, his functions were to be of an extremely limited kind. Over the whole of Victoria's private life the Baroness reigned supreme; and she had not the slightest intention of allowing that supremacy to be diminished by one iota. Since the accession, her power had greatly increased. Besides the undefined and enormous influence which she exercised through her management of the Queen's private correspondence, she was now the superintendent of the royal establishment and controlled the important office of Privy Purse. Albert very soon perceived that he was not master in his own house. Every detail of his own and his wife's existence was supervised by a third person: nothing could be done until the consent of Lehzen had first been obtained. And Victoria, who adored Lehzen with unabated intensity, saw nothing in all this that was wrong.

Nor was the Prince happier in his social surroundings. A shy young foreigner, awkward in ladies' company, unexpansive and self-opinionated, it was improbable that, in any circumstances, he would have been a society success. His appearance, too, was against him. Though in the eyes of Victoria he was the mirror of manly beauty, her subjects, whose eyes were of a less Teutonic cast, did not agree with her. To them—and particularly to the high-born ladies and gentlemen who naturally saw him most—what was immediately and distressingly striking in Albert's face and figure and whole demeanour was his un-English look. His features were regular, no doubt, but there was something smooth and smug about them; he was tall, but he was clumsily put together, and he walked with a slight slouch. Really, they thought, this youth was more like some kind of foreign tenor than anything else. These were serious disadvantages; but the line of conduct which the Prince adopted from the first moment of his arrival was far from calculated to dispel them. Owing partly to a natural awkwardness, partly to a fear of undue familiarity, and partly to a desire to be absolutely correct, his manners were infused with an extraordinary stiffness and formality. Whenever he appeared in company, he seemed to be surrounded by a thick hedge of prickly etiquette. He never went out into ordinary society; he never walked in the streets of London; he was invariably accompanied by an equerry when he rode or drove. He wanted to be irreproachable and, if that involved friendlessness, it could not be helped. Besides, he had no very high opinion of the English. So far as he could see, they cared for nothing but fox-hunting and Sunday observances; they oscillated between an undue frivolity and an undue gloom; if you spoke to them of friendly joyousness they stared; and they did not understand either the Laws of Thought or the wit of a German University. Since it was clear that with such people he could have very little in common, there was no reason whatever for relaxing in their favour the rules of etiquette. In strict privacy, he could be natural and charming; Seymour and Anson were devoted to him, and he returned their affection; but they were subordinates—the receivers of his confidences and the agents of his will. From the support and the solace of true companionship he was utterly cut off.

A friend, indeed, he had—or rather, a mentor. The Baron, established once more in the royal residence, was determined to work with as wholehearted a detachment for the Prince's benefit as, more than twenty years before, he had worked for his uncle's. The situations then and now, similar in many respects, were yet full of differences. Perhaps in either case the difficulties to be encountered were equally great; but the present problem was the more complex and the more interesting. The young doctor who, unknown and insignificant, had nothing at the back of him but his own wits and the friendship of an unimportant Prince, had been replaced by the accomplished confidant of kings and ministers, ripe in years, in reputation, and in the wisdom of a vast experience. It was possible for him to treat Albert with something of the affectionate authority of a father; but, on the other hand, Albert was no Leopold. As the Baron was very well aware, he had none of his uncle's rigidity of ambition, none of his overweening impulse to be personally great. He was virtuous and well-intentioned; he was clever and well-informed; but he took no interest in politics, and there were no signs that he possessed any commanding force of character. Left to himself, he would almost certainly have subsided into a high-minded nonentity, an aimless dilettante busy over culture, a palace appendage without influence or power. But he was not left to himself: Stockmar saw to that. For ever at his pupil's elbow, the hidden Baron pushed him forward, with tireless pressure, along the path which had been trod by Leopold so many years ago. But, this time, the goal at the end of it was something more than the mediocre royalty that Leopold had reached. The prize which Stockmar, with all the energy of disinterested devotion, had determined should be Albert's was a tremendous prize indeed.

The beginning of the undertaking proved to be the most arduous part of it. Albert was easily dispirited: what was the use of struggling to perform a rôle which bored him and which, it was quite clear, nobody but the dear good Baron had any desire that he should take up? It was simpler, and it saved a great deal of trouble, to let things slide. But Stockmar would not have it. Incessantly, he harped upon two strings—Albert's sense of duty and his personal pride. Had the Prince forgotten the noble aims to which his life was to be devoted? And was he going to allow himself, his wife, his family, his whole existence, to be governed by Baroness Lehzen? The latter consideration was a potent one. Albert had never been accustomed to giving way; and now, more than ever before, it would be humiliating to do so. Not only was he constantly exasperated by the position of the Baroness in the royal household; there was another and a still more serious cause of complaint. He was, he knew very well, his wife's intellectual superior, and yet he found, to his intense annoyance, that there were parts of her mind over which he exercised no influence. When, urged on by the Baron, he attempted to discuss politics with Victoria, she eluded the subject, drifted into generalities, and then began to talk of something else. She was treating him as she had once treated their uncle Leopold. When at last he protested, she replied that her conduct was merely the result of indolence; that when she was with *him* she could not bear to bother her head with anything so dull as politics. The excuse was worse than the fault: was he the wife and she the husband? It almost seemed so. But the Baron declared that the root of the mischief was Lehzen: that it was she who encouraged the Queen to have secrets; who did worse— undermined the natural ingenuousness of Victoria, and induced her to give, unconsciously no doubt, false reasons to explain away her conduct.

Minor disagreements made matters worse. The royal couple differed in their tastes. Albert, brought up in a régime of Spartan simplicity and early hours, found the great Court functions intolerably wearisome, and was invariably observed to be nodding on the sofa at half-past ten; while the Queen's favourite form of enjoyment was to dance through the night, and then, going out into the portico of the Palace, watch the sun rise behind St. Paul's and the towers of Westminster. She loved London and he detested it. It was only in Windsor that he felt he could really breathe; but Windsor too had its terrors: though during the day he could paint and walk and play on the piano, after dinner black tedium descended like a pall. He would have liked to summon distinguished scientific and literary men to his presence, and after ascertaining their views upon various points of art and learning, to set forth his own; but unfortunately Victoria 'had no fancy to encourage such people'; knowing that she was unequal to taking a part in their conversation, she insisted that the evening routine should remain unaltered; the regulation interchange of platitudes with official persons was followed as usual by the round table and the books of engravings, while the Prince, with one of his attendants, played game after game of double chess.

It was only natural that in so peculiar a situation, in which the elements of power, passion, and pride were so strangely apportioned, there should have been occasionally something more than mere irritation— a struggle of angry wills. Victoria, no more than Albert, was in the habit of playing second fiddle. Her arbitrary temper flashed out. Her vitality, her obstinacy, her overweening sense of her own position, might well have beaten down before them his superiorities and his rights. But she fought at a disadvantage; she was, in very truth, no longer her own mistress; a profound preoccupation dominated her, seizing upon her inmost purposes for its own extraordinary ends. She was madly in love. The details of those curious battles are unknown to us; but Prince Ernest, who remained in England with his brother for some months, noted them with a friendly and startled eye. One story, indeed, survives, ill-authenticated and perhaps mythical, yet summing up, as such stories often do, the central facts of the case. When, in wrath, the Prince one day had locked himself into his room, Victoria, no less furious, knocked on the door to be admitted. 'Who is there?' he asked. 'The Queen of England' was the answer. He did not move, and again there was a hail of knocks. The question and the answer were repeated many times; but at last there was a pause, and then a gentler knocking. 'Who is there?' came once more the relentless question. But this time the reply was different. 'Your wife, Albert.' And the door was immediately opened.

Very gradually the Prince's position changed. He began to find the study of politics less uninteresting than he had supposed; he read Blackstone, and took lessons in English Law; he was occasionally present when the Queen interviewed her Ministers; and at Lord Melbourne's suggestion he was shown all the despatches relating to Foreign Affairs. Sometimes he would commit his views to paper, and read them aloud to the Prime Minister, who, infinitely kind and courteous, listened with attention, but seldom made any reply. An important step was taken when, before the birth of the Princess Royal, the Prince, without any opposition in Parliament, was appointed Regent in case of the death of the Queen. Stockmar, owing to whose intervention with the Tories this happy result had been brought about, now felt himself at liberty to take a holiday with his family in Coburg; but his solicitude, poured out in innumerable letters, still watched over his pupil from afar. 'Dear Prince,' he wrote, 'I am satisfied with the

news you have sent me. Mistakes, misunderstandings, obstructions, which come in vexatious opposition to one's views, are always to be taken for just what they are—namely, natural phenomena of life, which represent one of its sides, and that the shady one. In overcoming them with dignity, your mind has to exercise, to train, to enlighten itself; and your character to gain force, endurance, and the necessary hardness.' The Prince had done well so far; but he must continue in the right path; above all, he was 'never to relax.'— 'Never to relax in putting your magnanimity to the proof; never to relax in logical separation of what is great and essential from what is trivial and of no moment; never to relax in keeping yourself up to a high standard — in the determination, daily renewed, to be consistent, patient, courageous.' It was a hard programme, perhaps, for a young man of twenty-one; and yet there was something in it which touched the very depths of Albert's soul. He sighed, but he listened—listened as to the voice of a spiritual director inspired with divine truth. 'The stars which are needful to you now,' the voice continued, 'and perhaps for some time to come, are *Love, Honesty, Truth*. All those whose minds are warped, or who are destitute of true feeling, will *be apt to mistake you*,' and to persuade themselves and the world that you are not the man you are—or, at least, may become. . . . Do you, therefore, be on the alert betimes, with your eyes open in every direction. . . . I wish for my Prince a great, noble, warm, and true heart, such as shall serve as the richest and surest basis for the noblest views of human nature, and the firmest resolve to give them development.'

Before long, the decisive moment came. There was a General Election, and it became certain that the Tories, at last, must come into power. The Queen disliked them as much as ever; but, with a large majority in the House of Commons, they would now be in a position to insist upon their wishes being attended to. Lord Melbourne himself was the first to realise the importance of carrying out the inevitable transition with as little friction as possible; and with his consent, the Prince, following up the *rapprochement*[1] which had begun over the Regency Act, opened, through Anson, a negotiation with Sir Robert Peel. In a series of secret interviews, a complete understanding was reached upon the difficult and complex question of the Bedchamber. It was agreed that the constitutional point should not be raised, but that on the formation of the Tory Government, the principal Whig ladies should retire, and their places be filled by others appointed by Sir Robert. Thus, in effect, though not in form, the Crown abandoned the claims of 1839, and they have never been subsequently put forward. The transaction was a turning point in the Prince's career. He had con-

ducted an important negotiation with skill and tact; he had been brought into close and friendly relations with the new Prime Minister; it was obvious that a great political future lay before him. Victoria was much impressed and deeply grateful. 'My dearest Angel,' she told King Leopold, 'is indeed a great comfort to me. He takes the greatest interest in what goes on, feeling with and for me, and yet abstaining as he ought from biasing me either way, though we talk much on the subject, and his judgment is, as you say, good and mild.' She was in need of all the comfort and assistance he could give her. Lord M. was going; and she could hardly bring herself to speak to Peel. Yes; she would discuss everything with Albert now!

Stockmar, who had returned to England, watched the departure of Lord Melbourne with satisfaction. If all went well, the Prince should now wield a supreme political influence over Victoria. But would all go well? An unexpected development put the Baron into a serious fright. When the dreadful moment finally came, and the Queen, in anguish, bade adieu to her beloved Minister, it was settled between them that, though it would be inadvisable to meet very often, they could continue to correspond. Never were the inconsistencies of Lord Melbourne's character shown more clearly than in what followed. So long as he was in office, his attitude towards Peel had been irreproachable; he had done all he could to

---

[1] *rapprochement:* reconciliation.

facilitate the change of government; he had even, through more than one channel, transmitted privately to his successful rival advice as to the best means of winning the Queen's good graces. Yet, no sooner was he in opposition than his heart failed him. He could not bear the thought of surrendering altogether the privilege and the pleasure of giving counsel to Victoria—of being cut off completely from the power and the intimacy which had been his for so long and in such abundant measure. Though he had declared that he would be perfectly discreet in his letters, he could not resist taking advantage of the opening they afforded. He discussed in detail various public questions, and, in particular, gave the Queen a great deal of advice in the matter of appointments. This advice was followed. Lord Melbourne recommended that Lord Heytesbury, who, he said, was an able man, should be made Ambassador at Vienna; and a week later the Queen wrote to the Foreign Secretary urging that Lord Heytesbury, whom she believed to be a very able man, should be employed 'on some important mission.' Stockmar was very much alarmed. He wrote a memorandum, pointing out the unconstitutional nature of Lord Melbourne's proceedings and the unpleasant position in which the Queen might find herself if they were discovered by Peel; and he instructed Anson to take this memorandum to the ex-Minister. Lord Melbourne, lounging on a sofa, read it through with compressed lips. 'This is quite an apple-pie opinion,' he said. When Anson ventured to expostulate further, suggesting that it was unseemly in the leader of the Opposition to maintain an intimate relationship with the Sovereign, the old man lost his temper. 'Eternally damn it!' he exclaimed, leaping up from his sofa, and dashing about the room. 'Flesh and blood cannot stand this!' He continued to write to the Queen, as before; and two more violent bombardments from the Baron were needed before he was brought to reason. Then, gradually, his letters grew less and less frequent, with fewer and fewer references to public concerns; at last, they were entirely innocuous. The Baron smiled; Lord M. had accepted the inevitable.

The Whig Ministry resigned in September, 1841; but more than a year was to elapse before another and an equally momentous change was effected—the removal of Lehzen. For, in the end, the mysterious governess was conquered. The steps are unknown by which Victoria was at last led to accept her withdrawal with composure—perhaps with relief; but it is clear that Albert's domestic position must have been greatly strengthened by the appearance of children. The birth of the Princess Royal had been followed in November, 1841, by that of the Prince of Wales; and before very long another baby was expected. The Baroness, with all her affection, could have but a remote share in such family delights. She lost ground perceptibly. It was noticed as a phenomenon that, once or twice, when the Court travelled, she was left behind at Windsor. The Prince was very cautious; at the change of Ministry, Lord Melbourne had advised him to choose that moment for decisive action; but he judged it wiser to wait. Time and the pressure of inevitable circumstances were for him; every day his predominance grew more assured—and every night. At length he perceived that he need hesitate no longer—that every wish, every velleity [1] of his had only to be expressed to be at once Victoria's. He spoke, and Lehzen vanished for ever. No more would she reign in that royal heart and those royal halls. No more, watching from a window at Windsor, would she follow her pupil and her sovereign walking on the terrace among the obsequious multitude, with the eye of triumphant love. Returning to her native Hanover, she established herself at Bückeburg in a small but comfortable house, the walls of which were entirely covered by portraits of Her Majesty. The Baron, in spite of his dyspepsia, smiled again: Albert was supreme.

IV

The early discords had passed away completely—resolved into the absolute harmony of married life. Victoria, overcome by a new, an unimagined revelation, had surrendered her whole soul to her husband. The beauty and the charm which so suddenly had made her his at first were, she now saw, no more than but the outward manifestation of the true Albert. There was an inward beauty, an inward glory which, blind that she was, she had then but dimly apprehended, but of which now she was aware in every fibre of her being—he was good—he was great! How could she ever have dreamt of setting up her will against his wisdom, her ignorance against his knowledge, her fancies against his perfect taste? Had she really once loved London and late hours and dissipation? She who now was only happy in the country, she who jumped out of bed every morning—oh, so early!—with Albert, to take a walk, before breakfast, with Albert alone! How wonderful it was to be taught by him! To be told by him which trees were which; and to learn all about the bees! And then to sit doing cross-stitch while he read aloud to her Hallam's *Constitutional History of England!* Or to listen to him playing on his new organ ('The organ is the first of instruments,' he said); or to sing to him a song by Mendelssohn, with a great deal of care over the time and the breathing, and only a very occasional false note! And, after dinner, too—oh, how good of him! He had given up his double chess! And so there could be round games at the round table, or everyone could spend the evening in the most amusing way imaginable—spinning counters and rings. When the babies came it was

[1] velleity: slightest wish.

still more wonderful. Pussy was such a clever little girl ('I am not Pussy! I am the Princess Royal!' she had angrily exclaimed on one occasion); and Bertie—well, she could only pray *most* fervently that the little Prince of Wales would grow up to 'resemble his angelic dearest Father in *every, every* respect, both in body and mind.' Her dear Mamma, too, had been drawn once more into the family circle, for Albert had brought about a reconciliation, and the departure of Lehzen had helped to obliterate the past. In Victoria's eyes, life had become an idyll, and, if the essential elements of an idyll are happiness, love and simplicity, an idyll it was; though, indeed, it was of a kind that might have disconcerted Theocritus.[1] 'Albert brought in dearest little Pussy,' wrote Her Majesty in her journal, 'in such a smart white merino dress trimmed with blue, which Mamma had given her, and a pretty cap, and placed her on my bed, seating himself next to her, and she was very dear and good. And, as my precious, invaluable Albert sat there, and our little Love between us, I felt quite moved with happiness and gratitude to God.' The past—the past of only three years since—when she looked back upon it, seemed a thing so remote and alien that she could explain it to herself in no other way than as some kind of delusion—an unfortunate mistake. Turning over an

[1] Theocritus: Greek pastoral poet of the third century, B.C. His idylls are notable for their realistic quality.

old volume of her diary, she came upon this sentence—'As for "the confidence of the Crown," God knows! No *Minister, no friend* EVER possessed it so entirely as this truly excellent Lord Melbourne possesses mine!' A pang shot through her— she seized a pen, and wrote upon the margin—'Reading this again, I cannot forbear remarking what an artificial sort of happiness *mine* was *then,* and what a blessing it is I have now in my beloved Husband *real* and solid happiness, which no Politics, no worldly reverses *can* change; it could not have lasted long as it was then, for after all, kind and excellent as Lord M. is, and kind as he was to me, it was but in Society that I had amusement, and I was only living on that superficial resource, which I *then fancied* was happiness! Thank God! for *me* and others, this is changed, and I *know what* REAL *happiness* is —V. R.' How did she know? What is the distinction between happiness that is real and happiness that is felt? So a philosopher—Lord M. himself perhaps—might have inquired. But she was no philosopher, and Lord M. was a phantom, and Albert was beside her, and that was enough.

Happy, certainly, she was; and she wanted everyone to know it. Her letters to King Leopold are sprinkled thick with raptures. 'Oh! my dearest uncle, I am sure if you knew *how* happy, how blessed I feel, and how *proud* I feel in possessing *such* a perfect being as my husband . . .' such ecstasies seemed to gush from her pen unceasingly and almost of their own accord. When, one day, without thinking, Lady Lyttelton described someone to her as being 'as happy as a queen,' and then grew a little confused, 'Don't correct yourself, Lady Lyttelton,' said Her Majesty. 'A queen *is* a very happy woman.'

But this new happiness was no lotus dream. On the contrary, it was bracing, rather than relaxing. Never before had she felt so acutely the necessity for doing her duty. She worked more methodically than ever at the business of State; she watched over her children with untiring vigilance. She carried on a large correspondence; she was occupied with her farm—her dairy—a whole multitude of household avocations—from morning till night. Her active, eager little body hurrying with quick steps after the long strides of Albert down the corridors and avenues of Windsor, seemed the very expression of her spirit. Amid all the softness, the deliciousness of unmixed joy, all the liquescence, the overflowings of inexhaustible sentiment, her native rigidity remained. 'A vein of iron,' said Lady Lyttelton, who, as royal governess, had good means of observation, 'runs through her most extraordinary character.'

Sometimes the delightful routine of domestic existence had to be interrupted. It was necessary to exchange Windsor for Buckingham Palace, to open Parliament, or to interview social personages, or, occasionally, to entertain foreign vis-itors at the Castle. Then the quiet Court put on a sudden magnificence, and sovereigns from over the seas—Louis Philippe, or the King of Prussia, or the King of Saxony—found at Windsor an entertainment that was indeed a royal one. Few spectacles in Europe, it was agreed, produced an effect so imposing as the great Waterloo banqueting hall, crowded with guests in sparkling diamonds and blazing uniforms, the long walls hung with the stately portraits of heroes, and the tables loaded with the gorgeous gold plate of the kings of England. But, in that wealth of splendour, the most imposing spectacle of all was the Queen. The little *hausfrau,* who had spent the day before walking out with her children, inspecting her livestock, practising shakes at the piano, and filling up her journal with adoring descriptions of her husband, suddenly shone forth, without art, without effort, by a spontaneous and natural transition, the very culmination of Majesty. The Tsar of Russia himself was deeply impressed. Victoria on her side viewed with secret awe the tremendous Nicholas. 'A great event and a great compliment *his* visit certainly is,' she told her uncle, 'and the people *here* are extremely flattered at it. He is certainly a *very striking* man; still very handsome. His profile is *beautiful,* and his manners *most* dignified and graceful; extremely civil—quite alarmingly so, as he is so full of attentions and *politeness*. But the expression of the *eyes* is *formidable,* and unlike anything I ever saw before.' She and Albert and 'the good King of Saxony,' who happened to be there at the same time, and whom, she said, 'we like much—he is *so* unassuming'—drew together like tame villatic[1] fowl in the presence of that awful eagle. When he was gone, they compared notes about his face, his unhappiness, and his despotic power over millions. Well! She for her part could not help pitying him, and she thanked God she was Queen of England.

When the time came for returning some of these visits, the royal pair set forth in their yacht, much to Victoria's satisfaction, 'I do love a ship!' she exclaimed, ran up and down ladders with the greatest agility, and cracked jokes with the sailors. The Prince was more aloof. They visited Louis Philippe at the Château d'Eu; they visited King Leopold in Brussels. It happened that a still more remarkable Englishwoman was in the Belgian capital, but she was not remarked; and Queen Victoria passed unknowing before the steady gaze of one of the mistresses in M. Héger's *pensionnat*.[2] 'A little stout, vivacious lady, very plainly dressed—not much dignity or pretension about her,' was Charlotte Brontë's[3] comment as the royal carriage and six flashed by her, making her wait on the pavement for a moment, and

interrupting the train of her reflections. Victoria was in high spirits, and even succeeded in instilling a little cheerfulness into her uncle's sombre Court. King Leopold, indeed, was perfectly contented. His dearest hopes had been fulfilled; all his ambitions were satisfied; and for the rest of his life he had only to enjoy, in undisturbed decorum, his throne, his respectability, the table of precedence, and the punctual discharge of his irksome duties. But unfortunately the felicity of those who surrounded him was less complete. His Court, it was murmured, was as gloomy as a conventicle, and the most dismal of all the sufferers was his wife. 'Pas de plaisanteries, madame!' he had exclaimed to the unfortunate successor of the Princess Charlotte, when, in the early days of their marriage, she had attempted a feeble joke. Did she not understand that the consort of a constitutional sovereign must not be frivolous? She understood, at last, only too well; and when the startled walls of the state apartments re-echoed to the chattering and the laughter of Victoria, the poor lady found that she had almost forgotten how to smile.

Another year, Germany was visited, and Albert displayed the beauties of his home. When Victoria crossed the frontier, she was much excited—and she was astonished as well. 'To hear the people speak German,' she noted in her diary, 'and to see the German soldiers, etc., seemed to me so singular.' Having recovered from this slight

---

[1] villatic: rural.
[2] *pensionnat:* girls' boarding school.
[3] Charlotte Brontë (1816–1855): English novelist whose best-known work is *Jane Eyre.*

shock, she found the country charming. She was fêted everywhere, crowds of the surrounding royalties swooped down to welcome her, and the prettiest groups of peasant children, dressed in their best clothes, presented her with bunches of flowers. The principality of Coburg, with its romantic scenery and its well-behaved inhabitants, particularly delighted her; and when she woke up one morning to find herself in 'dear Rosenau, my Albert's birthplace,' it was 'like a beautiful dream.' On her return home, she expatiated, in a letter to King Leopold, upon the pleasures of the trip, dwelling especially upon the intensity of her affection for Albert's native land. 'I have a feeling,' she said, 'for our dear little Germany, which I cannot describe. I felt it at Rosenau so much. It is a something which touches me, and which goes to my heart, and makes me inclined to cry. I never felt at any other place that sort of pensive pleasure and peace which I felt there. I fear I almost like it too much.'

v

The husband was not so happy as the wife. In spite of the great improvement in his situation, in spite of a growing family and the adoration of Victoria, Albert was still a stranger in a strange land, and the serenity of spiritual satisfaction was denied him. It was something, no doubt, to have dominated his immediate environment; but it was not enough; and, besides, in the very completeness of his success, there was a bitterness. Victoria idolised him; but it was understanding that he craved for, not idolatry; and how much did Victoria, filled to the brim though she was with him, understand him? How much does the bucket understand the well? He was lonely. He went to his organ and improvised with learned modulations until the sounds, swelling and subsiding through elaborate cadences, brought some solace to his heart. Then, with the elasticity of youth, he hurried off to play with the babies, or to design a new pigsty, or to read aloud the *Church History of Scotland* to Victoria, or to pirouette before her on one toe, like a ballet-dancer, with a fixed smile, to show her how she ought to behave when she appeared in public places. Thus did he amuse himself; but there was one distraction in which he did not indulge. He never flirted—no, not with the prettiest ladies of the Court. When, during their engagement, the Queen had remarked with pride to Lord Melbourne that the Prince paid no attention to any other woman, the cynic had answered, 'No, that sort of thing is apt to come later'; upon which she had scolded him severely, and then hurried off to Stockmar to repeat what Lord M. had said. But the Baron had reassured her; though in other cases, he had replied, that might happen, he did not think it would in Albert's. And the Baron was right. Throughout their married life no rival female charms ever had cause to give Victoria one moment's pang of jealousy.

What more and more absorbed him—bringing with it a curious comfort of its own—was his work. With the advent of Peel, he began to intervene actively in the affairs of the State. In more ways than one—in the cast of their intelligence, in their moral earnestness, even in the uneasy formalism of their manners—the two men resembled each other; there was a sympathy between them; and thus Peel was ready enough to listen to the advice of Stockmar, and to urge the Prince forward into public life. A royal commission was about to be formed to enquire whether advantage might not be taken of the rebuilding of the Houses of Parliament to encourage the Fine Arts in the United Kingdom; and Peel, with great perspicacity, asked the Prince to preside over it. The work was of a kind which precisely suited Albert: his love of art, his love of method, his love of coming into contact—close yet dignified—with distinguished men—it satisfied them all; and he threw himself into it *con amore*. Some of the members of the commission were somewhat alarmed when, in his opening speech, he pointed out the necessity of dividing the subjects to be considered into "categories"—the word, they thought, smacked dangerously of German metaphysics; but their confidence returned when they observed His Royal Highness's extraordinary technical acquaintance with the processes of fresco paint-

ing. When the question arose as to whether the decorations upon the walls of the new buildings should, or should not, have a moral purpose, the Prince spoke strongly for the affirmative. Although many, he observed, would give but a passing glance to the works, the painter was not therefore to forget that others might view them with more thoughtful eyes. This argument convinced the commission, and it was decided that the subjects to be depicted should be of an improving nature. The frescoes were carried out in accordance with the commission's instructions, but unfortunately before very long they had become, even to the most thoughtful eyes, totally invisible. It seems that His Royal Highness's technical acquaintance with the processes of fresco painting was incomplete.

The next task upon which the Prince embarked was a more arduous one: he determined to reform the organisation of the royal household. This reform had been long overdue. For years past the confusion, discomfort, and extravagance in the royal residences, and in Buckingham Palace particularly, had been scandalous; no reform had been practicable under the rule of the Baroness; but her functions had now devolved upon the Prince, and in 1844, he boldly attacked the problem. Three years earlier, Stockmar, after careful inquiry, had revealed in an elaborate memorandum an extraordinary state of affairs. The control of the household, it appeared, was divided in the strangest manner between a number of authorities, each independent of the other, each possessed of vague and fluctuating powers, without responsibility, and without co-ordination. Of these authorities, the most prominent were the Lord Steward and the Lord Chamberlain—noblemen of high rank and political importance, who changed office with every administration, who did not reside with the Court, and had no effective representatives attached to it. The distribution of their respective functions was uncertain and peculiar. In Buckingham Palace, it was believed that the Lord Chamberlain had charge of the whole of the rooms, with the exception of the kitchen, sculleries, and pantries, which were claimed by the Lord Steward. At the same time, the outside of the Palace was under the control of neither of these functionaries—but of the Office of Woods and Forests; and thus, while the insides of the windows were cleaned by the Department of the Lord Chamberlain—or possibly, in certain cases, of the Lord Steward—the Office of Woods and Forests cleaned their outsides. Of the servants, the housekeepers, the pages, and the housemaids were under the authority of the Lord Chamberlain; the clerk of the kitchen, the cooks, and the porters were under that of the Lord Steward; but the footmen, the livery-porters, and the under-butlers took their orders from yet another official—the Master of the Horse. Naturally, in these circumstances the service was extremely defective and the lack of discipline among the servants disgraceful. They absented themselves for as long as they pleased and whenever the fancy took them; 'and if,' as the Baron put it, 'smoking, drinking, and other irregularities occur in the dormitories, where footmen, etc., sleep ten and twelve in each room, no one can help it.' As for Her Majesty's guests, there was nobody to show them to their rooms, and they were often left, having utterly lost their way in the complicated passages, to wander helpless by the hour. The strange divisions of authority extended not only to persons but to things. The Queen observed that there was never a fire in the dining-room. She enquired why. The answer was 'the Lord Steward lays the fire, and the Lord Chamberlain lights it'; the underlings of those two great noblemen having failed to come to an accommodation, there was no help for it—the Queen must eat in the cold.

A surprising incident opened everyone's eyes to the confusion and negligence that reigned in the Palace. A fortnight after the birth of the Princess Royal the nurse heard a suspicious noise in the room next to the Queen's bedroom. She called to one of the pages, who, looking under a large sofa, perceived there a crouching figure 'with a most repulsive appearance.' It was 'the boy Jones.' This enigmatical personage, whose escapades dominated the newspapers for several ensuing months, and whose motives and character remained to the end ambiguous, was an undersized lad of 17, the son of a tailor, who had apparently gained admittance to the Palace by climbing over the garden wall and walking in through an open window. Two years before he had paid a similar visit in the guise of a chimney-sweep. He now declared that he had spent three days in the Palace, hiding under various beds, that he had 'helped himself to soup and other eatables,' and that he had 'sat upon the throne, seen the Queen, and heard the Princess Royal squall.' Every detail of the strange affair was eagerly canvassed. *The Times* reported that the boy Jones had 'from his infancy been fond of reading.' but that 'his countenance is exceedingly sullen.' It added: 'The sofa under which the boy Jones was discovered, we understand, is one of the most costly and magnificent material and workmanship, and ordered expressly for the accommodation of the royal and illustrious visitors who call to pay their respects to Her Majesty,' The culprit was sent for three months to the 'House of Correction.' When he emerged, he immediately returned to Buckingham Palace. He was discovered, and sent back to the 'House of Correction' for another three months, after which he was offered £4 a week by a music hall to appear upon the stage. He refused this offer, and shortly afterwards was found by the police loitering round Buckingham Palace. The authorities acted vigorously,

and, without any trial or process of law, shipped the boy Jones off to sea. A year later his ship put into Portsmouth to refit, and he at once disembarked and walked to London. He was re-arrested before he reached the Palace, and sent back to his ship, the *Warspite*. On this occasion it was noticed that he had 'much improved in personal appearance and grown quite corpulent'; and so the boy Jones passed out of history, though we catch one last glimpse of him in 1844 falling overboard in the night between Tunis and Algiers. He was fished up again; but it was conjectured—as one of the *Warspite's* officers explained in a letter to *The Times*—that his fall had not been accidental, but that he had deliberately jumped into the Mediterranean in order to 'see the life-buoy light burning.' Of a boy with such a record, what else could be supposed?

But discomfort and alarm were not the only results of the mismanagement of the household; the waste, extravagance, and peculation that also flowed from it were immeasurable. There were preposterous perquisites and malpractices of every kind. It was, for instance, an ancient and immutable rule that a candle that had once been lighted should never be lighted again; what happened to the old candles, nobody knew. Again, the Prince, examining the accounts, was puzzled by a weekly expenditure of thirty-five shillings on "Red Room Wine." He enquired into the matter, and after great difficulty discovered that in the time of George III a room in Windsor Castle with red hangings had once been used as a guard-room, and that five shillings a day had been allowed to provide wine for the officers. The guard had long since been moved elsewhere, but the payment for wine in the Red Room continued, the money being received by a half-pay officer who held the sinecure position of under-butler.

After much laborious investigation, and a stiff struggle with the multitude of vested interests which had been brought into being by long years of neglect, the Prince succeeded in effecting a complete reform. The various conflicting authorities were induced to resign their powers into the hands of a single official, the Master of the Household, who became responsible for the entire management of the royal palaces. Great economies were made, and the whole crowd of venerable abuses was swept away. Among others, the unlucky half-pay officer of Red Room was, much to his surprise, given the choice of relinquishing his weekly emolument or of performing the duties of an under-butler. Even the irregularities among the footmen, etc., were greatly diminished. There were outcries and complaints; the Prince was accused of meddling, of injustice, and of saving candle-ends; but he held on his course, and before long the admirable administration of the royal household was recognised as a convincing proof of his perseverance and capacity.

At the same time his activity was increasing enormously in a more important sphere. He had become the Queen's Private Secretary, her confidential adviser, her second self. He was now always present at her interviews with Ministers. He took, like the Queen, a special interest in foreign policy; but there was no public question in which his influence was not felt. A double process was at work; while Victoria fell more and more absolutely under his intellectual predominance, he, simultaneously, grew more and more completely absorbed by the machinery of high politics—the incessant and multifarious business of a great State. Nobody any more could call him a dilettante; he was a worker, a public personage, a man of affairs. Stockmar noted the change with exultation. 'The Prince,' he wrote, 'has improved very much lately. He has evidently a head for politics. He has become, too, far more independent. His mental activity is constantly on the increase, and he gives the greater part of his time to business, without complaining.' 'The relations between husband and wife,' added the Baron, 'are all one could desire.'

Long before Peel's ministry came to an end, there had been a complete change in Victoria's attitude towards him. His appreciation of the Prince had softened her heart; the sincerity and warmth of his nature, which, in private intercourse with those whom he wished to please, had the power of gradually dissipating the awkwardness of his manners, did the rest. She came in time to regard him with intense feelings of respect and attachment. She spoke of 'our worthy Peel,' for whom, she said, she had 'an *extreme* admiration' and who had shown himself 'a man of unbounded *loyalty, courage,* patriotism, and *high-mindedness,* and his conduct towards me has been *chivalrous* almost, I might say.' She dreaded his removal from office almost as frantically as she had once dreaded that of Lord M. It would be, she declared a *great calamity.* Six years before, what would she have said, if a prophet had told her that the day would come when she would be horrified by the triumph of the Whigs? Yet there was no escaping it; she had to face the return of her old friends. In the ministerial crises of 1845 and 1846, the Prince played a dominating part. Everybody recognised that he was the real centre of the negotiations—the actual controller of the forces and the functions of the Crown. The process by which this result was reached had been so gradual as to be almost imperceptible; but it may be said with certainty that, by the close of Peel's administration, Albert had become, in effect, the King of England.

VI

With the final emergence of the Prince came the final extinction of Lord Melbourne. A year after his loss of office, he had been struck down by a paralytic seizure; he had apparently recovered, but his old elasticity had gone for ever. Moody, restless, and unhappy, he wandered like a ghost about the town, bursting into soliloquies in public places, or asking odd questions, suddenly, *à propos de bottes.*[1] 'I'll be hanged if I'll do it for you, my Lord,' he was heard to say in the hall at Brooks's, standing by himself, and addressing the air after much thought. 'Don't you consider,' he abruptly asked a fellow-guest at Lady Holland's, leaning across the dinner-table in a pause of the conversation, 'that it was a most damnable act of Henri Quatre to change his religion with a view to securing the Crown?' He sat at home, brooding for hours in miserable solitude. He turned over his books—his classics and his Testaments—but they brought him no comfort at all. He longed for the return of the past, for the impossible, for he knew not what, for the devilries of Caro, for the happy platitudes of Windsor. His friends had left him, and no wonder, he said in bitterness—the fire was out. He secretly hoped for a return to power, scanning the newspapers with solicitude, and occasionally making a speech in the House of Lords. His correspondence with the Queen continued, and he appeared from time to time at Court; but he was a mere simulacrum of his former self; 'the dream,' wrote Victoria, 'is *past.*' As for his political views, they could no longer be tolerated. The Prince was an ardent Free Trader, and so, of course, was the Queen; and

[1] *à propos de bottes:* about nothing.

when, dining at Windsor at the time of the repeal of the Corn Laws, Lord Melbourne suddenly exclaimed, 'Ma'am, it's a damned dishonest act!' everyone was extremely embarrassed. Her Majesty laughed and tried to change the conversation, but without avail; Lord Melbourne returned to the charge again and again with—'I say, Ma'am, it's damned dishonest!' —until the Queen said 'Lord Melbourne, I must beg you not to say anything more on this subject now'; and then he held his tongue. She was kind to him, writing him long letters, and always remembering his birthday; but it was kindness at a distance, and he knew it. He had become 'poor Lord Melbourne.' A profound disquietude devoured him. He tried to fix his mind on the condition of Agriculture and the Oxford Movement. He wrote long memoranda in utterly undecipherable handwriting. He was convinced that he had lost all his money, and could not possibly afford to be a Knight of the Garter. He had run through everything, and yet—if Peel went out, he might be sent for—why not? He was never sent for. The Whigs ignored him in their consultations, and the leadership of the party passed to Lord John Russell. When Lord John became Prime Minister, there was much politeness, but Lord Melbourne was not asked to join the Cabinet. He bore the blow with perfect amenity; but he understood, at last, that that was the end. For two years more he lingered,

sinking slowly into unconsciousness and imbecility. Sometimes, propped up in his chair, he would be heard to murmur, with unexpected appositeness, the words of Samson:—

So much I feel my genial spirits droop,
My hopes all flat, nature within me
   seems
In all her functions weary of herself;
My race of glory run, and race of
   shame,
And I shall shortly be with them that
   rest.[1]

A few days before his death, Victoria, learning that there was no hope of his recovery, turned her mind for a little towards that which had once been Lord M. 'You will grieve to hear,' she told King Leopold, 'that our good, dear, old friend Melbourne is dying. . . . One cannot forget how good and kind and amiable he was, and it brings back so many recollections to my mind, though, God knows! I never wish that time back again.'

She was in little danger. The tide of circumstance was flowing now with irresistible fullness towards a very different consummation. The seriousness of Albert, the claims of her children, her own inmost inclinations, and the movement of the whole surrounding world, combined to urge her forward along the narrow way of public and domestic duty. Her family steadily increased. Within eighteen months of the birth of the Prince of Wales the Princess Alice appeared, and a

[1] Lines are from John Milton's *Samson Agonistes*.

year later the Prince Alfred, and then the Princess Helena, and, two years afterwards, the Princess Louise; and still there were signs that the pretty row of royal infants was not complete. The parents, more and more involved in family cares and family happiness, found the pomp of Windsor galling, and longed for some more intimate and remote retreat. On the advice of Peel they purchased the estate of Osborne, in the Isle of Wight. Their skill and economy in financial matters had enabled them to lay aside a substantial sum of money; and they could afford, out of their savings, not merely to buy the property but to build a new house for themselves and to furnish it at a cost of £200,000. At Osborne, by the seashore, and among the woods, which Albert, with memories of Rosenau in his mind, had so carefully planted, the royal family spent every hour that could be snatched from Windsor and London—delightful hours of deep retirement and peaceful work. The public looked on with approval. A few aristocrats might sniff or titter; but with the nation at large the Queen was now once more extremely popular. The middle-classes, in particular, were pleased. They liked a love-match; they liked a household which combined the advantages of royalty and virtue, and in which they seemed to see, reflected as in some resplendent looking-glass, the ideal image of the very lives they led themselves. Their own existences, less exalted, but oh! so soothingly similar, acquired an added excellence, an added succulence, from the early hours, the regularity, the plain tuckers, the round games, the roast beef and Yorkshire pudding of Osborne. It was indeed a model Court. Not only were its central personages the patterns of propriety, but no breath of scandal, no shadow of indecorum, might approach its utmost boundaries. For Victoria, with all the zeal of a convert, upheld now the standard of moral purity with an inflexibility surpassing, if that were possible, Albert's own. She blushed to think how she had once believed—how she had once actually told *him*— that one might be too strict and particular in such matters, and that one ought to be indulgent towards other people's dreadful sins. But she was no longer Lord M.'s pupil: she was Albert's wife. She was more— the embodiment, the living apex of a new era in the generations of mankind. The last vestige of the eighteenth century had disappeared; cynicism and subtlety were shrivelled into powder; and duty, industry, morality, and domesticity triumphed over them. Even the very chairs and tables had assumed, with a singular responsiveness, the forms of prim solidity. The Victorian Age was in full swing.

VII

Only one thing more was needed: material expression must be given to the new ideals and the new forces so that they might stand revealed, in visible glory, before the eyes of an astonished world. It was for Albert to supply this want. He mused, and was inspired: the Great Exhibition came into his head.

Without consulting anyone, he thought out the details of his conception with the minutest care. There had been exhibitions before in the world, but this should surpass them all. It should contain specimens of what every country could produce in raw materials, in machinery and mechanical inventions, in manufactures, and in the applied and plastic arts. It should not be merely useful and ornamental; it should teach a high moral lesson. It should be an international monument to those supreme blessings of civilisation— peace, progress, and prosperity. For some time past the Prince had been devoting much of his attention to the problems of commerce and industry. He had a taste for machinery of every kind, and his sharp eye had more than once detected, with the precision of an expert, a missing cog-wheel in some vast and complicated engine. A visit to Liverpool, where he opened the Albert Dock, impressed upon his mind the immensity of modern industrial forces, though in a letter to Victoria describing his experiences, he was careful to retain his customary lightness of touch. 'As I write,' he playfully remarked, 'you will be making your evening toilette, and not be ready in time for dinner. I must set about the same task, and not, let me hope, with the same re-

sult. . . . The loyalty and enthusiasm of the inhabitants are great; but the heat is greater still. I am satisfied that if the population of Liverpool had been weighed this morning, and were to be weighed again now, they would be found many degrees lighter. The docks are wonderful, and the mass of shipping incredible.' In art and science he had been deeply interested since boyhood; his reform of the household had put his talent for organisation beyond a doubt; and thus from every point of view the Prince was well qualified for his task. Having matured his plans, he summoned a small committee and laid an outline of his scheme before it. The committee approved, and the great undertaking was set on foot without delay.

Two years, however, passed before it was completed. For two years the Prince laboured with extraordinary and incessant energy. At first all went smoothly. The leading manufacturers warmly took up the idea; the colonies and the East India Company were sympathetic; the great foreign nations were eager to send in their contributions; the powerful support of Sir Robert Peel was obtained, and the use of a site in Hyde Park, selected by the Prince, was sanctioned by the Government. Out of 234 plans for the exhibition building, the Prince chose that of Joseph Paxton, famous as a designer of gigantic conservatories; and the work was on the point of being put in hand when a series of unexpected difficulties arose. Opposition to the whole scheme, which had long been smouldering in various quarters, suddenly burst forth. There was an outcry, headed by *The Times,* against the use of the park for the exhibition; for a moment it seemed as if the building would be relegated to a suburb; but, after a fierce debate in the House, the supporters of the site in the Park won the day. Then it appeared that the project lacked a sufficient financial backing; but this obstacle, too, was surmounted, and eventually £200,000 was subscribed as a guarantee fund. The enormous glass edifice rose higher and higher, covering acres and enclosing towering elm trees beneath its roof: and then the fury of its enemies reached a climax. The fashionable, the cautious, the Protectionists, the pious, all joined in the hue and cry. It was pointed out that the Exhibition would serve as a rallying point for all the ruffians in England, for all the malcontents in Europe; and that on the day of its opening there would certainly be a riot and probably a revolution. It was asserted that the glass roof was porous, and that the droppings of fifty million sparrows would utterly destroy every object beneath it. Agitated nonconformists declared that the Exhibition was an arrogant and wicked enterprise which would infallibly bring down God's punishment upon the nation. Colonel Sibthorpe, in the debate on the Address, prayed that hail and lightning might descend from heaven on the accursed thing. The Prince,

with unyielding perseverance and infinite patience, pressed on to his goal. His health was seriously affected; he suffered from constant sleeplessness; his strength was almost worn out. But he remembered the injunctions of Stockmar and never relaxed. The volume of his labours grew more prodigious every day; he toiled at committees, presided over public meetings, made speeches, and carried on communications with every corner of the civilised world—and his efforts were rewarded. On May 1, 1851, the Great Exhibition was opened by the Queen before an enormous concourse of persons, amid scenes of dazzling brilliancy and triumphant enthusiasm.

Victoria herself was in a state of excitement which bordered on delirium. She performed her duties in a trance of joy, gratitude, and amazement, and, when it was all over, her feelings poured themselves out into her journal in a torrential flood. The day had been nothing but an endless succession of glories—or rather one vast glory —one vast radiation of Albert. Everything she had seen, everything she had felt or heard, had been so beautiful, so wonderful that even the royal underlinings broke down under the burden of emphasis, while her remembering pen rushed on, regardless, from splendour to splendour—the huge crowds, so well-behaved and loyal—flags of all the nations floating—the inside of the building, so immense, with myriads of people and the sun shining through the roof—a little side room, where we left our shawls— palm-trees and machinery—dear Albert—the place so big that we could hardly hear the organ— thankfulness to God—a curious assemblage of political and distinguished men—the March from Athalie—God bless my dearest Albert, God bless my dearest country! —a glass fountain—the Duke and Lord Anglesey walking arm in arm —a beautiful Amazon, in bronze, by Kiss—Mr. Paxton, who might be justly proud, and rose from being a common gardener's boy—Sir George Grey in tears, and everybody astonished and delighted.

A striking incident occurred when, after a short prayer by the Archbishop of Canterbury, the choir of 600 voices burst into the 'Hallelujah Chorus.' At that moment a Chinaman, dressed in full national costume, stepped out into the middle of the central nave, and, advancing slowly towards the royal group, did obeisance to Her Majesty. The Queen, much impressed, had no doubt that he was an eminent mandarin; and, when the final procession was formed, orders were given that, as no representative of the Celestial Empire was present, he should be included in the diplomatic cortège. He accordingly, with the utmost gravity, followed immediately behind the Ambassadors. He subsequently disappeared, and it was rumoured, among ill-natured people, that, far from being a mandarin, the fellow was a mere impostor. But nobody ever really discovered the nature of the comments that had been lurking behind the matchless impassivity of that yellow face.

A few days later Victoria poured out her heart to her uncle. The first of May, she said, was 'the *greatest* day in our history, the most *beautiful* and *imposing* and *touching* spectacle ever seen, and the triumph of my beloved Albert. . . . It was the *happiest, proudest* day in my life, and I can think of nothing else. Albert's dearest name is immortalised with this *great* conception, *his* own, and my *own* dear country *showed* she was *worthy* of it. The triumph is *immense.*'

It was. The enthusiasm was universal; even the bitterest scoffers were converted, and joined in the chorus of praise. Congratulations from public bodies poured in; the City of Paris gave a great *fête* to the Exhibition committee; and the Queen and the Prince made a triumphal progress through the North of England. The financial results were equally remarkable. The total profit made by the Exhibition amonted to a sum of £165,000, which was employed in the purchase of land for the erection of a permanent National Museum in South Kensington. During the six months of its existence in Hyde Park over six million persons visited it, and not a single accident occurred. But there is an end to all things; and the time had come for the Crystal Palace to be removed to the salubrious seclusion of Sydenham. Victoria, sad but resigned, paid her final visit. 'It looked so beautiful,' she said. 'I could not believe it was the last time I was to see it. An organ, accompanied by a fine and powerful wind instrument called the sommerophone, was being played, and it nearly upset me. The canvas is very dirty, the red curtains are faded and many things are very much soiled, still the effect is fresh and new as ever and most beautiful. The glass fountain was already removed . . . and the sappers and miners were rolling about the little boxes just as they did at the beginning. It made us all very melancholy.' But more cheerful thoughts followed. When all was over, she expressed her boundless satisfaction in a dithyrambic [1] letter to the Prime Minister. Her beloved husband's name, she said, was for ever immortalised, and that this was universally recognised by the country was a source to her of immense happiness and gratitude. 'She feels grateful to Providence,' Her Majesty concluded, 'to have permitted her to be united to so great, so noble, so excellent a Prince, and this year will ever remain the proudest and happiest of her life. The day of the closing of the Exhibition (which the Queen regretted much she could not witness), was the twelfth anniversary of her betrothal to the Prince, which is a curious coincidence.'

[1] dithyrambic: wildly emotional.

Chapter 5

Lord Palmerston

I

In 1851 the Prince's fortunes reached their high-water mark. The success of the Great Exhibition enormously increased his reputation and seemed to assure him henceforward a leading place in the national life. But before the year was out another triumph, in a very different sphere of action, was also his. This triumph, big with fateful consequences, was itself the outcome of a series of complicated circumstances which had been gathering to a climax for many years.

The unpopularity of Albert in high society had not diminished with time. Aristocratic persons continued to regard him with disfavour; and he on his side, withdrew further and further into a contemptuous reserve. For a moment, indeed, it appeared as if the dislike of the upper classes was about to be suddenly converted into cordiality; for they learnt with amazement that the Prince, during a country visit, had ridden to hounds and acquitted himself remarkably well. They had always taken it for granted that his horsemanship was of some second-rate foreign quality, and here he was jumping five-barred gates and tearing after the fox as if he had been born and bred in Leicestershire. They could hardly believe it; was it possible that they had made a mistake, and that Albert was a good fellow after all? Had he wished to be thought so he would certainly have seized this opportunity, purchased several hunters, and used them constantly. But he had no such desire; hunting bored him, and made Victoria nervous. He continued, as before, to ride, as he himself put it, for exercise or convenience, not for amusement; and it was agreed that though the Prince, no doubt, could keep in his saddle well enough, he was no sportsman.

This was a serious matter. It was not merely that Albert was laughed at by fine ladies and sneered at by fine gentlemen; it was not merely that Victoria, who before her marriage had cut some figure in society, had, under her husband's influence, almost completely given it up. Since Charles the Second the sovereigns of England had, with a single exception, always been unfashionable; and the fact that the exception was George the Fourth seemed to give an added significance to the rule. What was grave was not the lack of fashion, but the lack of other and more important qualities. The hostility of the upper classes was symptomatic of an antagonism more profound than one of manners or even of tastes. The Prince, in a word, was un-English. What that word precisely meant it was difficult to say; but the fact was patent to every eye. Lord Palmerston, also, was not fashionable; the great Whig aristocrats looked askance at him, and

tolerated him as an unpleasant necessity thrust upon them by fate. But Lord Palmerston was English through and through; there was something in him that expressed, with extraordinary vigour, the fundamental qualities of the English race. And he was the very antithesis of the Prince. By a curious chance it so happened that this typical Englishman was brought into closer contact than any other of his countrymen with the alien from over the sea. It thus fell out that differences which, in more fortunate circumstances, might have been smoothed away and obliterated, became accentuated to the highest pitch. All the mysterious forces in Albert's soul leapt out to do battle with his adversary, and, in the long and violent conflict that followed, it almost seemed as if he was struggling with England herself.

Palmerston's whole life had been spent in the government of the country. At twenty-two he had been a Minister; at twenty-five he had been offered the Chancellorship of the Exchequer, which, with that prudence which formed so unexpected a part of his character, he had declined to accept. His first spell of office had lasted uninterruptedly for twenty-one years. When Lord Grey came into power he received the Foreign Secretaryship, a post which he continued to occupy, with two intervals, for another twenty-one years. Throughout this period his reputation with the public had steadily grown, and when, in 1846, he became Foreign

Secretary for the third time, his position in the country was almost, if not quite, on an equality with that of the Prime Minister, Lord John Russell. He was a tall, big man of sixty-two, with a jaunty air, a large face, dyed whiskers, and a long sardonic upper lip. His private life was far from respectable, but he had greatly strengthened his position in society by marrying, late in life, Lady Cowper, the sister of Lord Melbourne, and one of the most influential of the Whig hostesses. Powerful, experienced, and supremely self-confident, he naturally paid very little attention to Albert. Why should he? The Prince was interested in foreign affairs? Very well, then; let the Prince pay attention to *him*—to him, who had been a Cabinet Minister when Albert was in the cradle, who was the chosen leader of a great nation, and who had never failed in anything he had undertaken in the whole course of his life. Not that he wanted the Prince's attention—far from it: so far as he could see, Albert was merely a young foreigner, who suffered from having no vices, and whose only claim to distinction was that he had happened to marry the Queen of England. This estimate, as he found out to his cost, was a mistaken one. Albert was by no means insignificant, and, behind Albert, there was another figure by no means insignificant either—there was Stockmar.

But Palmerston, busy with his plans, his ambitions, and the management of a great department,

brushed all such considerations on one side; it was his favourite method of action. He lived by instinct—by a quick eye and a strong hand, a dexterous management of every crisis as it arose, a half-unconscious sense of the vital elements in a situation. He was very bold; and nothing gave him more exhilaration than to steer the ship of state in a high wind, on a rough sea, with every stitch of canvas on her that she could carry. But there is a point beyond which boldness becomes rashness—a point perceptible only to intuition and not to reason; and beyond that point Palmerston never went. When he saw that the case demanded it, he could go slow—very slow indeed; in fact, his whole career, so full of vigorous adventure, was nevertheless a masterly example of the proverb, *tout vient à point à qui sait attendre*.[1] But when he decided to go quick, nobody went quicker. One day, returning from Osborne, he found that he had missed the train to London; he ordered a special, but the station-master told him that to put a special train upon the line at that time of day would be dangerous, and he could not allow it. Palmerston insisted, declaring that he had important business in London, which could not wait. The station-master, supported by all the officials, continued to demur; the company, he said, could not possibly

---

[1] *tout vient à point à qui sait attendre:* everything comes in time to one who knows how to wait.

take the responsibility. 'On *my* responsibility, then!' said Palmerston, in his off-hand, peremptory way; whereupon the station-master ordered up the train, and the Foreign Secretary reached London in time for his work, without an accident. The story is typical of the happy valiance with which he conducted both his own affairs and those of the nation. 'England,' he used to say, 'is strong enough to brave consequences.' Apparently, under Palmerston's guidance, she was. While the officials protested and shook in their shoes, he would wave them away with his airy '*My* responsibility!' and carry the country swiftly along the line of his choice, to a triumphant destination,—without an accident. His immense popularity was the result partly of his diplomatic successes, partly of his extraordinary personal affability, but chiefly of the genuine intensity with which he responded to the feelings and supported the interests of his countrymen. The public knew that it had in Lord Palmerston not only a high-mettled master, but also a devoted servant—that he was, in every sense of the word, a public man. When he was Prime Minister, he noticed that iron hurdles had been put up on the grass in the Green Park; he immediately wrote to the Minister responsible, ordering, in the severest language, their instant removal, declaring that they were 'an intolerable nuisance,' and that the purpose of the grass was 'to be walked upon freely and without restraint by the people, old

and young, for whose enjoyment the parks are maintained.' It was in this spirit that, as Foreign Secretary, he watched over the interests of Englishmen abroad. Nothing could be more agreeable for Englishmen; but foreign governments were less pleased. They found Lord Palmerston interfering, exasperating, and alarming. In Paris they spoke with bated breath of 'ce terrible milord Palmerston'; and in Germany they made a little song about him—

> *Hat der Teufel einen Sohn,*
> *So ist er sicher Palmerston.*[1]

But their complaints, their threats, and their agitations were all in vain. Palmerston, with his upper lip sardonically curving, braved consequences, and held on his course.

The first diplomatic crisis which arose after his return to office, though the Prince and the Queen were closely concerned with it, passed off without serious disagreement between the Court and the Minister. For some years past a curious problem had been perplexing the chanceries of Europe. Spain, ever since the time of Napoleon a prey to civil convulsions, had settled down for a short interval to a state of comparative quiet under the rule of Christina, the Queen Mother, and her daughter Isabella, the young Queen. In 1846, the question of Isabella's marriage, which had for long been the subject of diplo-

---

[1] If the Devil has a son,
He is surely Palmerston.

matic speculations, suddenly became acute. Various candidates for her hand were proposed—among others, two cousins of her own, another Spanish prince, and Prince Leopold of Saxe-Coburg, a first cousin of Victoria's and Albert's; for different reasons, however, none of these young men seemed altogether satisfactory. Isabella was not yet sixteen; and it might have been supposed that her marriage could be put off for a few years more; but this was considered to be out of the question. It might also have been supposed that the young Queen's marriage was a matter to be settled by herself, her mother, and the Spanish Government; but this again was far from being the case. It had become, by one of those periodical reversions to the ways of the eighteenth century, which, it is rumoured, are still not unknown in diplomacy, a question of dominating importance in the foreign policies both of France and England. For several years, Louis Philippe and his Prime Minister Guizot had been privately maturing a very subtle plan. It was the object of the French King to repeat the glorious *coup* of Louis XIV, and to abolish the Pyrenees by placing one of his grandsons on the throne of Spain. In order to bring this about, he did not venture to suggest that his younger son, the Duc de Montpensier, should marry Isabella; that would have been too obvious a move, which would have raised immediate and insurmountable opposition. He therefore proposed that Isabella should marry her cousin, the Duke of Cadiz, while Montpensier married Isabella's younger sister, the Infanta Fernanda; and pray, what possible objection could there be to that? The wily old King whispered into the chaste ears of Guizot the key to the secret; he had good reason to believe that the Duke of Cadiz was incapable of having children, and therefore the offspring of Fernanda would inherit the Spanish crown. Guizot rubbed his hands, and began at once to set the necessary springs in motion; but, of course, the whole scheme was very soon divulged and understood. The English Government took an extremely serious view of the matter; the balance of power was clearly at stake, and the French intrigue must be frustrated at all hazards. A diplomatic struggle of great intensity followed; and it occasionally appeared that a second War of the Spanish Succession was about to break out. This was avoided, but the consequences of this strange imbroglio were far-reaching and completely different from what any of the parties concerned could have guessed.

In the course of the long and intricate negotiations there was one point upon which Louis Philippe laid a special stress—the candidature of Prince Leopold of Saxe-Coburg. The prospect of a marriage between a Coburg Prince and the Queen of Spain was, he declared, at least as threatening to the balance of power in Europe as that of a marriage between the Duc de

Montpensier and the Infanta; and, indeed, there was much to be said for this contention. The ruin which had fallen upon the House of Coburg during the Napoleonic wars had apparently only served to multiply its vitality, for that princely family had by now extended itself over Europe in an extraordinary manner. King Leopold was firmly fixed in Belgium; his niece was Queen of England; one of his nephews was the husband of the Queen of England, and another the husband of the Queen of Portugal; yet another was Duke of Würtemberg. Where was this to end? There seemed to be a Coburg Trust ready to send out one of its members at any moment to fill up any vacant place among the ruling families of Europe. And even beyond Europe there were signs of this infection spreading. An American who had arrived in Brussels had assured King Leopold that there was a strong feeling in the United States in favour of monarchy instead of the misrule of mobs, and had suggested, to the delight of His Majesty, that some branch of the Coburg family might be available for the position. That danger might, perhaps, be remote; but the Spanish danger was close at hand; and if Prince Leopold were to marry Queen Isabella, the position of France would be one of humiliation, if not of positive danger. Such were the asseverations of Louis Philippe. The English Government had no wish to support Prince Leopold, and though Albert and Vic-

toria had some hankerings for the match, the wisdom of Stockmar had induced them to give up all thoughts of it. The way thus seemed open for a settlement: England would be reasonable about Leopold, if France would be reasonable about Montpensier. At the Château d'Eu, the agreement was made, in a series of conversations between the King and Guizot on the one side, and the Queen, the Prince, and Lord Aberdeen on the other. Aberdeen, as Foreign Minister, declared that England would neither recognise nor support Prince Leopold as a candidate for the hand of the Queen of Spain; while Louis Philippe solemnly promised, both to Aberdeen and to Victoria, that the Duc de Montpensier should not marry the Infanta Fernanda until after the Queen was married and had issue. All went well, and the crisis seemed to be over, when the whole question was suddenly re-opened by Palmerston, who had succeeded Aberdeen at the Foreign Office. In a despatch to the English Minister at Madrid, he mentioned, in a list of possible candidates for Queen Isabella's hand, Prince Leopold of Coburg; and at the same time he took occasion to denounce in violent language the tyranny and incompetence of the Spanish Government. This despatch, indiscreet in any case, was rendered infinitely more so by being communicated to Guizot. Louis Philippe saw his opportunity and pounced on it. Though there was nothing in

Palmerston's language to show that he either recognised or supported Prince Leopold, the King at once assumed that the English had broken their engagement, and that he was therefore free to do likewise. He then sent the despatch to the Queen Mother, declared that the English were intriguing for the Coburg marriage, bade her mark the animosity of Palmerston against the Spanish Government, and urged her to escape from her difficulties and ensure the friendship of France by marrying Isabella to the Duke of Cadiz and Fernanda to Montpensier. The Queen Mother, alarmed and furious, was easily convinced. There was only one difficulty: Isabella loathed the very sight of her cousin. But this was soon surmounted; there was a wild supper-party at the Palace, and in the course of it the young girl was induced to consent to anything that was asked of her. Shortly after, and on the same day, both the marriages took place.

The news burst like a bomb on the English Government, who saw with rage and mortification that they had been completely outmanœuvred by the crafty King. Victoria, in particular, was outraged. Not only had she been the personal recipient of Louis Philippe's pledge, but he had won his way to her heart by presenting the Prince of Wales with a box of soldiers and sending the Princess Royal a beautiful Parisian doll with eyes that opened and shut. And now insult was added to injury. The Queen of

the French wrote her a formal letter, calmly announcing, as a family event in which she was sure Victoria would be interested, the marriage of her son, Montpensier— 'qui ajoutera à notre bonheur intérieur, le seul vrai dans ce monde, et que vous, madame, savez si bien apprécier.'[1] But the English Queen had not long to wait for her revenge. Within eighteen months the monarchy of Louis Philippe, discredited, unpopular, and fatally weakened by the withdrawal of English support, was swept into limbo, while he and his family threw themselves as suppliant fugitives at the feet of Victoria.

II

In this affair both the Queen and the Prince had been too much occupied with the delinquencies of Louis Philippe to have any wrath to spare for those of Palmerston; and, indeed, on the main issue, Palmerston's attitude and their own had been in complete agreement. But in this the case was unique. In every other foreign complication— and they were many and serious— during the ensuing years, the differences between the royal couple and the Foreign Secretary were constant and profound. There was a sharp quarrel over Portugal, where violently hostile parties were flying

[1] *qui ajoutera à notre bonheur intérieur, le seul vrai dans ce monde, et que vous, madame, savez si bien apprécier:* which will add to our domestic happiness, the only true happiness in the world, and that you, Madame, know so well how to value.

at each other's throats. The royal sympathy was naturally enlisted on behalf of the Queen and her Coburg husband, while Palmerston gave his support to the progressive elements in the country. It was not until 1848, however, that the strain became really serious. In that year of revolutions, when, in all directions and with alarming frequency, crowns kept rolling off royal heads, Albert and Victoria were appalled to find that the policy of England was persistently directed—in Germany, in Switzerland, in Austria, in Italy, in Sicily—so as to favour the insurgent forces. The situation, indeed, was just such an one as the soul of Palmerston loved. There was danger and excitement, the necessity of decision, the opportunity for action, on every hand. A disciple of Canning, with an English gentleman's contempt and dislike of foreign potentates deep in his heart, the spectacle of the popular uprisings, and of the oppressors bundled ignominiously out of the palaces they had disgraced, gave him unbounded pleasure, and he was determined that there should be no doubt whatever, all over the Continent, on which side in the great struggle England stood. It was not that he had the slightest tincture in him of philosophical radicalism; he had no philosophical tinctures of any kind; he was quite content to be inconsistent—to be a Conservative at home and a Liberal abroad. There were very good reasons for keeping the Irish in their places; but what had that to do

with it? The point was this—when any decent man read an account of the political prisons in Naples his gorge rose. He did not want war; but he saw that without war a skilful and determined use of England's power might do much to further the cause of the Liberals in Europe. It was a difficult and a hazardous game to play, but he set about playing it with delighted alacrity. And then, to his intense annoyance, just as he needed all his nerve and all possible freedom of action, he found himself being hampered and distracted at every turn by . . . those people at Osborne. He saw what it was; the opposition was systematic and informed, and the Queen alone would have been incapable of it; the Prince was at the bottom of the whole thing. It was exceedingly vexatious; but Palmerston was in a hurry, and could not wait; the Prince, if he would insist upon interfering, must be brushed on one side.

Albert was very angry. He highly disapproved both of Palmerston's policy and of his methods of action. He was opposed to absolutism; but in his opinion Palmerston's proceedings were simply calculated to substitute for absolutism, all over Europe, something no better and very possibly worse—the anarchy of faction and mob violence. The dangers of this revolutionary ferment were grave; even in England Chartism was rampant—a sinister movement, which might at any moment upset the Constitution and abolish the Monarchy. Surely, with such dangers at home, this was a very bad time to choose for encouraging lawlessness abroad. He naturally took a particular interest in Germany. His instincts, his affections, his prepossessions, were ineradicably German; Stockmar was deeply involved in German politics; and he had a multitude of relatives among the ruling German families, who, from the midst of the hurly-burly of revolution, wrote him long and agitated letters once a week. Having considered the question of Germany's future from every point of view, he came to the conclusion, under Stockmar's guidance, that the great aim for every lover of Germany should be her unification under the sovereignty of Prussia. The intricacy of the situation was extreme, and the possibilities of good or evil which every hour might bring forth were incalculable; yet he saw with horror that Palmerston neither understood nor cared to understand the niceties of this momentous problem, but rushed on blindly, dealing blows to right and left, quite—so far as he could see—without system, and even without motive—except, indeed, a totally unreasonable distrust of the Prussian State.

But his disagreement with the details of Palmerston's policy was in reality merely a symptom of the fundamental differences between the characters of the two men. In Albert's eyes Palmerston was a coarse, reckless egotist, whose combined arrogance and ignorance must inevitably have their issue in folly and disaster. Nothing could be more antipathetic to him than a mind so strangely lacking in patience, in reflection, in principle, and in the habits of ratiocination. For to him it was intolerable to think in a hurry, to jump to slap-dash decisions, to act on instincts that could not be explained. Everything must be done in due order, with careful premeditation; the premises of the position must first be firmly established; and he must reach the correct conclusion by a regular series of rational steps. In complicated questions—and what questions, rightly looked at, were not complicated?—to commit one's thoughts to paper was the wisest course, and it was the course which Albert, laborious though it might be, invariably adopted. It was as well, too, to draw up a reasoned statement after an event, as well as before it; and accordingly, whatever happened, it was always found that the Prince had made a memorandum. On one occasion he reduced to six pages of foolscap the substance of a confidential conversation with Sir Robert Peel, and, having read them aloud to him, asked him to append his signature; Sir Robert, who never liked to commit himself, became extremely uneasy; upon which the Prince, understanding that it was necessary to humour the singular susceptibilities of Englishmen, with great tact dropped that particular memorandum into the fire. But as for Palmerston, he never even gave one so much as a chance to read him a memorandum; he positively seemed to dislike discussion; and, before one knew where one was, without any warning whatever, he would plunge into some hare-brained, violent project which, as likely as not, would logically involve a European war. Closely connected, too, with this cautious, painstaking reasonableness of Albert's, was his desire to examine questions thoroughly from every point of view, to go down to the roots of things, and to act in strict accordance with some well-defined principle. Under Stockmar's tutelage he was constantly engaged in enlarging his outlook and in endeavouring to envisage vital problems both theoretically and practically—both with precision and with depth. To one whose mind was thus habitually occupied, the empirical activities of Palmerston, who had no notion what a principle meant, resembled the incoherent vagaries of a tiresome child. What did Palmerston know of economics, of science, of history? What did he care for morality and education? How much consideration had he devoted in the whole course of his life to the improvement of the condition of the working-classes and to the general amelioration of the human race? The answers to such questions were all too obvious; and yet it is easy to imagine, also, what might have been Palmerston's jaunty comment. 'Ah! your Royal Highness is busy with fine schemes and beneficent calculations—exactly! Well, as for me, I must say I'm quite satisfied with my morning's work—I've had the iron hurdles taken out of the Green Park.'

The exasperating man, however, preferred to make no comment, and to proceed in smiling silence on his inexcusable way. The process of 'brushing on one side' very soon came into operation. Important Foreign Office despatches were either submitted to the Queen so late that there was no time to correct them, or they were not submitted to her at all; or, having been submitted, and some passage in them being objected to and an alteration suggested, they were after all sent off in their original form. The Queen complained; the Prince complained; both complained together. It was quite useless. Palmerston was most apologetic—could not understand how it had occurred—must give the clerks a wigging—certainly Her Majesty's wishes should be attended to, and such a thing should never happen again. But, of course, it very soon happened again, and the royal remonstrances redoubled. Victoria, her partisan passions thoroughly aroused, imported into her protests a personal vehemence which those of Albert lacked. Did Lord Palmerston forget that she was Queen of England? How could she tolerate a state of affairs in which despatches written in her name were sent abroad without her approval or even her knowledge? What could be more derogatory to her position than to be obliged to receive indignant letters from the crowned heads to whom those despatches were addressed—letters which she did not know how to answer, since she so thoroughly agreed with them? She addressed herself to the Prime Minister. 'No remonstrance has any effect with Lord Palmerston,' she said. 'Lord Palmerston,' she told him on another occasion, 'has as usual pretended not to have had time to submit the draft to the Queen before he had sent it off.' She summoned Lord John to her presence, poured out her indignation, and afterwards, on the advice of Albert, noted down what had passed in a memorandum: 'I said that I thought that Lord Palmerston often endangered the honour of England by taking a very prejudiced and one-sided view of a question; that his writings were always as bitter as gall and did great harm, which Lord John entirely assented to, and that I often felt quite ill from anxiety.' Then she turned to her uncle. 'The state of Germany,' she wrote in a comprehensive and despairing review of the European situation, 'is dreadful, and one does feel quite ashamed about that once really so peaceful and happy country. That there are still good people there I am sure, but they allow themselves to be worked upon in a frightful and shameful way. In France a crisis seems at hand. *What* a very bad figure we cut in this mediation! Really it is quite immoral, with Ireland quivering in our grasp and ready to throw off her allegiance at any moment, for us to force Aus-

tria to give up her lawful possessions. What shall we say if Canada, Malta, etc., begin to trouble us? It hurts me terribly.' But what did Lord Palmerston care?

Lord John's position grew more and more irksome. He did not approve of his colleague's treatment of the Queen. When he begged him to be more careful, he was met with the reply that 28,000 despatches passed through the Foreign Office in a single year, that, if every one of these were to be subjected to the royal criticism, the delay would be most serious, that, as it was, the waste of time and the worry involved in submitting drafts to the meticulous examination of Prince Albert was almost too much for an overworked Minister, and that, as a matter of fact, the postponement of important decisions owing to this cause had already produced very unpleasant diplomatic consequences. These excuses would have impressed Lord John more favourably if he had not himself had to suffer from a similar neglect. As often as not Palmerston failed to communicate even to him the most important despatches. The Foreign Secretary was becoming an almost independent power, acting on his own initiative, and swaying the policy of England on his own responsibility. On one occasion, in 1847, he had actually been upon the point of threatening to break off diplomatic relations with France without consulting either the Cabinet or the Prime Minister. And such incidents were constantly recurring. When this became known to the Prince, he saw that his opportunity had come. If he could only drive in to the utmost the wedge between the two statesmen, if he could only secure the alliance of Lord John, then the suppression or the removal of Lord Palmerston would be almost certain to follow. He set about the business with all the pertinacity of his nature. Both he and the Queen put every kind of pressure upon the Prime Minister. They wrote, they harangued, they relapsed into awful silence. It occurred to them that Lord Clarendon, an important member of the Cabinet, would be a useful channel for their griefs. They commanded him to dine at the Palace, and, directly the meal was over, 'the Queen,' as he described it afterwards, 'exploded, and went with the utmost vehemence and bitterness into the whole of Palmerston's conduct, all the effects produced all over the world, and all her own feelings and sentiments about it.' When she had finished, the Prince took up the tale, with less excitement, but with equal force. Lord Clarendon found himself in an awkward situation; he disliked Palmerston's policy, but he was his colleague, and he disapproved of the attitude of his royal hosts. In his opinion, they were 'wrong in wishing that courtiers rather than Ministers should conduct the affairs of the country,' and he thought that they 'laboured under the curious mistake that the Foreign Office was their peculiar department, and that

they had the right to control, if not to direct, the foreign policy of England.' He, therefore, with extreme politeness, gave it to be understood that he would not commit himself in any way. But Lord John, in reality, needed no pressure. Attacked by his Sovereign, ignored by his Foreign Secretary, he led a miserable life. With the advent of the dreadful Schleswig-Holstein question—the most complex in the whole diplomatic history of Europe —his position, crushed between the upper and the nether mill-stones, grew positively unbearable. He became anxious above all things to get Palmerston out of the Foreign Office. But then—supposing Palmerston refused to go?

In a memorandum made by the Prince, at about this time, of an interview between himself, the Queen, and the Prime Minister, we catch a curious glimpse of the states of mind of those three high personages—the anxiety and irritation of Lord John, the vehement acrimony of Victoria, and the reasonable animosity of Albert—drawn together, as it were, under the shadow of an unseen Presence, the cause of that celestial anger—the gay, portentous Palmerston. At one point in the conversation Lord John observed that he believed the Foreign Secretary would consent to a change of offices; Lord Palmerston, he said, realised that he had lost the Queen's confidence—though only on public, and not on personal, grounds. But on that, the Prince noted, 'the Queen interrupted Lord

John by remarking that she distrusted him on *personal* grounds also, but I remarked that Lord Palmerston had so far at least seen rightly; that he had become disagreeable to the Queen, not on account of his person, but of his political doings—to which the Queen assented.' Then the Prince suggested that there was a danger of the Cabinet breaking up, and of Lord Palmerston returning to office as Prime Minister. But on that point Lord John was reassuring: he 'thought Lord Palmerston too old to do much in the future (having passed his sixty-fifth year).' Eventually it was decided that nothing could be done for the present, but that the *utmost secrecy* must be observed; and so the conclave ended.

At last, in 1850, deliverance seemed to be at hand. There were signs that the public were growing weary of the alarums and excursions of Palmerston's diplomacy; and when his support of Don Pacifico, a British subject, in a quarrel with the Greek Government, seemed to be upon the point of involving the country in a war not only with Greece but also with France, and possibly with Russia into the bargain, a heavy cloud of distrust and displeasure appeared to be gathering and about to burst over his head. A motion directed against him in the House of Lords was passed by a substantial majority. The question was next to be discussed in the House of Commons, where another adverse vote was not improbable, and would seal the doom of the Minister. Palmerston received the attack with complete nonchalance, and then, at the last possible moment, he struck. In a speech of over four hours, in which exposition, invective, argument, declamation, plain talk and resounding eloquence were mingled together with consummate art and extraordinary felicity, he annihilated his enemies. The hostile motion was defeated, and Palmerston was once more the hero of the hour. Simultaneously, Atropos [1] herself conspired to favour him. Sir Robert Peel was thrown from his horse and killed. By this tragic chance, Palmerston saw the one rival great enough to cope with him removed from his path. He judged —and judged rightly—that he was the most popular man in England; and when Lord John revived the project of his exchanging the Foreign Office for some other position in the Cabinet, he absolutely refused to stir.

Great was the disappointment of Albert; great was the indignation of Victoria. 'The House of Commons,' she wrote, 'is becoming very unmanageable and troublesome.' The Prince, perceiving that Palmerston was more firmly fixed in the saddle than ever, decided that something drastic must be done. Five months before, the prescient Baron had drawn up, in case of emergency, a memorandum, which had been carefully docketed, and placed

1 Atropos: one of the three Fates, who cuts off the thread of life.

in a pigeon-hole ready to hand. The emergency had now arisen, and the memorandum must be used. The Queen copied out the words of Stockmar, and sent them to the Prime Minister, requesting him to show her letter to Palmerston. 'She thinks it right,' she wrote, 'in order *to prevent any mistake* for the *future,* shortly to explain *what it is she expects from her Foreign Secretary.* She requires: (1) That he will distinctly state what he proposes in a given case, in order that the Queen may know as distinctly to *what* she has given her Royal sanction; (2) Having *once given* her sanction to a measure, that it be not arbitrarily altered or modified by the Minister; such an act she must consider as failing in sincerity towards the Crown, and justly to be visited by the exercise of her Constitutional right of dismissing that Minister.' Lord John Russell did as he was bid, and forwarded the Queen's letter to Lord Palmerston. This transaction, which was of grave constitutional significance, was entirely unknown to the outside world.

If Palmerston had been a sensitive man, he would probably have resigned on the receipt of the Queen's missive. But he was far from sensitive; he loved power, and his power was greater than ever; an unerring instinct told him that this was not the time to go. Nevertheless, he was seriously perturbed. He understood at last that he was struggling with a formidable adversary, whose skill and strength, un-

less they were mollified, might do irreparable injury to his career. He therefore wrote to Lord John, briefly acquiescing in the Queen's requirements—'I have taken a copy of this memorandum of the Queen and will not fail to attend to the directions which it contains'—and at the same time, he asked for an interview with the Prince. Albert at once summoned him to the Palace, and was astonished to observe, as he noted in a memorandum, that when Palmerston entered the room 'he was very much agitated, shook, and had tears in his eyes, so as quite to move me, who never under any circumstances had known him otherwise than with a bland smile on his face.' The old statesman was profuse in protestations and excuses; the young one was coldly polite. At last, after a long and inconclusive conversation, the Prince, drawing himself up, said that, in order to give Lord Palmerston 'an example of what the Queen wanted,' he would 'ask him a question point-blank.' Lord Palmerston waited in respectful silence, while the Prince proceeded as follows:— 'You are aware that the Queen has objected to the Protocol about Schleswig, and of the grounds on which she has done so. Her opinion has been overruled, the Protocol stating the desire of the Great Powers to see the integrity of the Danish monarchy preserved has been signed, and upon this the King of Denmark has invaded Schleswig, where the war is raging. If Holstein is attacked also, which is likely, the Germans will not be restrained from flying to her assistance; Russia has menaced to interfere with arms, if the Schleswigers are successful. What will you do, if this emergency arises (provoking most likely an European war), and which will arise very probably when we shall be at Balmoral and Lord John in another part of Scotland? The Queen expects from your foresight that you have contemplated this possibility, and requires a categorical answer as to what you would do in the event supposed.' Strangely enough, to this point-blank question, the Foreign Secretary appeared to be unable to reply. The whole matter, he said, was extremely complicated, and the contingencies mentioned by His Royal Highness were very unlikely to arise. The Prince persisted; but it was useless; for a full hour he struggled to extract a categorical answer, until at length Palmerston bowed himself out of the room. Albert threw up his hands in shocked amazement: what could one do with such a man?

What indeed? For, in spite of all his apologies and all his promises, within a few weeks the incorrigible reprobate was at his tricks again. The Austrian General Haynau, notorious as a rigorous suppressor of rebellion in Hungary and Italy, and in particular as a flogger of women, came to England and took it into his head to pay a visit to Messrs. Barclay and Perkins's brewery. The features of 'General Hyæna,' as he was everywhere called—his grim thin face, his enormous pepper-and-salt moustaches—had gained a horrid celebrity; and it so happened that among the clerks at the brewery there was a refugee from Vienna, who had given his fellow-workers a first-hand account of the General's characteristics. The Austrian Ambassador, scenting danger, begged his friend not to appear in public, or, if he must do so, to cut off his moustaches first. But the General would take no advice. He went to the brewery, was immediately recognised, surrounded by a crowd of angry draymen, pushed about, shouted at, punched in the ribs, and pulled by the moustaches until, bolting down an alley with the mob at his heels brandishing brooms and roaring 'Hyæna!' he managed to take refuge in a public house, whence he was removed under the protection of several policemen. The Austrian Government was angry and demanded explanations. Palmerston, who, of course, was privately delighted by the incident, replied regretting what had occurred, but adding that in his opinion the General had 'evinced a want of propriety in coming to England at the present moment'; and he delivered his note to the Ambassador without having previously submitted it to the Queen or to the Prime Minister. Naturally, when this was discovered, there was a serious storm. The Prince was especially indignant; the conduct of the draymen he regarded, with disgust and alarm, as 'a slight foretaste of what an unregulated mass of illiterate people is capable'; and Palmerston was requested by Lord John to withdraw his note, and to substitute for it another from which all censure of the General had been omitted. On this the Foreign Secretary threatened resignation, but the Prime Minister was firm. For a moment the royal hopes rose high, only to be dashed to the ground again by the cruel compliance of the enemy. Palmerston, suddenly lamblike, agreed to everything; the note was withdrawn and altered, and peace was patched up once more.

It lasted for a year, and then, in October, 1851, the arrival of Kossuth in England brought on another crisis. Palmerston's desire to receive the Hungarian patriot at his house in London was vetoed by Lord John; once more there was a sharp struggle; once more Palmerston, after threatening resignation, yielded. But still the insubordinate man could not keep quiet. A few weeks later a deputation of Radicals from Finsbury and Islington waited on him at the Foreign Office and presented him with an address, in which the Emperors of Austria and Russia were stigmatised as 'odious and detestable assassins' and 'merciless tyrants and despots.' The Foreign Secretary in his reply, while mildly deprecating these expressions, allowed his real sentiments to appear with a most undiplomatic insouciance.[1] There was an immediate scandal, and the Court flowed

[1] insouciance: indifference.

over with rage and vituperation. 'I think,' said the Baron, 'the man has been for some time insane.' Victoria, in an agitated letter, urged Lord John to assert his authority. But Lord John perceived that on this matter the Foreign Secretary had the support of public opinion, and he judged it wiser to bide his time.

He had not long to wait. The culmination of the long series of conflicts, threats, and exacerbations came before the year was out. On December 2, Louis Napoleon's *coup d'état* took place in Paris; and on the following day Palmerston, without consulting anybody, expressed in a conversation with the French Ambassador his approval of Napoleon's act. Two days later, he was instructed by the Prime Minister, in accordance with a letter from the Queen, that it was the policy of the English Government to maintain an attitude of strict neutrality towards the affairs of France. Nevertheless, in an official despatch to the British Ambassador in Paris, he repeated the approval of the *coup d'état* which he had already given verbally to the French Ambassador in London. This despatch was submitted neither to the Queen nor to the Prime Minister. Lord John's patience, as he himself said, 'was drained to the last drop.' He dismissed Lord Palmerston.

Victoria was in ecstasies; and Albert knew that the triumph was his even more than Lord John's. It was his wish that Lord Granville, a young man whom he believed to be pliant to his influence, should be Palmerston's successor; and Lord Granville was appointed. Henceforward, it seemed that the Prince would have his way in foreign affairs. After years of struggle and mortification, success greeted him on every hand. In his family, he was an adored master; in the country, the Great Exhibition had brought him respect and glory; and now in the secret seats of power he had gained a new supremacy. He had wrestled with the terrible Lord Palmerston, the embodiment of all that was most hostile to him in the spirit of England, and his redoubtable opponent had been overthrown. Was England herself at his feet? It might be so; and yet . . . it is said that the sons of England have a certain tiresome quality: they never know when they are beaten. It was odd, but Palmerston was positively still jaunty. Was it possible? Could he believe, in his blind arrogance, that even his ignominious dismissal from office was something that could be brushed aside?

III

The Prince's triumph was short-lived. A few weeks later, owing to Palmerston's influence, the Government was defeated in the House, and Lord John resigned. Then, after a short interval, a coalition between the Whigs and the followers of Peel came into power, under the premiership of Lord Aberdeen. Once more, Palmerston was in the Cabinet. It was true that he did not return to the Foreign Office; that

was something to the good; in the Home Department it might be hoped that his activities would be less dangerous and disagreeable. But the Foreign Secretary was no longer the complacent Granville; and in Lord Clarendon the Prince knew that he had a Minister to deal with, who, discreet and courteous as he was, had a mind of his own.

These changes, however, were merely the preliminaries of a far more serious development. Events, on every side, were moving towards a catastrophe. Suddenly the nation found itself under the awful shadow of imminent war. For several months, amid the shifting mysteries of diplomacy and the perplexed agitations of politics, the issue grew more doubtful and more dark, while the national temper was strained to the breaking-point. At the very crisis of the long and ominous negotiations, it was announced that Lord Palmerston had resigned. Then the pent-up fury of the people burst forth. They had felt that in the terrible complexity of events they were being guided by weak and embarrassed counsels; but they had been reassured by the knowledge that at the centre of power there was one man with strength, with courage, with determination, in whom they could put their trust. They now learnt that that man was no longer among their leaders. Why? In their rage, anxiety, and nervous exhaustion, they looked round desperately for some hidden and horrible explanation of what had occurred. They suspected plots, they smelt treachery in the air. It was easy to guess the object upon which their frenzy would vent itself. Was there not a foreigner in the highest of high places, a foreigner whose hostility to their own adored champion was unrelenting and unconcealed? The moment that Palmerston's resignation was known, there was a universal outcry and an extraordinary tempest of anger and hatred burst, with unparalleled violence, upon the head of the Prince.

It was everywhere asserted and believed that the Queen's husband was a traitor to the country, that he was a tool of the Russian Court, that in obedience to Russian influences he had forced Palmerston out of the Government, and that he was directing the foreign policy of England in the interests of England's enemies. For many weeks these accusations filled the whole of the press; repeated at public meetings, elaborated in private talk, they flew over the country, growing every moment more extreme and more improbable. While respectable newspapers thundered out their grave invectives, halfpenny broadsides, hawked through the streets of London, re-echoed in doggerel vulgarity the same sentiments and the same suspicions.[1] At last

the wildest rumours began to spread.

In January, 1854, it was whispered that the Prince had been seized, that he had been found guilty of high treason, that he was to be committed to the Tower. The Queen herself, some declared, had been arrested, and large crowds actually collected round the Tower to watch the incarceration of the royal miscreants.[2]

These fantastic hallucinations, the result of the fevered atmosphere of approaching war, were devoid of any basis in actual fact. Palmerston's resignation had been in all probability totally disconnected with foreign policy; it had certainly been entirely spontaneous, and had surprised the Court as much as the nation. Nor had Albert's influence been used in any way to favour the interests of Russia. As often happens in such cases, the Government had been swinging backwards and

> *Chorus*
> 'We'll send him home and make him
>   groan,
>   Oh, Al! you've played the deuce
>   then;
> The German lad has acted sad
>   And turned tail with the Russians.'
>   —*Lovely Albert!*

---

[1] 'The Turkish war both far and near
   Has played the very deuce then,
And little Al, the royal pal,
   They say has turned a Russian;
Old Aberdeen, as may be seen,
   Looks woeful pale and yellow,
And Old John Bull had his belly full
   Of dirty Russian tallow.

[2] 'You Jolly Turks, now go to work,
   And show the Bear your power.
It is rumoured over Britain's isle
   That A—— is in the Tower;
The postmen some suspicion had,
   And opened the two letters,
'Twas a pity sad the German lad
   Should not have known much
   better!'
            —*Lovely Albert!*

forwards between two incompatible policies—that of non-interference and that of threats supported by force—either of which, if consistently followed, might well have had a successful and peaceful issue, but which, mingled together, could only lead to war. Albert, with characteristic scrupulosity, attempted to thread his way through the complicated labyrinth of European diplomacy, and eventually was lost in the maze. But so was the whole of the Cabinet; and, when war came, his anti-Russian feelings were quite as vehement as those of the most bellicose of Englishmen.

Nevertheless, though the specific charges levelled against the Prince were without foundation, there were underlying elements in the situation which explained, if they did not justify, the popular state of mind. It was true that the Queen's husband was a foreigner, who had been brought up in a foreign Court, was impregnated with foreign ideas, and was closely related to a multitude of foreign princes. Clearly this, though perhaps an unavoidable, was an undesirable, state of affairs; nor were the objections to it merely theoretical; it had in fact produced unpleasant consequences of a serious kind. The Prince's German proclivities were perpetually lamented by English Ministers; Lord Palmerston, Lord Clarendon, Lord Aberdeen, all told the same tale; and it was constantly necessary, in grave questions of national policy, to combat the prepossessions of a Court in which German views and Ger-

man sentiments held a disproportionate place. As for Palmerston, his language on this topic was apt to be unbridled. At the height of his annoyance over his resignation, he roundly declared that he had been made a victim to foreign intrigue. He afterwards toned down this accusation; but the mere fact that such a suggestion from such a quarter was possible at all showed to what unfortunate consequences Albert's foreign birth and foreign upbringing might lead.

But this was not all. A constitutional question of the most profound importance was raised by the position of the Prince in England. His presence gave a new prominence to an old problem—the precise definition of the functions and the powers of the Crown. Those functions and powers had become, in effect, his; and what sort of use was he making of them? His views as to the place of the Crown in the Constitution are easily ascertainable; for they were Stockmar's; and it happens that we possess a detailed account of Stockmar's opinions upon the subject in a long letter addressed by him to the Prince at the time of this very crisis, just before the outbreak of the Crimean War. Constitutional Monarchy, according to the Baron, had suffered an eclipse since the passing of the Reform Bill. It was now 'constantly in danger of becoming a pure Ministerial Government.' The old race of Tories, who 'had a direct interest in upholding the prerogatives of the Crown,' had died out; and the Whigs were 'nothing but partly conscious, partly unconscious Republicans, who stand in the same relation to the Throne as the wolf does to the lamb.' There was a rule that it was unconstitutional to introduce 'the name and person of the irresponsible Sovereign' into parliamentary debates on constitutional matters; this was 'a constitutional fiction, which, although undoubtedly of old standing, was fraught with danger'; and the Baron warned the Prince that 'if the English Crown permit a Whig Ministry to follow this rule in practice, without exception, you must not wonder if in a little time you find the majority of the people impressed with the belief that the King, in the view of the law, is nothing but a mandarin figure, which has to nod its head in assent, or shake it in denial, as his Minister pleases.' To prevent this from happening, it was of extreme importance, said the Baron, 'that no opportunity should be let slip of vindicating the legitimate position of the Crown.' 'And this is not hard to do,' he added, 'and can never embarrass a Minister where such straightforward loyal personages as the Queen and the Prince are concerned.' In his opinion, the very lowest claim of the Royal Prerogative should include 'a right on the part of the King to be the permanent President of his Ministerial Council.' The Sovereign ought to be 'in the position of a permanent Premier, who takes rank above the temporary head of the Cabinet, and

in matters of discipline exercises supreme authority.' The Sovereign 'may even take a part in the initiation and the maturing of the Government measures; for it would be unreasonable to expect that a king, himself as able, as accomplished, and as patriotic as the best of his Ministers, should be prevented from making use of these qualities at the deliberations of his Council.' 'The judicious exercise of this right,' concluded the Baron, 'which certainly requires a master mind, would not only be the best guarantee for Constitutional Monarchy, but would raise it to a height of power, stability, and symmetry, which has never been attained.'

Now it may be that this reading of the Constitution is a possible one, though indeed it is hard to see how it can be made compatible with the fundamental doctrine of ministerial responsibility. William III presided over his Council, and he was a constitutional monarch; and it seems that Stockmar had in his mind a conception of the Crown which would have given it a place in the Constitution analogous to that which it filled at the time of William III. But it is clear that such a theory, which would invest the Crown with more power than it possessed even under George III, runs counter to the whole development of English public life since the Revolution; and the fact that it was held by Stockmar, and instilled by him into Albert, was of very serious importance. For there was good reason to believe not only that these doctrines were held by Albert in theory, but that he was making a deliberate and sustained attempt to give them practical validity. The history of the struggle between the Crown and Palmerston provided startling evidence that this was the case. That struggle reached its culmination when, in Stockmar's memorandum of 1850, the Queen asserted her 'constitutional right' to dismiss the Foreign Secretary if he altered a despatch which had received her sanction. The memorandum was, in fact, a plain declaration that the Crown intended to act independently of the Prime Minister. Lord John Russell, anxious at all costs to strengthen himself against Palmerston, accepted the memorandum, and thereby implicitly allowed the claim of the Crown. More than that; after the dismissal of Palmerston, among the grounds on which Lord John justified that dismissal in the House of Commons he gave a prominent place to the memorandum of 1850. It became apparent that the displeasure of the Sovereign might be a reason for the removal of a powerful and popular Minister. It seemed indeed as if, under the guidance of Stockmar and Albert, the 'Constitutional Monarchy' might in very truth be rising 'to a height of power, stability, and symmetry, which had never been attained.'

But this new development in the position of the Crown, grave as it was in itself, was rendered peculiarly disquieting by the unusual circumstances which surrounded it. For the functions of the Crown were now, in effect, being exercised by a person unknown to the Constitution, who wielded over the Sovereign an undefined and unbounded influence. The fact that this person was the Sovereign's husband, while it explained his influence and even made it inevitable, by no means diminished its strange and momentous import. An ambiguous, prepotent figure had come to disturb the ancient, subtle, and jealously guarded balance of the English Constitution. Such had been the unexpected outcome of the tentative and faint-hearted opening of Albert's political life. He himself made no attempt to minimise either the multiplicity or the significance of the functions he performed. He considered that it was his duty, he told the Duke of Wellington in 1850, to 'sink his *own individual* existence in that of his wife . . . —assume no separate responsibility before the public, but make his position entirely a part of hers—fill up every gap which, as a woman, she would naturally leave in the exercise of her regal functions—continually and anxiously watch every part of the public business, in order to be able to advise and assist her at any moment in any of the multifarious and difficult questions or duties brought before her, sometimes international, sometimes political, or social, or personal. As the natural head of her family, superintendent of her household, manager of her private affairs, sole *confidential* adviser in politics, and only assistant in her communications with the officers of the Government, he is, besides, the husband of the Queen, the tutor of the royal children, the private secretary of the Sovereign, and her permanent minister.' Stockmar's pupil had assuredly gone far and learnt well. Stockmar's pupil!—precisely; the public, painfully aware of Albert's predominance, had grown, too, uneasily conscious that Victoria's master had a master of his own. Deep in the darkness the Baron loomed. Another foreigner! Decidedly, there were elements in the situation which went far to justify the popular alarm. A foreign Baron controlled a foreign Prince, and the foreign Prince controlled the Crown of England. And the Crown itself was creeping forward ominously; and when, from under its shadow, the Baron and the Prince had frowned, a great Minister, beloved of the people, had fallen. Where was all this to end?

Within a few weeks Palmerston withdrew his resignation, and the public fenzy subsided as quickly as it had arisen. When Parliament met, the leaders of both the parties in both the Houses made speeches in favour of the Prince, asserting his unimpeachable loyalty to the country and vindicating his right to advise the Sovereign in all matters of State. Victoria was delighted. 'The position of my beloved lord and master,' she told the Baron, 'has been defined for *once and all* and his merits have been acknowl-

edged on all sides most duly. There was an immense concourse of people assembled when we went to the House of Lords, and the people were very friendly.' Immediately afterwards, the country finally plunged into the Crimean War. In the struggle that followed, Albert's patriotism was put beyond a doubt, and the animosities of the past were forgotten. But the war had another consequence, less gratifying to the royal couple: it crowned the ambition of Lord Palmerston. In 1855, the man who five years before had been pronounced by Lord John Russell to be 'too old to do much in the future,' became Prime Minister of England, and, with one short interval, remained in that position for ten years.

✖ *Chapter* **6**

Last Years of Prince Consort

I

The weak-willed youth who took no interest in politics and never read a newspaper had grown into a man of unbending determination whose tireless energies were incessantly concentrated upon the laborious business of government and the highest questions of State. He was busy now from morning till night. In the winter, before the dawn, he was to be seen, seated at his writing-table, working by the light of the green reading-lamp which he had brought over with him from Germany, and the construction of which he had much improved by an ingenious device. Victoria was early too, but she was not so early as Albert; and when, in the chill darkness, she took her seat at her own writing-table, placed side by side with his, she invariably found upon it a neat pile of papers arranged for her inspection and her signature. The day, thus begun, continued in unremitting industry. At breakfast, the newspapers—the once hated newspapers—made their appearance, and the Prince, absorbed in their perusal, would answer no questions or, if an article struck him, would read it aloud. After that there were ministers and secretaries to interview; there was a vast correspondence to be carried on; there were numerous memoranda to be made. Victoria, treasuring every word, preserving every letter, was all breathless attention and eager obedience. Sometimes Albert would actually ask her advice. He consulted her about his English: 'Lese recht aufmerksam, und sage wenn irgend ein Fehler ist,'[1] he would say; or, as he handed her a draft for her signature, he would observe, 'Ich hab' Dir hier ein Draft gemacht, lese es mal! Ich dächte es wäre recht so.'[2] Thus the diligent, scrupulous, absorbing hours passed by. Fewer and fewer grew the moments of recreation and of exercise. The demands of society were narrowed down to the smallest limits, and even then but grudgingly attended to. It was no longer a mere pleasure, it was a positive necessity, to go to bed as early as possible in order to be up and at work on the morrow betimes.

The important and exacting business of government, which became at last the dominating preoccupation in Albert's mind, still left unimpaired his old tastes and interests; he remained devoted to art, to science, to philosophy; and a multitude of subsidiary activities showed how his energies increased as the demands upon them grew. For whenever duty called, the Prince was all alertness. With indefatigable perseverance he opened museums, laid the foundation stones of hospitals, made speeches to the Royal Agricultural Society, and attended meetings of the British Association. The National Gallery particularly interested him: he drew up careful regulations for the arrangement of the pictures according to schools; and he attempted—though in vain—to have the whole collection transported to South Kensington. Feodora now the

---

[1] Lese recht aufmerksam, und sage wenn irgend ein Fehler ist: Read this carefully, and tell me if there are any mistakes in it.

[2] Ich hab' Dir hier ein Draft gemacht, lese es mal! Ich dächte es wäre recht so: Here is a draft I have made for you. Read it! I should think this would do.

Princess Hohenlohe, after a visit to England, expressed in a letter to Victoria her admiration of Albert both as a private and a public character. Nor did she rely only on her own opinion. 'I must just copy out,' she said, 'what Mr. Klumpp wrote to me some little time ago, and which is quite true—'Prince Albert is one of the few Royal personages who can sacrifice to any principle (as soon as it has become evident to them to be good and noble) all those notions (or sentiments) to which others, owing to their narrow-mindedness, or to the prejudices of their rank, are so thoroughly inclined strongly to cling.'— 'There is something so truly religious in this,' the Princess added, 'as well as humane and just, most soothing to my feelings which are so often hurt and disturbed by what I hear and see.'

Victoria, from the depth of her heart, subscribed to all the eulogies of Feodora and Mr. Klumpp. She only found that they were insufficient. As she watched her beloved Albert, after toiling with state documents and public functions, devoting every spare moment of his time to domestic duties, to artistic appreciation, and to intellectual improvements; as she listened to him cracking his jokes at the luncheon table, or playing Mendelssohn on the organ, or pointing out the merits of Sir Edwin Landseer's pictures; as she followed him round while he gave instructions about the breeding of cattle, or decided that the Gainsboroughs must be hung higher up so that the Winterhalters might be properly seen— she felt perfectly certain that no other wife had ever had such a husband. His mind was apparently capable of everything, and she was hardly surprised to learn that he had made an important discovery for the conversion of sewage into agricultural manure. Filtration from below upwards, he explained, through some appropriate medium, which retained the solids and set free the fluid sewage for irrigation, was the principle of the scheme. 'All previous plans,' he said, 'would have cost millions; mine costs next to nothing.' Unfortunately, owing to a slight miscalculation, the invention proved to be impracticable; but Albert's intelligence was unrebuffed, and he passed on, to plunge with all his accustomed ardour into a prolonged study of the rudiments of lithography.[1]

But naturally it was upon his children that his private interests and those of Victoria were concentrated most vigorously. The royal nurseries showed no sign of emptying. The birth of the Prince Arthur in 1850 was followed, three years later, by that of the Prince Leopold; and in 1857 the Princess Beatrice was born. A family of nine must be, in any circumstances, a grave responsibility; and the Prince realised to the full how much the high destinies of his offspring intensified the need of parental care. It was inevitable that he should

[1] lithography: a method of printing.

believe profoundly in the importance of education; he himself had been the product of education; Stockmar had made him what he was; it was for him, in his turn, to be a Stockmar—to be even more than a Stockmar—to the young creatures he had brought into the world. Victoria would assist him; a Stockmar, no doubt, she could hardly be; but she could be perpetually vigilant, she could mingle strictness with her affection, and she could always set a good example. These considerations, of course, applied pre-eminently to the education of the Prince of Wales. How tremendous was the significance of every particle of influence which went to the making of the future King of England! Albert set to work with a will. But, watching with Victoria the minutest details of the physical, intellectual, and moral training of his children, he soon perceived, to his distress, that there was something unsatisfactory in the development of his eldest son. The Princess Royal was an extremely intelligent child; but Bertie though he was good-humoured and gentle, seemed to display a deep-seated repugnance to every form of mental exertion. This was most regrettable, but the remedy was obvious; the parental efforts must be redoubled; instruction must be multiplied; not for a single instant must the educational pressure be allowed to relax. Accordingly, more tutors were selected, the curriculum was revised, the time-table of studies was re-arranged, elaborate memoranda dealing with every possible contingency were drawn up. It was above all essential that there should be no slackness: 'work,' said the Prince, 'must be work.' And work indeed it was. The boy grew up amid a ceaseless round of paradigms, syntactical exercises, dates, genealogical tables, and lists of capes. Constant notes flew backwards and forwards between the Prince, the Queen, and the tutors, with inquiries, with reports of progress, with detailed recommendations; and these notes were all carefully preserved for future reference. It was, besides, vital that the heir to the throne should be protected from the slightest possibility of contamination from the outside world. The Prince of Wales was not as other boys; he might, occasionally, be allowed to invite some sons of the nobility, boys of good character, to play with him in the garden of Buckingham Palace; but his father presided, with alarming precision, over their sports. In short, every possible precaution was taken, every conceivable effort was made. Yet, strange to say, the object of all this vigilance and solicitude continued to be unsatisfactory—appeared, in fact, to be positively growing worse. It was certainly very odd: the more lessons that Bertie had to do, the less he did them; and the more carefully he was guarded against excitements and frivolities, the more desirous of mere amusement he seemed to become. Albert was deeply grieved and Victoria was sometimes very angry; but grief and anger produced no more effect than supervision and time-tables. The Prince of Wales, in spite of everything, grew up into manhood without the faintest sign of 'adherence to and perseverance in the plan both of studies and life'—as one of the Royal memoranda put it—which had been laid down with such extraordinary forethought by his father.

II

Against the insidious worries of politics, the boredom of society functions, and the pompous publicity of state ceremonies, Osborne had afforded a welcome refuge; but it soon appeared that even Osborne was too little removed from the world. After all, the Solent was a feeble barrier. Oh, for some distant, some almost inaccessible sanctuary, where, in true domestic privacy, once could make happy holiday, just as if—or at least very, very, nearly—one were anybody else! Victoria, ever since, together with Albert, she had visited Scotland in the early years of her marriage, had felt that her heart was in the Highlands. She had returned to them a few years later, and her passion had grown. How romantic they were! And how Albert enjoyed them too! His spirits rose quite wonderfully as soon as he found himself among the hills and the conifers. 'It is a happiness to see him,' she wrote. 'Oh, What can equal the beauties of nature!' she exclaimed in her journal, during one of these visits.

'What enjoyment there is in them! Albert enjoys it so much; he is in ecstasies here.' 'Albert said,' she noted next day, 'that the chief beauty of mountain scenery consists in its frequent changes. We came home at six o'clock.' Then she went on a longer expedition—up to the very top of a high hill. 'It was quite romantic. Here we were with only this Highlander behind us holding the ponies (for we got off twice and walked about). . . . We came home at half-past eleven,—the most delightful, most romantic ride and walk I ever had. I had never been up such a mountain, and then the day was so fine.' The Highlanders, too, were such astonishing people. They 'never make difficulties,' she noted, 'but are cheerful, and happy, and merry, and ready to walk, and run, and do anything.' As for Albert he 'highly appreciated the good-breeding, simplicity, and intelligence, which make it so pleasant and even instructive to talk to them.' 'We were always in the habit,' wrote Her Majesty, 'of conversing with the Highlanders—with whom one comes so much in contact in the Highlands.' She loved everything about them—their customs, their dress, their dances, even their musical instruments. 'There were nine pipers at the castle,' she wrote, after staying with Lord Breadalbane! 'sometimes one and sometimes three played. They always played about breakfast-time, again during the morning, at luncheon, and also whenever we went in and out;

again before dinner, and during most of dinner-time. We both have become quite fond of the bag-pipes.'

It was quite impossible not to wish to return to such pleasures again and again; and in 1848 the Queen took a lease of Balmoral House, a small residence near Braemar in the wilds of Aberdeenshire. Four years later she bought the place outright. Now she could be really happy every summer; now she could be simple and at her ease; now she could be romantic every evening, and dote upon Albert, without a single distraction, all day long. The diminutive scale of the house was in itself a charm. Nothing was more amusing than to find oneself living in two or three little sitting-rooms, with the children crammed away upstairs, and the minister in attendance with only a tiny bedroom to do all his work in. And then to be able to run in and out of doors as one liked, and to sketch, and to walk, and to watch the red deer coming so surprisingly close, and to pay visits to the cottagers! And occasionally one could be more adventurous still—one could go and stay for a night or two at the Bothie at Alt-na-giuthasach —a mere couple of huts with 'a wooden addition'—and only eleven people in the whole party! And there were mountains to be climbed and cairns to be built in solemn pomp. 'At last, when the cairn, which is, I think, seven or eight feet high was nearly completed, Albert climbed up to the top of it, and placed the last stone; after

which three cheers were given. It was a gay, pretty, and touching sight; and I felt almost inclined to cry. The view was so beautiful over the dear hills; the day so fine; the whole so *gemüthlich*.'[1] And in the evening there were sword-dances and reels.

But Albert had determined to pull down the little old house, and to build in its place a castle of his own designing. With great ceremony, in accordance with a memorandum drawn up by the Prince for the occasion, the foundation-stone of the new edifice was laid, and by 1855 it was habitable. Spacious, built of granite in the Scotch baronial style, with a tower 100 feet high, and minor turrets and castellated gables, the castle was skilfully arranged to command the finest views of the surrounding mountains and of the neighbouring river Dee. Upon the interior decorations Albert and Victoria lavished all their care. The wall and the floors were of pitch-pine, and covered with specially manufactured tartans. The Balmoral tartan, in red and grey, designed by the Prince, and the Victoria tartan, with a white stripe designed by the Queen, were to be seen in every room: there were tartan curtains, and tartan chair-covers, and even tartan linoleums. Occasionally the Royal Stuart tartan appeared, for Her Majesty always maintained that she was an ardent Jacobite. Watercolour sketches by Victoria hung

[1] *gemüthlich*: agreeable; cozy.

upon the walls, together with innumerable stags' antlers, and the head of a boar, which had been shot by Albert in Germany. In an alcove in the hall, stood a life-sized statue of Albert in Highland dress. Victoria declared that it was perfection. 'Every year,' she wrote, 'my heart becomes more fixed in this dear paradise, and so much more so now, that *all* has become my dear Albert's *own* creation, own work, own building, own lay-out; . . . and his great taste, and the impress of his dear hand, have been stamped everywhere.'

And here, in very truth, her happiest days were passed. In after years, when she looked back upon them, a kind of glory, a radiance as of an unearthly holiness, seemed to glow about these golden hours. Each hallowed moment stood out clear, beautiful, eternally significant. For, at the time, every experience there, sentimental or grave, or trivial, had come upon her with a peculiar vividness like a flashing of marvellous lights. Albert's stalkings—an evening walk when she lost her way—Vicky sitting down on a wasps' nest—a torchlight dance —with what intensity such things, and ten thousand like them, impressed themselves upon her eager consciousness! And how she flew to her journal to note them down! The news of the Duke's[1] death! What a moment!—when, as she sat sketching after a picnic by a loch in the lonely hills, Lord

Derby's letter had been brought to her, and she had learnt that '*England's,* or rather *Britain's* pride, her glory, her hero, the greatest man she had ever produced, was no more!' For such were her reflections upon the 'old rebel' of former days. But that past had been utterly obliterated—no faintest memory of it remained. For years she had looked up to the Duke as a figure almost superhuman. Had he not been a supporter of good Sir Robert? Had he not asked Albert to succeed him as commander-in-chief? And what a proud moment it had been when he stood as sponsor to her son Arthur, who was born on his eighty-first birthday! So now she filled a whole page of her diary with panegyrical regrets. 'His position was the highest a subject ever had—above party,—looked up to by all,—revered by the whole nation,—the friend of the Sovereign . . . The Crown never possessed,— and I fear never *will*—so *devoted,* loyal, and faithful a subject, so staunch a supporter! To *us* his loss is *irreparable* . . . To Albert he showed the greatest kindness and the utmost confidence . . . Not an eye will be dry in the whole country.' These were serious thoughts; but they were soon succeeded by others hardly less moving—by events as impossible to forget—by Mr. MacLeod's sermon on Nicodemus,—by the gift of a red flannel petticoat to Mrs. P. Farquharson, and another to old Kitty Kear.

But, without doubt, most memorable, most delightful of all were

[1] The Duke of Wellington (1769-1852).

the expeditions—the rare, exciting expeditions up distant mountains, across broad rivers, through strange country, and lasting several days. With only two gillies—Grant and Brown—for servants, and with assumed names . . . it was more like something in a story than real life. 'We had decided to call ourselves *Lord and Lady Churchill and party*—Lady Churchill passing as *Miss Spencer* and General Grey as *Dr. Grey!* Brown once forgot this and called me "Your Majesty" as I was getting into the carriage, and Grant on the box once called Albert "Your Royal Highness," which set us off laughing, but no one observed it.' Strong, vigorous, enthusiastic, bringing, so it seemed, good fortune with her—the Highlanders declared she had 'a lucky foot'—she relished everything—the scrambles and the views and the contretemps and the rough inns with their coarse fare and Brown and Grant waiting at table. She could have gone on for ever and ever, absolutely happy with Albert beside her and Brown at her pony's head. But the time came for turning homewards; alas! the time came for going back to England. She could hardly bear it; she sat disconsolate in her room and watched the snow falling. The last day! Oh! If only she could be snowed up!

III

The Crimean War brought new experiences, and most of them were pleasant ones. It was pleasant to be patriotic and pugnacious, to look out appropriate prayers to be read in the churches, to have news of glorious victories, and to know oneself, more proudly than ever, the representative of England. With that spontaneity of feeling which was so peculiarly her own, Victoria poured out her emotion, her admiration, her pity, her love, upon her 'dear soldiers.' When she gave them their medals her exultation knew no bounds. 'Noble fellows!' she wrote to the King of the Belgians. 'I own I feel as if these were *my own children;* my heart beats for *them* as for my *nearest and dearest.* They were so touched, so pleased; many, I hear, cried—and they won't hear of giving up their medals to have their names engraved upon them for fear they should *not* receive the *identical one* put into *their hands by me,* which is quite touching. Several came by in a sadly mutilated state.' She and they were at one. They felt that she had done them a splendid honour, and she, with perfect genuineness, shared their feeling. Albert's attitude towards such things was different; there was an austerity in him which quite prohibited the expansions of emotion. When General Williams returned from the heroic defence of Kars and was presented at Court, the quick, stiff, distant bow with which the Prince received him struck like ice upon the beholders. He was a stranger still.

But he had other things to occupy him, more important, surely, than the personal impressions of military officers and people who went to Court. He was at work—ceaselessly at work—on the tremendous task of carrying through the war to a successful conclusion. State papers, despatches, memoranda, poured from him in an overwhelming stream. Between 1853 and 1857 fifty folio volumes were filled with the comments of his pen upon the Eastern question. Nothing would induce him to stop. Weary ministers staggered under the load of his advice; but his advice continued, piling itself up over their writing-tables, and flowing out upon them from red box after red box. Nor was it advice to be ignored. The talent for administration which had reorganised the royal palaces and planned the Great Exhibition asserted itself no less in the confused complexities of war. Again and again the Prince's suggestions, rejected or unheeded at first, were adopted under the stress of circumstances and found to be full of value. The enrolment of a foreign legion, the establishment of a depôt for troops at Malta, the institution of periodical reports and tabulated returns as to the condition of the army at Sebastopol—such were the contrivances and the achievements of his indefatigable brain. He went further: in a lengthy minute he laid down the lines for a radical reform in the entire administration of the army. This was premature, but his proposal that 'a camp of evolution' should be created, in which troops should be concentrated and drilled, proved to be the germ of Aldershot.

Meanwhile Victoria had made a new friend: she had suddenly been captivated by Napoleon III. Her dislike of him had been strong at first. She considered that he was a disreputable adventurer who had usurped the throne of poor old Louis Philippe; and besides he was hand-in-glove with Lord Palmerston. For a long time, although he was her ally, she was unwilling to meet him; but at last a visit of the Emperor and Empress to England was arranged. Directly he appeared at Windsor her heart began to soften. She found that she was charmed by his quiet manners, his low, soft voice, and by the soothing simplicity of his conversation. The good-will of England was essential to the Emperor's position in Europe, and he had determined to fascinate the Queen. He succeeded. There was something deep within her which responded immediately and vehemently to natures that offered a romantic contrast with her own. Her adoration of Lord Melbourne was intimately interwoven with her half-unconscious appreciation of the exciting unlikeness between herself and that sophisticated, subtle, aristocratical old man. Very different was the quality of her unlikeness to Napoleon; but its quantity was at least as great. From behind the vast solidity of her respectability, her conventionality, her established happiness, she peered out with a strange delicious pleasure at that unfamiliar, darkly-glittering foreign object, moving so meteorically before her, an ambiguous creature of wilfulness and Destiny. And, to her surprise, where she had dreaded antagonisms, she discovered only sympathies. He was, she said, 'so quiet, so simple, *naïf* even, so pleased to be informed about things he does not know, so gentle, so full of tact, dignity, and modesty, so full of kind attention towards us, never saying a word, or doing a thing, which could put me out . . . There is something fascinating, melancholy, and engaging, which draws you to him, in spite of any *prévention* [1] you may have against him and certainly without the assistance of any outward appearance, though I like his face.' She observed that he rode 'extremely well, and looks well on horseback, as he sits high.' And he danced 'with great dignity and spirit.' Above all, he listened to Albert; listened with the most respectful attention; showed, in fact, how pleased he was 'to be informed about things he did not know'; and afterwards was heard to declare that he had never met the Prince's equal. On one occasion, indeed—but only on one— he had seemed to grow slightly restive. In a diplomatic conversation, 'I expatiated a little on the Holstein question,' wrote the Prince in a memorandum, 'which appeared to bore the Emperor as *très-compliquée.*' [2]

Victoria, too, became much attached to the Empress, whose looks and graces she admired without a touch of jealousy. Eugénie, indeed, in the plenitude of her beauty, exquisitely dressed in wonderful Parisian crinolines which set off to perfection her tall and willowy figure, might well have caused some heartburning in the breast of her hostess, who, very short, rather stout, quite plain, in garish middle-class garments, could hardly be expected to feel at her best in such company. But Victoria had no misgivings. To her it mattered nothing that her face turned red in the heat and that her purple pork-pie hat was of last year's fashion, while Eugénie, cool and modish, floated in an infinitude of flounces by her side. She was Queen of England, and was not that enough? It certainly seemed to be; true majesty was hers, and she knew it. More than once, when the two were together in public, it was the woman to whom, as it seemed, nature and art had given so little, who, by the sheer force of an inherent grandeur, completely threw her adorned and beautiful companion into the shade.

There were tears when the moment came for parting, and Victoria felt 'quite *wehmüthig,*' [3] as her guests went away from Windsor. But before long she and Albert paid a return visit to France, where everything was very delightful, and she drove incognito through the streets of Paris in a 'common bonnet,' and saw a play in the theatre at St. Cloud, and, one evening, at a

---

[1] *prévention:* presupposition; prejudice.
[2] *très-compliquée:* very complicated.

[3] quite *wehmüthig:* quite melancholy.

great party given by the Emperor in her honour at the Château of Versailles, talked a little to a distinguished-looking Prussian gentleman, whose name was Bismarck. Her rooms were furnished so much to her taste that she declared they gave her quite a home feeling— that, if her little dog were there, she should really imagine herself at home. Nothing was said, but three days later her little dog barked a welcome to her as she entered the apartments. The Emperor himself, sparing neither trouble nor expense, had personally arranged the charming surprise. Such were his attentions. She returned to England more enchanted than ever. 'Strange indeed,' she exclaimed, 'are the dispensations and ways of Providence!'

The alliance prospered, and the war drew towards a conclusion. Both the Queen and the Prince, it is true, were most anxious that there should not be a premature peace. When Lord Aberdeen wished to open negotiations Albert attacked him in a *'geharnischten'* [1] letter, while Victoria rode about on horseback reviewing the troops. At last, however, Sebastopol was captured. The news reached Balmoral late at night, and 'in a few minutes Albert and all the gentlemen in every species of attire sallied forth, followed by all the servants, and gradually by all the population of the village—keepers; gillies, workmen —up to the top of the cairn.'

---

[1] *geharnischten*: stinging; biting.

A bonfire was lighted, the pipes were played, and guns were shot off. 'About three-quarters of an hour after, Albert came down and said the scene had been wild and exciting beyond everything. The people had been drinking healths in whisky and were in great ecstasy.' The 'great ecstasy,' perhaps, would be replaced by other feelings next morning; but at any rate the war was over—though, to be sure, its end seemed as difficult to account for as its beginning. The dispensations and ways of Providence continued to be strange.

IV

An unexpected consequence of the war was a complete change in the relations between the royal pair and Palmerston. The Prince and the Minister drew together over their hostility to Russia, and thus it came about that when Victoria found it necessary to summon her old enemy to form an administration she did so without reluctance. The premiership, too, had a sobering effect upon Palmerston; he grew less impatient and dictatorial; considered with attention the suggestions of the Crown, and was, besides, genuinely impressed by the Prince's ability and knowledge. Friction, no doubt, there still occasionally was, for, while the Queen and the Prince devoted themselves to foreign politics as much as ever, their views, when the war was over, became once more antagonistic to those of the Prime Minister. This was especially the case with regard to Italy. Albert, theoretically the friend of constitutional government, distrusted Cavour, was horrified by Garibaldi, and dreaded the danger of England being drawn into war with Austria. Palmerston, on the other hand, was eager for Italian independence; but he was no longer at the Foreign Office, and the brunt of the royal displeasure had now to be borne by Lord John Russell. In a few years the situation had curiously altered. It was Lord John who now filled the subordinate and the ungrateful rôle; but the Foreign Secretary, in his struggle with the Crown, was supported, instead of opposed, by the Prime Minister. Nevertheless the struggle was fierce, and the policy, by which the vigorous sympathy of England became one of the decisive factors in the final achievement of Italian unity, was only carried through in face of the violent opposition of the Court.

Towards the other European storm-centre, also, the Prince's attitude continued to be very different to that of Palmerston. Albert's great wish was for a united Germany under the leadership of a constitutional and virtuous Prussia; Palmerston did not think that there was much to be said for the scheme, but he took no particular interest in German politics, and was ready enough to agree to a proposal which was warmly supported by both the Prince and the Queen—that the royal Houses of England and Prussia should be united by the marriage of the Princess Royal with the Prussian Crown Prince. According-

ly, when the Princess was not yet fifteen, the Prince, a young man of twenty-four, came over on a visit to Balmoral, and the betrothal took place. Two years later, in 1857, the marriage was celebrated. At the last moment, however, it seemed that there might be a hitch. It was pointed out in Prussia that it was customary for Princes of the blood royal to be married in Berlin, and it was suggested that there was no reason why the present case should be treated as an exception. When this reached the ears of Victoria, she was speechless with indignation. In a note, emphatic even for Her Majesty, she instructed the Foreign Secretary to tell the Prussian Ambassador 'not to *entertain* the *possibility* of such a question. . . . The Queen *never* could consent to it, both for public and for private reasons, and the assumption of its being *too much* for a Prince Royal of Prussia to *come* over to marry *the Princess Royal of Great Britain* in England is too *absurd* to say the least. . . . Whatever may be the usual practice of Prussian princes, it is not *every* day that one marries the eldest daughter of the Queen of England. The question must therefore be considered as settled and closed.' It was, and the wedding took place in St. James's Chapel. There were great festivities—illuminations, state concerts, immense crowds, and general rejoicings. At Windsor a magnificent banquet was given to the bride and bridegroom in the Waterloo room, at which, Victoria noted in her diary, 'everybody was most friendly and kind about Vicky and full of the universal enthusiasm, of which the Duke of Buccleuch gave us most pleasing instances, he having been in the very thick of the crowd and among the lowest of the low.' Her feelings during several days had been growing more and more emotional, and when the time came for the young couple to depart she very nearly broke down—but not quite. 'Poor dear child!' she wrote afterwards. 'I clasped her in my arms and blessed her, and knew not what to say. I kissed good Fritz and pressed his hand again and again. He was unable to speak and the tears were in his eyes. I embraced them both again at the carriage door, and Albert got into the carriage, an open one, with them and Bertie. . . . The band struck up. I wished good-bye to the good Perponchers. General Schreckenstein was much affected. I pressed his hand, and the good Dean's, and then went quickly upstairs.'

Albert, as well as General Schreckenstein, was much affected. He was losing his favourite child, whose opening intelligence had already begun to display a marked resemblance to his own—an adoring pupil, who, in a few years, might have become an almost adequate companion. An ironic fate had determined that the daughter who was taken from him should be sympathetic, clever, interested in the arts and sciences, and endowed with a strong taste for memoranda, while not a single one of these qualities could be discovered in the son who remained. For certainly the Prince of Wales did not take after his father. Victoria's prayer had been unanswered, and with each succeeding year it became more obvious that Bertie was a true scion of the House of Brunswick. But these evidences of innate characteristics only served to redouble the efforts of his parents; it still might not be too late to incline the young branch, by ceaseless pressure and careful fastenings, to grow in the proper direction. Everything was tried. The boy was sent on a continental tour with a picked body of tutors, but the results were unsatisfactory. At his father's request he kept a diary which, on his return, was inspected by the Prince. It was found to be distressingly meagre: what a multitude of highly interesting reflections might have been arranged under the heading: 'The First Prince of Wales visiting the Pope!' But there was not a single one. *'Le jeune prince plaisit à tout le monde,'* old Metternich reported to Guizot, *'mais avait l'air embarrassé et très triste.'* [1] On his seventeenth birthday a memorandum was drawn up over the names of the Queen and the Prince informing their eldest son that he was now entering upon the period of manhood, and directing him henceforward to perform the duties of a Christian gentleman. 'Life is com-

---

[1] *Le jeune prince plaisit à tout le monde . . . mais avait l'air embarrassé et très triste:* The young prince pleases everyone . . . but has a shy and very melancholy manner.

posed of duties,' said the memorandum, 'and in the due, punctual and cheerful performance of them the true Christian, true soldier, and true gentleman is recognised. . . . A new sphere of life will open for you in which you will have to be taught what to do and what not to do, a subject requiring study more important than any in which you have hitherto been engaged.' On receipt of the memorandum Bertie burst into tears. At the same time another memorandum was drawn up, headed 'confidential: for the guidance of the gentlemen appointed to attend on the Prince of Wales.' This long and elaborate document laid down 'certain principles' by which the 'conduct and demeanour' of the gentlemen were to be regulated 'and which it is thought may conduce to the benefit of the Prince of Wales.' 'The qualities which distinguish a gentleman in society,' continued this remarkable paper, 'are:—

(1) His appearance, his deportment and dress.

(2) The character of his relations with, and treatment of, others.

(3) His desire and power to acquit himself creditably in conversation or whatever is the occupation of the society with which he mixes.'

A minute and detailed analysis of these subheadings followed, filling several pages, and the memorandum ended with a final exhortation to the gentlemen: 'If they will duly appreciate the responsibility of their position, and taking the points above laid down as the outline, will

exercise their own good sense in acting *upon all occasions* upon these principles, thinking no point of detail too minute to be important, but maintaining one steady consistent line of conduct they may render essential service to the young Prince and justify the flattering selection made by the royal parents.' A year later the young Prince was sent to Oxford, where the greatest care was taken that he should not mix with the undergraduates. Yes, everything had been tried—everything . . . with one single exception. The experiment had never been made of letting Bertie enjoy himself. But why should it have been? 'Life is composed of duties.' What possible place could there be for enjoyment in the existence of a Prince of Wales?

The same year which deprived Albert of the Princess Royal brought him another and a still more serious loss. The Baron had paid his last visit to England. For twenty years, as he himself said in a letter to the King of the Belgians, he had performed 'the laborious and exhausting office of a paternal friend and trusted adviser' to the Prince and the Queen. He was seventy; he was tired, physically and mentally; it was time to go. He returned to his home in Coburg, exchanging, once and for all, the momentous secrecies of European statecraft for the tittle-tattle of a provincial capital and the gossip of family life. In his stiff chair by the fire he nodded now over old stories—not of emperors and generals—but of neighbours and relatives and the domestic adventures of long ago—the burning of his father's library —and the goat that ran upstairs to his sister's room and ran twice round the table and then ran down again. Dyspepsia and depression still attacked him; but, looking back over his life, he was not dissatisfied. His conscience was clear. 'I have worked as long as I had strength to work,' he said, 'and for a purpose no one can impugn. The consciousness of this is my reward —the only one which I desired to earn.'

Apparently, indeed, his 'purpose' had been accomplished. By his wisdom, his patience, and his example he had brought about, in the fullness of time, the miraculous metamorphosis of which he had dreamed. The Prince was his creation. An indefatigable toiler, presiding, for the highest ends, over a great nation—that was his achievement; and he looked upon his work and it was good. But had the Baron no misgivings? Did he never wonder whether, perhaps, he might have accomplished not too little but too much? How subtle and how dangerous are the snares which fate lays for the wariest of men! Albert, certainly, seemed to be everything that Stockmar could have wished—virtuous, industrious, persevering, intelligent. And yet—why was it? —all was not well with him. He was sick at heart.

For in spite of everything he had never reached to happiness. His work, for which at last he came to crave with an almost morbid appetite, was a solace and not a cure; the dragon of his dissatisfaction devoured with dark relish that evergrowing tribute of laborious days and nights; but it was hungry still. The causes of his melancholy were hidden, mysterious, unanalysable perhaps—too deeply rooted in the innermost recesses of his temperament for the eye of reason to apprehend. There were contradictions in his nature, which, to some of those who knew him best, made him seem an inexplicable enigma: he was severe and gentle; he was modest and scornful; he longed for affection and he was cold. He was lonely, not merely with the loneliness of exile but with the loneliness of conscious and unrecognised superiority. He had the pride, at once resigned and overweening, of a doctrinaire. And yet to say that he was simply a doctrinaire would be a false description; for the pure doctrinaire rejoices always in an internal contentment, and Albert was very far from doing that. There was something that he wanted and that he could never get. What was it? Some absolute, some ineffable sympathy? Some extraordinary, some sublime success? Possibly, it was a mixture of both. To dominate and to be understood! To conquer, by the same triumphant influence, the submission and the appreciation of men—that would be worth while indeed! But, to such imaginations, he saw too clearly how faint were

the responses of his actual environment. Who was there who appreciated him, really and truly? Who
could appreciate him in England?
And, if the gentle virtue of an inward excellence availed so little,
could he expect more from the hard
ways of skill and force? The terrible land of his exile loomed before
him a frigid, an impregnable mass.
Doubtless he had made some slight
impression: it was true that he had
gained the respect of his fellow
workers, that his probity, his industry, his exactitude, had been recognised, that he was a highly influential, an extremely important man.
But how far, how very far, was all
this from the goal of his ambitions!
How feeble and futile his efforts
seemed against the enormous coag-
ulation of dullness, of folly, of
slackness, of ignorance, of confusion that confronted him! He
might have the strength or the ingenuity to make some small change
for the better here or there—to re-
arrange some detail, to abolish some
anomaly, to insist upon some obvious reform; but the heart of the
appalling organism remained un-
touched. England lumbered on, impervious and self-satisfied, in her
old intolerable course. He threw
himself across the path of the monster with rigid purpose and set
teeth, but he was brushed aside.
Yes! even Palmerston was still un-
conquered—was still there to afflict
him with his jauntiness, his mud-
dle-headedness, his utter lack of
principle. It was too much. Neither

nature nor the Baron had given
him a sanguine spirit; the seeds of
pessimism, once lodged within him,
flourished in a propitious soil. He

> questioned things, and did not find
> One that would answer to his mind;
> And all the world appeared unkind.

He believed that he was a failure
and he began to despair.

Yet Stockmar had told him that
he must 'never relax,' and he never
would. He would go on, working
to the utmost and striving for the
highest, to the bitter end. His industry grew almost maniacal. Earlier and earlier was the green lamp
lighted; more vast grew the correspondence; more searching the examination of the newspapers; the
interminable memoranda more
punctilious, analytical, and precise.
His very recreations became duties.
He enjoyed himself by time-table,
went deer-stalking with meticulous
gusto, and made puns at lunch—it
was the right thing to do. The
mechanism worked with astonishing efficiency, but it never rested
and it was never oiled. In dry exactitude the innumerable cog-wheels
perpetually revolved. No, whatever
happened, the Prince would not relax; he had absorbed the doctrines
of Stockmar too thoroughly. He
knew what was right, and, at all
costs, he would pursue it. That was
certain. But alas! in this our life
what are the certainties? 'In nothing be over-zealous!' says an old
Greek. 'The due measure in all the
works of man is best. For often one

who zealously pushes towards some excellence, though he be pursuing a gain, is really being led utterly astray by the will of some Power, which makes those things that are evil seem to him good, and those things seem to him evil that are for his advantage.' Surely, both the Prince and the Baron might have learnt something from the frigid wisdom of Theognis.[1]

Victoria noticed that her husband sometimes seemed to be depressed and overworked. She tried to cheer him up. Realising uneasily that he was still regarded as a foreigner, she hoped that by conferring upon him the title of Prince Consort (1857) she would improve his position in the country. 'The Queen has a right to claim that her husband should be an Englishman,' she wrote. But unfortunately, in spite of the Royal Letters Patent, Albert remained as foreign as before; and as the years passed his dejection deepened. She worked with him, she watched over him, she walked with him through the woods at Osborne, while he whistled to the nightingales, as he had whistled once at Rosenau so long ago. When his birthday came round, she took the greatest pains to choose him presents that he would really like. In 1858, when he was thirty-nine, she gave him 'a picture of Beatrice, life-size, in oil, by Horsley, a complete collection of photographic

views of Gotha and the country round, which I had taken by Bedford, and a paper-weight of Balmoral granite and deers' teeth, designed by Vicky.' Albert was of course delighted, and his merriment at the family gathering was more pronounced than ever: and yet . . . what was there that was wrong?

No doubt it was his health. He was wearing himself out in the service of the country; and certainly his constitution, as Stockmar had perceived from the first, was ill-adapted to meet a serious strain. He was easily upset; he constantly suffered from minor ailments. His appearance in itself was enough to indicate the infirmity of his physical powers. The handsome youth of twenty years since with the flashing eyes and the soft complexion had grown into a sallow, tired-looking man, whose body, in its stoop and its loose fleshiness, betrayed the sedentary labourer, and whose head was quite bald on the top. Unkind critics, who had once compared Albert to an operatic tenor, might have remarked that there was something of the butler about him now. Beside Victoria, he presented a painful contrast. She, too, was stout, but it was with the plumpness of a vigorous matron; and an eager vitality was everywhere visible—in her energetic bearing, her protruding, enquiring glances, her small, fat, capable, and commanding hands. If only, by some sympathetic magic, she could have conveyed into that portly, flabby figure, that

[1] Theognis: a Greek poet of the sixth century, B.C. Elegies ascribed to him express a reliance on political conservatism and practicality.

desiccated and discouraged brain, a measure of the stamina and the self-assurance which were so pre-eminently hers!

But suddenly she was reminded that there were other perils besides those of ill-health. During a visit to Coburg in 1860, the Prince was very nearly killed in a carriage accident. He escaped with a few cuts and bruises; but Victoria's alarm was extreme, though she concealed it. 'It is when the Queen feels most deeply,' she wrote afterwards, 'that she always appears calmest, and she could not and dared not allow herself to speak of what might have been, or even to admit to herself (and she cannot and dare not now) the entire danger, for her head would turn!' Her agitation, in fact, was only surpassed by her thankfulness to God. She felt, she said, that she could not rest 'without doing something to mark permanently her feelings,' and she decided that she would endow a charity in Coburg. '£1,000, or even £2,000, given either at once, or in instalments yearly, would not, in the Queen's opinion, be too much.' Eventually, the smaller sum having been fixed upon, it was invested in a trust, called the 'Victoria-Stift,' in the name of the Burgomaster and chief clergyman of Coburg, who were directed to distribute the interest yearly among a certain number of young men and women of exemplary character belonging to the humbler ranks of life.

Shortly afterwards the Queen underwent, for the first time in her life, the actual experience of close personal loss. Early in 1861 the Duchess of Kent was taken seriously ill, and in March she died. The event overwhelmed Victoria. With a morbid intensity, she filled her diary for pages with minute descriptions of her mother's last hours, her dissolution, and her corpse, interspersed with vehement apostrophes, and the agitated outpourings of emotional reflection. In the grief of the present the disagreements of the past were totally forgotten. It was the horror and the mystery of Death—Death, present and actual —that seized upon the imagination of the Queen. Her whole being, so instinct with vitality, recoiled in agony from the grim spectacle of the triumph of that awful power. Her own mother, with whom she had lived so closely and so long that she had become a part almost of her existence, had fallen into nothingness before her very eyes! She tried to forget, but she could not. Her lamentations continued with a strange abundance, a strange persistency. It was almost as if, by some mysterious and unconscious precognition, she realised that for her, in an especial manner, that grisly Majesty had a dreadful dart in store.

For indeed, before the year was out, a far more terrible blow was to fall upon her. Albert, who had for long been suffering from sleeplessness, went, on a cold and drenching day towards the end of November, to inspect the buildings for the new Military Academy at Sandhurst. On his return, it was clear that the fatigue and exposure to which he had been subjected had seriously affected his health. He was attacked by rheumatism, his sleeplessness continued, and he complained that he felt thoroughly unwell. Three days later a painful duty obliged him to visit Cambridge. The Prince of Wales, who had been placed at that University in the previous year, was behaving in such a manner that a parental visit and a parental admonition had become necessary. The disappointed father, suffering in mind and body, carried through his task; but, on his return journey to Windsor, he caught a fatal chill. During the next week he gradually grew weaker and more miserable. Yet, depressed and enfeebled as he was, he continued to work. It so happened that at that very moment a grave diplomatic crisis had arisen. Civil war had broken out in America, and it seemed as if England, owing to a violent quarrel with the Northern States, was upon the point of being drawn into the conflict. A severe despatch by Lord John Russell was submitted to the Queen; and the Prince perceived, that if it was sent off unaltered, war would be the almost inevitable consequence. At seven o'clock on the morning of December 1, he rose from his bed, and with a quavering hand wrote a series of suggestions for the alteration of the draft, by which its language might be softened, and a way left open for a peaceful solution of the question. These changes were accepted by the Government, and war was averted. It was the Prince's last memorandum.

He had always declared that he viewed the prospect of death with equanimity. 'I do not cling to life,' he had once said to Victoria. 'You do; but I set no store by it.' And then he had added: 'I am sure, if I had a severe illness, I should give up at once, I should not struggle for life. I have no tenacity of life.' He had judged correctly. Before he had been ill many days, he told a friend that he was convinced he would not recover. He sank and sank. Nevertheless, if his case had been properly understood and skilfully treated from the first, he might conceivably have been saved; but the doctors failed to diagnose his symptoms; and it is noteworthy that his principal physician was Sir James Clark. When it was suggested that other advice should be taken, Sir James pooh-poohed the idea: 'there was no cause for alarm,' he said. But the strange illness grew worse. At last, after a letter of fierce remonstrance from Palmerston, Dr. Watson was sent for; and Dr. Watson saw at once that he had come too late. The Prince was in the grip of typhoid fever. 'I think that everything so far is satisfactory,' said Sir James Clark.

The restlessness and the acute suffering of the earlier days gave place to a settled torpor and an ever-deepening gloom. Once the failing patient asked for music—'a fine chorale at a distance'; and a piano having been placed in the adjoining room, Princess Alice played on it some of Luther's hymns, after which the Prince repeated 'The Rock of Ages.' Sometimes his mind wandered; sometimes the distant past came rushing upon him; he heard the birds in the early morning, and was at Rosenau again, a boy. Or Victoria would come and read to him *Peveril of the Peak,* and he showed that he could follow the story, and then she would bend over him, and he would murmur *'liebes Frauchen'* [1] and *'gutes Weibchen,'* [2] stroking her cheek. Her distress and her agitation were great, but she was not seriously frightened. Buoyed up by her own abundant energies, she would not believe that Albert might prove unequal to the strain. She refused to face such a hideous possibility. She declined to see Dr. Watson. Why should she? Had not Sir James Clark assured her that all would be well? Only two days before the end, which was seen now to be almost inevitable by everyone about her, she wrote, full of apparent confidence, to the King of the Belgians: 'I do not sit up with him at night,' she said, 'as I could be of no use; and there is nothing to cause alarm.' The Princess Alice tried to tell her the truth, but her hopefulness would not be daunted. On the morning of December 14, Albert, just as she had expected, seemed to be better; perhaps the crisis was over. But in the course of the day there was a serious relapse. Then at last she allowed herself to see that she was standing on the edge of an appalling gulf. The whole family was summoned, and, one after another, the children took a silent farewell of their father. 'It was a terrible moment,' Victoria wrote in her diary, 'but, thank God! I was able to command myself, and to be perfectly calm, and remained sitting by his side.' He murmured something, but she could not hear what it was; she thought he was speaking in French. Then all at once he began to arrange his hair, 'just as he used to do when well and he was dressing.' *'Es ist kleines Frauchen,'* [3] she whispered to him; and he seemed to understand. For a moment, towards the evening, she went into another room, but was immediately called back; she saw at a glance that a ghastly change had taken place. As she knelt by the bed, he breathed deeply, breathed gently, breathed at last no more. His features became perfectly rigid; she shrieked one long wild shriek that rang through the terror-stricken castle—and understood that she had lost him for ever.

[3] *Es ist kleines Frauchen:* It is your little wife.

[1] *liebes Frauchen:* dear little woman.
[2] *gutes Weibchen:* good little wife.

✖ Chapter 7

Widowhood

I

The death of the Prince Consort was the central turning-point in the history of Queen Victoria. She herself felt that her true life had ceased with her husband's, and that the remainder of her days upon earth was of a twilight nature—an epilogue to a drama that was done. Nor is it possible that her biographer should escape a similar impression. For him, too, there is a darkness over the latter half of that long career. The first forty-two years of the Queen's life are illuminated by a great and varied quantity of authentic information. With Albert's death a veil descends. Only occasionally, at fitful and disconnected intervals, does it lift for a moment or two; a few main outlines, a few remarkable details may be discerned; the rest is all conjecture and ambiguity. Thus, though the Queen survived her great bereavement for almost as many years as she had lived before it, the chronicle of those years can bear no proportion to the tale of her earlier life. We must be content in our ignorance with a brief and summary relation.

The sudden removal of the Prince was not merely a matter of overwhelming personal concern to Victoria; it was an event of national, of European importance. He was only forty-two, and in the ordinary course of nature he might have been expected to live at least thirty years longer. Had he done so it can hardly be doubted that the whole development of the English polity would have been changed. Already at the time of his death he filled a unique place in English public life; already among the inner circle of politicians he was accepted as a necessary and useful part of the mechanism of the State. Lord Clarendon, for instance, spoke of his death as 'a national calamity of far greater importance than the public dream of,' and lamented the loss of his 'sagacity and foresight,' which, he declared, would have been 'more than ever valuable' in the event of an American war. And, as time went on, the Prince's influence must have enormously increased. For, in addition to his intellectual and moral qualities, he enjoyed, by virtue of his position, one supreme advantage which every other holder of high office in the country was without: he was permanent. Politicians came and went, but the Prince was perpetually installed at the centre of affairs. Who can doubt that, towards the end of the century, such a man, grown grey in the service of the nation, virtuous, intelligent, and with the unexampled experience of a whole life-time of government, would have acquired an extraordinary prestige? If, in his youth, he had been able to pit the Crown against the mighty Palmerston and to come off with equal honours from the contest, of what might he not have been capable in his old age? What Minister, however able, however popular, could have withstood the wisdom, the irreproachability, the vast prescriptive authority, of the venerable Prince? It is easy to imagine how, under such a ruler, an attempt might have been made to convert England into a State as exactly organised, as elaborately trained, as efficiently equipped, and as autocratically controlled, as Prussia herself. Then perhaps, eventually, under some powerful leader— a Gladstone or a Bright—the democratic forces in the country might have rallied together, and a struggle might have followed in which the Monarchy would have been shaken to its foundations. Or, on the other hand, Disraeli's hypothetical prophecy might have come true. 'With Prince Albert,' he said, 'we have buried our sovereign. This German Prince has governed England for twenty-one years with a wisdom and energy such as none of our kings have ever shown. . . . If he had outlived some of our "old stagers" he would have given us the blessings of absolute government.'

The English Constitution—that indescribable entity—is a living thing, growing with the growth of men, and assuming ever-varying forms in accordance with the subtle and complex laws of human character. It is the child of wisdom and chance. The wise men of 1688 moulded it into the shape we know; but the chance that George I could not speak English gave it one of its essential peculiarities—the system of a Cabinet independent of the Crown and subordinate to the Prime Minister. The wisdom of Lord Grey saved it from petrification and destruction, and set it upon the path of Democracy. Then chance intervened once more; a female sovereign happened to marry an able and pertinacious man; and it seemed likely that an element which had been quiescent within it for years—the element of irresponsible administrative power—was about to become its predominant characteristic and to change completely the direction of its growth. But what chance gave chance took away. The Consort perished in his prime; and the English Constitution, dropping the dead limb with hardly a tremor, continued its mysterious life as if he had never been.

One human being, and one alone, felt the full force of what had happened. The Baron, by his fireside at Coburg, suddenly saw the tremendous fabric of his creation crash down into sheer and irremediable ruin. Albert was gone, and he had lived in vain. Even his blackest hypochondria had never envisioned quite so miserable a catastrophe. Victoria wrote to him, visited him, tried to console him by declaring with passionate conviction that she would carry on her husband's work. He smiled a sad smile and looked into the fire. Then he murmured that he was going where Albert was—that he would not be long.

He shrank into himself. His children clustered round him and did their best to comfort him, but it was useless: the Baron's heart was broken. He lingered for eighteen months, and then, with his pupil, explored the shadow and the dust.

II

With appalling suddenness Victoria had exchanged the serene radiance of happiness for the utter darkness of woe. In the first dreadful moments those about her had feared that she might lose her reason, but the iron strain within her held firm, and in the intervals between the intense paroxysms of grief it was observed that the Queen was calm. She remembered, too, that Albert had always disapproved of exaggerated manifestations of feeling, and her one remaining desire was to do nothing but what he would have wished. Yet there were moments when her royal anguish would brook no restraint. One day she sent for the Duchess of Sutherland, and, leading her to the Prince's room, fell prostrate before his clothes in a flood of weeping, while she adjured the Duchess to tell her whether the beauty of Albert's character had ever been surpassed. At other times a feeling akin to indignation swept over her. 'The poor fatherless baby of eight months,' she wrote to the King of the Belgians, 'is now the utterly heartbroken and crushed widow of forty-two! My *life* as a *happy* one is *ended!* The world is gone for *me!* . . . Oh! to be cut off in the prime of life—to see our pure, happy, quiet, domestic life, which *alone* enabled me to bear my *much* disliked position, CUT OFF at forty-two—when I *had* hoped with such instinctive certainty that God never *would* part us, and would let us grow old together (though *he* always talked of the shortness of life) —is *too awful,* too cruel!' The tone of outraged Majesty seems to be discernible. Did she wonder in her heart of hearts how the Deity could have dared?

But all other emotions gave way before her overmastering determination to continue, absolutely unchanged, and for the rest of her life on earth, her reverence, her obedience, her idolatry. 'I am anxious to repeat *one* thing,' she told her uncle, 'and *that one* is *my firm* resolve, *my irrevocable decision, viz.,* that *his* wishes—*his* plans—about everything, *his* views about *every* thing are to be *my law!* And *no human power* will make me swerve from *what he* decided and wished.' She grew fierce, she grew furious, at the thought of any possible intrusion between her and her desire. Her uncle was coming to visit her, and it flashed upon her that *he* might try to interfere with her and seek to 'rule the roost' as of old. She would give him a hint. 'I am *also determined,'* she wrote, 'that *no one* person—may *he* be ever so good, ever so devoted among my servants—is to lead or guide or dictate *to me.* I know *how he* would disapprove it . . . Though miserably weak and utterly shattered, my spirit rises when I think *any* wish or plan of his is to be touched or changed, or I am to be *made to do* anything.' She ended her letter in grief and affection. She was, she said, his 'ever wretched but devoted child, Victoria R.' And then she looked at the date: it was the 24th of December. An agonising pang assailed her, and she dashed down a postscript.—'What a Xmas! I won't think of it.'

At first, in the tumult of her distresses, she declared that she could not see her Ministers, and the Princess Alice, assisted by Sir Charles Phipps, the keeper of the Privy Purse, performed, to the best of her ability, the functions of an intermediary. After a few weeks, however, the Cabinet, through Lord John Russell, ventured to warn the Queen that this could not continue. She realised that they were right: Albert would have agreed with them; and so she sent for the Prime Minister. But when Lord Palmerston arrived at Osborne, in the pink of health, brisk, with his whiskers freshly dyed, and dressed in a brown overcoat, light grey trousers, green gloves, and blue studs, he did not create a very good impression.

Nevertheless, she had grown attached to her old enemy, and the thought of a political change filled her with agitated apprehensions. The Government, she knew, might fall at any moment; she felt she could not face such an eventuality; and therefore, six months after the death of the Prince, she took the unprecedented step of sending a private message to Lord Derby, the leader of the Opposition, to tell him that she was not in a fit state of mind or body to undergo the anxiety of a change of Government, and that if he turned the present Ministers out of office it would be at the risk of sacrificing her life— or her reason. When this message reached Lord Derby he was considerably surprised. 'Dear me!' was his cynical comment. 'I didn't think she was so fond of them as *that.*'

Though the violence of her perturbations gradually subsided, her cheerfulness did not return. For months, for years, she continued in settled gloom. Her life became one of almost complete seclusion. Arrayed in thickest *crêpe,* she passed dolefully from Windsor to Osborne, from Osborne to Balmoral. Rarely visiting the capital, refusing to take any part in the ceremonies of state, shutting herself off from the slightest intercourse with society, she became almost as unknown to her subjects as some potentate of the East. They might murmur, but they did not understand. What had she to do with empty shows and vain enjoyments? No! She was absorbed by very different preoccupations. She was the devoted guardian of a sacred trust. Her place was in the inmost shrine of the house of mourning—where she alone had the right to enter, where she could feel the effluence of a mysterious presence, and interpret, however faintly and feebly, the promptings of a still living soul. That, and that only was her glorious, her terrible duty. For terrible indeed it was. As the years passed her depression seemed to deepen and her loneliness to grow more intense. 'I am on a dreary sad pinnacle of solitary grandeur,' she said. Again and again she felt that she could bear her situation no longer—that she would sink under the strain. And then, instantly, that Voice spoke: and she braced herself once more to perform, with minute conscientiousness, her grim and holy task.

Above all else, what she had to do was to make her own the master-impulse of Albert's life—she must work, as he had worked, in the service of the country. That vast burden of toil which he had taken upon his shoulders it was now for her to bear. She assumed the gigantic load; and naturally she staggered under it. While he had lived, she had worked, indeed, with regularity and conscientiousness; but it was work made easy, made delicious, by his care, his forethought, his advice, and his infallibility. The mere sound of his voice, asking her to sign a paper, had thrilled her; in such a presence she could have laboured gladly for ever. But now there was a hideous change. Now there were no neat piles and docketings under the green lamp; now there were no simple explanations of difficult matters; now there was nobody to tell her what was right and what was wrong. She had her secretaries, no doubt: there were Sir Charles Phipps, and General Grey, and Sir Thomas Biddulph; and they did their best. But they were mere subordinates: the whole weight of initiative and responsibility rested upon her alone. For so it had to be. 'I am *determined*'—had she not declared it?—'that *no one* person is to lead or guide or dictate to *me*'; anything else would be a betrayal of her trust. She would follow the Prince in all things. He had refused to delegate authority; he had examined into every detail with his own eyes; he had made it a rule never to sign a paper without having first, not merely read it, but made notes on it too. She would do the same. She sat from morning till night surrounded by huge heaps of despatch-boxes, reading and writing at her desk—at her desk, alas! which stood alone now in the room.

Within two years of Albert's death a violent disturbance in foreign politics put Victoria's faithfulness to a crucial test. The fearful Schleswig-Holstein dispute, which had been smouldering for more than a decade, showed signs of bursting out into conflagration. The complexity of the questions at issue was indescribable. 'Only three people,' said Palmerston, 'have ever really understood the Schleswig-Holstein business—the Prince Consort, who is dead—a German professor, who has gone mad—and I, who have forgotten all about it.' But, though the Prince might be dead, had he not left a vicegerent behind him? Victoria threw herself into the seething embroilment with the vigour of inspiration. She devoted hours daily to the study of the affair in all its windings; but she had a clue through the labryrinth: whenever the question had been discussed, Albert, she recollected it perfectly, had always taken the side of Prussia. Her course was clear. She became an ardent champion of the Prussian point of view. It was a legacy from the Prince, she said. She did not realise that the Prussia of the Prince's day was dead, and that a new Prussia, the Prussia of Bismarck, was born. Perhaps Palmerston, with his queer prescience, instinctively apprehended the new danger; at any rate, he and Lord John were agreed upon the necessity of supporting Denmark against Prussia's claims. But opinion was sharply divided, not only in the country but in the Cabinet. For eighteen months the controversy raged; while the Queen, with persistent vehemence, opposed the Prime Minister and the Foreign Secretary. When at last the final crisis arose—when it seemed possible that England would join forces with Denmark in a war against Prussia—Victoria's agitation grew febrile in its intensity. Towards her German relatives she preserved a discreet appearance of impartiality; but she poured out upon her Ministers a flood of appeals, protests, and expostulations. She invoked the sacred cause of Peace. 'The only chance of preserving peace for Europe,' she wrote, 'is by not assisting Denmark, who has brought this entirely upon herself. . . . The Queen suffers much, and her nerves are more and more totally shattered. . . . But though all this anxiety is wearing her out, it will not shake her firm purpose of resisting any attempt to involve this country in a mad and useless combat.' She was, she declared, 'prepared to make a stand,' even if the resignation of the Foreign Secretary should follow. 'The Queen,' she told Lord Granville, 'is completely exhausted by the anxiety and suspense, and misses her beloved husband's help, advice, support, and love in an overwhelming manner.' She was so worn out by her efforts for peace that she could 'hardly hold up her head or hold her pen.' England did not go to war, and Denmark was left to her fate; but how far the attitude of the Queen contributed to this result it is impossible, with our present knowledge, to say. On the whole, however, it seems probable that the determining factor in the situation was the powerful peace party in the Cabinet rather than the imperious and pathetic pressure of Victoria.

It is, at any rate, certain that the Queen's enthusiasm for the sacred cause of peace was short-lived. With a few months her mind had completely altered. Her eyes were opened to the true nature of Prussia, whose designs upon Austria were about to culminate in the Seven Weeks' War. Veering precipitately from one extreme to the other, she now urged her Ministers to interfere by force of arms in support of Austria. But she urged in vain.

Her political activity, no more than her social seclusion, was approved by the public. As the years passed, and the royal mourning remained as unrelieved as ever, the animadversions grew more general and more severe. It was observed that the Queen's protracted privacy not only cast a gloom over high society, not only deprived the populace of its pageantry, but also exercised a highly deleterious effect upon the dressmaking, millinery, and hosiery trades. This latter consideration carried great weight. At last, early in 1864, the rumour spread that Her Majesty was about to go out of mourning, and there was much rejoicing in the newspapers; but unfortunately it turned out that the rumour was quite without foundation. Victoria, with her own hand, wrote a letter to *The Times* to say so. 'This idea,' she declared, 'cannot be too explicitly contradicted. The Queen,' the letter continued, 'heartily appreciates the desire of her subjects to see her, and whatever she *can* do to gratify them in this loyal and affectionate wish, she *will* do. . . . But there are other and higher duties than those of mere representation which are now thrown upon the Queen, alone and unassisted—duties which she cannot neglect without injury to the public service, which weigh unceasingly upon her, overwhelming her with work and anxiety.' The justification might have been considered more cogent had it not been known that those 'other and higher duties' emphasised by the Queen consisted for the most part of an attempt to counteract the foreign policy of Lord Palmerston and Lord John Russell. A large section —perhaps a majority—of the nation were violent partisans of Denmark in the Schleswig-Holstein quarrel; and Victoria's support of Prussia was widely denounced. A wave of unpopularity, which reminded old observers of the period preceding the Queen's marriage more than twenty-five years before, was beginning to rise. The press was rude; Lord Ellenborough attacked the Queen in the House of Lords; there were curious whispers in high quarters that she had had thoughts of abdicating—whispers followed by regrets that she had not done so. Victoria, outraged and injured, felt that she was misunderstood. She was profoundly unhappy. After Lord Ellenborough's speech, General Grey declared that he 'had never seen the Queen so completely upset.' 'Oh, how fearful it is,' she herself wrote to Lord Granville, 'to be suspected—uncheered—unguided and unadvised —and how alone the poor Queen feels!' Nevertheless, suffer as she might, she was as resolute as ever; she would not move by a hair's breadth from the course that a supreme obligation marked out for her; she would be faithful to the end.

And so, when Schleswig-Holstein was forgotten, and even the image of the Prince had begun to grow dim in the fickle memories of men, the solitary watcher remained immutably concentrated at her peculiar task. The world's hostility, steadily increasing, was confronted and outfaced by the impenetrable weeds of Victoria. Would the world never understand? It was not mere sorrow that kept her so strangely sequestered; it was devotion, it was self-immolation; it was the laborious legacy of love. Unceasingly the pen moved over the black-edged paper. The flesh might be weak, but that vast burden must be borne. And fortunately, if the world would not understand, there were faithful friends who did. There was Lord Granville, and there was kind Mr. Theodore Martin. Perhaps Mr. Martin, who was so clever, would find means to make people realise the facts. She would send him a letter, pointing out her arduous labours and the difficulties under which she struggled, and then he might write an article for one of the magazines. It is not, she told him in 1863, 'the Queen's *sorrow* that keeps her secluded. . . . It is her *overwhelming work* and her health, which is greatly shaken by her sorrow, and the totally overwhelming amount of work and responsibility —work which she feels really wears her out. Alice Helps was wonderfully struck at the Queen's room; and if Mrs. Martin will look at it, she can tell Mr. Martin what surrounds her. From the hours she gets out of bed till she gets into it again there is work, work, work,—letterboxes, questions, &c., which are dreadfully exhausting—and if she had not comparative rest and quiet in the evening she would most likely not be *alive*. Her brain is constantly overtaxed.' It was too true.

III

To carry on Albert's work—that was her first duty; but there was another, second only to that, and yet nearer, if possible, to her heart —to impress the true nature of his genius and character upon the minds of her subjects. She realised that during his life he had not been properly appreciated; the full extent of his powers, the supreme quality of his goodness, had been necessarily concealed; but death had removed the need of barriers, and now her husband, in his magnificent entirety, should stand revealed to all. She set to work methodically. She directed Sir Arthur Helps to bring out a collection of the Prince's speeches and addresses, and the weighty tome appeared in 1862. Then she commanded General Grey to write an account of the Prince's early years—from his birth to his marriage; she herself laid down the design of the book, contributed a number of confidential documents, and added numerous notes; General Grey obeyed, and the work was completed in 1866. But the principal part of the story was still untold, and Mr. Martin was forthwith instructed to write a complete biography of the Prince Consort. Mr. Martin laboured for fourteen years. The mass of material with which he had to deal was almost incredible, but he was extremely industrious, and he enjoyed throughout the gracious assistance of Her Majesty. The first bulky volume was published in 1874; four others slowly followed; so that it was not until 1880 that the monumental work was finished.

Mr. Martin was rewarded by a knighthood; and yet it was sadly evident that neither Sir Theodore nor his predecessors had achieved the purpose which the Queen had in view. Perhaps she was unfortunate in her coadjutors, but, in reality, the responsibility for the failure must lie with Victoria herself. Sir Theodore and the others faithfully carried out the task which she had set them—faithfully put before the public the very image of Albert that filled her own mind. The fatal drawback was that the public did not find that image attractive. Victoria's emotional nature, far more remarkable for vigour than for subtlety, rejecting utterly the qualifications which perspicuity, or humour, might suggest, could be satisfied with nothing but the absolute and the categorical. When she disliked, she did so with an unequivocal emphasis which swept the object of her repugnance at once and finally outside the pale of consideration; and her feelings of affection were equally unmitigated. In the case of Albert her passion for superlatives reached its height. To have conceived of him as anything short of perfect—perfect in virtue, in wisdom, in beauty, in all the glories and graces of man—would have been an unthinkable blasphemy: perfect he was, and perfect

he must be shown to have been. And so, Sir Arthur, Sir Theodore, and the General painted him. In the circumstances, and under such supervision, to have done anything else would have required talents considerably more distinguished than any that those gentlemen possessed. But that was not all. By a curious mischance Victoria was also able to press into her service another writer, the distinction of whose talents was this time beyond a doubt. The Poet Laureate,[1] adopting, either from complaisance or conviction, the tone of his sovereign, joined in the chorus, and endowed the royal formula with the magical resonance of verse. This settled the matter. Henceforward it was impossible to forget that Albert had worn the white flower of a blameless life.

The result was doubly unfortunate. Victoria, disappointed and chagrined, bore a grudge against her people for their refusal, in spite of all her efforts, to rate her husband at his true worth. She did not understand that the picture of an embodied perfection is distasteful to the majority of mankind. The cause of this is not so much an envy of the perfect being as a suspicion that he must be inhuman; and thus it happened that the public, when it saw displayed for its admiration a figure resembling the sugary hero of a moral story-book rather than a fellow man of flesh and blood,

[1] The Poet Laureate: Alfred, Lord Tennyson (1809–1892).

turned away with a shrug, a smile, and a flippant ejaculation. But in this the public was the loser as well as Victoria. For in truth Albert was a far more interesting personage than the public dreamed. By a curious irony an impeccable waxwork had been fixed by the Queen's love in the popular imagination, while the creature whom it represented—the real creature, so full of energy and stress and torment, so mysterious and so unhappy, and so fallible and so very human—had altogether disappeared.

IV

Words and books may be ambiguous memorials; but who can misinterpret the visible solidity of bronze and stone? At Frogmore, near Windsor, where her mother was buried, Victoria constructed, at the cost of £200,000, a vast and elaborate mausoleum for herself and her husband. But that was a private and domestic monument, and the Queen desired that wherever her subjects might be gathered together they should be reminded of the Prince. Her desire was gratified; all over the country—at Aberdeen, at Perth, and at Wolverhampton—statues of the Prince were erected; and the Queen, making an exception to her rule of retirement, unveiled them herself. Nor did the capital lag behind. A month after the Prince's death a meeting was called together at the Mansion House to discuss schemes for honouring his memory. Opinions, however, were divided upon the sub-ject. Was a statue or an institution to be preferred? Meanwhile a subscription was opened; an influential committee was appointed, and the Queen was consulted as to her wishes in the matter. Her Majesty replied that she would prefer a granite obelisk, with sculptures at the base, to an institution. But the committee hesitated: an obelisk, to be worthy of the name, must clearly be a monolith; and where was the quarry in England capable of furnishing a granite block of the required size? It was true that there was granite in Russian Finland; but the committee were advised that it was not adapted to resist exposure to the open air. On the whole, therefore, they suggested that a Memorial Hall should be erected, together with a statue of the Prince. Her Majesty assented; but then another difficulty arose. It was found that not more than £60,000 had been subscribed—a sum insufficient to defray the double expense. The Hall, therefore, was abandoned; a statue alone was to be erected; and certain eminent architects were asked to prepare designs. Eventually the committee had at their disposal a total sum of £120,000, since the public subscribed another £10,000, while £50,000 was voted by Parliament. Some years later a joint stock company was formed and built, as a private speculation, the Albert Hall.

The architect whose design was selected, both by the committee and by the Queen, was Mr. Gilbert Scott, whose industry, conscientiousness, and genuine piety had brought him to the head of his profession. His lifelong zeal for the Gothic style having given him a special prominence, his handiwork was strikingly visible, not only in a multitude of original buildings, but in most of the cathedrals of England. Protests, indeed, were occasionally raised against his renovations; but Mr. Scott replied with such vigour and unction in articles and pamphlets that not a Dean was unconvinced, and he was permitted to continue his labours without interruption. On one occasion, however, his devotion to Gothic had placed him in an unpleasant situation. The Government offices in Whitehall were to be rebuilt; Mr. Scott competed, and his designs were successful. Naturally, they were in the Gothic style, combining 'a certain squareness and horizontality of outline' with pillar-mullions, gables, high-pitched roofs, and dormers; and the drawings, as Mr. Scott himself observed, 'were, perhaps, the best ever sent in to a competition, or nearly so.' After the usual difficulties and delays the work was at last to be put in hand, when there was a change of Government and Lord Palmerston became Prime Minister. Lord Palmerston at once sent for Mr. Scott. 'Well, Mr. Scott,' he said, in his jaunty way, 'I can't have anything to do with this Gothic style. I must insist on your making a design in the Italian manner, which I am sure you can do very cleverly.' Mr. Scott was appalled; the style of the Italian renaissance was not only unsightly, it was positively immoral, and he sternly refused to have anything to do with it. Thereupon Lord Palmerston assumed a fatherly tone. 'Quite true; a Gothic architect can't be expected to put up a Classical building; I must find someone else.' This was intolerable, and Mr. Scott, on his return home, addressed to the Prime Minister a strongly-worded letter, in which he dwelt upon his position as an architect, upon his having won two European competitions, his being an A.R.A., a gold medallist of the Institute, and a lecturer on architecture at the Royal Academy; but it was useless—Lord Palmerston did not even reply. It then occurred to Mr. Scott that, by a judicious mixture, he might, while preserving the essential character of the Gothic, produce a design which would give a superficial impression of the Classical style. He did so, but no effect was produced upon Lord Palmerston. The new design, he said, was 'neither one thing nor 'tother—a regular mongrel affair—and he would have nothing to do with it either.' After that Mr. Scott found it necessary to recruit for two months at Scarborough, 'with a course of quinine.' He recovered his tone at last, but only at the cost of his convictions. For the sake of his family he felt that it was his unfortunate duty to obey the Prime Minister; and, shuddering with horror, he constructed the Government offices in a strictly Renaissance style.

Shortly afterwards Mr. Scott found some consolation in building the St. Pancras Hotel in a style of his own.

And now another and yet more satisfactory task was his. 'My idea in designing the Memorial,' he wrote, 'was to erect a kind of ciborium [1] to protect a statue of the Prince; and its special characteristic was that the ciborium was designed in some degree on the principles of the ancient shrines. These shrines were models of imaginary buildings, such as had never in reality been erected; and my idea was to realise one of these imaginary structures with its precious materials, its inlaying, its enamels, &c. &c.' His idea was particularly appropriate since it chanced that a similar conception, though in the reverse order of magnitude, had occurred to the Prince himself, who had designed and executed several silver cruet-stands upon the same model. At the Queen's request a site was chosen in Kensington Gardens as near as possible to that of the Great Exhibition; and in May, 1864, the first sod was turned. The work was long, complicated, and difficult; a great number of workmen were employed, besides several subsidiary sculptors and metalworkers under Mr. Scott's direction, while at every stage sketches and models were submitted to Her Majesty, who criticised all the details with minute care, and constantly suggested improvements. The frieze, which encircled the base of the monument, was in itself a very serious piece of work. 'This,' said Mr. Scott, 'taken as a whole, is perhaps one of the most laborious works of sculpture ever undertaken, consisting, as it does, of a continuous range of figure-sculpture of the most elaborate description, in the highest *alto-relievo* [2] of life-size, of more than 200 feet in length, containing about 170 figures, and executed in the hardest marble which could be procured.' After three years of toil the memorial was still far from completion, and Mr. Scott thought it advisable to give a dinner to the workmen, 'as a substantial recognition of his appreciation of their skill and energy.' 'Two long tables,' we are told, 'constructed of scaffold planks, were arranged in the workshops, and covered with newspapers, for want of table-cloths. Upwards of eighty men sat down. Beef and mutton, plum pudding and cheese were supplied in abundance, and each man who desired it had three pints of beer, ginger-beer and lemonade being provided for the teetotalers, who formed a very considerable proportion. . . . Several toasts were given and many of the workmen spoke, almost all of them commencing by "Thanking God that they enjoyed good health"; some alluded to the temperance that prevailed amongst them, others observed how little swearing was ever heard, whilst all

---

[1] ciborium: a canopy or roof resting on four pillars.

[2] *alto-relievo*: sculpture in such high relief as to be partially detached from the background.

said how pleased and proud they were to be engaged on so great a work.'

Gradually the edifice approached completion. The one hundred and seventieth life-size figure in the frieze was chiselled, the granite pillars arose, the mosaics were inserted in the allegorical pediments, the four colossal statues representing the greater Christian virtues, the four other colossal statues representing the greater moral virtues, were hoisted into their positions, the eight bronzes representing the greater sciences—Astronomy, Chemistry, Geology, Geometry, Rhetoric, Medicine, Philosophy, and Physiology—were fixed on their glittering pinnacles, high in air. The statue of Physiology was particularly admired. 'On her left arm,' the official description informs us, 'she bears a new-born infant, as a representation of the development of the highest and most perfect of physiological forms; her hand points towards a microscope, the instrument which lends its assistance for the investigation of the minuter forms of animal and vegetable organism.' At last the gilded cross crowned the dwindling galaxies of superimposed angels, the four continents in white marble stood at the four corners of the base, and, seven years after its inception, in

July, 1872, the monument was thrown open to the public.

But four more years were to elapse before the central figure was ready to be placed under its starry canopy. It was designed by Mr. Foley, though in one particular the sculptor's freedom was restricted by Mr. Scott. 'I have chosen the sitting posture,' Mr. Scott said, 'as best conveying the idea of dignity befitting a royal personage.' Mr. Foley ably carried out the conception of his principal. 'In the attitude and expression,' he said, 'the aim has been, with the individuality of portraiture, to embody rank, character, and enlightenment, and to convey a sense of that responsive intelligence indicating an active, rather than a passive, interest in those pursuits of civilisation illustrated in the surrounding figures, groups, and relievos. . . . To identify the figure with one of the most memorable undertakings of the public life of the Prince—the International Exhibition of 1851—a catalogue of the works collected in that first gathering of the industry of all nations, is placed in the right hand.' The statue was of bronze gilt and weighed nearly ten tons. It was rightly supposed that the simple word 'Albert,' cast on the base, would be a sufficient means of identification.

✂ Chapter 8

Mr. Gladstone and
Lord Beaconsfield [1]

I

Lord Palmerston's laugh—a queer metallic 'Ha! ha! ha!' with reverberations in it from the days of Pitt and the Congress of Vienna —was heard no more in Piccadilly; Lord John Russell dwindled into senility; Lord Derby tottered from the stage. A new scene opened; and new protagonists—Mr. Gladstone and Mr. Disraeli—struggled together in the limelight. Victoria, from her post of vantage, watched these developments with that passionate and personal interest which she invariably imported into politics. Her prepossessions were of an unexpected kind. Mr. Gladstone had been the disciple of her revered Peel, and had won the approval of Albert; Mr. Disraeli had hounded Sir Robert to his fall with hideous virulence, and the Prince had pronounced that he 'had not one single element of a gentleman in his composition.' Yet she regarded Mr. Gladstone with a distrust and dislike which steadily deepened, while upon his rival she lavished an abundance of confidence, esteem, and affection such as Lord Melbourne himself had hardly known.

Her attitude towards the Tory Minister had suddenly changed when she found that he alone among public men had divined her feelings at Albert's death. Of the others she might have said 'they pity me and not my grief'; but Mr. Disraeli had understood; and all his condolences had taken the form of reverential eulogies of the departed. The Queen declared that he was 'the only person who appreciated the Prince.' She began to show him special favour; gave him and his wife two of the coveted seats in St. George's Chapel at the Prince of Wales's wedding, and invited him to stay a night at Windsor. When the grant for the Albert Memorial came before the House of Commons, Disraeli, as leader of the Opposition, eloquently supported the project. He was rewarded by a copy of the Prince's speeches, bound in white morocco, with an inscription in the royal hand. In his letter of thanks he 'ventured to touch upon a sacred theme,' and, in a strain which reechoed with masterly fidelity the sentiments of his correspondent, dwelt at length upon the absolute perfection of Albert. 'The Prince,' he said, 'is the only person whom Mr. Disraeli has ever known who realised the Ideal. None with whom he is acquainted have ever approached it. There was in him an union of the manly grace and sublime simplicity, of chivalry with the intellectual splendour of the Attic Academe. The only character in English history that would, in some

---

[1] Benjamin Disraeli became the first Earl of Beaconsfield in 1876.

respects, draw near to him is Sir Philip Sidney: the same high tone, the same universal accomplishments, the same blended tenderness and vigour, the same rare combination of romantic energy and classic repose.' As for his own acquaintance with the Prince, it had been, he said, 'one of the most satisfactory incidents of his life: full of refined and beautiful memories, and exercising, as he hopes, over his remaining existence, a soothing and exalting influence.' Victoria was much affected by 'the depth and delicacy of these touches,' and henceforward Disraeli's place in her affections was assured. When, in 1866, the Conservatives came into office, Disraeli's position as Chancellor of the Exchequer and leader of the House necessarily brought him into a closer relation with the Sovereign. Two years later Lord Derby resigned, and Victoria, with intense delight and peculiar graciousness, welcomed Disraeli as her First Minister.

But only for nine agitated months did he remain in power. The Ministry, in a minority in the Commons, was swept out of existence by a general election. Yet by the end of that short period the ties which bound together the Queen and her Premier had grown far stronger than ever before; the relationship between them was now no longer merely that between a grateful mistress and a devoted servant: they were friends. His official letters, in which the personal element had always been percep-

tible, developed into racy records of political news and social gossip, written, as Lord Clarendon said, 'in his best novel style.' Victoria was delighted; she had never, she declared, had such letters in her life, and had never before known *everything*. In return, she sent him, when the spring came, several bunches of flowers, picked by her own hands. He despatched to her a set of his novels, for which, she said, she was 'most grateful, and which she values much.' She herself had lately published her *Leaves from the Journal of Our Life in the Highlands,* and it was observed that the Prime Minister, in conversing with Her Majesty at this period, constantly used the words 'we authors, ma'am.' Upon political questions, she was his staunch supporter. 'Really there never was such conduct as that of the Opposition,' she wrote. And when the Government was defeated in the House, she was 'really shocked at the way in which the House of Commons go on; they really bring discredit on Constitutional Government.' She dreaded the prospect of a change; she feared that if the Liberals insisted upon disestablishing the Irish Church, her Coronation Oath might stand in the way. But a change there had to be, and Victoria vainly tried to console herself for the loss of her favourite Minister by bestowing a peerage upon Mrs. Disraeli.[1]

[1] Disraeli wanted to remain in the House of Commons at this time, so when

Mr. Gladstone was in his shirt-sleeves at Hawarden, cutting down a tree, when the royal message was brought to him. 'Very significant,' he remarked, when he had read the letter, and went on cutting down his tree. His secret thoughts on the occasion were more explicit, and were committed to his diary. 'The Almighty,' he wrote, 'seems to sustain and spare me for some purpose of His own, deeply unworthy as I know myself to be. Glory be to His name.'

The Queen, however, did not share her new Minister's view of the Almighty's intentions. She could not believe that there was any divine purpose to be detected in the programme of sweeping changes which Mr. Gladstone was determined to carry out. But what could she do? Mr. Gladstone, with his daemonic energy and his powerful majority in the House of Commons, was irresistible; and for five years (1869–74) Victoria found herself condemned to live in an agitating atmosphere of interminable reform—reform in the Irish Church and the Irish land system, reform in education, reform in parliamentary elections, reform in the organisation of the Army and the Navy, reform in the administration of justice. She disapproved, she struggled, she grew very angry; she felt that if Albert had been living things would never have happened so; but her protests and her

complaints were alike unavailing. The mere effort of grappling with the mass of documents which poured in upon her in an ever-growing flood was terribly exhausting. When the draft of the lengthy and intricate Irish Church Bill came before her, accompanied by an explanatory letter from Mr. Gladstone covering a dozen closely-written quarto pages, she almost despaired. She turned from the Bill to the explanation, and from the explanation back again to the Bill, and she could not decide which was the most confusing. But she had to do her duty: she had not only to read, but to make notes. At last she handed the whole heap of papers to Mr. Martin, who happened to be staying at Osborne, and requested him to make a précis of them. When he had done so, her disapproval of the measure became more marked than ever; but, such was the strength of the Government, she actually found herself obliged to urge moderation upon the Opposition, lest worse should ensue.

In the midst of this crisis, when the future of the Irish Church was hanging in the balance, Victoria's attention was drawn to another proposed reform. It was suggested that the sailors in the Navy should henceforward be allowed to wear beards. 'Has Mr. Childers ascertained anything on the subject of the beards?' the Queen wrote anxiously to the First Lord of the Admiralty. On the whole, Her Majesty was in favour of the change.

offered a peerage, he requested that it be given to his wife.

'Her own personal feeling,' she wrote, 'would be for the beards without the moustaches, as the latter have rather a soldierlike appearance; but then the object in view would not be obtained, viz. to prevent the necessity of shaving. Therefore it had better be as proposed, the entire beard, only it should be kept short and very clean.' After thinking over the question for another week, the Queen wrote a final letter. She wished, she said, 'to make one additional observation respecting the beards, viz. that on no account should moustaches be allowed without beards. That must be clearly understood.'

Changes in the Navy might be tolerated; to lay hands upon the Army was a more serious matter. From time immemorial there had been a particularly close connection between the Army and the Crown; and Albert had devoted even more time and attention to the details of military business than to the processes of fresco-painting or the planning of sanitary cottages for the deserving poor. But now there was to be a great alteration: Mr. Gladstone's fiat had gone forth, and the Commander-in-Chief was to be removed from his direct dependence upon the Sovereign, and made subordinate to Parliament and the Secretary of State for War. Of all the liberal reforms this was the one which aroused the bitterest resentment in Victoria. She considered that the change was an attack upon her personal position—al-most an attack upon the personal position of Albert. But she was helpless, and the Prime Minister had his way. When she heard that the dreadful man had yet another reform in contemplation—that he was about to abolish the purchase of military commissions—she could only feel that it was just what might have been expected. For a moment she hoped that the House of Lords would come to the rescue; the Peers opposed the change with unexpected vigour; but Mr. Gladstone, more conscious than ever of the support of the Almighty, was ready with an ingenious device. The purchase of commissions had been originally allowed by Royal Warrant; it should now be disallowed by the same agency. Victoria was faced by a curious dilemma: she abominated the abolition of purchase; but she was asked to abolish it by an exercise of sovereign power which was very much to her taste. She did not hesitate for long; and when the Cabinet, in a formal minute, advised her to sign the Warrant, she did so with a good grace.

Unacceptable as Mr. Gladstone's policy was, there was something else about him which was even more displeasing to Victoria. She disliked his personal demeanour towards herself. It was not that Mr. Gladstone, in his intercourse with her, was in any degree lacking in courtesy or respect. On the contrary, an extraordinary reverence impregnated his manner, both in his conversation and his correspondence with the Sovereign. Indeed, with that deep and passionate conservatism which, to the very end of his incredible career, gave such an unexpected colouring to his inexplicable character, Mr. Gladstone viewed Victoria through a haze of awe which was almost religious—as a sacrosanct embodiment of venerable traditions—a vital element in the British Constitution—a Queen by Act of Parliament. But unfortunately the lady did not appreciate the compliment. The well-known complaint—'He speaks to me as if I were a public meeting'—whether authentic or no —and the turn of the sentence is surely a little too epigrammatic to be genuinely Victorian—undoubtedly expresses the essential element of her antipathy. She had no objection to being considered as an institution; she was one, and she knew it. But she was a woman too, and to be considered *only* as an institution —that was unbearable. And thus all Mr. Gladstone's zeal and devotion, his ceremonious phrases, his low bows, his punctilious correctitudes, were utterly wasted; and when, in the excess of his loyalty, he went further, and imputed to the object of his veneration, with obsequious blindness, the subtlety of intellect, the wide reading, the grave enthusiasm, which he himself possessed, the misunderstanding became complete. The discordance between the actual Victoria and this strange Divinity made in Mr. Gladstone's image produced disastrous results. Her discomfort and dislike turned at last into positive animosity, and, though her manners continued to be perfect, she never for a moment unbent; while he on his side was overcome with disappointment, perplexity, and mortification.

Yet his fidelity remained unshaken. When the Cabinet met, the Prime Minister, filled with his beatific vision, would open the proceedings by reading aloud the letters which he had received from the Queen upon the questions of the hour. The assembly sat in absolute silence while, one after another, the royal missives, with their emphases, their ejaculations, and their grammatical peculiarities, boomed forth in all the deep solemnity of Mr. Gladstone's utterance. Not a single comment, of any kind, was ever hazarded; and, after a fitting pause, the Cabinet proceeded with the business of the day.

II

Little as Victoria appreciated her Prime Minister's attitude towards her, she found that it had its uses. The popular discontent at her uninterrupted seclusion had been gathering force for many years, and now burst out in a new and alarming shape. Republicanism was in the air. Radical opinion in England, stimulated by the fall of Napoleon III and the establishment of a republican government in France, suddenly grew more extreme than it ever had been since 1848. It also became for the first time almost respectable. Chartism had been entirely an affair of the lower classes; but now Members of Parliament, learned professors, and ladies of title openly avowed the most subversive views. The monarchy was attacked both in theory and in practice. And it was attacked at a vital point: it was declared to be too expensive. What benefits, it was asked, did the nation reap to counterbalance the enormous sums which were expended upon the Sovereign? Victoria's retirement gave an unpleasant handle to the argument. It was pointed out that the ceremonial functions of the Crown had virtually lapsed; and the awkward question remained whether any of the other functions which it did continue to perform were really worth £385,000 per annum. The royal balance-sheet was curiously examined. An anonymous pamphlet entitled 'What does she do with it?' appeared, setting forth the financial position with malicious clarity. The Queen, it stated, was granted by the Civil List £60,000 a year for her private use; but the rest of her vast annuity was given, as the Act declared, to enable her 'to defray the expenses of her royal household and to support the honour and dignity of the Crown.' Now it was obvious that, since the death of the Prince, the expenditure for both these purposes must have been very considerably diminished, and it was difficult to resist the conclusion that a large sum of money was diverted annually from the uses for which it had been designed by Parliament, to swell the private fortune of Vic-

toria. The precise amount of that private fortune it was impossible to discover; but there was reason to suppose that it was gigantic; perhaps it reached a total of five million pounds. The pamphlet protested against such a state of affairs, and its protests were repeated vigorously in newspapers and at public meetings. Though it is certain that the estimate of Victoria's riches was much exaggerated, it is equally certain that she was an exceedingly wealthy woman. She probably saved £20,000 a year from the Civil List, the revenues of the Duchy of Lancaster were steadily increasing, she had inherited a considerable property from the Prince Consort, and she had been left, in 1852, an estate of half a million by Mr. John Neild, an eccentric miser. In these circumstances it was not surprising that when, in 1871, Parliament was asked to vote a dowry of £30,000 to the Princess Louise on her marriage with the eldest son of the Duke of Argyle, together with an annuity of £6,000, there should have been a serious outcry.

In order to conciliate public opinion, the Queen opened Parliament in person, and the vote was passed almost unanimously. But a few months later another demand was made: the Prince Arthur had come of age, and the nation was asked to grant him an annuity of £15,000. The outcry was redoubled. The newspapers were filled with angry articles; Bradlaugh thundered against 'princely paupers' to one of the largest crowds that had ever been seen in Trafalgar Square; and Sir Charles Dilke expounded the case for a republic in a speech to his constituents at Newcastle. The Prince's annuity was ultimately sanctioned in the House of Commons by a large majority; but a minority of fifty members voted in favour of reducing the sum to £10,000.

Towards every aspect of this distasteful question, Mr. Gladstone presented an iron front. He absolutely discountenanced the extreme section of his followers. He declared that the whole of the Queen's income was justly at her personal disposal, argued that to complain of royal savings was merely to encourage royal extravagance, and successfully convoyed through Parliament the unpopular annuities, which, he pointed out, were strictly in accordance with precedent. When, in 1872, Sir Charles Dilke once more returned to the charge in the House of Commons, introducing a motion for a full enquiry into the Queen's expenditure with a view to a root and branch reform of the Civil List, the Prime Minister brought all the resources of his powerful and ingenious eloquence to the support of the Crown. He was completely successful; and amid a scene of great disorder the motion was ignominiously dismissed. Victoria was relieved; but she grew no fonder of Mr. Gladstone.

It was perhaps the most miserable moment of her life. The Ministers, the press, the public, all conspired to vex her, to blame her, to misinterpret her actions, to be unsympathetic and disrespectful in every way. She was 'a cruelly misunderstood woman,' she told Mr. Martin, complaining to him bitterly of the unjust attacks which were made upon her, and declaring that 'the great worry and anxiety and hard work for ten years, alone, unaided, with increasing age and never very strong health' were breaking her down, and 'almost drove her to despair.' The situation was indeed deplorable. It seemed as if her whole existence had gone awry; as if an irremediable antagonism had grown up between the Queen and the nation. If Victoria had died in the early seventies, there can be little doubt that the voice of the world would have pronounced her a failure.

III

But she was reserved for a very different fate. The outburst of republicanism had been in fact the last flicker of an expiring cause. The liberal tide, which had been flowing steadily ever since the Reform Bill, reached its height with Mr. Gladstone's first administration; and towards the end of that administration the inevitable ebb began. The reaction, when it came, was sudden and complete. The General Election of 1874 changed the whole face of politics. Mr. Gladstone and the Liberals were routed; and the Tory party, for the first time for over forty years, attained an unquestioned supremacy in England. It was obvious that their surprising triumph was pre-eminently due to the skill and vigour of Disraeli. He returned to office, no longer the dubious commander of an insufficient host, but with drums beating and flags flying, a conquering hero. And as a conquering hero Victoria welcomed her new Prime Minister.

Then there followed six years of excitement, of enchantment, of felicity, of glory, of romance. The amazing being, who now at last, at the age of seventy, after a lifetime of extraordinary struggles, had turned into reality the absurdest of his boyhood's dreams, knew well enough how to make his own, with absolute completeness, the heart of the Sovereign Lady whose servant, and whose master, he had so miraculously become. In women's hearts he had always read as in an open book. His whole career had turned upon those curious entities; and the more curious they were, the more intimately at home with them he seemed to be. But Lady Beaconsfield, with her cracked idolatry, and Mrs. Brydges-Williams, with her clogs, her corpulence, and her legacy, were gone: an even more remarkable phenomenon stood in their place. He surveyed what was before him with the eye of a past-master; and he was not for a moment at a loss. He realised everything—the interacting complexities of circumstance and character, the pride of place mingled so inextricably with personal arrogance, the superabundant emotionalism, the ingenuousness of outlook, the solid, the laborious respectability, shot

through so incongruously by temperamental cravings for the coloured and the strange, the singular intellectual limitations, and the mysteriously essential female elements impregnating every particle of the whole. A smile hovered over his impassive features, and he dubbed Victoria 'the Faery.' The name delighted him, for, with that epigrammatic ambiguity so dear to his heart, it precisely expressed his vision of the Queen. The Spenserian allusion was very pleasant— the elegant evocations of Gloriana; [1] but there was more in it than that: there was the suggestion of a diminutive creature, endowed with magical—and mythical—properties, and a portentousness almost ridiculously out of keeping with the rest of her make-up. The Faery, he determined, should henceforward wave her wand for him alone. Detachment is always a rare quality, and rarest of all, perhaps, among politicians; but that veteran egotist possessed it in a supreme degree. Not only did he know what he had to do, not only did he do it; he was in the audience as well as on the stage; and he took in with the rich relish of a connoisseur every feature of the entertaining situation, every phase of the delicate drama, and every detail of his own consummate performance.

The smile hovered and vanished, and, bowing low with Oriental gravity and Oriental submissive-

[1] Gloriana: the title figure in Edmund Spenser's *The Faery Queene*.

ness, he set himself to his task. He had understood from the first that in dealing with the Faery the appropriate method of approach was the very antithesis of the Gladstonian; and such a method was naturally his. It was not his habit to harangue and exhort and expatiate in official conscientiousness; he liked to scatter flowers along the path of business, to compress a weighty argument into a happy phrase, to insinuate what was in his mind with an air of friendship and confidential courtesy. He was nothing if not personal; and he had perceived that personality was the key that opened the Faery's heart. Accordingly, he never for a moment allowed his intercourse with her to lose the personal tone; he invested all the transactions of State with the charms of familiar conversation; she was always the royal lady, the adored and revered mistress, he the devoted and respectful friend. When once the personal relation was firmly established, every difficulty disappeared. But to maintain that relation uninterruptedly in a smooth and even course a particular care was necessary: the bearings had to be most assiduously oiled. Nor was Disraeli in any doubt as to the nature of the lubricant. 'You have heard me called a flatterer,' he said to Matthew Arnold, 'and it is true. Everyone likes flattery; and when you come to royalty you should lay it on with a trowel.' He practised what he preached. His adulation was incessant, and he applied it in the

very thickest slabs. 'There is no honor and no reward,' he declared, 'that with him can ever equal the possession of your Majesty's kind thoughts. All his own thoughts and feelings and duties and affections are now concentrated in your Majesty, and he desires nothing more for his remaining years than to serve your Majesty, or, if that service ceases, to live still on its memory as a period of his existence most interesting and fascinating.' 'In life,' he told her, 'one must have for one's thoughts a sacred depository, and Lord Beaconsfield ever presumes to seek that in his Sovereign Mistress.' She was not only his own solitary support; she was the one prop of the State. 'If your Majesty is ill,' he wrote during a grave political crisis, 'he is sure he will himself break down. All, really, depends upon your Majesty.' 'He lives only for Her,' he asseverated, 'and works only for Her, and without Her all is lost.' When her birthday came he produced an elaborate confection of hyperbolic compliment. 'Today Lord Beaconsfield ought fitly, perhaps, to congratulate a powerful Sovereign on her imperial sway, the vastness of her Empire, and the success and strength of her fleets and armies. But he cannot, his mind is in another mood. He can only think of the strangeness of his destiny that it has come to pass that he should be the servant of one so great, and whose infinite kindness, the brightness of whose intelligence and the firmness of whose will, have enabled him to undertake labours to which he otherwise would be quite unequal, and supported him in all things by a condescending sympathy, which in the hour of difficulty alike charms and inspires. Upon the Sovereign of many lands and many hearts may an omnipotent Providence shed every blessing that the wise can desire and the virtuous deserve!' In those expert hands the trowel seemed to assume the qualities of some lofty masonic symbol—to be the ornate and glittering vehicle of verities unrealised by the profane.

Such tributes were delightful, but they remained in the nebulous region of words, and Disraeli had determined to give his blandishments a more significant solidity. He deliberately encouraged those high views of her own position which had always been native to Victoria's mind and had been reinforced by the principles of Albert and the doctrines of Stockmar. He professed to a belief in a theory of the Constitution which gave the Sovereign a leading place in the councils of government; but his pronouncements upon the subject were indistinct; and when he emphatically declared that there ought to be 'a real Throne,' it was probably with the mental addition that that throne would be a very unreal one indeed whose occupant was unamenable to his cajoleries. But the vagueness of his language was in itself an added stimulant to Victoria. Skilfully confusing the woman and the Queen, he threw, with a grandiose gesture, the govern-

ment of England at her feet, as if in doing so he were performing an act of personal homage. In his first audience after returning to power, he assured her that 'whatever she wished should be done.' When the intricate Public Worship Regulation Bill was being discussed by the Cabinet, he told the Faery that his 'only object' was 'to further your Majesty's wishes in this matter.' When he brought off his great *coup* over the Suez Canal, he used expressions which implied that the only gainer by the transaction was Victoria. 'It is just settled,' he wrote in triumph; 'you have it, Madam . . . Four millions sterling! and almost immediately. There was only one firm that could do it—Rothschilds. They behaved admirably; advanced the money at a low rate, and the entire interest of the Khedive is now yours, Madam.' Nor did he limit himself to highly-spiced insinuations. Writing with all the authority of his office, he advised the Queen that she had the constitutional right to dismiss a Ministry which was supported by a large majority in the House of Commons; he even urged her to do so, if, in her opinion, 'your Majesty's Government have from wilfulness, or even from weakness, deceived your Majesty.' To the horror of Mr. Gladstone, he not only kept the Queen informed as to the general course of business in the Cabinet, but revealed to her the part taken in its discussions by individual members of it. Lord Derby, the son of the late Prime Minister and

Disraeli's Foreign Secretary, viewed these developments with great mistrust. 'Is there not,' he ventured to write to his Chief, 'just a risk of encouraging her in too large ideas of her personal power, and too great indifference to what the public expects? I only ask; it is for you to judge.'

As for Victoria, she accepted everything—compliments, flatteries, Elizabethan prerogatives—without a single qualm. After the long gloom of her bereavement, after the chill of the Gladstonian discipline, she expanded to the rays of Disraeli's devotion like a flower in the sun. The change in her situation was indeed miraculous. No longer was she obliged to puzzle for hours over the complicated details of business, for now she had only to ask Mr. Disraeli for an explanation, and he would give it her in the most concise, in the most amusing, way. No longer was she worried by alarming novelties; no longer was she put out at finding herself treated, by a reverential gentleman in high collars, as if she were some embodied precedent, with a recondite knowledge of Greek. And her deliverer was surely the most fascinating of men. The strain of charlatanism, which had unconsciously captivated her in Napoleon III, exercised the same enchanting effect in the case of Disraeli. Like a dram-drinker, whose ordinary life is passed in dull sobriety, her unsophisticated intelligence gulped down his rococo allurements with peculiar zest. She became intoxicated, entranced. Believing all that he told her of herself, she completely regained the self-confidence which had been slipping away from her throughout the dark period that followed Albert's death. She swelled with a new elation, while he, conjuring up before her wonderful Oriental visions, dazzled her eyes with an imperial grandeur of which she had only dimly dreamed. Under the compelling influence, her very demeanour altered. Her short, stout figure, with its folds of black velvet, its muslin streamers, its heavy pearls at the heavy neck, assumed an almost menacing air. In her countenance, from which the charm of youth had long since vanished, and which had not yet been softened by age, the traces of grief, of disappointment, and of displeasure were still visible, but they were overlaid by looks of arrogance and sharp lines of peremptory hauteur. Only, when Mr. Disraeli appeared, the expression changed in an instant, and the forbidding visage became charged with smiles. For him she would do anything. Yielding to his encouragements, she began to emerge from her seclusion; she appeared in London in semi-state, at hospitals and concerts; she opened Parliament; she reviewed troops and distributed medals at Aldershot. But such public signs of favour were trivial in comparison with her private attentions. During his hours of audience, she could hardly restrain her excitement and delight. 'I can only describe my reception,' he wrote to a friend on one occasion, 'by telling you that I really thought she was going to embrace me. She was wreathed with smiles, and, as she tattled, glided about the room like a bird.' In his absence, talked of him perpetually, and there was a note of unusual vehemence in her solicitude for his health. 'John Manners,' Disraeli told Lady Bradford, 'who has just come from Osborne, says that the Faery only talked of one subject, and that was her Primo. According to him, it was her gracious opinion that the Government should make my health a Cabinet question. Dear John seemed quite surprised at what she said; but you are more used to these ebullitions.' She often sent him presents; an illustrated album arrived for him regularly from Windsor on Christmas Day. But her most valued gifts were the bunches of spring flowers which, gathered by herself and her ladies in the woods at Osborne, marked in an especial manner the warmth and tenderness of her sentiments. Among these it was, he declared, the primroses that he loved the best. They were, he said, 'the ambassadors of Spring,' 'the gems and jewels of Nature.' He liked them, he assured her, 'so much better for their being wild; they seem an offering from the Fauns and Dryads of Osborne.' 'They show,' he told her, 'that your Majesty's sceptre has touched the enchanted Isle.' He sat at dinner with heaped-up bowls of them on every side, and told his guests that 'they were all sent to me this morning by the Queen from Osborne, as she knows it is my favorite flower.'

As time went on, and as it became clearer and clearer that the Faery's thraldom was complete, his protestations grew steadily more highly-coloured and more unabashed. At last he ventured to import into his blandishments a strain of adoration that was almost avowedly romantic. In phrases of baroque convolution, he conveyed the message of his heart. The pressure of business, he wrote, had 'so absorbed and exhausted him, that towards the hour of post he has not had clearness of mind, and vigour of pen, adequate to convey his thoughts and facts to the most loved and illustrious being, who deigns to consider them.' She sent him some primroses, and he replied that he could 'truly say they are "more precious than rubies," coming, as they do, and at such a moment, from a Sovereign whom he adores.' She sent him snowdrops, and his sentiment overflowed into poetry. 'Yesterday eve,' he wrote, 'there appeared, in Whitehall Gardens, a delicate-looking case, with a royal superscription, which, when he opened, he thought, at first, that your Majesty had graciously bestowed upon him the stars of your Majesty's principal orders. And, indeed, he was so impressed with this graceful illusion, that, having a banquet, where there were many stars and ribbons, he could not resist the temptation, by placing some snowdrops on his heart, of showing that, he, too, was decorated by a gracious Sovereign.

'Then, in the middle of the night, it occurred to him, that it might all be an enchantment, and that, perhaps, it was a Faery gift and came from another monarch: Queen Titania,[1] gathering flowers, with her Court, in a soft and sea-girt isle, and sending magic blossoms, which, they say, turn the heads of those who receive them.'

A Faery gift! Did he smile as he wrote the words? Perhaps; and yet it would be rash to conclude that his perfervid declarations were altogether without sincerity. Actor and spectator both, the two characters were so intimately blended together in that odd composition that they formed an inseparable unity, and it was impossible to say that one of them was less genuine than the other. With one element, he could coldly appraise the Faery's intellectual capacity, note with some surprise that she could be on occasion 'most interesting and amusing,' and then continue his use of the trowel with an ironical solemnity; while, with the other, he could be overwhelmed by the immemorial panoply of royalty, and, thrilling with the sense of his own strange elevation, dream himself into a gorgeous phantasy of crowns and powers and chivalric love. When he told Victoria that 'during a somewhat romantic and imaginative life, nothing has ever occurred to

him so interesting as this confidential correspondence with one so exalted and so inspiring,' was he not in earnest after all? When he wrote to a lady about the Court, 'I love the Queen—perhaps the only person in this world left to me that I do love,' was he not creating for himself an enchanted palace out of the Arabian Nights, full of melancholy and spangles, in which he actually believed? Victoria's state of mind was far more simple; untroubled by imaginative yearnings, she never lost herself in that nebulous region of the spirit where feeling and fancy grow confused. Her emotions, with all their intensity and all their exaggeration, retained the plain prosaic texture of everyday life. And it was fitting that her expression of them should be equally commonplace. She was, she told her Prime Minister, at the end of an official letter, 'your aff'ly V. R. and I.' In such a phrase the deep reality of her feeling is instantly manifest. The Faery's feet were on the solid earth; it was the *rusé*[2] cynic who was in the air.

He had taught her, however, a lesson, which she had learnt with alarming rapidity. A second Gloriana, did he call her? Very well, then, she would show that she deserved the compliment. Disquieting symptoms followed fast. In May, 1874, the Tsar, whose daughter had just been married to Victoria's second son, the Duke of Edinburgh, was in London, and, by an unfor-

[1] Titania: Queen of the Fairies in Shakespeare's *A Midsummer Night's Dream*.

[2] *rusé*: artful.

tunate error, it had been arranged that his departure should not take place until two days after the date on which his royal hostess had previously decided to go to Balmoral. Her Majesty refused to modify her plans. It was pointed out to her that the Tsar would certainly be offended, that the most serious consequences might follow; Lord Derby protested; Lord Salisbury, the Secretary of State for India, was much perturbed. But the Faery was unconcerned; she had settled to go to Balmoral on the 18th, and on the 18th she would go. At last Disraeli, exercising all his influence, induced her to agree to stay in London for two days more. 'My head is still on my shoulders,' he told Lady Bradford. 'The great lady has absolutely postponed her departure! Everybody had failed, even the Prince of Wales; . . . and I have no doubt I am not in favour. I can't help it. Salisbury says I have saved an Afghan War, and Derby compliments me on my unrivalled triumph.' But before very long, on another issue, the triumph was the Faery's. Disraeli, who had suddenly veered towards a new Imperialism, had thrown out the suggestion that the Queen of England ought to become the Empress of India. Victoria seized upon the idea with avidity, and, in season and out of season, pressed upon her Prime Minister the desirability of putting his proposal into practice. He demurred; but she was not to be baulked; and in 1876, in spite of his own unwillingness and that of

his entire Cabinet, he found himself obliged to add to the troubles of a stormy session by introducing a bill for the alteration of the Royal Title. His compliance, however, finally conquered the Faery's heart. The measure was angrily attacked in both Houses, and Victoria was deeply touched by the untiring energy with which Disraeli defended it. She was, she said, much grieved by 'the worry and annoyance' to which he was subjected; she feared she was the cause of it; and she would never forget what she owed to 'her kind, good, and considerate friend.' At the same time, her wrath fell on the Opposition. Their conduct, she declared, was 'extraordinary, incomprehensible, and mistaken,' and, in an emphatic sentence which seemed to contradict both itself and all her former proceedings, she protested that she 'would be glad if it were more generally known that it was *her* wish, as people *will* have it, that it has been *forced upon her!*' When the affair was successfully over, the imperial triumph was celebrated in a suitable manner. On the day of the Delhi Proclamation, the new Earl of Beaconsfield went to Windsor to dine with the new Empress of India. That night the Faery, usually so homely in her attire, appeared in a glittering panoply of enormous uncut jewels, which had been presented to her by the reigning Princes of her *Raj*. At the end of the meal the Prime Minister, breaking through the rules of etiquette, arose, and in a flowery oration proposed the health of the Queen-Empress. His audacity was well received, and his speech was rewarded by a smiling curtsey.

These were significant episodes; but a still more serious manifestation of Victoria's temper occurred in the following year, during the crowning crisis of Beaconsfield's life. His growing imperialism, his desire to magnify the power and prestige of England, his insistence upon a 'spirited foreign policy,' had brought him into collision with Russia; the terrible Eastern Question loomed up; and when war broke out between Russia and Turkey, the gravity of the situation became extreme. The Prime Minister's policy was fraught with difficulty and danger. Realising perfectly the appalling implications of an Anglo-Russian war, he was yet prepared to face even that eventuality if he could obtain his ends by no other method; but he believed that Russia in reality was still less desirous of a rupture, and that, if he played his game with sufficient boldness and adroitness, she would yield, when it came to the point, all that he required without a blow. It was clear that the course he had marked out for himself was full of hazard, and demanded an extraordinary nerve; a single false step, and either himself, or England, might be plunged in disaster. But nerve he had never lacked; he began his diplomatic egg-dance with high assurance; and then he discovered that, besides the Russian Government, besides the Liberals and Mr. Gladstone, there were two additional sources of perilous embarrassment with which he would have to reckon. In the first place there was a strong party in the Cabinet, headed by Lord Derby, the Foreign Secretary, which was unwilling to take the risk of war; but his culminating anxiety was the Faery.

From the first, her attitude was uncompromising. The old hatred of Russia, which had been engendered by the Crimean War, surged up again within her; she remembered Albert's prolonged animosity; she felt the prickings of her own greatness; and she flung herself into the turmoil with passionate heat. Her indignation with the Opposition—with anyone who ventured to sympathise with the Russians in their quarrel with the Turks—was unbounded. When anti-Turkish meetings were held in London, presided over by the Duke of Westminster and Lord Shaftesbury, and attended by Mr. Gladstone and other prominent Radicals, she considered that 'the Attorney-General ought to be set at these men'; 'it can't,' she exclaimed, 'be constitutional.' Never in her life, not even in the crisis over the Ladies of the Bedchamber, did she show herself a more furious partisan. But her displeasure was not reserved for the Radicals; the back-sliding Conservatives equally felt its force. She was even discontented with Lord Beaconsfield himself. Failing entirely to appreciate the delicate complexity of his policy, she constantly assailed him with demands for vigorous action, interpreted each finesse as a sign of weakness, and was ready at every juncture to let slip the dogs of war. As the situation developed, her anxiety grew feverish. 'The Queen,' she wrote, 'is feeling terribly anxious lest delay should cause us to be too late and lose our prestige for ever! It worries her night and day.' 'The Faery,' Beaconsfield told Lady Bradford, 'writes every day and telegraphs every hour; this is almost literally the case.' She raged loudly against the Russians. 'And the language,' she cried, 'the insulting language—used by the Russians against us! It makes the Queen's blood boil!' 'Oh,' she wrote a little later, 'if the Queen were a man, she would like to go and give those Russians, whose word one cannot believe, such a beating! We shall never be friends again till we have it out. This the Queen feels sure of.'

The unfortunate Prime Minister, urged on to violence by Victoria on one side, had to deal, on the other, with a Foreign Secretary who was fundamentally opposed to any policy of active interference at all. Between the Queen and Lord Derby he held a harassed course. He gained, indeed, some slight satisfaction in playing off the one against the other—in stimulating Lord Derby with the Queen's missives, and in appeasing the Queen by repudiating Lord Derby's opinions; on one occasion he actually went so far as to compose, at Vic-

toria's request, a letter bitterly attacking his colleague, which Her Majesty forthwith signed, and sent, without alteration, to the Foreign Secretary. But such devices only gave a temporary relief; and it soon became evident that Victoria's martial ardour was not to be sidetracked by hostilities against Lord Derby; hostilities against Russia were what she wanted, what she would, what she must, have. For now, casting aside the last relics of moderation, she began to attack her friend with a series of extraordinary threats. Not once, not twice, but many times she held over his head the formidable menace of her imminent abdication. 'If England,' she wrote to Beaconsfield, 'is to kiss Russia's feet, she will not be a party to the humiliation of England and would lay down her crown,' and she added that the Prime Minister might, if he thought fit, repeat her words to the Cabinet. 'This delay,' she ejaculated, 'this uncertainty by which, abroad, we are losing our prestige and our position, while Russia is advancing and will be before Constantinople in no time! Then the Government will be fearfully blamed and the Queen so humiliated that she thinks she would abdicate at once. Be bold!' 'She feels,' she reiterated, 'she cannot, as she before said, remain the Sovereign of a country that is letting itself down to kiss the feet of the great barbarians, the retarders of all liberty and civilisation that exists.' When the Russians advanced to the outskirts of Constantinople she fired off three letters in a day demanding war; and when she learnt that the Cabinet had only decided to send the Fleet to Gallipoli she declared that 'her first impulse' was 'to lay down the thorny crown, which she feels little satisfaction in retaining if the position of this country is to remain as it is now.' It is easy to imagine the agitating effect of such a correspondence upon Beaconsfield. This was no longer the Faery; it was a genie whom he had rashly called out of her bottle, and who was now intent upon showing her supernal power. More than once, perplexed, dispirited, shattered by illness, he had thoughts of withdrawing altogether from the game. One thing alone, he told Lady Bradford, with a wry smile, prevented him. 'If I could only,' he wrote, 'face the scene which would occur at headquarters if I resigned, I would do so at once.'

He held on, however, to emerge victorious at last. The Queen was pacified; Lord Derby was replaced by Lord Salisbury; and at the Congress of Berlin *der alte Jude* [1] carried all before him. He returned to England in triumph, and assured the delighted Victoria that she would very soon be, if she was not already, the 'Dictatress of Europe.'

But soon there was an unexpected reverse. At the General Election of 1880 the country, mistrust-ful of the forward policy of the Conservatives, and carried away by Mr. Gladstone's oratory, returned the Liberals to power. Victoria was horrified, but within a year she was to be yet more nearly hit. The grand romance had come to its conclusion. Lord Beaconsfield, worn out with age and maladies, but moving still, an assiduous mummy, from dinner-party to dinner-party, suddenly moved no longer. When she knew that the end was inevitable, she seemed, by a pathetic instinct, to divest herself of her royalty, and to shrink, with hushed gentleness, beside him, a woman and nothing more. 'I send some Osborne primroses,' she wrote to him with touching simplicity, 'and I meant to pay you a little visit this week, but I thought it better you should be quite quiet and not speak. And I beg you will be very good and obey the doctors.' She would see him, she said, 'when we come back from Osborne, which won't be long.' 'Everyone is so distressed at your not being well,' she added; and she was, 'Ever yours very aff'ly, V.R.I.' When the royal letter was given him, the strange old comedian, stretched on his bed of death, poised it in his hand, appeared to consider deeply, and then whispered to those about him, 'This ought to be read to me by a Privy Councillor.'

[1] *der alte Jude:* the old Jew (Disraeli was Jewish by descent, though not by religion).

Chapter 9

Old Age

I

Meanwhile in Victoria's private life many changes and developments had taken place. With the marriages of her elder children her family circle widened; grandchildren appeared; and a multitude of new domestic interests sprang up. The death of King Leopold in 1865 had removed the predominant figure of the older generation, and the functions he had performed as the centre and adviser of a large group of relatives in Germany and in England devolved upon Victoria. These functions she discharged with unremitting industry, carrying on an enormous correspondence, and following with absorbed interest every detail in the lives of the ever-ramifying cousinhood. And she tasted to the full both the joys and the pains of family affection. She took a particular delight in her grandchildren, to whom she showed an indulgence which their parents had not always enjoyed, though, even to her grandchildren, she could be, when the occasion demanded it, severe. The eldest of them, the little Prince Wilhelm of Prussia, was a remarkably headstrong child; he dared to be impertinent even to his grandmother; and once, when she told him to bow to a visitor at Osborne, he dis-

obeyed her outright. This would not do: the order was sternly repeated, and the naughty boy, noticing that his kind grandmama had suddenly turned into a most terrifying lady, submitted his will to hers, and bowed very low indeed.

It would have been well if all the Queen's domestic troubles could have been got over as easily. Among her more serious distresses was the conduct of the Prince of Wales. The young man was now independent and married; he had shaken the parental yoke from his shoulders; he was positively beginning to do as he liked. Victoria was much perturbed, and her worst fears seemed to be justified when in 1870 he appeared as a witness in a society divorce case. It was clear that the heir to the throne had been mixing with people of whom she did not at all approve. What was to be done? She saw that it was not only her son that was to blame —that it was the whole system of society; and so she despatched a letter to Mr. Delane, the editor of *The Times,* asking him if he would 'frequently *write* articles pointing out the *immense* danger and evil of the wretched frivolity and levity of the views and lives of the Higher Classes.' And five years later Mr. Delane did write an article upon that very subject. Yet it seemed to have very little effect.

Ah! if only the Higher Classes would learn to live as she lived in the domestic sobriety of her sanctuary at Balmoral! For more and more did she find solace and refreshment in her Highland domain; and twice yearly, in the spring and in the autumn, with a sigh of relief, she set her face northwards, in spite of the humble protests of Ministers, who murmured vainly in the royal ears that to transact the affairs of State over an interval of six hundred miles added considerably to the cares of government. Her ladies, too, felt occasionally a slight reluctance to set out, for, especially in the early days, the long pilgrimage was not without its drawbacks. For many years the Queen's conservatism forbade the continuation of the railway up Deeside, so that the last stages of the journey had to be accomplished in carriages. But, after all, carriages had their good points; they were easy, for instance, to get in and out of, which was an important consideration, for the royal train remained for long immune from modern conveniences, and when it drew up, on some border moorland, far from any platform, the highbred dames were obliged to descend to earth by the perilous foot-board, the only pair of folding steps being reserved for Her Majesty's saloon. In the days of crinolines such moments were sometimes awkward; and it was occasionally necessary to summon Mr. Johnstone, the short and sturdy Manager of the Caledonian Railway, who, more than once, in a high gale and drenching rain with great difficulty 'pushed up'—as he himself described it—some unlucky Lady Blanche or Lady Agatha into her compartment. But Victoria cared for none of these things. She was only intent upon regaining, with the utmost swiftness, her enchanted Castle, where every spot was charged with memories, where every memory was sacred, and where life was passed in an incessant and delightful round of absolutely trivial events.

And it was not only the place that she loved; she was equally attached to 'the simple mountaineers,' from whom, she said, 'she learnt many a lesson of resignation and faith.' Smith and Grant and Ross and Thompson—she was devoted to them all; but, beyond the rest, she was devoted to John Brown. The Prince's gillie had now become the Queen's personal attendant—a body servant from whom she was never parted, who accompanied her on her drives, waited on her during the day, and slept in a neighbouring chamber at night. She liked his strength, his solidity, the sense he gave her of physical security; she even liked his rugged manners and his rough unaccommodating speech. She allowed him to take liberties with her which would have been unthinkable from anybody else. To bully the Queen, to order her about, to reprimand her —who could dream of venturing upon such audacities? And yet, when she received such treatment from John Brown, she positively seemed to enjoy it. The eccentricity appeared to be extraordinary; but, after all, it is no uncommon thing for an autocratic dowager to allow some trusted indispensable servant to adopt towards her an attitude of authority which is jealously forbidden to relatives or friends: the power of a dependent still remains, by a psychological sleight-of-hand, one's own power, even when it is exercised over oneself. When Victoria meekly obeyed the abrupt commands of her henchman to get off her pony or put on her shawl, was she not displaying, and in the highest degree, the force of her volition? People might wonder; she could not help that; this was the manner in which it pleased her to act, and there was an end of it. To have submitted her judgment to a son or a Minister might have seemed wiser or more natural; but if she had done so, she instinctively felt, she would indeed have lost her independence. And yet upon somebody she longed to depend. Her days were heavy with the long process of domination. As she drove in silence over the moors she leaned back in the carriage, oppressed and weary; but what a relief!—John Brown was behind on the rumble, and his strong arm would be there for her to lean upon when she got out.

He had, too, in her mind, a special connection with Albert. In their expeditions the Prince had always trusted him more than anyone; the gruff, kind, hairy Scotsman was, she felt, in some mysterious way, a legacy from the dead. She came to believe at last—or so it appeared—that the spirit of Albert was nearer when Brown was near.

Often, when seeking inspiration over some complicated question of political or domestic import, she would gaze with deep concentration at her late husband's bust. But it was also noticed that sometimes in such moments of doubt and hesitation Her Majesty's looks would fix themselves upon John Brown.

Eventually, the 'simple mountaineer' became almost a state personage. The influence which he wielded was not to be overlooked. Lord Beaconsfield was careful, from time to time, to send courteous messages to 'Mr. Brown' in his letters to the Queen, and the French Government took particular pains to provide for his comfort during the visits of the English Sovereign to France. It was only natural that among the elder members of the royal family he should not have been popular, and that his failings —for failings he had, though Victoria would never notice his too acute appreciation of Scotch whisky—should have been the subject of acrimonious comment at Court. But he served his mistress faithfully, and to ignore him would be a sign of disrespect in her biographer. For the Queen, far from making a secret of her affectionate friendship, took care to publish it to the world. By her orders two gold medals were struck in his honour; on his death, in 1883, a long and eulogistic obituary notice of him appeared in the *Court Circular;* and a Brown memorial brooch—of gold, with the late gillie's head on one side and the royal monogram on the other—was designed by Her Majesty for presentation to her Highland servants and cottagers, to be worn by them on the anniversary of his death, with a mourning scarf and pins. In the second series of extracts from the Queen's Highland Journal, published in 1884, her 'devoted personal attendant and faithful friend' appears upon almost every page, and is in effect the hero of the book. With an absence of reticence remarkable in royal persons, Victoria seemed to demand, in this private and delicate matter, the sympathy of the whole nation; and yet—such is the world!—there were those who actually treated the relations between their Sovereign and her servant as a theme for ribald jests.

II

The busy years hastened away; the traces of Time's unimaginable touch grew manifest; and old age, approaching, laid a gentle hold upon Victoria. The grey hair whitened; the mature features mellowed; the short firm figure amplified and moved more slowly, supported by a stick. And, simultaneously, in the whole tenour of the Queen's existence an extraordinary transformation came to pass. The nation's attitude towards her, critical and even hostile as it had been for so many years, altogether changed; while there was a corresponding alteration in the temper of Victoria's own mind.

Many causes led to this result.

Among them were the repeated strokes of personal misfortune which befell the Queen during a cruelly short space of years. In 1878 the Princess Alice, who had married in 1862 the Prince Louis of Hesse-Darmstadt, died in tragic circumstances. In the following year the Prince Imperial, the only son of the Empress Eugénie, to whom Victoria, since the catastrophe of 1870, had become devotedly attached, was killed in the Zulu War. Two years later, in 1881, the Queen lost Lord Beaconsfield, and, in 1883, John Brown. In 1884 the Prince Leopold, Duke of Albany, who had been an invalid from birth, died prematurely, shortly after his marriage. Victoria's cup of sorrows was indeed overflowing; and the public, as it watched the widowed mother weeping for her children and her friends, displayed a constantly increasing sympathy.

An event which occurred in 1882 revealed and accentuated the feelings of the nation. As the Queen, at Windsor, was walking from the train to her carriage, a youth named Roderick Maclean fired a pistol at her from a distance of a few yards. An Eton boy struck up Maclean's arm with an umbrella before the pistol went off; no damage was done, and the culprit was at once arrested. This was the last of a series of seven attempts upon the Queen—attempts which, taking place at sporadic intervals over a period of forty years, resembled one another in a curious manner. All, with a single exception, were perpetrated by adolescents, whose motives were apparently not murderous, since, save in the case of Maclean, none of their pistols was loaded. These unhappy youths, who, after buying their cheap weapons, stuffed them with gunpowder and paper, and then went off, with the certainty of immediate detection, to click them in the face of royalty, present a strange problem to the psychologist. But, though in each case their actions and their purposes seemed to be so similar, their fates were remarkably varied. The first of them, Edward Oxford, who fired at Victoria within a few months of her marriage, was tried for high treason, declared to be insane, and sent to an asylum for life. It appears, however, that this sentence did not commend itself to Albert, for when, two years later, John Francis committed the same offence, and was tried upon the same charge, the Prince pronounced that there was no insanity in the matter. 'The wretched creature,' he told his father, was 'not out of his mind, but a thorough scamp.' 'I hope,' he added, 'his trial will be conducted with the greatest strictness.' Apparently it was; at any rate, the jury shared the view of the Prince, the plea of insanity was set aside, and Francis was found guilty of high treason and condemned to death; but, as there was no proof of an intent to kill or even to wound, this sentence, after a lengthened deliberation between the Home Secretary and the Judges, was commuted for one of transportation for life. As the law stood, these assaults, futile as they were, could only be treated as high treason; the discrepancy between the actual deed and the tremendous penalties involved was obviously grotesque; and it was, besides, clear that a jury, knowing that a verdict of guilty implied a sentence of death, would tend to the alternative course, and find the prisoner not guilty but insane—a conclusion which, on the face of it, would have appeared to be the more reasonable. In 1842, therefore, an Act was passed making any attempt to hurt the Queen a misdemeanour, punishable by transportation for seven years, or imprisonment, with or without hard labour, for a term not exceeding three years—the misdemeanant, at the discretion of the Court, 'to be publicly or privately whipped, as often, and in such manner and form, as the Court shall direct, not exceeding thrice.' The four subsequent attempts were all dealt with under this new law; William Bean, in 1842, was sentenced to eighteen months' imprisonment; William Hamilton, in 1849, was transported for seven years; and, in 1850, the same sentence was passed upon Lieutenant Robert Pate, who struck the Queen on the head with his cane in Piccadilly. Pate, alone among these delinquents, was of mature years; he had held a commission in the Army, dressed himself as a dandy, and was, the Prince declared, 'manifestly deranged.' In 1872 Arthur O'Connor, a youth of seventeen, fired an unloaded pistol at the Queen outside Buckingham Palace; he was immediately seized by John Brown, and sentenced to one year's imprisonment and twenty strokes of the birch rod. It was for his bravery upon this occasion that Brown was presented with one of his gold medals. In all these cases the jury had refused to allow the plea of insanity; but Roderick Maclean's attempt in 1882 had a different issue. On this occasion the pistol was found to have been loaded, and the public indignation, emphasised as it was by Victoria's growing popularity, was particularly great. Even for this or for some other reason the procedure of the last forty years was abandoned, and Maclean was tried for high treason. The result was what might have been expected: the jury brought in a verdict of 'not guilty, but insane'; and the prisoner was sent to an asylum during Her Majesty's pleasure. Their verdict, however, produced a remarkable consequence. Victoria, who doubtless carried in her mind some memory of Albert's disapproval of a similar verdict in the case of Oxford, was very much annoyed. What did the jury mean, she asked, by saying that Maclean was not guilty? It was perfectly clear that he was guilty—she had seen him fire off the pistol herself. It was in vain that Her Majesty's constitutional advisers reminded her of the principle of English law which lays down that no man can be found guilty of a crime unless he be proved to have had a criminal

intention. Victoria was quite unconvinced. 'If that is the law,' she said, 'the law must be altered': and altered it was. In 1883 an Act was passed changing the form of the verdict in cases of insanity, and the confusing anomaly remains upon the Statute Book to this day.

But it was not only through the feelings—commiserating or indignant—of personal sympathy that the Queen and her people were being drawn more nearly together; they were beginning, at last, to come to a close and permanent agreement upon the conduct of public affairs. Mr. Gladstone's second administration (1880–85) was a succession of failures, ending in disaster and disgrace; liberalism fell into discredit with the country, and Victoria perceived with joy that her distrust of her Ministers was shared by an ever-increasing number of her subjects. During the crisis in the Sudan, the popular temper was her own. She had been among the first to urge the necessity of an expedition to Khartoum, and, when the news came of the catastrophic death of General Gordon, her voice led the chorus of denunciation which raged against the Government. In her rage, she despatched a fulminating telegram to Mr. Gladstone, not in the usual cypher, but open; and her letter of condolence to Miss Gordon, in which she attacked her Ministers for breach of faith, was widely published. It was rumoured that she had sent for Lord Hartington, the Secretary of State for War, and vehemently upbraided him. 'She rated me,' he was reported to have told a friend, 'as if I'd been a footman.' 'Why didn't she send for the butler?' asked his friend. 'Oh,' was the reply, 'the butler generally manages to keep out of the way on such occasions.'

But the day came when it was impossible to keep out of the way any longer. Mr. Gladstone was defeated, and resigned. Victoria, at a final interview, received him with her usual amenity, but, besides the formalities demanded by the occasion, the only remark which she made to him of a personal nature was to the effect that she supposed Mr. Gladstone would now require some rest. He remembered with regret how, at a similar audience in 1874, she had expressed her trust in him as a supporter of the throne; but he noted the change without surprise. 'Her mind and opinions,' he wrote in his diary afterwards, 'have since that day been seriously warped.'

Such was Mr. Gladstone's view; but the majority of the nation by no means agreed with him; and, in the General Election of 1886, they showed decisively that Victoria's politics were identical with theirs by casting forth the contrivers of Home Rule—that abomination of desolation—into outer darkness, and placing Lord Salisbury in power. Victoria's satisfaction was profound. A flood of new unwonted hopefulness swept over her, stimulating her vital spirits with a surprising force. Her habit

of life was suddenly altered; abandoning the long seclusion which Disraeli's persuasions had only momentarily interrupted, she threw herself vigorously into a multitude of public activities. She appeared at drawing-rooms, at concerts, at reviews; she laid foundation-stones; she went to Liverpool to open an international exhibition, driving through the streets in her open carriage in heavy rain amid vast applauding crowds. Delighted by the welcome which met her everywhere, she warmed to her work. She visited Edinburgh, where the ovation of Liverpool was repeated and surpassed. In London, she opened in high state the Colonial and Indian Exhibition at South Kensington. On this occasion the ceremonial was particularly magnificent; a blare of trumpets announced the approach of Her Majesty; the 'National Anthem' followed; and the Queen, seated on a gorgeous throne of hammered gold, replied with her own lips to the address that was presented to her. Then she rose, and, advancing upon the platform with regal port, acknowledged the acclamations of the great assembly by a succession of curtseys, of elaborate and commanding grace.

Next year was the fiftieth of her reign, and in June the splendid anniversary was celebrated in solemn pomp. Victoria, surrounded by the highest dignitaries of her realm, escorted by a glittering galaxy of kings and princes, drove through the crowded enthusiasm of the capital to render thanks to God in Westminster Abbey. In that triumphant hour the last remaining traces of past antipathies and past disagreements were altogether swept away. The Queen was hailed at once as the mother of her people and as the embodied symbol of their imperial greatness; and she responded to the double sentiment with all the ardour of her spirit. England and the people of England, she knew it, she felt it, were, in some wonderful and yet quite simple manner, *hers*. Exultation, affection, gratitude, a profound sense of obligation, an unbounded pride—such were her emotions; and, colouring and intensifying the rest, there was something else. At last, after so long, happiness—fragmentary, perhaps, and charged with gravity, but true and unmistakable none the less—had returned to her. The unaccustomed feeling filled and warmed her consciousness. When, at Buckingham Palace again, the long ceremony over, she was asked how she was, 'I am very tired, but very happy,' she said.

III

And so, after the toils and tempests of the day, a long evening followed—mild, serene, and lighted with a golden glory. For an unexampled atmosphere of success and adoration invested the last period of Victoria's life. Her triumph was the summary, the crown, of a greater triumph—the culminating prosperity of a nation. The solid splendour of the decade between Victoria's two jubilees can hardly be paralleled in the annals of England. The sage counsels of Lord Salisbury seemed to bring with them not only wealth and power, but security; and the country settled down, with calm assurance, to the enjoyment of an established grandeur. And—it was only natural—Victoria settled down too. For she was a part of the establishment—an essential part as it seemed —a fixture—a magnificent, immovable sideboard in the huge saloon of state. Without her the heaped-up banquet of 1890 would have lost its distinctive quality—the comfortable order of the substantial unambiguous dishes, with their background of weighty glamour, half out of sight.

Her own existence came to harmonise more and more with what was around her. Gradually, imperceptibly, Albert receded. It was not that he was forgotten—that would have been impossible—but that the void created by his absence grew less agonising, and even, at last, less obvious. At last Victoria found it possible to regret the bad weather without immediately reflecting that her 'dear Albert always said we could not alter it, but must leave it as it was'; she could even enjoy a good breakfast without considering how 'dear Albert' would have liked the buttered eggs. And, as that figure slowly faded, its place was taken, inevitably, by Victoria's own. Her being, revolving for so many years round an external object, now changed its motion and found its centre in itself. It had to be so: her domestic position, the pressure of her public work, her indomitable sense of duty, made anything else impossible. Her egotism proclaimed its rights. Her age increased still further the surrounding deference; and her force of character, emerging at length in all its plenitude, imposed itself absolutely upon its environment by the conscious effort of an imperious will.

Little by little it was noticed that the outward vestiges of Albert's posthumous domination grew less complete. At Court the stringency of mourning was relaxed. As the Queen drove through the Park in her open carriage with her Highlanders behind her, nursery-maids canvassed eagerly the growing patch of violet velvet in the bonnet with its jet appurtenances on the small bowing head.

It was in her family that Victoria's ascendency reached its highest point. All her offspring were married; the number of her descendants rapidly increased; there were many marriages in the third generation; and no fewer than thirty-seven of her great-grandchildren were living at the time of her death. A picture of the period displays the royal family collected together in one of the great rooms at Windsor—a crowded company of more than fifty persons, with the imperial matriarch in their midst. Over them all she ruled with a most potent sway. The small concerns of the youngest aroused her passionate interest; and the oldest she treated as if they were children still. The Prince of Wales, in particular, stood in tremendous awe of his mother. She had steadily refused to allow him the slightest participation in the business of government; and he had occupied himself in other ways. Nor could it be denied that he enjoyed himself—out of her sight; but, in that redoubtable presence, his abounding manhood suffered a miserable eclipse. Once, at Osborne, when, owing to no fault of his, he was too late for a dinner party, he was observed standing behind a pillar and, wiping the sweat from his forehead, trying to nerve himself to go up to the Queen. When at last he did so, she gave him a stiff nod, whereupon he vanished immediately behind another pillar, and remained there until the party broke up. At the time of this incident the Prince of Wales was over fifty years of age.

It was inevitable that the Queen's domestic activities should occasionally trench upon the domain of high diplomacy; and this was especially the case when the interests of her eldest daughter, the Crown Princess of Prussia, were at stake. The Crown Prince held liberal opinions; he was much influenced by his wife; and both were detested by Bismarck, who declared with scurrilous emphasis that the Englishwoman and her mother were a menace to the Prussian State. The feud was still further intensified when, on the death of the old Emperor (1888), the Crown Prince succeeded to the throne. A family entanglement brought on a violent crisis. One of the daughters of the new Empress had become betrothed to Prince Alexander of Battenberg, who had lately been ejected from the throne of Bulgaria owing to the hostility of the Tsar. Victoria, as well as the Empress, highly approved of the match. Of the two brothers of Prince Alexander, the elder had married another of her grand-daughters, and the younger was the husband of her daughter, the Princess Beatrice; she was devoted to the handsome young man; and she was delighted by the prospect of the third brother—on the whole the handsomest, she thought, of the three—also becoming a member of her family. Unfortunately, however, Bismarck was opposed to the scheme. He perceived that the marriage would endanger the friendship between Germany and Russia, which was vital to his foreign policy, and he announced that it must not take place. A fierce struggle between the Empress and the Chancellor followed. Victoria, whose hatred of her daughter's enemy was unbounded, came over to Charlottenburg to join in the fray. Bismarck, over his pipe and lager, snorted out his alarm. The Queen of England's object, he said, was clearly political—she wished to estrange Germany and Russia—and very likely she would have her way. 'In family matters,' he added, 'she is not used to contradiction'; she would 'bring the parson with her in her travelling bag and the bride-groom in her trunk, and the marriage would come off on the spot.' But the man of blood and iron was not to be thwarted so easily, and he asked for a private interview with the Queen. The details of their conversation are unknown; but it is certain that in the course of it Victoria was forced to realise the meaning of resistance to that formidable personage, and that she promised to use all her influence to prevent the marriage. The engagement was broken off; and in the following year Prince Alexander of Battenberg united himself to Fräulein Loisinger, an actress at the court theatre of Darmstadt.

But such painful incidents were rare. Victoria was growing very old; with no Albert to guide her, with no Beaconsfield to enflame her, she was willing enough to abandon the dangerous questions of diplomacy to the wisdom of Lord Salisbury, and to concentrate her energies upon objects which touched her more nearly and over which she could exercise an undisputed control. Her home—her court—the monuments at Balmoral—the livestock at Windsor—the organisation of her engagements—the supervision of the multitudinous details of her daily routine—such matters played now an even greater part in her existence than before. Her life passed in an extraordinary exactitude. Every moment of her day was mapped out beforehand; the succession of her engagements was immutably fixed; the dates of her journeys—to Osborne, to Balmoral, to the South of France, to Windsor, to London—were hardly altered from year to year. She demanded from those who surrounded her a rigid precision in details, and she was preternaturally quick in detecting the slightest deviation from the rules which she had laid down. Such was the irresistible potency of her personality, that anything but the most implicit obedience to her wishes was felt to be impossible; but sometimes somebody was unpunctual; and unpunctuality was one of the most heinous of sins. Then her displeasure—her dreadful displeasure—became all too visible. At such moments there seemed nothing surprising in her having been the daughter of a martinet.

But these storms, unnerving as they were while they lasted, were quickly over, and they grew more and more exceptional. With the return of happiness a gentle benignity flowed from the aged Queen. Her smile, once so rare a visitant to those saddened features, flitted over them with an easy alacrity; the blue eyes beamed; the whole face, starting suddenly from its pendulous expressionlessness, brightened and softened and cast over those who watched it an unforgettable charm. For in her last years there was a fascination in Victoria's amiability which had been lacking even from the vivid impulse of her youth. Over all who approached her—or very nearly all—she threw a peculiar spell. Her grandchildren adored her; her ladies waited upon her with a reverential love. The honour

of serving her obliterated a thousand inconveniences—the monotony of a court existence, the fatigue of standing, the necessity for a superhuman attentiveness to the minutiæ of time and space. As one did one's wonderful duty one could forget that one's legs were aching from the infinitude of the passages at Windsor, or that one's bare arms were turning blue in the Balmoral cold.

What, above all, seemed to make such service delightful was the detailed interest which the Queen took in the circumstances of those around her. Her absorbing passion for the comfortable commonplaces, the small crises, the recurrent sentimentalities, of domestic life constantly demanded wider fields for its activity; the sphere of her own family, vast as it was, was not enough; she became the eager confidante of the household affairs of her ladies; her sympathies reached out to the palace domestics; even the housemaids and scullions—so it appeared—were the objects of her searching inquiries, and of her heartfelt solicitude when their lovers were ordered to a foreign station, or their aunts suffered from an attack of rheumatism which was more than usually acute.

Nevertheless the due distinctions of rank were immaculately preserved. The Queen's mere presence was enough to ensure that; but, in addition, the dominion of court etiquette was paramount. For that elaborate code, which had kept Lord Melbourne stiff upon the sofa and ranged the other guests in silence about the round table according to the order of precedence, was as punctiliously enforced as ever. Every evening after dinner, the hearth-rug, sacred to royalty, loomed before the profane in inaccessible glory, or, on one or two terrific occasions, actually lured them magnetically forward to the very edge of the abyss. The Queen, at the fitting moment, moved towards her guests; one after the other they were led up to her; and, while dualogue followed dualogue in constraint and embarrassment, the rest of the assembly stood still, without a word. Only in one particular was the severity of the etiquette allowed to lapse. Throughout the greater part of the reign the rule that ministers must stand during their audiences with the Queen had been absolute. When Lord Derby, the Prime Minister, had an audience of Her Majesty after a serious illness, he mentioned it afterwards, as a proof of the royal favour, that the Queen had remarked 'How sorry she was she could not ask him to be seated.' Subsequently, Disraeli, after an attack of gout and in a moment of extreme expansion on the part of Victoria, had been offered a chair; but he had thought it wise humbly to decline the privilege. In her later years, however, the Queen invariably asked Mr. Gladstone and Lord Salisbury to sit down.

Sometimes the solemnity of the evening was diversified by a concert, an opera, or even a play. One of the most marked indications of Victoria's enfranchisement from the thraldom of widowhood had been her resumption—after an interval of thirty years—of the custom of commanding dramatic companies from London to perform before the Court at Windsor. On such occasions her spirits rose high. She loved acting; she loved a good plot; above all, she loved a farce. Engrossed by everything that passed upon the stage she would follow, with childlike innocence, the unwinding of the story; or she would assume an air of knowing superiority and exclaim in triumph, 'There! You didn't expect *that,* did you?' when the *dénouement* came. Her sense of humour was of a vigorous though primitive kind. She had been one of the very few persons who had always been able to appreciate the Prince Consort's jokes; and, when those were cracked no more, she could still roar with laughter, in the privacy of her household, over some small piece of fun—some oddity of an ambassador, or some ignorant Minister's *faux pas.* When the jest grew subtle she was less pleased; but, if it approached the confines of the indecorous, the danger was serious. To take a liberty called down at once Her Majesty's most crushing disapprobation; and to say something improper was to take the greatest liberty of all. Then the royal lips sank down at the corners, the royal eyes stared in astonished protrusion, and in fact the royal countenance became inauspicious in the highest degree. The transgressor shuddered into silence, while the awful 'We are not amused' annihilated the dinner table. Afterwards, in her private entourage, the Queen would observe that the person in question was, she very much feared, 'not discreet'; it was a verdict from which there was no appeal.

In general, her æsthetic tastes had remained unchanged since the days of Mendelssohn, Landseer, and Lablache. She still delighted in the roulades of Italian opera; she still demanded a high standard in the execution of a pianoforte duet. Her views on painting were decided; Sir Edwin, she declared, was perfect; she was much impressed by Lord Leighton's manners; and she profoundly distrusted Mr. Watts. From time to time she ordered engraved portraits to be taken of members of the royal family; on these occasions she would have the first proofs submitted to her, and, having inspected them with minute particularity, she would point out their mistakes to the artists, indicating at the same time how they might be corrected. The artists invariably discovered that Her Majesty's suggestions were of the highest value. In literature her interests were more restricted. She was devoted to Lord Tennyson; and, as the Prince Consort had admired George Eliot, she perused *Middlemarch*: she was disappointed. There is reason to believe, however, that the romances of another female writer, whose popularity among the humbler classes of Her Majesty's subjects was at one time enormous, secured, no less, the approval of Her Majesty. Otherwise she did not read very much.

Once, however, the Queen's attention was drawn to a publication which it was impossible for her to ignore. *The Greville Memoirs*, filled with a mass of historical information of extraordinary importance, but filled also with descriptions, which were by no means flattering, of George IV, William IV, and other royal persons, was brought out by Mr. Reeve. Victoria read the book, and was appalled. It was, she declared, a 'dreadful and really scandalous book,' and she could not say 'how *horrified* and *indignant*' she was at Greville's 'indiscretion, indelicacy, ingratitude towards friends, betrayal of confidence and shameful disloyalty towards his Sovereign.' She wrote to Disraeli to tell him that in her opinion it was *'very important* that the book should be severely censured and discredited.' 'The tone in which he speaks of royalty,' she added, 'is unlike anything one sees in history even, and is most reprehensible.' Her anger was directed with almost equal vehemence against Mr. Reeve for his having published 'such an abominable book,' and she charged Sir Arthur Helps to convey to him her deep displeasure. Mr. Reeve, however, was impenitent. When Sir Arthur told him that, in the Queen's opinion, 'the book degraded royalty,' he replied: 'Not at all; it elevates it by the contrast it offers between the present and the defunct state of affairs.' But this adroit defence failed to make any impression upon Victoria; and Mr. Reeve, when he retired from the public service, did not receive the knighthood which custom entitled him to expect. Perhaps if the Queen had known how many caustic comments upon herself Mr. Reeve had quietly suppressed in the published Memoirs, she would have been almost grateful to him; but, in that case, what would she have said of Greville? Imagination boggles at the thought. As for more modern essays upon the same topic, Her Majesty, it is to be feared, would have characterised them as 'not discreet.'

But as a rule the leisure hours of that active life were occupied with recreations of a less intangible quality than the study of literature or the appreciation of art. Victoria was a woman not only of vast property but of innumerable possessions. She had inherited an immense quantity of furniture, of ornaments, of china, of plate, of valuable objects of every kind; her purchases, throughout a long life, made a formidable addition to these stores; and there flowed in upon her, besides, from every quarter of the globe, a constant stream of gifts. Over this enormous mass she exercised an unceasing and minute supervision, and the arrangement and the contemplation of it, in all its details, filled her with an intimate satisfaction. The collecting instinct has its roots in the very depths of human nature; and, in the case of Victoria, it seemed to owe its force to two of her dominating impulses—the intense sense, which had always been hers, of her own personality, and the craving which, growing with the years, had become in her old age almost an obsession, for fixity, for solidity, for the setting up of palpable barriers against the outrages of change and time. When she considered the multitudinous objects which belonged to her, or, better still, when, choosing out some section of them as the fancy took her, she actually savoured the vivid richness of their individual qualities, she saw herself deliciously reflected from a million facets, felt herself magnified miraculously over a boundless area, and was well pleased. That was just as it should be; but then came the dismaying thought—everything slips away, crumbles, vanishes; Sèvres dinner-services get broken; even golden basins go unaccountably astray; even one's self, with all the recollections and experiences that make up one's being, fluctuates, perishes, dissolves . . . But no! It could not, should not be so! There should be no changes and no losses! Nothing should ever move—neither the past nor the present—and she herself least of all! And so the tenacious woman, hoarding her valuables, decreed their immortality with all the resolution of her soul. She would not lose one memory or one pin.

She gave orders that nothing should be thrown away—and nothing was. There, in drawer after drawer, in wardrobe after wardrobe, reposed the dresses of seventy years. But not only the dresses—the furs and the mantles and subsidiary frills and the muffs and the parasols and the bonnets—all were ranged in chronological order, dated and complete. A great cupboard was devoted to the dolls; in the china room at Windsor a special table held the mugs of her childhood, and her children's mugs as well. Mementoes of the past surrounded her in serried accumulations. In every room the tables were powdered thick with the photographs of relatives; their portraits, revealing them at all ages, covered the walls; their figures, in solid marble, rose up from pedestals, or gleamed from brackets in the form of gold and silver statuettes. The dead, in every shape—in miniatures, in porcelain, in enormous life-size oil-paintings—were perpetually about her. John Brown stood upon her writing-table in solid gold. Her favourite horses and dogs, endowed with a new durability, crowded round her footsteps. Sharp, in silver gilt, dominated the dinner table; Boy and Boz lay together among unfading flowers, in bronze. And it was not enough that each particle of the past should be given the stability of metal or of marble: the whole collection, in its arrangement, no less than its entity, should be immutably fixed. There might be additions, but there might never be alterations. No chintz might change, no carpet, no curtain, be replaced by another; or, if long use at last made it necessary, the stuffs and the patterns must be so identically reproduced that the keenest eye might not detect the difference. No new picture could be hung upon the walls at Windsor, for those already there had been put in their places by Albert, whose decisions were eternal. So, indeed, were Victoria's. To ensure that they should be the aid of the camera was called in. Every single article in the Queen's possession was photographed from several points of view. These photographs were submitted to Her Majesty, and when, after careful inspection, she had approved of them, they were placed in a series of albums, richly bound. Then, opposite each photograph, an entry was made, indicating the number of the article, the number of the room in which it was kept, its exact position in the room and all its principal characteristics. The fate of every object which had undergone this process was henceforth irrevocably sealed. The whole multitude, once and for all, took up its steadfast station. And Victoria, with a gigantic volume or two of the endless catalogue always beside her, to look through, to ponder upon, to expatiate over, could feel, with a double contentment, that the transitoriness of this world had been arrested by the amplitude of her might.

Thus the collection, ever multiplying, ever encroaching upon new fields of consciousness, ever rooting itself more firmly in the depths of instinct, became one of the dominating influences of that strange existence. It was a collection not merely of things and of thoughts, but of states of mind and ways of living as well. The celebration of anniversaries grew to be an important branch of it—of birthdays and marriage days and death days, each of which demanded its appropriate feeling, which, in its turn, must be itself expressed in an appropriate outward form. And the form, of course—the ceremony of rejoicing or lamentation—was stereotyped with the rest: it was part of the collection. On a certain day, for instance, flowers must be strewn on John Brown's monument at Balmoral; and the date of the yearly departure for Scotland was fixed by that fact. Inevitably it was around the central circumstance of death— death, the final witness to human mutability—that these commemorative cravings clustered most thickly. Might not even death itself be humbled, if one could recall enough?— if one asserted, with a sufficiently passionate and reiterated emphasis, the eternity of love? Accordingly, every bed in which Victoria slept had attached to it, at the back, on the right-hand side, above the pillow, a photograph of the head and shoulders of Albert as he lay dead, surmounted by a wreath of immortelles. At Balmoral, where memories came crowding so closely, the solid signs of memory appeared in surprising profusion. Obelisks, pyramids, tombs, statues, cairns, and seats of inscribed granite, proclaimed Victoria's dedication to the dead. There, twice a year, on the days that followed her arrival, a solemn pilgrimage of inspection and meditation was performed. There, on August 26—Albert's birthday—at the foot of the bronze statue of him in Highland dress, the Queen, her family, her Court, her servants, and her tenantry, met together and in silence drank to the memory of the dead. In England the tokens of remembrance pullulated hardly less. Not a day passed without some addition to the multifold assemblage—a gold statuette of Ross, the piper—a life-sized marble group of Victoria and Albert, in medieval costume, inscribed upon the base with the words: 'Allured to brighter worlds and led the way' —a granite slab in the shrubbery at Osborne, informing the visitor of 'Waldmann: the very favourite little dachshund of Queen Victoria; who brought him from Baden, April, 1872; died July 11, 1881.'

At Frogmore, the great mausoleum, perpetually enriched, was visited almost daily by the Queen when the Court was at Windsor. But there was another, a more secret and a hardly less holy shrine. The suite of rooms which Albert had occupied in the Castle was kept for ever shut away from the eyes of any save the most privileged. Within those precincts everything remained as it had been at the Prince's death; but the mysterious preoccupation of Victoria had commanded that her husband's clothing should be laid afresh, each evening, upon the bed, and that, each evening, the water should be set ready in the basin, as if he were still alive; and this incredible rite was performed with scrupulous regularity for nearly forty years.

Such was the inner worship; and still the flesh obeyed the spirit; still the daily hours of labour proclaimed Victoria's consecration to duty and to the ideal of the dead. Yet, with the years, the sense of self-sacrifice faded; the natural energies of that ardent being discharged themselves with satisfaction into the channel of public work; the love of business which, from her girlhood, had been strong within her, reasserted itself in all its vigour, and, in her old age, to have been cut off from her papers and her boxes would have been, not a relief, but an agony to Victoria. Thus, though toiling Ministers might sigh and suffer, the whole process of government continued, till the very end, to pass before her. Nor was that all; ancient precedent had made the validity of an enormous number of official transactions dependent upon the application of the royal sign-manual; and a great proportion of the Queen's working hours was spent in this mechanical task. Nor did she show any desire to diminish it. On the contrary, she voluntarily resumed the duty of signing commissions in the army, from which she had been set free by Act of Parliament, and from which, during the years of middle life, she had abstained. In no case would she countenance the proposal that she should use a stamp. But, at last, when the increasing pressure of business made the delays of the antiquated system intolerable, she consented that, for certain classes of documents, her oral sanction should be sufficient. Each paper was read aloud to her, and she said at the end 'Approved.' Often, for hours at a time, she would sit, with Albert's bust in front of her, while the word 'Approved' issued at intervals from her lips. The word came forth with a majestic sonority; for her voice now—how changed from the silvery treble of her girlhood!—was a contralto, full and strong.

IV

The final years were years of apotheosis. In the dazzled imagination of her subjects Victoria soared aloft towards the regions of divinity through a nimbus of purest glory. Criticism fell dumb; deficiencies which, twenty years earlier, would have been universally admitted, were now as universally ignored. That the nation's idol was a very incomplete representative of the nation was a circumstance that was hardly noticed, and yet it was conspicuously true. For the vast changes which, out of the England of 1837, had produced the England of 1897, seemed scarcely to have touched the Queen. The immense industrial development of the period, the significance of which had been so thoroughly understood by Albert, meant little indeed to Victoria. The amazing scientific movement, which Albert had appreciated no less, left Victoria perfectly cold.

Her conception of the universe, and of man's place in it, and of the stupendous problems of nature and philosophy remained, throughout her life, entirely unchanged. Her religion was the religion which she had learnt from the Baroness Lehzen and the Duchess of Kent. Here, too, it might have been supposed that Albert's views might have influenced her. For Albert, in matters of religion, was advanced. Disbelieving altogether in evil spirits, he had had his doubts about the miracle of the Gaderene Swine. Stockmar, even, had thrown out, in a remarkable memorandum on the education of the Prince of Wales, the suggestion that while the child 'must unquestionably be brought up in the creed of the Church of England,' it might nevertheless be in accordance with the spirit of the times to exclude from his religious training the inculcation of a belief in 'the supernatural doctrines of Christianity.' This, however, would have been going too far; and all the royal children were brought up in complete orthodoxy. Anything else would have grieved Victoria, though her own conceptions of the orthodox were not very precise. But her nature, in which imagination and subtlety held so small a place, made her instinctively recoil from the intricate ecstasies of High Anglicanism; and she seemed to feel most at home in the simple faith of the Presbyterian Church of Scotland. This was what might have been expected; for Lehzen was the daughter of a Lutheran pastor, and the Lutherans and the Presbyterians have much in common. For many years Dr. Norman Macleod, an innocent Scotch minister, was her principal spiritual adviser; and, when he was taken from her, she drew much comfort from quiet chats about life and death with the cottagers at Balmoral. Her piety, absolutely genuine, found what it wanted in the sober exhortations of old John Grant and the devout saws of Mrs. P. Farquharson. They possessed the qualities, which, as a child of fourteen, she had so sincerely admired in the Bishop of Chester's *Exposition of the Gospel of St. Matthew;* they were 'just plain and comprehensible and full of truth and good feeling.' The Queen, who gave her name to the Age of Mill and of Darwin, never got any further than that.

From the social movements of her time, Victoria was equally remote. Towards the smallest no less than towards the greatest changes she remained inflexible. During her youth and middle age smoking had been forbidden in polite society, and so long as she lived she would not withdraw her anathema against it. Kings might protest; bishops and ambassadors, invited to Windsor, might be reduced, in the privacy of their bedrooms, to lie full-length upon the floor and smoke up the chimney—the interdict continued. It might have been supposed that a female sovereign would have lent her countenance to one of the most vital of all the reforms to which her epoch gave birth—the emancipation of women—but, on the contrary, the mere mention of such a proposal sent the blood rushing to her head. In 1870, her eye having fallen upon the report of a meeting in favour of Women's Suffrage, she wrote to Mr. Martin in royal rage— 'The Queen is most anxious to enlist everyone who can speak or write to join in checking this mad, wicked folly of "Woman's Rights," with all its attendant horrors, on which her poor feeble sex is bent, forgetting every sense of womanly feeling and propriety. Lady —— ought to get a *good whipping*. It is a subject which makes the Queen so furious that she cannot contain herself. God created men and women different—then let them remain each in their own position. Tennyson has some beautiful lines on the difference of men and women in "The Princess." Woman would become the most hateful, heartless, and disgusting of human beings were she allowed to unsex herself; and where would be the protection which man was intended to give the weaker sex? The Queen is sure that Mrs. Martin agrees with her.' The argument was irrefutable; Mrs. Martin agreed; and yet the canker spread.

In another direction Victoria's comprehension of the spirit of her age has been constantly asserted. It was for long the custom for courtly historians and polite politicians to compliment the Queen upon the correctness of her attitude towards the Constitution. But such praises seem hardly to be justified by the facts. In her later years Victoria more than once alluded with regret to her conduct during the Bedchamber crisis, and let it be understood that she had grown wiser since. Yet in truth it is difficult to trace any fundamental change either in her theory or her practice in constitutional matters throughout her life. The same despotic and personal spirit which led her to break off the negotiations with Peel is equally visible in her animosity towards Palmerston, in her threats of abdication to Disraeli, and in her desire to prosecute the Duke of Westminster for attending a meeting upon Bulgarian atrocities. The complex and delicate principles of the Constitution cannot be said to have come within the compass of her mental faculties; and in the actual developments which it underwent during her reign she played a passive part. From 1840 to 1861 the power of the Crown steadily increased in England; from 1861 to 1901 it steadily declined. The first process was due to the influence of the Prince Consort, the second to that of a series of great Ministers. During the first, Victoria was in effect a mere accessory; during the second, the threads of power, which Albert had so laboriously collected, inevitably fell from her hands into the vigorous grasp of Mr. Gladstone, Lord Beaconsfield, and Lord Salisbury. Perhaps, absorbed as she was in routine, and difficult as she found it to distinguish at all clearly between the trivial and the essential, she was only dimly aware of what was happening. Yet, at the end of her reign, the Crown was weaker than at any other time in English history. Paradoxically enough, Victoria received the highest eulogiums for assenting to a political evolution, which, had she completely realised its import, would have filled her with supreme displeasure.

Nevertheless it must not be supposed that she was a second George III. Her desire to impose her will, vehement as it was, and unlimited by any principle, was yet checked by a certain shrewdness. She might oppose her Ministers with extraordinary violence; she might remain utterly impervious to arguments and supplications; the pertinacity of her resolution might seem to be unconquerable; but, at the very last moment of all, her obstinacy would give way. Her innate respect and capacity for business, and perhaps, too, the memory of Albert's scrupulous avoidance of extreme courses, prevented her from ever entering an *impasse*. By instinct she understood when the facts were too much for her, and to them she invariably yielded. After all, what else could she do?

But if, in all these ways, the Queen and her epoch were profoundly separated, the points of contact between them also were not few. Victoria understood very well the meaning and the attractions of power and property, and in such learning the English nation, too, had grown to be more and more proficient. During the last fifteen years of the reign—for the short Liberal Administration of 1892 was a mere interlude—imperialism was the dominant creed of the country. It was Victoria's as well. In this direction, if in no other, she had allowed her mind to develop. Under Disraeli's tutelage the British Dominions over the seas had come to mean much more to her than ever before, and, in particular, she had grown enamoured of the East. The thought of India fascinated her; she set to, and learnt a little Hindustani; she engaged some Indian servants, who became her inseparable attendants, and one of whom, Munshi Abdul Karim, eventually almost succeeded to the position which had once been John Brown's. At the same time, the imperialist temper of the nation invested her office with a new significance exactly harmonising with her own inmost proclivities. The English polity was in the main a common-sense structure; but there was always a corner in it where common-sense could not enter—where, somehow or other, the ordinary measurements were not applicable and the ordinary rules did not apply. So our ancestors had laid it down, giving scope, in their wisdom, to that mystical element which, as it seems, can never quite be eradicated from the affairs of men. Naturally it was in the Crown that the mysticism of the English polity was concentrated —the Crown, with its venerable antiquity, its sacred associations, its imposing spectacular array. But, for nearly two centuries, common-sense had been predominant in the great building, and the little, unexplored, inexplicable corner had attracted small attention. Then, with the rise of imperialism, there was a change. For imperialism is a faith as well as a business; as it grew, the mysticism in English public life grew with it; and simultaneously a new importance began to attach to the Crown. The need for a symbol—a symbol of England's might, of England's worth, of England's extraordinary and mysterious destiny—became felt more urgently than ever before. The Crown was that symbol: and the Crown rested upon the head of Victoria. Thus it happened that while by the end of the reign the power of the sovereign had appreciably diminished, the prestige of the sovereign had enormously grown.

Yet this prestige was not merely the outcome of public changes; it was an intensely personal matter, too. Victoria was the Queen of England, the Empress of India, the quintessential pivot round which the whole magnificent machine was revolving—but how much more besides! For one thing, she was of a great age—an almost indispensable qualification for popularity in England. She had given proof of one of the most admired characteristics of the race—persistent vitality. She had reigned for sixty years, and she was not out. And then, she was a character. The outlines of her nature were firmly drawn, and, even through the mists which envelop royalty, clearly visible. In the popular imagination her familiar figure filled, with satisfying ease, a distinct and memorable place. It was, besides, the kind of figure which naturally called forth the admiring sympathy of the great

majority of the nation. Goodness they prized above every other human quality; and Victoria, who had said that she would be good at the age of twelve, had kept her word. Duty, conscience, morality—yes! in the light of those high beacons the Queen had always lived. She had passed her days in work and not in pleasure—in public responsibilities and family cares. The standard of solid virtue which had been set up so long ago amid the domestic happiness of Osborne had never been lowered for an instant. For more than half a century no divorced lady had approached the precincts of the Court. Victoria, indeed, in her enthusiasm for wifely fidelity, had laid down a still stricter ordinance: she frowned severely upon any widow who married again. Considering that she herself was the offspring of a widow's second marriage, this prohibition might be regarded as an eccentricity; but, no doubt, it was an eccentricity on the right side. The middle classes, firm in the triple brass of their respectability, rejoiced with a special joy over the most respectable of Queens. They almost claimed her, indeed, as one of themselves; but this would have been an exaggeration. For, though many of her characteristics were most often found among the middle classes, in other respects—in her manners, for instance—Victoria was decidedly aristocratic. And, in one important particular, she was neither aristocratic nor middle-cless: her attitude toward herself was simply regal.

Such qualities were obvious and

important; but, in the impact of a personality, it is something deeper, something fundamental and common to all its qualities, that really tells. In Victoria, it is easy to discern the nature of this underlying element: it was a peculiar sincerity. Her truthfulness, her single-mindedness, the vividness of her emotions and her unrestrained expression of them, were the varied forms which this central characteristic assumed. It was her sincerity which gave her at once her impressiveness, her charm, and her absurdity. She moved through life with the imposing certitude of one to whom concealment was impossible—either towards her surroundings or towards herself. There she was, all of her—the Queen of England, complete and obvious; the world might take her or leave her; she had nothing more to show, or to explain, or to modify; and, with her peerless carriage, she swept along her path. And not only was concealment out of the question; reticence, reserve, even dignity itself, as it sometimes seemed, might be very well dispensed with. As Lady Lyttelton said: 'There is a transparency in her truth that is very striking—not a shade of exaggeration in describing feelings or facts; like very few other people I ever knew. Many may be as true, but I think it goes often along with some reserve. She talks all out; just as it is, no more and no less.' She talked all out; and she wrote all out, too. Her letters, in the surprising jet of their expression, remind one of a turned-on tap. What is within pours forth in an immediate, spontaneous rush. Her utterly unliterary style has at least the merit of being a vehicle exactly suited to her thoughts and feelings; and even the platitude of her phraseology carries with it a curiously personal flavor. Undoubtedly it was through her writings that she touched the heart of the public. Not only in her 'Highland Journals,' where the mild chronicle of her private proceedings was laid bare without a trace either of affectation or of embarrassment, but also in those remarkable messages to the nation which, from time to time, she published in the newspapers, her people found her very close to them indeed. They felt sincerity, and they responded. And in truth it was an endearing trait.

The personality and the position, too—the wonderful combination of them—that, perhaps, was what was finally fascinating in the case. The little old lady, with her white hair and her plain mourning clothes, in her wheeled chair or her donkey-carriage—one saw her so; and then —close behind—with their immediate suggestion of singularity, of mystery, and of power—the Indian servants. That was the familiar vision, and it was admirable; but, at chosen moments, it was right that the widow of Windsor should step forth apparent Queen. The last and the most glorious of such occasions was the Jubilee of 1897. Then, as the splendid procession passed along, escorting Victoria through the thronged re-echoing streets of London on her progress of thanksgiving to St. Paul's

Cathedral, the greatness of her realm and the adoration of her subjects blazed out together. The tears welled to her eyes, and, while the multitude roared around her, 'How kind they are to me! How kind they are!' she repeated over and over again. That night her message flew over the Empire: 'From my heart I thank my beloved people. May God bless them!' The long journey was nearly done. But the traveller, who had come so far, and through such strange experiences, moved on with the old faltering step. The girl, the wife, the aged woman, were the same: vitality conscientiousness, pride, and simplicity were here to the latest hour.

✗ *Chapter* 10

The End

The evening had been golden; but, after all, the day was to close in cloud and tempest. Imperial needs, imperial ambitions, involved the country in the South African War. There were checks, reverses, bloody disasters; for a moment the nation was shaken, and the public distresses were felt with intimate solicitude by the Queen. But her spirit was high, and neither her courage nor her confidence wavered for a moment. Throwing herself heart and soul into the struggle, she laboured with redoubled vigour, interested herself in every detail of the hostilities, and sought by every means in her power to render service to the national cause. In April 1900, when she was in her eighty-first year, she made the extraordinary decision to abandon her annual visit to the South of France, and to go instead to Ireland, which had provided a particularly large number of recruits to the armies in the field. She stayed for three weeks in Dublin, driving through the streets, in spite of the warnings of her advisers, without an armed escort; and the visit was a complete success. But, in the course of it, she began, for the first time, to show signs of the fatigue of age.

For the long strain and the unceasing anxiety, brought by the war, made themselves felt at last. Endowed by nature with a robust constitution, Victoria, though in periods of depression she had sometimes supposed herself an invalid, had in reality throughout her life enjoyed remarkably good health. In her old age, she had suffered from a rheumatic stiffness of the joints, which had necessitated the use of a stick, and, eventually, a wheeled chair; but no other ailments attacked her, until, in 1898, her eyesight began to be affected by incipient cataract. After that, she found reading more and more difficult, though she could still sign her name, and even, with some difficulty, write letters. In the summer of 1900, however, more serious symptoms appeared. Her memory, in whose strength and precision she had so long prided herself, now sometimes deserted her; there was a tendency towards aphasia; [1] and, while no specific disease declared itself, by the autumn there were unmistakable signs of a general physical decay. Yet, even in these last months, the strain of iron held firm. The daily work continued; nay, it actually increased; for the Queen, with an astonishing pertinacity, insisted upon communicating personally with an ever-growing multitude of men and women who had suffered through the war.

By the end of the year the last remains of her ebbing strength had almost deserted her; and through the early days of the opening century it was clear that her dwindling forces were only kept together by an effort of will. On January 14, she had at Osborne an hour's interview with Lord Roberts, who had returned victorious from South Africa a few days before. She inquired with acute anxiety into all the details of the war; she appeared to sustain the exertion successfully; but, when the audience was over, there was a collapse. On the following day her medical attendants recognized that her state was hopeless; and yet, for two days more, the indomitable spirit fought on; for two days more she discharged the duties of a Queen of England. But after that there was an end of working; and then, and not till then, did the last optimism of

those about her break down. The brain was failing, and life was gently slipping away. Her family gathered round her; for a little more she lingered, speechless and apparently insensible; and, on January 22, 1901, she died.

When, two days previously, the news of the approaching end had been made public, astonished grief had swept over the country. It appeared as if some monstrous reversal of the course of nature was about to take place. The vast majority of her subjects had never known a time when Queen Victoria had not been reigning over them. She had become an indissoluble part of their whole scheme of things, and that they were about to lose her appeared a scarcely possible thought. She herself, as she lay blind and silent, seemed to those who watched her to be divested of all thinking—to have glided already, unawares, into oblivion. Yet, perhaps, in the secret chambers of consciousness, she had her thoughts, too. Perhaps her fading mind called up once more the shadows of the past to float before it, and retraced, for the last time, the vanished visions of that long history—passing back and back, through the cloud of years, to older and ever older memories—to the spring woods at Osborne, so full of primroses for Lord Beaconsfield —to Lord Palmerston's queer clothes and high demeanour, and Albert's face under the green lamp, and Albert's first stag at Balmoral, and Albert in his blue and silver uniform, and the Baron coming in through a doorway, and Lord M. dreaming at

[1] aphasia: a brain condition resulting in a loss of power to use or understand words.

Windsor with the rooks cawing in the elm-trees, and the Archbishop of Canterbury on his knees in the dawn, and the old King's turkey-cock ejaculations, and Uncle Leopold's soft voice at Claremont, and Lehzen with the globes, and her mother's feathers sweeping down towards her, and a great old repeater-watch of her father's in its tortoise-shell case, and a yellow rug, and some friendly flounces of sprigged muslin, and the trees and the grass at Kensington.

AFTERWORD

Lytton Strachey published his first biographical work, *Eminent Victorians,* in 1918. It was a time when all youngish intellectuals felt profoundly disillusioned. The old men and their ideas had between them brought about the Great War, in which millions of young men had perished. The notion of a gradual but inevitable progress, so widely accepted during the Victorian Age, had now begun to seem ridiculous. It appeared that poison gas, tanks, and bombing planes could be part of progress too. All the old overoptimistic talk about an approaching era of universal peace seemed nonsensical or wicked now that Europe was one vast slaughterhouse. It was the typical Victorians who had been the supremely confident optimists. They had established the values, had written and talked the rubbish which had been blown to dust on the Western Front. So Lytton Strachey sharpened his pen and wrote biographical studies of four famous Victorians: two heroic figures, General Gordon and Florence Nightingale; two revered figures, Cardinal Manning and Dr. Arnold, headmaster of Rugby and the originator of the "character-building" style of education. Strachey announced quite frankly in his Introduction that he was following a French tradition of biography, not the dull and routine English manner:

> Those two fat volumes, with which it is our custom to commemorate the dead—who does not know them, with their ill-digested masses of material, their slipshod style, their tone of tedious panegyric, their lamentable lack of selection, of detachment, of design? They are as familiar as the *cortège* of the undertaker, and wear the same air of slow, funereal barbarism . . .

It is quite clear from the above that Strachey is ready to claim for his own biographical method the virtues of selection, detachment, design.

Selection and design are obvious in *Eminent Victorians*. But their author cannot justly claim to be detached. Indeed, his selection and design are often used quite unscrupulously to produce not a truthful portrait but a brilliant caricature. It is not that he tells lies about his subjects. But by ignoring some facts and by emphasizing and highlighting others, all very adroitly, he creates the effect he has decided from the first to create, like an artful prosecuting counselor addressing a jury. These studies in *Eminent Victorians* are astonishingly brilliant performances: the first, and probably still the best, of their kind in English. But they must be recognized for what they are—biography as caricature.

Their success was immediate and enormous. So was their influence. A term was found for the method—it "debunked." And because both writers and readers in the 1920's were in a "debunking" mood, then very soon "debunking" biographies, which instead of plastering their subjects with praise now rushed them into the prisoner's dock and began prosecuting them, became all the fashion, both in Britain and America. But most of these "debunking" biographers had not a tenth of Strachey's knowledge, skill, and wit, could offer only the clumsiest imitation of his manner; and the result was, with a very few exceptions, a number of books forgotten now—and best forgotten. On the other hand, it is only fair to Strachey to add that not only are these original biographical studies of his not forgotten, for they have been reprinted over and over again, but that he has had a good as well as a dubious influence upon succeeding English and American biographers, encouraging them to avoid "ill-digested masses of material," "slipshod style," "tedious panegyric," and to try to achieve a rigorous selection of facts, design, ease, and wit. Politicians, generals, and tycoons may still have their lives dully chronicled in the same fat volumes, but nearly all biographers with any pretensions to literary merit, writing during the last thirty or forty years, owe something to Strachey's influence.

Now my guess—and it is frankly a guess, for I have no direct evidence to offer—is that when Strachey decided to write a life of Queen Victoria, he saw himself presenting her in the style of the *Eminent Victorians*. Fortunately for him, and for us, when he actually set to work, faced with the task (a very formidable task) of transforming thousands of notes into an easy, continuous narrative, he changed his mind and his method. I say "fortunately" not because I regard Victoria as a semisacred subject, not to be made fun of, but simply because the earlier style, designed for short studies or sketch portraits, would have been intolerable in such a narrative, covering one of the longest reigns in history. Not that he entirely abandoned his earlier manner, with its bland mocking irony. It keeps appearing, especially when he is dealing with Albert, the Prince Consort, whom he regards with no admiration whatever. Here is a good example of this manner:

As she watched her beloved Albert, after toiling with State documents and public functions, devoting every spare moment of his time to domestic duties, to artistic appreciation, and to intellectual improvements; as she listened to him cracking his jokes at the luncheon-table, or playing Mendelssohn on the organ, or pointing out the merits of Sir Edwin Landseer's pictures; as she followed him round while he gave instructions about the breeding of cattle, or decided that the Gainsboroughs must be hung higher up so that the Winterhalters might be properly seen—she felt perfectly certain that no other wife had ever had such a husband. His mind was apparently capable of everything, and she was hardly surprised to learn that he had made an important discovery for the conversion of sewage into agricultural manure. . . .

Nobody should mistake the nature of this passage: it is, as women often say, thoroughly "catty." He is telling us that Albert was an industrious, solemn prig, without taste and artistic judgment.

It is generally believed that Strachey largely dropped his "debunking" manner because he began to feel both respect and affection for Victoria. My own view is that he had good literary reasons for changing his manner, as I have already suggested, and that it is only at the end of his story, when Victoria is very old, that he begins to show signs of respect and affection. I find little evidence of them in the earlier chapters. On the other hand, he is not as critical of her as he might have been. This is what struck me first, on rereading the book after many years. In spite of his mockery and irony and dislike of her beloved Albert, he is kinder to her than he need have been, than I would have been if I had been writing the life of this queen. It is not that he is too directly sympathetic, for he sees and indicates her limitations and faults quite clearly, but that he tends to ignore or to minimize the harmful consequences of these limitations and faults.

A strong case can be made against Queen Victoria. She had character and courage but she was narrow and rather stupid. Her accession, as Strachey points out, represented a triumph of the new middle class; and she soon became almost the symbolic figure of this class, itself narrow, smug, complacent, detested by every major Victorian writer. Too much German influence came in through her unbounded adoration of Albert. (Here is one small instance: the Christmas tree, which we consider now to be typically Victorian, was borrowed from Germany. I am not denouncing this charming object, only showing how widespread this German influence was.) Her retirement from public life for years after Albert's death was self-indulgent; it encouraged prejudice against the Crown. She wanted to be a queen in private but not in public, an unreasonable desire that many of her subjects rightly resented. She should have left foreign affairs entirely to her ministers or, if she was determined to interfere in them, she should have tried to understand them properly and not to regard them as a mere extension of royal family affairs. Her political views were too easily influenced by what she felt personally about her leading statesmen. One of them, that master of flattery, Disraeli, invented for her, against the feeling of Parliament, the title of Empress of India, and this, together with the Jubilee celebrations, strengthened the whole Imperial idea, and in the end did Britain more harm than good. Finally, her immense personal influence, used on behalf of a narrow unenlightened idea of the arts, morals, and manners, kept Victorianism, the outlook of a smug middle class, triumphant too long. The reaction against it was equally extreme and uncivilized. So, during the second half of Victoria's reign, London was the most hypocritical and the most vicious city in Europe.

There, briefly, is the case against Victoria. Strachey, of course, was not ignorant of it; there is no statement of mine he could not easily have amplified. But he does seem to me to be too ready to glide over it, not, I believe, out of sympathy with his subject herself, for that sympathy only arrives at the end, but largely, I think, because any close presentation of the case against her would not have been in agreement with his general design and manner. After rereading him, I have a further criticism. While there is a great deal of political history in this biography, and perhaps rather too much, it seems to me to be curiously weak and inadequate in its social history, in those very regions where Victoria's personal influence was strongest. It might be said that there is too much about foreign advisers, prime ministers, and foreign secretaries in the narrative, and far too little about culture and social life, morals and manners, and the relation between the Queen and her ordinary subjects. And this is odd because Strachey himself was anything but a conventional historian, and was in fact a literary critic and biographer who happened to have chosen as his subject a historical personage. Perhaps he felt, as authors often do in these circumstances when they are a little outside their own field, that he had to resist his own inclinations, to be a political historian, for once, at all costs.

These reservations, however, do nothing to change my opinion that we have here a masterpiece of biography. The enormous mass of material has been miraculously transformed into a continuously fascinating narrative, moving with lightness and ease down all the years. The longest reign in English history, beginning in the world of *Pickwick Papers* and ending in the world of Wells's *The First Men in the Moon,* a giant age crowded with great personalities and events, becomes an absorbing life story. We see the fair rosy girl, crowned in 1837, gradually change into the indomitable little old woman, a figure of legend, that we discover at the end of the tale. And what a wonderful piece of writing that final chapter is!

Here, condensed into four superb paragraphs, are the pathos and the wonder, the glory and the mystery of this woman's life—and indeed, in essence, of all our lives.

STUDY QUESTIONS

1. What aspects of Victoria's early childhood does Strachey emphasize in his account? To what extent was Victoria exposed to treatment and training markedly different from that given any little rich girl?

2. In what particular ways do you think that Victoria's education influenced her actions and decisions as Queen of England?

3. In Chapters 1 and 2 ("Antecedents" and "Childhood") the reader is supplied with considerable information about various members of the royal family, their personalities, and their problems. These chapters seem to be largely pre-Victorian. In what ways do they turn out to be important to our understanding of the central subject of the biography?

4. With what examples of Victoria's strength of will, as it was evident prior to her marriage, does Strachey supply us?

5. One of the significant experiences of Victoria's early life seems, by Strachey's account, to have been the struggle between her mother and the Baroness Lehzen. What is the history of this contest? What part did Victoria play in it?

6. Queens must, within certain limitations, choose their mates and initiate their own proposals of marriage. What were the limitations which controlled Victoria's courtship? Through what stages did Victoria's attitude toward Albert pass before their marriage? What, according to Strachey, seem to have been her reasons for falling in love with him?

7. Strachey assures us, on page 505, that Albert was not in love with his fiancée. How can such an assertion be supported or attacked on the evidence recorded in this biography?

8. Consider the history, personality, and status of Baron Stockmar. What was the nature of his influence on the Queen and Prince Consort?

9. What specific changes did Albert make in the daily life of Victoria's household? Which of his personal characteristics prompted these changes?

10. In our century the term *Victorian* has been widely used to imply prudishness, stuffiness, and an excessive concern with ignoring many of the basic realities of human life. (It is, for example, *Victorian* to call legs *limbs,* or to avoid the barnyard term *bull.* The clothing that we are accustomed to wear in warm weather and at the beach is not *Victorian,* to say the least.) From Strachey's report of her life and influence, what justification do you find for attaching the Queen's name to this meaning?

11. What impressions of the royal couple's artistic tastes and recreational preferences do we receive from Strachey's description of Balmoral?

12. Strachey tells us that Albert, at

the height of his public importance in England, still wanted "to dominate and to be understood." To what extent did he come to dominate his wife? To what extent did she ever understand him?

13. Describe Albert's relationships with the various classes of people in his adopted country. What tastes and qualities does Strachey note in Albert as being un-English? By what elements of the population was he apparently appreciated most? Why?

14. "For suave malice nothing in English exceeds the portrait of Albert" (William York Tindall). What do you think of this appraisal of Strachey's treatment of the Prince Consort? You may note that from the beginning Strachey depicts an Albert who took himself very seriously indeed; a man who spent himself strenuously and sometimes absurdly on a number of mistaken or unimportant causes. But are there grounds for arguing that Strachey also shows, at times, sympathy and admiration for Albert?

15. Frank Swinnerton, in his book, *The Georgian Scene,* writes: "quite half the pleasure we obtain from Strachey is due to the fact that he amuses us at the expense of others." To what extent do you think that Strachey makes Victoria amusingly ridiculous? Using as an example Strachey's depiction of an evening's entertainment in the royal household (485–486), demonstrate certain of his methods for amusing us at the expense of others.

16. Strachey tells us that "from 1840 to 1861 the power of the Crown steadily increased in England; from 1861 to 1901 it steadily declined." We note, of course, that 1861 was the year of Prince Albert's death. How important does Strachey feel this event

was in the decline of royal power? What other factors does he supply as causes for this decline?

17. How close, according to the evidence before us, was Queen Victoria to the lives and affairs of her subjects? Did she, apparently, know a good deal more about some parts of English society than others? What abilities and disabilities in her character and background affected her knowledge of her people?

18. Although Strachey's style is ordinarily detached and ironic, there are scenes in this biography which apparently drew out the romantic in him. Consider, for example, his descriptions of the respective deathbeds of Victoria and Albert. What elements in these presentations suggest strong feeling, perhaps even sentimentality? On the other hand, is ironic detachment entirely absent from them?

19. What was Victoria's attitude toward Albert's illness up to his final relapse? How was this attitude characteristic of her?

20. Unlike James Boswell, Lytton Strachey did not have a personal acquaintance with his famous subject. His information comes from reports, letters, memoirs, and, occasionally, indirect hearsay. Yet most readers agree that *Queen Victoria* seems an intimate, personal picture of an individual. What techniques does Strachey use in order to achieve this effect?

21. One of the stylistic characteristics of *Queen Victoria* is the frequent appearance of French and German terms, phrases, and quotations. With two exceptions, Strachey did not choose to translate these himself, although they have, in most cases, been translated in the footnotes of this edition. What are the various circumstances under which this English bi-

ographer uses foreign languages? What seem to be the effects that he is attempting?

22. Of all her prime ministers, Lord Melbourne and Mr. Disraeli were the most intimate and personally influential with their queen. What notable similarities and differences were there between the two men as Strachey pictures them? Compare and contrast particularly their methods of getting along with the sovereign.

23. What were Mr. Gladstone's problems in dealing with the Queen? How does Strachey's account of her reactions toward this prime minister help characterize her as a person?

24. Describe in sequence Victoria's relations with Lord Palmerston. In what ways was his effect on her and on her reign different from that of any other of her ministers?

25. On at least one notable occasion Victoria changed her preference in political parties. This is not surprising, since parties and problems changed considerably during her long reign. What evidence do you find in this biography, however, that she maintained a fairly consistent basic political philosophy throughout her adult life? To what extent was she really interested in politics?

26. What were Victoria's reactions to the loss of Albert as they continued, with some variation, through her widowhood? Which of them particularly suggest the extraordinariness (or, perhaps, peculiarity) of the Queen? What effects did these reactions have on her social and political life?

27. In what particulars did Victoria, in her old age, replace and surpass the role formerly enacted by her uncle, King Leopold of Belgium?

28. While Strachey deals amply with Victoria's mistakes, absurdities, and limitations, by the end of the book it is perfectly evident that he admires her. On what qualities is this admiration based?

The Edge of Day

A Boyhood in the West of England

by Laurie Lee

THE EDGE OF DAY by Laurie Lee is a poet's account of his childhood. It contrasts very sharply with the other three works in this volume. They are biographies; this is an autobiography. They are on a very broad scale, showing the life of a master dramatist, a literary dictator, a famous queen; this is on a very narrow scale, offering us a few years in the life of a small boy. They are filled with public personages and events; this is all very private. But being a poet's book, this one brings us far nearer to the actual sight, sound, feel, quality of *living*.

Laurie Lee was born in 1914. I have no need to describe his early life because here it is in this autobiography. He was educated at local schools and never went to a university. For some years before the war, he lived—in a kind of "offbeat" fashion, for he is, in the better sense of that term, something of an "offbeat" character—in various places along the shores of the Mediterranean, accompanied by a guitar. During the war and afterward, he worked for various film units. He has published several books of poems, and an enchanting little book about Spain, *A Rose for Winter*.

He is, to my mind, one of the best lyrical poets we have now in England. His poetry comes out of a whole style of life and outlook that are essentially poetic. There are some poets who can look and behave like bank managers, but Laurie Lee is not one of them, belonging to the other and older tradition, poets who seem to sing—and almost live—like birds. He is a slightly built man, with a sensitive and humorous face, and engaging, unconventional manners. He is one of those men, like the Pied Piper, who instantly fascinate children. With *The Edge of Day*—very successful in Britain as *Cider with Rosie*—he has fascinated many thousands of readers.

✖ First Light

I was set down from the carrier's cart at the age of three; and there with a sense of bewilderment and terror my life in the village began.

The June grass, amongst which I stood, was taller than I was, and I wept. I had never been so close to grass before. It towered above me and all around me, each blade tattooed with tiger skins of sunlight. It was knife-edged, dark, and a wicked green, thick as a forest and alive with grasshoppers that chirped and chattered and leapt through the air like monkeys.

I was lost and didn't know where to move. A tropic heat oozed up from the ground, rank with sharp odours of roots and nettles. Snow clouds of elderblossom banked in the sky, showering upon me the fumes and flakes of their sweet and giddy suffocation. High overhead ran frenzied larks, screaming, as though the sky were tearing apart.

For the first time in my life I was out of the sight of humans. For the first time in my life I was alone in a world whose behaviour I could neither predict nor fathom: a world of birds that squealed, of plants that stank, of insects that sprang about without warning. I was lost and I did not expect to be found again. I put back my head and howled, and the sun hit me smartly on the face, like a bully.

From this daylight nightmare I was wakened, as from many another, by the appearance of my sisters. They came scrambling and calling up the steep, rough bank and, parting the long grass, found me. Faces of rose, familiar, living; huge shining faces hung up like shields between me and the sky; faces with grins and white teeth (some broken) to be conjured up like genii with a howl, brushing off terror with their broad scoldings and affection. They leaned over me—one, two, three—their mouths smeared with red currants and their hands dripping with juice.

'There, there, it's all right; don't you wail anymore. Come down 'ome and we'll stuff you with currants.'

And Marjorie, the eldest, lifted me into her long brown hair, and ran me jogging down the path and through the steep rose-filled garden, and set me down on the cottage doorstep, which was our home, though I couldn't believe it.

That was the day we came to the village, in the summer of the last year of the first World War. To a cottage that stood in a half acre of garden on a steep bank above a lake; a cottage with three floors and a cellar and a treasure in the walls, with a pump and apple trees, syringa and strawberries, rooks in the chimneys, frogs in the cellar, mushrooms on the ceiling, and all for three and sixpence a week.

I don't know where I lived before then. My life began on the carrier's cart which brought me up the long, slow hills to the village, and dumped me in the high grass, and lost me. I had ridden wrapped up in a Union Jack to protect me from the sun, and when I rolled out of it, and stood piping loud among the buzzing jungle of that summer bank, then, I feel, was I born. And to all the rest of us, the whole family of eight, it was the beginning of a life.

But on that first day we were all lost. Chaos was come in cartloads of furniture, and I crawled the kitchen floor through forests of upturned chair legs and crystal fields of glass. We were washed up in a new land, and began to spread out, searching its springs and treasures. The sisters spent the light of that first day stripping the fruit bushes in the garden. The currants were at their prime, clusters of red, black, and yellow berries all tangled up with wild roses. Here was bounty the girls had never known before, and they darted squawking from bush to bush, clawing the fruit like sparrows.

Our mother too was distracted from duty, seduced by the rich wilderness of the garden so long abandoned. All day she trotted to and fro, flushed and garrulous, pouring flowers into every pot and jug she could find on the kitchen floor. Flowers from the garden, daisies from the bank, cow parsley, grasses, ferns, and leaves—they flowed in armfuls through the cottage door until its dim interior seemed entirely possessed by the world outside—a still green pool flooding with honeyed tides of summer.

I sat on the floor on a raft of muddles and gazed through the green window which was full of the rising garden. I saw the long black stockings of the girls, gaping with white flesh, kicking among the currant bushes. Every so often one of them would dart into the kitchen, cram my great mouth with handfuls of squashed berries, and run out again. And the more I got, the more I called for more. It was like feeding a fat young cuckoo.

The long day crowed and chirped and rang. Nobody did any work, and there was nothing to eat save berries and bread. I crawled about among the ornaments on the unfamiliar floor—the glass fishes, china dogs, shepherds and shepherdesses, bronze horsemen, stopped clocks, barometers, and photographs of bearded men. I called on them each in turn, for they were the shrines and faces of a half-remembered landscape. But as I watched the sun move around the walls, drawing rainbows from the cut-glass jars in the corner, I longed for a return of order.

Then, suddenly, the day was at an end, and the house was furnished. Each stick and cup and picture was nailed immovably in place; the beds were sheeted, the windows curtained, the straw mats laid, and the house was home. I don't remember seeing it happen, but suddenly the inexorable tradition of the house, with its smell, chaos, and complete logic, occurred as though it had never been otherwise. The furnishing and founding of the house came like the nightfall of that first day. From that uneasy loneliness of objects strewn on the kitchen floor, everything flew to its place and was never again questioned.

And from that day we grew up. The domestic arrangement of the house was shaken many times, like a snowstorm toy, so that beds and chairs and ornaments swirled from room to room, pursued by the gusty energies of Mother and the girls. But always these things resettled within the pattern of the walls, nothing escaped or changed, and so it remained for twenty years.

Now I measured that first growing year by the widening fields that became visible to me, the new tricks of dressing and getting about with which I became gradually endowed. I could open the kitchen door by screwing myself into a ball and leaping and banging the latch with my fist. I could climb into the high bed by using the ironwork as a ladder. I could whistle, but I couldn't lace my shoes. Life became a series of experiments which brought grief or the rewards of accomplishment: a pondering of patterns and mysteries in the house, while time hung golden and suspended, and one's body, from leaping and climbing, took on the rigid insanity of an insect, petrified, as it were, for hours together, breathing and watching. Watching the grains of dust fall in the sunny room, following an ant from its cradle to the grave, going over the knots in the bedroom ceiling—knots that seemed to dilate and run in the half-light of dawn and form the fluid shapes of monsters, or moved stealthily from board to board; but which settled again in the wax light of day no more monstrous than fossils in coal.

These knots on the bedroom ceiling were the whole range of a world, and over them my eyes went endlessly voyaging in that long primeval light of waking to which a child is condemned. They were archipelagoes in a sea of blood-coloured varnish, they were armies grouped and united against me, they were the alphabet of a macabre tongue, the first book I ever learned to read.

Radiating from that house, with its crumbling walls, its thumps and shadows, its fancied foxes under the floor, I moved along paths that lengthened inch by inch with my mounting strength of days. From stone to stone in the trackless yard I sent forth my acorn shell of senses, moving unfathomable oceans like a South Sea savage island-hopping across the Pacific. Antennae of eyes and nose and grubbing fingers captured a new tuft of grass, a fern, a slug, the skull of a bird, a grotto of bright snails. Through the long summer ages of those first few days I enlarged my world and mapped it in my mind: its secure havens, its dust-deserts and puddles, its peaks of dirt and flag-flying bushes. Returning too, dry-throated, over and over again, to its several well-prodded horrors: the bird's gaping bones in its cage of old sticks; the black flies in the corner, slimy dead; dry rags of snakes; and the crowded, rotting, silent-roaring city of a cat's grub-captured carcass.

Once seen, these relics passed within the frontiers of the known lands, to be remembered with a buzzing in the ears, to be revisited when the stomach was strong. They were the first tangible victims of that destroying force whose job I knew went on both night and day, though I could never catch him at it. Nevertheless I was grateful for them. Though they haunted my eyes and stuck in my dreams, they reduced for me the first infinite possibilities of horror. They chastened the imagination with the proof of a limited frightfulness.

From the harbour mouth of the scullery door I learned the rocks and reefs and the channels where safety lay. I discovered the physical pyramid of the cottage, its stores and labyrinths, its centres of magic, and of the green, sprouting island-garden upon which it stood. My mother and sisters sailed past me like galleons in their busy dresses, and I learned the smells and sounds which followed in their wakes, the surge of breath, air of carbolic, song and grumble, and smashing of crockery.

How magnificent they appeared, full-rigged, those towering girls, with their flying hair and billowing blouses, their white-mast arms stripped for work or washing. At any moment one was boarded by them, bussed and buttoned, or swung up high like a wriggling fish to be hooked and held in their lacy linen.

The scullery was a mine of all the minerals of living. Here I discovered water—a very different element from the green crawling scum that stank in the garden tub. You could pump it in pure blue gulps out of the ground; you could swing on the pump handle and it came out sparkling like liquid sky. And it broke and ran and shone on the tiled floor, or quivered in a jug, or weighted your clothes with cold. You could drink it, draw with it, froth it with soap, swim beetles across it, or fly it in bubbles in the air. You could put your head in it, and open your eyes, and see the sides of the bucket buckle, and hear your caught breath roar, and work your mouth like a fish, and smell the lime from the ground. Substance of magic—which you could tear or wear, confine or scatter, or send down holes, but never burn or break or destroy.

The scullery was water, where the old pump stood. And it had everything else that was related to water: thick steam of Mondays, edgy with starch; soapsuds boiling, bellying and popping, creaking and whispering, rainbowed with light and winking with a million windows. Bubble, bubble, toil and grumble, rinsing and slapping of sheets and shirts, and panting Mother rowing her red arms like oars in the steaming waves. Then the linen came up on a stick out of the pot, like pastry, or woven suds, or sheets of moulded snow.

Here, too, was the scrubbing of floors and boots, of arms and necks, of red and white vegetables. Walk into the morning disorder of this room and all the garden was laid out dripping on the table. Chopped carrots like copper pennies, radishes and chives, potatoes dipped and stripped clean from their coats of mud, the snapping of tight pea pods, long shells of green pearls, and the tearing of glutinous beans from their nests of wool.

Grown stealthy, marauding among these preparations, one nibbled one's way like a rat through roots and leaves. Peas rolled under the tongue, fresh cold, like solid water; teeth chewed green peel of apples, acid sharp, and the sweet white starch of swedes. Beaten away by wet hands gloved with flour, one returned in a morose and speechless lust. Slivers of raw pastry, moulded, warm, went down in the shapes of men and women—heads and arms of un-salted flesh seasoned with nothing but a dream of cannibalism.

Large meals were prepared in this room, cauldrons of stew for the in-satiate hunger of eight. Stews of all that grew on these rich banks, fla-voured with sage, coloured with Oxo and laced with a few bones of lamb. There was, it is true, little meat at those times; sometimes a pound of bare ribs for boiling, or an occasional rabbit dumped at the door by a neighbour. But there was green food of great weight in season, and lentils and bread for ballast. Eight to ten loaves came to the house every day, and they never grew dry. We tore them to pieces with their crusts still warm, and their monotony was brightened by the objects we found in them—string, nails, paper, and once a mouse; for those were days of happy-go-lucky baking. The len-tils were cooked in a great pot which also heated the water for the Satur-day night baths. Our small wood fire could heat sufficient water to fill one bath only, and this we shared in turn. Being the youngest but one, my water was always the dirtiest but one, and the implications of this privilege remain with me to this day.

Waking one morning in the white-washed bedroom, I opened my eyes and found them blind. Though I stretched them and stared where the room should be, nothing was visible but a glare of gold, flat on my throbbing eyelids. I groped for my body and found it there. I heard the singing of birds. Yet there was noth-ing at all to be seen of the world save this quivering yellow light. Was I dead? I wondered. Was I in heaven? Whatever it was, I hated it. I had wakened too soon from a dream of crocodiles and I was not ready for this further outrage. Then I heard the girls' steps on the stairs. 'Our Marge!' I shouted. 'I can't see nothing!' And I began to give out my howl.

A slap of bare feet slithered across the floor, and I heard sister Mar-jorie's giggle.

'Just look at him,' she said. 'Pop and fetch a flannel, Doth—'is eyes've got stuck down again.'

The cold edge of the flannel passed over my face, showered me with water, and I was back in the world. Bed and beams, and the sun-square window, and the girls bending over me grinning.

' 'Oo did it?' I yelled.

'Nobody, silly. Your eyes got bunged up, that's all.'

The sweet glue of sleep; it had happened before but somehow I always forgot. So I threatened the girls I'd bung theirs up too; I was awake, I could see, I was happy. I lay looking out of the small green window. The world outside was crimson and on fire. I had never seen it looking like that before.

'Doth?' I said. 'What's happening to them trees?'

Dorothy was dressing. She leaned out of the window, slow and sleepy, and the light came through her nightdress like sand through a sieve.

'Nothing's happening,' she said.

'Yes it is then,' I said. 'They're falling to bits.'

Dorothy scratched her dark head, yawning wide, and white feathers floated out of her hair.

'It's only the leaves droppin'. We're in autumn now. The leaves always drop in autumn.'

Autumn? In autumn. Was that where we were? Where the leaves always dropped and there was always this smell. I imagined it continuing, with no change, for ever, these wet flames of woods burning on and on like the bush of Moses, as natural a part of this new-found land as the eternal snows of the poles. Why had we come to such a place?

Marjorie, who had gone down to help with the breakfast, suddenly came tumbling back up the stairs.

'Doth,' she whispered; she seemed excited and frightened; 'Doth . . . 'e's turned up again. 'Elp on Loll with 'is clothes and come on down, quick.'

We went down and found him sitting by the fireside, smiling, wet and cold. I climbed up to the breakfast table and stared at him, the stranger. To me he did not so much appear to be a man as a conglomeration of woody things. His face was red and crinkled, brilliant like fungus. There were leaves in his mud-matted hair, and leaves and twigs on his crumbling clothes, and all over him. His boots were like the black pulp you find when you dig under a tree. Mother gave him porridge and bread and he smiled palely at us all.

'It must have been cruel in the wood,' said our mother.

'I've got some sacks, ma'am,' he said, spooning his porridge. 'They keep out the wet.'

They wouldn't; they'd suck it up like a wick and wrap him in it.

'You oughtn't to live like that,' said Mother. 'You ought to get back to your home.'

'No,' smiled the man. 'That wouldn't do. They'd jump on me before you could say "knife." '

Mother shook her head sadly, and sighed, and gave him more porridge. We boys adored the look of the man; the girls, fastidious, were more uncertain of him. But he was no tramp or he wouldn't be in the kitchen. He had four bright medals in his pocket, which he would produce and polish and lay on the table like money. He spoke like nobody else we knew; in fact we couldn't understand many of his words. But Mother seemed to understand him, and would ask him questions, and look at the photographs he carried in his shirt and sigh and shake her head. He talked something of battles and of flying in the air, and it was all wonderful to us.

He was no man from these parts. He had appeared on the doorstep one early morning, asking for a cup of tea. Our mother had brought him in and given him a whole breakfast. There had been blood on his face and he had seemed very weak. Now he was in a kitchen with a woman and a lot of children, and his eyes shone brightly, and his whiskers smiled. He told us he was sleeping in the wood, which seemed to me a good idea. And he was a soldier, because Mother had said so.

I knew about war; all my uncles were in it; my ears from birth had been full of the talk of it. Sometimes I used to climb into the basket chair by the fire and close my eyes and see brown men moving over a field in battle. I was three, but I saw them grope and die and felt myself older than they.

This man did not look like a soldier. He had a beard and his khaki was torn. But the girls insisted he was a soldier, and said it in whispers, like a secret. And when he came down to our house for breakfast, and sat hunched by the fire, steaming with damp and coated with leaves and dirt, I thought of him sleeping up there in the wood. I imagined him sleeping, then having a go at the battle, then coming down to us for a cup of tea. He was the war, and the war was up there; I wanted to ask, 'How's the war in that wood?'

But he never told us. He sat drinking his tea, gulping and gasping, the fire drawing the damp out of his clothes as if ghosts were rising from him. When he caught our eyes, he smiled from his beard. And when brother Jack shot at him with a spoon, saying, 'I'm a sodger,' he replied softly, 'Aye, and you'd make a better one than me, son, any day.'

When he said that, I wondered what had happened to the war. Was he in those rags because he was such a bad soldier? Had he lost the war in the wood?

When he didn't come any more, I knew he had. The girls said some policemen had taken him away in a cart. And Mother sighed and was sad over the poor man.

In weather that was new to me, and cold, and loud with bullying winds, my mother disappeared to visit my father. This was a long way off, out of sight, and I don't remember her going. But suddenly there were only the girls in the house, tumbling about with brooms and dishcloths, arguing, quarrelling, and putting us to bed at random. House and food had a new smell, and meals appeared like dismal conjuring tricks: cold, raw, or black with too much fire. Marjorie was breathless and everywhere; she was fourteen, with all the family in her care. My socks slipped down, and stayed down. I went unwashed for long periods of time. Black leaves swept into the house and piled up in the corners; it rained, and the floors sweated, and washing filled all the lines in the kitchen and dripped sadly on one and all.

But we ate; and the girls moved about in a giggling flurry, exhausted at their losing game. As the days went by, such a tide of muddles mounted in the house that I didn't know which room was which. I lived free, grubbing outside in the mud till I was black as a badger. And my nose ran free, as unchecked as my feet. I sailed my boots down the drain, I cut up sheets for puttees and marched like a soldier through the swamps of leaves. Sensing my chance, I wandered far, eating all manner of raw objects: coloured berries, twigs and grubs; sick every day, but with a sickness of which I was proud.

All this time the sisters went through the house, darting upstairs and down, beset on all sides by the rain coming in, boys growing filthier, sheets scorching, saucepans burning, and kettles boiling over. The doll's house became a madhouse, and the girls frail birds flying in a wind of chaos. Doth giggled helplessly, Phyl wept among the vegetables, and Marjorie would say, when the day was over: 'I'd lie down and die, if there was a place to lie down in.'

I was not at all surprised when I heard of the end of the world. Everything pointed to it. The sky was low and whirling with black clouds; the woods roared night and day, stirring great seas of sound. One night we sat round the kitchen table, cracking walnuts with the best brass candlestick, when Marjorie came in from the town. She was shining with rain and loaded with bread and buns. She was also very white.

'The war's over,' she said. 'It's ended.'

'Never,' said Dorothy.

'They told me at the Stores,' said Marjorie. 'And they were giving away prunes.' She gave us a bagful, and we ate them raw.

The girls got tea and talked about it. And I was sure it was the end of the world. All my life was the war, and the war was the world. Now the war was over. So the end of the world was come. It made no other sense to me.

'Let's go out and see what's happening,' said Doth.

'You know we can't leave the kids,' Marge said.

So we went too. It was dark, and the gleaming roofs of the village echoed with the buzz of singing. We went hand in hand through the rain, up the bank and down the street. A bonfire crackled in one of the gardens, and a woman jumped up and down in the light of it, red as a devil, a jug in her hand, uttering cries that were not singing. All down the other gardens there were other bonfires too. And a man came up and kissed the girls and hopped in the road and twisted on one toe. Then he fell down in the mud and lay there, working his legs like a frog and croaking a loud song.

I wanted to stop. I had never seen a man like this, in such a wild good humour. But we hurried on. We got to the pub and stared through the windows. The bar seemed on fire with its many lamps. Rose-coloured men, through the rain-wet windows, seemed to bulge and break into flame. They breathed out smoke, drank fire from golden jars, and I heard their great din with awe. Now anything might happen. And it did. A man rose up and crushed a glass like a nut between his hands, then held them out laughing for all to see his wounds. But the blood was lost in the general light of blood. Two other men came waltzing out of the door, locked in each other's arms. Fighting and cursing, they fell over the wall and rolled down the bank in the dark.

There was a screaming woman we could not see. 'Jimmy! Jimmy!' she wailed. 'Oh, Jimmy! Thee s'll kill 'im! I'll fetch the vicar, I will! Oh, Jimmy!'

'Just 'ark at 'em,' said Dorothy, shocked and delighted.

'The kids ought to be in bed,' said Marjorie.

'Stop a minute longer. Only a minute. It wouldn't do no 'arm.'

Then the schoolhouse chimney caught fire. A fountain of sparks shot high into the night, writhing and sweeping on the wind, falling and dancing along the road. The chimney hissed like a firework, great rockets of flame came gushing forth, emptying the tiny house, so that I expected to see chairs and tables, knives and forks, radiant and burning, follow. The moss-tiles smouldered with sulphurous soot, yellow jets of smoke belched from cracks in the chimney. We stood in the rain and watched it, entranced, as if the sight had been saved for this day. As if the house had been saved, together with the year's bad litter, to be sent up in flames and rejoicing.

How everyone bellowed and scuffled and sang, drunk with their beer and the sight of the fire. But what would happen now that the war was over? What would happen to my uncles who lived in it?—those huge remote men who appeared suddenly at our house, reeking of leather and horses. What would happen to our father, who was khakied like every other man, yet special, not like other men? His picture hung over the piano, trim, haughty, with a badged cap and a spiked moustache. I confused him with the Kaiser. Would he die now the war was over?

As we gazed at the flaming schoolhouse chimney, and smelt the burning throughout the valley, I knew something momentous was occurring. At any moment I looked for a spectacular end to my already long life. Oh, the end of the war and the world! There was rain in my shoes, and Mother had disappeared. I never expected to see another day.

First Names

Peace was here; but I could tell no difference. Our mother returned from far away with excited tales of its madness, of how strangers had stopped and kissed each other in the streets and climbed statues shouting its name. But what was peace anyway? Food tasted the same, pump water was as cold, the house neither fell nor grew larger. Winter came in with a dark, hungry sadness, and the village filled up with unknown men who stood around in their braces and khaki pants, smoking short pipes, scratching their arms, and gazing in silence at the gardens.

I could not believe in this peace at all. It brought no angels or explanations; it had not altered the nature of my days and nights, nor gilded the mud in the yard. So I soon forgot it, and went back to my burrowing among the mysteries of indoors and out. The garden still offered its corners of weed, blackened cabbages, its stones and flower stalks. And the house its areas of hot and cold, dark holes and talking boards, its districts of terror and blessed sanctuary, together with an infinite range of objects and ornaments that folded, fastened, creaked and sighed, opened and shut, tinkled and sang, pinched, scratched, cut, burned, spun, toppled, or fell to pieces. There was also a pepper-smelling cupboard, a ringing cellar and a humming piano, dry bunches of spiders, colliding brothers, and the eternal comfort of the women.

I was still young enough then to be sleeping with my mother, which to me seemed life's whole purpose. We slept together in the first-floor bedroom on a flock-filled mattress in a bed of brass rods and curtains. Alone, at that time, of all the family, I was her chosen dream companion, chosen from all for her extra love; my right, so it seemed to me.

So in the ample night and the thickness of her hair I consumed my fattened sleep, drowsed and nuzzling to her warmth of flesh, blessed by her bed and safety. From the width of the house and the separation of the day, we two then lay joined alone. That darkness to me was like that fruit of sloes, heavy and ripe to the touch. It was a darkness of bliss and simple languor, when all edges seemed rounded, apt, and fitting; and the presence for whom one had moaned and hungered was found not to have fled after all.

My mother, freed from her noisy day, would sleep like a happy child, humped in her nightdress, breathing innocently, and making soft drinking sounds in the pillow. In her flights of dream she held me close, like a parachute, to her back; or rolled and enclosed me with her great tired body so that I was snug as a mouse in a hayrick.

They were deep and jealous, those wordless nights, as we curled and muttered together, like a secret I held through the waking day which set me above all others. It was for me alone that the night came down, for me, the prince of her darkness, when only I would know the huge helplessness of her sleep, her dead face, and her blind bare arms. At dawn, when she rose and stumbled back to the kitchen, even then I was not wholly deserted, but rolled into the valley her sleep had left, lay deep in its smell of lavender, deep on my face to sleep again in the nest she had made my own.

The sharing of her bed at that three-year-old time, I expected to last for ever. I had never known, or could not recall, any night spent away from her. But I was growing fast; I was no longer the baby; brother Tony lay in wait in his cot. When I heard the first whispers of moving me to the boys' room, I simply couldn't believe it. Surely my mother would never agree? How could she face night without me?

My sisters began by soothing and flattering; they said, 'You're a grown big man.' 'You'll be sleeping with Harold and Jack,' they said. 'Now what d'you think of that?'—What was I supposed to think? To me it seemed outrageous. I affected a brainstorm and won a few extra nights, my last nights in that downy bed. Then the girls changed their tune: 'It'll only be for a bit. You can come back to Mum later on.' I didn't quite believe them, but Mother was silent, so I gave up the struggle and went.

I was never recalled to my mother's bed again. It was my first betrayal, my first dose of aging hardness, my first lesson in the gentle, merciless rejection of women. Nothing more was said, and I accepted it. I grew a little tougher, a little colder, and turned my attention more towards the outside world, which by now was emerging visibly through the mist. . . .

The yard and the village manifested themselves at first through magic and fear. Projections of their spirits and of my hallucinations sketched in the first blanks with demons. The thumping of heartbeats which I heard in my head was no longer the unique ticking of a private clock but the marching of monsters coming in from outside. They were creatures of the 'world' and they were coming for me, advancing up the valley with their heads stuck in breadbaskets, grunting to the thump of my blood. I suppose they were a result of early headaches, but I spent anxious days awaiting them. Indefatigable marchers though they were, they never got nearer than the edge of the village.

This was a daylight uneasiness which I shared with no one; but night, of course, held various others about which I was far more complaining—dying candles, doors closed on darkness, faces seen upside down, night holes in the ground where imagination seethed and sent one shrieking one's chattering head off. There were the Old Men too, who lived in the walls, in floors, and down the lavatory; who watched and judged us and were pitilessly spiteful, and were obviously gods gone mouldy. These Old Men never failed to control us boys, and our sisters conjured them shamelessly, and indeed in a house where no father ruled they were the perfect surrogates.

But there was one real old pagan of flesh and blood who ruled us all for a while. His visits to the village were rare yet deliberate; and when he appeared it was something both sovereign and evil that walked among us, though it was the women who were most clearly affected.

The first time I actually saw him myself had a salt taste I still remember. It was a frost-bright, moon-cold night of winter, and we were sitting in the kitchen as usual. The fire boiled softly, the candles quivered, the girls were drowsily gossiping. I had fallen half-asleep across the table when Marjorie suddenly said, 'Ssssh! . . .'

She had heard something; of course, somebody was always hearing something; so I woke up and listened vaguely. The others were in attitudes of painful attention; they would listen at the drop of a feather. I heard nothing at first. An owl cried in the yew trees and was answered from another wood. Then Dorothy said 'Hark!' And Mother said 'Hush!' And the alarm had us all in its grip.

Like a stagless herd of hinds and young our heads all went up together. We heard it then, far away down the lane, still faint but unmistakable—the drag of metal on frosty ground and an intermittent rattle of chains.

The girls exchanged looks of awful knowledge, their bright eyes large with doom. 'It's him!' they whispered in shaky voices. 'He's broke out again! It's him!'

It was him all right. Mother bolted the door and blew out the lamps and candles. Then we huddled together in the fire-flushed darkness to await his ominous coming.

The drag of the chains grew louder and nearer, rattling along the night, sliding towards us up the distant lane to his remorseless, moon-lit tread. The girls squirmed in their chairs and began giggling horribly; they appeared to have gone off their heads.

'Hush,' warned our Mother. 'Keep quiet. Don't move . . .' Her face was screwed in alarm

The girls hung their heads and waited, shivering. The chains rattled nearer and nearer. Up the lane, round the corner, along the top of the bank—then with a drumming of feet, he was here. . . . Frantic, the girls could hold out no longer; they leapt up with curious cries, stumbled their way across the firelit kitchen and clawed the dark curtains back. . . .

Proud in the night the beast passed by, head crowned by royal horns, his milky eyes split by strokes of moonlight, his great frame shaggy with hair. He moved with stiff and stilted strides, swinging his silvered beard, and from the tangled strength of his thighs and shoulders trailed the heavy chains he'd broken.

'Jones's goat!' our Dorothy whispered; two words that were almost worship. For this was not just a straying animal but a beast of ancient dream, the moonlight walker of the village roads, half captive, half king. He was huge and hairy as a Shetland horse and all men were afraid of him; Squire Jones, in fact, kept him chained to a spike driven five feet into the ground. Yet when nights were bright with moon or summer, neither spike nor chains could hold him. Then he snorted and reared, tore his chains from the ground, and came trailing his lust through the village.

I had heard of him often; now I saw him at last, striding jerkily down the street. Old as a god, wearing his chains like a robe, he exuded a sharp whiff of salt, and every few steps he sniffed the air as though seeking some friend or victim. But he walked alone, he encountered no one, he passed through an empty village. Daughters and wives peeped from darkened bedrooms; men waited in the shadows with axes. Meanwhile, reeking with power and white in the moon, he went his awesome way. . . .

'Did you ever see a goat so big?' asked Dorothy with a sigh.

'They knocks you down and tramples you. I heard he knocked down Miss Cohen.'

'Just think of meeting him, coming home alone . . .'

'Whatever would you do?'

'I'd have a fit. What would you do, Phyl?'

Phyl didn't answer: she had run away, and was having hysterics in the pantry.

Jones's terrorist goat seemed to me a natural phenomenon of that time, part of a village which cast up beasts and spirits as casually as human beings. All seemed part of the same community, though their properties varied widely—some were benevolent, some strictly to be avoided; there were those that appeared at different shapes of the moon, or at daylight or midnight hours, that could warn or bless or drive one mad according to their different natures. There was the Death Bird, the Coach, Miss Barraclough's Goose, Hangman's House, and the Two-Headed Sheep.

There is little remarkable about a two-headed sheep, except that this one was old and talked English. It lived alone among the Catswood larches and was only visible during flashes of lightning. It could sing harmoniously in a double voice and cross-question itself for hours; many travellers had heard it when passing that wood, but few, naturally enough, had seen it. Should a thunderstorm ever have confronted you with it, and had you had the presence of mind to enquire, it would have told you the date and nature of your death—at least so people said. But no one quite relished the powers of this beast. And when the sheep-lightning flickered over the Catswood trees, it was thought best to keep away from the place.

The Bulls Cross Coach was another ill omen, and a regular midnight visitor. Bulls Cross was a saddle of heath land set high at the end of the valley, once a crossing of stage roads and cattle tracks which joined Berkeley to Birdlip, and Bisley to Gloucester-Market. Relics of the old stage roads still imprint the grass as well as the memories of the older villagers. And up here, any midnight, but particularly New Year's Eve, one could see a silver-grey coach drawn by flaring horses thundering out of control, could hear the pistol crack of snapping harness, the screams of the passengers, the splintering of wood, and the coachman's desperate cries. The vision recalled some ancient disaster, and was rehearsed every night, at midnight.

Those who hadn't seen it boasted they had, but those who had seen it, never. For the sight laid a curse upon talkative witnesses, a curse we all believed in—you went white in the night, and your teeth fell out, and later you died by trampling. So news of the phantom usually came secondhand. 'They sin that Coach agen last night. 'Arry Lazbury sin it, they says. He was comin' from Painsick a-pushin' 'is bike. 'E dropped it, an run 'ome crazy.' We committed poor Harry to his horrible end, while the Coach ran again through our minds, gliding white on its rocking wheels, as regular as the Post.

As for the tiny tragedy behind the phantom, it had been jealously remembered to haunt us. The tilted coach, the splintered shafts, the wheels crooked against the moon, the sobbing horses kicking out each other's brains, the passengers dying on the moor—the image of that small but local disaster still possesses qualities to appal which the more grandiose carnage of recent times has never quite overshadowed.

As for Bulls Cross—the ragged wildness of windbent turves—I still wouldn't walk there at midnight. It was a curious tundra, a sort of island of nothing set high above the crowded valleys. Yet its hollows and silences, bare of all habitations, seemed stained by the encounters of strangers. At this no-man's crossing, in the days of footpads and horses, travellers would meet in suspicion, or lie in wait to do violence on each other, to rob or rape or murder. To the villages around, it was a patch of bare skyline, a baldness among the woods, a wind-scarred platform which caught everybody's eye, and was therefore just the place for a gibbet. A gibbet, consequently, had stood there for years, which the old folk could still remember.

Below Bulls Cross stood a dank yellow wood which we knew as Deadcombe Bottom. My brothers and I discovered a cottage down there, roof-fallen, in a garden run wild. We played there often among its rotting rooms, running up the littered stairs, picking and gorging on the small sharp apples which hung round the shattered windows. It was a damp dark ruin in the damp depth of the wood; its rooms reeked of old beds and fungus. And behind the door, blood red with rust, hung a naked iron hook.

To this silent, birdless, sunless shambles, we returned again and again. We could do what we liked here, wreak what damage we wished and, strangely enough, no one disturbed us. Only later did we learn the history of the place: that it had been the home of the Bulls Cross hangman, that he had lived here with his son, and worked at his trade, and had later killed himself here.

The cottage in the wood had been specially chosen, close to his work, yet hidden. The times were hungry, his days were busy; he was a discreet and skilful man. Night after night he strolled up the hill to load the gallows with local felons. After a routine summons one storm-black evening, he was handed a shivering boy. Used to working in darkness, he dispatched the lad quickly, then paused to light up his pipe. He was turning to go when a cloud moved from the moon and lit up the gallows clearly, and in the rain-washed face that stared crookedly down at him the hangman saw his son. To the men who stood by he said nothing at all. He just walked back to his cottage, drove a hook into the wall, fixed up a noose, and hanged himself.

Since then, no one had lived in Hangman's House, which crumbled in Deadcombe Bottom, where we played, and chewed apples, and swung from that hook, and kicked the damp walls to pieces. . . .

From the age of five or so I began to grow acquainted with several neighbors—outlaws, most of them, in dress and behaviour—whom I remember both by name and deed. There was Cabbage-Stump Charlie, Albert the Devil, and Percy-from-Painswick, to begin with.

Cabbage-Stump Charlie was our local bruiser—a violent, gaitered, gaunt-faced pigman, who lived only for his sows and for fighting. He was a nourisher of quarrels, as some men are of plants, growing them from nothing by the heat of belligerence and watering them daily with blood. He would set out each evening with his cabbage stalk, ready to strike down the first man he saw. 'What's up then, Charlie? Got no quarrel with thee.' 'Wham!' said Charlie, and hit him. Men fell from their bicycles or backpedalled violently when they saw old Charlie coming. With his hawk-brown nose and whiskered arms he looked like a landlocked Viking; and he would take up his stand outside the pub, swing his great stump round his head, and say 'Wham! Bash!' like a boy in a comic, and challenge all comers to battle. Often bloodied himself, he left many a man bleeding before crawling back home to his pigs. Cabbage-Stump Charlie, like Jones's Goat, set the village to bolting its doors.

Albert the Devil was another alarmer—a deaf-mute beggar with a black beetle's body, short legs, and a mouth like a puppet's. He had soft-boiled eyes of unusual power which filled every soul with disquiet. It was said he could ruin a girl with a glance and take the manhood away from a man, or scramble your brains, turn bacon green and effect other domestic disorders. So when he came to the village on a begging trip, and we heard his musical gurgle approaching, money and food were put on the tops of the walls and then people shut themselves up in their privies.

Percy-from-Painswick, on the other hand, was a clown and a ragged dandy, who used to come over the hill, dressed in frock coat and leggings, looking for local girls. Harmless, half-witted, he wooed only with his tongue; but his words were sufficient to befuddle the girls and set them shrieking with pleasure and shock. He had a sharp pink face and a dancer's light body and the girls used to follow him everywhere, teasing him on into cheekier fancies and pinning ribbons to his swallowtail coat. Then he'd spin on his toes, and say something quick and elaborate, uttered smoothly from smiling teeth—and the girls would run screaming down over the bank, red-faced, excited, incredulous, hiding in bushes to exclaim to each other: Was it possible what Percy just said? He was a gentle, sharp, sweet-moving man, but he died of his brain soon after.

Then there was Willy the Fish, who came round on Fridays, mongering from door to door, with baskets of mackerel of such antiquity that not even my family could eat them. Willy was a loose-lipped, sad-eyed man who had lost his girl to his trade. He would lean by our door, and blow and scratch, and lament how it was he'd lost her. But transport was bad, and the sea far away; and the truth was, poor Willy stank.

Among others I remember was Tusker Tom, who sold sacks of tree roots for burning. And Harelip Harry, Davis the Drag, Fisty Fill, and the Prospect Smiler. The first-named three were orbiting tramps, but the last was a manic farmer. Few men, I think, can have been as unfortunate as he; for on the one hand he was a melancholic with a loathing for mankind, on the other, some paralysis had twisted his mouth into a permanent and radiant smile. So everyone he met, being warmed by this smile, would shout him a happy greeting. And beaming upon them with his sunny face he would curse them all to hell.

Bulls Cross itself had two daylight familiars: John-Jack and Emmanuel Twinning. John-Jack spent his time by the Bulls Cross signpost staring gloomily into Wales. Emmanuel Twinning, on the other hand, was gentle and very old, and made his own suits out of hospital blankets, and lived nearby with a horse.

Emmanuel and the skewbald had much in common, including the use of the kitchen, and one saw their grey heads, almost any evening, poking together out of the window. The old man himself, when seen alone, seemed to inhabit unearthly regions, so blue and remote that the girls used to sing:

'O come, O come, E-mah-ah-ah-new-el!
An' ransom captive Is-rah-ah-ah-el! . . .'

At this he would nod and smile gently upon us, moving his lips to the hymn. He was so very old, so far and strange, I never doubted that the hymn was his. He wore sky-blue blankets, and his name was Emmanuel; it was easy to think he was God.

In the long, hot summer of 1921 a serious drought hit the country.

Springs dried up, the wells filled with frogs, and the usually sweet water from our scullery pump turned brown and tasted of nails. Although this drought was a relief to my family, it was a scourge to the rest of the village. For weeks the sky hung hot and blue, trees shrivelled, crops burned in the fields, and the old folk said the sun had slipped in its course and that we should all of us very soon die. There were prayers for rain; but my family didn't go, because it was rain we feared most of all.

As the drought continued, prayer was abandoned and more devilish steps adopted. Finally soldiers with rifles marched to the tops of the hills and began shooting at passing clouds. When I heard their dry volleys, breaking like sticks in the stillness, I knew our long armistice was over. And sure enough—whether from prayers or the shooting, or by a simple return of nature—the drought broke soon after and it began to rain as it had never rained before.

I remember waking in the night to the screams of our mother, and to rousing alarms of a howling darkness and the storm-battered trees outside. Terror, the old terror, had come again and, as always, in the middle of the night.

'Get up!' cried Mother. 'It's coming in! Get up or we'll all be drowned!'

I heard her banging about and beating the walls in accents of final doom. When Mother gave her alarms one didn't lie back and think, one didn't use reason at all; one bristled with fright, leapt out of bed and scrambled downstairs with the others.

Our predicament was such that we lived at nature's mercy; for the cottage, stuck on its steep bank, stood directly in the path of the floods. All the spouts of the heavens seemed to lead to our door, and there was only one small drain to swallow them. When this drain blocked up, as it did in an instant, the floods poured into our kitchen—and as there was no back door to let them out again, I felt it natural, at the time, we should drown.

'Hell in Heaven!' wailed Mother. 'Damn it and cuss! Jesus have mercy on us!'

We grizzled and darted about for brooms, then ran out to tackle the storm. We found the drain blocked already and the yard full of water. The noise of the rain drowned our cries and whimpers, and there was nothing to do but sweep.

What panic those middle-night rousings were, those trumpet calls murdering sleep; with darkness, whirlwind and invisible rain, trees roaring, clouds bursting, thunder crashing, lightning crackling, floods rising, and our Mother demented. The girls in their nightdresses held spitting candles while we boys swept away at the drain. Hot rods of rain struck straight through our shirts; we shivered with panic and cold.

'More brooms!' shouted Mother, jumping up and down. 'Run someone, in the name of goodness! Sweep harder, boys! Sweet saints above, it's up to the doorstep already!'

The floodwater gurgled and moved thickly around us, breeding fat yellow bubbles like scum, skipping and frothing where bullet rain hit it, and inching slowly towards the door. The drain was now hidden beneath the water and we swept at it for our lives, the wet candles hissed and went out one by one, Mother lit torches of newspaper, while we fought knee-deep in cries and thunder, splashing about, wet through, half-weeping, overwhelmed by gigantic fears.

Sometimes, in fact, the water did get in; two or three inches of it. It slid down the steps like a thick cream custard and spread all over the floor. When that happened Mother's lamentations reached elegiac proportions, and all the world was subpoenaed to witness. Dramatic apostrophes rang through the night; the gods were arraigned, the saints called to order, and the fates severely ticked off.

There would be a horrible mess in the kitchen next morning, mud and slime all over the matting, followed by the long, depressed drudgery of scraping it up and carrying it away in buckets. Mother, on her knees, would wring her hands and roll her eyes about.

'I can't *think* what I've done to be so troubled and tried. And just when I got the house straight. Neither saints nor angels would keep their patience if they had such things to put up with. . . . My poor, poor children, my precious darlings —you could die in this filthy hole. No one would care—not a bell-ess-ed soul. Look out with that damn-and-cuss bucket!'

Apart from the noise and the tears and the dirt, these inundations were really not much. But I can't pretend they didn't scare me stiff. The thought that the floodwaters should actually break into our house seemed to me something worse than a fire. At the mid-hour of night, when the storms really blew, I used to lie aghast in my bed, hearing the rain claw the window and the wind slap the walls, and imagining the family, the house, and all the furniture being sucked down the eternal drain.

It was not till much later that I reasoned things out: that our position on the hillside made it unlikely we should drown, that Mother's frenzies and scares belonged to something else altogether, and that it was possible after all to sleep through rain in peace. Even so, to this day, when the skies suddenly darken, and a storm builds up in the west, and I smell rain on the wind and hear the first growl of thunder, I grow uneasy, and start looking for brooms.

✖ Village School

The village to which our family had come was a scattering of some twenty to thirty houses down the southeast slope of a valley. The valley was narrow, steep, and almost entirely cut off; it was also a funnel for winds, a channel for the floods, and a jungly, bird-crammed, insect-hopping sun trap whenever there happened to be any sun. It was not high and open like the Windrush country, but had secret origins, having been gouged from the escarpment by the melting ice caps some time before we got there. The old flood terraces still showed on the slopes, along which the cows walked sideways. Like an island, it was possessed of curious survivals—rare orchids and Roman snails; and there were chemical qualities in the limestone springs which gave the women pre-Raphaelite goitres. The sides of the valley were rich in pasture and the crests heavily covered in beech woods.

Living down there was like living in a bean pod; one could see nothing but the bed one lay in. Our horizon of woods was the limit of our world. For weeks on end the trees moved in the wind with a dry roaring that seemed a natural utterance of the landscape. In winter they ringed us with frozen spikes, and in summer they oozed over the lips of the hills like layers of thick green lava. Mornings, they steamed with mist or sunshine, and almost every evening threw streamers above us, reflecting sunsets we were too hidden to see.

Water was the most active thing in the valley, arriving in the long rains from Wales. It would drip all day from clouds and trees, from roofs and eaves and noses. It broke open roads, carved its way through gardens, and filled the ditches with sucking noises. Men and horses walked about in wet sacking, birds shook rainbows from sodden branches, and streams ran from holes, and back into holes, like noisy underground trains.

I remember, too, the light on the slopes, long shadows in tufts and hollows, with cattle, brilliant as painted china, treading their echoing shapes. Bees blew like cake crumbs through the golden air, white butterflies like sugared wafers, and when it wasn't raining a diamond dust took over, which veiled and yet magnified all things.

Most of the cottages were built of Cotswold stone and were roofed by split-stone tiles. The tiles grew a kind of golden moss which sparkled like crystallized honey. Behind the cottages: fruit bushes, roses, rabbit hutches, earth closets, bicycles, and pigeon lofts. In the very sump of the valley wallowed the Squire's Big House—once a fine, though modest, sixteenth-century manor, to which a Georgian façade had been added.

The villagers themselves had three ways of living: working for the Squire, or on the farms, or down in the cloth mills at Stroud. Apart from the Manor, and the ample cottage gardens—which were an insurance against hard times—all other needs were supplied by a church, a chapel, a vicarage, a manse, a wooden hut, a pub—and the village school.

The village school at that time provided all the instruction we were likely to ask for. It was a small stone barn divided by a wooden partition into two rooms—the Infants and the Big Ones. There was one dame teacher, and perhaps a young girl assistant. Every child in the valley came crowding there, remained till he was fourteen years old, then was presented to the working field or factory with nothing in his head more burdensome than a few mnemonics, a jumbled list of wars, and a dreamy image of the world's geography. It seemed enough to get by with, in any case; and was one up on our poor old grandparents.

This school, when I came to it, was at its peak. Universal education and unusual fertility had packed it to the walls with pupils. Wild boys and girls from miles around—from the outlying farms and half-hidden hovels way up at the ends of the valley—swept down each day to add to our numbers, bringing with them strange oaths and odours, quaint garments, and curious pies. They were my first amazed vision of any world outside the womanly warmth of my family; I didn't expect to survive it for long, and I was confronted with it at the age of four.

The morning came, without any warning, when my sisters surrounded me, wrapped me in scarves, tied up my boot laces, thrust a cap on my head, and stuffed a baked potato in my pocket.

'What's this?' I said.

'You're starting school today.'

'I ain't. I'm stopping 'ome.'

'Now, come on, Loll. You're a big boy now.'

'I ain't.'

'You are.'

'Boo-hoo.'

They picked me up bodily, kicking and bawling, and carried me up to the road.

'Boys who don't go to school get put into boxes, and turn into rabbits, and get chopped up Sundays.'

I felt this was overdoing it rather, but I said no more after that. I arrived at the school just three feet tall and fatly wrapped in my scarves. The playground roared like a rodeo, and the potato burned through my thigh. Old boots, ragged stockings, torn trousers and skirts, went skating and skidding round me. The rabble closed in; I was encircled; grit flew in my face like shrapnel. Tall girls with frizzled hair, and huge boys with sharp elbows, began to prod me with hideous interest. They plucked at my scarves, spun me round like a top, screwed my nose, and stole my potato.

I was rescued at last by a gracious lady—the sixteen-year-old junior teacher—who boxed a few ears and dried my face and led me off to the Infants. I spent that first day picking holes in paper, then went home in a smouldering temper.

'What's the matter, Loll? Didn't he like it at school, then?'

'They never give me the present!'

'Present? What present?'

'They said they'd give me a present.'

'Well, now, I'm sure they didn't.'

'They did! They said: "You're Laurie Lee, ain't you? Well, just you sit there for the present." I sat there all day but I never got it. I ain't going back there again!'

But after a week I felt like a veteran and grew as ruthless as anyone else. Somebody had stolen my baked potato, so I swiped somebody else's apple. The Infant Room was packed with toys such as I'd never seen before—and coloured shapes and rolls of clay, stuffed birds and men to paint. Also a frame of counting beads which our young teacher played like a harp, leaning her bosom against our faces and guiding our wandering fingers. . . .

The beautiful assistant left us at last, and was replaced by an opulent widow. She was tall, and smelt like a cartload of lavender; and wore a hair net, which I thought was a wig. I remember going close up and having a good look—it was clearly too square to be hair.

'What are you staring at?' the widow enquired.

I was much too softhearted to answer.

'Go on. Do tell. You needn't be shy.'

'You're wearing a wig,' I said.

'I can assure you I'm not!' She went very red.

'You are. I seen it.' I said.

The new teacher grew flustered and curiously cross. She took me upon her knee.

'Now look very close. Is that really a wig?'

I looked hard, saw the net, and said, 'Yes.'

'Well, really!' she said, while the Infants gaped. 'I can assure you it's *not* a wig! And if only you could watch me getting dressed in the morning you'd know it wasn't one either.'

She shook me from her knee like a sodden cat, but she'd stirred my imagination. To suggest I might watch her getting dressed in the morning seemed to me both outrageous and wonderful.

This tiny, whitewashed Infants' Room was a brief but cozy anarchy. In that short time allowed us we played and wept, broke things, fell asleep, cheeked the teacher, discovered the things we could do to each other, and exhaled our last guiltless days.

My desk companions were those two blond girls, already puppishly pretty, whose names and bodies were to distract and haunt me for the next fifteen years of my life. Rosie and Jo were limpet chums; they sat holding hands all day; and there was a female self-possession about their pink sticky faces that made me shout angrily at them.

Vera was another I studied and liked; she was lonely, fuzzy, and short. I felt a curious compassion for stumpy Vera; and it was through her, and no beauty, that I got into trouble and received the first public shock of my life. How it happened was simple, and I was innocent, so it seemed. She came up to me in the playground one morning and held her face close to mine. I had a stick in my hand, so I hit her on the head with it. Her hair was springy, so I hit her again and watched her mouth open with a yell.

To my surprise a commotion broke out around me, cries of scandal from the older girls, exclamations of horror and heavy censure mixed with Vera's sobbing wails. I was intrigued, not alarmed, that by wielding a beech stick I was able to cause such a stir. So I hit her again, without spite or passion, then walked off to try something else.

The experiment may have ended there and, having ended, would have been forgotten. But no; angry faces surrounded me, very red, all spitting and scolding.

'Horrid boy! Poor Vera! Little monster! Urgh! We're going to tell teacher about you!'

Something was wrong, the world seemed upset; I began to feel vaguely uneasy. I had only hit Vera on her wiry black hair, and now everybody was shouting at me. I ran and hid, feeling sure it would pass, but they hunted me down in the end. Two big righteous girls hauled me out by the ears.

'You're wanted in the Big Room, for 'itting Vera. You're 'alf going to cop it!' they said.

So I was dragged to that Room, where I'd never been before and, under the savage eyes of the older children, Teacher gave me a scalding lecture. I was confused by now and shaking with guilt. At last I smirked and ran out of the room. I had learnt my first lesson, that I could not hit Vera, no matter how fuzzy her hair. And something else too: that the summons to the Big Room, the policeman's hand on the shoulder, comes almost always as a complete surprise, and for the crime that one has forgotten.

My brother Jack, who was with me in the Infants, was too clever to stay there long. Indeed, he was so bright he made us uncomfortable, and we were all of us glad to get rid of him. Sitting pale in his pinafore, gravely studying, commanding the teacher to bring him fresh books, or to sharpen his pencils, or to make less noise, he was an Infant freak from the start. So he was promoted to the Big Room with unprecedented promptness, given a desk and a dozen atlases to sit on, from which he continued to bully the teachers in that cold, clear voice of his.

But I, myself, was a natural Infant, content to serve out my time, to slop around and whine and idle; and no one suggested I shouldn't. So I remained long after bright Jack had moved on, the fat lord of my nursery life, skilled at cutting out men from paper, chalking suns on the walls, making snakes from clay, idling voluptuously through the milky days with a new young teacher to feed on. But my time was slowly running out; my Big Room bumps were growing. Suddenly, almost to my dismay, I found that I could count up to a hundred, could write my name in both large and small letters, and subtract certain numbers from each other. I had even just succeeded in subtracting Rosie from Jo, when the call came down from on high. Infant no longer, I was being moved up—the Big Room was ready for me.

I found there a world both adult and tough, with long desks and inkwells, strange maps on the walls, huge boys, heavy boots, scratching pens, groans of labour, and sharp and sudden persecutions. Gone for ever were the infant excuses, the sanctuary of lisping charms. Now I was alone and unprotected, faced by a struggle which required new techniques, where one made pacts and split them, made friends and betrayed them, and fought for one's place near the stove.

The stove was a symbol of caste among us, the tub of warmth to which we cleaved during the long seven months of winter. It was made of cast iron and had a noisy mouth which rattled coke and breathed out fumes. It was decorated by a tortoise labelled 'Slow But Sure,' and in winter it turned red hot. If you pressed a pencil against it, the wood burst into flames; and if you spat on the top, the spit hopped and gambolled like tiny ping-pong balls.

My first days in the Big Room were spent in regret for the young teacher I'd left in the Infants, for her braided breasts and unbuttoning hands and her voice of sleepy love. Quite clearly the Big Room boasted no such comforts; Miss B., the Head Teacher, to whom I was now de-livered, being about as physically soothing as a rake.

She was a bunched and punitive little body and the school had christened her Crabby; she had a sour yellow look, lank hair coiled in earphones, and the skin and voice of a turkey. We were all afraid of the gobbling Miss B.; she spied, she pried, she crouched, she crept, she pounced—she was a terror.

Each morning was war without declaration; no one knew who would catch it next. We stood to attention, half-crippled in our desks, till Miss B. walked in, whacked the walls with a ruler, and fixed us with her squinting eye. 'Good a-morning, children!' 'Good morning, Teacher!' The greeting was like a rattling of swords. Then she would scowl at the floor and begin to growl 'Ar Farther . . .'; at which we said the Lord's Prayer, praised all good things, and thanked God for the health of our King. But scarcely had we bellowed the last Amen than Crabby coiled, uncoiled, and sprang, and knocked some poor boy side-ways.

One seldom knew why; one was always off guard, for the punishment preceded the charge. The charge, however, followed hard upon it, to a light shower of angry spitting.

'Shuffling your feet! Playing with the desk! A-smirking at that miserable Betty! I will not have it. I'll not, I say. I repeat—I will not have it!'

Many a punch-drunk boy in a playground battle, outnumbered and beaten to his knees, would be heard to cry: 'I will not have it! I'll not, I say! I repeats I will not have it.' It was an appeal to the code of our common suffering, and called for immediate mercy.

So we did not much approve of Crabby—though she was responsible for our excellent reflexes. Apart from this, her teaching was not memorable. She appears in my recollection as merely a militant figure, a hunched-up little creature all spring coils and slaps—not a monster by any means, but a natural manifestation of what we expected of school.

For school in my day, that day, Crabby's day, seemed to be designed simply to keep us out of the air and from following the normal pursuits of the fields. Crabby's science of dates and sums and writing seemed a typical invention of her own, a sour form of fiddling or prison labour like picking oakum or sewing sacks.

So while the bright times passed, we sat locked in our stocks, our bent backs turned on the valley. The June air infected us with primitive hungers, grass seed and thistledown idled through the windows, we smelt the fields and were tormented by cuckoos, while every out-of-door sound that came drifting in was a sharp nudge in the solar plexus. The creaking of wagons going past the school, harness jingle and the cries of the carters, the calling of cows from the seventeen-acre, Fletcher's chattering mower, gunshots from the warrens—all tugged and pulled at our active wishes till we could

have done Miss B. a murder.

And indeed there came the inevitable day when rebellion raised its standard, when the tension was broken and a hero emerged whom we would willingly have named streets after. At least, from that day his name was honoured, though we gave him little support at the time. . . .

Spadge Hopkins it was, and I must say we were surprised. He was one of those heavy, full-grown boys, thick-legged, red-fisted, bursting with flesh, designed for the great outdoors. He was nearly fourteen by then, and physically out of scale—at least so far as our school was concerned. The sight of him squeezed into his tiny desk was worse than a bullock in ballet shoes. He wasn't much of a scholar; he groaned as he worked, or hacked at his desk with a jackknife. Miss B. took pleasure in goading him, in forcing him to read out loud; or in asking him sudden unintelligible questions which made him flush and stumble.

The great day came; a day of shimmering summer, with the valley outside in a state of leafy levitation. Crabby B. was at her sourest, and Spadge Hopkins had had enough. He began to writhe in his desk, and roll his eyes, and kick with his boots, and mutter: 'She'd better look out. 'Er—Crabby B. She'd better, that's all. I can tell you . . .'

We didn't quite know what the matter was, in spite of his meaning looks. Then he threw down his pen, got up, and walked to the door.

'And where are you going, young man, may I ask?' said Crabby with her awful leer.

Spadge paused and looked her straight in the eye.

'If it's any business of yourn.'

We shivered with pleasure at this defiance. Spadge leisurely made for the door.

'Sit down this instant!' Crabby suddenly screamed. 'I won't have it!'

'Ta-ta,' said Spadge.

Then Crabby sprang like a yellow cat, spitting and clawing with rage. She caught Spadge in the doorway and fell upon him. There was a shameful moment of heavy breathing and scuffling, while the teacher tore at his clothes. Spadge caught her hands in his great red fists and held her at arm's length, struggling.

'Come and help me, someone!' wailed Crabby, demented. But nobody moved; we just watched. We saw Spadge lift her up and place her on the top of the cupboard, then walk out of the door and away. There was a moment of silence, then we all laid down our pens and began to stamp on the floor in unison. Crabby stayed where she was, on top of the cupboard, drumming her heels and weeping.

We expected some terrible retribution to follow, but nothing happened at all. Not even the trouble-spark, Spadge, was called to account—he was simply left alone. From that day Crabby never spoke to him, or crossed his path, or denied him anything at all. He perched idly in his desk, his knees up to his chin, whis-tling in a world of his own. Sometimes Miss B. would consider him narrowly, and if he caught her glance he just winked. Otherwise he was free to come and go, and to take time off as he pleased.

But we never rebelled again; things changed. Crabby B. was replaced by a new Head Teacher—a certain Miss Wardley from Birmingham. This lady was something quite new in our lives. She wore sharp glass jewellery which winked as she walked, and she sounded her 'gees' like gongs. But she was fond of singing and she was fond of birds, and she encouraged us in the study of both. She was more sober than Crabby, her reins looser but stronger; and after the first hilarity of her arrival and strangeness, we accepted her proper authority.

Not that she approved very much of me. 'Fat-and-Lazy,' was the name she called me. After my midday dinner of baked cabbage and bread I would often nod off in my desk. 'Wake up!' she would cry, cracking my head with a ruler. 'You and your little red eyes!' She also took exception to my steady sniff, which to me came as natural as breathing. 'Go out into the road and have a good blow, and don't come back in till you're clear.' But I wouldn't blow, not for anyone on earth, especially if ordered to do so; so I'd sit out on the wall, indignant and thunderous, and sniff away louder than ever. I wouldn't budge either, or come back in, till a boy was sent to fetch me. Miss Wardley would greet me with freezing brightness.

'A little less beastly now? How about bringing a hanky tomorrow? I'm sure we'd all be grateful.' I'd sit and scowl, then forget to scowl, and would soon be asleep again. . . .

My brothers, by this time, were all with me at school. Jack, already the accepted genius, was long past our scope or help. It was agreed that his brains were of such distinction that they absolved him from mortal contacts. So he was left in a corner where his flashes of brilliance kept him twinkling away like a pin-table. Young Tony came last, but he again was different, being impervious either to learning or authority, importing moreover a kind of outrageous cheekiness so inspired that it remained unanswerable. He would sit all day picking holes in blotting paper, his large eyes deep and knowing, his quick tongue scandalous, his wit defiant, his will set against all instruction. There was nothing anyone could do about him, except to yelp at the things he said.

I alone, the drowsy middleman of these two, found it hard to win Miss Wardley's approval. I achieved this in the end by writing long faked essays on the lives and habits of otters. I'd never seen an otter, or even gone to look for one, but the essays took her in. They were read out aloud, and even earned me medals, but that's nothing to boast about.

Our village school was poor and crowded, but in the end I relished it. It had a lively reek of steaming life: boys' boots, girls' hair, stoves and sweat, blue ink, white chalk and shavings. We learnt nothing abstract or tenuous there—just simple patterns of facts and letters, portable tricks of calculation, no more than was needed to measure a shed, write out a bill, read a swine-disease warning. Through the dead hours of the morning, through the long afternoons, we chanted away at our tables. Passers-by could hear our rising voices in our bottled-up room on the bank: 'Twelve-inches-one-foot. Three-feet-make-a-yard. Fourteen-pounds-make-a-stone. Twelve-stone-a-hundred-weight.' We absorbed these figures as primal truths declared by some ultimate power. Unhearing, unquestioning, we rocked to our chanting, hammering the gold nails home. 'Twice-two-are-four. One-God-is-Love. One-Lord-is-King. One-King-is-George. One-George-is-Fifth . . .' So it was always, had been, would be for ever; we asked no questions; we didn't hear what we said; yet neither did we ever forget it.

So do I now, through the reiterations of those days, recall that schoolroom which I scarcely noticed— Miss Wardley in glory on her high desk throne, her long throat tinkling with glass. The bubbling stove with its chink of red fire; the old world map as dark as tea; dead field flowers in jars on the windowsills; the cupboard yawning with dog-eared books. Then the boys and the girls, the dwarfs and the cripples; the slow, fat ones and the quick, bony ones; giants and louts, angels and squinters—Walt Kerry, Bill Timbrell, Spadge Hopkins, Clergy

Green, the Ballingers and Browns, Betty Gleed, Clarry Hogg, Sam and Sixpence, Rosie and Jo—were ugly and beautiful, scrofulous, warted, ringwormed and scabbed at the knees; we were noisy, crude, intolerant, cruel, stupid, and superstitious. But we moved together out of the clutch of the fates, inhabitors of a world without doom; with a scratching, licking, and chewing of pens, a whisper and passing of jokes, a titter of tickling, a grumble of labour, a vague stare at the wall in a dream. . . .

'Oh, miss, please miss, can I go round the back?'

An unwilling nod permits me. I stamp out noisily into a swoop of fresh air and a musical surge of birds. All around me now is the free green world, with Mrs. Birt hanging out her washing. I take stock of myself for a moment, alone. I hear the schoolroom's beehive hum. Of course I don't really belong to that lot at all; I know I'm something special, a young king perhaps placed secretly here in order to mix with the commoners. There is clearly a mystery about my birth, I feel so unique and majestic. One day, I know, the secret will be told. A coach with footmen will appear suddenly at our cottage, and Mother (my mother?) will weep. The family will stand very solemn and respectful, and I shall drive off to take up my throne. I'll be generous, of course, not proud at all; for my brothers there shall be no dungeons. Rather will I feed them on cakes and jellies, and I'll provide all my

sisters with princes. Sovereign mercy shall be their portion, little though they deserve it. . . .

I return to the schoolroom and Miss Wardley scowls (she shall curtsy when I am king). But all this is forgotten when Walt Kerry leans over and demands the results of my sums. 'Yes, Walt. Of course, Walt. Here, copy them out. They ain't hard; I done 'em all.' He takes them, the bully, as his tributary right, and I'm proud enough to give them. Then little Jim Fern, sitting beside me, looks up from his ruined pages. 'Ain't you a good scholar! You and your Jack. I wish I was a good scholar like thee!' He gives me a sad, adoring look, and I begin to feel much better.

Playtime comes and we charge outdoors, releasing our steamed-up cries. Somebody punches a head. Somebody bloodies their knees. Boys cluster together like bees. 'Let's go round the back then, shall us, eh?' To the dark, narrow alley, rich with our mysteries, we make our clattering way. Over the wall is the girls' own place, quite close, and we shout them greetings.

'I 'eard you, Bill Timbrell! I 'eard what you said! You be careful, I'll tell our teacher!'

Flushed and refreshed, we stream back to the playground, whistling, indivisibly male.

'D'you 'ear what I said then? Did you then, eh? *I* told 'em! They 'alf didn't squeal!'

We all double up; we can't speak for laughing, we can't laugh without hitting each other.

Miss Wardley was patient, but we weren't very bright. Our books showed a squalor of blots and scratches as though monkeys were being taught to write. We sang in sweet choirs, and drew like cave men, but most other faculties escaped us—apart from poetry, of course, which gave no trouble at all. I can remember Miss Wardley, with her squeaking chalk, scrawling the blackboard like a shopping list:

'Write a poem—which *must* scan —on one or more of the following: A Kitten. Fairies. My Holidays. An Old Tinker. Charity. Sea Wreck . . .' ('What's that, miss?')

But it was easy in those days; one wrote a dozen an hour, one simply didn't hesitate, just began at the beginning and worked steadily through the subjects, ticking them off with indefatigable rhymes.

Sometimes there was a beating, which nobody minded—except an occasional red-faced mother. Sometimes a man came and took out our teeth. ('My mum says you ain't to take out any double-'uns. . . .' '. . . . Fourteen, fifteen, sixteen, seventeen . . .' 'Is they all double-'uns?' 'Shut up, you little horror.') Sometimes the Squire would pay us a visit, hand out prizes and make a misty-eyed speech. Sometimes an Inspector arrived on a bicycle and counted our heads and departed. Meanwhile Miss Wardley moved jingling amongst us, instructing, appealing, despairing:

'You're a grub, Walter Kerry. You have the wits of a hen. You're a great hulking lout of an oaf. You can just stay behind and do it over again. You can all stay behind, the lot of you.'

When lessons grew too tiresome, or too insoluble, we had our traditional ways of avoiding them.

'Please, miss, I got to stay 'ome tomorrow, to 'elp with the washing —the pigs—me dad's sick.'

'I dunno, miss; you never learned us that.'

'I 'ad me book stole, miss. Carry Burdock pinched it.'

'Please, miss, I got a gurt 'eadache.'

Sometimes these worked, sometimes they didn't. But once, when some tests hung over our heads, a group of us boys evaded them entirely by stinging our hands with horseflies. The task took all day, but the results were spectacular—our hands swelled like elephants' trunks. ' 'Twas a swarm, please, miss. They set on us. We run, but they stung us awful.' I remember how we groaned, and that we couldn't hold our pens, but I don't remember the pain.

At other times, of course, we forged notes from our mothers, or made ourselves sick with berries, or claimed to be relations of the corpse at funerals (the churchyard lay only next door). It was easy to start wailing when the hearse passed by. 'It's my auntie, miss—it's my cousin Wolf—can I go miss, please miss, can I?' Many a lone coffin was followed to its grave by a straggle of long-faced children, pinched, solemn, raggedly dressed, all strangers to the astonished bereaved.

So our schoolwork was done—or where would we be today? We would be as we are: watching a loom or driving a tractor, and counting in images of fives and tens. This was as much as we seemed to need, and Miss Wardley did not add to the burden. What we learned in her care were the less formal truths—the names of flowers, the habits of birds, the intimacy of objects in being set to draw them, the treacherous innocence of boys, the sly charm of girls, the idiot's soaring fancies, and the tongue-tied dunce's informed authority when it came to talking about stoats. We were as merciless and cruel as most primitives are. But we learnt at that school the private nature of cruelty; and our inborn hatred for freaks and outcasts was tempered by meeting them daily.

There was the gypsy boy, Rosso, who lived up the quarry where his tribe had encamped for the summer. He had a chocolate-smooth face and crisp black curls, and at first we cold-shouldered him. He was a real outsider (they ate snails, it was said) and his slant Indian eyes repelled us. Then one day, out of hunger, he stole some sandwiches and was given the cane by Miss Wardley. Whatever the rights and wrongs of the case, that made him one of us.

We saw him run out of school, grizzling from the beating, and kneel down to tie up his boots. The shopkeeper's wife, passing by at that moment, stopped to preach him a little sermon. 'You didn't have to steal, even if you was that hungry. Why didn't you come to me?' The boy gave her a look, picked himself up, and ran off without a word. He knew, as we did, the answer to that one: we set our dogs on the gypsies here. As we walked back home to our cabbage dinners, we were all of us filled with compassion. We pictured poor Rosso climbing back to his quarry, hungry to his miserable tents, with nothing but mud and puddles to sit in and the sour banks to scavenge for food. Gypsies no longer seemed either sinister or strange. No wonder they eat snails, we thought.

The narrow school was just a conveyor belt along which the short years drew us. We entered the door marked 'Infants,' moved gradually to the other, and were then handed back to the world. Lucky, lucky point of time; our eyes were on it always. Meanwhile we had moved to grander desks, saw our juniors multiplying in number; Miss Wardley suddenly began to ask our advice and to spoil us as though we were dying. There was no more to be done, no more to be learned. We began to look round the schoolroom with nostalgia and impatience. During playtime in the road we walked about gravely, patronizing the younger creatures. No longer the trembling, white-faced battles, the buttering-up of bullies; just a punch here and there to show our authority, then a sober stroll with our peers.

At last Miss Wardley was wringing our hands, tender and deferential. 'Good-bye, old chaps, and jolly good luck! Don't forget to come back and see me.' She gave each one of us a coy sad glance. She knew that we never would.

✗ The Kitchen

Our house, and our life in it, is something of which I still constantly dream, helplessly bidden, night after night, to return to its tranquillity and nightmares: to the heavy shadows of its stone-walled rooms creviced between bank and yew trees, to its boarded ceilings and gaping mattresses, its bloodshot geranium windows, its smells of damp pepper and mushroom growths, its chaos, and rule of women.

We boys never knew any male authority. My father left us when I was three, and apart from some rare and fugitive visits he did not live with us again. He was a knowing, brisk, evasive man, the son and the grandson of sailors; but having himself no stomach for the sea, he had determined to make good on land. In his miniature way he succeeded in this. He became, while still in his middle teens, a grocer's assistant, a local church organist, an expert photographer, and a dandy. Certain portraits he took of himself at that time show a handsome though threadbare lad, tall and slender, and much addicted to gloves, high collars, and courtly poses. He was clearly a cut above the average, in charm as well as ambition. By the age of twenty he

had married the beautiful daughter of a local merchant, and she bore him eight children—of whom five survived—before dying herself, still young. Then he married his housekeeper who bore him four more, three surviving, of which I was one. At the time of his second marriage he was still a grocer's assistant, and earning nineteen shillings a week. But his dearest wish was to become a civil servant and he studied each night to this end. The first World War gave him the chance he wanted, and though properly distrustful of arms and battle he instantly sacrificed both himself and his family, applied for a post in the Army Pay Corps, went off to Greenwich in a bulletproof vest, and never permanently lived with us again.

He was a natural fixer, my father was, and things worked out pretty smoothly. He survived his clerkstool war with a War Office pension (for nervous rash, I believe), then entered the civil service, as he had planned to do, and settled in London for good. Thus enabling my mother to raise both his families, which she did out of love and pity, out of unreasoning loyalty and a fixed belief that he would one day return to her. . . .

Meanwhile, we lived where he had left us, a relic of his provincial youth; a sprawling, cumbersome, countrified brood too incongruous to carry with him. He sent us money, and we grew up without him; and I, for one, scarcely missed him. I was perfectly content in this world of women, muddleheaded though it might be, to be bullied and tumbled through the hand-to-mouth days, patched or dressed up, scolded, admired, swept off my feet in sudden passions of kisses, or dumped forgotten among the unwashed pots.

My three half sisters shared much of Mother's burden, and were the good fortune of our lives. Generous, indulgent, warm-blooded, and dotty, these girls were not hard to admire. They seemed wrapped, as it were, in a perpetual bloom, the glamour of their grown-up teens, and expressed for us boys all that women should be in beauty, style, and artifice.

For there was no doubt at all about their beauty, or the naturalness with which they wore it. Marjorie, the eldest, a blond Aphrodite, appeared quite unconscious of the rarity of herself, moving always to measures of oblivious grace and wearing her beauty like a kind of sleep. She was tall, long-haired, and dreamily gentle, and her voice was low and slow. I never knew her to lose her temper, or to claim any personal justice. But I knew her to weep, usually for others, quietly, with large blue tears. She was a natural mother, and skilled with her needle, making clothes for us all when needed. With her constant beauty and balanced nature she was the tranquil night light of our fears, a steady flame reassuring always, whose very shadows seemed thrown for our comfort.

Dorothy, the next one, was a wispy imp, pretty and perilous as a firework. Compounded equally of curiosity and cheek, a spark and tinder for boys, her quick dark body seemed writ with warnings that her admirers did well to observe. 'Not to be held in the hand,' it said. 'Light the touch paper, but retire immediately.' She was an active forager who lived on thrills, provoked adventure, and brought home gossip. Marjorie's were the ears to which most of it came, making her pause in her sewing, open wide her eyes, and shake her head at each new revelation. 'You don't mean it, Doth! He *never*! NO! . . .' was all all I seemed ever to hear.

Dorothy was as agile as a jungle cat, quick-limbed, entrancing, noisy. And she protected us boys with fire and spirit, and brought us treasures from the outside world. When I think of her now, she is a coil of smoke, a giggling splutter, a reek of cordite. In repose she was also something else: a fairy-tale girl, blue as a plum, tender and sentimental.

The youngest of the three was cool, quiet Phyllis, a tobacco-haired, fragile girl, who carried her good looks with an air of apology, being the junior and somewhat shadowed. Marjorie and Dorothy shared a natural intimacy, being closer together in age, so Phyllis was the odd one, an unclassified solitary, compelled to her own devices. This she endured with a modest simplicity quick to admire and slow to complain. Her favourite chore was putting us boys to bed, when she emerged in a strange light of her own, revealing a devout, almost old-fashioned watchfulness, and gravely singing us to sleep with hymns.

Sad Phyllis, lit by a summer night, her tangled hair aglow, quietly sitting beside our beds, hands folded, eyes far away, singing and singing of 'Happy Eden,' alone with her care over us—how often to this did I drop into sleep, feel the warmth of its tide engulf me, steered by her young, hoarse hymning voice and tuneless reveries? . . .

These half sisters I cherished; and apart from them I had two half brothers also. Reggie, the first-born, lived apart with his grandmother; but young Harold, he lived with us. Harold was handsome, bony, and secretive, and he loved our absent father. He stood somewhat apart, laughed down his nose, and was unhappy more often than not. Though younger than the girls, he seemed a generation older, was clever with his hands, but lost.

My own true brothers were Jack and Tony, and we three came at the end of the line. We were of Dad's second marriage, before he flew, and were born within the space of four years. Jack was the eldest, Tony the youngest, and myself the protected centre. Jack was the sharp one, bright as a knife, and was also my close companion. We played together, fought and ratted, built a private structure around us, shared the same bed till I finally left home, and lived off each other's brains. Tony, the

baby—strange and beautiful waif—was a brooding, imaginative solitary. Like Phyllis, he suffered from being the odd one of three; worse still, he was the odd one of seven. He was always either running to keep up with the rest of us or sitting alone in the mud. His curious, crooked, suffering face had at times the radiance of a saint, at others the blank watchfulness of an insect. He could walk by himself or keep very still, get lost or appear at wrong moments. He drew like an artist, wouldn't read or write, swallowed beads by the boxful, sang and danced, was quite without fear, had secret friends, and was prey to terrible nightmares. Tony was the one true visionary amongst us, the tiny hermit no one quite understood. . . .

With our mother, then, we made eight in that cottage and disposed of its three large floors. There was the huge white attic which ran the length of the house, where the girls slept on fat striped mattresses; an ancient, plaster-crumbling room whose sloping ceilings bulged like tent cloths. The roof was so thin that rain and bats filtered through, and you could hear a bird land on the tiles. Mother and Tony shared a bedroom below; Jack, Harold, and I the other. But the house had been so patched and parcelled, that it was now almost impossible to get to one's own room without first passing through someone else's. So each night saw a procession of pallid ghosts, sleepily seeking their beds, till the candle-snuffed darkness laid us out in rows, filed away in our allotted sheets, while snores and whistles shook the old house like a roundabout getting up steam.

But our waking life, and our growing years, were for the most part spent in the kitchen; and until we married, or ran away, it was the common room we shared. Here we lived and fed in a family fug, not minding the little space, trod on each other like birds in a hole, elbowed our ways without spite, all talking at once or all silent at once, or crying against each other, but never, I think, feeling overcrowded, being as separate as notes in a scale.

That kitchen, worn by our boots and lives, was scruffy, warm, and low, whose fuss of furniture seemed never the same but was shuffled around each day. A black grate crackled with coal and beech twigs; towels toasted on the guard; the mantel was littered with fine old china, horse brasses, and freak potatoes. On the floor were strips of muddy matting, the windows were choked with plants, the walls supported stopped clocks and calendars, and smoky fungus ran over the ceilings. There were also six tables of different sizes, some armchairs gapingly stuffed, boxes, stools, and unravelling baskets, books and papers on every chair, a sofa for cats, a harmonium for coats, and a piano for dust and photographs. These were the shapes of our kitchen landscape, the rocks of our submarine life, each object worn smooth by our

constant nuzzling, or encrusted by lively barnacles, relics of birthdays and dead relations, wrecks of furniture long since foundered, all silted deep by Mother's newspapers which the years piled round on the floor.

Waking up in the morning I saw squirrels in the yew trees nibbling at the moist red berries. Between the trees and the window hung a cloud of gold air composed of floating seeds and spiders. Farmers called to their cows on the other side of the valley and moor hens piped from the ponds. Brother Jack, as always, was the first to move, while I pulled on my boots in bed. We both stood at last on the bare wood floor, scratching and saying our prayers. Too stiff and manly to say them out loud, we stood back to back and muttered them, and if an audible plea should slip out by chance, one just burst into song to cover it.

Singing and whistling were useful face-savers, especially when confounded by argument. We used the trick readily, one might say monotonously, and this morning it was Jack who began it.

'What's the name of the King, then?' he said, groping for his trousers.

'Albert.'

'No, it's not. It's George.'

'That's what I said you, didn't I? George.'

'No, you never. You don't know. You're feeble.'

'Not so feeble as you be, any road.'

'You're balmy. You got brains of a bedbug.'

'Da-da-di-da-da.'

'I said you're brainless. You can't even count.'

'Turrelee-turrelee . . . Didn't hear you.'

'Yes, you did then, blockhead. Fat and lazy. Big faa—'

'Dum-di-dah! . . . Can't hear. . . . Hey nonnie! . . .'

Well, that was all right; honours even, as usual. We broke the sleep from our eyes and dressed quickly.

Walking downstairs there was a smell of floor boards, of rags, sour lemons, old spices. The smoky kitchen was in its morning muddle, from which breakfast would presently emerge. Mother stirred the porridge in a soot-black pot, Tony was carving bread with a ruler, the girls in their mackintoshes were laying the table, and the cats were eating the butter. I cleaned some boots and pumped up some fresh water; Jack went for a jug of skimmed milk.

'I'm all behind,' Mother said to the fire. 'This wretched coal's all slack.'

She snatched up an oilcan and threw it all on the fire. A belch of flame roared up the chimney. Mother gave a loud scream, as she always did, and went on stirring the porridge.

'If I had a proper stove,' she said. 'It's a trial getting you off each day.'

I sprinkled some sugar on a slice of bread and bolted it down while I could. How different again looked the kitchen this morning, swirling with smoke and sunlight. Some cut-glass vases threw jagged rainbows across the piano's field of dust, while Father in his pince-nez up on the wall looked down like a scandalized god.

At last the porridge was dabbed on our plates from a thick and steaming spoon. I covered the smoky lumps with treacle and began to eat from the sides to the middle. The girls round the table chewed moonishly, wrapped in their morning stupor. Still sick with sleep, their mouths moved slow, hung slack while their spoons came up; then they paused for a moment, spoon to lip, collected their wits, and ate. Their vacant eyes stared straight before them, glazed at the sight of the day. Pink and glowing from their dreamy beds, from who knows what arms of heroes, they seemed like mute spirits hauled back to the earth after paradise feasts of love.

'Golly!' cried Doth. 'Have you seen the time?'

They began to jump to their feet.

'Goodness, it's late.'

'I got to be off.'

'Me too.'

'Lord, where's my things?'

'Well, ta-ta, Ma; ta boys—be good.'

'Anything you want up from the stores? . . .'

They hitched up their stockings, patted their hats, and went running up the bank. This was the hour when walkers and bicyclists flowed down the long hills to Stroud, when the hooters called through the morning dews and factories puffed out their plumes. From each crooked corner of Stroud's five valleys girls were running to shops and looms, with sleep in their eyes, and eggy cheeks, and in their ears night voices fading. Majorie was off to her milliner's store, Phyllis to her boots-and-shoes, Dorothy to her job as junior clerk in a decayed cloth mill by a stream. As for Harold, he'd started work already; his day began at six, when he'd leave the house with an angry shout for the lathe work he really loved.

But what should we boys do, now they had all gone? If it was schooltime, we pushed off next. If not, we dodged up the bank to play, ran snail races along the walls, or dug in the garden and found potatoes and cooked them in tins on the rubbish heap. We were always hungry, always calling for food, always seeking it in cupboards and hedges. But holiday mornings were a time of risk, there might be housework or errands to do. Mother would be ironing, or tidying up, or reading books on the floor. So if we hung round the yard, we kept our ears cocked; if she caught us, the game was up.

'Ah, there you are, son. I'm needing some salt. Pop to Vick's for a lump, there's a dear.'

Or: 'See if Granny Trill's got a screw of tea—only ask her nicely, mind.'

Or: 'Run up to Miss Turk and try and borrow half crown; I didn't know I'd got so low.'

'Ask our Jack, our Mother! I borrowed the bacon. It's blummin'-well his turn now.'

But Jack had slid off like an eel through the grass, making his sly getaway as usual. He was jumpy, shifty, and quick off the mark, an electric flex of nerves, skinny compared with the rest of us, or what farmers might call a 'poor doer.' If they had, in fact, they would have been quite wrong, for Jack did himself very well. He had developed a mealtime strategy which ensured that he ate for two. Speed and guile were the keys to his success, and we hungry ones called him the Slider.

Jack ate against time; that was really his secret; and in our house you had to do it. Imagine us all sitting down to dinner; eight round a pot of stew. It was lentil stew usually, a heavy brown mash made apparently of plastic studs. Though it smelt of hot stables, we were used to it, and it was filling enough—could you get it. But the size of our family outstripped the size of the pot, so there was never quite enough to go round.

When it came to serving, Mother had no method, not even the law of chance—a dab on each plate in any old order and then every man for himself. No grace, no warning, no starting gun; but the first to finish what he'd had on his plate could claim what was left in the pot. Mother's swooping spoon was breathlessly watched—let the lentils fall where they may. But starveling Jack had worked it all out; he followed the spoon with his plate. Absent-mindedly Mother would give him first dollup, and very often a second, and as soon as he got it he swallowed it whole, not using his teeth at all.

'More please, I've finished'—the bare plate proved it, so he got the pot scrapings too. Many's the race I've lost to him thus, being just that second slower. But it left me marked with an ugly scar, a twisted, food-crazed nature, so that I am calling for whole rice puddings and big pots of stew in the night.

The day was over and we had used it, running errands or prowling the fields. When evening came we returned to the kitchen, back to its smoky comfort, in from the rapidly cooling air to its wrappings of warmth and cooking. We boys came first, scuffling down the bank, singly, like homing crows. Long tongues of shadows licked the curves of the fields and the trees turned plump and still. I had been off to Painswick to pay the rates, running fast through the long wet grass, and now I was back, painting hard, the job finished, with hayseeds stuck to my legs. A plate of blue smoke hung above our chimney, flat in the motionless air, and every stone in the path as I ran down home shook my bones with arriving joy.

We chopped wood for the night and carried it in; dry beech sticks as brittle as candy. The baker came down with a basket of bread slung carelessly over his shoulder. Eight quartern loaves, cottage-size, black-crusted, were handed in at the door. A few crisp flakes of pungent crust still clung to his empty basket, so we scooped them up on our spit-wet fingers and laid them upon our tongues. The twilight gathered, the baker shouted good night, and whistled his way up the bank. Up in the road his black horse waited, the cart lamps smoking red.

Indoors, our Mother was cooking pancakes, her face aglow from the fire. There was a smell of sharp lemon and salty batter, and a burning hiss of oil. The kitchen was dark and convulsive with shadows, no lights had yet been lit. Flames leapt, subsided, corners woke and died, fires burned in a thousand brasses.

'Poke round for the matches, dear boys,' said Mother. 'Damn me if I know where they got to.'

We lit the candles and set them about, each in its proper order: two on the mantelpiece, one on the piano, and one on a plate in the window. Each candle suspended a ball of light, a luminous, fragile glow, which swelled and contracted to the spluttering wick or leaned to the moving air. Their flames pushed weakly against the red of the fire, too tenuous to make much headway, revealing our faces more by casts of darkness than by any clear light they threw.

Next we filled and lit the tall iron lamp and placed it on the table. When the wick had warmed and was drawing properly, we turned it up full strength. The flame in the funnel then sprang alive and rose like a pointed flower, began to sing and shudder and grow more radiant, throwing pools of light on the ceiling. Even so the kitchen remained mostly in shadow, its walls a voluptuous gloom.

The time had come for my violin

practice. I began twanging the strings with relish. Mother was still frying and rolling up pancakes; my brothers lowered their heads and sighed. I propped my music on the back of a chair and sliced through a Russian Dance while sweet smells of resin mixed with lemon and fat as the dust flew in clouds from my bow. Now and then I got a note just right, and then Mother would throw me a glance. A glance of piercing, anxious encouragement as she side-stepped my swinging arm. Plump in her slippers, one hand to her cheek, her pan beating time in the other, her hair falling down about her ears, mouth working to help out the tune—old and tired though she was, her eyes were a girl's, and it was for looks such as these that I played.

'Splendid!' she cried. 'Top hole! Clap-clap! Now give us another, me lad.'

So I slashed away at 'William Tell' and when I did that, plates jumped; and Mother skipped gaily around the hearthrug, and even Tony rocked a bit in his chair.

Meanwhile Jack had cleared some boots from the table and started his inscrutable homework. Tony, in his corner, began to talk to the cat and play with some fragments of cloth. So with the curtains drawn close and the pancakes coming, we settled down to the evening. When the kettle boiled and the toast was made, we gathered and had our tea. We grabbed and dodged and passed and snatched, and packed our mouths like pelicans.

Mother ate always standing up, tearing crusts off the loaf with her fingers, a hand-to-mouth feeding that expressed her vigilance, like that of a wireless operator at sea. For most of Mother's attention was fixed on the grate, whose fire must never go out. When it threatened to do so, she became seized with hysteria, wailing and wringing her hands, pouring on oil and chopping up chairs in a frenzy to keep it alive. In fact it seldom went out completely, though it was very often ill. But Mother nursed it with skill, banking it up every night and blowing hard on the bars every morning. The state of our fire became as important to us as it must have been to a primitive tribe. When it sulked and sank, we were filled with dismay; when it blazed, all was well with the world; but if—God save us—it went out altogether, then we were clutched by primeval chills. Then it seemed that the very sun had died, that winter had come for ever, that the wolves of the wilderness were gathering near, and that there was no more hope to look for. . . .

But tonight the firelight snapped and crackled, and Mother was in full control. She ruled the range and all its equipment with a tireless, nervous touch. Eating with one hand, she threw on wood with the other, raked the ashes and heated the oven, put on a kettle, stirred the pot, and spread out some more shirts on the guard. As soon as we boys had finished our tea, we pushed all the crockery aside, piled it up roughly at the far end of the table, and settled down under the lamp. Its light was warm and live around us, a kind of puddle of fire of its own. I set up my book and began to draw. Jack worked at his notes and figures. Tony was playing with some cotton reels, pushing them slowly round the table.

All was silent except for Tony's voice, softly muttering his cotton-real story.

'. . . So they come out of this big hole see, and the big chap said fie he said we'll kill 'em see, and the pirates was waiting up 'ere, and they had this gurt cannon and they went bang fire and the big chap fell down wheeee! and rolled back in the 'ole and I said we got 'em and I run up the 'ill and this boat see was comin' and I jumped on board whooosh cruump and I said now I'm captain see and they said fie and I took me 'achet 'ack 'ack and they all fell plop in the sea wallop and I sailed the boat round 'ere and round 'ere and up 'ere and round 'ere and down 'ere and up 'ere and round 'ere and down 'ere . . .'

Now the girls arrived home in their belted mackintoshes, flushed from their walk through the dark, and we looked up from our games and said: 'Got anything for us?' And Dorothy gave us some liquorice. Then they all had their supper at one end of the table while we boys carried on at the other. When supper was over and cleared away, the kitchen fitted us all. We drew together round the evening lamp, the vast and easy time. . . . Marjorie be-

gan to trim a new hat, Dorothy to write a love letter, Phyllis sat down with some forks and spoons, blew ah! and sleepily rubbed them. Harold, home late, cleaned his bike in a corner. Mother was cutting up newspapers.

We talked in spurts, in lowered voices, scarcely noticing if anyone answered.

'I turned a shaft to a thou' today,' said Harold.

'A what?'

'He said a "thou".'

Chairs creaked awhile as we thought about it. . . .

'Charlie Revell's got a brand-new suit. He had it made to fit. . . .'

'He half fancies himself.'

'Charlie Revell! . . .'

Pause.

'Look, Doth, I got these bits for sixpence. I'm going to stitch 'em all round the top here.'

'Mmmmm. Well. Tcch-tcch. S'alright . . .'

'Dr. Green came up to the shop this morning. Wearing corduroy bloomers. Laugh! . . .'

'Look, Ma, look! I've drawn a church on fire. Look, Marge, Doth! Hey, look! . . .'

'If x equals x, then y equals z—shut up!—if x is y . . .'

'O Madeline, if you'll be mine, I'll take you o'er the sea, di-dah . . .'

'Look what I've cut for my scrapbook, girls—a Beefeater—isn't he killing?'

'Charlie Revel cheeked his dad today. He called him a dafty. He . . .'

'. . . You know that boy from the Dairy, Marge—the one they call Barnacle Boots? Well, he asked me to go to Spot's with him. I told him to run off home.'

'No! You never!'

'I certainly did. I said I don't go to no pictures with butter-wallopers. You should have seen his face . . .'

'Harry Lazbury smells of chicken-gah. I had to move me desk.'

'Just hark who's talking. Dainty Dick.'

'I'll never be ready by Sunday . . .'

'I've found a lovely snip for my animal page—an old seal—look girls, the expression! . . .'

'So I went round 'ere, and down round 'ere, and he said fie so I went 'ack 'ack . . .'

'What couldn't I do to a nice cream slice . . .'

'Charlie Revell's had 'is ears syringed . . .'

'Do you remember, Doth, when we went to Spot's, and they said, "Children in Arms Not Allowed," and we walked little Tone right up the steps and he wasn't even two? . . .'

Marge gave her silky, remembering laugh and looked fondly across at Tony. The fire burned clear with a bottle-green light. Their voices grew low and furry. A farm dog barked far across the valley, fixing the time and distance exactly. Warned by the dog and some hooting owls, I could sense the night valley emptying, stretching in mists of stars and water, growing slowly more secret and late.

The kitchen, warm and murmuring now, vibrated with rosy darkness. My pencil began to wander on the page, my eyes to cloud and clear. I thought I'd stretch myself out on the sofa—for a while, for a short while only. The girls' muted chatter went on and on; I struggled to catch the drift. 'Sh! . . . Not now . . . When the boys are in bed . . . You'll die when you hear . . . Not now . . .'

The boards on the ceiling were melting like water. Words broke and went floating away. Chords of smooth music surged up in my head, thick tides of warmth overwhelmed me, I was drowning in languors of feathered seas, spiralling cozily down. . . .

Once in a while I was gently roused to a sound amplified by sleep: to the fall of a coal, the sneeze of the cat, or a muted exclamation. 'She couldn't have done such a thing. . . . She did. . . . Done what? . . . What thing? . . . Tell, tell me. . . .' But helpless I glided back to sleep, deep in the creviced seas, the blind waters stilled me, weighed me down, the girls' words floated on top. I lay longer now, and deeper far; heavier weeds were falling on me. . . .

'Come on, Loll. Time to go to bed. The boys went up long ago.' The whispering girls bent over me; the kitchen returned upside down. 'Wake up, lamb. . . . He's wacked to the wide. Let's try and carry him up.'

Half-waking, half-carried, they got

me upstairs. I felt drunk and tattered with dreams. They dragged me stumbling round the bend in the landing, and then I smelt the sweet blankets of bed.

It was cold in the bedroom; there were no fires here. Jack lay open mouthed, asleep. Shivering, I swayed while the girls undressed me, giggling around my buttons. They left me my shirt and my woolen socks, then stuffed me between the sheets.

Away went the candle down the stairs, boards creaked, and the kitchen door shut. Darkness. Shapes returning slow. The window a square of silver. My bed-half was cold—Jack hot as a bird. For a while I lay doubled, teeth chattering, blowing, warming against him slowly.

'Keep yer knees to yerself,' said Jack, turning over. He woke. 'Say, think of a number!'

' 'Leven-hundred and two,' I groaned, in a trance.

'Double it,' he hissed in my ear.

Double it . . . twenty-four hundred and what? Can't do it. Something or other . . . A dog barked again and swallowed a goose. The kitchen still murmured downstairs. Jack quickly submerged, having fired off his guns, and began snorkling away at my side. Gradually I straightened my rigid limbs and hooked all my fingers together. I felt wide awake now. I thought I'd count to a million. 'One, two . . .' I said; that's all.

✖ Grannies in the Wainscot

Our house was seventeenth-century Cotswold, and was handsome as they go. It was built of stone, had hand-carved windows, golden surfaces, moss-flaked tiles, and walls so thick they kept a damp chill inside them whatever the season or weather. Its attics and passages were full of walled-up doors which our fingers longed to open—doors that led to certain echoing chambers now sealed off from us for ever. The place had once been a small country manor, and later a public beerhouse; but it had decayed even further by the time we got it, and was now three poor cottages in one. The house was shaped like a T, and we lived in the downstroke. The top stroke—which bore into the side of the bank like a rusty, expanded shell—was divided separately between two old ladies, one's portion lying above the other's.

Granny Trill and Granny Wallon were rival ancients and lived on each other's nerves, and their perpetual enmity was like mice in the walls and absorbed much of my early days. With their sickle-bent bodies, pale pink eyes, and wild wisps of hedgerow hair, they looked to me the very images of witches and they were also much alike. In all their time as such close neighbours they never exchanged a word. They communicated instead by means of boots and brooms—jumping on floors and knocking on ceilings. They referred to each other as 'Er-Down-Under' and 'Er-Up-Atop, the Varmint'; for each to the other was an airy nothing, a local habitation not fit to be named.

Er-Down-Under, who lived on our level, was perhaps the smaller of the two, a tiny white shrew who came nibbling through her garden, who clawed, squeaking with gossip at our kitchen window, or sat sucking bread in the sun; always mysterious and self-contained and feather-soft in her movements. She had two names, which she changed at will according to the mood of her day. Granny Wallon was her best, and stemmed, we were told, from some distinguished alliance of the past. Behind this crisp, trotting body were certainly rumours of noble blood. But she never spoke of them herself. She was known to have raised a score of children. And she was known to be very poor. She lived on cabbage, bread, and potatoes—but she also made excellent wines.

Granny Wallon's wines were famous in the village, and she spent a large part of her year preparing them. The gathering of the ingredients was the first of the mysteries. At the beginning of April she would go off with her baskets and work round the fields and hedges, and every fine day till the end of summer would find her somewhere out in the valley. One saw her come hobbling home in the evening, bearing her cargoes of crusted flowers till she had buckets of cowslips, dandelions, elderblossom crammed into every corner of the house. The elder-flower, drying on her kitchen floor, seemed to cover it with a rancid carpet, a crumbling rime of grey-green blossom fading fast in a dust of summer. Later the tiny grape clusters of the elderberry itself would be seething in purple vats, with daisies and orchids thrown in to join it, even strands of the dog-rose bush.

What seasons fermented in Granny Wallon's kitchen, what summers were brought to the boil, with limp flower heads piled around the floor holding fast to their clotted juices— the sharp spiced honey of those cowslips first, then the coppery, reeking dandelion, the bitter poppy's whiff of powder, the cat's breath, death-green elder. Gleanings of days and a dozen pastures, strippings of lanes and hedges—she bore them home to her flag-tiled kitchen, sorted them each from each, built up her fires and loaded her pots, and added her sugar and yeast. The vats boiled daily in suds of sugar, revolving petals in throbbing water, while the air, aromatic, steamy, embalmed, distilled the hot dews and flowery soups and ran the wine down the dripping walls.

And not only flower heads went into these brews; the old lady used parsnips, too, potatoes, sloes, crab apples, quinces, in fact, anything she could lay her hands on. Granny Wallon made wine as though demented, out of anything at all; and no doubt, if given enough sugar and yeast, could have made a drink out of a box of old matches.

She never hurried or hoarded her

wines, but led them gently through their natural stages. After the boiling they were allowed to settle and to work in the cool of the vats. For several months, using pieces of toast, she scooped off their yeasty sediments. Then she bottled and labelled each liquor in turn and put them away for a year.

At last one was ready, then came the day of distribution. A squeak and a rattle would shake our window, and we'd see the old lady, wispily grinning, waving a large white jug in her hand.

'Hey there, missus! Try thi'n, then. It's the first of my last year's cowslip.'

Through the kitchen window she'd fill up our cups and watch us, head cocked, while we drank. The wine in the cups was still and golden, transparent as a pale spring morning. It smelt of ripe grass in some faraway field and its taste was as delicate as air. It seemed so innocent, we would swig away happily and even the youngest guzzled it down. Then a curious rocking would seize the head; tides rose from our feet like a fever, the kitchen walls began to shudder and shift, and we all fell in love with each other.

Very soon we'd be wedged, tight-crammed, in the window, waving our cups for more, while our mother, bright-eyed, would be mumbling gaily:

'Lord bless you, Granny. Fancy cowsnips and parsney. You must give me the receipt, my dear.'

Granny Wallon would empty the jug in our cups, shake out the last

drops on the flowers, then trot off tittering down the garden path leaving us hugging ourselves in the window.

Whatever the small indulgences with which Granny Wallon warmed up her old life, her neighbour, Granny Trill, had none of them. For Er-Up-Atop was as frugal as a sparrow and as simple in her ways as a grub. She could sit in her chair for hours without moving, a veil of blackness over her eyes, a suspension like frost on her brittle limbs, with little to show that she lived at all save the gentle motion of her jaws. One of the first things I noticed about old Granny Trill was that she always seemed to be chewing, sliding her folded gums together in a daylong ruminative cud. I took this to be one of the tricks of age, a kind of slowed-up but protracted feasting. I imagined her being delivered a quartern loaf—say, on a Friday night—then packing the lot into her rubbery cheeks and chewing them slowly through the week. In fact she never ate bread at all—or butter, or meat, or vegetables; she lived entirely on tea and bisquits, and on porridge sent up by the Squire.

Granny Trill had an original sense of time which seemed to obey some vestigial pattern. She breakfasted, for instance, at four in the morning, had dinner at ten, took tea at two-thirty, and was back in her bed at five. The régime never varied either winter or summer, and belonged very likely to her childhood days when she lived in the woods with her father. To me it seemed a monstrous arrangement, upsetting the roots of order. But Granny Trill's time was for God, or the birds, and although she had a clock, she kept it simply for the tick, its hands having dropped off years ago.

In contrast to the subterranean, almost cavernous, life which Granny Wallon lived down under, Granny Trill's cottage door was always open and her living room welcomed us daily. Not that she could have avoided us anyway, for she lay at our nimble mercy. Her cottage was just outside our gate and there were geraniums in pots round the door. Her tiny room opened straight onto the bank and was as visible as a last year's bird's nest. Smells of dry linen and tea caddies filled it, together with the sweeter tang of old flesh.

'You at home, Granny Trill? You in there, Gran?'

Of course—where else would she be? We heard her creaking sigh from within.

'Well, I'll be bound. That you varmints again?'

'We come on a visit, Gran.'

'Just mind them pots then, or I'll cut you to pieces.'

The three of us clumped indoors. Granny Trill was perched in the window sill, combing her thin white hair.

'What you doing, Gran?'

'Just biding still. Just biding and combing me bits.'

The room was blue and hazy with wood smoke. We prowled slowly around its treasures, opening boxes, filling teapots with cotton reels, skimming plates along the floor. The old lady sat and watched us mildly, taking very little notice, while her dry yellow arm swept up and down, and the black-toothed comb, as it slid through her hair, seemed to be raking the last ash of a fire.

'You going bald, Gran?'

'I still got me bits.'

'It's coming out.'

'No, it ain't.'

'Look at that dead stuff dropping out of yer comb.'

'That's healthy. It makes room for more.'

We didn't think it mattered; it was merely conversation, any subject at all would do. But suddenly the old lady skipped out of her seat and began to leap up and down on the floor.

'Er down there! I got more than er; Er's bald as a tater root! Wicked old lump, I'll see er gone. Er's failing, you mark my words.'

When the spasm was over, she was back in the window, winding her hair into a fragile bun. Beautiful were the motions of her shrunken hands, their movements so long rehearsed; her fingers flew and coiled and pinned, worked blind without aid of a mirror. The result was a structure of tight perfection, a small, shining ball of snow.

'Get yer hands from me drawers! Them's female things!'

She sat relaxed now her hair was done, put on her cracked and steel-rimmed glasses, unhooked the almanac from the wall, and began to read bits out loud. She read in a clear and solemn voice, as though from the Holy Writ.

' "Tragic Intelligence of a Disaster at Sea, in the Region of the Antipoods." That's for June; poor creatures, with their families an' all. "A Party of Scientists Will Slip down a Crevice, with Certain Resultant Fatalities. . . ." Oh, dear, oh well, if they must poke round them places. "A Murdered Cadaver Will Be Shockingly Uncovered in a Western Industrial Town." There, what did I tell you? I knew that'd come. I been expecting that.' She began to skip pages, running through the months, but giving weights to the warnings that struck her. ' "Crisis in Parliament . . ." "House Struck by Fireball . . ." "Riots . . ." "A Royal Surprise . . ." "Turkish Massacre . . ." "Famine . . ." "War . . ." "The King Will Suffer a Slight Infirmity . . ." ' The catalogue of disasters seemed to give her peace, to confirm her sense of order. In Old Moore's pages she saw the future's worst, saw it and was not dismayed. Such alarums were neither threats nor prophecies but simply repetitions; were comforting, frightful, and familiar, being composed of all that had fashioned her long past, the poisoned cuds she had so patiently chewed, swallowed, and yet survived.

'Ah, well,' she said placidly, as she lay down the book. 'He foresees some monstrous doings. A terrible year it looks to be. And he says we'll have hail on Tuesday. . . .'

We boys took up the almanac and leafed through the pages, seeking the more ominous pictures. We saw drawings of skies cracked across by lightning, of church towers falling, multitudes drowning, of men in frock coats shaking warning fingers, of coffins laden with crowns. The drawings were crude but jaggedly vital, like scratches on a prison wall. We relished them much as did Granny Trill, as signs of an apocalypse which could not touch us. In them we saw the whole outside world—split, convulsive, and damned. It had nothing, of course, to do with our village; and we felt like gods, both compassionate and cruel, as we savoured these bloody visions.

Granny Trill used the almanac as an appetizer; now she shifted to her table for dinner. She sopped a few biscuits in a cup of cold tea and scooped the wet crumbs into her mouth, then began grinding away with such an effort of gums one would have thought she was cracking bones. She wore, as usual, her black net dress, but her bright old head rose out of it. Her brow was noble, her pink eyes glittered, her nose swooped down like a finger; only the lower part of her face was collapsed and rubbery, but then that did all the work.

'You a hundred yet, Granny?'

'Nigh on—nigh on.'

'Have you got a dad?'

'Bless you, no; he died long since. He was killed by a tree over Elcombe.'

She often told us the story of this, and now she told us again. Her father had been a woodcutter, strong as a giant—he could lift up a horse and wagon. From the age of five, when she lost her mother, she lived with him in the woods. They used to sleep in a tent, or a kind of wigwam of pine branches, and while her father was tree-felling, the little girl made baskets and sold them around the village. For ten years they lived this life together and were perfectly contented. She grew up into a beautiful young girl— 'Some'ow I seemed to send men breathless'—but her father was careful, and when the timbermen came, he used to hide her under piles of sacking.

Then one day—she was fifteen years old at the time—a tree fell on her father. She heard him shout and ran up the thicket and found him skewered into the ground with a branch. He was lying face down and couldn't see her. 'I'm going, Alice,' he said. She clawed a hole with her hands and lay down beside him, and held him until he died. It took twenty-four hours, and she never moved, nor did he speak again.

When at last some carters discovered them, she was still lying with the body. She watched them roll the tree off him, and straighten his limbs, then she ran up the scrubs and hid. She hid for a week near some foxholes there, and neither ate nor drank. Then the Squire sent out some men to look for her, and when they found her she fought like a savage. But they managed to carry her down to the manor, where she was given a bath and a bed.

'That was the first bath I ever had,' said Granny. 'It took six of 'em to get me soaped.' But they nursed her and pacified her, and gave her housework to do, and later married her to George Trill, the gardener. 'He were a good man, too; he settled me. I was about sixteen years at the time. He was much like me dad, only a good bit slower—and a lot older than I, of course.'

When she finished her story, her chin was resting in her cup and her features were abstracted and bright. Sharp little veins crackled around her eyes, and her skull pushed hard through the skin. Could she ever have been that strapping Alice whom the carters had chased through the woods?—a girl of sixteen whom men washed and married?—the age of our sister Dorothy? . . .

'Me dad planted that tree,' she said absently, pointing out through the old cracked window.

The great beech filled at least half the sky and shook shadows all over the house. Its roots clutched the slope like a giant hand, holding the hill in place. Its trunk writhed with power, threw off veils of green dust, rose towering into the air, branched into a thousand shaded alleys, became a city for owls and squirrels. I had thought such trees to be as old as the earth; I never dreamed that a man could make them. Yet it was Granny Trill's dad who had planted this tree, had thrust in the seed with his finger. How old must he have been to leave such a mark? Think of Granny's age, and add his on top, and you were back at the beginning of the world.

'He were a young man then, a-course,' said Granny. 'He set it afore he got married.' She squinted up at the height of the tree, and sat there nodding gently, while a branch of green shadows, thrown by its leaves, moved softly across her face.

'I got to see to summat!' she said abruptly, slipping creakily down from her chair. She left us then, gathered up her skirts, and trotted lightly along to the wood. We saw her squatting among the undergrowth, bright-eyed, like a small black partridge. Old age might compel her to live in a house, but for comfort she still went to the woods.

Granny Trill and Granny Wallon were traditional ancients of a kind we won't see today, the last of that dignity of grandmothers to whom age was its own embellishment. The grandmothers of those days dressed for the part in that curious but endearing uniform which is now known to us only through the music hall. And our two old neighbours, when setting forth on errands, always prepared themselves scrupulously so. They wore high-laced boots and long muslin dresses, beaded chokers and candlewick shawls, crowned by tall poke bonnets tied with trailing ribbons and smothered with inky sequins. They looked like starlings, flecked with jet, and they walked in a tinkle of darkness.

Those severe and similar old bodies enthralled me when they dressed that way. When I finally became king (I used to think) I would command a parade of grandmas, and drill them, and march them up and down—rank upon rank of hobbling boots, nodding bonnets, flying shawls, and furious, chewing faces. They would be gathered from all the towns and villages and brought to my palace in wagonloads. No more than a monarch's whim, of course, like eating cocoa or drinking jellies; but far more spectacular any day than those usual trudging guardsmen.

In spite of their formal dressing up, the two old ladies never went very far—now and again to church for the sermon, and to the village shop once a week. Granny Wallon went for her sugar and yeast; Granny Trill for her tuppence of snuff.

Snuff was Granny T.'s one horrible vice, and she indulged it with no moderation. A fine brown dust coated all her clothes and she had nostrils like badger holes. She kept her snuff in a small round box, made of tin and worn smooth as a pebble. She was continually tapping and snapping it open, pinching a nailful, gasping *Ah!* flicking her fingers and wiping her eyes, and leaving on the air a faint dry cloud like an explosion of fungoid dust.

The snuffbox repelled and excited us boys and we opened its lid with awe. Reeking substance of the underworld, clay-brown dust of decay, of powdered flesh and crushed old bones, rust-scrapings and the rubbish of graves. How sharp and stinging was this fearful spice, eddying up from its box, animating the air with tingling fumes like a secret breath of witchery. Though we clawed and sniffed it, we could not enjoy it, but neither could we leave it alone.

'You at me snuff agen, you boys? I'll skin yer bottoms, I will!'

We looked up guiltily, saw her cackling face, so took a big pinch between us. With choking tears and head-rocking convulsions we rolled across the floor. The old lady regarded us with pleasure; our paroxysms shook the house.

'That'll learn you, I reckon; you thieving mites. Here, give it to me; I'll show' ee.'

She took up the box and tapped the lid, then elegantly fed her nose. A shudder of ecstasy closed her eyes. She was borne very far away.

One morning our mother was paring apples, so we boys settled down to the peelings. They lay in green coils upon the table, exuding their tart, fresh odours. Slowly we chewed through the juicy ribbons, mumbling our jaws as we went.

'I'm old Granny Trill, a-eating her dinner,' said Jack, sucking peel through his gums. A great joke, this; we chewed and moaned, making much of the toothless labour.

'Don't mock,' said our mother. 'The poor, poor soul—alone by herself all day.'

We glanced at our sisters to share our wit but got no encouragement there. They were absorbed as usual in some freakish labour, stitching dead birds on canvas hats.

'The poor lone creature,' our mother went on, lowering her voice out of charity. 'It's a sin and a shame!' She raised it again. 'That's what it is—a crime! You girls ought to pop up and pay her a visit. You know how she dotes on you all.'

Our sisters had reached the impressive stage; they talked carefully and dressed in splendour—as fine, that is, as they were able to do with the remnants that fell to their hands. With a short length here, a bit of tulle there, a feather picked up at a sale, a hedgehog of needles, a mouthful of pins, a lot of measuring, snipping, and arguing—it was remarkable what raiment they managed to conjure considering what little they had.

They were always willing to put on a show, so they accepted Mother's suggestion. They decided to deck themselves out in their best and to give Gran Trill a treat. The attics were ransacked, the cupboards breached, and very soon all was uproar. Quarreling, snatching, but smoothly efficient, they speedily draped themselves; took a tucket in here, let a gusset out there, spliced a waist or strapped up a bodice; in no time at all they were like paradise birds, and off they minced to see the old lady.

Enthralled as ever by their patchwork glories, I followed them closely behind. Beautiful Marge led the way up the path and rapped elegantly on Granny's door. Meanwhile Doth and Phyl hitched their slipping girdles, pushed the bandeaux out of their eyes, stood hands on hips making light conversation —two jazz-debs bright in the sun.

For once Granny Trill seemed hard of hearing, though the girls had knocked three times. So with a charming shrug and a fastidious sigh Marge swung a great kick at the door.

'Who's that?' came a frightened yelp from within.

'It's only us,' trilled the girls.

They waltzed through the door, apparitions of rose, striking postures straight out of *Home Notes*. 'How do we look then, Gran?' asked Marjorie. 'This line is the mode, you know. We copied it out of that pattern book. It's the rage in Stroud, they say.'

Riffling their feathers, arching their necks, catching coy reflections in mirrors, they paraded the room, three leggy flamingoes, each lit by a golden down. To me they were something out of the sky, airborne visions of fairy light; and with all the enthusiasm they were capable of, they gave the old lady the works. Yet all was clearly not going well. There was a definite chill in the air. . . .

Granny watched them awhile, then her jaws snapped shut; worse still, her gums stopped chewing. Then she clapped her hands with a terrible crack.

'You baggages! You jumped-up varmints! Be off, or I'll fetch me broom!'

The girls retreated at the dainty double, surprised but in no way insulted. Their sense of fashion was unassailable, for were they not up with the times? How could the old girl know about belts and bandeaux? After all, she was only a peasant. . . .

But later Gran Trill took our mother aside and spoke grimly of her concern.

'You better watch them gels of yourn. They'll bring shame on us one of these days. Strutting and tennis playing and aping the gentry —it's carnal and blasphemy. Just you watch 'em, missus; I don't like their doings. Humble gels got to remember their stations.'

Mother, I fancy, was half with her there; but she wouldn't have dreamed of interfering.

For several more years the lives of the two old ladies continued to revolve in intimate enmity around each other. Like cold twin stars, linked but divided, they survived by a mutual balance. Both of them reached back similarly in time, shared the same modes and habits, the same sense of feudal order, the same rampaging, terrible God. They were far more alike than unalike, and could not abide each other.

They arranged things, therefore, so that they never met. They used separate paths when they climbed the bank, they shopped on different days, they relieved themselves in different areas, and staggered their church-going hours. But each one knew always what the other was up to, and passionately disapproved.

Granny Wallon worked at her flowering vats, boiling and blending her wines; or crawled through her cabbages; or tapped on our windows, gossiped, complained, or sang. Granny Trill continued to rise in the dark, comb her waxen hair, sit out in the wood, chew, sniff and suck up porridge, and study her almanac. Yet between them they sustained a mutual awareness based solely on ear and nostril. When Granny Wallon's wines boiled, Granny Trill had convulsions; when Granny Trill took snuff, Granny Wallon had strictures; and neither let the other forget it. So all day they listened, sniffed, and pried, rapping on floors and ceilings, and prowled their rooms with hawking coughs, chivvying each other long range. It was a tranquil, bitter-pleasant life, perfected by years of custom; and to me they both seemed everlasting, deathless crones of an eternal mythology; they had always been somewhere there in the wainscot and I could imagine no world without them.

Then one day, as Granny Trill was clambering out of her wood, she stumbled and broke her hip. She went to bed then for ever. She lay patient and yellow in a calico coat, her combed hair fine as a girl's. She accepted her doom without complaint, as though some giant authority—Squire, father, or God—had ordered her there to receive it.

'I knowed it was coming,' she told our mother, 'after that visitation. I saw it last week sitting at the foot of me bed. Some person in white; I dunno . . .'

There was a sharp, early rap on our window next morning. Granny Wallon was bobbing outside.

'Did you hear him, missus?' she asked knowingly. 'He been a-screeching round since midnight.' The death bird was Granny Wallon's private pet and messenger, and she gave a skip as she told us about him. 'He called three-a-four times. Up in them yews. Her's going, you mark my words.'

And that day indeed Granny Trill died, whose bones were too old to mend. Like a delicate pale bubble, blown a little higher and further than the other girls of her generation, she had floated just long enough for us to catch sight of her, had hovered for an instant before our eyes; and then had popped suddenly, and disappeared for ever, leaving nothing on the air but a faint-drying image and the tiniest cloud of snuff.

The little church was packed for her funeral, for the old lady had been a landmark. They carried her coffin along the edge of the wood and then drew it on a cart through the village. Granny Wallon, dressed in a shower of jets, followed some distance behind; and during the service she kept to the back of the church and everybody admired her.

All went well till the lowering of the coffin, when there was a sudden and distressing commotion. Granny Wallon, ribbons flying, her bonnet awry, fought her way to the side of the grave.

'It's a lie!' she screeched, pointing down at the coffin. 'That baggage were younger'n me! Ninety-five, she says!—ain't more'n ninety, an' I gone on ninety-two! It's a crime you letting 'er go to 'er Maker got up in such brazen lies! Dig up the old devil! Get 'er brass plate off! It's insulting the living church! . . .'

They carried her away, struggling and crying, kicking out with her steel-sprung boots. Her cries grew fainter and were soon obliterated by the sounds of the grave-diggers' spades. The clump of clay falling on Granny Trill's coffin sealed her with her inscription for ever; for no one knew the truth of her age, there was no one old enough to know.

Granny Wallon had triumphed; she had buried her rival; and now there was no more to do. From then on she faded and diminished daily, kept to her house and would not be seen. Sometimes we heard mysterious knocks in the night, rousing and summoning sounds. But the days were silent, no one walked in the garden, or came skipping to claw at our window. The wine fires sank and died in the kitchen, as did the sweet fires of obsession.

About two weeks later, of no special disease, Granny Wallon gave up in her sleep. She was found on her bed, dressed in bonnet and shawl, with her signalling broom in her hand. Her open eyes were fixed on the ceiling in a listening stare of death. There was nothing, in fact, to keep her alive; no cause, no bite, no fury. Er-Down-Under had joined Er-Up-Atop, having lived closer than anyone knew.

✖ Public Death, Private Murder

Soon after the first World War a violent event took place in the village which drew us together in a web of silence and cut us off for a while almost entirely from the outside world. I was too young at the time to be surprised by it, but I knew those concerned and learned the whole story early. Though it was seldom discussed—and never with strangers—the facts of that night were familiar to us all, and common consent buried the thing down deep and raked out the tracks around it. So bloody, raw, and sudden it was, it resembled an outbreak of family madness which we took pains to conceal, out of shame and pride, and for the sake of those infected.

The crime occurred a few days before Christmas, on a night of deep snow and homecoming; the time when the families called in their strays for an annual feast of goose. The night was as cold as Cotswold cold can be, with a wind coming straight from the Arctic. We children were in bed blowing hard on our knees; wives toasted their feet by the fires; while the men and youths were along at the pub, drinking hot-pokered cider, cutting cards for crib, and watching their wet boots steam.

But few cards were dealt or played that night. An apparition intervened. The door blew open to a gust of snow and a tall man strode into the bar. He seemed to the drinkers both unknown and familiar; he had a sharp tanned face, a nasal twang, and, convinced of his welcome, he addressed everyone by name, while they lowered their eyes and nodded. Slapping the bar, he ordered drinks all round, and then he began to talk.

Everyone, save the youths, remembered this man; now they studied the change within him. Years ago, as a pale and bony lad, he had been packed off to one of the colonies, sent by subscription and the prayers of the Church, as many a poor boy before him. Usually they went, and were never heard from again, and their existence was soon forgotten. Now one of them had returned like a gilded ghost, successful and richly dressed; had come back to taunt the stay-at-homes with his boasting talk and money.

He had landed that morning, he said, at Bristol, from an Aukland mutton boat. The carriage he'd hired had broken down in the snow, so he was finishing his journey on foot. He was on his way to his parents' cottage to give them a Christmas surprise; another mile up the valley, another mile in the snow—he couldn't pass the old pub, now, could he?

He stood feet apart, his back to the bar, displaying himself to the company. Save for his yelping voice, the pub was silent, and the drinkers watched him closely. He'd done pretty well out there, he said; raised cattle, made a heap of money. It was easy enough if you just had the guts and weren't stuck in the bogs like some. . . . The old men listened, and the young men watched, with the oil lamps red in their eyes. . . .

He sent round more drinks and the men drank them down. He talked of the world and its width and richness. He lectured the old ones for the waste of their lives and the youths for their dumb contentment. They slogged for the Squire and the tenant farmers for a miserable twelve bob a week. They lived on potatoes and by touching their caps, they hadn't a sovereign to rub between them, they saw not a thing save muck and each other—and perhaps Stroud on a Saturday night. Did they know what he'd done? what he'd seen? what he'd made? His brown face was aglow with whisky. He spread a sheaf of pound notes along the bar and fished a fat gold watch from his pocket. That's nothing, he said, that's only a part of it. They should see his big farm in New Zealand—horses, carriages, meat every day, and he never said 'sir' to no one.

The old men kept silent, but drank their free drinks and sniggered every so often. The youths in the shadows just gazed at the man, and gazed at his spinning watch, and as he grew more drunk, they looked at each other, then stole away one by one. . . .

The weather outside had suddenly hardened into a blizzard of cutting snow; the night shut down to the blinding cold and the village curled up in its sheets. When the public house closed and turned down its lamps, the New Zealander was the last to leave. He refused a lantern, said he was born here, wasn't he? and paid for his bill with gold. Then he buttoned his coat, shouted good night, and strode up the howling valley. Warm with whisky and nearing home, he went singing up the hill. There were those in their beds who heard his last song, pitched wailing against the storm.

When he reached the stone cross, the young men were waiting, a bunched group, heads down in the wind.

'Well, Vincent?' they said; and he stopped, and stopped singing.

They hit him in turn, beat him down to his knees, beat him bloodily down in the snow. They beat and kicked him for the sake of themselves, as he lay there face down, groaning. Then they ripped off his coat, emptied his pockets, threw him over a wall, and left him. He was insensible now from his wounds and the drink; the storm blew all night across him. He didn't stir again from the place where he lay; and in the morning he was found frozen to death.

The police came, of course, but discovered nothing. Their enquiries were met by stares. But the tale spread quickly from mouth to mouth, was deliberately spread amongst us, was given to everyone, man and child, that we might learn each detail and hide it. The police left at last with the case unsolved; but neither we nor they forgot it. . . .

About ten years later an old lady lay dying, and towards the end she grew lightheaded. The subject of her wandering leaked out somehow: she seemed to be haunted by a watch. 'The watch,' she kept mumbling, 'they maun find the watch. Tell the boy to get it hid.' A dark-suited stranger, with a notebook in his hand, appeared suddenly at her bedside. While she tossed and muttered, he sat and waited, head bent to her whispering mouth. He was patient, anonymous, and never made any fuss; he just sat by her bed all day, his notebook open, his pencil poised, the blank pages like listening ears.

The old lady at last had a lucid moment and saw the stranger sitting beside her. 'Who's this?' she demanded of her hovering daughter. The girl leaned over the bed. 'It's all right, Mother,' said the daughter distinctly. 'It's only a police station gentleman. He hasn't come to make any trouble. He just wants to hear about the watch.'

The old lady gave the stranger a sharp, clear look and uttered not another word; she just leaned back on the pillow, closed her lips and eyes, folded her hands, and died. It was the end of the weakness that had endangered her sons; and the dark-suited stranger knew it. He rose to his feet, put his notebook in his pocket, and tiptoed out of the room. This old and wandering dying mind had been their final chance. No other leads appeared after that, and the case was never solved.

But the young men who had gathered in that winter ambush continued to live among us. I saw them often about the village: simple jokers, hard-working, mild—the solid heads of families. They were not treated as outcasts, nor did they appear to live under any special strain. They belonged to the village and the village looked after them. They are all dead now anyway.

Grief or madness were not so private, though they were kept within the village, playing themselves out before our eyes to the accompaniment of lowered voices. There was the case of Miss Fluck, the Elcombe suicide, a solitary, off-beat beauty, whose mute, distressed, life-abandoned image remains with me till this day.

Miss Fluck lived up on the other side of the valley in a cottage which faced the Severn, a cottage whose rows of tinted windows all burst into flame at sundown. She was tall, consumptive and pale as thistledown, a flock-haired pre-Raphaelite stunner, and she had a small wind harp which played tunes to itself by swinging in the boughs of her apple trees. On walks with our mother we often passed that way, and we always looked out for her. When she saw strangers coming, she skipped at the sight of them—into her cellar or into their arms. Mother was evasive when we asked questions about her, and said, 'There are others more wicked, poor soul.'

Miss Fluck liked us boys, and gave us apples and stroked our hair with her long yellow fingers. We liked her too, in an eerie way—her skipping, her hair, her harp in the trees, her curious manners of speech. Her beauty for us was also remarkable, there was no one like her in the district; her long, stone-white and tapering face seemed as cool as a churchyard angel.

I remember the last time we passed her cottage, our eyes cocked as usual for her. She was sitting behind the stained-glass window, her face brooding in many colours. Our mother called brightly: 'Yoo-hoo, Miss Fluck! Are you home? How are you keeping, my dear?'

Miss Fluck came out with a skip to the door, stared down at her hands, then at us.

'Such cheeky boys,' I heard her say. 'The image of Morgan they are.' She lifted one knee and pointed her toe. 'I've been bad, Mrs. Er,' she said.

She came swaying towards us, twisting her hair with her fingers and looking white as a daylight moon. Our mother made a clucking, sympathetic sound, and said the west wind was bad for the nerves.

Miss Fluck embraced Tony with a kind of abstract passion and stared hard over our heads at the distance.

'I've been bad, Mrs. Er—for the things I must do. It's my mother again, you know. I've been trying to keep her sick spirit from me. She don't let me alone at nights.'

Quite soon we were hurried off down the lane, although we were loath to go. 'The poor, poor soul,' Mother sighed to herself; 'and she half gentry, too. . . ."

A few mornings later we were sitting round the kitchen, waiting for Fred Green to deliver the milk. It must have been a Sunday because the breakfast was spoilt, and on weekdays that didn't matter. Everybody was grumbling; the porridge was burnt, and we hadn't yet had any tea. When Fred came at last, he was an hour and a half late, and he had a milk-wet look in his eyes.

'Where were you, Fred Green?' our sisters demanded; he'd never been late before. He was a thin, scrubby lad in his middle teens, with a head like a bottle brush. But the cat didn't coil round his legs this morning, and he made no reply to the girls. He just ladled us out our usual jugful and kept sniffling and muttering.

'What's up then, Fred?' asked Dorothy.

'Ain't nobody told you?' he asked. His voice was hollow, amazed, yet proud, and it made the girls sit up. They dragged him indoors and poured him a cup of tea and forced him to sit down a minute. Then they all gathered round him with gaping eyes, and I could see they had sniffed an occurrence.

At first Fred could only blow hard on his tea and mutter, 'Who'd a thought it?' But slowly, insidiously, the girls worked on him, and in the end they got his story. . . .

He'd been coming from milking; it was early, first light, and he was just passing Jones's pond. He'd stopped for a minute to chuck a stone at a rat—he got tuppence a tail when he caught one. Down by the lily weeds he suddenly saw something floating. It was spread out white in the water. He'd thought at first it was a dead swan or something, or at least one of Jones's goats. But when he went down closer, he saw, staring up at him, the white drowned face of Miss Fluck. Her long hair was loose—which had made him think of a swan—and she wasn't wearing a stitch of clothes. Her eyes were wide open and she was staring up through the water like somebody gazing through a window. Well, he'd got such a shock he dropped one of his buckets, and the milk ran into the pond. He stood there a bit, thinking, 'That's Miss Fluck'; and there was no one but him around. Then he'd run back to the farm and told them about it, and they'd come and fished her out with a hay rake. He'd not waited to see any more, not he; he'd got his milk to deliver.

Fred sat for a while, sucking his tea, and we gazed at him with wonder. We all knew Fred Green, we knew him well, and our girls often said he was soppy; yet only two hours ago, and only just down the lane, he'd seen drowned Miss Fluck with no clothes on. Now he seemed to exude a sort of salty sharpness so that we all wished to touch and taste him; and the excited girls tried to hold him back and make him go through his story again. But he finished his tea, sniffed hard, and left us, saying he'd still got his milk-round to do.

The news soon spread around the village, and women began to

gather at their gates.

'Have you heard?'

'No. What?'

'About poor Miss Fluck . . . Been and drowned herself down in the pond.'

'You just can't mean it!'

'Yes. Fred Green found her.'

'Yes—he just been drinking tea in our kitchen.'

'I can't believe it. I only saw her last week.'

'I know; I saw her just yesterday. I said, "Good morning, Miss Fluck"; and she said, "Good morning, Mrs. Ayres,"—you know, like she always did.'

'But she was down in the town only Friday, it was! I saw her in the Home-and-Colonial.'

'Poor, sad creature—whatever made her do it?'

'Such a lovely face she had.'

'So good to our boys. She was kindness itself. To think of her lying there.'

'She had a bit of a handicap, so they say.'

'You mean about those fellows?'

'No, more'n that.'

'What was it?'

'Ssssh!'

'Well, not everyone knows, of course. . . .'

Miss Fluck was drowned. The women looked at me listening. I stole off and ran down the lane. I was dry with excitement and tight with dread; I just wanted to see the pond. A group of villagers, including my sisters, stood gaping down at the water. The pond was flat and green and empty, and a smudge of milk clung to the reeds. I hid in the rushes, hoping not to be seen, and stared at that seething stain. This was the pond that had choked Miss Fluck. Yet strangely, and not by accident. She had come to it naked, alone in the night, and had slipped into it like a bed; she lay down there, and drew the water over her, and drowned quietly away in the reeds. I gazed at the lily roots coiled deep down, at the spongy weeds around them. That's where she lay, a green foot under, still and all night by herself, looking up through the water as though through a window and waiting for Fred to come by. One of my knees began to quiver; it was easy to see her there, her hair floating out and white eyes open, exactly as Fred Green had found her. I saw her clearly, slightly magnified, and heard her vague dry voice: 'I've been mad, Mrs. Er. It's my mother's spirit. She won't let me bide at night. . . .'

The pond was empty. She'd been carried home on a hurdle, and the women had seen to her body. But for me, as long as I can remember, Miss Fluck remained drowned in that pond.

As for Fred Green, he enjoyed for a day a welcome wherever he went. He repeated his story over and over again and drank cups of tea by the dozen. But his fame turned bad, very suddenly; for a more sinister sequel followed. The very next day, on a visit to Stroud, he saw a man crushed to death by a wagon.

'Twice in two days,' the villagers said. 'He'll see the Devil next.'

Fred Green was avoided after that. We crossed roads when we saw him coming. No one would speak to him or look him in the eyes, and he wasn't allowed to deliver milk any more. He was sent off instead to work alone in a quarry, and it took him years to re-establish himself.

The murder and the drowning were long ago, but to me they still loom large; the sharp death-taste, tooth-edge of violence, the yielding to the water of that despairing beauty, the indignant blood in the snow. They occurred at a time when the village was the world and its happenings all I knew. The village, in fact, was like a deep-running cave still linked to its antic past, a cave whose shadows were cluttered by spirits and by laws still vaguely ancestral. This cave that we inhabited looked backwards through chambers that led to our ghostly beginnings; and had not, as yet, been tidied up, or scrubbed clean by electric light, or suburbanized by a Victorian Church, or papered by cinema screens.

It was something we just had time to inherit, to inherit and dimly know —the blood and beliefs of generations who had been in this valley since the Stone Age. That continuous contact has at last been broken, the deeper caves sealed off for ever. But arriving, as I did, at the end of that age, I caught whiffs of something old as the glaciers. There were ghosts in the stones, in the trees, and the wells, and each field and hill had several. The elder people knew about these things and would refer to them in personal terms, and there were certain landmarks about the valley— tree clumps, corners in woods—that bore separate, antique, half-muttered names that were certainly older than Christian. The women in their talk still used these names which are not used now any more. There was also a frank and unfearful attitude to death, and an acceptance of violence as a kind of ritual which no one accused or pardoned.

In our grey stone village, especially in winter, such stories never seemed strange. When I sat at home among my talking sisters, or with an old woman sucking her jaws, and heard the long details of hapless suicides, of fighting men loose in the snow, of witch-doomed widows disembowelled by bulls, of child-eating sows, and so on, I would look through the windows and see the wet walls streaming, the black trees bend in the wind, and I saw these things happening as natural convulsions of our landscape, and though dry-mouthed, I was never astonished.

Being so recently born, birth had no meaning; it was the other extreme that enthralled me. Death was absorbing, and I saw much of it; it was my childhood's continuous fare. Somebody else had gone, they had gone in the night, and nobody tried to hide it. Old women, bright-eyed, came carrying the news; the corpse was praised and buried; while Mother and the girls at their kitchen chorus went over the final hours. 'The poor old thing. She fought to the last. She didn't have the strength left in her.' They wept easily, sniffing, and healthily flushed; they could have been mourning the death of a dog.

Winter, of course, was the worst time for the old ones. Then they curled up like salted snails. We called one Sunday on the old Davies couple who lived along by the shop. It had been a cold, wet January, a marrow-bone freezer, during which three old folk, on three successive Saturdays, had been carried off to their graves. Mr. and Mrs. Davies were ancient too, but they had a stubborn air of survival; and they used to watch each other, as I remember, with the calculating looks of cardplayers. This morning the woman began to discuss the funerals, while we boys sat down by the fire. Mrs. Davies was jaunty, naming each of the mourners and examining their bills of health. She rocked her white head, shot her husband a glance, and said she wondered who would be next.

The old man listened, fed some sticks to the fire, then knocked out his pipe on his leggings.

'You best fasten the windows, missus,' he said. 'The Old Bugger seems to snatch 'em week ends.'

He wheezed at that, and coughed a bit, then relapsed into a happy silence. His wife considered him brightly for a moment, and then turned with a sigh to our mother.

'Once you had to run to keep up with him,' she said. 'You can talk to him now all right. He's no longer the way as I remember. The years have slowed him down.'

Her husband just cackled and stared at the fire bars as though he'd still a few cards up his sleeve. . . .

A week or two later he took to his bed. He was bad and was said to be wasting. We went up again to the bankside cottage to enquire how the old man was. Mrs. Davies, looking frisky in a new yellow shawl, received us in her boxlike kitchen—a tiny smoked cave in which had been gathered a lifetime of fragile trophies, including some oddments of china, an angel clock, a text on a string by the fireplace, a bust of Victoria, some broken teapots and pipes, and an engraving of Redcoats at bay.

Mrs. Davies was boiling a pot of gruel, her thin back bent like an eel cage. She bade us sit down, stirred the pot madly, then sank into a wicker chair.

'He's bad,' she said, jerking her head upstairs, 'and you can't really wonder at it. He's had ammonia for years . . . his lungs is like sponges. He don't know it, but we reckon he's sinking.'

She handed us boys some hard peas to chew and settled to talk to our mother.

'It was like this, Mrs. Lee. He took ill on the Friday. I sent for me daughter Madge. We fetched him two doctors, Dr. Wills and Dr. Packer, but they fell out over the operation. Dr. Wills, you see, don't believe in cutting, so he gave him a course of treatment. But Dr. Packer, he got into a pet over that, being a rigid one for the knife. But Albert wouldn't be messed about. He said he'd no mind to be butchered. "Give me a bit of boiled bacon and let me bide," he said. I'm with him there, of course. It's true, you know—once you've been cut, you're never the same again.'

'Let me finish the gruel,' said Mother, standing up. 'You're trying to do too much.'

Mrs. Davies surrendered the ladle vaguely, and shook out her shawl around her.

'D'you know, Mrs. Lee, I was setting here last night just counting all them as been took; and from Farmer Lusty's up to the Memorial I reckoned t'were nigh on a hundred.' She folded her hands into a pious box and settled her eyes on the ceiling. 'Give me the strength to fight the world, and that what's to come upon us. . . .'

Later we were allowed to climb up the stairs and visit the old man in his bed. Mr. Davies was sinking, that was only too clear. He lay in the ice-cold poky bedroom, his breath coming rough and heavy, his thin brown fingers clutching the sheets like hooks of copper wire. His face was a skull wrapped in yellow paper, pierced by two brilliant holes. His hair had been brushed so that it stuck from his head like frosted grass on a stone.

'I've brought the boys to see you!' cried Mother; but Mr. Davies made no answer; he just stared away at some shiny distance, at something we could not see. There was a long, long silence, smelling of cologne and bed dust, of damp walls and apple-sweet fever. Then the old man sighed and shrank even smaller, a bright wetness against the pillow. He licked his lips, shot a glance at his wife, and gave a wheezy, half-giggling cough.

'When I'm gone,' he said, 'see I'm decent, missus. Wrap up me doings in a red silk handkerchief . . .'

The wet winter days seemed at times unending, and quite often they led to self-slaughter. Girls jumped down wells, young men cut their veins, spinsters locked themselves up and starved. There was something spendthrift about such gestures, a scorn of life and complaining, and those who took to them were never censured, but were spoken about in a special voice as though their actions raised them above the living and defeated the misery of the world. Even so, such outbursts were often contagious and could lead to waves of throat-cutting; indeed, during one particularly gloomy season even the coroner did himself in.

But if you survived melancholia and rotting lungs, it was possible to live long in this valley. Joseph and Hannah Brown, for instance, appeared to be indestructible. For as long as I could remember they had lived together in the same house by the common. They had lived there, it was said, for fifty years; which seemed to me for ever. They had raised a large family and sent them into the world, and had continued to live on alone, with nothing left of their noisy brood save some dog-eared letters and photographs.

The old couple were as absorbed

in themselves as lovers, content and self-contained; they never left the village or each other's company; they lived as snug as two podded chestnuts. By day blue smoke curled up from their chimney, at night the red windows glowed; the cottage, when we passed it, said, 'Here live the Browns,' as though that were part of nature.

Though white and withered, they were active enough, but they ordered their lives without haste. The old woman cooked, and threw grain to the chickens, and hung out her washing on bushes; the old man fetched wood and chopped it with a billhook, did a bit of gardening now and then, or just sat on a seat outside his door and gazed at the valley, or slept. When summer came they bottled fruit, and when winter came they ate it. They did nothing more than was necessary to live, but did it fondly, with skill—then sat together in their clock-ticking kitchen enjoying their half century of silence. Whoever called to see them was welcomed gravely, be it man or beast or child; and to me they resembled two tawny insects, slow but deft in their movements; a little foraging, some frugal feeding, then any amount of stillness. They spoke to each other without raised voices, in short chirrups as brief as bird song, and when they moved about in their tiny kitchen, they did so smoothly and blind, gliding on worn, familiar rails, never bumping or obstructing each other. They were fond, pink-faced, and alike as cherries, having taken and merged, through their years together, each other's looks and accents.

It seemed that the old Browns belonged for ever, and that the miracle of their survival was made commonplace by the durability of their love —if one should call it love, such a balance. Then suddenly, within the space of two days, feebleness took them both. It was as though two machines, wound up and synchronized, had run down at exactly the same time. Their interdependence was so legendary we didn't notice their plight at first. But after a week, not having been seen about, some neighbours thought it best to call. They found old Hannah on the kitchen floor feeding her man with a spoon. He was lying in a corner, half-covered with matting, and they were both too weak to stand. She had chopped up a plate of peelings, she said, as she hadn't been able to manage the fire. But they were all right really, just a touch of the damp; they'd do, and it didn't matter.

Well, the Authorities were told; the Visiting Spinsters got busy; and it was decided they would have to be moved. They were too frail to help each other now, and their children were too scattered, too busy. There was but one thing to be done; it was for the best; they would have to be moved to the Workhouse.

The old couple were shocked and terrified, and lay clutching each other's hands. 'The Workhouse'— always a word of shame, grey shadow falling on the close of life, most feared by the old (even when called the Infirmary); abhorred more than debt, or prison, or beggary, or even the stain of madness.

Hannah and Joseph thanked the Visiting Spinsters but pleaded to be left at home, to be left as they wanted, to cause no trouble, just simply to stay together. The Workhouse could not give them the mercy they needed, but could only divide them in charity. Much better to hide, or die in a ditch, or to starve in one's familiar kitchen, watched by the objects one's life had gathered—the scrubbed empty table, the plates and saucepans, the cold grate, the white stopped clock. . . .

'You'll be well looked after,' the Spinsters said, 'and you'll see each other twice a week.' The bright busy voices cajoled with authority and the old couple were not trained to defy them. So that same afternoon, white and speechless, they were taken away to the Workhouse. Hannah Brown was put to bed in the Women's Wing, and Joseph lay in the Men's. It was the first time, in all their fifty years, that they had ever been separated. They did not see each other again, for in a week they both were dead.

I was haunted by their end as by no other, and by the kind, killing Authority that arranged it. Divided, their life went out of them, so they ceased as by mutual agreement. Their cottage stood empty on the edge of the common, its front door locked and soundless. Its stones grew rapidly cold and repellent with its life so suddenly withdrawn. In a year it fell down, first the roof, then the walls, and lay scattered in a tangle of briars. Its decay was so violent and overwhelming, it was as though the old couple had wrecked it themselves.

Soon all that remained of Joe and Hannah Brown, and of their long close life together, were some grass-grown stumps, a garden gone wild, some rusty pots, and a dog rose.

Mother

My mother was born near Gloucester, in the village of Quedgeley, sometime in the early 1880's. On her own mother's side she was descended from a long static line of Cotswold farmers who had been deprived of their lands through a monotony of disasters in which drink, simplicity, gambling, and robbery played more or less equal parts. Through her father, John Light, the Berkeley coachman, she had some mysterious connection with the Castle, something vague and intimate, half-forgotten, who knows what?—but implying a blood link somewhere. Indeed, it was said that a retainer called Lightly led the murder of Edward II—at least, this was a local scholar's opinion. Mother accepted the theory with both shame and pleasure—as it has similarly confused me since.

But whatever the illicit grandeurs of her forbears, Mother was born to quite ordinary poverty, and was the only sister to a large family of boys, a responsibility she discharged somewhat wildly. The lack of sisters and daughters was something Mother always regretted; brothers and sons being her lifetime's lot.

She was a bright and dreamy child, it seemed, with a curious, hungry mind; and she was given to airs of incongruous elegance which never quite suited her background. She was the pride, nonetheless, of the village schoolmaster, who did his utmost to protect and develop her. At a time when country schooling was little more than a cane-whacking interlude in which boys picked up facts like bruises and the girls scarcely counted at all, Mr. Jolly, the Quedgeley schoolmaster, found this solemn child and her ravenous questioning both rare and irresistible. He was an elderly man who had battered the rudiments of learning into several generations of farm hands. But in Annie Light he saw a freak of intelligence which he felt bound to nurture and cherish.

'Mr. Jolly was really educated,' Mother told us. 'And the pains he took with poor me.' She giggled. 'He used to stop after school to put me through my sums—I was never any good at figures. I can see him now, parading up and down, pulling at his little white whiskers. "Annie," he used to say, "you've got a lovely fist. You write the best essays in class. But you can't do sums. . . ."' And I couldn't, either; they used to tie me in knots inside. But he was patience itself; he *made* me learn; and he used to lend me all his beautiful books. He wanted me to train to be a teacher, you see. But of course Father wouldn't hear of it. . . .'

When she was about thirteen years old, her mother was taken ill, so the girl had to leave school for good. She had her five young brothers and her father to look after, and there was no one else to help. So she put away her books and her modest ambitions as she was naturally expected to do. The schoolmaster was furious and called her father a scoundrel, but was helpless to interfere. 'Poor Mr. Jolly,' said Mother, fondly. 'He never seemed to give up. He used to come round home when I was doing the washing and lecture me on Oliver Cromwell. He used to sit there so sad, saying it was a sinful shame, till Father used to dance and swear. . . .'

There was probably no one less capable of bringing up five husky brothers than this scatterbrained, half-grown girl. But she did what she could, at least. Meanwhile, she grew into tumble-haired adolescence, slapdashing the housework in fits of abstraction and sliding into trances over the vegetables. She lived by longing rather than domestic law: Mr. Jolly and his books had ruined her. During her small leisure hours she would put up her hair, squeeze her body into a tight-boned dress, and either sit by the window, or walk in the fields—getting poetry by heart, or sketching the landscape in a delicate snowflake scribble.

To the other village girls Mother was something of a case, yet they were curiously drawn towards her. Her strain of fantasy, her deranged sense of fun, her invention, satire, and elegance of manner, must have intrigued and perplexed them equally. One gathered that there were also quarrels at times, jealousies, name-callings and tears. But there existed a coterie among the Quedgeley girls of which Mother was the exasperating centre. Books were passed round, excursions arranged, boys confounded by witty tongues. 'Beatie Thomas, Vi Phillips—the laughs we used to have. The things we did. We were *terrible*.'

When her brothers were big enough to look after themselves, Mother went into domestic service. Wearing her best straw hat and carrying a rope-tied box, seventeen and shapely, half wistful, half excited, she set out alone for that world of great houses which in those days absorbed most of her kind. As scullery maid, housemaid, nursemaid, parlour maid, in large manors all over the west, she saw luxuries and refinements she could never forget, and to which in some ways she naturally belonged.

The idea of the gentry, like love or the theatre, stayed to haunt her for the rest of her life. It haunted us too, through her. 'Real gentry wouldn't hear of it,' she used to say. 'The gentry always do it like this.' Her tone of voice, when referring to their ways, was reverent, genteel, and longing. It proclaimed standards of culture we could never hope to attain and mourned their impossible perfections.

Sometimes, for instance, faced by a scratch meal in the kitchen, Mother would transform it in a trance of memory. A gleam would come to her hazy eyes and a special stance to her body. Lightly she would deploy a few plates on the table and curl her fingers airily. . . .

'For dining, they'd have every place just *so;* personal cruets for every guest. . . .' Grimly we settled to our greens and bacon: there was no way to stop her now. 'The silver and napery must be arranged in order, a set for each separate dish.' Our old bent forks would be whisked into line, helter-skelter along the table. 'First of all, the butler would bring in the soup (scoop-scoop) and begin by serving the ladies. There'd be river trout next, or fresh salmon (flick-flick) lightly sprinkled with herbs and sauces. Then some woodcock perhaps, or a guinea fowl!—oh, yes, and a joint as well. And a cold ham on the sideboard, too, if you wished. For the gentlemen only, of course. The ladies never did more than pick at their food—' 'Why not?' '—Oh, it wasn't thought proper. Then Cook would send in some violet cakes, and there'd be walnuts and fruit in brandy. You'd have wine, of course, with every dish, each served in a different glass. . . .' Stunned, we would listen, grinding our teeth and swallowing our empty hungers. Meanwhile Mother would have completely forgotten our soup, which then boiled over, and put out the fire.

But there were other stories of Big House life which we found somewhat less affronting. Glimpses of balls and their shimmering company, the chandeliers loaded with light. ('We cleared a barrel of candle ends next morning.') And then Miss Emily's betrothal. ('What a picture she was—we were allowed a peep from the stairs. A man came from Paris just to do her hair. Her dress had a thousand pearls. There were fiddlers in black perched up in the gallery. The gentlemen all wore uniform. Then the dances—the polka, the two-step, the schottische—oh, dear, I was carried away. We were all of us up on the top landing, listening; I was wicked in those days, I know. I seized hold the pantry boy and said, "Come on Tom," and we danced up and down the passage. Then the butler found us and boxed our ears. He was a terrible man, Mr. Bee. . . .')

The long hard days the girls had of it then: rising before dawn, all feathered with sleep, to lay twenty or thirty fires; the sweeping, scrubbing, dusting, and polishing that was done but to be done again; the scouring of pyramids of glass and silver; the scampering up and down stairs; and those irritable little bells that began ringing in tantrums just when you'd managed to put up your feet. There was a five-pound-a-year wage, a fourteen-hour day, and a small attic for ravenous sleep; for the rest, the sub-grandees of the servants' hall with a caste system more rigid than India's.

All the same, belowstairs was a lusty life, an underworld of warmth and plenty, huge meals served cozily cheek by jowl, with roast joints and porter for all. Ruled by a despotic or gin-mellow butler and a severe or fun-fattened cook, the young country girls and the grooms and the footmen stirred a seething broth together. There were pursuits down the passages, starched love in the laundry, smothered kisses behind green-baize doors—such flights and engagements filled the scrambling hours when the rows of brass bells were silent.

How did Mother fit in to all this, I wonder? And those neat-fingered parlour queens, prim over-housemaids, reigning cooks, raging nannies who ordered her labours—what could they have made of her? Mischievous, muddle-headed, full of brilliant fancies, half witless, half touched with wonder; she was something entirely beyond their ken and must often have been their despair. But she was popular in those halls, a kind of mascot or clown; and she was beautiful, most beautiful at that time. She may not have known it, but her pictures reveal it; she herself seemed astonished to be noticed.

Two of her stories which reflect this astonishment I remember very well. Each is no more than an incident, but when she told them to us, they took on a poignancy which prevented us from thinking them stale. I must have heard them many times, right on into her later years, but at each retelling she flushed and shone, and looked down at her hands in amazement, recalling again those two magic encounters which raised her for a moment from Annie Light the housemaid to a throne of enamelled myrtles.

The first one took place at the end

of the century, when Mother was at Gaviston Court. 'It was an old house, you know; very rambling and dark; a bit primitive, too, in some ways. But they entertained a lot—not just gentry, but all sorts, even black men, too, at times. The Master had travelled all round the world and he was a very distinguished gentleman. You never quite knew what you were going to run into—it bothered us girls at times.

'Well, one winter's night they had this big house party and the place was packed right out. It was much too cold to use the outside privy but there was one just along the passage. The staff wasn't supposed to use it, of course; but I thought, Oh, I'll take a chance. Well, I'd just got me hand on the privy door when suddenly it flew wide open. And there, large as life, stood an Indian prince, with a turban, and jewels in his beard. I felt awful, you know—I was only a girl—and I wished the ground to swallow me up. I just bobbed him a curtsy and said, "Pardon, your Highness"—I was paralyzed, you see. But he only smiled, and then folded his hands, and bowed low and said, "Please, madame, to enter." So I held up my head, and went in, and sat down. Just like that. I felt like a queen. . . .'

The second encounter Mother always described as though it had never happened—in that special, morning, dream-telling voice that set it apart from all ordinary life. 'I was working at the time in a big red house at a place called Farnhamsurrey. On my Sundays off I used to go into Aldershot to visit my friend Amy Frost—Amy Hawkins that was, from Churchdown you know, before she got married, that is. Well, this particular Sunday I'd dressed up as usual, and I do think I looked a picture. I'd my smart lace-up boots, stripped blouse, and choker, a new bonnet and crochet-work gloves. I got into Aldershot far too early so I just walked about for a bit. We'd had rain in the night and the streets were shining, and I was standing quite alone on the pavement. When suddenly round the corner, without any warning, marched a full-dress regiment of soldiers. I stood transfixed; all those men and just me; I didn't know where to look. The officer in front—he had beautiful whiskers—raised his sword and cried out "Eyes right!" Then, would you believe, the drums started rolling, and the bagpipes started to play, and all those wonderful lads as they went swinging by snapped to attention and looked straight in my eyes. I stood all alone in my Sunday dress; it quite took my breath away. All those drums and pipes, and that salute just for me—I just cried, it was so exciting. . . .'

Later, our grandfather retired from his horses and went into the liquor business. He became host at The Plough, a small Sheepscombe inn, and when Grandmother died, a year or two afterwards, Mother left service to help him. Those were days of rough brews, penny ales, tuppenny rums, homemade cider, the staggers, and violence. Mother didn't altogether approve of the life, but she entered the calling with spirit. 'That's where I learned the frog march,' she'd say, 'and there were plenty of those who got it! Pug Sollars, for instance; the biggest bully in Sheepscombe—cider used to send him mad. He'd pick up the tables and lay about him like an animal while the chaps hid behind the piano. "Annie" they'd holler. "For the Lord's sake save us!" I was the only one could handle Pug. Many's the time I've caught him by the collar and run him along the passage. Others, too—if they made me wild, I'd just throw them out in the road. Dad was too easy, so it was me had to do it. . . . They smirk when they see me now.'

The Plough Inn was built as one of the smaller stages on the old coach road to Birdlip; but by Mother's time the road had decayed and was no longer the main route to anywhere. One or two carters, impelled by old habits, still used the lane and the inn, and Mother gave them ale and bacon suppers and put them to sleep in the stables. Otherwise, few travellers passed that way, and the lane was mostly silent. So through the long afternoons Mother fell into dreams of idleness, would dress in her best and sit out on the terrace, reading, or copying flowers. She was a lonely young woman, mysteriously detached, graceful in face and figure. Most of the village boys were afraid of her, of her stormy temper, her superior wit, her unpredictable mental exercises.

Mother spent several odd years in that village pub, living her double life, switching from barroom rages to terrace meditations, and waiting while her twenties passed. Grandfather, on the other hand, spent his time in the cellars playing the fiddle across his boot. He held the landlordship of an inn to be the same as Shaw's definition of marriage—as something combining the maximum of temptation with the maximum of opportunity. So he seldom appeared except late in the evening, when he'd pop up through a hole in the floor, his clothes undone, his face streaming with tears, singing 'The Warrior's Little Boy.'

Mother stuck by him faithfully, handled the drunks, grew older, and awaited deliverance. Then one day she read in a local paper: 'Widower (4 Children) Seeks Housekeeper.' She had had enough of Pug Sollars by now, and of fiddle tunes in the cellar. She changed into her best, went out onto the terrace, sat down, and answered the advertisement. A reply came back, an appointment was made; and that's how she met my father.

When she moved into his tiny house in Stroud, and took charge of his four small children, Mother was thirty and still quite handsome. She had not, I suppose, met anyone like him before. This rather priggish young man, with his devout gentility, his airs and manners, his music and ambitions, his charm, bright talk, and undeniable good looks, overwhelmed her as soon as she saw him. So she fell in love with him immediately, and remained in love for ever. And herself being comely, sensitive, and adoring, she attracted my father also. And so he married her. And so later he left her—with his children and some more of her own.

When he'd gone, she brought us to the village and waited. She waited for thirty years. I don't think she ever knew what had made him desert her, though the reasons seemed clear enough. She was too honest, too natural for this frightened man; too remote from his tidy laws. She was, after all, a country girl: disordered, hysterical, loving. She was muddled and mischievous as a chimney jackdaw, she made her nest of rags and jewels, was happy in the sunlight, squawked loudly at danger, pried and was insatiably curious, forgot when to eat or ate all day, and sang when sunsets were red. She lived by the easy laws of the hedgerow, loved the world and made no plans, had a quick, holy eye for natural wonders and couldn't have kept a neat house for her life. What my father wished for was something quite different, something she could never give him—the protective order of an unimpeachable suburbia, which was what he got in the end.

The three or four years Mother spent with my father she fed on for the rest of her life. Her happiness at that time was something she guarded as though it must ensure his eventual return. She would talk about it almost in awe, not that it had ceased but that it had happened at all.

'He was proud of me then. I could make him laugh. "Nance, you're a killer," he'd say. He used to sit on the doorstep quite helpless with giggles at the stories and things I told him. He admired me too; he admired my looks; he really loved me, you know. "Come on Nance," he'd say, "take out your pins. Let your hair down—let's see it shine!" He loved my hair; it had gold lights in it then and it hung right down my back. So I'd sit in the window and shake it over my shoulders—it was so heavy you wouldn't believe—and he'd twist and arrange it so that it caught the sun, and then sit and just gaze and gaze. . . .

'Sometimes, when you children were all in bed, he'd clear all his books away—"Come on, Nance," he'd say. "I've had enough of them. Come and sing us a song!" We'd go to the piano, and I'd sit on his lap, and he'd play with his arms around me. And I'd sing him "Killarney" and "Only a Rose." They were both his favourites then. . . .'

When she told us these things it was yesterday and she held him again in her enchantment. His later scorns were stripped away and the adored was again adoring. She'd smile and look up the weed-choked path as though she saw him coming back for more.

But it was over all right, he'd gone for good, we were alone and that was that. Mother struggled to keep us clothed and fed, and found it pretty hard going. There was never much money, perhaps just enough, the few pounds that Father sent us; but it was her own muddlehead that

Mother was fighting, her panic and innocence, forgetfulness, waste, and the creeping tide of debt. Also her outbursts of wayward extravagance which splendidly ignored our needs. The rent, as I said, was only three shillings sixpence a week but we were often six months behind. There would be no meat at all from Monday to Saturday, then on Sunday a fabulous goose; no coal or new clothes for the whole of the winter, then she'd take us all to the theatre; Jack, with no boots, would be expensively photographed; a new bedroom suite would arrive; then we'd all be insured for thousands of pounds and the policies would lapse in a month. Suddenly the iron-frost of destitution would clamp down on the house, to be thawed only by another orgy of borrowing, while harsh things were said by our more sensible neighbours and people ran when they saw us coming.

In spite of all this, Mother believed in good fortune, and especially in newspaper competitions. She was also convinced that if you praised a firm's goods, they would shower you with free samples and money. She was once paid five shillings for such a tribute which she had addressed to a skin-food firm. From then on she bombarded the market with letters, dashing off several each week. Ecstatically phrased and boasting miraculous cures, they elegantly hinted at new dawns opened up because of, or salvations due only to: headache-powders, limejuice-bottlers, corset-makers, beef-extractors, sausage-stuffers, bust-improvers, eyelash-growers,

soap-boilers, love-mongerers, statesmen, corn-plasterers, and kings. She never got another penny from any of these efforts; but such was her style, her passion and conviction, that the letters were often printed. She had bundles of clippings lying all over the house, headed 'Grateful Sufferer' or 'After Years of Torture' or 'I Used to Groan Myself to Sleep till I Stumbled on Your Ointment.' . . . She used to read them aloud with a flush of pride, quite forgetting their original purpose.

Deserted, debt-ridden, flurried, bewildered, doomed by ambitions that never came off, yet our mother possessed an indestructible gaiety which welled up like a thermal spring. Her laughing, like her weeping, was instantaneous and childlike, and switched without warning—or memory. Her emotions were entirely without reserve; she clouted you one moment and hugged you the next—to the ruin of one's ragged nerves. If she knocked over a pot, or cut her finger, she let out a blood-chilling scream—then forgot about it immediately in a hop and skip or a song. I can still seem to hear her blundering about the kitchen: shrieks and howls of alarm, an occasional oath, a gasp of wonder, a sharp command to things to stay still. A falling coal would set her hair on end, a loud knock made her leap and yell; her world was a maze of small traps and snares acknowledged always by cries of dismay. One couldn't help jumping in sympathy with her, though one learned to ignore these alarms. They were, after all, no more than formal salutes to the devils that dogged her heels.

Often, when working and not actually screaming, Mother kept up an interior monologue. Or she would absent-mindedly pick up your last remark and sing it back at you in doggerel. 'Give me some tart,' you might say, for instance. 'Give you some tart? Of course . . . Give me some tart! O give me your heart! Give me your heart to keep! I'll guard it well, my pretty Nell, As the shepherd doth guard his sheep, tra-la. . . .'

Whenever there was a pause in the smashing of crockery, and Mother was in the mood, she would make up snap verses about local characters that could stab like a three-pronged fork:

'Mrs. Okey
Makes me chokey:
Hit her with a mallet!—croquet.'

This was typical of their edge, economy, and freedom. Mrs. Okey was our local postmistress. . . .

Mother, like Gran Trill, lived by no clocks, and unpunctuality was bred in her bones. She was particularly offhand where buses were concerned and missed more than she ever caught. In the free-going days when only carrier carts ran to Stroud, she would often hold them up for an hour, but when the motorbus started, she saw no difference and carried on in the same old way. Not till she heard its horn winding down from Sheepscombe did she ever begin to get ready. Then she would cram on her hat and fly round the kitchen with habitual cries and howls.

'Where's my gloves? Where's my handbag? Damn and cuss—where's my shoes? You can't find a thing in this hole! Help me, you idiots— don't just jangle and jarl—you'll all make me miss it, I know. Scream! There it comes! Laurie, run up and stop it. Tell 'em I won't be a minute. . . .'

So I'd tear up the bank, just in time as usual, while the packed bus steamed to a halt.

'. . . Just coming, she says. Got to find her shoes. Won't be a minute, she says. . . .'

Misery for me; I stood there blushing; the driver honked on his horn, while all the passengers leaned out of the windows and shook their umbrellas crossly.

'Mother Lee again. Lost 'er shoes again. Come on, put a jerk in it there!'

Then sweet and gay from down the bank would come Mother's placating voice.

'I'm coming—yo-hoo! Just mislaid my gloves. Wait a second! I'm coming, my dears.'

Puffing and smiling, hat crooked, scarf dangling, clutching her baskets and bags, she'd come hobbling at last through the stinging nettles and climb hiccoughing into her seat. . . .

When neither bus nor carrier cart were running, Mother walked the four miles to the shops, trudging back home with her baskets of groceries and scattering packets of tea in the mud. When she tired of this, she'd borrow Dorothy's bicycle, though she never quite mastered the machine. Happy enough when the thing was in motion, it was stopping and starting that puzzled her. She had to be launched on her way by running parties of villagers; and to stop, she rode into a hedge. With the Stroud Co-op Stores, where she was a registered customer, she had come to a special arrangement. This depended for its success upon a quick ear and timing, and was a beautiful operation to watch. As she coasted downhill towards the shop's main entrance, she would let out one of her screams; an assistant, specially briefed, would tear through the shop, out the side door, and catch her in his arms. He had to be both young and nimble, for if he missed her, she piled up by the police station.

Our mother was a buffoon, extravagant and romantic, and was never wholly taken seriously. Yet within her she nourished a delicacy of taste, a sensibility, a brightness of spirit, which, though continuously bludgeoned by the cruelties of her luck, remained uncrushed and unembittered to the end. Wherever she got it from, God knows—or how she managed to preserve it. But she loved this world and saw it fresh with hopes that never clouded. She was an artist, a light-giver, and an original, and she never for a moment knew it. . . .

My first image of my mother was of a beautiful woman, strong, bounteous, but with a gravity of breeding that was always visible beneath her nervous chatter. She became, in a few years, both bent and worn, her healthy opulence quickly gnawed away by her later trials and hungers. It is in this second stage that I remember her best, for in this stage she remained the longest. I can see her prowling about the kitchen, dipping a rusk into a cup of tea, with hair loose-tangled and shedding pins, clothes shapelessly humped round her, eyes peering sharply at some revelation of the light, crying 'Ah' or 'Oh' or 'There,' talking of Tonks or reciting Tennyson and demanding my understanding.

With her love of finery, her unmade beds, her litters of unfinished scrapbooks, her taboos, superstitions, and prudishness, her remarkable dignity, her pity for the persecuted, her awe of the gentry, and her detailed knowledge of the family trees of all the Royal Houses of Europe, she was a disorganized mass of unreconciled denials, a servant girl born to silk. Yet in spite of all this, she fed our oafish wits with steady, imperceptible shocks of beauty. Though she tortured our patience and exhausted our nerves, she was, all the time, building up around us, by the unconscious revelations of her loves, an interpretation of man and the natural world so unpretentious and easy that we never recognized it then, yet so true that we never forgot it.

Nothing now that I ever see that

has the edge of gold around it—the change of a season, a jewelled bird in a bush, the eyes of orchids, water in the evening, a thistle, a picture, a poem—but my pleasure pays some brief duty to her. She tried me at times to the top of my bent. But I absorbed from birth, as now I know, the whole earth through her jaunty spirit.

Not until I left home did I ever live in a house where the rooms were clear and carpeted, where corners were visible and window seats empty, and where it was possible to sit on a kitchen chair without first turning it up and shaking it. Our mother was one of those obsessive collectors who spend all their time stuffing the crannies of their lives with a ballast of wayward objects. She collected anything that came to hand, she never threw anything away; every rag and button was carefully hoarded as though to lose it would imperil us all. Two decades of newspapers, yellow as shrouds, was the dead past she clung to, the years saved for my father, maybe something she wished to show him. . . . Other crackpot symbols also littered the house: chair springs, boot lasts, sheets of broken glass, corset bones, picture frames, fire dogs, top hats, chessmen, feathers, and statues without heads. Most of these came on the tides of unknowing, and remained as though left by a flood. But in one thing—old china—Mother was a deliberate collector and in this had an expert's eye.

Old china to Mother was gambling, the bottle, illicit love, all stirred up together; the sensuality of touch and the ornament of a taste she was born to but could never afford. She hunted old china for miles around, though she hadn't the money to do so; haunted shops and sales with wistful passion, and by wheedling, guile, and occasional freaks of chance, carried several fine pieces home.

Once, I remember, there was a big auction at Bisley, and Mother couldn't sleep for the thought of its treasures.

'It's a splendid old place,' she kept telling us. 'The Delacourt family, you know. Very cultivated they were—or *she* was, at least. It would be a crime not to go and look.'

When the sale day arrived, Mother rose right early and dressed in her auction clothes. We had a cold scratch breakfast—she was too strung up to cook—then she edged herself out through the door.

'I shall only be looking. I shan't buy, of course. I just wanted to see their Spode. . . .'

Guiltily she met our expressionless eyes, then trotted away through the rain. . . .

That evening, just as we were about to have tea, we heard her calling as she came down the bank.

'Boys! Marge—Doth! I'm home! Come and see!'

Mud-stained, flushed, and just a little shifty, she came hobbling through the gate.

'Oh, you *should* have been there. Such china and glass. I never saw anything like it. Dealers, dealers all over the place—but I did 'em all in the eye. Look, isn't it beautiful? I just had to get it . . . and it only cost a few coppers.'

She pulled from her bag a bone cup and saucer, paper-thin, exquisite, and priceless—except that the cup and its handle had parted company, and the saucer lay in two pieces.

'Of course, I could get those bits riveted,' said Mother, holding them up to the sky. The light on her face was as soft and delicate as the eggshell chips in her hand.

At that moment two carters came staggering down the path with a huge packing case on their shoulders.

'Put it there,' said Mother, and they dumped it in the yard, took their tip, and departed groaning.

'Oh, dear,' she giggled. 'I'd quite forgotten. . . . *That* went with the cup and saucer. I had to take it, it was all one lot. But I'm sure we'll find it helpful.'

We broke open the crate with a blow from the chopper and gathered to inspect the contents. Inside was a ball cock, a bundle of stair rods, an aigrette, the head of a spade, some broken clay pipes, a box full of sheep's teeth, and a framed photograph of Leamington Baths. . . .

In this way and others, we got some beautiful china, some of it even perfect. I remember a Sèvres clock once, pink-crushed with angels, and a set of Crown Derby in gold, and some airy figures from Dresden or somewhere that were like pieces of bubble-blown sunlight. It was never quite clear how Mother came by them all, but she would stroke and dust them, smiling to herself, and place them in different lights; or just stop and gaze at them, broom in hand, and sigh and shake with pleasure. They were all to her as magic casements, some cracked, some gravelled with faults, but each opening out on that secret world she knew intuitively but could never visit. She couldn't keep any of them long, however. She just had time to look them up in books, to absorb their shapes and histories, then guilt and necessity sent her off to Cheltenham to sell them back to the dealers. Sometimes—but rarely—she made a shilling or two profit, which eased her mind a little. But usually her cry was, 'Oh, dear, I *was* foolish! I should really have asked them double. . . .'

Mother's father had a touch with horses; she had the same with flowers. She could grow them anywhere, at any time, and they seemed to live longer for her. She grew them with rough, almost slapdash love, but her hands possessed such an understanding of their needs they seemed to turn to her like another sun. She could snatch a dry root from field or hedgerow, dab it into the garden, give it a shake—and almost immediately it flowered. One felt she could grow roses from a stick or chair leg, so remarkable was this gift.

Our terraced strip of garden was Mother's monument, and she worked it headstrong, without plan. She would never control or clear this ground, merely cherish whatever was there; and she was as impartial in her encouragement to all that grew as a spell of sweet, sunny weather. She would force nothing, graft nothing, nor set things in rows; she welcomed self-seeders, let each have its head, and was the enemy of very few weeds. Consequently our garden was a sprouting jungle and never an inch was wasted. Syringa shot up, laburnum hung down, white roses smothered the apple tree, red flowering-currants (smelling sharply of foxes) spread entirely along one path; such a chaos of blossom as amazed the bees and bewildered the birds in the air. Potatoes and cabbages were planted at random among foxgloves, pansies, and pinks. Often some species would entirely capture the garden—forget-me-nots one year, hollyhocks the next, then a sheet of harvest poppies. Whatever it was, one let it grow, while Mother went creeping round the wilderness, pausing to tap some odd bloom on the head, as indulgent, gracious, amiable, and inquisitive as a queen at an orphanage.

Our kitchen extended this outdoor profusion, for it was always crammed with bunches. In the green confines of that shadowy place, stockaded by leaves and flowers, the sun filtering dimly through the plant-screened windows, I often felt like an ant in a jungle overwhelmed by its opulent clusters. Almost anything that caught her wandering eye, Mother gathered and brought indoors. In bottles, teapots, dishes, and jugs, in anything old or beautiful, she'd put roses, beech boughs, parsley, hellebore, garlic, cornstalks, and rhubarb. She also grew plants in whatever would hold them—saucepans, tea caddies, or ash tins. Indeed, she once raised a fine crop of geraniums in a cast-iron water softener. We boys had found it thrown away in a wood—but only she knew what use to give it.

Although there was only one man in my mother's life—if he could ever be said to have been in it—she often grew sentimental about her girlhood suitors and liked to tell of their vanquished attentions. The postman she rejected because of his wig, the butcher who bled from her scorn, the cowman she'd shoved into Sheepscombe brook to cool his troublesome fires—there seemed many a man up and down the valleys whose love she once had blasted. Sometimes, out walking, or trudging from Stroud with our heads to the blowing rain, some fat whiskered farmer or jobbing builder would go jingling past in his trap. Then Mother would turn and watch him go, and shake the rain from her hat. 'You know, I could have married that man,' she'd murmur, 'if only I'd played my cards right. . . .'

Mother's romantic memories may not have all been reliable, for their character frequently changed. But of the stories she told us, about herself and others, the one of the Blacksmith and Toffeemaker was true. . . .

Once, she said, in the village of C——, there lived a lovelorn blacksmith. For years he had loved a local spinster, but he was shy, as most blacksmiths are. The spinster, who eked out a poor existence by boiling and selling toffee, was also lonely, in fact desperate for a husband, but too modest and proud to seek one. With the years the spinster's desperation grew, as did the blacksmith's speechless passion.

Then one day the spinster stole into the church and threw herself down on her knees. 'Oh Lord!' she prayed. 'Please be mindful of me, and send me a man to marry!'

Now the blacksmith by chance was up in the belfry, mending the old church clock. Every breathless word of the spinster's entreaties rose clearly to where he was. When he heard her praying, 'Please send me a man!' he nearly fell off the roof with excitement. But he kept his head, tuned his voice to Jehovah's, and boomed 'Will a blacksmith do?'

'Ern a man's better than nern, dear Lord!' cried the spinster gratefully.

At which the blacksmith ran home, changed into his best, and caught the spinster on her way out of church. He proposed, and they married, and lived forever contented, and used his forge for boiling their toffee.

In trying to recapture the presence of my mother, I am pulling at broken strings. The years run back through the pattern of her confusions. Her flowers and songs, her unshaken fidelities, her attempts at order, her relapses into squalor, her near madness, her crying for light, her almost daily weeping for her dead child-daughter, her frisks and gaieties, her fits of screams, her love of man, her hysterical rages, her justice towards each of us children —all these rode my mother and sat on her shoulders like a roosting of ravens and doves. Equally I remember her occasional blooming, when she became secretly beautiful and alone. And those summer nights— we boys in bed—when the green of the yew trees filled the quiet kitchen, and she would change into her silk, put on her bits of jewellery, and sit down to play the piano.

She did not play well; her rough fingers stumbled, they trembled to find the notes—yet she carried the music with little rushes of grace, half-faltering surges of feeling, that went rippling out through the kitchen windows like signals from a shuttered cage. Solitary, eyes closed, in her silks and secrets, tearing arpeggios from the yellow keys, yielding, through dusty but golden chords, to the peak of that private moment, it was clearly then, in the twilit tenderness she created, that the man should have returned to her.

I would lie awake in my still-light bedroom and hear the chime of the piano below: a ragged chord, a poignant pause, then a twinkling wagtail run. Brash yet melancholy, coarse yet wistful, it would rise in a jangling burst, then break and shiver as soft as water and lap round my listening head. She would play some waltzes, and of course 'Killarney'; and sometimes I would hear her singing—a cool lone voice, uncertainly rising, addressed to her own reflection. They were sounds of peace, half-edged with sleep, yet disturbing, almost shamefully moving. I wanted to run to her then, and embrace her as she played. But somehow I never did.

As time went on Mother grew less protesting. She had earned acquiescence and wore it gratefully. But as we children grew up, leaving home in turn, so her idiosyncrasies spread; her plant pots and newspapers, muddles and scrapbooks extended further throughout the house. She read more now and never went to bed, merely slept upright in a chair. Her nights and days were no longer divided nor harassed by the wants of children. She would sleep for an hour, rise and scrub the floor, or go wooding in the middle of the night. Like Granny Trill, she began to ignore all time and to do what she would when she wished. Even so, whenever we returned for a visit, she was ready, fires burning, to greet us. . . .

I remember coming home in the middle of the war, arriving about two in the morning. And there she was, sitting up in her chair, reading a book with a magnifying glass.

'Ah, son,' she said—she didn't know I was coming—'come here, take a look at this. . . .' We examined the book, then I went up to bed and fell into an exhausted sleep. I was roused at some dark, cold hour near dawn by Mother climbing the stairs. 'I got you your dinner, son,' she said, and planked a great tray on the bed. Aching with sleep, I screwed my eyes open —veg soup, a big stew, and a pudding. The boy had come home and he had to have supper, and she had spent half the night preparing it. She sat on my bed and made me eat it all up—she didn't know it was nearly morning.

So with the family gone, Mother lived as she wished, knowing she'd done what she could: happy to see us, content to be alone, sleeping, gardening, cutting out pictures, writing us letters about the birds, going for bus rides, visiting friends, reading Ruskin or the lives of the saints. Slowly, snugly, she grew into her background, warm on her grassy bank, poking and peering among the flowery bushes, dishevelled and bright as they. Serenely unkempt were those final years, free from conflict, doubt, or dismay, while she reverted gently to a rustic simplicity as a moss rose reverts to a wild one.

Then suddenly our absent father died—cranking his car in a Morden suburb. And with that, his death, which was also the death of hope, our mother gave up her life. Their long separation had come to an end, and it was the coldness of that which killed her. She had raised his two families, faithfully and alone; had waited thirty-five years for his praise. And through all that time she had clung to one fantasy—that aged and broken, at last in need, he might one day return to her. His death killed that promise, and also ended her reason. The mellow tranquillity she had latterly grown forsook her then forever. She became frail, simple-minded, and returned to her youth, to that girlhood which had never known him. She never mentioned him again, but spoke to shades, saw visions, and then she died.

We buried her in the village, under the edge of the beechwood, not far from her four-year-old daughter.

✖ Winter and Summer

The seasons of my childhood seemed (of course) so violent, so intense and true to their nature, that they have become for me ever since a reference of perfection whenever such names are mentioned. They possessed us so completely they seemed to change our nationality; and when I look back to the valley, it cannot be one place I see, but village-winter or village-summer, both separate. It becomes increasingly easy in urban life to ignore their extreme humours, but in those days winter and summer dominated our every action, broke into our houses, conscripted our thoughts, ruled our games, and ordered our lives.

Winter was no more typical of our valley than summer, it was not even summer's opposite; it was merely that other place. And somehow one never remembered the journey towards it; one arrived, and winter was here. The day came suddenly when all details were different and the village had to be rediscovered. One's nose went dead so that it hurt to breath, and there were jigsaws of frost on the window. The light filled the house with a green polar glow; while outside —in the invisible world—there was a strange hard silence, or a metallic creaking, a faint throbbing of twigs and wires.

The kitchen that morning would be full of steam, billowing from kettles and pots. The outside pump was frozen again, making a sound like broken crockery, so that the girls tore icicles from the eaves for water and we drank boiled ice in our tea.

'It's wicked,' said Mother. 'The poor, poor birds.' And she flapped her arms with vigour.

She and the girls were wrapped in all they had, coats and scarves and mittens; some had the shivers and some drops on their noses, while poor little Phyllis sat rocking in a chair, holding her chilblains like a handful of bees.

There was an iron-shod clatter down the garden path and the milkman pushed open the door. The milk in his pail was frozen solid. He had to break off lumps with a hammer.

'It's murder out,' the milkman said. 'Crows worryin' the sheep. Swans froze in the lake. An' tits droppin' dead in midair. . . .' He drank his tea while his eyebrows melted, slapped Dorothy's bottom, and left.

'The poor, poor birds,' Mother said again.

They were hopping round the window sill, calling for bread and fats—robins, blackbirds, woodpeckers, jays, never seen together save now. We fed them for a while, amazed at their tameness, then put on our long wool mufflers.

'Can we go out, Mother?'

'Well, don't catch cold. And remember to get some wood.'

First we found some old cocoa tins, punched them with holes, then packed them with smouldering rags. If held in the hand and blown on occasionally, they would keep hot for several hours. They were warmer than gloves, and smelt better too. In any case, we never wore gloves. So armed with these, and full of hot breakfast, we stepped out into the winter world.

It was a world of glass, sparkling and motionless. Vapours had frozen all over the trees and transformed them into confections of sugar. Everything was rigid, locked up and sealed, and when we breathed the air, it smelt like needles and stabbed our nostrils and made us sneeze.

Having sucked a few icicles, and kicked the water butt—to hear its solid sound—and breathed through the frost on the windowpane, we ran up into the road. We hung around, waiting for something to happen. A dog trotted past like a ghost in a cloud, panting his aura around him. The distant fields in the low, weak sun were crumpled like oyster shells.

Presently some more boys came to join us, wrapped like Russians, with multicoloured noses. We stood round in a group and just gasped at each other, waiting to get an idea. The thin ones were blue, with hunched-up shoulders, hands deep in their pockets, shivering. The fat ones were rosy and blowing like whales; all of us had wet eyes. What should we do? We didn't know. So the fat ones punched the thin ones, who doubled up. Then the thin ones punched the fat ones, who half died, coughing. Then we all jumped up and down for a bit, flapped our arms, and blew on our cocoa tins.

'What we goin' to *do,* then, eh?'

We quieted down to think. A shuddering thin boy, with his lips drawn back, was eating the wind with his teeth. 'Giddy up,' he said suddenly, and sprang into the air and began whipping himself, and whinnying. At that we all galloped away down the road, bucking and snorting, tugging invisible reins, and lashing away at our hindquarters.

Now the winter's day was set in motion and we rode through its crystal kingdom. We examined the village for its freaks of frost, for anything we might use. We saw the frozen spring by the side of the road, huge like a swollen flower. Water wagtails hovered above it, nonplussed at its silent hardness, and again and again they dropped down to drink, only to go sprawling in a tumble of feathers. We saw the stream in the valley, black and halted, a tarred path threading through the willows. We saw trees lopped off by their burdens of ice, cow tracks like potholes in rock, quiet lumps of sheep licking the spiky grass with their black and rotting tongues. The church clock had stopped and the weathercock was frozen, so that both time and the winds were stilled; and nothing, we thought, could be more exciting than this: interference by a hand unknown, the winter's No! to routine and laws—sinister, awesome, welcome.

'Let's go an' 'elp Farmer Wells,' said a fat boy.

'You can—I ain't,' said a thin one.

'If you don't I'll give thee a clip in the yer'ole.'

'Gurt great bully.

'I ain't.'

'You be.'

So we went to the farm on the lip of the village, a farm built from a long-gone abbey. Wells, the farmer, had a young, sick son more beautiful than a girl. He waved from his window as we trooped into the farmyard, and wouldn't live to last out the winter. The farmyard muck was brown and hard, dusted with frost like a baked bread-pudding. From the sheds came the rattle of morning milking,

chains and buckets, a cow's deep sigh, stumbling hooves, and a steady munching.

'Wan' any 'elp, Mr. Wells?' we asked.

He crossed the yard with two buckets on a yoke; as usual he was dressed in dung. He was small and bald, but had long, sweeping arms that seemed stretched from his heavy labours.

'Well, come on,' he said. 'But no playing the goat. . . .'

Inside the cowsheds it was warm and voluptuous, smelling sweetly of milky breath, of heaving hides, green dung and udders, of steam and fermentations. We carried cut hay from the heart of the rick, packed tight as tobacco flake, with grass and wild flowers juicily fossilized within—a whole summer embalmed in our arms.

I took a bucket of milk to feed a calf. It opened its mouth like a hot, wet orchid. It began to suck at my fingers, gurgling in its throat and raising its long-lashed eyes. The milk had been skimmed for making butter and the calf drank a bucket a day. We drank the same stuff at home sometimes; Mr. Wells sold it for a penny a jug.

When we'd finished the feeding, we got a handful of apples and a baked potato each. The apples were so cold they stung the teeth, but the potatoes were hot, with butter. We made a dinner of this, then scuffled back to the village, where we ran into the bully, Walt Kerry.

'Wan' a know summat?' he asked.

'What?'

'Shan't tell ya.'

He whistled a bit, and cleaned his ears. He gave out knowledge in very small parcels.

'Well, if you *wan'* a know, I may's well . . .'

We waited in a shivering lump.

'Jones's pond is bearing,' he said at last. 'I bin a-slidin' on it all mornin'. Millions bin comin' wi 'orses an' traps an' skates an' things an' all.'

We tore away down the frosty lane, blood up, and elbows well out.

'Remember I told ya. An' I got there fust. An' I'll be back when I've 'ad me tea!'

We left him standing in the low, pink sun, small as a cankered rose, spiky, thorny, a thing of dread, only to be encountered with shears.

We could hear the pond as we ran down the hill, the shouts that only water produces, the squeal of skates, the ring of the ice and its hollow, heaving grumble. Then we saw it: black and flat as a tray, the skaters rolling round it like marbles. We broke into a shout and charged upon it and fell sprawling in all directions. This magic substance, with its deceptive gifts, was something I could never master. It put wings on my heels and gave me the motions of Mercury, then threw me down on my nose. Yet it chose its own darlings, never the ones you supposed, the dromedary louts of the schoolroom, who came skating past with one leg in the air, who twirled and simpered, and darted like swifts; and never fell once—not they.

I was one of the pedestrians, and we worked up a slide across the polished darkness. So smooth that to step on it was to glide away, while the valley slid past like oil. You could also lie prone and try to swim on the ice, kicking your arms and legs. And you saw deep down, while in that position, little bubbles like cold green stars, jagged, ominous cracks, dead ribbons of lilies, drowned bulrushes loaded like rockets.

The frozen pond on such a winter's evening was a very treadmill of pleasure. Time was uncounted; we played ourselves into exhaustion. We ran and slid till we dripped with sweat; our scarves were pearled with our breath. The reeds and horsetails at the pond's grey edge smelt as pungent as old men's fingers. Hanging branches of willow, manacled in the ice, bloomed like lilac in the setting sun. Then the frost moon rose through the charcoal trees, and we knew that we'd played too long.

We had promised Mother we would fetch some wood. We had to get some each day in winter. Jack and I, hands in pockets, mooched silently up the lane; it was night now, and we were frightened. The beech wood was a cavern of moonlight and shadows, and we kept very close together.

The dead sticks on the ground were easily seen, glittering with the night's new frost. As we ripped them from the earth, scabbed with soil and leaves, our hands began to burn with the cold. The wood was silent and freezing hard, white and smelling of wolves. Such a night as lost hunters must have stared upon when first they wandered north into the Ice Age. We thought of caves, warm skins, and fires, grabbed our sticks and tore off home.

Then there were 'Where've-you-beens? Never-minds, Oh-Dears, and Come-by-the-fire-you-look-half-dead.' First, the long slow torment as our hands thawed out, a quiet agony of returning blood. Worse than toothache it was; I sat there sobbing, but gradually the pain wave passed. Then we had jugs of tea, hot toast and dripping; and later our sisters came.

'It was murder in Stroud. I fell down twice—in the High Street—and tore my stockings. It was terrible, Ma. And a horse went through Maypole's window. And old Mr. Fowler couldn't get down the hill and had to sit on his bottom and slide. It's freezing harder than ever now. We won't none of us be able to budge tomorrow.'

They sat at their tea and went on talking about it in their singsong disaster voices. And we boys were content to know the winter had come, total winter, the new occupation. . . .

Later, towards Christmas, there was heavy snow, which raised the roads to the tops of the hedges. There were millions of tons of the lovely stuff, plastic, pure, all-purpose, which nobody owned, which one could carve or tunnel, eat, or just throw about. It covered the

hills and cut off the villages, but nobody thought of rescues; for there was hay in the barns and flour in the kitchens, the women baked bread, the cattle were fed and sheltered—we'd been cut off before, after all.

The week before Christmas, when snow seemed to lie thickest, was the moment for carol-singing; and when I think back to those nights it is to the crunch of snow and to the lights of the lanterns on it. Carol-singing in my village was a special tithe for the boys; the girls had little to do with it. Like hay-making, black-berrying, stone-clearing, and wishing-people-a-happy-Easter, it was one of our seasonal perks.

By instinct we knew just when to begin it; a day too soon and we should have been unwelcome, a day too late and we should have received lean looks from people whose bounty was already exhausted. When the true moment came, exactly balanced, we recognized it and were ready.

So as soon as the wood had been stacked in the oven to dry for the morning fire, we put on our scarves and went out through the streets, calling loudly between our hands, till the various boys who knew the signal ran out from their houses to join us.

One by one they came stumbling over the snow, swinging their lanterns round their heads, shouting and coughing horribly.

'Coming carol-barking then?'

We were the Church Choir, so

no answer was necessary. For a year we had praised the Lord out of key, and as a reward for this service—on top of the Outing—we now had the right to visit all the big houses, to sing our carols and collect our tribute.

To work them all in meant a five-mile foot journey over wild and generally snowed-up country. So the first thing we did was to plan our route; a formality, as the route never changed. All the same, we blew on our fingers and argued; and then we chose our leader. This was not binding, for we all fancied ourselves as leaders, and he who started the night in that position usually trailed home with a bloody nose.

Eight of us set out that night. There was Sixpence the Simple, who had never sung in his life (he just worked his mouth in Church); the brothers Horace and Boney, who were always fighting everybody and always getting the worst of it; Clergy Green, the preaching maniac; Walt the bully, and my two brothers. As we went down the lane, other boys, from other villages, were already about the hills, bawling 'Kingwenslush,' and shouting through keyholes 'Knock on the knocker! Ring at the bell! Give us a penny for singing so well!' They weren't an approved charity as we were, the Choir; but competition was in the air.

Our first call as usual was the house of the Squire, and we trooped nervously down his drive. For light we had candles in marmalade jars suspended on loops of string, and they threw pale gleams on the towering snowdrifts that stood on each side of the drive. A blizzard was blowing but we were well wrapped up, with army puttees on our legs, woollen hats on our heads, and several scarves around our ears.

As we approached the Big House across its white silent lawns, we too grew respectfully silent. The lake nearby was stiff and black, the waterfall frozen and still. We arranged ourselves shuffling around the big front door, then knocked and announced the Choir.

A maid bore the tiding of our arrival away into the echoing distances of the house, and while we waited, we cleared our throats noisily. Then she came back, and the door was left ajar for us, and we were bidden to begin. We brought no music; the carols were in our heads. 'Let's give 'em "Wild Shepherds,"' said Jack. We began in confusion, plunging into a wreckage of keys, of different words and tempos; but we gathered our strength; he who sang loudest took the rest of us with him, and the carol took shape, if not sweetness.

This huge stone house, with its ivied walls, was always a mystery to us. What were those gables, those rooms and attics, those narrow windows veiled by the cedar trees? As we sang 'Wild Shepherds' we craned our necks, gaping into the lamplit hall which we had never entered; staring at the muskets and untenanted chairs, the great tapestries furred by dust—until suddenly, on the stairs, we saw the old Squire himself standing and listening with his head on one side.

He didn't move until we'd finished; then slowly he tottered towards us, dropped two coins in our box with a trembling hand, scratched his name in the book we carried, gave us each a long look with his moist blind eyes, then turned away in silence.

As though released from a spell, we took a few sedate steps, then broke into a run for the gate. We didn't stop till we were out of the grounds. Impatient, at last, to discover the extent of his bounty, we squatted by the cowsheds, held our lanterns over the book, and saw that he had written 'Two Shillings.' This was quite a good start. No one of any worth in the district would dare to give us less than the Squire.

So with money in the box, we pushed on up the valley, pouring scorn on each other's performance. Confident now, we began to consider our quality and whether one carol was not better suited to us than another. Horace, Walt said, shouldn't sing at all; his voice was beginning to break. Horace disputed this and there was a brief token battle—they fought as they walked, kicking up divots of snow, then they forgot it, and Horace still sang.

Steadily we worked through the length of the valley, going from house to house, visiting the lesser and the greater gentry—the farmers, the doctors, the merchants, the majors, and other exalted persons. It was freezing hard and blowing too; yet not for a moment did we feel the cold. The snow blew into our faces, into our eyes and mouths, soaked through our puttees, got into our boots, and dripped from our woollen caps. But we did not care. The collecting box grew heavier, and the list of names in the book longer and more extravagant, each trying to outdo the other.

Mile after mile we went, fighting against the wind, falling into snowdrifts, and navigating by the lights of the houses. And yet we never saw our audience. We called at house after house; we sang in courtyards and porches, outside windows, or in the damp gloom of hallways; we heard voices from hidden rooms; we smelt rich clothes and strange hot food; we saw maids bearing in dishes or carrying away coffee cups; we received nuts, cakes, figs, preserved ginger, dates, cough drops, and money; but we never once saw our patrons. We sang, as it were, at the castle walls and, apart from the Squire, who had shown himself to prove that he was still alive, we never expected it otherwise.

As the night drew on there was trouble with Boney. 'Noel,' for instance, had a rousing harmony which Boney persisted in singing, and singing flat. The others forbade him to sing it at all, and Boney said he would fight us. Picking himself up, he agreed we were right, then he disappeared altogether. He just turned away and walked into the snow and wouldn't answer when we called him back. Much later, as we reached a far point up the valley, somebody said 'Hark!' and we stopped to listen. Far away across the fields from the distant village came the sound of a frail voice singing, singing 'Noel,' and singing it flat—it was Boney, branching out on his own.

We approached our last house high up on the hill, the place of Joseph the farmer. For him we had chosen a special carol, which was about the other Joseph, so that we always felt that singing it added a spicy cheek to the night. The last stretch of country to reach his farm was perhaps the most difficult of all. In these rough, bare lanes, open to all winds, sheep were buried and wagons lost. Huddled together, we tramped in one another's footsteps, powdered snow blew into our screwed-up eyes, the candles burnt low, some blew out altogether, and we talked loudly above the gale.

Crossing, at last, the frozen mill-stream—whose wheel in summer still turned a barren mechanism— we climbed up to Joseph's farm. Sheltered by trees, warm on its bed of snow, it seemed always to be like this. As always it was late; as always this was our final call. The snow had a fine crust upon it, and the old trees sparkled like tinsel.

We grouped ourselves round the farmhouse porch. The sky cleared, and broad streams of stars ran down over the valley and away to Wales. On Slad's white slopes, seen through the black sticks of its woods, some red lamps still burned in the windows.

Everything was quiet; everywhere there was the faint crackling silence of the winter night. We started singing, and we were all moved by the words and the sudden trueness of our voices. Pure, very clear, and breathless we sang:

'As Joseph was a-walking
He heard an angel sing;
"This night shall be the birth-time
Of Christ the Heavenly King.

' "He neither shall be borned
In Housen nor in hall,
Nor in a place of paradise
But in an ox's stall. . . ." '

And two thousand Christmases became real to us then; the houses, the halls, the places of paradise had all been visited; the stars were bright to guide the kings through the snow; and across the farmyard we could hear the beasts in their stalls. We were given roast apples and hot mince pies; in our nostrils were spices like myrrh, and in our wooden box, as we headed back for the village, there were golden gifts for all.

Summer, June summer, with the green back on earth and the whole world unlocked and seething—like winter, it came suddenly and one knew it in bed, almost before waking up; with cuckoos and pigeons hollowing the woods since daylight and the chipping of tits in the pear blossom.

On the bedroom ceiling, seen first through sleep, was a pool of expanding sunlight—the lake's reflection thrown up through the trees by the rapidly climbing sun. Still drowsy, I watched on the ceiling above me its glittering image reversed, saw every motion of its somnambulant waves and projections of the life upon it. Arrows ran across it from time to time, followed by the far call of a moor hen; I saw ripples of light around each root of the bulrushes; every detail of the lake seemed there. Then suddenly the whole picture would break into pieces, would be smashed like a molten mirror and run amok in tiny globules of gold, frantic and shivering; and I would hear the great slapping of wings on water, building up a steady crescendo, while across the ceiling passed the shadows of swans off into the heavy morning. I would hear their cries pass over the house and watch the chaos of light above me, till it slowly settled and re-collected its stars and resumed the lake's still image.

Watching swans take off from my bedroom ceiling was a regular summer wakening. So I woke and looked out through the open window to a morning of cows and cockerels. The beech trees framing the lake and valley seemed to call for a royal hunt; but they served equally well for climbing into, and even in June you could still eat their leaves—a tight-folded salad of juices.

Outdoors, one scarcely knew what had happened or remembered any other time. There had never been rain, or frost, or cloud; it had always been like this. The heat from the ground climbed up one's legs and smote one under the chin. The garden, dizzy with scent and bees, burned all over with hot white flowers, each one so blinding an incandesence that it hurt the eyes to look at them.

The villagers took summer like a kind of punishment. The women never got used to it. Buckets of water were being sluiced down paths, the dust was being laid with grumbles, blankets and mattresses clung like tongues from the windows, panting dogs crouched under the rain tubs. A man went by and asked 'Hot enough for 'ee?' and was answered by a worn-out shriek.

In the builder's stable, well out of the sun, we helped to groom Brown's horse. We smelt the burning of his coat, the horn of his hooves, his hot leather harness and dung. We fed him on bran, dry as a desert wind, till both we and the horse half-choked. Mr. Brown and his family were going for a drive, so we wheeled the trap into the road, backed the blinkered horse between the shafts, and buckled his jingling straps. The road lay deserted in its layer of dust and not a thing seemed to move in the valley. Mr. Brown and his best-dressed wife and daughter, followed by his bowler-hatted son-in-law, climbed one by one into the high-sprung trap and sat there with ritual stiffness.

'Where we goin' then, Father?'

'Up the hill for some air.'

'Up the hill? He'll drop down dead.'

'Bide quiet,' said Mr. Brown, already dripping with sweat. 'Another word, and you'll go back 'ome.'

He jerked the reins and gave a flick of the whip and the horse broke into a saunter. The women clutched their hats at the unexpected movement, and we watched them till they were out of sight.

When they were gone there was nothing else to look at; the village slipped back into silence. The untarred road wound away up the valley, innocent as yet of motorcars; wound empty away to other villages, which lay empty too, the hot day long, waiting for the sight of a stranger.

We sat by the roadside and scooped the dust with our hands and made little piles in the gutters. Then we slid through the grass and lay on our backs and just stared at the empty sky. There was nothing to do. Nothing moved or happened, nothing happened at all except summer. Small heated winds blew over our faces, dandelion seeds floated by, burnt sap and roast nettles tingled our nostrils together with the dull rust smell of dry ground. The grass was June high and had come up with a rush, a massed entanglement of species, crested with flowers and spears of wild wheat, and coiled with clambering vetches, the whole of it humming with blundering bees and flickering with scarlet butterflies. Chewing grass on our backs, the grass scaffolding the sky, the summer was all we heard; cuckoos crossed distances on chains of cries, flies buzzed and choked in the ears, and the saw-toothed chatter of mowing machines drifted on waves of air from the fields.

We moved. We went to the shop and bought sherbet and sucked it through sticks of liquorice. Sucked gently, the sherbet merely dusted the tongue; too hard, and you choked with sweet powders; or if you blew back through the tube, the sherbet bag burst and you disappeared in a blizzard of sugar. Sucking and blowing, coughing and weeping, we scuffled our way down the lane. We drank at the spring to clean our mouths, then threw water at each other and made rainbows. Mr. Jones's pond was bubbling with life, and covered with great white lilies—they poured from their leaves like candle fat, ran molten, then cooled on the water. Moor hens plopped, and dabchicks scooted, insects rowed and skated. New-hatched frogs hopped about like flies, lizards gulped in the grass. The lane itself was crusted with cow dung, hard-baked and smelling good.

We met Sixpence Robinson among the bulrushes, and he said, 'Come and have some fun.' He lived along the lane just past the sheep wash in a farm cottage near a bog. There were five in his family, two girls and three boys, and their names all began with S. There was Sis and Sloppy, Stosher and Sammy, and our good friend Sixpence the Simple. Sis and Sloppy were both beautiful girls and used to hide from us boys in the gooseberries. It was the brothers we played with; and Sammy, though a cripple, was one of the most agile lads in the village.

Theirs was a good place to be at any time, and they were good to be with. (Like us, they had no father; unlike ours, he was dead.) So today, in the spicy heat of their bog, we sat round on logs and whistled, peeled sticks, played mouth organs, dammed up the stream, and cut harbours in the cool clay banks. Then we took all the pigeons out of their dovecots and ducked them in the water butt, held them under till their beaks started bubbling, then threw them up in the air. Splashing spray from their wings, they flew round the house, then came back to roost like fools. (Sixpence had a one-eyed pigeon called Spike who he boasted could stay under longest, but one day the poor bird, having broken all records, crashed for ever among the cabbages.)

When all this was over, we retired to the paddock and played cricket under the trees. Sammy, in his leg irons, charged up and down. Hens and guinea fowl took to the trees. Sammy hopped and bowled like murder at us, and we defended our stumps with our lives. The cracked bat clouting; the cries in the reeds; the smells of fowls and water; the long afternoon with the steep hills around us watched by Sloppy still hid in the gooseberries—it seemed down here that no disasters could happen, that nothing could ever touch us. This was Sammy's and Sixpence's: the place past the sheep wash, the hide-out unspoiled by authority, where drowned pigeons flew and cripples ran free; where it was summer, in some ways, always.

Summer was also the time of these: of sudden plenty, of slow hours and actions, of diamond haze and dust on the eyes, of the valley in post-vernal slumber; of burying birds saved from seething corruption; of Mother sleeping heavily at noon; of jazzing wasps and dragonflies, hay stooks and thistle seeds, snows of white butterflies, skylarks' eggs, bee orchids and frantic ants; of wolf-cub parades, and boy scouts' bugles; of sweat running down the legs; of boiling potatoes on bramble fires, of flames glass-blue in the sun; of lying naked in the hill-cold stream; begging pennies for bottles of pop; of girls' bare arms; of unripe cherries, green apples, and liquid walnuts; of fights and falls and new-scabbed knees, sobbing pursuits and flights; of picnics high up in the crumbling quarries, of butter running like oil, of sunstroke, fever, and cucumber peel stuck cool to one's burning brow. All this, and the feeling that it would never end, that such days had come for ever, with the pump drying up and the water butt crawling, and the chalk ground hard as the moon. All sights twice-brilliant and smells twice-sharp, all game-days twice as long. Double charged as we were, like the meadow ants, with the frenzy of the sun, we used up the light to its last violet drop, and even then couldn't go to bed.

When darkness fell, and the huge moon rose, we stirred to a second life. Then boys went calling along the roads, wild, slit-eyed animal calls, Walt Kerry's naked nasal yodel,

Boney's jackal scream. As soon as we heard them we crept outdoors, out of our stifling bedrooms, stepped out into moonlight warm as the sun to join our chalk-white, moon-masked gang.

Games in the moon. Games of pursuit and capture. Games that the night demanded. Best of all, Fox and Hounds—go where you like, and the whole of the valley to hunt through. Two chosen boys loped away through the trees and were immediately swallowed in shadow. We gave them five minutes, then set off after them. They had church-yard, farmyard, barns, quarries, hill-tops, and woods to run to. They had all night, and the whole of the moon, and five miles of country to hide in. . . .

Padding softly, we ran under the melting stars, through sharp garlic woods, through blue-blazed fields, following the scent by the game's one rule, the question and answer cry. Every so often, panting for breath, we paused to check on our quarry. Bullet heads lifted, teeth shone in the moon. 'Whistle-or-'OLLER! Or-we-shall-not-FOL–LER!' It was a cry on two notes, prolonged. From the other side of the hill, above white fields of mist, the faint fox-cry came back. We were off again then, through the waking night, among sleepless owls and badgers, while our quarry slipped off into another parish and would not be found for hours.

Round about midnight we ran them to earth, exhausted under a haystack. Until then we had chased them through all the world, through jungles, swamps, and tundras, across pampas, plains, and steppes of wheat and plateaux of shooting stars, while hares made love in the silver grasses, and the large, hot moon climbed over us, raising tides in my head of night and summer that move there even yet.

✖ Sick Boy

As a child I used to boast the rare distinction of having been christened twice. The second time, which took place in church, was a somewhat rowdy affair; I was three years old and I cheeked the parson and made free with the holy water. But my first anointing was much more solemn and occurred immediately after my birth. I had entered the world in doubt and silence, a frail little life-less lump; and the midwife, after one look at my worn-out face, said I wouldn't last the day. Everybody agreed, including the doctor, and they just waited for me to die.

My mother, however, while resigned to my loss, was determined I should enter heaven. She remembered those tiny anonymous graves tucked away under the churchyard laurels, where quick-dying infants— behind the vicar's back—were stowed secretly among the jam-jars. She said the bones of her son should rest in God's own ground and not rot with those pitiful heathens. So she summoned the curate, who came and called out my Adam, baptized me from a teacup, admitted me to the Church, and gave me three names to die with.

This flurried christening proved unnecessary, however. Something—who knows what?—some ancestral toughness maybe, saw me safely through the first day. I remained seriously ill for many months, inert, unnoticing, one of life's bad debts, more or less abandoned by all. 'You never moved or cried,' said my mother. 'You just lay where I put you, like a little image, staring up at the ceiling all day.' In that motionless swoon I was but a clod, a scarce-breathing parcel of flesh. For a year I lay prone to successive invasions, enough to mop up an orphanage—I had diphtheria, whooping cough, pleurisy, double pneumonia, and congestion of the bleeding lungs. My mother watched, but could not help me; waited, but could not hope. In those days young children dropped dead like chickens, their diseases not well understood; families were large as though by compensation; at least a quarter were not expected to survive. My father had buried three of his children already, and was quite prepared to do the same by me.

But secretly, silently, aided by unknown forces, I hung on—though it was touch and go. My most perilous moment came when I was eighteen months old, at the hands of Mrs. Moore, a neighbour. My mother was in bed for the birth of my brother—we were all born at home those days. Mrs. Moore had been called in to help, to scrub the children and to cook them soups. She was a jolly, eye-bulging, voodoolike creature who took charge of us with primitive casualness. While still in her care I entered a second bout of pneumonia. What followed I was told much later. . . .

It seems that brother Tony was but two days born and Mother just beginning to take notice. Eleven-year-old Dorothy came upstairs to see her, played awhile with the baby, nibbled some biscuits, then sat in the window and whistled.

'How you all getting on?' Mother asked.

'Oh, all right,' said Dorothy.

'You behaving yourselves?'

'Yes, Ma.'

'And what you all up to?'

'Nothing much.'

'Where's Marjorie then?'

'Out in the yard.'

'And Phyllis?'

'She's peeling spuds.'

'What about the others?'

'Harold's cleaning his trolley. And Jack and Frances is sitting on the steps.'

'And Laurie? . . . How's Laurie?'

'Oh, Laurie's dead.'

'What!'

'He turned yellow. They're laying him out. . . .'

Giving one of her screams, Mother leapt out of bed.

'No one's going to lay out our Laurie!'

Gasping, she groped her way downstairs and staggered towards the kitchen; and lo, there I was, stretched naked on the table, yellow, just as Dorothy said. Mrs. Moore, humming gaily, was sponging my body as though preparing a chicken for dinner.

'What you think you're doing?' my mother shouted.

'Poor boy, he's gone,' crooned Mrs. Moore. 'Gone fled to the angels— thought I'd wash him for the box— just didn't want to bother you, mum.'

'You cruel, wicked woman! Our Laurie ain't dead—just look at his healthy colour.'

Mother plucked me from the table, wrapped me up in a blanket, and carried me back to my cot— cursing Mrs. Moore for a snatcher of bodies and asking the saints what they thought they were up to. Somehow, I lived—though it was a very near thing, a very near thing indeed. So easy to have succumbed to Mrs. Moore's cold sponge. Only Dorothy's boredom saved me.

It was soon after this that my sister Frances died. She was a beautiful, fragile, dark-curled child, and my mother's only daughter. Though only four she used to watch me like a nurse, sitting all day beside my cot and talking softly in a special language. Nobody noticed that she was dying herself; they were too much concerned with me. She died suddenly, silently, without complaint, in a chair in the corner of the room. An ignorant death which need never have happened—and I believe that she gave me her life.

But at least she was mourned. Not a day passed afterwards but that Mother shed some tears for her. Mother also grew jealous for the rest of us, more careful that we should survive. So I grew to be, not a pale, wasting boy, but sickly in another way, switching regularly from a swaggering plumpness—a tough equality with other boys—to a monotonous return of grey-ghosted illness, hot and cold, ugly-featured and savage. When I was well, I could hold my own; no one spared me, because I didn't look delicate. But when I was ill, I just disappeared from the scene and remained out of sight for weeks. If it were summer when the fever caught me, I lay and sweated in my usual bed, never quite sure which of us was ill, me or the steaming weather. But in winter a fire was lit in the bedroom, and then I knew I was ill indeed. Washbasins could freeze, icicles hang from the ornaments, our bedrooms remained normally unheated; but the lighting of a fire especially in Mother's room, meant that serious illness had come.

As soon as I recognized the returning face of my sickness—my hand light as feathers, a swaying in the head, and lungs full of pulsing thorns—the first thing I did was to recall my delusions and send messages to the anxious world. As I woke to the fever, I thought of my subjects, and their concern always gave me comfort. Signals in Morse, tapped out on the bedrail, conveyed brief and austere intelligences. 'He is ill.' (I imagined the first alarm.) 'He has told his mother.' (Some relief.) 'He is fighting hard.' (Massed prayers in the churches.) 'He is worse.' (Cries of doom in the streets.) There were times I was almost moved to tears at the thought of my anxious people, the invisible multitudes up and down the land joined in grief at this threat to their king. How piteously they awaited each sombre bulletin, and how brave I was meanwhile. Certainly I took pains to give them something to be anxious about, but I also bid them be strong. 'He wishes no special arrangements made. Only bands and tanks. A parade or two. And perhaps a three minutes' silence.'

This would occupy my first morning, with the fever still fresh; but by nightfall I was usually raving. My limbs went first, splintering like logs, so that I seemed to grow dozens of arms. Then the bed no longer had limits to it and became a desert of hot, wet sand. I began to talk to a second head laid on the pillow, my own head once removed; it never talked back but just lay there, grinning very coldly into my eyes. The walls of the bedroom were the next to go; they began to bulge and ripple and roar, to flap like pastry, melt like sugar, and run bleeding with hideous hues. Then out of the walls, and down from the ceiling, advanced a row of intangible smiles; easy, relaxed, in no way threatening at first, but going on far too long. Even a maniac's smile will finally waver, but these just continued in silence, growing brighter, colder, and ever more humourless till the sick blood roared in my veins. They were Cheshire-cat smiles, with no face or

outlines, and I could see the room clearly through them. But they hung above me like a stain on the air, a register of smiles in space, smiles without pity, smiles without love, smiling smiles of unsmiling smileness; not even smiles of strangers but smiles of no one, expanding in brilliant silence, persistent, knowing, going on and on . . . till I was screaming and beating the bedrails.

At my scream all the walls shook down like a thunderclap and everything was normal again. The kitchen door opened, feet thumped up the stairs, and the girls bustled into the room. 'He's been seeing them faces again,' they whispered. 'It's all right!' they bawled. 'There, there! You won't see any more. Have a nice jug of lemon.' And they mopped me, and picked up the bedclothes. I lay back quietly while they fussed around; but what could I say to them? That I hadn't seen faces—that I'd only seen smiles? I tried that, but it got me nowhere.

Later, as the red night closed upon me, I was only barely conscious. I heard myself singing, groaning, talking, and the sounds were like hands on my body. Blood boiled, flesh crept, teeth chattered and clenched, my knees came up to my mouth; I lay in an evil swamp of sweat which alternately steamed and froze me. My shirt was a kind of enveloping sky wetly wrapping my goosey skin, and across which, at intervals, hot winds from Africa and Arctic blizzards blew. All objects in the room became molten again, and the pictures repainted themselves; things ran about, changed shape, grew monstrous, or trailed off into limitless distances. The flame of the candle threw shadows like cloaks which made everything vanish in turn, or it drew itself up like an ivory saint, or giggled and collapsed in a ball. I heard voices that couldn't control themselves, that either whispered just out of sound, or suddenly boomed some great echoing word, like 'Shovel!' or 'Old-men's-ears!' Such a shout would rouse me with terrible echoes, as though a piano had just been kicked by a horse.

It was myself, no doubt, who spoke these words, and the monologue went on for hours. Sometimes I deliberately answered back, but mostly I lay and listened, watching while the room's dark crevices began to smoke their ash-white nightmares. . . . Such a night of fever slowed everything down as though hot rugs had been stuffed in a clock. I went gliding away under the surface of sleep, like a porpoise in tropic seas, heard the dry house echoing through caves of water, followed caverns through acres of dreams, then emerged after fathoms and years of experience, of complex lives and deaths, to find that the moon on the window had not moved an inch, that the world was not a minute older.

Between this sleeping and waking I lived ten generations and grew weak on my long careers; but when I surfaced at last from its endless delirium, the real world seemed suddenly dear. While I slept, it had been washed of fever and sweetened, and now wrapped me like a bell of glass. For a while, refreshed, I heard its faintest sounds: streams running, trees stirring, birds folding their wings, a hill-sheep's cough, a far gate swinging, the breath of a horse in a field. Below me the kitchen made cozy murmurs, footsteps went up the road, a voice said good night, a door creaked and closed—or a boy suddenly hollered, animal-clear in the dark, and was answered far off by another. I lay moved to stupidity by these precious sounds as though I'd just got back from the dead. Then the fever returned as it always did, the room began its whisper and dance, the burnt-down candle spat once and shuddered, and I saw its wick fold and go out. . . . Then darkness hit me, a corroding darkness, a darkness packed like a box, and a row of black lanterns swung down from the ceiling and floated towards me, smiling. And once more I was hammering the bedrails in terror, screaming loudly for sisters and light.

Such bouts of delirium were familiar visitations, and my family had long grown used to them. Jack would enquire if I needed to groan quite so much, while Tony examined me with sly speculation; but for the most part I was treated like a dog with distemper and left to mend in my own good time. The fevers were dramatic, sudden, and soaring, but they burnt themselves out very quickly. There would follow a period of easy convalescence, during which I lived on milk custards and rusks; then I'd begin to feel bored, I'd get up and go out, start a fight, and my sickness was closed. Apart from the deliriums, which puzzled and confused me, I never felt really ill; and in spite of the whispers of scarred lungs and t.b., it never occurred to me I might die.

Then one night, while sweating through another attack, which seemed no different from any of the others, I was given a shock which affected me with an almost voluptuous awe. As usual my fever had flared up sharply, and I was tossing in its accustomed fires, when I woke up, clearheaded, somewhere in the middle of the night, to find the whole family round my bed. Seven pairs of eyes stared in dread surmise, not at me but at something in me. Mother stood helplessly wringing her hands, and the girls were silently weeping. Even Harold, who could usually shrug off emotion, looked pale and strained in the candlelight.

I was surprised by their silence and the look in their eyes, a mixture of fear and mourning. What had suddenly brought them in the dark of the night to stand blubbing like this around me? I felt warm and comfortable, completely relaxed, and amused as though somehow I'd fooled them. Then they all started whispering, around me, across me, but never directly to me.

'He's never been like this before,' said one. 'Hark at his awful rattle.'

'He never had that ghastly colour, either.'

'It's cruel—the poor little mite.'

'Such a gay little chap he was, boo-hoo.'

'There, there, Phyl; don't you fret.'

'D'you think the vicar would come at this hour?'

'Someone better run and fetch him.'

'We'd better knock up Jack Halliday, too. He could bike down and fetch the doctor.'

'We'll have to sit up, Ma. His breathing's horrible.'

'Perhaps we should wire his dad. . . .'

Perfectly conscious, I heard all this, and was tempted to join in myself. But their strangeness of tone compelled my silence; some peculiar threat in their manner, and a kind of fearful reverence in their eyes and voices as though they saw in me shades of the tomb. It was then that I knew I was very ill; not by pain, for my body felt normal. Silently the girls began to prepare for their vigil, wrapping their shawls round them. 'You go get some rest, Ma—we'll call you later.' They disposed themselves solemnly round the bed, folded their hands in their laps, and sat watching my face with their hollow eyes for the first sign of fatal change. Held by the silence of those waiting figures in that icy mid-hour of the night, it came to me then, for the first time in my life, that it was possible I might die.

I remember no more of that sombre occasion; I think I just fell asleep —my eyelids closing on a shroud of sisters which might well have been my last sight on earth. When I woke next morning, to their surprise, the crisis was apparently over. And save for that midnight visitation, and for the subsequent behaviour of the village, I would never have known my danger.

I remained in Mother's bedroom for many weeks, and a wood fire burned all day. Schoolfriends, as though on a pilgrimage, came in their best clothes to bring me flowers. Girls sent me hen's eggs pencilled with kisses; boys brought me their broken toys. Even my schoolteacher (whose heart was of stone) brought me a bagful of sweets and nuts. Finally Jack, unable to keep the secret any longer, told me I'd been prayed for in church, just before the collections, twice, on successive Sundays. My cup was full, I felt immortal; very few had survived that honour.

This time my convalescence was even more indulgent. I lived on Bovril and dry sponge cakes. I was daily embalmed with camphorated oils and hot-poulticed with thermogene. Lying swathed in these pungent and peppery vapours, I played through my hours and days, my bed piled high with beads and comics, pressed flowers, old cartridges, jackknives, sparking plugs, locusts, and several stuffed linnets.

I took every advantage of my spoiled condition and acted simple when things got tough. Particularly when it came to taking my medicine, a hell-draught of unspeakable vileness.

It was my sisters' job to get this down, and they would woo me with outstretched spoon.

'Now come on, laddie—One! Two! Three . . .'

'You can clean out the jam pot after. . . .'

'We'll peg up your nose. You won't taste it at all.'

I crossed my eyes and looked vacant.

'Be a good boy. Just this once. Come on.'

'Archie says no,' I said.

'What?'

'Archie,' I said, 'does not want the dose. Archie does not like the dose. And Archie will not have the dose. Says Archie.'

'Who's Archie?' they whispered, shaking their heads at each other. They usually left me then.

After fever my body and head felt light, like a piece of dew-damp vegetable. The illness had emptied me so completely, now I seemed bereft of substance. Being so long in that sunless, fever-spent room, I was filled with extraordinary translations. I felt white and blood-drained, empty of organs, transparent to colour and sound, while there passed through my flesh the lights of the window, the dust-changing air, the fire's bright hooks, and the smooth lapping tongues of the candle. Heat, reflections, whispers, shadows, played around me as though I were glass. I seemed to be bodiless, printed flat on the sheets, insubstantial as a net in water. What gross human wastes, dull jellies, slack salts I had been purged of I could not say; but my senses were now tuned to such an excruciating awareness that they vibrated to every move of the world, to every shift and subsidence both outdoors and in, as though I were renewing my entire geography.

When I woke in the mornings, damp with weakness, the daylight was milk of paradise; it came through the windows in beaming tides, in currents of green and blue, bearing debris of bird song, petals, voices, and the running oils of the sky. Its light washed the room of night and nightmare and showed me the normal day, so that waking was a moment of gratitude that savages must have felt. The bedroom objects removed their witch masks and appeared almost sheepishly ordinary. The boarded walls shone with grains and knots; the mirror recorded facts; the pictures, framed in the morning's gold, restored me their familiar faces. I sighed and stretched like a washed-up sailor who feels the earth safe beneath him, wild seas wiped away, green leaves around, deliverance miraculously gained.

So each morning at dawn I lay in a trance of thanks. I sniffed the room and smelt its feathers, the water in the wash jug, the dust in the corners, kind odours of glass and paper, the dry stones facing the window sills, bees bruising the geranium leaves, the pine in the pencil beside my bed, the dead candle and the fire in the matchstick. But I also sensed, without needing to look, the state of the early day: the direction of the wind, how the trees were blowing, that there were cows in the fields or not, whether the garden gate was open or shut, whether the hens had yet been fed, the weight of the clouds in the invisible sky, and the exact temperature of the air. As I lay in my bed, I could sense the whole valley by the surfaces of my skin, the turn of the hour, the set of the year, the weather and the life to come. A kind of pantheist grandeur made me one with the village, so that I felt part of its destination; and washed of my fevers, ice-cold but alive, it seemed I would never lose it again. . . .

Then Mother would come carolling upstairs with my breakfast, bright as a wind-blown lark.

'I've boiled you an egg, and made you a nice cup of cocoa. And cut you some lovely thin bread and butter.'

The fresh-boiled egg tasted of sun-warmed manna, the cocoa frothed and steamed, and the bread and butter—cut invalid fashion—was so thin you could see the plate through it. I gobbled it down, looking weak and sorry, while Mother straightened the bed, gave me my pencil and drawing book, my beads and toys, and chattered of treats to come.

'I'm going to walk into Stroud and buy you a paintbox. And maybe some liquorice allsorts. All kinds of people have been asking about you. Even Miss Cohen!—Just fancy that.'

Mother sat on the bed and looked at me proudly. All was love; and I could do no wrong. When I got up I would not have to chop any firewood, and nobody would be cross for a month. Oh, the fatal weakness that engaged me then, to be always and for ever ill. . . .

Pneumonia was the thing for which I was best known, and I made a big drama out of it. But it was not by any means my only weapon; I collected minor diseases also, including, in the space of a few short years, bouts of shingles, chicken pox, mumps, measles, ringworm, adenoids, nosebleed, nits, earache, stomach-ache, wobbles, bends, scarlet fever, and catarrhal deafness.

Then finally, as though to round the lot off, I suffered concussion of the brain. I was knocked down by a bicycle one pitch-dark night and lay for two days unconscious. By the time I came to, all battered and scabbed, one of my sisters was in love with the bicyclist—a handsome young stranger from Sheepscombe way who had also knocked down my mother.

But my boyhood career of shocks and fevers confirmed one thing at least: had I been delicate I would surely have died, but there was no doubt about my toughness. Those were the days, as I have already said, when children faded quickly, when there was little to be done, should the lungs be affected, but to burn coal tar and pray. In those cold valley cottages, with their dripping walls, damp beds, and oozing floors, a child could sicken and die in a year, and it was usually the strongest who went. I was not strong; I was simply tough, self-inoculated by all the plagues. But sometimes, when I stop to think about it, I feel it must have been a very close call.

Strangely enough it was not illness, but the accident, which I believe most profoundly marked me. That blow in the night, which gave me concussion, scarred me, I think, for ever—put a stain of darkness upon my brow and opened a sinister door in my brain, a door through which I am regularly visited by messengers whose words just escape me, by glimpses of worlds I can never quite grasp, by grief, exultation, and panic. . . .

✖ The Uncles

Our family was large, even by the full-bred standards of those days, and we were especially well endowed with uncles. Not so much by their numbers as by their qualities of behaviour, which transformed them for us boys into figures of legend, and filled the girls with distress and excitement. Uncle George —our father's brother—was a thin, whiskered rogue, who sold newspapers in the streets, lived for the most part in rags, and was said to have a fortune in gold. But on my mother's side there were these five more uncles: squat, hard-hitting, heavy-drinking heroes whom we loved and who were the kings of our youth. For the affection we bore them and the pride we took in them, I hope they'll not be displeased by what follows.

Grandfather Light—who had the handsomest legs of any coachman in Gloucestershire—raised his five sons in a world of horses; and they inherited much of his skill. Two of them fought against the Boers; and all five were cavalrymen in the first World War, where they survived the massacres of Mons and Ypres, quick-witted their way through some others, and returned at last to peace and salvation with shrapnel in each of their bodies. I remember them first as khaki ghosts coming home on leave from the fighting, square and huge with their legs in puttees, smelling sweetly of leather and oats. They appeared as warriors stained with battle; they slept like the dead all day, then blackened their boots and brassed their buttons and returned again to the war. They were men of great strength, of bloody deeds, a fist of uncles aimed at the foe, riders of hell and apocalypse, each one half man, half horse.

Not until after the war did that brotherhood of avengers detach itself in my mind, so that I was able to see each one separate and human and to know at last who they were. The sons of John Light, the five Light brothers, illuminated many a local myth, were admired for their wildness, their force of arms, and for their leisurely, boasting wit. 'We come from the oldest family in the world. We're down in the Book of Genesis. The Almighty said: "Let there be Light"—and *that* was long afore Adam. . . .'

The uncles were all of them bred as coachmen and intended to follow their father; but the army released them to a different world, and by the time I was old enough to register what they were up to, only one worked with horses; the others followed separate careers: one with trees, one with motors, another with ships, and the last building Canadian railways.

Uncle Charlie, the eldest, was most like my grandfather. He had the same long face and shapely gaitered legs, the same tobacco-kippered smell about him, the same slow story-telling voice heavy with Gloucester bass notes. He told us long tales of war and endurance, of taming horses in Flanders mud, of tricks of survival in the battlefield which scorned conventional heroism. He recounted these histories with stone-faced humour, with a cool, self-knowing dryness, so that the surmounting of each of his life-and-death dilemmas sounded no more than a slick win at cards.

Now that he had returned at last from his mysterious wars, he had taken up work as a forester, living in the depths of various local woods with a wife and four beautiful children. As he moved around, each cottage he settled in took on the same woody stamp of his calling, putting me in mind of charcoal burners and the lost forest huts of Grimm. We boys loved to visit the Uncle Charles family, to track them down in the forest. The house would be wrapped in aromatic smoke, with winter logs piled in the yard, while from eaves and doorposts hung stoats' tails, fox skins, crow bones, gin traps, and mice. In the kitchen there were axes and guns on the walls, a stone jar of ginger in the corner, and on the mountainous fire a bubbling stew-pot of pigeon or perhaps a new-skinned hare.

There was some curious riddle about Uncle Charlie's early life which not even our mother could explain. When the Boer War ended, he had worked for a time in a Rand diamond town as a barman. Those were wide-open days when a barman's duties included an ability to knock drunks cold. Uncle Charlie was obviously suited to this, for he was a lion of a man in his youth. The miners would descend from their sweating camps, pockets heavy with diamond dust, buy up barrels of whisky, drink themselves crazy, then start to burn down the saloon. . . . This was where Uncle Charles came in, the kingfish of those swilling bars, whose muscled bottle-swinging arm would lay them out in rows. But even he was no super-man and suffered his share of damage. The men used him one night as a battering ram to break open a liquor store. He lay for two days with a broken skull, and still had a fine bump to prove it.

Then for two or three years he disappeared completely and went underground in the Johannesburg stews. No letters or news were received during that time, and what happened was never explained. Then suddenly, without warning, he turned up in Stroud, pale and thin and penniless. He wouldn't say where he'd been, or discuss what he'd done, but he'd finished his wan-derings, he said. So a girl from our district, handsome Fanny Causon, took him and married him.

He settled then in the local forests and became one of the best woods-men in the Cotswolds. His employ-er flattered, cherished, and under-paid him; but he was content among his trees. He raised his fam-ily on labourer's pay, fed them on game from the woods, gave his daughters no discipline other than his humour, and taught his sons the skill of his heart.

It was a revelation of mystery to see him at work, somewhere in a cleared spread of the woods, han-dling seedlings like new-hatched birds, shaking out delicately their fibrous claws, and setting them firmly along the banks and hollows in the nests that his fingers had made. His gestures were caressive yet instinctive with power, and the plants settled ravenously to his touch, seemed to spread their small leaves with immediate life and to become rooted for ever where he left them.

The new woods rising in Horsley now, in Sheepscombe, in Rend-combe and Colne, are the forests my Uncle Charlie planted on thirty-five shillings a week. His are those man-sions of summer shade, lifting sky-lines of leaves and birds, those blocks of new green now climbing our hills to restore their remembered perspec-tives. He died last year, and so did his wife—they died within a week of each other. But Uncle Charlie has left a mark on our landscape as permanent as he could wish.

The next of the Lights was Uncle Tom, a dark, quiet talker, full of hidden strength, who possessed a way with women. As I first remember him, he was coachman-gardener at an old house in Woodchester. He was married by then to my Auntie Minnie—a tiny, pretty, parted-down-the-middle woman who resembled a Cruickshank drawing. Life in their small, neat stable yard—surrounded by potted ferns, high-stepping ponies, and bright-painted traps and carriages—always seemed to me more toylike than human, and to visit them was to change one's scale and to leave the ponderous world behind.

Uncle Tom was well-mannered, something of a dandy, and he did peculiar things with his eyebrows. He could slide them independently up and down his forehead, and the habit was strangely suggestive. In moments of silence he did it constantly, as though to assure us he wished us well; and to this trick was ascribed much of his success with women—to this and to his dignified presence. As a bachelor he had suffered almost continuous pursuit; but, though slow in manner, he was fleet of foot and had given the girls a long run. Our mother was proud of his successes. 'He was a cut above the usual,' she'd say. 'A proper gentleman. Just like King Edward. He thought nothing of spending a pound.'

When he was young the girls died for him daily and bribed our Mother to plead their cause. They were always inviting her out to tea and things, and sending him messages, and ardent letters, wrapped up in bright scarves for herself. 'I was the most popular girl in the district,' she said. 'Our Tom was so refined. . . .'

For years Uncle Tom played a wily game and avoided entanglements. Then he met his match in Effie Mansell, a girl as ruthless as she was plain. According to Mother, Effie M. was a monster, six foot high and as strong as a farm horse. No sooner had she decided that she wanted Uncle Tom than she knocked him off his bicycle and told him. The very next morning he ran away to Worcester and took a job as a tram conductor. He would have done far better to have gone down the mines, for the girl followed hot on his heels. She began to ride up and down all day long on his tram, where she had him at her mercy; and what made it worse, he had to pay her fares; he had never been so humiliated. In the end his nerve broke, he muddled the change, got the sack, and went to hide in a brick quarry. But the danger passed, Effie married an inspector, and Uncle Tom returned to his horses.

By now he was chastened, and the stables reassured him—you could escape on a horse, not a tram. But what he wished for more than anything was a good woman's protection; he had found the pace too hot. So very soon after, he married the Minnie of his choice, abandoned his bachelor successes, and settled for good with a sigh of relief and a few astonishing runs on his eyebrows.

From then on Uncle Tom lived quietly and gratefully, like a prince in deliberate exile, merely dressing his face, from time to time, in those mantles of majesty and charm, those solemn winks and knowing convulsions of the brow which were all that remained of past grandeurs. . . .

My first encounter with Uncle Ray—prospector, dynamiter, buffalo fighter, and builder of transcontinental railways—was an occasion of memorable suddenness. One moment he was a legend at the other end of the world, the next he was in my bed. Accustomed only to the satiny bodies of my younger brother and sisters, I awoke one morning to find snoring beside me a huge and scaly man. I touched the thick legs and knotted arms and pondered the barbs on his chin, felt the crocodile flesh of this magnificent creature and wondered what it could be.

'It's your Uncle Ray come home,' whispered Mother. 'Get up now and let him sleep.'

I saw a rust-brown face, a gaunt Indian nose, and smelt a reek of cigars and train oil. Here was the hero of our school boasting days, and to look on him was no disappointment. He was shiny as iron, worn as a rock, and lay like a chieftain sleeping. He'd come home on a visit from building his railway, loaded with money and thirst, and the days he spent at our house that time were full of wonder and conflagration.

For one thing he was unlike any other man we'd ever seen—or heard of, if it came to that. With his leather-beaten face, wide, teeth-crammed mouth, and far-seeing ice-blue eyes, he looked like some wigwam warrior stained with suns and heroic slaughter. He spoke the Canadian dialect of the railway camps in a drawl through his resonant nose. His body was tattooed in every quarter —ships in full sail, flags of all nations, reptiles, and round-eyed maidens. By cunning flexings of his muscled flesh he could sail these ships, wave the flags in the wind, and coil snakes round the quivering girls.

Uncle Ray was a gift of the devil to us, a monstrous toy, a good-natured freak, more exotic than a circus ape. He would sit quite still while we examined him and absorb all our punishment. If we hit him he howled, if we pinched him he sobbed; he bore our aches and cramps like a Caliban. Or at a word he'd swing us round by our feet, or stand us upon his stomach, or lift us in pairs, one on either hand, and bump our heads on the ceiling.

But sooner or later he always said: 'Waal, boys, I gotta be going.'

He'd stand up and shake us off like fleas and start slowly to lick his lips.

'Where you got to go to, Uncle?'

'See a man 'bout a mule.'

'You ain't! Where you going? What for?'

'Get my fingers pressed. Tongue starched. Back oiled.'

'It ain't true! You're fibbing! Uncle! . . .'

'Just *got* to, boys. See you all in the oven. Scrub yer elbows. Be good. So long.'

Off he'd go at a run, though the Lord knew where; *we* couldn't think of any place to go to. Then he'd come back much later, perhaps the following night, wet through, with a doglike grin. He'd be unable to see properly, couldn't hang up his coat, couldn't find the latch on the door. He'd sit by the fire and steam and sing and flirt with the squawking girls. 'You'd best get to bed,' Mother would say severely; at which he'd burst into theatrical sobs. 'Annie, I can't! I can't move an inch. Got a bone in me leg. . . . Mebbe two.'

One night, after he'd been missing for a couple of days, he came home on a bicycle, and rode it straight down the bank in the stormy darkness and crashed into the lavatory door. The girls ran out and fetched him indoors, howling and streaming with blood. They lay him full-length on the kitchen table, then took off his boots and washed him. 'What a state he's in,' they giggled, shocked. 'It's whisky or something, Mother.' He began to sing, 'O, Dolly dear . . .' then started to eat the soap. He sang and blew bubbles, and we crowded round him, never having had any man in our house like this.

Word soon got round that Ray Light was home, laden with Canadian gold. He was set on by toughs, hunted by girls, and warned several times by the police. He took most of this in his powerful stride, but the girls had him worried at times. A well-bred young seamstress whom he was cuddling in the picture palace stole his dollar-crammed purse in the dark. Then one morning Beatie Burroughs arrived on our doorstep and announced that he'd promised to marry her. Under the Stroud Brewery arches, she said— just to clinch it. He had to hide for three days in our attic. . . .

But drunk or sober, Uncle Ray was the same; a great shaggy animal wagging off to his pleasures; a helpless giant, amiable, naïve, sentimental, and straightforwardly lustful. He startled my sisters, but even so they adored him; as for us boys, what more could we want? He even taught us how to tie him up, boasting that no knots could hold him. So we tied him one night to a kitchen chair, watched him struggle, and then went to bed. Mother found him next morning on his hands and knees, still tied up and fast asleep.

That visit of Uncle Ray's, with its games and exhibitions, was like a prolonged Christmas Day in the house. Routine, discipline, and normal behaviour were suspended during that time. We stayed up late, took liberties, and shared his intoxications; while he bounded about, disappeared on his errands, returned in a tousled daze, fumbled the girls, sang songs, fell down, got up, and handed dollars all round. Mother was by turns prim and indulgent with him, either clicking her tongue or giggling. And the girls were as excited and assailed as we, though in a different, whispering way; saying, 'Would you believe it?' 'I never!' 'How awful!' or, 'Did you hear what he said to me then?'

When he got through his money, he went back to Canada, back to the railway camps, leaving behind him several broken heads, some fat innkeepers and well-set-up girls. Soon after, while working in the snow-capped Rockies, he blew himself up with dynamite. He fell ninety feet down the Kicking Horse Pass and into a frozen lake. A Tamworth schoolteacher—now my Auntie Elsie —travelled four thousand miles to repair him. Having plucked him from the ice and thawed him out, she married him and brought him home. And that was the end of the pioneer days of that bounding prairie dog, without whom the Canadian Pacific Railroad would never have reached the Pacific—at least, so we believe.

Moody, majestic Uncle Sid was the fourth, but not least, of the brothers. This small, powerful man, at first a champion cricketer, had a history blighted by rheumatism. He was a bus driver, too, after he left the army, put in charge of our first double-deckers. Those solid-tyred, open-topped, passenger chariots were the leviathans of the roads at that time, staggering seige-towers which often ran wild and got their top decks caught under bridges. Our Uncle Sid, one of the élite of the drivers, became a famous sight in the district. It was a thing of pride and some alarm to watch him go thundering by, perched up high in his reeking cabin, his face sweating beer and effort, while he wrenched and wrestled at the steering wheel to hold the great bus on its course. Each trip through the town destroyed roof tiles and gutters and shook the gas mantles out of the lamps, but he always took pains to avoid women and children and scarcely ever mounted the pavements. Runaway roarer, freighted with human souls, stampeder of policemen and horses—it was Uncle Sid with his mighty hands who mastered its mad career. Uncle Sid's story, like Uncle Charlie's, began in the South African War. As a private soldier he had earned a reputation for silence, cunning, and strength. His talent for cricket, learned on the molehills of Sheepscombe, also endowed him with special privileges. Quite soon he was chosen to play for the army and was being fed on the choicest rations. The hell-bent technique of his village game worked havoc among the officers. On a flat pitch at last, with scorched dry wicket, after the hillocks and cow dung of home, he was projected straightaway into regions of greatness and broke records and nerves galore. His murderous bowling reduced heroes to panic; they just waved him good-bye and ran; and when he came in to bat, men covered their heads and retired piecemeal to the boundaries. In an old Transvaal newspaper, hoarded by my mother, I once found a score card which went something like this:

Army v. Transvaal. Pretoria. 1899.

ARMY

Col. 'Tigger' Ffoukes-Wyte	1
Brig. Fletcher	0
Maj. T.W.G. Staggerton-Hake	12
Capt. V. O. Spillingham	0
Major Lyle (not)	31
Pte. S. Light (not)	126
Extras	7
Total for 4 dec.	177

TRANSVAAL   21 all out (Pte S. Light 7 for 5)

I can picture that squat little whizzing man knocking the cricket ball out of the ground, his face congested with brick-red fury, his shoulders bursting out of his braces. I can see him crouch for the next delivery, then spin on his short bowed legs, and clout it again halfway to Johannesburg while he heard far-off Sheepscombe cheer. This was probably the peak of Uncle Sid's glory, the time he would most wish to remember. From then on his tale shows a certain fall—though it still flared up on occasions.

There was, for instance, the day of the Outing, when our village took three charabancs [1] to Clevedon, with Uncle Sid driving the leading one, a crate of beer at his feet. 'Put her in top, Uncle Sid!' we cried, as we roared through the summer country. Guzzling with one hand, steering with the other, he drove through the flying winds, while we bounced and soared above the tops of the hedges,

[1] charabancs: large excursion buses.

made airborne by this man at the wheel. . . .

Then on our way home, at the end of the day, we were stopped by a woman's screams. She stood by the roadside with a child in her arms, cringing from a threatening man. The tableau froze for us all to see: the wild-haired woman, the wailing child, the man with his arm upraised. Our charabancs came to a shuddering halt and we all started shouting at once. We leaned over the sides of our open wagons and berated the man for a scoundrel. Our men from their seats insulted him roundly; they suggested he leave the poor woman alone. But our Uncle Sid just folded his coat, climbed down from his cab without speaking, walked up to the bully, swung back his arm, and knocked the man straight through the hedge. Life to him was black and white and he had reacted to it simply. Scowling with pride he returned to the wheel and drove us home, a hero.

Uncle Sid differed in no way from his other brothers in chivalry, temper, and drink. He could knock down a man or a glass of beer as readily and as neatly as they. But his job as a bus driver (and his rheumatism) both increased—and obstructed—his thirst. The result exposed him to official censure, and it was here that the fates laid him low.

When he married my Aunt Alice, and became the father of two children, his job promised to anchor his wildness. But the law was against him and he soon got into scrapes.

He was the best double-decker driver in Stroud, without doubt; even safer, more inspired, when he drank. Everybody knew this—except the bus company. He began to get lectures, admonitions, stern warnings, and finally suspensions without pay.

When this last thing happened, out of respect for Aunt Alice, he always committed suicide. Indeed he committed suicide more than any man I know, but always in the most reasonable manner. If he drowned himself, then the canal was dry; if he jumped down a well, so was that; and when he drank disinfectant, there was always an antidote ready, clearly marked, to save everyone trouble. He reasoned, quite rightly, that Aunt Alice's anger, on hearing of another suspension, would be swallowed up by her larger anxiety on finding him again near to death. And Auntie Alice never failed him in this, and forgave him each time he recovered.

The bus company were almost equally forgiving; they took him back again and again. Then one night, having brought his bus safely home, they found him fast asleep at the wheel, reeking of malt and stone-jar cider; and they gave him the sack for good.

We were sitting in the kitchen rather late that night, when a loud knock came at the door. A hollow voice called 'Annie! Annie!' and we knew that something had happened. Then the kitchen door crept slowly open and revealed three dark-clad figures. It was Auntie Alice and her two small daughters, each dressed in their Sunday best. They stood at the foot of the kitchen steps, silent as apparitions, and Auntie Alice's face, with its huge drawn eyes, wore a mantle of tragic doom.

'He's done it this time,' she intoned at last. 'That's what. I know he has.'

Her voice had a churchlike incantation which dropped crystals of ice down my back. She held the small, pretty girls in a majestic embrace while they squirmed and sniffed and giggled.

'He never came home. They must have give him the sack. Now he's gone off to end it all.'

'No, no,' cried our mother. 'Come and sit down, my dear.' And she drew her towards the fire.

Auntie Alice sat stiffly, like a Gothic image, still clutching her wriggling children.

'Where else could I go, Annie? He's gone down to Deadcombe. . . . He always told me he would. . . .'

She suddenly turned and seized Mother's hands, her dark eyes rolling madly.

'Annie! Annie! He'll do himself in. Your boys—they just *got* to find him! . . .'

So Jack and I put on caps and coats and went out into the half-moon night. From so much emotion I felt lightheaded; I wanted to laugh or hide. But Jack was his cool, intrepid self, tight-lipped as a gunboat commander. We were men in a crisis, on a secret mission; life and death seemed to hang on our hands. So we stuck close together and trudged up the valley, heading for

Deadcombe Wood.

The wood was a waste of rotting silence, transformed by its mask of midnight; a fine rain was falling, wet ferns soaked our legs, leaves shuddered with owls and water. What were we supposed to do, we wondered. Why had we come, anyway? We beat up and down through the dripping trees, calling 'Uncle!' in chill, flat voices. . . . What should we find? Perhaps nothing at all. Or worse, what we had come to seek. . . . But we remembered the women, waiting fearfully at home. Our duty, though dismal, was clear.

So we stumbled and splashed through invisible brooks, followed paths, skirted ominous shadows. We poked bits of stick into piles of old leaves, prodded foxholes, searched the length of the wood. There was nothing there but the fungoid darkness, nothing at all but our fear.

We were about to go home, and gladly enough, when suddenly we saw him. He was standing—tiptoe under a great dead oak with his braces around his neck. The elastic noose, looped to the branch above him, made him bob up and down like a puppet. We approached the contorted figure with dread; saw his baleful eye fixed on us.

Our Uncle Sid was in a terrible temper.

'You've been a bloody long time!' he said.

Uncle Sid never drove any buses again but took a job as a gardener in Sheepscombe. All the uncles now, from their wilder beginnings, had resettled their roots near home—all, that is, save Insurance Fred, whom we lost through prosperity and distance. These men reflected many of Mother's qualities, were foolish, fantastical, moody; but in spite of their follies they remained for me the true heroes of my early life. I think of them still in the image they gave me; they were bards and oracles each, like a ring of squat megaliths [1] on some local hill, bruised by weather and scarred with old glories. They were the horsemen and brawlers of another age, and their lives spoke its long farewell. Spoke, too, of campaigns on desert marches, of Kruger's [2] cannon and Flanders mud; of a world that still moved at the same pace as Caesar's, and of that empire greater than his—through which they had fought, sharp-eyed and anonymous, and seen the first outposts crumble. . . .

Outings and Festivals

The year revolved around the village, the festivals round the year, the church round the festivals, the Squire round the church, and the village round the Squire. The Squire was our centre, a crumbling moot

1 megaliths: prehistoric monuments of stone.

2 Kruger, Paul (1825–1904): president of the Transvaal against whom the English fought in the Boer War.

tree; and few indeed of our local celebrations could take place without his shade. On the greater occasions he let us loose in his gardens, on the smaller gave us buns and speeches; and at historic moments of national rejoicing—when kings were born, enemies vanquished, or the Conservatives won an election—he ransacked his boxrooms for fancy dresses that we might rejoice in a proper manner.

The first big festival that I can remember was Peace Day in 1919. It was a day of magical transformations, of tears and dusty sunlight, of bands, processions, and buns by the cartload; and I was so young I thought it normal. . . .

We had all been provided with fancy dress, and that seemed normal, too. Apart from the Squire's contributions Marjorie had been busy for weeks stitching up glories for ourselves and the neighbours. No makeshift, rag-bag cobbling either; Marjorie had worked as though for a wedding.

On the morning of the feast Rosie Burdock came to the house to try on her angel's dress. She was five years old and about my size. She had russet curls like apple peelings, a polished pumpkin face, a fruity air of exploding puddings, and a perpetual cheeky squint. I loved her, she was like a portable sweetshop. This morning I watched my sisters dress her. She was supposed to represent a spirit. They'd made her a short, frilly frock, a tin-foil helmet, cardboard wings, and a wand with a star. When they'd clothed her, they stood her up on the mantlepiece and had a good look at her. Then they went off awhile on some other business and left us alone together. 'Fly!' I commanded. 'You got wings, ain't you?'

Rosie squirmed and wiggled her shoulders.

I grew impatient and pushed her off the mantelpiece, and she fell with a howl into the fireplace. Looking down at her, smudged with coal and tears, her wand and wings all crumpled, I felt nothing but rage and astonishment. She should have been fluttering round the room.

They sponged and soothed her, and Rosie trotted home, her bent wand clutched in her hand. Then shapes and phantoms began to run through the village, and we started to get ready ourselves. Marge appeared as Queen Elizabeth, with Phyllis her lady in waiting. Marjorie, who was sixteen and at her most beautiful, wore a gown of ermine, a brocaded bodice, and a black cap studded with pearls. She filled the kitchen with such a glow of grace that we just stood and gaped at her. It was the first time I had seen Queen Elizabeth, but this was no sharp-faced Tudor. Tender and proud in her majestic robes, she was the Queen of Heaven, risen from the dust, unrecognizable as Marge till she spoke, and her eyes shone down on us from her veils of ermine like emeralds laid in snow. Thirteen-year-old Phyllis, with finery of her own, skipped like a magpie round her, wearing a long chequered dress of black and white velvet, and a hat full of feathers and moths.

The rest of us, whom Marjorie had dressed, were the result of homespun inspirations. Dorothy, as 'Night,' was perhaps the most arresting; an apparition of unearthly beauty, a flash of darknes, a strip of nocturnal sky, mysteriously cloaked in veils of black netting entangled with silver paper. A crescent moon lay across her breast, a comet across her brow, and her long, dark curls fell in coils of midnight and were sprinkled with tinsel dust. I smelt frost when I saw her and heard a crackling of stars; familiar Dorothy had grown far and disturbing.

Brother Jack had refused to be dressed up at all, unless in some aspect of recognized valour. So they hung him in green, gave him a bow and arrow, and he called himself Robin Hood. Little Tony was dressed as a market girl, curly-headed and pretty as love, bare-armed and bonneted, carrying a basket of flowers, but so proud we forgave him his frock.

As for me, a squat neck and solid carriage made the part I should play inevitable. I was John Bull—whoever he was—but I quickly surmised his importance. I remember the girls stuffing me into my clothes with many odd squeals and giggles. Gravely I offered an arm or leg, but remained dignified and aloof. Marjorie had assembled the ritual garments with her usual flair and cunning. I wore a top hat and choker, a Union Jack waistcoat, a frock coat, and pillowcase breeches. But I'd been finished off hurriedly with gaiters of cardboard fastened loosely together with pins—a slovenly makeshift which offended my taste, and which I was never able to forgive.

This Peace Day I remember as a blur of colour, leading from fury to triumph. There was a procession with a band. I walked alone solemnly. Fantastic disguises surrounded me; every single person seemed covered with beards, false noses, bootblack, and wigs. We had not marched far when my boots fell off, followed by my cardboard gaiters. As I stopped to find them, the procession swept over me. I sat down by the roadside and howled. I howled because I could hear the band disappearing, because I was John Bull and it should not have happened. I was picked up by a carriage, restored to the procession, then placed on a trolley and pulled. Cross-legged on the trolley, bare-footed and gaiterless, I rode like a prince through the village.

Dusty, sweating from its long-route march, the procession snaked round the houses. The old and infirm stood and cheered from the gutters; I nodded back from my trolley. At last we entered the cool beech wood through which the Squire's drive twisted. The brass band's thunder bounced back from the boughs. Owls hooted and flapped away.

We came out of the wood into the Big House gardens, and the sun returned in strength. Doves and pigeons flew out of the cedars. The swans took off from the lake. On the steps of the Manor stood the wet-eyed Squire, already in tears at the sight of us. His mother, in a speech from a basket chair, mentioned the glory of God, the Empire, us; and said we weren't to touch the flowers.

With that the procession dispersed, I was tipped off the trolley, and I wandered away through the grounds. Flags and roses moved against the sky, bright figures among the bushes. Japanese girls and soot-faced savages grew strangely from banks of lilac. I saw Charlie Chaplin, Peter the Pieman, a collection of upright tigers, a wounded soldier about my age, and a bride on the arm of a monkey.

Later I was given a prize by the Squire and was photographed in a group by a rockery. I still have that picture, all sepia shadows, a leaf ripped from that summer day. Surrounded by girls in butter muslin, by Druids and eastern kings, I am a figure rooted in unshakable confidence, oval, substantial, and proud. About two feet high and two feet broad, my breeches like slack balloons, I stand, top-hatted, with a tilted face as severe as on a Roman coin. Others I recognize are gathered round me, all marked by that day's white dust. Tony has lost his basket of flowers, Jack his bow and arrow. Rosie Burdock has had her wings torn off and is grasping a broken lily. She stands beside me, squinting fiercely, ruffled a bit by the heat, and the silver letters across her helmet—which I couldn't read then—say 'PEACE.'

Our village outings were both sacred and secular, and were also far between. One seldom, in those days, strayed beyond the parish boundaries, except for the annual Choir Outing. In the meantime we had our own tribal wanderings, unsanctified though they were, when a sudden fine morning would send us forth in families for a day's nutting or blackberrying. So up we'd go to the wider end of the valley, to the bramble-entangled scrubs, bearing baskets and buckets and flasks of cold tea, like a file of foraging Indians. Blackberries clustered against the sky, heavy and dark as thunder, which we plucked and gobbled, hour after hour, lips purple, hands stained to the wrists. Or later, mushrooms, appearing like manna, buttoning the shaggy grass, found in the mists of September mornings with the wet threads of spiders on them. They came in the night from nowhere, rootless, like a scattering of rubber balls. Their suckers clung to the roots of grass and broke off with a rubbery snap. The skin rubbed away like the bark of a birch tree, the flesh tasted of something unknown. . . . At other times there would be wild green damsons, tiny plums, black sloes, pink crab apples —the free waste of the woods, an unpoliced bounty, which we'd carry back home in bucketfuls. Whether we used them for jam or jellies or pies, or just left them to rot, didn't matter.

Then sometimes there'd be a whole day's outing, perhaps to Sheepscombe to visit relations—a four-mile walk, which to our short

legs seemed further, so that we needed all day to do it. We would start out early, with the sun just rising and the valley wrapped in mist.
. . .

'It's going to be hot,' says our mother brightly, and usually she is right. We climb up slowly towards Bulls Cross, picking up the bushes for birds' nests. Or we stop to dig holes or to swing on gates while Mother looks back at the view. 'What a picture,' she murmurs. 'Green as green . . . And those poppies, red as red.' The mist drags the treetops, flies away in the sky, and there is suddenly blue air all around us.

Painswick sprawls white in the other valley, like the skeleton of a foundered mammoth. But active sounds of its working morning—carts and buzz saws, shouts and hammering—come drifting in gusts towards us. The narrow lane that leads to Sheepscombe bends steeply away on our right. 'Step out, young men!' our mother says crisply. She begins to teach us a hymn; the kind that cries for some lost land of paradise, and goes well with a tambourine. I've not heard it before (nor ever since) but it entirely enshrines our outing—the remote, shaggy valley in which we find ourselves, the smell of hot straw on the air, dog roses and distances, dust and spring waters, and the long day's journey, by easy stages, to the sheepfolds of our wild relations.

They are waiting for us with warm ginger beer, and a dinner of broad beans and bacon. Auntie Fan

says, 'Annie, come in out of the sun. You must be ready to drop.' We go indoors and find our Uncle Charlie hacking at the bacon with a billhook. Young cousin Edie and her cautious brothers seem to be pondering whether to punch our heads. Our gramp comes in from his cottage next door, dressed in mould-green corduroy suiting. We sit down and eat, and the cousins kick us under the table, from excitement rather than spite. Then we play with their ferrets, spit down their well, have a fight, and break down a wall. Later we are called for and given a beating, then we climb up the tree by the earth closet. Edie climbs highest, till we bite her legs, then she hangs upside down and screams. It has been a full, far-flung, and satisfactory day; dusk falls, and we say good-bye.

Back down the lane in the thick, hot darkness we walk drowsily, heavy with boots. Night odours come drifting from woods and gardens; sweet musks and sharp green acids. In the sky the fat stars bounce up and down, rhythmically, as we trudge along. Glowworms, brighter than lamps or candles, spike the fields with their lemon fires, while huge horned beetles stumble out of the dark and buzz blindly around our heads.

Then Painswick appears—a starfish of light dilating in a pool of distance. We hurrry across the haunted common and come at last to the top of our valley. The village waterfall, still a mile away, lifts its cool, familiar murmur. We are nearing home, we are almost there; Mother starts to recite a poem. 'I remember, I re-member, the house where I was born . . .' She says it right through, and I tag beside her watching the trees walk past in the sky. . . .

The first Choir Outing we ever had was a jaunt in a farm wagon to Gloucester. Only the tenors and bas-ses and the treble boys were included in that particular treat. Later, with the coming of the horse-brake and charabanc, the whole village took part as well. With the help of the powerful new charabanc we even got out of the district altogether, rat-tling away to the ends of the earth, to Bristol or even further.

One year the Outing was to Wes-ton-super-Mare, and we had saved up for months to be worthy of it. We spent the night before preparing our linen and the girls got up at dawn to make sandwiches. The first thing I did when I came down that morning was to go out and look at the weather. The sky was black, and Tony was behind the lavatory pray-ing hard through his folded hands. When he saw that I'd seen him, he began to scratch and whistle, but the whole thing was a very bad sign.

We couldn't eat breakfast, the por-ridge was like gravel; so Jack and I ran up the bank to see what was go-ing on. Families were already gath-ering for the charabancs, so we ran back down again. The girls were ready, and Tony was ready. Mother was raking under the piano with a broomstick.

'Come on, our Mother! They'll go without us!'

'I've just got to find my corsets.'

She found them; then started very slowly to wash, like a duck with all summer to do it. We stood round and nagged her, rigid with nerves.

'Run along—you're under my feet.'

So we left her, and scampered along to the Woolpack. The whole village was waiting by now; mothers with pig-buckets stuffed with pic-nics, children with cocoa-tin spades, fathers with bulging overcoats lined entirely with clinking bottles. There was little Mrs. Tulley collecting fares and plucking at her nervous cheeks; Mr. Vick, the shopkeeper, carrying his keys in a basket; the two dress-makers in unclaimed gowns; and Lily Nelson, a fugitive from her brother, whispering, 'You mustn't tell Arnold—he'd kill me.' The Squire's old gardener had brought a basket of pigeons which he planned to release from the pier. And the postman, having nobody to deliver his letters to, had dumped them, and was coming along too.

Faces looked pale in the early light. Men sniffed and peered at the sky. 'Don't look too good, do it?' 'Can't say it do.' 'Bloody black over Stroud.' 'Might clear though . . .' Teeth were sucked in, heads doubt-fully shaken; I felt the doom of storm-sickness on me.

The vicar arrived to see us off—his pyjamas peeping out from his raincoat. 'There's a very nice church near the Promenade. . . . I trust you will all spare a moment. . . .' He issued each choirboy with his shilling for dinner, then dodged back home to bed. The last to turn up was Herbert the gravedigger, with something queer in a sack. The last, that is, except our Mother, of whom there was still no sign.

Then the charabancs arrived and everyone clambered aboard, fighting each other for seats. We abandoned our mother and climbed aboard too, feeling guilty and miserable. The charabancs were high, with broad open seats and with folded tarpaulins at the rear, upon which, as choirboys, we were privileged to perch and to fall off and break our necks. We all took our places, people wrapped themselves in blankets, horns sounded, and we were ready. 'Is everyone present?' piped the choirmaster. Shamefully, Jack and I kept silent.

Our Mother, as usual, appeared at that moment, a distant trotting figure, calling and waving her handbags gaily to disarm what impatience there might be. 'Come on, Mother Lee! We near went without you!' Beaming, she climbed aboard. 'I just had to wash out my scarf,' she said, and tied it on the windscreen to dry. And there it blew like a streaming pennant as we finally drove out of the village.

In our file of five charabancs, a charioted army, we swept down the thundering hills. At the speed and height of our vehicles the whole valley took on new dimensions; woods rushed beneath us, and fields and flies were devoured in a gulp of air. We were wind-borne now by motion and pride, we cheered everything, beast and fowl, and taunted with heavy ironical shouts those unfortunates still working in the fields. We kept this up till we had roared through Stroud, then we entered the stranger's country. It was no longer so easy to impress pedestrians that we were the Annual Slad Choir Outing. So we settled down, and opened our sandwiches, and began to criticize the farming we passed through.

The flatness of the Severn Valley now seemed dull after our swooping hills, the salmon-red sandstone of the Clifton Gorges too florid compared with our chalk. Everything began to appear strange and comic, we hooted at the shapes of the hayricks, laughed at the pitiful condition of the cattle—'He won't last long— just look at 'is knees.' We began to look round fondly at our familiar selves, drawn close by this alien country. Waves of affection and loyalty embraced us. We started shouting across the seats. 'Harry! Hey, Harry! Say, whatcher, Harry! Bit of all right, ain't it, you? Hey, Bert! 'Ow's Bert? 'Ow you doin' ole sparrer? Where's Walt? Hey there, Walt! Whatcher!'

Mile after rattling mile we went, under the racing sky, flying neckties and paper kites from the back, eyes screwed in the weeping wind. The elders, protected in front by the windscreen, chewed strips of bacon, or slept. Mother pointed out landmarks and lectured the sleepers on points of historical interest. Then a crawling boy found the basket of pigeons and the coach exploded with screams and wings. . . .

The weather cleared as we drove into Weston, and we halted on the

Promenade. 'The seaside,' they said; we gazed round us, but saw no sign of the sea. We saw a vast blue sky and an infinity of mud stretching away to the shadows of Wales. But rousing smells of an invisible ocean astonished our landlocked nostrils: salt, and wet weeds, and fishy oozes; a sharp difference in every breath. Our deep-ditched valley had not prepared us for this, for we had never seen such openness; the blue windy world seemed to have blown quite flat, bringing the sky to the level of our eyebrows. Canvas booths flapped on the edge of the Prom, mouths crammed with shellfish and vinegar; there were rows of prim boarding-houses (each the size of our vicarage); bath chairs, carriages, and donkeys; and stilted far out on the rippled mud a white pier like a sleeping dragon.

The blue day was ours; we rattled our money and divided up into groups. 'Hey, Jake, Steve; let's go have a wet'—and the men shuffled off down a side street. 'I'm beat after that, Mrs. Jones, ain't you?—there's a clean place down by the band-stand.' The old women nodded, and went seeking their comforts; the young ones stared at the policemen.

Meanwhile, we boys just picked up and ran; we had a world of mud to deal with. The shops and streets ended suddenly, a frontier to the works of man; and beyond—the mud, salt winds, and birds, a kind of double ration of light, a breathless space neither fenced nor claimed, and far out a horizon of water. We whinnied like horses and charged up and down, every hoof-mark written behind us. If you stamped in this mud, you brought it alive, the foot-print began to speak, it sucked and sighed and filled with water, became a foot cut out of the sky. I dug my fingers into a stretch of mud to see how deep it was, felt a hard, flat pebble and drew it out and examined it in the palm of my hand. Suddenly, it cracked, and put out two claws; I dropped it in horror, and ran. . . .

Half the village now had hired themselves chairs and were bravely facing the wind. Mrs. Jones was complaining about Weston tea: 'It's made from drains, I reckon.' The Squire's old gardener, having lost his pigeons, was trying to catch gulls in a basket; and the gravedigger (who appeared to have brought his spade) was out on the mud digging holes. Then the tide came in like a thick red sludge, and we all went on the pier.

Magic construction striding the waves, loaded with freaks and fancies, water chutes, and crumpled mirrors, and a whole series of nightmares for a penny. One glided secretly to one's favourite machine, the hot coin burning one's hand, to command a murder, a drunk's delirium, a haunted grave, or a Newgate hanging. This last, of course, was my favourite; what dread power one's penny purchased—the painted gallows, the nodding priest, the felon with his face of doom. At a touch they jerked through their ghastly dance, the priest, the hangman, and the convict, joined together by rods and each one condemned, as it were, to perpetual torment. Their ritual motions led to the jerk of the corpse; the figures froze, and the lights went out. Another penny restored the lights, brought back life to the cataleptic trio, and dragged the poor felon once more to the gallows to be strangled all over again.

That white pier shining upon the waves seemed a festive charnel house. With our mouths hanging open, sucking gory sticks of rock, we groped hungrily from horror to horror. For there were side shows too, as well as the machines, with hair-raising freaks under glass—including a towheaded Indian, a seven-legged sheep, and a girl's eye with a child coiled inside it.

We spent more time on that turgid pier than anywhere else in Weston. Then the tide went out, and evening fell, and we returned to the waiting charabancs. People came wandering from all directions, with bags full of whelks and seaweed, the gravedigger was dragged from his holes in the sand, and our numbers were checked and counted. Then we were all in our seats, the tarpaulins pulled over us, and with a blast of horns we left.

A long homeward drive through the red of the twilight, through landscapes already relinquished, the engines humming, the small children sleeping, and the young girls gobbling shrimps. At sunset we stopped at a gaslit pub for the men to have one more drink. This lasted till all of them turned bright pink and started embracing their wives. Then we repacked the charabancs, every-one grew drowsy, and we drove through the darkness beyond Bristol. The last homestretch; someone played a harmonica; we boys groped for women to sleep on, and slept, to the sway and sad roar of the coach and the men's thick, boozy singing.

We passed Stroud at last and climbed the valley road, whose every curve our bodies recognized, whose every slant we leaned to, though still half-asleep, till we woke to the smell of our houses. We were home, met by lanterns—and the Outing was over. With subdued good nights we collected into families, then separated towards our beds. Where soon I lay, my head ringing with sleep, my ears full of motors and organs, my shut eyes printed with the images of the day—mud, and red rock, and hangmen.

The Parochial Church Tea and Annual Entertainment was the village's winter treat. It took place in the schoolroom, round about Twelfth Night, and cost us a shilling to go. The Tea was an orgy of communal gluttony, in which everyone took pains to eat more than his money's worth and the helpers ate more than the customers. The Entertainment which followed, home-produced and by lamplight, provided us with sufficient catch phrases for a year.

Regularly, for a few weeks before the night, one witnessed the same scenes in our kitchen, the sisters sitting in various corners of the room, muttering secretly to themselves, smiling, nodding and making lah-di-dah gestures with a kind of intent and solitary madness. They were rehearsing their sketches for the Entertainment, which I found impossible not to learn too, so that I would be haunted for days by three nightmare monologues full of one-sided, unanswered questions.

On the morning of the feast we got the school ready. We built a stage out of trestles and planks. Mr. Robinson was in the cloakroom slicing boiled ham, where he'd been for the last three days, and three giggling helpers were now forking the meat and slapping it into sandwiches. Outside in the yard John Barraclough had arrived and set up his old field kitchen, had broken six hurdles across his knee and filled up the boiler with water. Laid out on the wall were thirty-five teapots, freshly washed and drying in the wind. The feast was preparing; and by carrying chairs, helping with the stage, and fetching water from the spring, Jack and I made ourselves sufficiently noticeable to earn a free ticket each.

Punctually at six, with big eating to be done, we returned to the lighted school. Villagers with lanterns streamed in from all quarters. We heard the bubbling of water in Barraclough's boiler, smelt the sweet wood smoke from his fire, saw his red face lit like a turnip lamp as he crouched to stoke up the flames.

We lined up in the cold, not noticing the cold, waiting for the doors to open. When they did, it was chins and boots and elbows, no queues; we just fought our way in. Lamplight and decorations had transformed the schoolroom from a prison into a banqueting hall. The long trestle tables were patterned with food: flycake, brown buns, ham sandwiches. The two stoves were roaring, reeking of coke. The helpers had their teapots charged. We sat down stiffly and gazed at the food; fidgeted, coughed, and waited. . . .

The stage curtains parted to reveal the Squire, wearing a cloak and a deer-stalking hat. He cast his dim, wet eyes round the crowded room, then sighed and turned to go. Somebody whispered from behind the curtain. 'Bless me!' said the Squire, and came back.

'The Parochial Church Tea!' he began, then paused. 'Is with us again . . . I suggest. And Entertainment. Another year! Another year comes round! . . . When I see you all gathered together here—once more—when I see—when I think . . . And here you all are! When I see you here—as I'm sure you all are —once again . . . It comes to me, friends!—how time—how you—how all of us here—as it were . . .' His moustache was quivering, tears ran down his face, he groped for the curtains and left.

His place was taken by the snow-haired vicar, who beamed weakly upon us all.

'What is the smallest room in the world?' he asked.

'A mushroom!' we bawled, without hesitation.

'And the largest, may I ask?'

'ROOM FOR IMPROVEMENT!'

'You know it,' he muttered cross-ly. Recovering himself, he folded his hands: 'And now O bountiful Father . . .'

We barked through grace and got our hands on the food and began to eat it in any old order. Cakes, buns, ham, it didn't matter at all, we just worked from one plate to the next. Folk by the fires fanned themselves with sandwiches, a joker fried ham on the stove, steaming brown teapots passed up and down, and we were so busy there was small conversa-tion. Through the lighted windows we could see snow falling, huge feathers against the dark. 'It's old Mother Hawkins a-plucking her geese!' cried someone; an excellent omen. Twelfth Night, and old Mother Hawkins at work, up in the sky with her birds; we loosened our belts and began to nod at each other; it was going to be a year of fat.

We had littered the tables with our messy leavings of cake crumbs and broken meat; some hands still went through the motions of eating, but clearly we'd had enough. The vicar rose to his feet again, and again we thanked the Lord. 'And now, my friends, comes the—er—feast for the soul. If you would care to—ah—take the air a moment, willing hands are waiting to clear the hall and prepare for the—um—Entertainment. . .'

We crowded outside and huddled in the snow while the tables were taken away. Inside, behind curtains, the actors were making up—and my moment, too, was approaching. The snow whirled about me and I began to sweat; I wanted to run off home. Then the doors reopened and I crouched by the stove, shivering and chattering with nerves. The curtains parted and the Entertainment began, with a comic I neither saw nor heard. . . .

'For the next item, ladies and gen-tlemen, we have an instrumental duet, by Miss Brown and—er—young Laurie Lee.'

Smirking with misery I walked to the stage. Eileen's face was as white as a minim. She sat at the piano, placed the music crooked, I straight-ened it, it fell to the ground. I groped to retrieve it; we looked at one an-other with hatred; the audience was still as death. Eileen tried to give me an *a,* but struck *b* instead, and I tuned up like an ape threading needles. At last we were ready, I raised my fiddle; and Eileen was off like a bolting horse. I caught her up in the middle of the piece—which I believe was a lullaby—and after play-ing the repeats, only twice as fast, we just stopped, frozen motionless, spent.

Some hearty stamping and whis-tling followed, and a shout of 'Give us another!' Eileen and I didn't ex-change a glance, but we loved each other now. We found the music of 'Danny Boy' and began to give it all our emotion, dawdling dreamily among the fruitier chords and scam-pering over the high bits; till the audience joined in, using their hymn-singing voices, which showed us the utmost respect. When it was over, I returned to my seat by the stove, my body feeling smooth and beautiful. Eileen's mother was weeping into her hat, and so was mine, I think. . . .

Now I was free to become one of the audience, and the Entertainment burgeoned before me. What had seemed to me earlier as the capering of demons now became a spectacle of human genius. Turn followed turn in variety and splendour. Mr. Crosby, the organist, told jokes and stories as though his very life depended on them, trembling, sweating, never pausing for a laugh, and rolling his eyes at the wings for rescue. We loved him, however, and wouldn't let him go, while he grew more and more hysterical, racing through monologues, gabbling songs about shrimps, skipping, mopping, and jumping up and down, as though humouring a tribe of savages.

Major Doveton came next, with his Indian banjo, which was even harder to tune than my fiddle. He straddled a chair and began wrestling with the keys, cursing us in English and Urdu. Then all the strings broke, and he snarled off the stage and started kicking the banjo round the cloakroom. He was followed by a play in which Marjorie, as Cinderella, sat in a goose-feathered dress in a castle. While waiting for the pumpkin to turn into a coach, she sang 'All Alone by the Telephone.'

Two ballads came next, and Mrs. Pimbury, a widow, sang them both with astonishing spirit. The first invited us to go with her to Canada; the second was addressed to a mushroom:

'Grow! Grow! Grow! Little mushroom, grow!
Somebody wants you soon.
I'll call again tomorrow morning—
See!
And if you've grown bigger you will just suit ME!
So Grow! Grow! Grow! little mushroom—Grow!'

Though we'd not heard this before, it soon became part of our heritage, as did the song of a later lady. This last—the Baroness von Hodenburg—sealed our entertainment with almost professional distinction. She was a guest star from Sheepscombe and her appearance was striking; it enshrined all the mystery of art. She wore a loose green gown like a hospital patient's, and her hair was red and long. 'She writes,' whispered Mother. 'Poems and booklets and that.'

'I am going to sink you,' announced this lady, 'a little ditty I convected myself. Bose vords und music, I may say, is mine—und zey refer to ziss pleasant valleys.'

With that she sat down, arched her beautiful back, raised her bangled wrists over the keyboard, then ripped off some startling runs and trills, and sang with a ringing laugh.

'Elfin volk come over the hill!
Come und dance, just vere you vill!
Brink your pipes, und brink your flutes,
Brink your sveetly soundink notes!
Come avay-hay! Life is gay-hay!
Life—Is—Gay!'

We thought this song soppy, but we never forgot it. From then on, whenever we saw the Baroness in the lanes, we used to bawl the song at her through the hedges. But she would only stop, and cock her head, and smile dreamily to herself. . . .

After these songs the night ended with slapstick; rough stuff about babies, chaps dressed as women, broad Gloucester exchanges between yokels and toffs, with the yokels coming off best. We ached with joy, and kicked at the chairs; but we knew the end was coming. The vicar got up, proposed a vote of thanks, and said oranges would be distributed at the gate. The national anthem was romped through, we all began coughing, then streamed outdoors through the snow.

Back home our sisters discussed their performances till the tears dripped off their noses. But to us boys it was not over, not till tomorrow; there was still one squeeze left in the lemon. Tomorrow, very early, we'd go back to the schoolroom, find the baskets of broken food—half-eaten buns, ham coated with cake crumbs—and together we'd finish the lot.

Last Days

The last days of my childhood were also the last days of the village. I belonged to that generation which saw, by chance, the end of a thousand years' life. The change came late to our Cotswold valley, didn't really show itself till the late 1920's; I was twelve by then, but during that handful of years I witnessed the whole thing happen.

Myself, my family, my generation, were born in a world of silence; a world of hard work and necessary patience, of backs bent to the ground, hands massaging crops, of waiting on weather and growth; of villages like ships in the empty landscapes and the long walking distances between them; of white narrow roads, rutted by hooves and cart wheels, innocent of oil or petrol, down which people passed rarely, and almost never for pleasure, and the horse was the fastest thing moving. Man and the horse were all the power we had—abetted by levers and pulleys. But the horse was king, and almost everything grew round him: fodder, smithies, stables, paddocks, distances, and the rhythm of our days. His eight-miles-an-hour was the limit of our movements, as it had been since the days of the Romans. That eight-miles-an-hour was life and death, the size of our world, our prison.

This was what we were born to, and all we knew at first. Then, to the scream of the horse, the change began. The brass-lamped motorcar came coughing up the road, followed by the clamorous charabanc; the solid-tyred bus climbed the dusty hills and more people came and went. Chickens and dogs were the early sacrifices, falling demented beneath the wheels. The old folk, too, had strokes and seizures, faced by speeds beyond comprehension. Then scarlet motor-bikes, the size of five-barred gates, began to appear in the village, on which our youths roared like rockets up the two-minute hills, then spent weeks making repairs and adjustments.

These appearances did not immediately alter our lives; the cars were freaks and rarely seen, the motor-bikes mostly in pieces, we used the charabancs only once a year, and our buses at first were experiments. Meanwhile Lew Ayres, wearing a bowler hat, ran his wagonette to Stroud twice a week. The carriage held six, and the fare was twopence, but most people preferred to walk. Mr. West, from Sheepscombe, ran a cart every day, and would carry your parcels for a penny. But most of us still did the journey on foot, heads down to the wet Welsh winds, ignoring the carters—whom we thought extortionate—and spending a long hard day at our shopping.

But the car-shying horses with their rolling eyes gave signs of the hysteria to come. Soon the village would break, dissolve, and scatter, become no more than a place for pensioners. It had a few years left, the last of its thousand, and they passed almost without our knowing. They passed quickly, painlessly, in motor-bike jaunts, in the shadows of the new picture palace, in quick trips to Gloucester (once a foreign city) to gape at the jazzy shops. Yet right to the end, like the false strength that precedes death, the old life seemed as lusty as ever.

The church, for instance, had never appeared more powerful. Its confident bell rang out each Sunday; the village heard it, asked no questions, put on satin and serge, filed into the pews, bobbed and nodded, frowned at its children, crouched and prayed, bawled or quavered through hymns, and sat in blank rows or jerkily slept while the curate reeled off those literary sermons which he had hired from the ecclesiastical library.

Sunday, far from being a day of rest, was in some ways tougher than a weekday; it was never torpid and it gave one a lift, being a combination of both indulgence and discipline. On that one day in seven—having bathed the night before—we were clean, wore our best, and ate meat. The discipline was Sunday School, learning the Collect, and worship both morning and evening. Neither mood nor inclination had any say in the matter, nor had doubt occurred to us yet.

Sunday mornings at home were the usual rush—chaos in the kitchen, shrill orders to wash, and everyone's eyes on the clock. We polished our hair with grease and water, and scrubbed ourselves under the pump. Being Sunday, there was a pound of large sausages for breakfast fried black and bursting with fat. One dipped them in pepper and ate them in haste, an open prayer book propped up by the plate.

'Heavens alive, you'll be late, our lad.'

Gobble, mumble, and choke.

'What *are* you up to? Get a move on, do.'

'Leave off—I'm learning the Collect.'

'What's that you say?'

'I-gotta-learn-me-Collect!'

'Hurry up and learn it then.'

'I can't hurry up! Not if you just keep on! . . .'

But it was really not difficult at all; ten inscrutable lines absorbed between mouthfuls, and usually on the run. Up the bank, down the road, the greasy prayer book in one hand, the remains of the sausage in the other: 'Almighty and Most Merciful Father, who alone worketh Great Marvels . . .' In five minutes it was all in my head.

At Sunday School Miss Bagnall, polishing her nose, said: 'The Collect—now who will oblige? . . .' I would jump to my feet and gabble, word-perfect, the half page of sonorous syllables. It came in through the eyes and out through the mouth, and left no trace of its passing. Except that I can never read a Collect today without tasting a crisp burnt sausage. . . .

After an hour of Sunday School we all went to the church, the choir going straight to the vestry. Here we huddled ourselves into our grimy robes, which only got washed at Easter. The parson lined us up and gave us a short, sharp prayer; then we filed into the stalls, took our privileged places, and studied the congregation. The Sunday School infants packed the bleak north wing, heads fuzzy as frosted flowers. The rest of the church was black with adults, solemn in cat's fur and feathers. Most were arranged in family groups, but here and there a young couple, newly engaged, sat red in the neck and hands. The leading benches contained our gentry, their pews marked with visiting cards— the lords of the manor, Squire Jones and the Croomes; then the army, the Carvosses and Dovetons; the rich settled spinsters, the Misses Abels and Bagnall; and finally the wealthier farmers. All were neatly arranged by protocol, with the Squire up front by the pulpit. Through prayers and psalms and rackety hymns he slept like a beaming child.

Morning service began with an organ voluntary, perhaps a Strauss waltz played very slow. The organ was old, and its creaks and sighs were often louder than the music itself. The organ was blown by an ordinary pump handle which made the process equally rowdy; and Rex Brown, the blower, hidden away in his box—and only visible to us in the choir—enlivened the service by parodying it in mime or by carving girls' names on the woodwork.

But in the packed congregation solemnity ruled. There was power, lamentation, full-throated singing, heavy prayers, and public repentance. No one in the village stayed away without reason, and no one yet wished to do so. We had come to the church because it was Sunday, just as we washed our clothes on Monday. There was also God taking terrible notes—a kind of squirearchical rent collector, ever ready to record the tenants' backsliding and to evict them if their dues weren't paid.

This morning service was also something else. It was a return to the Ark of all our species in the face of the ever-threatening flood. We are free of that need now and when the flood does come shall drown proud and alone, no doubt. As it was, the lion knelt down with the lamb, the dove perched on the neck of the hawk, sheep nuzzled wolf, we drew warmth from each other and knew ourselves beasts of one kingdom. . . .

That was Sunday morning. With the service over there was gossip among the gravestones, a slow walk home to roasted dinners, then a nap with 'The News of the World.' The elders dozed through the fat afternoon, while the young went again to Sunday School. Later came Evensong, which was as different from Matins as a tryst from a Trafalgar Square rally. The atmosphere was gentler, moonier, more private; the service was considered to be voluntary. We choirboys, of course, were compelled to go, but for the rest, they went who would.

The church at night, in the dark of the churchyard, was just a strip of red-fired windows. Inside, the oil lamps and motionless candles narrowed the place with shadows. The display of the morning was absent now; the nave was intimate and sleepy. Only a few solitary worshippers were present this time, each cloaked in a separate absorption: Miss Bagnall, Widow White, the church cleaning woman, a widower, and the postman at the back. The service was almost a reverie, our hymns nocturnal and quiet, the psalms traditional and never varying so that one could sing them without a book. The scattered faithful, half-obscured by darkness, sang them as though to themselves. 'Lord, now lettest Thou Thy servant depart in peace. . . .' It was sung, eyes closed, in trembling tones. It could not have been sung in the morning.

From our seats in the choir we watched the year turn: Christmas, Easter and Whitsun, Rogation Sunday and prayers for rain; the church following the plough very close. Harvest Festival perhaps was the one we liked best, the one that came nearest home. Then how heavily and abundantly was our small church loaded; the cream of the valley was used to decorate it. Everyone brought of his best from field and garden; and to enter the church on harvest morning was like crawling headfirst into a horn of plenty, a bursting granary, a vegetable stall, a grotto of bright flowers. The normally bare walls sprouted leaves and fruits, the altar great stooks of wheat, and ornamental loaves as big as cart wheels stood parked by the communion rails. Bunches of grapes, from the Squire's own vines, hung blue from the lips of the pulpit. Gigantic and useless marrows abounded, leeks and onions festooned the pews, there were eggs and butter on the lectern shelves, the windows were heaped with apples, and the fat round pillars which divided the church were skirted with oats and barley.

Almost everyone in the congregation had some hand in these things. Square-rumped farmers and ploughmen in chokers, old gardeners and poultry keepers, they nodded and pointed and prodded each other to draw attention to what they had brought. The church was older than its one foundation, was as old as man's life on earth. The seed of these fruits, and the seed of these men, still came from the same one bowl; confined to this valley and renewing itself here, it went back to the days of the Ice. Pride, placation, and the continuity of growth were what we had come to praise. And even when we sang 'All is safely gathered in,' knowing full well that some of Farmer Lusty's oats still lay rotting in the fields, the discrepancy didn't seem important.

I remember one particular Harvest Festival which perfectly summed up this feeling. I was not old enough then to be in the choir, and I was sitting beside Tony, who was three. It was his first Harvest Festival, but he'd heard much about it and his expectations were huge. The choir, with banners, was fidgeting in the doorway, ready to start its procession. Tony gazed with glittering eyes around him, sniffing the juicy splendours. Then, in a moment of silence, just before the organ crashed into the hymn, he asked loudly, 'Is there going to be drums?'

It was a natural question, innocent and true. For neither drums, nor cymbals, nor trumpets of brass would have seemed out of place at that time.

The death of the Squire was not the death of the church, though they drew to their end together. He died, and the Big House was sold by auction and became a Home for Invalids. The lake silted up, the swans flew away, and the great pike choked in the reeds. With the Squire's hand removed, we fell apart—though we were about to do so anyway. His servants dispersed and went into the factories. His nephew broke up the estate.

Fragmentation, free thought, and new excitements came now to intrigue and perplex us. The first young couple to get married in a registry office was roundly denounced from the pulpit. 'They who play with fire shall be consumed by fire!' stormed the vicar. 'Ye mark my words!' Later he caught me reading Sons and Lovers and took it away and destroyed it. This may well have been one of his last authoritative gestures. A young apologist succeeded him soon.

Meanwhile the old people just dropped away—the white-whiskered, gaitered, booted and bonneted, ancient-tongued last of their world, who thee'd and thou'd both men and beast, called young girls 'damsels,' young boys 'squires,' old men 'masters,' the Squire himself 'He,' and who remembered the Birdlip stagecoach. Kicker Harris, the old coachman, with his top hat and leggings, blew away like a torn-out page. Lottie Escourt, peasant shoot of a Norman lord, curled up in her relics and died. Others departed with hardly a sound. There was old Mrs. Clissold, who sometimes called us for errands: 'Thee come up our court a minute, squire; I wants thee to do I a mission.' One ran to the shop to buy her a packet of bull's-eyes and was rewarded in the customary way. Bull's-eye in cheek, she'd sink back in her chair and dismiss one with a sleepy nod. 'I ain't nurn a aypence about I just now—but Mrs. Crissole'll recollect 'ee. . . .' We wrote her off as the day's good deed, and she died still recollecting us.

Now the last days of my family, too, drew near, beginning with the courting of the girls.

I remember very clearly how it started. It was summer, and we boys were sitting on the bank watching a great cloud of smoke in the sky.

A man jumped off his bike and cried, 'It's the boilerworks!' and we ran the four miles to see it.

There was a fire at the boilerworks almost every year. When we got there, we found it a particularly good one. The warehouse, as usual, was sheathed in flame, ceilings and floors fell in, firemen shouted, windows melted like icicles, and from inside the building one heard thundering booms as the boilers started crashing about. We used up a lot of the day at this, cheering each toppling chimney.

When we got back to the village, much later in the evening, we saw a strange man down in our garden. We studied him from a distance with some feeling of shock. No one but neighbours and visiting relations had ever walked there before. Yet this ominous stranger was not only wandering free, he was being accompanied by all our women.

We rushed down the bank and burst roughly upon them, to find everyone crackjawed with politeness.

Our sisters cried 'La' when they saw us coming, and made us welcome as though we'd been around the world. Marjorie was particularly soft and loving, the others beamed anxiously at us; Mother, though not smart, was in her best black dress, and the stranger was twisting his hat.

'These are our brothers,' said Marjorie, grabbing two of us close to her bosom. 'This is Jackie and Loll, and that one's Tone. They're all of them terrible bad.'

There was nervous laughter and relief at this, as though several dark ghosts had been laid. We smirked and wriggled, aped and showed off, but couldn't think what was going on. In fact, the day of that boilerworks fire marked a beacon in the life of our girls. It was the day when their first young man came courting, and this stranger was he, and he was Marjorie's, and he opened a path through the garden.

He was handsome, curly-haired, a builder of barges, very strong, and entirely acceptable. His name was Maurice, and we boys soon approved him and gave him the run of the place. He was followed quite quickly by two other young men, one each for Dorothy and Phyllis. Dorothy got Leslie, who was a shy local scoutmaster, at least until he met her; Phyllis in turn produced Harold the bootmaker, who had fine Latin looks, played the piano by ear, and sang songs about old-fashioned mothers. Then Harold, our brother, got the infection too, mended our chairs, reupholstered the furniture, and brought home a girl for himself.

At these strokes our home life changed for ever; new manners and notions crept in; instead of eight in the kitchen there were now a round dozen, and so it stayed till the girls started marrying. The young men called nightly, with candles in jars, falling headlong down our precipitous bank; or came pushing their bikes on summer evenings, loitering with the girls in the lanes; or sat round the fire talking slowly of work; or sat silent, just being there; while the sewing machine hummed, and Mother rambled, and warm ripples of nothing lapped round them. They were wary of Mother, unsure of her temper, though her outbursts were at the world, not people. Leslie was tactful and diffident, giving short, sharp laughs at her jokes. Maurice often lectured her on 'The Working Man Today,' which robbed her of all understanding. Phyl's Harold would sometimes draw up to the piano, strike the keys with the strength of ten, then charm us all by bawling 'Because' or 'An Old Lady Passing By.'

Then there was cheese and cocoa, and 'Good night all,' and the first one got up to leave. There followed long farewells by the back-kitchen door, each couple taking their turn. Those waiting inside had to bide their time. 'Our Doth! Ain't you finished yet?' 'Shan't be a minute.' Yum-yum, kiss-kiss. 'Well, hurry up, do! You're awful.' Five more minutes of silence outside, then Marge shakes the latch on the door. 'How much longer, our Doth? You been there all night. There's some

got to work tomorrow.' 'All right, don't get ratty. He's just off now. Night-night, my beautiful bab.' One by one they departed; we turned down the lights, and the girls heaved themselves to bed.

Sundays, or Bank Holidays, were daylong courtships, and then the lovers were all over us. When it rained it was hopeless and we just played cards, or the boy friends modelled for dressmaking. When fine, perhaps Mother would plan a small treat, like a picnic in the woods.

I remember a sweltering August Sunday. Mother said it would be nice to go out. We would walk a short mile to a nice green spot and boil a kettle under the trees. It sounded simple enough, but we knew better. For Mother's picnics were planned on a tribal scale, with huge preparations beforehand. She flew round the kitchen issuing orders and the young men stood appalled at the work. There were sliced cucumbers and pots of paste, radishes, pepper and salt, cakes and buns and macaroons, soup plates of bread and butter, jam, treacle, jugs of milk, and several fresh-made jellies.

The young men didn't approve of this at all, and muttered it was blooming mad. But with a 'You carry that now, there's a dear boy,' each of us carried something. So we set off at last like a frieze of Greeks bearing gifts to some woodland god —Mother, with a tea cloth over her head, gathering flowers as she went along, the sisters following with cakes and bread, Jack with the kettle, Tony with the salt, myself with a jug of milk; then the scowling youths in their blue serge suits carrying the jellies in open basins—jellies which rapidly melted in the sun and splashed them with yellow and rose. The young men swapped curses under their breath, brother Harold hung back in shame, while Mother led the way with prattling songs, determined to make the thing go.

She knew soon enough when people turned sour and moved mountains to charm them out of it, and showed that she knew by a desperate gaiety and by noisy attacks on silence.

'Now come along, Maurice, best foot forward, mind how you go, tee-hee. Leslie! just look at those pretty what-d'you-call-'ems—those what's-its—*aren't* they a picture? I said Leslie, look, aren't they pretty, my dear? Funny you don't know the name. Oh, isn't it a scrumptious day, tra-la? Boys, isn't it a scrumptious day?'

Wordy, flustered, but undefeated, she got us to the woods at last. We were ordered to scatter and gather sticks and to build a fire for the kettle. The fire smoked glumly and stung our eyes, the young men sat round like martyrs, the milk turned sour, the butter fried on the bread, cake crumbs got stuck to the cucumbers, wasps seized the treacle, the kettle wouldn't boil, and we ended by drinking the jellies.

As we boys would eat anything, anywhere, none of this bothered us much. But the young courting men

sat on their spread silk handkerchiefs and gazed at the meal in horror. 'No thanks, Mrs. Lee. I don't think I could. I've just had me dinner, ta.'

They were none of them used to such disorder, didn't care much for open-air picnics—but most of all they were wishing to be away with their girls, away in some field or gully, where summer and love would be food enough, and an absence of us entirely.

When the girls got engaged, heavy blushes followed as the rings were shown to the family. 'Its a cluster of brilliants. Cost more than two pounds. He got it at Gloucester Market.' Now that things were official, there was more sitting in the dark and a visible increase in tensions. The girls were now grown and they wished to be gone. They were in love and had found their men. Meanwhile, impatience nagged at them all, till in one case it suddenly exploded. . . .

It was evening. I was drawing at the kitchen table. One of the girls was late. When she came at last, we had finished supper. She arrived with her boy, which seemed unusual, as it wasn't his calling night.

'Well, take your coat off,' said Mother. 'Sit down.'

'No, thank you,' he answered frozenly.

'Don't just stand there—stiff as stiff can be.'

'I'm all right, Mrs. Lee, I assure you.'

'Ma, we've been thinking—' the

sister began. Her voice was level and loud.

I always went still at the sound of trouble, and didn't turn or look. I just worked at my drawing, and each line and detail became inscribed with the growing argument. A penciled leaf, the crook of a branch, each carried a clinging phrase: 'Don't talk so daft. . . . You're acting very funny. . . . You don't none of you know what I feel. . . . It's cruel to hear you talk like that. . . . I never had a proper chance. . . . Oh, come and sit down and don't act so silly. . . . It's no good, we made up our minds. . . . She's just about had enough, Mrs. Lee, it's time she was out of it all. . . .' My pencil paused; what did they mean?

The other girls were indignant, Mother sad and lost, the argument rose and fell. 'Well, that's what *we* think, anyway. It's a scandal, you coming like this. What about him? —he just walks in—who does he think he is? What about you, if it comes to that? Well, what about us —we're listening. You think the whole place is run just for you. We don't! You do! We never! Well, come on girl. I've had enough!' Shocked pause, aghast. 'You dare!'

I was listening with every nerve and muscle of my back. Nothing happened; words flared and died. At last we boys went up to bed, undressed, and lay in the dark. As we lay, still listening, the kitchen grew quieter, the trouble seemed to fade to a murmur. . . . Suddenly, there was uproar, the girls screaming, Mother howling, and a scuffling and crashing of furniture. Jack and I sprang instantly from our beds and tore downstairs in our shirts. We found Mother and two sisters at the young man's throat, bouncing him against the wall. The other girl was trying to pull them away. The whole was a scene of chaos. Without hesitation, and in spite of the congestion, we sprang at the young man too.

But by the time we reached him, the battle was over, the women had broken off. The young man stood panting, alone in the corner. I gave him a shove, he gave me a swipe, then he bent down to look for his hat.

He had tried to carry off our willing sister and we had all of us very near killed him. Now, just as suddenly, everybody was kissing each other, weeping, embracing, forgiving. Mother put her arm round the young man's neck and nearly strangled him afresh with affection. The whole party moved out into the dark back-kitchen, sniffing, mumuring: 'There, there. It's all right. We're all friends now, aren't we? Dear boy. . . . Oh, Mother. . . . There, there . . .'

A moment before I'd been blind with anger, ready to slay for the family. Now the rage was over, cancelled, let down. I turned in disgust from their billing and cooing; went up to the fire, lifted my nightshirt, and warmed my bare loins on the fireguard. . . .

The girls were to marry; the Squire was dead; buses ran and the towns were nearer. We began to shrug off the valley and look more to the world, where pleasures were more anonymous and tasty. They were coming fast, and we were nearly ready for them. Each week Miss Bagnall held her penny dances, where girls' shapes grew more familiar. For a penny one could swing them through lancers and two-steps across the resinous floor of the Hut —but if one swung them entirely off their feet, then Miss Bagnall locked the piano and went home. . . .

Time squared itself, and the village shrank, and distances crept nearer. The sun and moon, which once rose from our hill, rose from London now in the east. One's body was no longer a punching ball, to be thrown against trees and banks, but a telescoping totem crying strange demands, few of which we could yet supply. In the faces of the villagers one could see one's change, and in their habits their own change also. The horses had died; few people kept pigs any more but spent their spare time buried in engines. The flutes and cornets, the gramophones with horns, the wind harps were thrown away—now wireless aerials searched the electric sky for the music of the Savoy Orpheans. Old men in pubs sang, 'As I Walked Out,' then walked out and never came back. Our mother was grey now, and a shade more lightheaded, talking of mansions she would never build.

As for me—for me, the grass grew longer and more sorrowful, and the trees were surfaced like flesh, and girls were no longer to be treated lightly but were creatures of commanding sadness, and all journeys through the valley were now made alone, with passion in every bush, and the motions of wind and cloud and stars were suddenly for myself alone, and voices elected me of all men living and called me to deliver the world, and I groaned from solitude, blushed when I stumbled, loved strangers and bread and butter, and made long trips through the rain on my bicycle, stared wretchedly through lighted windows, grinned wryly to think how little I was understood, and lived in a state of raging excitement.

The sisters, as I said, were about to get married. Harold was working at a factory lathe. Brother Jack was at grammar school, and his grammar was excellent; and Tony still had a fine treble voice. My mother half-knew me, but could not help; I felt doomed, and of all things wonderful.

It was then that I began to sit on my bed and stare out at the nibbling squirrels, and to make up poems from intense abstraction, hour after unmarked hour, imagination scarcely faltering once, rhythm hardly skipping a beat, while sisters called me, suns rose and fell, and the poems I made, which I never remembered were the first and last of that time. . . .

AFTERWORD

The first point I want to make about *The Edge of Day* is this: the village it describes was old-fashioned even for forty years ago. I can say this because I am exactly twenty years older than Laurie Lee and therefore was a grown man when he was a small child. And by the time the first World War was over, I came across few villages that were like Laurie Lee's. Not that I think he is not being truthful about his village; I am sure he is. The point I am making is that so far as my memory serves me, the kind of village he describes was not typical of English country life in the early 1920's. The final changes he mentions had taken place much earlier, before the first World War, in most parts of the country. His bit of Gloucestershire had defied change—or escaped its attention—longer than most. But he really makes the point himself:

> The last days of my childhood were also the last days of the village. I belonged to that generation which saw, by chance, the end of a thousand years' life. The change came late to our Cotswold valley, didn't really show itself till the late 1920's; I was twelve by then, but during that handful of years I witnessed the whole thing happen.
>
> Myself, my family, my generation, were born in a world of silence; a world of hard work and necessary patience, of backs bent to the ground, hands massaging crops, of waiting on weather and growth; of villages like ships in the empty landscapes and the long walking distances between them; of white narrow roads, rutted by hooves and cart wheels, innocent of oil or petrol, down which people passed rarely, and almost never for pleasure, and the horse was the fastest thing moving. Man and the horse were all the power we had—abetted by levers and pulleys. But the horse was king, and almost everything grew round him: fodder, smithies, stables, paddocks, distances, and the rhythm of our days. His eight-miles-an-hour was the limit of our movements, as it had been since the days of the Romans. That eight-miles-an-hour was life and death, the size of our world, our prison.

All this I understand and appreciate, but in the places I knew, the change came before the first World War. What that war did, in my part of England, was simply to complete the change, to stamp and seal it.

Like many people of my generation I have spent a good deal of time comparing the past—let us say, fifty years ago—with the present. In theory and on paper, the present cannot even be challenged. Everything seems to be better. People work shorter hours for far more money; they are healthier, better housed, better clothed; their opportunities for recreation and travel are beyond anything their grandfathers dreamt about; and so on and so forth. There have been some solid gains, and I would never attempt to deny them. But we are very foolish if we imagine, as too many people seem to, that it has been all gain, without any losses. This denial of any loss is not only foolish but dangerous. Indeed, we are beginning to suffer from what has been perhaps a deliberate blindness. We are now living in a society that is to some extent sick from having moved too quickly, having done too much in too short a time. Too many people now feel empty and lost because they cannot catch up with themselves.

Here is one simple example of this change and its possible consequences. Imagine a boy of fifty years ago traveling by horse and buggy, perhaps twelve miles, to a market town. Now think of a boy today who climbs into a jet airliner and is carried across whole continents at more than five hundred miles an hour. At first glance, there seems no possible comparison between the two styles of life, the one so narrow, restricted, dull, and the other so astonishing in its achievement and its possibilities. But we must not simply compare a body moving at eight miles an hour with a body being carried at five hundred; after all, we are spirits, not parcels. If, for example, the horse-and-buggy boy has his mind filled with wonder and delight during his twelve-mile journey, and if the boy in the jet plane feels nothing but a mixture of boredom and apprehension, then which is the more satisfying and rewarding journey? And some things I know from my own experience. I can remember the enormous zest and enthusiasm, the curiosity and wonder, of people in my youth who merely made short journeys by train or in a wagonette. On the other hand, during a number of long-distance flights I have made, including one right round the world by jet plane, I have always been struck by the absence of any signs of curiosity, wonder, and delight on the part of my fellow travelers, who always looked either bored or anxious.

No doubt people ought to make the most of either type of journey, the twelve-mile trot, the five-thousand-mile flight; but only a person touched with poetic genius—perhaps our friend Laurie Lee—would probably be capable of it. For most people, speed destroys curiosity, wonder, poetic observation, and feeling. Moreover, the easier communications are, the more "progress" they bring, the more all the differences that surprised and delighted the old traveler tend to disappear. By the time we can travel anywhere in an hour or two, it will not be worthwhile going anywhere, all places looking alike. Stagecoaches set out from and arrived at cities and towns that looked widely different; railroad stations were more alike but yet had some character of their own; whereas airports— and I know them from Alaska to Chile, Bangkok to Iceland—look almost identical and are very boring. A widening of horizons can bring a narrowing of real interests. So there are plenty of people now in America and Britain who, through the press, radio, television, know what is happening on the other side of the world but neither know nor care what is happening to their next-door neighbors. And there is a profound difference between mere *news* and genuine personal exprience. Indeed, sometimes I feel that people these days take in so much on this abstract, flavorless *news* level that the quality of their genuine personal experience is rapidly declining. But this applies more to men than to women, who keep closer to earth, to the color, scent, flavor, and feel of actuality.

Now let us return to *The Edge of Day*. This is an account of what was, in contemporary terms, a shockingly limited, downright "underprivileged" childhood. There was poor Mrs. Lee, in her half of a tumble-down old house, trying to bring up this brood on the equivalent of three or four dollars a week. (It is doubtful now if she would even be allowed to try.) These children were fed anyhow, poorly dressed, hardly ever went anywhere, obtained such scraps of education as they could pick up, and there, in their remote, old-fashioned village, might almost have been living in the Middle Ages. *In theory* the limitations of their life were appalling. But in practice they were not entirely a bad thing. As I suggested before, there may have been some loss, as well as gain, when the change, the improvements, the progress, finally arrived. To begin with, these children made the most of their family life. They may have seen little but the village and the surrounding countryside, but—and this is certainly true of Laurie Lee himself—what they saw and knew they *really* saw and knew, as many urban people now never see or know anything. The color, the flavor, the richness, the wonder of life, were all experienced and enjoyed.

What seems to me chiefly missing now for vast masses of people—and in much of the writing about those people—is a whole dimension in depth. Their lives may be broader, freed from the severe limitations, the old rural narrowness we discover here, but they are also much shallower. Their actual experience, not what happens to their bodies but what happens inside their heads, is therefore less exciting, stimulating, satisfying, spiritually rewarding. The modern craze for speed—and here in Britain we have hordes of young men who do not really want to go anywhere or see anything but only to go faster and faster on their motorcycles—is a kind of protest against this decline in the quality of experience, an attempt, one might almost say, to get out of the trap. Now open this book of Laurie Lee's anywhere and you will at once discover this dimension in depth, as this very fine passage, coming after his account of the uncles:

> These men reflected many of Mother's qualities, were foolish, fantastical, moody; but in spite of their follies they remained for me the true heroes of my early life. I think of them still in the image they gave me; they were bards and oracles each, like a ring of squat megaliths on some local hill, bruised by weather and scarred with old glories. They were the horsemen and brawlers of another age, and their lives spoke its long farewell. Spoke, too, of campaigns on desert marches, of Kruger's cannon and Flanders

mud; of a world that still moved at the same pace as Caesar's, and of that empire greater than his—through which they had fought, sharp-eyed and anonymous, and seen the first outposts crumble. . . .

It is this dimension in depth, with its sense of time and feeling for what is symbolical, that gives such passages as this, of which there are scores in these chapters, their beauty, their poignancy, their magic.

But Laurie Lee is a poet, I shall be told, and poets are exceptional men. They should be exceptional, however, not in what they think and feel but in their capacity to make words express, and therefore communicate, what they think and feel. And it may well be that life lived in one way, no matter how narrow and limited it may appear to be, is more likely to offer nourishment to poets and the readers of their poetry than are other styles of life superficially broader, freer, on a newer, higher level of our civilization. It may be that it is here where the losses overtake the gains. Now, of the four works in this volume, this may well appear to be the slightest, merely a few chapters about a childhood in a village; but it is to my mind the one that makes me feel the most and think the hardest. I could recommend it—as indeed I do, with enthusiasm—as a piece of autobiography unusual in its charm, zest, gaiety of spirit, beauty of phrase. But my last words on it in this place are these: when you have read it and have enjoyed these exceptional qualities, read it again and begin to think about these gains and losses of ours, about the way life is going, and begin to question yourself and others.

STUDY QUESTIONS

1. In "First Light" Laurie Lee describes his home in the Cotswold hills as he first knew it. He does not translate what he remembers into adult perceptions and sensations, but attempts to reproduce those of the three-year-old he was at the time. How does he achieve this in his account of being first set down from the carrier's cart into the high June grass? How does his extended simile likening his mother and sisters to galleons under sail help support this depiction of an infant consciousness?

2. Consider the details of the incident of the ragged man whom his mother feeds in the kitchen. Again we are told only what the little boy saw and heard. What can we infer from this evidence as to who the man was and what he had done?

3. What impressions did the end of the war make on Laurie? What is the ironic force of these impressions when they are considered in the light of more mature knowledge?

4. "The yard and the village manifested themselves through magic and

fear." Magic and fear, myth and a sense of the catastrophic, are basic in the life of a child. They are necessities to the poet, and important to all aware human beings. The concrete terms in which they appear, however, vary greatly with time, place, circumstance, and the individual consciousness. What are the particular ways in which the magic and fear to which Laurie Lee refers entered his life? How did these particular ways reflect the world immediately around him?

5. After the author describes the wild and heroic battles waged by the Lee family against floods of rain water, he notes that afterward he came to realize that there had been no actual danger and that "Mother's frenzies and scares belonged to something else altogether." What was that something else? How does he demonstrate that the danger was real enough in one sense?

6. What were the specific deficiencies of the village school and its program? What advantages, if any, did this schooling provide for Laurie Lee?

7. Why did Laurie hit Vera on the head with a stick? What were the results of hitting her? What lessons did he learn from the incident? What is demonstrated here about the difference between the world of very little children and that of grownups?

8. What might a child learn about the grownup world from witnessing the rebellion of Spadge Hopkins? What was, in fact, the response of the children who did witness it?

9. "With our mother, then, we made eight in that cottage . . ." Who were Laurie's brothers and sisters? How was each one different from the others? Which of them seems to have left the deepest impression on the au-

thor? Which of the other children in the cottage seems to interest him the least? Why?

10. How did the two grannies, "Er-Down-Under" and "Er-Up-Atop," communicate with each other? By what means are we shown how closely their lives were bound together? In what ways were they different? In what ways were they alike? Are their differences or their similarities more important to the author? Why did he include so much about them in a book supposedly about himself?

11. The fate of Vincent, the wild colonial boy, is at once strange and familiar, brutal and human. In what sense was his end a "private murder"? In what sense was it a "public death"? Who killed him? Why? Explain what became of the killers afterwards.

12. "There was also a frank and unfearful attitude to death, and an acceptance of violence as a kind of ritual which no one accused or pardoned." Laurie Lee supports this general statement with a number of scenes and instances. What specific differences is he pointing up between his childhood village and the modern world as most of us know it?

13. Laurie Lee tells us that he was haunted by the end of Joe and Hannah Brown as by no other. Various strange and violent deaths are described in the book. Why should the quiet passing of this aged couple be so memorable? What does this suggest to us about the author?

14. What were the various significant experiences in Mother Lee's life before the family moved to the Cotswold cottage? What part did each of these play in the life of the family there? What were her deficiencies as the head of a household? What were

her particular talents and superiorities? What qualities of hers does Laurie Lee appear to have inherited?

15. We are given limited information about Laurie Lee's father. What picture of the man and his life can we infer from it? What was Laurie's childhood attitude toward his father?

16. In "Winter and Summer," the author describes characteristic out-of-school activities of the boys in his village. These things were done for fun, but were not particularly easy or comfortable things to do. They were not done simply at the choice of the boys; other factors allowed or, sometimes, demanded them. What are the activities described in this chapter? What are the discomforts and difficulties involved? What control by outside forces is stated or implied? How do these recreations differ from characteristic recreations of boys in the world we know? How are they similar?

17. Laurie Lee deals, half-humorously, with the practical advantages that a child can gain from being sick to the point of death. What were these advantages in his case? Which were valuable simply from the little boy's point of view? Which seem to the author, in retrospect, to have been additions to life as a whole?

18. Some of "Sick Boy" is not half-humorous, but heart-rending or terrifying. What is particularly moving about the description of the little sister, Frances? What horrible imaginings are suggested in the little boy's feverish vision of the second head laid on his pillow, his own head once removed, that "just lay there grinning very coldly into my eyes"? What is suggested by the "row of intangible smiles"?

19. What was the particular significance of his bicycle accident as Laurie Lee looks back on it?

20. The author speaks of his uncles as the heroes of his boyhood. From the boy's point of view, what were the heroic qualities that they shared? Does the author regard them with admiration in retrospect? What note of melancholy is evident in his treatment of them and their lives?

21. The "fist of uncles" had certain general qualities in common. Each of the four with whom Laurie Lee deals in detail, however, had some broadly comic individual quirk of personality or special experience which set him apart. How were Charlie, Tom, Ray, and Sid each thus distinguished?

22. Each of the events described in "Outings and Festivals" had some institutional basis. That is, Laurie participated in each of them because he belonged unquestioningly and unquestionably to a particular group which traditionally did these things in prescribed ways. What were the groups? How were they related, one to another? How does the author show us the traditional, seemingly inevitable, quality of each festival and outing? What became of these rites and practices? Why?

23. What were some of the most pleasurable incidents for Laurie in the festivals and outings? What relation had ordinary life in the village to his enjoyment of them?

24. How did each of the following circumstances contribute to the end of village life as Laurie Lee once knew it?

    a. The supremacy of the motor vehicle
    b. The death of the Squire
    c. The courting of the Lee sisters

25. What were the real deprivations endured by the Lee family dur-

ing their life together in the Cotswold cottage? To what extent does the author suggest that these deprivations were due to the social system in force at the time and place? To what extent do they seem to have been the results of chance and the individual personalities involved?

26. Here are some examples of figurative language selected from *The Edge of Day*. What, in each case, do the passages describe? Explain, with attention to specific details, the appropriateness of the direct and implied comparisons.

a. ". . . a deep-running cave still linked to its antic past, a cave whose shadows were cluttered by spirits and by laws vaguely ancestral. This cave that we inhabited looked backwards through chambers that led to our ghostly beginnings; and had not, as yet, been tidied up . . ."

b. "Miss Wardley, in glory on her high desk throne, her long throat tinkling with glass. The bubbling stove with its chink of red fire; the old world map as dark as tea . . . the cupboard yawning with dog-eared books."

c. "They were the horsemen and brawlers of another age, and their lives spoke its long farewell. Spoke, too, of campaigns on desert marches, of Kruger's cannon and Flanders mud; of a world that still moved at the same pace as Caesar's, and of that empire greater than his . . . through which they had fought, sharp-eyed and anonymous, and seen the first outposts crumble."

FINAL AFTERWORD

A surprisingly long span of English life and history can be discovered in this volume. We begin in the middle of the sixteenth century and end about 1930. There are gaps, of course; a particularly long one between the death of Shakespeare in 1616 and the birth of Johnson in 1709. But apart from these 93 years we are never off the stage of English life and history for very long. And up to the death of Queen Victoria, we are involved in quite a parade, quite a pageant. A film that attempted anything on this scale would probably cost 50 million dollars, and even then fail in its attempt. We have only to settle down in a quiet corner with this volume, and several different Englands, down the centuries, come alive for us.

Here are three Londons. First, the London of the Elizabethan Theater, tremendously alive, magnificent, and riotous with color, tumult, and great words; the London that Shakespeare knew, although, unlike his fellow dramatists, he never wrote a single scene that openly represented it. Next, the London where Dr. Johnson lived and dominated his fellow authors, where Boswell—fortunately for us—came so often to make his notes, where Burke and Gibbon and Goldsmith and Reynolds and Sheridan met at the Literary Club. Then the London that Queen Victoria knew, as a girl queen, an adoring young wife, a widow, a small but terrifying old lady; the London of Lord Melbourne, Sir Robert Peel, Lord Palmerston, Gladstone, and Disraeli; the London of the Great Exhibition and so many glittering state occasions. And then, when we have come to the end of these Londons, we have little Laurie Lee in the heart of rural Gloucestershire, lost in the grass:

> It towered above me and all around me, each blade tattooed with tiger-skins of sunlight. It was knife-edged, dark and a wicked green, thick as a forest and alive with grasshoppers that chirped and chattered and leapt through the air like monkeys.

This account of a poet's childhood is of course a work of art, with all the resources of color and cadence in prose brought to the aid of memory. (Make no mistake about the art here. Strachey's *Queen Victoria,* with its carefully organized prose, *looks* well written, whereas a young and inexperienced reader might imagine that *The Edge of Day* had written itself. I can assure such a reader that it is much harder to write like Laurie Lee than it is to write like Strachey.) This autobiography is at the opposite extreme from what still remains the most famous autobiography in the English language: Pepys's *Diary.* There is some art in Samuel Pepys but not much. His secret is his complete frankness. Whatever happened to him, he noted it in his diary, which was not intended for publication and indeed was written in a kind of cipher-shorthand difficult to transcribe. This diary covers the years 1660–69 and is of great historical interest (Pepys was an important government official), a wonderfully realistic and closely detailed account of social life under Charles II, and a most entertaining revelation of one man's opinions, prejudices, habits, manners, morals, all his little weaknesses. Room could not be found for Pepys in this volume, but selections from the *Diary* are easy to find and are delightful reading.

I must add a word about Daniel Defoe. He lived the life of what we should call now a free-lance journalist and literary hack, though a man of great talent, and original, too; and he specialized in mock autobiographies, the first and most successful of them being his famous *Robinson Crusoe.* They were actually works of fiction masquerading as autobiographies, and because they had to look like the life stories of various fairly simple persons, they had to be realistic. Even if he had wished to be, Defoe in these works could not afford to be fanciful and extravagant; he was compelled to give them the appearance of actuality. And so, by way of these mock autobiographies and Daniel Defoe, realism came into the English novel.

There is no space here fore even the briefest catalogue of readable and enduring biographies and autobiographies in English literature. It is very rich in them, especially from about the middle of the eighteenth century onward; and, I am happy to add, new works of distinction are constantly appearing in our own time. Two particularly fine autobiographies that have arrived since the war are Neville Cadus' *Autobiography,* a big and beautifully written book, and *Over the Bridge,* an account of his childhood in London by Richard Church. Women writers have been producing some of the best historical biographies, notably Cecil Woodham Smith's *Life of Florence Nightingale* and Elizabeth Jenkins' biography of Elizabeth the First.

Our species loves to give an account of itself, and certainly the British specimens of it are no exceptions to the rule. From the mighty Shakespeare so long ago to little Laurie Lee, staring at the grass, after the first World War, from Sam Johnson in Fleet Street to Queen Victoria at Windsor or Balmoral, we have offered you here a tasting sample of English autobiography and biography that is in itself several substantial meals. We hope you have enjoyed the fare and will ask for more.